THE AMERICAN CHALLENGE:
A New History of the United States, Vol I
Fifth Edition

THE AMERICAN CHALLENGE:
A New History of the United States, Vol I
Fifth Edition

Michael Phillips
>   Collin College
>   Plano, Texas

Austin Allen
>   University of Houston-Downtown
>   Houston, Texas

Roger Ward
>   Collin College
>   Plano, Texas

Andrew C. Lannen
>   Stephen F. Austin State University
>   Nacogdoches, Texas

Doug Cantrell
>   Elizabethtown Technical & Community College
>   Elizabethtown, Kentucky

Edited by
Keith J. Volanto
Michael Phillips

Abigail Press   Wheaton, IL 60189

Design and Production: Abigail Press
Typesetting: Abigail Press
Typeface: AGaramond
Cover Art: Sam Tolia

THE AMERICAN CHALLENGE:
A New History of the United States, Vol. I

Fifth Edition, 2019
Printed in the United States of America
Translation rights reserved by the authors
ISBN 1-890919-72-1 ISBN 978-1-890919-72-6

Contents in Brief

Contents

MAPS & TABLES

Preface

Every nation encounters challenges during its existence. Some are common to all countries, some are quite unique. How a people rise to overcome these challenges, or fail in their attempts to address them adequately, engenders much of that country's history. Americans experienced a series of internal and external challenges over the past 500 years even before the creation of the United States: exploration of unknown lands, intense military conflicts, demanding technological problems, divisive political battles, and epic social upheavals, just to name a few. This textbook is an attempt to relay how Americans have risen to their own set of challenges and either prevailed over them or continue to deal with those not yet overcome.

The work's subtitle—"A New History of the United States"—refers to the effort by the authors to synthesize the latest historical scholarship (and borrow, when pertinent, from other disciplines) to provide a fresh account of this country's national story. Unlike many older textbooks originally produced during the Cold War era and simply updated with token changes, the authors of *The American Challenge* have written their chapters entirely from the perspective of the early twenty-first century. At the conclusion of each chapter, the authors have included a list of suggested readings consisting of a few classic works and numerous recent publications that influenced their interpretation of a particular period. These books can also provide an important starting point for students interested in delving deeper into the introduced topics.

Every textbook contains a tremendous amount of information. To guide the retention of material, the authors of *The American Challenge* have emboldened key terms to aid readers in distinguishing the most important persons, events, and concepts appearing in each chapter. A glossary at the end of the book serves as a compilation of all bold terms, providing informative descriptions. To further help digest the information, each chapter also contains a chronology to act as a quick-guide for those wishing to keep track of key events over time, and a set of five summary review questions that students should feel comfortable answering before moving on to the next chapter. To enhance the overall learning experience, all chapters include helpful maps, interesting photographs of noteworthy people and everyday scenes, and other enlightening illustrations relevant to a particular period. A reader for *The American Challenge*, containing primary source documents and an assortment of vignettes, is available from Abigail Press.

I am very proud to be associated with the fine group of scholars who authored *The American Challenge*. Each professor channeled their broad experiences as academics and classroom educators to produce a book that not only reflects the latest historical scholarship, but also written in a compelling manner which will resonate with today's college students. My colleague at Collin College, Michael Phillips, earned his Ph.D. in History from the University of Texas at Austin. His teaching and books on race in Dallas and Texas House Speakers demonstrate his strong interest and expertise in American government as well as race, class, and gender issues. Doug Cantrell holds the rank of Professor of History and chairs the History Department at the Elizabethtown Community and Technical College where he has taught for the past 25 years. Professor Cantrell studied at the University of Kentucky and has authored numerous articles and book reviews in academic journals and encyclopedias in the field of immigration and ethnic history. Austin Allen received his Ph.D. from the University of Houston and is an Associate Professor of History at the University of Houston-Downtown where he has taught since 2002. A specialist in the legal history of the antebellum United States, Austin has written a book detailing the origins of the Dred Scott Case and is presently working on a book about the Fugitive Slave Law. Andrew Lannen is an expert on colonial and revolutionary America who received his Ph.D. from Louisiana State University. His publications have focused on the Native American experience and colonial warfare. He has taught American history for over 15 years and is currently an assistant professor of history at Stephen F. Austin University. Andrew's colleague at Stephen F. Austin, Scott Sosebee, received his Ph.D. from Texas Tech University. In addition to his position as Associate Professor of History, he currently serves as the Executive Director of the East Texas Historical Association. Dr. Sosebee's published works and research interests focus on twentieth century economic and political history, centered on Texas and the American South. Roger Ward completed his Ph.D. coursework at the University of Kentucky before becoming Professor of History at Collin

College where he has taught for over ten years. A specialist of the early American Republic, his research focus is on nineteenth century race and class, as well as rural history, especially with regard to Appalachia. Finally, I received my Ph.D. in American history from Texas A&M University and currently serve as Professor of History and Chair of the History Department at Collin College. I have taught American and Texas history for the past 20 years and published a book as well as a dozen articles reflecting my interests in twentieth century American politics and race relations. The authors hope you enjoy this effort and welcome feedback from our readers. We wish to acknowledge the assistance of James Page, North Central Texas College, faculty members from Collin College, and our students for all of their feedback. Also, we appreciate the love, support, and patience of our family members during the long publication process.

Keith J. Volanto

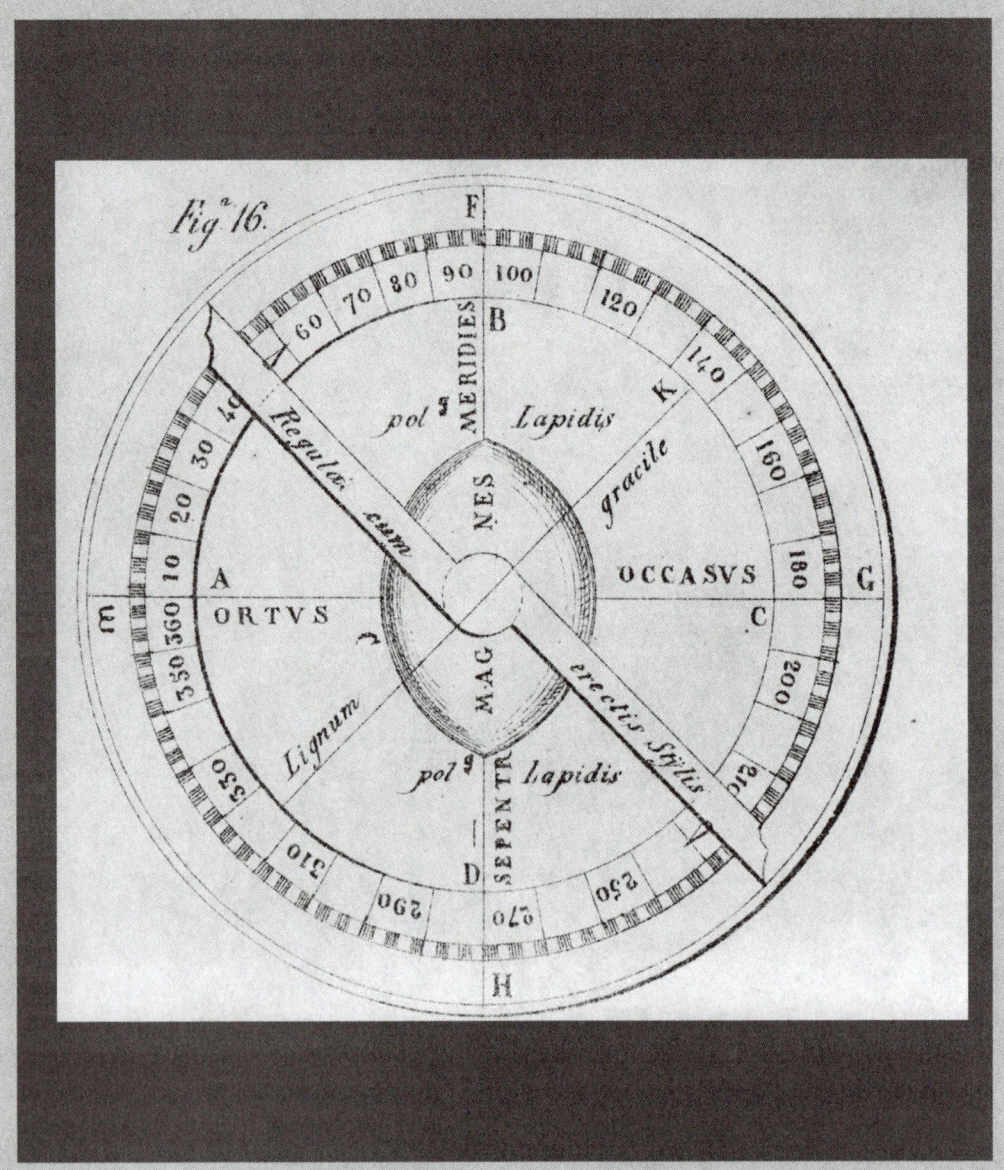

A MARINER'S COMPASS

Chapter One

NATIVE AMERICANS AND THE EUROPEAN CONQUEST

On the morning of October 12, 1492, Taíno men, women, and children awoke to find European ships, with their sun-bleached sails billowing in the light breeze, anchored off the coast of their homeland, one of the many islands making up the Bahamas. Awestruck, these Arawak-speaking people emerged from their homes and walked to the island's sandy beaches to get a closer look at the strange boats, which were much larger than the native canoes they were accustomed to seeing. Suddenly, strange men emerged from the boats. Their skin was light, their dress seemed odd, and they spoke a language the natives could not understand. Following their custom, the Taíno greeted the strangers and brought them food and water. They then gave the newcomers gifts—parrots, balls of cotton, spears, and other items commonly found in the Bahamas. In return, the Europeans, led by a Genoese sailor, Cristoforo Colombo (Christopher Columbus), gave the Arawaks glass beads, hawks' bells, and other trinkets.

After this initial meeting, Columbus described these people in his journal as generous and handsome. He wrote: "… they willingly traded everything they owned…. They were well-built, with good bodies and handsome features…." However, new arrivals did not hold this view for long. Instead of returning the Taínos' hospitality and generosity, Columbus and his men later enslaved them, viewing the natives as ignorant, uncivilized, and fit only for servile roles. In another journal entry, Columbus wrote: "They do not bear arms, and do not know them, for I showed them a sword, they took it by the edge and cut themselves out of ignorance. They have no iron. Their spears are made of cane…. They would make fine servants…. With fifty men we could subjugate them all and make them do whatever we want."

For their part, the Taínos initially seemed to like the Europeans and viewed their first encounter as an opportunity to increase trade. They were puzzled, however, by one question the Spanish repeated over and over: "*Dónde está el oro?*" (Where is the gold?) Unfamiliar with these words, the Taíno could not understand what the explorers wanted. Finally, the natives understood that Columbus and the others were interested in the small gold earrings, with which the Taíno adorned themselves. Although they were willing to give the visitors these earrings, the Taíno could not satisfy the newcomers' desire to know the source of the gold used to make the jewelry. Promised 10 percent of the profits from all gold and spices that he brought back to the Spanish government by King Ferdinand and Queen Isabella, Columbus began to fantasize about vast gold fields that would make him rich beyond his dreams. Unable to get an answer to his question, Columbus took many Taínos prisoner aboard his ships. Eventually, Columbus took his captives to Hispaniola (the name Spain gave to the island that today consists of Haiti and the Dominican Republic), all the time insisting that he be shown the source of the gold.

Three years later, on his second expedition to the Caribbean region, Columbus led a party of twelve hundred men who accompanied him to enslave as many natives as they could find. Raiding parties captured approximately fifteen hundred Arawak men, women, and children. These people were then confined in outdoor pens and guarded twenty-four hours a day by vicious dogs and soldiers. Five hundred natives, those considered to be the finest slave material, were eventually chained in the hold of ships and transported to Spain to be sold by a Catholic archdeacon. Only three *hundred captives survived the trip, the remainder succumbing to poor food, stale air, cramped living quarters, and harsh treatment. The Taínos who remained on the islands fought back, but to no avail. Their forces faced armored and mounted Spanish soldiers armed with muskets and steel swords. Many prisoners that the Spanish captured were either hanged or burned alive. Thousands more fell to smallpox and other diseases inadvertently brought to the New World by the Spanish. When resistance failed, those Taínos who could escape fled from their islands. Still others committed suicide by cassava poisoning, loving their freedom so much they killed their precious babies to save them from captivity.*

THE FIRST INHABITANTS: ASIAN MIGRATIONS

The ancestors of the Taíno and other native peoples that Columbus encountered began arriving in North America during a massive migration from central Asia across the Bering Strait during the last Ice Age about 20,000 years ago. At that time, massive glaciers lay upon the earth's surface, creating a land bridge that nomadic hunters from modern-day Siberia used to cross into North America while searching for large game. Geologists generally believe that this land bridge, which was perhaps 600 miles wide, afforded easy passage between Asia and North America. Although paleoanthropologists disagree on the precise timing of this migration, most likely the bulk of it occurred between eleven and fifteen thousand years ago. By about 8,000 B.C. these people reached the southern-

most parts of South America. Although scholars disagree, one estimate is that fifty to sixty million people inhabited the Western Hemisphere at the end of the fifteenth century when the Spanish invasion occurred. In comparison, about eighty to ninety million people lived in Europe and about seventy million in Africa at the same time.

Recent scholarship indicates that the Amerindians, a term anthropologists use to describe Native Americans, developed approximately 2,000 distinct cultures, displaying a rich variety of social systems, forms of religion, structures of government, and aspects of economic life. In fact, the Amerindians were as different from each other as they were from the Europeans they encountered.

Because of their common Asian ancestry and certain physical features, dark skin, straight black hair, and high cheekbones they shared, Europeans disregarded the cultural and linguistic differences among tribes. Europeans usually thought of Native Americans as being alike in most respects. The Amerindians, however, had no reason to think of themselves as a singular, undifferentiated people. Each group was a separate entity that referred to itself by a different name. For example, the Cherokee called themselves Ani-yun-wiya (the real people), the Mohawk called themselves Kaniengehaga (people of the place of flint), the Pawnee called themselves Chahiksichahiks (men of men), and the Cheyenne called themselves Dzi-tsistas (our people).

The forerunners of modern Native Americans, referred to as Paleo-Indians by archaeologists, lived as nomadic hunters and gatherers of wild plants. They moved about the land in extended families called bands.

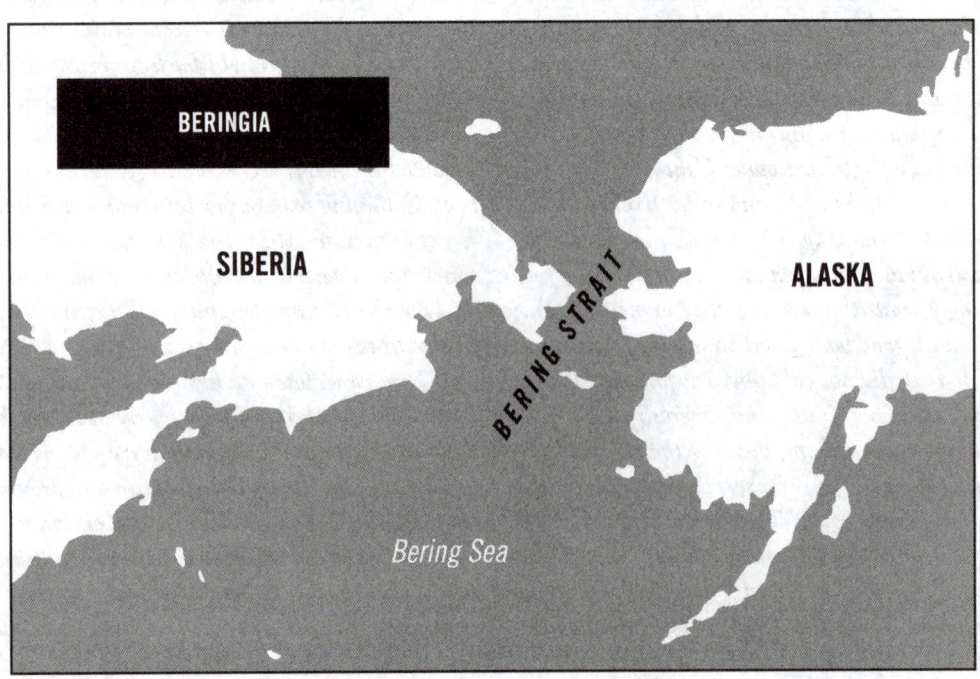

Map 1.1 Location of the Bering Land Bridge

Later, tribes formed when various bands created alliances to protect each other from attacks by other peoples. The earliest archaeological evidence of the presence of Paleo-Indians in the Western Hemisphere dates to about 28,000 years ago. At sites throughout North and South America, archaeologists have unearthed artifacts, including stone projectile points attached to wooden shafts used to hunt and butcher wildlife.

One of the most important technological developments in the hunting practices of Paleo-Indians was the **Clovis point,** a distinctive projectile tip formed by pressure-flaking the sides of a stone blade and using a concave base to fit onto the end of a spear. Named for the site of its initial discovery at Clovis, New Mexico in 1929, archaeological evidence suggests that the Paleo-Indians starting employing Clovis points about 12,000 years ago, and their use spread rapidly across North America. Clovis point hunters were mobile people who traveled in bands of thirty to fifty individuals tied together by kinship. Each group claimed territory as large as several hundred square miles and moved from camp to camp, season after season, returning to previous encampments at different times. They generally built camps near sources of water attractive to game animals that were subsequently driven into swamps and bogs to be slaughtered.

The Agricultural Revolution

Paleo-Indians had to change their nomadic lifestyle when the Ice Age ended and large mammals such as the woolly mammoth disappeared. Deprived of their primary source of meat, Paleo-Indians had to find an alternative means of survival. They turned to agriculture, especially the cultivation of maize (corn), beans, and squash. The development of agriculture was the most important change to take place among Paleo-Indians because it allowed the human population to increase and people to establish permanent villages.

Agricultural development in the Western Hemisphere seems to have first occurred in Mexico about eight thousand years ago. Paleo-Indians in the highlands of Mexico

Clovis Points

developed a wild grass into corn. Maize agriculture then became their dominant means of support. The cultivation of corn eventually spread across North and South America, transforming bands of nomadic hunters and gatherers into village farmers. Everywhere that the transformation occurred, vast changes in human society took place. As more established villages appeared, religious beliefs became ordered around elements of nature such as the sun, moon, rain, and the seasons. Work roles increasingly became separated by gender with men hunting, fishing, and preparing the fields for crops while women engaged in child rearing, planting, weeding, food preparation, and harvesting.

GREAT CIVILIZATIONS OF MEXICO AND SOUTH AMERICA

The development of agriculture enabled some indigenous peoples to create large and urban civilizations that rivaled those existing in Europe and Asia. Residents of these societies were capable of producing art, creating rituals and ceremonies, and accumulating wealth because they no longer had to devote most of their energy to acquiring the materials necessary for survival.

Several complex cultures eventually arose in Mexico and South America. Centered in the Yucatan Peninsula, the **Maya** civilization was the most important early society to develop in Mexico, with archaeological finds placing its origins before 1500 B.C. By the time of the Classic Period (250-900), Maya cities were substantial in size, containing large temples and pyramids. A creative people who valued learning, the Maya created the first system of hieroglyphic writing in the Western Hemisphere, enabling scribes to record their history and other aspects of their culture. Interested in science, Maya mathematicians discovered the usefulness of the number zero long before the Arabs and Europeans. Their astronomers could calculate the beginnings of eclipses and track the movement of the moon and major planets in the sky. The Maya also developed the most accurate calendar in the entire world at that time, enabling them to predict the arrival of the seasons among other benefits. Maya craftspeople created jewelry from gold and silver, and merchants developed extensive trading networks throughout Central America.

Similar to the social structure of the later Aztecs, Maya society was highly stratified into various classes—royalty, priests, merchants, and slaves—and their religious activities made use of blood sacrifices. Warfare contributed to the decline of the Maya. About one thousand years ago, leaders of Maya city-states fought each other for dominance. When no king could subjugate the other city-states, the Maya civilization began to decline. Aggravating the decline was overpopulation and possibly a famine or other agricultural catastrophe. Whatever the exact causes (which archaeologists continue to investigate), when the Spanish *conquistadores* arrived in Mexico, the Mayan civilization had largely disappeared.

A major trading partner of the Maya, the city-state of Teotihuacan (before it was abandoned and later rebuilt by the Aztecs) reached an estimated population of over 100,000 at its zenith around 600. Initially settled 2,200 years ago in the valley of Mexico, the city served as a major center of commerce. Sellers from Teotihuacan traveled hundreds of miles in all directions trading a variety of items, including obsidian—a dark, volcanic glass that thousands of craft workers in Mexico labored to convert into arrowheads, cutting blades, and decorative items. Teotihuacan also served as a center of religious worship. Native Americans traveled great distances to worship the feathered serpent god, Quetzalcoatl, at the Pyramids of the Sun and the Moon.

The **Aztecs** of central Mexico proved to be the most powerful native civilization at the time of European arrival. According to an oral tradition and Aztec chronicles, people who referred to themselves as *Mexica* (hence the word Mexico) migrated into the region during the twelfth century. There they found a large city that had been abandoned for almost two centuries. Huitzilopochtli, the Aztec Sun and War god, ordered his people to construct their capital on an island in the middle of an immense lake where they saw an eagle eating a snake. This city, named Tenochtitlán, became the center of a vast Aztec empire. Tenochtitlán's population surpassed 200,000 by 1500, making it one of the largest cities in the world, rivaling major European population centers such as Paris, London, and Rome. At the height of Aztec civilization in the fifteenth century, the empire's total population numbered about five million. The Aztecs were an aggressive people who dominated their neighbors, fostering hatred because of the frequent demands for tribute, including captives to be used in ritualistic religious sacrifices. The Aztecs believed that Huitzilopochtli demanded a steady diet of human hearts, which were torn from live victims' chests with sharpened obsidian knives. At the coronation of the Emperor Moctezuma II in the year that the Aztecs called Ten Rabbit (1502, according to the European calendar), five thousand were sacrificed to Huitzilopochtli. At one temple dedication at a later time, reports indicate that Aztec priests sacrificed twenty thousand victims. When Spanish invaders arrived, tribes subjugated by the Aztecs, not surprisingly, helped the Spanish destroy their oppressors.

Perhaps the most advanced of all Native American civilizations was the **Inca** of present-day Peru. This society became prominent about 1100 in the Andes Mountains. At its height, the Inca Empire contained six to seven million people. The Incas constructed an elaborate system of roads that connected every vital location in the realm. Inca craftspeople were extremely skilled metallurgists, fashioning weapons, tools, and jewelry from materials such as gold, silver, copper, and bronze. In fact, the Incas were far wealthier than the Aztecs, at least by European standards. They valued gold and silver, which were mined in large amounts, later making them an attractive target for Spanish *conquistadores* searching for precious metals.

Inca society, like that of the Aztecs, was militant. All young males were required to undergo military training to become warriors to protect the empire and their emperors who were believed to be gods. Although elites enjoyed the benefits of their privileged states—all riches belonged to the Inca ruler, while chiefs and warriors lived more comfortably than most of the people—Inca society also took care of the less fortunate. Incas believed their government should care for the aged, poor, and ill. Consequently, the Inca government operated a type of welfare system that enabled the physically handicapped, the mentally ill, and individuals suffering from chronic illness to have an adequate lifestyle.

NORTH AMERICAN PEOPLES AND SOCIETIES

Pre-Columbian Mound Builders

When Europeans first arrived in the sixteenth century, there were perhaps eight million Native American inhabitants within what is now the United States. Differences in climate and geography contributed to the evolution of distinct cultures with widely varying customs and lifestyles.

Two of the most prominent civilizations that existed in North America prior to the arrival of Europeans were the **Adena and Hopewell Cultures** of the Ohio River Valley. The earlier Adena culture developed about 1000 B.C. and survived until 200 B.C. The latter and more advanced Hopewell culture, which retained many characteristics of the Adena people, thrived until approximately 500. The most distinctive feature of these societies was the construction and use of earthen mounds as burial sites and places of worship. As a result, these ancient peoples are frequently referred to as mound builders. At the center of Adena and Hopewell communities stood relatively small earthen mounds used to intern the dead. Higher status individuals, such as chiefs and priests,

Photograph of a Cahokia mound in Illinois, c. 1907

were generally buried within the mounds along with important personal possessions, such as ceremonial axes and pipes, while common people were buried around the mounds' periphery. Occasionally, larger burial mounds were constructed. The 1,350-foot-long Great Serpent Mound in Ohio is perhaps the best example of such a mound. Adena and Hopewell people were farmers, traders, craftspeople, and hunters. Hopewell trade networks extended over most of the central and eastern United States. (Their trade goods have been unearthed in archaeological excavation sites from the Great Lakes to the Gulf of Mexico.)

Another mound building culture that developed in North America was the Mississippian. This society, which began to thrive around 800, lasted until approximately 1400. Like the Adena and Hopewell cultures that preceded them, Mississippian people were traders who had extensive contact with large numbers of Native American groups across the eastern half of the continent. Heavily engaged in the cultivation of corn to support their populations, the Mississippian people constructed substantial cities. The largest was located at Cahokia, in present-day southern Illinois near St. Louis, where by the year 1250, as many as 25,000 people lived. The Mississippians constructed much larger mounds than did the people of the Adena and Hopewell cultures. Mississippian mounds generally had elaborate temples at their top where priests resided. Eighty-five large mounds stood at Cahokia, with the largest surpassing the size of the

great pyramids constructed in ancient Egypt. For reasons not clearly understood by scholars, Mississippian society disintegrated before significant contact with Europeans occurred. However, several modern Native American tribes appear to be direct descendants of the Mississippian culture, including the Shawnee, Choctaw, Creeks, Natchez, and Caddo. These tribes built mounds and buried their dead in ways similar to the Mississippians.

Native American Diversity at the Time of Columbus

By the time of European contact, a great diversity of life existed in North America. Native groups spoke over five hundred distinct languages across the continent. Each people developed a lifestyle best suited to meet survival needs in its environment. In the Pacific Northwest, the Chinooks, Nez Perce, and Nootka relied primarily upon salmon fishing, whereas in the Great Plains the Kiowa, Comanche, Sioux, Cheyenne, Pawnee, and Arapaho hunted wild animals within set territorial boundaries. In the desert Southwest, the Navajo, Ute, Hopi, Zuni, and Apache farmed the land through use of irrigation because the arid climate created a scarcity of animal life, which limited hunting. In the New England and Mid-Atlantic regions, the Micmac, Abenaki, Iroquois, Wampanoag, Patuxet, and Pamunkey relied upon fishing, hunting, and gathering due to the relatively cold, harsh climate and short growing season. Southeastern peoples, including

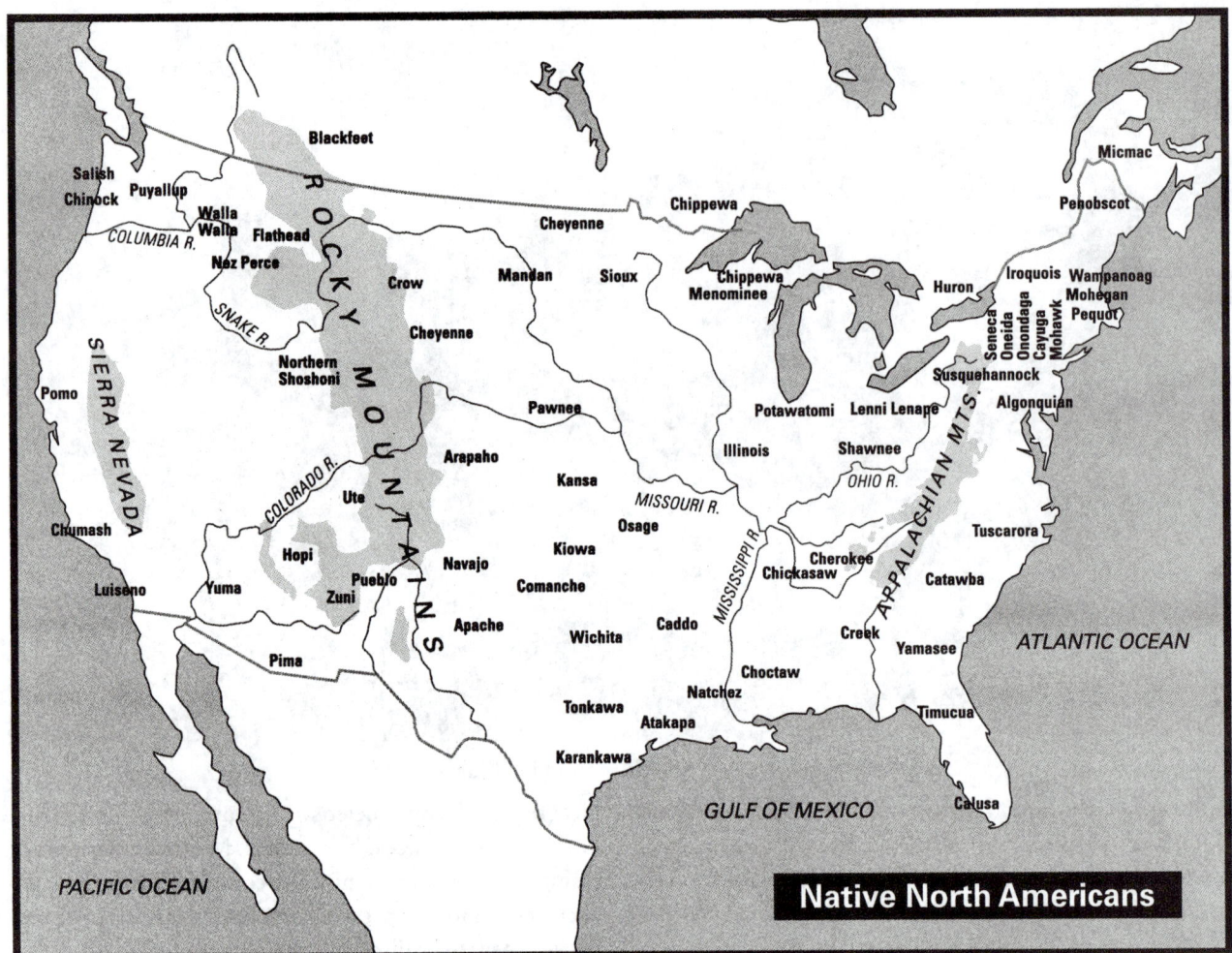

Map 1.2 Location of Native North Americans

the Cherokee, Chickasaw, Shawnee, Choctaw, Creek, and Tuscarora, were primarily agricultural, because the warm climate, long growing season, and rich, thick topsoil were conducive to farming. Native Americans along the Gulf Coast and Florida, in particular the Natchez and Seminole, like the groups residing in the Pacific Northwest, largely fished because the sea offered a bountiful harvest.

Governments varied by Native American group. Some societies had governments that were relatively open and democratic, while others had single authoritarian leaders. Generally, tribes that relied upon hunting and gathering had governments in which the power of the ruler derived from the consent of the population, while groups depending upon agriculture often had inherited rulers or a select group of influential leaders. Among the Muskogean people, for example, government consisted of a twenty-to-thirty-man elected council empowered to make all decisions affecting the tribe. In contrast, the Natchez, an agricultural tribe inhabiting lands in the Mississippi River Delta region, were governed by a chief called the Great Sun who ruled more like a dictator.

Treated royally by his subjects, he resembled the great pharaohs of ancient Egypt. Believed by his people to be a god, the Great Sun was carried on a litter born by servants whenever in public, with the pathways swept clean before him by an array of servants and wives who accompanied him. Noble families, whose position in society was based on heredity, comprised the Great Sun's council, which appointed village chiefs.

Native American peoples sometimes exhibited a high degree of political unity and organization. The Cherokee, Choctaw, Chickasaw, Creeks, and Iroquois formed strong confederacies. Among the Cherokee, over sixty villages were united in the Appalachian region of present-day Tennessee and Georgia governed by councils of elderly men and women. Five Iroquois nations, the Mohawks, Oneidas, Onondagas, Cayugas, and Senecas, were united in 1451 by Chief Deganawida, the Law Giver, to control violence and warfare and regulate the economy among them. According to oral histories taken during the nineteenth century, Deganawida caused the sun to become dark to demonstrate his power and convince tribal leaders to join the confederacy. Assisting Deganawida was the great Iroquois orator Hiawatha. His elaborate words are said to have helped convince various chiefs to support participation in the Iroquois Confederation. Within this alliance, local communities were relatively autonomous, but the central government brokered disputes among member villages and organized the five nations to wage war on enemy tribes such as the Hurons, Petuns, and Eries, who also organized confederacies of their own to defend against Iroquois aggression.

Like governmental systems, forms of shelter also varied by native group. The chosen type of housing usually reflected the Native Americans' use of the resources present within the territory they inhabited. Nomadic tribes of the Great Plains usually fashioned dwellings from animal skins stretched over wooden frames. These "teepees" were light in weight and mobile, enabling inhabitants to dismantle them quickly when it became necessary to move the village after game and plant life became scarce in one location. Despite their ease of construction and weight, teepees were comfortable dwelling structures. A hole at the top enabled light to enter and smoke from fires to exit.

More settled agricultural tribes constructed larger and more elaborate houses than the mobile teepee. The Iroquois built a dwelling structure called a longhouse from tree bark. These houses, measuring about 800 feet long and 25 feet wide, contained five or six fireplaces and provided living quarters for two nuclear families. Pueblo and Navajo tribes in the desert Southwest constructed houses from mud and stone called adobe. These structures were stacked on top of each other and interconnected with hallways. Meanwhile, Muskogean, Caddo, and Algonquians residing in the present-day American Southeast lived in dwellings consisting of a wooden frame covered with thatch.

Native American Women

Within North American native groups, a division of labor existed along gender lines. Hunting and gathering peoples often assigned the hunting to men while the gathering, food processing and preservation, clothes-making, and child-rearing responsibilities fell to the women. Agricultural societies differed in this regard. Among the Pueblo people in the desert Southwest, for example, men performed the planting, cultivating, and harvesting of crops, while among eastern farming groups, such as the Iroquois, women held these responsibilities. In Iroquois society, men hunted wild game and cleared the land, usually by burning trees, for agriculture.

In some agricultural groups, such as the Algonquian, Iroquois, Muskogean, and Pueblo, for example, family lineage was defined matrilineally with ancestry traced through female lines of descent. Kinship was thus defined along matriarchal lines, with property inherited through the mother's side of the family. Extended families generally were comprised of a mother, their married daughters, their husbands, and all children produced by the daughters' marriages. At the time of marriage, husbands left the home of their mothers to live with the mother of their wife. These extended families were also linked into clans along matrilineal lines. Conversely, more nomadic groups, such as those roaming the Great Plains, usually traced their lineage patrilineally. The Sioux, Cheyenne, Kiowa, Comanche, Pawnee, and Arapaho lacked permanent villages and constituted themselves into small bands of family members related to the group's father who moved four or five times a year, depending on the availability of game within a given territory.

Among Native American peoples, a degree of sexual equality existed that was unknown in European cultures. Women in matrilineal societies could initiate divorce proceedings simply by setting the husband's possessions outside the lodge door. Among the Cherokee, whose rulers could be either male or female, women controlled both household and village life. Each year different Cherokee villagers met in tribal councils that lasted several days or, on occasion, several weeks. At these meetings all tribal members, both men and women, were allowed to speak. Women owned property in some Native American tribes. Pueblo peoples in Arizona and New Mexico, for example, developed an economic system in which women owned the fields, the crops, the tools used in cultivation, and the family house. Within this system, men hunted game and worked the corn, bean, and squash fields, which they did not own, coming home to houses owned by their wives.

Women in some Native American groups wielded much political power. Among the Iroquois, the village council, consisting of men, sat in a circle to discuss issues and make decisions relating to war, diplomacy, and other things affecting the people. Behind the circle of male chiefs stood the village women who gave advice to the chiefs, often persuading them to vote one way or another. Political influence and power in Iroquois society was often the result of age. Even though Iroquois chiefs were men, older women in the village chose the leaders. Chiefs who displeased Iroquois women were subject to removal by the female council who had appointed them. In some Native American groups, such as the Algonquian, women served as chiefs. Powerful women leaders could also be found among tribes dwelling in the area encompassed presently by the southeastern United States. In western South Carolina during the 1550s, a female chief called the Lady of Cofitachequi by Spanish explorers ruled over several villages.

Common Native American Beliefs

Though countless cultural, social, and political distinctions among North America Indians at the time of European arrival can be noted, some important commonalities among native groups did exist, tracing their origin back to the common ancestors who trekked across the Siberian land bridge thousands of years earlier. Among their core values, native peoples held a deep respect for nature. Plant and animal life were treated with reverence. Unlike their European counterparts, Native Americans emphasized cooperation with nature rather than control over it. They typically did not, for example, attempt to control flooding rivers with dams or level mountaintops to build cities, as Europeans would do after they took control of the Western Hemisphere.

Since Native Americans lived in harmony with their environment, their religions were nature-based. Most believed that every living thing, including plants and trees, contained spirits that governed animal and plant behavior. Humans were only allowed to kill enough animals or gather enough plants for survival. Greed on the part of human beings would anger the animal and plant spirits, which would direct the life forms to stop growing and reproducing or cause them to leave tribal lands, resulting in human starvation. Native Americans also did not value the acquisition of great personal wealth because doing so violated the natural balance present in the world.

Within each group a holy figure, or "**shaman**," served as an elite religious figure believed by the people to have been given enormous powers to communicate with the spiritual world. In this capacity, the shaman relayed to the people the wishes of spirits, which eventually developed into rules, values, mores, and taboos regarding the relationship between humans and the natural world.

Individual ownership of land was an alien concept to Native Americans. Like the air they breathed, the land was believed to belong to everyone within the group. Fencing land to deny people and animals use of it was a concept that natives rejected. Tribal boundaries usually consisted of an area large enough to amply supply the needs of the people. Wars undertaken simply to enlarge territory were not part of the Native American mindset since taking more than needed was believed to bring disaster to the group. Native Americans sometimes waged war against each other, but intertribal warfare was usually short-lived. Two or three small battles between bands of wandering warriors numbering between twenty and forty individuals might occur within the space of several months. Very few lives were lost in these engagements, and chiefs often ended the conflict by negotiating an oral peace agreement.

Native American societies emphasized cooperation over individualism. The achievements of one person were not valued as highly as group accomplishments. This idea was particularly evident in sporting contests. Events, such as lacrosse matches, were team-centered. Native peoples around the Great Lakes, the Mid-Atlantic coast, and the American Southeast formed lacrosse teams that competed with members of different groups. The victor was not any individual or team, but the tribe. The same principle held true for other types of competition. Archery contests, as well as spear and tomahawk throwing events, often pitted one group against another for tribal fame rather than personal glory.

During the centuries that North and South America were inhabited before Europeans invaded, Native American cultures, in all their sophistication and splendor, thrived. The hundreds of distinctive societies that developed among native people were designed to suit the particular environment they lived in. These societies continued to develop unimpeded until European nations began to conquer and destroy them after 1492.

EUROPE ON THE EVE OF EXPLORATION

Approximately one thousand years ago, during the time that the mound builders of the Mississippi River Valley were constructing elaborate cities at Cahokia and elsewhere, Europeans were in the midst of a languishing period that historians call the Middle Ages (the period between the fall of the Roman Empire and the birth of modern Europe from about 400 to 1400). During this time, political and economic power resided with the Byzantine Empire, which controlled vast territories in Eastern Europe, the Balkans, and Turkey, while Islamic civilizations dominated North Africa and the Middle East. At this time, Western Europe consisted of agricultural societies with large numbers of peasant workers. Politically, the region was controlled by an economic and social system called feudalism. European nations divided land into many small units owned and governed by noblemen who wielded absolute power over the peasants living on their land. The nobles demanded labor from the peasant farmers, taking a portion of the crops produced each year as rent, and provided basic protection in return. Within this system, the landowners accumulated large estates and much wealth, allowing them to build huge castles overlooking their vast holdings.

Poor nutrition, overcrowding, and lack of sanitation often contributed to high death rates due to disease. The most devastating epidemic to strike European societies during the Middle Ages, however, the **Bubonic Plague**, was a bacterial infection spread by parasitic fleas on rats. This disease, which first hit Europe in 1347, most likely originated in China and was carried to Italy by rodents living on trading vessels. The "Black Death," as the Bubonic Plague was commonly called, killed about one-third of Europe's population by the end of the 1370s.

The Impact of Trade

After surviving the Bubonic Plague, Western Europe emerged from the Middle Ages. Several developments occurred that eventually played a role in European exploration of territory lying westward across the Atlantic. During the fourteenth century, trade routes with Asia opened. Products from India and China, including silk, jewels, and spices, were sold in Europe while copper, wood, iron, armor, lead, tin, and other products were carried to Asia along a trade route known as the Silk Road. Chinese, Italian, and Arab traders who handled this trade made vast fortunes. Spices from Asia proved to be the most important commodity that Europeans received in this intercontinental trade. In Europe, Asian spices were literally worth their weight in gold. Wealthy Europeans believed spices were necessary for a comfortable life. They retarded spoilage, relieved the bland taste of local foods, and hid the poor quality of meat before refrigeration was developed. Most of these spices, such as cinnamon, cloves, black pepper, and nutmeg, could only be acquired from Asia.

The European trade with Asia led to development of a new economic system, capitalism, which eventually replaced feudalism. Before the spice trade developed, kings and nobles held merchants in contempt, often using the power of government to suppress them. Trade with Asia changed European attitudes toward profit making. Rulers began to rely upon wealthy traders to provide money to pay debts or equip the king's army with weapons. In return for financial assistance, European monarchs ended the oppression of merchants, enacted new laws granting various privileges to them, and used armies and navies to protect trade. This, in turn, caused religious leaders, who had previously declared profit making sinful, to ease their views on lending, interest, and earning money through investment.

The Euro-Asian trade also helped end the feudal system. Before Europeans had economic contact with Asia, manorial estates that nobles and peasants resided on were largely self-sufficient, producing virtually all items their residents needed for survival. Trade with Asia caused European nobles to desire the wonderful luxuries of the Orient. Since silk and spices could not be produced on manorial lands, nobles needed cash, which was difficult to acquire within the feudal economy, because payments were received in the form of goods and services produced locally. Because nobles now needed cash, they began to alter rules governing the feudal system, allowing peasants to leave the land so that it could be sold or leased to others for money.

The growth of urban areas proved to be another factor that characterized Europe on the eve of exploration. The Euro-Asian trade caused new cities to arise and old ones to increase in size and population. As peasants became free, they moved to urban areas and worked as wage laborers. Not only did cities attract former serfs, they also attracted educated people who wanted to enjoy the company of others and take advantage of learning and entertainment opportunities that urban areas offered. The migration to urban centers caused problems. As more people arrived in cities, overcrowding became commonplace, leading to increased unemployment and the spread of diseases, which caused some urban residents to desire to leave the cities. Many such people later moved to European colonies in North and South America to escape chronic unemployment and unhealthy living conditions.

The Rise of Nation States

Western Europe also experienced an important political transformation during the two centuries before the invasion of the Americas in the form of the creation of modern nation states. These countries arose largely because capitalism could not function smoothly in feudal lands. The powerful manor lords who controlled the land made it difficult for merchants to move their products easily. Most required merchants to pay extravagant fees to cross their lands, an act that cut into already thin profits. At the same time, nobles refused to pay taxes to monarchs. Able to use peasants as soldiers, nobles often had stronger armies than kings, which meant that rulers could not always enforce their laws or collect taxes. To combat this situation, some merchants and monarchs joined forces. Merchants provided capital that kings used to form larger and stronger armies than any forces that noblemen could raise. In return, merchants wanted protection, stability, and an end to feudalism. Merchants and burghers (town residents) were opposed to the feudal system because it created disorder and chaos that interfered with trade. Capitalistic merchants preferred a centralized government that could protect them and ensure the safety of goods being transported over long distances.

Kings also preferred centralized government. By using merchant capital, monarchs could free themselves from reliance on priests and bishops to carry out administrative tasks and hire professional clerks who were more loyal to the king than the church. Centralized government also enabled kings to impose and collect national taxes, which fattened the coffers of monarchs, enabling them to sponsor national projects such as overseas exploration. By 1500, the modern nation state, complete with its powerful armies and navies and the ability to mobilize vast resources to undertake large projects to promote national interests, had replaced the inefficient feudal system throughout Western Europe.

The most important nation state formed in Western Europe was Spain. In 1469, the marriage of Ferdinand of Aragon to Isabella of Castile began the process of nationalism on the Iberian Peninsula. Ferdinand and Isabella had sufficient capital to equip an army powerful enough to subdue defiant nobles. After bringing the feudal lords under their control, these strong monarchs crushed the power of the Moors, a Muslim people from North Africa who had occupied much of the peninsula for centuries. At the same time, Isabella and Ferdinand, in conjunction with the Roman Catholic Church, began the infamous Spanish Inquisition, using torture against individuals with questionable Catholic loyalties. By 1500, they succeeded in tying the allegiance of the Spanish citizenry to the monarchs rather than feudal estate owners. All residents of Spain were required to exhibit loyalty to the nation and serve the Crown.

Other European nations underwent nationalistic movements. During the 1380s, John I consolidated power in a divided Portugal (a Catholic kingdom located on the western coast of the Iberian Peninsula). National unification helped to fuel Portuguese exploration. King John had sufficient resources afterwards to support efforts by his son, **Prince Henry the Navigator**, to explore parts of the world unknown to Europeans. Prince Henry established an academy at Sagres, Portugal, to train ship captains in the art of exploration. Financed by King John's money, Prince Henry outfitted ships and sent them on exploratory missions. Information from these voyages was used to draw more accurate maps, compose manuals on sailing tactics and navigational techniques, and design ships better suited for transoceanic voyages. Initially, Prince Henry was concerned with learning more about the world and spreading Christianity. As exploration led to trade opportunities with other nations, Prince Henry and Portugal became less concerned with gaining knowledge and proselytizing, and more concerned with profit.

England and France were also changed by nationalism. Louis XI successfully subdued French nobles in the 1460s after ending the Hundred Years War with England. Henry VII (Henry Tudor) united England in 1485 after two powerful manorial families, the Yorks and Lancasters, destroyed themselves in the War of the Roses from 1455 to 1485. Henry VII greatly diminished the power of the English nobility, helping to turn England into a modern nation while also preparing his country for overseas expansion.

The formation of nation states was critical to the beginning of European exploration. Without a centralized government with the power to raise tremendous sums of money through taxation, Christopher Columbus and other early mariners could not have secured sufficient financial backing to undertake long, expensive voyages across the ocean.

The Renaissance: New Thought and Technologies

Contact between Europeans, Asians, and the Middle East sparked a revolution in thought, the flowering of knowledge known as the **Renaissance**, which led to important new technological developments in overseas navigation and exploration. While scholars disagree about the exact dates that the Renaissance took place, the period encompassed parts of the fourteenth through seventeenth centuries and began in the Italian cities of Venice, Genoa, and Pisa as a result of the spice trade. Contact with Muslim civilizations gave Europeans access to ancient writings from the Egyptians, Greeks, Romans, and Arabs found in libraries at Alexandria, Egypt, and Baghdad, Iraq, which had not been read in Europe for several centuries. The rediscovery of these documents sparked an interest in classical antiquity that eventually spread via trade routes throughout Western Europe. Literature, philosophy, science, mathematics, and art were just some of the more important aspects of life affected by this revival of learning.

Generally speaking, the Renaissance was a celebration of human accomplishment and potential, which can be illustrated in many facets. Artists, for example, used light and shadow techniques to focus on the human body, producing paintings and sculptures showing humans as heroes rather than as the degraded beings common in medieval works. Changes in architecture also reflected the change in thought. Medieval buildings of the Gothic style were gradually replaced with architectural styles heavily influenced by the ancient Greeks and Romans.

The new artistic and architectural styles were part of a broader movement within the Renaissance known as humanism that revolted against religious orthodoxy. While art, literature, and architectural styles during the Middle Ages focused on religion, depictions of Heaven, and the afterlife, Renaissance art, literary works, and architecture emphasized human life on Earth. Through its inherent arousing of curiosity, this new outlook on life helped to stimulate overseas exploration.

The development of the printing press helped to spread Renaissance ideas from Italy to other European nations. In ancient and medieval times, books were extremely rare and expensive because each page had to be laboriously copied by hand. Given the high cost of books, it is not surprising that a high degree of illiteracy existed in Europe. With the exception of Catholic priests, church officials, and nobles, most Europeans could neither read nor write. Trade with Asia and the Middle East had, however, created a need for literacy within the merchant class due to the need to keep accurate records of business transactions. Though the high cost of producing the written word prevented the rapid spread of literacy and knowledge, this situation was about to change. Since at least the seventh century, the Chinese used a means of printing an entire page of paper or cloth using a carved block of wood. By 1050, Chinese craftsmen had developed a basic moveable type system. Four hundred years later, the German smith **Johannes Gutenberg** independently devised a printing press using moveable type. Pages could now be mechanically printed from individual letter blocks that could be set to form words and sentences then reused. Printing was to change the world forever.

Printing houses opened everywhere. A new profession had been created; by 1500, about 1200 printers were operating throughout Western Europe. These early printers published about 35,000 different books, issuing a total of eight million copies on subjects including science, history, philosophy, religion, exploration, trade, and travel. Some of the books sparked an interest by Europeans in overseas exploration. The most important was Marco Polo's *Travels*. First published in 1477, this work, which detailed a Venetian merchant's travels in China during the thirteenth century, was widely read by educated Europeans. Polo stimulated interest in oceanic travel by stating that an ocean bounded China on the east,

Engraving of Johannes Gutenberg taking the first proof from his printing press.

convincing many traders that there might be a way to circumvent Arabs who controlled the Silk Road to China and thus European access to Asian products. If Polo was correct about an ocean lying east of China, then it should be possible to navigate directly to Asia by ship. The only problem was that the ocean was largely unexplored.

Before significant oceanic exploration could occur, improvements in navigation and technology had to take place. Prior to the Renaissance, navigational methods were primitive. Viking sailors, the best mariners that Europe had produced by 1000, simply calculated their position on the ocean by viewing the sun with the naked eye. They could only guess at the speed their ships traveled and the distance covered. However, all this had changed by the time Columbus made his first voyage in 1492.

By the late 1400s, European sailors had begun to use a myriad of mechanical devices to help with navigation on the open seas. The most important navigational device proved to be the **compass**. First invented by the Chinese, the compass was a simple tool that consisted of a magnetic needle fastened to a piece of wood marked with directions. Since the needle always pointed toward the earth's magnetic North Pole, navigators could always determine the direction their ship was traveling.

In addition to being able to mechanically determine direction of travel, ship captains could also fix their precise location on the ocean's surface by using the astrolabe, quadrant, and sextant. All three instruments enabled navigators to measure the altitude and position of stars in relation to the earth's surface and thus precisely locate a ship's location on a map. Used in conjunction with the compass, ship captains could correctly and accurately record direction, distance, location, and speed.

Not only were improvements in navigation made, but Europeans also benefited from better ships. The medieval ship was a relatively small vessel with one sail, high sides, wide bodies, and a steering rudder on its side. The sail was useful only if the wind blew from behind the ship, because it could not be rotated. For locomotion, these ships often relied upon slaves to man oars. Over time, modifications in ship design occurred. Important changes included more, larger, and adjustable sails. By using a sailing technique called "tacking" along with the lateen sail, an ancient form of rigging whose effective use by the Arabs led to its wider dissemination across the Mediterranean Sea, ships could position various sails to travel into the wind. No longer did ships have to travel in the same direction that the wind blew—now they could even move against it. In addition to improved sail technology, European ships in the fifteenth and sixteenth centuries became longer, sleeker, faster, and more stable. Also, more advanced rudder designs made them more maneuverable. Such improvements were first manifest in Portuguese caravels and carracks during the 1400s and in Portuguese, Spanish, French, Dutch, and English galleons in the 1500s and 1600s. These ships, and the navigational devices incorporated into them, made possible European exploration of North and South America. Without this technology, Europeans would have been stuck on their side of the Atlantic, lacking the equipment, knowledge, and confidence to make long voyages across the ocean.

EUROPEAN EXPLORATION AND EXPANSION

The Viking Explorations

Contrary to popular belief, Christopher Columbus and his crew were not the first Europeans to reach the Western Hemisphere. About 1000, Scandinavian sailors explored portions of eastern Canada. These Norse adventurers, often called **Vikings**, were Europe's foremost seafarers. In 984 a group of Vikings led by Erik the Red sailed westward across the Atlantic from Iceland to a large island. Erik the Red, who had been banished from Norway after committing murder, called the island he reached Greenland, in an attempt to attract settlers to his colony. Greenland was not an appropriate name for this island because it is ice bound for much of the year due to its location in the far northern latitudes. Several years later, Erik the Red's son, Leif Ericson, led an expedition of Norsemen from Greenland to present-day Newfoundland and Labrador.

Ericson had apparently heard about lands that lay west of Greenland from Bjarni Herjolfsson, captain of a Viking ship blown off course en route to Greenland from Iceland. According to Herjolfsson, he sighted land but did not stop on it. Instead, he rushed back to Greenland. Excited by the story, Ericson purchased Herjolfsson's ship and, with a crew of thirty-five, sailed westward in 1001. The first landing was at a site Ericson named Helluland or Flat Rock Land. Modern scholars believe the site to be Baffin Island in Canada. Sailing south, the Vikings then reached the eastern coast of Canada, which they called Markland or Woodland. From there, Ericson sailed southeast for two days, most likely reaching Newfoundland. Since Newfoundland had an abundance of wild grapes, the Vikings called the land Vinland.

Ericson and his Norse mariners established short-lived colonies in Vinland before returning to Greenland. The job of colonizing the land that Ericson reached fell to his younger brother, Thorvald. However, things did not go well. The first contact with Native Americans resulted in bloodshed after the Vikings captured and enslaved several local Indians. One slave escaped and later returned with an armed war party. A battle ensued, and Thorvald was killed when an arrow pierced his heart. He became the first known European to be buried in North American soil. After the battle, the Vikings abandoned their settlement and returned to Greenland.

Norse colonies did not thrive because there was no strong expansionist nation-state supporting them, poor communications with their homeland, political problems in Norway, and hostile encounters with Native Americans.

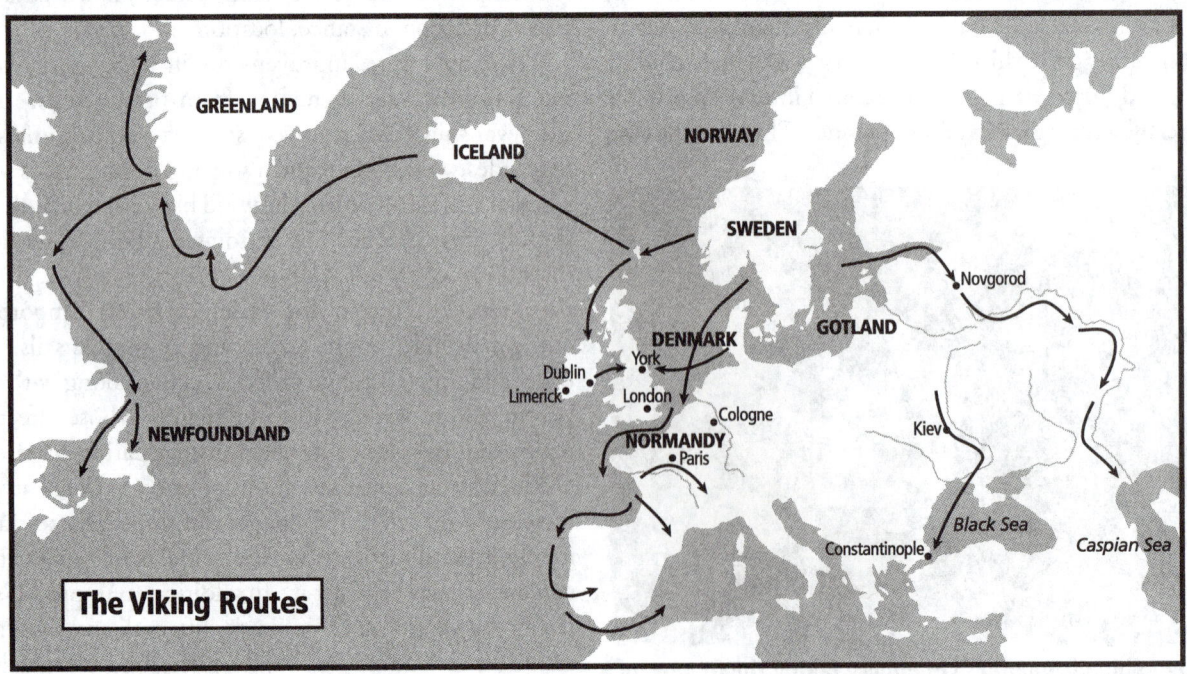

Map 1.3 The Viking Exploration Routes

In fact, the Viking explorations were largely forgotten after their North American settlements were abandoned. If not for oral history, saga, and song, record of these accomplishments likely would have been lost.

During the twentieth century, archaeologists unearthed additional evidence of the Norse presence in North America, discovering the ruins of a Viking settlement in 1960 at L'Anse aux Meadows in Newfoundland. At the site, scientists uncovered eight Norse sod houses along with jewelry, tools, slag iron, and coal.

Portuguese Explorations

The modern age of European exploration began with Portuguese efforts during the late fifteenth century originating with the aforementioned Prince Henry the Navigator's quest to learn more about the world, establish trade relations with distant peoples, and spread Christianity. In pursuit of the latter, Henry wished to make contact with the fabled nation of Prester John, a Catholic priest who according to legend governed a Christian state somewhere in Africa or Asia. A devout Catholic, Prince Henry wanted to contact Prester John in hopes of forming a Christian alliance that would encircle Muslim nations. To achieve all these objectives, Prince Henry undertook major explorations along Africa's western coast. Although he personally did not sail on any of these voyages, his financial assets were critical to their success. Portuguese explorers, who may or may not have believed in the existence of Prester John, soon realized there were vast profits to be made in Africa. Paid handsomely by their royal benefactor, Portuguese captains pushed farther south and west, discovering the island of Madeira to the southwest of Portugal in 1420 and the Azores archipelago to the west of Portugal in 1427, leading to the establishment of colonies in both locations. On a voyage in 1445, Dinis Dias sailed around Cape Verde and passed beyond the Sahara Desert. Ten years later, Alvise da Cadamosto sailed up the mouth of the Senegal and Gambia Rivers and discovered the Cape Verde Islands.

After Prince Henry died in 1460, his exploration program continued under various Portuguese monarchs. The new goal became to find the southern tip of Africa, sail around it, and reach India, China, and Japan. Consequently, merchants began to invest heavily in Portuguese exploration, willing to risk large sums on these exploratory voyages upon the promise of trade monopolies granted by the government. If Portugal could discover a water route to Asia, it could control the spice trade, which had been dominated by Italian and Arab traders for centuries. By bypassing Italian and Muslim middlemen, Portugal could reduce the cost of importing silk, spices, perfumes, and other Asian luxuries. Not only would this make Portuguese merchants rich, it would make Portugal one of the strongest nations in Europe.

In 1488 Portugal achieved its goal of sailing around Africa. **Bartolomé Dias** rounded the Cape of Good Hope at the southern tip of Africa and saw the Indian Ocean for the first time. Dias had to turn back before reaching Asia because his sailors were afraid to go farther, but ten years later Vasco da Gama found Portugal's ocean route to Asia. Setting sail in 1497 and intending to go beyond the Cape of Good Hope, he arrived in India the next year. Subsequent expeditions soon began sailing into the ports of China. Portugal had finally achieved its goal of controlling the spice trade and began to build a commercial empire in Africa and Asia by establishing trading posts at São Tomé, the Cape Verde Islands, Ceylon, and Malabar, India. In 1509, the Portuguese solidified control over their Indian Ocean trade route with a decisive naval victory over a Muslim fleet at Diu off the coast of western India. This triumph ensured that Portugal would be the dominant European power in Asia during the sixteenth century. By 1550, Portugal had a world monopoly on the spice trade with an empire stretching from the Persian Gulf to the Pacific Ocean. The Portuguese sent Catholic missionaries to convert native peoples to Christianity. In Africa, converted natives sometimes married Portuguese traders. The ethnically mixed society they formed became important in securing captives for the Atlantic slave trade begun by Portugal.

After discovering an oceanic route to Asia, Portugal largely lost interest in further western explorations across the Atlantic. However, in 1500, a storm blew the ships of Pedro Álvares Cabral so far off course that he reached the coast of Brazil, which eventually became a Portuguese colony. With the exception of Brazil, Portugal established few colonies in the Western Hemisphere. Exploration and colonization of North and South America was largely left to other European countries.

Spain's Empire in the Americas

Spain eventually emerged as the most important nation involved in the exploration and colonization of the Western Hemisphere. Jealous of Portugal's success and fearful of its power, Spanish monarchs wished to challenge Portuguese mastery of the seas. Like Portugal, Spain sought an ocean route to the riches of Asia but first had to win back its territory on the Iberian Peninsula from the Moors, a feat finally accomplished in 1492 when the forces of the Spanish monarchs Ferdinand and Isabella conquered the southern province of Granada. With the defeat of the Moors, Spain could focus on challenging Portugal.

Christopher Columbus, an experienced Italian sea captain from Genoa, eventually persuaded Ferdinand and Isabella in 1492 that a second ocean trade route to Asia could be discovered. Sixteen years earlier, Columbus had been shipwrecked near Prince Henry the Navigator's school at Sagres. After being rescued, he lived with his brother who labored as a mapmaker in Lisbon. Columbus later married and lived in the Portuguese colony of Madeira where he worked as a sailor. During this time, his study of inaccurate maps, belief in others' miscalculations, and acceptance of the plausibility of certain popular folk tales convinced him that a new route could be found by sailing only a few thousand miles westward across the Atlantic. Contrary to popular belief, Columbus was not the only European who believed the Earth was round. In fact, most educated Europeans accepted the ancient Greek idea that the world was oval. After all, Aristotle had proven it mathematically. In actuality, Columbus based his theory on false premises and convinced himself that the Earth was far smaller than its actual size, and thus the Asian continent was much closer to the west of Europe than previously believed. These misconceptions convinced Columbus that the Atlantic Ocean was small enough to cross after a short voyage, never suspecting that the Western Hemisphere lay between Europe and Asia.

At first, Columbus tried to convince Portugal to finance his voyage in search of a westward route to the riches of Asia. When the mariner presented his ideas to Portuguese government officials in 1484, they politely listened but turned him down because their primary interest lay in finding a southern route around Africa. Columbus then tried to arouse other European monarchs, but all rejected his ideas because royal geographic advisors determined, correctly as it turned out, that Columbus had miscalculated the distance to Asia.

Columbus's last hope of achieving royal backing for his scheme lay with Ferdinand and Isabella. At first, the Spanish monarchs were no more interested in his ideas than other European rulers. However, fear of Portugal's increasing power, coupled with Columbus's promises of gold, glory, and colonies, caused the Spanish rulers to change their minds and take a chance on this Italian sailor. Provided with three ships, the *Niña, Pinta,* and *Santa Maria,* Columbus set sail for China in August 1492. After stopping for repairs and supplies in the Canary Islands, he sailed across the Atlantic for just over a month before spotting a small, flat island in the Bahamas, either Samana Cay or San Salvador Island. Erroneously believing that he had found the East Indies near the Asian mainland, Columbus began to call the native peoples that he en-

Replica of the *Pinta,* one of Columbus's caravels.

countered *indios* (the Spanish term for Indian). He then explored the islands of Cuba and Hispaniola (modern-day Haiti and the Dominican Republic). After capturing several Native Americans to prove that he had reached Asia, Columbus returned triumphantly to Spain. There he was knighted, made governor of the Indies, and given the title "Admiral of the Ocean Sea." For a while, Ferdinand and Isabella believed that Spain now possessed a short route to the wealth of Asia. To resolve potential disputes over the newly discovered lands, Spain and Portugal negotiated the Treaty of Tordesillas in 1494, creating a longitudinal demarcation line 370 leagues (approximately 1,100 miles) west of the Cape Verde Islands with Spain being granted all the lands to the west of the boundary (and thus, most of the Americas) while giving Portugal all the lands in the eastern zone (thus securing exclusive rights to the eastern water route to Asia).

Columbus's first voyage did not produce the wealth that he had promised Ferdinand and Isabella because the mariner found no large hordes of gold, silver, spices, or gems. He did report that natives on Hispaniola wore gold earrings leading him to order the construction of a fort to be manned by a small contingent of men with instructions to find the source. In fact, the small amounts of jewelry that Native Americans wore infected Columbus and his sailors with gold fever. Afterwards, the Spanish spent most of their time and energy searching for the precious metal.

In 1493, Ferdinand and Isabella provided Columbus with seventeen ships and 1,500 men to begin colonization of the islands that he had discovered. Their primary orders were to locate the sources of the gold that the natives used to fashion their jewelry. When this expedition reached Hispaniola, Columbus discovered that the fort erected during his first voyage had been destroyed and his men killed by the Taíno who were unwilling to tolerate Spanish brutality in their pursuit of gold, as well as being disgusted by the Spanish pursuit of Taíno women. Columbus responded by destroying villages, demanding gold as tribute, and beginning the practice of enslaving natives.

Columbus made two additional voyages to the Americas in 1498 and 1502, respectively, exploring numerous Caribbean islands and portions of the coastal mainland. On his third trek, Columbus reached the northern coast of Venezuela in South America. After this voyage, however, Ferdinand and Isabella ordered him arrested and shipped back to Spain in chains for brutality and mismanagement of the colonies while serving as governor. After being cleared of wrongdoing (though never reinstated as governor), Columbus received funding for one final expedition, which reached the eastern coast of Central America, briefly exploring modern-day Honduras, Nicaragua, Costa Rica, and Panama.

Even before Columbus died in 1506, some Europeans realized what he had accomplished: that he had not reached Asia but an entirely "new world" previously unknown to the Europeans. Among those understanding the magnitude of Columbus's find was Amerigo Vespucci, an Italian mariner who joined a 1499 Portuguese expedition that explored the eastern coast of South America. In 1500, he published a series of vivid and largely fictional descriptions of the areas that he visited. Vespucci was the first European to describe the lands that Columbus reached as a *mundus novus*, or "new world." In 1507, a geographer named Martin Waldseemuller published a map depicting lands west of Europe as a separate continent, which he labeled America in honor of Vespucci. Perhaps not having the lands he discovered named after him was the ultimate insult to Columbus. This aside, Columbus paved the way for later exploration that gave Spain control of much of the Western Hemisphere.

Largely as a result of Columbus's journeys, Spain replaced Portugal as Europe's most dominant nation. One century before the English founded their first permanent colony at Jamestown, Spain already possessed a New World empire. In 1521-22, **Ferdinand Magellan**, a Portuguese navigator sailing for Spain, accomplished what Columbus failed to do—find an Atlantic Ocean route to Asia. Magellan sailed around a passage at the tip of South America into the Pacific Ocean, later named the Straits of Magellan in his honor. Magellan eventually reached the Philippine Islands where he died during a fight with

Christopher Columbus

"Thursday October 11"

The course was W.S.W. [west-southwest], and there was more sea than there had been during the whole of the voyage. They saw sand-pipers, and a green reed near the ship. Those of the caravel Pinta saw a cane and a pole, and they took up another small pole which appeared to have been worked with iron; also another bit of cane, a land-plant, and a small board. The crew of the caravel Niña also saw signs of land, and a small branch covered with berries. Everyone breathed afresh and rejoiced at these signs. The run until sunset was 27 leagues.

After sunset the Admiral returned to his original west course, and they went along at the rate of 12 miles an hour. Up to two hours after midnight they had gone 90 miles, equal to 22 1/2 leagues. As the caravel Pinta was a better sailer, and went ahead of the Admiral, she found the land, and made the signals ordered by the Admiral. The land was first seen by a sailor named Rodrigo de Triana. But the Admiral, at ten o'clock, being on the castle of the poop, saw a light, though it was so uncertain that he could not affirm it was land. He called Pedro Gutierrez, a gentleman of the King's bedchamber, and said that there seemed to be a light, and that he should look at it. He did so, and saw it. The Admiral said the same to Rodrigo Sanchez of Segovia, whom the King and Queen had sent with the fleet as inspector, but he could see nothing, because he was not in a place whence anything could be seen.

After the Admiral had spoken he saw the light once or twice, and it was like a wax candle rising and failing. It seemed to few to be an indication of land; but the Admiral made certain that land was close. When they said the **Salve** *(Salve Regina, a Catholic hymn), which all the sailors were accustomed to sing in their way, the Admiral asked and admonished the men to keep a good lookout on the forecastle, and to watch well for land; and to him who should first cry out that he saw land, he would give a silk doublet, besides the other rewards promised by the Sovereigns, which were 10,000 maravedis to him who should first saw it. At two hours after midnight the land was sighted at a distance of two leagues.*

Source: "Christopher Columbus Discovers America, 1492," Columbus's journal appears in Olson, Julius, *The Northmen, Columbus and Cabot, 985-1503* (1926). EyeWitness to History, www.eyewitnesstohistory.com (2004).

Amerigo Vespucci

Other Spanish explorers became part of a group called the *conquistadores*, or conquerors, who began the process whereby Native American peoples and their societies were systematically destroyed over the next four centuries. Before 1510, *conquistadores* generally operated in the Caribbean, where they sought out Native Americans in their attempts to find gold, silver, and spices. To deceive the intruders, many Native Americans often lured the Spanish away by enticing them with stories about enormous cities filled with gold somewhere else in the Americas. After 1510, the *conquistadores* moved onto the mainland of North and South America. In 1513, the Spanish explorer Vasco Nuñez de Balboa led an expedition across the Isthmus of Panama, becoming the first Europeans to see the Pacific Ocean. During that same year, Juan Ponce de León, the governor of Puerto Rico, claimed Florida for Spain as an expedition he led trekked across portions of the peninsula, fighting Native Americans along the way, during a fruitless search for a Fountain of Youth that Taínos on Puerto Rico described to him.

Hernán Cortés, a government official in Cuba, became the most famous *conquistador* after leading six hundred men into Mexico upon hearing Native American stories about gold, silver, and precious gems located there. In 1519, Cortés landed in eastern Mexico, soon finding the great civilization established by the Aztecs. Though greatly outnumbered by Aztec warriors, the Spanish soldiers had gunpowder, muskets, and horses to give them a tactical military advantage. Especially terrifying to Aztecs were soldiers mounted on horses, which they believed were four-legged monsters. Native American

natives. One of his ships sailed around the tip of Africa and returned to Spain, thus completing the first voyage to circumnavigate the globe.

groups subservient to the Aztecs also helped Cortés in his plans of conquest. Further benefiting the Spanish invaders was an Aztec prophecy predicting that, about the time the *conquistador* appeared, a powerful god arriving on a great white bird would destroy their world. The Aztecs and their emperor Moctezuma II mistook Cortés for the revered deity Quetzalcoatl, who they thought had returned to destroy them. The Spaniards' ships were believed to be the white birds foretold in the divine prediction. Moctezuma responded by trying to bribe Cortés with vast amounts of gold and silver, hoping that the great god would not destroy Tenochtitlán. The sight of vast amounts of gold and silver, however, only whetted the Spanish appetite for more wealth. Rather than withdrawing from the Aztec capital, Cortés attacked and captured Moctezuma, holding him for ransom. In 1520, the Aztecs drove Cortés out of their city, with Moctezuma dying in the process. The Spanish returned the next year, however, and recaptured Tenochtitlán with the help of other Native Americans and the onset of smallpox among the Aztecs, which had been brought earlier inadvertently by the Spanish. Soon, the Aztec empire lay in ruins.

Cortés's success in finding riches led other *conquistadores* to search for new sources of gold, with **Francisco Pizarro** proving to be the most ruthless. In 1531, Pizarro commanded an expedition following rumored cities of gold in the Andes Mountains. After a year of searching, Pizarro found the mountain homeland of the Incas. After

Francisco Pizarro

a forty-five day climb up the high Andes, Pizarro and his force of 168 men reached Peru, encountering the Incas led by Atahualpa. Like the Aztecs, the Incas regarded the Spanish as vengeful gods and thus feared that their empire would be destroyed. Through emissaries, Pizarro told Atahualpa that the Spanish meant the Incas no harm—that they were simply exploring, and intended to remain among the Incas only a few days. Believing what Pizarro said, Atahualpa allowed the *conquistador* to enter the Inca capital of Cuzco. After being welcomed, Pizarro turned on his Inca benefactors, killing more than five thousand Inca warriors and capturing Atahualpa. To gain his freedom, the emperor offered Pizarro a room full of gold and silver. Pizarro agreed to set Atahualpa free once the precious metals were transferred to him, but he lied. Once he had the treasure safely in hand, Pizarro tied Atahualpa to a stake and executed him by strangulation. With the help of traitors in the Inca royal family, Pizarro completely conquered the Inca Empire, destroying a great civilization. All Inca resistance crumbled when the Spanish survived a siege at Cuzco in 1533. After acquiring Inca lands, the Spanish Empire stretched along the entire length of the western coast of South America.

The last great Native American civilization destroyed by the Spanish was the Maya of the Yucatan Peninsula. Spain could not conquer the Maya as quickly as the Aztecs and Incas because the Maya had a loose confederation

Lithograph depicting Moctezuma's reception of Hernán Cortés.

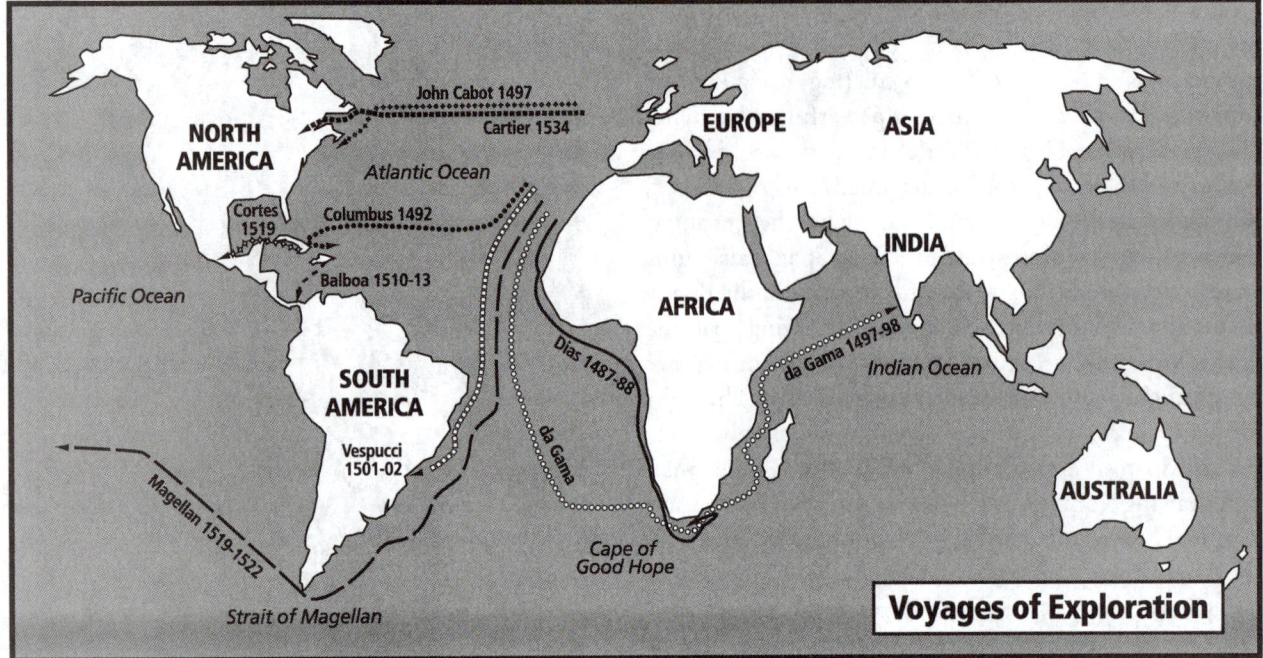

Map 1.4 Voyages of Exploration

of city-states rather than a centralized seat of authority. Beginning in 1527, Spanish forces fought for twenty years before finally defeating the Maya and securing dominance over the region.

After establishing dominance over much of Central and South America, Spanish rulers began to devise a system to keep order, enforce its laws, and prevent other nations from encroaching on its vast territorial holdings. Spain established two agencies in Madrid to control its American colonies. The House of Trade was placed in charge of economic policy, while the Council for the Indies handled governmental administrative duties. To help supervise the empire, the Council of the Indies created four territorial regions called viceroyalties, governed by viceroys who consulted with a council of appointed officials called *audiencias*. Democracy did not exist in the viceroyalties—only full-blooded Spaniards could serve as government officials, and they were appointed rather than elected by ordinary citizens.

The Spanish who came to the Americas faced a tremendous labor shortage. To overcome this deficit, Spain devised the **encomienda system**, whereby the Spanish government rewarded *conquistadores* by giving them title to vast tracts of land, including Native American villages and the territories surrounding them. As part of the system, the *encomendero*, or landlord, was required to civilize, Christianize, and educate Native Americans living on his land. In return, the landowner was allowed to enslave the natives. Thousands of Native Americans had their freedom taken away and were greatly abused by the Spanish who could buy and sell them like livestock.

Execution awaited anyone who resisted. Despite the death penalty, Native Americans occasionally revolted against their enslavement. The Carib people, for example, defended their islands from Spanish invasion until the end of the sixteenth century. In Mexico, the Chichimec people also resisted enslavement for over a hundred years.

A former *conquistador* who rejected his previous ways to become a Dominican friar, Bartolomé de Las Casas gained notoriety for his impassioned protests against Spanish rule in the New World. In a book entitled *The Destruction of the Indies,* Las Casas indicted the Spanish for their brutal conquests and subsequent enslavement of the Native Americans, demanding that all people should be treated humanely. Published in 1522, his work was subsequently translated into several languages, earning him a place among the great humanitarian leaders.

In 1542, the Spanish government finally outlawed the *encomienda* system. Despite the government's best intentions, things changed little for Native Americans. Government officials simply replaced the *encomienda* system with the *hacienda* system. Spanish settlers were still given large land grants called *haciendas,* with enslavement replaced by debt peonage. Henceforth, natives had to borrow money from Spanish landlords and were forced to produce crops given to the *hacienda* master to help discharge the debt, which usually grew larger with each passing year. For Native Americans, this system was often little better than slavery.

Because Native American mortality rates were high, the Spanish could not meet their labor needs entirely from the native population. Spain began to import Afri-

---

Bartolomé de Las Casas, Brief Account of the Devastation of the Indies (1542)

The Indies were discovered in the year one thousand four hundred and ninety-two. In the following year a great many Spaniards went there with the intention of settling the land. Thus, forty-nine years have passed since the first settlers penetrated the land, the first so claimed being the large and most happy isle called Hispaniola, which is six hundred leagues in circumference. Around it in all directions are many other islands, some very big, others very small, and all of them were, as we saw with our own eyes, densely populated with native peoples called Indians. This large island was perhaps the most densely populated place in the world. There must be close to two hundred leagues of land on this island, and the seacoast has been explored for more than ten thousand leagues, and each day more of it is being explored. And all the land so far discovered is a beehive of people; it is as though God had crowded into these lands the great majority of mankind. And of all the infinite universe of humanity, these people are the most guileless, the most devoid of wickedness and duplicity, the most obedient and faithful to their native masters and to the Spanish Christians whom they serve. They are by nature the most humble, patient, and peaceable, holding no grudges, free from embroilments, neither excitable nor quarrelsome. These people are the most devoid of rancors, hatreds, or desire for vengeance of any people in the world. And because they are so weak and complaisant, they are less able to endure heavy labor and soon die of no matter what malady. The sons of nobles among us, brought up in the enjoyments of life's refinements, are no more delicate than are these Indians, even those among them who are of the lowest rank of laborers. They are also poor people, for they not only possess little but have no desire to possess worldly goods. For this reason they are not arrogant, embittered, or greedy. Their repasts are such that the food of the holy fathers in the desert can scarcely be more parsimonious, scanty, and poor. As to their dress, they are generally naked, with only their pudenda covered somewhat. And when they cover their shoulders it is with a square cloth no more than two yards in size. They have no beds, but sleep on a kind of matting or else in a kind of suspended net called bamacas. They are very clean in their persons, with alert, intelligent minds, docile and open to doctrine, very apt to receive our holy Catholic faith, to be endowed with virtuous customs, and to behave in a godly fashion. And once they begin to hear the tidings of the Faith, they are so insistent on knowing more and on taking the sacraments of the Church and on observing the divine cult that, truly, the missionaries who are here need to be endowed by God with great patience in order to cope with such eagerness. Some of the secular Spaniards who have been here for many years say that the goodness of the Indians is undeniable and that if this gifted people could be brought to know the one true God they would be the most fortunate people in the world.

Yet into this sheepfold, into this land of meek outcasts there came some Spaniards who immediately behaved like ravening wild beasts, wolves, tigers, or lions that had been starved for many days. And Spaniards have behaved in no other way during the past forty years, down to the present time, for they are still acting like ravening beasts, killing, terrorizing, afflicting, torturing, and destroying the native peoples, doing all this with the strangest and most varied new methods of cruelty, never seen or heard of before, and to such a degree that this Island of Hispaniola once so populous (having a population that I estimated to be more than three million), has now a population of barely two hundred persons.

---

can slaves to its American colonies in 1501. Slavery was an evil and brutal institution in New Spain. *Hacienda* owners preferred young males who were often worked so hard they collapsed and died from exhaustion. Slaves did, however, have some protection. Spanish law and Catholic authority forbade brutality, at least in theory. Because the church wanted all souls to be saved, slave marriage was recognized as a sacrament. This meant that slaves could wed, raise families, and their marriages could not dissolve when one party was sold. Under Spanish law, slaves could buy their freedom. While the work was grueling, slaves in New Spain actually possessed more legal rights than those in the later English colonies located farther north.

The Spanish discriminated against slaves on the basis of skin pigmentation. Those in bondage with lighter-colored skin received better treatment than those with darker skin tones. In fact, Spain created a racial pyramid in its American colonies. At the top of society were pureblooded Spanish born in Spain called *peninsulares*, who had more rights and privileges in society than all other people. Next were the *creoles*, pure-blooded Spanish born in the New World. Beneath the *creoles* was a class called *mestizos*, which consisted of offspring produced by the sexual union of Spanish males and Native American females. Finally, there were the *mulattoes*, products of Spanish males and African females. The lower an individual's position on the racial pyramid, the less status and fewer privileges they retained in society.

The Spanish Empire used slave labor to ensure that wealth flowed to the mother country from the colonies, which existed primarily to benefit Spain. New World wealth made Spain the envy of all European nations and spawned rivalries. Other nations, England, France, and the Netherlands, were determined to plant colonies in the New World and gain riches from America for themselves.

The Impact of the Protestant Reformation

Beginning in the early 1500s, European history became forever altered by the **Protestant Reformation**. This religious upheaval shattered the previous unity of Europe provided under the auspices of the Roman Catholic Church, provoking major conflicts across much of the continent. Prior to the Reformation, the Roman Catholic Church reigned as the most powerful and dominant institution in Western Europe. All nations, their rulers as well as ordinary citizens, were Catholic. Those daring to challenge church orthodoxy risked imprisonment, torture, or death if they refused to publicly recant their heretical views.

Circumstances changed in 1517 when an obscure German monk, Martin Luther, openly challenged numerous teachings of the Catholic Church by nailing his "Ninety-five Theses" to a church door in Wittenberg. Luther's actions began a religious revolt against Catholicism that profoundly changed the Western world. Luther believed that the Catholic Church had become corrupt and proposed to cleanse the Church of its degeneracy by following Scripture and returning it to a pure form of worship as practiced by first-century Christians.

By the 1520s, another branch of Protestantism also appeared in France, where the Catholic Church persecuted those who observed the teachings of the dissenting theologian Jean Calvin (John Calvin). Fleeing France, Calvin settled in Geneva, Switzerland where he and his followers eventually gained control of the city. A lawyer by profession, he developed a strict set of theological principles for his followers published in his famous *Institutes of the Christian Religion* in 1536. From the 1560s to the late 1590s, France experienced forty years of religious strife between Huguenots (as Calvin's adherents who gained influence and displayed their faith openly came to be called) and supporters of the French government who had become one of the most ardent foes of Protestantism in Europe. A degree of peace returned in 1598 when the Edict of Nantes declared Catholicism to be the official state religion of France but also granted religious and political freedoms to the Protestants.

LUTHER SCHLÄGT DIE 90 SÄTZE AN.

Life of M...

Print depicting Martin Luther nailing his Ninety-five Theses to a church door in Wittenberg, Germany.

England, like France and Germany, underwent its own Reformation, but the Anglican reformation was more the result of politics than religious dissent. Henry VIII, the English king from 1509 to 1547, was a devout Catholic. Henry had published *Defense of the Seven Sacraments*, which attacked Luther's idea that Christians should only accept two sacraments. For this, the Pope had given Henry the title "Defender of the Faith." Henry, however, encountered a political problem that conflicted with his religious loyalties. He had no male heir to assume the throne when he died. Henry and his wife Catherine of Aragon (daughter of Isabella and Ferdinand) had six children, but only one, Mary, survived childhood. Henry needed a son to sustain the Tudor family dynasty. In 1527, he requested that Pope Clement VIII annul his marriage to Catherine. The Pope refused, leading Henry to renounce his Catholic faith and to sever all ties with the Roman church. Henry then created the Anglican Church, making it the official state religion of England.

The Protestant Reformation broke the power of the papacy in Europe. Spain, Ireland, France, and the Italian States resisted the Reformation, remaining Catholic, while England, Scotland, Switzerland, the Netherlands, the Scandinavian countries, and much of Germany became largely Protestant. The Reformation also caused much violence, with Protestants and Catholics slaughtering each other in the name of God. The Reformation also fostered a strong interest in colonization as both Catholics and Protestants established colonies in North America to escape religious persecution.

English Exploration

Five years after Columbus's initial voyage, England sent Giovanni Caboto (**John Cabot**), a Venetian sea captain, on a New World expedition via a northern Atlantic route. From 1497 to 1498, Cabot explored the Atlantic coastline of North America from Newfoundland to Chesapeake Bay. Like Columbus, he sought a westward oceanic route to Asia across the Atlantic—a "Northwest Passage." Cabot's 1497 voyage represented the first recorded transatlantic trek by an English ship, although some evidence indicates that English fishermen might have accidentally landed in Nova Scotia and Newfoundland in the 1480s. Regardless, the English based their territorial claims in the New World upon Cabot's voyages. After Cabot died on his second voyage to America in 1498, his son Sebastian continued England's explorations. In 1508 and 1509, he sailed across the Atlantic attempting to find the elusive Northwest Passage. Along the way, he explored the Hudson Bay area, claiming the region for England.

After the Cabots failed to find a Northwest Passage, England lost interest in the New World for the next seventy-five years as it contended with the internal strife caused by the Reformation and related foreign conflicts, especially with Spain whose rulers vowed to bring England back to Catholicism. When Henry VIII's daughter Elizabeth I assumed the throne, English overseas exploration witnessed a revival, with **Sir Humphrey Gilbert** proving to be a driving force. Originally, he wanted to continue the search for a Northwest Passage, publishing a book on the subject, which included speculations about where such a waterway might be located. Gilbert also promised readers, who might be potential investors in an expedition to find a northern route to Asia, that wealth awaited those smart enough to find a new trade route. In 1576, he convinced the Crown that it was in England's national interest to find a Northwest Passage. At this time, England was experiencing economic difficulties due to the Calvinist Dutch rebellion against Catholic Spain. The Spanish crushed this revolt, destroying the city of Antwerp and taking away England's primary marketplace for textiles on the European continent. Consequently, English merchants began to form joint-stock companies to develop trade with other parts of the world. These corporations allowed individuals to invest small amounts of capital to finance huge undertakings with little overall risk. Not only did the joint-stock companies undertake trade expeditions throughout the world, but they also

Sir Francis Drake

financed English privateers like **Francis Drake** and John Hawkins. On one particular voyage from 1577 to 1580, Drake sailed around the globe, attacking Spanish ports and ships wherever he found them. Upon his return to England (in which Drake returned a 4,600 percent profit for his investors, including the queen), Elizabeth knighted him for becoming the first Englishman to circumnavigate the Earth.

In addition to facing economic pressure, many among the English gentry sought exploration and settlement because of their concern for their younger sons who could not legally inherit their family estates. They often pressured Elizabeth I to claim land in the New World so their sons would have a place to build estates of their own. A growing population and limited economic opportunities among the poor also fueled a desire to explore and settle North America as an outlet for immigration.

Because of these pressures, Elizabeth was ready to challenge Spain's supremacy in the Americas. In 1576, at the behest of Gilbert, the Queen sent **Martin Frobisher** to seek a Northwest Passage. Sailing to the island of Labrador, Frobisher captured an Inuk (a member of the Inuit people who inhabit the northern part of modern-day Canada) and his kayak before returning to England with his captive and what he believed was a small sample of gold ore. After finding assayers to claim that the sample was gold, Elizabeth organized a joint-stock company to construct a fort and begin mining operations in Labrador. This company financed two expeditions by Frobisher in 1577 and 1578. During these trips, Frobisher captured three more Inuit and brought back two thousand tons of ore. The Inuit like the first one captured in 1576, died soon after arriving in England. Meanwhile, the ore from Labrador proved not to be gold after all, but only iron pyrite ("fools gold"). This mistake forever ruined Frobisher's reputation.

Distrusting Frobisher, Humphrey Gilbert had refused to invest in his expeditions. After Frobisher's fall from grace, Gilbert took advantage of the explorer's misfortune and persuaded Elizabeth to grant him a charter to explore, settle, and govern all territory in North America not occupied by Christian people. The English charter completely disregarded all claims that Native Americans had upon their land. For some time, Gilbert had tried to convince the queen that England should be more interested in land than gold. Although he probably harbored hopes that he might find another Peru or Mexico, Gilbert convinced Elizabeth that establishing colonies in North America would enable England to relieve population pressures, which had resulted in people crowding into English cities where many committed crimes out of desperation. Gilbert hoped to settle these people on land in North America.

What Gilbert envisioned was the resurrection of a form of feudalism in North America. His plans called for providing settlers with free land, farm tools, and a governmental framework consisting of a governor and thirteen advisors chosen by settlers. He saw himself and other gentry as manorial lords, ruling colonies of tenants who paid rent by giving the lord a portion of crops they produced.

Gilbert set sail in 1583, reaching Nova Scotia before aborting the expedition due to bad weather. On the return voyage, Gilbert's ship sank during a storm. His death prompted his stepbrother, Sir Walter Raleigh, to attempt to colonize the New World for England. Raleigh received permission from Elizabeth I to explore and establish a colony in North America, resulting in the ill-fated adventures at Roanoke Island (discussed in Chapter Two). England's next attempt at North American colonization at Jamestown in 1607 would prove to be more successful.

The French and Dutch Footholds in North America

The English had rivals for control of North America. Both France and the Netherlands explored and established colonies in the New World. French claims in North America were based on explorations by Giovanni da Verrazzano in 1524 and Jacques Cartier ten years later. Verrazzano sailed westward across the Atlantic under authority of Frances I, exploring the eastern coastline of North America from present-day South Carolina to New England, claiming the entire territory for France. Following in Verrazzano's wake, Cartier led three expeditions between 1534 and 1542 through the St. Lawrence River Valley, reaching sites of present-day Montreal and Quebec. Cartier established the first French colony in 1541, but the effort failed due to political upheaval in France. Not until 1608 did the French successfully established a settlement in Canada when Samuel de Champlain built a fort at Quebec on the St. Lawrence River.

Fort Quebec served primarily as a trading post. Unlike the Spanish and English who sought gold and land, the French desired to trade with Native Americans for valuable furs. Champlain realized that he could make a substantial profit from trade. Wealthy Europeans had an almost insatiable desire for furs, especially beaver pelts, used to make stylish hats and other clothing apparel. Likewise, Native Americans developed a great interest in European products, such as metal tools, firearms, and woolen blankets, which could provide security from rival tribes and improve their quality of life. Following Champlain's lead, French trappers and traders explored vast territories throughout eastern Canada, the Great Lakes region, the Ohio River Valley, parts of New England, and the Mississippi River, claiming the land for France. Because they were primarily interested in trade, the French generally established harmonious relations with Native Americans. Sometimes, French settlers fought alongside favored Native Americans in tribal wars in order to gain and maintain trading partners.

Dutch claims to North American territory were based upon the explorations of **Henry Hudson**, an English sea captain. In 1609, Hudson, in the employ of the Netherlands, was sent to search for a Northwest Passage. Along the way, he explored the Hudson River and Hudson Bay, which were later named in his honor. As the French, Hudson was interested in establishing a fur-trading network with Native Americans. To achieve this objective, the Dutch in 1624 established forts on Manhattan Island and at Albany, which they called New Amsterdam and Fort Orange, respectively. For a time, the two outposts prospered, with the Iroquois people supplying furs in return for Dutch trade goods, until England forcefully seized the colony in 1664.

THE COLUMBIAN EXCHANGE

Contact between Europeans and the New World produced what historian Alfred W. Crosby first labeled the **"Columbian Exchange"** to refer to the biological and environmental impact of Columbus's exploration of America. With the breakdown of the previous isolation of

Depiction of Jacques Cartier's first interview with the Indians of Hochelaga (now Montreal) in 1535.

the Eastern and Western Hemispheres caused by the vastness of the Atlantic and Pacific Oceans, a great exchange of plants, animals, and microorganisms began to take place impacting societies on both sides of the globe. While both Europeans and Native Americans realized advantages and disadvantages from the Columbian Exchange, Native Americans generally suffered more harm and Europeans reaped more benefits from this development.

One consequence of the Columbian Exchange that greatly harmed Native Americans was the arrival of deadly diseases. Because of their separation from Asia, Africa, and Europe when ocean levels rose following the end of the last Ice Age, Native Americans were not afflicted with diseases that existed in the Old World. Smallpox, measles, pneumonia, influenza, and malaria were unknown in the Americas. Without previous exposure, Native Americans had no antibody resistance to the microbes that caused these illnesses.

As Europeans inadvertently brought these diseases to the Amerindians, the results were devastating. Spanish contact with Native Americans triggered the largest population decline in recorded history. When Europeans arrived in the Western Hemisphere, about sixty million Native Americans were scattered throughout North and South America. After contact with foreign microbes, the native population declined by about 90 percent within the span of one century, a relatively short time taken within the wide expanse of human history. By 1600, only about six million Native Americans had survived the biological onslaught. On the island of Hispaniola, for example, there were about one million Taínos when Columbus arrived in 1492. Forty years later, only 14,000 remained alive. In Mexico, about twenty-five million Aztecs resided when Cortés landed. Within twenty years, 50 percent of the population had died of disease. After the passage of a century, only about one million Aztecs

existed. A similar fate befell the Incas of Peru. In all areas where Europeans contacted Native Americans, the same catastrophe occurred. Diseases played a major role in European powers being able to defeat, conquer, and destroy Native American civilizations. In fact, diseases were more important than firearms in the European conquest of the New World. After contact with Europeans, Native Americans spread disease inter-tribally. Economic and social contact among various Native American groups caused millions of people who had never seen a European to die of smallpox or some other disease in what Native Americans call "the great dying." By the time English settlers arrived at Jamestown, three epidemics had already swept through the Chesapeake region.

Epidemics completely devastated Native American societies. Because of the precipitous drop in population, political, governmental, social, religious, and economic institutions were upended. Native American religion and shamans were hit especially hard. Most religious systems in the Americas depended on priestly mysticism and ability to influence nature, including the ability to cure disease and heal wounds. These talents were called into question after European diseases began to ravage native peoples. Eventually, entire societies collapsed from lack of people to make institutions within native civilizations function.

Europeans also lacked immunity to infectious diseases present in the New World but suffered far less devastation than did Native Americans. Syphilis was perhaps the worst disease Europeans contracted from the intercontinental exchange. A few years after Columbus's four voyages, a virulent form of syphilis broke out in Europe, quickly spreading across the continent. Thousands of Europeans contacted this venereal disease, dying a slow death before doctors knew what caused it and how to prevent its spread. Recent scientific evidence has shown, contrary to what scientists previously believed, syphilis did indeed exist in the Old World before 1492. Corpses of individuals in Europe known to have died before Columbus's voyages have now been discovered. What is known, however, is that syphilis, not a common killer before 1492, soon thereafter became a noticeable illness that Europeans began to associate with the New World.

The movement of diseases became only part of the Columbian Exchange. The Old and New Worlds also experienced a transfer of plant and animal life. Since Europe was separated from the Americas by a great ocean, evolution created vastly different ecosystems. Large, domesticated mammals, such as cattle and horses, were present in Europe but unknown in North and South America. The largest beasts of burden found in the Western Hemisphere were dogs and llamas. When contact occurred between Europe and the Americas, Europeans introduced horses, mules, oxen, sheep, and cows. Horses had a particularly important impact on some Native American cultures. Native Americans acquired horses after Spanish *conquistadores* introduced them into the New World. Nomadic tribes of the Great Plains, including the Cheyenne, Apaches, Comanche, and Sioux, who hunted bison came to rely upon the horse as an essential tool to support their lifestyle. Not only did these tribes use equines for hunting, food, and transportation, but they also used them as a source of exchange. The nature of warfare among nomadic tribes was altered by use of horses. Rather than fighting on foot, these skilled equestrians engaged the enemy on horseback. Even women's work became easier after introduction of the horse. Females no longer had to carry the tribe's possessions strapped to their backs when villages were moved to better hunting territory; now, they loaded belongings on horses. Great Plains tribes also largely abandoned agriculture after acquiring horses. Prior to introduction of equines, these natives had hunted various animals, gathered food plants, and produced agricultural crops. This traditional mode of subsistence among plains tribes gave way to a lifestyle that was almost totally dependent on hunting buffalo.

Domesticated animals harmed Native Americans in other ways. In parts of the Americas, herds of sheep, cattle, and goats destroyed native agriculture. Usually, Native American farming practices were destroyed because livestock did much environmental damage. European ranchers and farmers often allowed large herds of animals to roam free across the landscape, resulting in overgrazing, which produced erosion and prevented Native Americans from farming this land. Other ranchers and farmers fenced in the land, placed "no trespassing" signs on it, and prevented native tribes from using the land for agriculture.

Not only was European livestock introduced into the Americas, there was an exchange of agricultural products. Vegetables that grew in North and South America, such as beans, corn, squash, and potatoes, were high in nutrition and produced greater yields than did traditional European crops such as wheat and rye. As a result, explorers carried American crops back to Europe with them. It became increasingly common for European farmers to grow crops native to the Americas. Maize, which was the staple crop for most Native American agricultural tribes, became an important food crop in Mediterranean countries, a feed crop for livestock in Western Europe, and the primary food source for slave ships crossing the Atlantic from Africa. Likewise, New World potatoes became a means of subsistence for peasant farmers in northern Europe, and tomatoes became one of the most important ingredients in Italian cuisine. New World crops enabled Europe to overcome the persistent problem of famine that had plagued the region before 1500. Largely as a result of the introduction of American agricultural crops, Europe's population doubled within the three centuries after Columbus's voyages. A downside existed, however, to the introduction of American agricultural crops in Europe. In some localities peasants became so dependent on New World crops that when these crops failed, starvation occurred. In Ireland during the middle decades of the nineteenth century, for example, the potato crop was wiped out by a devastating fungal blight. The subsequent food shortages led to a million deaths and an outward migration of a million more as the island experienced a 25 percent reduction in population.

One plant that Europeans encountered had a devastating effect on Old World people—tobacco. Native to the New World, tobacco had been cultivated and used by Native Americans for centuries before European arrival. At first, tobacco, called the "stinking weed" by James I of England, was believed to have medicinal effects. Smoking or chewing the plant became popular in Europe during the sixteenth and seventeenth centuries. Tobacco cultivation in Virginia and other southern colonies provided a living for many English settlers, making some of them rich. Only in the twentieth century did medical science discover the link between tobacco use and cancer, heart disease, and other ailments. Presently, tobacco use is responsible for countless deaths annually throughout the world and costs governments and individuals billions of dollars. Tobacco-related deaths since contact between Europe and the Americas have numbered in the millions. Most likely, the number of deaths from tobacco use among Europeans equals those of Native Americans from Old World microbes. King James I of England was correct in 1604 when he published an essay denouncing tobacco use as "loathsome to the eye, hatefull (sic) to the Nose, harmfull (sic) to the brain, dangerous to the Lungs."

European agricultural products also came to the New World. Rice, sugar, coffee, wheat, and rye are examples of crops exported from Europe to the Americas. The introduction of these crops to the Western Hemisphere created new industries. Sugar produced in the Americas became an important crop. Portugal first produced sugar in the lowlands of Brazil in the sixteenth century. By 1570 Brazil produced six million pounds of sugar annually; by 1635 the output totaled 32 million pounds. Sugar production impacted Native Americans negatively. England, Holland, France, Spain, and Portugal all produced sugar on various Caribbean islands. In most places, sugar plantation owners enslaved Native American workers. The few natives who escaped enslavement were scattered, their cultures and societies destroyed by the European sweet tooth.

The New World provided Europe with an influx of gold and silver, mostly plundered from Native Americans or mined by them under forced-labor conditions in Mexico and Peru. The amount of specie circulating in Europe tripled during the first half of the sixteenth century and then tripled again from 1550-1600. European economies faced runaway inflation because so much gold and silver was placed in circulation, causing business profits to increase while simultaneously lowering living standards for common people. The buying power of European workers was depressed by 50 percent due to rising prices during the 1500s. Artisans, laborers, and farmers, who comprised the vast majority of Europe's population, suffered deprivation when wages did not keep pace with inflation. A common complaint voiced by artisans was that despite their skills, the lifestyle they led was hardly better than that of a common beggar. Although European economies were wrecked by the inflation, some economic historians believe American gold and silver was the most important factor in the development of capitalism.

European attempts to export religion harmed Native Americans. Many Christian missionaries tried to force native people to abandon traditional religious beliefs and practices. When such efforts failed, Christian missionaries sometimes launched attacks on Native American religious institutions. Soldiers were sent to destroy American temples and religious artifacts contained within them. Diego de Landa, a Catholic bishop in the Yucatan, burned thousands of Mayan books because he wanted to stop what he viewed as idolatry. Consequently, modern scholars have limited knowledge about the Mayan civilization.

Not all aspects of the Columbian Exchange were intentional. Europeans inadvertently carried germs, seeds, plant spores, and pestilent animals when they came to the New World. The process also worked in reverse when Europeans returned home. The destruction of Native American crafts by the introduction of European manufactured products was also unintentional. European products replaced native products, and tribal craftspeople eventually lost the ability to make traditional items previously common in the Americas.

NEW CULTURES

The European exploration of America began a process in which numerous Native American cultures were almost completely destroyed by the time English American colonists declared their independence in 1776. Within a span of three centuries, Europeans destroyed what it took Native Americans thousands of years to construct. By the end of the sixteenth century, the population of the Americas was less than it had been when Columbus first made contact in 1492. Though the seemingly unlimited wealth of the Aztec and Inca empires amazed the Spanish, the invaders tore down native temples, using the stones to construct churches in which the Christian god was worshipped. Native Americans were enslaved along with Africans and employed to work the fields and mines Europeans established in the Western Hemisphere. It is doubtful that Columbus ever realized the changes his voyage across the Atlantic would set in motion. At the same time Native American cultures were being destroyed, European nations were establishing new societies on their ruins.

Though October 12 has been commemorated annually as "Columbus Day" in the United States, Spain, and numerous Latin American countries to celebrate the "discovery" of the Western Hemisphere, many have criticized the holiday as a chauvinistic tribute honoring a daring seafarer that totally disregards the immense upheaval experienced by the indigenous peoples of America due to the subsequent European expansion and domination. Further, far from being an unwitting tool of this onslaught, critics point out that Columbus was an active member of this vanguard, callously disregarding the Native Americans' well-being while taking part in their destruction as he ambitiously sought wealth and power. Nevertheless, even if one could remove all moral contexts surrounding the date, October 12, 1492, ranks as one of the monumental days in world history marking the beginning of a vast European territorial expansion that profoundly impacted the entire globe, most immediately affecting the Native Americans whose civilizations crumbled under the collective weight of European guns, germs, and steel.

Chronology

c.20,000 B.C.E. Migration across the Bering Strait begins.

c.1000 B.C.E. Adena culture begins in North America.

500-1400 Middle Ages in Europe.

600-900 Maya civilization reaches its zenith.

1001 Vikings reach North America.

1100-1400 Mississippian culture at its height in North America.

1325 Founding of the Aztec capital of Tenochtitlán.

1450s Johannes Gutenberg invents a printing press.

1488 Bartolomé Dias reaches the Indian Ocean by sailing around Africa.

1492 Moors defeated in Spain; Christopher Columbus's first voyage.

1497 John Cabot reaches North America.

1498 Vasco de Gama reaches India.

1517 Protestant Reformation begins.

1519 Hernán Cortés invades Mexico.

1521-22 Magellan sails around tip of South America into Pacific Ocean, one of his ships circumnavigates the globe.

1532-1533 Francisco Pizarro subjugates the Inca.

1536 Calvin publishes *Institutes of the Christian Religion*.

1583 Humphrey Gilbert reaches Nova Scotia.

1587-1590 Second Roanoke Island colony vanishes.

1607 Jamestown settlement established.

SUGGESTED READINGS

C. R. Boxer, *The Portuguese Seaborne Empire, 1415-1825* (1972).

Carl Bridenbaugh, *Vexed and Troubled Englishmen, 1500-1642* (1968).

Inga Clendinnen, *Aztecs* (1991).

Alfred W. Crosby, *The Columbian Exchange: Biological and Cultural Consequences of 1492* (1972).

Basil Davidson, *The African Genius* (1969).

Jared Diamond, *Guns, Germs, and Steel: The Fates of Human Societies* (1997).

Brian Fagan, *The Great Journey: The Peopling of Ancient America* (1987).

Felipe Fernandez-Armesto, *Columbus* (1991).

Melvin Fowler, *Cahokia: Ancient Capital of the Midwest* (1974).

Charles Gibson, *Spain in America* (1966).

Karen O. Kupperman, *Roanoke, the Abandoned Colony* (1984).

Paul E. Lovejoy, *Transformations in Slavery: A History of Slavery in Africa* (1983).

Kenneth Macgowan and Joseph A. Hester, Jr., *Early Man in the New World* (1983).

Samuel Eliot Morison, *The European Discovery of America: The Northern Voyages, A.D. 1500-1600* (1971).

——, *The European Discovery of America: The Southern Voyages, A.D. 1492-1616* (1971).

Richard Olaniyan, *African History and Culture* (1982).

William and Carla Phillips, *The Worlds of Christopher Columbus* (1992).

David B. Quinn, *North America from Earliest Discovery to First Settlement: The Norse Voyages to 1612* (1977).

Kirkpatrick Sale, *The Conquest of Paradise: Christopher Columbus and the Columbus Legacy* (1990).

Linda Schele and David Friedel, *A Forest of Kings* (1990).

Zvi Dor Ner and William Scheller, *Columbus and the Age of Discovery* (1991).

Jacques Soustelle, *The Olmecs: The Oldest Civilization in Mexico* (1984).

David E. Stannard, *American Holocaust: Columbus and the Conquest of the New World* (1992).

David J. Weber, *The Spanish Frontier in North America* (1992).

John Noble Wilford, *The Mysterious History of Columbus* (1991).

Review Questions

1. Explain the advantages that the Europeans had in their conquest of North and South America, with a focus on technology, disease, religion, and conflicts among Native Americans.

2. What events prompted the Portuguese, Spanish, French, English and Dutch explorations of the 1400s and 1500s?

3. How did European attitudes towards Native Americans evolve in the fifteenth and sixteenth centuries?

4. In what ways did the conquests of North and South America undermine the European economy and how did the introduction of horses and European manufactured goods shape the Native American way of life?

5. Discuss the impact of the Columbian Exchange on Native American and European societies in terms of diet and the natural environment.

Glossary of Important People and Concepts

Adena and Hopewell Cultures
Aztecs
Bubonic Plague
John Cabot
Clovis point
Columbian Exchange
Christopher Columbus
Compass
Hernán Cortés
Bartolomé Dias
Francis Drake
Encomienda system
Martin Frobisher
Sir Humphrey Gilbert
Johannes Gutenberg
Prince Henry the Navigator
Henry Hudson
Inca
Ferdinand Magellan
Maya
Francisco Pizarro
Protestant Reformation
Renaissance
Shaman
Vikings

NOVA BRITANNIA.

OFFERING MOST

Excellent fruites by Planting in
VIRGINIA.

Exciting all such as be well affected
to further the same.

LONDON
Printed for SAMVEL MACHAM, and are to besold at
his Shop in Pauls Church-yard, at the
Signe of the Bul-head.
1609.

Virginia Company pamphlet, 1609

Chapter Two

THE SOUTHERN COLONIES

In May 1587, three ships carrying 115 settlers departed England bound for North America to establish a new colony. One of the passengers on board the largest of the ships, the **Lyon***, was nineteen-year-old Eleanor Dare. She was six months pregnant and facing an arduous and dangerous future. Sir Walter Raleigh, the financial supporter of the colonial venture, had specifically recruited women and children to send to the new settlement in order to give it a more peaceful and permanent appearance. Eleanor's father, John White, had been chosen as governor of the yet to be constructed town. Her husband, Ananias Dare, was a London bricklayer by trade, but in the New World would serve as one of Governor White's official assistants. Also on board with the Dares were two Croatoan Indians, Manteo and Towaye, who would serve as translators and friendly Native American contacts for the colonists.*

Like everyone else on board, Eleanor was probably filled with a strange mixture of hope, fear, and excitement. They all knew that a 1585 colonial effort on Roanoke Island had run into such serious problems with food shortages and negative relations with neighboring tribes that the earlier setters had abandoned that colony and returned to England. Fifteen men had been left behind to maintain England's claim to the land. Given the number of hostile natives that surrounded the fifteen men, their safety was very much in doubt. Eleanor could take some comfort in knowing that her colony would settle far away from the danger zone of the old colony. The three ships would stop on Roanoke Island only briefly to pick up the fifteen men, and then proceed a hundred miles up the

coast to a fresh start among tribes either friendly or at least neutral toward England.

During the ocean crossing, Governor White frequently argued with Simon Fernandez, the pilot in charge of the ships. These disagreements were very public, and on a small ship it meant that Eleanor knew nearly every detail of her father's troubles. When the fleet finally arrived at Roanoke Island, Eleanor watched while her father and a group of other men went ashore to pick up and evacuate the 15 settlers left behind. The search party found only a single skeleton and began to return to the ships empty-handed. Eleanor was shocked when Fernandez, however, refused to let White and the men return to the ships, instead ordering her and the remaining colonists to disembark onto the island. Fernandez was a pirate and privateer, and was eager to sail south to plunder Spanish shipping and settlements. The ships remained anchored off shore while unloading the colony's supplies, but Fernandez absolutely refused to let any of the settlers back on board. Under these trying circumstances, on August 18, 1587, Eleanor gave birth to a daughter named Virginia, after the territory in which their colony was located. Virginia Dare was the first English child born in America.

Eleanor knew that the colony was in severe danger. The local tribes were almost all hostile due to their experiences with earlier English settlers. Plus, someone or something had killed the fifteen Englishmen—the colonists were convinced that they had been murdered by Indians. Everyone's fear of an Indian attack was confirmed when one of their fellow colonists was killed while searching for oysters along the shore. Just days after Eleanor gave birth to Virginia, the entire colony asked her father, the governor, to travel to England and bring help. Only a direct intervention from the mother country could save them. After much arguing, Governor White finally convinced Fernandez to give him the smallest one of the three boats for the voyage back to England. Eleanor, Ananias, and newborn Virginia all said goodbye to Eleanor's father and watched him sail away on August 28, 1587. None of them realized at the time that it would be the final time that the entire family would be together. When Governor White returned after three long years, his daughter Eleanor, granddaughter Virginia, son-in-law Ananias, and all the other colonists had vanished. Various theories have been put forward over the centuries to explain the mystery. Some experts believe the colonists were attacked and killed by enemy Indian tribes. Others believe the missing people moved in with Manteo and the friendly Croatoans, and, when no one from England came for them, eventually were adopted into the tribe. No trace of the Dare family or the others has ever been found, and to the present day their settlement is known as the "Lost Colony of Roanoke." The story of Eleanor and her family makes clear how dangerous it could be to settle in a strange and distant land.

INITIAL ENGLISH SETTLEMENTS

Due in part to the turmoil of the Protestant Reformation in the early sixteenth century and to brutal fighting between English and Irish armies in Ireland, England lagged behind Spain and Portugal in the exploration and settlement of the New World. **Queen Elizabeth I**'s ascension to the throne in 1558 brought with it stability and a renewed interest in exploration and expansion. Spain was by then the dominant force in the Americas, and so a relatively smaller power like England had to approach carefully. Elizabeth dispatched multiple naval expeditions to give England an initial presence. (See Chapter 1)

England had numerous complex motives for pursuing colonization of the New World. Part of the equation was rivalry with the Spanish. Yet another part was pure desire for money. But England was also facing a demographic challenge that left it with a large surplus population. The English population boomed after 1500, jumping from 3 million to 4 million in 1600. At the same time, wealthy English landlords had begun an enclosure movement, evicting small farmers from their lands and blocking access to previously public lands. This benefited the landlords, who could then exploit larger holdings for greater profits, but it left tens of thousands of English families landless, unemployed, and impoverished. Some moved to cities, creating an urban underclass and driving down wages due to increased competition for jobs. Others roamed the countryside looking for employment, with a few turning to banditry to support themselves. Some historians estimate that up to half of the English population in the late sixteenth century lived at or below the poverty level. One potential solution to this social crisis was for unemployed people to leave England and live in colonies.

Roanoke

After the failure of Humphrey Gilbert, his half-brother, Sir **Walter Raleigh**, stepped in to continue English colonization efforts. He had accompanied his brother on earlier voyages but had missed Gilbert's final, fatal voyage due to a lack of supplies on board his vessel. Raleigh first sent an expedition to scout the Carolina region in 1584, believing that the climate of the area would be far more hospitable than more northern reaches. In 1585, he sent settlers to **Roanoke** Island, off the coast of what is today North Carolina. Raleigh named the region "Virginia" in honor of "Virgin" Queen Elizabeth, who never married nor bore children, and whom English society therefore considered to be a lifelong virgin. The Roanoke settlement was poorly planned from the start. The colonists were all military men who lacked the variety of professions and skills needed for a permanent civilian settlement. In particular, they had no knowledge of or interest in farming, and instead expected that nearby Indian tribes would give them food. Local natives, however, had not expected the English arrival and had no extra food to trade. The absence of women and children made the English presence look more like a military invasion than a peaceful civilian colony, making Indians immediately distrustful of the newcomers. The leaders of the colony badly botched efforts at establishing a good working relationship with nearby tribes. After one goodwill visit to a native village, a silver cup turned up missing. The English were convinced that one of the natives had stolen it, so they returned to the village and burned it to the ground in retaliation (but never found the cup). Facing hunger and starvation, the Englishmen began to attack local villages to steal food. Through it all, only the Roanoke Indians who shared the island with the English had remained friendly. The English settlers began to view that friendliness with suspicion since every other nearby group had turned hostile. The settlers grew convinced that the Roanoke natives were treating them kindly in order to hide some secret planned attack against the fort, so the colonists launched a preemptive attack of their own, killing the tribe's chief and displaying his head on a stick. Within a short period of time, the English colony was at war with nearly every surrounding native group.

Roanoke Mystery Solved? The Dare Stones

Few mysteries have enthralled historians as much as the disappearance of the entire Roanoke colony in the 1580s. Over 100 English men, women, and children vanished, leaving behind some carefully disassembled buildings and some of their possessions, but there were no signs of struggle or violence. Among the missing were Eleanor Dare, the daughter of the governor, Ananais Dare, her husband, and their daughter Virginia Dare, who had been the first English child born in the New World. Most scholars believe that the settlers moved in with a nearby Indian tribe, but there is no clear evidence as to which tribe nor how long the missing settlers survived. One possible explanation was uncovered in 1608 when Chief Powhatan told John Smith and the settlers at Jamestown that he had ordered the killing of the surviving Roanoke colonists just a year or two earlier, whom the Native leader said had lived with a rival tribe. No evidence of this event, however, could be found either at the time or by later archaeological investigations.

Over three hundred years later, in 1937, a California tourist named Louis E. Hammond appeared to have solved at least part of the mystery. According to Hammond, he found an odd looking 21-pound stone while picking nuts along a roadway in North Carolina, and then brought the stone to Emory University in Atlanta to be examined by historian Haywood Pearce. The stone contained an inscription purportedly written by Eleanor Dare in 1591, explaining that the colonists had moved inland to a new site. However, war and illness killed the majority of the colonists, leaving only 24 alive after a few years. Then, in 1591, an Indian attack killed almost all the remaining colonists, including Eleanor's husband and child. The inscription explained that Eleanor left this inscribed stone next to a larger rock that served as a gravestone for her family. Professor Pearce believed the stone to be authentic and published his initial findings in a scholarly journal. Hammond, however, proved unable to lead Emory experts back to the exact place where he found the stone, but Pearce continued to search fruitlessly around the road and the surrounding countryside for the Dare grave or any other markers left by Eleanor Dare. Frustrated by his inability to find further evidence, Pearce decided that publicity could help his cause, and so publicly offered a $500 reward for information leading to the Dare gravestone.

Slightly more than one year later, a farmer named William Eberhardt brought Pearce three inscribed stones dated 1589 and supposedly inscribed by Eleanor Dare, found some 300 miles away in South Carolina. Pearce took these stones, but said that the reward would only be paid for the Dare gravestone. A short time later, Eberhardt turned in a Dare gravestone for the reward. Pearce became very excited at the discovery and put out a call to search for even more stones and offering more cash. Eberhardt found a total of 42 stones, collecting around $2,000. A few other individuals also found stones and turned them in for rewards. In all, a total of 48 stones were found from 1937 to 1940. Collectively, they told an epic story of a trek from Roanoke in North Carolina to South Carolina and then to Georgia. According to the stones, Eleanor Dare married a local Indian king in 1598 and bore him a daughter before herself dying in 1599. The Smithsonian Institution commissioned an investigation by a team of historians who in 1940 pronounced the 48 stones to be authentic.

*However, the stones and their story unraveled quickly due to a magazine article written in 1941 by **Saturday Evening Post** journalist Boyden Sparkes. Sparkes hired detectives to try and track down Hammond in California, but their search came up empty. Boyden discovered that, except for Hammond, all of the people who found stones were friends of William Eberhardt, and further discovered that Eberhardt was not just a farmer but also a stone cutter with the skill to create newly inscribed stones. What's more, Eberhardt had in the past created fake "ancient" Indian stones to sell as antiques. Sparkes's conclusion was that the whole episode was a hoax, and that Pearce was somehow knowingly involved in the deception. Pearce would later claim to have been blackmailed by Eberhardt into participating, but in any case, the Dare stones became a nationwide laughingstock as everyone seemingly agreed that they were fake.*

Historical stories rarely have a neat and tidy ending, and this one is no exception. Since the 1940s, the stones have resided in the collection of Brenau University, which was founded and run by Professor's Pearce's father. In 2016, a team of university researchers conducted geological and mineral tests on the first (Hammond) stone. They concluded that the stone came from Virginia and that the aging on the inscription was consistent with having been carved in the 1500s. As of 2019, Brenau University hopes to conduct further tests to try and prove that the first stone at least was authentic.

After a harsh winter, and finding no gold or other easy sources of profit, the settlers quickly agreed to return to England in 1586 when Francis Drake arrived to survey the location as a possible future base.

Raleigh was surprised by the sudden abandonment of the colony but soon began organizing another attempt. In 1587, he sent over more than one hundred new settlers. This effort contained a mixture of both men and women, plus a wider variety of professions to help sustain a permanent base. They were supposed to build their new settlement further up the coast in the Chesapeake region, where more peaceful relations had been successfully established with Native Americans. A series of disagreements between the colonists and the captain of their transport ships, however, led to the settlers being deposited back on Roanoke Island at the site of the earlier failed settlement. The new arrivals had limited supplies, the use of only one small vessel, and were surrounded by Native Americans who were hostile due to their prior experience with the English. Feeling their situation to be desperate, the colonists sent their governor, John White, back to England to plead for assistance. White hoped to quickly bring back a small flotilla of ships to evacuate the settlers to a new location, as well as bring additional supplies they would need to survive. White's hopes for rapid assistance were quickly dashed. In 1588, Spain launched a massive fleet, the Spanish Armada, in an attempt to invade and conquer England. A combination of battle losses and storms quickly diminished the Armada's strength. The outnumbered English navy, using superior speed and maneuverability, forced the remnants of the devastated Spanish fleet to abandon the attempt and return home to Spain. However, no one in England was sure whether Spain would make a second attempt at an invasion. Until the danger fully passed, every seaworthy ship was pressed into service defending England's coastline.

Not until 1590 was White able to return at the head of a rescue effort. What he found is still a source of mystery and speculation to the present day. Roanoke's settlers had vanished, among them Governor White's daughter Eleanor and young granddaughter Virginia. The buildings were still standing, and there were no bodies or signs of violence. The word "Croatoan" had been carved into a fence post by one of the English settlers, the name of a nearby island and Indian tribe located to the south. Bad weather, however, forced White and the rescue effort to return to England before they could follow the lead, and no further serious attempt was made to find the Lost Colony.

The Roanoke disaster caused Raleigh to give up on his American dreams, but writers in England kept interest in colonization alive. In particular, geographer

Richard Hakluyt became a leading advocate for what he called "plantations" of colonists in America. Hakluyt's publications in the 1580s and 1590s made appeals to both the public and to Queen Elizabeth. America, he was convinced, contained vast riches, both in the form of gold and in the promise of increased trade. Many of Hakluyt's economic observations were grounded in the theory of mercantilism, which was dominant throughout Europe at the time. Mercantilists believed that a nation only became richer by taking wealth from another nation. This was most easily achieved by exporting goods to other countries while importing as little as possible. In this type of system, colonies were essential as providers of raw materials that otherwise would have to be imported by the mother country. Hakluyt also made a moral appeal in favor of English colonization, criticizing Spain's brutal treatment of Native Americans. England, he claimed, would be greeted as liberators by the Native peoples of America. In reality, the English would mostly replicate the Spanish behavior of brutalizing indigenous peoples and taking their land.

Jamestown

Queen Elizabeth I died in 1603 without a direct heir, so her cousin and closest relative, James VI of Scotland, suddenly found himself crowned King James I (1603-1625) of England. In 1606, James issued charters to two private **joint stock companies** who sold shares to investors to raise the money needed for colonization efforts. The English Virginia claim at the time stretched nearly the entirety of North America, from Canada south to Carolina, and from the Atlantic Ocean west to the Pacific Ocean. The **Virginia Company of London** was granted the right to settle the southern portion of this vast territory while the Plymouth Company had rights to the north. Though the English government surrendered direct control over newly established colonies, it also meant that private investors rather than the Crown would bear all the costs, risks, and rewards (if any) of settlement in the New World. The companies were instructed by the King to convert Native Americans to Christianity as part of their missions, but at heart they were driven by a desire for profit.

The Plymouth Company in early 1607 sent 120 male settlers to what is today Maine to settle the Popham colony, so named after its leader George Popham. Their intent was to use the area's extensive virgin forests to build large sailing ships. The Popham colonists, though, failed to establish a productive relationship with the local Abenaki Indians, depriving the colony of the opportunity to trade for much needed food. Many of the colonists returned to England at the end of 1607 to escape starvation.

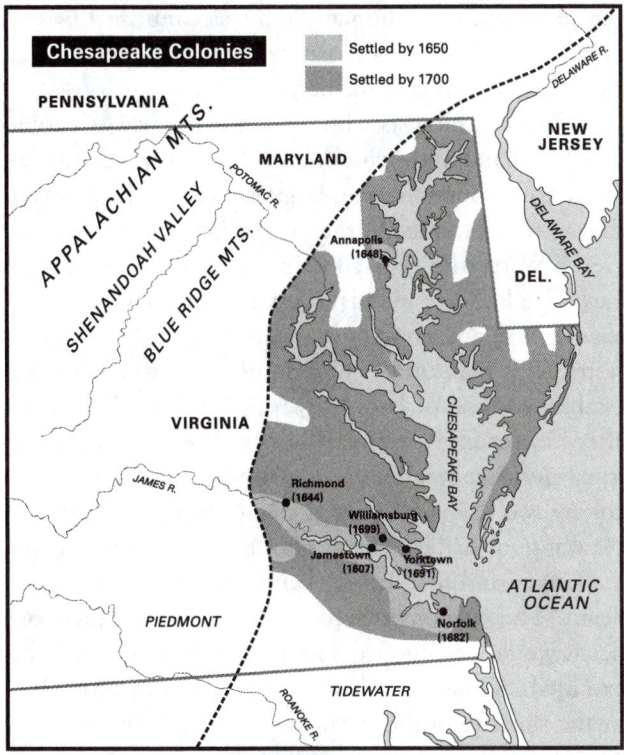

Map 2.1 Chesapeake Colonies

The rest remained to wait out the winter. In early 1608, Popham died—the lone colonist to die in the settlement. In the spring, the survivors decided to leave the colony and return to England. The only tangible result they had to show for their efforts was a 30-ton ship that they had built, the first European ship constructed in America. The Plymouth Company never managed to piece together the money or people for a second try. While this northern push failed, the Virginia Company succeeded further south in establishing the first permanent English settlement in America, **Jamestown**.

In late 1606, three ships, the *Susan Constant, Godspeed,* and *Discovery,* left England bound for Virginia. On board were 144 men and boys intended to be the first settlers in the Virginia Company's colony. They discovered the dangers of their task during the voyage itself. The ships were buffeted by storms and the passengers afflicted by illness. After a long journey of four months, the three ships finally sighted the coast of North America. Thirty-nine of the settlers, though, had died during the voyage. The 105 survivors decided to build a fort on a small peninsula about 40 miles up one of the rivers that emptied into Chesapeake Bay. Their distance from the coast would hide them from potential discovery and military attack by the Spanish, who also claimed the same land, and presumably the river would grant the colonists easy access to fresh water. In tribute to their monarch, they named the river the James River, and the fort Jamestown.

The colonists did not realize it at the time, but their timing and choice of location could hardly have been worse. The Chesapeake area was suffering through a severe drought, making it difficult to grow crops and adding an increased physical strain on the inhabitants. The selected land was both low-lying and swampy, creating ideal conditions for mosquitos and mosquito-borne illnesses. Wave after wave of fevers and malaria devastated the first colonists and then those who arrived in subsequent years. The waters of the river and surrounding swamp had high salinity levels during part of the year, adding salt toxicity to an already deadly mix of environmental hazards. The behavior of this first wave of settlers made the situation even worse. Instead of trying to grow their own food or dig wells for fresh water, many of the men instead spent their days searching for gold in the hopes of making an instant fortune for themselves and the company. They found no gold but did find an abundance of death. By January 1608, only 38 of the original 105 colonists were still alive. Such appalling death rates remained a constant feature of early Virginia life. At least 8,000 people moved to Virginia between 1607 and 1624. In 1624, the surviving population stood at only 1,200.

Jamestown's situation was made even more precarious by the close proximity of the largest and most powerful Native American confederacy in the region whose leader, **Powhatan**, had united some 200 villages containing a total population between 10,000 and 20,000 people. The English at first tried to live by eating turtles, fish, oysters, and various birds. They quickly realized, though, that their long-term survival rested on establishing a good trading relationship with Powhatan to ensure a steady supply of maize for eating and planting. Powhatan was not certain, at first, how he should react to the presence of outsiders. On the one hand, they had shown up and built a settlement without permission. If he chose to use it, he had the military might to easily wipe out the survivors of that first winter and end this English colonization effort. On the other hand, the English seemed to be in a deplorable condition and unable to take care of themselves. After consideration, Powhatan decided to take pity on the English settlers and open up trade with them. By doing so, he hoped to demonstrate that the Powhatan Confederacy was stronger than the English and worthy of respect from future European settlers. Powhatan would later regret his decision to help the Jamestown settlement.

While there was a seven-man council set up to govern Jamestown, they spent more time dealing with illnesses or arguing with each other than governing. In 1608, one of the councilors, twenty-eight-year-old **John Smith,** emerged as the most important leader in Jamestown.

Despite his young age, he had already acquired a wide reputation as a traveler and mercenary soldier. Smith instilled military discipline into the colony and forced everyone to work. Those who did not work would be denied food. He led efforts to trade with local natives. When those efforts failed, he led the English on raids to steal their food. At one point, Smith noticed that the Powhatan left the swampy area along the river each spring and summer, and further noted that the Indians died at much lower rates than the English. Even though Smith did not understand why this was the case, he nevertheless decided to copy the natives and dispersed his colonists during the hot months of the year. By doing so, Smith reduced salt toxicity and the frequency of malaria outbreaks, though he did not recognize the cause and effect pattern. The result was that the English death rate temporarily plummeted. It was largely through Smith's leadership that the colony made its first halting steps towards permanence.

Despite Jamestown's improving prospects, Smith was extremely unpopular in the colony. Many residents of the colony were upper-class "gentlemen" who resented the lower-class "commoner" Smith giving them orders. Smith's abrasive and prickly personality certainly did not win him many friends. Smith was injured in a 1609 gunpowder explosion and had to return to England for treatment. While officially the explosion was classified as an accident, many experts think it might have been an assassination attempt against Smith. Smith's departure was one of several events in 1609 that combined to push Jamestown to the brink of failure.

The Virginia Company in 1609 sent over an unusually large group of setters, some 600 in all, plus enough food to last them several months. Their ships were struck by severe storms during the Atlantic crossing, and not all of them arrived at Jamestown. Those ships that did finish the journey lost much of their food in the bad weather, which meant that the colony suddenly had a large number of new mouths to feed and insufficient food. In addition, the already rocky relationship between the English and Powhatan took a sharp turn for the worse once Smith left for England, and the Powhatan besieged Jamestown. The combination of severe food shortages and war with the Powhatan Confederacy led to incredible suffering in the colony over the 1609-1610 winter. English settlers ate everything they could: dogs, cats, dirt, shoes, even candles, which at the time were made using animal fat. Approximately 500 colonists were in Jamestown at the start of winter. By spring, only 60 were left alive. That winter became known as the "starving time," during which some of the survivors turned to cannibalism to stay alive. There had been some doubts about the reports of cannibalism both at the time and in later centuries, but

the consumption of human flesh was confirmed by the discovery in 2012 of human skeletal remains that had clear carving marks in the bone.

The few colonists who remained in early 1610 decided to abandon the colony and headed towards Chesapeake Bay in order to sail to England. On the James River they were intercepted by their first official governor, Lord De La Warr, who ordered them to turn around and go back. De La Warr and his successors kept colonists from abandoning Jamestown by implementing even more harsh restrictions than under John Smith. In 1612, Virginia established a set of laws known as Dale's Code, named after Lieutenant Governor Thomas Dale. The laws punished any discontent or disorder harshly. One man in the colony was caught stealing a small amount of oatmeal. He was punished by having a hot needle shoved through his tongue and then being chained to a tree to starve to death. Those who criticized the colony's government officials would be whipped and repeat offenders would be executed. These stern laws were repealed in 1618, but in the short term did what they had been intended to do—prevent people from undermining Virginia.

Stability and Expansion

Two events in 1614 helped improve the fortunes of Jamestown. Both involved a planter named **John Rolfe**, who arrived in the colony in 1610. In 1614, Rolfe exported Virginia's first tobacco crop to England, turning a substantial profit and giving the colony a new economic future. Tobacco had long been grown by Chesapeake Indian tribes and used in ceremonial situations. However, the extremely harsh taste of tobacco caused Europeans to cough and gag. Rolfe's breakthrough came from importing a strain of tobacco much more sweet and mild than indigenous varieties. That same year, Rolfe married **Pocahontas**, the daughter of Powhatan, who had been kidnapped and held hostage by the settlers for protection from attack. John Smith had met her years earlier, according to his autobiography, when she intervened with her father to save his life after Smith's capture during a foraging expedition. (Many historians believe this first meeting between Smith and Pocahontas was a product of Smith's imagination rather than a real event.) Afterwards, Pocahontas frequently played a role in mediating differences between her people and the English. Living amongst the English, she eventually adapted many of their ways, including conversion to Christianity. The union between Rolfe and Pocahontas ushered in a period of relative peace. (In 1616, a year after the birth of their only child, the couple traveled to England. The following year, after meeting the king and other dignitaries,

Pocahontas fell ill at the beginning of the return voyage and soon died at the age of 21.)

To encourage further population growth, the Virginia Company implemented the **headright system** in 1618. The company would grant 50 acres to everyone who paid their own way to Virginia, plus an additional 50 acres for each person they brought with them. The colony also eased up on the harsh military discipline that had been in place ever since John Smith had imposed it, believing that many people would not move to a colony with such strict rules. The first women had arrived in 1609, but the sex ratio remained heavily skewed towards men, so the company made a particular effort to send single women to Jamestown to create more opportunities for marriages and families.

Two developments occurred in 1619 that had tremendous consequences for the future. The first African slaves arrived to be purchased and forced to labor on farms and tobacco plantations. In the same year, the company created the **House of Burgesses**, the first legislative body in America. The legislature would be elected by landowners and have the power to write and pass local rules for approval by the company. Both events set crucial precedents for later British colonies. Every British colony founded after Virginia would have both legal slavery and also an elected local government.

Powhatan's death in 1618 and the expansion of English settlements into Native American lands soon brought the peace to an end. Powhatan's brother and successor **Opechancanough** launched a surprise attack against Virginia in 1622, killing around one-third of the English settlers, nearly 350 in all, including John Rolfe. The Virginia colony, though, had grown in strength during the years of peace. With help from reinforcements from England, the English were able to recover from the

Painting of Pocahontas while in England.

initial massacre and launch a counterattack that destroyed every Powhatan village near Jamestown. The English army destroyed Indian food supplies to starve the Powhatan into submission. Opechancanough and his Powhatan Confederacy launched one final war in 1644 to push back the tide of European settlement, but already the balance of power in Virginia had shifted to the English. By 1669,

Print depicting Captain John Smith's story of Pocahontas's intervention, saving him from execution.

Pocahontas

No Native American figure from early America has drawn as much attention and interest as Pocahontas. She has appeared as a character in hundreds of plays, books, and films. She also represents an important key in understanding the relationship between early English settlers and Native peoples.

She was born around 1596. Her birth name was Matoaka, but she acquired the nickname Pocahontas ("playful one") as a child. Her father, Powhatan, was the Chief of the largest Indian confederacy in the region, but there is no record of her mother. The English arrived and settled Jamestown in May 1607, but young Pocahontas did not meet her first Englishman until near the end of that year when John Smith was brought before Powhatan. This first meeting, recounted by Smith for the first time many years later, has entered into legend. According to Smith, Powhatan had Smith's head forced down onto the ground on top of two rocks, and an executioner was about to smash Smith's head with a club. Suddenly, Pocahontas rushed over and placed her head on top of Smith's, preventing the execution from proceeding. Many historians believe the scene was invented by Smith, and certainly a romance between Smith and Pocahontas, often depicted in later popular culture, never happened (Smith was at the time 27 years old and Pocahontas around 10 or 11).

Despite her young age, Pocahontas entered into a diplomatic role, learning to speak English, and often visiting Jamestown to bring gifts or negotiate. Her visits to Jamestown stopped when war broke out between the Powhatan and the English in 1609. In 1613, she was visiting one of the villages of her father's confederacy when she was taken captive by the English, who intended to use her as leverage to negotiate an end to the war. During her year-long captivity, she converted to Christianity and was baptized and renamed "Rebecca." At some point, she met planter John Rolfe and the two married in April 1614, and their son Thomas was born early the following year. The marriage between an English planter and the favorite daughter of Powhatan brought the war to an end.

The Virginia Company, who ran the Jamestown settlement, decided to bring Pocahontas to England to show off the colony's success in civilizing and converting Native Americans. She, Rolfe, Thomas, and several other Powhatan arrived in London in 1616. The presence of an "Indian Princess" generated a great deal of interest in English society, and Pocahontas spent many days and nights at social gatherings, including a meeting with King James I. She also had an emotional reunion with John Smith, whom she had not seen for a decade and had believed to be dead. According to Smith, Pocahontas was friendly towards him but also criticized him for the way he and the English had treated the Powhatan people.

In March 1617, John and Rebecca Rolfe boarded a ship to return to Virginia. They left behind their son Thomas, who was sickly as an infant, to be raised in England. Before they departed, however, Pocahontas fell seriously ill and was moved to shore. There she died at of an unidentified illness at the age of 21. Her interracial marriage had built a temporary bridge between Europeans and Indians, but as often happened throughout early American history, the bridge soon came crashing down as John Rolfe died in a Powhatan attack in 1622.

The wedding of Pocahontas and John Rolfe. 1614

Print depicting Lord Calvert's presentation of the 1649 Act of Toleration establishing civil and religious liberty in Maryland.

the local Native American population had plummeted from 20,000 to a mere 2,000. By contrast, the English population in the Chesapeake had grown to 35,000.

The Second Anglo-Powhatan War that began in 1622 did not destroy Virginia, but it did spell the end of the Virginia Company. Despite tobacco's introduction, the colony had never turned a profit for its shareholders. Only in the aftermath of the Powhatan war did the English government and public learn the full truth about the colony's horrific death rates. With its reputation and finances in ruin, the company dissolved in 1624, and Virginia became a royal colony. The monarch would now appoint Virginia's governor, but the citizens of Virginia retained a measure of self-government through the House of Burgesses.

In 1634, a new group of colonists arrived in the Chesapeake and established the colony of Maryland. The settlement was first envisioned by George Calvert, first Lord Baltimore. Calvert was a Catholic, and he intended for his settlement to be a refuge for fellow English Catholics who often found themselves persecuted as a religious minority in England. However, Calvert died in 1632 before his colony became a reality. King Charles I (1625-1649) instead granted the colonial charter to George's son Cecil Calvert, the second Lord Baltimore. Maryland would be a **proprietary colony**, in which one person and his heirs had ultimate authority over the colony. Because the new settlement desperately needed immigrants, Calvert was willing to accept people of all religious backgrounds, and so Maryland developed into a Protestant majority colony rather than an exclusively Catholic one. Catholics still held a number of political

offices in Maryland, but the colony's Protestant population resented any Catholic influence. Religious disputes became a fundamental feature of Maryland life, and even the passage of a broad religious toleration law granting freedom of worship to all Christians in 1649 could not end the religious strife.

Inhabitants of Maryland quickly adopted tobacco as their staple crop, and under pressure from Protestant colonists, the Calverts quickly established an elected legislature, granting Marylanders the same type of self-government that existed in Virginia. Facing a labor shortage on tobacco plantations, Maryland adopted a headright system to encourage migration, and when that failed to provide the needed labor supply, Maryland planters turned to African slavery. In short, Maryland's economy and society rapidly grew to resemble those of Virginia.

The English Civil War and Restoration

The English Civil War (1642-1651) and its aftermath had a tremendous impact on both the mother country and its overseas colonies. The war pitted King Charles I against the Parliament for supreme authority in England. Charles had dismissed Parliament in 1629 and for more than a decade governed the country without any representative input. Religion figured prominently in the struggle. Charles implemented a number of reforms in the Church of England, such as common forms of prayer and worship, which were deeply unpopular among some Protestant groups in Scotland and England. Despite the fact that Charles was king of both Scotland and England,

Scottish armies invaded England in both 1639 and 1640 in order to force changes to Anglican religious policies. Irish Catholics also rose in rebellion around the same time. These international crises caused Charles to reconvene an assembly, and Parliament and the Crown then became locked in a struggle for power.

The King's cause was supported by most mainstream Church of England authorities and also by many Catholics. His Queen, Henrietta Maria, was a French-born Catholic, and royal authorities had shown great toleration towards English Catholics. Parliament's side was dominated by Puritans, Protestants who followed the teachings of the French theologian John Calvin (see Chapter 1) and believed that England and the Anglican Church needed to be thoroughly purified of all Catholic influences. In 1645, a Parliamentary army led by the Puritan Oliver Cromwell decisively defeated the main royalist army. After a series of royalist uprisings encouraged by the king and his supporters, Parliament tried Charles I for treason and beheaded him in 1649.

To replace the monarchy, Parliament established a Republican Commonwealth. During its brief existence, the Commonwealth could not afford to spend much time on trying to secure and govern its American colonies. Most of the Commonwealth government's efforts were put towards fighting European enemies and dealing with royalist plots and uprisings. In 1651, Charles II, the king-in-exile, and his newly recruited army unsuccessfully invaded from Scotland, which had switched sides and now supported the royalist cause. War then broke out the following year with the Netherlands, and then in 1654 with Spain.

English colonies were forced to choose sides in the struggle between the Crown and Parliament. The Puritan colonies in New England (see Chapter 3) strongly backed Parliament, and some colonists even traveled back to England to take part in the fighting. Virginia and many Caribbean colonies, which had been largely settled by mainstream Anglicans, sided with the King. Maryland, with its competing Protestant and Catholic factions, nearly ripped itself apart. The Calverts and the Catholic population sided with the King, Maryland's Protestants mostly with Parliament, and the colony as a result fought a small-scale civil war of its own. In 1644, Parliamentary forces in the colony captured Maryland's capital and forced Governor Leonard Calvert to flee to neighboring Virginia. Two years later Calvert put together an armed force and recaptured Maryland's capital. The back-and-forth struggle continued sporadically for more than a decade.

The Maryland civil war came to a close only with the Restoration of the monarchy in England in 1660, when Charles II ascended to the throne. The Commonwealth had increasingly devolved into a dictatorship under Cromwell, but his death in 1658 deprived England of its strongest leader, and his son Richard did not instill confidence in the country's military or in Parliament. After getting Charles II to agree to pardon most of those who had fought against the Crown in the Civil War, Parliament invited the king to return and resume the throne. The Restoration also ushered in a new period of overseas colonial expansion and regulation as the Crown attempted to more firmly establish its authority both in England and its numerous colonies.

Tobacco Society and Culture

Tobacco production in the Chesapeake boomed from 1620-1660, and demand for the crop in England was high. King James I had warned that the "stinking weed" was bad for people's lungs, but the public as a whole ignored the warning. The influx of tobacco taxes also helped to ease the King's criticism. Tobacco became the region's staple crop—an agricultural product that was a basic and fundamental part of daily life. Exports grew from 2,000 pounds in 1615 to 500,000 pounds in 1626. By 1660, exports totaled 10 million pounds per year. Tobacco gained such importance in the Chesapeake that it was used as a substitute for money, with people buying goods and paying taxes using units of tobacco instead of cash. Wealthy planters, the gentry, began to use their riches to accumulate larger and larger plantations. The gentry also asserted their control over colonial government and filled nearly every leadership position in society from legislators to judges to tax collectors.

The shift to a tobacco economy had other major effects. Tobacco is a particularly labor intensive crop, and as a result, planters were in constant need of more labor. Tobacco plantations were for much of the seventeenth century worked primarily by white **indentured servants**, individuals who voluntarily agreed to work for free for a planter for a number of years, usually four or five, in return for the planter paying the cost of the servant's passage to America. The majority of immigrants to the Chesapeake during its first century were such servants, and these were overwhelmingly male, cementing the imbalance between men and women as a long-term feature of tobacco society. During the early years of the tobacco boom, an indentured servant could within a few years earn a planter back several times the cost of the servant's passage. With the high death rates in the region, however, masters could never predict how long servants would live. Over fifty percent of male servants died before completing their indenture. Masters frequently exploited servants to extract maximum profits in a hurry, forcing servants to work abnormally long hours and beating them if the pace of work slackened. Indentured women found themselves vulnerable to sexual abuse by male masters. Servants who ran away to escape abuse could be taken to court by their masters, where judges, almost all of whom had indentured servants of their own, could punish the wayward laborers by extending the length of their contracts. Though on the surface the servant-master relationship appeared to be equally beneficial, bad treatment caused a great deal of anger and resentment among servants.

By 1660, the tobacco boom was over, undone in large measure by soil exhaustion and overproduction. Prices and profits entered a prolonged period of decline. The largest tobacco plantations still managed to make money, but barely. For non-elites, the outlook was more bleak. Indentured servants who survived to the end of their contract usually wanted land of their own. The rich lands of the eastern tidewater, however, were all taken. This forced the ex-servants to move to the frontier, where indigenous peoples controlled the land. Native tribes pushed back against the growing wave of white settlement, and over time the friction between landless men and Native Americans continued to grow. By the 1670s, a quarter of all white men in Virginia were landless, and most of these were looking for ways to pry land away from native peoples, including by force. The Chesapeake underclass blamed their unhappy circumstances on the wealthy English gentry who monopolized power.

Bacon's Rebellion

The late seventeenth century discontent and social unrest in the Chesapeake boiled over into a violent outburst in the 1670s that became known as **Bacon's Rebellion**. One of the uprising's targets was Sir William Berkeley, the royal governor of Virginia. Berkeley first took office in 1642, and he remained governor with only one interruption (during the English Civil War) until 1677. As governor, he aligned himself with the wealthy coastal gentry, and his administration's policies were crafted to favor their interests. Berkeley oversaw the implementation of new property requirements that restricted voting only to landowners, stripping political rights away from part of the unhappy white underclass in the colony. He also acquired a reputation for corruption, handing out large land grants, tax exemptions, and political appointments to his friends and allies. Elections occurred only rarely, and the seated Burgesses overwhelmingly came from the ranks of the eastern elite. Taxes had gone up to pay for fortifications, but those were mostly being built to pro-

tect lands along the coast rather than inland. Governor Berkeley strongly supported Indian treaties guaranteeing the territorial integrity of tribal lands, not because he loved Native Americans, but because stability increased tobacco profits and allowed the governor to control the lucrative fur trade. The governor's Indian policy, however, greatly limited the ability of lower class whites to acquire land and start farms of their own. Poor white colonists demanded that Berkeley declare war on neighboring Indian tribes in order to seize their land.

Violence broke out in late 1675 when a minor dispute between a white planter and some Native Americans led to the murder of an indentured servant. White vigilantes in return killed some 30 Indians. Enraged, multiple tribes carried out revenge attacks against white settlements. Berkeley tried to halt the fighting, but colonists did not want the fighting to end until they had destroyed the major native groups in the region. Defying the governor's order to disband, small farmers and servants formed a 1,000-man militia force with the goal of pursuing all-out war against the Native Americans. The head of the army was young Nathaniel Bacon, a distant relative of the governor and a member of the governor's council. Bacon had arrived very recently, fleeing a financial scandal in England. His connections had gotten him a position in the Virginia government, but he lacked the real influence that he desired because Berkeley hoarded most of the power in the colony. Bacon saw the fighting as a way to carve out a new power base for himself among small farmers and ex-servants. Berkeley favored a peaceful settlement, while Bacon advocated a genocidal policy towards the indigenous people and led the militia army to attack native tribes along the Virginia frontier. Eager for Indian lands, the army attacked both hostile and friendly Native Americans alike.

When Bacon refused to follow government orders to disband his army, Berkeley had Bacon declared a rebel and arrested. What began as an Indian war now became a full uprising against the colonial government. The rebel army pressured Berkeley into freeing their leader and then into holding new legislative elections, in which the pro-Bacon faction did shockingly well. Bacon had managed to enlist a number of substantial landowners to his cause, at least enough to win a substantial number of seats in the legislature. He and his followers demanded lower taxes, wider voting rights, and the conquest of lands currently held by native tribes. When the governor tried to block the assembly's actions and re-arrest Bacon, the rebel army marched on the capital at Jamestown and burned it to the ground. Berkeley was forced to flee to the other side of Chesapeake Bay. At the height of his power, Bacon issued a "Declaration of the People" in which he railed against excessive taxation and Berkeley's corruption. However, the tide soon turned against the uprising. Bacon fell ill with fever and died in October 1676, leaving the army and the rebellion without a strong leader. Pro-government reinforcements sent by the King also arrived from England, allowing Berkeley safely to return and reassert control over Virginia. Berkeley confiscated the lands of leading rebels and hanged twenty-three men before the reprisals stopped. Authorities in England felt Berkeley's actions were excessive and removed him as governor, finally bringing the violence to a halt.

Bacon's Rebellion was an important turning point in American history. Rich planters recognized that they needed to make more common cause with middle and lower class whites to prevent further violence. The gentry continued to maintain their political and social dominance, but they lowered taxes, appointed selected small farmers to public office, and pushed Native Americans off their lands to pave the way for white ownership. Planters reduced the number of poor white immigrants by hiring fewer indentured servants. Instead, plantation owners would increasingly use African slaves to fill their labor needs. In 1675, there were only about 5,000 slaves in the entire Chesapeake region. By 1700, that number had jumped to 13,000, and by 1770, had skyrocketed to 250,000. In contrast to white servants, Africans would never become free and demand land for themselves, and the presence of so many black slaves helped to unite poor and rich whites in racial solidarity. This transition from servitude to enslavement made African slavery a fundamental feature of American life.

THE ATLANTIC SLAVE TRADE

The **Atlantic slave trade** was one of the most important developments in world history, and its impact continues to be felt throughout the entirety of the Western Hemisphere. Nearly every African who arrived in the New World from 1492 to 1888, when Brazil ended slavery, did so as a slave. A total of twelve million Africans were taken by force from Africa to the Americas. Slaves provided much of the labor of colonization. Every European colonial nation took part in the buying, transporting, or selling of Africans. The vast majority of slaves were sent to South America and the Caribbean. About half a mil-

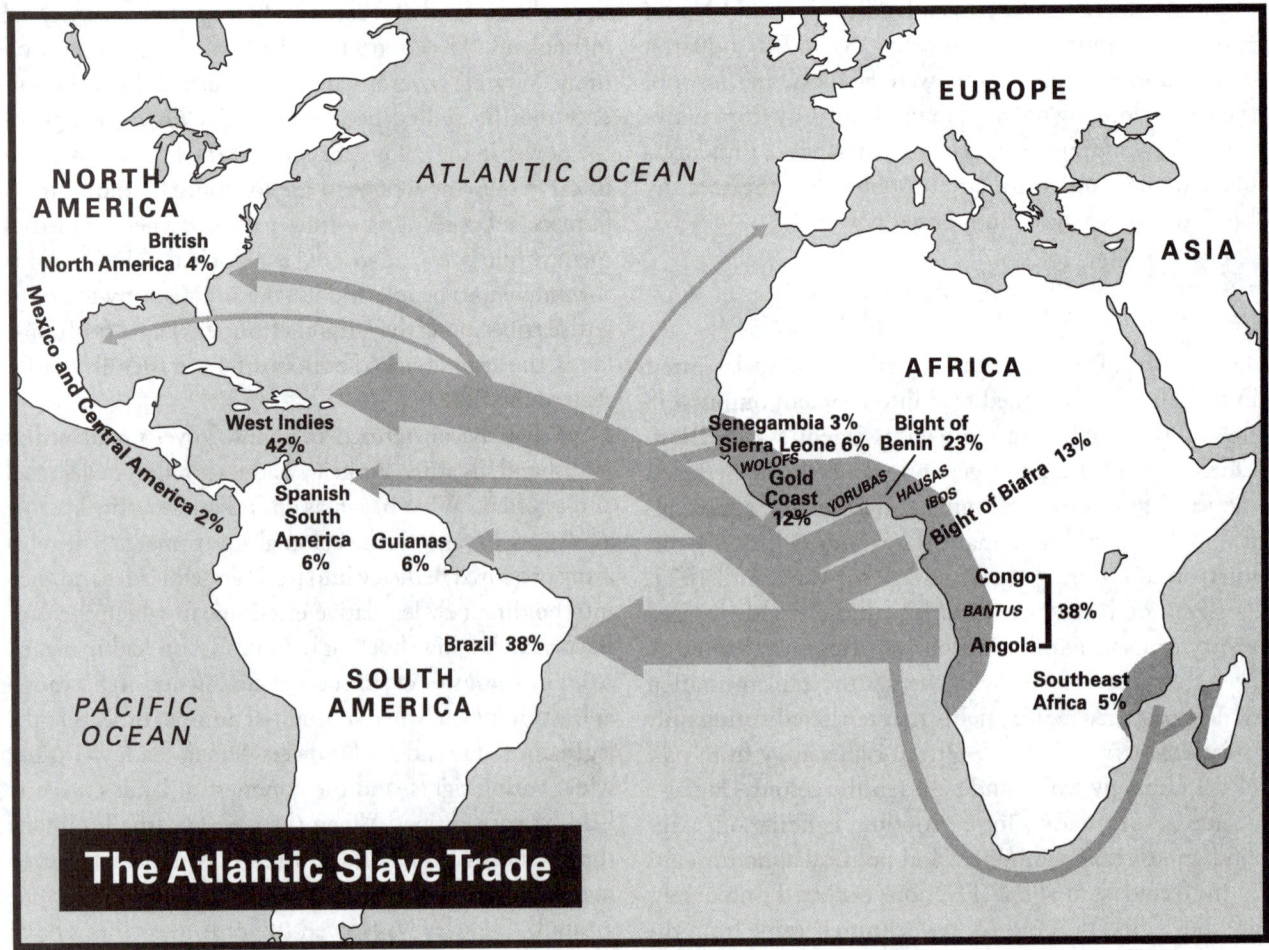

Map 2.2 The Atlantic Slave Trade

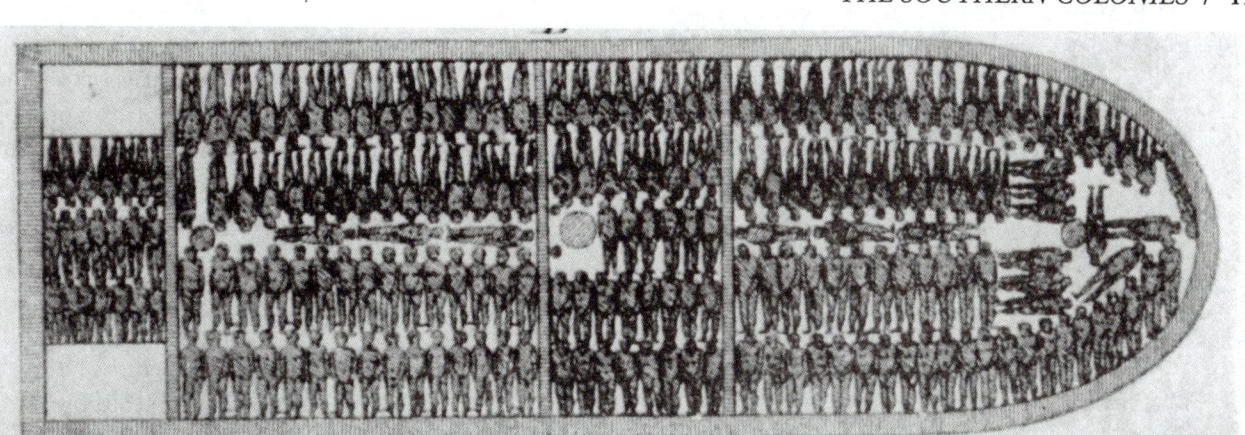

This eighteenth-century engraving shows the horrors of slavery. The slaves were marched to ships and tightly packed below the deck of the vessel.

lion of the slaves were carried to British North America, the area later to become the United States.

Two main factors explain the rise of African slavery in the Americas: economics and race. Most colonial agricultural products were labor intensive, and labor shortages were an endemic part of settlement. African slaves filled these colonial labor needs. Slavery had long been a part of human history. What set African slavery apart from earlier types of slavery was its racialized dimension. Europeans justified the enslavement of Africans because Africans were "primitive" and "heathens." Dark skin was equated with savagery, laziness, evil, and ignorance. Colonists came to believe that slavery was the natural condition of Africans and that the institution of slavery in fact helped slaves to become civilized. Most Europeans came to view race-based slavery as a normal part of everyday life. Not until the end of the eighteenth century did there emerge any sustained European or American critique of slavery's morality.

Most slaves in the slave trade originally came from West Africa. Though often referred to by the blanket term "Africans," these individuals came from dozens of different nations and cultures, and spoke as many as fifty different languages. West African kingdoms often had a rigid political and social hierarchy, with nobles and religious men at the top ruling over the common people. Beneath the commoners were a variety of unfree peoples such as captives, criminals, and slaves. Slavery in Africa operated on different principles than did New World slavery. Slavery within Africa was considered frequently a temporary condition, and children born to slave parents were not automatically slaves themselves as was the case in the Americas.

Rivalries and warfare were common parts of African life, just as they were frequent features in European history. African kingdoms often enslaved captives in war, and that process fed into and was accelerated by the transatlantic

slave system developed by Europeans. African nations at first began selling some of their war prisoners to European slave merchants, who would then ship them to the Americas. European nations then sold guns to rival African kingdoms to accelerate the process of war and enslavement. Some African kings began going to war specifically to raid or conquer their neighbors in order to acquire slaves to sell to Europeans.

Slaves taken in this way were marched to coastal ports and loaded onto European slave ships. The long journey across the Atlantic Ocean from the coast of Africa to the Americas became known as the **middle passage**. The ships were often overcrowded and the captives underfed since merchants engaged in the trade tried to spend as little money as possible on the well being of slaves. The journey could take anywhere from one month to a few months depending on wind and weather. Feces and urine built up in the cargo holds, creating a highly unsanitary environment that all but guaranteed outbreaks of serious illness. About 1.5 million slaves died in the middle passage alone. So much refuse and so many bodies were dumped overboard that sharks usually circled around slave ships for the entirety of the voyage. Some captives jumped overboard and committed suicide rather than endure such conditions. This became a frequent enough occurrence for some slave ships to install netting around the entirety of the ship's decks to prevent anyone from jumping overboard. Other slaves attempted to rebel and seize control of the ship. About 10 percent of slaving voyages experienced an uprising on board, though not all of these were successful.

Once the slaves arrived in the New World, they found their ordeal just beginning. Though slaves often arrived sick and covered with sores from the conditions of the middle passage, slave traders would rub grease on the skin of their captives. This did nothing to improve the health of the slaves but rather was to fool potential bidders as

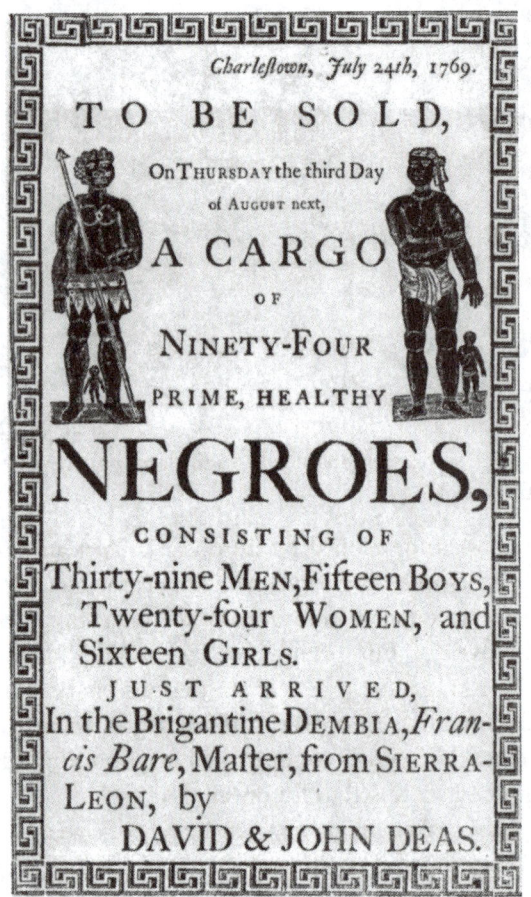

they made inspections. Auctioneers paid no attention to family connections, and if any families managed to make it intact across the ocean, they might easily be divided if purchased by different owners. Africans caught up in this transatlantic system faced slavery not only for themselves, but for all of their descendants as well—generations of whippings, beatings, sexual assaults, and backbreaking labor. New World slavery was explicitly lifelong and hereditary, and only a tiny percentage of slaves ever managed to achieve their freedom in the British colonies.

The Atlantic slave trade irrevocably altered the destiny of the Americas, but also of West Africa as well. The slave trade provided a new source of wealth for some Africans but created a world of miseries for others. By the eighteenth century, slaves were the continent's leading export. Because of the focus on slave exports, other economic avenues were not seriously pursued, leading to long-term economic and technological stagnation. In addition to the loss of 12 million people, Africa suffered high death totals from warfare and slave raids. Since slavers preferred male captives, who fetched higher prices at auction, sex ratios on the West African coast became skewed with women greatly outnumbering men. The resulting demographic shifts undermined traditional social and political relationships. Some kingdoms became predators, growing in power by draining the strength of their neighbors. Other

kingdoms became insular, limiting contact with others in an attempt to protect their people from slavery. By the nineteenth century, the slave trade had left large portions of Africa disorganized and weakened, no longer able to repel large-scale European colonization efforts.

The English Caribbean

At the same time that English settlement took hold in North America during the early seventeenth century, a massive wave of settlement also flowed into the islands of the Caribbean. For the first 130 years after Columbus, Spain had controlled nearly the entirety of the West Indies. The British, however, claimed Barbados in 1625 and began settling other islands soon after. During the 1630s, about half of all British emigrants to the Americas chose the Caribbean as their new home rather than North America. Puritan emigrants set up new colonies on Providence Island, off the coast of Nicaragua, and in the Bahamas. In 1655, an English military expedition invaded and captured Jamaica from Spain. The newly established English authorities invited privateers to move into the coastal town of Port Royal. For more than two decades, Jamaica would serve as a base from which buccaneers such as Bartholomew Sharp and Henry Morgan raided the Spanish Main.

Privateering and piracy, however, did not make for a very complete economy, and a continued British presence in the West Indies depended on finding an economic basis for maintaining permanent colonies. Settlers on Barbados at first tried to grow tobacco as in the Chesapeake, but the crop turned out not to be as profitable in the climate. However, the introduction of sugar in the 1640s gave the British West Indies their staple crop. Sugar grew superbly in the warm tropics, and Europeans of all backgrounds seemed to have an unquenchable taste for sweets. Sugar cane plantations rapidly spread to most islands in the Caribbean, grown in British, Spanish, French, and Dutch colonies alike.

Tobacco was considered a labor-intensive crop, but sugar was even more so. Sugar production required three times the number of workers as tobacco. To meet these intense labor requirements, sugar planters relied from the beginning on African slaves brought over via the middle passage. White indentured servants were usually used only for skilled positions. Though slaves were more expensive than indentured servants, black slaves worked for a lifetime, generating far more profits for their owners. The concentration on sugar cultivation and its reliance on black slaves meant that the black population in Caribbean colonies outnumbered the white population. The Royal African Company during the 1680s, when it

Map 2.3 European Possessions in the Caribbean in the Seventeenth Century

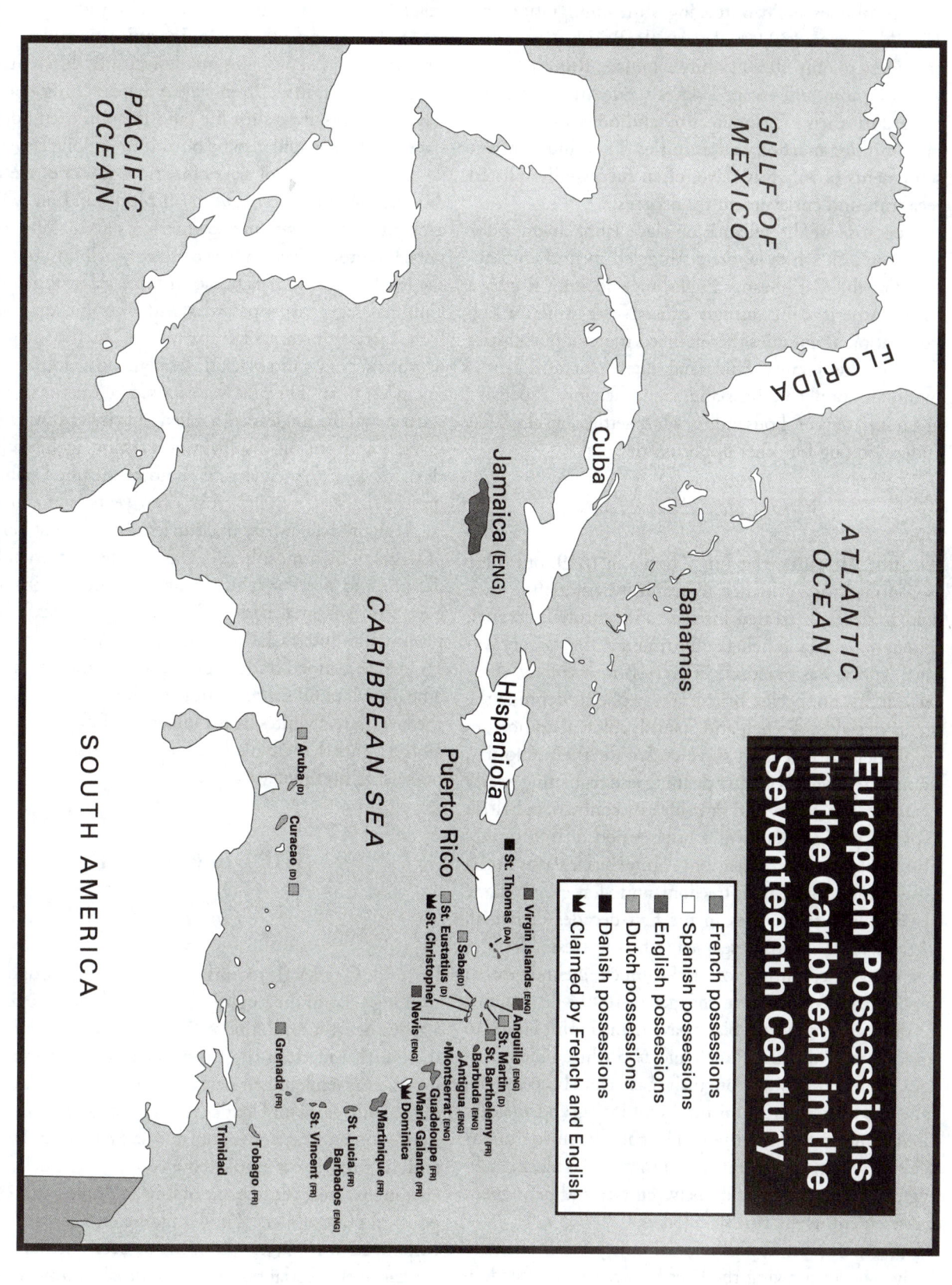

European Possessions in the Caribbean in the Seventeenth Century

- ■ French possessions
- □ Spanish possessions
- ■ English possessions
- ■ Dutch possessions
- ■ Danish possessions
- ■ Claimed by French and English

PACIFIC OCEAN

GULF OF MEXICO

FLORIDA

ATLANTIC OCEAN

Cuba

Bahamas

Jamaica (ENG)

Hispaniola

Puerto Rico

CARIBBEAN SEA

SOUTH AMERICA

Aruba (D)

Curacao (D)

St. Thomas (DA)

Virgin Islands (ENG)

Saba(D)

St. Eustatius (D)

St. Christopher

Nevis (ENG)

Anguilla (ENG)

St. Martin (D)

St. Barthelemy (FR)

Barbuda (ENG)

Antigua (ENG)

Montserrat (ENG)

Guadeloupe (FR)

Marie Galante (FR)

Dominica

Grenada (FR)

Martinique (FR)

St. Lucia (FR)

Barbados (ENG)

St. Vincent (FR)

Trinidad

Tobago (FR)

held a monopoly over the English portion of the slave trade, transported an average of 5,000 slaves per year to British colonies, easily outpacing white immigration. By 1713, there were 130,000 slaves in the British West Indies compared to only 30,000 white colonists. Running away was common, and escaped slaves tended to congregate in hard to reach interior areas of and other island provinces forming **maroon communities**. These independent settlements of runaway slaves often successfully resisted recapture and enslavement for decades.

Because of the reliance on slave labor, many poor and common white laborers struggled to find employment in the Caribbean. Englishmen looking to move to the Americas increasingly chose North America as a destination as colonies there offered more opportunities for white immigrants. Since land suitable for farming was in limited supply on the islands, and, therefore, expensive as a result, tens of thousands of white settlers left the West Indies looking for other opportunities.

British Colonial Slave Laws

The first Africans arrived in Virginia in 1619, but there is contradictory evidence regarding whether they were sold as slaves or treated instead as indentured servants. Though the default belief at the time was that slavery was legal, and it was practiced in every British colony, there were at first no specific British laws explicitly defining the status of slaves. French and Spanish colonial authorities implemented extensive **slave codes** for their colonies, comprehensive sets of laws defining and regulating nearly every facet of slavery and slave life. By contrast, in British North America there was a brief period of uncertainty and flexibility in race relations. Some black slaves in the Chesapeake earned their freedom, and a few even became slave owners themselves in the first decades of British settlement. Virginians seemed at first to treat slavery as a temporary condition for blacks, much like indentured servitude for whites. That changed in 1640, when a court in Virginia sentenced a black slave named John Punch to enslavement for life. Punch and two white indentured servants had run away from their master and been caught. The two whites were punished by whipping and an additional four years of servitude. The court justified Punch's lifelong sentence by pointing out that he was black, making explicit the connection between race and permanent enslavement in the British colonies.

From then on, British colonial society became increasingly rigid in drawing the lines between white freedom and black chattel slavery. In 1641, Massachusetts became the first British colony to specifically pass a law making lifelong slavery legal. As the colonies became more committed to the institution, the law increasingly equated blackness with slavery. A 1663 Maryland statue declared that all Africans who arrived in the colony were presumed to be slaves, and other colonies quickly implemented similar laws. A 1664 Virginia law clearly differentiated indentured servitude from slavery by declaring that enslavement was always for life, and that children born to slave mothers would also be born into lifelong slavery.

As the number of slaves in British colonies grew, so did the racial divide between all blacks and all whites, even though some whites owned no slaves. White settlers as a group lived in fear of slave rebellions and used the legal system to try and control the slave population. Colonial legislatures passed statutes prohibiting slaves from carrying firearms for any reason. In 1663, a group of white servants and black slaves planned a violent uprising in Virginia. The plot was exposed before the uprising started, and the ringleaders hanged. Their heads were then severed and put on display as a warning against future slave resistance. Such violent theatrics became a standard part of the slave system. Just a few years later, Virginia implemented a new law making legal the "casual killing" of slaves. This atmosphere of fear and distrust led to laws designed to prevent whites from ever interacting with blacks on an equal basis. Colonial legislatures banned black-white interracial marriages, and Massachusetts in 1673 even banned trade between whites and free blacks. The overall trend throughout the colonial period was for the law to treat whites by default as free Englishmen with all the rights that entailed and blacks by default as slaves possessing no rights whatsoever.

THE DEEP SOUTH

Carolina

In 1663, Charles II, recently restored to his throne after the long years of the English Civil War, decided to reward a group of eight royal supporters with a piece of land along the North American coast to the south of Virginia. The proprietors named their new colony Carolina, a variation of the Latin word for Charles. The first step was to draw up a government structure for the new settlement, and to that end the proprietors employed a young John Locke, who later in his career became one of England's most influential political philosophers. The Fundamental Constitutions, completed in 1669, tried to set up a governmental system similar to the feudal system of medieval Europe, though with some republican touches. The proprietors would act as nobles, holding much of the land in Carolina and exercising much of the political power. Commoners, who would own much smaller pieces of land, would be allowed an elected legislative assembly, but would be expected to defer to the nobility in most matters. The document also envisioned an entire class of landless peasants who worked as laborers on the estates of the nobles.

None of the proprietors had any interest in living in America, so they recruited others to settle the colony on their behalf. In 1670, they moved 200 wealthy planters from Barbados, along with some of their slaves, to establish Charles Town (modern Charleston). For the next decade, most of the white immigrants to the colony came from the British West Indies. Carolina thus started more as an extension of the English Caribbean than as an extension of the mother country. The northern part of the colony, covered by thick pine forests, developed an economy based on a mixture of tobacco, lumber, turpentine, and pine tar (hence the origin of the nickname "tarheel"). These activities turned a profit, but not a large one.

Some colonists in the southern area began searching for a staple crop that could earn a higher return. The climate was not ideal for either tobacco or for sugar, but southern planters eventually settled on a staple of rice. Rice cultivation required a heavy initial investment in land, slaves, and construction but returned high levels of profit. Planters quickly determined that European workers would not succeed on rice plantations. The damp rice paddies were fertile breeding grounds for mosquitos, which in turn spread malaria and yellow fever, both of which killed white servants quickly. Africans, however, had been exposed to both diseases in Africa, so had a built-in level of inherited resistance. Therefore, rice planters had to rely almost completely on enslaved laborers rather than free ones. Africans from the Guinea Coast had cultivated rice for centuries and passed this information along to white masters and overseers who did not have much experience with the grain. Carolina planters used hollowed out logs as pipes to move water between dammed areas of rice fields, a technique pioneered in Africa. African slaves also very likely brought the red variety of rice grown early in the colony's history. South Carolina, like the British Caribbean colonies, became a majority black society.

The other major staple crop grown in South Carolina was indigo, a plant that produces a blue dye that could be used in clothing. The dye was so highly prized that a pound of it was worth more than a pound of sugar, a crop that itself generated massive profits. A female planter, Eliza Lucas Pinckney, introduced indigo to South Carolina. She arrived as a teenager from the island of Antigua. With her mother deceased and her father absent for much of the time from South Carolina, Pinckney managed his three plantations in the province. She left behind a detailed record of her management decisions

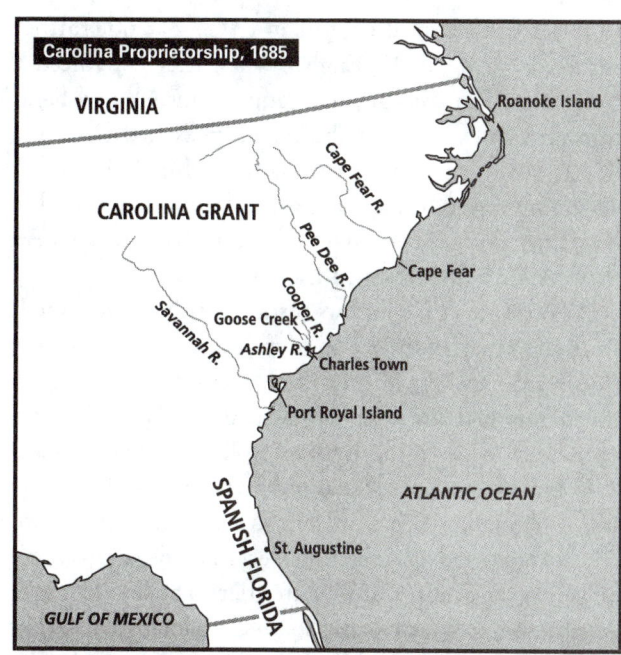

Map 2.4 Carolina Proprietorship, 1685

and experiments with indigo in an extensive book that today still represents one of the most important sources for understanding the roles of colonial women.

Carolina planters attempted to supplement their work force by enslaving Indians in addition to Africans. English settlers armed friendly native tribes and encouraged them to attack their enemies and sell the resulting captives in an **Indian slave trade**. English-allied Indians, like the Yamasee and the Creek, raided as far away as Florida to acquire slaves to trade or sell to white planters. Carolinians used some Indians on rice plantations but began exporting most native captives to other British colonies, both in the Caribbean and on the mainland. Over 30,000 Indians were enslaved in Carolina between 1670 and 1715.

In addition to providing captives for the Indian slave trade, the Yamasee also proved crucial to defending Carolina against the strong Tuscarora people, who posed a legitimate threat to the English colony's existence in the early eighteenth century. The Tuscarora had been steadily losing control of their lands to the encroachment of white farmers, and some of the tribe members had been captured and sold into slavery by the English. In fact, the Tuscarora had petitioned the colony of Pennsylvania to take them in as refugees, feeling that only such a drastic move might save the rest of the them from being enslaved. The Tuscarora struck suddenly in 1711 under the leadership of "King Hancock" (as the British called him), attacking multiple settlements simultaneously, driving the English backwards, and killing over 100 white colonists. The northern portion of Carolina was jolted into a state of utter panic by the early Tuscarora victories. The Yamasee came to Carolina's rescue by sending a 500-warrior army to counterattack the Tuscarora in 1712. The tide further turned in favor of the English when they convinced a rival chief, Tom Blount, to capture Hancock and hand him over for execution. The Tuscarora experienced total defeat in the war. After the war ended in 1715, a few Tuscarora stayed in Carolina with Blount as their leader, but the majority of survivors moved to New York where they settled amongst allied Indian tribes.

The same year that the Tuscarora tribe surrendered, Carolina experienced yet another Indian war. This time it was against their former allies, the Yamasee. English merchants had for years imposed unfair trading terms on natives, causing the Yamasee to fall deeply into debt. The Yamasee in 1715 killed several members of an English diplomatic delegation sent to negotiate with them. Then, supported by several smaller tribes, began to attack all across the South Carolina frontier. The first Yamasee advance was so effective that South Carolinians feared that their entire colony would be wiped from existence. The colonial government went to the extraordinary length of recruiting 400 African slaves into military service. The colony was assisted by the arrival of a contingent of troops from Virginia and a group of 100 Tuscarora warriors—those who had sided with the English after the Tuscarora War—from North Carolina. The war ended in 1717, when the powerful Creek, Cherokee, and Chickasaw, whom the Yamasee had been trying to recruit in the Indian alliance, instead signed a treaty with the English. The Yamasee then realized that they no longer had any hope of victory and retreated south into Spanish Florida. Some the Yamasee continued the fight, however, using Florida as a base to raid Carolina settlements throughout the 1720s.

The bloody and destructive war against the Yamasee in 1715 successfully convinced South Carolina to abandon the Indian slave trade and focus on rice production. In recognition of the very different economies of the northern and southern portions of the colony, the proprietors in 1712 began the process of dividing the territory into two separate provinces, North Carolina and South Carolina, a process officially concluded in 1729.

By 1729, the proprietors were gone. The colonists had chafed from the start under the unusual constitution shaped by the proprietors and in the early eighteenth-century, there was a major push by colonists to get the two colonies taken over by the Crown. A series of crises in the early eighteenth century led to the end of proprietary rule. Early in Carolina's history, general religious toleration had been the rule, and there was no officially established church in the province. As a result, a number of dissenting Protestants had moved in and made a home for themselves. In 1699, the proprietors' officials estab-lished the Church of England as the only legal church and began taxing inhabitants to pay for it. Colonial officials also expelled all religious dissenters from government offices. The controversy erupted into a brief shooting match in North Carolina in 1711 between two English factions. This chaos was followed in quick order by both the Tuscarora and Yamasee Wars, during which the Lords Proprietors did very little to assist the colony militarily. In 1719, after the conclusion of the two Indian wars, colonists successfully petitioned the King to make South Carolina and North Carolina royal colonies.

Men, Women, and Families in British Plantation Colonies

The high death rates in British plantation colonies—the Chesapeake, Carolinas, West Indies—in the seventeenth-century deeply affected the structure of colonial families. Since effective birth control was largely unknown (natural methods used by colonists did not work), a typical family tended to have multiple pregnancies, with slightly more than half resulting in successful live births. In the malaria- and yellow fever-ridden southern colonies, approximately 40 percent of children died in infancy, taking a devastating emotional and psychological toll on survivors. One family had eleven children, four of whom lived to survive to become adults. One of those four fathered sixteen children, only six of whom reached the age of 18. Disease and poor health claimed fathers and mothers in addition to children. In addition to diseases, adult men were more likely to die in warfare and work accidents. Women faced increased risk of mortality from childbirth. A typical Virginian who reached the age of 18 at the end of the seventeenth century had less than a 1-in-3 chance of having both birth parents still living.

For adult colonists, widowhood and remarriage was the rule rather than the exception. Fresh European immigrants into the southern colonies underwent a period known as the "seasoning"—a nearly guaranteed bout of illnesses within weeks of arrival. If a person survived that initial period, they were then "seasoned" colonists. Individual examples can show how quickly marriages could be disrupted and formed again. Virginia planter John Rolfe died at 37 years of age, having been married three times. His first two wives (including Pocahontas) lived only a combined total of five years. Each time that he became a widower, he remarried within a couple of years. He married his third wife in 1619 and himself died three years later in the 1622 Indian uprising, leaving her a widow. The result of this pattern was that extended families took on a brand new importance compared to nuclear families. Adult colonists normally had a mismatched collection of siblings, half-siblings, step-parents, and—as they aged—children and step-children. Communities were forced by necessity to address orphanhood, which may have affected as many as 20 percent of children in some southern areas. Parents often made provisions for surviving children in wills, sometimes specifying a particular relative who should gain custody, and some went even further and proscribed the conduct of their child's named guardians to ensure that their children would not be left destitute by an ill-intentioned caretaker. Courts frequently required guardians of orphaned children to take out performance bonds to guarantee good conduct towards their charges.

Early English colonies in the West Indies and in New England had, from the start, relatively even ratios of men and women, making the initial formation of families easier. By contrast, in the seventeenth-century Chesapeake colonies, men always outnumbered women. The early waves of settlement were almost entirely male. The Virginia Company had belatedly tried to address the situation by sending over 147 single young women from 1619-21. However, the company's actions were too little, too late. The sexual imbalance continued due to the nature of a tobacco plantation economy that prized indentured (and later enslaved) male labor above all else. Marriage was further delayed in the Chesapeake because indentured servants were forbidden from marrying, so men and women who arrived under such terms would have to complete their lengthy contracts before seeking a husband or wife. In such conditions, pre-marital sex was far more widespread than in other English colonies, much to the consternation of religious authorities. Because of their relative scarcity, Chesapeake women had more ability to select their husbands and greater economic independence than colonial women elsewhere. These relative advantages did not, however, translate into greater political or legal rights for women in society. It was not until about 1700 that the percentage of females in Chesapeake society reached 40 percent, allowing for more widespread marriage and family stability.

The French South

The French, in contrast to both the Spanish and the English, placed very few settlers in the south during the seventeenth century. Beginning with Quebec in 1609, France had first focused its colonial efforts to the north in Canada (see Chapter 1). The French had made an effort in the 1560s to place a settlement called Fort Caroline along the southern Atlantic coast, but that was destroyed by Spanish troops. The French shied away from the area for most of the next century. Only near the end of the seventeenth century did French explorers and colonists show renewed interest in the southern reaches of North America. **René-Robert Cavelier, Sieur de La Salle** had become convinced in the 1660s that the Mississippi River, which the French had been exploring from the North, emptied into the Gulf of Mexico. His belief was proven correct by the 1673 Joliet-Marquette expedition. In 1682, La Salle made his way down the Illinois River to the Mississippi, then on to the latter river's mouth. La Salle claimed for France all of the lands drained by the river. He did not realize at the time that such a claim amounted to almost a third of the continent.

La Salle then returned to France to outfit an expedition to settle where the Mississippi met the Gulf of Mexico. In 1684, he left France with four ships and 300 settlers and entered the Gulf of Mexico. La Salle had previously seen the mouth of the Mississippi from the river side rather than from out in the Gulf, and due to storms, navigational errors, and unfamiliarity the Gulf shoreline, the expedition sailed right past the river. La Salle instead landed at Matagorda Bay in Texas and built Fort St. Louis. At the time, he believed it was the mouth of the Mississippi, but in reality, he was over 400 miles off course. He was also hampered by French maps that had drawn the course of Mississippi River based on mistaken assumptions rather than solid information. La Salle was disappointed by his failure to find the river but still determined to locate it and proceed with his original settlement plan. The expedition, though, was

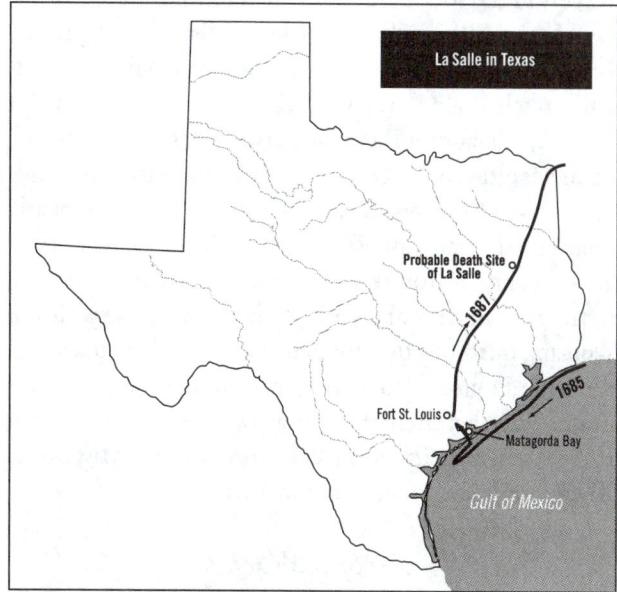

Map 2.5 **La Salle was the first European to descend the Mississippi all the way to the Gulf of Mexico in 1682. He claimed the entire Mississippi River Valley for France, naming the entire region "Louisiana" in honor of his king, Louis XIV.**

rapidly running out of a necessary resource—ships. One of his ships had been lost on the voyage due to Spanish privateers. Another grounded on a sandbar at the mouth of Matagorda Bay. A number of disillusioned sailors and colonists used the third ship to return to France, leaving La Salle with only a single ship, *Belle*. In 1686, the *Belle* wrecked during a storm, severing the French colony's last lifeline to the outside world.

La Salle attempted to explore overland to find the Mississippi River, first heading west in 1685, perhaps reaching as far as the Rio Grande. He realized that he was too far west and instead, needed to head east. He made two separate overland attempts to make his way. During the second of these search efforts, in 1687, one of La Salle's men mutinied and murdered him. Six survivors eventually managed to make their way up through the continent to safety in Canada. By this time, various misfortunes had greatly reduced the number of colonists left alive at Fort St. Louis. In late 1688, the colony was overrun by Karankawa natives who the French had quarreled with since their arrival. The Spanish had been looking for the French colony since it was built on land claimed by Spain. Spanish military expeditions eventually located the remains of the fort and rescued a handful of French children who had been taken captive by Indians. The French had their own "Lost Colony," though it was lost under less mysterious circumstances than Roanoke.

Not until the end of the 1600s, decades after the Spanish and English, did the French achieve colonial success in the south. In 1699, the French brothers Pierre Le Moyne d'Iberville and Jean-Baptiste Le Moyne de Bienville founded the colony of Louisiana, which eventually stretched along the Gulf coast as far as modern day Mobile, Alabama. Bienville personally selected the site of the capital, New Orleans, proclaiming it to be completely safe from hurricanes. Louisiana was very nearly established as an English colony. When Bienville traveled downriver from New Orleans shortly after arriving in the region, he found an English colonizing expedition scouting out a location for a town. Bienville managed to bluff the English into leaving by claiming that there was a large French military force nearby. The English decided to flee, and the site of the encounter on the Mississippi River is still known as "English Turn."

The Spanish South

While the English were settling along the eastern seaboard during the seventeenth century, the Spanish were also expanding into the southern reaches of what would later become the United States. In 1513, Spain spent Ponce de Leon to explore the region now known as Florida, and in 1521, he tried unsuccessfully to plant a colony in Southwest Florida. Spanish conquistadores were not discouraged by this failure, however. In 1528, Panfilo de Narvaez landed near what today is Tampa with around 400 men. His object was to search for and conquer Native American cities such as those in the Aztec and Incan empires farther to the south. He did not realize that there were no such cities in Florida. Narvaez's expedition soon got separated from his ships, then ran low on food and supplies, and in desperation he and his men had to try and make their way to the nearest Spanish settlement, which was thousands of miles away in Mexico. Eight years later, four survivors (Narvaez not among them) staggered out of the wilderness on the Pacific coast of Mexico. The expedition's surviving treasurer, Cabeza de Vaca, published a detailed account of their harrowing journey. This expedition was followed in 1539 by the conquistador Hernando de Soto, who again landed near Tampa. De Soto was much more prepared for a long trek, and spent the next three years exploring the American southeast. He became the first European to cross the Mississippi River, and after his death due to disease in 1542, his men explored as far west as Texas before making their way to Spanish settlements in Mexico in 1543. Together the de Leon, Narvaez, and de Soto expeditions had found little in the way of gold or other easily exploited valuables. Nevertheless, Spain maintained an interest in the region, eventually establishing in 1565 the first permanent European settlement in what became the mainland United States: St. Augustine, Florida.

At the same time, Spain also took an interest in what is now the American Southwest. From 1540-1542, Francisco Vasquez de Coronado led an exploration of what are today the states of Arizona, New Mexico, Texas, Oklahoma, and Kansas, hoping they would yield gold and silver. When those hopes faded, Spain looked towards the Pueblo Indians as a potential source of trade and profit. Spanish priests also began building a series of church missions stretching across large areas of the American south. The Catholic Church declared that Christianizing the Indians was going to be a principal goal of New World settlement. By the 1590s, Franciscan friars were building missions in both Florida and the desert Southwest. In 1610, Spanish settlers established the town of Santa Fe, which served as the capital of the newest province in the Spanish empire. New Mexico's European population grew steadily, reaching 10,000 by the end of the century. In addition to seeking a profit, the Spanish settlers were also supposed to force the Native peoples to convert to Catholicism and away from "heathen" ways. In 1675, Spanish authorities arrested dozens of Pueblo medicine men for practicing sorcery. Three were executed, one committed suicide in prison, and the others were whipped

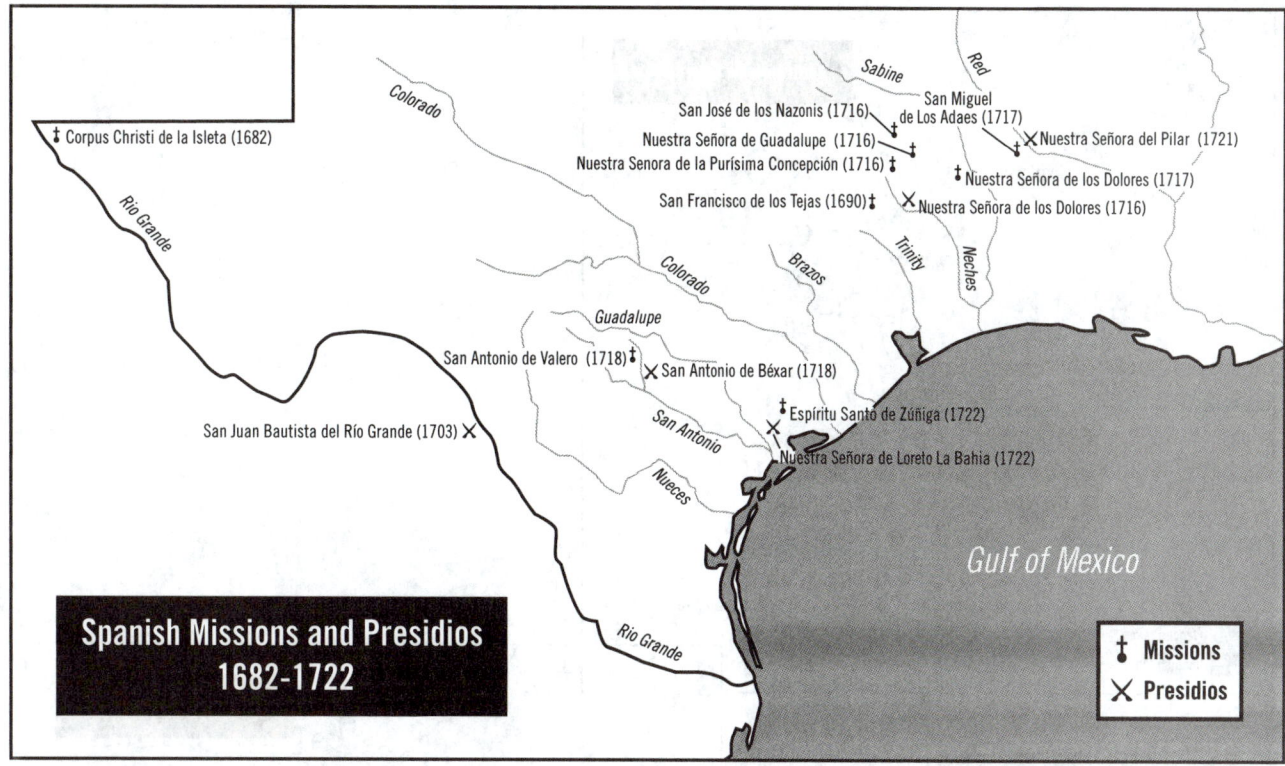

Map 2.6 Spanish Missions and Presidios, 1682-1722

as punishment for unchristian behavior. Pueblo leaders objected to this European attack on their traditions. In particular, the Pueblo leader Popé sought to lead his people back to the beliefs of their ancestors, believing that the Spanish presence had brought with it nothing but misery and misfortune. In 1680, the Pueblo launched an attack against the Spanish in New Mexico. The **Pueblo Revolt** at first achieved significant success. In the early fighting, the Pueblo drove out as many as two thousand Spanish colonists. However, a combination of drought and attacks by the rival Navajo and Apache tribes weakened the Pueblo, and in 1692, the Spanish managed to return and reassert control.

The relationship between the Spanish and Pueblo mirrored that of the English and Powhatan in many ways. European settlers had originally been welcomed by Native peoples, but when those same Native peoples felt abused at the hands of Europeans, they struck back militarily. The Pueblo in New Mexico and the Powhatan in Virginia both achieved early success in their wars, but each had been weakened by their interaction with Europeans. The Spanish and English were too numerous and too powerful to defeat militarily.

By 1675, there were four Spanish mission provinces in Florida to complement the permanent Spanish town of St. Augustine. As in New Mexico, Franciscan priests tried to dismantle traditional Indian cultures and turn the Natives towards Christianity. The ongoing Spanish presence in Florida served as constant thorn in the side of southern English colonies during the late seventeenth century and early eighteenth century. Spanish military forces in the region constantly threatened to invade the Carolinas and the Chesapeake. The Spanish also encouraged slaves to run away from British masters and flee to Florida, where they could gain freedom by converting to Catholicism. Spain did not want to end slavery; instead, it merely wanted to weaken the British colonies. So many slaves took this offer that the Spanish put together an entire army regiment of former slaves.

La Salle's failed 1685 French colony helped change the course of Spanish settlement in North America. It ushered in a contest between the two countries for control over the Gulf Coast. Up to that point, Spain had expanded out of Mexico almost entirely out west, towards California and New Mexico. Since the failed expeditions of Narvaez and de Soto in the 1530s and 1540s, the Spanish had largely avoided the northern Gulf Coast. French interest in the area, however, prompted Spain to establish a more formidable presence. Spanish authorities began to build a series of missions throughout the region, of which San Francisco de los Tejas in 1690 was the first in East Texas. That this first expedition was a direct response to La Salle could not be more clear—the first stop after leaving Mexico was at the abandoned remnants of Fort St.

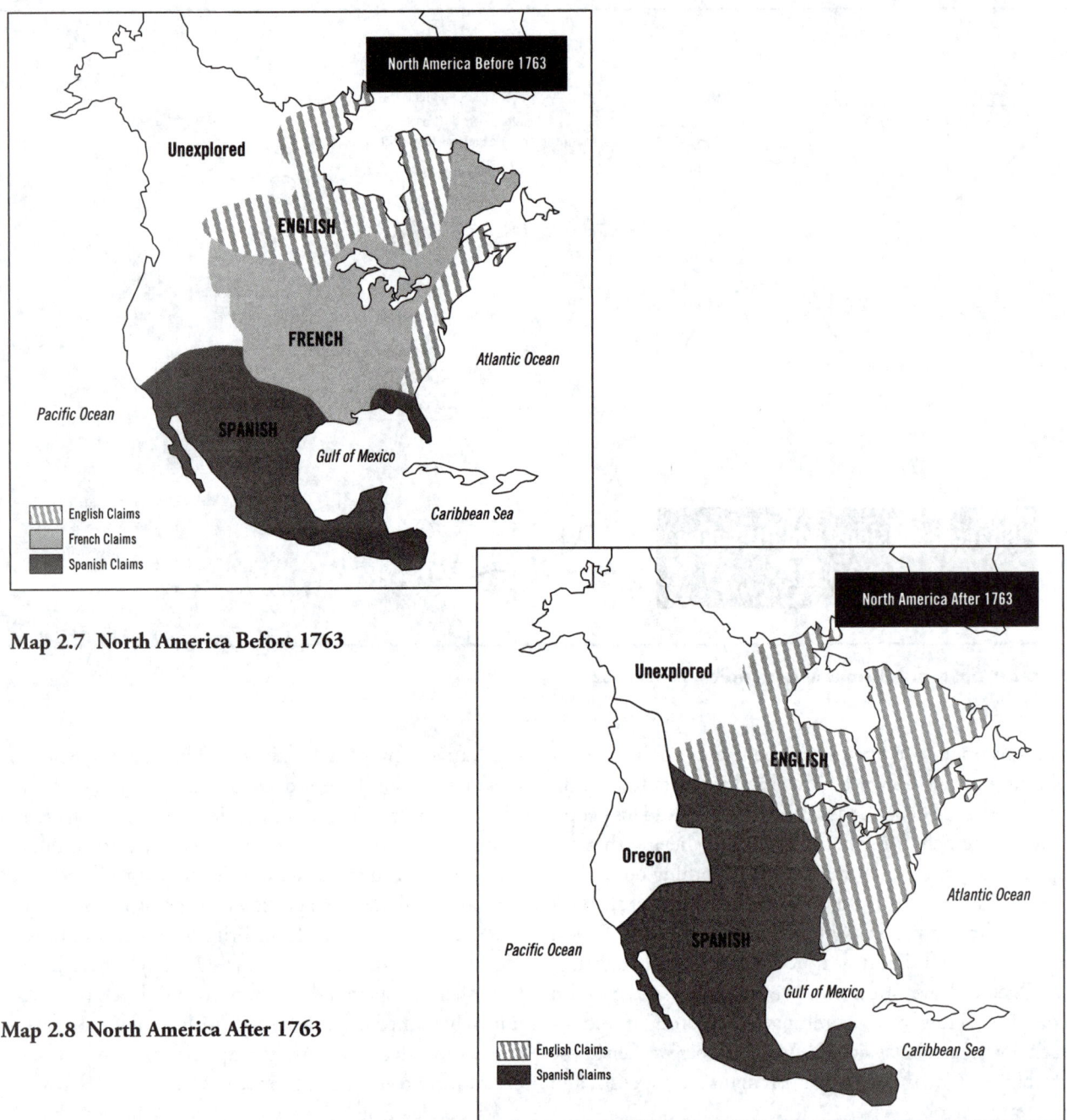

Map 2.7 North America Before 1763

Map 2.8 North America After 1763

Louis to burn the remaining French buildings. Though the mission was abandoned in 1693, rebuilt in 1716 and abandoned yet again, Spain continued to build missions and presidios, or fortified military outposts, throughout the early eighteenth century in response to French encroachments. The effort to settle the eastern portion of Texas led to the founding of San Antonio in 1718 to serve as a waystation for the long overland trip from Mexico.

Georgia

The experience of colonial Georgia demonstrates just how deeply ingrained certain colonial traditions had become in British America. Parliament in 1732 granted a group of Trustees in England the right to settle a colony south of Carolina. The Trustees, made up of a hodgepodge of religious, political, and philanthropic gentlemen, drew up plans for a settlement radically different than other British colonies. Slavery would be illegal in Georgia. This was done not out of respect for the rights of slaves, but rather to motivate white settlers to do more work themselves rather than rely on slaves for labor. The colony would also be a military buffer to guard against invasion from Spanish Florida, and the trustees felt that slaves would present an internal danger if the Spanish ever did send an army into the province.

The colony placed sharp limitations on land, with most families given only 50 acres of land and no one given more than 500 acres. To prevent the resale of land to others, the Trustees in England would retain actual ownership of all the land rather than the farmers who worked it. This would prevent the accumulation of vast planter estates like those in the Caribbean, the Chesapeake, and the Carolinas. All farmers were required to devote at least part of their land to silk production, which English authorities believed would be less labor intensive than staple crops like tobacco and rice grown in other colonies. Finally, Georgia settlers would be denied any self-government. There would be no governor and no elected assembly, just a few, minor appointed officials with limited powers. All significant decisions would be made in England. The **Georgia Trustees** envisioned a utopian colony of white farmers toiling away on small farms, living simply, and paying due obedience to their superiors across the ocean.

The Georgia plan went awry very quickly. Settlement began in 1733 when a group of colonists led by James Oglethorpe founded the city of Savannah, which would serve as Georgia's capital. Without clearly defined political leaders, colonists squabbled and feuded over nearly everything with no real system to resolve disagreements. As the only Trustee to ever travel to Georgia, Oglethorpe wielded tremendous unofficial influence over the settlers, but the Trust specifically denied him both the title and the powers of a governor. In any case, due to the threat posed by the Spanish in Florida, Oglethorpe had to spend a large percentage of his time on military defenses and preparations rather than on civil affairs. When war erupted in 1739, Oglethorpe could devote even less time to political or economic leadership. He launched two unsuccessful expeditions against Spanish St. Augustine, and then, disgusted by his experiences in America, sailed for England in 1743 never to return.

Georgians led a political campaign to remove all of the burdensome restrictions placed on them by the Trustees, even sending an agent to London to lobby Parliament into revoking the colonial charter and making their colony a royal one. Colonists had no desire to raise silk nor did most have any understanding of silk worms or how to care for them. What's more, the land ownership restrictions served as a disincentive for farmers. Why should individuals invest money and time into cultivating land that they did not truly own and could not pass along to their children? They demanded clear title to lands and an end to the 500-acre limit on holdings. The Trustees gave in on land titles but still tried to limit the amount of land any one person could control. At a distance of thousands of miles, however, London officials could do little to investigate or punish those who accumulated excess property.

The two most controversial restrictions were the absence of representative government and the ban on slavery. Georgia farmers pointed to both their own labor shortage and to the profitability of slavery in other British colonies as proof that slavery was an absolute necessity. Outlawing slavery in the province, they argued, had condemned white settlers to a life of poverty. Colonists further complained that the Trust's officials were both inadequate and incompetent. Oglethorpe had become a near dictator by the end of his time in the province, and after his absence the colonists now faced the opposite problem—there was a leadership vacuum because the Trust insisted on running the colony from afar. Colonists demanded to be allowed an elected legislature so that they could govern themselves. Every other British colony already enjoyed such an assembly, and Georgia was going against over a century of precedent in being denied one. The Trustees fought back against the complaints and tried to maintain their original vision, but by 1751, slavery was legal and the first colonial assembly met. In 1752, the Trust surrendered its charter and Georgia became a royal colony. Relieved planters quickly abandoned silk in favor of rice cultivation, and Georgia soon developed a plantation economy like those of Carolina and the Chesapeake. The Trustees had tried to swim against the colonial current and failed. Georgia settlers, on the other hand, were happy to make Georgia look just like its British colonial neighbors.

THE GROWTH OF ENGLISH COLONIES

In the sixteenth century, England lagged far behind Spain, Portugal, and France in the race to explore and settle the Americas. England's first attempts to plant a colony went poorly, and Jamestown survived only through the continual arrival of new colonists to replace the thousands who died. Once England managed to establish a permanent presence, English colonies expanded rapidly, both on the mainland and in the Caribbean. In the process, England's southern colonies set in place precedents that affected the course of history. Staple crops, representative government, the slave trade, and class and racial divisions all came to characterize the American south for not only the entirety of the colonial period, but also far beyond.

Chronology

1558	Queen Elizabeth I crowned.
1585-1590	Roanoke colony founded and then vanished.
1607	Jamestown established.
1614	John Rolfe exports tobacco, marries Pocahontas.
1619	First Africans arrive in Virginia. House of Burgesses first meets.
1622	Opechancanough launches series of attacks in Virginia.
1624	The Crown assumes direct control of Virginia.
1625	Establishment of Barbados
1632	King Charles I grants Lord Baltimore land for the colony of Maryland.
1642-1651	English Civil War
1644	Opechancanough's second uprising against Virginia colonists.
1660	Restoration of Charles II
1663	First Carolina charter granted.
1670	First English settlement established in South Carolina.
1675-76	Bacon's Rebellion in Virginia.
1680	Pueblo Revolt in New Mexico.
1685	La Salle attempts to establish a French colony in present-day Texas.
1699	Louisiana established by the French.
1705	Virginia adopts comprehensive slave code.
1715	Yamasee War in South Carolina.
1732	Charter issued for the Georgia colony.

SUGGESTED READINGS

David Armitage and Michael J. Braddick, eds., *The British Atlantic World, 1500-1800* (2002).

Ira Berlin, *Many Thousands Gone: The First Two Centuries of Slavery in North America* (1998).

Richard S. Dunn, *Sugar and Slaves: The Rise of the Planter Class in the English West Indies, 1624-1713* (1972).

Allan Gallay, *The Indian Slave Trade: The Rise of the English Empire in the American South, 1670–1717* (2003).

Frederic W. Gleach, *Powhatan's World and Colonial Virginia: A Conflict of Cultures* (1997).

Winthrop Jordan, *White over Black: American Attitudes Toward the Negro, 1550-1812* (1968).

Allan Kulikoff, *Tobacco and Slaves: The Development of the Southern Cultures in the Chesapeake, 1680-1800* (1986).

David C. Littlefield, *Rice and Slaves: Ethnicity and the Slave Trade in Colonial South Carolina* (1981).

Peter C. Mancall, *Hakluyt's Promise: An Elizabethan's Obsession for an English America* (2007).

Gloria L. Main, *Tobacco Colony: Life in Early Maryland, 1650-1720* (1982).

Sidney Mintz, *Sweetness and Power: The Place of Sugar in Modern History* (1985).

Edmund S. Morgan, *American Slavery, American Freedom: The Ordeal of Colonial Virginia* (1975).

Anthony S. Parent, *Foul Means: The Formation of a Slave Society in Virginia, 1660-1740* (2003).

David Price, *Love and Hate in Jamestown: John Smith, Pocahontas, and the Start of a Nation* (2003).

Alan Taylor, *The American Colonies* (2001).

John Thornton, *Africa and Africans in the Making of the Atlantic World, 1400-1800* (1992).

Wilcomb E. Washburn, *The Governor and the Rebel: A History of Bacon's Rebellion in Virginia* (1957).

Richard Waterhouse, *A New World Gentry: The Making of a Merchant and Planter Class in South Carolina, 1670-1770* (1989).

Peter H. Wood, *Black Majority: Negroes in Colonial South Carolina from 1670 through the Stono Rebellion* (1974).

Review Questions

1. How well did English colonists and Native Americans get along? Which issues caused the most tension or disagreement between the two groups?

2. Discuss the causes and consequences of slavery and the Atlantic slave trade for both the Americas and Africa.

3. Compare and contrast English colonization efforts in the New World with those of the Spanish and French.

4. Why did Bacon's rebellion happen? Why is it seen as such a key event in the history of colonial America?

5. What were some of the common social, economic, and political features of the southern British colonies? Why were these features important?

Glossary of Important People and Concepts

Atlantic Slave Trade
Bacon's Rebellion
Elizabeth I
Georgia Trustees
Richard Hakluyt
Headright System
House of Burgesses
Indentured Servants
Indian Slave Trade
Jamestown
Joint Stock Company
René-Robert Cavelier, Sieur de La Salle
London or Virginia Company
Maroon communities
Middle Passage
Opechancanough
Pocahontas
Powhatan
Proprietary Colony
Pueblo Revolt
Walter Raleigh
Roanoke
John Rolfe
Slave Codes
John Smith

The *Mayflower*, 1620

Chapter Three

THE NORTHERN COLONIES

In early 1692, the small village of Salem, Massachusetts was gripped by panic. A group of young girls had manifested strange symptoms, including intense pain, muscle spasms, seizures, and incoherent speech. They claimed to be pinched and poked by unseen forces. When asked what was ailing them, the girls accused three local women of afflicting them through black magic. An audience gathered at Nathaniel Ingersoll's tavern to question the girls and hear their accusations. Among the crowd were Giles and Martha Corey, a recently married elderly couple who lived in town. Martha was suspicious of the girls and publicly questioned in the meeting whether the girls were sincerely the victims of witchcraft. After they left the tavern, Martha advised her husband to stop attending any further examinations of the girls, as she was sure nothing good would come from it.

After the evening at the tavern, one of the girls accused Martha Corey of casting evil spells on them. When the two town leaders arrived at the Corey house, Martha said she already knew why they had come. "Ye are come to talk with me about being a witch," she said, "but I am none." She smiled and then accused the girls of being up to no good. There were no witches in the village she said, and she, a church member in good standing and a follower of Christ, had nothing to fear from lying children. The magistrates departed with new doubts in their heads. They asked the afflicted girls again whether they were sure Martha was a witch. The girls accused Martha of appearing to them at night and temporarily blinding them with magic.

A week later, officials swore out a warrant for Martha Corey's arrest. However, the day was a Sunday, and by tradition no warrants could be enforced on the Sabbath. Martha knew full well that she would be arrested on Monday morning, but she proudly and defiantly attended church services that Sunday while the entire church congregation gawked at the supposed witch in their midst. On Monday she was taken into custody and interrogated in court in the presence of the young witchcraft victims. Immediately after the court's opening prayer, the afflicted girls fell on the ground and began thrashing around in pain, and continued to do this throughout most of the questioning. The magistrates repeatedly asked Martha to explain how and why she was doing this to the girls, but she insisted on her innocence and said that she was doing absolutely nothing to them. At one point, an afflicted girl interrupted the judges and cried out that there was an invisible black man whispering in Martha Corey's ear. This alarmed the judges, who demanded that Martha tell them immediately what the invisible being was whispering to her. When she replied that there was no man whispering in her ear, the girls intensified their screaming and writhing.

The magistrates demanded that Martha confess to practicing witchcraft. She continued to insist, however, that she was innocent and that God would protect her. The judges read statements from several other witnesses willing to testify that Martha was a witch. In response, she laughed, saying that some of her enemies in town were clearly conspiring against her. Her laughter was a mistake, and one of the judges angrily asked how she could laugh at the sufferings of the children unless she was in fact causing their pain. Martha, continuing to laugh, declared her belief that there were no witches at all in Salem and that the girls were faking their symptoms. The afflicted girls then cried out that a yellow bird that only they could see was at that very moment sucking blood out from between Martha's fingers and that the invisible man was still whispering in her ear. To the judges, this was conclusive proof of Martha Corey's guilt, and they ordered that a full trial be held for her.

During the investigation, Giles Corey spoke up in defense of his wife's innocence. The Coreys had only recently married, and their short relationship had admittedly been troubled by arguments, but he was convinced that Martha was not a witch. This put him in direct opposition to the witchcraft victims. One of the afflicted girls then claimed that Giles's spirit had visited her and asked her to sign her soul over to the Devil. The other girls quickly spoke up to agree that his specter had appeared to them as well and attacked them. Giles Corey was arrested and accused of being a wizard. Numerous witnesses testified against him, with two women in the village claiming that they had seen him at a massive gathering with over fifty other witches.

Both Martha and Giles Corey were held over for formal trial. On September 9, Martha Corey and five other accused witches were found guilty and sentenced to death by hanging. When a minister came to her in jail and told her that she had been excommunicated by her church, she scornfully told him to stop pestering her and just let her die in peace. She was executed on September 22, 1692, at the age of 72. By that time, her husband Giles was already dead. When indicted for witchcraft, Giles refused to participate at all in his trial. He insisted on his innocence but refused to put in an official plea of not guilty. Without a plea, the trial could not legally begin. This was important for Corey because had he been convicted (a near certainty given the outcomes of other trials), his lands would have been confiscated by the court. In order to force him to enter his plea, the court ordered him to be tortured by "pressing."

On September 17, he was lain down on the ground face up with wooden boards placed across his stomach and chest. Sheriff George Corwin and his men then began piling heavy stones on the platform, occasionally pausing to give Giles food and water. He remained completely silent as the rocks began to slowly crush him. The process dragged out for two days. Three times the sheriff asked him to enter a plea of guilty or not guilty. Each time, Giles told the men "more weight!" though that may have been less an act of defiance than his desire to die faster rather than slowly. Giles Corey died at the age of 81 on September 19 without ever entering a plea, and his property was passed along to his children. Through his actions, he managed to secure a future for his family. According to witnesses, just moments before dying, Corey placed a curse on the sheriff. Sheriff Corwin died four years later of a heart attack at only 30 years of age.

THE FOUNDING OF NEW ENGLAND

The Pilgrims and Plymouth

After the failure of the 1607 Popham colony in Maine (discussed in Chapter 2), efforts to establish English colonies in the northern reaches of America slowed. John Smith, after recovering from the wounds that he suffered in Jamestown, had taken an exploratory journey in 1614 to the area located east of the Hudson River and had been favorably impressed by the fertility of the land and the climate of the region that he became the first to name "New England." But, his journey resulted in no colonization effort. Instead, the story of New England's founding took a circuitous route from the small English village of Scrooby to the European mainland before finally reaching across the Atlantic to the New World.

By the early 1600s, all men and women in England were required to attend the religious services of the Church of England, also known as the Anglican Church, as well as pay taxes to financially support its ministers. Religious dissenters who opposed church doctrines could be fined, imprisoned, or worse. One group of dissenters, the **Puritans**, believed that the Protestant Reformation had not gone far enough in England. These English followers of the French theologian John Calvin (see Chapter 1) objected to Anglican prayers, holidays, ceremonies, and church hierarchies that still resembled those of the Catholic Church. Puritans also pitted themselves against the traditional festive culture of English commoners. In the age of Shakespeare, Puritans called for playhouses to shut down, arguing that public performances promoted moral degeneracy. They opposed gambling and most popular forms of sport like football or bull baiting, where dogs were released to attack and bring down a chained or roped bull. Such sporting events often took place on Sundays, the one day of the week that most laborers had free from work, and Sabbath desecration was deeply offensive to Puritans.

Within Puritanism, there were two main groups. The largest group consisted of non-Separatists who continued to obey the law and worked to reform the Anglican Church from within even as they criticized it. A smaller, more radical camp of Puritans were **Separatists** who believed that the Church of England was so corrupt that it could not be reformed at all and that the only solution was to abandon the church and establish separate worship services. Doing so, however, violated the law and was a direct challenge to the authority of the monarch, who in England also served as head of the church. If people could reject the spiritual authority of the king, perhaps they might also reject his secular

Puritans going to church

authority as well. Queen Elizabeth's successor, James I, disliked Puritan beliefs as a whole, correctly believing them to be potentially revolutionary, but he reserved his most extreme hatred for Separatists, swearing that he would force the Separatists to either obey him or drive them out of England entirely. James even commissioned a new version of the Scripture—the King James Bible—that placed greater emphasis on obedience to kings in order to counter Puritan sermons that questioned the monarch's supreme authority.

The small village of Scrooby in the East Midlands of England was home to one of these separatist congregations. As a result of their religious beliefs, they were constantly threatened with arrest and punishment. Puritans sometimes named their female children after the emotion felt by the parents at the time of the child's birth. In 1606, elder William Brewster named his newborn daughter Fear. The Scrooby Separatists, therefore, resolved to leave England and flee to the Netherlands, which had a reputation for accepting dissenting religious groups of all varieties. In 1608, they made their way to the city of Leiden, Holland, where they settled down and tried to maintain their community and their beliefs. Over the course of more than a decade, however, they encountered a number of difficulties that made them increasingly unhappy with their new home. As refugees and outsiders, most of them were unable to find high-paying employment. They also grew concerned at the long-term influence that the more permissive Dutch society was having on their children. Finally, the English church had been lobbying the Dutch government to disrupt the emigrant group's printing ef-

forts, as the Separatists had continued to send dissenting religious tracts back into England for public distribution. By 1619, those diplomatic efforts had begun to pay off, and the Puritans in Leiden feared being arrested by Dutch authorities.

Some of the Separatists began looking for an alternative location to live. Many of them feared returning to England since James I was still the king. Most other European countries were officially Catholic and, therefore, also undesirable. England by 1619, however, had established the Jamestown colony, which gave the Separatists a new possibility. Several of the Leiden congregation successfully petitioned the Virginia Company for the right to settle in America. In September 1620, the *Mayflower* sailed from Plymouth, England. On board were thirty-five Scrooby **"Pilgrims"** plus an additional sixty-seven others sent over on behalf of the company. They originally intended to land and settle near the Hudson River in what is today New York, but they were concerned that the location might be too close to existing English and Dutch colonial settlements. The Separatists did not want to experience the same outside cultural influences as they had encountered in England or Holland. The Pilgrims eventually came ashore in present-day Massachusetts. They had landed in an area that was not included in the Virginia Company's grant, but the travelers ultimately decided to plant their colony right there anyway. The advantage was that they would not have to follow any of the Virginia Company's rules. Despite the fact that two-thirds of the passengers were not Separatist Puritans, the Separatist leader William Bradford insisted that all the men sign the Mayflower Compact before they would be allowed off the ship. This document established a new government to oversee their colony, which they named Plymouth. The colony held annual elections for government offices, and Bradford, widely admired by his fellow colonists, was elected governor a remarkable thirty times.

The Pilgrims landed in December and thus had no time to rest and prepare before being battered by the harsh New England winter. Half of the colonists died within a few months from starvation and exposure. By the time spring arrived, the colonists were exhausted, and their future was very much in doubt. Plymouth owed much of its long-term success to the local Native American population. The area that the Pilgrims settled had already been cleared by the Patuxet Indians, so the fields were ready for planting. The Patuxet, however, were nowhere to be seen. A horrific plague brought by European fishermen had swept through the tribe in 1617 and killed them all. Only one Patuxet survived and only because he was thousands of miles away at the time. His name was **Squanto**, and he provided essential assistance to the English settlers

Plymouth Rock: The Story of a Stone

*Each November, millions of school children around the United States celebrate the Pilgrims. Kids dress in Pilgrim outfits for school plays that reenact the Thanksgiving gathering between New England settlers and Native Americans. Student learn about the voyage of the **Mayflower**, the ship that carried the Pilgrims from Europe to their new homes in the New World. And they are also taught that the first landing site of the Pilgrims was Plymouth Rock. Today, Plymouth Rock is a famed symbol of America's beginnings that resides in its own monumental structure along the waterfront in Plymouth, Massachusetts. How did a simple stone reach such lofty symbolic heights, and importantly, has it always been held in such reverence?*

According to the traditional story, the Pilgrims set foot in New England on December 26, 1620, and first stepped directly on a massive granite boulder that would later be known as Plymouth Rock. However, such a stone does not appear in any of the eyewitness accounts of the landing. The artifact's story really begins in 1741, over a century after the Pilgrim landing, when townspeople in Plymouth began construction of a new wharf that would cover the ten-ton boulder. A teary-eyed 94-year old church elder named Thomas Faunce asserted that his father had told him that the boulder in question was in fact the site of the first Pilgrim arrival in New England. There were, however, problems with the claim. Faunce had been born almost 30 years after the Pilgrim embarkation, and Faunce's father had moved to the colony from Europe only in 1623, and so therefore also could not have witnessed the 1620 landing. Due to Faunce's age and passionate speech, however, the townspeople accepted his identification as truth and built the dock in such a way that Plymouth Rock was left untouched. Plymouth Rock had begun its career.

With rebellion brewing between the colonists and the mother country in 1774, townspeople attempted to move the boulder from the waterfront into the town square to use as a symbol of resistance to British policies. In the process, however, the rock broke into two pieces. The bottom half was left in place, while the top half was moved next to the town's liberty pole. During the American Revolution, the stone became a symbol of the split from old England. It remained in the town square until 1834, when it was moved to a building known as Pilgrim Hall. In that move, it again broke into two smaller pieces. In 1867, an arched canopy was built to house the lower part of the rock, which was still near the waterfront. Unfortunately, the rock was too large for the structure, and so clever townspeople decided to smash several hundred pounds off the sides of the stone to make it fit. Some of those smashed pieces were put to use as doorstops. Several years later, in 1880, the remaining part of the top was moved from Pilgrim Hall to be rejoined with the bottom half.

Probably few precious historical artifacts have been moved around and damaged as frequently as Plymouth Rock. When the top and bottom halves were rejoined in 1880, the town decided to carve the date "1620" into the stone, perhaps under a delusion that such a carving would enhance the boulder's claim to historical authenticity. Until around 1900, it had been common practice for tourists and visitors to chisel off pieces of the rock to keep as souvenirs. As a result, Plymouth Rock today is only about 1/3 the size of the original. That type of treatment hardly indicates reverence for a treasured artifact.

Whether or not it was the actual site of the Pilgrim landing, Plymouth Rock still holds a prime spot in America's national consciousness. Many visitors come to celebrate the accomplishments of the Pilgrims. Native American activists hold a vigil at the rock each year to commemorate the tragic European displacement of Indian peoples. Regardless of their personal views of the stone and what it represents, approximately 1 million visitors per year come to see it and remember its place in history.

who now lived on his extinct tribe's land. Squanto had been kidnapped by an English sailor in 1614 and taken to Spain to be sold as a slave. After Spanish priests rescued him, he made his way to England where he worked for a few years before being carried back to Massachusetts on an English expedition in 1619. Squanto approached the Plymouth settlers in 1621 and operated as a tutor and guide. He taught the Pilgrims how the natives planted fish in the soil to fertilize crops, and within a few months the colony had grown its own corn. He also served as a translator and liaison between the English and the local Wampanoag Chief Massasoit (the Patuxet were one of several tribes that made up the Wampanoag confederation). Seeking an alliance of his weakened confederacy with the English to help stave off the rival Narragansett people of present-day Rhode Island, Massasoit spread word through the region that the English should be treated as friends, not enemies. The early results of their efforts

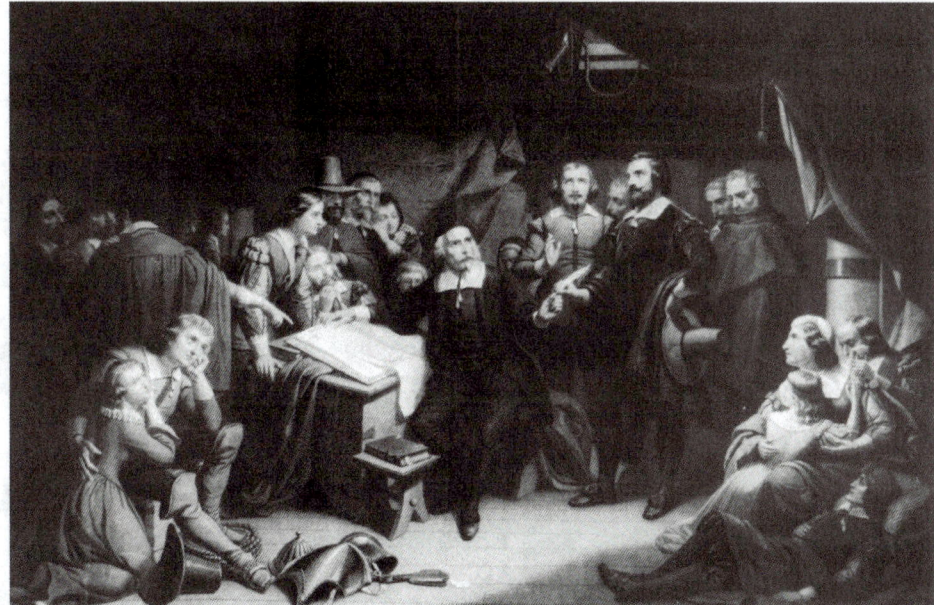

The Pilgrims signing the Mayflower Compact, November 11, 1620

were so positive that the colonists invited Indian guests to a celebration of thanksgiving in the fall of 1621. In 1622, on one of his diplomatic missions between Massasoit and the Pilgrims, Squanto fell ill of fever and died, but not before he had brought much needed stability to the young separatist colony. The Plymouth colony lasted until 1691, when it was merged with Massachusetts. The colony remained relatively small throughout its existence, never numbering more than 7,000 people at its height. The Pilgrims had moved to America to isolate themselves from the rest of the world and its influences. Little did they realize that they were about to be quickly overshadowed and outnumbered by a much larger Puritan colony established just to their north.

The first Thanksgiving, 1621.

The Massachusetts Bay Colony and the New England Way

In 1629, a group of Puritan gentlemen in England formed the Massachusetts Bay Company, a joint-stock company granted royal permission to set up a colony north of Plymouth. Unlike the Pilgrims, these Puritans were non-Separatists who remained legally within the Church of England. Though they did not face the same extreme treatment as did the Separatists, James I and his successor **Charles I** had increased the pressure on all Puritans during the 1620s. The company settlers elected lawyer **John Winthrop** as their governor, and in 1630 put together an impressive colonial expedition consisting of 17 ships and almost 1,000 people. England had never before started off a new settlement on such a large scale, and the colony's fast start continued throughout the decade. During the 1630s, about 80,000 people left England, moving to Ireland, the Netherlands, and America in what became known as the **Great Migration**. A large number of them settled in the Caribbean, but about 20,000 settlers, not all of them Puritans, arrived in Massachusetts. Boston was the largest town and served as the capital of the province, but given the explosive population growth, later groups of settlers soon began to establish towns up and down the coast and throughout the countryside. Winthrop and the others wisely took their company charter to America with them, which they then used as the basis for a constitution. Since the colony's charter was physically located in America, it meant that their corporate headquarters would be 3,000 miles away from the direct influence of the King or Parliament. This granted Massachusetts a much greater degree of independence than enjoyed in other English colonies.

Wood engraving showing Massasoit and his warriors visiting the Pilgrims at Plymouth.

Winthrop and the others viewed their settlement as different from other English colonies. Virginia had been based on the profit motive. The Pilgrims had largely been trying to avoid the rest of the world. The Massachusetts Puritans, however, had a very different goal in mind. This group of colonists was going to save the world. They were about to launch an ambitious religious experiment, and America was their laboratory. Their plan was to build a perfect biblical commonwealth based on the word of God and on Puritan principles. The colonists and the perfect society they built would serve as a model for everyone else on Earth to copy. In a famous speech made during the ocean crossing, Winthrop told the passengers: "We shall be as a **City upon a Hill,** the eyes of all people are upon us."

Once in Massachusetts, the Puritans set up a government to reflect their conception of a godly commonwealth. Colonial Massachusetts was in most ways a theocracy in which the church and state were so interlinked that they often seemed wholly the same. Rejecting any move towards religious toleration, Puritanism was enshrined as the state religion, and all other faiths were prohibited. Church attendance was mandatory for all inhabitants. While ministers were not allowed to hold official positions in the government—due to the fear that politics might corrupt them—they were supposed to guide and advise government officials in their duties. The legal system's main task was to punish religious dissenters and others whose personal behavior acted contrary to the Bible. For example, blasphemy, adultery, and failure to respect one's parents were all legally punishable by death. However, the death penalty was rarely applied to any of these particular crimes, and the threat of such a severe punishment was designed more to intimidate people into obedience. Civil magistrates had a duty to enforce God's law, and most early Massachusetts statutes cited specific Bible verses as justification for their enactment.

Participation in politics was more widespread in Massachusetts than in most other colonies. The governor, deputy governor, and the Council of Assistants (the upper house of the legislature) were elected annually. In theory, all the freemen—or male property owners—made up the lower house colonial legislative assembly, but as the population of the colony grew larger that system became unworkable, so voters began to choose a lesser number of representatives. Towns and villages held annual meetings at which male residents elected all of their town aldermen (known as selectmen) and other officials. There were limits, however, to Massachusetts's democracy. Women could not vote, and in keeping with strict adherence to Puritanism, colonists changed the rules for male voting so that only fully admitted church members could cast ballots. Though church attendance was required, full membership in a Puritan church was often determined by religious leaders and difficult to obtain. Applicants who desired full church membership had to undergo a rigorous conversion experience and be questioned and judged by those who were already full members. Despite

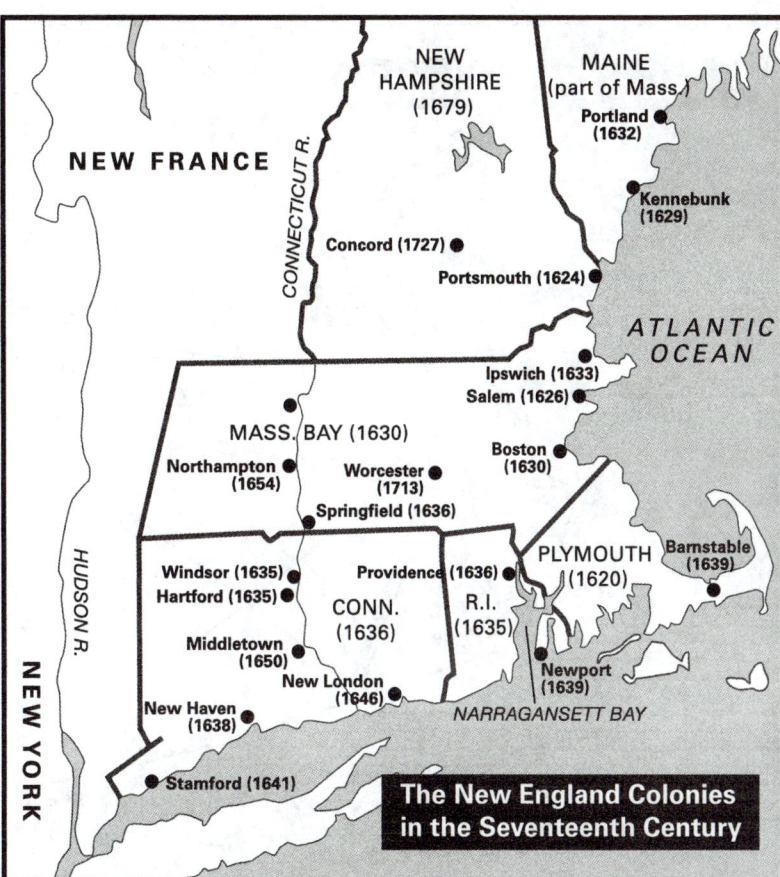

Map 3.1 The New England Colonies in the Seventeenth Century

these voting restrictions, a far higher percentage of the population enjoyed the franchise in Massachusetts than in England.

Puritan New England placed special emphasis on literacy and the ability of individuals to read Scripture. As a result, New Englanders had a much higher literacy rate than inhabitants of other seventeenth-century colonies. In 1636, the colonial government granted a charter to Harvard University to train a new generation of ministers. Two years later, Harvard became home to the first printing press in America. The Old Deluder Satan Act of 1647 further specified that every town had to either appoint a schoolteacher or build a schoolhouse, depending on the size of the town, in order to teach children to read Scripture. Literacy would then protect them from being tricked by the devil.

Massachusetts's churches remained formally within the Church of England, but Puritans disliked almost every feature of Anglican structure and governance. In England, everyone had to obey the dictates of the King and the Archbishop of Canterbury, even if groups or individuals believed those dictates to be wrong. New England Puritans instead practiced congregationalism, a decentralized system where each individual church congregation had a great deal of independence and did not have to answer to any formal higher authority such as a bishop. Lay members of each church congregation had

authority to hire and fire their minister if they disapproved of his teachings. Each church would have its own elders and deacons responsible for their congregation's good order. Though such a decentralized system potentially served as fertile ground for religious disagreements and disorder, Puritans believed they could guarantee purity and stability by giving power only to full church members who had undergone the conversion experience and been identified as one of God's chosen "saints"—individuals predestined from birth to receive God's grace and salvation. This would supposedly ensure that religious dissenters and troublemakers could never hold any real power and, therefore, could be easily isolated and dispatched. Everyone in a community was thus part of a holy covenant to monitor their own behavior and that of the community as a whole to ensure compliance with God's Word. This informal system of control became known as the "New England Way."

LIFE AND LABOR IN NEW ENGLAND

Daily life in New England was influenced heavily by both the spiritual nature of the Puritan mission and by the climate of the region. Colonists preferred to form close communities of family members and friends who worked and prayed together. In these small villages and towns,

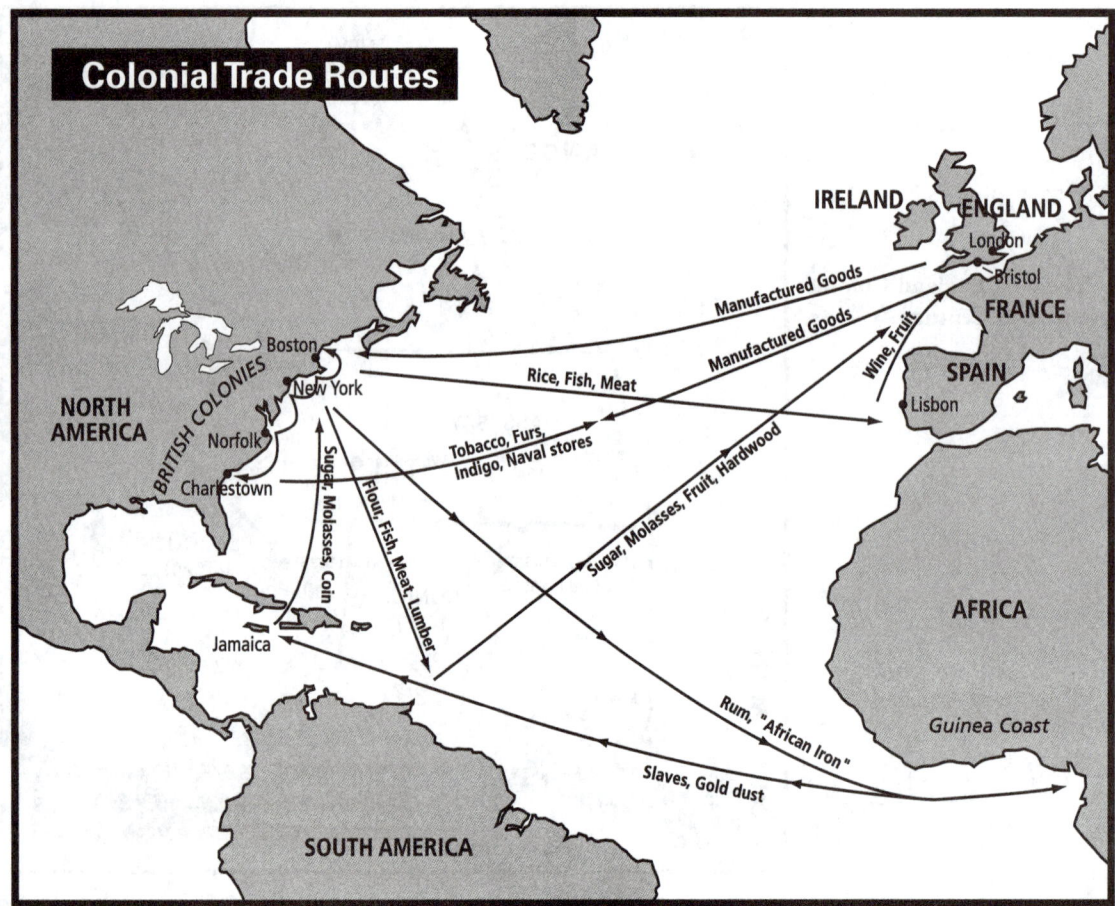

Map 3.2 Colonial Trade Routes

they could also watch over each other more closely. This town-based settlement pattern was reinforced by New England's rocky and glaciated soil. Staple crops and large-scale plantations such as those in the Chesapeake region were not economically feasible. Farmers grew a variety of grains such as wheat, corn, and barley. Part of a farmer's land would typically be given over to raising cattle, sheep, or pigs. Slavery was legal in New England and slaves were imported in small numbers to labor as personal servants and dock workers, but there was never an economic basis for the development of large-scale slavery as there was in the agricultural export-oriented southern provinces.

Most towns were constructed to enhance a sense of community. In the center would be the church and the village common. Around those were the various homes and shops of residents, and beyond those the fields of those who resided in the town. In a nod to the extremes of winter, roofs on the houses were sharply angled to keep snow from building up, giving early New England homes a distinctive appearance. The town church doubled as the meeting house and where the adult men often gathered to elect local officials and settle both major and minor issues confronting the community. Towns rarely expanded in size beyond the range of church bells. When a community

got too large, it typically split, with some of its residents breaking away to start a brand new town.

Unlike the seventeenth-century southern colonies, New England migration was dominated by whole families moving together. Thus, the region never experienced wide gender imbalances and the instability that derived from them. Nor did New England, with its milder summers, suffer the same extraordinary death rates experienced in the southern colonies. In late-seventeenth-century Virginia, a typical adult male would live on average to the age of fifty. For southern women, average life expectancy was only 40 years due to deaths related to childbirth. In New England at the end of the 1600s, the life expectancies for men and women were 69 and 62, respectively. These were longer lifespans than people who lived in England. Better health and more stable family units contributed to New England's natural population increase. Infant mortality was low, so more children survived to have children of their own, and more of their children then survived to procreate. Grandparents become a feature of New England life but were exceedingly rare elsewhere in the English-speaking world. Puritan families tended to run large. The famous Bostonian Paul Revere fathered sixteen children, and Massachusetts Governor William

Phips had twenty-five brothers and sisters. Such examples are extreme, to be sure, but indicative of New England fertility rates. The typical New England family might have between five to seven children all reach adulthood.

New Englanders referred to family as a "little commonwealth." Within the family, each member had a role to fulfill. A wife was supposed to obey her husband. In turn, a husband was bound to respect and protect his wife and family. Wives were, along with female children, in charge of household tasks such as cooking, cleaning, spinning, and sewing. Women also tried to produce trade goods within the household that could then be exchanged with neighbors for products such as eggs or cheese. Husbands and male children were expected to do farm labor or to bind themselves to a trade in order to provide an income. Marriage was not a relationship of equals anywhere in the colonies, north or south. English law specified that a married woman fell under the legal doctrine of **coverture**. Under the doctrine, a married woman's legal rights were removed and given to her husband. A wife had no independent legal existence of her own. In the eyes of society, man and wife became a single person and that person was the husband.

Women also took a subservient position in the church. Though technically women who were full church members were considered spiritual equals to men, Puritan ministers stressed the guilt of women in man's moral fall, starting with Eve who led Adam to sin and both of them expelled from the Garden of Eden. Women were, therefore, considered in Puritan teachings to be more susceptible to temptation and sin than men. Women could not preach or vote on church business. They were expected to worship silently and let their husbands speak for them, though they could, of course, influence men unofficially.

In addition to small farmers and craftsmen, New England's diversified economy also relied on the nearby presence of the sea. Even before the Pilgrims landed, the region had been a major fishing area for European vessels. Cape Cod got its name from the thick schools of codfish that thrived near the shore. Puritan settlers quickly took to mining the fishy gold mines of New England. More daring fishermen even hunted whales for oil that could be used in lighting or perfumes, though the New England whaling industry did not truly take off until the nineteenth century. The smell of rotting fish was an everyday part of the ambience of sea towns.

New England was, and still is, blessed with an abundance of natural harbors. Boston was at the time a peninsula connected to the mainland only by a thin neck of land. Rhode Island is essentially one massive harbor with a bit of land sprinkled around its edges. With its thick old growth forests, New England became a major entrant into the shipbuilding and sea trade business. By the end of the 1600s, English shipbuilders began to complain about high levels of competition from the colonies. It was much cheaper to build ships in America where there was lumber rather than send the wood to England for construction. Ship construction in turn drove a number of other related industries: timbering, sawmills, carpentry, sail crafting, and rope making among them. A single ship could require the efforts of dozens of skilled craftsmen to build. New England built and manned ships that carried livestock, timber, slaves, and other cargoes back and forth across the Atlantic. Fishing and shipping became central to the region's economy.

PURITAN ORTHODOXY AND DISSENT

Rhode Island and Connecticut

Though Massachusetts Bay enjoyed strong social and religious unity in its initial years, it did not take long for cracks to begin appearing on its surface. The colony tried to deal with dissension first through informal interventions by ministers who attempted to steer stray individuals or congregations back to the proper path. Only if informal efforts failed did the government take more decisive, official action in the name of true religion. One example is the case of **Roger Williams**, a young separatist Puritan minister with a gift for public speaking who arrived in 1631. He was offered a position as a junior minister in a Boston church but declined it since the church was still affiliated with the Church of England. He believed that the Anglican Church was thoroughly corrupt and that worshippers needed to completely separate themselves from its influence in order to achieve true purity and Godliness. In his view, religion was between the individual and God, with no role for any earthly institution. He not only advocated for complete freedom of religion but also for a strict separation of church and state. Government, he believed, could corrupt true worship just as much as could an established church.

Williams spent some time preaching in the Plymouth Colony, but he believed that even his fellow Separatists were too beholden to earthly authority. He wrote a pamphlet attacking the right of the king to issue colonial charters and further doubted whether the Plymouth and Massachusetts colonies had a right to any land that had not been directly purchased from native peoples. After taking a position as a minister in Salem, Williams was called before the Massachusetts General Court multiple times to be questioned for his "erroneous" views. The

General Court at first tried to pressure him to abandon his opinions, and only when those efforts failed did the government take more direct action. The government ordered Salem to fire him as minister and refused to seat Salem's elected representatives in the legislature until it was done. The Salem congregation, however, balked at such an intrusion into their independence. Finally, out of lesser options, Massachusetts put Williams on trial in 1635 for sedition and heresy. He was found guilty and punished by banishment on pain of death, meaning that if he ever returned to Massachusetts, he would face certain execution. Williams was supposed to be sent back to England the following spring, but in early 1636, he and some of his devout followers slipped away and escaped southward. Williams purchased land from the Wampanoag and Narragansett tribes and founded the colony of Providence, later to become Rhode Island. In Williams's new colony, church and state would be strictly separated, and all individuals would have the freedom to worship as they pleased. Over the years Rhode Island became a refuge for numerous religious refugees cast out of the other New England colonies. He also used his influence to try and protect the rights of non-English people. Residents were prohibited from invading or molesting native peoples, and in 1652, the colony passed a law limiting the institution of African slavery to a fixed 10-year term, though there was no effort made to enforce it.

In 1643, Williams traveled to England to seek an official charter for his new colony. During his brief one year stay in the mother country, he published two influential books. The first, *A Key into the Language of America* (1643), was the first Native American language dictionary ever published. The second book, *The Bloudy Tenent of Persecution for Cause of Conscience* (1644), proved much more controversial. Williams advocated complete religious freedom of worship, including non-Christian religions. Williams strongly condemned the efforts of governmental authorities in both Britain and America to enforce religious conformity. The book argued that the relationship between an individual and God was highly personal and should not be subject to any human earthly interference, and thus there should be a "wall of separation" between church and state. Though condemned by Parliament at the time of its publication, *Bloudy Tenent's* ideas about the relationship between religion and government nevertheless became enormously influential in the seventeenth and eighteenth centuries.

The same year that Roger Williams founded Rhode Island, another new colony also got its start due to discord in Massachusetts. Thomas Hooker had fled from England to escape the persecution of Puritans but encountered similar persecution in Massachusetts. In religious terms,

Depiction of Anne Hutchinson preaching in her Boston home.

he was very orthodox in his views, and he supported close cooperation between the church and the state. He served as a judge in the trials of other religious dissenters, including Roger Williams and Anne Hutchinson. Hooker, though, strongly disagreed with restricting the right to vote to property-holding church members. He believed in the enfranchisement of all Christian men regardless of church status or property. In a holy experiment such as theirs that relied so heavily on the faith and consent of the people, it was important for all Christian men to have a voice. Though his disagreements with Massachusetts's government were less severe than those of Williams, Hooker nevertheless felt compelled to leave Massachusetts. He and his supporters founded the colony of Connecticut, which granted far wider voting rights.

Anne Hutchinson

The Massachusetts Puritans struggled to cope with Roger Williams's ideas, but they soon faced an even greater challenge from another dissident—**Anne Hutchinson**—who had emigrated to Boston along with her family in 1634. Her husband was a successful businessman, and she was highly educated and eloquent in addition to being trained as a midwife, an essential medical position in any community. As a result, the Hutchinsons quickly rose to prominence in the settlement. At some point, Anne started to hold religious gatherings in her home attended by a mixed group of men and women. Such Bible study sessions were not uncommon in the colony, but what was said and done at her meetings resulted in tremendous controversy. She preached that salvation was achieved solely through God's direct grace and that ministers, churches, and governments did not matter at all. She criticized the notion that public displays of piety or good works did anything to prepare the chosen for salvation. To Hutchinson, ministers were at best useless, attempting to help others to be holy but not actually achieving anything. At worst, she said, most ministers and government magistrates could actually do harm by spreading false messages and leading people away from righteousness. She singled out several ministers by name who she felt were guilty of leading their parishioners away from God.

Hutchinson's views deeply disturbed Massachusetts authorities. Their biblical commonwealth rested on close cooperation between the state and the church, on religious and political leaders together monitoring and enforcing the covenant that bound them all in their experiment. Mainstream Puritanism insisted that ministers were absolutely necessary to interpret God's will for the general public. Hutchinson's insistence that saved people did not have to obey moral laws undermined the colony's legal code, which was based around moral laws drawn from the Bible. Additionally, many ministers were uncomfortable seeing any woman emerge as a religious teacher, a role traditionally reserved for men only. In addition, her views seemed to be gaining in popularity. Her meetings overflowed with wives, husbands, farmers, merchants, and craftsmen. Even the young Governor Henry Vane, only 23 years of age, began to attend. In the eyes of the colony's elder leaders, Hutchinson and her followers were trying to destroy the fundamental stability of their society. At first, informal pressure was applied to try and get her to conform. She was visited multiple times by groups of ministers and politicians who urged her to retract her more controversial statements or even stop holding her meetings entirely. Hutchinson, however, was undeterred and continued speaking her mind at her religious gatherings.

In 1637, Hutchinson's opponents moved against her. That year, Vane lost the governor's election to John Winthrop, who held more conventional theological views and had already expressed his opposition to Hutchinson's teachings. Vane's defeat and subsequent departure for England cost Hutchinson her most powerfully positioned defender. Later that same year, she was arrested and brought to trial before the General Court, presided over by Governor Winthrop. Among the charges against her were slandering ministers and spreading ideas that disturbed the peace of the colony. Her opinions were called "vomit" and compared to gangrene and leprosy in their effects. Over two days of interrogation, Hutchin-

A portrait of Governor John Winthrop flanked by statues of a Native American on the left and a Puritan on the right.

son more than held her own against some of the most respected and prominent men in the colony. She denied holding heretical views and quoted Bible verses back to the prosecution to defend her conduct. Winthrop, one of her most ardent critics, described her as "a woman of ready wit and a bold spirit," though he also considered her to be "an instrument of Satan." Exasperated, and probably exhausted from the extensive questioning, Hutchinson bluntly told the court at one point that God protected her, that its members had no power over her, and that God would punish them for persecuting her. Winthrop interpreted the remark as a confession to the charges and asked the assembly to vote. She was found guilty of being a heretic who was, as one leading minister said, "raised up by Satan amongst us to raise up divisions and contentions." She was later also convicted in a religious trial. Her combined sentence was both excommunication from the church and banishment from Massachusetts. Shortly after her church trial, Hutchinson suffered a miscarriage, which Winthrop viewed as God's definitive judgment of her guilt. Hutchinson lived for a time in Rhode Island, then, after her husband's death in 1642, moved to the Dutch colony of New Netherland where she died in an Indian attack.

PURITANS AND NATIVES

Pequot War

The Pequot of Connecticut were a major Indian power numbering some 8,000 people, and they exercised control over dozens of smaller tributary tribes. They were rivals of several other groups in the region for control over the lucrative fur trade, which generated profits for Native Americans, the Dutch, and the English. As New England Puritans expanded into Pequot territory during the 1630s, it was only a matter of time until conflict flared. In 1633, the Pequot were hit with an epidemic, probably smallpox, that killed over half of their people, which they blamed on the Europeans. In 1634, the Niantic people, a client tribe of the Pequot, murdered an English trader. The Pequot claimed that they had believed the man to be Dutch and had, in a case of mistaken identity, killed him in retaliation for the earlier Dutch murder of one of the principal Pequot chiefs. Connecticut officials rejected this explanation and demanded that the Pequot hand over the Niantic killers for trial and execution. While that controversy dragged on, a Massachusetts trader named John Oldham was killed in 1636, near the coast of Rhode Island. Though Oldham's murderers were from a different tribe, they fled to the Pequot seeking refuge. In response to this new killing, Massachusetts sent an expedition to the coast of Connecticut where English soldiers burned down and looted a Pequot village.

Up to this point, there had been serious tensions between the Pequot and New Englanders, but cooler heads had maintained the peace. The 1636 Massachusetts raid ended the peace and sparked the **Pequot War**. During the winter of 1636-37, the Pequot lay siege to the English Fort Saybrook, at the mouth of the Connecticut River, killing 20 Englishmen in the process. During the following spring, the Pequot launched a wider series of attacks on English villages, carrying the war directly to the doorsteps of their Puritan enemies. The New England Puritans looked around for allies and recruited the Mohegan and Narragansett, both traditional rivals of the Pequot, to assist them. A combined Connecticut and native force launched an attack against Mystic village, one of two fortified towns in Pequot territory. The town held about 500 Pequot, most of whom were women, children, or elderly since the tribe's warriors were away at war. The English force surrounded the town and set it on fire. As the flames grew, Pequot villagers ran out the gates of the palisade only to be shot or stabbed by the English. Only a handful of the Pequot survived the massacre. One of the leaders of the English force, John Mason, declared that it was God's will to make Mystic into "a firey Oven." The Mohegan and Narragansett, who had sided with the English, were appalled by the Puritan brutality, but it was too late for them to do anything to stop the killing.

The destruction of Mystic broke the back of Pequot resistance, leading many to abandon their villages and try to flee west for safety among the Mohawk. Mason and his army surrounded the retreating Pequot, killing 100 warriors and taking 700 prisoners. One of the Pequot chiefs reached the Mohawk but rather than granting him protection, the Mohawk cut off his head and sent it to the English as proof of their neutrality in the conflict. Many of the Pequot prisoners were sold as slaves in the Caribbean. Others were handed over to the Mohegan and Narragansett as slaves. The English then declared that no Indian could ever again call themselves Pequot, thus attempting to make the group extinct. Not until 1983 did the descendants of the Pequot regain recognition as a tribe.

Praying Towns

The excessive violence of the Pequot War led to much criticism in England. As a result, some Puritans felt the need to adopt a new, more peaceful approach to interacting with the native population of New England. Conversion of the Native Americans to Christianity had been one of the stated goals of the first wave of Puritan settlers. The Seal of the Massachusetts Bay Colony features

The Seal of the Massachusetts Bay Colony.

the figure of an Indian standing with open arms asking for white Englishmen to "Come Over and Help Us." In 1646, the Reverend John Eliot preached a sermon to a group of natives in Massachusetts. He failed to win any converts, thus joining a long list of earlier, unsuccessful Puritan missionaries. Rather than giving up, he decided to do something that his predecessors had not seriously attempted—to preach to natives in their own language. All of the local native groups spoke dialects of the Algonquian language, so Eliot, with the help of a former Pequot captured in 1637, sat down to learn how to translate Scripture into a language that they could read. This was an immense challenge since Algonquian was strictly a spoken language, with no written letters or symbols. Eliot relied on writing out phonetic spellings of spoken words. In 1663, he produced a 1,200-page Algonquian language translation of the entire Bible. Through these painstaking efforts, he succeeded in converting a number of natives to Christianity.

For Eliot and other Puritans, however, just changing indigenous religious beliefs was insufficient. They believed that Native Americans had to abandon their old ways of life, including traditional clothing and common rituals, while adopting English-style customs. Christian Indians caught breaking the rules were fined or whipped. To make sure that converts did not slip back into their old "savage" customs, Eliot insisted that they be segregated into "**Praying Towns**." By 1675, fourteen such towns containing 1,100 Native American converts had been es-

tablished by the Massachusetts government and more were under construction. Most of the residents were survivors of coastal tribes devastated by waves of disease. Praying towns could elect their own leaders, but they would still be subject to English laws and rules of conduct. For example, hair was closely regulated. Men were required to wear their hair short, while women were required to wear theirs long. If either gender wore their hair incorrectly, they would be fined. The lifestyle transformation was uneven at best. Though Eliot urged residents to build English style housing, most built traditional wigwams. Accustomed to a society based on reciprocal and close personal interaction, the Native Americans were unable to fully grasp the more legalistic and institutional basis of English society. Some of them only pretended to convert, fearing that otherwise they would suffer the same fate as the Pequot.

King Philip's War

While some New England natives converted to Christianity, others believed that their best hope for the future was to unite against the English. Disease had reduced the indigenous population of New England from 125,000 in 1600 to a mere 10,000 in 1675. At the same time, the ever-expanding Puritan population had continually encroached on Indian lands. Refusal to conform to English religion also became one of the central features of native resistance in the 1670s. Many Indian tribes felt that their traditional way of life was in danger of disappearing forever. Metacom (nicknamed King Philip by the English), the Sachem of the Wampanoag and the son of Massasoit, began organizing smaller tribes into an anti-English alliance.

In 1675, Plymouth executed three Wampanoags for the killing of a Christian Indian, igniting **King Philip's War**. The belligerents in this conflict were more evenly matched on the battlefield than in the earlier Pequot War because the Indians had acquired firearms. About two-thirds of New England tribes supported Metacom in his rebellion, and to the surprise of the English, Metacom won several early battles against Plymouth forces. The fighting quickly devolved into a series of massacres and atrocities. Massachusetts and Connecticut soldiers launched attacks against the Narragansett, who were technically neutral. In the Great Swamp Fight of 1675, several hundred Narragansett nevertheless were massacred. Metacom's warriors and their allies attacked 52 New England towns, destroying twelve completely, and in the process killed over 1,000 settlers. The tide finally turned in favor of the Puritans in 1676, when the English convinced the Mohawks to ambush and kill Metacom. New

Map 3.3 King Philip's War

Englanders and their Indian allies then hunted down and killed even more of their Native American enemies, not all of whom had taken part in the uprising. Metacom's head was severed and displayed on a pole in Plymouth for two decades. Hundreds of surviving Indians were sold into slavery, among them Metacom's wife and son.

THE MIDDLE COLONIES

New Netherland and New Sweden

While England was settling colonies in Virginia and New England during the early seventeenth century, other European nations were also planting roots on the North American coast. As mentioned in Chapter 1, English explorer Henry Hudson, on a mission for the Dutch, sailed along the coastline and up the river that still bears his name in search of a Northwest Passage. He did not find the hoped-for route to Asia, but his glowing reports about the land did pave the way for Dutch settlement in the area. The Dutch built a trading post along the Hudson River in 1614 in order to tap into the lucrative Indian fur trade. The colony was given the name **New Netherland**. The Dutch presence was minimal until investors formed the Dutch West India Company in 1621. The company had far ranging business and territorial interests with jurisdiction over portions of Brazil, the Caribbean, and

North America. The company took over Portugal's slave trading fortresses on the West African coast and, for a time, dominated the Atlantic slave trade. By contrast, the North Atlantic coast drew a much smaller portion of the company's money and resources.

In 1626, Peter Minuit was named Director of New Netherland and sent to negotiate a lease or purchase of land on Manhattan Island near the mouth of the Hudson River. Minuit purchased the entire island for trade goods amounting to the modern equivalent of around $1,000. Ever since, numerous observers have remarked on the astonishingly low sales price. However, this simplistic view overlooks the differences between European and native societies. Native Americans did not conceive land ownership in the same way as people from Europe, where individuals had exclusive and permanent rights to plots of land. The local natives on the island most likely saw the deal not as full sale and transfer of the land, but rather as an agreement for them both to share the land. In return, they gained not only the trade goods but also the Dutch as potential allies against rival tribes. Fort Orange was established near present-day Albany, 150 miles north of Manhattan, to serve as the main trading post for Native Americans bringing in furs. The town of New Amsterdam was soon built on Manhattan to serve as the capital.

Growth was slow in the New Netherland. By 1629, only about 300 Dutch lived in trading posts or on Man-

Map 3.4 The Middle Colonies in the Seventeenth Century

hattan. In a bid to gain more settlers, the company opened up the colony to almost any immigrant regardless of their origins. As a result, the province gained an ethnically varied population: Germans, French Huguenots, Danes, Finns, Scots, Jews, Muslims, and African slaves. In 1638, a group of Swedish merchants moved to the Delaware River region and established New Sweden. Minuit, who had been fired from his position in the Dutch company, served as the Swedish colony's first governor. New Sweden remained small, however, with never over 400 inhabitants. In 1655, the Dutch conquered the colony and absorbed it into New Netherland, further boosting both the population and diversity of that province.

In the 1630s, the Dutch trade with Native Americans increasingly involved muskets. The Iroquois in particular used Dutch-provided muskets to expand their involvement in the acquisition of furs. The **Iroquois Confederacy** was a league made up of some 12,000 members who dominated the inland areas of New Netherland. Since the fur trade was unregulated, native and European hunters could rapidly strip all the fur-bearing animals out of an area. Therefore, parties in the fur trade were always in search of virgin lands whose animal populations were still intact. In a series of "Beaver Wars," the Iroquois defeated French-backed tribes to gain access to animal-laden lands in Canada, Michigan, and modern Tennessee. Eventually, the French-supported natives pushed back against the Iroquois and forced a peace in 1701. These conflicts helped to cement a lasting friendship between the French and various native peoples of the Great Lakes region. The French-Indian alliance would have major consequences in the eighteenth century for the British North American colonies.

Despite continued efforts, New Netherland never really became profitable for the Dutch West India Company. In 1640, the company declared the region to be a free trade zone, signaling their intention not to invest more money in its maintenance or expansion. Dutch Governor William Kieft tried to cover the colony's administrative costs by forcing local tribes to pay tribute. This triggered a bloody Indian war that lasted from 1643-45. In early 1643, Dutch forces massacred 120 natives, mainly women and children. In response, a large Indian force invaded New Netherland, destroying farms and killing settlers, including the Puritan dissident Anne Hutchinson. Kieft was recalled to Holland and peace temporarily restored, but the experience showed that the Dutch were no more successful than the English at establishing long-lasting positive relationships with Native Americans.

New York and New Jersey

In 1664, an English fleet forced the Dutch to surrender New Amsterdam. Though the Dutch briefly recaptured the city in 1673, the English regained control and added it to their growing colonial presence on the Atlantic coast. Charles II granted his brother James, Duke of York, control over the territory, which was renamed New York. New Amsterdam was rechristened New York City.

New York still held a very substantial Dutch population, and integrating them was a top priority. English authorities tried to be gentle and forgiving towards the Dutch, despite their previous status as enemies. Any Dutch settler who wished could emigrate and take all their possessions with them. Those who stayed would retain their lands and be allowed to worship as they pleased rather than be required to conform to the Church of England. Dutch law continued to be used in portions of the English colony for decades. New York's governors often turned a blind eye to illicit trade between New York's Dutch merchants and the Netherlands, fearing that a ban on such trade would wreck the colony's economy. Despite these conciliatory policies, there were very real cultural differences between the English and Dutch that made the relationship between the two groups difficult. Some English merchants resented the continuing trade with Holland, feeling that it gave Dutch merchants an unfair competitive advantage. When Dutch inhabitants in 1673 refused to resist an invasion from the Netherlands, it convinced many English colonists to push for greater reductions in the influence of what they considered to be untrustworthy Dutch colonists. Friction between Dutch and English settlers remained an important feature of the province's society and politics until well into the eighteenth century.

James appointed a governor and an advisory council for his proprietary colony but did not establish a representative assembly. The governor and appointed council would have taxing authority over the colonists. This was a bold departure from English colonial precedent and sparked an outcry among English inhabitants. The Dutch, who had not had a representative government previously, were less disturbed. This political arrangement was so unlike the English tradition, however, that New York had difficulty attracting English settlers, who preferred to go to other colonies that did enjoy representative government. Fearing that English settlers would begin emigrating from New York in large numbers, James finally, in 1683, allowed an assembly to convene.

James gave some of his southern land to two close political friends, who named their new colony New Jersey. This colony had an unsteady early history. It was split into two separate regions, East Jersey and West Jersey. The two Jerseys answered to different proprietors and frequently disagreed with each other, including the exact location of the border between them. Anti-proprietor movements in both colonies created additional instability until they were taken over by the Crown and reunited in 1702. New Jersey, like New York, had a sizable Dutch population. It also drew in a significant number of Quakers who had found themselves unwelcomed in the Puritan New England colonies. Their arrival starting in the 1660s was a preview of a much larger migration of Quakers into another new colony, Pennsylvania, just a few years later.

Quakerism and William Penn

The colony of Pennsylvania was founded as a refuge for a group of English Protestants, the Society of Friends. Commonly known as **Quakers**, their denomination began in seventeenth-century England under the leadership of its founder, George Fox. During the English Civil War, Fox had a revelation that individuals could have a direct connection with Christ, and that ordained ministers were not necessary. People instead needed to follow their "Inner Light"—Christ's presence within them. Quakers rejected the Puritan notion of predestination, instead believing that all people contained a spark of divinity and could achieve salvation. In social terms, they rejected many class and gender distinctions common to the rest of society. Quakers did away with gestures of rank, such as bowing and the doffing of caps to social superiors. In weekly religious meetings, Quakers sat in silence until individual members began to speak whenever they felt moved to do so. (Misconceptions about this practice led many in England to believe that the Society's members felt their bodies being taken over by spirits at their meetings, forcing them to speak in tongues and lose control

William Penn

The Life and Death of Mary Dyer

The life and death of Mary Dyer illustrates just how seriously early New Englanders took their commitment to religious orthodoxy. Mary Barrett was born in England in 1611. Not much is known about her early years, but she was described at the time as being highly educated. She was married in London in 1633 to William Dyer, a milliner (hatmaker). Mary and William were both Puritans who joined the Great Migration of the 1630s and moved to New England. Settling in Boston, both became strong supporters of the controversial Anne Hutchinson. Mary was in the audience of Hutchinson's church trial, and when Hutchinson was formally sentenced to excommunication and banishment from Massachusetts, Mary took her hand and walked out of the church with her. During this same time period, Mary had given birth to a deformed, stillborn baby, and for the remainder of her life she was known in the colony as the mother of the monster. Due to his support of the Hutchinson heresy, her husband William was stripped of his voting rights in Massachusetts. Mary and William decided to join Hutchinson in exile in Rhode Island where they could practice their religious beliefs more freely.

The Dyers lived quietly through the 1640s, but in 1651, the couple traveled to England. William, by then a government official in Rhode Island, returned about a year later after concluding some official colonial business. Mary stayed for five years. During her time in England, she converted to Quakerism, a religion established in England just a few years earlier. Quakers believed that all men and women contained an "Inner Light," denounced ordained ministers as unnecessary, and demanded a separation of church and state. To Puritans, who had no real separation of church and state and among whom clergy members wielded great influence, Quakers were perhaps the worst possible heretics. Massachusetts passed multiple laws making Quakerism illegal and punishable by banishment or death.

Mary returned to Boston in 1657. She was identified as a Quaker, arrested, and expelled from Massachusetts. She then became a traveling Quaker missionary, spreading her faith to towns and villages throughout New England. Her husband had not become a Quaker but seems to have supported her efforts. She was at home recovering from a serious illness in 1658 when she heard that three male Quakers had been arrested in Boston and their right ears sliced off as punishment for their refusal to accept banishment. Along with several other Quakers, Mary traveled to Boston to visit the men and ended up once again arrested and banished. When she returned to Boston yet another time in 1659, she and two other Quakers were sentenced to death for her refusal to stay out of Massachusetts.

On October 27, 1659, the day of her execution, she walked hand-in-hand to the gallows with her fellow Quakers. Dyer watched as each of the other two men was hanged and their bodies taken down. She was then hooded and set in place for her own hanging. Instead, authorities announced a reprieve from her sentence, which had been arranged by the intervention of her husband and son. She was led back to prison in the hope that she would finally accept banishment. Instead, she asked for her execution to go forward. Massachusetts authorities declined to hang her and now expelled her for a third time. She had to be tied to a horse in order to get her to leave the colony. Undeterred, she again traveled to Boston in 1660, specifically to seek her own execution and demonstrate to the world how unjustly Quakers were treated. She was arrested and brought before the Governor, who again passed a sentence of death. This time, there would be no reprieve. Mary died on the gallows on June 1, 1660 and is today considered one of the most respected martyrs in Quakerism. The clergy and government officials in Massachusetts were willing to execute her in order to defend their religious beliefs, and Mary was willing to die for hers.

of their bodies—shaking and "quaking" about the room. The term "Quaker" also possibly was popularized by George Fox's admonition that people should "tremble at the Word of the Lord.") Women enjoyed nearly full equality in worship, and some of them, like Mary Dyer, became respected missionaries of the faith. Quakers also preached pacifism, rejecting violence and war. Fox wandered throughout England, the Netherlands, and even traveled to several American colonies to spread his faith. By 1660, there were some 60,000 Quakers in England and Wales and a slowly growing number in the Americas.

Because Quakers dissented from the Church of England's mandated forms of worship, they frequently faced persecution and punishment. Quaker religious meetings were prohibited by law. Many in England viewed Quakers not only as heretics, but traitors as well, since they refused to swear oaths, including oaths of fealty to the King. Fox was in and out of prison regularly from 1650 onwards. One of Quakerism's converts during this troubled period was **William Penn**, the son of a prominent English family headed by Admiral Sir William Penn. The younger Penn found that his family's influence, however, did not protect him from the Anglican Church or the laws against Quaker worship. Penn wrote several pamphlets in the 1660s in

Table 3.1	England's Principal Mainland Colonies				
Name	Original Purpose	Date of Founding	Principal Founder	Major Export	Estimated Population c. 1700
Virginia	Commercial venture	1607	Captain John Smith	Tobacco	64,560
New York	Commercial venture	1664	Peter Stuyvesant, (Duke of York)	Furs, grain	19,107
New Hampshire	Commercial venture	1623	John Mason	Wood, naval stores	4,958
Massachusetts Bay Company	Refuge for English Puritans	1628	John Winthrop	Grain, wood, fish	55,941
Maryland	Refuge for English Catholics	1634	Lord Baltimore (George Calvert)	Tobacco	34,100
Connecticut	Expansion of Massachusetts	1635	Thomas Hooker	Grain	25,970
Rhode Island	Refuge for dissenters from Massachusetts	1636	Roger Williams	Grain	5,894
Delaware	Commercial venture	1638	Peter Minuit William Penn	Grain	2,470
North Carolina	Commercial venture	1653	Anthony Ashley Cooper	Wood, naval stores, tobacco	10,720
South Carolina	Commercial venture	1663	Anthony Ashley Cooper	Naval stores, rice, indigo	5,720
New Jersey	Consolidation of new English territory, Quaker settlement	1664	Sir George Cartaret	Grain	14,010
Pennsylvania	Refuge for English Quakers	1682	William Penn	Grain	18,950
Georgia	Discourage Spanish expansion; charity	1732	James Oglethorp	Silk, rice, wood, naval stores	5,200 (in 1750)

which he attacked the Catholic Church, the Church of England, and Puritanism, for which he spent eight months in solitary confinement in the Tower of London. Though released from confinement, he was repeatedly arrested and jailed in subsequent years for practicing Quakerism. In court, he refused to remove his cap, angering judges who saw his refusal as a sign of disrespect for the court and the law. His family's influence helped to protect him from the most extreme legal consequences until he inherited a massive estate and became wealthy in his own right.

During the 1670s, Penn looked to America as a potential place of safety for Quakers. In 1677, Penn and a group of fellow Quakers purchased the colony of West Jersey from its proprietor. Penn and Fox envisioned a far larger colony, however, and in 1681, Penn received a new colonial charter from Charles II in part to settle a debt that the King owed to his deceased father but most probably to simply remove many troublesome Quakers from England. Pennsylvania, as it would be called, would be wedged in between the existing colonies of Maryland and New York. Penn insisted on traveling to the settlement himself to personally oversee its construction.

Pennsylvania was the most meticulously planned English colonial effort up to that point. In 1682, Penn

Unlike the Puritans (and other Christian denominations), the Quakers believed in female equality, even allowing women to speak at their meetings as depicted in this scene.

laid out the highly structured pattern of the provincial capital, Philadelphia ("Brotherly Love"). The design, with its regimented street grid and frequent green parks, would, he hoped, bring order and harmony to this colonial effort. Above all, Penn hoped that Pennsylvania could avoid the factionalism and infighting that had reigned in places like Virginia and New England. The colony's laws were remarkably lenient, mandating the death penalty for only two offenses (treason and murder) versus two hundred offenses in English law. As a Quaker, Penn set up his colony along religious principles different than most others. Pennsylvania was to be Penn's "holy experiment," where Quaker sensibilities would lead to a harmonious and unified colony. He declared complete religious toleration, meaning that all dissenting Protestants, not just Quakers, would flock to the colony. Penn also insisted that, despite his royal charter, the land still belonged to the local indigenous peoples, so he made sure to fairly compensate them for their land. Penn even learned several Indian dialects since he wanted to speak to the natives without an interpreter, an unusual effort for someone as lofty as a colonial proprietor. As a result, early Pennsylvania did not experience warfare with Native Americans, as was the case in virtually every other British colony. In fact, Penn and his fellow Quakers were so equitable in their treatment of Native peoples that some tribes moved into the colony from elsewhere to make it their home.

By 1687, nearly 8,000 settlers had arrived in Pennsylvania. By 1700, about half of the Quakers in England had left for America, with Pennsylvania being the most popular destination. Penn published pamphlets in French and German to attract additional Protestant migrants, and in 1683, a large group of immigrants from Saxony established Germantown, near Philadelphia. Thousands of additional Germans followed, attracted not only by religious toleration but also by economic opportunity. Pennsylvania's rich flat fields were well suited to grow wheat and other grains to feed the booming populations of other British provinces, especially those in the West Indies. By the mid-eighteenth century, Philadelphia was one of the busiest ports in the British Empire.

Penn's Experiment: Success or Failure?

Pennsylvania did disappoint its founder in some ways. As proprietor, Penn had absolute power in the colony and his use of that power caused resentment from colonists who believed they deserved to make significant decisions for themselves. Penn returned to England in 1684 to address a border dispute with Maryland, but during his long absence from America, he continued to favor Quakers when making appointments to the most important and influential government positions in the colony. The political constitution was drafted and redrafted many times before reaching its final form. Voting rights for Pennsylvania's elected legislative assembly were very generous and nearly every adult male could vote. Women were denied the franchise, which shows that Quaker gender equality was largely restricted to religious matters.

The first legislature had limited powers, and it too was dominated by Quakers, much to the frustration of other Protestants. Very quickly, the province began to splinter along pro-Penn and anti-Penn lines. Opponents criticized Penn's control over foreign trade and protested the Quaker dominance of government. The disputes became so bitter that the speaker of the assembly was imprisoned briefly over a political disagreement. Penn sent over a carefully selected governor in 1688 with instructions to settle colonial tempers and heal the breaches between different factions. The governor resigned a year later, declaring that Pennsylvanians were more interested in preying on their fellow man than praying for him.

A conflict within the colony's Quaker population in the 1690s caused a few members of the Society of Friends to emigrate and slowed down the rate of new Quaker arrivals. Not even the Quaker community, it seemed, could maintain total harmony. Under pressure from his critics, Penn in 1701 issued a Charter of Liberties, limiting his own authority (and that of his heirs) and authorizing the election of a more fully empowered representative assembly. He even surrendered the right to veto legislation passed in the colony. These final constitutional revisions gave Pennsylvania one of the most democratic governments in all of colonial America. Penn's move to further decentralize power also led to the creation of a separate colony, Delaware, which split off in 1703 and formed its own assembly. The region had been populated mostly by Swedes, Finns, and Dutch rather than English Quakers. The breakaway colony's independence was limited, however, as whoever was appointed as Pennsylvania's governor also served as governor of Delaware, a situation that continued throughout the colonial period.

Pennsylvania disappointed its founder in one other significant way. Penn had hoped to turn a profit on the colony through a combination of land sales and quitrents—annual charges paid on occupied land in the colony. However, land did not sell for as much as he hoped, and colonial protests led to the elimination of quitrents. Meanwhile, the costs of administering the colony grew along with its population. Though Pennsylvania was not his only financial misfortune, it nevertheless was a burden rather than a boon to Penn. Penn suffered a financial collapse in the early 1700s and in 1708 was briefly committed to a debtor's prison. He then attempted to sell Pennsylvania to the Crown and had nearly succeeded when negotiations were derailed by a serious stroke he suffered in 1712. Penn ultimately died in poverty in 1718.

PURITANISM IN CRISIS

Decline of Old School Puritanism

In the wake of the English Civil War, Puritans in New England were in a state of crisis. The overthrow of the English monarchy that had been aided by a large number of Puritans and resulted in the execution of Charles I, had been undone with the restoration of Charles II to the throne in 1660. Puritanism had failed to revolutionize England. Likewise, John Winthrop's inspirational "City upon A Hill" had not become a model for the rest of the world to follow. Religious disagreements had troubled the Puritan experiment from the start, and extended non-Puritan migration had by the 1660s begun to undermine the Puritan sense of mission. Full church membership steadily declined among Puritan children and grandchildren who did not feel the same religious zeal as had the original generation of settlers. Younger New Englanders were not willing to undergo the arduous conversion experience and interrogation required for full admittance to the congregation. The decline in church membership shrank the pool of both eligible voters and officeholders. At the same time, the growing non-Puritan population began demanding access to voting rights and representative government. Puritan leaders were not willing to make full church membership easier to obtain, so New England leaders in 1662 settled upon a compromise known as the **Halfway Covenant**. Under the agreement, the children and grandchildren of church members could be baptized into the church and granted a partial church membership without having to undergo a conversion experience. They would not, however, enjoy the same rights and powers as full members. This arrangement temporarily extended the control of Puritan ministers over the New England colonies by bringing more people into a halfway church membership but did not completely reverse the long-term trend of declining religious zeal and falling full church membership.

Starting in the 1650s, publicly delivered Puritan sermons began to bemoan the decline of Puritan morality. These jeremiads—moralistic texts lamenting the supposed declension of society—criticized wickedness in colonial communities and predicted New England's downfall. Indian wars, crop failures, bad weather, and disease outbreaks were blamed on immoral and irreligious behavior in the community. The declines in full church membership and the institution of the Halfway Covenant were held up as further proof that Puritans had gone astray. However, these jeremiads did offer hope: if the people repented and recommitted themselves to God, they would be spared their future sufferings. Though such sermons exaggerated the extent of religious decline (New Englanders remained far more religious than most other colonial Americans), they nevertheless fueled a growing fear of failure.

The Dominion of New England

Charles II had become increasingly unhappy with the Puritan New England colonies. They often ignored English law when they judged it contrary to Scripture, and Massachusetts did not pay much heed to royal efforts in favor of broader religious toleration. In 1683, the Crown insisted that Massachusetts change its charter to remove church membership requirements for voting. When the colony refused, the Crown revoked the Bay Colony's charter. During these back and forth actions, there was also a changeover in the monarchy. James II, a Catholic and a proponent of absolute monarchy, ascended to the throne in 1685. He desired a more tightly controlled and regulated empire. In order to directly control the northern colonies, James combined Massachusetts, Rhode Island, Connecticut, Plymouth, New Jersey, and New York into a single colony, the **Dominion of New England**. As king, James would exercise near total control by replacing the existing governments of these colonies with one of his own choosing.

Edmund Andros, a former soldier, was chosen to lead the Dominion. He would be advised by an appointed royal council, but there would be no elected assembly. Taxes would be imposed without the consent of the governed, and colonists who refused to pay would be jailed. Andros chose Boston for his headquarters. Many New England residents, who already distrusted James II, hated the Dominion, and Andros's arrogant personality cemented and strengthened the opposition. He sided with the mainstream Church of England to the point of forcing a Boston Puritan church to hand over its building for Anglican services. He sharply limited town meetings and placed restrictions on colonial courts and newspapers. He insisted that New England farmers take out new titles to their lands and begin making annual quitrent payments where previously there had been none. Andros also cracked down on smuggling, a practice that had become widespread among colonial merchants as they tried to evade what they viewed as harmful imperial trade restrictions. In short order, Andros managed to alienate nearly every segment of New England society.

The Glorious Revolution

English Protestants in the mother country were deeply fearful of James II. His absolutist tendencies had been widely known for years, and his conversion to Catholicism in the 1670s alienated much of the English population. From 1679 to 1681, Parliament had unsuccessfully tried to exclude James from the royal succession due to his religion. Once he became the king, James installed Catholic allies in many top political and military positions. The main hope of English Protestants was that James's reign would be short (he was 52 years old), and, since he had no sons, the throne would then pass to a Protestant family member. Then, in 1688, the Queen had a son who would be raised in the Catholic Church, meaning that the next monarch would be Catholic as well. This event triggered what became known as the **Glorious Revolution**. Parliament invited Mary, James's Protestant daughter, and her husband William of Orange, stadholder of the Netherlands, to take the throne. In November 1688, William landed in England, and most of the English army defected to him rather than support a Catholic dynasty. James fled to France. Though the revolution was bloodless, it nevertheless had profound consequences in both England and America. The new monarchs approved an Act of Toleration for all Protestant faiths. While the Church of England remained the officially established state church, the act gave freedom of worship to religious dissenters. Catholics, however, were not covered by the new tolerance. William and Mary also approved a Bill of Rights that guaranteed Parliament's essential role in the government of England. The Bill of Rights specified individual rights possessed by all English men and women, including the right to trial by jury. To people in England and in her colonies, the Glorious Revolution was a firm rejection of absolutism and an enthusiastic celebration of liberty.

The Glorious Revolution was justified in the writings of political philosopher **John Locke**, particularly his *Two Treatises on Government* (1690). Locke had lived in exile during the monarchy of James II and returned during the Glorious Revolution. Locke rejected the theory of divine right monarchy that had been espoused by James II, instead writing that governments owed their authority to the consent of the governed. The proper role of government was to secure the fundamental rights of citizens: life, liberty, and property. Locke's writings had a significant impact on how American colonists thought about individual rights and representative government, and later would be used to provide a justification for revolution in the colonies.

When word arrived in the colonies of the Glorious Revolution in England, colonists moved to eject officials who had been aligned with James II. A Boston mob numbering 1,000 people formed in early 1689 to strike at the hated Dominion of New England. Among the throng were a number of prominent Puritan ministers and merchants—leaders in the community. Their goal was to seize Governor Andros and restore the old government of Massachusetts. Andros was caught trying to flee the city, arrested, and held in prison for nearly a year before being sent back to England for trial.

In New York, there was a similar uprising. New York City was the home of Andros's Lieutenant Governor, Francis Nicholson. An organization of merchants and artisans formed to defend their colony from the "papist" threat of James and his officials. Leisler's Rebellion in New York was led by German-born Jacob Leisler, a merchant and militia officer. He forced Nicholson to flee and the successful rebels then set up their own committee to run the colony until William and Mary sent new Protestant officials to America. Initially popular, Leisler was closely aligned with the Dutch faction in New York politics, and eventually English New Yorkers turned against his leadership. Leisler clamped down on his critics, imprisoning many of them, and even his Dutch allies began to drop their support. When the new governor arrived in 1691, Leisler hesitated to hand the colony over to him, fearing that he was being tricked by an agent of the deposed James II. After proving his legitimacy and taking the reins of power, the new governor had Leisler tried on charges of treason in front of a jury packed with Leisler's enemies. Leisler was convicted and hanged, drawn, and quartered, the most extreme punishment available.

Maryland, whose politics were already complicated by tensions between Catholics and Protestants, also experienced a series of tumults during the period. Lord Baltimore sent over a Catholic governor in 1688 while James II was still on the throne. The governor quickly alienated Maryland's Protestant population. In the summer 1689, Marylanders formed the Protestant Association to deal with rumors that Catholic spies were trying to organize an Indian attack on the colony. The association raised its own army and overthrew the proprietary government without bloodshed, forming a Protestant government that ruled for two years. Maryland was then made into a royal colony controlled by the Crown. It reverted to proprietary control only in 1715 after the noble title of Lord Baltimore passed to a Protestant heir.

William and Mary abolished the Dominion of New England, but they did not allow the respective colonies to fully return to their old ways. Plymouth lost its independence and was absorbed into Massachusetts, which in turn would no longer have its own corporate charter but would instead become a royal colony with a governor appointed by the Crown rather than elected. Suffrage was legally separated from church membership, and voting rights extended to all free males who met a property requirement. Finally, religious toleration had to be extended to all Protestants. The Puritan ideal of a place where only full church saints had a voice—already strained by earlier religious, social, and economic developments—was now lost.

Witchcraft at Salem

New England had suffered two major crises in short succession: King Philip's War in the 1670s and the Glorious Revolution in the 1680s. News of the new Massachusetts charter and new governor arrived in January 1692. At the same time, Puritan jeremiads continued to blame such events on the immorality and religious indifference of the colonial population. This tense atmosphere contributed to one of the most famous and troubling episodes of mass panic in American history—the **Salem Witchcraft Hysteria**—that led to the execution of twenty people and the imprisonment of dozens more.

Witchcraft persecutions were common at the time in Europe, and among both common people and educated leaders there was a belief that magic was real. Those views were carried over into American settlements, and by the 1690s, there had already been a number of witchcraft trials in both the northern and southern colonies. The Puritan worldview stressed the everyday reality of the supernatural. Puritans believed that they lived in "worlds of wonder" where witches, demons, fairies, monstrous births, portents, curses, miracles, and other magical phenomena were real and affected human beings. Some forms of magic, such as hanging a horseshoe over a door for good luck, were seen as largely harmless. Others, though, were seen as malicious. Whenever tragedy struck—fires, disease, death, flooding—New England colonists frequently looked for supernatural explanations. The majority of individuals accused of practicing witchcraft were women, since according to Puritan teachings, women were more susceptible to moral corruption by Satan. Witchcraft accusations also largely targeted those on the outer edges of society: the poor, the elderly, those in trouble with the law, or women who acted in ways that society considered improper for their sex. In the case of Salem, all of these things were true, but charges of witchcraft also traveled well up the social ladder and a number of prominent men and women were accused of using evil magic.

In late January 1692, nine-year-old Elizabeth Parris and eleven-year-old Abigail Williams began acting strangely. They had seizures during which their bodies contorted into strange positions. They screamed, uttered strange noises, and complained of being pinched by unseen hands and poked with invisible pins. Both girls were relatives of Salem's minister, Samuel Parris. As the symptoms worsened, Reverend Parris summoned a doctor to examine the girls. The doctor determined that there was no physical cause for the girls' behavior, and therefore, the cause must be supernatural. Parris consulted with ministers from surrounding towns, who concurred in the diagnosis. Shortly afterwards, several other girls in Salem began manifesting similar symptoms. When interviewed by local magistrates, the girls accused three women in town of bewitching them. One was Tituba, a Caribbean Indian slave belonging to the Parris family. The other two were Sarah Good, a homeless woman, and Sarah Osborn, who was elderly and poor.

The three accused witches were arrested and interrogated in court. During the interrogations, the afflicted girls would periodically go into fits, screaming and writhing in agony. Good and Osborn declared their innocence, but Tituba confessed to telling fortunes and conducting witchcraft ceremonies. The urge to confess—even falsely—would have been strong. Confessed witches could escape a death sentence by acting as informers and testifying against other accused witches. Those who maintained their innocence would be put on trial and, if found guilty, hanged. Tituba named not only Good and Osborn as fellow witches but also backed up allegations made against other townspeople that the afflicted girls accused of sorcery.

Several of the other accused witches in town likewise confessed and began to name others. Interrogations entered into a standard routine. The accused witch would be brought in front of the magistrates and the afflicted girls. Every time the accused would look at the girls or gesture with his or her hands, the girls would fall down screaming and thrashing. The number of accused witches grew rapidly, including the four-year-old daughter of Sarah Good, who confessed to having a black pet snake that spoke to her and drank blood from her finger. When the judges examined the little girl's finger, they found a red mark the size of a fleabite, which they took as conclusive evidence of the girl's supernatural powers. The girls also pointed to former Salem minister George Burroughs as one of their tormentors. Burroughs, who was at the time living hundreds of miles away in Maine, was arrested and brought to Massachusetts for questioning. The girls claimed that Burroughs flew through the air from Maine to Massachusetts to torment them. Anyone who spoke up in defense of accused witches, or questioned whether the afflicted girls were being truthful, often found themselves also arrested for practicing dark magic. The spiraling number of cases soon began to overwhelm the local legal system.

Print depicting a witchcraft trial in Salem, Massachusetts.

In May, the new royal Governor Sir William Phips arrived in Boston. He brought with him the new charter and the responsibility for implementing it despite the unpopularity of some of its provisions. His first challenge was this growing witchcraft situation in Salem. He considered trying to stop or reduce the accusations but perhaps was concerned about losing popularity among the populace while being so new to his position. Phips instead appointed a special tribunal to investigate and try the various accused witches. At that point, 62 people had been arrested in just three months. The court considered multiple types of evidence before reaching a verdict. One type of evidence was eyewitness statements, often people describing how some misfortune—an illness or the death of a farm animal for example—befell them within days or weeks of encountering an accused witch. A second type of evidence was a visual inspection of an accused witch, looking for marks or blemishes where an animal might have feasted on the witch's blood. It was a common belief at the time that the Devil gave each witch an animal familiar, and it was from that familiar that the witch derived his or her powers. Familiars in return had to be fed the witch's blood. Another type of evidence was to ask the accused to read a passage from the Bible or say the Lord's Prayer, which supposedly would be impossible if the accused was a servant of Satan.

One final type of evidence at the trials was particularly controversial. The judges approved what was called spectral evidence. If one of the afflicted girls or an eyewitness said that they had seen the invisible ghost or image of one of the accused, it was evidence that the accused was indeed guilty of witchcraft. Only witches had the power to send their specters out of their body to torment people at a distance. The esteemed Reverend **Cotton Mather** was considered an expert on witchcraft after writing a book about another witchcraft case in 1689. Mather defended the use of spectral evidence at the trials, admitting that while it had limitations, it ultimately was as reliable as any other type of evidence available to the court. A few individuals spoke out in opposition to spectral evidence, though not loudly, and then typically only after the worst of the hysteria had already passed. One of those who eventually spoke out against spectral evidence was Reverend Increase Mather, Cotton's father and the President of Harvard. In the latter stages of the trials, he published a book in which he stated "it were better that ten suspected witches should escape, than that one innocent person should be condemned." Despite Increase Mather's reservations about the use of spectral evidence, however, like his son he was a strong defender of the trials themselves.

The first formal conviction came on June 2, 1692, and eight days later Bridget Bishop was hanged. One of the judges, Nathaniel Saltonstall, resigned from the court after the first execution feeling that the court was not granting fair trials, but the court continued on without him. The special court convicted every accused witch who stood trial before it, and the number of accusations continued to mount. Several more individuals were executed in July and August. During a three-day span in September, the court executed nine accused witches, including Giles Corey, who was pressed to death by stones. One of those executed over the summer was the Reverend Burroughs, who stunned eyewitnesses by giving a perfect recitation of the Lord's Prayer on the gallows. The crowd of onlookers began to wonder if they should halt the hanging, since only an innocent man could have done that. However, some of the afflicted girls were in attendance and claimed to see the Devil whispering the words in Burroughs's ear. Cotton Mather, who was also in attendance, agreed with the girls that the Devil could indeed assist a witch in saying prayers correctly. The execution proceeded as planned.

Governor Phips had for months been absent from the colony on a military expedition to Maine. He returned in October to find the situation spiraling out of control, with even his own wife falling under suspicion of witchcraft. Phips dismissed the special court and suspended any further arrests. The trials resumed in January 1693, under a different court with more strict standards of evidence—spectral evidence was not accepted. Under the new rules, fifty-three trials ended in not guilty verdicts. In only three cases did the new court convict an accused witch. Phips stepped in and pardoned the three convicted witches, plus those who had been convicted under the previous court and who had not yet been executed. After several more acquittals, the court dismissed all remaining charges of witchcraft, even refusing to indict Tituba, whose confession had been instrumental at the very beginning of the episode. In all, 185 people had been accused of witchcraft and twenty executed. Seven other accused witches died in prison. In the years that followed, inhabitants concluded that a great injustice had occurred and that many, perhaps even all, of those accused and convicted were in fact innocent. In 1711, Massachusetts reversed the convictions of 22 witches and granted monetary compensation to their families.

Though there is still an active debate over why the Salem accusations reached such heights, many people see the hysteria as an example of Puritans looking for someone or something to blame for their own social, cultural, and economic insecurities.

LAYING FOUNDATIONS FOR THE AMERICAN NATION

England's two northern colonial regions—New England and the Middle Colonies—in many ways stand in sharp contrast to each other. New England's population consisted almost entirely of English men and women, making it ethnically homogenous and largely distrustful of outsiders. Church and state were far more intertwined in New England than in their neighboring colonies. The Middle Colonies were settled by a diverse group of people from multiple nationalities and ethnicities. By both plan and by necessity, New York, Pennsylvania, and the other mid-Atlantic colonies were more open and accepting of religious and cultural differences than were their neighbors to the north.

Yet despite the many differences, there were a surprising number of commonalities between the two regions. Massachusetts and Pennsylvania had both been established as utopian religious experiments, and in the eyes of their founders, both failed to reach their goals. Northern colonies also prospered much more quickly than did England's southern colonies, assisted by a far healthier disease environment and more dedicated planning. All of the northern colonies relied heavily on a combination of farming and maritime activities for their economic survival. New England and the Middle Colonies alike showed a stubborn commitment to representative self-government, a trend that had first been established at Jamestown farther to the south.

By the 1700s, England's northern colonies were prospering and in many ways challenging the mother country that spawned them. Northern colonial shipbuilding and shipping competed directly with London companies. Ships based in Philadelphia, Boston, New York, Newport, and other northern seaports were carrying goods to and from every corner of the Atlantic basin. American colonists had shown a distinct tendency to ignore or overturn laws and instructions that they disliked. That undercurrent of colonial rebelliousness was a sour note in an otherwise happy relationship between England and her colonies at the close of the seventeenth century.

Chronology

1620   Pilgrims adopt and settle Plymouth.

1621   Dutch West India Company chartered.

1624   Peter Minuit purchases Manhattan Island.

1630   Puritans settle Massachusetts Bay.

1636   Harvard University opens its doors.
Roger Williams founds Providence colony.
Anne Hutchinson banished from
Massachusetts Bay Colony.
Pequot War begins.

1638   Pierre Minuit founds New Sweden.

1653   Oliver Cromwell becomes Lord Protector
of England.

1662   Charles II grants Rhode Island charter.
Halfway Covenant implemented in New
England.

1663   Charles II grants Connecticut charter.

1664   England takes New Netherland from the
Dutch and renames it New York.

1675-76 King Philip's War.

1681-82 William Penn receives charter to
establish Pennsylvania.

1684   Massachusetts charter revoked.

1686   King James II creates the Dominion of New
England.

1688-89 The Glorious Revolution in England.

1691   Jacob Leisler executed.

1692-93 Witchcraft hysteria in Salem, Massachusetts.

SUGGESTED READINGS

Victoria D. Anderson, *New England's Generation: The Great Migration and the Formation of Society and Culture in the Seventeenth Century* (1991).

Bernard Bailyn, *The New England Merchants in the Seventeenth Century* (1955).

——, *The Peopling of British North America* (1986).

Patricia Bonomi, *Under the Cope of Heaven: Religion, Society, and Politics in the Seventeenth Century* (1986).

William Cronon, *Changes in the Land: Colonists and the Ecology of New England* (1983).

John Demos, *A Little Commonwealth: Family Life in Plymouth Colony* (1971).

David D. Hall, *Worlds of Wonder, Days of Judgment: Popular Religious Belief in Early New England* (1989).

Stephen Innes, *Creating the Commonwealth: The Economic Culture of Puritan New England* (1995).

Richard R. Johnson, *Adjustment to Empire: The New England Colonies, 1675-1715* (1981).

Jill Lepore, *The Name of War: King Philip's War and the Origin of American Identity* (1998).

Perry Miller, *The New England Mind: The Seventeenth Century* (1939).

John A. Moretta, *William Penn and the Quaker Legacy* (2007).

Edmund S. Morgan, *The Puritan Family* (1944).

——, *Visible Saints: The History of a Puritan Idea* (1963).

Gary B. Nash, *Quakers and Politics: Pennsylvania, 1681-1726* (1968).

Mary Beth Norton, *In the Devil's Snare: The Salem Witchcraft Crisis of 1692* (2002).

Carla G. Pestana, *The English Atlantic in an Age of Revolution, 1640-1661* (2001).

Owen Stanwood, *The Empire Reformed: English America in the Age of the Glorious Revolution* (2011).

Alan Taylor, *American Colonies* (2001).

Review Questions

1. In what significant ways did English colonization in the northern colonies differ from that in southern colonies?

2. What factors caused dissension in New England? What consequences did religious and social dissent have on the New England colonies?

3. Discuss William Penn's idea of Pennsylvania as a "Holy Experiment." How did Penn's idea differ from John Winthrop's vision of Massachusetts as a glorious "City upon a Hill"?

4. Discuss the relationship between the New England Puritans and Native Americans in the region. Why was the relationship so hostile?

5. What effects did the ascension of James II to the throne and the subsequent Glorious Revolution have on the American colonies?

Glossary of Important People and Concepts

Edmund Andros
Charles I
"City upon a Hill"
Coverture
Dominion of New England
Glorious Revolution
Great Migration
Halfway Covenant
Anne Hutchinson
Iroquois Confederacy
King Philip's War
John Locke
Cotton Mather
New Netherland
William Penn
Pequot War
Pilgrims
Praying Towns
Puritans
Quakers (The Society of Friends)
Salem Witchcraft Hysteria
Separatists
Squanto
Roger Williams
John Winthrop

Benjamin Franklin of Philadelphia, between 1763 and 1785

Chapter Four

CREATING AN AMERICAN PEOPLE, 1700-1763

An invisible killer stalked the streets of Boston in 1721. In April, a ship arrived in Massachusetts from Barbados, bringing trade goods for sale in the city along with an unseen passenger in the form of the smallpox virus. When the ship's sailors first began to show symptoms of the disease, city officials quickly put them in quarantine, fervently hoping to protect the city of 11,000 people. However, Boston's preventative measures were too little, too late. During the disease's incubation period, the ill sailors had circulated throughout the town for several days, and the disease quickly took root and began to flower. By June, the virus had spread to almost every corner of the tightly packed city. Boston's citizens had good reason to be terrified since in earlier centuries smallpox had wiped out entire native tribes. Those of European descent had more built-in resistance to this Old World disease, but based on Boston's five previous smallpox outbreaks, the city could expect at least half its citizens to fall ill and as many as 20 percent of those infected would die. True to form, by the time this particular epidemic had run its course, it ranked as one of the deadliest in eighteenth-century America.

A common view in this Puritan city in 1721 was that the plague was a sign of God's displeasure and divine judgment. Many people argued that people should just brace for the worst, pray for forgiveness, and accept their just punishment, believing that any effort to stop the spread of smallpox might anger God even more and thus make the situation worse. On the other hand, there were a small number of leading citizens who disagreed with the divine punishment view of the outbreak. They instead embraced the Enlightenment's more scientific approach, concluding that the epidemic had natural causes and could, therefore, be fought through the implementation of rational, empirical solutions. Among

this Enlightenment group was the illustrious minister Cotton Mather, perhaps most famous for his earlier involvement in the very unscientific Salem Witchcraft Trials. Mather knew of a procedure—inoculation—that could limit the impact of smallpox. Inoculation involved deliberately infecting a healthy person with a mild case of smallpox via the insertion of infected blood or pus through a needle or cut. When the person recovered from the mild form of the illness, they would have lifelong immunity to the more virulent strains. Mather had learned of the procedure many years earlier from one of his slaves, Onesimus, who had been inoculated in Africa as a child and remembered the procedure. Curious, Mather had researched inoculation in subsequent years through correspondence with English scientific societies, and over time became convinced that it was scientifically sound. He reached out to Boston's medical community but was disappointed to find that almost all the city's physicians were hostile to the idea. After much effort, Mather finally convinced Dr. Zabdiel Boylston to try inoculation on the physician's son and on two slaves. All three patients survived, offering clear proof of the procedure's soundness. Dr. Boylston then began to inoculate hundreds of others who came to him, including Reverend Mather's son.

Public criticism of Mather, Boylston, and their experiment with inoculation was intense. Many physicians and politicians feared that inoculation would spread smallpox (and other diseases like syphilis) even faster than would otherwise happen. There was some logical basis to this criticism as the blood or pus exchanged during inoculation could transmit additional infectious diseases from one person to another. Furthermore, an inoculated person's smallpox case did become contagious for the duration of their resulting illness. Finally, inoculation could not always guarantee that the deliberate infection would be of the mild variety, and some inoculated individuals could and did die as a result of their inoculation. Among the loudest critics of inoculation was Dr. William Douglass, the only physician in Boston who had a medical degree. Douglass opposed inoculation on both religious and scientific grounds, in particular strongly believing that deliberately infecting healthy people would cause even more deaths rather than save lives. He also argued that since the procedure had been used by primitive heathens in Africa, it was therefore not fit for civilized and Christian Englishmen. Mather, by contrast, defended African medical practices, saying that regardless of social and cultural prejudices, inoculation as a procedure had been scientifically proven in Africa by the observation of its effects.

Douglass's scathing criticisms, as well as those of like-minded Bostonians, frequently appeared in the **New England Courant**, a newspaper published by printer James Franklin and his 16-year-old brother Benjamin. Anonymous articles each week attacked Mather, Boylston, and Boston's clergy, many of whom had come around to the support of Mather. As Boston's death toll climbed throughout the summer and fall, the newspaper's war of words became increasingly heated and personal. Insults flew in both directions, but insults were the least of Mather's troubles. In November, someone threw a crude incendiary bomb through the window of Mather's home. It landed in a front room near where his son was playing. Fortunately for the Mather family, the bomb's fuse burned out and the device did not explode. Attached was a message: "Cotton Mather, you dog, dam you! I'll inoculate you with this; with a pox to you." Undeterred, Mather and Boylston continued to promote smallpox inoculation.

By the early part of 1722, the epidemic was over, and Boston was finally smallpox free. During the crisis, 4917 people had been infected, and 842 died, a mortality rate of nearly 15 percent. By comparison, Boylston had personally inoculated 287 people, of whom only 6 died, a mortality rate of just over 2 percent. Inoculation had proven so successful during the 1721 epidemic that even Douglass at last admitted its effectiveness, and in later years he wrote pamphlets promoting the procedure. The young printer Benjamin Franklin, whose newspaper had published many vicious attacks on inoculation and on Mather, would also later become one of inoculation's most ardent proponents. In the age of the Enlightenment, evidence and reason had won out over prejudice and fear.

REGULATING THE EMPIRE

By 1700, the British American colonies were enmeshed in a complex and interconnected trade network that flowed to and from every corner of the Atlantic Ocean. Each year, massive quantities of Virginia tobacco, Carolina rice and indigo, and Caribbean sugar departed for European ports, where at the same time vessels were loading on European clothing, salt, wine, and manufactured goods for shipment to the American colonies. Ships carrying Pennsylvania grains, North Carolina timber, Massachusetts dried fish, and Georgia rice made their way south to the British sugar islands of the Caribbean, then returning home with cargo holds full of molasses. Slave ships plied their trade back and forth across the middle passage, carrying with them millions of terrible and tragic stories into the New World. As testimony to the centrality of maritime trade, one of the most critical sections in colonial newspapers was the announcement of arriving and departing ships. In a very real and immediate way, trade was life for the colonies. Without trade, overseas colonies would have no economic basis for existing. If cut off from commerce, most colonies would not be able to produce for themselves the full range of materials needed to survive, let alone prosper. Of all the trade routes, the one with the mother country was culturally and economically the most vital of all, and many people in America communicated as regularly with people in England as they did people in neighboring colonies.

Even in Puritan New England, which had been established mainly for religious reasons rather than economic ones, trade increasingly took on an importance rivaling that of faith. Ministers often complained of congregants skipping church on Sundays in order to put additional time into their work. The shift from an insular and religious society in New England to a more cosmopolitan and profit-driven one has been called a shift from "Puritan to Yankee." By the early 1700s, that cultural transformation

Cotton Mather

was almost complete. When one minister tried to exhort his listeners to embrace old time Puritan zeal, he was flatly told by one prominent citizen that whatever the motives of previous generations, that now the "main end was to catch fish."

The Navigation Acts

Authorities in England tried with mixed success to impose order on the chaos of colonial commerce. The main goal of the British mercantilist system was to enrich the mother country, and under such an approach, only secondarily would any economic benefits accrue to English colonies. Colonies would provide raw materials and agricultural products that England would otherwise have to import from foreign nations. Economists at the time believed that buying from other countries made the purchasing nation poorer. Any excess colonial materials that England did not use could be sold to other countries, thus bringing in cash that would enrich the mother country. To ensure that all trade would enrich England, in 1651, Parliament began passing a series of **Navigation Acts**. The first such law mandated that any trade with England or its colonies had to be carried in English or colonial cargo vessels, thus eliminating ships from other nations—particularly the Netherlands—from even participating as shippers. Later versions of the laws added requirements that the ship crews had to be mostly Englishmen and that all goods from other European nations that were intended for sale in English colonies had to first be shipped through England. The goods would be unloaded by English dockworkers, taxed by English officers, and then reloaded onto English-owned vessels. Certain enumerated goods shipped from America (including rice and tobacco) also had to first land in England before being sold in other European ports. After the Act of Union in 1707, which united Scotland, England, and Wales into the nation of Great Britain, cargo was allowed to land in Scottish ports. This transit system helped people in Great Britain at almost every step but increased the expenses of colonial merchants. The resulting higher prices on foreign imported goods encouraged colonists to purchase from England rather than from other European nations.

Enforcement of the Navigation Acts was uneven from the start. Some colonial merchants evaded the laws by smuggling items into and out of the colonies. Parliament passed multiple amendments to the acts trying to close loopholes and tighten enforcement. By the end of the seventeenth century, imperial authorities had to send customs officials to try and force colonists to obey trade restrictions. Colonial authorities and citizens, however, often tacitly supported smuggling, since it resulted in

cheap goods flowing into and out of colonial ports, greatly boosting local economies. Even on occasions when customs officials managed to apprehend and prosecute an accused smuggler, it was a challenge to get a conviction from American juries in colonial courts. Many jury members voted to acquit smugglers regardless of the evidence against them.

The Molasses Act of 1733 demonstrated both the desire in England to capture the colonial trade, and also the determination of colonists to pursue profit even if it meant skirting the law. The act placed a heavy tax on foreign imported molasses. The French sugar islands in particular produced molasses at lower prices than the British-held islands. The intent of the law was to protect the interest of British sugar planters by taxing French molasses so much as to make it unaffordable. The booming New England rum industry relied on the cheaper French molasses to make rum, and the law threatened to disrupt the economy of the English mainland colonies. Instead of obeying the act, colonial merchants started bribing customs officers to look the other way when ships arrived carrying French molasses. The tax, if collected, would have been six pennies per gallon. The going rate for a bribe was only a half-penny per gallon. Even with the expense of the bribe, smuggled French molasses was less expensive than British molasses. Even if customs officials remained honest and vigilant, they were always too few in number to be able to effectively monitor the thousands of miles of America's coastline and block smugglers. Even in times of war, when the English navy took a more direct role in blockading foreign colonies, colonial ships still found clever ways to continue the illicit trade in Spanish and French sugar. One popular tactic was to stage fake prisoner exchanges. A British merchant would pass through a British blockade under these false pretenses, dock in a French sugar colony, and then depart with a cargo hold full of molasses instead of redeemed prisoners of war.

Parliament also passed a series of laws designed to protect manufacturing in England against competition from English colonies. In 1699, a new law prohibited American colonies from exporting any wool. All wool sheared in America had to be used within the boundaries of the colony where it was produced. In 1732 and 1750, Parliament similarly prohibited the exporting of American-made hats and finished iron products so as to make sure that colonial manufacturers would not undercut similar industries in Great Britain. The ultimate intent of all such laws was to dissuade American businessmen from entering certain businesses. Instead, colonists would have to purchase goods from England rather than produce them locally.

Though the imperial trade system was always messy and drew its share of grumbles from both sides of the Atlantic, by and large it led to prosperity for the mother country and the colonies. By 1700, England was the world's leading maritime power. London, the primary trade port for American merchants, became the largest and most wealthy city in Europe. British merchants extended generous amounts of credit for Americans who purchased goods from England. By the time of the American Revolution, millions of pounds of British goods were imported to the American colonies each year, bringing about a consumer product revolution. In American communities, displaying the latest clothing, furniture, or tableware from London became a marker of social status. The British colonial standard of living far exceeded that in French and Spanish colonies, and was as high or higher than many areas of the English countryside. The volume of imports from England to America also served to reinforce the common British cultural heritage of both the mother country and her colonies.

Piracy in the Americas

Since trade was so vital to the British Empire's well-being, any threat to commerce was dealt with swiftly and severely. One such threat in the early eighteenth century was piracy. England, France, and the Netherlands during the sixteenth and seventeenth centuries had relied heavily on private ship captains to supplement their navies in the New World. These privateers were given letters of marque and reprisal granting legal permission to wage war on and plunder the issuing country's rivals. While the letter would provide a legal shield in friendly ports, if privateers were caught by their enemies, they were considered common pirates and punished accordingly. Some ship captains fully embraced piracy by disregarding the restrictions outlined in their privateering letters and plundering any ship regardless of its national origin. By 1700, the nations of the world had begun to turn against illegal piracy, with England leading the way. England declared total war on pirates, proclaiming them to be "*hostis humani generis*," or "enemies of mankind."

For a time in the 1690s, Britain's North American colonies offered save havens from which pirates could sail. Pirate ships left towns like Boston or New York to cross the Atlantic Ocean, then down and around the coast of Africa, and toward the Indian Ocean and Red Sea. After loading up on riches, these pirate ships would return to their home bases in America to sell off their goods. Some colonial governors willingly accepted the presence of pirates because the sale of stolen goods benefited the immediate community. The most famous colonial pirate of the 1690s was Captain William Kidd of New York, whose expeditions were funded and supported by a number of government officials, including the governor. Kidd sailed into the Indian Ocean in 1697 as a legal privateer but soon exceeded his authority by seizing ships that were not enemies of England. Upon his return to New York he was arrested, sent to London for trial, and, in 1701, hanged as a pirate. His body was put on display to emphasize that England had a zero tolerance policy towards pirates or anyone who supported them. Any colonial governors who tolerated pirates in the future would face immediate dismissal from office. Kidd's very high profile trial and execution, however, did not spell the end for piracy.

From 1716-1726, the Caribbean Sea and the Atlantic Ocean experienced what has become known as the **Golden Age of Piracy**. Initially using the Bahamas as a base, pirates raided and plundered any ship they could catch. Though many of the captains were British, their crews were multinational, including many of European and African descent. National loyalties no longer mattered to those who "went on the account." Pirate crews often signed formal articles that acted as constitutions for the ship, and most issues or disputes were solved by majority vote of the crew. Captains were elected and ruled by consent of the governed rather than acting as dictators. Famous buccaneers such as Bartholomew Roberts, Benjamin Hornigold, and Edward England attacked shipping across vast ranges of ocean stretching from the coast of Canada down to Brazil, and then across to the west coast of Africa. Edward Teach, better known as Blackbeard, put together a large fleet and boldly blockaded the harbor of Charleston, South Carolina in 1718. Piratical activity on such a scale severely disrupted the intricate British trade system and thus required decisive government action. Using a combination of naval power and strategically offered pardons, England first took control of the Bahamas, depriving pirates of their one safe haven in the Americas. The British navy and privateer pirate hunters then tracked down and methodically brought pirate crews to justice. Blackbeard was killed in combat off the coast of North Carolina in 1718, and one by one other famous pirate captains met the same fate. By 1726, the British had hanged hundreds of pirates, and the Golden Age of Piracy came to an end. The oceans were once again safe for commerce.

Colonial Government

In the same way that London authorities attempted to regulate colonial trade, so too did the mother country try to impose order on colonial politics and government. By 1700, most colonies were either proprietary or royal

Past and Present Collide: The Controversial Ship *Whydah Gally*

In 1984, an expedition led by underwater explorer Barry Clifford uncovered a shipwreck off the coast of Cape Cod. Along this rocky shoreline, famous for its sudden shifts in weather, underwater wrecks were far from rare. Clifford, however, was using a hand-drawn eighteenth century map to search for one particular ship that sank during a major storm in colonial Massachusetts waters in 1717. In 1985, Clifford's dive team brought up a ship's bell that confirmed that they had found the object of their quest. Across the bronze bell was an inscription reading: WHYDAH GALLY, 1716. This was the long-lost shipwreck of the notorious pirate Sam Bellamy, and the first ever confirmed recovery of a lost pirate ship from the 18th century Golden Age of Piracy. The excavation of nearly 200,000 artifacts continued over the course of many years, with ship's cannon, sailing equipment, clothing, and finally thousands of gold and silver coins coming up from the bottom of the ocean. Little did anyone at the time of the wreck's rediscovery realize how controversial these artifacts would become.

In 1992, Clifford teamed up with a group of developers to plan a Whydah Complex, a multi-story pirate museum and entertainment complex that would feature artifacts from the shipwreck as well as a full-scale replica of the ship. Developers pitched the idea to city leaders in Tampa, Florida, which was chosen as a site both because of its year-round warm weather and because the ship had been initially captured by Bellamy in southern waters. The city of Tampa already had cultural traditions tied into piracy—there was and still is an annual pirate-themed Gasparilla parade through downtown, and the area's NFL football team was named the Buccaneers. The museum development company was willing to fund almost the entire project, but needed the city to give them authorization to purchase and develop land along the Tampa waterfront. However, the development company found that the history of the ship was complex and hotly contested. The **Whydah Gally** had been constructed and launched in 1716 as a slave ship. It left London and traveled to the west coast of Africa, where the ship's crew traded for and loaded on board approximately 500 African slaves. The ship then crossed the Atlantic Ocean to the Americas, a trip known in the history of the slave trade as the "Middle Passage." Off the coast of the Bahamas, it was captured by Bellamy in February 1717 and made into the pirate's new flagship. Bellamy then sailed up the coast of North America where his pirate ship met its fate in the April 1717 storm, sinking and killing all but two of the 150 crew members on board.

The proposed museum and entertainment complex around the **Whydah** artifacts was originally designed to focus entirely on pirates and piracy. Some African-American leaders in the Tampa area were concerned about the proposed erasure of the ship's history in the slave trade. A group of black scholars and business leaders conditionally supported the project as long as developers agreed to re-formulate the concept into a "Slavery and Piracy" museum to give equal attention to the ship's two roles during its short lifespan. Other African-American leaders opposed the museum altogether regardless of any changes made in the exhibits, arguing that it was inappropriate to let a for-profit enterprise exploit the history of slavery for entertainment and greed. Making things even more complex was the fact that this was not the first time that racial tensions over piracy had flared in Tampa. Until the 1980s, the private community group that staged the annual Gasparilla pirate parade had bylaws banning minorities from participating in the parade. Even though the bylaws had been deleted, not until 1991 were any black community members allowed to join the parade, which was all the more galling since 18th century pirate crews (including Bellamy's) had often contained sizable numbers of freed African slaves. The anger generated by this earlier controversy was still very fresh in 1992-1993 and complicated the situation surrounding the proposed Whydah Gally Complex. Frustrated by months of controversy and halted progress, the Whydah museum developers stopped communicating with African-American community groups, and bluntly announced their intention to press forward with an entertainment complex that focused on pirate history. Tampa groups opposed to the proposed museum organized a series of protest marches that eventually successfully convinced city officials to kill the project entirely. A much smaller Whydah Pirate Museum finally opened in Yarmouth, Massachusetts in 2016. Even though the capture and subsequent sinking of the slave and pirate ship had occurred nearly 300 years earlier, the ship's history still burned bright in the present.

colonies. Thus, the typical American provincial government consisted of a governor appointed in England, a council (often made up of prominent local citizens) appointed by the governor, and an assembly elected by local voters. One of the dominant themes in colonial politics during the late seventeenth and early eighteenth centuries was the struggle for power between imperial authorities in London and the colonial assemblies in America. Leaders in England wanted to centralize as much control as possible in the mother country, while leaders in colonial assemblies wanted greater freedom to make decisions themselves. Over time, colonists began to see their assemblies as miniature Parliaments defending colonial liberty against excessive encroachment from central authority. The most contentious issue of all was, unsurprisingly, money. Colonial assemblies insisted that any tax bills had to originate with them rather than with governors, councils, or officials in England.

Colonists also argued that appointed governors needed to respect the role of provincial assemblies in much the same way that the English monarch had been forced by the English Civil War to respect Parliament. On paper, colonial governors wielded considerable power in America. Governors typically had the right to veto all colonial legislation and to form or dissolve assemblies. This last power in particular could be open to abuse. Should a governor disapprove of a colonial assembly's actions, the governor had every right simply to dissolve it and call for new elections. In reality, however, governors were strongly motivated to work cooperatively with assemblies because the governor's salary was approved and paid by the legislature. Appointed officials who alienated elected colonial representatives could find their paychecks withheld as punishment.

While colonial assemblies claimed to represent all the people of a given province, the structure of politics greatly limited the number of people allowed to formally participate in the political system. As in England, most colonies restricted voting to white male property owners, though because land was much more obtainable in America, a majority of white colonial men enjoyed the right to vote. Elected positions, however, had higher property ownership requirements, and many voters were ineligible to run for public office. Assemblymen were not paid a salary, which meant that only those with significant independent wealth could afford to serve. The result was that elected representatives were almost exclusively chosen from the most wealthy and powerful families in a colony. This same small pool of elite families also normally held the bulk of appointed offices. In America, the elite were very much in charge of local government. Despite these various class-based limitations in the system, colonial assemblies still were the only structures in America that could claim to represent the will of the people.

Officials in London worked to limit the role of legislatures in making major governmental decisions. The English Crown in 1696 established the **Board of Trade** to monitor and regulate colonial commerce and governance. While the board had few formal powers, it served as an important source of advice for the King and others who could take action. The board's effectiveness rested entirely on the energy and commitment of its individual members, and quite often appointees did not take their positions seriously. Thus, the period from 1690 to 1763 has often been called a time of **salutary neglect**—a period where London authorities took a lax attitude towards colonial deviations from British law and custom. As a result, provincial politics developed with only sporadic interference from the mother country. A switch to more direct imperial intervention in colonial trade and government after 1763 marked a major shift in the colonial relationship and became one of the contributing factors that led to the American Revolution.

THE PEOPLING OF EIGHTEENTH-CENTURY BRITISH AMERICA

Rapid Population Growth

After 1700, the British colonies experienced an incredible rate of growth, roughly doubling in size every 25 years. In 1700, there were approximately 250,000 inhabitants of the thirteen mainland colonies that later made up the United States, compared to the mother country's 5 million people. By 1775, the number stood at nearly 2.5 million, compared to a population in Great Britain of 7.5 million. Meanwhile, France and Spain's North American colonies had populations only a small fraction of this size. Some of the American population growth was due to a positive birth rate. American colonists married earlier, had more children, and lived longer than Europeans. Since land was plentiful and fertile, famine was rare in America after the first years of settlement. Firewood was also cheap and easily obtained, which made winters easier to survive. In Europe, someone was considered prosperous in life if they had enough food to eat and were warm in the winter. By that material standard, almost every white colonist was considered well off.

Natural population increase, however, was only part of the picture. The main driver of population growth was immigration from all across Europe and by slaves from Africa. Indeed, the large majority of new arrivals in the eighteenth century were non-English, usually refugees fleeing economic troubles or religious strife. In Europe, land was expensive and unemployment was high. In the New World, land was cheap, and there was always a need for more workers. These conditions created a strong draw for individuals in search of a fresh start in life. In many ways, America developed into a "melting pot" of different languages, cultures, and nationalities.

The single largest group of immigrants were the Scots-Irish, of whom some 250,000 made their way to the colonies. These people were descendants of Presbyterian

Scots (followers of John Calvin) who settled in Northern Ireland in the seventeenth century and who grew to think of themselves as a distinct group different from both the Scottish and the Irish. Ireland in the early 1700s witnessed a dramatic increase in land rents, causing many hard-pressed farmers to seek cheaper land elsewhere, such as America. In the colonies, the Scots-Irish developed a reputation for restlessness and combativeness. The latter trait was particularly evident in their often harsh and violent attitudes toward native populations on the frontier.

The second largest ethnic group of voluntary immigrants were approximately 100,000 Germans, who arrived from numerous principalities and countries in central Europe. Most were Protestants who feared living in regions where the Catholic Church dominated. Others were simply refugees from war-ravaged areas. Most of the German arrivals were poor, and many made the journey to America as indentured servants. Philadelphia served as the biggest port of entry for most of these immigrants to the colonies. New England received very few immigrants since its society was in many ways unwelcoming toward outsiders. The Deep South drew in more people than did New England, but with slaves doing much of the labor in coastal areas, the eastern portions of those colonies were seen as less desirable for those seeking economic opportunity. Not all immigrants stayed in Pennsylvania, but enough did so that by the 1760s less than half of the colony's population was English. So many Germans settled in Pennsylvania that in some western parts of the province, it was difficult to locate someone fluent in English. The "Pennsylvania Dutch" (derived from the fact that they spoke Deutsch, or German) alone made up over 30 percent of Pennsylvania's population. While they were happy to find refuge in America, most German settlers had no real personal loyalty towards the British king and no deep-seeded attachment to British culture and traditions. The arrival so many non-English families sparked concern and resentment in some English settlers. Benjamin Franklin, for example, publicly worried that there were so many Germans in his home colony that the population might become Germanized and adopt German ways of life rather than English.

There were in addition a variety of smaller yet still significant groups of immigrants. Tens of thousands of Scots fled to America following failed rebellions against the British King in 1715 and 1745. Most of the thousands of Irish newcomers were Catholics who felt mistreated by Protestant English authorities. A visitor to the colonies in the eighteenth century could also find French Huguenots, Dutch, Jews, Finns, Swedes, Swiss, and even a small number of Poles. Collectively, the American colonies had one of the most diverse populations in the world.

Occupying the Backcountry

By the time most eighteenth-century colonial immigrants arrived, land along the coast was already occupied. New arrivals instead had to settle further inland in the backcountry of the various colonies. Hundreds of thousands of immigrants spread out along the frontier, many of them following an inland road that led south from Philadelphia, skirted along the edge of the Appalachian Mountains, and then ended in the Deep South. Migrants along this Great Wagon Road traveled until they found an area that suited them and then stopped to settle down. One of the most famous migrants down the road was Daniel Boone. Born into a Pennsylvania Quaker household, Boone and his family had traveled down the Great Wagon Road when he was a teenager, settling in the North Carolina backcountry. They later led the way for Americans who pushed even farther to the west in search of land. Some backcountry settlers legally took out ownership grants for the land on which they settled, but others merely squatted and lived on lands they neither owned nor rented. Since backcountry settlers were far away from coastal elites and seaports, they collectively developed a strong sense of rugged independence. They often resented the actions of colonial governments, which all seemed to prioritize the needs and wishes of coastal areas above those of inland regions.

Voting and representation were crucial complaints among backcountry immigrants. In addition to colonial assembly district boundaries often being drawn to give political power to coastal districts regardless of the actual pattern of residents, slaves (much more numerous in the coastal areas) were also counted on an equal basis with whites for representation purposes. As a result, backcountry areas typically had fewer representatives than they deserved based on population. For example, the backcountry areas of South Carolina had approximately half the colony's white population but elected only about 5 percent of the colonial assembly's members. On top of that inequity, legislative and court sessions usually took place on the coast, meaning that backcountry representatives needed to travel great distances to take part in their government or in legal proceedings. Tax revenues were also a source of contention as taxes collected from backcountry farmers and hunters were mostly spent improving life for those who lived along the coast. In protest against their mistreatment, backcountry inhabitants in the 1760s in both South and North Carolina formed bands of local vigilantes called "Regulators," who saw their role as providing local law and order in the absence of any real interest by the legal colonial government. Colonial governments viewed the Regulator movement as an armed rebellion and eventually suppressed it, but the conflict took years and much bloodshed to resolve. The events, though, did pay some long term dividends in that backcountry areas were given more equitable representation in the South Carolina legislature.

Another source of backcountry anger arose from the presence of Indians on the frontier. White settlers and Native Americans were rivals for land, and many poor western colonists believed that the only way they could obtain land for themselves was to take it away from native groups. As a result, western violence between whites and natives was frequent, and whenever war broke out, frontier whites would insist that attacks on indigenous peoples had to be the top military priority regardless of whether there was a legitimate Indian threat or not. In 1763, a group of western Pennsylvania farmers known as the **Paxton Boys** reacted to the outbreak of an Indian war by shifting blame to nearby peaceful natives. The mob attacked and massacred a group of Christian Indians allied with the English. In early 1764, shortly after the massacre, a crowd of about 250 Paxton Boys marched against Philadelphia to demand the resignation of pacifist Quakers from the government and to demand that colonial authorities turn over a large group of Native Americans who had fled to the capitol for protection. The marchers intended to execute the natives and then take control of the government in order to use Pennsylvania's power to make further war on native tribes. The rebellion was averted by a settlement negotiated in large part by Benjamin Franklin, who rode out to meet the Paxton Boys before they reached Philadelphia. In the final deal, the backcountry areas would receive greater representation in the colonial government, and no one would be prosecuted for the murder of the peaceful Indians. For the Paxton Boys, it was a nearly complete victory.

Colonial Cities

By the 1770s, there were still only five population centers that held over 5,000 residents and could be called cities: Philadelphia, New York, Boston, Newport, and Charleston. Despite its late start, Philadelphia had become the largest at 40,000 residents, followed by New York (25,000), Boston (15,000), and Newport (11,000). Though in total these urban spaces held just a small fraction of the overall colonial population, they nevertheless had an importance far exceeding their size. As seaports, they served as focal points of communication and trade between merchants in the provinces and those in the mother country. These seaports served as points of arrival for immigrants, books, magazines, and news from abroad. For much of the colonial period, urban centers

usually held weekly market days that spread economic benefits to nearby smaller communities who used the opportunity to sell their goods in the city. Cities also were the home of many of colonial America's printing presses and newspapers, which gave the cities further importance in education, politics, and religion.

Many people in colonial cities were employed as craftsmen and artisans, whose skills were often learned through a system of apprenticeship similar to that existing in Europe. Young men in their early teens were usually handed over to a master for three or four years, providing their labor in return for education in the chosen profession. The population in these cities grew in large part through immigration, meaning that colonial cities contained a diverse array of ethnicities and religions. Because of their size and cosmopolitanism, cities offered a wide range of culture and entertainment not readily available to rural dwellers. Sports, concerts, theaters, libraries, and educational lectures were all features of colonial cities.

Despite their attractions, colonial cities also faced unique dangers. In such cramped conditions, fires were a major concern. Since most buildings were wooden, fires easily jumped from structure to structure and could burn a major part if not all of a city. Cities provided fire ladders and water buckets for citizens to fight fires, but such simple tools proved inadequate for serious blazes. Boston was a leader in forming fire clubs and brigades, men who agreed to train and work together to combat fires more effectively, some of them even using water pumps and engines imported from Europe. Cities were also sites of regular outbreaks of epidemic diseases. Illnesses could easily arrive on an incoming ship and spread rapidly throughout the concentrated population before authorities became aware of the exposure.

Slavery and Resistance

About 140,000 newcomers to eighteenth-century North America arrived involuntarily from Africa, and by 1775, 500,000 slaves (20 percent of the colonial population) lived in the colonies. There was also a small free black population, totaling perhaps 50,000, as well. While the slave trade accounted for some of that total, there was a natural increase through childbirth. The long-term result of this increased birth rate was the development of a creole slave population that had no firsthand knowledge of free life in Africa. Their culture became African-American instead of just African. Slaves could be found in every British colony, though they were more numerous in the southern provinces and in cities. In Philadelphia and New York, about 15 to 20 percent of the population was unfree in the mid-eighteenth century. Some urban slaves served alongside skilled artisans in their trade, but even more were personal servants of the rich city elites.

Despite efforts made by slave owners to control their slaves, slaves continued to seek ways to resist their bondage. Some slowed down the pace of work, pretended to be sick, or broke important tools as gestures of defiance against their masters. Thousands of slaves ran away from their masters, even though there were few places for them to hide since slavery was legal in every colony. Some managed to find refuge in Spanish Florida or with native tribes on the frontier, while others merely attempted to survive on their own in the wilderness. The most dramatic, and most rare, type of slave resistance was armed rebellion. Slave revolts faced impossible odds, as slaves had little access to weapons, and secrecy was almost impossible to maintain during the planning stage. Despite their hopeless chances of success, some slaves rebelled nevertheless.

New York City had experienced two large-scale rebellion scares during the eighteenth century. In 1712, a group of bondsmen set a building on fire and then killed nine white townspeople who came to fight it. In the aftermath, twenty-one slaves were executed, twenty of them by burning and one through breaking on the wheel. Both forms of execution were no longer in use against whites but were unleashed on blacks out of fear. The city faced another panic in 1741 as rumors spread through the city that a large number of slaves and poor white indentured servants had joined forces to rise up and kill the city's free population. Though it is still far from clear whether there was indeed a planned slave rebellion, a series of unexplained fires taking place early that year convinced white New Yorkers that the threat was real. About 200 slaves and white servants were arrested. Many of them were executed, while the remainder were deported or banished.

The most violent and deadly slave rebellion to occur in the mainland colonies took place in 1739 north of the Stono River in South Carolina. During the **Stono Rebellion**, a group of twenty slaves broke into a general store to arm themselves with guns and promptly killed several whites that they encountered. Their plan was to escape to Spanish-held Florida. The rebels marched in plain sight with drums playing loudly, trying to draw new recruits into their fight for freedom. The impromptu slave army grew as large as one hundred before South Carolina's militia and Indian allies defeated them within a week and restored order, but not until 50 whites and several dozen black slaves were dead. The rebellion failed, but it dramatically demonstrated that African slaves maintained their desire for freedom.

While slavery gained widespread acceptance in white society during the colonial era, there were at least scattered examples of antislavery sentiment by the 1770s. Samuel Sewall, who had previously served as a judge during the Salem Witchcraft Trials in 1692, wrote in 1700 that all men had an equal right to liberty regardless of their skin color. Quakers, too, were predisposed towards antislavery beliefs. One of the central tenants of their faith was that all people carried an inner divine spark, slaves included. Some Quakers still embraced slavery and the profits that could be gained from the institution, but many others spoke out against it. As far back as 1688, the Quakers of Germantown, Pennsylvania, had written and endorsed a petition against slavery. While these voices of liberty were small in number and rarely heard during the colonial period, they foreshadowed the emergence of a stronger abolitionist movement in the nineteenth century.

THE ENLIGHTENMENT IN AMERICA

The **Enlightenment**—an intellectual movement which rejected superstition in favor of more rational and scientific explanations of the world—flourished in Europe and America during the seventeenth and eighteenth centuries. Praising mankind's ability to reason and acquire knowledge through education, experimentation, and observation, the Enlightenment led some religious authorities within the Anglican Church to reject doctrinarism and fanaticism and embrace a more rational Christian piety. Scientific authors explored the meaning of Sir Isaac Newton's laws of motion and gravity, not just for the world of physics, but in terms of humanity's understanding of the universe. Francis Bacon's commitment to empiricism ushered in an age in which thinkers based conclusions not on hunches or whims, but on careful observation, inductive reasoning, and a methodical approach to deriving answers. Bacon became known as the father of the scientific method. Political philosophers like John Locke and David Hume approached government and society as well through a more rational, enlightened lens to discover natural laws of government that could in turn guide the actions and decisions of society. All of these thinkers helped to undermine the authority of monarchs and established religions by convincing people to rely on their own intellect, not just on their political leaders or on God.

Though overall the Enlightenment undermined many traditional religious beliefs, some intellectuals, among them Benjamin Franklin, Thomas Jefferson, and Thomas Paine, managed to maintain their own personal religious beliefs. Franklin and Jefferson identified themselves nominally as Christian, but they rejected the idea of divine intervention and the presence of the supernatural. If the Bible clashed with science and reason, they believed

John Locke

that a person should follow the dictates of their own reason. Jefferson, for example, produced his own edition of the New Testament in which he edited out all reference to Christ's divinity and to the existence of miracles. This naturalistic view of Christianity was known as **Deism**. Deists believed that God created a perfect universe and then left it alone to run according to natural laws that man could discover and understand. They often spoke of God as the Great Clockmaker who set in motion a creation that needed no further effort to operate smoothly.

The Enlightenment also emphasized the concept of progress in human society. Intellectuals believed that advances in knowledge would directly translate into improvements in the human condition, and that the march of time would inexorably lead to a brighter future. Since there was such extensive communication between England and her overseas colonies, it was inevitable that Enlightenment thinking would cross over the Atlantic Ocean to America.

Colonial Print Culture

America's print culture helped to spread Enlightenment ideas throughout the English colonies. The British American colonies had a very high literacy rate, though literacy was more common among men than women. By the mid-eighteenth century, well over half of all white colonial men could read and write. This paved the way for the mass consumption of books, pamphlets, and newspapers in the provinces. The first colonial newspaper, *Publick Occurrences*, began publication in Boston in 1690. By 1760, nearly every sizable city or town had a weekly newspaper. Colonial newspapers spent much of their space covering European events, only rarely devoting time to local matters, but were nonetheless critical sources of information about the outside world. By the mid-1700s,

as the colonies grew in both size and confidence, more newspapers started to pay attention to colonial controversies and developments.

Aside from the Bible, the most popular type of book in America was the almanac. Hundreds of different editions circulated throughout the colonial period, and nearly every literate household had at least one. Geared towards common farmers, almanacs attempted to make predictions about weather events for the upcoming year, thus allowing readers to plan ahead in their agricultural efforts. Almanacs also contained practical advice on planting, doses of humor, and even medical advice. The most famous and successful of these was Benjamin Franklin's *Poor Richard's Almanac*, published in Philadelphia starting in 1732. The title came from the pen name, Richard Saunders, that Franklin used for the yearly editions. The book was updated and published annually for twenty-five years, with sales reaching as many as 10,000 copies per year.

Poetry proved to be perhaps the most popular literary form in the colonies, and America produced a number of prominent poets. The Puritan Anne Bradstreet's poetry starting in 1650 reflected the Puritan view of the importance of God in the triumphs and tragedies of daily life. Whether the subject of one of her poems was the birth of a child, a family member's absence, the death of an infant, or the burning of her family's home, she expressed in her work that everything was the will of God. Though Bradstreet's work attracted some positive attention, some critics believed that women should not be writers. Phyllis Wheatley not only had to deal with critics of her gender, but of her race as well. Born in Africa and transported to Boston as a slave child in 1761, Wheatley's master's family taught her to read and write, and in her teen years she began to write poems. The idea that a female slave might compose profound poetry was met with such disbelief that Wheatley had to prove her authorship to a special panel of Bostonians. Among those on the panel were the Massachusetts colony's governor, Thomas Hutchinson, and respected merchant John Hancock. Wheatley drew such fascination that even Hutchinson and Hancock—two men who deeply disagreed with each other's politics—could agree to temporarily put aside their differences to study her poetry. Perhaps the most popular poet of the colonial era was the minister Michael Wigglesworth, whose 1662 epic poem *The Day of Doom*, a piece which dwells on the inevitability that sinners would be doomed to hell, was a best seller for the next century.

The American colonies were the site of a critical development in the history of journalism. The trial of **John Peter Zenger** in 1735 helped to enshrine the principle of freedom of the press. The case revolved around the

A depiction of Harvard College in 1726.

recently appointed royal governor of New York, William Cosby, who quickly became a controversial leader, accused by his critics of being incompetent, corrupt, and dictatorial. Cosby's opponents used Zenger's newspaper, the *New York Weekly Journal*, as a venue to publish news stories and letters critical of the governor. In late 1734, Governor Cosby ordered Zenger arrested and copies of his newspaper burned. Zenger was charged with seditious libel, the publishing of material that caused members of the public to dislike or distrust the government. At the time, the truth or falsity of negative statements about politicians did not matter, only whether they had been published in the newspaper. Truth, therefore, was not legally supposed to be considered a defense against charges of seditious libel. To further rig the case against Zenger, Cosby's government disbarred lawyers who attempted to defend Zenger. Zenger's supporters had to hire an out-of-colony attorney, Andrew Hamilton, who Cosby could not legally disbar. Hamilton argued that the jury in the case ought to disregard what the law said, and choose to not punish publishers for the writings in their newspapers unless the contents could be proven false. The lawyer's closing statement appealed to the jury's sense of liberty, stating that a free press was an essential bulwark against abusive or tyrannical government officials. The jury agreed and found Zenger not guilty.

Education

From the beginning, American colonists showed a strong commitment to education, particularly religious education. In early New England, schooling was seen as an absolute necessity to enable individuals to read and study the Bible. Quakers, too, saw education as vital and operated schools for both adults and children. Harvard had been established in 1636 to train ministers for the pulpit.

By the end of the seventeenth century, education had taken on an importance far beyond just religious training. William and Mary College was formed in 1693, Yale in 1701, and Princeton in 1746. Though each was founded by religious individuals, their curriculums emphasized Enlightenment principles. Students studied philosophy, history, mathematics, classics, Latin, and Greek. Two colleges founded in the 1750s, King's College (now Columbia University) and the University of Pennsylvania, were established with largely secular curriculums. By the mid-eighteenth century, most leading colonial families chose to educate their sons in American colleges rather than sending them to England.

Though some forms of education were widely available, some groups had more limited opportunities than others. Free blacks had very limited access to education in colonial society, and slaves had nearly none. Among white colonists, economics was a major factor. There were very few public school systems, and those that did exist were very rudimentary. Education, therefore, often involved hiring a private teacher or tutor to work directly with a family's children. The result was that formal schooling was largely restricted to upper- and middle-class households, and college education was a possibility only for the wealthiest of families. Even within households that could afford a teacher for their children, boys and girls experienced schooling differently. From an early age, boys learned math, science, Latin, and Greek. These were seen as essential to an eventual business or political role when males reached adulthood. While girls did learn some of the same subjects as boys, they were also taught more "practical arts" such as sewing, cooking, art, and music. These skills would assist women in their expected adult roles—housewives and mothers. Even with these caveats, the eighteenth century British colonies were as educated as any societies in the western world.

Science and Technology

Another manifestation of the Enlightenment in America was a growing interest in science. Most colonial colleges, regardless of whether they were religious institutions or not, typically had permanent faculty members who researched and taught biology, physics, and astronomy. Towns and cities formed philosophical and scientific societies where amateur members could compare their observations and experiments. Interested colonial individuals made a special effort to correspond with the Royal Society of London, England's chief scientific society. Through such correspondence Cotton Mather had become convinced that inoculation could defend against smallpox epidemics like the one that raged through Boston in 1721.

John Winthrop, American Scientist

One of the foremost American scientists of the eighteenth century was John Winthrop, but today he is largely unknown. Born in Boston in 1714, he was named for his famous great-great-grandfather who had led the Massachusetts Bay Puritans to New England. While the younger Winthrop was a religious man, he was deeply influenced by the Enlightenment, and he blended together his faith with a scientific approach to understanding the universe. God existed, he believed, but the world he created operated under natural rules and laws. Winthrop graduated from Harvard College at age 18, and six years later the university named him Professor of Mathematics and Natural Philosophy, a contemporary field that covered chemistry, physics, and astronomy. Late in life, he even twice served as the acting President of Harvard.

Winthrop first developed a keen interest in astronomy, making early observations on the phenomenon of sun spots in 1739. In 1740, he observed a transit of Mercury across the sun, and his written comments about the event were well received and published in London. He then began a decades long project to chart daily temperature and weather patterns, perhaps a nod to the particular importance of weather to an agricultural society. In 1761, he mounted a voyage to Newfoundland in order to observe a transit of Venus, one of the first explicitly scientific overseas expeditions in colonial America. He rejected the supernatural idea that comets were signs of prophecy from God, instead agreeing with the scientific view that comets were naturally occurring astronomical objects that traveled in a fixed orbit around the sun and whose returns could therefore be predicted in advance.

On November 18, 1755, a small earthquake shook New England. Though there were no deaths and mostly just damage to chimneys, stone fences, church steeples, and sets of family dishes, the rattling did spark an outpouring of responses attributing the event to supernatural causes. Among these was a published work by minister Thomas Prince, who argued that the earthquakes were acts of God to show his displeasure. Winthrop, however, gave a lecture just days after the earthquake at which he theorized that the shaking was caused by heat and chemical reactions under the earth's surface. Prince and Winthrop argued the causes of the earthquake for months in the **Boston Gazette**. *Winthrop did not deny that God could begin earthquakes but insisted that even if God did so, it would be through natural processes and causes. Some scholars have argued on that basis that he should be considered one of the founders of modern seismology.*

Professor Winthrop died in 1779, having influenced an entire generation of young American scientists and leaders. Benjamin Franklin was one of his admirers, as was the young John Adams, who took Winthrop's classes at Harvard. He was one of the first American scientists to gain a positive reputation in Europe. More importantly, Winthrop was a crucial advocate for the importance of the Enlightenment, education, and scientific knowledge in the American colonies.

Naturalists like Mark Catesby and John Bartram focused their efforts on the study of America's plant and animal life. Some scientists in Europe viewed the New World as savage and uncivilized, and therefore predicted that any plants or animals found there would be inferior to European ones. American naturalists set out to prove them wrong, collecting, classifying, and examining the properties of samples from across the continent. North America, it turned out, was the home of hundreds of animal and plant species previously unknown to European scientists. Some plants in America even turned out to have medicinal properties unlike any counterpart in Europe. The abundance of animal life in America allowed naturalists to make brand new observations about animal behavior. Catesby, whose detailed and precise drawings still impress viewers even today, was one of the first scholars to describe the migration patterns of birds. America was also in some ways the birthplace of paleontology. A French military expedition in 1739, in what is now Kentucky, found a large number of tusks, teeth, and massive bones at a site later named Big Bone Lick. The remains were those of wooly mammoths, and the fossils caused a frenzy of excitement in both America and Europe. Some American scientists believed the Big Bone Lick fossils proved that America's natural history was every bit the equal of Europe's, if not superior.

No American colonist represented the Enlightenment ideal more fully than **Benjamin Franklin**. Born into a Boston Puritan family in 1706, Franklin later in life turned against his upbringing and became a free-thinking Deist. He had no taste or tolerance for strict religious orthodoxy or doctrinal conflicts. As a teenager, he apprenticed in his brother's print shop and remained a printer through his early adult life. He retired at age 42 and devoted the remainder of his life to social progress and scientific advancement, helping to found the American Philosophical Society, a university, the first lending library in America, and a local fire company in Philadelphia.

Franklin consumed any reading material that came his way dealing with scientific topics. In 1727, he co-founded the **Junto Society of Philadelphia** so he and other educated individuals could exchange their insights on interesting moral and scientific questions.

Franklin spent much of his life tinkering with scientific experiments and inventions. During his many trips back and forth across the Atlantic Ocean, Franklin could often be seen lowering a thermometer into the water from the deck of his ship in order to chart the course of the Gulf Stream. His most famous experiment—involving flying a kite in a lightning storm—helped to reveal the basic principles of electricity, and still gives us much of the terminology we use today (battery, positive, and negative). Franklin constantly looked for ways to translate scientific knowledge into practical applications to improve people's lives. He experimented with using electric batteries to cook turkey. Franklin also developed the lightning rod, which greatly reduced the risk of fires caused by lightning strikes, which had been a constant source of worry in cities. He developed a new model oven that retained more heat without belching smoke into the home (the Franklin stove); invented the first eyeglasses with bifocal lenses; and created a glass harmonica all while serving as an international diplomat, postmaster general, and as a drafter of the the Declaration of Independence and the U.S. Constitution. Above all else, Franklin approached his very full life with a curious mixture of rationalism and optimism that led him to believe that, as long as humanity maintained its focus on science and reason, each generation would live better than the previous one.

Colonial Medicine

The Enlightenment brought a number of beneficial ideas to America, though some fields of study benefited more than others. Medicine changed only slightly in the eighteenth century. Colonial medicine had long tolerated a variety of oddball ideas and crackpot theories. Some people believed that the positions of the planets and stars affected the health of individuals. This view was popularized in almanacs, which often included an illustrated "Zodiac Man" with advice on which astrological sign corresponded with a particular medical ailment. By the mid-eighteenth century, almanacs included these pictures solely out of tradition rather than belief since the Enlightenment rejected astrology. Individuals who practiced folk medicine or herbalism sometimes offered foul smelling concoctions—some including feces or urine—as treatments or cures for serious illnesses. One suggested cure for blindness was to dry out dog droppings, then grind them into a powder, and finally rub the dung powder into the blind person's eyes on a daily basis. Such cures usually did little except offend the patient's senses.

In some ways, medical theory had not advanced much since the ancient period, when Hippocrates believed that the human body was made up of four different fluids (blood, yellow bile, black bile, and phlegm) that he called "humors." Though incorrect, this theory of **humoralism** continued to dominate the thinking of physicians in the colonial period. If a person was ill, the humors needed to be restored to a state of balance by removing excess fluids from the body. Hence tools to induce vomiting and bleeding were considered important parts of a physician's craft. The practice of bloodletting was particularly common and was often a prescribed treatment for infections. Doctors made sure to carry knives, lancets, and leeches for the task. Physicians believed that even mental illness could be cured by continual purging and opening up of veins to let out bad blood. In reality, bleeding did nothing positive at all, and usually weakened the patients further, increasing the chances of death. In fact, many historians and physicians today believe that George Washington's death in 1799 was caused by physicians bleeding him excessively in response to a simple throat infection.

Since it was very rare to see a college-trained doctor in the colonial period, women played a significant part in colonial medicine. Female midwives attended to women in childbirth and frequently were called in to treat a variety of "female" illnesses. Such women were paid just like professionals and were often quite respected in their communities. Male doctors, however, frowned on the idea of women in medicine, and by the end of the eighteenth century pushed for a greater professionalization of medicine. Doing so would exclude women from medical roles since women lacked access to higher education. Social mores at the time, however, made it difficult for male doctors to treat female issues. Men were not supposed to see the private parts of women; so male doctors who attended to childbirth frequently did so with the woman fully covered by a blanket. The doctor would never physically look at the act of birth. In any case, the beginnings of medical professionalization came only late in the colonial era, with the first medical school not opening until 1766.

THE GREAT AWAKENING

At the same time that many upper-class colonists embraced the rationalism and scientific view of the world espoused by the Enlightenment, others joined in a fervent religious revival appealing to faith and emotion rather than reason that swept through the colonies. The movement first hit New England, where ministers had long bemoaned what they felt was an upsurge in secularism and a corresponding decline in religious zeal. Beginning in the late 1600s, influential minister Solomon Stoddard began preaching with a style that stressed making emotional connections with his listeners. Viewing the pastor's role as being more than a conduit for bringing God's Word to church members, he also sought to elicit passionate responses ("awakenings") from his audiences through vivid descriptions of eternal bliss in Heaven along with graphic depictions of spending an eternity in the depths of Hell. A Calvinist who firmly believed in divine predestination regarding one's salvation, Stoddard agreed with other Puritan theologians in the concept of "preparation," whereby individuals must first actively prepare their hearts to receive the grace of God. In practice, people were expected to understand their utter helplessness to achieve salvation on their own—good works alone or even devout faith would not produce salvation. Such an understanding then typically generated an intense sense of despair and doubt. While some never emerged from the depths of desolation induced by such preoccupation (even to the point of committing suicide), many others experienced a profound and liberating ecstasy they identified as God's saving grace—the "New Birth"—that confirmed to the individual that they were indeed one of God's "elect." During the sixty years that Stoddard preached, his Northampton parish underwent six sporadic revivals (in 1679, 1683, 1696, 1712, 1718, and 1727, respectively) characterized by large waves of conversions. Other congregations across New England experienced their own revivals, but they occurred less frequently than in Northampton and took place independently from other churches.

The larger, sustained intercolonial religious revival known as the **Great Awakening**, which began in the 1730s and 1740s and lasted through the 1770s, took place as evangelical ministers crossed denominational lines to make contact with each other and publicized their congregation's success in achieving conversions. In New England, one of the most influential preachers proved to be Solomon Stoddard's grandson, the reverend **Jonathan Edwards** of Connecticut. Edwards rejected any move towards universal salvation, instead embracing a strict Calvinist position that God had determined the fate of everyone and that human beings were totally at his mercy. In his most famous sermon entitled "Sinners in the Hands of an Angry God," first delivered in 1741 and soon reprinted throughout the colonies, Edwards conjured up the image of Hell for his listeners, warning them that only God stood between them and eternal torment. His audience was encouraged to feel both terror and hope, and to channel those powerful emotions into their worship.

Even more influential than Edwards was **George Whitefield**. Born and trained in England, his religious views were originally quite conventional. He had a short and unpleasant experience in the infant colony of Georgia and returned to England frustrated at his failure to bring religion to the province. In England, he got caught up in a religious revival and became a follower of John Wesley, the founder of Methodism. Wesley had founded a Holy Club at Oxford University whose members fasted or lay prostrate for hours on end while praying. Critics gave the movement its name when they mocked the fervent and exacting methods of worshipers. In 1740, Whitefield carried this sense of religious zeal back to the American colonies, traveling extensively up and down the Atlantic coast and speaking wherever he could draw an audience. Such itinerant preachers were a crucial part of spreading the Great Awakening's reach, and Whitefield was tireless. He made seven separate trips to the American colonies from 1737 to 1770, at times delivering multiple sermons a day every day during the week. Between his time in England and America, he may have delivered as many as 18,000 sermons to a total of 10 million people. As he became more famous, Whitefield created a sensation whenever he came to a town. When he traveled to Boston, over 20,000 people gathered to hear him speak—a remarkable crowd given that the city's population was only 15,000.

Whitefield had a grand sense of the dramatic, and he rehearsed his sermons to exacting standards. Every gesture and inflection had to be perfect in order to draw out maximum emotion from the crowd. To guarantee large audiences, he often arranged to have posters and advertisements placed ahead of his arrival. Colonial newspapers, desperate for stories to print each week, were more than happy to cover his travels and the controversy he generated. Witnesses who heard Whitefield speak claimed that his voice had a unique clarity and that it could be heard without amplification even from the very back rows of massive crowds. Through a combination of his voice and his theatrics, Whitefield could entrance even the most skeptical audience members. His listeners wept, shouted, and sometimes collapsed to the ground overwhelmed with emotions. During a revival in Philadelphia, the deist Benjamin Franklin decided to attend a Whitefield sermon out of curiosity, but he swore that he would not give the preacher any money in the collection plate when asked. During the course of the sermon, Franklin found himself so moved that he first put all his copper coins in the collection plate, then his silver, and finally all his gold. One of Franklin's likeminded skeptics had come to the gathering with no money at all and was so moved that he begged others for a loan so that he could donate money to Whitefield. Franklin soon began an odd friendship with the preacher that lasted through the rest of the minister's life, and the well-known deist skeptic became one of Whitefield's most ardent supporters despite their radically different approaches to religious worship.

The Great Awakening generated a great deal of controversy throughout the colonies. Ministers opposed to the evangelical movement, known as "**Old Lights**," were appalled by the shouting, wailing, and weeping at revival sermons. Such unbridled passions, they believed, ought to be controlled and restrained, and certainly never unleashed on purpose. They also strongly objected to the revival's willingness to allow women to speak during religious services—a role traditionally reserved solely for men. Those who embraced the Awakening, known as "**New Lights**," in turn criticized the stodgy, emotionless version of religion preached by Old Lights.

Many of the Old Lights were men of influence in established colonial churches and government, and they used that influence to try to undercut the Great Awakening. Connecticut passed a law forbidding ministers from delivering a sermon in a town or village without first receiving specific permission from the established minister of that church. Anyone who delivered an unauthorized sermon would be subject to arrest and imprisonment. The idea, of course, was that permission would always be denied to evangelical ministers. To evade such laws, itinerant ministers often gave impromptu sermons in open fields outside the boundaries of the town.

Old Lights attempted to discredit the Great Awakening by highlighting the movement's excesses. In 1742, South Carolina planter Hugh Bryan began ministering to his slaves. In the process, Bryan became convinced that he, like Moses, had been chosen to free the slaves. He attempted to part the waters of the Savannah River so that he could lead slaves to Georgia where the institution was then illegal, and instead fell in and had to be rescued by his brother. In New England, James Davenport began to denounce ministers by name who he believed were unsaved and who therefore were leading entire congregations towards damnation. Davenport organized a massive bonfire upon which he encouraged his followers to burn the books of leading ministers as well as any other worldly objects they believed interfered with religious devotion. In a dramatic gesture, Davenport took off his pants and threw them into the fire, proclaiming that clothes were an unnecessary vanity that interfered with true religion. He was arrested and declared insane. Later, he sheepishly apologized and blamed his strange behavior on the Devil.

The Great Awakening undermined established churches by urging converts to drop out and establish separatist New Light congregations. These new churches would then refuse to pay religious taxes to support the established church of the colony. One result of the Great Awakening was a rift in the Anglican Church and Presbyterianism between old and new views, weakening those churches and paving the way for new sects to rise in popularity. Some existing congregations—Baptists and Methodists in particular—embraced the revival and saw a rapid rise in church attendance.

Another impact of the Great Awakening was a spread in higher education. Older institutions like Harvard and Yale favored the Old Light perspective. As a result, evangelicals started the College of New Jersey (now Princeton University) in 1746, and the college in turn helped to bring warring factions of the Presbyterian Church back together. Baptists (who promoted adult baptism) founded the College of Rhode Island (now Brown University) in 1764, and Dutch Reformed evangelicals in New Jersey two years later built Queen's College (now Rutgers University). Minister Eleazer Wheelock even started a charity school to train native preachers. The idea drew so much financial support that Wheelock used some of the money to found Dartmouth in 1769. The Old Lights did not remain static, however, setting up the University of Pennsylvania and King's College (now Columbia University). The religious conflict between Old and New Lights, for all of its messiness, was undoubtedly a boon for higher education.

The appeal of the Great Awakening reached members of all social classes, but was particularly strong to lower-status families, representing a broad and subversive challenge to traditional sources of authority. By stressing the importance of individual faith and worship, the revival placed even humble citizens on an equal religious footing with powerful political rulers and clergymen. In southern colonies, mainstream Old Light church services often included ritual displays of power by elite community members who marched in unison to take their reserved seats at the start of Sunday services. New Light Baptist ministers did away with social distinctions in church, urging attendees to call each other brothers and sisters. Lower class colonists eagerly embraced the notion that all people were equal in church, but such a doctrine of equality threatened to spill out into society at large—what might happen to society if poor people thought of themselves as equal outside the church as well? Some Baptist minsters even spread their message of religious equality among the southern slave population. Established authorities viewed New Lights as a threat to the entire fabric of their society and feared that religious revivals could lead to anarchy. Their response to their fears could be quite violent. In Virginia, a group of Anglican elite planters pulled a Baptist minister off the stage at a religious meeting and horsewhipped him in front of his audience.

THE WARS FOR EMPIRE

During the late seventeenth century and much of the eighteenth century, Spain, France, and England fought a series of wars that collectively decided the future of North America. England had by far the largest colonial population and that advantage grew over time. Spain and France, however, had more extensive Indian alliances to help balance out the population gap. While some of the wars began in Europe, they nevertheless all spilled over into colonies in the New World.

King William's and Queen Anne's Wars

The first of the imperial wars began in 1688, immediately following England's Glorious Revolution. Newly crowned as the King of England, William joined a large coalition of nations fighting against Louis XIV of France. Most of the fighting in the War of the League of Augsburg (1688-1697) took place in Europe, but there was also a theatre in America where the war became known as King William's War. The colonial battles pitted not just the French against the English, but also the French-backed Wabanaki Confederation against the English-backed Iroquois. Much of the fighting consisted of native raids against the settlements of the other side. English colonists failed in their attempts at capturing Quebec and Montreal, but they did launch multiple successful raids against French settlements and military installations in Acadia and Newfoundland. No territory was won or lost in the peace treaty, but the Iroquois suffered heavily and felt abandoned by their English allies. In later wars, the Iroquois would declare their neutrality instead of supporting the English.

Peace lasted only a few years until the outbreak of the War of the Spanish Succession (1702-1713), called Queen Anne's War in America, which pitted England against both Spain and France. The war was not only longer, but the fighting in both Europe and North America was more intense. As in the previous war, the European theatre was still the main focus. Unlike before, however, the peace treaty did begin to shift the balance of power in the colonies. Spanish forces in Florida and English forces in Carolina launched a series of brutal invasions and counter-invasions that, while unsuccessful in capturing and holding any major enemy towns, devastated the Spanish and Native American populations in Florida. The damage was so severe that it permanently weakened Spain's

two hundred-year-hold on Florida. In the North, British colonists repeatedly tried and failed to capture the French capital of Quebec, though the peace treaty did grant Acadia to Great Britain, which was then renamed Nova Scotia.

Queen Anne's War also involved Indian raiding against colonial settlements of Spain, France, and England. The most famous example was a combined French and Native American strike against the English town of Deerfield, Massachusetts in 1704. The attack killed over 50 townspeople, and more than 100 others were taken captive. Among the captives was the prominent minister John Williams, who later published a book titled *The Redeemed Captive* about the experiences of his family. Two of his children, one aged six and the other just six weeks old, were killed in the initial attack. His wife was then executed on the march to Canada. Williams and four of his children were released after nearly three years of captivity. His daughter Eunice, however, married a Mohawk man and resisted all her family's pleas for her to return to English society.

King George's War

Large-scale warfare stayed away from the British North American colonies for more than two decades, during which time English settlements continued to expand in size and population. The peace came to an end due to a strange, seemingly minor incident. The English ship *Rebecca*, captained by Robert Jenkins, was stopped in 1731 by Spanish authorities off the coast of Cuba on suspicion of smuggling. The Spanish found no contraband on board, but during their interrogation of Jenkins, they tortured him and sliced off part of his ear. Seven years later, Jenkins testified in Parliament about his ordeal and for dramatic effect produced his preserved severed ear. A wave of outrage led England in 1739 to seek reprisal against Spain through military action. The initial stage of the fighting (1739-1744) is today known as the War of Jenkins's Ear. The conflict later expanded in scope and became known as King George's War (1744-1748).

The first English actions came in the Caribbean. British Vice Admiral Edward Vernon captured the Spanish town of Portobello, on the Panama coast. Though the fighting was very light and the British did not keep the city—abandoning it after plundering and damaging its infrastructure—the victory was elevated to the realm of legend. Vernon was hailed as a conquering hero and commemorations of the battle began to appear on hundreds of different household items. "Rule Britannia," which became one of England's most beloved patriotic songs, was first played in 1740 in celebration of the Battle of Portobello. Many in England were convinced

Table 4.1	Major English Wars, 1689 - 1763			
Dates	European Name	American Name	Major Allies	Treaty
1689-1697	War of the League of Augsburg	King William's War	Britain, Holland, Spain, their colonies and Native American allies against France, its colonies and Native American allies	Treaty of Ryswick (1697)
1702-1713	War of the Spanish Succession	Queen Anne's War	Britain, Holland, their colonies and Native American allies against France, Spain, their colonies and Native American allies	Treaty of Utrecht (1713)
1739-1748	War of Jenkins's Ear	King George's War	Britain, its colonies and Native American allies, and Austria against France, Spain, their Native American allies, and Prussia	Treaty of Aix-la-Chappelle (1748)
1740-1748	War of the Austrian Succession			
1756-1763	Seven Years' War	French and Indian War	Britain, its colonies and Native American allies against France, its colonies and Native American allies	Peace of Paris (1763)

that the war would lead to the complete conquest of all Spanish settlements in the Caribbean.

Vernon used his newfound fame to mount an even larger offensive against the Spanish, this time targeting the heavily fortified city of Cartagena. The admiral's combined land and naval forces consisted of over 25,000 men, including a contingent of some 3,500 volunteers who had been recruited from the North American mainland colonies. The expedition became one of the largest invasion efforts of the entire colonial period. The expedition was beset from the start by numerous delays and bitter squabbles between officers, and steadily the Caribbean climate and disease began to take a toll on the British force. So many sailors died of yellow fever and smallpox that many of the American colonials were split up among the fleet and pressed into naval service over their objections—they had been promised that they would serve together as a unit. By the time Vernon lifted the siege, about 10,000 of his men were dead and most of the survivors ill with disease. Of the 3,500 colonists, only a few hundred lived to return home. One of the survivors was Lawrence Washington, who named his family's Virginia plantation Mount Vernon after the admiral. The home eventually was inherited by his more famous half-brother, George Washington.

On the mainland, most of the early fighting took place along the Georgia-Florida border. In 1740, a British army under the command of James Oglethorpe invaded Florida with the intent of capturing the main Spanish stronghold at St. Augustine. The invasion failed due in part to feuding between the Georgia and South Carolina troops. Two years later, in 1742, the Spanish launched their own invasion of Georgia. Despite outnumbering the English soldiers in the province, the Spanish army lost a battle on St. Simon's Island in Georgia. Afterward, Oglethorpe tricked the Spanish commander into thinking that a fleet full of reinforcements had arrived from Britain, causing the Spanish general to panic and retreat back to Florida. Oglethorpe tried to follow up the success by mounting a new invasion of Florida, but the effort quickly failed and that particular theater of war wound down into a stalemate.

The dimensions of the colonial war changed in 1744. Already there had been an ongoing war in Europe, the War of the Austrian Succession (1740-1748). In 1744, France and Spain became allies and began cooperating in America against the British. The French entry in the fighting changed the geographic focus of the war. France was seen as the most dangerous enemy, so the English colonial war effort shifted towards the northern reaches of America. Operating from their main fortress of Louisbourg in Newfoundland, French forces and their Indian allies began to attack English colonial outposts and towns along the Atlantic coast. British colonists realized that Louisbourg was essential to the French war effort so New England troops mounted a major siege, forcing the fort to surrender in 1745. The colonists suffered heavy losses due to combat and then to disease while manning the fortress walls. The French tried repeatedly to recapture the fort, making it necessary for colonial troops to continue manning it in large numbers until regular British units arrived from the mother country.

In response to the fall of Louisbourg, the French-backed Abenaki attacked English towns in western New York and Massachusetts, rolling back the tide of British settlement. The New England colonies were hardest hit during King George's War, losing thousands of soldiers and civilians to warfare and disease. Colonists began to grumble about England's lack of support for the colonial theater of the war, as many Americans had hoped to follow up the capture of Louisbourg with an invasion of Canada. However, no land or naval forces arrived from England to assist them. An English fleet finally arrived at the end of 1747, but rather than help the colonists, the commander began to force colonists into naval service against their will, sparking three days of rioting in Boston. When the war ended in 1748, negotiators in Europe agreed to reset colonial borders to their pre-war state, meaning that Louisbourg was handed back to France. American colonists were outraged that their most significant achievement in the war—paid for by both sweat and blood—had been undone with a stroke of a pen. Worse, New Englanders knew that in the next war, they would have to capture the French strongpoint of Louisbourg all over again. Some colonists felt as though they had been abandoned and betrayed during the war by their own imperial government in England.

The Path to World War

Despite all the bloodshed of King George's War, the conflict had settled none of the complex colonial questions facing the Spanish, French, and British North American empires. Though weakened, Spain maintained a significant presence in Florida and on the Gulf Coast, and threatened the British colonies from the south. France had two strong colonies: Canada, located to the north of the British mainland colonies, and Louisiana, located on the Gulf Coast and along a thin, tenuous line of trading stations and small outposts stretching up the Mississippi and Ohio Rivers through the interior of the continent. The situation in New England was particularly confusing. The French and British kept expanding toward each other. By 1750, the frontier between Canada and New England was marked by tangled, overlapping British and French military forts. The stage was set for an ultimate showdown over the fate of North America.

During the 1750s, Virginia had begun to send settlers to plant roots in the Ohio River Valley in territory previously claimed by the French. Virginia's initial land grant in 1606 had included the vast majority of land in North America, and the colony's inhabitants planned to start collecting it. A group of Virginia colonists formed the **Ohio Company**, whose plan was to develop hundreds of thousands of acres of land west of Pennsylvania. France was enraged by this move since the British company was claiming land that had for decades been considered part of the French colonial empire.

Anticipating an eventual war, British colonists moved to strengthen their positions. Colonial diplomats tried to repair the British relationship with the Iroquois Confederacy, whose members were also concerned by French expansion along their own borders. The English promised friendship and protection to the Iroquois and swore that British settlers would never move onto their lands. The effort at rekindling the English-Iroquois alliance failed. The Iroquois did not trust the English any more than they trusted their longtime enemies, the French.

Representatives from seven British colonies met in Albany, New York in the summer of 1754 to work out a plan for strengthening themselves in the event of a war with France. Though the Albany Congress was supposed to also discuss diplomacy with Indian tribes and plan a number of defensive military measures that required intercolonial cooperation, the delegates spent much of their time instead debating a bold plan put forward by Benjamin Franklin. Franklin proposed the **Albany Plan of Union** that would unite the various colonies under a single central government led by a President-General. The central government would also have a legislature with representatives elected by each colonial assembly. The government would have the power to coordinate military defense, engage in diplomacy, regulate trade, and collect taxes to support its activities. As Franklin expressed in an editorial cartoon, where the various colonies represented the disjointed parts of the body of snake, the colonies must "Join or Die." The plan met the approval of the assembled delegates but proved unpopular to the colonial governments. Colonial assemblies had pushed for decades to increase their own legislative powers and were reluctant to now surrender some of them to a centralized government in America. The Albany Plan of Union was soundly rejected in the 1750s, but it later would serve as a model during the American Revolution.

The French in Canada moved to block Virginia's westward expansion by building a fort in the Ohio region, at the site of what is today Pittsburgh. In 1753, Virginia sent young militia Major **George Washington** to warn the French to give up the effort. Despite being only twenty-one years of age, Washington was very familiar with the territory since he had done survey work there for the Ohio Company. The French, however, refused to engage with the youngster, saying that they had orders to proceed. They invited Washington to travel to Canada and take it up with authorities there but suggested in the meantime that the Virginian leave them alone. Washington carried the news back to Virginia, where the governor decided to send Washington, now promoted to lieutenant colonel, back at the head of a larger military force to build a fort of his own and intimidate the French into vacating the region immediately. No one at the time could have predicted that this would start a worldwide war. The Seven Years' War (which actually lasted nine years), also known as the **French & Indian War**, would once and for all determine whether Britain or France would be the supreme power in America.

Washington headed towards the French with about 150 militiamen and a handful of native scouts, building a road as they went so that future troops and settlers could follow more easily. When he arrived, he realized that the French fortifications were already complete and that the French garrison outnumbered his force. Though his orders gave him wide latitude to act as he saw fit, Washington initially decided to act conservatively, establish a base camp, build a fort (Fort Necessity), and then wait for reinforcements from Virginia before proceeding further. The French commander in the meantime had sent out a party of 35 French Canadians to find Washington and deliver him a message ordering the Virginian to get out of French territory. The French party's mission was thus similar to the one Washington had undertaken the previous year and could be interpreted as a diplomatic effort rather than a military one. The young Washington sensed an unexpected opportunity for victory and decided to ambush the French on May 28, 1754. Most of the French in the party were either killed or captured, with eyewitnesses claiming that some of the French of-

Benjamin Franklin's warning to the British colonies in America to "join or die," exhorting them to unite against the French and the natives, shows a segmented snake, "S.C., N.C., V., M., R., N.J., N.Y., [and] N.E."

ficers were executed by Washington's Indian allies after surrendering. Washington's ambush was the final step along the route to global war.

Washington completed Fort Necessity in June, shortly after his ambush of the French party. The fort was hastily constructed and primitive, consisting of a ditch and a seven-foot-high wooden stockade. It had been built in a dubious position, in a low area surrounded on most sides by tree-covered hills. Washington's Indian allies, seeing that multiple mistakes had been made in the military expedition, abandoned him. Washington did, however, receive some reinforcements from Virginia, and the size of his force grew to perhaps four hundred. In early July, a French army numbering seven hundred French and Indians surrounded Fort Necessity. Washington's men were mostly untrained, rain had wetted the English gunpowder, and the French were able to fire into the fort from the relative safety of the wooded hills. After a brief battle, one-third of Washington's men lay dead or wounded. The situation was untenable, and Washington knew it. The French offered generous surrender terms. The Virginians would be allowed to march away and return to their colony. Washington surrendered the fort and headed back to his home. His military career had just begun with a total defeat. Much to his amazement, the Governor of Virginia did not blame Washington, but rather placed the blame on other colonies for their refusal to assist Virginia. Lieutenant Colonel Washington would thus be given a chance to redeem himself.

Braddock's Defeat

When news of the fighting reached England, the government decided to send a strong military force from Great Britain to America to push the French back. The officer chosen to command this expedition was Major General

Edward Braddock, who despite a 44-year career in the British Army had rarely seen combat. Nor did he have any experience in America, and thus he was unfamiliar with both the terrain and with the complicated web of colonial relationships and Indian alliances critical to a war effort. One trait that Braddock did have in abundance was confidence, and he was convinced that the French and their Indian allies would run away at the approach of the regular British army. He arrived in America with two regiments totaling about 1,350 men and began collecting additional volunteers in the colonies to supplement his force. One such volunteer was George Washington, who joined Braddock's staff. Even before his departure for the Ohio region, Braddock had made an unfavorable impression on many colonial leaders who felt that he was too arrogant and overconfident. He also had made no serious attempt to enlist native tribes on his side to serve as scouts or warriors, a failure that cost his expedition dearly.

The 1755 Braddock expedition first had to cross over 100 miles of dense forest, building a road as they went so that heavy equipment and cannon could follow. The march thus proceeded very slowly. Frustrated with the pace, Braddock decided to split his force in two—he would lead a lightly equipped and faster force of about 1,300 men, while 800 would stay behind to move the baggage and equipment. Because of a lack of Indian scouts, Braddock's men marched right into an ambush. They were suddenly hit from all sides by a large group of French soldiers and their Indian allies. The trained British officers and soldiers did not panic, but they were surrounded and confused by the suddenness of the attack. Braddock died while trying to rally his men to maintain good order, and as the casualties mounted, the British retreat became more disorderly. A handful of officers, including Washington, managed to maintain some semblance of order and cover the retreat of the survivors.

Braddock's force lost 914 men out of 1,373. Among the dead were 63 out of 86 officers. In addition, the ambushers got valuable information and vital supplies: cannons, letters, orders, correspondence, and maps. When news of the disaster reached Virginia, everyone was stunned. Braddock had believed the British Army to be invincible and clearly too had many American colonists. Those illusions were shattered in Braddock's defeat. Washington's second military expedition had ended in a defeat almost as total as his first. He could take little comfort in the fact that this particular outcome was not his fault. He actually somehow emerged from the battle with his reputation improved since he had kept his cool during the retreat despite every reason to panic. Still, Washington was devastated and disheartened because he knew at that point that the war would last a long time.

All hopes for a quick and easy end to the war had died with Braddock.

The French and Indian War

For the first two years, fighting was confined entirely to North America, but in 1756, England and France formally declared war on each other. The European War became known as the Seven Years' War, while the longer American colonial conflict became known as the French and Indian War. The global war spanned not only Europe and North America, but also extended to Africa and India. In the American theatre, the British had a clear advantage in numbers. There were 1.5 million people in the British colonies as compared to 80,000 French colonists. However, the French had the most powerful tribes in the region as their allies. Everyone at the time understood that the war's outcome was very much in doubt, and it would come down to which side had the better leadership.

After Braddock's defeat, the French and their allies went on the offensive, attacking along the frontier and throughout the Ohio and Great Lakes regions. Canada's governor, the Marquis de Vaudreuil, ordered an attack on a British supply depot in the winter of 1756, destroying a massive stockpile of British gunpowder. The French military commander, Major General Louis-Joseph de Montcalm, further capitalized on British errors. The British had left Fort William Henry in western New York isolated. Montcalm besieged it in 1757 and forced the 2,500-man garrison to capitulate. After the surrender of the fort, some of the departing English soldiers were ambushed and massacred by French-allied Indians. Though the Indians may have committed the massacre without Montcalm's approval, the incident hardened British hatred of the French.

Two new leaders emerged in England during the war. The first was the rise of Secretary of State (later prime minister) **William Pitt**, who took over the English war effort starting in 1757. Pitt believed that, unlike the previous wars, America would be the decisive theater rather than a sidelight. From his position in London, he funneled far more military and economic resources into the American colonies than had any earlier British leader. Pitt's support of the American war effort made him a beloved figure in America, and he returned the affection in later years, becoming a sometimes lonely advocate for the colonies during the imperial troubles in the 1760s and 1770s. The other new British leader in these years was King George III, who ascended to the throne in 1760. Though the bulk of the fighting had already concluded by the time he became king, George III's youthful enthusiasm cemented—for a time—the colonists' love and devotion to Great Britain.

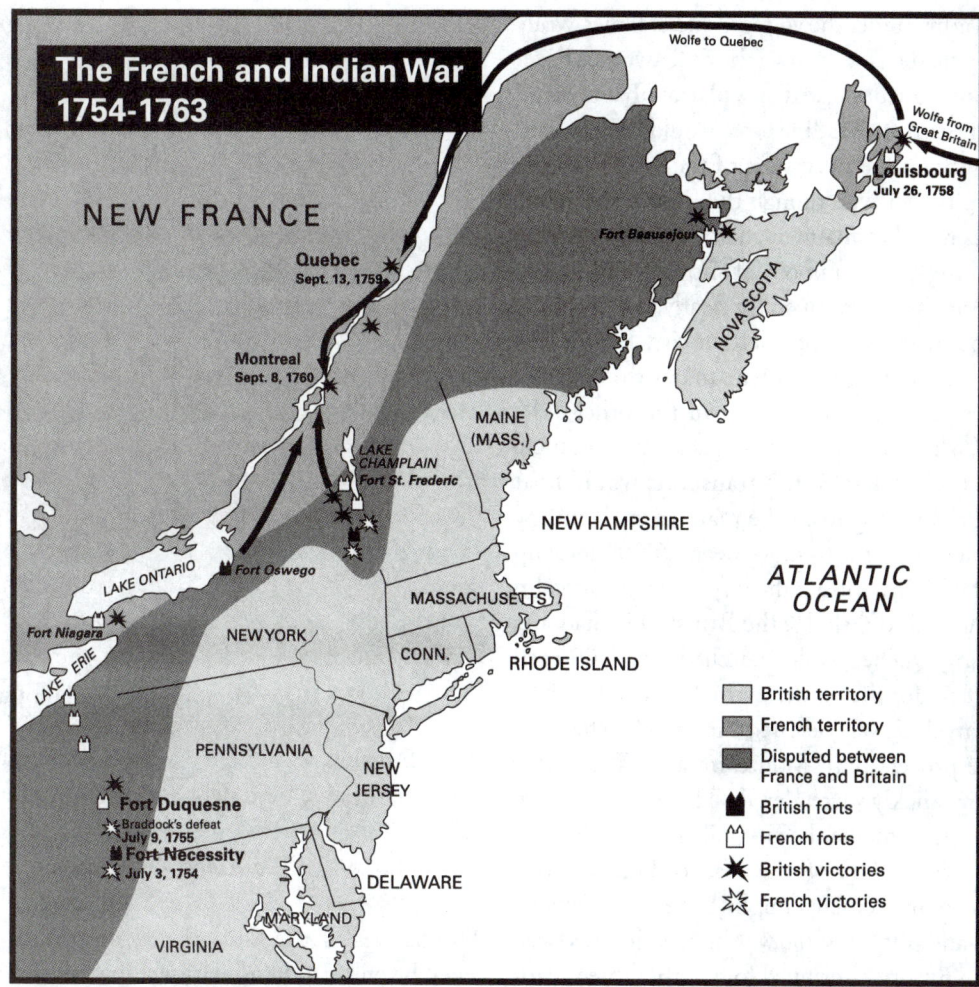

Map 4.1 The French and Indian War

Changing Tides of War

In 1758, William Pitt's commitment to America began to turn the war in favor of the British. A British blockade of Canada prevented the French from reinforcing or resupplying any of their military forces. The French supply problems were made worse by a poor harvest and an outbreak of smallpox among allied native tribes. General Montcalm was forced back onto the defensive, merely hoping to hold strong points at Louisbourg and Quebec. Pitt's plan had three parts: seize Fort Duquesne to expel the French from Ohio, capture the fortress at Louisbourg on the Atlantic coast, and then proceed with an invasion targeting Quebec, the capital of Canada.

A major expedition of 6,000 troops marched into Ohio to confront the French. Part of the force consisted of a unit of Virginians under Washington. The British slowly and steadily put pressure on the outnumbered French in the region. The 600 French soldiers had only two hopes for holding on—the strength of their forts (including Duquesne) and their Native American allies. The British, however, concluded a treaty in October 1758,

with thirteen different Indian nations who declared that they would not fight on behalf of the French in the current war. With their Indian allies abandoning them, the French had no choice but to abandon Fort Duquesne and withdraw from Ohio. Fort Duquesne was destroyed and replaced by Fort Pitt, later to become Pittsburgh, named in honor of Secretary of State Pitt. On the coast, a 26,000-man British expedition besieged and captured Louisbourg, where once again the French defenders were overwhelmingly outnumbered. Pitt's emphasis on the American theater of war was working. The last remaining stage was an invasion into Canada to capture the capital of Quebec. A British attempt to invade overland from New York failed in 1758, when General Montcalm defeated the British invasion force despite the British having a 6:1 advantage on the battlefield. The British invasion would have to wait until the British army had generals who could equal Montcalm in battle.

The final push of the war came in 1759. Britain sent two armies to attack Canada. One army, under General Jeffery Amherst, made its way through New York toward Montreal, capturing French positions along the way. A second British army under the young General James Wolfe simultaneously made its way down the St. Lawrence River towards Quebec. Quebec rested on a plateau that towered well over the river. Any invading force would have to land and make its way up the steep sides of the heights before getting at the city. So even though the French defenders were outnumbered, they maintained hope that they could hold out until the British ran out of supplies and had to retreat. The British siege went on for nearly three months while Wolfe found a way to approach the city. He decided to float a force past the city at night under the cover of darkness in order to ascend a road on the other side. The plan was risky and depended on achieving complete surprise since the helpless British transports would float right under the French guns. The plan worked, and by dawn Wolfe had managed to move nearly 5,000 men up the slope to the plains outside the city walls. Montcalm realized that he had to dislodge the British if he had any chance of saving Quebec, so he marched his 3,500 men out onto the plain for the battle. In the Battle of Quebec, the British Army decisively defeated the French defenders, though in the process both Montcalm and Wolfe were killed. Quebec quickly surrendered. The following year, a French attempt to retake the city failed, and a decisive defeat of the French Navy off the coast of France ended any hope that reinforcements might be sent to Canada. For all intents and purposes, the war in America was over. The fighting in Europe continued for another three years, but that too turned against the French and their Spanish allies, who had entered the war in 1762.

The Treaty of Paris was signed on February 10, 1763. France's North American Empire was wiped out. The majority of it, including Canada, was transferred to the British. Most of French Louisiana, including New Orleans, was handed over to Spain as compensation since Spain had lost Florida to Great Britain. The French were not pleased by the losses but were consoled that they managed to keep their lucrative Caribbean sugar colonies. French allied Native Americans, however, faced a bleak future. They had counted on the French presence to counter English expansion since they did not have the numbers to fight England and her colonies by themselves.

British authorities, on the other hand, were ecstatic now that both their northern and southern colonial flanks in North America were more secure. The British colonists in North America were excited to see so much land open to the possibility of future settlement. There were, however, lingering problems from the war. Great Britain's finances had been wrecked, and the British government was faced with crippling levels of debt. The British military also had to guard and garrison all the newly acquired territory, which was quite an expensive proposition. Lead-

The Right Honourable William Pitt

ers in England would have to find some way to pay for both the massive total debt and higher annual expenses.

Pontiac's Rebellion

The natives of the Great Lakes and Ohio regions had relied heavily on their relationship with the French. The French & Indian War, however, had decisively removed the French from North America. In their place would be the British, who had a much more confrontational history with Native Americans and who claimed under the terms of the Treaty of Paris to own all native lands east of the Mississippi. Fearing for the future of native groups under British colonial rule, the Ottawa chief Pontiac declared war in 1763, in a desperate attempt to keep British settlement out of the continent's interior. **Pontiac's Rebellion** at first achieved significant success as the British military was taken completely by surprise. Allied Indians overran most of the British outposts west of the Appalachian Mountains and lay siege to Fort Detroit, the strongest remaining English fortification. Warriors struck as far east as Maryland, Pennsylvania, and Virginia. The war then turned against Pontiac and his alliance. A smallpox epidemic broke out among the native besiegers of Fort Detroit, perhaps aided by the distribution of contaminated blankets. The failure at Detroit caused the native alliance to negotiate an end to the war, and the resulting peace agreement confirmed British control over the Ohio Valley.

To try and keep future peace with the Indians of North America, King George III's government issued

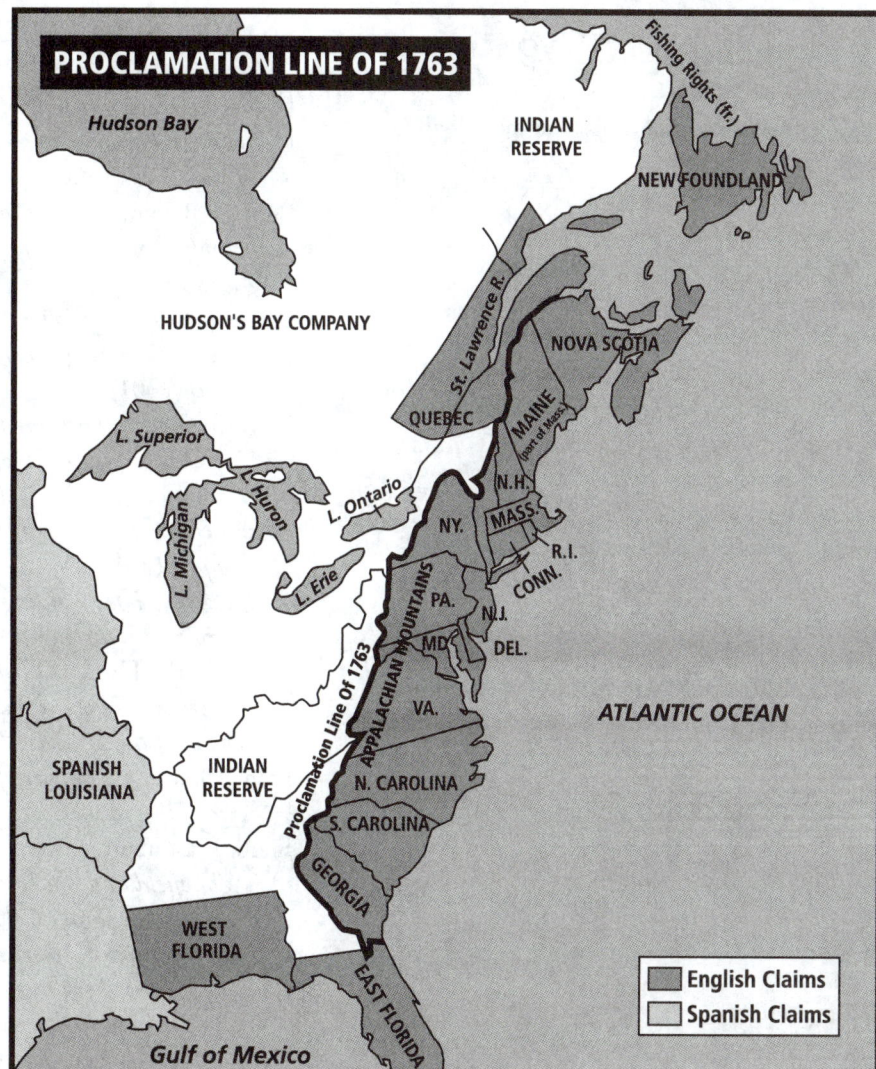

Map 4.2
Proclamation Line
of 1763

ECHOES OF THE FRENCH AND INDIAN WAR

the **Proclamation Line of 1763**. This created a dividing line in the continent running along the course of the Appalachian Mountains from Canada south to Georgia. All lands west of the line would be reserved for Native Americans, and white settlers were forbidden from entering the territory. The British government then sent thousands of soldiers to enforce the restriction on colonial expansion. British colonists were outraged that their own leaders would deny them the spoils of war by prohibiting settlers from moving on to the newly acquired lands. American colonists instead chose to ignore the proclamation line and began moving onto Indian lands, thus guaranteeing future bloodshed with native peoples.

ECHOES OF THE FRENCH AND INDIAN WAR

By 1763, Great Britain's colonies in North America had reached a level of development that rivaled anywhere in Europe. The colonial population was growing by leaps and bounds and the colonies offered an abundance of opportunity to immigrants from across Europe. Americans had already begun challenging imperial control and pushing for greater economic and political self-determination. The provinces were highly educated, with an expanding number of colleges and a thriving print culture. Colonial scientists regularly exchanged ideas with their counterparts in Europe, strengthening the advance of knowledge in both the Old World and New. British colonists were also newly self-confident after having emerged victorious from nearly a century of warfare between England and France over the fate of North America. All in all, white colonists were pleased with their place in the world. They were proud to be a part of an empire dedicated to liberty and prosperity, in which they enjoyed fundamental freedoms unheard of in the colonies of other nations. No one in 1763, whether in England or America, could have predicted that the relationship between the mother country and the colonies would degenerate so quickly that war and revolution were just barely a decade away.

Chronology

1651	First Navigation Acts passed by Parliament.
1696	Board of Trade established to oversee colonial commerce.
1707	Act of Union combining England, Scotland, and Wales into Great Britain.
1712	York City slave rebellion.
1716-1726	Golden Age of Piracy.
1721	Smallpox inoculations introduced in Boston.
1733	Molasses Act passed.
1735	John Peter Zenger trial.
1739	Stono Rebellion in South Carolina.
1740	George Whitefield preaches in North America.
1741	Jonathan Edwards delivers his sermon *Sinners in the Hands of an Angry God.* New York slave conspiracy.
1745	New England militia capture Louisbourg during King George's War.
1754	George Washington attacks French patrol near the forks of the Ohio River. Albany Congress proposes plan for colonial union. French and Indian War begins.
1755	General Braddock killed and his force defeated by French and Indian forces.
1757	William Pitt becomes Secretary of State.
1758	British take Fort Duquesne and Louisbourg.
1759	Battle of Quebec.
1760	Montreal falls to the British. King George III gains throne of Great Britain.
1763	Peace of Paris ends the Seven Years' War. Pontiac's Rebellion. Proclamation Line of 1763.

SUGGESTED READINGS

Fred Anderson, *Crucible of War: The Seven Years' War and the Fate of Empire in British North America, 1754-1766.* (2000).

Bernard Bailyn, *Voyagers to the West: A Passage in the Peopling of American on the Eve of the Revolution.* (1986);

——, *The Origins of American Politics.* (1968).

Jon Butler, *Becoming America: The Revolution before 1776* (2001).

David Hancock, *Citizens of the World: London Merchants and the Integration of the British Atlantic Community, 1735-1785* (1997).

Mark G. Hanna, *Pirate Nests and the Rise of the British Empire* (2015).

Tom Hatley, *The Dividing Paths: Cherokees and South Carolinians through the Era of Revolution.* (1993).

Peter Charles Hoffer, *When Benjamin Franklin Met the Reverend Whitefield: Enlightenment, Revival, and the Power of the Printed Word* (2011).

Francis Jennings, *Empire of Fortune: Crowns, Colonies, and Tribes in the Seven Years' War in America* (1988).

Frank J. Lambert, *"Pedlar in Divinity": George Whitefield and the Transatlantic Revivals.* (1994).

Ned Landsman, *From Colonials to Provincials: Thought and Culture in America: 1680-1770.* (1998).

Jill Lepore, *New York Burning: Liberty, Slavery, and Conspiracy in Eighteenth-Century Manhattan* (2005).

George M. Marsden, *Jonathan Edwards: A Life* (2003).

Susan Scott Parrish, *American Curiosity: Cultures of Natural History in the Colonial British Atlantic World* (2006)

James Pritchard, *In Search of Empire: The French in the Americas, 1670-1730.* (2004).

Peter Silver, *Our Savage Neighbors: How Indian War Transformed Early America.* (2007).

Stephanie E. Smallwood, *Saltwater Slavery: A Middle Passage from Africa to American Diaspora.* (2007).

Ian K. Steele, *An Exploration of Communication and Community* (1986).

Alan Taylor, *American Colonies: The Settling of North America* (2001).

W.R. Ward, *The Protestant Evangelical Awakening* (1992).

Richard White, *The Middle Ground: Indians, Empires, and Republics in the Great Lakes Region, 1650-1815.* (1991).

Peter H. Wood, *Black Majority: Negroes in Colonial South Carolina from 1670 Through the Stono Rebellion.* (1996).

Serena Zabin, *Dangerous Economies: Status and Commerce in Imperial New York.* (2009).

Review Questions

1. How did slaves resist their condition in the eighteenth century British colonies? What obstacles would prevent an armed rebellion from succeeding?

2. What were the causes of the Great Awakening? Did the religious movement leave the colonies more united or more divided?

3. What were the basic tenets of the Enlightenment? What impact did it have on the colonies?

4. Why did the British government seek more control over colonial trade and government? What areas of disagreements arose before 1763 in the relationship between the colonies and Great Britain?

5. Discuss the causes of the conflict between Spain, France, and England in the Americas. Why was the French and Indian War so important for both Great Britain and the colonies?

Glossary of Important People and Concepts

Albany Plan of Union
Board of Trade
Edward Braddock
Deism
Jonathan Edwards
Enlightenment
Benjamin Franklin
French and Indian War
Golden Age of Piracy
Great Awakening
Humoralism
Junto Society of Philadelphia
Navigation Acts
"New Lights"
Ohio Company
"Old Lights"
Paxton Boys
William Pitt
Pontiac's Rebellion
Proclamation Line of 1763
"Salutary neglect"
Stono Rebellion
George Washington
George Whitefield
John Peter Zenger

Chapter Five

ORIGINS OF THE AMERICAN REVOLUTION

In 1776, Thomas Jefferson wrote the most famous words of America's revolutionary era. "All men are created equal," he stated in the Declaration of Independence. All men, and women, however, were certainly not treated as equals in America, either in the years leading up to the Revolution or just after its conclusion in the early 1780s. Taught by their ministers that to "spare the rod" was to "spoil the child," parents punished wayward children with physical violence. Husbands were given license to physically discipline wives who they believed acted disrespectfully toward them. During the 1780s, almost one-third of the American population toiled as slaves or indentured servants. They too suffered physical beatings, while the women among them were sometimes raped.

Until the eve of the American Revolution, American schools, the Anglican Church, and the prevailing legal system taught the average person in the colonies that the division of humanity into the nobility and the commoners and the rule of kings was part of the divine order, as historian Gordon S. Wood notes in his book **The Radicalism of the American Revolution**: "[Future leader of the American Revolution] John Adams recalled that in the early 1760s the Massachusetts authorities had . . . introduced new 'scenary' in the Supreme Court —of scarlet and sable robes . . . and enormous tie wigs—in order to create a more 'theatrical' and 'ecclesiastical' setting for the doing of justice.' Full-length, gold-framed portraits of [English kings] Charles II and James II, said Adams, were 'hung up on the most conspicuous sides' of the courtroom 'for the admiration and imitation of all men.' 'The colors of the royal ermines and long flowing robes were the most glowing, the figures the most noble and graceful, the features the most distinct and characteristic—these portraits of these particular Stuart kings were designed to overawe.'"

Men who would later fight for the cause of liberty against a British tyrant held the lower classes in contempt. John Adams referred to the "common herd of mankind" and dismissed the "vulgar, rustic Imaginations" of the working poor, who had "no Idea of Learning, Eloquence and Genius." Elites even assumed that the poor were biologically closer to animals. The poor and the working class were expected to show constant deference to their social "betters." The average person had obedience literally beaten into him in some cases. Fear and awe often defined the relationship between rich and poor. A Maryland doctor named Alexander Hamilton (not the same person who later served as the United States' first Secretary of the Treasury) observed that people of the lower class glanced downward "like sheep" when addressing the powerful and wealthy. One man, George Hewes of Massachusetts, remembered decades later how he trembled and was "scared to death" when he made a visit as a cobbler's apprentice to the stately home of future leader of the Revolution John Hancock.

The concept of equality percolated slowly in English society back in the homeland and in the American colonies. In much of Europe the Catholic Church taught its faithful that kings ruled by divine right. "Why, even the hairs of your head are all numbered," said the Gospel of Luke, so it was inconceivable to the Church that God would allow anyone to serve as monarch over a Christian kingdom without divine approval. The king, therefore, ruled as God's representative politically, as the Pope ruled over the church. The English king, however, never enjoyed the absolute rule held by monarchs in France and Spain. Since Henry VIII established the Church of England, the king ruled not only over an Earthly kingdom, but he also became the nation's religious leader as well. The Church of England portrayed the Pope as the Anti-Christ, an earthly embodiment of satanic evil. This made the English king the defender of the faith. Even the most powerful of the nobility, such as those serving in Parliament, were not citizens but subjects, occupying a lower place on a God-created hierarchy of power.

The idea that God appointed Christian kings and placed them on top of a chain of being in which nobles ruled over commoners, and men over women, began to slowly unravel when the Stuart dynasty assumed the English throne in the 1600s. The Stuarts sought to achieve absolute authority like their European counterparts. They wished to reign without the consultation with Parliament. Meanwhile, the Stuart family had many marital connections to the Catholic French monarchy. James II (who reigned from 1685-1688) proposed that the British government legally tolerate Catholics, which raised the suspicions of the fiercely anti-Catholic Puritan faction in the Parliament. These differences led to violence between the Stuart King Charles I and the Parliament in 1642-1651 (which led to the beheading of the king in 1649) and in the so-called Glorious Revolution in 1688 that led to the overthrow of James II. These anti-royal rebellions posed a major challenge to the idea of the divine right of kings. If God placed the Stuarts on the English throne, then the successful parliamentary rebels had twice made themselves enemies of God. As historian Edmund S. Morgan notes in his book **Inventing the People: The Rise of Popular Sovereignty in England and America**, English philosophers like John Locke turned the concept of Divine Right of Kings on its head, arguing that the British people, in some distant, primeval past, had expressed God's will by creating the monarchy. This was a subtle but important change that provided an important rationale for the American Revolution. God had acted through the "people," not the king. The king was obligated to rule in the will of the populace. A king who did not serve the greater interests, whose rule failed to guarantee the life, liberty and property of the people, was no longer legitimate and the people as a whole were morally justified in ending that king's rule. The question now was how to define "the people." When privileged Virginia slave owner and plantation master Thomas Jefferson wrote, "All men are created equal," he certainly wasn't referring to women, the poor, commoners, or African Americans. The common people, Jefferson wrote at one point, "must never be considered when we calculate the national character." Jefferson's words, however, acted as a solvent on the Old World hierarchy. In

the coming decades, slavery opponents would insist that the "peculiar institution" made a mockery of Jefferson's words. When women met in Seneca Falls to demand suffrage rights in 1848, they would draft "The Declaration of Sentiments" in conscious imitation of the Declaration of Independence, and paraphrase Jefferson in proclaiming "that all men and women are created equal; that they are endowed by their Creator with certain inalienable rights; that among these are life, liberty, and the pursuit of happiness . . ." Much of American political history from the 1770s on would be a struggle over how inclusive the United States would be when the nation defined "the people."

THE COMING OF THE AMERICAN REVOLUTION

The Sugar and Currency Acts

After the French and Indian War, the British government experienced dire financial circumstances. Years of waging war, and the victories in Canada and the West Indies, had added millions of pounds to the national debt. The British sent 10,000 troops to North America to defend their new conquests in Canada and the Ohio Country. Those soldiers had to be paid, fed, clothed, and armed, which added further to the British government's fiscal burdens. Reduced purchases of military supplies, meanwhile, increased colonial unemployment. A post-war recession caused tax revenues to decline, while government expenditures continued to climb. The poor and working class in England rioted in some cases over taxes, high prices, and growing unemployment. Meanwhile, the rich landowners who dominated the Parliament selfishly voted themselves a 25 percent tax cut, worsening the deficit.

The British prime minister, **George Grenville** (in office from 1763-1765), looked for ways to raise revenue and cut expenses, eventually deciding to focus on taxing overseas commerce and the American colonists (who previously never had to pay revenue taxes to the British Treasury). In 1764, he steered through Parliament a series of revenue bills, including the **Sugar Act**. Previously-existing high tariffs on foreign molasses within the empire, often evaded by smugglers, had originally been intended to protect British sugar producers from foreign competition. The Sugar Act actually lowered these rates, but it tightened procedures for enforcement of the duties by customs officers. The act also allowed customs officers to prosecute smugglers in vice admiralty courts before royally appointed judges, rather than in local courts under colonial judicial systems. Grenville feared that local judges and local juries would sympathize with the smugglers and

Map 5.1 The Thirteen Colonies

find them not guilty, regardless of the evidence. For the smugglers, the days of benign neglect by imperial authorities were at an end. Overall, the British government hoped by reducing smuggling, revenues into the Treasury would increase even though the tax rates had been cut. In so doing, however, the nature of this particular Navigation Act governing molasses had been fundamentally altered from a basic trade regulation controlling the flow of legal trade to a law designed simply to accumulate revenues for the British Treasury.

At the same time, Parliament also passed a new Currency Act, which prohibited the colonies from issuing paper money as legal tender. British merchants and lenders had often sought to keep colonial debts from being repaid in depreciated colonial currency, and the new legislation responded to their petitions. It also guarded against inflation, but forcing all colonists to rely on limited supplies of specie (gold and silver) to pay their bills deepened the predicaments of the many debtors in the colonies.

The Stamp Act

Though the Sugar and Currency Acts began to generate sporadic protests in the colonies, the impending confrontation would eventually shake the British Empire to its core, leaving its rule over the North American colonies

fatally undermined. A strange paradox began to characterize relations between the king and his subjects in North America. In spite of the political alienation between Great Britain and the thirteen colonies, social, economic and cultural ties between the home country and its overseas possessions across the Atlantic actually strengthened. The rapid growth of the colonies encouraged higher volumes of transatlantic trade, bringing not only goods, capital, and immigrants, but also news, political commentary, fashion trends, and even religious movements—such as the evangelical Great Awakening. Wealthy colonial planters and merchants sought to imitate English standards of refined living and sent their sons to London to become socially polished and professionally trained. But were the colonists truly Englishmen? Were they even, as one New Hampshire newspaper editor stated, "British brothers"?

One of Benjamin Franklin's friends observed in a letter to Franklin that the tortured relationship between Britain and the American colonies was based on the fact that neither actually knew much about the other. Great Britain was also a dynamic, changing society. For a recently united kingdom now realizing unprecedented commercial wealth from its command of a global empire, the evolving meaning of "Britishness" was inseparable from the experience of imperial conquest and subjugation of others. Already, as of the 1760s, English news-

Burning of the Stamp Act in Boston

papers referred to the colonists by the term "Americans," a terminology not yet widely adopted by the colonists themselves.

Familiarity gave way to mutual estrangement. First-time colonial visitors to the mother country confronted an array of disorienting spectacles. As much as Philadelphia had grown, by the late-colonial period, London was twenty times larger. England outdid its colonies in terms of the ostentatious wealth, mass poverty, magnificence, and squalor on display. Social networks with elaborate rituals and pecking orders tended to exclude even eminent visiting young colonials. (In 1761, after two years of legal studies at the Inns of Court, Charles Carroll, who would later sign the Declaration of Independence, wrote to his father in Maryland, "I am intimate with nobody.") Colonials in Great Britain often felt they were strangers in a strange land.

The political system was perhaps most alien of all. In theory, the Houses of Parliament embodied the will of the British people—both lords and commoners. While Parliament swore allegiance to the king, its political supremacy supposedly protected the historic liberties of Englishmen from any potential tyrant. In reality, Parliament was anything but a straightforward, well-ordered system of representation. Elections to the House of Commons were held in constituencies that varied drastically in size, population, and qualifications for voting.

"Rotten boroughs"—former towns or onetime settlements that still retained ancient charters entitling them to elect members—were controlled by local noble men, or others with cash to spend and a desire for influence in the Commons. Bribery was the normal means of doing business for faction leaders. Far fewer people enjoyed the right to vote in England than in the colonies. While both the colonies and Great Britain required that a male citizen hold a certain amount of property to vote or run for office, the requirements were much higher in the mother country, effectively disfranchising about two-thirds of the male adult population in Great Britain but only an average of one-fourth in the American colonies.

In early 1765, Grenville moved forward with a proposal for "Stamp Duties" on the colonies. As already required in the British Isles, all printed materials, including legal documents, books, newspapers, magazines, and playing cards were to be made with special paper stamped in London and distributed in the colonies by authorized tax collectors. As with the Sugar Act, vice-admiralty courts were empowered to handle cases of violation. Meeting with a group of colonial agents that included Benjamin Franklin, Grenville gently insisted that the colonies must help pay the costs of their own defense and refused to hear arguments challenging the authority of Parliament to impose any kind of tax on the colonies. The House of Commons also ignored protest petitions from the colonial assemblies. On March 22, Parliament passed the **Stamp Act**, with its provisions due to start taking effect on November 1, 1765.

Patrick Henry Rails against the Stamp Act

Within the colonies, the response would not be a quiet one. In Williamsburg, Virginia, news of the Stamp Act's passage arrived toward the end of the spring session of the House of Burgesses, the elected Virginia assembly. **Patrick Henry** was a young, new member but already a successful trial attorney known for his courtroom eloquence. The tobacco planters who dominated the Virginia legislature generally opposed the imposition of taxes by Parliament and had protested the Sugar Act, but Henry's brand of opposition went further. On May 29, he and his allies proposed a set of seven resolutions, and a fiery debate consumed the chamber for three days. Together the "Virginia Resolves" denounced the Stamp Act, not as merely an unfair policy but as unconstitutional, illegitimate, tyrannical, and void.

The colonists were not represented in the Parliament and, therefore, were not allowed a voice in legislation directly affecting their pocketbooks. Taxation of the people by their own elected officials was "the distinguishing characteristic of British Freedom, without which the ancient Constitution cannot exist," according to Henry. Defenders of the tax, however, would argue that the colonies were "virtually represented" because members of Parliament supposedly represented not only their particular districts but also all the citizens of the British Empire. Men like Henry found these arguments unconvincing and "No taxation without representation" became a rallying cry for the growing American resistance. The seventh and last of the "resolves" even deemed any supporter of the Stamp Act to be "an enemy to this His Majesty's colony." Only four of the Resolves were actually approved by the burgesses (and a fifth was passed but rescinded after Henry had left for home), but all seven were printed in the newspapers.

This represented the boldest challenge yet by the colonists to the authority of Parliament. As the shock waves spread, Henry gained fame for his own speech during the Resolves debate. According to one observer, Henry called out names of tyrannical kings and the rebel leaders who overthrew them, noting for instance that "Caesar had his Brutus," and then said he "did not Doubt that some American would stand up, in favour of his Country." Cut off by cries of "Treason," Henry affirmed his loyalty to the King. But Henry maintained that if he had gone too far, it was because of "the Interest of his Countrys Dying liberty which he had at heart." Henry had mastered the hellfire-and-brimstone sermonizing style of evangelical preachers that had fired the Great Awakening, and his eloquence won a large audience for the cause of resistance to Parliament.

Stamp Act Protests in Boston

In Massachusetts, a democratic culture was evolving, reflected by the institution of the town meeting where citizens of all walks of life (but not women) gathered together to decide political issues. Town meetings in Boston included the wealthy, the middling, and even some of the "working artificers, seafaring men, and low sorts of people" (as an irate governor of the colony once observed). An organized faction called the Caucus, led by a group of master craftsmen and lesser merchants who called themselves the Loyal Nine, claimed to represent the workingmen and controlled the town meeting with their votes. At the same time, some colonists remained deeply loyal to imperial authority.

The leading example of this was Thomas Hutchinson, a successful merchant and a descendant of Anne Hutchinson who had challenged the original Puritan leadership of Massachusetts in the 1600s. Never widely popular but always politically ambitious, Hutchinson cultivated

connections with successive royally appointed governors of Massachusetts, and he secured many of the colony's other high offices for himself and his relatives. During the early 1760s, Hutchinson repeatedly urged Governor Francis Bernard to abolish Boston's town meeting and establish a local council that he, his relatives, and their friends could control.

Among the local leaders who resisted Hutchinson's efforts was **James Otis Jr.**, an unpredictable but brilliant lawyer and scholar who helped to unify the rest of the opposition. Otis was driven by a private feud with Hutchinson, but he could channel personal grievance into principled arguments. Rising to defend the interests of Boston's merchants, he boldly denounced policies such as the use of broad search warrants to seek evidence of smuggling, and the Sugar Act itself. Like Patrick Henry, Otis put narrow legal arguments aside and characterized the imperial customs laws as unconstitutional, tyrannical violations of the colonists' fundamental rights.

At the same time, he reached out to the Loyal Nine and their followers, attacking Hutchinson as an aristocratic pretender and an enemy of the common folk. Increasingly, the leadership of the town meeting became an alliance of merchants, artisans, and laborers who viewed their elite adversaries as tools of the Parliament who would usurp the self-governing powers of all colonists. By 1765, opposing Parliament, in the minds of many in Massachusetts, equaled supporting the rights of the people.

Boston's response to the Stamp Act was slow in coming but explosive. Newspapers in Massachusetts reprinted the Virginia Resolves. Hutchinson claimed to oppose the law but refused to deny Parliament's authority to pass it. His brother-in-law, Andrew Oliver, was appointed as stamp distributor for Massachusetts. On the morning of August 14, 1765, an ominous sight appeared, under one of Boston's largest elm trees: a figure representing Oliver, hanging by his neck from a branch. Suspended alongside Oliver's effigy was a boot (a symbolic reference to the Earl of Bute, once an adviser to **King George III**) with its sole painted green (and with a helpful sign bearing the word "Green-ville").

Hutchinson, as lieutenant governor of the colony, ordered the local sheriff to cut down the effigy, but a crowd of workingmen, led by a poor shoemaker named Ebenezer McIntosh, surrounded the tree. That night they took down the figures themselves, carried them through the city streets to the stamp distributor's office, tore down the office building, built a bonfire from its timbers, "stamped" on Oliver's effigy with their own boots, and beheaded it by the light of the flames. Then they stormed through Oliver's own house, leaving its interior partially gutted. Oliver pledged the next day to resign the stamp distributorship. Twelve nights later, McIntosh and the crowd reassembled at the houses of several other officials, including Hutchinson's own grand mansion, intent on destroying everything. Hutchinson and his family fled for their lives. A mob broke into, vandalized, and burned his mansion. He lost a fortune in worldly possessions (for which he compiled a detailed inventory, and eventually was compensated) including a draft of an extensive history of the colony that he had been working on for many years but maintained his dignified composure, as well as his network of political connections.

More than the material losses, the collapse of law and order left Hutchinson, the royal governor, and other respectable men most shaken. Members of local militias given the duty of maintaining crowd control had participated in the violence. Such mobs, however, had long been a local tradition. Crowds, sometimes including well-off men dressed as poor folk, assembled to force the closing down of houses of prostitution and to drive contagious smallpox sufferers out of town. Ritual mobs gave humble people roles in the maintenance of local traditions.

For decades, in Boston, on November 5 ("Pope's Day"), crowds took over the streets, lit bonfires, and paraded with effigies of the Pope as the Devil, to express hatred of the Catholic Church and its minions. (Pope's Day, also known as "Guy Fawkes Day," commemorates an incident in which Catholic conspirators failed to set off a bomb intended to blow up King James I and the Parliament at the start of the 1605 legislative session.) A violent routine even developed in which rival mobs from opposite sides of town battled in the streets, seeking to capture each other's effigies. (Ebenezer McIntosh was the elected leader of the South End's Pope's Day Company.) Additionally, at times of grain shortage, crowds in Boston and elsewhere gathered to force merchants to keep the price of bread within financial reach. A tradition of rough street politics was thus well established in Boston by the 1760s. By the time of the Stamp Act riot, for the struggling mass of people in Boston, the authority of the royally connected, socially condescending, tax-collecting leaders of the colony was no longer legitimate.

Stamp Act Resistance Spreads

Together, Patrick Henry's inflammatory rhetoric and the explosion of the Boston mob helped spread flames of protest across the colonies. In July, Otis had called for a Stamp Act Congress of delegates from all the colonies. Representatives from nine colonies convened in New York in October and issued more resolutions. Like the Virginia Resolves, the Congress invoked the historic rights and liberties of British subjects. Others went about it differently. Local politicians organized demonstrations, which turned into riots in Newport, Rhode Island, in several Connecticut towns, and in New York City, where crowds seized the colonial governor's coach, burned it, and sacked the home of a commander of the local British garrison manning the harbor. In each of the colonies, stamp distributors either resigned their commissions on their own or were forced to do so by mobs.

The spirit of rebellion turned out to be difficult to contain, and even whites leading the opposition to the Stamp Act became nervous as they feared that their slaves might also rise up. In Charles Town, South Carolina, white artisans had marched with their effigies on the local stamp distributor's home, chanting and waving flags bearing the word "Liberty." Whites were a minority in the city; most of the residents were black slaves. Whites began to fear that the African Americans would attempt a revolt of their own. As a white resident of Charles Town later said on one January day in 1766, "some negroes, apparently in thoughtless imitation, began to cry 'Liberty,'" and almost simultaneously more than one hundred slaves escaped from plantations outside the city. "The city was thrown in arms for a week," and slave masters, frightened for their lives, warned each other of an impending revolt and braced themselves for possible bloodshed. As the protests echoed up and down the Atlantic seaboard, elite protest leaders sought greater control over the forces they had unleashed. In Boston, shortly after stating their disapproval and regret over the destruction of Hutchinson's mansion, the Loyal Nine rebranded themselves as the **"Sons of Liberty"** (using a phrase from a speech delivered in the House of Commons) and focused on sustaining the opposition movement while calming its penchant for violence. Opposition leaders quickly adopted the name in other colonies. The Sons of Liberty made political inroads in Boston, organizing well-attended protest meetings and conducting mock trials of British officials under the shade of the same elm tree (now widely known as the "Liberty Tree" or "Liberty Hall") where the protests had started. With funds contributed by the wealthy merchant John Hancock, they bought a general's fine uniform for McIntosh and arranged for him to lead both of the Pope's Day companies in a more orderly celebration. (The Sons of Liberty proved to be fair-weather friends. McIntosh went broke several years later, and when a court tossed him into debtor's prison, no member of the group offered to bail him out.)

Meanwhile, in late 1765, merchants in New York, Boston, and Philadelphia organized a boycott of British goods, which proved crucial in killing the hated Stamp Act. Increased wealth during the previous decades fueled consumer demand for British-made goods, but as the economy soured, fewer customers could afford imported products. Merchants decided they had little to lose by joining the boycott and selling off the British imports that remained on store shelves. Sons of Liberty enforced the boycott, which proved to be a turning point. Meanwhile, back in London, Grenville had angered King George over an unrelated issue, and the monarch fired the minister in July 1765. The newly installed government felt no obligation to maintain the stamp tax and proved receptive to petitions it received from distressed British merchants who complained that Grenville's policies had hurt their bottom line. Franklin, still in London, offered testimony before Parliament that shrewdly emphasized colonial loyalty as well as economic grievances. The parliament repealed the Stamp Act in March 1766. An accompanying Declaratory Act, however, set an ominous tone, insisting that Parliament retained "full power and authority" to make laws binding the colonies "in all cases whatsoever."

The Townshend Acts

The colonists' rejoicing over the death of the Stamp Act proved to be short-lived. The Declaratory Act cast a shadow over their celebrations from the start, with its defiant message that many of the colonists' arguments had been heard but not accepted. The sugar taxes remained in place. Moreover, the budgetary problems facing His Majesty's government had hardly disappeared with the Stamp Act's repeal. Barely a year later, an entirely new tax scheme reopened the entire dispute. Another turnover of ministries placed responsibility for government finances in the hands of Charles Townshend, a clever politician, who became Chancellor of the Exchequer (the British equivalent of Treasury Secretary). He felt forced to seek revenues from America. **Townshend's Revenue Act of 1767** placed new import duties on goods colonial consumers relied on, such as lead, paint, glass, paper, and tea. The revenue yield would not be great, but Townshend viewed it as a first step. Perhaps more important, it would cover salaries for royal governors and magistrates. Townshend packaged his revenue act with other laws aimed at strengthening the authority of royal customs collectors and punishing New York for failing to pay for housing British army forces.

In the colonies, few were truly eager for renewed conflict, and at first the response to the Townshend Acts was muted. For the colonists, the issue remained not the amount of the tax but that the colonies had no voice in the debate about the Townshend duties. The Townshend taxes might be a small burden, but the colonists could

see clearly enough how they could create a precedent for future taxes imposed by an unresponsive Parliament across the Atlantic Ocean.

Once again, Boston took the lead. An outspoken voice from the Sons of Liberty, **Samuel Adams**, assumed center stage. Uniquely well suited to the leadership role, Adams was respectable yet humble, the son of a prosperous tradesman (and maltster, a provider of malted grains—not a brewer as legend has it, although close). An unsuccessful businessman, Adams had led a humble life not completely by choice. As Otis became more unstable, he still commanded the respect of the rank and file with his powerful speaking talents. Adams, however, gained influence by treating Caucus supporters as equals, regardless of wealth, and by proving his unshakable commitment to changing British policies. Holding a seat in the Massachusetts colonial legislature, Adams secured its approval of a letter to "sister colonies," presenting the case against the Townshend Acts as "infringements of their natural and constitutional rights."

The Massachusetts Circular Letter stirred a renewal of opposition throughout the colonies. In Boston, it led to the suspension of the legislature itself (by Royal Governor Francis Bernard, acting on orders from London). As royal customs commissioners attempted to enforce the duties, ominous crowds again filled the streets. At "Liberty Hall," under the tree branches, the Sons of Liberty convened official town meetings and passed resolutions condemning the governor. The newly arrived customs commissioners appealed for armed support, reporting to London that, "the Governor and Magistracy have not the least Authority or power in this place." Their request was heard. In October 1767, transport ships arrived from Canada carrying four regiments of British army regulars. Boston was now a city under military occupation.

As accounts of strife in Boston spread through the colonies, resistance took on a more urgent character. Townshend and his successors in London had no intention of surrendering the king's authority over the colonies, and they ordered royal governors to shut down any legislature voicing support for the Massachusetts Circular Letter. Cut off from expressing opposition through their established institutions, colonists resorted to more extreme tactics. Once again, the colonists turned to non-importation of British goods, the same tactic that had proven so successful during the Stamp Act crisis. The central government in London, however, proved more determined this time, and carrying out the new boycott became a bigger challenge. Merchants had suffered economically during previous boycotts, and they wanted to spread the pain of resistance around more broadly. In each of the seaport cities, artisans—often having struggled for years to com-

Paul Revere's famously skewed version of the Boston Massacre, 1770

pete with imported British products—now emerged in a critical role. Under pressure from Samuel Adams and his followers, Boston merchants reluctantly agreed in August 1768 to cease shipments of most British goods. Artisans, rice farmers, and others aggrieved by the new taxes joined together in Charles Town, making similar demands. But, as opponents organized, they also began looking beyond the merchants and toward consumers, toward the broader public itself. Boston officials incited "Persons of all Ranks" to sign a public pledge to "encourage the Use and Consumption of all Articles manufactured in any of the British American Colonies" and to refuse to buy "Articles from abroad." So-called "Subscription lists"—lists of boycotted goods—quickly spread beyond Boston as well.

By 1769, while "committees of inspection" in each colony enforced the non-importation campaign among merchants, the consumer boycott movement had extended the resistance movement into colonial communities and households. A decision not to buy imported articles—or a pledge not to do so—made one a participant in the broader struggle against British tyranny. Spending money on luxury items took on a new political meaning, making one a traitor to a virtuous cause. Peter Oliver (the brother of Boston stamp distributor Andrew Oliver) ridiculed the boycott, snidely suggesting that Massachusetts' common folk couldn't afford the items on the subscription list anyway. "Among the various prohibited Articles, were

Silks, Velvets, Clocks, Watches, Coaches & Chariots; & it was highly diverting, to see the names & marks, of Porters & Washing Women." For Oliver, a statement "signed" by humble and illiterate folk meant that the movement represented little more than a mob action. Unscrupulous boycott leaders, he suggested, had manipulated the lower classes into an act of disloyalty. The class diversity of boycott participants, however, suggested how deep the opposition to British government policies had grown.

The Boston Massacre

In an overheated political environment like Boston, the British decision to send an occupying force of "Redcoat" soldiers could only escalate tensions. Quartered on private properties seized from the city, guarded by sentries who challenged townsfolk at will, these soldiers inevitably provoked resentment by their mere presence. British soldiers received paltry pay, so they took side jobs placing them in direct competition with local workers. Fights with civilians led to prosecutions of soldiers in local courts, where convictions and fines confirmed the army's sense of being surrounded by enemies. Townsfolk, frustrated by what they feared was a failing boycott, threatened merchants they suspected of breaking the non-importation pact. Boston residents then vented their frustrations on the British soldiers. Anger exploded into violence one moonlit night on March 5, 1770, when an angry crowd in front of the Boston customhouse faced off against an army patrol led by Captain Thomas Preston. The crowd began to throw snowballs, some containing rocks. One chunk of ice struck a soldier, causing him to slip and fall. The sight of a fallen soldier caused panic and someone fired a musket. Believing that they were under attack, the British soldiers standing in formation also fired, aiming at the crowd and hitting eleven men. The volley killed five, including Crispus Attucks, a dockworker descended from Africans and Wampanoag Indians. (Historians are uncertain whether Attucks was a slave or free.) Hutchinson, then serving as acting governor of the colony, faced the furious crowd the following day, promised justice, and managed to prevent further bloodshed.

The "**Boston Massacre**" had immediate local consequences. The British troops were redeployed to an island fortress in Boston Harbor. Samuel Adams and other non-importation leaders exploited the tragedy for propaganda purposes, depicting the incident as an intentional attack by heavily armed troops on defenseless civilians. This version of the story resulted in the famous engraving by local silversmith Paul Revere soon distributed across the colonies. Revere depicted Captain Preston coldly ordering his troops to fire into a group of unthreatening bystanders. Preston and his men were held and later tried in colonial court, defended by **John Adams**, Samuel's second cousin. John Adams was equally dedicated to the opposition movement but, as an attorney, believed in the principle of a fair trial. Adams secured acquittals of all the defendants on murder charges (although two of the privates were convicted of manslaughter and released after being branded with an iron).

Beyond Boston, the incident coincided with a partial reversal of imperial policy toward the colonies. A new government installed in London decided to modify the Townshend revenue plan mainly due to pressure from unhappy London merchants. The boycott had undermined Townshend's goal of raising revenues, and the idea that the duties would ease the way to future taxes had been shattered in the ugly colonial climate following the Boston shootings. The latest prime minister, Lord Frederick North, persuaded Parliament to repeal most of the Townshend duties, but his government continued the levy on tea, intended to fund the salaries of royal governors and other colonial officials. North assumed (correctly as it turned out) that a partial repeal of the Townshend duties would calm colonists, reduce the risk of further violence, and undermine a continuation of the non-importation campaign. By July 1770, New York merchants overrode the objections of the local Sons of Liberty chapter and announced that they would resume importing British goods. The momentum gone, colonial resistance ebbed, and in October of that year Boston merchants also began importing British products. For a moment, reconciliation seemed within grasp. A new equestrian statue of King George III arose on Bowling Green at the tip of Manhattan, to the cheers of crowds. North seemed to have brought law and order back to the North American colonies. Nevertheless, Samuel Adams, among others, continued to organize colonists. Creating "committees of correspondence," these leaders spread information within their colonies and established contact with leaders in other colonies in an effort to maintain due diligence against any future provocative actions by the British government.

The Boston Tea Party

A deceptively quiet pause of three years ensued, a time that encouraged complacency on the part of government ministers in London but frustrated firebrands like Sam Adams. In fact, discontent and frustration with imperial rule continued to fester, sustained by minor incidents in the absence of major provocations such as the Townshend Acts. (In one notable incident taking place in 1772, angry locals burned a British customs patrol vessel—the *H.M.S. Gaspée*—after the anti-smuggling schooner ran aground

off the Rhode Island coast.) The relationship between colonies and mother country had already been altered forever, though most in America and Great Britain did not realize it at the time.

The **Tea Act** shattered the surface calm, and set in motion a final sequence of events leading to war and independence. Lord North really had no intention of demonstrating imperial power over the colonies. His attitude toward the colonies was relatively conciliatory. The British Empire, however, still badly needed revenues to pay its expenses, and the leadership of that Empire remained adamantly opposed to allowing any self-rule for the colonies or their representation in the Parliament. Then, a new fiscal problem arose. The British East India Company, a vast commercial enterprise controlling British trade with India and the Far East that heavily impacted the overall British economy, teetered on the edge of bankruptcy. The company wielded great influence in Parliament, and government ministers basically granted the company more favorable terms for the importation of its Indian tea to the American colonies. Because of this legislation, the company could now completely bypass Great Britain and avoid paying British import duties while directly supplying colonial merchants. This meant that American customers could now buy tea at lower prices, even with the Townshend tax included. Americans would pay a lower price, but the East India Company would be able to undersell smugglers and would eventually achieve a monopoly that could come back to haunt the colonies. Again, the colonists continued to object to a tax that had been passed without their consultation, whatever the amount of the duty. Tea represented a major issue. Americans preferred tea to coffee and quaffed gallons of it. North received advice that the existing tea duty remained a sensitive issue and that the Tea Act risked stirring new controversy if the duty were maintained. But as a continuing source of funds for payment of royal officials, North reasoned that the duty was too valuable to be abandoned.

Responses to the Tea Act in the colonial ports of entry were decisive, reflecting the underlying strength and renewed intensity of the opposition movement. Special circumstances made Boston's response uniquely provocative. As colonial newspapers published the Tea Act's provision, the Sons of Liberty encouraged followers to not fall for the latest British "trick," one designed to dupe colonists to accept the tea tax. The Sons of Liberty attacked the East India Company as a greedy monopoly whose claws would now grip Boston and other American cities. Merchants realized they could lose their lucrative profits from tea smuggling and feared they would be muscled out of legitimate trade by East India Company assignment agents. Merchants again found themselves allied with planters and artisans. The Sons of Liberty gently—or not so gently—persuaded local recipients of the company's tea consignment rights to resign their commissions. Incoming tea ships attempting to dock in New York and Philadelphia received warnings about a possibly hostile local welcome and turned back toward England with unsold cargoes still on board. But Governor Hutchinson—who, true to form, had secured company commissions for his two sons—insisted on allowing three Boston-bound vessels to enter the port. As the casks of tea remained on board, a standoff developed between the ship owner and consignment agents, who wanted the vessels unloaded, and Adams and the other leaders of the Boston town meeting.

Boston again boiled like a tea kettle as the city's committee of correspondence helped organize mass meetings at "Liberty Hall" and the Old South Church. These events drew thousands of townfolk. Meanwhile, mass gatherings in the surrounding counties joined the chorus demanding that the tea ships turn back to England. A legal deadline, however, loomed—one that empowered the governor to confiscate the cargo of the East India Company vessels and bring the tea ashore. Dozens of men disguised as Native Americans raided three ships on the night of December 16, 1773, smashing open the casks and tossing the tea into the harbor. The event, later called the **"Boston Tea Party,"** had one long-term cultural impact on the future United States, marking when Americans would begin to favor coffee over tea.

The Intolerable Acts

English responses to the Boston Tea Party reflected how much political, economic, and emotional distance had grown between Boston and London. Even British politicians and intellectuals who had sympathized with the colonial grievances expressed confusion over an American protest against what amounted to a tax cut. A council of ministers summoned Benjamin Franklin, ostensibly in England to defend a petition from Boston. Instead Franklin had to stand silently while his own character was impugned in extravagant terms, obviously in retaliation for Boston's collective action. (Franklin remained in England for another year, then left, never to return, and soon became a leader in the revolutionary cause.) For North, at this point, the only issue now involving the colonies was "whether we have, or have not, any authority in that country."

Parliament quickly approved a package of proposals known as the **Coercive Acts**. (In the colonies, they were derisively referred to as the "**Intolerable Acts**"). These new laws included the Boston Port Act, which closed the port to all commerce until the destroyed tea was paid for; the Massachusetts Government Act, which unilaterally rewrote the colony's charter to strengthen the governor's powers and limited town meetings to once a year; and new procedures for royal officials accused of crimes, allowing their trials to be held in England, which amounted to a grant of impunity, since witnesses for the prosecution were unlikely to be able to afford attending the proceedings. The Crown appointed General Thomas Gage, a highly experienced army commander who previously served on the colonial western frontier, as military governor of Massachusetts, and dispatched him to Boston to command a 4,000-strong force of regular troops.

The British Parliament stirred further resentments with another law, the Quebec Act, which stirred deep anti-Catholic and anti-Indian feelings from New England to Georgia. The legislation mostly pertained to the governances of what was once French Canada. Under the law, the Parliament furthermore expanded the province's boundaries south to the Ohio River, and the western border to the Mississippi River. Much of this land had previously been granted to New York, Pennsylvania, and Virginia. The British government, however, now set aside much of this sought-after real estate for the Iroquois nations. The Iroquois had traditionally lived in New York but had migrated west because of pressure from white encroachment. Many Iroquois would now occupy new territory in a greatly expanded Quebec and enjoy greater protection against white squatters. The British government also hoped that providing the Iroquois territory would ensure peace with one of the most populous Native American nations within their empire, allowing the army to focus more attention on the threat posed by the French and the Spanish in other parts of the world. On the other hand, the Quebec Act harmed the financial interests of colonial land speculators whose previously-laid claims were now overturned. The colonists had few sympathizers in the Parliament, which had grown tired of the constant discontent across the Atlantic Ocean. Legislators proved eager to put the colonists in their place. The Quebec Act further granted freedom of worship to French Catholics living in the province and ended the requirement that Catholics renounce their faith before they could serve in public office. This expression of religious tolerance infuriated many in the thirteen colonies, especially in Puritan New England, where anti-Catholic prejudice burned the brightest.

The British government could hardly have done anything more to confirm the colonists' worst suspicions. Admittedly, even now, at least some divisions persisted among colonists. Significant minorities of Boston merchants, facing the extinction of the city as a trading center, were willing to offer payment for the tea destroyed during the Tea Party and beg for mercy. Others elsewhere remained reluctant to go back to non-importation. But the Intolerable Acts seemed far more of an immediate threat. As the Boston Port Act took effect, with its catastrophic economic consequences for the city, colonists in other places recognized Boston as a martyr in a common cause. In Williamsburg, Virginia, Patrick Henry and a young burgess named Thomas Jefferson proposed a "Day of Fasting, Humiliation, and Prayer" for their fellow colonists facing a "hostile invasion." John Murray, the Fourth Earl of Dunmore and the royal governor of Virginia, generally known as **Lord Dunmore**, then promptly dissolved the legislature. Once again, denied a legal framework to express their grievances, the colonists turned to each other and acted outside of the law.

The Disintegration of Authority

In September 1774, the First Continental Congress convened in Philadelphia with delegates from twelve colonies appointed by legislatures when possible and by unofficial conventions when necessary. (Georgia was the one colony that failed to participate.) Behind closed doors, seven intense weeks of debate and committee work resolved differences over tactics and smoothed out differences between boycott advocates and southern planters dependent on British manufactured goods. Ultimately, they found common ground, endorsing a declaration of rights; agreements on non-importation, non-exportation, and nonconsumption of tea; and a network of "committees of safety," to be elected "in every county, city, and town," which would enforce the agreements. A Second Continental Congress was also scheduled for the following year.

Though the meeting of the Congress held much importance, the most crucial developments may have been those assemblages occurring within local communities, particularly those well outside the seaport cities whose merchants, artisans, and laborers had long provided much of the leadership and support for the colonial resistance. In long-settled farming regions and in the backcountry, in small villages and in the sprawling countryside, among the small landowning and tenant families who constituted 70 percent of the white population of the colonies, participation in the resistance developed slowly. Even in rural eastern Massachusetts, Boston's fights with Redcoats and customs commissioners seemed distant. Humble farming folk, however, were hardly cut off from the surrounding world. They read newspapers, attended evangelical revivals, and traded surplus crops for consumer goods, some even imported, but compared to city folk, their exposure

(as producers or as consumers) to the impact of imperial tax policies was limited.

When the shift finally came, the most important factor proved to be the passage of the Coercive Acts. The extreme punishment inflicted by the British blockade on Boston and that city's masses of impoverished artisans and hungry laborers evoked an emotional response and a tide of donations from throughout the colonies. (In rural Maryland, a member of a relief committee explained "those who cannot give money, can give corn.") Participation in the charitable campaign created new networks of correspondence and led to further commitments to a common cause. Moreover, for farmers within the colony, the Massachusetts Government Act posed an even more direct threat. Appointments to colonial offices by General Gage under the terms of the act were seen as intrusions into local government by an illegitimate pretender. As villagers began withholding taxes, assembling in crowds to shut down county courts, and disabling other functions of the colonial government, the committees of safety mandated by the Continental Congress began filling the vacuum. Farmers began joining the boycotts, watched their neighbors for signs of disloyalty, took charge of local militia units, and sought what one county committee called "a well-ordered resistance." The revolt against the British had moved from the cities to the countryside.

As Gage's appointees and others loyal to his government fled the rural areas for the safety of Boston, the governor recognized that his authority outside the city had disintegrated. An unauthorized Massachusetts Provincial Congress featuring Sam Adams and other resistance leaders now held sessions in Cambridge, across the river from Boston. Other colonial governors found themselves similarly isolated. In New York and Philadelphia, as large-scale committees of safety dominated by merchants and artisans asserted power, long-established colonial legislatures adjourned quietly and disappeared. In Virginia, Lord Dunmore grimly acknowledged that local committees of safety were now the acting government of the colony. By early 1775, opposition to British authority, once the distinct preoccupation of merchants, artisans, and leading planters had emerged as a defining feature of American patriots.

All the preliminaries for war had been set except for the actual shooting. This was especially true in Massachusetts, where armed rival governments now squared off. Gage kept his forces stationed in Boston throughout the winter, as he urgently requested more troops, considered tactics, and awaited clear orders from London. Across the surrounding countryside, in towns and villages, militia companies held drills, and local volunteers enlisted as so-called minutemen, ready for military duty upon a

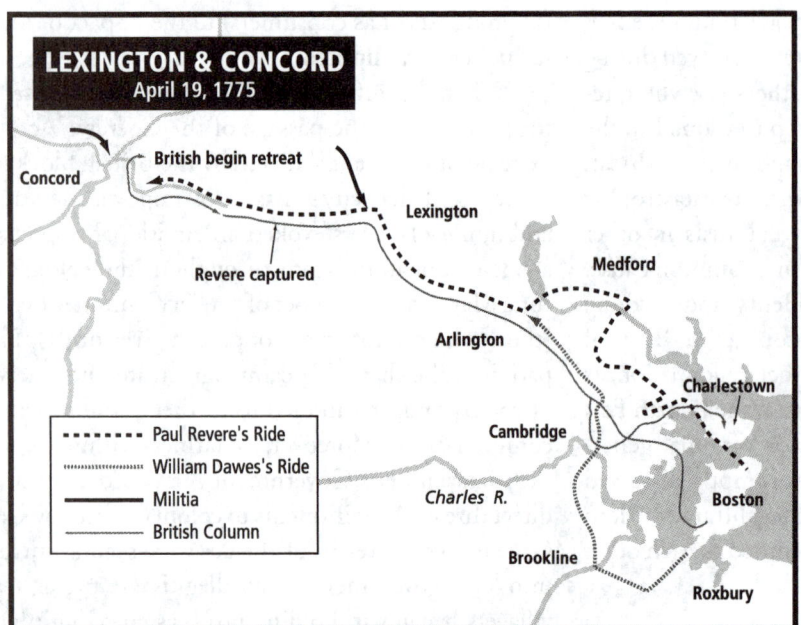

Map 5.2 Lexington & Concord

moment's notice. Meanwhile, a surprisingly sophisticated network of spies closely watched the movements of Gage's troops. In the city itself, Paul Revere, William Dawes, and other unemployed artisans kept watch in shifts.

In London, Lord North and his fellow minister William Legge, the 2nd Earl of Dartmouth and the secretary of state for the colonies, fumed over Gage's inaction. Dispatching new instructions to Gage in late January that ignored the general's request for more troops, Dartmouth demanded strong action "to defend the Constitution & to restore the Vigour of Government," never believing that the expanding Massachusetts resistance represented anything other than "a rude Rabble" that posed no serious threat to the British Army. In his opinion—"in which His Majesty concurs"—the most appropriate response was to capture and imprison the leadership of the Massachusetts Provincial Congress.

THE REVOLUTION BEGINS

Lexington, Concord, and Bunker Hill

The arrival of Dartmouth's letter in April 1775 forced Gage's hand. The general organized an expedition to seize militia arms and ammunition believed to be held in the town of Concord. Gage's own scouting patrols alerted the patriot militias to the impending action. Late on the evening of April 18, on Boston Common, Gage assembled a detachment of select infantrymen from different regiments. In the middle of the night, they rowed across the bay separating Boston from its hinterlands and advanced along the Concord road.

The British troops intended to arrest Samuel Adams and John Hancock, who they regarded as the leaders of a treasonous movement. Revere ordered associates to hang signal lanterns in the Old North Church steeple to send a warning then made his own crossing to the mainland with William Dawes. The two men scurried on horseback along a designated route through a succession of towns leading toward Concord, rousing the minutemen and sending other riders on their way. In Lexington, he awakened Adams and Hancock, who (after some hours of delay and debate) agreed to head for safety.

Ultimately, a British advance patrol caught Revere before he reached Concord but not before the alarm system was fully operational. By the time that the red-coated troops reached Lexington shortly after four in the morning, the village militia stood assembled on the green, some seventy men strong. As the regular infantrymen arranged themselves in battle formation, the minutemen attempted an orderly withdrawal with their arms. Just then, a shot rang out—the famous "Shot Heard Round the World," probably fired by a colonist located somewhere off the green. The British troopers responded by exchanging volleys with the militiamen before charging with their bayonets. At the end of the brief skirmish, sometimes referred to as the "**Battle of Lexington**," eight of the Lexington men lay dead and ten were wounded (including the militia commander, Captain John Parker). The war had begun. More than six years of bloodshed lay ahead.

Marching onward, the British infantry reached **Concord** later in the morning and searched the town. Failing to find any large cache of weapons (they had been

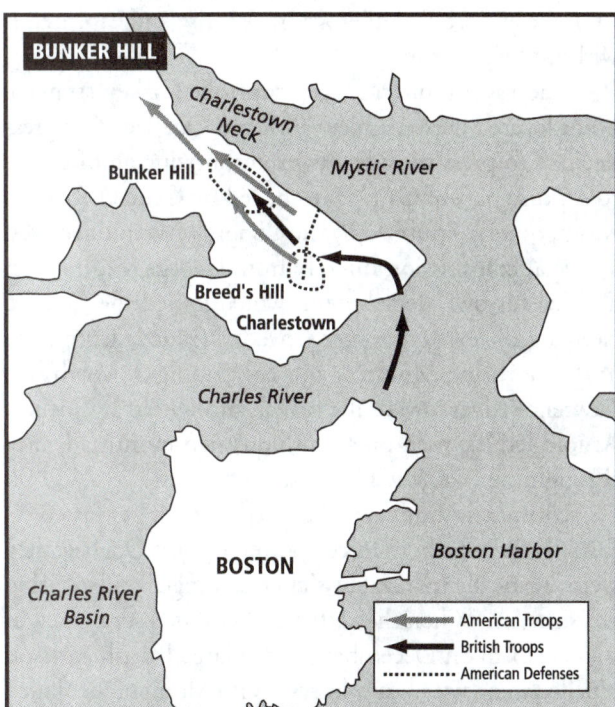

Map 5.3 Battle of Bunker Hill

on the colonies, new volunteers enthusiastically enlisted in militia companies.

General Gage, still under intense pressure to show results, recognized that militia forces on the ridges overlooking the Boston peninsula and its rivers and harbor might soon encircle his army. With his own reinforcements now arriving, Gage planned to secure the Charlestown Peninsula close to the North End of Boston, but he found himself beaten by a quick deployment of Massachusetts militia forces led by Colonel William Prescott. As Prescott hastily fortified his positions on the high ground above Charlestown—two ridge tops named Bunker Hill (the larger, but located farther away from Boston) and Breed's Hill (where most of the subsequent fighting would take place)—Gage and his lieutenants prepared an assault. With a total force of approximately 2,000, General William Howe led the British troops as they crossed the Charles River from Boston on June 17 and advanced up the hills. Armed with bayonets, the British forces charged against the patriot fortifications on Breed's Hill, marching directly into a deadly hail of musket fire. Suffering heavy losses, Howe still organized a second assault; this advance too dissolved in the face of what one British officer later called "an incessant stream of fire." Prescott's undersupplied militia, however, ran out of ammunition, allowing Howe's men to capture the top of Breed's Hill on the third try. The famously misidentified "**Battle of Bunker Hill**" resulted in a thousand British casualties (226 killed and 828 wounded). The casualties included many of Howe's subordinate officers who were sons of members of Parliament. About 140 Americans died, and about 360 suffered injuries in fighting on Bunker Hill during the patriot retreat to nearby Cambridge. The British government blamed Gage for the high losses. Three days after Dartmouth received the general's report on the battle, he requested the general's resignation.

The Second Continental Congress

Initially, the **Second Continental Congress** had been envisioned, like the First, as a kind of inter-colonial treaty conference working out a common response among the colonies to new actions by the British government. But when delegates convened in Philadelphia in May 1775, the colonies were already in a state of undeclared war against the world's leading imperial power. Instead of convening for a brief, intense assembly, delegates prepared for prolonged legislative debates and the difficult task of managing the war. The ultimate objective of the colonial resistance continued to divide the delegates. During its opening months, the new congress attempted, as John

long-since removed), they set a few buildings on fire, perhaps by accident. Unwilling to reenact the bloody scene in Lexington, the residents of Concord had initially evacuated to a nearby hillside until they saw the billowing smoke column rising from the town. Arriving on one side of the Concord River across from the main body of British troops, a group of Concord minutemen fired on three isolated companies of infantrymen, which had crossed one of the village bridges, sending them in retreat across the river. Suddenly, the momentum shifted. As the infantry column marched back to Boston, it found itself facing a gauntlet of militiamen along both sides of the road, shooting from behind trees and fences, and attacking stragglers with hatchets and clubs. The British troopers defended themselves with bayonets and returned fire, but what had been an intimidating show of force became a bloody ordeal. By the time they reached safety, the British forces had suffered nearly three hundred killed and wounded. Militia casualties numbered less than one hundred.

Events in Lexington and Concord reverberated across the colonies. "This accident has cut off our last hope of reconciliation," Jefferson wrote in a letter, "and a phrenzy of revenge seems to have seized all ranks of people." News of the "twin battles changed the instruments of War from the pen to the sword," John Adams later wrote. Supportive of the patriot cause, the colonial press mostly depicted the violent but inconclusive events in Lexington and Concord as an unmitigated disaster for the British. Believing that Great Britain had started a war

Adams put it, "to hold the sword in one hand, and the olive branch in the other."

George Washington, who had commanded frontier troops and militiamen during the French and Indian War, arrived as a uniformed representative for Virginia—the largest colony—and appeared as an indispensable man at a critical moment. On June 14, the Congress created the Continental Army, to be made up of new recruits from Pennsylvania, Maryland, and Virginia, along with the New England militia around Boston. Washington humbly accepted Congress's selection of him to be the Army's commander and immediately left for Massachusetts. The Virginian had earned the trust not only of fierce advocates of independence, such as John Adams (who had nominated him), but also supporters of continued efforts at negotiation with Britain, including **John Dickinson** of Pennsylvania, the leading advocate of reconciliation, who voted in favor of the army's creation and Washington's appointment as commanding general.

Perhaps in return for his cooperation, Dickinson secured the delegates' signatures to an "**Olive Branch Petition**" addressed to King George III, professing their loyalty as faithful subjects. The deferential prose of the petition, which described the conflict between the colonies and Great Britain as painful and blamed the impasse on devious ministers and "artful and cruel enemies," offers a window into the mindset of colonial moderates honestly torn between loyalty to England and sympathy with colonial complaints. In London, as Adams, Franklin, and other independence advocates could clearly see, none of it mattered. In November, intermediaries on behalf of the colonies presented the Olive Branch Petition to George III. The king refused to receive it.

The Colonists Take the Offensive: The Invasion of Canada and the Siege of Boston

Waging war brought its own kinds of disappointments. In late 1775, the Congress supported an ambitious effort to expel British forces from Quebec, bring the formerly French Canadians into the common struggle against London, and remove Canada as a source of likely threats to the colonies from the north and west. The patriots seized a chance for victory early in the war at Fort Ticonderoga, on Lake Champlain in northern New York. Ethan Allen, a legendary frontiersman, land speculator, and self-styled philosopher, led a militia called the Green Mountain Boys. They undertook a campaign to capture the fort. They were joined by **Benedict Arnold**, a Connecticut merchant and militia leader who had concocted a similar plan. Allen and Arnold caught the small British force at Fort Ticonderoga by surprise and captured it without firing a shot.

The revolutionaries now controlled a key strategic point located between New York and Quebec. Congress decided to press the advantage, authorizing an offensive to capture part of Canada, to be led by General Richard Montgomery. Snubbed by the Congress, Arnold received a special commission directly from George Washington and led his own detachment, which joined the Quebec campaign. As Montgomery invaded Canada from New York, capturing Montreal and continuing down the St. Lawrence River toward the British stronghold at Quebec, Arnold led his men on an arduous two-month advance through the Maine wilderness.

Ultimately, both expeditions proved to be wasted effort. By the time both forces converged near Quebec, they were drastically reduced by sickness, hunger, and expiring enlistments. When they attacked the city in the midst of a snowstorm on December 31, the large British garrison repelled them with heavy losses. With Montgomery killed in combat, Arnold maintained a semblance of a siege with his few surviving men. Eventually the American forces wore out their welcome among French-speaking colonists, and the entire venture collapsed.

George Washington's military campaigns that winter were less colorful but had much more positive outcomes. Battered by the Battle of Bunker Hill, General Howe's forces struggled to recover, giving officers in the Continental Army time to focus on teaching basic skills and imposing discipline on their largely amateur troops. Washington lacked an experienced officer corps and adequately trained soldiers, but he did the best with what he had. He decided, in early March 1776, that his army was ready for a major test. Exercising a skillful set of maneuvers, he successfully captured Dorchester Heights, which like Bunker Hill and Breed's Hill overlooked Boston. He then shocked the British, his men rapidly installing artillery seized at Fort Ticonderoga and hidden behind portable fortifications. Facing a possible gun barrage, Howe opted to not attempt another costly uphill attack against defended positions. Instead, Howe ordered his men to evacuate Boston and retreat to the safety of Nova Scotia, Canada. Washington and his men watched from high ground, and on March 17, the Continental Army triumphantly left the city. At that point, no British occupying armies remained in the thirteen colonies.

George III Throws Down the Gauntlet

A Congress that could approve a document such as the Olive Branch Petition was clearly not yet ready to declare independence. Indeed, a major reason for the petition was to defend the Congress against accusations of disloyalty. The Adams cousins from volatile, radical Massachusetts continued to bide their time and avoided provoking their colleagues. Yet, the mood in America changed quickly in the months that followed. The experience of being at war, under attack by British soldiers supposedly sent to defend the colonies, had a profound impact upon the colonists. If George III felt they were behaving disloyally, the colonists themselves felt betrayed. The colonists also recoiled at the king's reaction to the Olive Branch Petition, which made a lasting impression. In fact, during the closing months of 1775, both king and Parliament added still further insults and injuries. In a speech to Parliament in October, George III charged that the colonial rebellion was "manifestly carried on for the purpose of establishing an independent empire." One last piece of punitive legislation remained as the Parliament in December enacted the American Prohibitory Act, which shut out the thirteen colonies to all legal commerce with the rest of the world and authorized the Royal Navy to seize not only American ships and their cargoes, but also those belonging to other nationalities caught trading with the colonies.

For white Southerners, the most serious provocation came at the hands of **Lord Dunmore**. Dunmore dissolved the House of Burgesses after that legislature condemned the Intolerable Acts. Nevertheless, Virginians, like colonists elsewhere, formed unsanctioned committees that claimed governmental authority in defiance of the Crown. Under orders from Lord Dartmouth, Dunmore tried to prevent elections for the Second Continental Congress from taking place, but this gesture put his life in danger. Dunmore declared that if any militia threatened him, he would "declare freedom to the slaves, and reduce the City of Williamsburg to ashes." He then fled to the safety of a Royal Naval frigate. In fact, Dunmore was himself a slave owner, but he placed military necessity ahead of his own interests. In May, he proposed to Dartmouth to "arm all my own Negroes and receive all others who come to me whom I shall declare free." Finally, in November 1775, Dunmore landed at Norfolk accompanied by two companies of British troops, affirmed his authority as the legal governor of Virginia, and offered freedom to slaves who "are able and willing to bear arms, they joining His Majesty's Troops as soon as may be, for the more speedily reducing the Colony to a proper sense of their duty."

For the Virginia planters now committed to the colonial resistance, Dunmore's proclamation, and the military campaign that followed, could hardly have been a deeper outrage or a graver threat. As in the days of the Stamp Act, as masters debated the defense of their liberties, slaves listened carefully and watched for opportunities for their own freedom. In fact, Dunmore's initial threats against Williamsburg were not his own idea. A group of local slaves had offered to "take up arms" against Williamsburg in the governor's defense. News of the British government's offer of freedom spread widely among excited Virginia slaves.

In the closing days of 1775, as Dunmore marched inland from Norfolk through Princess Anne County, crowds of escaped slaves, including many women and children, flocked to his standard. With hundreds of new volunteers, Dunmore's officers formed a new "Ethiopian Regiment." Their uniforms included sashes bearing the inscription "Liberty to Slaves." (A second, smaller regiment was composed of white volunteers.) The Virginia committee of safety sent a force of militiamen and a Continental Army regiment. In the first major battle of the war in the South, at the hamlet of Great Bridge, on December 9, Dunmore's regular troops and volunteers attacked but failed to overrun the patriot position. Falling back on Norfolk, they were soon forced to withdraw to Royal Navy ships in the harbor. Dunmore attempted to maintain the Ethiopian Regiment offshore, but smallpox swept through the crowded vessels. Ultimately, the surviving members of the regiment were assigned to scattered locations, including Bermuda, Florida, and British regular forces later occupying New York.

Throughout the colonies, slaves spread word about Dunmore, the "African Hero." While gathered in cities or isolated on their own estates, masters active in the patriot struggle lived in fear. Thomas Jeremiah, a free African-American fisherman and boat pilot in South Carolina, faced accusations in August 1775 of plotting a slave insurrection. Jeremiah supposedly conspired to guide Royal Naval vessels into Charles Town harbor so they could help the slave rebels. Jeremiah, who owned slaves himself, had grown rich and probably stood out to white slave owners because of his business success, which made a mockery of the theory of white supremacy upon which slavery rested. Despite flimsy evidence, a kangaroo court quickly convicted Jeremiah, who was hanged. Escape plots, fears of insurrection, and the threat of British forces together preoccupied white Southerners. Even in the North, with significant concentrations of slaves in port cities and a vastly larger proportion of free black residents, rumors of slave conspiracies terrified local elites. Yet, in the seaport cities where artisans actively involved in politics had fostered the resistance movement, free blacks were well represented in the artisanal communities. Many black militiamen fought courageously at Bunker Hill and Breed's Hill. When Washington, owner of a large number of slaves, arrived outside Boston, he found himself in the ironic position of commanding black troops. He feared the threat that black soldiers might pose to the future of slavery but also could not spare the African-American soldiers he had under his command. So, he tried to split the difference, adopting a policy later ratified by the Congress. He ended the recruitment of "Slaves and Vagabonds" into the Continental Army but would allow black soldiers already serving to remain in uniform. In some regiments, such as in Connecticut, slaves took advantage of an offer of freedom in return for military service from the colonial authorities. Many dropped the slave names imposed by their masters and took new last names like "Liberty" or "Freedman" or even "Washington" to celebrate their new personal independence.

Common Sense

A significant number of Americans had traveled a long philosophical distance from when they considered themselves loyal British subjects. Beginning in January 1776, copies of **Thomas Paine**'s pamphlet **Common Sense** began to circulate throughout the colonies. Over the year that followed, the pamphlet was reprinted no fewer than twenty-five times, with roughly half a million individual copies made. Paine was a virtually penniless Englishman fleeing to America from a failed career as a corset-maker and tax collector, but along with a letter of introduction from Franklin, he brought a style of written expression that was clear, sharp, elegant, and fearless. In Philadelphia, he found work as an editor, but he would make his mark as an author of one of the clearest arguments for the colonies' political independence.

With his skeptical, scientific mind and his uncompromising temperament, Paine saved no respect for sacred traditions in his blunt pamphlet. His complete lack of deference was breathtaking. "The royal brute of Great Britain" was no guardian of his subjects' liberties. England was corrupt, not as a result of recent missteps or individually bad government ministers, but because kings by their nature tended to be corrupt tyrants. Governments existed to serve the people, not the other way around, and the British regime could not meet that basic requirement. "A government of our own," he proclaimed, "is our natural right." British rule brought no practical benefits, recent British military attacks made reconciliation unthinkable, and independence was no more likely to lead to intervention by foreign powers or civil wars among the colonies. Paine was not only angry at injustice; his pamphlet offered a vision of an optimistic American future. In his scripture-quoting yet fundamentally secular way, Paine reimagined America, as had earlier Puritans, as a shining city on a hill, a light to the rest of humanity:

O! ye that love mankind! Ye that dare oppose not only the tyranny but the tyrant, stand forth! Every spot of the old world is overrun with oppression. Freedom hath been hunted round the Globe. Asia and Africa have long expelled her. Europe regards her like a stranger, and England hath given her warning to depart. O! receive the fugitive, and prepare in time an asylum for mankind.

Common Sense captured a growing public mood and helped to seal a permanent shift away from olive branches and petitions to the king to demands for a separate, new American nation.

Debating "Independency"

The streets of Philadelphia turned out to be predictably hot, dusty, and smelly as the summer of 1776 dragged on. This oppressive atmosphere even permeated the interiors of the city's grand brick buildings. In the Pennsylvania state house, in a stifling hall filled for a second consecutive summer by weary delegates from thirteen colonies, the windows had to be closed to keep out the biting horseflies.

Some hoped the Congress would launch not just a war of political independence but a more profound social revolution as well. In writing to her husband John in March of that year, **Abigail Adams** had playfully instructed him, as he and the rest of the Congress drafted the Declaration of Independence, to "remember the Ladies, and be more generous and favourable to them than your Ancestors. . . . If perticuliar care and attention is not paid to the Laidies we are determined to foment a Rebellion, and will not hold ourselves bound by any Laws in which we have no voice, or Representation." John's response betrayed mild indignation. America's revolution would in many ways be a conservative one, aimed at replacing one government ruled by rich elites with one headed by a different, local set of the privileged. Gender, racial and class inequality were not on the table in Philadelphia.

Some delegates still held out hope for reconciliation at the beginning of this summit, but those who advocated what they called "Independency" carried the day. The Second Continental Congress appointed a small committee in early June to draft a proposed declaration. Preferring to work alone, Thomas Jefferson of Virginia retreated to his boarding house, where he agonized over the document. Jefferson hated speaking in public but as a writer he soared, and he made a forceful but precise case for American independence with his pen. Taking his wording sometimes directly from the English philosopher John Locke, Jefferson's declaration argued that "life, liberty and the pursuit of happiness" were natural rights

Peter Buckminster: A Muslim Patriot in the American Revolution?

Even if paintings from the 1700s and 1800s depicting the American Revolutionary War portray the American army as an exclusively white force, slaves in the North often fought for the independence cause in return for the promise of freedom. Though it is almost completely forgotten today, some of those slaves seeking freedom were Muslims.

For instance, General Thomas Sumter in South Carolina employed a Muslim man named Yusuf Ben Ali as an aide. Although his religious beliefs are now a matter of debate among historians, a slave named Peter Salem, thought to be a Muslim, became one of the least famous heroes of the American Revolution.

Born around 1750 in Framingham, Massachusetts, Peter Buckminster began life as the human property of an army captain, Jeremiah Belknap. We know nothing of his childhood, but records show that his master sold Peter to Major Lawson Buckminster in 1775, just as the War for Independence was beginning in Lexington and Concord. Massachusetts authorities, fearing that armed blacks might rise up violently against slavery, had prohibited African Americans from serving in the colonial militia back in 1656. The need for soldiers in the war against the powerful British Army, however, led the Committee on Public Safety to allow free African Americans to serve in the militia. Committed to the patriot cause, Buckminster freed Peter so he could join the militia. Upon freedom, Peter dropped his slave name and changed his last name to "Salem," similar to the Arabic word "salam," which means "peace."

There are no records indicating what religion Salem embraced. Whites in the eighteenth century had little interest in recording the biographies of black men and women. He may have simply named himself after the Massachusetts town Salem. However, an expert on American Muslims in early American history, Amir Muhammad, points out that about 30 percent of slaves imported to the thirteen British colonies from Africa practiced Islam and argues that the Arabic origin of Salem's adopted last name provides an important clue as to his faith.

What is beyond dispute is Salem's war record. One of few black so-called "minutemen," Salem fought in the Revolutionary War's first two battles, at Lexington and Concord. He achieved fame as a marksman during fighting at Breed's Hill, during what later became known as the Battle of Bunker Hill. Reportedly, the man leading the Redcoat assault on the well-defended patriot position on the summit, Major John Pitcairn, had just shouted, "The day is ours," when Salem took aim and fired a fatal shot at him. As a reward for his role in the important but indecisive battle, Salem was later introduced to General George Washington.

Just as historians argue over whether Salem was a Muslim, they also are unsure if he is the black soldier depicted in one of the most famous paintings of a Revolutionary War battle, John Trumbull's "The Death of General Warren at the Battle of Bunker Hill." (Trumbull lived near the scene of the battle, interviewed soldiers present at the battle, and may have met Salem.)

Salem also fought at other battles that marked key turning points in the war, including the Battle of Saratoga, a major British defeat in 1777, and the Battle of Stony Point, another American victory also earned in New York. Salem did not receive his discharge until 1780, as the war neared its climax. After his military career, he built a cabin in Leicester, Massachusetts but could eke out only a meager living as a gardener and basket weaver. In spite of his service and his heroics, Salem died in a poorhouse back in Framingham August 16, 1816. His hometown, appreciating his role in the American crusade for independence, placed a memorial to him at the Framingham Old Burying Ground and in 1882 inaugurated the first of the annual "Peter Salem Day" celebrations held on June 17. In the early twenty-first century, when many political figures have declared that the United States is locked in a "war of civilizations" against Islam and in which the opening of mosques became controversial in several American cities, it is fascinating to consider that perhaps the most famous black soldier to battle for the country's independence may have regarded the Koran as his holy book.

possessed by all people and that governments that failed to protect those rights were no longer legitimate. The declaration listed alleged acts of tyranny committed by the British king and the Parliament: the closure of Boston Harbor after the Tea Party protest; the suspension of the right of trial by jury for cases involving smugglers; closing elected colonial assemblies; using foreign mercenaries to attack the colonists; and so on. Jefferson wrote that as a result of these violations of rights, the bonds between the British government and the colonies had been "dissolved."

After Jefferson's fellow committee members (John Adams and Benjamin Franklin) suggested some minor changes, the Congress received his draft on June 28 and proceeded to fiercely debate its contents for several days in the nearly airless room. Eventually, the Congress reduced

The "Regulator" Rebellion

A violent sideshow to the French and Indian War, the 1759-1761 Cherokee War in South Carolina's backcountry spawned crime and social chaos in its aftermath. A 1760s uprising there and in North Carolina, characterized by racism, the anger of poor and struggling whites against wealthy elites, and resentments over political disenfranchisement, followed the local war. These simultaneous rebellions, instigated by the so-called Regulator movement, in many ways foreshadowed the American Revolution of the 1770s.

Approximately 8,000 Cherokee lived near the Appalachian and Piedmont mountains on land stretching from Virginia to the Carolinas. Those Cherokee fought alongside the British and the North American colonists against the French and their indigenous allies.

Rather than being rewarded for their service, the Cherokee soon became targets of economically struggling newcomers who had arrived in the region from Scotland and Germany and who sought control of the Native American land. After months of small-scale violent encounters, indigenous warriors, fresh from battle against French forces, returned to Virginia only to be waylaid by these European immigrants in 1759.

Colonist militias massacred Native warriors, raped indigenous women, and kidnapped Indian leaders, provoking a full-fledged war that spread into North and South Carolina. By July 1761, the colonists had destroyed Cherokee crops, driving them to hunger, and vanquished them on the battlefield. The Cherokee had been forced off of much of their traditional land. But even though the colonizers had triumphed, the Carolina backcountry sank into violent lawlessness, the region convulsed by sexual assault, robbery, and murder.

The anarchy stemmed from a lack of organized government in the backwoods. The colonial assembly, and the nearest courts, jails, and organized law enforcement often were too distant to be effective because of the slow transportation of that time. In the mid- to late-1760s, when wealthy whites became targets of crime, the backcountry upper class formed vigilante groups. Middling to prosperous landowners and often slave masters, these so-called "Regulators" sought vengeance against those they saw as lower-class renegades.

The Regulators in South Carolina took out their frustration on the Scottish and German immigrants, lashing them and dragooning them into labor battalions. The South Carolina Assembly clearly sympathized with the Regulators, essentially deputizing them to act as law enforcement by late 1767.

However, the excesses of the Regulators led to a backlash, with another set of well-off growers forming a group called the "Moderators" who were opposed to the militias. Tensions escalated to the edge of armed conflict, with weapons-bearing Regulators and Moderators facing off in 1769 near the Saluda River in the western part of South Carolina. Only an intervention by the royal governor prevented more bloodshed, with a plan implemented to provide courts, sheriffs, and other instruments of law and order on the colony's troubled frontier.

Backwoods people lived in counties badly underrepresented in both the North and South Carolina assemblies and resented having little voice on matters like local taxes. A poll tax to fund the construction of a new government building in New Bern, sarcastically called "Tryon's Palace," in reference to royal governor William Tyron, was particularly unpopular with supporters of the Regulator movement in North Carolina.

The colonial government taxed less fertile land near the mountains at the same rate it taxed the well-irrigated, rich soils the wealthiest planters controlled in the coastal plains. In North Carolina, Regulators suspected that colonial elites were using government revenues to enrich themselves, their families, and their friends. Religious differences also stirred conflict. Religious dissenters such as Baptists and other new sects distrusted a colonial government dominated by members of the establishment Church of England, seen as too closely resembling the Catholic faith by many living in the backwoods.

In 1768, Regulators launched a revolt, refusing to pay taxes. Three years later, after a courthouse was seized and Regulators vandalized government documents, Tyron responded by dispatching a well-supplied militia to the backwoods. Tyron's troops overwhelmed an armed Regulator force at what became known as the "Battle of Alamance." Nine government troops died, prompting Tyron to convene a military court. Authorities eventually hanged six of the Regulators. Tyron crushed the rebellion, with many in the backwoods fleeing the colony to seek a safe refuge.

The two Regulator revolts make clear that deep cleavages between whites and indigenous people, between rich and poor, and among different faiths tore at the fabric of American colonial society even as a deeper conflict between the colonists and the English homeland loomed on the horizon. These divisions would resurface with the pitched battles between colonists supporting and opposing independence in the American Revolution later in the 1770s.

the length of the Declaration by one-fourth, eliminating Jefferson's more controversial passages condemning King George III for encouraging the transatlantic slave trade. Even though Jefferson himself owned slaves, he frequently attacked the institution of slavery as immoral: "[H]e [the king] has waged cruel war against human nature itself, violating its most sacred rights of life & liberty in the persons of a distant people, who never offended him, captivating and carrying them into slavery in another hemisphere, or to incur miserable death in their transportation thither . . . determined to keep a market where MEN should be bought and sold." Jefferson then condemned the king for "suppressing every legislative attempt to prohibit or to restrain this execrable commerce . . ." Southern members of the Continental Congress, particularly from South Carolina and Georgia, disdained the argument that slavery was in any way "execrable" and insisted on deletion of this passage. Meanwhile, some Congressmen did not support slavery per se, but feared Jefferson's words would undermine support for independence on the part of both southern slave owners and New England merchants profiting from the slave trade. Some acknowledged the contradiction of proclaiming the universal right to liberty while holding human beings as property but decided the time to push for abolition of slavery had not arrived and that political independence from Great Britain remained the more important cause. However, they did not remove a reference to Lord Dunmore's offer of freedom to slaves who escaped from their masters and served in the British military or of the recent slave revolt supposedly plotted by Thomas Jeremiah. The final draft of the Declaration condemned the king for "inciting treasonable insurrections of our fellow citizens" and exciting "domestic insurrections among us." Regardless of the arguments it engendered about slavery, the Declaration itself had been improved in many ways from Jefferson's original draft.

After four intense days, delegates came to a consensus on the central issue—"that these United Colonies are, and of right ought to be, Free and Independent States." The delegates voted to approve the Declaration of Independence on July 2, 1776. In a letter to his wife Abigail in Massachusetts, Adams confidently predicted that day, July 2, would become a national holiday, "celebrated, by succeeding Generations, as the Great anniversary Festival. . . . It ought to be solemnized with Pomp and Parade, with Shows, Games, Sports, Guns, Bells, Bonfires and Illuminations from one End of this Continent to the other from this Time forward forever more." The Congress, however, quibbled about wording for another two days before ratifying a final draft on July 4 and sending the text to a printer. The die was cast. The "American Revolution" would not uproot society, but it would become one

of those rare points at which startling new possibilities existed, and the range of possible outcomes stretched the limits of human imagination.

CREATING AMERICANS

Colonial newspapers did not begin to use the term "American" until the French and Indian War (1754-1763). During that conflict, leaders like Benjamin Franklin bemoaned how poorly the colonies cooperated with each other and would urge his peers to form a confederacy like that established by the Iroquois nation in New York. In September 1762, when Bostonians learned of the French surrender in the French and Indian War, a wild street party broke out with drunken revelers drinking toasts to King George III and celebrating the joys of being British, which to them meant being the freest people on Earth. It was a short distance geographically from that Boston scene to Lexington Green thirteen years later, but for many, a psychological chasm separated the two events. In Massachusetts and Virginia, in South Carolina and in New Hampshire, commoner and elite alike contemplated a life not as Englishmen. Their new identities remained to be determined.

Only about 40 percent of Americans supported independence while about 20 percent considered themselves British loyalists. The remainder sat nervously in the middle, not opposed to independence but still hopeful for reconciliation with the throne. Regardless, the pro-independence forces won a rhetorical war. Those rebelling against the British government called themselves the "Patriots," thus making those loyal to the home country traitors or worse. In many ways, the American Revolution became a civil war, with the Patriots often torturing their opponents, whom they smeared as "Tories." Many Tories suffered the agonies of tarring and feathering. In these ritual punishments, "The offender was stripped to the waist, sometimes shorn, and daubed with hot tar and pitch," wrote historian Ann Fairfax Withington in her book *Towards a More Perfect Union: Virtue and the Formation of the American Republic*. "Then a pillow of goose feathers (or sometimes turkey or buzzard feathers, which had a stronger smell) was emptied over him, and he was carted through town . . ."

One Tory was made to walk from New Milford, Connecticut, to Litchfield, about twenty miles, carrying one of his own geese the whole way. He was then tarred, made to pluck his own goose, feathered, drummed out of town, and forced to kneel down and thank the crowd for its leniency . . . [A tax collector in Pennsylvania was led to a duck hole] . . . where he was dunked for some time.

Finally they tied him up with [a] grapevine and forced him . . . to praise the Americans as a generous, spirited, and much injured people.

No punishment for opposition to the Patriot cause was more creative or grotesque than that suffered by Jesse Dunbar of Halifax, Massachusetts. Dunbar had bought cattle from men who had accepted royal government appointments and, thus to some, was a traitor. They sewed him in the carcass of an ox that had just been slaughtered and skinned, and carried him in a cart that shook and rattled on a very bumpy four-mile ride. The mob then demanded he pay a dollar to the people of Kingston. He was carted four more miles to Duxbury where he was made to pay another dollar in ransom. Finally, he reached the house of one of the royal appointees, where he was made to pay one last dollar and was dumped on the roadside. In other cases, Patriots sought to humiliate Tories by chaining them to slaves, implying that they were slaves to the king in the way African Americans were the property of whites. Patriots celebrated liberty, but during the war, there would be little tolerance for pro-British dissent.

Protestants formed an overwhelming majority in the new American nation, but the Revolutionary War still opened up religious fissures. On Guy Fawkes Day on November 5, 1775, George Washington ordered his soldiers not to engage in "the ridiculous and childish custom of burning the Effigy of the Pope." Washington feared that such anti-Catholic merriment would alienate potential allies in the former French colony in Quebec. Even though Catholics were a tiny minority in Revolutionary America (around 35,000 out of the total of just under 4 million), Washington hoped that toleration would win this group over to the Revolutionary cause, particularly in states where Catholics were more numerous, such as Maryland. "At such a juncture, and in such circumstances, to be insulting their Religion, is so monstrous, as not to be suffered or excused," Washington wrote to his officers. Nevertheless, only three of the thirteen colonies granted the right to vote to Catholics, and only in North and South Carolina and Rhode Island could Catholics hold public office. The law banned the opening of Catholic schools everywhere but Pennsylvania, and Virginia law stipulated that priests who entered its borders were subject to arrest. The Patriots celebrated freedom of conscience, but they did not yet embrace religious diversity.

The American Revolution would reveal not only the deep divisions between Tories and Patriots, and Protestants and Catholics, but also blacks and whites. If whites thought they fought for freedom by resisting the Crown, many African Americans fought for their freedom by accepting British offers of emancipation in return for service in the royal army. Approximately 50 percent of the slaves in Georgia and 25 percent in South Carolina enlisted with the British. The issue of slavery would not be resolved until after the Civil War, with the ratification of the Thirteenth Amendment abolishing involuntary servitude in 1865. African Americans would be given the right to vote during Reconstruction, but that right for many blacks would quickly be stolen and not returned for another hundred years, until the Voting Rights Act of 1965. The Patriots boldly faced off the king and the Royal Army, but they ducked the issue of slavery and black rights, leaving another generation to fight a war over the issue—a war that would claim about 750,000 lives according to current estimates.

A deep divide separated men and women as well. Women remained without property rights. Any property they brought into a marriage passed to the ownership of their husbands. Laws barred women from seeking divorce even from abusive husbands, and, in the rare cases where divorces were granted (an action that usually required the approval of the state legislature), men almost always gained custody of the children. The Patriot faction answered to the need of merchants and farmers but ignored the pleas of women like Abigail Adams.

The United States in many ways was an accidental nation, the product of a long series of British mistakes. Even though the Parliament was less than representative in England itself, not granting the colonists in North America representation in that body proved to be a fatal mistake. Successive British governments had boxed themselves in, facing riots from the masses in England who already bore a heavy cost for the greatly expanded empire. Unable to raise taxes at home, the British had no choice but to shift some of the burden to the Americans. However, the Parliament proved unwilling to grant representation to the colonies, thus delegitimizing any taxes Parliament would impose, even if the funds went toward the colonies' defense.

Foolish measures by the British government to ensure compliance with the new taxes, like requiring accused tax dodgers to face trial in military courts where they would be denied their accustomed right to a trial by jury, only alienated the colonists further. When the British shut down uncooperative elected assemblies that protested the taxes, as happened in New York, it only granted further credence to the extremists like Samuel Adams who argued that the colonists were treated like second-class citizens and denied basic freedoms guaranteed by Britain's unwritten constitution. As hypocritical as the complaint was when voiced by white Americans, many thought it was no exaggeration that the colonists were being "enslaved" by the Crown.

The colonists knew what they opposed. Across the colonies, the so-called Patriots rose up against British taxes and British military occupation. On the other hand, it was not always altogether clear for what larger purpose the colonists were pledging "their lives, their liberties, and their sacred honor," to quote the Declaration of Independence. The new nation waging a War of Independence from Great Britain between 1775 and 1783 called itself the "United States," but these former colonies were united in name only. Even militarily, the states would frequently not cooperate, with several refusing to contribute a fair share of soldiers or the tax money requested by the Continental Congress needed to supply Washington's army. Defining what was meant by the word "American" and who constituted "the people" who supposedly held sovereignty in the new republic, remained a work in progress.

Chronology

1764 Parliament enacts the Sugar Act.
Parliament enacts the Currency Act.

1765 Parliament enacts the Stamp Act.
Virginia Resolves protest the Stamp Act.
Stamp Act Congress convenes in New York City.
Sons of Liberty protest against British taxes.

1766 Parliament repeals the Stamp Act and
passes the Declaratory Act.

1767 Parliament enacts the Townshend Acts.
Massachusetts Circular Letter stirs opposition
to the Townshend Acts.

1770 The "Boston Massacre" takes place.
Parliament repeals most of the Townshend Acts.

1772 *H.M.S. Gaspée* burned.

1773 Parliament implements the Tea Act.
The "Boston Tea Party" takes place.

1774 Parliament passes the "Intolerable Acts."
Parliament passes the Quebec Act.
Lord Dunmore dissolves the Virginia legislature.
The First Continental Congress convenes.

1775 Violence at Lexington and Concord.
Second Continental Congress convenes,
creates the Continental Army, and appoints
George Washington to be its commander.
The Battle of Bunker Hill takes place.
George III rejects the Olive Branch Petition.
Parliament passes the Prohibitory Act.
Lord Dunmore proclaims freedom for
defecting slaves.
Americans lose the Battle of Quebec.

1776 *Common Sense* published.
The British withdraw from Boston.
The Second Continental Congress approves
the Declaration of Independence.

SUGGESTED READINGS

Fred Anderson, *Crucible of War: The Seven Years' War and the Fate of Empire in British North America, 1754-1766* (2000).

Bernard Bailyn, *The Ideological Origins of the American Revolution* (1967).

___, *The Ordeal of Thomas Hutchinson* (1976).

Colin Bonwick, *The American Revolution* (1991).

___, *English Radicals and the American Revolution* (2011).

Steven Brumwell. *Redcoats: The British Soldier and the War in the Americas, 1755-1763* (2002).

Edward Countryman, *The American Revolution* (1985).

Marc Egnal, *A Mighty Empire: The Origins of the American Revolution* (1988).

Herbert Gutman, et al, *Who Built America?: Working People & The Nation's Economy, Politics, Culture & Society, Volume I: From Conquest and Colonization Through Reconstruction and the Great Uprising of 1877* (1989).

J. William Harris, *The Hanging of Thomas Jeremiah: A Free Black Man's Encounter With Liberty* (2011).

Merrill Jensen, *The Founding of a Nation: A History of the American Revolution, 1763-1776* (1968).

Pauline Maier, *From Resistance to Revolution: Colonial Radicals and the Development of the American Opposition to Britain, 1765-1776* (1972).

___, *American Scripture: Making the Declaration of Independence* (1997).

Edmund S. Morgan, *Birth of the Republic, 1763-1789* (1956).

___, *Inventing the People: The Rise of Popular Sovereignty in England and America* (1988).

Gary B. Nash, *The Urban Crucible: Social Change, Political Consciousness and the Origins of the American Revolution* (1979).

Thomas Paine, *Common Sense* (1776).

William Randolph Ryan, *The World of Thomas Jeremiah: Charles Town on the Eve of the American Revolution* (2012).

Sharon Salinger, *"To Serve Well and Faithfully": Labor and Indentured Servants in Pennsylvania, 1682-1800* (1987).

Paul Spickard, *Almost All Aliens: Race and Colonialism in American History and Identity* (2007).

Ann Fairfax Withington, *Toward a More Perfect Union: Virtue and the Formation of American Republics* (1991).

Gordon S. Wood, *The Radicalism of the American Revolution* (1991).

Review Questions

1. What motivated the British to pass such laws as the Sugar Act, the Stamp Act, and the Townshend Revenue Act? How did these laws mark a break from the traditional policy of salutary neglect?

2. Why were the new British taxation laws so controversial in the colonies? What arguments did men like Patrick Henry make against such legislation, and what was the response of the British government to these criticisms?

3. How did the implementation of the Tea Act lead to the "Boston Tea Party"? What was the reaction to that event in England?

4. How does the career of John Dickinson reveal the uncertainty Americans felt toward the British government and the possibility of revolution during the 1770s?

5. When do you think was the "point of no return" when the revolution became all but inevitable?

Glossary of Important People and Concepts

Abigail Adams
John Adams
Samuel Adams
Benedict Arnold
Boston Massacre
Boston Tea Party
Battle of Bunker Hill
Common Sense
John Dickinson
Lord Dunmore
George III
George Grenville
Patrick Henry
"Intolerable Acts" (Coercive Acts)
Lexington and Concord
Olive Branch Petition
James Otis, Jr.
Thomas Paine
Second Continental Congress
Sons of Liberty
Stamp Act
Sugar Act
Tea Act
Townshend Revenue Act
George Washington

George Washington and the Marquis de Lafayette at Valley Forge

Chapter Six

THE UNITED STATES AND THE AGE OF REVOLUTION

A *"mini ice age"* had gripped the Earth by the time of the American Revolution. This period of unusually cold weather began roughly in the mid-1300s and lasted until the mid-1800s. The global drop in temperatures was one reason that the Delaware River had frozen before General George Washington's famous crossing the night of December 25-26 and his attack on Hessian mercenaries stationed in Trenton. The plummet in temperatures accounted for the harsh weather that tormented Washington's troops at the Valley Forge encampment in Pennsylvania from December 19, 1777 until June 19, 1778.

Many remember Valley Forge as an American low point during the War for Independence. Marching soldiers lacking shoes left behind bloody footprints in the snow. The army's horses starved. Soldiers' meals, for days at a time, consisted of nothing but "firecake," an untasty, thin bread made mostly of water mixed with tiny amounts of flour.

The United States Congress operated under the Articles of Confederation, a document that did not give the legislature the power to tax, meaning the federal government constantly scrambled for money to fund its army. Members of Congress told Washington to simply take what he needed from local residents by force if he had to, but Washington knew this could spell disaster for the Revolution. Washington hoped he could maintain the support of the people by treating them fairly.

The villages near the city of Philadelphia had filled with refugees, so Washington also declined to seize control of buildings to house his soldiers, who were forced upon arrival to construct a series of huts 14 feet wide by 16 feet long by 6.5 feet tall. Until they completed construction, the men lived in tents as the ice on the ground alternately melted and froze and kept their threadbare uniforms damp in the bitter winds. Washington himself, in an expression of sympathy, remained outdoors as well and slept in his own tent.

Washington worried about the poor training of his Continental Army, its lack of discipline when marching in formation, the frequency with which soldiers disobeyed orders, and the high desertion rate. Volunteer militias not part of Washington's professional army in particular drove the general to distraction. As Washington and his forces struggled to discipline and adequately train their men, the militias undermined much of their efforts.

In Paris, American ambassador Benjamin Franklin believed he had found a solution to the Continental Army's lack of professionalism in the person of **Friederich Wilhelm Ludolf Gerhard Augustin von Steuben**. The Prussian, a self-proclaimed German nobleman, had little working knowledge of English, but with a letter of introduction from Franklin, he made a big impression. In fact, "Baron von Steuben" was a bit of a con artist and had no title but was an impoverished Prussian army veteran and soldier of fortune who had served in the Seven Years' War (1754-1761) in Europe during which Russian troops took him prisoner. He later served in the army of Prussian King Frederick II, reaching the rank of captain. He then served in the military of the prince of Hohenzollern-Hechingen.

Franklin heard stories about von Steuben's military skills. For his part, the Prussian falsely claimed not only that he was a baron but also that he was a general. Nevertheless, von Steuben possessed a genuine mastery of advanced methods of drill and training. Franklin begged the Continental Congress to offer von Steuben a position on the army's general staff. Franklin explained to von Steuben that the Americans would be unable to grant him a commission as a top officer or to *even pay him a salary, which von Steuben accepted. However, when Franklin informed him that the cash-strapped Congress would not even be able to pay for his transportation to the United States, von Steuben declined the offer.*

Von Steuben planned to work for another German prince in Baden when a letter accusing him of homosexual behavior while in the service of Frederick II was placed in the hands of the prince of Hohenzollern-Hechingen. The relationship supposedly took place while von Steuben served in the Prussian military. This would be the first of many times such accusations dogged him. This charge represented a possible death sentence in Europe at the time. Even if von Steuben never faced criminal prosecution, the scandal would ruin his military career on the continent. To avoid humiliation, von Steuben left for America.

Sensitive about his army's shortcomings though unable to solve many of them, Washington accepted the Baron at face value and appointed him as acting inspector general. The German translator who had been provided him was ignorant of military terminology, so von Steuben had to speak in French and rely on men like Washington's chief of staff Alexander Hamilton to relay the messages. Von Steuben didn't like what he saw when he watched the troops drill. Von Steuben immediately began authoring the first American army drill book, writing each chapter in French, and letting subordinate officers skilled in that language translate and hand-copy the text into English.

Von Steuben quickly earned the affection of his troops. He insisted on leading drills himself, memorizing the English terms such as "fix bayonets" and "charge." The troops saw von Steuben as one of them in spite of the language barrier. When troops made mistakes, he peppered his rants with one of the few English words he knew, "goddamn," and asked his translators to transmit his other more colorful curse words in English. His men came to love him because they saw him as an officer who could lead them to victory.

Within weeks, the troops were all following the Baron's precise instructions. Soon discipline and morale were improving as well. New recruits arrived during the spring, and news of the French alliance, arriving in May, provided further encouragement. Money from the French finally made it possible to pay von Steuben a salary. The Continental Army that faced the next year's campaign was much improved.

The "Baron" became a bona fide major general and also wrote a comprehensive set of training instructions and standard regulations, which was published by Congress in 1779 and served as the U.S. Army's official manual until 1812. Von Steuben's talents probably saved the American struggle for independence, but this did not lead to an acceptance of gays in the military. Just sixteen days after von Steuben's arrival, the army dismissed Lieutenant Gotthold Frederick Enslin for homosexual conduct after a military court found him guilty of sodomy and perjury. As Enslin stood in front of a formation of drummers, his sword was broken in half over his head as the drummers banged out a slow beat and his signs of rank were torn from his uniform. It could have been much worse for Enslin. Military regulations allowed soldiers convicted of sodomy to be imprisoned or hanged. In the same era, Virginia state law called for those convicted of sodomy to be executed, although Thomas Jefferson had proposed reducing the penalty to castration.*

Von Steuben retired to a farm in upstate New York, living off a military pension. He wrote a proposal for a military academy that led to the establishment of West Point in 1802. In Washington, D.C., a monument to his service stands across from the White House in Lafayette Square. A fort in Ohio and the town of Steubenville are also named in his honor.

THE BALANCE SHEET: BRITISH AND AMERICAN STRENGTHS AND WEAKNESSES

Before he signed the Declaration of Independence as the Second Continental Congress wrapped up its business in July of 1776, Ben Franklin, famous for his wit, engaged in a grim bit of literal gallows humor. Urging his Revolutionary comrades to stay united, Franklin said, "We must, indeed, all hang together, or most assuredly we shall all hang separately."

The prospect that the Americans might lose the Revolutionary War to Great Britain, and that the leaders of the revolt like Franklin, John Adams and George Washington might soon be swinging from a rope for treason against King George III must have seemed like a realistic possibility as the momentous year 1776 drew to a close. When Washington assumed command of the Continental Army in the summer of 1775, there must have been times when he questioned his sanity. The British advantages seemed overwhelming.

The British had built a world empire over the past century, repeatedly defeating European powerhouses like France and Spain. They controlled Canada and islands in the Caribbean, and held outposts in West Africa, India and South America. The British enjoyed a 2-1 population advantage over the Americans, with more than 8 million living in England, Scotland and Wales compared to just under 4 million in the thirteen American colonies. The British had an existing professional army.

However, in spite of having a larger overall population, the British never turned that into a military manpower advantage. Poor and working class people held military careers in low esteem and were not eager to sign up for a war against their cousins in America. At the start of the

Revolutionary War, the British standing army was small, and it fell behind in its recruiting goals. In one three-month period during the war, only 200 British citizens enlisted in the armed forces. "The ardor of this nation in this cause has not risen to the pitch one could wish," **Lord Frederick North**, the head of the British cabinet, said following the battles of Lexington and Concord.

The British government began hiring mercenaries—paid soldiers not part of the regular British army, especially from six German states whose princes received compensation for use of their soldiers. (The Prince of Brunswick, for example, got seven pounds for every soldier provided and another seven pounds for each one who died in service.) The largest group, the "**Hessians**," came from Hesse-Kassel. The princes profited from the arrangement, but the soldiers themselves lacked motivation. The 30,000 German mercenaries constituted about one-third of the total British forces during the Revolution. Of these, 12,000 did not survive and 5,000 deserted their posts in order to live permanently in America. The British use of such a large number of hired guns probably backfired, underscoring the feeling of Americans that the British themselves had become an invading foreign force rather than countrymen. Eventually the British government built its regular army to full, wartime size, fielding 90,000 regulars and mercenaries, but after a while the American armed forces reached a similar size.

The growing empire, connected and maintained by the most powerful navy on Earth, left the British rich in resources. In spite of their debts from previous imperial wars, the British also had one of the wealthiest and perhaps the most sophisticated banking system in the world. They had an established, strong currency. The Industrial Revolution had already started in England, and British factories made the Empire's soldiers some of the best equipped in the world. The officer corps of the British Army and Navy had excellent training and extensive wartime experience.

The British also had a strong central government, which could have allowed for a clear chain of command and efficient decision-making. However, the government was financially strapped, and unfortunately for Great Britain, mediocrities filled the nation's leadership positions. When he ascended to the throne in 1760, George III sought to assert greater royal power than his predecessor on the throne, his grandfather George II. Hampering his efforts, George suffered a major disability as the result of a blood disease, porphyria, which caused fits that his doctors interpreted as madness. At times George would be bound in a straitjacket and tied to a chair so he wouldn't be injured during his ravings. Some report that George suffered an early bout of this disease during the controversy

over the Stamp Act in 1765, though he would mainly be afflicted with bouts of irrationality and delusions in his fifties, after the Revolutionary War ended. Doctors today think that medicines George took, which contained high levels of arsenic, may have triggered the porphyria, which usually doesn't affect behavior in men.

George resented strong personalities who challenged his authority, thus he appointed to the government's key ministries less talented men who paid him deference. Hence, Lord North reigned as prime minister from 1770 to 1782, during the critical final five years before the American Revolution and during the entire combat phase of that war. Throughout his tenure, North repeatedly begged King George to relieve him of his duties. North knew he was in over his head. In one letter he wrote to the monarch, he argued that the first minister should be "a man of great abilities, who can choose decisively and carry his determination authoritatively into execution . . . and be capable of forming wise plans and of combing and connecting the whole force and operations of government . . . I am not that man."

Lethargic in temperament, North had developed a habit of falling asleep during debates while he served in Parliament. Fat and thick-tongued, North bore an unfortunate resemblance to George III, which led to jokes that he was the king's illegitimate son. Though he received a quality education at Eton and Oxford University, had traveled and achieved fluency not just in French, German and Italian, but also classic Greek and Latin, and had a sense of humor, North had a hard time asserting himself in the cabinet and was plagued by self-doubts. He had urged King George to avoid war with the Americans if at all possible. Even as the Parliament debated sending three regiments across the Atlantic to supplement General Thomas Gage's force in New England, North proposed what he called the Conciliatory Proposition, which would have exempted any colony from taxation provided it paid for its own expenses for governance and defense at amounts the Parliament and the King approved. The Parliament rejected the proposed compromise, and North, out of unwavering loyalty, backed his king's decision to declare the colonies in a state of rebellion and to respond militarily. Charles James Fox, who served with him in the cabinet, described him as lacking an air of authority. He was "far from leading the opinions of the other ministers that he seldom gave his own and generally slept the greater part of the time he was with them."

Another key player in the British government, George Germain, the secretary of state for the American Department, had been court-martialed and kicked out of the military during the Seven Years' War when he refused to follow the orders of a superior officer he personally disliked in the Battle of Minden in 1759 in modern-day Germany. Germain would be in charge of promoting and demoting generals and managing logistics, and helped form the British government's war plans. He reinforced North in some of his worst miscalculations, including that Britain could win the war by the conventional means that had brought victory previously against European powers. Germain also poorly communicated his intentions to officers, which would play a major role in the decisive British loss at the Battle of Yorktown in 1781.

Perhaps the most serious British shortcoming in the war was simple overconfidence. The British had defeated several vastly richer and more militarily powerful European rivals like France, the Netherlands, and Spain in the past century, and the British military and government never took George Washington's Continental Army seriously. The British military command had been unimpressed with the performance of the American militias in the French and Indian War and had not been particularly awed by George Washington's performance as an officer in that conflict. Unable to conceive that the Americans could win the Revolution, the British never fully committed their potentially vast resources to the war.

While the Americans had gifted leaders like **George Washington**, John Adams and Benjamin Franklin, they faced their own extensive challenges. The white American population was thinly stretched along the Eastern seaboard, extending deeply inland, where they faced a threat not only from the vast British military forces, but also from hostile Indian nations who had seen land confiscated and their peoples slaughtered for almost two centuries by the white conquerors. About 20 percent of the white colonists opposed the Revolution, and whites always had to worry, particularly in the South, about the potential revolt of 600,000 abused and exploited slaves, many of whom had already signed up with the British armed forces in exchange for emancipation. The American military was improvised. The Americans had no navy. The Americans had no banking system to fund the war or even a currency. Gold and silver were in short supply in the thirteen would-be independent states. The United States was still overwhelmingly a rural nation, with a microscopic manufacturing base to arm its troops compared to the British juggernaut.

On top of all this, the Americans labored under one of the weakest central governments ever devised by humanity. The American government had no chief executive. The Continental Congress made military decisions by committee. Given no power to tax directly, the Congress could only plead with each state to contribute a proportionate share of the cost and military manpower. The states, however, often functioned like thirteen separate republics. Each state had its own financial hardships and was reluctant to send desperately needed funds to the Congress. States also worried about the safety of their own borders and often put local needs ahead of the needs of the embryonic nation. In Vermont, Ethan Allen and his Green Mountain Boys militia ostensibly fought for the American cause, but they were embroiled in a secessionist struggle with New York and during the Revolution secretly negotiated with the British government about the possibility of becoming a separate province of the Empire.

On the plus side of the ledger, the Americans possessed one powerful psychological advantage. The war would be fought on their turf, on familiar terrain. Already deeply in debt, the British would spend a fortune transporting troops and supplies across the Atlantic and from battlefield to battlefield. British soldiers found themselves mostly surrounded by unfriendly locals who gave emotional and material support, and military intelligence, to the American troops. Communications with the British government were slow, with transatlantic voyages taking six or more weeks. Sometimes, months elapsed before officers in the field received orders from the government. American soldiers likely were more motivated throughout the war, because the British threatened their farms and homes. They also saw themselves fighting for political independence and liberty, which probably meant more to them than maintaining an Empire meant to the so-called "Redcoats." Finally, British victory depended on holding large swaths of American territory. The British lost political control of an area the moment they left. Fighting at home, George Washington and other American commanders could afford to avoid major direct battles with the British, striking only when an advantage arose, and then disappearing into the vast American forests. This led to a long war, with mounting costs and casualties ultimately sapping the British will to fight.

DISASTER, RETREAT, AND RECOVERY

New York City Falls to the British

The Revolutionary War, nevertheless, started out badly. "These are the times that try men's souls," wrote Thomas Paine, in an essay called appropriately *The American Crisis*, printed in Philadelphia on December 19, 1776. "The summer soldier and the sunshine patriot will, in this crisis, shrink from the service of his country; but he that stands it NOW, deserves the love and thanks of man and woman." Paine scribbled out his ringing sentences at one of the grimmest junctures in the war. Just months earlier the British had captured New York City, and it appeared that General Washington was on the run.

Following the withdrawal of British troops from Boston in the spring of 1776, Washington relocated his 19,000-man force to New York City. He knew New York would be a major objective for the British General **William Howe**. The British hoped to put a quick end to the American rebellion that had begun in Lexington and Concord, Massachusetts, on April 19 of the previous year by cutting off the colonies from trade with the outside world. They planned to do this by occupying important port cities like New York. Once they strangled the United States economically, overwhelming Washington's disorganized and poorly trained forces would—theoretically—be easy. Washington felt he had no choice but to make a defensive stand in New York, despite being outnumbered on land and sea. He worried about the general public who might interpret the loss of such a major city as a dangerous blow. Yet Washington was hampered by illness among his soldiers and by faulty intelligence. Unable to predict where Howe would strike, he divided his already smaller force, sending half to fortifications in Brooklyn Heights and the other half to **Long Island**. Washington hoped to re-create the conditions that led to numerous British casualties when the Redcoats attempted to scramble up Bunker Hill while facing murderous American fire.

Even as the Continental Congress put the finishing touches on the Declaration of Independence in Philadelphia on July 2, British General William Howe landed an invading force that eventually numbered 30,000 British regulars and hired guns from Germany at Staten Island. As was his custom, Howe waited before his attack. Finally, on August 27, Hessians faked a major frontal assault while Howe's main force bypassed the Heights through an unguarded, wooded Jamaica Pass and attacked the Americans from the left and the rear. Fearing they were

Thomas Paine's essays on freedom rallied tens of thousands to the cause of American independence.

surrounded, the Americans panicked. Washington uncharacteristically lost control and began beating officers and common soldiers who ran too near to him with his riding crop. He undertook a Herculean effort to restore order as his forces withdrew across the East River to Manhattan. For the first of many times in his career, Washington got a break. The always-lumbering Howe failed to pursue Washington's men, or to cut off their path of retreat with his Navy fleet (commanded by his brother Richard Howe) when they were most vulnerable, letting the Continental Army live to fight another day.

Howe had reasons not to take up the chase. "In common with his governmental superiors overseas, Howe believed that the rebellion had been fomented by a few desperate men, who had terrorized the American majority, which still loved their sovereign," Washington biographer James Thomas Flexner wrote. Howe hoped his military victories would convince that silent majority to abandon the rebels and reassert the loyalty of the colonies to the king. In fact, during the struggle in New York, secret negotiations had taken place with representatives of the Continental Congress and representatives of the British government, but the talks failed because the Americans insisted on recognition of their political independence. There would be no easy way out of the struggle for either side.

As the British took control of most of New York City, a devastating fire, most likely from accidental causes, raged the night of September 21. High winds and dry weather fed the flames. The blaze obliterated up to a fourth of the city. Both the British and the Americans accused each other of deliberately starting the inferno. The fire forced British troops to quarter themselves in private homes, which caused resentment, especially when **Tories**—Americans loyal to Great Britain—began to pour into the city, which would remain partly in ruins and would suffer from poor sanitation for the rest of the war. New York was a port city that suffered economically from the colonies' loss of trade with Britain. In a sign of how badly divided the city was on whether to support the war, when the Howe brothers offered amnesty to New Yorkers who would lay down their arms and swear allegiance, thousands took up the offer.

Howe again waited, this time until November 16, when he finally forced the rest of Washington's men out of Manhattan but for two encampments, Fort Washington on the highest point in Manhattan overlooking the Hudson River and Fort Lee on the New Jersey side of the waterway. Howe crushed the 3,000-man force in northern Manhattan, attacking the fortress from three sides. He paid for this victory dearly, however, with the loss of almost 500 men, though a much heavier cost

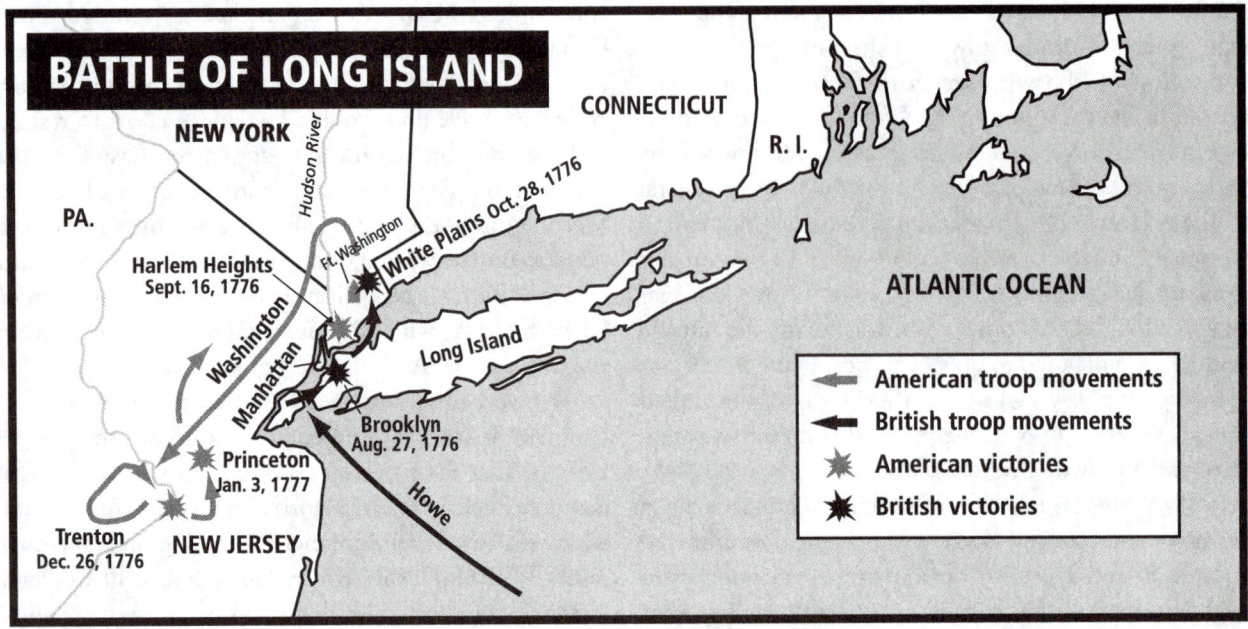

BATTLE OF LONG ISLAND

NEW YORK

CONNECTICUT

R. I.

Hudson River

PA.

Ft. Washington

Harlem Heights
Sept. 16, 1776

White Plains Oct. 28, 1776

ATLANTIC OCEAN

Washington

Long Island

Manhattan

Brooklyn
Aug. 27, 1776

Princeton
Jan. 3, 1777

Howe

Trenton
Dec. 26, 1776

NEW JERSEY

American troop movements
British troop movements
American victories
British victories

Map 6.1 Battle of Long Island and Washington's Retreat from New York

awaited the Americans. Resentful soldiers killed some Americans who surrendered to the British, while others were packed onto prison ships in New York harbor where more than 11,000 imprisoned soldiers and civilians died in horrific squalor during the war. Washington himself, from the New Jersey side of the river, watched helplessly. Self-control was everything to him, even though at times he struggled to keep his temper in check. But now, for once, he lost his composure completely and as one of his aides later admitted "wept, with the tenderness of a child."

A Surprise Comeback: The Attack on Trenton

To many observers, the loss of New York City looked like a grave defeat for the colonial rebels, but Washington soon began to implement his primary strategy: prolonging the conflict. While avoiding direct confrontations with larger and superior British forces, he would instead attack smaller enemy contingents when the opportunity presented itself and gradually reduce England's desire to continue. Washington's army slipped across the Hudson River into the woods of New Jersey, eventually crossing the Delaware River into Pennsylvania. One of General William Howe's chief subordinates, **Lord Charles Cornwallis**, crossed the Hudson with some 5,000 British and Hessian troops and maintained the pursuit. As New Jersey fell under British control, Patriots fled, Loyalists re-emerged, and many switched sides. Richard Stockton, a New Jersey delegate to Congress and a signer of the Declaration of Independence, was captured by a Loyalist band, imprisoned in New York, and persuaded to pledge his allegiance to the King as a condition of amnesty.

Meanwhile, Washington's still mostly green, untested army shrank with each mile it marched, men deserting because of the miserably cold weather and poor morale or leaving once their enlistment period ended. On December 2, 1776, as Washington's remaining units began arriving at the Delaware River crossing at Trenton, they numbered little more than 3,000 men. Pennsylvania militiamen arriving to help the army across the river were shocked to find the men of the Continental Army staggering onward, covered in sores and clothed in tattered rags.

When the British and Hessians arrived in Trenton on December 8, the American forces in Philadelphia, a short distance down river, faced immediate danger. Among those suddenly fleeing the city was the Second Continental Congress, which reconvened in Baltimore. "'Tis surprising," Paine wrote, "to see how rapidly a panic will sometimes run through a country." Despite Cornwallis's proximity to Washington's disheveled force, the British general once again failed to pursue Washington's men, allowing them to escape and missing an opportunity for a knockout blow.

Howe and Cornwallis planned to end their campaign for the year without invading Pennsylvania and forcing another battle. The chase had served their purpose well, and they had reason to hope that the Continental Army might keep fading away on its own, but Howe would be disappointed. As news spread about the conditions of Washington's men, Patrick Henry (now Virginia's governor under its new constitution as an independent state) ordered militia leaders in each county to gather blankets from residents "and draw upon me for the Amount of the

Purchase." On December 20 and 23, two vessels arrived in Philadelphia from the West Indies loaded with blankets and woolens, as well as arms and munitions. Captained by commissioned officers of the small Continental Navy, they had successfully run the Royal Navy's blockade of the Atlantic coast.

As desperately needed supplies arrived, brigades of troops previously assigned by Washington to other commanders arrived in Pennsylvania as reinforcements. In fact, new infantry units were also on the horizon, as appeals by Washington and his officers to the various states recruited more men than anticipated. Making use of lessons learned the hard way, Washington reorganized his forces to improve command and control. Henry Knox, a self-taught artillery expert, attached companies with field guns to each of the new infantry brigades. Morale began to recover. Soldiers were given newly printed copies of Paine's *American Crisis* and read them out loud to their comrades gathered in small crowds.

Unlike Howe, Washington felt too much political pressure to wait out the winter. The general feared that his tenacious fighting men were doomed unless they could fight and actually win. Many enlistments were also due to expire at the end of the year, which would further reduce his forces. Thus, he decided to make the first of many timely surprise attacks during the Revolution, leading his men in a perilous crossing of the ice-clogged Delaware River on Christmas night to seize Trenton, New Jersey, from a Hessian garrison.

Washington's men set out when the bitterly cold winds "blew a hurricane," in the words of one soldier. Arriving at the ferry for the crossing at 6 p.m., Washington divided his men into three groups who crossed at different points along the river. As they crossed, the rain and sleet turned to snow, the temperature dropped sharply, and the waters, roiling at first, became choked with drifting ice. Massachusetts infantrymen who worked at home as fishermen and seamen, standing in several inches of freezing water, rowed Washington across the river. Then he stood by the shore, watched, and waited as the other boats struggled through the ice, marveling as his men crossed without the loss of a soldier or being discovered by the nearby Hessians.

About 2,400 Americans arrived at Trenton in the morning light and found it nearly unguarded. Knox positioned the field cannons within the town and began firing at point-blank range. Many of the Hessians' heads ached with hangovers from the previous evening's Christmas celebrations. The shells exploding all around them probably made the pain worse. In the chaos, the Hessian commander could not organize a successful counterattack. The battle itself turned out to be far less dramatic than the river crossing. The Americans caught the Hessians by surprise, with many sleeping when gunfire erupted. A fierce snowstorm made it hard to see where the American fire came from. Surrender came quickly.

Washington's men killed twenty-two of the German soldiers of fortune and wounded ninety-eight, while capturing about one thousand prisoners and laying their hands on badly needed muskets, gunpowder and artillery pieces. In combat, the Americans suffered only four wounded (one of whom was future president James Monroe, who received a musket ball in his shoulder), though a number comparable to the Hessian losses may have died in the coming days from illness brought on from exposure to extreme cold. Nevertheless, Washington described his losses as "trifling." The Battle of Trenton held minimal to no strategic significance, but it greatly improved the spirits of the fighting men and increased the confidence of civilians in the Continental Army's prospects. The psychological impact was electric. Many throughout the states viewed it as providential, a deliverance from evil by the grace of God. Others who had lost faith in the army and its commander, in the midst of defeat and retreat, now gained a lasting confidence in both. Before returning to Philadelphia, John Hancock addressed Washington on behalf of the Continental Congress. "Troops properly inspired, and animated by a just confidence in their leader will often exceed expectation, or the limits of probability,"

Washington's *Victory at Princeton*

Washington still worried about the number of soldiers whose enlistment would expire in a matter of days. He was aware of his emotional effect on the troops, and their growing devotion to him. The Massachusetts soldiers who had rowed him across the Delaware River were among those whose enlistments were expiring at year's end. Scrambling for cash, Washington managed to pull together a bounty (a cash reward of ten dollars in hard coins) for those who re-enlisted, but he also held a ceremonial meeting with regiments from New England and appealed personally to his men, all of them now veterans, acknowledging their bravery and hardships. He led his men in a crossing back across the Delaware to return them to the scene of their recent victory in order to add emotional power to his pleas. "My brave fellows," Washington said, "You have done all I have asked you to do, and more than could be reasonably expected, but your country is at stake; your wives, your houses, and all that you hold dear. You have worn yourself out with fatigues and hardships, but we know not how to spare you . . . The present is emphatically the crisis which is to decide our destiny." More than half of his men would re-enlist.

Of those who committed to stay on during this pep talk near the Delaware River, nearly half would be killed in battle or by disease without ever making it back home.

Meanwhile, the British made a serious effort finally to battle Washington and his men before winter conditions ended hostilities for the season. General Cornwallis led 8,000 British regulars and Hessians south from New York to, as the British say, "bag the fox." Eager to avenge the embarrassment at Trenton, Cornwallis's troops quick-marched and located Washington's camp right before sundown the evening of January 2, 1777. Yet again, a British general paused. Cornwallis waited until sunrise when his men would have light to see their foes, but by the time the British awakened for their assault and reached the American encampment, they found nothing but lonely, burning campfires. Washington had evacuated his troops during the dark hour, muffling the wheels of his wagons and artillery to conceal the noise, and quietly slipped around Cornwallis, heading down a back road toward New Jersey. He left a handful of soldiers behind in the dead of the night to keep the campfires roaring and lull the British into thinking their prey remained nearby.

Washington's unconventional escape, which took him in the opposite direction of Patriot-held territory and supplies, flabbergasted Cornwallis. But Washington simply made use of the surprising advantages that came from having a lighter-armed, smaller, unconventional force. Washington introduced Cornwallis to the harsh realities of what would come to be known as guerilla war, a concept difficult for the traditional British military to grasp, so accustomed to the tradition of tightly aligned formations facing each other on open ground. Officers like Cornwallis did not know it, but an older era of warfare had ended and a new one had begun.

Washington led his men toward **Princeton, New Jersey**. As the sun rose January 3, Washington's men happened upon another isolated British regiment, commencing a quick battle in which the Continental Army enjoyed a 5-1 advantage. In a closely fought battle, with Washington appearing on horseback at the head of the Pennsylvania infantry, the General rallied the men forward against the British line marching into Princeton to score a second startling victory within two weeks. For a moment Washington got greedy, wishing to plan further attacks, but his lieutenants pointed out "the harassed state of our own troops . . . and the danger of losing the advantage we had gained by aiming at too much." Still keeping clear of Cornwallis's main force, the army set off for the mountains of northern New Jersey, settling there for the rest of the winter.

For many Americans, Washington was already passing into the realm of legend. General Howe, meanwhile, had retreated to New Brunswick, New Jersey, more than sixty miles northeast of Philadelphia, which remained safe for the time being. For Howe and his superiors in London, the year 1776 had ended badly, given the scale and expense of the British effort. The real purpose of the British winning successive battles, and conquering and occupying territory, was to discourage and demoralize the "damned Rebels," and inspire the Loyalists, so that the army, the Continental Congress, state governments, and the Patriot cause would all collapse on their own. For a time it had appeared to be working, but no longer.

In American minds, the New York-New Jersey campaign in 1776 captured the agony and the ecstasy of the entire revolutionary experience: humiliating retreats, barely avoided disasters, lucky breaks, inexplicable British blunders, and victories pulled off by Washington like rabbits from a magician's hat. The next six years would be grueling and would indeed try men's souls, but Washington's greatest accomplishment was not any particular successful battle plan so much as it was his ability to keep an army together with its most determined core motivated until the British will to fight finally collapsed.

As indispensable as Washington was, even the leadership of the Continental Army, like the Revolution itself, represented a collective effort. The commander-in-chief was overworked and constantly had to consider the delicate political implications of some of the most mundane tasks. Dealing with the egos of Congress alone could have been a full-time job for the thinly stretched commander. Some, like John Adams, were jealous. Adams had pushed for Washington's appointment, but he felt flashes of resentment when he saw the adulation showered on the general even at the beginning of the war. On June 23, 1775, when Washington received a big parade to mark his departure from Philadelphia to assume his duties as commander-in-chief in Massachusetts, Adams steamed. "Such is the pride and pomp of war," he wrote privately in his study. "I, poor creature worn out with scribbling for my bread and my liberty, low in spirits and weak in health, must leave others to wear the laurels which I have sown."

Sometimes, the laurels must have seemed like a crown of thorns. Some members of Congress were constant critics, looking for an excuse to sack him. Pressure came not just from his political superiors in the Congress, but also sometimes from his fellow officers. Congress offered high-ranking commissions and responsibilities to individuals such as Charles Lee, who led a portion of the army in the New York campaign, and Horatio Gates, then stationed at Ticonderoga who had little respect for Washington and allowed this to become known. Lee had acquired a not entirely deserved reputation for military genius, and he had many supporters in Congress who wanted him to be commander-in-chief instead of Washington. Lee did have more military experience, having served with distinction in the British regular army before offering his services as a major general in Poland and having advised the Russians in combat against the Turks.

Fortunately for the American side, however, Washington recognized some of his own limitations, and he found subordinate officers who were loyal and capable, and he listened to their advice. Over time, the officer corps became a training ground for future national leaders. One of the most exceptional examples would be Alexander Hamilton, a native of the West Indies island of Nevis who was studying at King's College (now Columbia University) in New York at the outbreak of the Revolution. Young Hamilton responded to an appeal for the defense of the city by recruiting a full company of artillerymen with himself as captain.

Hamilton had no prior military training or experience (apart from a great deal of reading), but through the campaign from New York to Trenton and Princeton, he led his men energetically and directed cannon fire with consummate skill. That winter, Washington asked him to join his staff as a personal assistant. Hamilton had a particularly brilliant mind regarding budgets and logistics. As Washington's irreplaceable aide still in his early twenties, he became notable himself. Able to anticipate the general's own thinking, he was soon relied upon to exercise his own judgment in drafting correspondence and offering advice. Hamilton rarely left Washington's side during the war. A man of enormous political and social ambition, he craved the social acceptance that would come with battlefield victories, but Washington repeatedly reminded him that he was too valuable making all the parts of the war machinery fit in the command center for his life to be risked on the battlefield.

SEEKING ALLIES

As the war progressed, American leaders sought, and sometimes received, assistance from the outside world. For the delegates in Congress, a major purpose of declaring independence was winning military and financial aid from foreign powers that would otherwise avoid interfering in what was basically a British civil war. Smuggled shipments of arms and supplies from the West Indies proved vital during the Battle of Trenton and other engagements, but Patriot leaders had little hope of prevailing in an extended war without help on a far larger scale. France had fought seven wars with England since 1627, and in the 1700s had been defeated by the English in the War of the Spanish Succession (1702-1713), the War of the Austrian Succession (1740-1748), and the French and Indian War (1754-1763). France and England battled for world supremacy, and their eighteenth-century wars had been global in scale. France might ally itself with the United States not because it supported the ideas of democracy and human equality called for in the Declaration of Independence (France was a monarchy where the king's power was considered absolute), but on the principle of "the enemy of my enemy is my friend."

Early in 1776, the delegates in the Continental Congress dispatched Silas Deane, a purchasing agent, to send out diplomatic feelers in Paris. Deane made little headway, so as the military situation grew grimmer, the Congress sent a member who had become a global celebrity, one of the Pennsylvania delegates, **Benjamin Franklin**. Franklin displayed dazzling diplomatic gifts in France, not only because of his fluency in French, his charm, and his sometimes-uproarious sense of humor, but also because a cult had grown up around him across the Atlantic. The French admired his literary skills and his role in the American Revolution thus far. His scientific experiments in electricity fascinated the French, who saw in him a harbinger of a more advanced age. "Franklin's . . . popularity was so widespread that it does not seem exaggerated to call it a mania," wrote European historian Simon Schama in his epic *Citizens: A Chronicle of the French Revolution.* "Mobbed wherever he went, and especially whenever he set his foot outside his house in Passy, he was probably better known by sight than the King [Louis XVI], and his likeness could be found on engraved glass, patterned porcelain, printed cottons, snuffboxes and inkwells . . . In June 1779 he wrote to his daughter that all of these likenesses 'have made your father's face as well known as that of the moon.'"

The French crowds loved Franklin's frequent affected rusticity, such as when he donned a beaver pelt cap. He seemed genuine, a perfect symbol of a people many French saw as natural. He contrasted nicely with the French nobility widely seen as wasteful, selfish, cynical, sexually promiscuous, and politically corrupt. Many French subjects hoped they saw in Franklin a glimpse of a more creative, honest future for their nation. The seeds of the French Revolution in 1789 had already found fertile soil by the time of Franklin's visit. The French did not immediately commit to support the American Revolution, but Franklin's proposed alliance intrigued them. The French needed to have more confidence that they would not lose yet another expensive war to the British before an alliance with the Americans could be forged. The French court waited on more American battlefield victories.

Outside of government ministries, however, the Declaration of Independence found an audience among French political thinkers and scientists. A well-known scholar of the French Enlightenment, Abbé Guillaume Raynal, found great importance in Jefferson's words, and gave several lectures on the American interpretation of the "rights of man." One admirer of the Declaration was an earnest young nobleman, Marie-Joseph Paul Yves Roch Gilbert du Motier, **Marquis de Lafayette**. "Lafayette" (as he would become known) decided that if the American cause was just, then he must do all that he personally could to help the revolutionaries triumph.

Lafayette contacted Silas Deane and was given a major general's commission in the Continental Army (albeit an unpaid one). He bought a ship, only to have it confiscated by agents of the king when his plans became known. Fleeing to Spain, he sailed from there, in disguise, and finally arrived in Philadelphia in July 1777. Delegates in Congress were bewildered by the young nobleman and skeptical of "French glory seekers." Washington, however, had been advised by Franklin to treat Lafayette with respect, as a possible means of encouraging French assistance in the war. When the Marquis presented himself at the Continental Army's headquarters, Washington told him that he could not offer him a position of command but would hold him in confidence "as friend and father." Indeed, like Hamilton, Lafayette saw in Washington a role model and father figure he had yearned for. Lafayette agreed to serve alongside Hamilton on Washington's personal staff.

1777: YEAR OF DISAPPOINTMENT AND HOPE

The Saratoga Campaign

The Patriot cause had narrowly survived the 1776 campaign, and the next year promised more grave threats. In New York, General Howe and his brother planned an attack on Philadelphia, which would drive away the Second Continental Congress and, he hoped, also lure Washington into another defensive battle in which the Patriot forces might finally be destroyed. The Howes wanted 20,000 more troops for this campaign, but nothing near this number was available to the military. Nevertheless, in London, King George, the Prime Minister (Lord North), and Lord Germain, the Secretary of State for the colonies, embraced a more ambitious plan involving an invasion route between northern New York and Canada. General **John Burgoyne** proposed to lead an army from Canada to Albany, on the upper Hudson River, where he would

fight to establish British control over the full length of the great waterway, cutting off New England from the other rebellious colonies and possibly deal a fatal blow to the Patriot war effort. The King and his ministers endorsed Burgoyne's plan, but failed to give Howe clear instructions to cooperate fully with the operation.

Burgoyne, meanwhile, led an army of 7,800 from Montreal toward Albany in early June, moving down Lake Champlain with forces that included British and German regulars and Iroquois allies, 130 artillery pieces, and a long supply train extending back into Canada. The general also brought his mistress, servants, feather bed, and other tasteful furnishings and culinary delicacies. ("Gentleman Johnny" was a brave and experienced officer who treated his men with consideration, but it never occurred to him to sacrifice his style of living, or that of his senior officers, even in a remote frontier campaign.) Burgoyne's men began the campaign by capturing Fort Ticonderoga, scene of the Patriots' earliest successes in the war, on June 2, 1777. A braggart, Burgoyne boasted in letters sent back to the rest of the world about his initial victory and proclaimed that his invasion was proceeding according to plan.

After this initial success, British plans went awry. Burgoyne carelessly overextended his supply lines, and his men suffered fatigue. According to plans hatched in London, Howe was supposed to send to Burgoyne men and supplies from New York. Instead, Howe launched his own mission and was leaving by sea for an invasion of Maryland and Pennsylvania.

Burgoyne would have to manage with the supplies he already possessed, or his men would have to forage for food in the wilderness. A further setback came when an expeditionary force led by British Colonel Barry St. Leger made a thrust through the Mohawk River Valley, but his Iroquois allies abandoned him when American General Benedict Arnold's forces confronted them in August, reducing St. Leger's forces by half and forcing a retreat back to Oswego in western New York.

Far from supply depots, Burgoyne split his forces, ordering 700 Hessians to hunt for supplies in the nearby Green Mountains. There, a 2,600-man New Hampshire militia led by John Stark launched a surprise attack from behind, ambushing the 700 mercenaries and killing or imprisoning almost the entire force. Another exchange between the New Hampshire militia and a different group of Hessians had similar results. Burgoyne's force limped toward Albany, his once considerable army much reduced. The American commander near Albany, Horatio Gates, now enjoyed a three-to-one manpower advantage. Unable to punch through Gates's lines to reach Albany, Burgoyne lost two disastrous battles thirty miles from the town on

September 19 and on October 7 (the latter initiated by Arnold against Gates's direct orders). Retreating to nearby **Saratoga**, Burgoyne surrendered on October 17. The British loss would have huge diplomatic consequences, convincing the French that the Revolution was not a lost cause and that the French could damage their British rivals by forming an alliance with the Americans.

Philadelphia Falls to the British

Still thinking in terms of conventional wars in Europe, General Howe placed great stock in capturing cities of economic and political significance rather than pursuing and destroying the enemy's main army. Trained in traditional army tactics, Washington still felt compelled to defend such points, especially a city as symbolically important as Philadelphia, which housed the Continental Congress. As the Saratoga campaign reached its dramatic climax, Washington was left to wage another defensive struggle against Howe's sizeable forces. In July, as Washington watched uneasily, Howe loaded some 18,000 troops onto transports in New York harbor, and then, instead of moving up the Hudson to support Burgoyne, the fleet headed out to the open sea.

Howe sailed to Chesapeake Bay, landing his forces in Maryland in late August. As the British army advanced on Philadelphia from the south, Washington marched from northern New Jersey to the lower Delaware Valley, gathering militia units along the way. Howe correctly surmised that Washington would not surrender the city without a fight and lured him into a direct confrontation that the colonial army could not hope to win.

Washington built defensive fortifications along the main road from Baltimore to Philadelphia at a fording site across Brandywine Creek. Yet despite these preparations, Howe used his superior reconnaissance to find a weakness in the Continental Army's position and utilized the maneuverability of his professional forces to exploit the opportunity. In the Battle of Brandywine Creek, on September 11, Howe outflanked Washington's men, forcing them back with heavy losses. Their line of retreat, however, was protected by General Nathanael Greene, one of Washington's most trusted lieutenants, and by Lafayette, who kept rallying troops even after he had been shot in the leg. In his report to Congress, Washington cited Lafayette for "bravery and military ardour" as he recommended the Frenchman for command of a division.

On September 26, Lord Cornwallis led a ceremonial entry into Philadelphia. One month previously, Washington had paraded the Continental Army through the city, on their way south. "Much yet remains to be done," John Adams then observed. "Our soldiers have not yet quite the air of soldiers. They don't step exactly in time. They don't hold up their heads quite erect.... They don't all of them cock their hats, and such as do, don't all wear them the same way." The occupying army now presented an entirely different spectacle, with British and German regulars in crisp uniforms, brass buttons and polished guns shining in the sunlight, marching to a band playing "God Save the King."

But with the news of Burgoyne's struggles now circulating, even the parade's spectators suspected that military professionalism could do only so much to restore British authority. Congress and many residents were forced to flee the city, but its conquest made far less of an impact on the Patriot cause than Howe had hoped.

With the Continental Army still attracting recruits, Washington observed the division of Howe's forces into scattered detachments. He attempted to coordinate an attack from different directions against the largest body of British troops under Howe's own command at Germantown, Pennsylvania, on the foggy morning of October 4. Washington had a bad habit of constructing battle plans far more complex than necessary, and such was the case in Germantown. The baffled Continental Army failed to execute their orders successfully, with some Patriot units accidentally firing on each other. After some initial success, Washington was forced to withdraw with the army suffering heavy casualties yet again. Still, "the retreat was extraordinary," observed Thomas Paine. "Nobody hurried themselves. Everyone marched his own pace.... They appeared to me to be only sensible of a disappointment, not a defeat."

Winter at Valley Forge

As Paine already recognized, the hard fighting of 1777 had profound consequences, which continued to develop as the battlefields fell silent for the cold season. As the third winter of the war set in, those who were committed to the Patriot cause once again found the reassurance they needed. Having escaped to York, Pennsylvania, the Second Continental Congress proclaimed December 18 a day for "solemn thanksgiving and praise" to Almighty God, seeing "that He hath been pleased ... to crown our arms with most signal success." Across the thirteen states, village and town churches marked the day of thanksgiving with formal services. Northwest of Philadelphia, in a hilly, forested area known as **Valley Forge**, chosen by Washington for the army's winter quarters, Reverend Israel Evans, the Continental Army chaplain, preached a sermon of thanksgiving. In many ways, it would be a winter of discontent, with Washington's soldiers freezing and barely fed, and members of Congress grumbling about

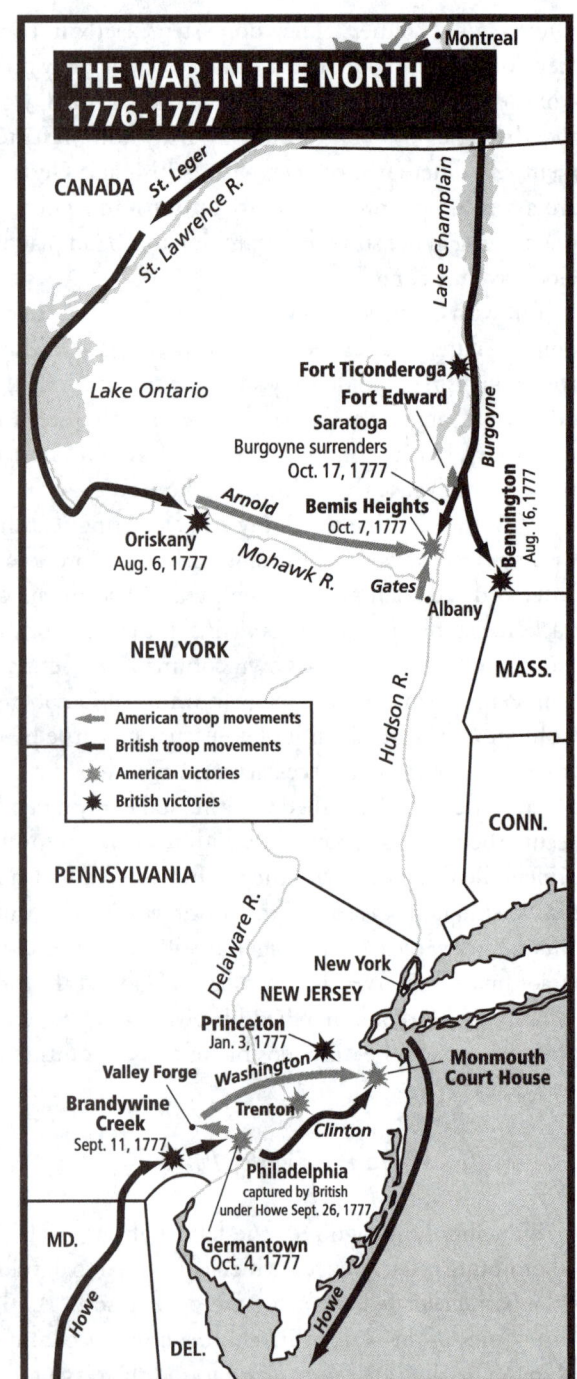

Map 6.2 The War in the North, 1776-1777

that Howe had taken Philadelphia, Franklin was said to have replied, "I beg your pardon, Philadelphia has taken Howe.") In fact, shortly after arriving, Howe sent off a letter of resignation as commander-in-chief. He left in the spring after British officials accepted his offer, but not before one last spectacular, unbelievably costly party thrown for him by his officers (featuring a musical parade of boats and costumed passengers on the Delaware, a medieval joust held in an amphitheater, a "magnificent bouquet of rockets" and fireworks shaped like "bursting balloons," and a banquet served by slaves in Turkish dress). As he must already have known, Howe would spend the next few years fighting to salvage his own reputation and fend off the blame for Burgoyne's disastrous fate. It would prove to be his last failed campaign, as he never would be able to clearly explain his own crucial errors of judgment.

France Enters the War

The most crucial results of the year's campaigns developed far away, in Paris, in the secret meetings and delicate conversations between the commissioners sent by Congress and the foreign ministry of Louis XVI. The British occupation of Philadelphia alarmed the French Foreign Minister, Comte de Vergennes, because he feared the Americans might surrender and the French would lose a chance to gain an advantage on their English enemy. News of the American victory at Saratoga, however, pleased Vergennes, convincing him that the Americans had a credible army after all. European politics rested upon a zero-sum game. What was bad for England was good for France, and Vergennes hoped to make the situation much worse for the enemy across the English Channel.

On February 6, 1778, the two sides finished negotiations and signed a pair of treaties. One established trade between the two nations, while the other created a military alliance. The French thus committed to independence for the United States. In an agreement that would pose difficulties for the United States in the 1790s, both nations pledged to help each other in the event either was attacked. "Neither of the two Parties shall conclude either Truce or Peace with Great Britain, without the formal consent of the other," stated the alliance treaty, "and they mutually engaged not to lay down their arms, until assured by the Treaty or Treaties that shall terminate the War."

The agreements with France transformed the conflict. What had begun as an American colonial rebellion against British imperial authority had become a global war, with England and France resuming their bloody struggle for supremacy over the Atlantic Ocean and in North America that had been in recess since the end of the French and Indian War fourteen years earlier.

Washington's performance. The criticism of Washington reached a crescendo after the almost simultaneous defeat of the commander-in-chief outside Philadelphia with Gates's smashing victory at Saratoga. A turning point had arrived, however, as Baron von Steuben arrived to professionalize the Continental Army and as a critical diplomatic victory occurred overseas.

Meanwhile, some twenty miles to the southeast, with the occupying British army comfortably settled in the city, English officers surrendered themselves to the strenuous demands of the winter social calendar. (When told

Like France, Spain also eagerly sought a chance to get even for previous military defeats at the hands of Great Britain. Worried if the United States succeeded in its revolt against England then restless Spanish colonists might follow the example and launch their own revolutions, the Spanish government never entered into a direct alliance with the United States government. Instead, Spain fought alongside the French and successfully battled to retake parts of Florida previously lost to England. The British military, already stretched thin, now had to fight along the Gulf Coast, in the Caribbean, and in Europe where the Spanish unsuccessfully tried to recapture the Strait of Gibraltar, which the Great Britain had controlled since the War of the Spanish Secession in 1704.

After the French alliance, seasoned European officers volunteered for service and eventually made up 20 percent of all officers in the Continental Army. In London, where the shock of Burgoyne's surrender had scarcely worn off, the announcement of the Paris treaties confirmed the worst fears of virtually everyone in Parliament and the king's cabinet. Great Britain itself was now in peril. With such great commitment of arms, men, and ships already made in North America, and a new, powerful enemy entering the conflict, no light at the end of the tunnel was even faintly in sight. Ironically, as the military and political situations got worse in North America, advocates for peace like Edmund Burke decided to keep their criticisms of the war effort to themselves and joined the call for national unity. The day belonged to George III who, stubborn as always, insisted that his ministers remain resolute.

The American strategy would continue to be simply to outlast the British by keeping the Continental Army intact and avoiding battles with the British when the numbers favored the enemy. British Secretary of State George Germain proposed the worst possible military strategy in response. He wanted to strike at the French, whom he saw as the greater threat to Britain. If British naval superiority could be maintained in American waters, then parts of the new British commander General **Henry Clinton**'s forces would be redeployed against other targets of opportunity, such as the French islands in the West Indies. However, this meant that Clinton would lack sufficient forces to hold onto Philadelphia, forcing him to withdraw from the American capital.

Meanwhile, Germain gave up on the idea of waging a campaign on land against Washington's army. Instead, after approving Howe's resignation, he instructed Clinton to withdraw from Philadelphia and return to New York. Troops would also be diverted to the southern states on the North American mainland, where ministers believed the British military would find a larger percentage of

American Loyalists who would support the troops from the homeland.

THE BATTLE OF THE CUPBOARDS: COLONIAL WOMEN ON THE HOMEFRONT

As their husbands, fathers, brothers, and sons went off to war, American women faced their own series of battles: to keep family businesses going; to manage plantations and workforces; to keep the family budget in the black; and to raise children. Their added duties during the Revolution did not mean they could neglect the ordinary housework that had always fallen to wives, mothers, and daughters in American society—feeding, bathing, doctoring and educating the children; gardening, milking cows; cleaning the henhouse; gathering eggs; plucking chickens; and gathering fuel and water. Greedy merchants did not make the endless chores any easier. Inflation ran rampant, and consumer goods were scarce. Some merchants exploited the uncertainty by outrageously overcharging their customers. Prices rose by 45 percent during one year of the Revolution.

Women occasionally formed their own battalions, sometimes joined by men, and organized attacks on unscrupulous shop owners, looting stores and emptying their shelves. This was a matter of justice and, for the poor, survival. More than thirty times between 1776 and 1779, food rioters confronted rapacious shopkeepers and merchants who were hoarding or overcharging. In one riot, women in Longmeadow, Massachusetts, in July 1776 wrapped themselves in blankets "like Indians," blackened their faces and presented a warning to businessmen selling rum, sugar, and molasses who had taken advantage of the embargo of British goods and the war to raise prices on their increasingly scarce goods:

Sirs, it is a matter of great grief that you Should give us cause to call upon you in this uncommon way . . . We find you guilty of very wrong behavior in selling at extravagant prices . . . This conduct tends to under-value paper currency which is very detrimental to the Liberties of America. We therefore as your offended Brethren demand satisfaction of you the offender for your past conduct and a Thorough reformation for time to Come.

The mob gave the businessmen a list of suggested prices for the goods they sold and gave them an hour to consider. Seeing the anger of the crowd, some retailers complied. Another Longmeadow merchant refused

Mercy Otis Warren, A Founding Mother

It is a cliché to refer to Revolutionary War leaders like George Washington, John Adams and Thomas Jefferson as "Founding Fathers" of the American nation. Mercy Otis Warren clearly qualifies as a "Founding Mother." A leading satirist, poet and playwright from the 1760s until her death in 1814, Warren disliked the original draft of the United States Constitution and wrote a list of suggested revisions that closely resembled what became known as the Bill of Rights—the constitution's first 10 amendments guided through Congress by James Madison. Warren also wrote one of the first published analyses of the War for Independence, the controversial three-volume **History of the Rise, Progress and Termination of the American Revolution**.

Warren was born in 1728 into a prominent Massachusetts family. Her brother, the mentally unbalanced but fierce advocate for American independence James Otis, Jr., coined the phrase, "Taxation without representation is tyranny." Warren, her brother, and her husband led opposition in the 1770s to the royal governor of Massachusetts Thomas Hutchinson as he implemented wildly unpopular policies like the Stamp Act and the Tea Act. Ahead of many of her male contemporaries, Mercy Warren supported American independence, a quest she celebrated in a 1768 poem, "Massachusetts Liberty Song." Seven years before soldiers fired the first shots in the Revolution in Lexington and Concord, Warren warned the British that "no cut-throats our spirits can tame, Nor hosts of oppressors shall smother the flames."

Warren's political satires, like the script for a play she called **The Adulateur,** appeared anonymously until 1790, in part because she worried about whether her audience would accept political satire and commentary written by a woman. Her writing career blossomed at a time when even upper-class women were expected to confine themselves to the roles of dutiful wives and devoted mothers.

The prevailing Puritan culture in her home state viewed the theater as immoral; thus her plays did not get performed. When she started writing scripts, Warren had never attended a play herself. Local newspapers, however, published the plays. One of Warren's biggest fans was John Adams. Adams and Warren exchanged letters for decades, and he described "The Squabble of the Sea Nymphs; or the Sacrifice of the Tuscararoes," a parody of events leading to the Boston Tea Party, as a work of "real genius." Whenever Warren told Adams she had no energy left for writing because of her domestic duties, her friend told her that the country needed her talents and he urged her to write a detailed history of the Revolutionary War.

Warren pushed against the narrow boundaries placed on women in 18th- and early 19th-century America, but she preferred to do so with subtlety, pushing for women's freedom while seeming to accommodate male sexism. "My dear, it may be necessary for you to seem inferior, but you need not be so," she wrote one young female friend. "Let them [men] have their little game, since it may have been so willed. It won't hurt you; it will amuse them."

Adams would regret his mentoring of Warren. In spite of her close friendship with John and especially his wife Abigail, the friends parted political ways during the 1787-1788 debate over the proposed new Constitution of the United States, with John Adams arguing for a stronger central government and supporting the idea of a powerful presidency, and Warren believing the Revolution had been about states' rights and limited executive power. When the Constitutional convention released its handiwork for ratification by the states, Warren expressed outrage that the document did not enumerate the rights of citizens.

Warren wrote a pamphlet, "Observations on the New Constitution," making this point, complaining that the Constitution placed too much power in the hands of the central government. The objections she raised in this pamphlet seem, to a remarkable degree, to have been addressed by the first ten amendments to the United States Constitution, and Warren may have been an unacknowledged inspiration for what came to be known as the "Bill of Rights."

In the 1790s, Adams became a leader of the new Federalist Party while Warren backed the Republican Party. By the time Warren wrote her history of the Revolution, she had concluded that her old friend Adams favored establishing an American monarchy and had forgotten the principles they had shared during the struggle against Great Britain. Adams believed she unfairly downplayed his role in the Revolution. Adams deeply resented Warren for years, though the two reconciled before the author's death in 1814.

Sadly, Warren's epochal history, published under her name in 1805, did not receive positive reviews from male critics, who questioned her qualifications to analyze the male worlds of politics and war. Relatively famous for her time, Warren's contributions to the revolutionary generation would be largely forgotten until after the rise of the modern feminist movement in the late twentieth century.

THE UNITED STATES AND THE AGE OF REVOLUTION | 147

to lower what the crowd saw as excessive prices, so the crowd emptied his stores' shelves and refused to return his goods until he repented. A few weeks later, however, the merchant (Samuel Colton) had inflated his prices again. A mob returned, smashed into his store, seized the rum, sugar, salt, and molasses and then looted Colton's house, which was attached to the store. Looters in these incidents accused greedy merchants of acting no different from the British oppressors and would call them unpatriotic.

The rioters came from all classes. In some cases, the mobs were led by the well-to-do, but it seems this was mostly a revolt of the poor and struggling against much better off merchants. The longer the Revolution lasted, the more the riots shifted from rural areas to cities. The food riots became more an expression of class struggle as the Revolution dragged on. Food riots in American cities intensified. Aimed at greedy merchants, these protests met with wide approval. As a Philadelphia newspaper reported, "[T]he People have always done themselves justice when the scarcity of bread has arisen from the avarice of forestallers. They have broken open magazines—appropriated stores to their own use without paying for them—and in some instances have hung up the culprits who created their distress."

Soldiers heard the complaints of their wives and mothers about widespread price gouging, leading the First Company of Philadelphia Artillery to petition the state assembly in May 1779 to crack down on exploitive merchants. In their petition, they threatened violence to "those who are avariciously intent upon amassing wealth by the destruction of the more virtuous part of the community." Residents of Philadelphia demanded an investigation of Robert Morris, a wealthy merchant and one of the chief American financiers of the Revolution, for reportedly hoarding food to increase prices.

Women took a leadership position in these riots. They may have lacked the right to vote but they successfully pressured New England legislatures to mandate that merchants accept paper currency as legal tender, set caps on the prices merchants could charge for a wide variety of domestic and imported goods, and outlaw hoarding. Meanwhile, average people began to organize boycotts of merchants who overcharged, just as elites had organized earlier boycotts of British goods. Fearing that the legislature would fail to enforce these laws, spontaneous gatherings of protestors continued to take the law into their own hands. In one incident on April 19, 1777, the second anniversary of the Battle of Lexington and Concord, a 500-person crowd in Boston grabbed five "Tory" merchants ("Tory" was another term for those Americans supporting the British), tossed them into a cart and intentionally rode them past a gallows, tipping the

cart over to dump them out and warning them to never return to the city again.

Once again, elites like John Adams worried that incidents like these suggested that the Revolution might spin out of control. The leaders of the Revolution wanted to transfer power from British to American hands but feared an uprising of poor Americans against their wealthy fellow citizens. A pushback against price controls began in the Continental Congress at the behest of affluent men like Dr. Benjamin Rush and in state legislatures. The well-to-do urged consumers to take their grievances to court, ignoring the fact that lawyers' fees might be beyond most families' reach. Women continued to press for price fairness. Far more powerful male politicians still found it difficult to roll back price controls or to condemn mob actions at the shop counters. However, the riots inspired anxiety in the hearts of elites, who started the Revolution committed to a more radical vision of equality but by the time of the Constitution had retreated to defense of the traditional hierarchy.

YEARS OF STALEMATE, 1778-1780

The British Evacuation of Philadelphia

During the Revolution, Washington faced constant trouble from his top officers. General Charles Lee in particular refused to submit to Washington's authority. Lee had never surrendered the idea that he was more brilliant and capable than Washington and every other military commander. While serving as the second-in-command during the Americans' retreat across New Jersey in late 1776, he was captured by the British at a tavern and then held in New York City where, according to later accusations, he offered his expert military advice to General Howe who befriended him. Lee may have entered into a conspiracy to betray the Continental Army. Yet, Washington still felt he needed the benefit of Lee's expertise. In early 1778, Lee obtained his release as part of a prisoner exchange. Lee's arrogance, however, would finally get him fired by his furious commander when he disobeyed battlefield orders after the British evacuated Philadelphia.

General Clinton began his withdrawal by sending shiploads of Loyalists and sick soldiers to New York City by sea. Clinton then transported the bulk of his forces in boats across the Delaware River and began a long march across New Jersey. With the British army and its long baggage train exposed, Washington looked for an opportunity to attack. On June 28, 1778, his troops, now executing maneuvers with precision learned from von Steuben's drills at Valley Forge, caught up with Clinton's rear guard, commanded by Lord Cornwallis, near Monmouth Court House. Over Lee's objections, Washington ordered his subordinate to mount an attack. Though the assault seemed to be succeeding, Lee mysteriously ordered a retreat. Confused, Lee's men reversed ground and the pullback turned into a panic when Clinton immediately counterattacked. The retreating Continentals ran straight into Washington himself, riding just ahead of the main body of the American army.

Furious, Washington demanded an immediate explanation from Lee, who had little to offer. Washington fired Lee on the spot and gave Lafayette command of Lee's men. Turning his back to Lee, Washington once again personally rallied his forces. The Americans quickly reestablished themselves in an orderly formation while under the fire of the approaching British troops. Their long hours of drill and training paid off in the moment of crisis. An admiring Lafayette later remembered "our beloved chief who, mounted on a splendid charger, rode along the ranks amid the shouts of the soldiers, cheering them by his voice and example, and restoring to our standard the fortunes of the fight."

The British charged the Patriot lines but failed to break through. That night, with both sides having lost hundreds of dead and wounded, and with the American side holding the battlefield, the British troops slipped away and resumed their march to New York City. Monmouth Court House would prove to be the last major battle of the Revolutionary War in the North. Though the battle was strategically inconclusive, the Americans claimed victory. "We forced the enemy from the field and encamped on their ground," Washington reported. A court martial later convicted Lee of insubordination and ended his service in the Continental Army.

Meanwhile, Lafayette, who had continued to rise through the ranks of Washington's senior officers, returned to France briefly in 1779, where crowds hailed him as a hero. With his popularity came influence with the French court, and Lafayette worked with Franklin to win new commitments of financial and military assistance for the war effort. The following year, he returned to America, followed by an army of 6,000 troops under French General Comte de Rochambeau.

For nearly three years, Washington kept the main body of his army near New York City, mostly watching and waiting. After the British withdrew from Newport, Rhode Island, Rochambeau established a base there for French land and sea forces before linking up with Washington's army in 1781. The two commanders formed a mutually respectful partnership. Meanwhile, Clinton had few options other than fortifying New York City and hoping the French and Americans would not attack.

The British commander had been ordered by North and Germain to send troops to other theaters of combat, so he appealed in vain for reinforcements and never felt he had sufficient numbers on hand to launch an offensive. The hard fighting now continued elsewhere. As` the war in the North settled into a long stalemate in late 1779, Clinton was assigned to supervise a new campaign in the southern states even as battles raged on America's western frontier.

THE WAR IN THE WEST

After the French and Indian War, the British had tried to draw a line at the Appalachian Mountains that they hoped would serve as the outer border dividing white settlement from "Indian Country." Always worried about France and Spain, the British did not want to be drawn into Indian wars in the American West. They also hoped to profit from trade with Native American groups. Many of the rebellious colonists, however, assumed they had a limitless claim on Indian land and saw British interference as a violation of their rights.

American whites poured over the imaginary border, establishing farms and communities on newly cleared lands and extending the lines of settlement and land claims ever westward. Ruthless land speculators joined them in this creeping conquest. The invaders collided with Native American peoples, many already displaced from their traditional lands farther east. Although many Indian bands tried to remain neutral, when the Revolution started, Native Americans inevitably got caught in the crossfire. The racism of white colonists, and their violence toward indigenous people, drove many Indians into supporting the British. In the West, the British Army was only too happy to ally itself with resisting Native American nations. The war in the West raged beyond the Appalachians, across vast stretches of the Mississippi and Ohio River Valleys (including much of the present-day states of Illinois, Indiana, and Kentucky) populated by Shawnee and other tribes and by isolated French-speaking settlers and soldiers stationed at British-held fortresses.

During the summer of 1778, **George Rogers Clark**, the young commander of the Virginia state militia in charge of defending the western counties, led some 200 volunteers far down the Ohio River and across hundreds of miles of forest, to Kaskaskia, originally a French colonial settlement and now a British army outpost on the Mississippi. Appearing unexpectedly with his armed company, and proclaiming the news of the Franco-American alliance to the local settlers, Clark occupied Kaskaskia without firing a shot and claimed it for Virginia.

Clark sent some of his men, as well as French settlers, back east to occupy Vincennes, the other main British outpost south of Detroit. Forced to act, the British commander in the frontier region, Lieutenant Governor Henry Hamilton, with a company of English soldiers and Shawnee warriors, retook Vincennes from the small detachment of Virginians, but he still failed to reckon fully with his adversary's ability to lead fighting frontiersmen on long, difficult treks. In February 1779, Clark again emerged at Vincennes, having marched through the snow from Kaskaskia with the rest of his militiamen and French volunteers. Clark ordered the killing, by tomahawk, of four captured Indians in full view of the British. Hamilton then agreed to surrender the fortress and his men.

Clark led repeated campaigns in the Ohio River region, attacking and burning Shawnee villages and cornfields, but he never managed to gather sufficient forces for his ultimate objective, which was crushing Indian resistance. Indian leaders like Mohawk Joseph Brant (Thayendanegea) emerged as a threatening force as confrontations between settlers and tribes turned into wars of extermination and elimination. In the North, where most of the Iroquois tribes elected to wage war alongside the British, outrage and fear prevailed among the American settlers of the Mohawk and upper Delaware River valleys. To reassert control of the region, Washington sent an expedition of several thousand Continental troops and militiamen in 1779, giving orders to the commander, General John Sullivan, to "rush on with the war whoop and the bayonet" and "make rather than receive attacks." Brant and other Indian warriors waged guerilla warfare, avoiding set battles. In response, Sullivan and his men focused mainly on the systematic destruction and burning of Iroquois villages and farmlands—literally a "scorched earth" campaign. During the winter of 1779-1780, thousands of homeless Iroquois villagers were forced to migrate to Fort Niagara, where British troops offered shelter. During the next year, however, with Sullivan and his troops reassigned to the war against the British in the south, the Iroquois mounted an equally fierce campaign of retaliation, destroying settlers' homes and farms throughout the Pennsylvania and New York frontier country.

Far to the south, on the Virginia frontier, the destruction was more one-sided. Cherokee communities were deeply split between young militants wanting to battle the Americans who had caused them so much loss and sorrow and older chiefs seeking accommodation with the settlers. However, in 1780 and 1781 Virginia militiamen attacked the friendly villages, destroying the tribe's "beloved town" of Chota and validating the fears of the younger Indian firebrands.

No uglier chapter in the American Revolution took place than the Gnadenhutten Massacre in the Ohio country. A group of Delawares who had been converted to Christianity by the Moravian sect for a time lived in the Moravian-established settlement in modern-day east central Ohio. The band had moved out of Gnadenhutten, but some had returned to harvest crops left behind. They came under attack on March 8-9, 1782 by Pennsylvania militiamen under the command of Captain David Williamson, who sought revenge after Native Americans had recently killed and kidnapped several whites in the region. The Delawares had not been involved, but they would pay the price for these earlier attacks.

When they reached the village on March 8, soldiers forced the men and women to separate at gunpoint and held them in separate buildings. The Pennsylvanians decided to execute the entire village the next morning. Informed of their fate, the women and children cried. The Delawares prayed and tried to rally their spirits with hymns. When morning came, the militia seized two natives at a time and battered their heads with mallets, killing 57 unarmed men and women and 39 children. Only two Delawares survived.

Essentially, the brutal episodes of the "War on the Frontier" were part of a larger pattern of conflict that continued long after the war for independence was settled. After the Revolution, the British ceded control of what they had intended to be Indian Country to the United States. They illegally retained forts in the "Northwest Country" and encouraged the natives living there to attack white settlements, providing them weapons until the end of the War of 1812. Nevertheless, the white conquest of the lands between the Appalachians and the Mississippi River would prove unstoppable. With the British no longer there to hold back the Americans, white invaders pushed into regions such as Kentucky, a favorite hunting ground of the Shawnees, and Indian groups would be forced at gunpoint to resettle farther west. Kentucky became infamous as "a dark and bloody ground" after the Revolution ended, yet, by the time of the first-ever United States federal census in 1790, 74,000 whites and their slaves had relocated to Kentucky and approximately half that number had made living in Tennessee, where the Cherokee had surrendered after defeat in a 1776 battle.

THE WAR MOVES SOUTH, 1780-1781

As the war among the European powers unfolded, the continuing struggle in North America became one piece of a much larger global conflict. British and French ships battled on the high seas, raiding each other's trading routes and imperial possessions around the Atlantic rim, focusing especially on the West Indies and India, where both empires had also established hugely important commercial interests. The Empress of Russia, Catherine the Great, even became involved, organizing on March 11, 1780 the League of Armed Neutrality, which opposed British efforts to cut off trade between the United States and northern European maritime powers. Already battling the Americans, the French and the Spanish, Britain declared war on the Dutch in December 1780 when the Netherlands threatened to join the league. The British now had to maintain naval forces in the North Sea to face a threat from their newest enemy.

Back in London, the global scope of the war stretched Secretary of State Germain and Prime Minister North's limited strategic and logistical talents to the breaking point. At the same time, Loyalists from Virginia and the Carolinas, now exiled in London, did what they could to influence the ministers. Encouraged to imagine the southern colonies overflowing with Loyalists patiently waiting for help, Germain hoped that a campaign there might re-establish royal authority while requiring fewer troops and arms than would a similar effort in troublesome New England.

Optimists like Germain hoped that the capture of Savannah, followed quickly by the rest of the colony, would rapidly lead to British re-conquest of the whole region. Clinton began dispatching his men south, leaving New York in the hands of Hessian troops. A British force of more than 31,000 troops began a siege of the weakly defended port city of Charles Town, South Carolina, shortly after landing on December 23, 1778. By January, Clinton arrived with an army of 8,000 men. General Benjamin Lincoln, the commander of the American southern forces, tried to prepare defenses with some 5,000 troops in the city, but Clinton's artillery pounded the city with heavy guns. Sparing the city and his men a blood-soaked finale, Lincoln surrendered on May 12, 1779, giving Clinton the largest British victory of the war.

As Lord Dunmore had done at the beginning of the war in 1775 in Virginia, Clinton tried to exploit the wedge between slave and master in South Carolina as a matter of military convenience rather than humanitarian concern. On June 30, 1779, from his headquarters near New York City, Clinton issued the "**Philipsburg Proclamation**," announcing that slaves who escaped from American rebels were eligible to serve in the British army—and that those captured from American rebels without having escaped would not be freed, but would instead be sold for the benefit of the British. Most important, Loyalists were allowed to keep all their slaves, with those escaping to be returned upon recapture.

Upon arriving in South Carolina, Clinton honored his promise to Loyalists, and sold off many captured slaves of rebels. Even so, the invading army again found that escaped slaves flooded into the area. Overall, the war in the South represented by far the largest uprising in the history of North American slavery. In South Carolina, out of a population of 80,000 slaves, perhaps up to 20,000 fled their plantation homes and sought refuge behind British lines. Unlike Dunmore, Clinton refused to set up an "Ethiopian Regiment," but escaped slaves instead provided the British army with a large population of attendants—some acting as servants, others as skilled craftsmen. Perhaps most important, British commanders were able to use refugees familiar with each locale to create effective foraging parties, enabling the army's movements across the countryside. For the refugees themselves, as with Dunmore's black soldiers, most if not all instances of liberation ended in tragedy. Smallpox outbreaks took a drastic toll. When the disease struck Charles Town after the British conquest, hundreds of sick refugees were expelled from the city and left to die in the surrounding woods.

Soon after taking Charles Town, Clinton returned north with 4,000 men, leaving General **Charles Cornwallis** and the rest of his army to occupy the rest of South Carolina. Taking advantage of the ample assistance offered by the escaped slaves, Cornwallis completed the assignment. In one infamous episode, on May 29, 1780, at Waxhaws near the state line, a group of 350 Continental soldiers attempted to retreat to North Carolina but were overtaken by mounted troops made up of enraged Loyalists who had suffered at the hands of the so-called Patriots. Lieutenant Colonel **Banastre Tarleton**, one of Cornwallis's officers, led them. As the surrendering soldiers held their hands up in the air, Tarleton coldly ordered his men to gun their captives down. This war crime became a major propaganda coup for the Revolutionary cause as Tarleton's brutality alienated South Carolinians previously uncommitted to the Revolution. The incident also inspired a battle cry. Since Tarleton had given no quarter to his defenseless prisoners, American militias often shouted "Tarleton's Quarter" when they subsequently butchered British or Loyalist troops attempting to surrender. The war turned more vindictive as Patriots destroyed the property of suspected Tories and vice versa, with both sides mutilating the corpses of their enemies.

Trying to restore colonial control in South Carolina, General **Horatio Gates**, the victor of Saratoga, led a hastily assembled army into the state in late July. Cornwallis confronted him at **Camden**, in the western backcountry, on August 16. When Gates attempted to fight the British in an open European-style battle, the result was a triumph for Cornwallis and another complete disaster for the Americans, as many of Gates's troops panicked, leading to the disintegration of his entire army. The bad news continued for the Americans when it was discovered that Benedict Arnold, who had been secretly negotiating with the British, switched sides in the war.

Passed over for promotions, court-martialed, and asked to return money to Congress when accused of misappropriating military funds for personal use, **Benedict Arnold** had grown so bitter against the American government and military command that he began selling military secrets to the British in 1779. After becoming commander of West Point on August 3, 1780, he offered to turn over the fortress to the British. His scheme was exposed when the American military captured a British spy, Major John André, carrying papers detailing the conspiracy. Hearing of André's arrest, Arnold fled and barely escaped arrest by George Washington's forces in New York. A military court sentenced André to death. Hoping to be executed by firing squad, as was the custom in the military for officers, he was hanged instead in Tappan, New York on October 2.

Meanwhile, the British military made Arnold a brigadier general and gave him a cash bonus. Prospects had looked bright for the Americans after the French alliance, but the battle for independence had hit another depressing low. The British had virtually destroyed the Continental Army in the South. "I have almost ceased to hope," Washington privately moaned during this string of disasters.

Settling Scores in the Carolinas

As the British had hoped, Loyalists emerged in significant numbers to support Cornwallis and the Crown. Whether Loyalist sentiments were uniquely widespread in the South remains unclear, but the collapse of the Continental Army and state governments brought the Tories out of the underground. The manipulative Philipsburg Proclamation succeeded in encouraging many slave owners to identify as Loyalists, but it also stoked the rage of Patriot masters against the British. Predating the war for independence were bitter divisions within the region such as the political feud between wealthy coastal planters (who had shaped the Patriot cause) and backcountry settlers (some of whom supported the king because of their grievances against the planters). But ultimately, the war cut across local communities and separated neighbor from neighbor.

Instead of revealing a Loyalist consensus, or enabling a secure re-conquest, British victories created a void in which Patriots (calling themselves Whigs) and Loyalists (or Tories) organized rival militias and paramilitary groups to defend themselves, kill each other, and seize each others' slaves. In this new, grim chapter of the war a new Patriot leader, **Francis Marion**, led a Whig militia, a fast-moving company of several dozen. "Marion's Men" made deadly surprise raids on larger groups of Tories and British regulars. Determined to eliminate Marion's Men, Tarleton chased them for nearly thirty miles, only to lose them in the swamps covering much of the South Carolina low country. "As for this damned old fox," Tarleton complained, "the Devil himself could not catch him."

Gaining notoriety as "the Swamp Fox," Marion continued to terrorize Tory militias and disrupt British lines of supply and communication. Soon, the Loyalist upsurge was starting to recede. After his victory at Camden, Cornwallis, still trailing a growing population of escaped slaves and taking advantage of their support, continued marching northward, intent on capturing North Carolina. But he could not mobilize the Tories without stirring up Whigs as well. At Kings Mountain, on the border between North and South Carolina, on October 7, converging Patriot militias attacked a Loyalist detachment led by Major Patrick Ferguson (one of Cornwallis's key officers). After killing Ferguson and winning the battle, the militiamen kept on shooting wounded soldiers and those trying to surrender. "Tarleton's quarter!" they shouted.

The Battles of Cowpens and Guilford Court House

Fierce Whig resistance prevented the restoration of British rule in the South. At the same time, with Lee and Gates discredited, Washington regained momentum with the appointment of a new, vastly more loyal core military leadership. After Gates's calamitous defeat in Camden, with Congress in despair, Washington recommended **Nathanael Greene**, who had combined field commands with the office of quartermaster general since Valley Forge and had performed heroically in the defeat at Camden. Brigadier General Daniel Morgan, the leader of the Virginia riflemen at Saratoga, came out of retirement and offered his services.

Taking the risk of dividing his own outnumbered forces, Greene supplied Morgan 700 men, giving them the mission of disrupting Cornwallis's supply lines, buying Greene more time to rebuild the rest of his army. Cornwallis dispatched Tarleton to destroy Morgan's detachment, now numbering about 1,000. But at Cowpens, South Carolina, on January 17, 1781, Morgan gained another measure of revenge for the Whigs and Continentals, striking another damaging blow to British control of the South.

Taking advantage of Tarleton's now-famous ferocity and aggressiveness, Morgan dispatched militiamen to advance against Tarleton. After firing two rounds, the infantrymen fell back. Tarleton pursued. Morgan had his troops fake a retreat, but with discipline and precision, they wheeled around against Tarleton's unprepared forces, who fell, under the withering line of fire. For the first time in the war, a significant force of British soldiers was almost completely destroyed in battle. Like Gates after Camden, Tarleton fled for his life and escaped with only a few of his men.

Undeterred by this serious setback, Cornwallis plunged into North Carolina, seeking to cut off the supplies that sustained Greene's forces and (he imagined) the rest of the American forces. Greene retreated quickly to the north, maintained his supply lines, and kept gathering reinforcements. At Guilford Court House, North Carolina, on March 15, the two armies faced off in battle for the only time. Although Cornwallis withstood fierce volleys and continued to advance, Morgan inflicted heavy casualties at a time when the war was becoming increasingly unpopular in Britain. Like Washington in previous battles, Greene kept his own army intact and left his opponent bleeding. "The enemy got the ground the other day, but we the victory," Greene proclaimed. "They had the splendor, we the advantage."

Both armies now turned away from each other and embarked on separate missions. Still searching for a way in which military power could resurrect British authority, Cornwallis looked farther north, toward Virginia, where he imagined uniting his forces with the rest of Clinton's army from New York. Greene envisioned something similarly ambitious but much more practical. Turning south, he set about clearing South Carolina of the occupying forces Cornwallis had left behind. Working closely with Whig militiamen under Marion and others—and taking advantage of collapsing Loyalist support—Greene coordinated a campaign of attacks on British garrisons. Despite several more hard-fought battles in which they held their ground, British unit commanders felt they had no choice but to abandon South Carolina's interior. By September 1781, like Clinton in New York, the British in South Carolina were confined to their stronghold in Charles Town.

Cornwallis Blunders—The Siege of Yorktown

Cornwallis yearned for a chance to battle the Continental Army face-to-face with his main army, a confrontation in which he thought British professionalism would prevail. In seeking this showdown, he unknowingly marched into a trap. In May, the general arrived in Petersburg, Virginia, and linked up with other British forces under the command of Benedict Arnold. Lafayette now commanded

the small army of Continentals based in Virginia while Cornwallis pondered his next move. Tarleton made another of his raids, chasing the Virginia legislature, which had moved from Richmond to Charlottesville. Tarleton and Arnold also staged a raid on Jefferson's estate at Monticello. They almost captured the revolutionary leader, then serving as governor of Virginia. Tarleton celebrated this humiliation of the author of the Declaration of Independence by helping himself to Jefferson's wine cellar.

In New York, Clinton struggled with formulating a plan to end the rebellion, unable to decide between sending the rest of his own forces, as Cornwallis hoped, to fight a decisive battle in Virginia and recalling troops from the South for a campaign in the North. In June, he ordered Cornwallis to find a defensible point on the Virginia coastline and set up a base that would accommodate naval forces. No final decision was ever reached about what purpose this base would ultimately serve, but in August, Cornwallis settled his army at **Yorktown**, a short distance up the York River from Chesapeake Bay—a site isolated on a peninsula between two rivers, but accessible to ships requiring deep-water clearance. As the British army and its trailing mass of escaped slaves began building fortress walls, Lafayette kept watch, reporting back to Washington.

Recognizing a precious opportunity, Washington seized it. Early in the year, he and Rochambeau agreed that any decisive move against British armies would require the participation of the French fleet in the West Indies, now commanded by Admiral Comte de Grasse. Washington had wanted to launch an operation against Clinton in New York, but Rochambeau suggested to de Grasse that an assault against Cornwallis in the Chesapeake region offered a better option. In mid-August, as word arrived from Lafayette about Cornwallis's base at Yorktown, a message also arrived from de Grasse that the greater part of the fleet was now bound for Chesapeake Bay. Washington's decision had been made for him. The long years of struggle, hardship, training, lessons learned from lost battles, and hard-won improvements in the Continental Army—as well as the arrival of French soldiers—all served as preparation for this moment.

Back in New York, Washington worked to deceive Clinton about his intentions. Within view of the British commander's scouts, American soldiers staged apparent preparations for a move against the British forces in Manhattan. Meanwhile, Washington and his staff wrote detailed instructions for the storage of supplies, repair of roads, and placement of boats along specific routes leading south. As late as the end of August, Clinton still believed Washington was repositioning his forces to attack New York. By then, however, the Continental and

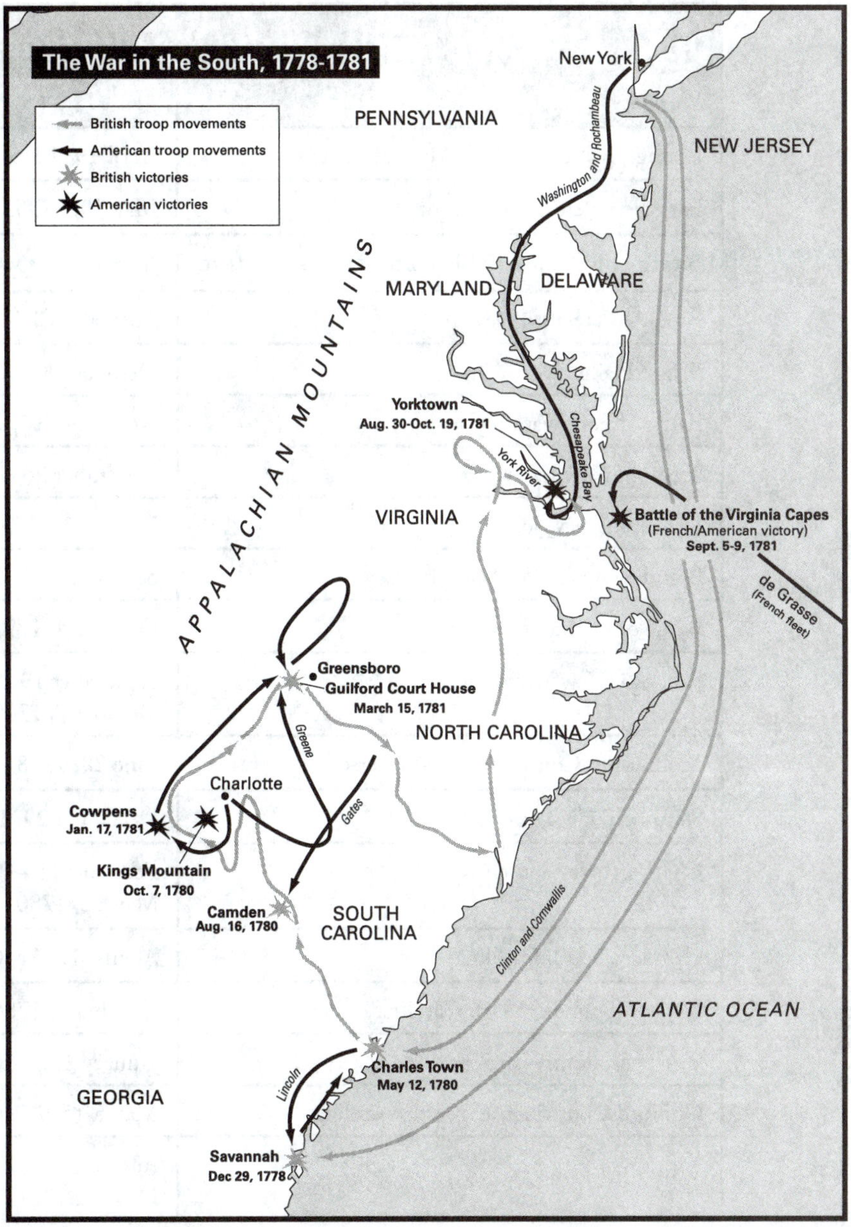

Map 6.3 The War in the South, 1778-1781

The War in the South, 1778-1781

Legend:
- British troop movements
- American troop movements
- British victories
- American victories

New York
PENNSYLVANIA
NEW JERSEY
Washington and Rochambeau
MARYLAND
DELAWARE
Yorktown
Aug. 30-Oct. 19, 1781
York River
Chesapeake Bay
VIRGINIA
Battle of the Virginia Capes
(French/American victory)
Sept. 5-9, 1781
de Grasse
(French fleet)
APPALACHIAN MOUNTAINS
Greensboro
Guilford Court House
March 15, 1781
Greene
NORTH CAROLINA
Gates
Charlotte
Cowpens
Jan. 17, 1781
Kings Mountain
Oct. 7, 1780
Camden
Aug. 16, 1780
SOUTH CAROLINA
Clinton and Cornwallis
ATLANTIC OCEAN
Charles Town
May 12, 1780
Lincoln
GEORGIA
Savannah
Dec 29, 1778

French troops had already passed through Trenton and were headed toward Virginia.

Shipping artillery and other heavy equipment on boats down the Delaware, they marched through Philadelphia on September 2, and then onward to the south, almost at running speed. Three weeks later they were in Williamsburg, Virginia, together with Lafayette, as well as French reinforcements from de Grasse and army and militia units arriving from throughout the states. By the end of the month, the expanded American and French armies had marched down the neck of the peninsula toward Yorktown and formed a semicircle around the British defenses. Cornwallis faced French and American troops on three sides on the ground while 300 warships commanded by Admiral de Grasse cut off an escape route by sea. Washington and Rochambeau received one more stroke of luck.

The British naval commander in the West Indies, Admiral George Brydges Rodney, 1st Baron Rodney, ordered a squadron led by Admiral Sir Samuel Hood to follow and intercept the French fleet. Hood's men, however, lost sight of the enemy's ships and arrived in the Chesapeake ahead of de Grasse's forces. Finding no French ships in Chesapeake Bay on August 25, Hood decided that the French were headed north to attack Clinton's army in New York City, and he directed his ships in that direction, away from the gathering French and American forces in Virginia. Back on Chesapeake Bay, the French fleet arrived unimpeded and landed troop reinforcements for Rochambeau.

On August 28, Admiral Hood arrived in New York and reported to Admiral Thomas Graves, commander-in-chief of the British naval forces in North America,

Table 6.1   Major Battles of the Revolutionary War

Battle	Date	Outcome
Lexington and Concord, Massachusetts	April 19, 1975	Contested
Fort Ticonderoga, New York	May 10, 1775	American victory
Breeds Hill ("Bunker Hill"), Boston, Massachusetts	June 17, 1775	Contested
Brooklyn Heights, New York	August 27, 1776	British victory
White Plains, New York	October 28, 1776	British victory
Battle of Fort Washington	November 16, 1776	British victory
Trenton, New Jersey	December 26, 1776	American victory
Princeton, New Jersey	January 3, 1777	American victory
Brandywine Creek, Pennsylvania	September 11, 1777	British victory
Battle of Germantown	October 4, 1777	British victory
Saratoga, New York	September 19 - October 7, 1777	American victory
Monmouth Court House, New Jersey	June 28, 1778	Contested
Savannah, Georgia	December 29, 1778	British victory
Charles Town, South Carolina	February 11 – May 12, 1780	British victory
Camden, South Carolina	August 16, 1780	British victory
Kings Mountain, South Carolina	October 7, 1780	American victory
Cowpens, South Carolina	January 17, 1781	American victory
Guilford Court House, North Carolina	March 15, 1781	Contested
Yorktown, Virginia	August 30 – October 19, 1781	American victory

that a French fleet from the West Indies was somewhere in American waters. Graves received intelligence that another French fleet had sailed from Newport, Rhode Island, and was headed south. Realizing Hood's mistake, Graves combined his forces with Hood's, and the British fleet redirected for Chesapeake Bay for what would be the most decisive naval confrontation of the war. On September 5, the combined forces of Graves and Hood appeared off the Virginia Capes. The French ships sailed hastily out to open water and into battle formation. As much as the outcome of the war depended on Washington's decisions and the Continental Army's abilities, it now rested as well on French naval strength. After long hours in which the opposing lines of ships maneuvered against each other and against the winds and the currents, then raked each other with cannon fire, the French maintained their line and the British failed to break through. As an east wind pushed the fleets farther out to sea, Graves decided to sail back to New York to try to organize a larger expedition. The bay remained under French control. Cornwallis and his army, in their fortress by the bay, remained cut off from the rest of the world.

In the final days at Yorktown, abandoning his headquarters in the city's grandest mansion, the British commander hid in a cave dug underneath a garden. Above ground, shells exploded and smashed against the crumbling fortress walls. In his last messages to Clinton, Cornwallis acknowledged the situation: "Against so powerful an attack, we cannot hope to make a very long resistance." Outside the city, Washington pressed for a rapid end to the siege, before another naval expedition

A Family Divided by Revolution:
Ben Franklin and His Tory Son

The American Revolution not only divided the United States between those supporting independence and supporters of the King, called Tories, it also tore apart one of the most famous families in the United States, dividing Benjamin Franklin from his estranged son William.

An author, inventor, and diplomat, the elder Franklin became perhaps the most famous American of the 18th century. As a signer of the Declaration of Independence and diplomat to France who secured a critical military alliance with that empire, Benjamin Franklin also served as one of the most important leaders of the independence cause.

Benjamin Franklin fathered William approximately in 1730, although the birth date and the identity of his mother is not entirely certain. William grew up with his father and Ben Franklin's common-law wife, Deborah Read, usually assumed to have been William's birth mother. William Franklin distinguished himself in the military, rising to the rank of captain while serving with Pennsylvania colonial troops during King George's War from 1744-1748.

His relationship with his father was not always troubled. Benjamin and William travelled together to England where the son earned a law degree. William also assisted his father during the latter's famous kite experiment in 1752 said to have conclusively demonstrated the electrical nature of lightning. When not keeping company, the two frequently exchanged letters and the two shared similar politics until critical events of 1775, when the battles of Lexington and Concord signaled the beginning of the revolution.

Both Franklins had won appointments from the British crown. The government named Ben Franklin Postmaster General of America in 1753, while in 1763, William had been appointed royal governor of New Jersey. In spite of his duties on this side of the Atlantic, Ben Franklin spent only two years in America in the 18-year period between 1757 and 1775, living most of those years in London. The Pennsylvania colony dispatched him there as its agent and for most of his tenure in the capital of the British Empire, Franklin remained a loyal subject of the crown.

That relationship strained as the British government passed a series of tax laws unpopular in the Thirteen Colonies such as the Stamp Act, the Sugar Act, and the Tea Act to defray the cost of defending its North American possessions against the French. Franklin became an open critic of these measures and subsequent actions such as the British Army's occupation of Boston.

British authorities sacked Ben Franklin in 1774 from his position as Postmaster when he was accused of revealing secret letters written by Massachusetts Governor Thomas Hutchinson that recommended the placement of more British troops in the colony and the suspension of traditional British liberties there in response to anti-tax resistance. The next year, he was appointed to represent Pennsylvania in the Second Continental Congress.

Benjamin urged William to resign the New Jersey governorship and enjoy life as a farmer. "'Tis an honester and a more honorable because more independent Employment," the father told his son. Ben and William Franklin reunited in 1775 at the home of a family friend and Ben discovered, to his fury, that the younger man remained loyal to the British government. William believed that the "patriots" were traitors to their country and that he was bound by honor to serve the king and what he still considered his country, Great Britain. The two had several shouting matches but William persisted, and by 1776, the year Benjamin served on the committee that drafted the Declaration of Independence and the Continental Congress approved it, William remained the last royal governor on duty.

Revolutionaries ousted William from power in June 1776, and he fled to Connecticut where he was soon placed under house arrest, but even there he managed to pass intelligence on to Tory forces. By May 1777, on the orders of the Continental Congress, authorities locked him in solitary confinement, placing him in a dirty cell that usually had been reserved for prisoners facing execution. William fell ill and lost his teeth before he was released as part of a prisoner exchange, and he crossed to greater safety in England.

Though they would meet again briefly in 1785, they never fully mended their relationship. "Indeed, nothing has ever hurt me so much and affected me with such keen Sensations, as to find myself deserted in my old Age by my only Son; and not only deserted, but to find him taking up Arms against me in a Cause wherein my good Fame, fortune, and Life were all at stake."

Ben Franklin cut William out of his will. Ben died in Philadelphia in 1790 at the age of 84, already an American icon and a revered international celebrity. William lived almost as long a life, passing away at age 83 and was buried in an unmarked grave in London, a now largely forgotten figure in his homeland. The political gulf between the two captured in microcosm the bitter divide in the United States during a revolution that in many ways was also the first American civil war.

could arrive from New York. (Graves did, in fact, arrive back in the Chesapeake, several days too late.)

Under General von Steuben's supervision, the American and French troops built a tightening ring of earthworks around Cornwallis's forces: parapets for reinforced shelter, batteries for gun emplacements, and redoubts for the massing of troops, all connected by lines of trenches. The network grew quickly once the American and French heavy artillery were fully in position and firing. Washington's right-hand man, Alexander Hamilton, who had spent years coveting battlefield glory, led an infantry brigade that stormed and seized a British redoubt, preparing the way for a final storming of the city. Cornwallis pre-empted the inevitable by asking on October 17 for peace terms. Too proud to capitulate to Washington, Cornwallis sent his deputy to present his sword as a gesture of surrender. Washington and Rochambeau, insulted by Cornwallis's absence, refused it, and directed that the sword be handed to one of the senior American officers, Benjamin Lincoln. The British taken prisoner numbered over 7,000 soldiers. As they were paraded between lines of American and French soldiers facing each other, a band played "The World Turned Upside Down."

THE WAR CONCLUDES

While the news from Yorktown sparked wild celebrations in Philadelphia and elsewhere across the former colonies, Washington immediately organized a return march to the encampments around New York City, where his forces remained for the next two years. In London, upon receiving the news of Cornwallis's surrender, Lord North cried out, "Oh, God, it's all over!" Determined to cut Britain's losses, the Parliament would not approve any further military attempts to prevent American independence. George III drafted a declaration of his abdication that he decided not to deliver, but he finally allowed North to resign as Prime Minister. A British envoy, Richard Oswald, came to Paris to meet with American and French delegates at a peace conference.

Even though the Congress directed the American peace delegation to follow the instructions of the French, American representative Benjamin Franklin focused on working out terms directly with Oswald. Ironically, British victories in 1782 over Admiral de Grasse in the Caribbean, and over Spanish attempts to reconquer Gibraltar, proved useful to the Americans, in that they persuaded France and Spain to wind down the war as well. On September 3, 1783, the American, British, and other European delegates signed treaties in Paris and Versailles. The **Treaty of Paris**, between Great Britain and the United

States, not only recognized American independence but also defined American territory as extending west all the way to the Mississippi River. Under the terms of the treaty, the Congress was to "earnestly recommend" that states return confiscated property to Loyalists, or provide compensation for their losses. The states, however, disregarded this provision. The British, meanwhile, ignored a provision requiring them to abandon military forts near the Great Lakes, which now lay within territory claimed by the United States. The British signed separate treaties with the French and the Spanish.

Cynically, and correctly, the French Foreign Minister Vergennes observed that the British "buy peace, rather than make it." Ministers in London soon realized that the former colonies would largely retain their traditional dependence on Britain's investment capital and export goods. The restoration of commercial ties between Britain and the newly independent states would restore many of the economic benefits of empire for the British. For the Americans, the uncertainty of the Revolutionary era seemed over. In the summer of 1776, when Howe's army conquered New York, Washington and the Continental Army seemed overmatched, and the war looked like a lost cause. Seven years later, the last British commander-in-chief to occupy Manhattan, Guy Carleton (who had succeeded Clinton the year before), received orders to evacuate. In addition to the remaining British and Hessian troops, the Royal Navy carried away some 29,000 Loyalists and also slaves liberated from Patriot masters (again technically violating the Treaty of Paris). On November 25, the last Union Jack (flag of the United Kingdom) was pulled down from a flagpole over lower Manhattan, and a cannon fired a final shot from one of the departing ships. Roughly 200,000 men (approximately half of those eligible by age) out of a total American population of between 3 to 4 million served at some point in the Continental Army or in state militia units.

American forces had lost approximately 25,000 dead, only 8,000 directly in combat with another 17,000 dying from exposure, disease, and the poor quality of medical care provided. Unaware of the existence of germs, Army doctors performed operations with unclean instruments. Believing that disease derived from an imbalance of body fluids, American medical doctors, like their British counterparts, would bleed patients, deliberately cutting a vein and draining blood to restore the correct ratio of blood, phlegm, and black and yellow bile. This procedure often killed badly dehydrated patients suffering influenza and other serious illnesses. An unknown but surely large number of deaths went unrecorded among soldiers and camp attendants. The total of deaths and injuries may have amounted to 1 in 4 of those who fought. The French lost about 2,000 in North America. Twenty thousand British soldiers died, as well as 7,600 German mercenaries; about 42,000 Redcoats and 5,000 Hessians deserted.

The long, brutal fight for independence had finally ended, but Americans would soon enter a rough adjustment period. In addition to persistent foreign policy issues with the major nations of Europe, the new republic would experience a host of internal problems spawned by the weakness of its new central government and exacerbated by the inherent differences among the former colonies. It remained to be seen how such a diverse nation would learn to endure without the common enemy of the British government providing the source of unity.

Chronology

1776   The Continental Congress approves the
Declaration of Independence.
Battle of Long Island
The American Crisis is published.
Battle of Trenton.

1777   Battle of Princeton.
Vermont abolishes slavery.
British troops enter Philadelphia.
Burgoyne surrenders at Saratoga.
Second Continental Congress approves
the Articles of Confederation.

1778   Winter at Valley Forge.
United States and France agree to a
military alliance.
Battle of Monmouth Court House.
Siege of Savannah.

1779   George Rogers Clark occupies Vincennes.
Benjamin Lincoln withdraws from Savannah.
Philipsburg Proclamation.

1780   Pennsylvania passes gradual emancipation law.
League of Armed Neutrality formed.
Waxhaw Massacre takes place.
Benedict Arnold given command at West Point
and betrays the American cause.
Cornwallis's forces overwhelm Gates's men in
Camden, South Carolina.

1781   Battles of Cowpens and Guilford
Courthouse.
Articles of Confederation ratified.
Elizabeth Freeman freed.
Siege of Yorktown.

1783   Treaty of Paris signed.

SUGGESTED READINGS

Carol Berkin, *Revolutionary Mothers: Women in the Struggle for American Independence* (2005).

Jeremy Black, *War for America: The Fight for Independence, 1775-1783* (1991).

Colin Calloway, *The American Revolution in the Indian Country: Crisis and Diversity in Native American Communities* (1995).

Stephen Conway, *The War of American Independence* (1995).

Edward Countryman, *The American Revolution* (1985).

Joseph Ellis, *American Sphinx: The Character of Thomas Jefferson* (1998).

___, *Founding Brothers: The Revolutionary Generation* (2000).

___, *His Excellency, George Washington* (2004).

David Hackett Fischer, *Washington's Crossing* (2004).

James Thomas Flexner, *Washington: The Indispensable Man* (1974).

Don Higgenbotham, *The War of American Independence, Policies and Practices 1763-1789* (1971).

Merrill Jensen, *The Founding of a Nation: A History of the American Revolution, 1763-1776* (1968).

Paul Douglas Lockhart, *The Drillmaster of Valley Forge: The Baron de Steuben and the Making of the American Army* (2008).

James Kirby Martin and Mark E. Lender, *A Respectable Army: The Military Origins of the Republic, 1763-1789* (1982.)

Robert Middlekauf, *The Glorious Cause: The American Revolution, 1763-1789* (1982).

Edward S. Morgan, *Birth of the Republic, 1763-1789* (1956).

Charles Royster, *A Revolutionary People at War: The Continental Army and American Character, 1775-1783* (1979).

Randy Shilts, *Conduct Unbecoming: Gays and Lesbians in the Military* (1993).

Barbara Clark Smith, *"Food Rioters and the American Revolution," The William and Mary Quarterly, 3rd Series, Volume II, No. 1* (January 1994).

Nancy Rubin Stuart, *The Muse of the Revolution: The Secret Pen of Mercy Otis Warren and the Founding of a Nation.* (2008).

Leonard E. Tise, *The American Counterrevolution: A Retreat from Liberty, 1783-1800* (1998).

Barbara W. Tuchman. *The March of Folly: From Troy to Vietnam.* (1984).

Review Questions

1. What strengths and weaknesses did each side possess during the Revolution? Ultimately, which factors proved decisive for the American victory?

2. What major flawed assumptions did the British military make in its war plans against the Continental Army?

3. Discuss the British efforts to undermine colonial resistance during the Revolution by the issuance of various proclamations dealing with slavery.

4. Discuss the impact of the Revolution on colonial women.

5. What role did international diplomacy play in securing a victory for the Americans in the Revolution?

Glossary of Important People and Concepts

Benedict Arnold
John Burgoyne
Battle of Camden
George Rogers Clark
Henry Clinton
Lord Charles Cornwallis
Benjamin Franklin
Horatio Gates
Nathanael Greene
Hessians
William Howe
Marquis de Lafayette
Battle of Long Island
Francis Marion
Lord Frederick North
Treaty of Paris
Philipsburg Proclamation
Battle of Princeton
Battle of Saratoga
Friederich Wilhelm Von Steuben
Tories
Valley Forge
Mercy Otis Warren
George Washington
Yorktown Siege

JOURNAL

OF THE

PROCEEDINGS

OF THE

CONGRESS,

Held at PHILADELPHIA,

September 5, 1774.

PHILADELPHIA:

Printed by WILLIAM and THOMAS BRADFORD,
at the *London Coffee-House.*

Chapter Seven

THE CRITICAL PERIOD, 1781-1789

A common plot device in science fiction films has been time travel. One of the most popular movies in this genre has been the trilogy that started with the 1985 film **Back to the Future**. In this story arc, the main character, Marty McFly, is accidentally dispatched 30 years into the past where he unintentionally prevents his parents, then teenagers, from meeting and falling in love. Unless he can correct this alteration in history, he and his brother and sister will never be born. In this film and two sequels, McFly continually alters the future in wildly unanticipated ways. As the scientific author Stephen Jay Gould writes, this film accurately captures the progress of history. The past is treated as contingent. Nothing is inevitable.

That is not how most of the public sees American history. The leaders of the American Revolution such as George Washington, Ben Franklin, Thomas Jefferson, and John Adams traditionally are imagined by the public to be uniquely farsighted, with the outcome of the American Revolution and the destiny of the country never really in doubt. In the early twenty-first century, conservative Christian evangelist and amateur historian David Barton argued in a series of bestselling books that God directly inspired the Founding Fathers. Many other Americans accepted the idea that the American Revolution, the writing of the Constitution, the Republic's increasingly democratic institutions, and the spreading of the United States from coast to coast were foreordained. Even some of the Founders convinced themselves of this.

Writing just after the Revolution ended in 1783, George Washington concluded that there must have been some divine plan in Americans being "placed in the most enviable condition, as the sole Lords and Proprietors of a vast Tract of Continent, comprehending all the various soils and Climates of the world, and abounding with all the necessaries and conveniences of life . . . [This] seems to be peculiarly designed by Providence for the display of human greatness and felicity." With hindsight, Washington seemed to suggest that the War for Independence could not have turned out any other way than with the United States triumphing over Great Britain.

Washington neglected to consider the Native Americans who still lived on the continent when he enthused about whites being the "sole Lords and proprietors" of North America. He also forgot his deep doubts and fears during the war over how the American Revolution would end and his own frequent sense that independence was a lost cause. Once the fighting was over, he could pretend that Americans had always been destined for greatness, that it had been part of God's plan from the beginning of time.

That kind of confidence faded once again in the first decade of independence. By the mid-1780s, many leaders wondered if the new American republic would survive the eighteenth century. As the country languished under its first constitution, the Articles of Confederation, John Adams feared the United States was doomed. With independence less than a half-decade old, he reflected on previous republics—the city-states in ancient Greece and medieval Italy, and the short-lived Roman Republic almost 2,000 years earlier. Adams shuddered as he considered how transitory those earlier experiments in republican government had been and contemplated *the vexing complications of governing a vast nation as diverse and complex as the United States. "The lawgivers of antiquity legislated for single cities . . . [but] who can legislate for 20 or 30 states, each of which is greater [in size] than Greece or Rome at those times?" he asked with despair.*

Adams was not alone in his pessimism. The Congress, the only branch of the federal government established under the Articles of Confederation, poorly managed the country and commanded little respect overseas. A depression ravaged America after the Revolution ended and lasted for most of the 1780s. A farmers' rebellion broke out in Massachusetts. Former Revolutionary War officers grumbled about the need to overthrow the Congress.

These men feared for the future, and they floundered for an answer. There were so many different paths American history could have taken. A coup led by former military officers could have installed Washington, if he accepted the post, as king or dictator. Several states could have seceded, asking for readmission to the British Empire or to become part of Spain's imperial realm. Farmers' revolts could have led to a second revolution, this one not managed by a relatively conservative moneyed elite but by the angry dispossessed. This second revolution could have been a full-scale class revolt and led in a more radical direction, as did the French Revolution that started in 1789. Nothing about the future was preordained in the 1780s.

To corral the chaos, the leading men of their times gathered in Philadelphia in 1787 to plot a non-violent overthrow of the existing government and write a new constitution that would re-establish what they saw as the proper social and economic order. The Framers of the Constitution were well off, but still a motley crew. These were not the demigods later depicted in national myth, but deeply flawed and uncertain men, philanderers and rogues like Gouverneur Morris of Pennsylvania, privileged bluebloods like George Mason of Virginia and Preston Butler of South Carolina, and cynical alcoholics like Luther Martin of Maryland. One cliché has it that one should never watch law or sausages being made, because the process is so unappetizing. These often less-than-heroic Framers of the Constitution were sausage-makers of the first degree. They cut moral corners and compromised principles, particularly on the issue of slavery, in writing the final document that became the Constitution of the United States.

At several points, the process almost completely fell apart, and several state delegations nearly stormed out of the Convention over the issue of slavery and representation in the new Congress that the delegates debated. It was messy and what would be created in Philadelphia was definitely not inevitable. A misstep at several points and the delegates in Philadelphia would have bequeathed to their descendants a very different future—one in which the new country would

have fragmented and failed. Convenience and chance ruled the day as much as inspiration.

THE RADICALISM OF THE AMERICAN REVOLUTION

The American Revolution was certainly about battles, but, more importantly, it was about ideas. As noted in the previous chapter, the concept of popular sovereignty (the idea that governments can rule legitimately only with the consent of the people and that governments existed solely to protect "life, liberty and the pursuit of property") had arisen in seventeenth-century England. This viewpoint suggested that governments failing to meet those ends lacked legitimacy and could be justly overthrown by the people. Such were the explanations offered to explain the overthrow and execution of Charles I in 1649 during the English Civil War, the overthrow and exile of the last Stuart king in England, James II, in 1688, and finally, the American Revolution.

The elites leading the American Revolution sought to create a republic in a world of kings, but the concept of the monarchy was already decaying in England and elsewhere in Europe and the Americas before shots were fired at Lexington and Concord in 1775. As the historian Gordon Wood wrote, "Republicanism seeped everywhere in the eighteenth-century Atlantic world, eroding monarchial society from within, wearing away all the traditional supports of kingship, ultimately desacralizing monarchy to the point where, as [eighteenth-century Scottish philosopher] David Hume observed, 'the mere name of king commands little respect; and to talk of a *king* as God's vice-regent on earth, or to give him any of those magnificent titles which formerly dazzled mankind, would but excite laughter in everyone.'"

The leaders of the American Revolution, however, took the ideas of the Enlightenment much further. The years from the French and Indian War in the 1750s and 1760s to the ratification of the United States Constitution in 1788 saw a subtle but important shift in the emerging United States in terms of class, the separation of church and state, slavery, and gender politics. The American Revolution started as a mere shift in who would rule—the British king or wealthy American oligarchs—but opened the door for later, more radical change.

The Revolution's Impact on Class and Family

After the Revolution, inheritance still mattered and the rich still ruled, but the aristocracy became markedly more open-ended. Lineage increasingly mattered less

Map 7.1 The United States (1787)

than financial independence, and men born to relatively humble means sometimes rose to the top of the social and political ladder. "There are but two *sorts* of men in the world, freemen and slaves," John Adams declared in 1775. The freemen, as Adams's English contemporary John Toland put it, were "men of property, or persons that are able to live of themselves." Those who derived their living by working for others were the ones Adams called slaves. Adams saw independent farmers, business owners and professionals like doctors, lawyers and the clergy as the freemen. The freemen's supposed independence from political blackmail and manipulation is the excuse the Founders used for limiting suffrage and the right to run for and hold public office to property owners. However, after the Revolution, Vermont extended the vote to all adult white men who were not slaves or indentured servants. Kentucky entered the Union in 1792, and its state constitution included no property requirements for voting or holding office. Other states generally reduced the property requirements for voting.

The Founders also made tentative steps towards expanding the freemen class. State legislatures began abolishing traditions that limited the number of self-sufficient property owners within families, customs such as **primogeniture** (in which only the oldest son inherits a father's estate) or entail (in which inheritance is limited to lineal descendants). Before the Revolution, widows usually were granted only lifetime use of their husband's estates. New state laws allowed widows to own outright one-third of their deceased spouses' property, giving them the freedom to dispense with this property as they pleased.

In the late 1700s, a revolution took place within the American family. Even as the just-born United States had severed its connection to the British king, the dictatorial authority of fathers within families noticeably loosened. This process began earlier in the 1700s when more Americans survived childhood, which left more adult children without estates due to primogeniture. As land became more expensive and there were more adults who could not count on inheriting an estate, more adult children moved away from their birth families. The number of marriages arranged by parents as business deals declined, and these newly independent young adults began to marry for personal reasons such as romance, sexual attraction, or unplanned pregnancies. Early American authors writing advice books urged their readers to have marriages based on affection, and told parents that they should rely less on harsh physical punishments and have more open, affectionate relationships with their children.

Changing Attitudes toward Women

Before the Revolution, women were universally portrayed as physically and morally weak. Sin came to the world and God cursed humanity with mortality because Eve succumbed to temptation by the serpent in the Garden of Eden, ministers insisted. After the Revolution, some men acknowledged the role women had played in the success of the war effort. Women had managed the family economy, run farms and businesses, and negotiated with merchants while their husbands were off to war. After the Revolution, the United States had a new, republican system of government in which the political leaders would not be assumed to hold office because God directly selected them. No one knew if a rotating cast of politicians who could be voted out of office, even (after 1789) the presidency, would command respect. Many men realized that women were the first and sometimes the only teachers children had, and it would be up to what were now called "**republican mothers**" to teach their children respect for the new form of government and loyalty to the new nation.

In sermons and in literature in the post-Revolution period, women were no longer portrayed as weaklings without character, but as bedrocks of virtue. Literacy among women in the Northeast skyrocketed. In New England, the literacy rate for women reached 45 percent, one of the highest levels in the world. More affluent women became the chief audience for a wildly popular art form, the novel, which often depicted virginal heroines rejecting the advances of scoundrels and, with grit, holding off marriage proposals until an equally pure hero arrived on the scene. Even as literature depicted women in a more positive light, by the 1790s, female academies began to appear in the United States, creating a better-educated population of women.

This softer attitude towards women, unfortunately, became a double-edged sword. America's patriarchy deemed that these brave, pure "republican mothers" had maintained their virtue precisely because, unlike men, they had been shielded from the supposedly corrupting world of business and politics. This became one more sexist reason for denying women a political voice and keeping them economically subordinate. In 12 of the 13 states women could not vote. In New Jersey, for a time women could vote if they were the heads of households, but by 1807, these women had been disenfranchised.

Separation of Church and State

The Revolution also marked the beginning of separation of church and state. In several of the thirteen colonies, the officially established faith had been the Church of England, an institution headed by the king. This name and this relationship became untenable in the new United States. In the United States, Anglican leaders dubbed their denomination the "**Episcopal Church**" and severed direct ties to the mother church in England. As the established religion, Anglican churches had been directly subsidized by taxpayers and the Church of England had the exclusive right to conduct marriage ceremonies. After the Revolution, across the South the Anglican Church was "**disestablished**," meaning it lost public funding and its special privileges. This began in Virginia in 1786 when the state passed the Thomas Jefferson-authored Statute for Religious Freedom, which announced in its preamble that, "God hath created the mind free."

The separation of church and state proceeded most slowly in New England, except in Rhode Island, which had established religious freedom for all Protestants in its original colonial charter. In states like Massachusetts, the Congregationalist Church (descended from the Puritan movement) had been established as the state religion by law, and ministers and churches still received tax support, a status not changed until 1818 in Connecticut and 1833 in Massachusetts. Most states continued to restrict office holding to Christians, or specifically Protestants, with many, for instance, having so-called "Jew bills" that required elected officials to affirm a belief in Jesus as savior. However, after the Revolution, the general public became less comfortable with religious coercion and marginally more tolerant of Jews and Catholics. For instance, just before the Revolution, American colonists held ferocious protests upon hearing that the British government had recognized the Catholic Church in the Quebec Act of 1774. A decade later, hardly a voice of opposition was heard when Pope Pius VI consecrated John Carroll of Maryland as the first Roman Catholic bishop in America during the 1780s.

The Revolution and Slavery

The struggle for independence transformed race relations in ways subtle but profound. After the Revolution, many whites felt painfully aware of the hypocrisy of a supposedly freedom-loving people embracing slavery. Constitutional protections aside, many masters began to emancipate their slaves. Not long after the Revolution, indentured servitude vanished, passing almost unnoticed in the 1820s. Within a decade after Yorktown, slavery had virtually disappeared in New England, and in the North would soon be confined primarily to port cities in New York and New Jersey. Vermont banned slavery in its new constitution in 1777. The Massachusetts Court of Common Pleas essentially ruled slavery unconstitutional four years later. **Elizabeth Freeman**, a slave, had filed a lawsuit arguing that her involuntary servitude violated the new Massachusetts state constitution which read, in part, "All men are born free and equal, and have certain natural, essential, and unalienable rights; among which may be reckoned the right of enjoying and defending their lives and liberties; that of acquiring, possessing, and protecting property; in fine, that of seeking and obtaining their safety and happiness." The court ruled for Freeman and another slave named Brom on August 21, 1781, and ordered them freed. Even though the decision pertained directly only to those two slaves, across Massachusetts and New Hampshire slaves abandoned their masters who, sensing how the tide of history had changed, did not seek to recapture them. Slavery essentially disappeared in those two states. Rhode Island banned slavery completely in 1784. Congress, with its powerful southern caucus, recognized that chattel slavery was likely doomed in the North and voted to abolish slavery in the newly organized Northwest Territory (modern-day Illinois, Indiana, Michigan, Ohio, and Wisconsin) in the Northwest Ordinance passed July 13, 1787.

Quakers began to insist that their members free their servants. Pennsylvania passed the world's first gradual emancipation law on March 1, 1780. The law did not emancipate those already enslaved but provided that the children of those slaves would be freed when they reached 28 years of age. Under the law it would potentially take decades for slavery to completely disappear and, tragically, some white masters determined not to lose their financial investment in their chattel auctioned off the slave offspring destined for emancipation to southern buyers before they reached their 28th birthday. Other whites kidnapped free blacks, smuggling them to the South for auction.

The Pennsylvania Abolition Society became one of the first anti-slavery organizations in the country, forming in 1774 to combat such horrific abuses of the law. By 1800, Philadelphia boasted the largest free black community in the country. The African-American community there had already built many of its own institutions, including political groups, churches, and poverty relief societies. The black community in Philadelphia would establish the African Methodist Episcopal Church in 1818, becoming one of the largest black denominations in the country.

For all its tragic flaws, Pennsylvania's emancipation statute provided a model for other northern states. New York and New Jersey adopted similar laws in 1799 and 1804, respectively. By 1830, the number of African Americans enslaved north of the Mason-Dixon Line dwindled to a mere 3,568, with more than 66 percent of that number confined to New Jersey. Even Upper South states like Maryland and Virginia experienced a wave of emancipation, with the legislatures allowing masters to free their slaves. Twenty percent of Maryland slaves had won their freedom by 1820.

Idealism did not motivate all of these emancipations. The price for tobacco had dropped worldwide, and Southerners had not yet found a replacement cash crop. By the 1790s, British industrialization had given birth to a massive textile industry, which in turn spurred an increased demand for cotton. Southern planters cultivated long-staple cotton, a fragile species that grew well only on the Sea Islands off Georgia and South Carolina. Long-staple cotton was easy for slaves to remove the seeds, but the crop did not thrive in most of the inland South. The hardier short-staple variety could grow anywhere in the South with at least 200 frost-free days a year, basically anywhere south of Virginia. The problem for growers was that short-staple cotton had much stickier seeds, making it difficult to remove by hand, a necessary step before the cotton could be processed. On average, one adult slave, working at top speed for an entire day, could clean only about one pound of short-staple cotton, a profit-destroying rate of return for the high labor costs. Absent a technological innovation, it was hard for many planters to see a future for slavery, which, in short, was becoming too expensive and providing too few returns. The loss of profits, most likely, inspired many of the emancipations in southern states like Maryland.

Another ten thousand slaves also received their emancipation papers in Virginia in the aftermath of the Revolution, including the three hundred owned by George Washington. As Washington got older, he sought to more closely match his claimed political principles with his personal life. With the exception of Ona Judge, a woman enslaved by his wife Martha who escaped and was tirelessly hunted by the couple as long as they lived, Washington became the only Founding Father from Virginia to emancipate all other slaves he personally owned. During his presidency, when the capital was located in Philadelphia, he penned a letter to the British agricultural expert Arthur Young, confessing a desire "more powerful than all the rest" to "liberate a certain species of property which I possess very repugnantly to my feelings, but which

Ona Judge Staines
and the Tireless Pursuit of Freedom

George Washington, at a minimum, left a mixed record regarding slavery. Washington and his wife Martha owned 317 slaves at the time of the first president's death in 1799. As commander of the Continental Army during the American Revolution, Washington only reluctantly accepted the service of African Americans from northern states who had enlisted in return for their emancipation, fearful of the impact these free men would have on slavery in the South. In his last years, Washington expressed doubts about the morality of slavery and, in his will, he freed slaves he personally owned. But that emancipation did not apply to the slaves owned by his wife and then her estate, and many of George's slaves had married Martha's and thus remained emotionally bound to the plantation. When some slaves escaped, Washington did not seek their recapture vigorously. There was at least one notable exception.

The Washingtons' obsessive search for one escaped servant of Martha's, Ona "Oney" Judge Staines, demonstrated clearly that slavery was no less cruel at Mount Vernon than anywhere else in pre-Emancipation America. The daughter of a white tailor and an enslaved African-American woman, Staines became a favorite of Martha Washington's and was prized for her sewing talents. When George became president, she became part of the small party of slaves brought by the First Couple to the original American capital in New York City and who then followed them when the capital moved to Philadelphia.

The Washingtons took care to never keep their slaves in Pennsylvania for more than six months at a time, because the state's gradual emancipation law might have resulted in their unintended freedom. Brought to Philadelphia at age 17, Staines spent her young adulthood in a city with a large Quaker population that had begun campaigning against slavery. Philadelphia was home to the Pennsylvania Abolition Society, and free African Americans formed a majority of the black population in the city. Staines often wandered without supervision, attending plays and visiting markets outside of the supervision of her masters.

In the last months of George Washington's presidency, the president's family planned to spend the summer at its estate in Mount Vernon in Virginia, a state with highly restrictive slave laws. The news that Martha Washington planned to will Staines to her emotionally volatile granddaughter Elizabeth Parke Custis after her death alarmed the young woman. On May 21, 1796, while the Washingtons ate dinner, Staines simply walked out of the president's residence and slipped from their control for the rest of her life. "I had friends among the colored people of Philadelphia, had my things carried there beforehand, and left Washington's house while they were eating dinner," she said in a later interview.

The Washingtons took out newspaper advertisements with descriptions of Staines seeking help in finding her. With help from friends, Staines boarded a ship that carried her to Portsmouth, New Hampshire. There, a friend of Martha's extended family recognized her and notified the Washingtons.

Upon hearing of her location, the president sought the help of Secretary of the Treasury Oliver Wolcott, Jr., to recapture her. A customs collector confronted Staines, but she warned him that local abolitionists might rise up if she were abducted and such a scene would badly damage the president's image. She would agree to return only if the Washingtons made an ironclad pledge to free her upon both of their deaths.

Judge's bold demands affronted President Washington, who could not believe a slave woman would dare set conditions for her return. She set a bad example for his remaining slaves, Washington worried, and endangered a fortune built on human bondage. Toward the end of Washington's presidency, his former chattel married a sailor, Jack Staines. In 1797, a nephew of the Washingtons, Burwell Bassett, Jr., plotted to kidnap Staines, but the scheme was thwarted when Staines was warned by New Hampshire Sen. John Langdon who, though he was a friend of the former president, found the planned abduction too disturbing to not intervene.

While the Washingtons pursued Ona, the now retired president, perhaps motivated by guilt, began to express to his friends qualms about owning human property. Yet, Staines never experienced legal emancipation, even after George died in 1799 and Martha passed away three years later. She remained a fugitive until her death in 1848 but, through her bravery and willingness to stand up to the most politically powerful man in the nation, she maintained her freedom and that of her children.

imperious necessity compels, and until I can substitute some other expedient by which expenses not in my power to avoid (however well disposed I may be to do it) can be defrayed."

Washington confided this desire to no one else. When he left the presidency in 1797, however, Washington let several slaves escape. In his will, drawn up in July 1799, he implemented his own gradual emancipation plan. The slaves he still had would be freed as soon as his wife Martha died. In that document, he also instructed his heirs to insure that elderly slaves unable to care for themselves would receive shelter, clothing, and food. Fearing that younger freed men and women would be kidnapped and sold by slavetraders to harsh sugar plantations in the Indies or elsewhere, he demanded that none of his former chattel be transported out of Virginia. Children abandoned by their parents or with parents unable to care for them, would be provided for until they were old enough to learn a trade and "be taught to read and write."

Greed and white fears about the presence of a large population of free black sparking an African American insurrection, however, dampened the post-Revolution spike in emancipations and most slave owners kept their chattel in chains

Emancipation was a complicated business, and most slave owners did not attempt it. Thomas Jefferson, whose words inspired the Revolution, and who often, unlike Washington, publicly condemned the trans-Atlantic slave trade and slavery itself, freed only two of his many slaves in his lifetime. Jefferson had a sexual and possibly romantic relationship with one of his house slaves, **Sally Hemings**, beginning during his diplomatic service in Paris when she was as young as sixteen. Hemings was the half-sister of Jefferson's late wife, Martha Skelton (they had the same father). Jefferson and Hemings had as many as six children together, and many contemporaries, especially his political opponents, remarked on how much the offspring resembled their master. Before his death, Jefferson freed Sally Hemings's older brothers Robert and James Hemings. He also freed five members of the Hemings family in his will, including his three surviving children by her: Madison, Eston, and Harriet. In spite of his familial relationship with African Americans and his apparently affectionate relationship with Sally Hemings, Jefferson demeaned the appearance of blacks and would never believe that "all men were created equally" in terms of intellect. As he wrote in his book, *Notes on the State of Virginia*, published in 1781:

> Comparing them [blacks to whites] by their faculties of memory, reason, and imagination, it appears to me, that in memory they are equal to the whites; in reason much inferior, as I think one [black] could scarcely be found capable of tracing and comprehending the investigations of Euclid; and that in imagination they are dull, tasteless, and anomalous.

Even if he saw blacks as an inferior race, and contended that orangutans were attracted to black women, in the same book Jefferson outlined a plan by which all African Americans born after 1800 would eventually be emancipated. In 1784, he proposed legislation to the Confederation Congress that would have prohibited slavery in all Western territories, a plan that failed by a single vote. Already, however, the Revolution had inspired a small minority of white Americans to call for an end to slavery immediately.

The Revolutionary generation more often responded to pragmatism than high-minded beliefs. Slavery would not be abolished until a bloody civil war seven decades later, because most slaveowners would not agree to peaceful abolition unless they were paid for their lost human property. Some advocated what came to be known as compensated emancipation, but any such scheme would have proven catastrophically expansive. A government program of paying masters to free their slaves would cost between $100 and $200 per slave (between $2,500 and $5,000 today). At the higher rate, the total cost for compensated emancipation for the entire slave population in the United States in 1790 would have reached $140 million (about $3.5 billion today). By contrast, the entire federal budget in 1790 came to less than $7 million ($175 million today). Furthermore, the cost of any plan for paying slave owners for liberated human property, only skyrocketed as the years went on. The slave population had climbed from 500,000 in 1776 to about 700,000 in 1790, according to the first federal census. At that rate, the slave population would double every two decades. It would be up to a later generation to pay for universal emancipation not in cash but in blood.

The American Revolution would inspire other major revolts in the coming decades. Bad harvests, widespread hunger, staggering national debt from their involvement in the American Revolution, and the rise of Enlightenment ideas that questioned the absolute power held by their monarchs led to the French Revolution, an epoch of violence, chaos and war beginning in 1789. The French revolutionaries sent King Louis XVI and his wife Marie Antoinette to the guillotine. By 1793, the French Convention and its "Committee of Public Safety" ruled France. With good cause, the committee believed that the Catholic Church had allied itself with the foreign

Benjamin Franklin at the Constitutional Convention.

powers trying to overthrow the government. The Convention ordered church property seized, and priests and nuns executed, along with much of the French nobility. Soon, even former leaders of the revolution fell under the suspicion of the government and were executed during what came to be known as the "Reign of Terror." As many as 50,000 died at the hands of the revolutionary government by the time the Terror ended in 1794.

In 1804, Haiti saw the conclusion of the first-ever successful slave revolt in the history of the world resulting in the establishment of a new nation. Formerly the French colony of Saint-Domingue, the island had been converted into a giant sugar plantation dependent on African slave labor. Conditions were so horrific that deaths from malnutrition, exhaustion, and exposure exceeded births each year. The uprising began in 1791. Within weeks, slaves avenged themselves against their abusive former masters, torturing some of their one-time tormentors, killing 4,000 whites and setting aflame 180 sugar plantations and scores of coffee and indigo plantations.

The **Haitian Revolution** set a frightening example for American slaves. American slaveowners worried that their human property would see the Haitian revolutionaries as role models. The United States would place an embargo on Haiti, causing the island nation much economic damage, and would not recognize its government until the Civil War in 1862. Jefferson once famously advocated

repeated revolutions as healthy for societies, suggesting that one was needed every 20 years. "The tree of liberty must be refreshed from time to time with the blood of patriots and tyrants," he famously said. He did not feel that way about slave revolts. The Haitian Revolution seemed to him to be a frightful prophecy of the United States' future, seeing only a racial Armageddon if blacks were to be free. As he wrote in *Notes on the State of Virginia*, "Deep rooted prejudices entertained by the whites; ten thousand recollections, by the blacks, of the injuries they have sustained; new provocations; the real distinctions which nature has made; and many other circumstances, will divide us into parties, and produce convulsions which will probably never end but in the extermination of the one or the other race." A racial revolution, one dreaded by many of the Founders of the American Republic, would unfold in ways they never anticipated, coming slowly and sweeping away the world inhabited by the Revolutionary generation. Revolutions, once started, are hard to stop.

The leaders of the Revolution had ended the rule over the colonies by a king and ushered in an era of revolts in France, Haiti, and elsewhere that more dramatically altered those societies. But the American Founders still created a new government in which Protestant white men of property held a monopoly of power, in which slavery thrived, in which women were disenfranchised and almost all were financially dependent on their nearest male relatives or husbands, and in which Native Americans continued to be the victims of imperialism and genocide.

Nevertheless, a door had been opened. Suffocating paternalism had weakened, and the groundwork had been laid for religious diversity and for generations of abolitionists and feminists. It was not even the beginning of the freedom revolutions that would mark the period from 1865 with the abolition of slavery to the gay rights triumphs in the early twenty-first century, but it was at least the beginning of the beginning.

CHAOS UNDER
THE ARTICLES OF CONFEDERATION

The Americans won the war, but they almost lost the peace. By 1787, six years after the victory at Yorktown secured the independence of the United States, many inside and outside of the country wondered if Americans could actually govern themselves. The country teetered on the edge of economic ruin, the political system lay in chaos, and everywhere lay signs that a second revolution loomed, this time aimed at overthrowing American elites.

Through the years of fighting, the United States lacked a fully functional national government. The

Second Continental Congress raised armies, approved officers' commissions, set policies on war and diplomacy, issued paper currency (basically IOU's, promising future redemption in hard cash) to pay for expenses, and declared independence, all in response to immediate practical necessities. Yet the Congress lacked other powers, most important among these the authority to impose taxes. On November 15, 1777, the delegates finally approved the **Articles of Confederation**, which served as the United States' first constitution.

Not until March 1, 1781, did the Articles of Confederation go into effect. Drafted at a time when the American political leadership blamed the American Revolution on a king they believed had assumed dictatorial powers and the British Parliament, which they thought overruled the authority of local elected governments, the Articles reflected a deep distrust of central government. The national government created under the Articles became one of the weakest in modern Western history.

The delegates in the Continental Congress wrote the Articles with the intention of placing strict limits on the national government's authority. They insisted on a written constitution. Many revolutionary leaders believed that England's unwritten "constitution" had allowed the Parliament and King George III too much opportunity to claim unchecked power. Not only the Congress but also the states started drafting written constitutions, seen as contracts between the national and state governments and the people as a whole, with the powers, responsibilities, and limitations of government bodies clearly spelled out.

Under the Articles, the Congress served as the only branch of government. There was no presidency under the Articles, no single executive who could transform into the tyrant George III had supposedly become. Each state delegation, regardless of size, got one vote in the Congress. The Congress was not completely impotent. The Articles gave the Congress authority to declare war and make peace, negotiate treaties with other nations and Native American peoples, conduct foreign policy, and formulate military strategy.

The Articles, however, placed severe limits on the Congress, which could not impose a military draft during the Revolution but could only request that the independent-minded states provide a fair share of troops based on their population. The idea of "states' rights"—the concept that state governments were more representative of the voters and should therefore enjoy sovereignty within their borders, granting only limited powers to the federal government—served as the governing principle of the Articles. The drafters of the Articles hoped that state legislatures would see the big picture and put the country ahead of local concerns. Unfortunately, states often worried more about their individual security, and congressional requisitions for troops often went unmet. In a critical error, the Articles provided Congress no power to tax. Again, Congress could only request each state to pay a fair share based on population. Facing financial problems of their own, the states often balked at congressional requests for funds, leaving Washington's Continental Army often underfed, underclothed, and underarmed. The Congress paid soldiers and sailors, as well as merchants selling goods to the military, in paper government notes to be redeemed at some vague future date. As more notes went into circulation, the paper became almost worthless. Washington, who became a bitter critic of the Articles, would say that this system of government almost caused the United States to lose the war.

Lacking the power of the purse also meant that the Congress had limited funds to build roads, bridges, and other infrastructure that not only served citizens but also were critical for the Continental Army's military operations. The Congress also could not regulate trade between the states. Some states passed burdensome taxes on goods that crossed their borders, leaving consumers in some parts of the country paying substantially higher prices for products than their neighbors. The Articles created no federal judiciary to settle conflicts between states over issues like taxes and boundaries or between citizens living in different states. The "United" States were united in name only and poorly functioned as a loose alliance of thirteen independent republics.

Such a weak government could not adequately respond to economic conditions after the combat phase of the Revolution ended in 1781. Following the war, commerce with America's chief trading partner, Great Britain, dropped to 40 percent of the pre-war level. The drop in trade created a post-war recession, which caused a drop in tax revenues. The United States ran up heavy debts to the French, the Dutch, and others during the war, and each year it borrowed more money because the individual states provided less money than requisitioned. Between 1781 and 1786, because of the shortfall of funds requested from the states, the Congress ran up a $2.3 million deficit in addition to the $37 million owed by the Congress for loans taken out to pay for the war (over $1 billion in 2012 dollars). The states owed approximately $14 million, or almost $400 million in today's dollars. By 1787, the Congress faced a day of reckoning as the interest on the foreign debt mushroomed and the principal on foreign loans came due.

Over time, the crushing burden of debt exposed the serious weakness of the American government under the Articles. Unable to tax, the Congress began printing

Table 7.1   The Articles of Confederation and the Constitution Compared

	Articles	Constitution
Power to Tax	No power to tax	Congress has right to levy taxes
Representation in Congress	Equal representation of states	Upper house (Senate) with 2 votes; lower house (House of Representatives) based on population
Amendment Process	Unanimous consent of the states	2/3 vote of both houses of Congress or a national convention plus 3/4 vote of state legislatures or state conventions
Executive Branch	None	Headed by President with defined powers and potential checks on power of the legislative and judicial branches
Federal Courts	None	Federal courts created to deal with issues between citizens and states; potential check on power of the legislative and executive branches
Federal Regulation of Trade	None	Congress given power to regulate foreign and domestic trade
Raising an Army	Dependent on states to contribute forces	Congress can raise an army to deal with military situations
Sovereignty	Sovereignty resides in the states	The Constitution, federal laws, and U.S. treaties declared the supreme law of the land
Passing Laws	9 states out of 13 required to approve legislation	Majority of both houses plus signature of the President

money, which fueled ruinous inflation. By July 1777, the dollar retained one-third of its face value. In other words, it took $3 in Continental currency to purchase $1 in gold coins. By January 1779, $1 in specie required $8 in Continental money. Two years later, it required $500.

The Newburgh Conspiracy

In 1781, after the successful siege of Yorktown, the French Navy headed back home, leaving the tiny American Navy to defend the long U.S. coastline. Unable to pay their soldiers but afraid to completely disband the armed forces in case Britain had second thoughts about ending the war, Congress refused to discharge enlisted men. Worried about their farms and businesses back home and missing their families, soldiers brimmed with resentment in the months after combat ended, inspiring a disturbing series of mutinies. In 1783, nearly all 500 men who enlisted in the Pennsylvania infantry units of the Continental Army, most of whom had served multiple terms of enlistment (and endured occasional hunger and harsh winters) rose up in anger and seized control of arms depots. Joined by soldiers from Maryland, on June 20, the mutineers blocked the exits from Independence Hall, where the Congress met. For a time they refused to let anyone leave unless they received full payment of back wages. With the Philadelphia Executive Council unable to ensure order, the Congress moved its base of operations to Princeton, New Jersey.

But Continental Army officers, not enlisted men, posed a serious threat that the civilian Congress, the new government of the United States, might be replaced with a military dictatorship or a monarchy. In May 1782, Colonel Lewis Nicola wrote a passionate letter to Washington urging him to assume power as king. A committee of disgruntled officers dispatched Washington's chief aide during the war, Alexander Hamilton, to meet with the general to see if he would support a possible *coup d'état* or at least not stand in the way of one. Hamilton sent Washington a letter warning him that the Army could no longer supply the men and "that by June [1782], the troops would have to take everything by bayonet point." Hamilton asked Washington, as historian James Flexner paraphrased it, "in a world of kings, why should not George Washington also be a king?" Washington took months to answer Hamilton, but in his reply he refused to endorse an overthrow of the Congress.

By the end of the war, the officer corps seethed over late pay and the lack of military pensions. Some men had served six years without compensation. A committee of officers presented soldiers' grievances to the Congress, without any apparent effect. On March 12, 1783, in the army's winter quarters in Newburgh, New York, an anonymous letter (actually written by an aide to General Horatio Gates) circulated. Venting fury over the treatment of the military, the author urged fellow officers to "assume a bolder tone" and tell leaders in Congress that if they conveyed disrespect to the army one more time, "you will retire to some unsettled country . . ." Deeply upset by the letter, Washington worried that what became known as the "**Newburgh Conspiracy**" would result in a civil war. "I cannot avoid apprehending that a train of evils will follow of a very serious and distressing nature," Washington wrote at one point as he contemplated the rising anger among his men.

The seditious spirit in the military continued to boil. If Washington would not lead a coup, some officers decided, they would try to persuade him to remain quiet and ask General Horatio Gates to serve as ruler instead. Washington called a meeting of officers in Newburgh, New York, for March 15, 1783. Washington assured his officers that he loved them and cared about their plight, but tried to convince them that the situation would resolve itself without a second revolution. Republics, he said, act with often frustrating deliberation rather than speed, but the Congress would ultimately do the right thing. A coup would "open the flood gates of civil discord, and deluge our rising empire in blood."

The audience seemed unimpressed until Washington tried to produce a calming letter from a congressman. He seemed disoriented and then pulled out his glasses, saying: "Gentlemen, you will permit me to put on my spectacles, for I have not only grown gray but almost blind in the service of my country." The moment inspired tears of compassion, admiration, and regret from those gathered.

The image of a frail Washington begging his men to not betray the Revolution broke the spell. The officers calmed. The air went out of the Newburgh Conspiracy, and the coup never took place. As Thomas Jefferson said, "The moderation and virtue of a single character probably prevented this Revolution from being closed, as most others have been, by a subversion of that liberty it was intended to establish." Washington yearned to return to private life, but he knew that the Articles of Confederation provided an unworkable form of government and endangered the future of the United States. He began a quiet campaign to replace the Articles with a new constitution.

Western Troubles

The United States' economic and political standing in the world continued to deteriorate. Unable to get states to deliver sufficient funds, Congress ceased interest payments on debts owed to France in 1785, and two years later defaulted on installments of principal. The likelihood of new foreign loans was now remote. With the navy fully dismantled and the U.S. Army (successor to the Continental Army) reduced to a few hundred men, other imperial powers began to take advantage of the country's military vulnerabilities. Sent to London by Congress to seek more favorable terms of commerce, John Adams found his diplomatic efforts undercut by individual states offering their own concessions. Spanish ministers also saw opportunities to exploit American weakness. Despite the provision of the Treaty of Paris allowing U.S. access to the Mississippi River, the separate treaty ending England's war with Spain reverted all of Florida, extending across the Gulf Coast west to the river, back to Spanish rule. Having ruled the Louisiana Territory since 1763, Spain now fully controlled the mouth of the Mississippi and, in 1784, closed it to U.S. shipping.

Farmers in Tennessee and Kentucky and other territories near the Mississippi River could not transport their harvests down the Mississippi. Instead, they had to pay high Spanish tariffs, continue using more expensive, difficult overland routes or simply forget participating in global markets. Doubting the ability of the U.S. government to defend their interests, some white settlers west of the Appalachian Mountains began negotiating secretly with the Spanish about handing over control of Tennessee and Kentucky to Spain. Not just rebellion, but treason was in the air.

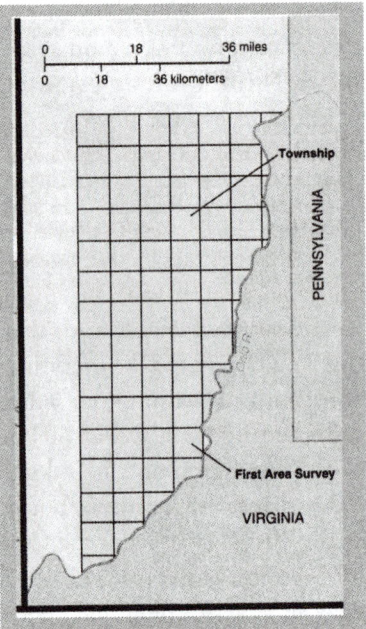

Map 7.2 The Northwest Territory

The Land Ordinance of 1785 created a rectangular grid pattern that was the model for future land surveyed in the public domain. A township was 36 square miles.

Shays's Rebellion

State governments were as weak as the federal government during the Articles period, with many having no governor or one who held only ceremonial duties, unable to veto laws or call the legislatures in sessions in emergencies. Members of many state legislatures had to run for re-election every year, and they proved reluctant to raise taxes to pay off their state's war debts or to fund government operations because taxes were always unpopular, especially during a recession like that gripping the United States in the 1780s.

Struggling to balance budgets, some states went on a spree printing local currency, a policy that worsened inflation. As state-issued bank notes and the Continental currency dropped in value, farmers struggled to pay their tax bills. To prevent a rebellion from the indebted masses, many of whom were war veterans who had not been paid their promised bonuses from the federal government, several states passed laws allowing farmers to delay paying debts. Still many former soldiers and other farmers lost their land because they could not pay their debts or state taxes.

The state of Massachusetts harshly rejected any debt holiday, refused to print more money, stepped up collection of back taxes, and raised taxes to record heights. Farmers in western Massachusetts particularly suffered. In 1786, some began arming themselves and seizing control of courthouses in Hampshire County, stopping judges from foreclosing on farm mortgages. In early 1787, a Revolutionary War veteran, Captain Daniel Shays, led an army of the indebted, who attacked the federal arsenal at Springfield.

Since local militiamen refused to suppress the uprising, Governor James Bowdoin was forced to raise an army with funds donated by his own merchant supporters. **"Shays's Rebellion"** quickly dissipated, as the rebels scattered instead of fighting a pitched battle with state forces. But politically, the episode continued to divide Massachusetts and reverberated throughout the states. Shortly afterward, Massachusetts's authorities indicted hundreds of rebels and barred thousands more from holding public office. Two convicted ringleaders were hanged, while others, including Shays himself, escaped and were condemned in absentia. But in the gubernatorial elections later that year, John Hancock, the first signer of the Declaration of Independence, soundly defeated Bowdoin, sweeping the state's rural votes. Hancock pardoned Shays, reduced payments on state debts, and lightened rural tax burdens. Nevertheless, the uprising alarmed Washington, Alexander Hamilton, and other leaders who worried that it foreshadowed a future of anarchy.

The Northwest Ordinance

After the American Revolution, whites from upstate New York and the eastern side of the Appalachian Mountains poured into the Old Northwest (the area bounded by the Great Lakes, the Ohio River, and the Mississippi River). In a series of laws the Congress politically organized the Northwest Territory, regulated how land would be allocated, and dealt with the issue of slavery in the region, one of the few major accomplishments by the United States Congress under the Articles of Confederation.

These achievements came at the price of human suffering. The Congress assumed that the region rightfully belonged to whites, and they sought to punish Indians who allied with the British during the Revolution. The Congress appointed negotiators to force Indians in the Northwest Territory to surrender land, and their methods often proved ruthless. The American diplomats even took hostages in order to coerce compliance with government demands. Groups such as the Iroquois, the Cherokee, the Choctaws and the Chickasaws continued to live in the Northwest but on ever-shrinking real turf surrounded by ever-increasing numbers of hostile white neighbors.

Some in the American government saw the potential of increased federal revenues by holding public sales of the newly acquired land, but private companies hoped to profit immensely by directly selling the land to potential settlers. Another complication arose because New York, Connecticut, Massachusetts, and Virginia all laid claims to parts of the Northwest Territory based on their colonial charters. The Congress eventually persuaded these states to surrender these claims. Meanwhile, whites, many of them poor and unable to afford land in the established states, started squatting in the Northwest. This alarmed members of Congress who feared the settlers would provoke new Indian wars. The Congress decided to impose legal order on the territory.

In 1784, the Congress appointed Thomas Jefferson to head a committee charged with planning how new states would be created in the territory. Jefferson's proposals became known as the Land Ordinance of 1784.

Jefferson's priority was to establish local control as soon as possible. He called for Congress to divide the territory into ten districts. Under Jefferson's plan, settlers could organize the districts into new states that could apply to join the union once they reached a population of 20,000. The local population would be given the freedom to write their own state constitutions, and these new states would have the same rights and powers under the United States Constitution as already-established states. The new states would also be responsible for paying their proportionate share of the national debt. Most controversially, the ordinance prohibited slavery in any states created in the Northwest Territory after 1800.

The Congress adopted the 1784 ordinance minus the language regarding slavery. The Congress then set the rules by which land would be distributed in the Land Ordinance of 1785. This law did away with Jefferson' numerous districts. The law required the survey of land in the Northwest Territory, setting up townships of six square miles each. Within each township, the land would be subdivided into 36 sections of 640-acre lots auctioned off at a minimum bid of $1 per acre. A purchaser thus would be required to spend more than $8,700 in modern dollars to buy any land in the territory. This provision eliminated a lot of poor potential buyers and heavily favored land speculators, but the always cash-starved U.S. government needed the revenues such a high price would generate. Rich land investors often divided their lots into smaller pieces and sold it to settlers at inflated costs. Under the ordinance, Congress set aside revenues from one acre at the center of each township for public education, marking the first federal investment in schools in United States history.

Even as the Constitutional Convention met in Philadelphia to draft a new constitution, the old Congress under the Articles of Confederation continued to tweak the laws governing the Northwest region. The Northwest Ordinance of 1787, adopted July 13, reset the number of states to be created from the Northwest Territory from only three to five. Regardless of the number, setting a limit on the number of states that could be created in the territory mollified Congressmen representing the original 13 states who feared the diminished influence they would have in the Congress in the future. The law provided for the Congress to appoint governors, a secretary and three judges to govern each territory. Once the population of a territory reached 5,000 free inhabitants, the local population could then elect a local assembly that could pass laws subject to approval by the appointed governor, who held veto power. Once the population of a territory reached 60,000, then the inhabitants could petition the Congress for admission to the union.

The Northwest Ordinance extended free speech, the right to a trial by a jury, the right to assembly, and other rights later embodied in the United States Constitution to those living in the Northwest. The legislation furthermore required the government to show "utmost good faith" towards the Native American population in the territory and banned the taking of Indian land without consent, though that provision was violated almost before the ink was dry on the legislation.

The Congress reversed itself on slavery, abolishing bondage within the region but at the same time established tighter restrictions on voting and on who was qualified to hold public office, for instance requiring any representative in the territorial assembly to own at least 200 acres of land. Southern representatives in the Congress agreed to the law, in spite of the ban on slavery, because they felt the new states would provide a buffer zone from potential Indian attacks. Southern congressmen also anticipated that most of the future inhabitants of the region would come from southern states, thus creating a section of the country sympathetic to southern interests. Eventually, five new states would be created from the Northwest Territory: Ohio (1803); Indiana (1816); Illinois (1818); Michigan (1837); and Wisconsin (1848).

Amid all the chaos unfolding under the Articles of Confederation, the series of laws regulating the Northwest marked a singular achievement in the pre-Constitution period: the law encouraged migration to the west, created a new class of landowners, added free states to the Union, provided an innovative method of funding public education, and extended the power and influence of the United States over the North American continent. In spite of the Congress' success in enacting these laws, however, the days of the Articles of Confederation were numbered.

The Movement to Replace the Articles

Following Yorktown, Alexander Hamilton settled in New York City and served as a member of the state's delegation in Congress. Hamilton had already decided that the Articles were a disaster and wanted to scrap the current government with a new system in which the federal government would take away powers from the individual states that had plunged the nation into what he saw as anarchy and would provide for a more powerful economy and military. James Madison, a young, quietly effective member of the Virginia legislature, also advocated replacing the Articles with the new constitution. As long as the country languished under the Articles, Madison wrote, "the states will continue to invade the national jurisdiction, to violate treaties and the law of nations,

and to harass each other with rival and spiteful measures dictated by mistaken views of interest." Hamilton tried to get the Articles amended to allow the Congress to assess and collect taxes, but his efforts failed, largely because of the requirement that any amendment be unanimously approved by the states.

Washington watched events in the national capital in Philadelphia and the rebellion in Western Massachusetts led by Shays with dismay. His life's work, the establishment of an American nation, seemed in jeopardy. Hoping for governmental reform, Washington invited representatives from Virginia and Maryland to his Mount Vernon estate to negotiate a boundary dispute involving shipping along the nearby Potomac River. Meanwhile, Madison persuaded his colleagues in the Virginia legislature to call for a meeting of the states to discuss adoption of "a uniform system in their commercial regulations." Madison and Washington hoped for much more out of this conference, but no one in leadership circles was ready to openly discuss doing away with the Articles of Confederation.

The **Annapolis Convention** met September 11-14, 1786, with only five state delegations (from Delaware, New Jersey, New York, Pennsylvania, and Virginia) attending. Hamilton, representing New York, wrote a resolution urging all the states to appoint delegates to another gathering to be held the following year, "to take into consideration the situation of the United States," and "devise such further provisions as shall appear to them necessary to render the constitution of the Federal Government adequate to the exigencies of the Union." This was the first public hint at the agenda that Washington, Madison and Hamilton shared. The Confederation Congress endorsed the Annapolis resolution several months later. The public still thought the Articles would only be modified. A secret consensus had already formed among the powerful, however, to start from scratch, a genteel conspiracy born of mistrust of the common man.

THE STRUGGLE TO CREATE THE CONSTITUTION

The Constitutional Convention of 1787

Thomas Jefferson held profoundly mixed feelings about the **Constitution of the United States**. Jefferson acknowledged the dangerous inefficiencies of the Articles but worried over the new Constitution's shift of powers away from the states to the federal government. Others saw the Constitution as a betrayal of the principles of the American Revolution. They feared that creating the office of the presidency would inevitably lead to tyranny.

They did not like the fact that the Constitution would not allow the people to vote directly for members of the newly created Senate (until the Seventeenth Amendment was ratified in 1913, senators were selected by state legislatures) or the president (selected to this day by the Electoral College).

The nation's Founders had adopted the Articles of Confederation in a fit of optimism about human nature, believing that the citizens of a free republic would always put the nation's interests ahead of provincial concerns and the needs of the community above selfish desires. Men like Washington, Hamilton, and Madison did not believe that events since the Articles went into effect in 1781 bore out that optimism. They saw states inconsistently contributing to the costs of running the republic and abandoning soldiers who had risked their lives and fortunes to create the nation. They saw events like Shays's Rebellion as the acts of an ungrateful rabble. Furthermore, they saw economic chaos and felt shame at the disrespect shown the United States by powers like Spain. The Articles had ushered in rule by the mob, Hamilton in particular believed. The Founders decided to retreat from their experiment in "radical democracy" and create a more hierarchical republic ruled by the supposed best and brightest.

"An Assembly of Demigods"

Once again, Philadelphia and the assembly room of the Pennsylvania State House hosted a fateful gathering. Seven of the thirteen states had agreed to attend what would be dubbed the **Constitutional Convention**, before Congress itself endorsed the convention in February. The sole holdout would be tiny Rhode Island, which refused to send a delegation. In mid-May, the Virginia delegation arrived, including George Washington, who had reluctantly agreed to leave his beloved Mount Vernon one more time to represent his state at the Convention.

The Convention would be the largest gathering of some of the most important figures in American history, including Washington, already a legend; fellow icon-in-his-lifetime Ben Franklin; future president James Madison; the man who would soon create the American economic system, Alexander Hamilton; Gouverneur Morris, who would end up writing the famous Preamble to the Constitution and later serve as senator; and scholarly attorney and future Supreme Court Justice James Wilson

It was a wealthy, well-connected gathering. Of the fifty-five delegates in total, forty-two had served at some point in the Second Continental Congress, or in the Congress created under the Articles. Apart from Washington and Franklin, most of the delegates who had served in

the military or in government during the independence struggle had done so as younger men. Nearly all were landowners, although only sixteen made their living mainly as planters. No fewer than twenty-nine had studied law. Perhaps most important, twenty-five of them, including the sixteen planters, all from the South, owned slaves.

John Adams and Thomas Jefferson were serving abroad as diplomats and so did not attend, while some other leading figures of the older generation, such as Patrick Henry, declined to leave their states. The delegates were not perfectly representative of the elite layer of American society, but they were almost all drawn from it. Jefferson referred to the delegates as "an assembly of demigods" in a letter to Adams.

The Virginia and New Jersey Plans and the Connecticut Compromise

After finally convening on May 25, the delegates quickly made several crucial decisions. Washington was immediately chosen as presiding officer. For the rest of the Convention he sat at the front of the room in an ornate Chippendale-style chair featuring a half-sun and its rays carved into its high back. Washington's chairmanship lent the controversial gathering a measure of credibility with a nervous public. The Convention voted not to allow outsiders to observe the proceedings and to keep no official records of the debates. Delegates wanted to be able to debate controversial issues without fear of suffering political harm. The Constitutional Convention met behind closed doors and kept shut all windows. Secrecy was strictly, and successfully, maintained. Several delegates, most notably Madison, kept notes during the Convention, which he amended years after the event and which did not become available to the public until the late 1830s. Robert Yates, a delegate from New York, Rufus King, from Massachusetts, and William Pierce, from Georgia, kept more sketchy records of the proceedings, but none of this material was published until after the participants had died. No complete, objective record of the Convention has ever been found. The creators of the republic were less than enthusiastic about the public's right to know.

By the time the delegates gathered in May 1787, the Articles of Confederation were a dead letter. The Articles could be amended, with unanimous consent of the states, but the Convention chose to ignore the Articles' existence. It would be a gentlemanly *coup d'état*. The delegates had lost the fear of executive power that had prevailed at the writing of the Articles, and a consensus formed behind creating a chief executive for the new government to be called a president. Whatever qualms they might have had that a president could transform into a kingly tyrant like George III, the Convention felt confident that the first president at least would respect constitutional limits. Everyone knew the first president would be Washington, a war hero trusted by all factions.

Revealing his distrust of the voting public, Alexander Hamilton proposed that the new office of president and members of an upper house of Congress called the Senate be appointed to lifetime terms. Presidents and senators could rule without worrying about the popular passions of the moment. Hamilton had more faith in the inherent wisdom of the wealthy and powerful who would fill these offices than most of his peers at the Convention, who rejected lifetime terms, though the idea would survive for federal judges.

Much of the summer centered on how much power large states and small states would have in a new, restructured Congress. On May 29, Edmund Randolph formally proposed the "**Virginia Plan**" drafted by **James Madison**. The plan proposed a three-branch government with two chambers: a lower house elected by the people, and a Senate elected by the lower house. Madison sought to practically eliminate the voices of the smaller states wanting both houses of congress to use population as the basis for dividing the seats among the states. In short, smaller states faced diminished representation in the Congress under this plan.

The Congress would also enjoy more powers than under the Articles. Under the Virginia Plan, the Congress would appoint the president and also a federal judiciary. The legislature would possess all the powers that the Congress had under the Articles but with enhanced authority over state affairs. In a significant retreat from the concept of "states' rights," the Congress would have gained the ability to legislate in all matters in which the individual states were "incompetent," such as in boundary disputes. In Madison's scheme, the Congress could veto state laws it considered unconstitutional. A peculiar oversight marked the Virginia Plan: it failed to call for giving the Congress the power to impose and collect taxes, perhaps the most serious flaw in the Articles.

On June 15, New Jersey delegate William Paterson proposed the "**New Jersey Plan**," or "small state" plan, which retained the basic structure of the Confederation Congress—one single chamber with each state given equal representation—albeit with enhanced powers, such as taxation and regulation of commerce. As different as these proposals were, they shared some basic features. Both aimed at vastly expanding the range and scope of federal powers at the expense of the states. Both would have created the office of a chief executive not chosen by the voters. The Virginia and the New Jersey Plans represented a retreat from the concept of popular sovereignty, the idea that the average person possessed ample civic virtue and could be trusted with a large voice in public matters.

Delegates from small states feared that their voices would be drowned out in the federal government if anything like the Virginia Plan won approval, with a Delaware delegate warning that if the Convention backed Randolph's proposed constitution, the small states would secede and seek admission into a foreign empire. Delegates from the large states countered that most of the population lived within their borders, so therefore fairness dictated that membership in the Congress should be based on proportional representation. By the end of June, one delegate said that the Convention was "at full stop."

Delegates gave the dispute to a committee made up of staunch small-state partisans and Virginia Plan advocates who were willing to make accommodations. Finally, **Roger Sherman** of Connecticut brokered the "**Connecticut Compromise**," (or "**Great Compromise**"), introduced July 5, which organized the lower house on the basis of population (with members chosen directly by each state's eligible voters) and the Senate reflecting equal representation by having two members (chosen by the state legislatures) per state.

Reflecting the writings of the French Enlightenment *philosophe* Montesquieu, the Framers divided the proposed national government's powers among three separate branches—legislative, executive, and judicial—in the hope of preventing a dangerous concentration of power in any single individual or group. By creating a system of "checks and balances," each branch could theoretically deny another branch complete control over an issue of public policy. As designed by the Constitution's creators, for example, only the legislative branch—the Congress—could pass national laws. However, the head of the executive branch—holding the newly established office of president—had the power to veto such legislation that could then only be overridden with a 2/3 vote in each house of Congress. Further, the federal courts had the final say in determining whether a portion of a law passed by Congress, or its entirety, was even allowed by the Constitution. Another noteworthy case involves the exercise of the life-and-death power to declare war, which was granted solely to the Congress. However, the Constitution empowers only the president to direct the military as commander-in-chief. Other examples of checks and balances imbedded into the document included the Senate's ability to confirm presidential nominees, ratify treaties negotiated by presidential representatives, and even remove an impeached president or federal judge found guilty of committing "treason, bribery, or high crimes and misdemeanors."

HANGING FOR PLEASURE AND EDUCATION

In the late 1700s and early 1800s, American elites worried about the corrupting influence of alcohol and prostitution on the public, but many of the same politicians and ministers embraced public executions as a platform for moral education. Meanwhile, those attending hangings seemed to enjoy the drama. The Revolutionary generation's elites didn't want rebellion against the British to translate into a class revolution, so they used the elaborate rituals of executions to teach the masses lessons about obedience. As one minister put it, "In civil society, the wicked would walk on every side, and the cry of the oppressed would be in vain, the foundations would be destroyed, [and] confusion and misery would prevail were punishment, capital punishment, never executed."

As with today, executions followed a strict protocol. Often the defendant would be led to a church in the morning where the minister would deliver a lengthy sermon on how the God of the Bible approved of capital punishment and the gift represented by the 10 Commandments. The last part of the sermon would be pointed directly at the prisoner, identified by name. The minister would note the condemned's sins and make clear that their gravity meant that God himself demanded the prisoner's death. After the service, the condemned would be walked or carried by cart to the gallows, his arms bound behind him. Sometimes prisoners rode on top of their future coffins on the way to the execution site. Upon reaching the top of the gallows, the prisoner would stand by while the sheriff or other official read the death warrant, then the prisoner would be given the chance to speak last words. It became common for the condemned to explain how they got to that spot, which temptations turned them to a life of crime, and then to repent.

Oddly, the condemned seemed to have willingly played their part in these dramatic execution productions. Typical were the gallows regrets expressed by two burglars hanged in Worcester, Massachusetts just after the war, June 19, 1783. "We pray that our unhappy fate may be a solemn Warning to Youth and induce them to forsake the paths of vice and immorality, and seek the road of virtue and happiness," one of the burglars said before his death. Another prisoner, a teenager hanged in Dedham, Massachusetts, warned the crowd, "Do not CHEAT—Do not STEAL—Do not LIE—Do not commit ADULTERY—Especially, do not destroy VIRGIN INNOCENCE—and, above all, do not KILL."

A hood would be placed on the condemned's head, he or she would be put on top of a trap door, and the prisoner's body would drop. The length of the rope was calculated so the condemned's neck would break, but the executioner sometimes made mistakes, which meant that the victim would slowly strangle to death. Often, the prisoner's "confession" would be printed in which the doomed person would beg the readers not to follow the path of sin and end up in a noose.

The condemned tended to be young. According to historian Louis Masur, the median age of those executed in his study sample was 25. The condemned also disproportionately came from the ranks of former soldiers, immigrants, people of color, and people without longstanding ties to communities. Soldiers received death sentences at a rate higher than average, perhaps, because of the practical fear that the low-paid servicemen might desert the Revolutionary Army and live a higher-paid life of crime. Authorities profiled African Americans, immigrants and strangers, probably as a result of the anxiety posed by the Revolution, as the former colonists traded in their status as Englishmen for an American identity not yet clearly defined.

Elites hoped that executions would deter future crimes, but also that the masses would learn, for their own sakes, to obey authority. Leaders worried constantly that the Revolution would spin out of control. In any case, the public hangings during the Revolutionary era and the early republic failed as a deterrent. There was no appreciable effect on the rate of homicides, robberies, rapes and other crimes then punishable by death—and the confused, crowded, excited atmosphere around the gallows during a hanging proved a magnet for pickpockets and other criminals.

The Constitution and Slavery

By the 1840s, the abolitionist William Lloyd Garrison derided the Constitution as a "covenant with death" and an "agreement with hell." What outraged Garrison was that the Framers not only failed to abolish slavery, which he saw as inescapably evil, but that they included provisions in the Constitution that guaranteed the institution's survival for decades.

Even though he owned more than a hundred slaves, Madison had been a major advocate for reigning in states' rights and shifting power to the federal government. Many southern delegates, however, feared the North would eventually dominate the new government and would, with expanded powers, be able to limit or even eliminate involuntary servitude. Speaking for increasingly uneasy slave owners, Charles Pinckney, of South Carolina, warned the Convention that unless he "received some security against an emancipation of slaves . . . he should be bound by duty to his State to vote against their Report." Despite some objections by northern delegates, the Convention was basically willing to give Pinckney the security he demanded.

Thus, six of the Constitution's eighty-four clauses pertained to slavery. Delegates added a provision that prohibited the federal government from passing any laws regarding slavery until 1808, two decades in the future. Big southern slave owners also worried because the continued importation of slaves from the Caribbean and from Africa, combined with the increase in the slave population from sexual reproduction, threatened to drive the value of slaves down. The bigger slave owners like Madison, who already had more than enough human property to turn a profit on tobacco and other cash crops, knew they would benefit economically by a slower growth in the slave population. Consequently, delegates to the Convention agreed to a ban on the international slave trade by 1808, a provision that on the surface seemed like a blow against slavery but in fact served as a big gift to the wealthiest southern planters.

A heated controversy erupted over the census. The Framers of the Constitution sought a nationwide census every 10 years, which would then allow the Congress to apportion the size of each state delegation to the United States House and the representation of each state in the Electoral College.

Southerners, fearing a small but rising tide of antislavery sentiment in the North, wanted to guarantee what they hoped would be a permanent strong influence over the new federal government. Southerners insisted that slaves be counted as part of a state's population during future federal censuses, even though slaves had no voting rights or civil liberties and essentially did not exist politically. Counting slaves, however, would give white Southerners a disproportionate voice in both the new House of Representatives and the Electoral College. Northern delegates wanted slaves not to count, so that only free whites would be considered when apportioning seats in the House and the Electoral College.

As a compromise, delegates agreed to count each slave as three-fifths of a person both when determining representation and in apportioning taxes. By guaranteeing white southern overrepresentation in the House, this "**Three-Fifths Compromise**" would hold profound electoral consequences for the next 70 years. In the first census year, 1790, for instance, even though southern whites made up only 40 percent of the total U.S. population, they held 47 percent of the seats in the U.S. House. Until 1861, when the southern states would secede from the Union over the supposed threat to slavery posed by newly elected President Abraham Lincoln, white southern men held sufficient power in the House of Representatives to force major concessions on any legislation regarding slavery.

The South would also possess sufficient votes in the Electoral College to block any presidential candidate unfriendly to slavery. No candidate could win the White House without substantial southern support until population growth in the North allowed Abraham Lincoln to be elected in 1860 without his name being placed on the ballot in a single southern state. Four of the first six presidents were from what was then the most populous slave state, Virginia. Eight of the first thirteen came from slave states.

Because of the influence Southerners had over the presidency, the South would deeply influence whom the president would appoint, with congressional approval, to the federal judiciary. Southerners and southern sympathizers dominated the Supreme Court for the first seven decades after the Constitution was ratified and usually ruled in favor of slave owner interests until the Civil War changed the regional balance of power.

The Constitution would serve as a shield protecting slavery, yet the authors avoided ever using that word or the word "slave" anywhere in the document. Instead, they employed elaborate euphemisms, such as in the provision regarding how slaves would be counted in the census in Article 1, Section 2 when they direct census takers to count "the whole number of Free Persons" but "three fifths of all other Persons." This cowardly verbal evasion reveals that many of the members of the Constitutional Convention knew that slavery could not be reconciled with the supposed ideals of the Revolution or the proposed new national charter. Winning ratification of the Constitution, however, would require southern support, and that goal, and not liberating millions of humans chained in the South, became the delegates' more pressing objective.

The Campaign for Ratification

By the middle of September, the substantive decisions were made. One last committee—the Committee of Style—re-edited the proposed preamble and all approved sections and rendered them in polished form. Three delegates who had made important contributions—George Mason and Edmund Randolph, from Virginia, and Elbridge Gerry of Massachusetts—citing their own reservations about the finished work, pronounced themselves unwilling to sign. But thirty-nine other delegates did add their names to the document. On the day of signatures and adjournment, September 17, 1787, in his final remarks, Benjamin Franklin told his fellow delegates that he had often looked at the half-sun carved on Washington's chair "without being able to tell if it was rising or setting. Now at length I have the happiness to know that it is a rising and not a setting sun."

Writing the Constitution represented one long, difficult political struggle, conducted within the secretive confines of a meeting room. A new and more difficult conflict over the country's future would now unfold in sometimes angry state conventions across the country. Under the Articles of Confederation, the document could be amended only through the unanimous consent of the states. The writers of the new Constitution specified a threshold of only nine states for ratification for the new charter. The Constitution required each state to elect special conventions, which were supposed to vote up or down on the text as proposed.

In a clever political move, supporters of ratification named themselves "**Federalists**." The term, implying respect for the division of authority between central and local institutions, minimized the impact of a Constitution that so sharply reduced the power of states. The name also attracted people who distrusted radical change but wanted a more effective government.

The opponents found themselves stuck with the label "**Anti-Federalists**," a negative term that revealed only what they opposed, not what they believed. The Anti-Federalists opposed the Constitution for a wide variety of reasons, but because of these divisions they had problems articulating a clear argument for rejecting ratification. When the Convention adjourned in September and presented the brief proposed Constitution to the public, every newspaper in the country printed a copy and invited readers to discuss it. The United States was a nation of newspaper readers, with taverns often providing dozens of publications for their clientele. Literate drinkers would read the newspapers out loud so all could hear the latest developments from Philadelphia. Only twelve newspapers outright opposed the new national charter, and editorial support was generally so enthusiastic that the Anti-Federalists complained that their arguments did not get a fair hearing in the press. Positive media coverage increased early support for ratification.

The ratification process at first looked like it would proceed with breakneck speed, with the Federalists winning approval in Delaware, Pennsylvania, New Jersey, Georgia and Connecticut. Ironically, given the initial resistance by small states to early drafts of the Constitution during the Convention in Philadelphia, smaller states now appreciated the advantages of a more centralized government. Under the Articles of Confederation, for instance, New Jersey had been squeezed by its neighbors, forced to pay taxes to bordering states on foreign goods imported through New York City and Philadelphia. Under the new Constitution, the federal government would levy a single import duty, thereby reducing the tax bill for New Jersey residents. If smaller states now believed that a more powerful central government would offer them greater protections, residents in larger states like Virginia believed they could survive as separate republics, and some became reluctant to surrender control.

The first big ratification battle took place in Massachusetts, the birthplace of the American Revolution. Many residents who had fought a war over taxes like the Stamp Act held suspicions about the new federal government they were asked to approve. The Federalists won the Massachusetts convention by a squeaky 187-168 margin in February 1788. That April and May, Federalists also carried the Maryland and South Carolina conventions. Now, eight of the required nine states had ratified the Constitution, but it would be an uphill struggle from there.

Conventions were scheduled almost simultaneously in New Hampshire, New York, North Carolina, and Virginia, and at the outset the Anti-Federalists carried a soft majority in each convention. As the public more closely read the Constitution, its anti-democratic elements became clearer to many. Anti-Federalists contended that the grant of powers to the Congress in the proposed Constitution was dangerously broad. Anti-Federalist writers portrayed the "consolidated" federal government as a kind of successor to Parliament—a distant, uncontrollable authority aiming to invade local jurisdictions and usurp the powers of familiar, established institutions. Anti-Federalists argued that a House of Representatives elected in districts of at least 30,000 people, as mandated by the Constitution, meant that elections would be expensive, guaranteeing that the House would be filled by an aristocracy of wealthy, remote men empowered to impose taxes on the common person and unanswerable to the public will.

Again, the slavery issue erupted, with public figures on both sides finding fault with the Constitution. Yankee abolitionists in Massachusetts and New York pointed to the continuation of the slave trade, and the silence of abolitionist delegates, as damning evidence of moral compromise. Luther Martin, a delegate from Maryland who had left the Convention without signing, actually published the text of a speech from the Constitutional Convention criticizing the failure to limit the slave trade. But, on the other hand, the ambiguity of the Constitution allowed some to criticize it for only weakly supporting slavery. Patrick Henry, after Washington the most respected Virginian Revolutionary leader, opposed the Constitution in the Virginia ratifying convention. Its omission of any explicit protection for slave property, in his words, "was done with design." For Henry, a strong central government that had not clearly committed to preserve slavery would inevitably come under pressure to limit or abolish it.

At the Convention, George Mason had urged the adoption of a **Bill of Rights** before the Constitution was submitted to the states, but Madison said this was unnecessary and he carried the day. That decision now haunted the Federalists as the lack of a Bill of Rights stoked much of the opposition. It was obvious that public fears would have to be allayed if the final hurdle to ratification were to be cleared. To get over the hump, three of the most prominent supporters of the new Constitution, Alexander Hamilton, James Madison and John Jay, authored a series of eighty-five eloquent essays supporting the Constitution originally printed in New York newspapers and then republished across the country. The trio addressed criticisms of the Constitution in detail in what came to be known as the "*Federalist Papers.*"

Some Anti-Federalists argued that the strong republican government outlined in the Constitution represented a dangerous experiment without historical precedent. The city-state republics of antiquity like Athens in ancient Greece had been small and culturally homogenous, promoting civic discourse and allowing the larger public more direct input to their government. Many feared that the United States would, as a large republic with a strong central government, become unstable and too vast to be socially cohesive. A powerful federal authority might be forced to impose authoritarian rule in order to preserve law and order. At a minimum, the central government would grow indifferent to local needs.

Madison flipped this argument on its head. He contended in one essay that the greatest threat to freedom came from the tyranny of local majorities. Such majorities formed more easily in small, economically and culturally similar societies. In a republic as massive and diverse as the United States, however, such a majority would have a hard time gaining control, Madison insisted. A large republic encompasses too many competing interests for any one faction to completely dominate. The new, strong central government could intervene in localities where tyrannical majorities reigned to ensure constitutional rights were protected. In addition to these arguments, Madison also promised he would author and propose to the Congress a series of amendments that would provide a Bill of Rights. A powerful national government, he suggested, rather than a weak confederation of separate states, would offer the best mechanisms for the fulfillment of the highest aspirations of the American Revolution.

The Anti-Federalists were never to mount a case as strong and well considered. In the end, the multiple problems the Articles had caused and the support of Washington, Franklin, and other prestigious national leaders for the new Constitution proved decisive. Following publication of *The Federalist Papers*, the Federalists prevailed over reluctance in the New Hampshire constitutional convention on June 21, 1788. The Constitution had been approved. Madison was able to carry the Virginia convention five days later. New York checked off a month later, then North Carolina by July 1788. On September 13, the Confederation Congress certified that the Constitution had been ratified. The new government assumed authority March 4, 1789. Rhode Island became the last state to ratify in May 1790. The United States Constitution thus became the law of the land. The controversies surrounding its writing and approval would be forgotten, and the document was on its way to becoming American scripture.

A RETREAT FROM DEMOCRACY

In many ways, the new Constitution made elected officials less answerable to their constituents. The Constitution's creators sought to limit the influence of the "mob" that had participated in uprisings like Shays's Rebellion—the uneducated voters supposedly swayed by immediate emotions. By doing so, the Framers sought to guarantee rule by men of their education, culture, and class.

Delegates set the terms for the House of Representatives at two years, instead of the one year required under the Articles of Confederation. Senate terms would last six years. That chamber would not be a democratic body, with senators appointed by state legislatures until the Seventeenth Amendment was ratified in 1913.

The Founders also devised a complicated method of choosing the president and vice president, the only two elected officials in the federal government who would represent the entire country. The president would serve for four years, could be re-elected an unlimited number of times, and would not have to grovel for votes from the common person but would be elected by a body of men called the **Electoral College**. State representation in the Electoral College would be based on the number of representatives and senators each state had in the Congress. The proposed Constitution would allow each state to determine how electors were chosen.

Under the original provisions of the Constitution, each elector would vote for two people in the presidential race. The elector could not vote for two candidates from his own state. The candidate with the most votes would gain the presidency, while the one earning the second most ballots would become vice president. This allowed for political opponents to serve in the top two offices in the government. This aspect of the presidential election process would prove troublesome, and electors would begin choosing presidents and vice presidents separately after the states ratified the Twelfth Amendment in 1804.

The judicial branch also displays elements of detachment from the general population. Federal judges who are empowered not only to interpret the constitutionality of federal laws and presidential actions but also state laws and actions, serve lifetime terms. Despite such power and the length of their tenures, they are not subject to election by the people. Rather, the Constitution grants the president sole power to appoint federal judges subject to Senate confirmation.

The procedure for amending the Constitution, while less demanding than the process under the Articles of Confederation which required unanimous state approval, nevertheless has proven to be a significant barrier for advocates of change. In addition to two-thirds approval from each house of Congress, a proposed amendment also needs ratification from three-quarters of the state legislatures or of special state constitutional conventions. As a result of the difficult hurdles the framers created, only 27 amendments have been adopted and only 17 since the Bill of Rights was ratified in 1791.

Though a majority of the early Republic's leaders favored the adoption of the Constitution, they had no way of knowing how the new national government would function and no guarantees that the document would endure. Many expressed doubts and wondered if in ten or twenty years, they would have to reconvene another convention and rework another constitution reflecting changing realities and additional lessons learned with the passage of time. Nevertheless, much depended upon how those chosen to lead the separate branches of the government would perform their tasks. No individual understood this more than George Washington, who came out of retirement to serve as the nation's first president.

Chronology

1783 George Washington thwarts the Newburgh Conspiracy
Treaty of Paris ends the war.

1784 Spain closes the Mississippi River to use by American ships.

1785 Confederation Congress suspends interest payments on a wartime loan from France.

1786 Shays's Rebellion begins.
The Annapolis Convention is held.
Virginia adopts Statute of Religious Freedom.

1787 Constitution Convention meets in Philadelphia.
Shays's Rebellion ends.
Northwest Ordinance implemented.
Delaware provides manumission law.

1788 United States Constitution ratified.

1789 New national government under the Constitution assumes authority.
Slavery ends in Massachusetts by judicial decision.

SUGGESTED READINGS

Akhil Reed Amar, *The Bill of Rights: Creation and Reconstruction* (1998).

Charles A. Beard, *An Economic Interpretation of the Constitution of the United States* (1913).

Carol Berkin, *Revolutionary Mothers: Women in the Struggle for American Independence* (2005).

Ron Chernow, *Alexander Hamilton* (2005).

James Thomas Flexner, *Washington: The Indispensable Man* (1974).

Annette Gordon-Reed, *The Hemingses of Monticello: An American Family* (2008).

Robert A. Hendrickson, *The Rise and Fall of Alexander Hamilton* (1981).

John P. Kaminski, ed., *A Necessary Evil? Slavery and the Debate Over the Constitution* (1995).

Susan Jacoby, *Freethinkers: A History of American Secularism* (2004).

Michael Kammen, *A Machine That Would Go By Itself: The Constitution in American Culture* (1986).

Richard H. Kohn, *Eagle and Sword: The Federalists and the Creation of the Military Establishment in America, 1783-1802* (1975).

Louis P. Masur, *Rites of Execution: Capital Punishment and the Transformation of American Culture, 1776-1865* (1989).

Jon Meacham, *American Gospel: The Founding Fathers, and the Making of a Nation* (2007).

Jack N. Rakove, *Original Meanings: Politics and Ideas in the Making of the Constitution* (1996).

Robert A. Rutland, *The Ordeal of the Constitution: The Anti-Federalists and the Ratification Struggle of 1787-1788* (1966).

Simon Schama, *Citizens: A Chronicle of the French Revolution* (1989).

Garry Wills, *Explaining America: The Federalist,* (1981).

___ , *A Necessary Evil: History of the American Distrust of Government,* (2002).

Ann Fairfax Withington, *Toward a More Perfect Union: Virtue and the Formation of the American Republic,* (1991)

Gordon S. Wood, *The Radicalism of the American Revolution,* (1991).

Review Questions

1.   Describe the Newburgh Conspiracy and its significance.

2.   What were the major flaws in the Articles of Confederation, why were they written that way, and what political and economic problems were caused by these flaws?

3.   What different proposals regarding representation in the Congress were made at the Constitutional Convention and how was the issue resolved?

4.   In what ways did the United States Constitution address the flaws of the Articles of Confederation? In what ways can the Constitution be seen as a retreat from democracy?

5.   In what ways did the Constitution strengthen and protect slavery? What were the political impacts of the so-called 3/5s Compromise?

Glossary of Important People and Concepts

Annapolis Convention
Anti-Federalists
Articles of Confederation
Bill of Rights
"Connecticut Compromise" (or "Great Compromise")
Constitution of the United States
Constitutional Convention
Disestablishment
Electoral College
Episcopal Church
Federalist Papers
Federalists
Elizabeth Freeman
Haitian Revolution
Alexander Hamilton
Sally Hemings
James Madison
Newburgh Conspiracy
New Jersey Plan
Primogeniture
"Republican Mothers"
Shays's Rebellion
Roger Sherman
Three-Fifths Compromise
Virginia Plan

George Washington

Chapter Eight

THE FEDERALIST ERA, 1789-1800

The Founding Fathers were very concerned about their public virtue. They strongly believed that leaders in a republic must exhibit virtue, or acting in the best interests of the common good rather than for their own self-interest. As such, Alexander Hamilton made great efforts in his public life to ensure that others viewed him as a virtuous man whose actions were without regard for his personal benefit.

In his private life, however, Hamilton had a weakness for women and had many affairs, possibly even with his wife's sister. His wife's knowledge of his affairs did not destroy his marriage and posed little threat to his public image as a virtuous man.

In 1791, with the government relocated to Philadelphia, Hamilton left his family in New York rather than move them to Philadelphia while he would have to be there for work as Secretary of the Treasury. While at his home in Philadelphia, a young woman named Maria Reynolds visited him. She proceeded to tell Hamilton a story of abuse and abandonment by her husband, James Reynolds. Learning that she was originally from New York, Hamilton offered to help her with the funds to return there. When Hamilton arrived at her home with the money, Maria led him upstairs, and it became clear to Hamilton that she was willing to repay him with something other than money—and he was willing to accept.

Having a taste of Maria's generosity, Hamilton began an affair with her that lasted for several months until her husband showed up at his door. James Reynolds produced a handful of love letters from Hamilton to Maria and de-manded money in return for his silence. (Indeed, Reynolds may have arranged the entire affair in order to later extort the Treasury Secretary.) Hamilton agreed to pay Reynolds but still could not resist Maria and continued their affair for several months after the blackmail began. When he finally sought to end the affair, however, Hamilton found that James Reynolds's demands would not cease, leading Hamilton ultimately to pay Reynolds more than $1,000.

When Reynolds got into trouble with the law, he sought help from Hamilton who refused. Reynolds then told some Republicans about the affair and how Hamilton had paid him off by providing him with insider knowledge that enabled him to become wealthy through speculation. Hamilton had seemingly violated the public trust in order to make a private problem go away.

Thomas Jefferson's friend James Monroe and two other congressmen confronted Hamilton. Meeting at Hamilton's house that night, he showed the men letters from Maria and James Reynolds to reveal the affair and subsequent blackmail, but made it clear that there had been no malfeasance by Hamilton. He then proceeded to tell them every sordid detail of the affair, making the men extremely uncomfortable before they agreed not to mention the relationship to anyone.

In 1797, in an effort to undermine the Federalist Party and Hamilton's power behind it, Republicans raised the issue of the Reynolds affair, suggesting that the Secretary diverted funds from the Treasury to pay off James Reynolds. In order to preserve his public virtue, Hamilton sacrificed his private virtue by publishing a 98-page pamphlet confessing to the affair but denying any malfeasance. He also submitted a meticulous financial record of his tenure as Secretary of the Treasury, which left little doubt that he was innocent of that charge. While he was able to preserve his public virtue, knowledge of the affair destroyed any chance of holding public office again and weakened his grip on the Federalist Party.

With the ratification of the Constitution by the summer of 1788, elections were set for a new government to be established by the following spring. Of utmost importance would be the selection of a president, as there had been no executive branch under the Articles of Confederation. The choice of that president, however, would provide little suspense—**George Washington** was still warmly regarded throughout the states for his military leadership during the American Revolution. Moreover, his willingness to resign his commission at the end of hostilities, rather than use his popularity and control of the army to take power for himself, allayed fears that he would try to rule as a despot. Washington was elected unanimously by the Electoral College, while John Adams received the most second-votes from the presidential electors (who originally cast two votes for president) and therefore became the vice president.

Washington certainly understood that every action that he performed as president would be a precedent to be noted and possibly emulated by future presidents, even minor details such as how formal state dinners were to be held. Other decisions by Washington, such as choosing to serve only two terms despite the Constitution allowing for repeated elections every four years for life would prove to be eminently more important. Washington also understood that through his actions hopefully the people would develop respect for the presidency while maintaining the republican principles upon which the nation was founded. When debate erupted around choosing a title for the president, some wanted that title to demonstrate the kind of respect held by European heads of state. After all, if the United States was to engage European powers as their equal, European leaders would have to regard the American president as their equal. John Adams proposed that the president's title should be "His Highness, the President of the United States and Protector of Their Liberties." For Washington, such titles suggested monarchy, which could undermine the republican foundations of the government and the people's faith in their president as protector of that republic. He chose a more simple title, "Mr. President."

A COMMON PURPOSE

The Constitutional Convention had exposed some deep divisions within the United States, especially between northern and southern states. The ratification debates made clear that sectional divisions might not, however, be the gravest threat to the young nation. The problems of the Confederation period had showed how inadequate the Articles of Confederation were and how the nation needed a stronger central government. The Constitution certainly addressed that problem but, with memories of British rule still vivid in citizens' minds, many feared that the new government could become too strong and abuse their rights as Americans just as the King and Parliament had abused their rights as Englishmen.

The nation's faith in George Washington may have helped to dispel fears in the short term, but much more important in Americans' minds was the possibility that sectional and other differences would ultimately result in the United States falling apart, with states becoming independent nations or creating regional alliances. Such an outcome would not bode well for their liberty as the powerful nations of Europe watched events in North America closely with an eye to pursuing their own advantages there. The collective power of the states, however, would provide a much greater hope of staving off European intrigues. As such, Anti-Federalists (who opposed ratification of the Constitution) joined with Federalists for the common purpose of making the government under the United States work.

For his part, George Washington tried to do his best to remain sensitive to the issues threatening to divide the nation. His cabinet reflected those efforts, as he chose individuals from different regions of the country as well as some who had been opposed to the Constitution, or at least been cautious in providing their support. He would often ask all of his cabinet officers to submit written opinions with justifications when important issues arose. This would allow Washington to better understand how different interests viewed those issues before he made a decision.

In addition to relying on the advice of his cabinet, he also sought the advice of others, most notably James Madison. A fellow Virginia planter, Madison had been the driving force at the Constitutional Convention. With Alexander Hamilton and John Jay, he wrote the most compelling arguments in favor of the Constitution. More than anyone else, Madison convinced Washington to serve as the presiding officer of the Constitutional Convention and would write most of his speeches early in Washington's presidency, even crafting a farewell address in 1792, as Washington seriously considered not seeking a second term.

ESTABLISHING A NATIONAL GOVERNMENT

George Washington's Executive Branch

While the Constitution established the basic parameters of the government, much was left to be determined as the first members arrived in New York City, the temporary seat of the new government. Congress had to pass enabling legislation to create the offices of a small but necessary bureaucracy. Most important were the executive branch departments whose appointed heads would become the president's **cabinet**. At the time there were only four departments (a fifth was the postal service but the Postmaster General would not serve in the president's cabinet). Washington looked to Virginians to head two of those departments, Thomas Jefferson (Secretary of State) and Edmund Randolph (Attorney General). Both men had initially expressed opposition to the Constitution, but by the time of ratification debates in Virginia they supported the document. Washington then looked to the northern states to fill the other positions with men who had served under Washington during the American Revolution—Henry Knox, an artillery general who had served as Secretary of War under the Confederation government was tabbed for the same role in the new government; and Alexander Hamilton, Washington's aide-de-camp, who agreed to serve as the nation's first Secretary of the Treasury.

For a young nation trying to establish itself with respect to European powers while still grappling with a large debt from its revolution, as well as the inadequacy of the Confederation government, Jefferson and Hamilton would serve as the most important department heads for the young country. They would also come to dominate American politics during the decade of the 1790s.

James Madison's Congress

As the most powerful leader in the first Congress, **James Madison** worked hard to achieve what he had sought to accomplish at the Constitutional Convention—create a national government with the power and respect to lead a truly united nation, as opposed to a confederation of sovereign states. In establishing the national government's authority over interstate and international trade, he helped pass a tariff law in 1789 that provided the young government with a steady source of revenue. Because the Constitution was silent on the specifics of the federal court system (beyond granting Congress the ability to create a Supreme Court), Madison pushed for passage of the **Judiciary Act of 1789.** This legislation established a six-member Supreme Court as well as a full federal judicial system with district courts and appeals courts. The law also extended federal power over the states by allowing for some state court decisions to be appealed to federal courts. To serve as the first chief justice, President Washington appointed John Jay, who had been temporarily serving as Secretary of State until Thomas Jefferson returned from France.

Madison's most important action in the first Congress was to personally take charge of adoption of a **bill of rights**, the unspoken promise of the ratification battles of 1788. While Madison had been opposed to adding a bill of rights during the ratification debates, by 1789, he had changed his position and became one its biggest supporters, ultimately viewing the Bill of Rights another way that the Constitution could protect individuals from the power and whim of popular majorities. While Congress considered many potential amendments, it ultimately passed twelve, ten of which were ratified by the states. Most of these amendments related to individual rights and harkened back to memories of British abuses under colonial rule (the freedom of speech, assembly, the press, and religion; prohibitions against quartering troops and unreasonable searches; trial by jury). In order to temper the thought that those were the only "natural" rights possessed by Americans, the Ninth Amendment stated that those rights listed in the first eight amendments were not an exhaustive list and, as such, the Constitution guaranteed other rights as well. Finally, the Tenth Amendment was a nod to those who feared that the new federal government might become too powerful—all powers not given to the federal government in the Constitution were reserved for the states and the people. In all, these amendments were seen as a means of limiting the power of the federal government. Interestingly, as the federal government has increasingly become the guarantor of those rights, against all who might try to limit those rights, the Bill of Rights has, in many ways, increased the power of the federal government.

COMPETING VISIONS FOR AMERICA

Those entering into service in the new government, whether elected or appointed, were committed to the survival of the United States. By the second year of George Washington's presidency, however, it was becoming clear that not all of those people had the same vision for the future of the United States. Two very different, seemingly incompatible, visions of America were emerging. As Secretaries of State and Treasury, respectively, Thomas Jefferson and Alexander Hamilton were certain to have a large impact on foreign and domestic policy for the young nation. They also soon were to become the leading political figures of the decade, heading political parties that promoted two different visions for America. They would often engage in a style of politics that would make many current politicians blush, but one must remember that at the time the survival of the United States was not a foregone conclusion. Members of the political parties that ultimately formed, the Democratic-Republicans (led by Jefferson) and the Federalists (led by Hamilton), truly believed that their experiment in republican government depended upon the visions of a future America that their leaders espoused.

The Hamiltonian Vision

While **Alexander Hamilton** was later trained as lawyer, he was born into poverty on the West Indian island of Nevis and raised by a single mother on St. Croix before she died of an illness when he was eleven. He then worked as an accounting clerk for a mercantile firm before being sent to New York by some influential men to attend college (he entered King's College, which later became Columbia University, in 1773). His commercial background and reading of Adam Smith and other Scottish Enlightenment thinkers served as a basis for his developing views on political economy, which were neither mercantilist nor free market but, rather, a blending of the two theories.

Soon after arriving in New York, Hamilton became involved in the patriot cause, writing essays in its support. A year later, he joined a New York militia and caught the eye of George Washington. For the remainder of the Revolution, he served as Washington's most reliable aide, writing much of the general's correspondence as well as reports on strategy and organization of the army. While serving under Washington, Hamilton began to recognize the inadequacy of the weak central government under the Articles of Confederation. When that dysfunction continued in peacetime, Hamilton became a driving force pushing for a stronger central government during the Constitutional Convention and afterward as he worked feverishly for its ratification.

Hamilton's desire for a stronger central government was most closely tied to his economic vision for America. That vision started to become clear when he, as Secretary of the Treasury, introduced plans for dealing with the national debt that the new government had inherited from the American Revolution and the Confederation government. At the request of Congress, in January 1790, Hamilton submitted a ***Report on the Public Credit.*** In it he detailed the total debt owed by the United States at $79 million, which included $25 million in debts owed by the states. Not all foreign creditors were pleased with the fact that Hamilton's plan called for paying the nearly $12 million of foreign debt in U.S. dollars as they were essentially worthless in Europe—forcing them to spend that money in the United States where it had clear value. But paying the debts, regardless of the currency used, would establish the young nation as credit-worthy with the nations of Europe. Gaining the respect of foreign creditors would ensure that the U.S. could borrow foreign money in the future if the need arose.

Hamilton proposed paying the remaining $67 million of federal and state debt in full, despite calls to discount the domestic debt. He understood that there was not yet widespread confidence in the government. To shirk that responsibility to those holding government notes would destroy any faith that there might be in the government—paying that debt in full would increase faith in the government. By extending that payment to state debts (which some states had been negligent in paying responsibly), Hamilton would further engender popular support for the national government.

In order to stabilize the nation's finances by creating a means of issuing bonds to pay debts that tariff revenue alone could not cover, as well as to extending loans to benefit the business community, Hamilton proposed the establishment of a national bank. The national bank would be a private institution chartered by the U.S. government with the federal government its largest partner. Throughout its twenty-year charter, the **Bank of the United States** would hold the deposits of the federal treasury, be the only institution with exclusive rights to issue U.S. bonds, and issue an extensive number of loans

Alexander Hamilton

to stimulate business activity in the young nation, especially to budding industries.

Hamilton's full vision for the future of America became clear in December 1791, when he submitted to Congress his *Report on Manufactures*. While he clearly saw the value of agriculture to the American economy—with vast land and European demand for American crops, agriculture would remain an important part of the American economy, but Hamilton felt that the United States would never achieve its full economic potential without expanding its fledgling manufacturing enterprises. In addition to national bank loans, he believed that the federal government needed to use its power and authority to aid and support manufacturing and trade through government policy in the form of subsidies designed to help upstart manufacturers compete with established European businesses (especially English), the building of roads and other infrastructure to better facilitate internal trade, and the imposition of selective tariffs to protect American manufactures from foreign competition.

Overall, Hamilton believed that his program would enable the United States to become economically independent of Europe while aiding in the promotion of economic stability. The plan would benefit manufacturers, but also farmers by enabling them to purchase cheaper, American-made goods while helping them better market their products due to an improved national infrastructure.

Thomas Jefferson and the Agrarian Republic

Unlike Hamilton, who grew up in a world of commercial trade, **Thomas Jefferson** came from the agricultural economy as a member of the Virginia planter class. That background, coupled with his devotion to republicanism, led him to develop an entirely different vision for the future of America than Hamilton's—one celebrating the creation of an **agrarian republic**.

Coming out of the American Revolution, the Founding Fathers embraced republican ideals. Their experiences with the British monarchy and reading of Enlightenment thinkers such as John Locke and David Hume led them to believe that while government was necessary, a republican form of government would provide societal order and ensure individual liberty. These men had seen the abuses of monarchy and did not trust democracy, as average Americans would likely pursue self-interest through government—and they saw this self-interestedness firsthand in the state governments during the Confederation period. A republican government led by virtuous men looking to the common good rather than promoting their own self-interest was the answer to the perils of abusive monarchy and self-interested democracy.

For Jefferson, the virtue necessary to sustain that government could be seen in his fellow farmers, men whose hard work reaped economic rewards. Hamilton's America would lead to the rise of business, banking, and high finance. To Jefferson, the men engaged in those occupations were simply not virtuous men. Those "stock jobbers" manipulated money and people to further enrich themselves at the expense of others. A government under their control would soon be acting in their self-interest at the expense of the common good. Virtue would become meaningless as they dominated the government and ruined the dream of an American republic. With abundant land, America had plenty of room to expand, and that physical growth would also lead to economic growth. More important to Jefferson, because most Americans would work in farming, they would develop the virtue necessary to maintain the republic.

Interestingly, Jefferson's vision of an agrarian republic was not one of plantation owners like himself, but of small, independent farmers. The self-reliance of being an independent farmer enabled them to live virtuous public lives. Meanwhile, a society based on manufacturing would lead to growing cities whose dependent workers would be incapable of voting politically against the interests of their employers for fear of losing their jobs. Regarding his views, Jefferson, while in Paris in 1787, wrote to James Madison: "I think our governments will remain virtuous for many centuries; as long as they are chiefly agricultural; and this will be as long as there shall be vacant lands in any part of America. When they get piled upon one another in large cities, as in Europe, they will become corrupt as in Europe."

The growth of manufacturing in America was a threat to his hope for a virtuous republic. Moreover, he felt it was unnecessary. America would be able to feed itself and still have plenty of agricultural products to trade to Europe. In return, Europe would send manufactured goods to America, freeing America from the dangers manufacturing posed to social order. When wheat prices increased by over 50 percent during the 1790s due to the beginning of hostilities in Europe, it further emboldened Jefferson's view.

A GROWING RIFT

Thomas Jefferson arrived in New York in February 1790 ready to assume his role as Secretary of State. By the end of the year, he was deeply involved in heated political disagreements with Alexander Hamilton over the proper direction of the country. He had seen the beginning of the **French Revolution** and his faith in republicanism was bolstered by what he observed. France, it seemed, had been inspired by the events taking place in America and was on its way to establishing a republican government under majority rule. With that experience in mind, his first impressions of the new government in America shocked and dismayed him. "When I arrived at New York in 1790 . . . being fresh from the French Revolution . . . I was astonished to find the general prevalence of monarchical sentiments [in the government]."

Jefferson, however, still had faith that majority rule and the republican system created by the Constitution would correct that problem, probably by the next election. Jefferson believed those men with "monarchical sentiments," many holding high positions in government, were "preachers without followers." The majority of Americans did not hold those views so they would be voted out of power in short order. "The happiness of governments like ours, wherein the people are truly the mainspring," he wrote, "is that they are never to be despaired of. When an evil becomes so glaring as to strike them generally, they arouse themselves, and it is redressed."

Not only did Jefferson begin to organize opposition to government actions that he viewed as a danger to republicanism, James Madison (who had worked closely with President Washington and Secretary Hamilton for the past three years) joined his friend from Virginia in the effort. For Jefferson and Madison, it was increasingly clear that Hamilton led a minority of elites seeking to undermine republican government, destroy checks and balances, and replace the American government with a British-style government—a governmental system for which Hamilton had more than once voiced his admiration.

Hamilton's Financial Program

Hamilton introduced his financial program as a means of dealing with the enormous debt the government inherited while also trying to establish the government on firm financial footing to allow for economic growth and respect from the powerful nations of Europe.

His first proposal was to pay the national debt of $54 million by redeeming existing government bonds and notes at full face value. This would seem a logical and necessary thing to ensure trust in future government bonds but it faced immediate criticism. With the value of those bonds severely depreciated during the Confederation period, many average bondholders (farmers and shopkeepers) saw those bonds as virtually worthless. But with the creation of the new government some speculators grew confident that the new government, with increased powers of raising revenue, would redeem those bonds. Therefore, they bought up as many bonds as they could

at deflated values, sometimes paying as little as 10 percent of the face value.

Jefferson and Madison believed that Hamilton's plan posed a two-fold problem. By paying the debt at face value, it would enrich those speculators at the expense of average Americans. Moreover, it would gain support for the government from the wealthy speculators whose wealth and power could generally increase the power of the federal government. Adding to their unease was the fact that more than half the members of Congress owned such bonds. Even Hamilton's Assistant Treasury Secretary held bonds valued at $4.6 million. That was the kind of self-interest that a virtuous republican government was intended to prevent.

Madison voiced immediate opposition in the House of Representatives, arguing that original bondholders should be identified and given their fair share of the value of those bonds. From Virginia, Patrick Henry argued that Hamilton's plan would "erect, and concentrate, and perpetuate a large monied interest" that would use government to serve its own ends without respect to the needs or wants of the people. Hamilton responded by stating that tracking down the original bondholders would be a herculean task nearly impossible to achieve and that the government must repay its debts in full to maintain respect and ensure creditworthiness if it ever wanted to borrow money in the future. With Hamilton's arguments, and many congressmen personally benefiting, the funding plan was approved.

To Jefferson, Hamilton's next proposal, the establishment of a national bank, posed an even greater risk to republicanism, potentially creating a concentration of wealth threatening to the interests of average Americans. For Jefferson, there was an even more dangerous issue based on the fact that the Constitution did not specifically authorize Congress to create a national bank. Hamilton argued that the power to do so was an "**implied power**" granted to the government through the necessary and proper clause—granting the government all other powers needed in order to carry out its assigned duties and functions. Jefferson feared that such an interpretation could stretch the limits on federal power beyond credulity.

In supporting Jefferson's position within the House, Madison was forced to depart from opinions regarding the Constitution that he had advanced in the *Federalist Papers*, where he had argued that the Constitution contain implied powers (those powers not specifically listed). In *Federalist # 44*, he argued that the Constitution granted the federal government the power to establish corporations, including banks. Jefferson and Madison were now taking a **strict constructionist** approach to the Constitution—if a power was not specifically enumerated in the Constitution, then the government did not have the legal right to perform certain actions based on that power.

Hamilton responded that to accept Jefferson's argument regarding the Constitution "would be to give [necessary] the same force as if the word absolutely or indispensably had been used." He further argued that implied powers were simply the means by which the various branches of the government could carry out the enumerated powers granted to them under the Constitution.

Hamilton marshaled support in Congress and, with many believing that George Washington supported Hamilton's position, it passed in the Senate by a mere voice vote. Despite Madison's efforts in the House, the bank bill passed there by a margin of 39-20. The emerging divisions were clear to President Washington. He asked Hamilton to write a justification while also asking Madison to compose a veto message. In his justification, Hamilton argued that to adhere to a strict constructionist view of the Constitution would leave federal authority so at the mercy of individual states that the nation would revert back to its condition under the Articles of Confederation. After reading both arguments, Washington sided more with Hamilton and signed the bill into law the next day.

Hamilton's victory proved to be short-lived. Madison was able to lead opposition to the portion of the Treasury Secretary's debt plan—federal government assumption of state debts—to defeat that proposal in the House by a vote of 32-29. An exasperated Hamilton approached Jefferson to see if he could convince Madison to reconsider to which Jefferson suggested that the three of them dine at Jefferson's house the next night. At that dinner, an important deal was struck. Madison agreed to withdraw his opposition to the assumption bill if Hamilton would support the Virginians on another issue that was being debated in Congress—a permanent location for the nation's capital.

The government had been seated in New York since its inception, and, certainly, New Yorkers wanted to see the capital remain there. But to Jefferson, that location placed the government too near powerful moneyed interests. A site along the Potomac River would put the government far from those moneyed interests while also placing it closer to the geographical center of the nation (and on the border of Virginia). The final deal was to move the government temporarily to Philadelphia (to appease some powerful Pennsylvanians who had been lobbying for that location as a permanent site) and, after ten years, a permanent relocation to a newly created city to be called Washington, in the District of Columbia. As soon as Congress approved the Residence Act relocating

the capital, Madison allowed the assumption bill to come up for a vote in which he and four of his supporters abstained, allowing the bill to pass. Hamilton had his plan enacted, but it had been a bitter pill for Jefferson and his supporters to swallow and the fight only intensified the growing political divisions in Congress and the country.

The Emergence of Political Parties

In 1789, Alexander Hamilton worked behind the scenes to establish a newspaper in New York City. The *Gazette of the United States*, edited by John Fenno, would allow Hamilton to celebrate and justify the actions of the new government, often by submitting his own articles under various pseudonyms. Meanwhile, Thomas Jefferson and James Madison realized that Hamilton had the support of the majority in Congress and began to develop a better organized opposition. Their first step was to counter the propaganda generated by Hamilton's newspaper. They identified an anti-Federalist newspaper editor in New York, Philip Freneau, moved him to Philadelphia where the government had relocated, and supported him economically where he began to publish a new newspaper called *National Gazette*. Jefferson and Madison also supplied Freneau with numerous articles that they anonymously authored. Like Fenno's journal, they shared articles with like-minded newspaper editors in other parts of the country.

Jefferson and Madison then went on a trip to northern New York for what they claimed was to study new flora and fauna in the region. The main purpose, however, was to cultivate relationships with powerful New York anti-Federalists who were suspicious of Hamilton and his motives, men like Robert Livingston, Aaron Burr, and Governor George Clinton. In doing so, they were creating the foundations of a new political party to counter the influence Hamilton held over the government.

Freneau and other newspaper editors supporting Jefferson began to refer to themselves as Republicans, implying that Hamilton and those who supported him did not favor a republican form of government. Although acting as an organized political entity, they did not formally form as a party until near the end of George Washington's second term, largely due to negative attitudes toward political parties at that time. They would eventually adopt the name **Democratic-Republicans**, though they often still referred to themselves simply as Republicans.

By 1792, Hamilton's supporters were referring to themselves as **Federalists**, adopting the name of the supporters of the Constitution during the ratification debates. This label suggested that they were the true defenders of the Constitution against those who would take America

THE EMERGENCE OF THE PARTISAN PRESS

In the years before the American Revolution, and continuing through the conflict, the press served to raise issues of British abuse and share information across the colonies in an effort to draw more people to the patriot cause. Newspapers and popular journals also gave leading colonists the ability to share ideas about their rights as Englishmen, their concepts of liberty, and the proper role and power of government. After independence, with the national government under the Articles of Confederation floundering and the ratification of the Constitution in doubt, supporters of the Constitution used the press as a means to rally public support for their cause.

Though the Constitution was ratified, by razor thin margins in some states, there were still many Americans who did not trust the new government. One of the leaders of that new government, Alexander Hamilton, turned to the press once again to win greater popular support, arranging the creation of a newspaper. The "Gazette of the United States" under its editor John Fenno essentially became a mouthpiece for the government, lauding government policies and actions. Hamilton himself submitted articles using pseudonyms.

Shortly after returning to America to serve as Secretary of State, and greatly alarmed by what he saw as a government headed toward aristocracy and monarchy, Thomas Jefferson, along with James Madison, worked to establish a newspaper to serve as a counterbalance to Hamilton's pro-government newspaper. They lured Philip Freneau, an anti-Federalist newspaper editor in New York, to Philadelphia to launch a new newspaper, the "National Gazette." Freneau had been a classmate of Madison's and had become known as the "Poet of the Revolution" for his satiric poetry and essays during that conflict. Madison was also a major contributor of essays, using pseudonyms, of course. To ensure that the paper would remain economically viable, Jefferson and Madison conducted a subscription drive and Jefferson provided Freneau with a job in the State Department as a translator (although the only language Freneau spoke was French, a language at which Jefferson was fluent).

With his finances secure, and little work for him to do at the State Department, Freneau spent his time writing his newspaper through which he attacked nearly every policy proposal from Hamilton. As Hamilton and Jefferson began to formalize their supporters into political parties, the attacks of their newspapers broadened. The criticisms could be based on principles or policy but also could be personal, with little regard for actual truth in trying to denigrate their political opponents. Even the widely-popular George Washington increasingly faced the wrath of Republican editors like Freneau and Benjamin Franklin Bache (who, while not a Republican partisan, was certainly an anti-Federalist). In one article and political cartoon published during the Whiskey Rebellion, Freneau satirically suggested that President Washington would be treated by the America people in the same way that the King of France had been – at the guillotine.

The partisan newspapers, however, did not only serve as vehicles for attacking political opponents. Springing up in cities and towns across the country, they allowed for a sharing of ideas among party leaders on the issues of the day and of their ideas about government. The newspapers helped the Federalists and Republicans develop more consistent ideologies that connected party members from different regions of the country. With the perception of virtue still so important to leaders of both parties, the newspapers also served as mouthpieces doing the dirty work of politics—campaigning— which allowed the candidates themselves to remain largely above the fray, maintaining their public virtue as servants of the people.

toward democracy (which at that time many thought was simply one step away from anarchy) and the chaos and associated bloodshed of the French Revolution.

EUROPE CREATES NEW PROBLEMS

With the government already dividing into two factions, the Washington administration faced new problems due to events occurring in Europe. In 1789, the French Revolution had erupted. Most Americans, including Thomas Jefferson, celebrated the revolt, as it appeared that France was following the example set by America in rising up against monarchical power. Initial developments seemed to indicate that France would adopt a constitutional monarchy. Even Jefferson seemed fine with this limited revolution, as he viewed King Louis XVI as much more reasonable than King George III of England.

Not everyone in France, however, was happy with the limits of the revolution and a second wave of revolutionary fervor arose to throw off the power of the king entirely. The new French Republic embraced a government based on democratic ideology. Frenchmen began referring to each other as citizen as a means of displaying their equality with each other. To prevent powerful groups with other interests in France from threatening that government, the revolutionary leadership began to execute political opponents in what were termed reigns of terror, beheading them at the guillotine.

As the French Revolution became more radical, feelings intensified in America. Some were shocked by the bloodshed; others were alarmed at the attack on property; while many others did not like the seeming attack on religion (the new government promoted a national religion based on rationalism and "natural morality"). Despite those issues, Jefferson and his supporters continued to support the revolution and the new French government that was spawned. Bloodshed in the cause of liberty was a small price to pay. Jefferson viewed the bloody revolutionaries in France "as the same as the Republican patriots in America. . . . The liberty of the whole earth was depending on the issue of the contest, and was there ever such a prize won with so little innocent blood." His newspaper editor, Philip Freneau, wrote more succinctly that the French Revolution killed "two or three thousand scoundrels to rescue the liberties of millions of honest men." The monarchies of Europe, however, were alarmed by the radical revolution, and France soon found itself at war with many of the major European powers, including England.

Proclamation of Neutrality

With France at war with England, Jefferson argued that the United States had a responsibility to aid France, based on the Treaty of 1778 in which the United States gained the support of France during the American Revolution. French aid was instrumental in America winning its independence from Britain, and now it was time for the United States to repay that debt.

Hamilton, however, did not want to engage in a war with Britain, America's most important trading partner. Not only would war hurt the American economy, the United States did not even have a standing army. Going to war against Britain might encourage British efforts to try to take their former colonies back. There was also much to be gained by staying out of the conflict. With Europe at war, the nations of Europe would need American trade more than ever and the war would be great for the American economy.

George Washington also did not want to get drawn into the war in Europe. The United States was a young nation just trying to get on its feet. Hardship at home as a result of war might lead to opposition to the government

that was still trying to establish itself. Nevertheless, he fretted about the implications of refusing to live up to the obligations of the treaty. Hamilton assured Washington that the U.S. had no responsibility with regard to the treaty that they entered with King Louis XVI because he was now dead, executed by the current government. With that assurance, Washington issued a **Proclamation of Neutrality** stating that America would not be going to war in Europe.

The Genêt Affair

Officials in the French revolutionary government were not pleased with U.S. neutrality. Greatly desiring American aid and believing that a majority of Americans would willingly help them as kindred republican spirits, the French laid the blame for the neutrality policy squarely on the Washington administration.

Because of that prevailing belief, the French government sent a minister to the U.S. named Edmond-Charles Genêt, known by the egalitarian moniker of **Citizen Genêt**, to promote support for American intervention on behalf of France. Rather than report directly to President Washington or Secretary of State Jefferson, Genêt landed in Charleston, South Carolina and began making direct appeals to the local people. In addition to rallying support for the French cause, he also carried with him letters of marque, which he began distributing to private ship captains and granted the captains permission by the French government to seize British ships.

Washington was infuriated by Genêt's actions. Not only was Genêt appealing directly to Americans in an effort to undermine his policy of neutrality, he was encouraging Americans to attack British ships, which could ultimately draw the United States into war with Britain. After a month in the country, Genêt finally arrived in Philadelphia where he was greeted by cheering crowds and the warm embrace of the Republican governor of Pennsylvania who had a long-standing animosity toward Washington. After two days in the city, Genêt finally met with Secretary of State Jefferson who then took him to meet the president. The meeting with Washington was short and cordial but firm and without a hint of warmth. Genêt, however, was prepared for that. In his earlier meeting with Jefferson, he had been warned that Hamilton retained great influence over the president and that, along with some other high government officials, they held pro-British views. Jefferson clearly thought that the popular fervor over Genêt's arrival would ultimately push the president to support France.

Encouraged by Jefferson and other Republicans, Genêt began to organize "**democratic societies**" in Philadelphia that spread to other parts of the country. He also sent a Frenchman to the Kentucky governor with a note of introduction from Jefferson asking Kentuckians to join with a French force in attacking Spanish New Orleans. This was very appealing to those in Kentucky as Spain had long threatened western trade with their control of the Mississippi. To top it off, American privateers, armed with French letters of marquee, began hauling British ships into American ports. One vessel was even brought into Philadelphia. Genêt then began to equip a captured British merchant ship with cannons in preparation to send it back to sea as a privateer. In a contentious cabinet meeting in which Jefferson did his best to defend Genêt, Secretary of War Henry Knox produced a copy of Freneau's latest edition. The piece included a satiric article titled *The Funeral Dirge of George Washington* depicting the president being prepared for execution at the guillotine because of his aristocratic pretensions. This insult was the last straw for Washington.

As Secretary of State, Jefferson was told to send a letter to the French government demanding that Genêt be recalled. Faced with the prospect of being sent back to France, Genêt became even more indignant and began openly courting the support of Republicans around the country. Hamilton arranged for an article to be published in a New York newspaper that demonstrated how Genêt was trying to appeal to the American people over the head of George Washington. Despite the emerging party tensions, Washington was still very popular, and the article helped to launch a groundswell of support for the president. Even Jefferson turned against Genêt as he had ceased to be an asset for the Republicans. After a new group seized power in France, the diplomat was replaced by a new minister from France. Fearing execution by the new group in power if he returned home, Genêt remained in the United States and was granted asylum by President Washington.

As the Genêt Affair came to a close, Thomas Jefferson submitted his resignation to the president. Within a year, Hamilton would also resign. Perhaps the battles of the past two years were wearing on both men, especially when it was becoming increasingly difficult to serve two masters—the Washington administration and their respective political parties. Of course, these moves would also free them to devote more time to organizing their parties in preparation for the next election, one in which George Washington would not be a candidate.

PROBLEMS IN THE WEST

The western frontier had posed a problem for the U.S. government dating back to the Confederation period. Westerners felt neglected by the national government, which was dominated by Easterners. The Jay-Gardoqui Treaty in 1786 offered to give up American navigation of the Mississippi River for twenty years in exchange for better trade with Spain from eastern ports. This was especially troubling for western farmers who primarily produced grains such as wheat and rye for export. Transporting those crops over the Appalachian Mountains was difficult and expensive. River trade was much cheaper but Spanish control of New Orleans, and therefore the Mississippi River, made it difficult to trade. The Jay-Gardoqui Treaty suggested that Easterners did not care about the problems of the West. The Confederation Congress failed to ratify that treaty, which probably kept Westerners from separating from the United States at that time, but trade through New Orleans would remain an important issue for western farmers.

Spain was not the only foreign nation creating problems for Westerners. In 1783, the British had agreed in the Treaty of Paris to cede all lands south of Canada and east of the Mississippi River to the United States, promising to remove British troops from forts in that region known as the Old Northwest. More than a decade later, British troops were still there, ostensibly because the United States had failed to ensure that London merchants were compensated for pre-Revolutionary debts owed to them by American citizens. The British military, in fact, had even established another fort in the region where they were aiding and encouraging Native American resistance to American expansion. To those Westerners, the federal government was unwilling or unable to force the British to leave and quell the Indian unrest. These were, however, issues of a failure of the government to act or of its weakness when it did act. By 1794, growing dissatisfaction in the West would turn into outright resistance because of a government action.

The Whiskey Rebellion

In an effort to better raise revenue to operate the government and service the debt, Secretary Hamilton proposed an excise tax on distilled spirits, including whiskey. This levy made sense to the Treasury Secretary, as raising tariff rates too high could lead other countries to retaliate with high tariff rates that would hurt the American economy. While he was proposing an internal tax, it faced little opposition when it was passed by Congress in 1791 (Jefferson and Madison both supported it at the time). When the government began sending revenue collectors to enforce the tax, however, there was immediate resistance.

Western farmers producing excess grain had difficulty trading their crops due to shipping costs and the uncertainty of trading through New Orleans. Many of them began to convert excess grain into whiskey that was easier and cheaper to transport for sale. When the government imposed an excise tax on distilled spirits but not other domestic products, the growers felt that they were asked to carry an unfair burden.

In Kentucky there was little overt resistance, largely because local officials and judges did little to enforce the tax. Hamilton complained bitterly about the ineffectiveness of the tax collectors there, but little changed. In western Pennsylvania, the situation was quite different. Farmers in the region evaded the tax and were often openly hostile to the tax collectors. In 1794, those disgruntled farmers became organized and armed themselves in protest against federal government authority known as the **Whiskey Rebellion**. In July, an army of fifty men confronted John Neville, the federal supervisor of tax collection in the region who had been extraordinarily ruthless in dealing with the farmers. They demanded access to all records related to the tax on whiskey. When he refused, shots were exchanged before the farmers quickly retreated. Several days later, an even larger rebel group of more than four hundred marched to Neville's home and again skirmished, this time setting Neville's property on fire as he escaped. On August 1, an army of nearly 7,000 whiskey rebels gathered at Braddock's Field in preparation of marching on the city of Pittsburgh and possibly capturing Fort Pitt, which housed a federal arsenal.

Officials in Philadelphia became increasingly alarmed about events in western Pennsylvania. They determined that they would not allow a group of citizens to openly resist the authority of the federal government, especially because the rebelliousness seemed to be spreading. People in backcountry Maryland, Virginia, and Kentucky were raising liberty poles and voicing their support for the rebels. President Washington believed this was a direct result of Citizen Genêt's intrigues and support for the creation of "democratic societies," as well as the Republican press. Memories of Shays' Rebellion also returned. Upon Hamilton's request, the president called up a militia of 13,000 men from Virginia, Maryland, Pennsylvania, and New Jersey. He placed Virginia Governor Henry "Lighthorse Harry" Lee in command but made a point of announcing that he would meet the army near Carlisle, Pennsylvania. It appeared that Washington might lead the army himself, which certainly must have unnerved some of the rebels. He inspected the troops in his old general's uniform before returning to Philadelphia, leaving Lee and Alexander Hamilton to lead them on to Pittsburgh. Washington then issued a proclamation calling on the support of all Americans in his efforts "to maintain the Constitution and the laws."

Jefferson and Madison were appalled by Washington's decision to use force against Americans and even more so by his attack on the "democratic societies." Madison, in reference to that attack, called it the "greatest error of his political life." To Jefferson, it was "one of the most extraordinary acts of boldness of which we have seen so many from the faction of the monocrats." Nevertheless, Washington's actions succeeded in ending the protest. After his proclamation, he received widespread support from all over the country. The whiskey rebels, facing a large federal expedition, began to disperse. The army rounded up 150 suspects, of whom twenty were transported to Philadelphia for treason trials. As a final effort

Home of Thomas Gaddis, one of the principal leaders of the "Whiskey Boys." During the short-lived revolt, Gaddis erected a "Liberty Pole" next to this cabin carrying a banner inscribed with the slogan "Liberty and No Excise," to rally support for the rebel cause.

to defuse the situation, Washington prudently pardoned all twenty.

THE FINAL SPLIT

While partisan newspapers continued their attacks, and the issues and events through the beginning of Washington's second term increasingly drove them apart, the supporters of Hamilton and Jefferson were still not identifying themselves as belonging to political parties. The idea of political parties still carried negative connotations for most Americans. George Washington was still widely respected, which probably delayed any formal creation of parties. But with their resignations by the summer of 1794, Jefferson and Hamilton were freer to focus on party organization. Growing tension with Britain, and U.S. efforts at quelling that tension, was the final straw.

The Jay Treaty

British government officials were not happy with the attacks on England's trading vessels by privateers that had been orchestrated by Genêt. Their belief in the U.S. government's acquiescence in the French emissary's intrigues, along with the known widespread pro-French sentiments among Republicans led by Jefferson and Madison, only intensified their anger. Despite the declared neutrality of the U.S. government, to the British, American actions and rhetoric did not seem very neutral.

With the war against France deepening, British officials began to press what had always been their biggest advantage over their rivals—its navy. With France in dire need of American crops to feed its large army, the British government issued the **Orders in Council**, authorizing British naval vessels and privateers to seize neutral (especially American) ships to prevent the transport of contraband to France or its West Indian colonies. The new regulations also expanded the concept of contraband, which by international law referred to war materiel, to also include vital food items such as corn, flour, and grain. England also signed a treaty with the Algerines, allowing these Barbary Coast pirates of North Africa to pass through the Straits of Gibraltar in order to attack American trading ships in the Atlantic.

Adding to the insulting British orders, the British Royal Navy, always short of sailors but even more so during times of war, began to fill its ranks through a practice known as **impressment**, which was essentially a draft. Press gangs would go into seaport towns in England and conscript people with seafaring experience into the British navy. Beginning in 1793, the British extended that practice to include American sailors, either pressed into service while in British ports or when their ships were seized on the high seas. These British actions caused increasing anger in America. This only added to American anger over Britain's failure to live up to all the terms of the 1783 Treaty of Paris.

The most important of those issues had to do with American sovereignty in the Old Northwest and continued British occupation of forts there, even expanding their occupation with construction of a new fort while aiding and encouraging Native American resistance to encroaching U.S. settlements. These actions galled western Americans. Coupled with impressment, it seemed to be a clear indication to Americans that Britain did not respect the United States as an independent nation. To Americans, England viewed America, at best, as a second-rate nation and, at worst, as a nominal British colony.

The Republicans, led by James Madison in Congress, pushed for a retaliatory tariff against Britain. In his last act as Secretary of State, Jefferson had submitted a report to Congress suggesting that trade with France could easily replace trade with Britain without any appreciable harm to the economy. Hamilton, however, understood economic issues far better than Jefferson and feared that a trade war with Britain would be devastating for the U.S. economy—and much worse if that trade war turned into an actual fighting war. He provided Federalists in Congress with all the ammunition they needed to defeat Madison's proposals. American exports to Britain were nearly $8.5 million, while exports to France were less than $5 million. Perhaps even more important, Americans imported over $15 million in goods from Britain but only a little over $2 million from France. In addition, British merchants had millions in cash reserves that they were more than willing to loan to Americans. Finally, trade with Britain benefited the American economy beyond just the value of the goods being carried. American ships were carrying a larger amount of those trade goods than any other nation—four times the amount carried on British ships. More than anything else, Hamilton wanted to secure and even improve that trade between the U.S. and Britain while also averting a war between the two countries.

Britain opened the door for negotiations with the U.S. when the British prime minister revoked an Order in Council that had prohibited trade with the French West Indies and promised that Americans harmed by the order would receive compensation. President Washington seized the opportunity by sending an envoy, Chief Justice John Jay, to England to discuss their differences. The choice of Jay caused immediate dissatisfaction by those who felt he would not represent the interests of all Americans. Westerners were especially upset, remembering how Jay had proposed giving up the right to navigate the Mississippi in preference to eastern trade with Europe.

Jay faced a bigger problem than unrest at home, however, as he had little leverage to pressure Britain to accede to American demands. In addition to the issues with regard to impressment, seizure of American ships, and British forts in the Old Northwest (along with British encouragement of Native American hostility there), Southerners also had been seeking British compensation for slaves taken during the Revolution since 1783 and wanted to use this treaty to accomplish that. Jay's position was so weak that he could achieve little, but he did enhance trade with Britain by guaranteeing Britain most-favored-nation status (ensuring low tariff rates for British goods). He also got a British concession to remove their troops from forts in the Old Northwest by June 1796 but a provision guaranteeing all Americans, British, and Indians across the boundary between the U.S. and British Canada made this essentially moot as the British would continue to aid and encourage Native American resistance in the region. Moreover, in order to get that concession, Jay agreed that any private pre-Revolution debts owed by Americans to British merchants or bankers would be paid by the U.S. Treasury.

To many Americans, what became known as the **Jay Treaty** provided little benefit for the U.S. while giving up much. For Republicans, the agreement was just more evidence that Hamilton and his Federalists would bow to Britain while working to create their own monarchy in America. The treaty also produced anger from some Federalists, especially northeastern merchants. Their right to trade in the British West Indies, an important trading partner, was restricted to small trade ships that effectively prevented most trade with the region. In cities across America, Jay was hung in effigy as street protests erupted. Republicans marshaled their forces to convince Washington not to sign the treaty. Failing in that, they sought to prevent ratification.

Hamilton, however, believed that Jay got everything he felt America *needed* out of the treaty, while other issues would work themselves out or be settled later. In his view, the treaty would promote American economic growth and keep America from getting dragged into a European war. As such, he used his influence with the Senate to ratify the treaty exactly by the necessary two-thirds majority. President Washington, realizing the position of weakness from which Jay was negotiating, and on Hamilton's advice, signed the treaty while believing it was the best deal that the U.S. could expect to receive.

Republicans responded by trying to defeat the treaty in another way, refusing to pass appropriation measures to fund the treaty. Federalists argued that once the president

signed the treaty and the Senate ratified it, the House had no choice but to pass enabling legislation. To Jefferson, that argument was a clear effort by the minority Federalists to undermine the will of the people as represented by the body of the federal government, which most closely reflected that will, the House of Representatives. It appeared that the large Republican majority in the House intended to embarrass the president by pushing the country toward war or dissolution. President Washington stood up to Congress as news reached Philadelphia indicating that popular opinion in support of the treaty was growing, in the form of large rallies favoring the treaty. Washington was also able to diminish the general angst that had developed over the Jay Treaty when he announced in February 1796 that the **Treaty of San Lorenzo**, also known as Pinckney's Treaty, had been negotiated with Spain and sent to the Senate for ratification. This agreement proved to be very favorable to the U.S., especially for Westerners, as the treaty secured American navigation of the Mississippi River as well as right of deposit for American goods in New Orleans. The large Republican majority began to melt away, and when Madison's resolution to withhold appropriations for carrying out terms of the Jay Treaty came up for a vote, the proposal lost by a narrow margin.

Political Parties Become Reality

George Washington had been convinced to serve a second term, but he refused to serve another. Some argued that with the rift between Federalists and Republicans, only Washington could keep the nation together. Given the increasingly bitter attacks, however, he doubted that he still had that much influence and had grown weary of the political battles in which he felt trapped. Any decision that he made was certain to lead to the enmity of one group or the other. In his farewell address, he did suggest that serious dangers lay ahead for America—in particular, he cautioned Americans to resist entanglement with European nations and to avoid the factionalism of political parties, which threatened to fracture the nation.

Despite Washington's pleas, the Jay Treaty had served only to intensify political organization. After efforts to thwart the treaty failed, Jefferson wrote: "Where the principle of difference is so substantial and as strongly pronounced as between the Republicans and Monocrats of our country, I hold it as honorable to take a firm and decided part, and as immoral to pursue a middle line, as between the parties of honest men and rogues, into which every country is divided." Jefferson was suggesting to Republicans that those who took "a middle line," or compromised with Federalists, were not men of honor. He now demanded strict party loyalty.

During the election year of 1796, Jefferson made it clear why he sought party loyalty—the Federalists were "an Anglican monarchical aristocratical party [which had] sprung up, whose avowed object [was] to draw us the substance, as they have already done the forms, of the British government." To the Federalists, the pro-French Republicans would take the country toward the disorder, violence, and near-anarchy of the French Revolution. The parties had drawn their lines and had formalized their existence. The year 1796 would see the first election in which these new political organizations promoted candidates and policies.

The Election of 1796

Political parties were a brand new institution in American electoral politics. As such, they had not developed formal systems for party nomination of candidates. While Hamilton and, even more so, Jefferson had worked hard to develop party unity, there were still some who might generally side with the party on many matters but refused to be bound by party loyalty on all issues. Hamilton, especially, faced such a problem, as John Adams was one of the leading candidates for president and was known to be an independent-minded politician who refused to be bound by party dictates.

The original Electoral College system for selecting the president did not have presidential and vice-presidential candidates run as a ticket. Therefore, each elector cast two votes for president. The person with the most electoral votes became president and the runner up became vice president. With Adams having strong Federalist support in New England, Hamilton worked behind the scenes to get a South Carolina Federalist, Thomas Pinckney, enough support among electors to win the presidency over Adams. Meanwhile, Thomas Jefferson and New Yorker Aaron Burr ran as the Republican choices for president.

Changing attitudes about the Jay Treaty and the overwhelming popularity of Pinckney's Treaty brought much support for Federalist office-seekers. Thanks in no small part to Hamilton's financial policies, the nation was doing well economically. The Federalists won control of both houses of Congress and the presidency. Hamilton's machinations, however, backfired on him. Figuring that northern Federalist electors would cast a vote for Adams, he worked to get them to cast their second ballot for Pinckney rather than one of a number of other potential candidates. He then worked to convince Federalist electors from South Carolina to cast one vote for Pinckney, and simply throw away their second vote. In this way, Pinckney would gain as many votes in New England, where Adams was popular, and win extra votes in the South

where Adams would garner less support. The eight South Carolina electors all cast a vote for Pinckney but supporters of Adams heard rumors of Hamilton's plan. As a result, twenty northern electors cast their vote for someone other than Pinckney, giving Adams the presidency with 71 electoral votes to Pinckney's 59. Even worse for Hamilton and the Federalists, with the loss of so many electors from the northern states, Jefferson came in second with 68 electoral votes, three votes behind Adams. The president and vice president were now members of the two opposing parties. John Adams, independent by nature, became even more so after he found out about the deception, calling Hamilton "the bastard brat of a Scotch pedlar."

THE ADAMS PRESIDENCY

John Adams faced incredible obstacles as he assumed the presidency. The nation was badly divided with the emergence of political parties, and Adams,—stubborn and independent—did not have the stature and popular support of George Washington. Domestic divisions, however, were the least of his problems. France was angry with the Jay Treaty. The U.S. had refused to live up to the 1778 treaty with France, preferring neutrality. To France, the Jay Treaty looked anything but neutral. If many Americans thought it favored Britain, France did even more so. In response, France began to attack American trading ships. They also refused to accept the new minister to France, Charles Cotesworth Pinckney.

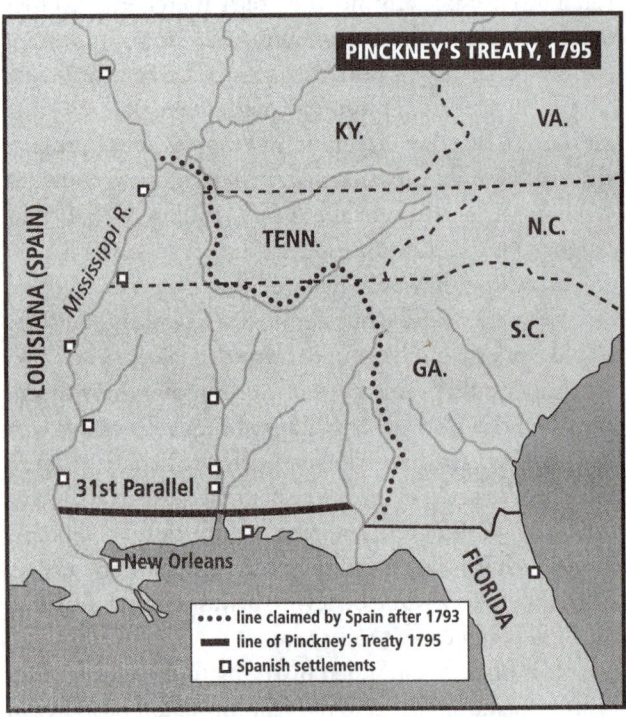

Map 8.1 Pinckney's Treaty, 1795

While most Federalists did not call for war, they did support taking a hard line with France and proposed military buildup in preparation for the possibility of a major conflict. Republicans, on the other hand, still supported the French government, seeing themselves and the French as fellow republicans—never mind that the revolutionary government had fallen only to be replaced by a government that made voting so convoluted that most Frenchmen had no real voice in the new government.

Intensified French attacks on American trade after March 1797 began what came to be known as the **Quasi-War**, an undeclared naval war between France and the U.S. that lasted until 1800. By the end of Adams's first year in office, over 300 American ships had been seized, and the nation saw a decrease in foreign trade over the previous year. The increased costs of shipping, including higher insurance rates, also weakened the American economy. Concerned with America's security and economy, the president adopted the Federalists' wishes for military preparation with increased spending on the army and the navy. This effort became part of a larger plan by Adams, however, to pursue peace with France. He believed that military preparations would strengthen the American hand during peace negotiations, which was Adams's ultimate goal. The president sought congressional approval for his plan and the Federalist-dominated Congress gave it to him over the sneers of angry Republicans who feared that Adams might form an alliance with Britain in order to pressure France.

Adams, however, truly desired peace. The United States, he believed, was in no position to go to war with any European power. The army had less than 3,500 poorly trained men, most of whom were busy fighting Native Americans on the frontier. The navy was also woefully inadequate. Congress had approved the building of six frigates in 1794, but budget cuts prevented their completion. Hamilton used his influence in Congress to get funding to complete three of the six ships, which included the *U.S.S. Constitution*, a powerful 44-gun, three-masted warship, but Congress was unwilling to raise the taxes necessary to build up the army.

In seeking peace, Adams planned to send a three-man commission to negotiate with France and wanted one of those diplomats to be a Republican. Not only was it politically smart at home, the commission was more likely to be received well by France than if it was only staffed by Federalists. Adams tried to convince Thomas Jefferson to go, and then James Madison, but both refused, and he ultimately turned to Massachusetts Republican Elbridge Gerry. He also chose a Federalist from Virginia, John Marshall, who would later become Chief Justice of the Supreme Court. The final member was Charles Cotes-

John Adams, Second President of the United States

worth Pinckney, the diplomat who France had refused to receive after Adams's election.

The XYZ Affair

The American commissioners arrived in France in October 1797 and met informally with French Foreign Minister Talleyrand, a man who had served as foreign minister to King Louis XVI and survived every change in government largely due to his diplomatic skills. Talleyrand instructed the commissioners to arrange a formal meeting with him through some intermediaries, who then informed the Americans that they would not be able to meet with Talleyrand until certain conditions were met. First, the U.S. must pay Talleyrand $250,000. Next, France would not be held liable for the claims of American shippers who had their ships seized by France. Finally, the U.S. government must provide France with a multi-million dollar loan.

Outraged, the demand for what amounted to a bribe for Talleyrand especially galled the commissioners. Pinckney responded, "No, no! Not a sixpence!" The practice of strong nations demanding such bribes from weaker nations was actually a common practice in Europe, but the implication that France viewed the U.S. as a second-rate nation was too much for the commissioners. The Americans tried to stall for time in order to give American ships a reprieve from French attacks by suggesting that they did not have the authority to make the deal. They would send for instructions from Philadelphia if France agreed to temporarily cease its attacks on American ships.

A CREATURE EMERGES IN MASSACHUSETTS

Most of the founders would have been suspicious of political parties yet, by the mid-1790s, a political party system was emerging in America. Leaders of both nascent parties used the press as a means of winning support for their positions while attacking the policies of their opponents—and often those opponents personally. Alexander Hamilton's Federalist Party had controlled the federal government since its inception and had even used its power within the federal government to undermine Thomas Jefferson's Democratic-Republican Party (for example, using the Alien and Sedition Acts to attack party newspapers). Clearly, such use of government to increase their own power were a staple of political parties from their very beginnings in America.

It was in that environment that Elbridge Gerry, who had maintained independence from the party system earlier, joined the Democratic-Republican Party by the late 1790's despite the fact that Massachusetts had solidly supported the Federalists during the previous decade. He unsuccessfully ran for governor of Massachusetts a number of times but saw his party gain increasing support in the state government. That growing support cut into the power of the Federalist Party in the state, eventually achieving a relative balance between the parties. Gerry finally won the governorship in 1810 but Federalists maintained a slim majority in the legislature. Gerry won re-election in 1811, this time with a slim Republican majority in the legislature.

With Republican control of the legislature and the governorship, the Republican Party worked to strengthen their control over the government despite the traditional balance between the parties. Gerry appointed a large number of Republicans to the state courts. At the same time, the legislature was mandated by the state constitution to re-draw legislative districts based on the recent census. The Republican legislature drew a new map of legislative districts, and Gerry signed it into law, aimed at undermining Federalist support, especially in traditionally-Federalist districts. For example, the five districts along the coast running from Boston to New Hampshire had consistently elected Federalists to the state legislature. With the new districts in place for the 1812 elections, three of the five new districts went to Republicans. Republicans also won 29 seats in the state senate compared to 11 for the Federalists despite the fact that the Federalists won more votes statewide, and Gerry was defeated by the Federalist candidate for governor.

In order to undercut the impact of popular support for the Federalists, Republicans drew some very oddly-shaped districts, including one north of Boston that was said to resemble a salamander. Since Gerry signed the new district map into law, he faced widespread criticism and drawing of that map became known as a Gerry-mander, combining the governor's name with salamander. Since then, the term gerrymander has referred to any drawing of a legislative map done specifically to give one party a political advantage.

Massachusetts Republicans did not invent the practice but Americans, building a young republic at the time, found the effort of those Republicans especially repugnant. It seemed to go against the very principles on which the nation was founded. Despite the response against that original gerrymander in 1812, it has maintained a long history in the United States and is still often used by political parties today in drawing state legislative districts.

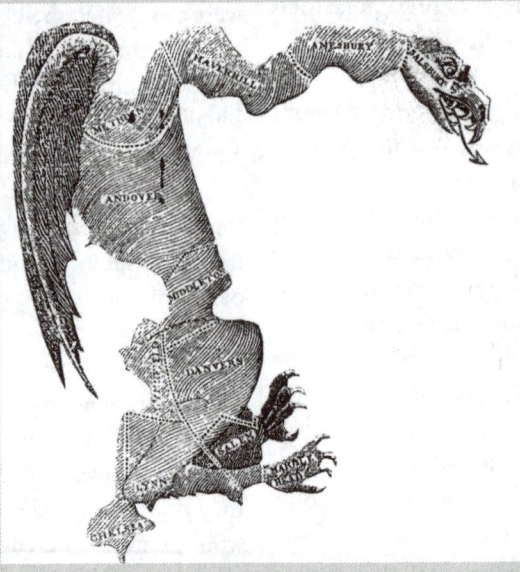

Talleyrand did not respond but, instead, sent more intermediaries with similar demands. After months of dealing with intermediaries and getting no closer to formal negotiations, John Marshall wrote a detailed report of their mission and the frustrated Federalists returned to the U.S. (Gerry remained in France believing he might actually get somewhere with the French but he was little more than a pawn in Talleyrand's skillful hands).

Meanwhile, with the Quasi-War inflicting real economic damage to America, Adams contemplated war and discussed the possibility with his cabinet. By that time (March 1798), the dispatches from Marshall arrived reporting the failure of the mission and the treatment of the American commissioners by Talleyrand. An enraged Adams prepared a declaration of war but instead of sending it to Congress he relayed a message relating the current state of affairs with France—that France and the U.S. were already at war on the seas, and that the American peace commission had failed. The president also asked Congress to begin preparing for war with new military expenditures.

Some Federalists began to call for hostilities with France, while Republicans countered that Adams and the Federalists were just using this episode as a means of drawing the United States closer to Britain. They argued that the dispatches would show a willingness on the part of France to negotiate being rebuffed by the commissioners. Interestingly, the pro-war Federalists joined with Republicans in passing a resolution demanding all of the correspondence from the diplomatic mission to France. The Federalists were hoping to bolster their justifications for war while the Republicans were trying to uncover what they viewed as a Federalist deception. Adams complied by sending Congress all of the documents related to the mission, redacting the names of the intermediaries and replaced them with X, Y, and Z, providing the name for what became known as the **XYZ Affair.** Republicans were amazed that the French had behaved as they did. The Federalist-controlled Senate voted to publish the documents and soon the entire country knew of the disrespect with which Talleyrand had treated the representatives of the United States.

Anti-French fervor erupted across the country, and the Federalists used the furor to their advantage. Rather than call for war, as hard-line Federalists wanted, they pushed for increased military preparation. In addition to completion of the three frigates already authorized, they added twelve new smaller gunships to the navy and created the Navy Department and the Marine Corps. They also authorized the arming of private merchant ships for self-defense. The U.S. was now fully engaged in the Quasi-War.

Response to the XYZ Affair also pushed support in Congress for increasing the size of the army to 10,000 men. Adams lured George Washington out of retirement to serve as the leader in charge of that larger standing army. The retired president dutifully complied with the request but wanted Hamilton to serve as his second-in-command. With Washington spending most of his time at his Virginia estate, Mount Vernon, Hamilton was effectively in command of the army.

Adams also responded to the XYZ Affair by formally recalling the peace commission from France in June (only Gerry remained by that time) and vowed never to send another diplomat to France "without assurances that he will be received, respected, and honored as the representative of a great, free, powerful, and independent nation." France, chagrined by the affair, ultimately dropped the demands that had led to the XYZ Affair. Hamilton's faction of the Federalist Party, known as the High Federalists, continued pushing for war, but Adams sought a middle course, even if it meant splitting the Federalist Party and costing him support for re-election in 1800. With a willing partner in France, negotiations reopened in 1799 with John Marshall (who had become Secretary of State), leading the American delegation that ultimately settled differences between the U.S. and France, ending the Quasi-War by 1800.

Alien and Sedition Acts

With anti-French sentiment high in the wake of the XYZ Affair in 1798, Hamilton and his supporters tried to benefit from the uproar through legislation that attempted to weaken their opponents and silence their anti-Federalist Party rhetoric. The Federalist-controlled Congress passed, and President Adams signed a series of laws known as the **Alien and Sedition Acts,** which would backfire on the Federalists and prove to be a huge political mistake by the otherwise shrewd Hamilton.

The Alien Acts dealt specifically with foreign nationals living in the United States. The legislation extended the time that an immigrant had to reside in the country before becoming eligible to apply for U.S. citizenship from five to fourteen years. The president was also authorized to arrest and deport, without trial, any foreigners deemed to be a threat to national security. With America effectively at war with France, these laws were clearly meant to prevent French nationals from stirring up government opposition, as Citizen Genêt had previously done.

The Sedition Act made it illegal to conspire to oppose government laws or to impede government officials from doing their jobs (a clear effort to prevent another Whiskey Rebellion). It would now be illegal to "write, print, utter or publish, or cause it to be done, or assist in it, any false, scandalous, and malicious writing against the government of the United States, or either House of Congress, or the President, with intent to defame, or bring either into contempt or disrepute, or to excite against either the hatred of the people of the United States, or to stir up sedition, or to excite unlawful combinations against the government, or to resist it, or to aid or encourage hostile designs of foreign nations." The Federalists believed that the law would serve two purposes. First, they thought that they could prevent Republicans from stirring up anti-government (really, anti-Federalist) sentiment. With the Federalists in control of both houses of Congress, majorities that grew even larger in 1798 due to the anti-French feelings generated by the XYZ Affair, they could now pursue their agenda with the opposition stifled by the Sedition Act. Second, they believed that the law could severely weaken, or even potentially destroy, Jefferson's Republican Party. Because political leaders in both parties still wanted to maintain the perception of virtue, newspapers had become the primary means of campaigning. Republican newspaper editors were now in jeopardy of being arrested for sedition when they criticized government policies or actions. Their only defense was truth, but with two very different views of the Constitution, truth was largely based on the perception of the jury.

The Republican response was swift, decrying a violation of freedom of speech and freedom of the press. In all, twenty-four arrests took place for violation of the Sedition Act. Most of those arrested were newspaper editors, although the law did not have the impact Federalists had hoped. Rather than silence those Republican newspapers, friends and family members often continued publishing them making a point of noting why the normal editors were not publishing the papers. A fiery Republican congressman from Vermont, Matthew Lyon, was also arrested for sedition—probably revenge for an earlier feud with a Connecticut congressman, Roger Griswold, which started when Lyon spit on Griswold. As an indication of how petty some Federalists could be, Luther Baldwin, a workingman in Newark, New Jersey, was drinking with friends in a tavern. After hearing a cannon salute offered to honor President Adams, one of the men suggested that the cannons were firing at the president's backside. Baldwin responded that maybe they should fire "through his arse." For that, Baldwin was arrested, found guilty, and fined $100, a considerable sum for a common workingman in the late 1790s.

The leaders of the party, Jefferson and Madison, felt it best if opposition to the law came from the states due to the nature of the federal system created in the Constitution. Each anonymously wrote a response to the Alien and Sedition Acts, which they had friends in the legislatures of Virginia and Kentucky submit for approval as resolutions that became known as the **Kentucky and Virginia Resolutions**. Madison's Virginia Resolution was highly critical of the acts through which, he argued, Congress was asserting "a power not delegated by the Constitution, but on the contrary, expressly and positively forbidden by one of the amendments thereto." Jefferson's Kentucky Resolution was more radical, although the two had spoken often while they were writing the documents, and Madison had tried to temper Jefferson's language. Jefferson argued that the states "being sovereign and independent, have the unquestionable right to judge of its infraction; and that a nullification, by those sovereignties, of all unauthorized acts done under colour of that instrument, is the rightful remedy." By suggesting that states had the power to nullify federal laws that they did not like, Jefferson was threatening the very existence of the federal government. If states had the power to ignore federal laws, the federal government would have no effective authority. The Kentucky legislature swore loyalty to the Union and did not invoke nullification, but raised that as a possible solution to states when they felt federal laws were "obnoxious" to the people of a state. Both resolutions called on other states to join them in questioning the federal government's use of power in the Alien and Sedition Acts. While there were popular protests against the acts throughout the country, no other state legislature joined them in protest. Nevertheless, the Resolutions served as good Republican Party propaganda and a rallying point for the upcoming presidential and congressional elections. For the Federalists, the political damage had been done. Their heavy-handed action in passing and enforcing the acts squandered popular support for the government and the Federalist Party after the XYZ Affair.

TOWARD THE ELECTION OF 1800

Passage of the Alien and Sedition Acts was not the only development turning popular opinion against the Federalists. The Republicans had long maintained that the Federalists were monarchists who wished to create a British-style government in the United States. To many Americans, the Alien and Sedition Acts were reminiscent of the abuses under the authority of British rule. Federalists had made it difficult to oppose unpopular laws with the threat of heavy fines and jail time. They had also dramatically increased the size of the army, using the Quasi-War with France as an excuse, with Alexander Hamilton, the leader of the High Federalists, as the *de facto* commander.

To pay for increasing the size of the army and navy, the Federalist-controlled Congress engineered a widely unpopular national property tax, which had little effect on the destitute and was aimed specifically at large landowners and slaveholders (slaves were taxed as well as land and homes). In 1799, John Fries, who was actually a Federalist, organized resistance against the tax in an area northeast of Philadelphia settled largely by German and Dutch immigrants. The rebels threatened tax assessors and refused to pay the tax. Adams saw the resistance of what became known as **Fries's Rebellion** as little more than a nuisance. He condemned the rebels and told the governor of Pennsylvania that he should call out the state militia to deal with it. Then he left Philadelphia for his home in Massachusetts, where he actually had spent much of his presidency. By that time, Fries had organized about 150 armed men and used them to march on a local jail and force the release of eighteen men who were being held for refusing to pay the tax. In Adams's absence, Hamilton convinced the cabinet to recommend to the president that 500 men from the army be sent to crush the rebellion, saying, "wherever the government appears in arms it ought to appear like a Hercules." The force was easily large enough to quell the unrest, but the heavy-handed actions of the commander of that force, General William MacPherson, only served to exacerbate the existing tensions. Fries and about sixty other rebels were arrested, and thirty were put on trial in federal court.

Most received fines, but Fries and two others were tried for treason and convicted, with Fries sentenced to death. Adams ultimately pardoned them, but the damage for Federalists had been done. The heavily Federalist region of Pennsylvania in which Fries and the other rebels lived voted overwhelmingly for Republicans in 1800.

The Election of 1800

The Federalist Party found itself badly divided by 1800. The independent-minded Adams had tried to steer a middle path. He still believed that the Republicans' strict interpretation of the Constitution undermine the Founders' purpose in creating a strong national government, but he also resented Hamilton's meddling in his administration and resisted the High Federalists' hard-line approach. Moderate Federalists supported Adams, leading Hamilton, once again, to try to orchestrate Adams's defeat in preference of a Federalist who Hamilton could better influence. Overall, Hamilton's clout by this time had been greatly diminished, and not just because of the split within the party. Hamilton had been involved in a scandalous extramarital affair while serving as Secretary of the Treasury. Her husband later blackmailed Hamilton and opponents suggested that Hamilton had used his position as Treasury Secretary to pay Reynolds off. Hamilton went public with a detailed recounting of the affair to exonerate himself of any wrongdoing as Treasury Secretary,

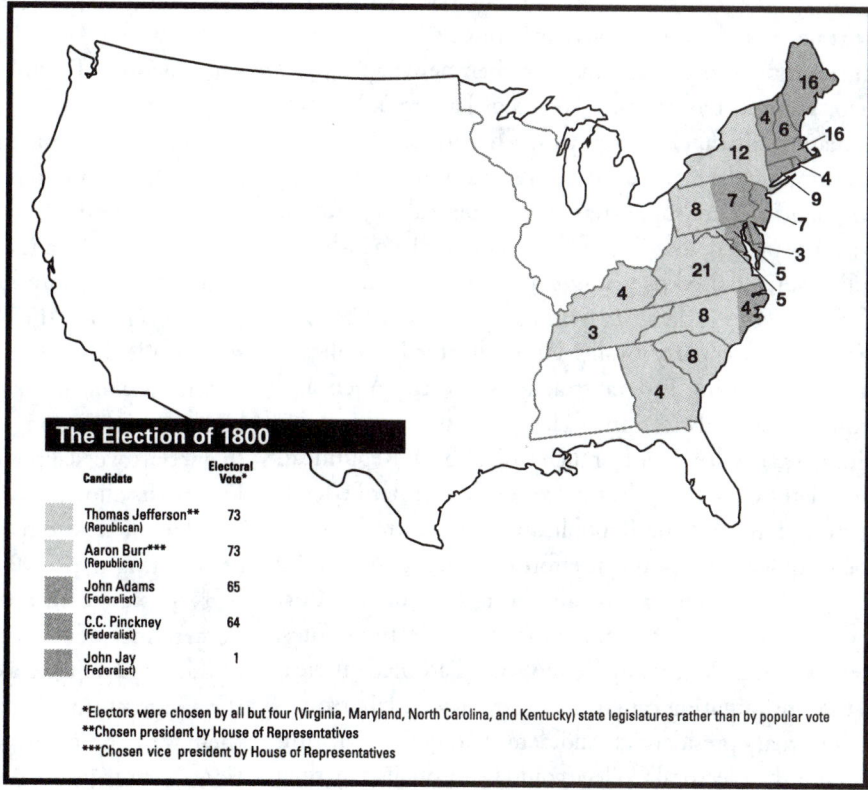

Map 8.2 The Election of 1800

The Election of 1800

Candidate	Electoral Vote*
Thomas Jefferson** (Republican)	73
Aaron Burr*** (Republican)	73
John Adams (Federalist)	65
C.C. Pinckney (Federalist)	64
John Jay (Federalist)	1

*Electors were chosen by all but four (Virginia, Maryland, North Carolina, and Kentucky) state legislatures rather than by popular vote
**Chosen president by House of Representatives
***Chosen vice president by House of Representatives

but while such personal drama was generally not spoken of by political opponents, the Republicans were all too happy to use the Reynolds affair to discredit Hamilton.

Adams won support in a May 1800 caucus to choose the Federalist candidates, along with Charles Cotesworth Pinckney. Because the system did not yet recognize specific presidential and vice presidential candidates, both were considered candidates for president with each elector casting two votes. As he had done in 1796, Hamilton worked to defeat Adams and get Pinckney elected instead. But this time he would do it publicly by writing a pamphlet that was a scathing indictment of Adams and his presidency. This act would further divide the Federalists and threaten their chances of success against their rivals for the presidency. The Republicans had once again nominated Thomas Jefferson and Aaron Burr as their presidential candidates.

This election, however, was not merely an election about policies or personalities, it was also about the type of country that the United States would ultimately become. Republicans continued the accusations of monarchy, even suggesting that Adams had tried to arrange a marriage between his son and a daughter of King George III of England. The Federalists referred to Republicans as Jacobins, in reference to the most radical French revolutionaries who had instituted the Reign of Terror. They pointed to the official name of Jefferson's party, the Democratic-Republican Party, as a sign that Jefferson intended to take the country toward democracy. Most landowners, the main people eligible to vote in much of the nation at the time, feared democracy as little more than mob rule. The election also got personal. In their newspapers, Jefferson's supporters accused Adams of having "a hideous hermaphroditical character, which has neither the force and firmness of a man, nor the gentleness and sensibility of a woman." Adams supporters, meanwhile, called Jefferson "a mean-spirited, low-lived fellow, the son of a half-breed Indian squaw, sired by a Virginia mulatto father."

While the Federalists were badly divided, Jefferson demanded strict party loyalty. Given that the Republicans had been fighting Federalist actions like the Alien and Sedition Acts and creation of a large standing army, maintaining that fealty became much easier. Both Republican candidates won more electoral votes than either Federalist candidate, and the Republicans won control of both houses of Congress, but the effort to ensure party loyalty neglected one important detail. Both Jefferson and Burr ended up winning the same number of electoral votes, seventy-three. While the Republicans had made it clear in their nominating caucus that they viewed Jefferson as their primary presidential candidate, neither the Constitution nor the Electoral College could be reconciled by their

intent. The tie would have to be decided by the procedure laid out in the Constitution, specifically, by the members of the House of Representatives voting as state blocs. A candidate needed need to win a majority of the delegations, or nine of the sixteen states, to be named president. Further, that vote would be performed by the current Federalist-controlled House and not the newly elected one soon to be dominated by Republicans. Meanwhile, the ambitious Aaron Burr infuriated Jefferson and other Republican leaders by refusing to declare publicly that he would not accept the presidency under any circumstances.

The House of Representatives proceeded to undertake 35 rounds of balloting, with Jefferson winning eight states on each one (Burr won six with two deadlocked among their even number of representatives), one short of the required nine. As much, if not more than any other Federalist, Alexander Hamilton truly hated Jefferson. Nevertheless, he still believed in the idea that government officials should possess virtue, especially those at the highest levels of government. To Hamilton, Burr did not possess a shred of virtue. Though Jefferson might pursue wrongheaded policies, they would be out of a sense of principled virtue. As the deadlock continued, Hamilton decided to use what influence he had remaining and convinced the Federalist congressmen from four states (two which had deadlocked and two that Burr had won) to abstain on the 36th ballot to ensure that Jefferson would become the next president.

The Revolution of 1800

The election of 1800 had resulted in a total change of power in the government. The Federalists, who had controlled the presidency and Congress since 1789, now found themselves out of power. As president, Thomas Jefferson would have Republican majorities in both houses, giving him the power to pursue whatever policies he and the Republicans deemed best. Jefferson referred to the election as the Revolution of 1800. What is most remarkable about the election, however, is not that the Republicans won such a resounding victory–the Federalists had helped that along with intra-party squabbling and by their controversial policies—but rather, that the outgoing Federalists allowed for a peaceful change of power.

The men who had become Federalists and Republicans during the 1790s and began the grand experiment in 1789 were committed to making it work. There was no certainty of success, and failure could mean the end of the United States as a nation. Sectional differences at the Constitutional Convention had made it clear that there were some deep divisions imbedded within the nation. Events of the 1790s had served to highlight those differences. Meanwhile, the biggest division had been an ideological battle over liberty and order. The Republicans erred on the side of liberty, which Federalists viewed as tantamount to democracy and anarchy. The Federalists erred on the side of order, which led to their opponents' cries of monarchy. With such clearly divergent visions for the future of America, both parties believed that the other would lead the nation toward ruin. Indeed, some Federalists, especially in New England, were so dismayed by the election that they made calls for secession. But those calls were silenced, and rather than use Hamilton's army to hold onto political power, the Republicans in March 1801, under Thomas Jefferson's leadership, assumed control of the government.

Chronology

1789 George Washington inaugurated first U.S. president.
Judiciary Act of 1789 establishes the Supreme Court and other federal courts.
French Revolution begins.

1790 Hamilton issues his *Report on Public Credit*.

1791 States ratify Bill of Rights.
Congress passes excise tax on whiskey.
Congress approves Hamilton's funding plan.
Hamilton issues his *Report on Manufactures*.
Congress creates the Bank of the United States.

1793 War breaks out in Europe.
George Washington issues Proclamation of Neutrality.
Citizen Genêt arrives in America

1794 Western unrest turns into whiskey rebellion.

1795 Jay's Treaty ratified.

1796 John Adams wins presidency.
Thomas Jefferson becomes vice president.

1797 Quasi-War begins with France.

1798 XYZ Affair erupts.
Alien and Sedition Acts enacted.
Virginia and Kentucky Resolutions passed.

1800 Thomas Jefferson elected third U.S. president.
Republicans end Federalist control of government

SUGGESTED READINGS

Joyce Appleby, *Capitalism and a New Social Order: The Republican Vision of the 1790s* (1984).

Alexander De Conde, *The Quasi-War: Politics and Diplomacy of the Undeclared War With France, 1797-1801* (1966).

Stanley Elkins and Eric L. McKittrick, *The Age of Federalism* (1993).

Thomas Fleming, *The Great Divide: The Conflict Between Washington and Jefferson that Defined a Nation* (2015).

Joanne B. Freeman, *Affairs of Honor: National Politics in the New Republic* (2001).

John Steele Gordon, *Hamilton's Blessing: The Extraordinary Life and Times of Our National Debt* (1997).

Frederick Hoxie, Ronald Hoffman, and Peter J. Albert, eds. *Native Americans and the Early Republic* (1999).

Stephen G. Kurtz, *The Presidency of John Adams* (1957).

Robert W.T. Martin, *Government by Dissent: Protest, Resistance, and Radical Democratic Thought in the Early American Republic* (2013).

David N. Mayer, *The Constitutional Thought of Thomas Jefferson* (1994).

Drew McCoy, *The Elusive Republic: Political Economy in Jeffersonian America* (1980).

John C. Miller, *Crisis in Freedom: The Alien and Sedition Acts* (1952)

___, *The Federalist Era, 1789-1801* (1960).

William Nestor, *The Hamiltonian Vision, 1789-1800: The Art of American Power During the Early Republic* (2012).

Jeffrey Pasley, et.al. eds., *Beyond the Founders: New Approaches to the Political History of the New Republic* (2004).

Thomas P. Slaughter, *The Whiskey Rebellion: Frontier Epilogue to the American Revolution* (1986).

William Stinchcombe, *The XYZ Affair* (1981).

Wiley Sword, *President Washington's Indian War: The Struggle for the Old Northwest, 1790-95* (1985).

David Waldsteicher, *In the Midst of Perpetual Fetes: The Making of American Nationalism, 1776-1820* (1997)

Phillip Ziesche, *Cosmopolitan Patriots: Americans in Paris in the Age of Revolution* (2009).

Review Questions

1.   Describe Alexander Hamilton's vision for America? How did he try to use government policies to achieve that vision?

2.   Describe Thomas Jefferson's vision for America? Why did Jefferson and his supporters believe government policies of the 1790s undermined that vision?

3.   How did George Washington as president try to maintain a balance between the two emerging political parties? How did the party leaders criticize government policies and/or leaders of the other party without discrediting themselves?

4.   Why did George Washington issue a Proclamation of Neutrality and urge against entangling alliances with European nations? Were his fears valid?

5.   What goals were the Federalists trying to accomplish with the Alien and Sedition Acts? How successful were they? What criticisms did the Republicans level against the acts?

Glossary of Important People and Concepts

John Adams
Alien Acts
Bank of the United States
Bill of Rights
Democratic-Republicans
Federalists
Edmund Genêt
Alexander Hamilton
Implied powers
Impressment
Jay's Treaty
Thomas Jefferson
Judiciary Act of 1789
James Madison
Orders in Council
Proclamation of Neutrality
Quasi-War
Report on Manufactures
Report on the Public Credit
San Lorenzo, Treaty of
Sedition Act
Strict Constructionist
Virginia and Kentucky Resolutions
George Washington
Whiskey Rebellion

Thomas Jefferson

Chapter Nine

JEFFERSONIAN AMERICA, 1801-1815

As America embarked on its grand experiment to create a republic, it was widely agreed that leaders of that republic must possess virtue so that the republic would not succumb to the corruption so evident in European governments. As such, those leaders took great pains to present themselves as virtuous men. If their honor was ever questioned, they believed that they were required to defend it vigorously. One way they did so was through the custom of dueling.

Whenever a gentleman in the early 1800s felt that his honor had been tarnished, he would likely demand a public apology. However, circumstances occasionally made it difficult for the other man to apologize without damaging his own honor. The duel allowed both men to preserve their sense of honor because it suggested that both were willing to die for it. While dueling could result in injury or even death, many such showdowns were settled without bloodshed. A man known as his second represented each combatant. They would communicate with each other before the scheduled duel date, trying to settle the dispute before the duel took place; or, failing that, they accompanied the combatants to ensure that the duel went according to the Code Duello (official rules of dueling codified in Ireland). Even after a duel commenced, the seconds were expected to attempt a reconciliation that would avoid violence. One way to avoid bloodshed was for one man to throw his shot away by firing into the ground. The other would then follow suit, and they could leave the dueling grounds with the honor of both men preserved.

Dueling remained popular in much of the country until after the Civil War, but by the 1790s, the practice was made illegal in a number of northeastern states. Even so, men in those states still often turned to dueling as a way of settling scores and preserving their honor. Unless someone was killed, charges were generally not brought for participating in them. During the 1790s, Alexander Hamilton was involved in a number of duels settled before shots were fired after both men had thrown their shots away.

In 1804, Hamilton again found himself fighting a duel, this time with Vice President Aaron Burr. There was long-standing tension between the two powerful politicians even though they had worked together on legal cases and engaged with the same man as a business partner. A dozen years earlier, Burr had defeated Hamilton's father-in-law for a U.S. Senate seat while Hamilton had engineered Jefferson's victory over Burr in the tied presidential election of 1800. With Burr's star in the Republican Party dimmed, he sought the governorship of New York in 1804 as a Federalist. Hamilton worked behind the scenes to convince his fellow Federalists to vote for Republican Morgan Lewis. After Burr was defeated, a letter written to Hamilton's father-in-law was published in a newspaper that revealed some things Hamilton had said about Burr at a dinner party. The letter said that Hamilton viewed Burr as a very dangerous man and that there was a "still more despicable" characterization that Hamilton said of Burr on which the writer did not elaborate (some historians believe that Hamilton suggested that Burr had an incestuous relationship with his own daughter).

Burr challenged Hamilton to a duel over these revelations and their seconds exchanged letters trying to settle matters.

He asked if Hamilton had said the "more despicable" thing and if he did to disavow it. Hamilton asked him to specify what it was he was to disavow, clearly wanting Burr to say out loud what had been only whispers. Unsatisfied with that, Burr pressed for a duel.

On July 11 they met on the same dueling ground in Weehawken, New Jersey where Hamilton's son Philip had been killed three years earlier (over an incident in which he had been defending his father's honor). After preparing Burr and Hamilton, the seconds turned their backs to offer them plausible deniability for their involvement in the duel. Hamilton fired first with his shot well high and to the side of his adversary. Burr either did not view the miss as Hamilton having thrown away his shot or he went to Weehawken fully intending to kill Hamilton. He took aim and fired, hitting Hamilton in the abdomen. He died the next day. Since the seconds had their backs turned, there is no way to know with certainty whether Hamilton had intentionally thrown away his shot. The only witness was Burr.

Burr fled to South Carolina, having been charged with murder in New York and New Jersey, before traveling to Washington, D.C. to finish his term as vice president, immune from prosecution there. By killing Hamilton, Burr had effectively killed his own political career. The duel also, in many ways, led to the death of the Federalist Party, left without its greatest political mind. Nevertheless, the practice of dueling as a means of preserving public honor would remain alive and well for years to come.

Thomas Jefferson believed that the Republican victories in the election of 1800 involved much more than winning control of the presidency and both houses of Congress, resulting for the first time in a change in power from one political party to another. As the incoming president summarized his views, the election "was as real a revolution in the principles of our government as that of 1776 was in its form." (The defeated principles to which he referred were those held by Alexander Hamilton.) However, for Jefferson, the "Revolution of 1800" was in reality, simply a return to the republican principles embraced by American revolutionaries in 1776 and enshrined in the Constitution. The Federalist ascendancy of the 1790s had moved the country away from that vision and toward what Republicans believed would be a British-style monarchy.

The electoral success of the Republicans in 1800, however, was not only due to agrarian supporters of Jefferson's republican ideology. Some were eager to engage in the expansive economy of the 1790s, but felt stymied by Federalist policies that failed to meet their needs. For them, the Federalists moved too slowly in adapting to the emerging commercial economy, and the powerful central government that the Federalists had tried to create sometimes got in the way of their pursuit of wealth. The Republican adherence to limited national government seemed to better satisfy their interests. Thus, Republican political power rested partly on the support of some of the very people whose activities threatened the Jefferson's hope that the United States would develop into an agrarian republic.

Most of the newly elected Republican leaders in Congress, nevertheless, embraced Jefferson's vision and viewed their victory in 1800 as more than a political triumph. They wanted to remake American society as well as the economy along Jeffersonian lines in order to preserve the new republic. Federalists also stressed the need for leaders to have virtue, but Republicans viewed agriculture as the best way to ensure that Americans remained virtuous. As it had become increasingly captivated by trade and manufacturing, Europe (and Europeans) had long since lost its virtue. When Jefferson spoke of European attitudes and economic activity spreading to America he referred them as "cankers" and "sores."

JEFFERSONIAN POLITICAL ECONOMY

The Agrarian Vision

Jefferson and the Republicans did not envision a nation consisting only of subsistence farmers, but rather, one filled with farmers who productively worked their land and sold surplus crops for profit. Productive farming instilled virtue. Those who thus labored helped to ensure their independence, because their ability to support themselves and their families derived from their own hard work. A lack of independence, they believed, undermined virtue, for both individuals and nations. Any growers involved in a dependent relationship had a lessened capacity to act virtuously. Jefferson's agrarians not only needed the independence to farm their land, but also for the ability to trade excess crops, thereby making their labor productive. The inability of farmers to trade their surplus production discouraged industrious behavior. As one Kentuckian said, "Without commerce to yield a market to the products of agriculture, that agriculture would languish, and the mass of society be thrown into a state of listless indolence and dissipation . . . The immense fertility of the soil, where human life is supported without that constant labor which requires an assiduous employment of time, would produce the same effect upon morals that acquired luxury does." In other words, the

MONTICELLO, THE EAST PORTICO.

The East Portico of Monticello, Thomas Jefferson's home

land in much of America (especially western regions like Kentucky) was so fertile that it required little effort, or moral discipline, to provide for basic subsistence.

Jefferson was also well aware of the writings of European intellectuals such as Thomas Malthus, whose ideas exhibited pessimism about the long-term success of republics partly because of his views on agricultural production. Malthus argued that the poverty, corruption, and decay of Europe was a natural development due to population growth. While increased food production could help a society improve its standard of living in the short term, the resulting abundance of food would inevitably lead to more population growth, with the end result being food shortages and social decline. To Jefferson, however, Malthus's ideas were not relevant to the situation in America, which made American crops all the more valuable. Jefferson's agrarian republic could be maintained "as long as there shall be vacant lands in any part of America."

Luckily for the Republicans, the United States by 1800 seemingly offered a much greater possibility for Jefferson's vision than for Alexander Hamilton's. Many Americans were still suspicious of a powerful federal government. More important to that agrarian vision, about 95 percent of Americans lived in rural areas, farms, and villages of fewer than 2,500 people. Even the cities were not large in comparison to the European cities that

Jefferson abhorred. Philadelphia and New York were the largest cities at 70,000 and 60,000 residents respectively. The next largest cities were Baltimore and Boston with about 25,000 residents each. There were, in fact, only twelve cities in America with populations larger than 5,000. By 1800, more Americans owned land than all Europeans combined despite Europe having thirty times the population of the United States. The demographics of America thus seemed to favor the development of Jefferson's agrarian republic.

The Role of the Carrying Trade

Commerce, especially the **carrying trade** (American ships transporting the products of southern export farmers, along with the goods of foreign nations and their colonies), had become a driving force in the U.S. economy by the end of the 1790s. American neutrality during Europe's many wars enhanced the profitability of that trade even more, especially after 1794 when Britain largely left American neutral trade uninterrupted. By the end of the 1790s, more American ships were involved in trading than the vessels of any European nation. Over half of that trade did not involve conveying American products, but instead, the re-exportation of goods to European colonies in the Caribbean as war-wracked European nations tried

CANE RIDGE CAMP MEETING

A major religious revival lasting for several days, known as a camp meeting because attendees actually camped at the site, occurred at Cane Ridge, Kentucky in August 1801. Historian Paul Conkin called it "the most important religious gathering in all of American history" because it sparked a period of religious fervor and revivalism, known as the Second Great Awakening, which lasted through much of the nineteenth century. But in 1801, America did not seem ripe for such a religious revival.

By the end of the 1790s, some religious leaders feared an impending crisis for their churches. The demise of the Anglican Church in America after the Revolution, coupled with disestablishment mandates in state constitutions as well as the First Amendment of the U.S. Constitution, offered fertile ground for other denominations (like Methodists, Baptists, and Presbyterians) to expand. One area that seemed like fertile ground for those denominations was a rapidly expanding western frontier. Regional and national synods sent preachers into the West to gain converts and establish churches. Since much of the region was still sparsely settled, those preachers often had to minister to multiple churches in what became known as circuits. Reports from western "circuit riders" were not promising. Methodist bishop Francis Asbury wrote of settlers in Tennessee, "that not one in a hundred came here to get religion, but rather to get plenty of good land." In the six years leading to 1800, the Methodist Church had seen a decline in its membership from nearly 68,000 to barely 61,000.

While the majority of western settlers were not church members at the time, some exhibited strong religious devotion. Presbyterian ministers held annual communion feasts, following Scottish tradition, which lasted for three to five days. Following the Scottish Presbyterian desire for order, these meetings were generally marked by quiet sermons and solemn prayer for the first two days but ended with celebratory feasts honoring the Last Supper. Presbyterian ministers on the frontier would often invite ministers from other denominations (Methodists and Baptists) to the communion meetings. Whether due to the more emotional nature of some Methodists and Baptists or the general influence of America, some Presbyterian ministers on the frontier dispensed with the Scottish desire for order and those meetings could take on a more emotional flavor. While these meetings were often small, they could see as many as 100 attendees.

In 1800, Barton W. Stone, the Presbyterian minister at Cane Ridge, Kentucky (about 20 miles east of Lexington), attended one such meeting in the western part of the state led by James McGready, an emotional and fiery Presbyterian minister. Not only were there over 100 attendees, some brought tents and camped at the meeting house for the duration. Stone also witnessed an emotional spirit that resulted in people crying and shouting; some even "fell to the floor in ecstasy." After witnessing the revival at McGready's church (considered to be the first camp meeting in America), he returned to his church at Cane Ridge and announced a communion service that would begin on August 6, inviting other Presbyterian ministers, as well as some from Methodist and Baptist churches.

Rain on the first day kept the numbers down, but Barton's church, which could accommodate 500 people standing, was full for the opening service. The next day began quietly as well with morning sermons, but by afternoon a storm of religious fervor swept the area. Preaching continued non-stop from within the church and a tent that had been set up outside the church. Others began preaching from tree stumps and anything else they might be able to stand on. The crowds had grown into the thousands, and many became caught up in the emotion of the moment. Amid the crying and shouting of the crowds (in both excitement and penitence) some began to fall to the ground with more than a few exhibiting uncontrollable body movements. The darkness of night did not dampen the enthusiasm as candles, lamps, and torches lit the area and preachers continued to shout their sermons. The scene lasted for days with the crowds ultimately swelling to between 10,000 and 20,000. As news of the camp meeting at Cane Ridge spread, it sparked similar revivals across the region ultimately leading to a religious fervor that lasted for decades.

to prevent the trade of their enemies. American shippers also carried goods from the Caribbean to American ports. Those ships often took on American goods with no intention of unloading the Caribbean goods. Then, using the cloak of neutrality, they would carry those goods on to Europe. By 1799, the carrying trade accounted for about one-fifth of the value of the American economy and earnings for shipping were more valuable than any single commodity exported from America.

Jeffersonian Republicans did not shun commerce, but viewed commercial activity only as a necessary means to achieving economic fulfillment of agriculture and honest industry. When commerce became an end unto itself, it led to speculation and avarice that would undermine the virtue of the republic and its people. For Republicans like Jefferson and his Secretary of Treasury Albert Gallatin, the carrying trade was overextended. More important, they believed that it was not crucial to American prosperity and, indeed, could possibly threaten it. Overextended shippers might demand naval protection from attacks by pirates and European nations at a great expense to the government. The resulting conflicts could then lead the country into wars that would be costly while also disrupting American economic activity.

Equally as important to Republicans was the impact that the carrying trade would have on the very republic they were trying to save. The economic impact would lead to risk-taking by speculators looking to get rich. They believed that the commercial speculator "often gets rich by accident, by imprudent and unfair venturing, by sudden exertions." In effect, it was like a lottery that would infect Americans with bad habits that would undermine steady growth and economic stability. By providing protection for that trade, the Federalist governments of the 1790s had encouraged that speculative behavior with all of the dangers inherent to the republic and its virtue. Republicans also had clear evidence that government protection of the overextended carrying trade would lead America into conflict with the nations of Europe with the Quasi-War with France.

The Quasi-War also led to increased military spending which posed another, maybe even larger, threat to the republic. A large standing army and navy could be used to oppress average Americans in the way, Republicans believed, the Federalists had during the Whiskey Rebellion and Fries' Rebellion.

The carrying trade, therefore, was important to Republicans but only as a means of facilitating the trade of American agricultural products. By limiting that trade to American products, the nation would see natural growth unlike the speculative growth of the 1790s. Because those ships would be limited primarily to American agricultural products, they would also be much less likely to face attacks by European nations. Other countries needed American agricultural products as well as the United States as a market for their manufactured goods (especially Britain). Republicans believed that the mutual needs of all of the parties involved would allow American trade to flourish unimpeded and the expanse of the Atlantic Ocean would also allow American agricultural production to grow without the interference of European intrigues.

REPUBLICANS IN POWER

Thomas Jefferson's inauguration day embodied the democratic ideals with which Jefferson is often associated. He walked from his boarding house to the Capitol rather than taking a carriage as both Washington and Adams had done to their inaugurals. Jefferson donned no ceremonial sword or any badges of status, instead choosing to wear the plain clothes of an average citizen. In fact, throughout his presidency, he dismissed much of the pomp and ceremony that had become standard for major federal government events during the 1790s. After arriving at the overflowing Senate chamber (with a reported crowd of over 1,000), he was sworn in by a distant cousin, the Federalist Chief Justice John Marshall. The new president proceeded to deliver an inaugural address in "so low a tone that few heard it." Fortunately, he had printed copies handed out to the audience, as well as published in newspapers.

In his speech, Jefferson touted the Republican triumph as the Revolution of 1800, but there was no gloating on that day. The election had been very bitter, and there were real threats that the nation may be torn apart by internal division. His address was one of modesty and unification, promising a "wise and frugal Government which shall restrain men from injuring one another." With regard to the bitter election, he assured Americans that "every difference of opinion is not a difference of principle. We have called by different names brethren of the same principle. We are all republicans, we are all federalists." Here he was not talking about political parties, but principles. They all favored a federal government with the power to serve its functions, and they all wanted that government to be a republic. Their similarities were much greater than their differences.

To a certain extent, Jefferson early in his presidency did practice the belief that members of the opposing political parties were more alike than they were different. Despite the wishes of some within his party, the new president refused to replace all of the non-elected federal government officials appointed by the Federalists with new Republican appointees (either as punishment to Federalists or rewards to Republicans). During his first two years in office, he removed about one-third of the government employees who made up the small federal bureaucracy, and made merit rather than party affiliation the determining factor. He did, however, fill his cabinet and other high government posts with strict party loyalists, including James Madison as the new Secretary of State and Albert Gallatin as Secretary of the Treasury.

Though he chose not to seek a premature end to the national bank before its charter expired in 1811 in order to cultivate favor with moderate Federalists, Jefferson also worked to instill in the government adherence to his principles, especially with regard to his strict constructionist views of the Constitution. He had watched Alexander Hamilton as Treasury Secretary hold sway over Congress. Jefferson believed that such a relationship violated the strict separation of powers between the executive and legislative branches. As president, he worked to establish a clearer separation of powers. Rather than presenting his State of the Union addresses to Congress in person, as both Washington and Adams had done, Jefferson sent written messages so that his physical presence in Congress would not be seen as an effort to exert influence in an area that the president had no constitutional role.

Despite his public modesty, Jefferson still managed to impact the proceedings in Congress. He held weekly dinners at the White House, inviting small groups of congressmen each week. The president may have been soft-spoken in public, but at the informal dinners he could engage congressmen in small groups, where his real political skills shone. He could thus influence legislation without openly pushing a particular agenda. Albert Gallatin, a former member of the House and Senate, also had a good working relationship with many in Congress, and served as an unofficial liaison between the president and that body. The caucus system that Republicans developed in Congress further allowed its members to work closely together in developing and carrying out their party's agenda, all while having a very clear idea of where their leader, Jefferson, stood on various issues.

Republican Policies

During Jefferson's first term, the Republican Party controlled both houses of Congress, with a large majority in the House but a smaller, 18 to 14, majority in the Senate. In power for the first time, the Republicans began their work by addressing especially obnoxious acts left over from the Federalist regime. Most parts of the Alien and Sedition Acts expired before the Republicans took power, but they repealed what remained while Jefferson pardoned all those convicted of violating the statutes and returned any fines they had paid with interest. Using the Quasi-War as justification, the Federalists had increased military spending, paying for that increase by passing a number of internal taxes. The Republicans repealed those as well, leaving the federal government's budget to rely almost entirely (about 90 percent) on tariffs as a source of revenue.

Treasury Secretary Gallatin worked with Congress to get support for Jefferson's goal of reducing the national debt, hoping to pay it off entirely within sixteen years.

Gallatin believed that eliminating the debt would also eliminate the need for most taxes. Being unburdened by taxes in normal times, he suggested, would make Americans more willing to pay them in emergency situations. Hamilton instead argued that eliminating debt and taxes entirely would also remove the need for the system under which debt can be incurred and taxes collected, making it difficult if not impossible to respond in emergency situations. With Congress already having eliminated a large source of revenue by repealing internal taxes, the Jefferson administration focused much on reducing spending, which fit naturally with Jefferson's desire for shrinking the size and influence of government. But as Gallatin began to scrutinize government spending meticulously, it became apparent that the Federalists had actually been pretty efficient, and there was little waste to cut.

The Republicans had the good fortune to come to power, however, just after the Quasi-War ended, with tensions between Britain and France temporarily cooling. Jefferson believed that the military created by the Federalists in 1798 was far too large for peacetime conditions. Congress agreed to reduce the size of the army from 5,500 to 3,300 men, reflecting the president's faith that the small national army could be supplemented by state militias in time of need. Congress did, however, establish a military academy at West Point, New York for the purpose of training U.S. Army officers. Meanwhile, Congress dramatically shrunk the size of the navy. After the Quasi-War's conclusion in 1800, Federalists had already reduced the navy down to six frigates (the best fighting ships of their class in the world), putting seven others in dry dock and selling off all other naval vessels. Once in power, congressional Republicans further limited the navy by putting the remaining frigates in dry dock and cutting annual appropriations from $3 million to $1 million, preferring smaller vessels to make up the bulk of a much smaller navy.

Critics complained that it was little more than a **"mosquito fleet"** but with America at peace the need for a larger navy did not seem pressing at the time. Moreover, the Republicans were only thinking of defense—protecting American harbors, which small ships could effectively do. A large navy on the open seas offered too many opportunities for one of the ships to get drawn into a conflict that might result in war.

Gallatin's efforts with regard to the debt did produce results. Jefferson left the presidency in 1809 with the debt reduced from $80 million to $57 million (with a $14 million surplus) while, as will be seen, doubling the size of the United States with the purchase of Louisiana from France. A big factor in their ability to achieve that, however, was the continuing success of the carrying trade, something that Jefferson and Gallatin both decried as having potential to undermine their virtuous republic.

The Midnight Appointments

Jefferson's Revolution of 1800 did not secure complete control over all branches of the federal government. Having lost control of the legislative and executive branches in the election of 1800, the outgoing Federalists made one last effort to maintain some influence in the federal government. In January 1801, two months before the newly elected Republicans would assume control of the government, Congress passed the Judiciary Act of 1801. The legislation created a number of new federal judicial positions and gave the president power to appoint as many federal magistrates for the District of Columbia as he felt necessary. In the final two months of his presidency, John Adams appointed a number of these new federal judges and magistrates whose appointments were quickly confirmed by the still-Federalist-controlled Senate. Because the judges could serve for life, the Adams appointments would ensure that federal cases would be presided over by men adhering to Federalist principles for years to come.

Republicans were outraged and decried Adams's last-minute maneuvers as the outgoing president's "**Midnight Appointments**," implying that Adams was signing appointment letters right up until midnight on his last day in office. Not only did they suggest that it was a desperate effort by Federalists to maintain power against the popular will, but also that the signing of late appointments was a sneaky action done in the dark of night. In January 1802, Senate Republicans introduced a bill to repeal the Judiciary Act of 1801, but with only a small majority in the Senate, the vote ended in a tie. (Aaron Burr, Jefferson's controversial vice president, actually cast the deciding vote against the bill.) Further debate and amendments ensued before the Judiciary Act was finally repealed by the Senate, followed quickly by a repeal vote in the House. Congress then passed a new judiciary act that incorporated parts of the original act that the Republicans liked.

Jefferson signed the new bill into law, giving the Republicans yet another victory over the old establishment. But Burr's vote against repeal of the 1801 act irreparably damaged what was left of any relationship between Jefferson and Burr (Jefferson had heard from many friends that Burr had conspired in 1801 to convince some in the House to vote him into the presidency rather than Jefferson). In 1804, Burr would not be the vice presidential candidate with Jefferson. He had destroyed his future prospects within the party. Even more important than the split with Burr, repeal of the 1801 act did nothing to rid the federal courts of Federalists already entrenched in the system.

John Marshall and Judicial Review

Congress stalled the Federalist-controlled Supreme Court by delaying their next meeting for a year. When the High Court next met, in February 1803, it had cases waiting to be decided that would dramatically reshape the power of the court and elevate it as a co-equal branch of government.

The Court was now led by recently appointed Chief Justice **John Marshall**, a Federalist who had served as John Adams' Secretary of State and was one of the president's midnight appointments. Before Marshall, the Court had seen a revolving door of chief justices presiding over what was widely viewed as a lesser branch of the government. During the 1790s, the Court had issued a number of rulings that affirmed federal supremacy over the states and hinted its role as the final arbiter with regard to the constitutionality of acts by the federal and state governments. But with the Court made up of strong individuals who each issued their own decisions, there was no one decision in those cases to serve as precedent.

John Marshall would change that. Using his natural political skills and the strength of his personality, he convinced his fellow justices to issue a single majority opinion rather than each justice writing their own opinion. And initially Marshall wrote nearly every majority decision himself. This allowed the Court to speak with one voice.

The first major case that the Supreme Court heard when it convened in 1803, *Marbury v. Madison*, involved the appointments made under the since-repealed Judiciary Act of 1801. William Marbury had been appointed by John Adams to serve as a magistrate in the District of Columbia, and the Senate confirmed his appointment. As appointments were confirmed, appointment letters were received by the Secretary of State's office for delivery. Those appointed could not assume their positions until they received their letters. John Marshall had been Adams's Secretary of State but was also one of the midnight appointments. Once appointed Chief Justice, he focused his attention on organizing the Court and neglected his duties in the final days of Adams's lame-duck presidency. Thus, appointment letters piled up on the desk of James Madison, Thomas Jefferson's Secretary of State, who assumed his position only to find a number of the letters waiting to be delivered. Madison did not dispense them; therefore, appointees such as Marbury did not receive their appointments. Marbury sued Madison, claiming that the Secretary was not doing his constitutional duty by refusing to deliver the letters.

When the case reached the Court, Justice Marshall was faced with quite a dilemma. If he ruled against Madison, he would have to expect the president to enforce his decision, something that Jefferson was unlikely to do, thus further weakening the Court. Ruling against Marbury, however, might encourage Republicans to further undermine Federalist influence in the federal courts. The Court's decision, which Marshall wrote himself, was a masterful stroke designed to establish the supremacy of the national government, the Constitution as the supreme law of the land, and the Supreme Court as the final word on the constitutionality of actions by the federal and state governments. In his decision, Marshall admitted that Marbury deserved his commission and that he did have legal recourse but the Court refused to issue a writ of mandamus (a judicial order to compel a government official to comply with a law) that would have forced Madison to deliver the appointment letter to Marbury. That portion of the decision satisfied Republicans, but did little with regard to the Court's power.

It was Marshall's reasoning for not issuing the writ that made the case one of the most important in American history. The Chief Justice argued that the Supreme Court did not have jurisdiction to issue the writ because the Constitution only gave the Court original jurisdiction over cases involving by ambassadors, public ministers, or consuls. The High Court only had appellate jurisdiction in other cases. Original jurisdiction in other cases was granted by Section 13 of the Judiciary Act of 1789, but Marshall ruled that Congress had erred and overstepped its constitutional authority with Section 13. Therefore, he declared, Section 13 was unconstitutional. The Constitution had not clearly defined the power of the federal courts, and specifically the Supreme Court, to interpret laws or actions of the other branches of the government (or of state governments when they conflicted with the Constitution). The ruling in *Marbury* established a legal precedent that recognized the role of the federal courts to interpret and uphold the Constitution by proclaiming, as Marshall wrote, that the courts had a duty to "say what the law is." Thus, he unequivocally promoted the principle of judicial review—the legal doctrine that only the federal judiciary could determine the constitutionality of laws passed by Congress. Marshall continued to serve as Chief Justice until his death in 1835, using judicial review to support the Supreme Court's ability to rule on many important cases that kept alive Federalist ideals long after the party ceased to exist.

Judicial Impeachments

Even with the repeal of the Judicial Act of 1801, the federal courts were primarily overseen by judges holding Federalist views, some of whom unabashedly expressed their political beliefs in their decisions. Faced with that fact, Republicans sought ways to diminish the impact of Federalist influence within the courts, but with federal judges serving for life there were few options. One possibility that they could pursue, however, was impeachment.

The Republicans' first target using the impeachment process was a federal district judge from New Hampshire named John Pickering. An especially obnoxious Federalist who often cited Federalist principles in his decisions, Pickering was also a drunk. In the view of many people at the time, he was also going insane. In March 1803, the House opened impeachment hearings against Pickering based on information provided to members of the House by Thomas Jefferson. The constitutional standard for impeachment is "treason, bribery, or other high crimes and misdemeanors," but Pickering's behavior did not meet that threshold. Nevertheless, the House impeached him by a vote of 45-8, and the Senate voted to remove him from office. While Pickering was clearly unfit to serve (his own clerks had asked for a temporary replacement because he was not able to hear cases due to his health), the move upset Federalists who argued that his impeachment exceeded the authority granted by the Constitution.

Federalists also feared that Republicans would use the impeachment process to remove other federal judges for no reason other than their political beliefs. The following year, Republicans attempted to do just that when they sought the removal of Supreme Court Justice **Samuel Chase** in 1804. Possessed with a brilliant legal mind, Chase was a staunch Federalist who was also forthright and bombastic in his attacks on Republicans. Republicans in the House of Representatives brought eight articles of impeachment against him, largely exhibiting displeasure with some of his judicial decisions that they viewed as politically biased. None of the charges against Chase rose to the level of "high crimes and misdemeanors," but the House voted for impeachment anyway. During the Senate trial, Chase's lawyer cautioned that his removal from office "will establish a most important precedent as to future cases of impeachment." If the standard for impeachment became simply one's political beliefs, then the independence of the judiciary created under the Constitution would be in jeopardy. The Senate acquitted Chase of all charges, and Republicans quickly dropped their efforts to further use impeachment as a tool to attack Federalist control of the courts.

FOREIGN AFFAIRS UNDER JEFFERSON

The Barbary Pirates

Thomas Jefferson's goal to create an agrarian republic was built on the belief that western expansion would help to preserve the republican virtue of Americans and the nation. With British Canada to the north, Spain on America's southern and western borders, and the need to trade surplus produce with Europe, Jefferson had to develop an assertive foreign policy that, at times, threatened the very independence necessary to maintain his republican vision. Thus, his foreign policy was rooted in the same republican ideas of virtue as his domestic policy. During the 1790s, he believed that the U.S. had refused to take the virtuous stand of living up to its 1778 treaty with France and instead opted for neutrality. He further believed that decision was based on America's financial relationship with Britain, which made America dependent upon British favor. Therefore, Jefferson embraced George Washington's warning to stay out of entangling alliances with Europe, but he also knew that he could not ignore Europe.

American prosperity and the future of Jefferson's agrarian republic were intricately tied to Europe, a primary market for southern and western crops. The ability to sell surplus crops ensured the productivity of farmers, a necessity for Jefferson's agrarian republic, and the wider prosperity of America. Republican virtue, therefore, was dependent upon foreign commerce, which was especially threatened in the West by Spanish control of New Orleans. If Spain or some other nation closed American trade through New Orleans, that development would threaten the civil society that Americans had built out of an otherwise savage wilderness.

Trade with Europe also benefited those regions of the country that did not produce large amounts of surplus crops. New England had developed a vibrant carrying trade, which had grown immensely due to America's neutrality during Europe's frequent wars. The neutral carrying trade, despite French attacks on it during the Quasi-War, had spurred dramatic economic growth in the United States during the 1790s. A large fleet of private American merchant ships provided the means of carrying crops to Europe while keeping more money at home in the U.S. (since those carrying that trade were Americans). As much as Jefferson and Gallatin believed that America's carrying trade was overextended, its necessity to their broader vision meant that they had little choice but to protect it when was threatened.

French attacks on American ships had ended when John Marshall negotiated an end to the Quasi-War. In addition, the Treaty of Amiens in 1802 ended hostilities between Britain and France, at least for the time being, offering relative calm on the Atlantic for American trade. American trading vessels, however, began to face increasing attacks from the **Barbary Pirates** operating out of Tripoli and other North African ports. Their relative proximity to the Mediterranean Sea's entrance at the Strait of Gibraltar enabled the pirates to control trade throughout the area by using pirates to threaten the vessels from countries whose governments had not paid them annual tribute payments in exchange for safe passage. The leaders of Britain and France decided that it was cheaper to pay the tribute rather than engage in a lengthy fight. After independence, the United States had done likewise, paying about $1 million per year. One of the reasons that Federalists had increased the size of the navy during the late 1790s was to better protect American trade in order to end such payments. While serving as Secretary of State to George Washington, Jefferson had advocated ending those payments, believing that they only encouraged further threats and higher demands for tribute.

Shortly after Jefferson was inaugurated, the Pasha of Tripoli (a man who killed his own brother so that he could assume power upon his father's death) demanded increased tribute from the U.S. and ordered his pirates to attack American ships. Jefferson immediately sent four ships to the region with orders to protect American trade but not to engage the pirates in outright war. He did this without informing Congress until the ships were too far away to be recalled. A year later Congress authorized Jefferson's use of force against the pirates while not going so far as to declare war.

The small fleet that Jefferson sent to North Africa, led by the *U.S.S. Constitution*, was not only able to successfully blockade Tripoli, but the ports of the other Barbary States as well, stopping the Barbary Pirates' attacks. Bad news struck, however, when the American frigate *Philadelphia* ran aground in Tripoli's harbor, leading to the crew's capture. Fearing that the ship might be used by pirates to attack the American blockade, a team led by Lieutenant Stephen Decatur slipped into the harbor at night using a smaller captured Arab vessel. Decatur and his crew destroyed the *Philadelphia* without losing a man. The conflict finally came to an end in 1805 when ten marines led a large group of Arab mercenaries overland into Tripoli, surprising a much larger force. The pasha entered into a treaty with the United States and the crew of the *Philadelphia* was released. Jefferson's strong action

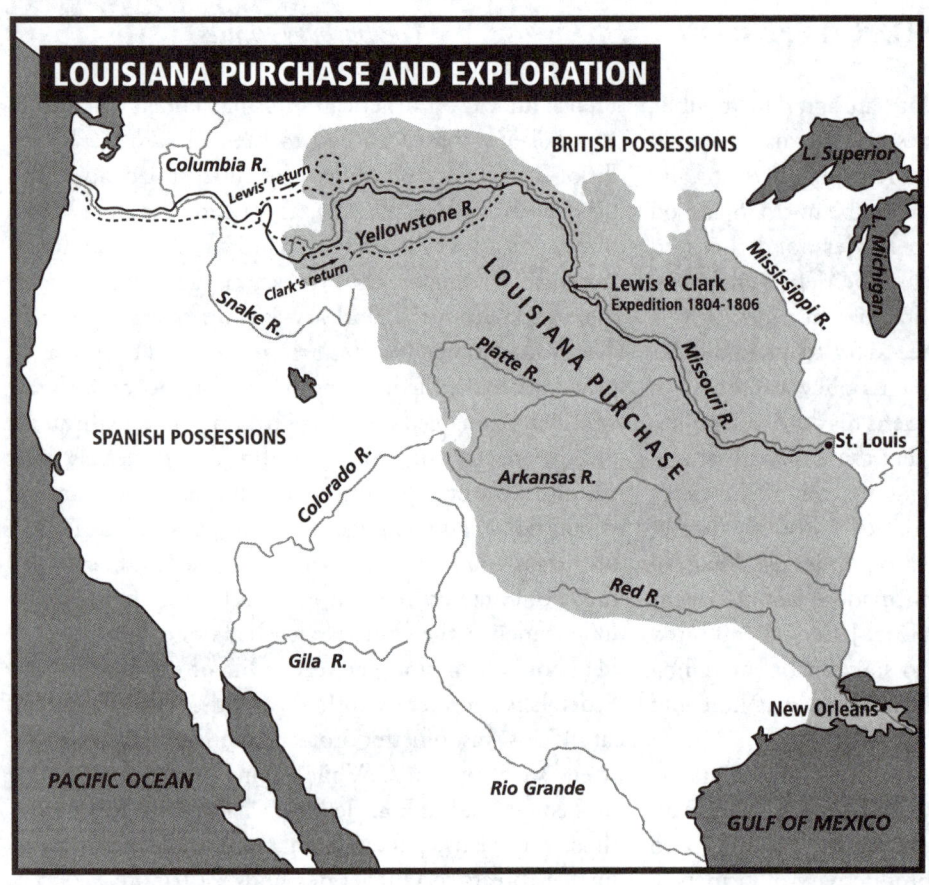

LOUISIANA PURCHASE AND EXPLORATION

BRITISH POSSESSIONS

Columbia R.

Lewis' return

Yellowstone R.

Clark's return

Snake R.

L. Superior

L. Michigan

Mississippi R.

LOUISIANA PURCHASE

Lewis & Clark
Expedition 1804-1806

Missouri R.

St. Louis

Platte R.

SPANISH POSSESSIONS

Arkansas R.

Colorado R.

Red R.

Gila R.

New Orleans

PACIFIC OCEAN

Rio Grande

GULF OF MEXICO

Map 9.1 Louisiana Purchase and Exploration Route of Lewis and Clark.

against the Barbary Pirates, and the success of the American blockade, served to broaden his popularity. His next major foray into foreign policy would produce an even greater effect.

The Louisiana Purchase

While protecting American trade served Jefferson's interests in developing his agrarian republic, expansion within America was an even bigger factor. Threats to the ability of western Americans to trade down the Mississippi River through New Orleans could discourage western expansion or, even worse, possibly encourage Westerners to split from the United States and join with Spain. With Britain and France both reaching out to each other in an effort to end the war that had been going on since 1793, the French leader, Napoleon Bonaparte, began to look to the Americas in order to expand his power and replenish his treasury.

His first goal was to reassert French control over **Saint-Domingue** (present-day Haiti), a sugar colony on the island of Hispaniola. Of incredible economic value to France because it produced more sugar and coffee than any other European colony (30 percent of the world's sugar and over half of its coffee), a slave revolt had erupted on the island in 1791, inspired in part by the ideals of the

French Revolution and led by a slave named Toussaint L'Ouverture. French leaders on the island legally ended slavery there in 1793 in order to get L'Ouverture's aid in turning back a British invasion, and the French government followed by ending slavery in all French colonies the following year. By 1799, Toussaint had written a new constitution making him the governor.

That same year, however, Napoleon led a coup in France ending the promise of republican rule there. He became determined to re-establish French control over Saint-Domingue. As tensions began to ease in Europe in 1801, he sent a force of 20,000 men (later reinforced by another 15,000) to retake the island. Napoleon also sought the aid of the U.S. in that effort. Jefferson agreed, under the condition that France reached peace with Britain first (Jefferson did not want to get dragged into a conflict with Britain). Jefferson was certainly glad to see France try to assert control over the island and destroy Toussaint's rebellion as the slave revolt had offered inspiration for American slaves, like the slave Gabriel who planned an uprising in Virginia in 1800. Jefferson assured Napoleon that once Britain and France were at peace, "nothing would be easier than to furnish your army and fleet with everything, and to reduce Toussaint to starvation." Napoleon also promised that American trade with the island would be respected.

General Charles Leclerc, Napoleon's brother-in-law, arrived in Saint-Domingue with a large force and convinced Toussaint to travel to Europe where he would be honored by Napoleon himself (unaware that the intended "honor" was to jail him in a prison cell). Leclerc's army then set out to reestablish French control over the island with the intention of re-introducing slavery. He also seized twenty American ships that were in port and jailed some of the captains of those ships. While the Jefferson administration issued a formal complaint, they were more pleased with French success on the island than indignant over the treatment of a few Americans.

What no one in Jefferson's administration knew at the time was that Napoleon had much bigger plans in the Americas than control of Saint-Domingue. He also wanted to gain control over Louisiana and Florida, and was preparing a force that would sail from Holland in the winter of 1802 with the goal of establishing military control of New Orleans. Control of New Orleans would give Napoleon power in the region while Louisiana would provide a source of grain to feed the slaves on Saint-Domingue so that the colony could once again produce sugar and coffee at the levels that it had been before the rebellion.

By March 1801, however, Americans were beginning to hear disturbing rumors. British officials were able to confirm the reports when they gained knowledge of a secret treaty between France and Spain signed in October 1800 in which Spain returned Louisiana to France and passed the information along to the American ambassador to England, Rufus King. The ambassador promptly forwarded the news to Secretary of State James Madison, along with warnings of French intent to occupy and control the entire Mississippi River Valley. Within a year, the treaty became public knowledge, leading to widespread concern, especially in the western United States.

Meanwhile, Jefferson had already been working to minimize the French threat to the region. Madison sent instructions to the American ambassador to France, Robert Livingston, to feel out French government officials about the rumored treaty. If it seemed clear that such a treaty had taken place, Livingston was asked to work with the French to secure the same protections for American trade in New Orleans that existed under Spanish rule. In April 1802, after the treaty's terms became known to the general public, Jefferson sent a letter to Livingston through a Frenchman, Pierre Samuel du Pont de Nemours. Before sealing the envelope, Jefferson asked du Pont to read the letter, assuming that its contents would, therefore, also be delivered to French officials. In the document, Jefferson wrote "there is on the globe one single spot, the possessor of which is our natural and habitual enemy. It

is New Orleans." If France took control of New Orleans, the United States would have to "marry ourselves to the British fleet and nation." France could avoid all of those headaches, he stated, if France simply ceded the territory to the U.S. The change from Spanish control to French control of New Orleans would be momentous. Spain was weak and posed no threat to America. If the city remained under French control, Jefferson had no doubt that it would ultimately become American territory, one way or another. But France was one of the most powerful nations in the world, with a leader who had already shown a desire for expansion. As much as Jefferson disliked the idea of a close relationship with Britain, the French threat to New Orleans might force America to take that course of action.

In October 1802, tensions grew when the Spanish governor in New Orleans suspended the American right to deposit goods there. Many Americans thought that France was behind the decision, which fanned anti-French flames that had subsided since the end of the Quasi-War (some historians believe it was done by the Spanish to cause problems for France). Jefferson then received word from du Pont that France might be willing to sell New Orleans to the U.S., although many scholars are unsure that du Pont had connections high enough in the French government to gain such knowledge (or that he had even delivered the information in Jefferson's letter to anyone of importance). Based on his correspondence with du Pont, Jefferson requested secret appropriations from Congress and sent James Monroe to France to join Livingston in negotiating such a sale.

Monroe's arrival in France served as perfect timing. Whether Napoleon had any intention to sell New Orleans when du Pont was communicating with Jefferson, by March 1803 the situation had changed dramatically. Toussaint's capture did not quell the rebellious slaves, who rose up against Leclerc's forces. The French forces on Saint-Domingue were also ravaged by an outbreak of yellow fever. After sending a second force to supplement the diminished French forces with no better result, it became clear to Napoleon that if victory even could be achieved it would take years to accomplish and would require a lot more men and resources. At the same time, the invasion force targeted for Louisiana that had been preparing to sail that winter got frozen in port in Holland due to unusually cold weather. With his plans not working as he intended, he is reported to have exclaimed: "Damn sugar! Damn coffee! Damn colonies!" In addition, the peace in Europe began to break down and it appeared that France and Britain would soon be at war once again. Napoleon thus had no further use for Louisiana and needed money for war in Europe. When Monroe and Livingston began discussions with French Foreign Minister Charles

Maurice de Talleyrand, he surprised them by offering all of Louisiana. Their amazement turned to pleasure when negotiations settled on a price of $15 million for the entire territory. The signed treaty would still need to be ratified by the Senate before becoming official.

Some Federalist senators immediately raised the issue of constitutionality. The Senate, however, was the least of the problems for the treaty. President Jefferson had some of the same qualms as those Federalists, and his views of the powers of the federal government were built on the strict constructionism that he had embraced during the 1790s–if the Constitution did not specifically grant a power, then the government did not possess that power. He discussed the constitutional difficulties with a number of close associates and felt that the best action would be to ask Congress to adopt an amendment to the Constitution granting the powers necessary to conduct the purchase. However, Livingston was reporting from France that Napoleon was having second thoughts about the deal, leading Madison and others to suggest that there was no time to pursue Jefferson's constitutional remedy. The treaty stipulated that the U.S. must ratify it within six months, and, if Napoleon was having second thoughts, a delay in ratification would give him the opportunity to back out. Jefferson sent the treaty to the Senate for ratification, relying on Hamilton's conception of implied powers to justify the purchase. He said to Madison, "I infer that the less we say about constitutional difficulties respecting Louisiana the better, and that what is necessary for surmounting them must be done." The treaty was ratified four days later.

Jefferson kept his constitutional reservations private. During his retirement, he justified the treaty to himself, writing: "A strict observance of the written laws is doubtless one of the highest duties of a good citizen, but it is not the highest. The laws of necessity, of self-preservation, of saving the country when in danger are of higher obligation." Jefferson certainly realized the benefits of the treaty for the U.S.—and for his agrarian republic. The treaty added 828,000 acres to the nation, doubling its size while removing a powerful nation from America's borders. Not only would there be room for his agrarian republic to grow, but those settling in the West would have unrestricted navigation of the Mississippi River and unrestricted trade through New Orleans.

The timing of the **Louisiana Purchase** also coincided with an exploratory mission of the lands west of the Mississippi River already in the planning stages and to be led by Meriwether Lewis and William Clark for the purposes of searching for potential trade routes to the Pacific, establishing relations with the Native American groups, and conducting a scientific study of the regional flora and fauna. At the time, Lewis and Clark had no expectation that they would be exploring American territory. Lewis, an army officer, had been serving more recently as Jefferson's private secretary. In January 1803, the president had requested $2,500 from Congress to fund an expedition across the continent. By the time that Lewis, along with Clark his second in command, left St. Louis in May 1804, the territory belonged to the United States. When the "Corps of Discovery" arrived back in St. Louis over two years later, they brought back a wealth of information about the region despite their inability to locate a viable trade route due to the Rocky Mountains providing too formidable a barrier.

Toward a Second Term

So much had gone right for Jefferson and the Republicans that they were virtually unbeatable in the election of 1804. They had increased their majorities in Congress during the midterm elections of 1802 and saw those margins only increase in 1804. By that time, they had conducted a successful blockade of the Barbary Pirates and were well on the way to defeating them. They also had doubled the size of the nation and, in the process, secured American navigation of the Mississippi River and control of New Orleans. They may have had some luck, but they also had the skill and good sense to take advantage of opportunities when they appeared.

The election of 1804 also saw the continuing decline of the Federalist Party. The party had begun to splinter by 1800 and did even more so after Jefferson's election. Some New England Federalists, known as the Essex Junto, were calling for New England to secede from the United States and tried to encourage New York to join them. Alexander Hamilton along with the High Federalists who supported him was opposed to any talk of secession. Hamilton had worked to take on the role of opposition to Jefferson's administration and led what remained of the party as the elections approached. He would be dead by mid-summer.

Aaron Burr, cast aside by Jefferson and the Republicans for another term as vice president, ran for governor of New York as a Federalist. As he had done in the presidential election of 1800, Hamilton privately lobbied against Burr, this time supporting the Republican candidate over him. During the months following the election, in which the Republican candidate won, tensions between the two politicians rose. On July 11, 1804, Burr and Hamilton fought a duel in which Burr shot and killed Hamilton, further speeding the end of the Federalist Party, which held on for a few more election cycles in control of some New England states.

Increasingly, however, many Federalists began to abandon the party and remake themselves as Republicans. John Quincy Adams, the son of the former president, became one of them.

JEFFERSON'S SECOND TERM

Jefferson had a very successful first term, in part due to the relative peace in Europe at the time. By his second term, Europeans were once again engulfed by war, leading to renewed opportunities for the U.S. to potentially benefit through trade while remaining neutral. Demand for American goods became economically favorable for the nation—because Europe was at war through much of the time period, American exports, especially food items, rose from $20 million in 1790 to over $138 million by 1807. This time, there was no desire on the part of Republicans to support France because any pretense of a republican France was shattered when Napoleon overthrew that government in a coup, declaring himself emperor.

European Attacks and
the American Response

Napoleon's army had been winning impressive victories across Europe and appeared unmatched on land. At the same time, the British navy crushed a combined French and Spanish fleet in November 1805 at the Battle of Trafalgar. Britain clearly controlled the seas, but the promise to allow American neutral ships to trade freely in Europe as long as they embarked from American ports was called into question. Since the U.S. carrying trade involved not just carrying goods produced in America, but also from European colonies, a stricter view by the British with regard to what constituted American trade could devastate that business.

During the early years of the Napoleonic Wars, England interfered with the ships of enemy nations but had agreed to respect American rights to trade in the Caribbean as a neutral nation. American shippers had been evading British prohibitions by bringing European colonial goods into U.S. ports, even though they had no intention of unloading any of that cargo, before heading to Europe. This became known as the principle of the broken voyage. As long as the trip from the Caribbean was broken up by a stop in an American port, that vessel could continue to Europe unmolested by British ships. That principle was challenged in a legal case involving an American trading vessel, the *Essex*, which had been seized by Britain, leading its captain to sue for damages.

In what became known as the *Essex Decision*, the British High Court of Admiralty dispensed with the traditional understanding of the broken voyage and determined that the captain would have to prove that the intent of the original voyage was to carry those goods to the U.S. and not to Europe. This ruling led to the increased capture of American merchant ships.

During 1806 and 1807, the British and French governments made a series of pronouncements that made it increasingly difficult for Americans to conduct trade into Europe. Britain began to conduct a blockade of 800 miles of European coastline. Meanwhile, both nations took an increasingly broad view of contraband. Contraband had traditionally been viewed as armaments of war, which they would be reasonable in preventing the delivery of to their enemy. Ultimately, they began to view almost all trade goods, including food, as contraband because of its use by armies.

Napoleon responded to the British blockade with the Berlin Decree, announcing a blockade of England and that all British goods were illegal. British leaders responded with its **Orders in Council** banning neutral trade with France and her allies. Neutral ships wishing to trade in European ports had to stop in a British port to have their cargo inspected, pay duties on those goods, and obtain a license from British authorities. Napoleon responded again, this time with the Milan Decree, which stated that any ships that obeyed the Orders in Council would be treated as a British ship and, therefore, be subject to attack by France.

Americans wishing to engage in the lucrative trade with Europe were thus placed in a situation where, regardless of what they did, they risked being attacked by at least one nation in Europe. The American navy had scant ability to protect that trade, as the efforts of Jefferson and Gallatin to reduce the debt had led to sharp cuts in naval spending and a navy built primarily around small gunboats for coastal defense. Nevertheless, because the European trade was so potentially lucrative, American merchants and shippers refused to abandon the effort.

Attacks on its trading vessels were not the only problem that American shippers faced. Britain had refused to end **impressment** in the Jay Treaty over a decade earlier. As the war in Europe intensified, so did British efforts to staff their navy through the impressment of American sailors. By the end of the Napoleonic Wars, Britain had forced as many as 15,000 Americans into service in the British navy. Impressment became an especially contentious issue for many Americans, as it served as clear evidence that Britain did not respect America's independence.

Anger toward Britain intensified in the summer of 1807 when British naval vessels pursued French ships off the coast of the U.S. to prevent them from obtaining American goods in violation of the British blockade of Europe. While in the area a number of British sailors deserted from their ships and rowed ashore at Norfolk, Virginia. One, Jenkin Ratford, joined the U.S. Navy aboard the **U.S.S. Chesapeake** and was very public about his "escape" from the British navy. British officers became aware of Ratford's boast and wanted to make an example of him to discourage the desertion of other sailors. A British frigate, the *HMS Leopard*, was sent to Norfolk and intercepted the *Chesapeake* headed to sea on its way to the Mediterranean. After an attempt to get the American commander to hand over the suspected deserters was rebuffed, the *Leopard* fired one shot across the bow of the *Chesapeake* (typically a warning shot in preparation for boarding) before opening a barrage of cannon fire into the side of the *Chesapeake*. Three Americans were killed and eighteen wounded before the dying American commander surrendered. The British captain boarded the ship to search for deserters. Ratford was grabbed along with three others who they claimed to be deserters, though they were actually Americans who had been impressed into the British navy prior to deserting. Ratford was hanged while the others were given 500 lashes.

News of the *Chesapeake* incident led to widespread calls for war in the United States. Reacting to the clamor, Jefferson said, "Never since the Battle of Lexington have I seen this country in such a state of exasperation as at present, and even that did not produce such unanimity." Jefferson, however, wished to avoid conflict. War was expensive and would undermine his efforts to reduce the debt. Moreover, the army and navy had already been gutted to save money. America was simply not prepared for war, militarily or economically. Nevertheless, something had to be done to make Britain pay for its constant acts of indignity toward the nation and its people.

Jefferson and congressional Republicans opted for economic sanctions that they hoped would pressure Britain and France to ease attacks on America trade due to each nation's reliance upon that trade. Congress had already attempted to use economic pressure against Britain with the Non-Importation Act of 1806, which prohibited importation of certain British goods. This time they opted for an embargo, which prohibited virtually all external trade. The **Embargo Act** was passed on December 21, 1807 and signed by Jefferson the following day. The legislation was a drastic step, as it had ramifications for the ability of southern and western farmers to sell their crops. The law would have an even greater impact in New England where so much of the economy was based on foreign trade.

President James Madison

The embargo did allow time for war fever to subside but did little to pressure Britain and France. American shippers prohibited from legally trading with Europe turned to illegal trade, smuggling goods into and out of the U.S. and on to Europe. In an effort to stop the smuggling, Jefferson sent a proposal, by way of Gallatin, to Congress. The Enforcement Act gave the government increased powers to enforce the embargo. First, it empowered customs collectors to seize cargos of suspected smugglers without warrant or the prospect of a trial, both violations of the Constitution. Jefferson wrote instructions to those collectors that suggested they be suspicious of the transportation of almost any trade, suggesting that they should "consider every shipment of provisions, lumber, flaxseed, tar, cotton, tobacco, etc. . . as sufficiently suspicious for detention. . . When you are doubtful, consider me as voting for detention." In a letter to state governors he said that he wanted to ensure that the real needs of citizens, such as food, were met but did not want people engaged in trade to be able to use that as "a cover for the crimes against their country." The act also gave the president the power to use the army and navy to enforce the embargo. While waiting for Congress to authorize him with that power, and angry over reports of widespread smuggling into Canada through the Lake Champlain region, Jefferson pressured the governors of New York and Vermont to use state militias to round up and detain suspected smugglers, arguing that a state of insurrection existed there.

Strong-armed enforcement led to some protests of the embargo, which had devastating effects on the U.S. economy. American exports totaling $108 million in 1807, fell to $22 million in 1808. In addition, farm prices fell, and tens of thousands of Americans engaged in trade (many of them sailors) found themselves out of work. As a result, the embargo became hugely unpopular, leading to a brief resurgence of the seemingly dead Federalist Party. Still, with no strong national organization, they lost the presidency by a wide margin to James Madison. Nonetheless, the Federalists were back in power in every northern state government except Pennsylvania and also won control of the lower house in Maryland. Further, they were able to gain at least 70 percent of the congressional seats from every state north of the Potomac River except Pennsylvania. The shift was especially clear to northern Republicans, who now faced real threats to their congressional seats. They led efforts in Congress, against Jefferson's wishes, to repeal the embargo (although it was set to expire in four months anyway). Jefferson was forced to bear the indignity of signing the repeal of the act that he was still trying to enforce until his last days in office.

THE WAR OF 1812

Toward War with Britain

James Madison won the presidency over his Federalist rival handily but soon realized that he would face some of the same resistance within the Republican Party that Jefferson had seen emerge in his last months in office. When Madison prepared to nominate Albert Gallatin as his Secretary of State, he faced a backlash in the Senate led by William Branch Giles of Virginia, as well as Robert and Samuel Smith of Maryland. In an effort to bring the party back together, Madison dropped his intention to appoint Gallatin as Secretary of State and instead appointed Robert Smith. Gallatin would remain in his cabinet as Secretary of Treasury, keeping the same position to which he had been nominated and confirmed in Jefferson's administration. Beyond keeping Gallatin, his trusted advisor, Madison was forced to appoint some less than qualified men for the sake of party unity. One contemporary critic called them a cabinet of nincompoops.

Madison's efforts at unity were largely a failure.

Map 9.2 The War of 1812

Some believed it was his influence that led Jefferson to depart from "pure" republicanism by taking harsh efforts to enforce the embargo (after all, Madison did support a federal government superior to the states during the 1780s). Many also distrusted Gallatin, a foreigner and a Jew, who had great influence upon Jefferson and Madison. For others, it was simply a matter of policy. Madison wanted to continue to use economic sanctions to buy time while preparing for the possibility of war. Others wanted to prepare for war immediately and dispense with diplomacy and economic coercion.

Madison's hands were initially tied by the outgoing Congress and Thomas Jefferson. The repeal of the embargo had been accompanied by a new law, the Non-Intercourse Act. Rather than prohibit all trade, this law only prohibited trade with Britain and France. The act was designed to ease some of the economic impact on Americans engaging in trade but did not even promise to be as effective as the largely ineffective embargo as Britain and France would still be able to get American trade through intermediaries. The weakness of the Non-Intercourse Act to pressure Britain to lift its Orders in Council angered Napoleon so much that he ordered attacks on American shipping to the extent that soon France was seizing more American ships than Britain.

The president proposed a new bill in March 1810, using North Carolina Representative Nathaniel Macon to introduce the measure, which would lift lessen restrictions on trade with Britain and France. Known as Macon's Bill No. 1, it would ban imports from either nation and would prohibit the ships of either nation from carrying American trade goods. Finally, if either nation lifted their edicts against neutral commerce, that nation would be relieved of the act's prohibitions. In this way, even if neither nation stopped their attacks on American shipping, at least Americans would get the economic benefit of the carrying trade.

Some Republicans itching for war joined with Federalists to defeat Madison's bill and replaced it with a new one called **Macon's Bill No. 2** (not because Macon introduced this one but likely because it was a perverted re-writing of the original bill). This bill lifted all trade restrictions. If either Britain or France revoked their edicts and the other nation failed to revoke theirs, the president would be empowered with re-imposing trade restrictions against that nation. Napoleon quickly agreed to the terms, but even three months later Britain had still refused. Despite Napoleon's promises, France was still seizing American ships. Beginning in early 1811, Madison cut off all trade with Britain and recalled the American minister there. The reluctance of Britain to respond affirmatively to Macon's Bill No. 2 only served to intensify anti-British sentiment in America in a growing chorus of calls for war.

Responding to those calls for war in Congress were a group of young congressmen from the southern and western frontier. **Henry Clay**, a first-term congressman from Kentucky, became the leading voice of those congressmen who became known as the "War Hawks." Clay was such a charismatic politician that he was chosen by his fellow congressmen to serve as Speaker of the House. They were not only angry with Britain over its refusal to revoke the Orders in Council but also over the long series of British degradations toward America that suggested that Britain did not respect American sovereignty. For many of these War Hawks, however, it was also due to issues related to the frontier regions from which they came.

Trouble on the Frontier

Americans had a long history of conflict with Native Americans on its western frontier. Those tensions were exacerbated by the presence of British troops still occupying forts in the Ohio River Valley region known as the Old Northwest (what would ultimately become the states of Ohio, Indiana, Illinois, Michigan, and Wisconsin). Perceiving that the United States government was not serious about honoring the provision of the Treaty of Paris calling for American citizens to honor their outstanding debts to British merchants, the British refused to respect the peace treaty's terms calling for the evacuation of British forces

Tecumseh

THE TREATY OF GREENVILLE

Americans had long desired expansion past the Appalachian Mountains. Those desires were a precipitating cause of the French and Indian War. After the French defeat, Native Americans in the region provided stiff resistance often organizing themselves collectively, as with Pontiac's Confederacy.

The American Revolution offered new opportunities for American settlers in the region to fight against Indian resistance, using the war against Britain as a premise. The Treaty of Paris ending the revolution ceded the land east of the Mississippi and south of Canada to the new United States, but Native Americans in the region did not recognize American sovereignty there, viewing the Ohio River as the boundary between Indian land and the United States.

In 1785, Little Turtle, chief of the Miamis, organized a confederacy of Indian nations in the region in an effort to thwart American expansion there while the U.S. government established policies for settling the region with the Northwest Ordinance. With the ratification of the Constitution, the federal government now had the authority to raise an army. In an effort to deal with the resistant Indians in the Ohio River Valley, President George Washington sent a small army into the region to break Indian resistance. The commanders of those militias, however, struggled to enlist enough men and those that did enlist were poorly trained, leading to American defeats in 1791 and 1792.

In 1793, President Washington placed General Anthony Wayne, experienced with fighting the Indians in the region, in command of the newly organized Legion of the United States. While the United States government spent 1793 trying to negotiate a treaty with Little Turtle's Western Confederacy, Wayne spent the year raising and training his army. When peace talks ended with no treaty, Wayne quickly moved to establish control in the region, finally defeating the Indians at the Battle of Fallen Timbers on August 20, 1794.

The following year a peace conference was held at Fort Greenville. Leaders from all of the member nations of the Western Confederacy were present. The resulting treaty took eight months to negotiate. Under the treaty, the Indian nations in the region ceded most of what today is Ohio along with other territory and the U.S. government agreed to cede all land north and west of the treaty line (with the exception of several forts already under American control and a number of trading posts to be established there). The nations would receive $20,000 worth of money and goods from the U.S. government along with annual payments (in money and goods) in perpetuity and would be permitted to continue to hunt in the land ceded to the U.S. All of this, however, was dependent upon continuing good behavior by the Indians. Little Turtle is reported to have remarked that he was the last to sign the treaty but would be the last to break it.

The treaty led to a decade-long period of relative peace in the region. With growing numbers of Americans flooding into the region, it was only a matter of time before they would cast their eyes on the territory guaranteed to the Indians. But there was also growing dissatisfaction among Native Americans who had seen the impact of American expansion before. In addition, with so many Americans clearing land for farming, the promise of continued Indian hunting in the region was clearly an empty one. The emergence of Tecumseh as a resistance leader brought renewed conflict to fruition.

from the lands given to the United States. The presence of those British troops had been a point of contention in the Treaty of Paris of 1783 and the Jay Treaty in 1794. Hostile Native American groups, aided and encouraged by the British remaining in the forts, discouraged growth into the western areas north of the Ohio River. In the early 1790s, President Washington sent militia troops under the command of army officers to protect the small but growing number of settlers and to bring Indian hostilities to an end. Those efforts failed miserably due to poorly trained militia soldiers and poor leadership. The Indians were organized into the Western Confederacy under the leadership of the Miami Chief Little Turtle and Shawnee Chief Blue Jacket. They were also aided by supplies from the British and, at times, direct military aid.

In 1792, President Washington commissioned General "Mad Anthony" Wayne to raise and train a professional army for the purpose of quelling the Indian hostilities. After training his army, known as the Legion of the United States, Wayne moved the force north from Cincinnati in 1793, establishing forts in the region where General Arthur St. Clair had been defeated two years earlier. Wayne's forts and supply trains to those forts often faced attack from Indians of the Western Confederacy, turning back a siege of about 2,000 Indian warriors in June 1794. Two months later, Wayne led an attack against those Indians, chasing them into an area of trees that had fallen during a previous tornado. The **Battle of Fallen Timbers** was a decisive victory for the American forces under Wayne's command, bringing an end to what is known as Little

Turtle's War. The following year, American officials met with leaders from the member nations of the Western Confederacy and reached an agreement that ended much of the fighting in the region for more than a decade. In the Treaty of Greenville, Native Americans ceded much of what today is Ohio and the Native American nations involved received annual grants of supplies and money. With the opening that region to settlement by Americans and the relative peace in the region, the population quickly grew, with Ohio becoming a state in 1803.

Tecumseh

By the time that Ohio joined the United States, some Native Americans in the West were beginning to show new signs of resistance to continuing American expansion. In 1805, a religious leader named **Tenskwatawa** emerged among the Shawnee. Having previously suffered from alcoholism, he claimed to have had a series of visions that ultimately depicted an Indian victory over Americans and Europeans. He quit drinking and became a religious leader, urging Native Americans to shun all American goods and reject all treaties made with America, returning instead to traditional native ways of life. He and his brother Tecumseh settled a village near the Tippecanoe River in what today is Indiana. Known as Prophetstown because Tenskwatawa was also referred to as the Prophet, the village grew into a large multi-tribal community. The Prophet not only shunned American ways, he also heavily criticized Native Americans who did not do the same, especially chiefs who continued to accept annual grant money under the Treaty of Greenville and urge cooperation with Americans.

While the Prophet was the religious leader of the community, **Tecumseh**, emerged as its political leader. Raised by another brother who was a war chief, Tecumseh learned to be a warrior at a young age. He fought at the Battle of Fallen Timbers and was present at the signing of the Treaty of Greenville though not as a signatory (a fact that he would later use to justify his refusal to obey its terms). A charismatic leader, he took advantage of the Prophet's popularity to push his idea for a pan-Indian alliance. While other Native American leaders called for accommodation and cultural adaptation, Tecumseh and the Prophet urged resistance.

Tecumseh began to emerge as an important figure in 1809. When the territorial governor of Indiana, **William Henry Harrison**, negotiated the Treaty of Fort Wayne, which ceded 3 million acres of Indian land to the Americans, Tecumseh voiced his opposition even though none of the land belonged to the Shawnee. He advocated the doctrine of common property, whereby Native American

Death of Tecumseh at the Battle of the Thames, October 18, 1813

groups owned the land collectively. Therefore, no land could be sold without the consent of all native groups. He split from Shawnee Chief Black Hoof over the latter's willingness to work with American leaders. Black Hoof had seen the strength of American military might at Fallen Timbers and believed that accommodation was in the best interests of Native Americans. Tecumseh suggested that collaborating Indian chiefs should be killed because of their unwillingness to stand up and defend their interests. His followers began conducting raids and killing some accommodationist Native Americans. He met with Harrison on a number of occasions as the governor hoped to subdue his resistance without force, but Tecumseh would not back down. Instead, he threatened Harrison, telling the governor that the Native Americans might be forced to ally themselves with the British.

Federal government leaders realized the dangers of Indian unrest in the Ohio River Valley. As tensions with Britain were growing, trouble with Native Americans would only complicate American interactions with Britain, especially if war came. Jefferson's Secretary of War, Henry Dearborn, urged American officials on the frontier to use prudence in dealing with Native Americans. After the Treaty of Fort Wayne, Madison ordered an end to the policy of extracting large land cessions.

Governor Harrison had a different view of the growing tensions resulting from increasing support for the Prophet and Tecumseh. He believed that if he could get friendly Indian chiefs to cede the remaining land in Indiana Territory, which included Prophetstown, he could evict the Prophet, Tecumseh, and their followers as trespassers. Such a course would ultimately require military force at some point. Tecumseh traveled with an army of over 700 warriors as he made extensive journeys across the region to bring other Native Americans into his confederacy and to secure arms and other supplies from the British. The territorial government, however, had no money with which to raise an army. Besides the lack of money, Indiana was sparsely settled and did not have enough manpower to field a militia large enough for the task.

With the support of territorial governors in Michigan, Missouri, and Illinois, Harrison requested federal troops that Madison grudgingly granted, with the caveat that hostilities be avoided unless "absolutely necessary." The governor then went to Kentucky to recruit volunteers from that state. By August 1811, Harrison had assembled a force of 400 regular army infantrymen and about 800 Indiana militiamen and volunteers from Kentucky, a total of about 1,200 men.

Two days after he received notification that he would be receiving federal troops, Harrison met one last time with Tecumseh. Neither man was willing to concede anything. Besides leaving Harrison with the warning of a British-Indian alliance, Tecumseh also suggested an even bigger threat. He would be traveling in the next few months to visit with Native Americans on the southern frontier (Creeks, Cherokees, and others) in order to bring them into his confederacy. For Harrison, the important information was not of a potentially large, resistant Indian confederation but that Tecumseh would be gone, providing the perfect opportunity to strike a blow at Prophetstown, which had grown to as many 3,000 inhabitants.

By the end of September, Harrison and his forces began moving northward toward Prophetstown. They built a fort on the Wabash River and reinforced their position while Harrison planned his attack. Ideally, the Prophet and his followers would have vacated the area, but they refused to leave. At the same time, the Prophet sent messengers to Harrison assuring him of their peaceful intentions. By November 6, Harrison and his men had moved within two miles of Prophetstown, encamping there along the Tippecanoe River. The Prophet sent another messenger requesting a meeting with Harrison on the next day. After surveying the terrain around Prophetstown and realizing that an attack on the village would be problematic, the governor was pleased that the threat of force seemed to have had its impact and hoped that his conference with the Prophet would resolve the issue without bloodshed.

With the meeting set for the next day, Harrison saw no need to reinforce his sentries. At about 4:30 on the morning of November 7, however, native warriors attacked, fighting largely by the light provided by dying campfires. Initially caught by surprise, Harrison's force was able to regroup and hold off their attackers for about two hours until the natives ran out of ammunition. As the sun began to rise, the warriors quickly fled, leaving 62 Americans killed and another 126 wounded (estimates placed the number of Indian dead as between 50 and 60, with another 70 to 80 wounded). After spending the day of November 7 tending to the wounded and fortifying defenses, Harrison took a force into Prophetstown and found the village deserted. He ordered his men to destroy the dwellings and declared the Battle of Tippecanoe a victory, believing that his show of military might had encouraged all but the most fervid followers of the Prophet and Tecumseh to return to their home villages.

There was reason to think that the battle had put the movement started by the Shawnee brothers on a rapid decline. Reports surfaced that some warriors at Prophetstown had become disillusioned with the Prophet when his magic did not protect them from American bullets. Those reports were premature, however, because the return of Tecumseh helped to keep the confederacy together.

Madison Asks for War

From late-1811 into the spring of 1812, James Madison faced increasing calls for war against England, from the War Hawks in Congress (led by Henry Clay and John Calhoun) as well as newspaper editors who whipped up public fervor. By April 1812, Clay's efforts paid off. Madison announced a temporary embargo so that American ships on the high seas would have time to return to the safety of American ports before war was declared. On June 1, Madison issued a message asking Congress for a declaration of war, outlining the many British degradations against American trade and American citizens (impressment). After spending much of his message on the maritime issues, he also mentioned British efforts to stir rebelliousness among the Native Americans on the frontier. He concluded by characterizing British actions as belligerent against the United States, whereas American actions had been nothing but peaceful. Congress soon voted in favor of war with Britain on June 18, 1812.

While Madison's focus may have been on maritime issues, and Americans certainly felt that British actions demonstrated a lack of respect for American independence, the issues on the frontier had a much larger impact on the war declaration than it seemed. Support for war was tepid among southern planters who benefited greatly from trade with Europe. There was also strong opposition to the war in New England where the economy was largely based on the carrying trade. While these groups did not like British attacks on American vessels, overseas trade was so lucrative that they were willing to accept lost cargos as the price of doing business. The embargo had hurt trade, but war would virtually end it by causing severe economic hardship, thus they did not feel war with Britain was worth that price.

The War Hawks, on the other hand, were a group of congressmen from southern and western frontier regions that were facing increasing rebelliousness among Native Americans. They believed much of that hostility was due to British aid and encouragement rather than anything the Americans had done. Calls for war after the Battle of Tippecanoe proved to be no surprise. By the end of the year, Congress authorized an increase in the army from less than 4,000 men to 35,000. At the same time, they resisted calls to increase the size of the U.S. Navy. The army would be needed to quell Indian unrest on the frontier and possibly lead an invasion into Canada, which some thought would encourage Canadians to separate from Britain and join the United States.

To those living on the frontier, the coming fight was not just a war against Britain, but also against the Native Americans, and the Westerners would take advantage of the war to open up more land for white settlement. Tecumseh's alliance with the English only made this attitude easier to hold in the Ohio River Valley. When the war began, the British established defenses along the southern border of Canada, joined by Tecumseh's confederacy, and vacated land in the valley, thereby making it easier for Americans on the frontier to establish control. When Tecumseh was killed at the Battle of the Thames in October 1813, it signaled the beginning of the end for Native Americans in that region.

The southern frontier also became an important battleground during the war. In that region, a group of Creek Indians calling themselves Red Sticks opposed assimilation or accommodation with Americans, shunning American ways much like the Prophet and Tecumseh had been preaching in the Ohio River Valley. The Creek leadership disagreed with them, but in an effort to thwart American expansion into the region, the British and the Spanish offered aid to the Red Sticks. In 1813, the Red Sticks used that support to rise up against accommodationist Creeks. Americans in Tennessee and the frontier settlements of the Mississippi Territory (the present-day states of Alabama and Mississippi) inserted themselves into the civil war by sending militias to help the Creeks. Of course, their real motive was to open more land in the region for settlement.

Andrew Jackson's 2,500-man militia was one of those forces sent into the region. In addition to being aided by Creek warriors, Jackson also had the support of the Cherokee. A Red Stick attack on a garrison named Fort Mims near Mobile deepened American involvement.

There, the Red Sticks slaughtered a small defensive force along with some white settlers and Creeks seeking refuge at the fort. In response to what Americans called the Fort Mims Massacre, the federal government sent regular army troops in February 1814 to supplement Jackson's force, bringing his numbers to about 5,000 men. On March 27, Jackson's forces crushed the Red Sticks at the **Battle of Horseshoe Bend** leaving 800 warriors dead. Four months later, Jackson pressured the Creeks to sign the Treaty of Fort Jackson, ceding over 21 million acres of land (including friendly Creek and Red Stick land). Jackson's other Indian allies, the Cherokee, would lose almost 2 million acres.

A Comedy of Errors

America was not ready for an extended military conflict when Congress approved Madison's war message. The president had a largely unqualified cabinet, and Congress at the time was badly divided (so divided that it took nearly three weeks to approve Madison's war message). The money that the treasury possessed was spent quickly and the established avenue for borrowing and issuing bonds, the national bank, had seen its twenty-year charter expire in 1811 without congressional renewal.

Congress had previously authorized an increase for the size of the army, but the U.S. Army still consisted of less than 8,000 men in 1812 (and would never have as many as 30,000 at any point during the war). Moreover, most of the men were recent enlistees, often on three- or six-month enlistments, meaning they were poorly trained. Filling the gap with state militiamen posed its own problems, as they were more concerned with state interests instead of national interests. In one instance, a regular army commander was preparing an invasion of Canada with a force supplemented by New York state militiamen. As he moved his army into Canada, the New Yorkers refused to cross the border. They were willing to defend New York, but had no interest in invading Canada.

The quality of military leadership was no better. Although West Point had been established to train officers, the rapid expansion of the army called for more officers than West Point could provide. As a result, many officers were political appointments with little training. William Hull, the sixty-year-old territorial governor of Michigan, was given command of the army at Fort Detroit although he had not led troops in battle since the American Revolution. Within the first months of the war Hull was tasked with an attack on Canada. He quickly retreated and was pursued to Fort Detroit by British General Isaac Brock. Hull became convinced that he could not hold the fort against Brock's forces, which Hull had learned was to receive the addition of "vast numbers of Indians" to his force. Without firing a shot, Hull surrendered Fort Detroit.

For the better part of two years, American and British forces (the latter mostly consisting of Canadian militiamen because the bulk of the English army was busy fighting Napoleon in Europe) tried unsuccessfully to launch invasions across the border. The Americans did briefly capture the Canadian capital of York (present-day Toronto), but since the city had no strategic significance, the Americans withdrew leaving buildings, including the legislature, in flames.

The biggest success that the Americans had in the fighting along the Canadian border occurred on the water. Commodore Oliver Hazard Perry was able to defeat the British on Lake Erie and controlled the lake throughout the war, a significant factor in William Henry Harrison's success at the Battle of the Thames leading to the recapture of Detroit. At Sackets Harbor, New York, where a shipbuilding operation was established, eleven warships constructed there during the war helped the Americans maintain control of Lake Ontario. Supremacy over the border lakes made British attempts to invade the U.S. difficult, even with the arrival of well-trained and battle-tested soldiers fresh off the defeat of Napoleon in April 1814.

The U.S. Navy also had great success in the Atlantic, especially the *U.S.S. Constitution*, which earned the nickname "Old Ironsides" because British cannonballs bounced off its sides during battle. That effect was actually the result of two factors: innovative tactics and superior materials. The commander of the *Constitution* had developed a maneuver whereby, instead of coming directly side-to-side with an enemy ship as was standard practice, he would make the *Constitution* approach the vessel at such a tight angle that it caused enemy cannonballs to bounce off the hard white oak of the ship's hull. The navy's operations were also supplemented by the use of privateers, many of them operating out of Baltimore. Privateers captured over 1,300 British merchant vessels during the war, as compared to only 250 captured by the U.S. Navy.

With the end of hostilities in Europe in April 1814, England was eager to end the war in North America. They entered into peace talks with representatives of the U.S. in the Belgian city of Ghent later that summer. The British government also wanted to push along negotiations by sending battle-tested troops to America. If they could turn the tide of the war, they could push the Americans to accept a peace that was more favorable to Britain. In particular, they wanted: an Indian state created in the American Northwest Territory; British right to navigate the Mississippi River; and a prohibition against American naval vessels on the Great Lakes. They sent one force to

Canada to launch an invasion of New York. The other force was sent to the Chesapeake Bay to deal a blow to the privateers operating out of Baltimore, a city that the British referred to as a "den of pirates."

The Chesapeake Bay expeditionary force arrived in August, with the British fleet facing little resistance. Once there, the British landed forces on the Maryland shore and moved inland towards Washington, D.C. An ineptly-led militia defended the approach to Washington at Bladensburg, Maryland. When the fighting began, the poorly-positioned Americans were fairly easily driven away by the experienced and determined British soldiers. The embarrassed American loss at the Battle of Bladensburg became derisively known as the "**Bladensburg races**." The British easily marched into Washington as government officials, including President Madison, fled into the countryside. First Lady Dolly Madison stayed behind to secure as many of the valuables in the White House as she could before the British arrived. Much like York had been for the Americans, Washington served no strategic value to the British, but in their desire to avenge York, the British left the city in flames as they prepared to move on their primary target, Baltimore.

Two weeks later, the British troops approached Baltimore with the intent of using the cannons on their ships to bombard the city in preparation for the land invasion. The commander at Fort McHenry, which guarded the entrance to the harbor, had sent his men to sink a line of merchant ships that prevented British ships from getting close enough to shell the city. At the same time, well-entrenched troops repulsed a British land attack. As British ships fired in vain on Fort McHenry for over 24 hours, an American lawyer named **Francis Scott Key** watched the battle from aboard the British flagship (he had gone aboard to seek the release of a man who had been detained by the English). When the morning arrived, Key spotted a large American flag still flying over Fort McHenry, signifying that it was still operational. Overwhelmed with patriotism, he felt inspired to begin writing a poem describing the bombardment and his emotions upon viewing the flag entitled "The Defense of Fort McHenry." When put to music (set to the tune of "To Anacreon in Heaven," a well-known contemporary English piece) and retitled "The Star-Spangled Banner," the song soon became an immensely popular song but was not made America's official national anthem until 1931.

After the British withdrawal from Baltimore, a second British attack launched from Canada into upstate New York also failed. The British made one final effort to gain a big victory that might force the Americans at Ghent to end the war with a treaty favorable to England, sending a force of nearly 15,000 men to New Orleans in early December 1814. Andrew Jackson, having recently concluded the Treaty of Fort Jackson, moved his force to defend New Orleans. He was joined by about 1,000 local militiamen from Louisiana (almost half of whom were free people of color), a group of Choctaw warriors, and even a contingent of local pirates led by Jean Lafitte who were promised immunity for past transgressions in exchange for volunteering to join the fight and donating their valuable ship's cannons to the defense of the city. Ultimately, Jackson's ragtag army numbered less than 5,000 men and consisted of less than one thousand regular army soldiers.

After some skirmishes through the first half of December, British forces were able to establish a camp about four miles from New Orleans by December 23. That night, Jackson attacked with about 2,000 men before withdrawing after about three hours of fighting. While Jackson had not won the fight, the move did cause the British to be excessively cautious afterward, giving Jackson's forces more time to set up their defenses outside of the city. Finally, on January 8, 1815, the British advanced on New Orleans with a force of 8,000 men. The British assault was badly coordinated, and by the end of the battle the British had suffered huge casualties (over 750 killed and captured, with 1,300 wounded). Jackson's losses were only 13 killed, 30 wounded, and 19 missing. Days later, the British force withdrew and the **Battle of New Orleans** became a huge victory for the United States.

Meanwhile, by the fall of 1814, British government leaders had grown impatient. They tried to send the Duke of Wellington, the general who defeated Napoleon, to the U.S. but he refused. He also suggested that Britain had no right to claim territory in the United States as a condition of the treaty since they had not been able to actually occupy such territory during the war. British negotiators dropped all their demands, and a treaty was reached on December 24, 1814. The **Treaty of Ghent** called for the status quo antebellum, essentially calling the war a tie. Neither nation would gain anything from the treaty other than producing an end to hostilities.

FINALLY, A NATION

While the Treaty of Ghent suggested that neither nation had won the war, Americans viewed things differently. All of the issues that had led to the war no longer existed, both Indian resistance and the attacks on ships and impressment. Additionally, the conflict had ended with a huge American victory at New Orleans. When the war began, Americans were divided over whether fighting a war with the English was wise. By the end of the war,

Americans were widely supportive, leading to a rising sense of national pride.

From the American Revolution up to 1812, Americans had generally been more loyal to their state than to the nation as a whole. That mindset began to change after the war. Because the war was seen as an American reaffirmation of their independence from Britain, it connected the nationalism fostered during the War of 1812 to the patriotism of the Revolution. Independence Day had not been regularly celebrated but became an annual celebration after the war, and, as previously mentioned, Francis Scott Key's "Star-Spangled Banner" became a widely popular patriotic song.

While a new sense of national pride might be deemed a big winner as a result of the war, there were losers as well. Native Americans located east of the Mississippi River had lost their last chance to stem the tide of American expansion. While some in frontier regions of the Northwest Territory tried to resist by force, most accepted their fate. Indian nations in the South saw little option but to appease American authority and cede increasingly portions of their land to allow for American expansion.

Another big loser from the war proved to be the Federalist Party. All but dead by the election of 1804, the Federalists made dramatic gains beginning in 1812. Nevertheless, they remained a regional party much stronger in New England than the rest of the country. Because the war was hardest economically on that region, strong opposition to the war developed there. By the fall of 1814, New Englanders grew gloomy about the war, upset about the economic impact that the conflict had on them. Federalist leaders soon called for a convention to discuss these matters, to be held in Hartford, Connecticut. Beginning in secret on December 15, 1814, the Hartford Convention was attended by 26 delegates, some of whom suggested that the New England states should secede from the Union and negotiate their own peace settlement with Britain. Moderate Federalists were able to quiet such talk of secession, but the convention's final report issued on January 5, 1815, two weeks after the Treaty of Ghent was signed and three days before Jackson's victory in New Orleans, openly condemned the war and proposed a series of constitutional amendments viewed as beneficial to New England, including the requirement of a two-thirds majority of Congress for the declaration of war, the admission of a new state, or interfering with foreign commerce. The timing could not have been worse for the Federalists who were now seen as unpatriotic at a time when the feelings of nationalism and patriotism were sweeping across America.

Oddly enough, the Republican Party could also be viewed as a loser, even though Republicans now had no viable political opponent. The Republican Party was largely born in the minds of Thomas Jefferson and James Madison, forming as an opposition party to the power that Hamilton was wielding in the young government. Because of their own party organization and Federalist missteps, they gained power in 1800. The Republican leadership, especially Jefferson and Madison, had to deal with the problem of ruling when the foundations of their party were oppositional in nature. The principles on which the party stood in the 1790s—strict construction of the Constitution and limited federal power—did not translate well to governing. They were faced with balancing an adherence to constitutional principles with serving the interests of the nation, resulting in the Republicans under Jefferson adopting some of the very political tactics they decried in the Federalist administrations of the 1790s. Hamilton's view of implied powers became a justification for Jefferson to purchase Louisiana, even if Jefferson would not admit to that. Washington's willingness to use military force to demand authority for federal law became Jefferson's strict enforcement and demand for respect of federal authority while enforcing the embargo. In a real twist of positions, some New England Federalists contemplated using Jefferson's conception of nullification against the embargo.

Without a well-organized opposition party, the Republicans would eventually begin to splinter from within, finding it difficult to demand party loyalty due to the weakness of the Federalists. Old Republicans resented what they saw as a shift away from their established principles. Those who had never adhered strictly to principles anyway saw fewer problems with the actions of Jefferson and Madison. By 1808, the party had seen an influx of former Federalists who did not adhere to those principles at all. Sectional and regional differences were also becoming more apparent. After the demise of the Federalists, the Republican Party would remain the only political party into the 1820s, but it ceased to be a unified party long before that as it became increasingly factionalized.

Few Americans, however, were lamenting the decline of the Republican Party in 1815. They had stood up to Britain and would never again have to prove their independence to that nation. Americans became imbued with a sense of confidence that would help to propel expansion and dramatic economic growth across the country in the coming years.

Chronology

1801 Jefferson inaugurated as 3rd U.S. President.
Jefferson sends four ships to fight Barbary Pirates.

1803 *Marbury v. Madison* decision.
The United States purchases Louisiana from France.
War in Europe resumes.

1804 Thomas Jefferson re-elected.
Lewis and Clark expedition departs.
Aaron Burr kills Alexander Hamilton in a duel.

1805 Justice Samuel Chase acquitted by the U.S. Senate.
Essex Decision delivered.

1806 Congress passes the Non-Importation Act.
Napoleon issues Berlin Decree.

1807 Congress passes the Embargo Act
British attack upon the *U.S.S. Chesapeake.*
Britain issues Orders in Council.

1808 James Madison elected 4th U.S. President.

1809 Congress passes the Non-Intercourse Act.

1810 Congress passes Macon's Bill No. 2.

1811 Battle of Tippecanoe.

1812 Congress declares war on Great Britain.
Hull surrenders Fort Detroit.

1813 Red Sticks conduct Fort Mims Massacre.
Oliver Hazard Perry wins on Lake Erie.

1814 Battle of Horseshoe Bend.
British burn Washington, D.C.
Battle of Baltimore.
Treaty of Ghent.

1815 Battle of New Orleans.
Hartford Convention ends.

SUGGESTED READINGS

Stephen Ambrose, *Undaunted Courage: Meriwether Lewis, Thomas Jefferson, and the Opening of the American West* (1996).

Lance Banning, *The Jeffersonian Persuasion: Evolution of a Party Ideology* (1978).

Troy Bickham, *The Weight of Vengeance: The United States, the British Empire, and the War of 1812* (2012).

Gregory Evans Dowd, *A Spiritual Resistance: The North American Indian Struggle for Unity, 1745-1815* (1992).

Don E. Fehrenbacher, *The Era of Expansion: 1800-1848* (1969).

Joseph J. Ellis, *American Sphinx: The Character of Thomas Jefferson* (1997).

Donald R. Hickey, *The War of 1812: A Forgotten Conflict* (1989).

Richard Hofstadter, *The Idea of a Party System: The Rise of Legitimate Opposition in the United States, 1780-1840* (1969).

Ralph Ketcham, *James Madison: A Biography* (1971).

Frank Lambert, *The Barbary Wars: American Independence in the Atlantic World* (2005)

Drew McCoy, *The Elusive Republic: Political Economy in Jeffersonian America* (1980).

Forrest McDonald, *The Presidency of Thomas Jefferson* (1976).

R. Kent Newmyer, *The Supreme Court Under Marshall and Taney* (1968).

Peter S. Onuf, *Jefferson's Empire: The Language of American Nationhood* (2000).

Bradford Perkins, *Prologue to War: England and the United States, 1805-1812* (1961).

James P. Ronda, *Lewis and Clark Among the Indians* (1984).

Adam Rothman, *Slave Country: American Expansion and the Origins of the Deep South* (2005).

Marshal Smelser, *The Democratic Republic, 1801-1815* (1968).

J.C.A. Stagg, *Mr. Madison's War: Politics, Diplomacy, and Warfare in the Early Republic, 1783-1830* (1983).

John Sugden, *Tecumseh's Last Stand* (1985).

Robert W. Tucker and David C. Hendrickson, *Empire of Liberty: The Statecraft of Thomas Jefferson.*

Steven Watts, *The Republic Reborn: War and the Making of Liberal America, 1790-1820* (1987).

Review Questions

1. Discuss Jefferson's views on republicanism and how they fit with his vision for an agrarian nation.

2. Discuss Chief Justice Marshall's decision in *Marbury* and its importance in American history.

3. How did America acquire Louisiana? Why did Jefferson have reservations about the purchase? How did he overcome those reservations?

4. What were the causes of the War of 1812? How did the U.S. respond to those issues in an effort to avoid war?

5. What impact did the War of 1812 have on America and Americans?

Glossary of Important People and Concepts

Barbary Pirates
Bladensburg races
Carrying trade
Samuel Chase
Henry Clay
Corps of Discovery
Embargo Act
Battle of Fallen Timbers
Albert Gallatin
William Henry Harrison
Impressment
Francis Scott Key
Louisiana Purchase
Macon's Bill Number 2
Marbury v. Madison
John Marshall
Midnight Appointments
"mosquito fleet"
Battle of New Orleans
Orders in Council
Sainte Domingue
Tecumseh
Tenskwatawa ("The Prophet")
U.S.S. Chesapeake
U.S.S. Constitution

Chief Justice John Marshall

Chapter Ten

THE "ERA OF GOOD FEELINGS"

As America emerged from the War of 1812 with a newfound sense of nationalism, the country was also experiencing dramatic changes to its economic system, often referred to as the Market Revolution. One of its driving forces was entrepreneurialism—a willingness of individuals to take risks in the drive to create more wealth. One of the men who embodied this entrepreneurial spirit was Timothy Dexter.

Dexter did not seem destined for great wealth as a young man. Working as an apprentice leather maker in the 1760s taught him a skill that would ultimately allow him to provide for a family but would not gain him wealth of any consequence, even after he opened his own business. His marriage to a wealthy widow, however, changed his fortunes. In the late 1780s, with her wealth at his disposal, Dexter followed the example of some of the wealthiest men in Boston, such as John Hancock, and speculated in government bonds. It was a risky endeavor at the time because there was no certainty those bonds would be redeemed by the young government. When Alexander Hamilton's financial plan went into effect in the early 1790s, Dexter found himself one of the wealthiest men in Boston.

To men of high social breeding, Dexter was a misfit, and they shunned him. As such, he relocated to Newburyport where he bought a large estate and entered business as a merchant like Hancock and the others that he tried to emulate in Boston, located 35 miles to the north. He used his wealth in an attempt to create even more wealth, buying a fleet of ships and establishing a mercantile house in the city. Other merchants disliked Dexter, possibly due to his low birth and eccentric behavior (he referred to himself as Lord Timothy Dexter, expecting others to do so as well, and once staged his own funeral just to see what others would say of him). They were also put off by the fact that Dexter assumed that he could

excel as a merchant with no background in, or understanding of, the business.

In an effort to see Dexter fail, other merchants supplied him with bad information. They suggested that there might be demand in the West Indies for bed warming pans (used to warm mattresses in the cold New England climate). He bought more than 40,000 of them to sell in the tropical location as his fellow merchants likely snickered with delight. While there was no use for bed warming pans in the West Indies, however, an enterprising worker in a sugar refinery saw that they could be useful as ladles in the refining process. Soon his pans were selling at a rapid pace as Dexter marked the prices up ever higher to increase his profit.

Other merchants were not to be deterred by Dexter's momentary luck. They soon suggested that he sell coal to Newcastle, England. Dexter did not realize that Newcastle was at the heart of England's coal mining region and sent off a large load of coal for sale there. Once again, he found good fortune as coal miners there went on strike while his ship was in route. On similar advice, he sent mittens to the West Indies, Bibles to the East Indies, and gloves to the South Seas always finding eager buyers where it would seem there would be no market for those goods. Dexter even managed to make a profit out of public service as he rid Newburyport of a large number of stray cats that had become a nuisance and sold them to a Caribbean island with a rat problem.

Dexter never became an important man like he had hoped. In fact, he serves as little more than a footnote to the history of his time, but he also represented the risk-taking individuals during that era who helped the conversion from a largely rural barter economy to the beginnings of a market system (and capitalism) that would become the hallmarks of the American economy ever since.

With the demise of the Federalist Party and the emergence of a widespread sense of nationalism, America was brimming with confidence in the years after the War of 1812—a period often referred to as the **Era of Good Feelings**. The political conflicts of the previous two decades had calmed. The United States had, for a second time, defended its independence against what many Americans viewed as British arrogance. Large parts of the West became open to expansion and settlement, and the economy grew stronger in the years after the war. For many Americans in 1815, the future looked very bright. Within a decade, however, some old divisions would re-emerge while new ones came to the surface. Nevertheless, looking forward from 1815, none of that was evident. For the first time, America was becoming a nation instead of merely a collection of states.

ECONOMIC NATIONALISM

Henry Clay's American System

The War of 1812 sped the development of manufacturing in America as the nation became isolated from British manufactured goods. Increased manufacturing offered the promise of greater economic independence from Britain (and Europe as a whole). As a result, **Henry Clay**, the powerful and influential Speaker of the House, looked to enhance that economic growth and independence. He adhered to many of Alexander Hamilton's views regarding the positive role that the government could, and should, play in fostering national economic development. He devised a program based on Hamiltonian principles, known as the **American System**, comprised of three main pillars designed to support economic growth by stabilizing the American economy with a national bank; protecting the budding manufacturing system from foreign competition through tariffs; and promoting internal trade by building infrastructure projects such as roads and bridges.

While manufacturing had expanded during the war, there was still danger of economic instability after the war due to lack of faith in state bank notes, so Clay moved to address that first. In 1811, the year before the war, the national bank's charter came up for renewal. The Republican-controlled Congress refused to issue a new charter for the bank, leaving it to state banks to fill the void. It became clear, however, that the financial system with bank notes issued by various state banks had become unstable. With Treasury Secretary Albert Gallatin and others calling for a new national bank, Clay led the way in Congress. The first Bank of the United States was chartered with largely northern support against opposition from southern Jeffersonians, but in March 1816, a new generation of Republicans from southern and western states, now embracing Hamiltonian loose constructionism supported the bank. On April 10, President James Madison signed the bill chartering the **Second Bank of the United States**. Traditional Republicans, like John Randolph of Roanoke, still opposed the national bank but voiced even greater criticism of the state banks.

The new national bank was very similar to the first Bank of the United States. Granted a twenty-year charter, it became the main depository for federal revenue. The federal government would also be its largest shareholder. The Bank would be headquartered in Philadelphia, but regional branches would be established across the country. Notes issued by the national bank would become legal tender for all transactions with the federal government, making them the basis for a national currency. By stabilizing the currency and restoring faith in the public credit, Clay believed that the Bank of the United States had solved the greatest threat to American economic growth.

The second part of Clay's American System, protection of American manufacturing from foreign competition, garnered much support in England. With Europe now at peace, America lost some of the advantages that it had gained while Europeans were at war. American shippers faced increased competition from European shippers, but the threat was greatest to the fledgling manufacturing sector in America, largely based in the Northeast. British manufacturers began to dump low-price textiles in the U.S., undermining the economic viability of that industry in America, which had not yet adopted the modern techniques used in Britain (improved spinning machinery and the power loom). British leaders knew that American businesses would never be able to invest in those changes while facing competition from cheaper English products. One member of the Parliament said that the glut of British textiles would "stifle in the cradle" the infant American textile industry. The problem of foreign competition was not just felt by New England textile manufacturers. Pennsylvania iron producers faced competition from Britain and Sweden. Corn growers were shut out by English Corn Laws. Kentuckians who spun hemp into cotton-picking sacks faced competition from the Scottish bagging industry. It was becoming increasingly clear that agricultural production and manufacturing production were increasingly tied together. Even Thomas Jefferson realized the changes, noting "We must now place the manufacturer by the side of the agriculturalist."

While approving the national bank charter, Congress also took up the issue of increasing the tariff in an effort to protect American producers from foreign competition

A RAISE FOR CONGRESS GETS A RISE OUT OF THE PEOPLE

In 1816, Congress voted to give itself a raise, and voters responded by throwing the majority of House members out of office. After the War of 1812, members of the Fourteenth Congress united to pass a flurry of legislation that would provide a foundation for a national market economy. Legislators passed a bill that created a new national bank, doing so with far less controversy than a similar bill had generated in the 1790s. They passed a tariff law to protect the Union's fledgling manufacturers. Many historians have termed this moment the "Era of Good Feelings" because policies that had once been deeply divisive sailed through the national legislature. That unity proved somewhat shallow as efforts to federally fund needed transportation infrastructure, for example, failed amidst sectional wrangling.

The reaction to the pay raise also revealed an undercurrent of disenchantment with political leaders. Members of Congress in 1816 did not receive much pay. They earned a $6 per diem, a rate that had been set in 1789 and which no longer met the cost of living in Washington, D.C. Representative Richard M. Johnson of Kentucky, the leading proponent of the bill that would provide members with a $1,500 annual salary instead of the per diem, considered this a modest increase. He noted that twenty-eight federal clerks would still be earning a larger salary even after the raise. Almost all members of Congress agreed that a raise was necessary, although they argued over the exact amount and whether the new salary should go into effect immediately or at the start of the next Congress. In the end, however, President Madison signed a bill that gave Congress a $1,500 annual salary, effective immediately.

Despite all of the potentially controversial legislation passed (and rejected) by the Fourteenth Congress, the Compensation Act grabbed public attention. Newspaper editors seized on the pay raise as an exorbitant increase in salary (a doubling or more by their calculations) and reported it as a sign that Congress had lost touch with the people and turned their backs on republican simplicity. Constituents held meetings across the country and issued resolutions criticizing not only those who voted for the raise but also those members who took the money. Crowds in Georgia even burned their House Representatives in effigy. During the next elections, voters turned out to punish the congressmen who had passed it. Johnson later said that the "poor compensation bill excited more discontent than . . . any one measure of the Government, from its existence." He may have overdramatized the situation at bit, but the public reaction had indeed been fierce. Voters returned only around 30 percent of House members to Congress (usually in this period around 50 percent of incumbent House members won election to the next Congress). The eighty-one members who voted in favor of the law suffered especially heavy losses: only fifteen (18.5 percent) of them returned. Congress grudgingly repealed the act in the next session, after a long debate about whether representatives were to follow their own understanding as to what was good policy or whether they were to bow to the wishes and instructions of their constituents.

In hindsight, voters' reaction to the Compensation Act of 1816 underscored a growing restlessness in the electorate and disenchantment with political leaders who held themselves aloof from the people (while expecting the public to pay for their extravagant lifestyles). That disenchantment over time would come to focus on some of the signature legislative achievements of this period—the Second Bank of the United States and protective tariffs—and transform them into deeply divisive political issues. Combined with the sectional divisions that had plagued the Union from the start but would by 1819 show themselves to be fearsomely intractable, these issues would transform American politics in the mid-nineteenth century. Ironically, these forces that would reshape national politics and ultimately lead to the Civil War were unleashed by political leaders (from all sections of the country) who made a genuine effort to come together and develop the United States in the wake of the War of 1812.

by passing the **Tariff of 1816**. The new law raised tariff rates by an average of 25 percent on a wide range of goods, including iron, leather, hats, paper, and sugar, but the biggest beneficiaries were textile manufacturers. High-quality textiles, which were not widely produced in the U.S., only saw a modest tariff. Coarse cotton cloth (the kind that most American manufacturers produced and which Britain was dumping in the United States at very low prices), however, saw tariff rates exceeding 100 percent.

The final pillar of Clay's American System was building a national infrastructure to facilitate internal trade.

If the U.S. was to truly become independent of Europe, protecting American producers from European competition was only half of the battle. Producers would also have to be able to trade their goods throughout the United States. American economic independence could thus be achieved through the mutual dependence of agriculture, manufacturing, and commerce. Long-distance transportation in the country could be very difficult at the time, even in the long-settled sections of the Northeast. With growing settlements in the nation now spreading from Georgia to Maine and from the Atlantic Ocean to the Mississippi River, interstate trade was becoming increasingly problematic. For many Americans, trade remained local, or at best regional, due to the poor infrastructure. Henry Clay, along with fellow War Hawk John C. Calhoun, saw the perfect opportunity for the federal government to take the lead in building the necessary infrastructure to fulfill the American System. The terms of the recently passed bank charter called for the national bank to pay the federal government three $1.5 million bonuses in its first years of operation. Calhoun proposed a system of well-made roads and canals connecting the country to be paid for by that bonus, along with dividends from government-held shares in the bank. His proposal did not receive the same level of support that the national bank or the tariff had received, largely due to regional differences and jealousies, but he and Clay did manage to get the bill narrowly passed on March 1, 1817, just before the congressional session ended.

President James Madison vetoed the bill on March 3, his final day in office. While Madison had supported re-chartering the national bank, he believed that federal programs to build national infrastructure was too great an expansion of government power. The Bank bill at least had a precedent in the form of the first national bank. There was no precedent for federally funded **internal improvements**, and Madison believed that there was also no constitutional grant of power within either the commerce clause or the general welfare clause. The outgoing president did urge his successor, James Monroe, to recommend that Congress propose a constitutional amendment granting that power, but Clay and Calhoun knew the low potential for success there after the difficulty they had in getting the original bill passed.

A Nationalist Supreme Court

While some Hamiltonian ideals were reborn by Clay and Calhoun in the American System, those ideals had remained alive and well in the Supreme Court under **John Marshall**. The Chief Justice had established the role of the Court as the final arbiter of the Constitution (and the supremacy of the national government) in *Marbury v. Madison* (see Chapter 9). He had further extended the High Court's authority to the review of state government actions when the Court overturned the repeal of the Yazoo land sales in *Fletcher v. Peck*. Even though those purchases had been proven to be the result of widespread bribery, Marshall argued that the state could not repeal the sales because that would violate the contract clause of the Constitution.

In 1812, Marshall gained an unlikely ally when James Madison appointed a former Republican congressman from Massachusetts, Joseph Story, to the Court. Like the Chief Justice, Story possessed a brilliant legal mind and over the next twenty years would ultimately write more decisions than any justice other than Marshall. Their discussions of cases before the Court served to sharpen their decisions. More importantly, Story and Marshall agreed on most legal positions.

The first decision written by Story, *Martin v. Hunter's Lessee* in 1816, strengthened the position of the Supreme Court, and the national government with regard to state governments. The Court had previously invalidated a Virginia law allowing for the confiscation and sale of land of British loyalists after the American Revolution as being in violation of federal law, in particular, the Jay Treaty, which promised the return of that land. The highest court in Virginia, the Virginia Court of Appeals, claimed that the Supreme Court lacked jurisdiction and refused to obey the decision. In the *Martin* case, Story argued that not only did the Court have the final word on constitutional issues raised in state court cases, but that the Constitution was a compact of the people rather than the states. Ten years earlier such an assertion would have raised alarm in the ranks of the Republican Party, but in 1816 the nation was riding the tide of nationalism so the scant criticism it received was meek.

In 1819, the Court further upheld the view that states could not take actions that undermined previously established contracts (as it had in *Fletcher*) in **Dartmouth College v. Woodward**. Dartmouth had been created as a private college under a charter granted by George III in 1769. The school continued to operate as a private institution until 1816 when the state of New Hampshire changed some terms of the charter effectively placing Dartmouth under state government control. Once again relying on the contract clause of the Constitution, Marshall argued that the original charter was a contract; therefore, the state could not take an action that would impair its terms. With businessmen at the time looking to limit the risks of expensive endeavors, some were asking states for charters of incorporation. If newly elected state governments could rewrite the terms of those charters, the practice could potentially stifle economic growth. Further, because some of those corporations chartered by states were canal, road, and bridge building companies (in the absence of federal support), such actions could have dealt a serious blow to the goals of Clay's American System.

Soon after the Dartmouth case, the Court handed down a decision involving the national bank in **McCulloch v. Maryland** that served to strengthen national supremacy over state governments while more directly supporting Clay's American System. The Bank had established a branch in Baltimore, Maryland issuing bank notes and performing other banking functions within

Table 10.1	**Major Decisions of the Marshall Court**	
Date	Case	Significance of Decision
1803	*Marbury v. Madison*	Introduced the doctrine of judicial review
1810	*Fletcher v. Peck*	Protected sanctity of legal contracts from impairment by the states; first time a state law ruled unconstitutional by the U.S. Supreme Court
1819	*Dartmouth College v. Woodward*	Held that private corporate charters are protected from state government interference
1819	*McCulloch v. Maryland*	Upheld the constitutionality of the National Bank, accepting the principle of implied powers; forbade the states from impeding valid constitutional exercises of federal power
1821	*Cohens v. Virginia*	State supreme court decisions in criminal law issues subject to High Court review; asserted the supremacy of federal law over state law, citing the Supremacy Clause of the Constitution
1824	*Gibbons v. Ogden*	States denied concurrent power to regulate interstate commerce with the federal government

the state but immediately found itself under attack from Jeffersonians who opposed its operation. They pushed a law through the legislature that imposed a tax on notes of all banks not chartered in the state of Maryland. Their motive was clear, as that branch of the national bank was the only bank operating within the state that did not have a charter from the state. When James W. McCulloch, the branch manager, appealed the ensuing fine to the Maryland Supreme Court, that court ruled that the bank was unconstitutional so Maryland did not have to respect its charter from the national government. John Marshall first argued that Congress had the power to establish the Bank based on the necessary and proper clause. In fact, he expanded Hamilton's reasoning of that clause by declaring that an act by the federal government was constitutional if it was taken in the course of the government's constitutional duties and it did not otherwise violate the Constitution. In addition to upholding the concept of implied powers, he also further upheld national supremacy over state governments. In reiterating Joseph Story's view of the Constitution as a compact of the people rather than the states, he also argued that state governments could not take actions that would undermine or harm the federal government, and the national bank was an agency of the national government. Excessive taxes could harm the national bank—as Marshall writes in the decision, "the power to tax is the power to destroy."

Another important case involved interstate trade. One primary hope of supporters of Clay's American Sys-

tem was to develop a system of national commerce tying the nation together in mutual economic interdependence. State governments, however, could undermine that dream if they restricted the flow of interstate trade. Just such a situation developed in New York. In an effort to promote the building and operation of steamboats, an expensive undertaking, the state of New York granted a monopoly on the operation of steamboats within the state. Eventually, that license was transferred to Aaron Ogden. When a competing steamboat operator, Thomas Gibbons, carried goods into New York City, Ogden sued in New York courts, which found in Ogden's favor and issued injunctions against Gibbons prohibiting him from engaging in trade into New York City. Gibbons subsequently appealed to the U.S. Supreme Court. In Gibbons v. Ogden, the Court clarified the commerce clause of the Constitution, giving Congress authority to regulate any trade that crosses state lines. This was an especially important decision coming at the dawn of an era of canal and road building that promised to better connect the commerce of the nation. If states could restrict trade (even if that was not their intent as in the case of steamboat operation in New York), that could undermine national efforts to expand domestic trade. Marshall ensured that would not be the case.

The Challenge of Transportation

Henry Clay's desire to aid the development of transportation systems through the federal government was a response to a serious impediment to the economic nationalism that he sought. Travel, even over relatively short distances, remained slow and difficult. The Northeast had the best road system in the nation. In 1790, the trip from Boston to New York took four to six days depending on the weather. By 1816, road improvements had reduced the trip's travel; time down to two days. With poorer roads elsewhere, travel outside of that region was more difficult. The West especially faced problems, as people there often had to travel over little more than narrow dirt paths. As hard as it was for people to move over those roads and trails, it was even harder to move goods. State governments tried to address the problem by granting charters to private stock companies for the purpose of building turnpikes (the best-made roads of the day), granting those companies the right to charge tolls. This type of public-private partnership did expand the road system across the East and even into the West, but travel was still slow with a stagecoach unable to travel much faster than six to eight miles per hour under the best conditions.

Due to the difficulty of travel on poor roads, especially west of the Appalachian Mountains, Westerners turned to waterways as a means of trade. If one could get to the Ohio and Mississippi Rivers, they could carry their goods to New Orleans by flatboat. The ability to engage in commerce downriver, however, did not dramatically improve trade between western farmers and eastern cities. In 1800, it took fifty days for goods leaving the Ohio River Valley by flatboat to reach New York by way of New Orleans at a cost that was greater than shipping goods to England. Because flatboats only traveled with the current, most Westerners trading through New Orleans sold their flatboats there and traveled back to their homes on foot. Some skilled boatmen used a variety of techniques to make it back up river with goods, but even then it was a three- or four-month trip. Thus, trade could flow out of the region on flatboats, but it trickled back in.

The steamboat, developed in 1807 by **Robert Fulton**, dramatically changed internal and coastal trade in America making it both faster and cheaper. By the 1820s, trade goods could be moved from the Ohio River Valley to New York in half the time it took by flatboat and sail. Steamboats also allowed trade to flow with equal ease and speed upriver. In 1817, a steamboat made the trip from New Orleans to Louisville, Kentucky in 25 days, more than three times as fast as the most experienced flatboat operators. Within a decade, the trip took only eight days. By then, the region was bustling with commercial activity.

Henry Clay certainly had to be pleased by the extent to which the West could now engage in the merging national economy, but his satisfaction must have been bittersweet. His own city of Lexington, Kentucky went into economic decline with the arrival of the steamboat in the West and never fully recovered. Central Kentucky farmers who had traded in Lexington now looked to Louisville and Cincinnati where they could connect directly with the steamboat trade. More important to the committed nationalist, with Madison's veto of the bill to build a national infrastructure to serve national interests, that infrastructure was now being built by state governments to serve state interests. Clay never gave up on that vision and would continue to push for all three pillars of his American System. (For the Erie Canal and the post-War of 1812 canal boom, see Chapter 12.)

THE MARKET REVOLUTION

During the first half of the nineteenth century, the United States was transformed from a nation relying largely on barter for trade (with the exception of eastern cities and cash crop farmers to a certain extent) to a budding capitalist nation, a change known as the Market Revolution. In some ways, Clay's American System was responding to economic changes already underway in the nations. As the United States emerged from the American Revolution, social, political, and economic life for most Americans was locally based. Economic activity in those rural communities relied on barter, with little need for money. Farms were largely self-sufficient, producing a wide range of crops and other farm products, bartering for most other things that the family needed. This system began to change slowly in the 1790s and early 1800s as men imbued with entrepreneurial spirit engaged in risk-taking in an effort to increase their wealth. Among the risks that they undertook were those involving investments in manufacturing, providing the necessary capital to jumpstart infant industries, especially those looking to rural America for buyers of their goods. With Americans increasingly beginning to conduct trade beyond their local communities in regional (and ultimately national and international) markets, barter no longer worked as an economic system. A medium of exchange that both parties engaging in trade could use and could trust became necessary, and that vehicle was money. No wonder that the first aspect of Clay's American System to be addressed was a national bank, whose notes would establish a stable medium of exchange for trade.

Northeastern manufacturing and the engagement of rural farmers in the market system went hand-in-hand. As manufacturing increased, so did the need for workers, followed by the growth of cities. With large numbers of factory workers living in the cities, a growing demand for food occurred. At the same time, rural farmers needed a means of acquiring money to buy the goods that eastern producers were looking to sell. The two needs met as farmers could sell surplus crops and other farm products, and then buy manufactured goods with the money that they gained by selling their excess farm production. Some farmers even began to expand production of certain crops because of the prices that they could command, further connecting them into the market system.

In addition to entrepreneurial spirit, an equally big factor driving the Market Revolution was innovation—new ways of doing things and, especially, inventions. Many of those inventions were related to transportation (such as the steamboat), and farming (like the cotton gin). As farmers became more productive and transportation became more reliable, many had become fully engaged in the market system (see Chapter 12 for a fuller discussion).

The Transformation of New England

As the nation expanded westward beyond the Mississippi River during the first half of the nineteenth century, the impact of the Market Revolution was uneven because of poor quality roads and limited routes for transportation. One region where the hand of the Market Revolution could clearly be seen was New England. Clay and other supporters who desired government support for the market economy must have been heartened by what they saw there, as specialized agriculture and manufacturing had become interdependent. This development suggested to them that, with government support of the American System, change could happen throughout the rest of the country in a rapid and orderly manner.

New England had a diversified economy throughout much of the colonial period, but the majority of its citizens were farmers. Despite the region's rocky soil, New England farmers engaged in mixed agriculture, growing a wide variety of crops (with grains being their primary crops) along with raising livestock and other farm animals. They also sometimes engaged in the production of other goods to supplement the family economy.

By the early nineteenth century, New England was changing dramatically. The rise of manufacturing, with an increasing number of non-agricultural workers in growing cities, finally gave subsistence farmers in the region a market to which they could sell farm produce. The combination of depleted soil and increasing competition from western grain farms made it difficult for them to rely on grains as a marketable commodity, leading many farmers to begin specializing in particular commodities. For many, this meant either livestock or perishable and bulky goods (for example, chicken, dairy products, fruits, and potatoes) that could not be easily or cheaply transported from the West. Farming and manufacturing had truly become interconnected. Farmers produced fresh produce and other farm goods for the growing urban population. Meanwhile, shoe and textile manufacturers bought leather and wool from cattle and sheep farmers. In return, farmers could now buy cheap, manufactured products that they previously would have produced on the farm or obtained through barter.

Many farm families still had to supplement the family income with other forms of production, but here they also looked to the shoe and other industries. While cotton mills began appearing in New England towns by the 1790s, most other manufacturing (like shoes, hats, and brooms) before the 1820s was performed in the homes of farm families during their spare time. While this practice did not replace farming as their primary source of support, it supplemented the economic benefits that they gained from farming. This means of production was

Wood engraving of slaves using the first cotton gin.

known as the **putting-out system**, whereby farm families produced one part of an item. One family would produce one portion of the finished product (they might cut soles for shoes to predetermined sizes) while other families would produce other important parts. Since none of the farmers needed to be a skilled shoemaker, the system provided them with an opportunity to do unskilled work to supplement the family economy while still maintaining their occupation (and identity) as a farmer. The distributor (usually a merchant) of the finished products also benefited because he could pay low wages for the work, as it did not require skilled labor. By the 1820s, however, factories increasingly replaced the putting out system as they gave distributors greater control over all aspects of production. Farmers either had to find a way to supplement family income or they would have to leave their farms and join the factory workforce.

Northern Manufacturing

Thomas Jefferson had feared that manufacturing would undermine his vision of an agrarian republic, but by 1820 he saw that domestic manufacturing could have a productive and vital role for the future of the United States. He had previously believed that Europe could supply all of America's needs for manufactured goods, with the sale of crops to Europe providing American farmers with the money needed to buy those European items. The War of 1812, however, had shown the need for domestic manufactures when the United States could not trade with Europe. Moreover, Jefferson's fear of industry leading to large cities seemed, at least at the time, to be unfounded. The water-powered cotton mills being built in New England during the 1790s and early 1800s were much smaller than British factories and were spread across the region rather than being congregated in large cities. Twenty-five years earlier, Jefferson and Alexander Hamilton had feuded largely because of their competing visions for America. Now it seemed as if their ideals, to a certain extent, might be able to coexist.

When Hamilton began working with other Founders to create a stronger national government, he envisioned a nation that included manufacturing. There was no certainty in 1787, however, that America would be able to develop anything besides small-scale manufacturing through the putting-out system, as the British possessed the most advanced knowledge about building and operating factories—and they were not sharing the information. They even passed laws to protect that knowledge, forbidding those employed in British factories from leaving the country for three years after their employment stopped. An Englishman, **Samuel Slater**, had been employed in

cotton mills since he was ten years old. At the age of twenty-one, he decided to head for the United States, having heard of some American cities offering rewards for the development of a successful factory. He was also well aware of English laws against the very sort of industrial espionage that he was about to undertake. As such, he memorized as much as he could about the design and operation of the factory.

When Slater arrived in the United States in 1790, he became acquainted with a wealthy Rhode Island merchant, Moses Brown, who provided the financial support for Slater to build the first successful cotton mill in the United States. It was smaller than the large factories of England and powered by water (England was beginning to shift to the newly invented power loom), but it proved effective in introducing textile manufacturing to the United States. Slater went into business with Brown and built several more cotton mills before establishing his own business using cotton mills, as well as producing the parts for other entrepreneurs interested in opening their own factories.

The establishment of Slater's first factory in Pawtucket led to the migration of a number of destitute New Englanders looking for work. Slater tried to address the problem of a poor community building up around a factory with the introduction of the **Rhode Island System**. Since the factories were small in comparison to British factories (none employed more than 100 workers), they did not need to be located in large cities to find a suitable workforce. In fact, most lived along waterways in rural areas where small villages developed around the factories.

Located in Pawtucket, Rhode Island, Slater Mill was the first cotton mill in the United States.

Generally, men worked on their own land (or on rented land) while women and children worked in the mills. In some cases, entire families were employed by the mills. In this way, Slater and other factory owners were simply centralizing the traditional function of the putting out system. This system of manufacture would remain in place through much of New England until the 1820s when factories began to adopt the power loom as well as new business techniques.

The Waltham System

In 1810, a wealthy merchant from Newburyport, Massachusetts, **Francis Cabot Lowell**, embarked on a two-year trip with his family to Scotland and England. While there, he toured factory towns and spent much of his time observing the factories, even arranging to be given factory tours. He also asked many questions. The British textile industry had changed dramatically since Samuel Slater had left there two decades earlier. In 1812, Lowell returned to the United States bringing with him knowledge that would reshape the American textile industry. Building a new factory that used British technology would be expensive. To accomplish his goal, he looked to the way that states were chartering corporations to undertake expensive projects like road and canal building. He created a corporation with the financial support of family and fellow merchants (at $1000 each), calling it the Boston Manufacturing Company. Lowell and his fellow shareholders became known as the Boston Associates. As they began construction of their first mill

in Waltham, Massachusetts, Lowell hired Paul Moody to set up the machinery in the new factory and build a power loom based on Lowell's descriptions (Lowell and Moody were awarded a patent for that design). By the 1820s, the factory became so successful that the Boston Associates expanded operations with an even larger factory complex on the Merrimack River and named the city of Lowell in honor Francis Lowell who had died five years earlier.

In addition to introducing the power loom, the Boston Associates also developed a new system of factory labor known as the **Waltham System**. Lowell had been struck by the harsh conditions in English factories. He was also sensitive to concerns that large factories, rather than the small rural factories centered within factory villages, would lead to the development of English-style cities with their inherent social problems. The Boston Associates mitigated those potential problems by composing their workforce almost entirely of young, single women. They recruited their workers, who became known as "**Lowell Girl**s," from rural New England farms where their labor was no longer needed. The girls were supervised and had to follow a strict code of conduct. If they were illiterate when they arrived at the mills, they were taught to read and write. All of the girls were encouraged to read and attend public lectures, which may have provided the encouragement that led the girls to begin publishing their own magazine with poetry, essays, and other musings.

In addition to ensuring the morality of the girls, the system ensured that the mills would get moral workers.

The putting-out system could not match the productivity of the new factories.

FROM CRAFTSMEN TO WORKERS

By the early 1800's, the market revolution was beginning to change life and work in America in dramatic ways. Nowhere is that change more apparent than in shoemaking. Shoemakers, known as cordwainers, were independent craftsmen in the 18th century who sold to local customers usually on a per order basis. By late in the century, cordwainers were making shoes by the order, known as "bespoke work," but also beginning to produce shoes to have on hand in their shops, which were known as "shop work." Those master craftsmen also employed apprentices (those learning the trade) and journeymen (those looking to improve their skills with the hope of one day becoming a master craftsman).

"Bespoke work" and "shop work" was generally of the same quality and journeymen were usually paid the same for either type of production – although journeymen would also produce lesser-quality shoes that they could sell in the public market to people too poor to buy shoes in the shop. In the late 1700's, masters and journeymen had similar interests in upholding standards of quality that prevented competition of inferior quality shoes to maintain the prices masters could charge and journeymen could expect to receive for each pair of shoes. By the early 1800's those common interests, and the relationship between master and journeyman, began to change.

Some master cordwainers, like John Bedford of Philadelphia, began contracting for sale of shoes in distant markets. In 1799, Bedford had excess shoes on hand so he travelled to Charleston, Norfolk, and Richmond to sell off that stock. He returned with $4,000 worth of orders. As Bedford and other master craftsmen began to look at selling shoes to distant markets, they were less concerned about the quality of those shoes and were unwilling to pay the same rates for this new "market" work that they paid for "bespoke" and "shop" work, even though it took journeymen nearly the same amount of time to make each different type of shoe.

Journeymen cordwainers had already begun to sense differing interests from masters when they organized the Federal Society of Journeymen Cordwainers in 1794. In response to the development of "market" work, at lower rates, the journeymen went on strike in 1805. The strike lasted nearly seven weeks. It ended when master cordwainers, including Bedford, pressured the city to charge the journeymen. In November 1805, eight journeymen were indicted for forming illegal combinations to force higher wages from the masters. The journeymen defended themselves with the ideals of republicanism but were found guilty in a precedent that was not overturned until 1842, making union organization difficult in America during that time.

By the 1810's, the shoe industry was moving farther away from the local shop that highlighted shoe production in the 1700's. Some master cordwainers with large amounts of capital, as well as other businessmen with no experience in shoemaking, began to contract with master cordwainers to produce large amounts of shoes for export to other markets, especially in the U.S. South and the Caribbean. This further removed the journeymen from consumers as now they were producing shoes for a master, who sold to a retailer, who then shipped those goods to distant markets. Some of these large shoe retailers even further undercut the ability of the journeymen to make a decent living by resorting to convict labor to produce shoes. At the time of the 1805 strike, journeymen were paid a standard rate of $2.75 per pair of boots. As a result of the changing nature of the shoe business, and the shift from journeyman to factory worker, they were paid just over $1.12 per pair of boots. As journeymen, they had an expectation that, through hard work and by refining their skills, they could one day become master craftsmen. That change was not lost on the journeymen. One of them, William Heighton, began publishing the Mechanics' Free Press and helped organize the Mechanics' Union of Trade Associations. Journeymen cordwainers were now creating unions and identifying as workers.

Because the girls would be expected to leave their factory jobs within about five years or less, a permanent laboring poor due to a permanent work force would not develop in the city. Finally, the company owners would not have to deal with labor unions and strikes because their labor force would be turning over so frequently.

Not all of the ideals of the Waltham System came to fruition. Working in the mills gave the girls a sense of independence and self-worth. Rather than return to the farms, many stayed in the cities carving out new lives there. Those who did return to their rural communities exhibited a sense of independence of which their mothers would not have dared. Some even remained in the mills, realizing that it was their work in the mills that gave them that independence. To the chagrin of the Boston Associates, they identified with each other as workers and went out on strike a number of times. They must have especially regretted educating the girls when one girl wrote, "When you sell your product you retain your person. But when you sell your labor, you sell yourself." Farming men largely saw the prospect of factory work as degrading but for the factory girls it was liberating.

POLITICAL AND DIPLOMATIC NATIONALISM

The Federalist Party had assured its own demise at the Hartford Convention (see Chapter 9). While the party ran a candidate for president in 1816, Rufus King from New York, Federalist politicians had already begun switching parties. For his part, King remained a Federalist. He ran for re-election to the U.S. Senate in 1819 as a Federalist and won, but in 1816 he was thoroughly routed for the presidency by **James Monroe**, losing by a margin of 183-34 in the Electoral College. Monroe ran unopposed in 1820 and won all but one electoral vote (when one elector refused to vote for Monroe because it would make him a unanimous president like Washington). Certainly some Republicans were upset by the so-called Virginia Dynasty, with Monroe being the third president in a row from that state and fourth out of five total. Republicans chafed at the use of the antiquated caucus system at a time when the nation was beginning to look toward more democratic processes. Monroe sought union rather than division. He planned to appoint cabinet officers from East, West, North, and South (failing to appoint one from the West when Henry Clay refused a position as Secretary of War). In his inaugural address, he endorsed the building of roads and canals (with constitutional sanction) and protection for domestic manufacturing. Thereafter, he went on a national tour of the United States, making a special point of traveling to New England where some Federalists had not fully accepted the reality of their party's future. Monroe spoke as if he wanted to be the president of all the people and many in New England appreciated his gesture of reconciliation. One Federalist newspaper in Boston suggested that the president's visit had ushered in an "Era of Good Feelings."

President Monroe certainly benefited from the spirit of nationalism that flooded the nation in the years after the War of 1812, but he also used it to gain universal support for his presidency and the government—opening old political wounds might bring that enthusiasm crashing down. Monroe's cabinet reflected the president's effort at representing different regions and ideals with the men he chose to fill those posts. With Clay declining Monroe's offer of Secretary of State, Monroe chose two Southerners, John Calhoun (Secretary of War) and William Crawford (Secretary of Treasury), but Calhoun was a strong nationalist while Crawford adhered to traditional Jeffersonian views regarding states' rights. His Postmaster General was John McLean from Ohio, a close associate of Calhoun. To represent northern interests, he opted against nominating a Federalist, instead choosing a former Federalist who also happened to be the son of former president John Adams—**John Quincy Adams**—who had split with the Federalist Party in 1808 but still embraced many of its views. Adams accepted Monroe's request to serve as Secretary of State. Eventually, he would become the most important member of Monroe's cabinet and one of the best Secretaries of State in U.S. history. With Adams, McLean, and Calhoun, Monroe's administration leaned more towards nationalism than to traditional Jeffersonian views, a perspective most evident in foreign policy.

Rapprochement with England

The War of 1812 signaled to leaders in Britain and the United States that a strong friendship was probably in the best interest of both nations. Monroe and Adams quickly moved to iron out what differences they could with the English, especially with regard to Canada. There was still tension on the border and competition over use of the Great Lakes could potentially ignite hostilities. In April 1817, the U.S. reached an accord with Britain, the Rush-Bagot Agreement, which began gradual naval disarmament on the Great Lakes. The deal also lessened the potential for a costly naval arms race between the countries.

The second agreement with Britain, the **Convention of 1818**, dealt with a number of pressing issues. One that appeased New Englanders involved protection for American fishing rights off Newfoundland and Labrador that had been guaranteed by the Treaty of Paris of 1783, which ended the American Revolution. The most important part of the treaty, however, dealt with the border between the United States and British territory in North America. Britain agreed to fix the boundary line between Louisiana and Canada at the 49th parallel from the western boundary of the Northwest Territory to the Rocky Mountains, a border that was much more beneficial to the United States than to England.

One final issue involved the Oregon Country. British and American fur trading companies had set up operations there, but the numbers of Americans and Brits in the region was very sparse. During the War of 1812, the American fur trader, John Jacob Astor, had sold his business and his fort named Astoria to a Canadian concern for fear that it might be captured by the British and he would lose his entire investment. The Americans, however, made no mention of that fact and the nations had agreed that any decision with regard to Oregon would be postponed for ten years, allowing both nations to jointly occupy the region until then. The United States had negotiated with the British as an equal and had won important concessions from them.

Spain and Florida

Spanish control of Florida had long concerned southern Americans. The territory had become a lure for runaway slaves who often settled in maroon communities near (or even among) Seminole Indians. At times, they would cross the border into the United States in order to attack American settlements. The Spanish colony had also become home to pirates and other ne'er-do-wells. Even more problematic was Spanish control of West Florida, which cut off river trade into the Gulf of Mexico east of New Orleans. That situation was precisely why Jefferson's commissioners to France in 1803 were tasked with acquiring New Orleans and West Florida. While still working to settle issues with Britain, the Monroe administration increasingly focused its efforts on Florida.

Tensions had been rising along the Florida border by the fall of 1817. In November 1817, American General Edmund Gaines, in an effort to force Creek Indians off land ceded to the United States in the Treaty of Fort Jackson, burned a Creek village located there. On November 30, Creeks from the village, aided by runaway slaves and Seminole Indians, struck back hard. They took forty U.S. soldiers and eleven of their dependents into Florida before killing most of them. Two weeks later, Secretary of War Calhoun instructed General Gaines to demand reparations from the Seminoles (the administration did not distinguish between runaway slaves and Indians in Florida, calling them all Seminoles). If they refused, he was to pursue them into Florida and attack. Gaines was told, however, not to threaten the Spanish forts there. Within weeks, **Andrew Jackson** was chosen to lead the mission instead of Gaines after the general was ordered to deal with troublesome pirates in eastern Florida.

On January 6, 1818, before Jackson knew of his own appointment, he sent a letter to President Monroe suggesting that Gaines's force could easily take the small Spanish garrison in Pensacola, delivering Florida to the United States with little trouble (approval of which, Jackson suggested, could be delivered to him secretly through a Tennessee congressman). Monroe did not respond to Jackson's letter but had composed another just one week earlier, after Monroe and Calhoun had decided to send Jackson on the mission. The document offered few specifics, but suggest that he undertake vigorous action. On April 6, Jackson led a force of 1,000 volunteers along with a force of friendly Creek Indians into Florida. After first seizing a Spanish fort to serve as a supply depot, Jackson moved on the Seminoles, easily defeating those who had not fled after detecting the approaching army. During the course of his foray, Jackson also found two British traders (one was also a Royal marine) who Jackson believed to be aiding and encouraging the Seminoles. After returning to the Spanish fort, he court-martialed the two Brits and ordered them to be executed. In May, Jackson moved on the Spanish capital of Pensacola. After briefly exchanging artillery fire, the Spanish governor surrendered. Jackson then appointed a territorial governor and collector of U.S. customs.

President Monroe may have encouraged Jackson's actions in Florida (the very choice of Jackson ensured that the mission would be carried out aggressively), but he was not prepared to deal with the firestorm it created with both Spain and Britain. Monroe gathered his cabinet to discuss a course of action. Secretary of War Calhoun, Jackson's direct superior, recommended court-martialing Jackson for disobeying orders. William Crawford and William Wirt agreed with Calhoun. The only member of the cabinet to oppose such drastic action toward Jackson was Secretary of State John Quincy Adams. He had no love for Jackson and believed that the general was prone to rash action. In this case, however, Jackson's actions in Florida could serve Adams in negotiations with Spain. Adams would argue that Jackson only went into Florida because Spain did not have a force there sufficient to control a lawless population that was wreaking havoc along the American border. That Spanish force was so weak that it surrendered without much of a fight. As such, if Spain was unwilling to place a force in Florida sufficient to control the population of the colony, they should sell the territory to the United States. Monroe subsequently announced that Jackson had exceeded his authority but that he had done so out of patriotism and based on credible information. That mild rebuke was much less than the censure he would have received if Monroe pursued Calhoun's course of action.

While Adams saw opportunity in Jackson's actions, there was still the potential of international outrage from governments in Britain and Spain. The protests from England, however, were little more than a whimper. The British had benefited greatly from the re-opening of trade with America after the War of 1812. With preparations for the Convention of 1818 under way, the British did not want to do anything that would undermine improving relations between the nations, especially over a couple of traders who were probably more rogues than gentlemen. Spanish anger also cooled when Monroe quickly restored Spanish control of Pensacola and the fort that Jackson had seized.

Adams then sent instructions to George Erving, the American ambassador to Spain, blaming the Florida incident on Spanish weakness and British meddling. This letter, however, was more for public consumption than for Erving's eyes. The Secretary of State made sure that

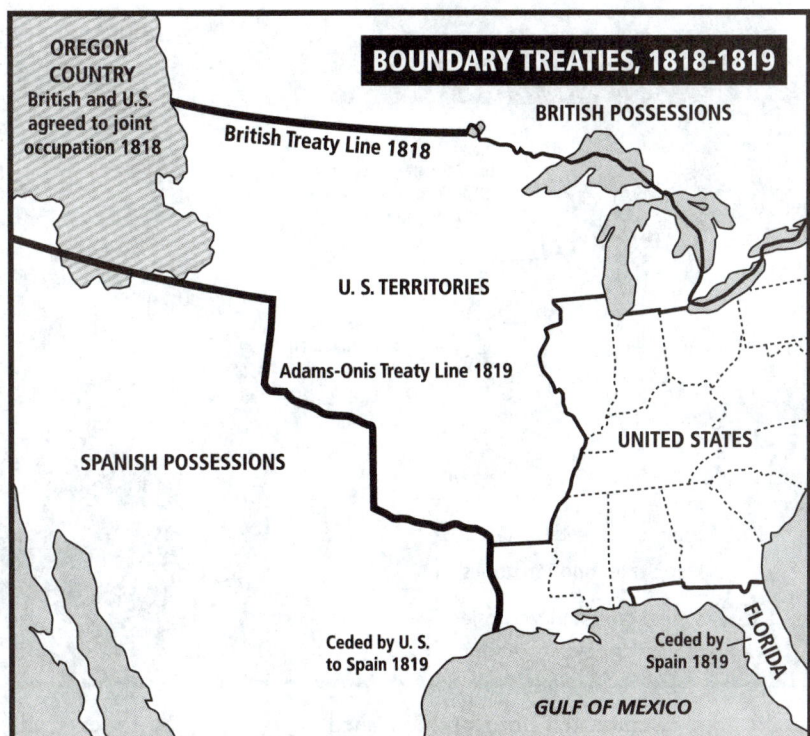

Map 10.1 Transcontinental Treaty, or the Adams-Onís Treaty

Britain, Spain, and the American public became aware of its contents. It stated that while the U.S. was graciously returning the Spanish territories that Jackson had taken, it might not do the same in the future. Adams also felt confident that he could deal strongly with Spain while that country was in the midst of attempting to suppress rebellions in its Latin American colonies. Florida was clearly of less importance to Spain than Mexico and its Caribbean colonies.

The Spanish Minister, Luis de Onís, returned to Washington in October 1818 to meet with Adams over the Florida incident. He had already been instructed to get the best deal possible for Florida while also settling disputes over the boundary between Louisiana and Spanish territory that bordered it. The issue of Florida was settled quickly with Spain ceding Florida to the United States and the U.S. paying off the $5 million dollars in claims that American citizens held against the Spanish government. The Louisiana border question was a bit trickier for Adams. He initially held to original American claims of the Colorado River, which would have given the U.S. much of eastern Texas, land that southern cotton growers were already eyeing. After months of negotiation over boundary lines in Texas, the Great Plains, and the Rocky Mountains, Adams suggested that the United States might be willing to accept the Spanish boundary of Texas at the Sabine River if Spain was willing to clarify the northern boundary of California and relinquish any Spanish claims north of that boundary. Onís quickly jumped at the offer, and the treaty was signed on February 22, 1819.

For Southerners, angry over what they viewed as the loss of Texas, Adams had traded Texas for claims to Oregon—criticism that was wrong on two counts. First, the cession of Florida was not an isolated event, but rather, integral to the treaty as a whole. Spain was not willing to cede Florida unless the U.S. settled the Louisiana boundary question. Second, Adams was well aware that the Spanish Empire was in the process of crumbling with its Latin American colonies declaring and winning their independence. While Adams could not know it at the time, Mexico would win its independence in the same year that the treaty was finally signed. The Secretary fully believed that as American expansion continued, sparsely settled neighboring territories would fall into American hands just like ripe fruit falling from a tree. The same was not true for Oregon, which lay on the western side of the Rocky Mountains. The claims to Oregon that the United States made connected the nation across the continent, hence the name often applied to this treaty, the **Transcontinental Treaty,** or the Adams-Onís Treaty made it a clear manifestation of the nationalist foreign policy of Monroe and Adams.

Before Monroe left office, he would produce a statement written by Adams that extended the ideals of a nationalist foreign policy to the entire Western Hemisphere. As Spain's empire crumbled, the king worked to establish a coalition that would help Spain restore its authority over the region. If Spain failed, a European land grab would likely occur which would almost certainly end in conflict between those nations (and the fledgling republics they

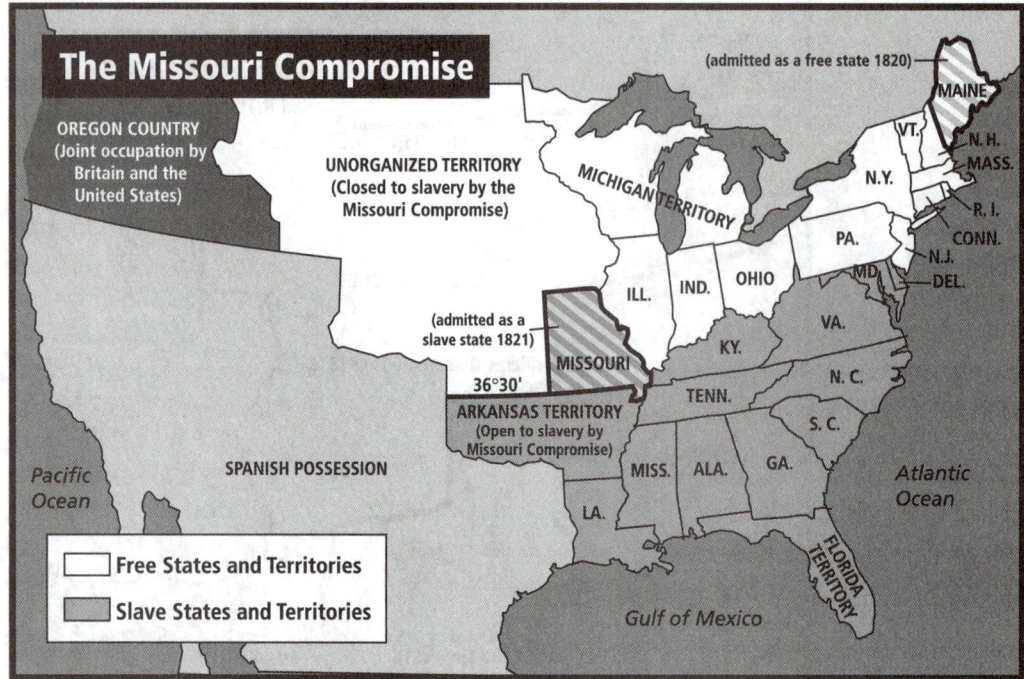

Map 10.2 The Missouri Compromise

NATIONALISM QUESTIONED

The Panic of 1819

might hope to colonize), bringing bloodshed along with vast political, social, and economic disruptions. The worst possibility of all would be if Britain began to covet new colonies in Latin America. Thus, in July 1822, the United States officially recognized a number of Latin American republics that had declared independence from Spain, with recognition of others following shortly afterward. Adams was especially pleased by British support for that action, further emboldening Adams and Monroe. Monroe's State of the Union message of December 1823 clarified the policy they had already been working to establish. Known as the **Monroe Doctrine**, the president declared that the colonies of the Western Hemisphere to be off limits to future European colonization. While the United States did not have the power to enforce the doctrine, the support of Britain provided at least some authority.

The nationalistic euphoria rising in the years after the War of 1812, along with the booming economy, led many Americans to try to take advantage of new opportunities, with the greatest for many average Americans being the abundance of public land for sale by the federal government. The national bank had been chartered and could offer loans for the purchase of that land, which could be repaid with any bank notes. By that time there were over 200 state banks in operation, more than double the number when the charter of the first Bank of the United States expired in 1811. One of the main purposes of the new national bank was to informally regulate those state banks. The main way that they could do so was to demand specie (gold or silver) from those banks whenever the national bank came into possession of a state bank's notes. This usually occurred when the federal treasury deposited a wide variety of notes from Americans who used them to pay taxes or to make land purchases. The national bank, however, tended to establish loose standards with regard to that practice leading to the money supply becoming severely inflated. With many of the eighteen national bank branches in the West overextending their specie reserves to support land sales, public land debt rose from $3 million in 1815 to $17 million in 1818. Thus, the nation faced two inflationary problems at once—in paper money and in land.

Exacerbating these problems was a dramatic drop in crop prices, especially cotton, which fell to almost half its previous value from 1818 to 1819. Part of this was due to the efforts of British manufacturers to replace American cotton with cotton from India. While the Indian cotton ultimately proved unsuitable for manufacturers in England, the damage to the American economy was already done. The decline in prices for American agriculture in Europe, however, was not limited to cotton. American agriculture sales to Europe had boomed after the war as Europeans tried to recover from the devastation of two decades of warfare. By 1819, European agricultural production was up and demand for American crops declined.

With the economic situation already unstable, a new national bank president, Langdon Cheves, tried to bring the excessive supply of bank notes under control. He adopted a tight money policy that saved the bank from failure but deepened the economic crisis known as the **Panic of 1819** as the number of bank notes in circulation dramatically declined. State banks failed and farmers who had borrowed heavily to purchase public land could not pay their annual installments. The nationalist faith that helped to undergird support for the second national bank was shaken. While the bank saw increasing criticism as a result of the crisis, it was not all bad for Henry Clay's American System, as support for both tariffs and internal improvements increased in response to the panic.

The Missouri Crisis

While the nation had been divided by party since the 1790s, much of these political oppositions had their roots in sectional differences. The demise of the two-party system did nothing to calm those tendencies. While Southerners pointed to economic and social differences, at its base, the primary cause of those sectional differences was slavery. Even at the height of postwar nationalism, southern opponents of Clay's American System saw threats to the institution of slavery in any expansion of federal government power. Western settlement hastened in the postwar years. By 1819, Missouri had a large enough population to apply for statehood.

Until this time, there had been little debate about the expansion of slavery in conjunction with the entry of new states into the Union. For the states entering from the Northwest Territory, there was no expectation of slavery. The Northwest Ordinance, which prohibited slavery in the region, was viewed as settled law. Moreover, many of the people moving into the area had migrated from northern states where slavery had either ended or was being ended through the process of gradual emancipation. Further, most Southerners who migrated into the region were yeoman farmers from Virginia and Kentucky who did not own any slaves. Meanwhile, little debate existed over whether slavery should expand into Alabama and Mississippi, as it was widely understood that slavery would expand with cotton production. Moreover, the entry of Indiana, Illinois, Mississippi, and Alabama in rapid succession between 1816 and 1819 brought two slave states and two free states into the Union, maintaining a seemingly natural balance.

Missouri's desire to enter the Union, however, raised a number of issues that the nation had not previously faced. There were no predetermined assumptions about the status of slavery in Missouri, which was settled not only by Northerners from Ohio, Indiana, and Illinois, but also by Southerners from Virginia, Tennessee, and Kentucky. Missouri's statehood also raised the issue of limits on the expansion of slavery. In the years after the Revolution, southern statesmen like Thomas Jefferson believed that slavery would and should end at some point. With slavery potentially expanding across the Mississippi River, it now seemed that the end of slavery was much farther away.

Rancorous debates in Congress, raising seemingly every sectional issue of the previous two decades, continued from December 1819 to March of 1820. Henry Clay worked to achieve passage of a bill that became known as the **Missouri Compromise**. Missouri would be admitted as a slave state based on the wishes of the state's residents as voiced by the recently adopted state constitution. To appease Northerners and maintain the relative balance that existed during the most recent admissions of new states, Maine was separated from Massachusetts and admitted as a free state. Finally, to prevent another debate each time that a new territory sought admission into the Union as a state, all land north of latitude 36° 30' within the Louisiana Purchase territory would be free of slavery (with the exception of Missouri). Clay's political skill had held the nation together, and the Missouri Compromise promised to settle the issue of slavery for the foreseeable future, but sectional tensions would not die so easily.

THE END OF THE ERA OF GOOD FEELINGS

If the period after the end of the War of 1812 was ever an Era of Good Feelings, by 1824 that era was clearly coming to an end. Faith in the national bank and economic nationalism was shaken by the Panic of 1819. Old sectional issues were revived anew with great vigor, and the end of the two-party system, which served as a basis for the spirit of nationalism abounding in 1816, may have posed the greatest threat to nationalism. The Republican Party was already beginning to splinter by the time of the war. Those inter-party divisions became clearer as nationalist Republicans like Clay and Calhoun dispensed with the principles of traditional Republicans when those ideas got in the way of accomplishing what the nationalists believed was in the best interest of the country. Adding to the emerging factionalism of the party, former Federalists were now adopting the mantle of the Republican Party without giving up their old Federalists beliefs. Furthermore, without an opposition party, there was no way to demand strict loyalty of party members. The problems of the Republican Party became evident in 1824. As for Clay's economic nationalism, despite his best efforts his American System would have no chance at ultimate success until the biggest issue dividing the nation—slavery—was settled by the Civil War.

Chronology

1790   Samuel Slater builds first cotton mill in U.S.

1807   Robert Fulton develops the first steamboat.

1813   The Waltham System introduced.

1816   Congress establishes the Second Bank of
the United States.
Congress passes Tariff of 1816.
James Monroe elected president.

1817   Rush-Bagot Agreement reached with England.

1818   Convention of 1818 with England.
Andrew Jackson invades Florida.

1819   The Panic of 1819 begins.
The U.S. and Spain agree to the Adams-Onís
Treaty or Transcontinental Treaty.
The Supreme Court decides *Dartmouth
College v. Woodward* and *McCulloch v.
Maryland* cases.

1820   Congress agrees to the Missouri Compromise.
James Monroe is elected president.

1823   The Monroe Doctrine is declared.

1824   The Supreme Court decides the
Gibbons v. Ogden case.

SUGGESTED READINGS

Samuel Flagg Bemis, *John Quincy Adams and the Foundations of American Foreign Policy* (1949).

Stuart Blumin, *The Emergence of the Middle Class: Social Experience in the City, 1760-1860* (1989).

Christopher Clark, *The Roots of Rural Capitalism: Western Massachusetts, 1780-1860* (1990).

George Dangerfield, *The Awakening of American Nationalism, 1815-1828* (1965).

Daniel Walker Howe, *What God Hath Wrought: The Transformation of America, 1815-1848* (2009).

Gerard Koeppel, *Bond of Union: Building the Erie Canal and the American Empire* (2010).

John Lauritz Larson, *The Market Revolution in America* (2001).

Bruce Laurie, *Artisans into Workers: Labor in Nineteenth-Century America* (1989).

Matthew Mason, *Slavery and Politics in the Early American Republic* (2008).

Ernest R. May, *The Making of the Monroe Doctrine* (1975).

Glover Moore, *The Missouri Compromise, 1819-1821* (1953).

Robert V. Remini, *Henry Clay: Statesman for the Union* (1991).

Kirkpatrick Sale, *The Fire of His Genius: Robert Fulton and the American Dream* (2001).

Charles G. Sellers, *The Market Revolution: Jacksonian America, 1815-1848* (1991).

Carol Sheriff, *The Artificial River: The Erie Canal and the Paradox of Progress, 1817-1862* (1996).

Francis N. Stites, *John Marshall: Defender of the Constitution* (1981).

George Rogers Taylor, *The Transportation Revolution, 1815-1860* (1951).

Sean Wilentz, *Chants Democratic: New York City and the Rise of the American Working Class, 1788-1850* (1984).

Review Questions

1.   What were the three pillars of Henry Clay's American System and what was he trying to achieve with it?

2.   Describe the problems of transportation in the United States after the War of 1812 and their impact on the American economy.

3.   Why is the post-war decade referred to as the "Era of Good Feelings?" How well does the name fit the time period?

4.   Describe the nationalist foreign policy of James Monroe and John Quincy Adams.

5.   Describe the issues leading to the Missouri Crisis. Did the Compromise resolve those issues?

Glossary of Important People and Concepts

John Quincy Adams
Adams-Onís (Transcontinental) Treaty
American System
Henry Clay
Convention of 1818
Dartmouth College v. Woodward
"Era of Good Feelings"
Robert Fulton
Internal Improvements
Andrew Jackson
Francis Cabot Lowell
Lowell Girls
John Marshall
McCulloch v. Maryland
Missouri Compromise
Monroe Doctrine
James Monroe
Panic of 1819
Putting-Out System
Rhode Island System
Rush-Bagot Agreement
Second Bank of the United States
Samuel Slater
Tariff of 1816
Waltham System

Andrew Jackson

Chapter Eleven

ANDREW JACKSON AND THE "WHITE MAN'S REPUBLIC"

To some of the nation's wealthy and most sophisticated, the event looked like the end of American civilization. The capital had never seen a presidential inauguration as emotional or as chaotic as on March 4, 1829, Supreme Court Chief Justice John Marshall swore in the man who would soon be his political enemy, Andrew Jackson, as the seventh President of the United States. Jackson had promoted the idea that his ascension to the presidency represented a new era. His supporters decorated the steamboat he rode up the Ohio River with brooms to symbolize how Jackson was going to "clean up the mess in Washington." It would be, his followers promised, a new age for the common man. Approximately 20,000 people had trekked to Washington, D.C., temporarily more than doubling the size of the city, to watch their hero grab the presidential reins. Some voyaged more than 500 difficult miles using primitive roads to reach the capital, where they paid $20 a week for rooms at boarding houses, about three times the normal rate, for the privilege of witnessing history.

Many visitors dressed in humble or even shabby clothes, used uneducated and even coarse language, and lacked the manners of the well-to-do. The crowd was like "an invasion of the northern barbarians into Rome," groused Senator Daniel Webster, who had supported Jackson's opponent, departing President John Quincy Adams. To accommodate the crowds, the inauguration moved outdoors to the more spacious grounds near the east portico of the Capitol. Jackson paid homage to the ordinary folk who had helped him reach the White House, removing his hat and bowing to the audience before taking his seat. A master of the populist gesture, he would bow again after finishing his speech and his oath of office.

Following the ceremony, the audience wanted to get closer, and they broke through the rope separating them from the new president, forcing Jackson to retreat back inside the Capitol. One wealthy Washington matron would later mourn that "The Majesty of the People had disappeared," pushed aside by an unruly "rabble, a mob of boys, of negroes, women, children scrambling, fighting, romping. What a pity. What a pity." An audience turned into a frenzied horde as hundreds followed Jackson, riding a white charger, with the bearing of a military hero, to his new residence, the White House. The throng stormed the White House, soiling the carpet and breaking cut glass and china. Jackson ended up retreating to the boarding house room he had rented for the week's festivities while the White House staff cleaned the mud stains on the rugs and drapes and dried up the pools of liquor spilled everywhere.

The inaugural madness symbolized for many in the American upper crust a disturbing trend in the country's politics personified by Jackson. He had defeated John Quincy Adams, a scion of the eastern establishment and the Harvard-educated son of a former president, in a rematch of their bitter, controversial 1824 presidential contest. A Tennessee planter, Jackson represented the loosening monopoly on economic and political power held by northeastern cities like Philadelphia, New York and Boston and by the largest Atlantic seaboard southern state, Virginia. Of the first six presidents, four had been from Virginia and two from Massachusetts. This east coast dominance no longer reflected the vastness of the country. The population of the United States almost had tripled from about 5 million in 1800 to around 13 million in 1830. The percentage of the population liv-

ing west of the Appalachian Mountains grew rapidly from 7 percent to 28 percent.

Jackson represented the rise of the West, but he also embodied the advance of what political reformers liked to call "universal manhood suffrage"—the idea that all white men, age 21 and older, should have the right to vote, whether or not they held property. Universal suffrage for adult white males had been achieved in the Northeast by the time Jackson left the White House in 1837. This dramatic expansion of eligible voters came to be known as "Jacksonian democracy," but the expansion of voting rights for white men came at the expense of free African Americans. Those new white voters saw their ballots as a matter of racial privilege. After the American Revolution, black men who owned property could vote in New England states such as Maine, Massachusetts, New Hampshire, and Vermont while New York and North Carolina gave suffrage rights to "all men" who met property qualifications. But as suffrage for white men spread in the first four decades of the nineteenth century, free African Americans lost access to the ballot in Connecticut, Maryland, New Jersey, New York, North Carolina, Pennsylvania, Maryland, and Tennessee.

As of 1840, 93 percent of African Americans in the North lived in states that had either severely restricted or completely eliminated the right to vote for blacks. Jacksonian democracy had no place for African Americans or Native Americans.

That republic was put on full display the day Andrew Jackson became president. White or not, to the wealthy and privileged on the Atlantic coast, and to their elected spokesman in Washington and in the media, this rabble was undesirable. As Supreme Court Justice Joseph Story described the scene after the inaugural throng had partly demolished the White House, "I never saw such a mixture. The reign of King Mob seemed triumphant."

JACKSON'S VIOLENT, TUMULTUOUS EARLY YEARS

Andrew Jackson shaped his era, and the era molded him. He was a violent man in a violent time, and a virulently racist one in a period defined by white supremacist dogma. He aggressively led the nation in an expansionist age. Impulsive and tumultuous, he perfectly reflected a transformative, unstable historical epoch. His parents, Scots-Irish immigrants Andrew Jackson, Sr., and Elizabeth Hutchison Jackson, were squatters, frontier people who settled on land for which no one held a legal title. They had settled in the Waxhaws region, a frontier so undefined by British colonial authorities that it is still unclear whether the future president was born on the North Carolina or South Carolina side of the border.

Andrew Jackson, Sr. died either just before or shortly after the birth of his namesake son as the result of a freak accident. A falling log killed him while he cleared land surrounding the Jackson home. His mother, Elizabeth, gave birth to Andrew on March 15, 1767, and raised him as a single widow.

Jackson was a rambunctious boy and not particularly studious during his early childhood. Nevertheless, Elizabeth scrimped and saved her meager earnings to pay for tutors. During the American Revolution, Jackson's mother and older brothers supported the Patriot cause. The eldest, Hugh, died from heat exhaustion at the Battle of Stono Ferry near Charles Town in 1779.

The Waxhaws would provide one of the most violent settings during the War for Independence. Using a force made up partly of Tories, British Lieutenant Colonel Banastre Tarleton fought a brutal war of vengeance against the American rebels in the South Carolina countryside, gunning down captured soldiers. Elizabeth Jackson, along with her surviving sons Andrew and Robert, nursed wounded Patriots, and the two young boys ran errands for the American forces in the area. British forces, including Tories, launched a surprise attack on the Waxhaws region in April 1781, taking eleven Patriot soldiers prisoner along with Andrew and Robert.

A British officer confronted Andrew, then 14, and demanded that the boy clean his muddy boots. Andrew refused, demanding proper treatment for a prisoner of war. The officer struck Jackson with his sword, Andrew protecting himself with his left hand. Jackson suffered gashes on his hand and head, wounds that would scar him for the rest of his life. More tragedy awaited the future president. While in a prisoner-of-war camp, both Jackson brothers contracted smallpox. Though Andrew survived, his brother died soon after his mother was able to secure the boys' release. Elizabeth Jackson then volunteered to care for Patriot prisoners held on ships moored in Charles Town Harbor where she contracted cholera and died in November 1781, leaving Andrew an orphan at age 14. "I felt utterly alone," Jackson later recalled. He moved from the home of one relative to another, often departing after an ugly argument. He spent his later teen years as a drifter, gambling, swearing, drinking and racing horses.

Dueling, Politics, and Slaveowning

Jackson received little formal education, but after his mother's death, in 1787 he relocated to Salisbury, North Carolina where he taught school. He then apprenticed for a lawyer, read legal books, and was admitted to the bar. When a friend was named Superior Court judge for the western district of North Carolina (later to become the state of Tennessee in 1796) by the legislature, Jackson secured an appointment to be the court's public prosecutor. Moving first to Jonesborough and then to Nashville, Jackson practiced as a country lawyer and began a lifelong custom of responding to perceived insults with violence or threatened violence. An opposing attorney named Waitstill Avery challenged Jackson in a way that offended him. "My character you have injured," Jackson wrote in a misspelled letter, "and further you have insulted me in the presence of the court and large audience. I therefore call upon you as a gentleman to give me satisfaction for the same." Jackson had challenged Avery to a duel and would engage in several similar face-offs in his life, some with consequences of injury and death. In this case, both parties satisfied honor by firing their pistols in the air.

By this time, Jackson already owned his first slave, a woman between the age of 18 and 20. Undereducated but sharply intelligent, Jackson plowed his legal earnings into land, becoming a successful speculator, with one of his big land investments eventually leading to the establishment of Memphis. While boarding with the widow of Revolutionary War General John Donelson, he met and became smitten with the woman's daughter, Rachel Donelson, the estranged wife of Captain Lewis Robards, a man subject to intense rages. At the time Robards still lived in Kentucky, but upon visiting Rachel in Nashville and seeing the attention that Jackson gave her, he sought a reconciliation that quickly failed. Jackson then arranged for Rachel to spend time away from Robards with friends in Natchez, Mississippi. Her husband eventually filed a divorce petition with the North Carolina legislature (which at the time alone had the power to grant divorces). Robards charged his wife with adultery and abandonment. He also placed an article in a newspaper openly declaring that he no longer held any financial responsibility for Rachel. Upon hearing a false rumor that Robards's request for a divorce had been granted (or so the Jacksons later claimed), Jackson and Donelson got married in Natchez in 1791 and returned to Nashville to live as husband and wife. When word reached Nashville three years later that the legislature had just approved Robards's divorce petition, the public became aware that Rachel had still been legally married to her first husband, thus making the Jacksons bigamists. Claiming an embarrassing misunderstanding had taken place, the couple remarried in 1794. The complicated beginning to their relationship would later politically haunt Jackson and his wife.

Rachel rose from an extensive clan, and this family network boosted Andrew's business and political career. Even though he struggled with a lifelong problem of drooling when he spoke, and he had a weak voice, Jackson would cast a giant shadow on the nation's political life from 1815 until he left the White House in 1837. His success as a lawyer and a businessman led to Jackson's election as a delegate to the 1796 Tennessee state constitutional convention. When Tennessee became a state later that year, he won election to the United States House. The Tennessee legislature appointed him to a United States Senate seat in September 1797,s but he wished to stay close to his business interests in Tennessee. His interest in the Senate quickly waned, especially after he encountered severe financial distress. Jackson passed notes to business associates from a bank that soon failed (an incident that permanently soured Jackson on all banks and paper money), leaving him with embarrassing debts. He resigned from the United States Senate after less than seven months and accepted a post as a justice on the Tennessee Supreme Court, a position he held until 1804.

Establishing a successful general store in Gallatin, Tennessee in 1803, he also developed a sprawling plantation he named the Hermitage, where eventually as many as 150 slaves at a time tended his cotton fields and maintained his household. Like other white men of his era, Jackson loved to speak of his own natural right to freedom but responded with cruelty when African Americans sought liberty themselves. Years later, taking out an advertisement for a runaway slave, Jackson offered a $50 reward for anyone capturing the escaped man (more than $800 today) plus "ten dollars extra, for every one hundred lashes any person will give him, to the amount of three hundred." Jackson did not blink at encouraging crippling and possibly lethal punishment for any black man who dared defy his will.

Jackson and the "Code of Honor"

For all his success in business and politics, Jackson seemed to derive the most pleasure from military service, particularly in battling Native Americans. Jackson saw Indian lands as a potential source for vast white wealth, and like many of his countrymen he desired their removal, through conquest and slaughter if necessary. Indians became a target of obsessive hatred for Jackson. He accused the natives of "savage murders & depredations," charged them with being deceitful and tricky and (ironically given the relentless white theft of Indian land and other resources) claimed they were guilty of "avarice." In his wars against Indians, he saw himself as an avenging angel, punishing Natives in the name of "our beloved wives and little prattling infants, butchered, mangled, murdered, and even torn to pieces by savage bloodhounds, and wallowing in their gore." In his career as a military officer and a politician, Jackson would more than make up for these often imagined offenses with a breathtaking record of genocide against Native Americans.

Jackson headed the Tennessee militia for a decade, leading battles against overwhelmed and demoralized Natives, fighting with a rage that one observer described as "mad upon his enemies." His Indian encounters, however, gave him little opportunity for the martial glory he deeply desired. Jackson became more deeply engaged in personal combat with Tennessee Governor John Sevier, a popular leader of a secession movement among western counties in North Carolina in the 1780s that briefly declared the creation of the never-officially-recognized state of Franklin. These counties later became the eastern part of Tennessee. Sevier was a war hero, having helped to annihilate a force of Loyalists at the Battle of King's Mountain during the American Revolution and gaining a reputation as a ruthless Indian fighter.

By the turn of the century, Jackson and Sevier had developed a budding rivalry. While serving as governor, Sevier thwarted Jackson's selection as commander of the Tennessee state militia. After leaving office due to term limits, Sevier competed with Jackson for the same post, but this time Jackson won out. When Sevier was eligible to run for governor again, Jackson helped to circulate a story that Sevier had engaged in land fraud—a charge that apparently had some merit. After winning reelection, Sevier confronted Jackson face-to-face over the issue on the streets of Knoxville and deliberately made reference to Jackson's earlier adulterous relationship with Rachel. Jackson immediately challenged Sevier to a duel, and the governor accepted. The two enemies planned to meet each other in the Tennessee woods, but Sevier's wagon stalled en route and he never showed. Jackson encountered him and his group while returning to Knoxville. He angrily drew his pistol on Sevier, who ran and hid behind a tree. When Sevier's son drew his weapon and aimed at Jackson, one of Jackson's friends pointed his pistol at the governor's son. After several tense moments, the parties decided to end the standoff without bloodshed.

Charles Dickinson would not be so lucky. A 25-year-old attorney, he had been overheard in May 1806 saying something unpleasant about Rachel Jackson and her sexual behavior after Jackson accused him of reneging on a horse race wager. Predictably, a duel challenge from Jackson resulted. During their face-off, Jackson (wearing a large overcoat to distort his frame) allowed Dickinson to fire the first shot. The bullet hit Jackson in the chest. Jackson survived, reeling for a time, but steadying himself, and holding one hand to his torso to slow the bleeding. According to dueling rules, Dickinson had to stand still while Jackson took a shot. Jackson cocked his pistol and squeezed the trigger, jamming the first time, but effectively executing his enemy on the second attempt. The bullet that hit Jackson landed close to his heart and could not

be removed safely, so the general carried this reminder of his encounter with Dickinson in his body for the rest of his life.

This was only the beginning of a career of gun battles. Later on, in September 1813, an argument over another duel in which Jackson served as a second (a backup) for one of his friends led to a Nashville barroom shootout between Jackson and future Missouri Senator Thomas Hart Benton and his brother Jesse. This brawl left Jackson with a bullet in the shoulder. This injury almost resulted in the amputation of his left arm, leaving the future president in considerable pain for the rest of his life. After migrating within his body for years, the bullet was finally removed by a doctor in 1832.

"Old Hickory"

Jackson had achieved wide fame in Tennessee but rose to national prominence as a result of his role in the War of 1812. Jackson never forgot the death of his brother and his mother. He had only to look at the wound on his hand to remember his near murder at the hands of the British military. So, he fought the War of 1812 against the hated English enemy and their Native American allies with particular relish.

In January 1813, Jackson led an army of 2,000 Tennessee volunteers who marched toward New Orleans with the goal of defending the lower Mississippi Valley. Reaching Natchez, Mississippi, Jackson received instructions from Madison's Secretary of War John Anderson to cancel the mission. Jackson disobeyed the order to immediately disband the force and instead led them on a march back to Nashville. His resilience on this physically difficult journey earned Jackson the nickname "Old Hickory," in reference to the hardness of the tree so common in Tennessee and the difficulty in cracking the tree's nuts.

In autumn 1813, Jackson finally received a command, getting orders to secure the border that Alabama and Georgia shared with Florida (then under Spanish control). After the horrific Fort Mims Massacre of over 250 settlers by Red Stick warriors, he needed little to encourage his genocidal longings towards Native Americans. Indians in the region would submit to his authority or face terrible consequences. At one Creek (Muskogee) village near Huntsville, Alabama, called Tallushatchee, about 1,000 of Jackson's men surrounded the 200 inhabitants and killed all the men. "We shot them like dogs," one of the soldiers, a not-yet-famous Davy Crockett, later recalled. Jackson's men then force-marched the Native American women and children back to the American camp, where they were held as prisoners. Jackson's men then slaughtered another 300 Red Sticks at Talladega, Alabama. Jackson followed up with a decisive victory against the Creeks at the Battle of Horseshoe Bend, an encounter in which his 4,000-man army, bolstered with pro-American Muskogee and Cherokee allies, thrashed 1,000 Red Sticks, ending in another massacre in which about 800 Red Sticks died.

Jackson, acting on behalf of President Madison, forced a peace agreement in which all Muskogee—friends and foes—surrendered 23 million acres of territory to the United States, more than half of all they possessed in Alabama and Georgia. This was typical of how Jackson would treat his Indian allies. The land would now be opened to white conquest. In most of his battles he received Native American help but that never mitigated Jackson's harshness toward Indians. As a reward for his victory, Jackson received a commission as a major general in the U.S. Army.

Jackson's successful defense of New Orleans in January 1815 made him a national hero, enhancing his largely undeserved military reputation and provided a launching pad for his three presidential bids in 1824, 1828, and 1832. From this moment on, Jackson would never be out of the national spotlight.

THE 1824 PRESIDENTIAL ELECTION

The Bank Issue

Like millions of Americans, Andrew Jackson suffered a financial crisis during the **Panic of 1819**. This economic downturn was caused in part by the rebound of European agriculture after economic chaos and trade disruptions caused by the Napoleonic Wars in Europe from 1803-1815. Officers in the Second Bank of the United States, just chartered in 1816, made the wobbly economy worse, because they were deeply involved in numerous shady corporations that quickly went belly-up, promoting a series of criminal investigations. Langdon Cheves, the president of the Bank of the United States, tried to tame inflation by tightening the availability of credit and demanding that all notes from other banks deposited with the national bank be paid back in precious metals.

State banks forced to pay back loans from the Bank of the United States demanded repayment from their customers, severely shrinking the money supply, suppressing consumer demand, and prompting a tide of businesses to go bankrupt. Businessmen filed more than 500 suits for debt in just one term of the county court in Nashville. Cities such as Philadelphia, where unemployment reached 75 percent, suffered the most. Almost 2,000 unemployed workers there were jailed for not paying off their debts. A total of a half-million workers nationwide lost their jobs, out of a population of nine million. Tent cities sprang up all over the United States.

Bankers were seen as the villains behind the financial collapse, and the Bank of the United States itself came to be referred to as "The Monster." Jackson co-wrote a manifesto in 1820 that blamed the economic disaster on "the largest emissions of paper from the banks." Back in Tennessee, Jackson ran again for the U.S. Senate on the issue of the national bank in 1822, winning his seat, which he saw as a springboard for a presidential campaign in 1824.

A Divided Republican Field

The Panic of 1819 and the earlier slavery-induced controversy over Missouri statehood opened fissures within the Jeffersonian Republican Party. The Federalist Party's frank elitism, opposition to increased white male suffrage and to immigration, and loud criticisms of the War of 1812 had killed the party by 1820, leaving the Republicans with a brief monopoly on power. Many former Federalists like John Quincy Adams joined the Republican ranks. Traditionally, Republicans had supported states' rights and an extremely limited role for the federal government—primarily providing for the national defense, conducting diplomacy and foreign policy, and delivering the mail. New Republicans such as Adams (soon to call themselves "**National Republicans**") believed the federal government should promote economic development by building turnpikes and canals, and creating institutions like the Second Bank of the United States that they believed would promote economic development and business growth.

More traditional Republicans like Jackson blamed the Panic of 1819 on Federalist-style big government represented by the chartering of the Second Bank of the United States three years earlier. The bitter 1819-1820 battle over the admission of Missouri as a slave state and the drawing of the Missouri Compromise line barring slavery in all new states north of the 36°30' parallel also alarmed southern slave owners like Jackson as a sign that power had shifted from the states to Washington, D.C.

These factions clashed in the highly contested 1824 presidential campaign, in which four Republican candidates—Monroe's Secretary of War William Crawford of Georgia, Secretary of State John Quincy Adams of Massachusetts, Speaker of the House **Henry Clay**, and the dark horse, General Andrew Jackson—faced off against each other in one of the most complex and hotly disputed White House races of all time. The Missouri crisis of 1819 still fractured the country regionally. Crawford's status as a southern slave owner dampened his appeal in the North. Adams's position as an elite Northerner made Southerners suspicious of him. Henry Clay's lead role in the Missouri Compromise, which admitted Missouri to the Union as a slave state but limited the growth of slavery elsewhere, damaged his standing in both the North and the South.

Jackson had the least governmental experience of any candidate, but in 1824, this was more an asset than a handicap. The Panic had led voters to see Washington as run by corrupt insiders willing to bankrupt the ordinary person in order to enrich themselves. As John C. Calhoun of South Carolina, then the Secretary of War, observed, voters throughout the nation believed that there was something "radically wrong with the administration of government" and the public was "ready to seize upon any event and looking out anywhere for a leader." The largest number saw that leader in Jackson, whose victory over the British in the Battle of New Orleans led many to admire him as a hero, regardless of region.

The "Corrupt Bargain"

The democratic revolution in American politics over the previous 24 years played a major role in the 1824 presidential election. Initially, a caucus of Republican congressmen selected Crawford to be their choice for president. While this method was the traditional procedure by which the party chose its nominee, many balked at the idea of Crawford, or any president, being selected in this manner. Without a Federalist Party opponent, whoever the congressmen selected would win the Electoral College vote by default without any consultation with the people. Thus, multiple candidates emerged to challenge Crawford's bid. Further, while six states still left the selection of members of the Electoral College in the hands of their state legislatures, eighteen states began to assign electors based on the popular vote. In the 1824 election, Jackson carried a clear plurality, 43 percent of the vote in those states compared to his nearest rival, Adams, who won only 31 percent. Clay got only 13 percent of the vote, and Crawford, who remained on the ballot even though he had suffered a stroke that left him half blind and temporarily paralyzed, won 13 percent.

The regional lines that would divide the country during the Civil War were already solidifying, with Adams carrying states only in his native New England and isolated electoral votes in other states in the North, Crawford's victories limited to the southern states of Georgia and Virginia, and Clay prevailing only in Ohio, Kentucky and Missouri. Jackson proved to be the sole national candidate, carrying 84 percent of the votes in the south-

west while winning outside of his home region victories in Pennsylvania, New Jersey, Indiana, and Illinois. Yet, no candidate had earned enough Electoral College votes to win the presidency. The election would have to be decided by the House of Representatives.

Since he had won both the most popular votes and the most Electoral College votes (99), and also enjoyed the widest geographic base of support, Jackson assumed he would prevail in the House. Under the Twelfth Amendment, the House would select the president from any of the top three candidates with the highest numbers of Electoral College votes (Jackson; Adams, who had 84; and Crawford, who had 41). Each state delegation would get one vote.

Clay, who finished fourth in the Electoral College, was ineligible, but as Speaker of the House, he carried considerable influence and threw enough support to Adams to win the New Englander the presidency. Adams won thirteen state delegations and Jackson won seven. The Speaker backed the candidate he most agreed with, and Adams believed that Clay's diplomatic skills, in evidence during the Missouri crisis, made him the most qualified person to be the nation's top diplomat. Upon assuming the presidency, Adams appointed Clay as Secretary of State. In the early nineteenth century, that office was seen as a steppingstone to the White House—Thomas Jefferson, James Madison and James Monroe, as well as John Quincy Adams, had served in that post. Certain that he deserved the White House and that the election had been stolen from him, Jackson furiously charged that Clay and Adams had made what Jackson called a "**corrupt bargain**." Clay had sold his support, Jackson charged, in return for his cabinet post. Referring to the disciple who betrayed Jesus in return for payment and then, in guilt, hanged himself, Jackson said of Clay, "So you see, the Judas of the West has closed the contract and will receive the thirty pieces of silver—his end will be the same."

THE JOHN QUINCY ADAMS PRESIDENCY AND THE LONG CAMPAIGN

Andrew Jackson never stopped running for president between his loss in 1824 and his eventual triumph in November 1828. Jackson relentlessly repeated the corrupt bargain charge and, with the help of crafty New York politician Martin Van Buren, a supporter of Crawford in 1824, built a formidable national political machine that would turn into the first modern American political party—the Democratic Party. Meanwhile, Adams's presidency was doomed at its inception. In a time of rising democratic sentiment, Adams gave his inauguration the

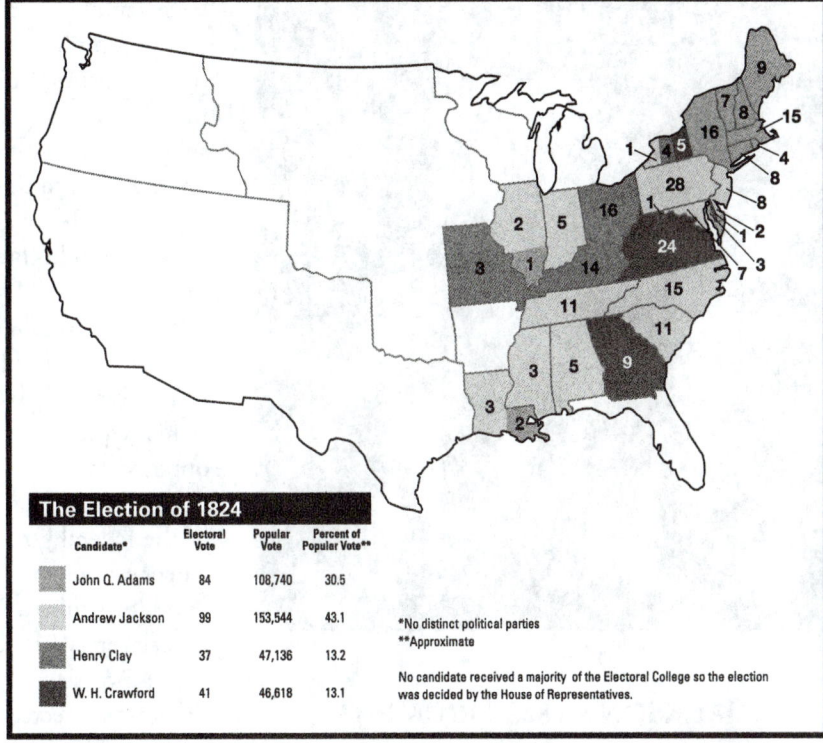

**Map 11.1
The Election of 1824**

The Election of 1824

Candidate*	Electoral Vote	Popular Vote	Percent of Popular Vote**
John Q. Adams	84	108,740	30.5
Andrew Jackson	99	153,544	43.1
Henry Clay	37	47,136	13.2
W. H. Crawford	41	46,618	13.1

*No distinct political parties
**Approximate

No candidate received a majority of the Electoral College so the election was decided by the House of Representatives.

air of a coronation and undermined his moral credibility. Senator John Randolph so loudly repeated the corrupt bargain charges that Clay challenged the Virginian to a duel. They met at Pimmit Rim in Virginia. Clay fired his pistol, the shot passing through Randolph's coat without causing any damage to the senator. Randolph had already confided to friends that he had no intention of harming Clay, who was married and a father. Randolph fired his gun harmlessly into the air above his head, ending the dangerous encounter. Clay's reputation, however, suffered permanent damage after the 1824 election and would shadow his unsuccessful presidential campaigns in 1832 and 1844.

John Quincy Adams had never strayed from the nationalist vision of his father (who died little more than a year into his son's presidency). In his annual message to Congress in December 1825, Adams asked for an ambitious federal program, including building a canal that would link the Potomac River that ran by Washington D.C. with the Ohio River, and the construction of a national road that would link the capital to New Orleans. He called for the creation of an Interior Department to handle public lands, a federal bankruptcy law, and the establishment of a national university, a naval academy, and a national observatory to make the United States a leader in astronomical sciences. Adams's vision was modern, would have stimulated the economy, improved commerce by easing the transportation of goods from one region to another, linked alienated regions more closely together,

and provided a great boost to American education, but it was completely out of step with the mood of the times.

After the bank failures of 1819 and the corruption charges surrounding the Second Bank of the United States, too many Americans distrusted the federal government and big institutions and had little appetite for new, ambitious programs coming out of Washington. Congress approved none of Adams's proposals. The hostile reaction to his ideas, Adams later said, caused him "protracted agony." The new president was largely miserable during his term. "I can scarcely conceive a more harassing, wearying, teasing condition of existence," Adams wrote in his diary about the agonies of being the president. "It literally renders life burdensome." The final *coup de grâce* to his administration came with his unpopular support of higher tariffs (taxes on foreign-made goods) as a means of aiding American manufacturing, a policy fiercely opposed in agricultural areas like the South where voters wanted access to cheaper foreign goods and feared foreign retaliation against American farm exports. His opponents called the proposal the "Tariff of Abomination," and the policy proved to be political poison in the South and the West when passed by the Congress in May 1828.

After this, Adams made no effort to prepare for a re-election campaign. The 1828 presidential campaign, one of the sleaziest in American history, would be a rematch between Adams and Jackson. Even before the contest started, however, there was little doubt, even on the part of the incumbent president, how it would turn out.

Henry Clay

JACKSON'S 1828 TRIUMPH

"The Little Magician": Martin Van Buren

The 1828, the original Jeffersonian Democratic-Republican Party ceased to exist. Nobody could afford to be associated with the name "Democratic-Republican" because of the controversy surrounding the 1824 election. John Quincy Adams and his followers adopted the name National Republicans (soon to be replaced). Those who supported Andrew Jackson became the Democratic Party. This new Democratic Party (still in existence today) was engineered by the clever and ambitious New York state politician, Martin Van Buren.

The son of a slave-owning tavern-keeper, Van Buren started his career in politics at a young age while building a law practice. Elected New York state attorney general in 1815 and to the state Senate in 1821, he became a leader of the so-called "Bucktail Faction" that successfully challenged the dominance of the state government by forces allied to DeWitt Clinton (who served at various times as governor and senator). In an era with only one national political party, Van Buren sought to clarify the lines dividing old Republicans and the former Federalists on various issues.

Unlike the Founding Fathers, who disdained political parties and believed that they only served to divide the country into uncompromising, bitter factions, Van Buren saw parties as healthy and vital for democracy. Parties, he wrote, "rouse the sluggish to exertion, give increased energy to the most active intellect . . . and prevent the apathy that has proved the ruin of Republics." "The Little Magician"

(as his admirers called him) sought to re-create what he had accomplished with his Bucktails in New York—a tightly organized, disciplined political machine with a clear message, whose members could be counted on for loyal support of a slate of candidates. Such an organization had never existed in the American Republic.

Van Buren was never explicitly pro-slavery, but not until later in his life did he become a critic of the institution. After the Missouri crisis he feared that the slavery controversy would block any national party from gaining traction and would eventually tear the nation apart. Van Buren, however, believed he could unite old-style, states' rights Republicans and farmers in the North (who often opposed tariffs) with southern planters by emphasizing their shared opposition to the supposed increasing power of the federal government. Van Buren urged his party, whenever possible, to avoid the issue of slavery altogether.

More subtly, Van Buren and his allies sought to link slavery with democracy. Van Burenites argued that because of slavery, white people would not have to do the least-respected, hardest work, and even the poorest white would never be the "mudsill" of society. Slavery and black inequality meant that all whites, theoretically, could be equal to each other, and the presence of slaves, supposedly, meant that all whites could possibly climb up the economic ladder. The Van Buren faction, who would in a few short years become the Democratic Party, supported expanding the franchise for white men. The old Federalists like Adams, on the other hand, tended to be suspicious or even hostile to expanding the number of eligible voters and consistently supported barriers to granting immigrants citizenship rights. The poorer voters and naturalized immigrants would gravitate toward the emerging Democrats, not just because that faction was perceived as friendlier to their interests, but also because of its perceived hostility to the African Americans, whom poor native whites and immigrants saw as economic rivals. Even before abolitionism became a major movement, many poor whites in the North opposed any move toward slave emancipation because free blacks might compete for the same low-wage jobs that poor whites and immigrants filled in northern society.

In spite of the dominance of wealthy southern slave owners within the Van Buren faction, the Democratic Party created in the 1830s would also position itself as the party of the white working man, a party of the producers who toiled in the fields and in the factories against parasites who made money off of trading paper, such as the bankers who engineered the Panic of 1819. The early nineteenth century marked one of the widest gaps between rich and poor in American history. Since the American Revolution, the share of the natural wealth held by the richest 10 percent climbed from almost 50 percent to nearly 75 percent by 1860. The economy, fueled by population growth and the transportation revolution, became supercharged during the Market Revolution. Business profits raced far ahead of workers' wages.

The genius of Jackson, Van Buren and others within the movement was to sell the Democratic Party, an institution controlled by slave owners like Jackson, as the voice of these frustrated working men, and to deflect their economic frustrations primarily toward even more powerless African Americans and Native Americans. The votes of working class white voters would be crucial to the 1828 election, as the percentage of eligible voters participating leaped from 27 percent four years earlier to 57 percent. The era of "mass politics" had begun, and Van Buren was well ahead of the curve.

The **Democratic Party** that Van Buren eventually formed, whose supporters initially threw their support to Andrew Jackson in 1828, would favor states' rights, oppose high tariffs, promote western expansion (because more land taken from Indians and placed under white control meant more farm land available for white farmers), and, just as important, was notoriously anti-black. This coalition became a major force in American politics from Jackson's election in 1828 until the eve of the Civil War three decades later.

The End of the "Era of Good Feelings"

Jackson had resigned from the United States Senate in 1825 so he would not be forced to vote on controversial issues. He returned to the Hermitage and followed the custom of presidential politics of the time and pretended not to be running for office. Starting in 1827, Van Buren tapped wealthy donors and began establishing pro-Jackson newspapers and political clubs across the country, with Jackson keeping close tabs on each development. John Quincy Adams thought such grubbing for votes was beneath the office of the president. He refused to use his power of appointment to reward friends and potential allies, or fire political enemies from the executive branch, insisting that character and qualifications were all that mattered. While this was admirable, his stance also showed obliviousness to the new politics of the day and the ability of the White House to use its powers to expand a political base.

Adams rarely went out to speak and, following the tradition begun by Jefferson, he sent his State of the Union Address to Congress to be read by the clerk. As carefully considered as his words usually were, the intellectual Adams only proved how out of touch he was when he spoke to the public through the written word. In his con-

troversial first annual message to the Congress, when he called for building a national university and other projects that came to be ridiculed, he—unintentionally or not—insulted the voting public, urging members of Congress not to be "palsied by the will of our constituents." Adams was asking the Congress not to worry about the priorities of voters when considering big projects, a comment that only solidified his image as an arrogant elitist who held the average person in disdain. It was exactly the wrong image to project in an era of expanded suffrage.

John Quincy Adams's father, the second president of the United States died, it seemed providentially, on July 4, 1826, the 50th anniversary of the Declaration of Independence, on the same day as his Revolutionary peer Thomas Jefferson. The younger Adams did not take this time to remind the nation of his family's role in founding the nation. Jackson, on the other hand, gladly took part in a celebration in New Orleans on January 8, 1828, the 13th anniversary of Jackson's defeat of the British army there. When Jefferson died, Jackson and his supporters forcefully depicted the Tennessee general as the rightful heir to the "Sage of Monticello." Meanwhile, the network of pro-Jackson newspapers that Van Buren helped create proved devastating to Adams's re-election efforts.

Van Buren organized committees of Jackson supporters within the Congress, on the state level within congressional districts, and even school districts. No campaign had ever so focused on the grassroots. Jackson organized nationally, whereas Adams had few advocates or even defenders in the South and the West. Jackson's men requested that friendly members of Congress raise funds for the campaign within their districts. With Van Buren at the helm, Jackson benefited from a sophisticated campaign structure that became a model for other presidential bids throughout the nineteenth century.

Newspapers and the Election of 1828

Newspapers became cheaper, printed news more quickly, and reached a broader audience by the 1820s. Relying on each other for content, editors simply copied stories from publications they received from across the country. The recent development of steamships, railroads, telegraph lines, and better roads increased the speed by which news traveled and reduced the costs, which promoted the birth of even more periodicals. Meanwhile, printing a paper became considerably cheaper. Publishers developed a process of making cheap newsprint from wood pulp to replace the more expensive recycled rags that had been used to make paper previously. Printers used new steam-operated web presses that allowed printing at higher speeds on continuous rolls of paper that were then cut into sheets. These reductions in production costs allowed the rise of what came to be known as the "penny press,"—newspapers sold at affordable prices aimed at the broadest possible audience.

Martin Van Buren realized the value of this new media market. In the late eighteenth and early nineteenth centuries, newspapers were often directly owned by political parties, or by supporters of particular candidates, and they made no pretense of objectivity. Newspapers assisted in organizing political party conventions and rallies, mobilized voters, promoted the views of candidates, and demonized opponents. Amos Kendall's newspaper, the *Argus of Western America,* in Frankfort, Kentucky, promoted the image of Jackson as a man who rose from humble circumstances to become a financial success and a war hero and farmer who had not forgotten his rural roots. Jacksonian-era editors rarely felt restrained in attacking the political opposition, with public figures often denounced harshly as cowards, traitors, or possibly insane.

In the lead-up to the 1828 election, pro-Jackson newspapers accused the exceedingly prudish president of having engaged in premarital relations with his wife and, when serving as ambassador to Russia, having acted as a pimp for the Czar and procuring American women for the Russian emperor. The Jackson papers made a big issue of a mistaken report filed by Adams's son, John Adams II, who worked as the president's secretary. The younger Adams accidentally reported the purchase of a billiard table, balls, and cues as a White House expense. The president had actually paid for the table himself. Jackson's critics accused the president of misspending the public's money and suggested that pool playing, often associated with drinking and gambling, raised doubts about Adams's morality. Such a pastime, said a North Carolina Congressman, could only "shock and alarm the religious, the moral and the reflective part of the community."

The pro-Adams newspapers probably hurt their cause more than they helped. The *New York Advocate* fully bared the anti-immigrant bigotry of the Adams faction with an ill-timed attack on the Irish. "When we look at the population of some districts of our country, mixtd [sic] up with the dregs of all nations; when we are told that we have among us half a million of Irishmen, and when we know that they are all linked, together and move in a phalanx, we are constrained to say, that the character of our country is being degraded with the connexion [sic]," one issue complained. Needless to say, with such sentiments expressed by Adams's surrogates, few citizens of Irish descent supported the president's re-election efforts.

The ugly attacks on Adams's character no doubt shocked and offended the proper New Englander. Adams likely had no direct involvement in the anti-Jackson smear

campaign that followed, but he hardly could have been unaware of it and he did not stop it. One of his allies in the press, Charles Hammond, editor of the *Cincinnati Gazette,* began publishing stories in 1827 claiming that Jackson had deliberately lured his wife, Rachel, while she was still married to Lewis Robards, and that the two had deliberately lived in adultery. It got worse. Hammond then charged in his paper "General Jackson's mother was a COMMON PROSTITUTE!" Hammond wrote that Jackson's mother had been "brought to this country by the British soldiers! She afterwards married a MULATTO [mixed-race] MAN, with whom she had several children, of which number General Jackson is one!!!" Another pro-Adams newspaper compared Rachel Jackson to a "dirty, black wench." Jackson's political advisors immediately worried because their candidate had already killed a man for making similar comments, and they feared that another homicide might prove a political liability for Jackson as a presidential candidate. They managed to convince Jackson to keep his pistol holstered even as Adams's men launched another assault, this time on his military reputation.

A Jackson foe, John Binn, published a campaign brochure decorated with boldfaced letters, a solemn, black border and coffins under the title of "Some Account of some of the Bloody Deeds of General Jackson." The coffins referred to six Tennessee militiamen whose terms of service were extended in 1814 and who then went "absent without leave" (AWOL) and were executed under signed orders by Jackson. The infamous "Coffin Handbill" portrayed Jackson as a cold-blooded killer, as did other Adams campaign literature that brought up his duel with Charles Dickinson and his shoot-out with the Benton brothers.

Jackson Emerges Victorious

The Adams campaign's election strategy backfired. Not for the last time, the public reacted with hostility when a politician tried to make the private life of an opponent a public issue. Andrew and Rachel Jackson's marriage had survived for almost 40 years by the time of the 1828 campaign, and Jackson supporters believed that their candidate had rescued an honorable woman from a cad of a first husband. They thought it was unmanly for the Adams forces to attack a candidate's wife. Most voters saw Jackson's many violent episodes as evidence of his bravery and virility. Jackson carried 80 percent of the popular vote in the South. Adams only won in New England, New Jersey, Delaware, and Maryland, plus he garnered 16 of New York's 36 Electoral College votes. Jackson won everywhere else, sweeping the Deep South, the West, Pennsylvania, and a majority of electoral votes

Benjamin Day and the Great Moon Hoax

On August 21, 1835, newspaper publisher Benjamin Day's **New York Sun** scooped its competition with a story guaranteed to change how human beings saw their place in the universe. The newspaper started running a six part series called "Great Astronomical Discoveries" and reported that a South African astronomer using the most powerful telescope in the world had discovered that forests and trees covered the surface of the moon and that animals resembling zebras and buffalo scampered across the lunar landscape. The astronomer had observed intelligent moon people through his lens, a species that looked human except that they flew using batlike wings. The story made a sensation, inspiring the printing of a bestselling booklet, even as rival newspapers tried to confirm the discovery of moon life or debunk it. Jacksonian era newspapers were no longer just about politics or dry information. They were about entertainment, and the crazier the content, the bigger the readership.

During New York City's cholera epidemic in 1832, Day wrestled with how to break into the metropolis' extremely competitive, cutthroat newspaper market. New publishing technology made printing newspapers extremely cheap, allowing publications to be sold at an affordable price to an ever-larger audience. As New York's population tripled to almost 313,000 between 1820 and 1840, the boroughs filled with low-wage, less educated workers, many of them new immigrants. Day sought to reach this potential audience. He pioneered the hiring of newspaper boys to sell copies of the publication at street corners. Most newspapers to that date had been owned by political organizations backing particular candidates. Highly partisan, they carried long, dry transcripts of debates in Congress, stump speeches and so on. Day realized that partisan newspapers did not sell copies to readers belonging to competing political parties and that working class readers might not be so obsessed with every detail of every public debate. His paper began to cover what was happening in the jailhouses, the workplace, and the bars, writing about the street life of a city that famously never slept.

One of his hires, George W. Wisner, became one of the first "beat writers" in American journalism history, a reporter who regularly covered a particular institution, in this case New York's always lively police courts. Presidential candidates and congress members had dominated press coverage, but Wisner filled the **Sun's** pages with tales of the prostitutes, beaten wives, the bank robbers, and pickpockets who appeared before judges in the city's crowded night court. Wisner became the **Sun's** star reporter and eventually rose to the position of co-publisher, but Day bought out his share in the paper when the writer became too loud an advocate for abolitionism. Day did not want the slave controversy to drive away any part of the **Sun's** enthusiastic readership.

Wisner's replacement, Richard Adam Locke, fabricated the story on the moon people, claiming that the most famous astronomer of the time, Sir John Herschel, had made the discovery. In the story, which Locke wrote anonymously, the writer described the bat-winged moon people as having built temples and other sophisticated structures. The story claimed the discoveries had been announced in a recent edition of the **Edinburgh Journal of Science**. A rival New York newspaper, the **Journal of Commerce**, apparently became the first publication to accuse the **Sun** of pulling a hoax, but the most thorough debunking came from James Gordon Bennett, the publisher of the **New York Herald**, who reported that the **Edinburgh Journal of Science** had ceased publication in 1833 and had never carried such an article. Bennett also pointed to Locke as the author of the stories, though Locke himself always denied it. Bennett later made the unproven claim that Locke had confessed to the fabrication in a letter addressed to him in November.

A reporter for the **Journal of Commerce** claimed that Locke made a confession while heavily drinking in a bar. Ten years later, the horror writer Edgar Allen Poe, claimed Locke had stolen the idea from a story of his, "The Unparalleled Adventure of One Hans Pfall," which featured a character who rode to the moon in a balloon, that had appeared in a publication called the **Southern Literary Messenger** three weeks before the **Sun's** series ran. In spite of these allegations, **The New York Sun**, never retracted the story. The astronomer Hershel laughed at first when shown news accounts of his alleged lunar findings but got angered as he kept getting pestered about the story.

Day bragged that the **Sun's** daily circulation increased from about 8,000 to about 20,000 as a result of the stories. In fact, the newspaper appeared to have a regular readership of about 20,000 and readership did not increase greatly because the moon stories got reprinted in rival dailies. However, the **Sun** did make a big profit when it reprinted the whole series, complete with elaborate illustrations of the lunar wildlife, as a pamphlet. The **Sun** sold 60,000 copies of the pamphlet. Day sold the **Sun** to his brother-in-law in 1838 for $40,000 (almost $850,000 today.) He died in 1889, eighteen years after Locke, the writer who made his publication infamous.

of New York. He even picked up an electoral vote in Maine. Overall, Jackson prevailed in the Electoral College by a tally of 178 to 83.

Unlike 1824, Jackson scored well throughout the country, winning an election shaped more by class than by region. It appeared that lower-income voters battled as foot soldiers in the Jacksonian Revolution. These rank-and-file supporters included both isolated frontiersmen and working class city dwellers. As one bitter friend of Henry Clay stated, "The ignorant and degraded class of our population are all against us." Such voters undoubtedly found allure in a party explicitly committed to the cause of white supremacy, a party that ostensibly made even the poorest white worker part of an aristocracy of color. Many whites might be poor and might have limited influence over their nation's politics, the Democratic appeal went, but no white was worse off than the most privileged Native American or African American.

Jackson's joy in his victory was short-lived. Rachel Jackson took the attacks on her husband during the campaign personally, and it seemed to affect her health. During the fall she suffered a heart attack. Still, she bought a gown for the Inaugural Ball. Reportedly, she had been shielded from the accusations regarding her personal life until after the election, but read some newspapers repeating the charges while on a shopping trip. She died a few days later, on December 22, 1828. Andrew Jackson entered the White House a bereaved husband and wore mourner's black the day he was sworn in for his first term. The new president would always blame his political enemies, like Clay, who was friends with the editor Hammond, for killing his wife. Much of his time in office, Jackson's relationship with his opponents was barely more civil than the Benton gun brawl.

John Quincy Adams, meanwhile, left the White House a bitter man, but his political life enjoyed a second act as Massachusetts voters returned him to Washington, D.C., this time as a member of the United States House of Representatives, where he served from 1831 until his death in 1848. He became the first and only former president to become a member of Congress.

JACKSON'S FIRST TERM

The Spoils System

Few doubted that Andrew Jackson would enthusiastically embrace presidential power. As a military commander, he had often gone beyond or ignored the commands of his civilian superiors, but Jackson always expected his edicts to be followed. Dealing with Congress and a strong-minded

opposition would not be easy, but Jackson would successfully assert his authority more often than not.

No president had used his veto power so generously before Jackson. Washington first used the presidential veto to reject an appropriations act in 1792. Since then, presidents had directly vetoed legislation passed by Congress eight times or "pocket vetoed" bills (by refusing to sign a bill when the Congress is in recess) twice. Jackson would directly veto five bills and pocket veto seven, more than all his predecessors combined.

If Adams had refused to exploit the patronage power of the presidency to extend his political influence, Jackson had no such scruples. He instituted what came to be derisively known as the "**spoils system,**" the term derived from the phrase delivered in a speech by a Jackson supporter, Senator William L. Marcy of New York, who proclaimed "to the victors belong the spoils." Jackson, certain that bureaucrats in the small executive branch might block implementation of his policy, began dismissing some federal employees and filling those posts with Jackson partisans. When government officers retired, they would also be replaced with Jackson loyalists. The federal government began to function more like the political machines that ran big cities, such as New York. Political advisors such as Martin Van Buren believed that federal patronage was a way to create an army of political activists personally loyal to the president.

Newspapers at the time claimed that the Jackson White House sacked hundreds of government workers in the first year the new administration took power, but that number most likely is partisan propaganda. Scholars estimate that the administration fired or accepted the resignations of 10 percent of the federal workforce. Qualifications for a particular federal job mattered less under this system than did devotion to Jackson and his ideas, campaign contributions to Jackson's political operations, and effectiveness at campaigning for the president and his allies. In spite of Jackson's devotion to small government, the executive branch would grow after the institution of the spoils system, in some cases jobs being created so they could be dispensed to political loyalists. Between 1832 and 1860, the number of positions in the executive branch increased threefold. The dispensing of jobs to supporters became both a burden and an instrument of political power for future presidents until civil service reforms in the 1880s.

The "Petticoat Affair"

Suspicion and resentment shaped the Jackson White House. In 1824, former Secretary of War and U.S. House Representative John C. Calhoun of South Caro-

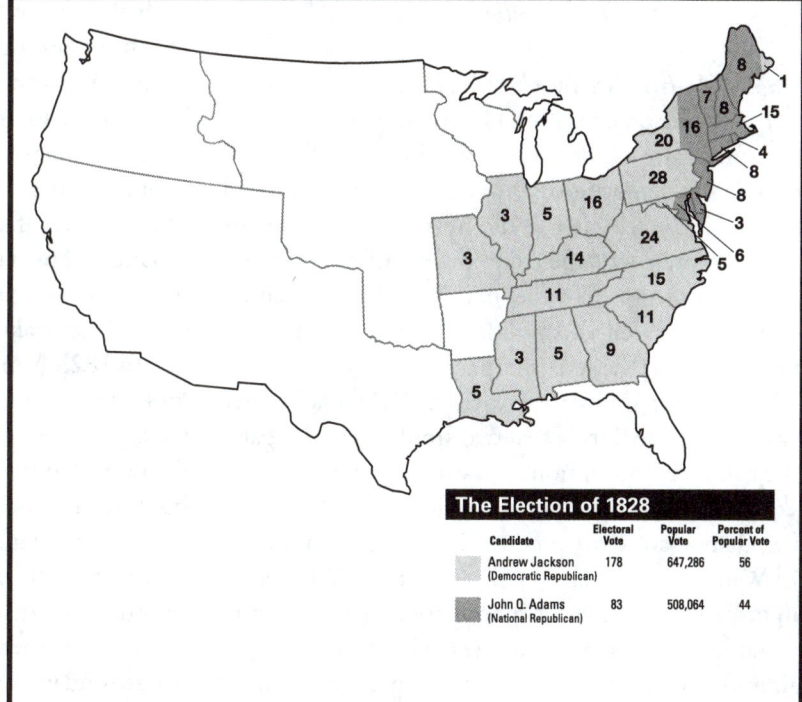

Map 11.2 The Election of 1828

lina considered a campaign for president but doubted he could prevail in the crowded field and instead ran for vice president, serving in that office under John Quincy Adams. Calhoun worked behind the scenes to undermine Adams, backing Jackson, but still hoping to one day win the White House himself. Jackson never trusted the vice president or many of the political insiders he appointed to his cabinet. This internal dissension only grew worse in the wake of a Washington soap opera surrounding the wife of Jackson's friend, Secretary of War John H. Eaton.

Eaton married Margaret **"Peggy" O'Neill Timberlake**, the daughter of a tavern keeper, less than a year after her first husband, a sailor, died. Rumor in Washington had it that John B. Timberlake had committed suicide after he learned of an affair between Eaton and Margaret. Gossip suggested Peggy had miscarried while her husband had long been out to sea. In any case, Washington society frowned upon such a hasty romance in what was supposed to be a time of mourning. Stories spread about Margaret's alleged sexual promiscuity. The marriage took place little more than two months before Jackson's inaugural. The wives of numerous cabinet officers, and particularly Floride Calhoun, the wife of the vice president, shunned her and refused to be introduced to her at inaugural festivities.

The rumors surrounding his close friend's wife provoked Jackson's famous temper and poured salt on some very fresh wounds. The president had just lost his wife, Rachel, who had been slandered as an adulteress and bigamist during the presidential campaign, and Jack-

son, drawn to Eaton because of her beauty and charm, rushed to her defense. Jackson also felt kinship, given his and Peggy Eaton's shared humble backgrounds and the privileged status of women like Floride Calhoun. Jackson also suspected that the whispered attacks on the Eatons constituted a subterranean attack on him launched by an ambitious Calhoun, who might want to trip up the president to serve his own political ambitions.

Jackson organized an investigation into the Eaton Affair (often referred to as the **"Petticoat Affair"**) and proved, to his own satisfaction, that the charges against the Eatons could not be true. He called a cabinet meeting, minus Eaton, to present the evidence. "She is chaste as a virgin," he declared to the stunned officials. The scandal did not die down, but the president presented an ultimatum, insisting that anyone who doubted John Eaton's honor was personally insulting Jackson and "had better withdraw" from the cabinet. Between May and August of 1831, Jackson's attorney general and secretaries of state, the treasury, and the Navy, as well as Eaton himself, all resigned. Van Buren, the secretary of state who resigned, had endeared himself to Jackson by supporting the Eatons and was rewarded with an appointment as ambassador to England. Calhoun, because of the Petticoat Affair, became *persona non grata*. Van Buren became a power within the administration. From that point on, Jackson would largely shun his official cabinet, except for Van Buren, and would heed the counsel primarily of his so-called "kitchen cabinet," consisting of longtime friends and confidantes.

The Tariff of Abominations

In 1832, Martin Van Buren cribbed an idea from the minor Anti-Masonic Party and helped organize the first-ever Democratic National Convention, which would nominate the Democratic Party choices for president and vice president. Delegates would hear dramatic speeches singing the praises of their nominees and hammer out an official platform. For the first time, the nomination of a major presidential candidate became a definable, galvanizing event, replete with pageantry.

More important for the future, the Democratic Party instituted a rule requiring that two-thirds of the delegates at the national convention support a candidate before he could become the nominee. This threshold required future Democratic Party presidential candidates, until the Civil War, to support slavery, or at least passively accept it, in order to get the party's nomination. After the war, it would require Democrats at the national level to be, at a minimum, passive partners in southern disenfranchisement of African Americans, segregation, and lynching.

Van Buren had few doubts that white Southerners would remain loyal to Jackson, who was one of their own, but he wanted to more firmly tie Southerners in the party to states' rights advocates in the North. Van Buren tried to do so by pushing through the Congress a policy most old-fashioned Jeffersonian Republicans would have abhorred: a higher federal tariff on foreign goods.

By 1830, the South had become an agricultural giant, growing cotton tended by slaves. That year, cotton exports were worth $30 million (more than $636 million today),

easily the United States' top export. The high profitability of cotton meant the South had invested little in manufacturing and relied on the North and industrialized nations like England for its factory-produced products. Southerners, therefore, preferred low tariffs (taxes) on foreign-made items, because the competition between European and northern manufacturers guaranteed them lower prices for products. Low tariffs would also prevent foreign governments from having a reason to slap high tariffs on American exports, especially cotton, entering their countries.

In 1828, Van Buren served as U.S. senator from New York and, as part of his national strategy to secure Jackson's victory in the presidential election, he convinced his allies in the Congress to pass a tariff bill that would heavily tax foreign-produced wool, flax, distilled spirits, iron, and hemp, giving aid to those industries in the North. Van Buren calculated Jackson's indirect support for the measure would increase his popularity in the northeast while Southerners would support him anyway, since they detested Adams. Van Buren underestimated the anger that the law would stir in the South, where the package of duties came to be known as the "**Tariff of Abominations.**" That anger reached a boiling point when Jackson failed, contrary to the expectations of the southern delegation, to even mention the tariff in his first two annual messages to Congress. The issue particularly resonated in South Carolina, which faced fierce competition from other cotton-growing states in the South, paid high tariffs on finished products made with the cotton it produced, and had been badly hit by the economic slump of the 1820s. South Carolinians like Vice President Calhoun saw the tariff as a serious roadblock to the state's recovery.

Lurking in the back of Calhoun's mind, and the minds of other Southerners, was fear of what the passage of the tariff meant concerning the power of northern states in the Congress and the implications this held for the future of slavery. Northerners now were a clear majority in the House of Representatives. The rate of population growth was larger in the North than the South, caused by both natural increase and foreign immigration. Immigrants from Ireland and elsewhere found the North, with its wider availability of jobs, more attractive and were turned off by the South's dependence on slavery. More than 7 million people lived in the free states by the 1830s, compared to 5 million in the slave states, and many of the Congressmen from free states began openly to oppose slavery. To men like Calhoun, the so-called Tariff of Abominations illustrated the power of the federal government to impose laws on the South, a power that might eventually be used to abolish slavery.

John C. Calhoun

Slave Rebels

Slavery had turned South Carolina into an armed camp by the 1820s, and state leaders used extreme measures to protect it. In 1822, a freed African American in Charles Town named **Denmark Vesey** concocted one of the most ambitious slave revolts in American history. A talented slave from the Caribbean, Vesey had convinced his owner to rent him out for work, with the earnings split between him and the master. Vesey used these earnings to purchase a city lottery ticket in 1799. He spent his winnings to buy his freedom, but he lacked the funds to purchase his wife and children. He went to work as a carpenter. He became a lay preacher at the local African Methodist Episcopal Church, which had approximately 6,000 members, mostly slaves.

Vesey's congregation became fascinated with the story in the Book of Exodus in the Christian Old Testament, which related how God led Moses and the children of Israel out of slavery in Egypt. Vesey believed God hated slavery and would save African Americans from bondage. One night, Vesey saw a comet in the sky, and he believed that this was a sign from God that a miracle of deliverance would soon unfold in South Carolina. Vesey's congregation believed that God would destroy the city of Charles Town just as he had the pagan city of Jericho in the Book of Joshua. The congregants were not content to wait for their earthly salvation, however, and they laid plans for an armed uprising in 1822. According to the plan, the plotters would seize the state arsenal and distribute the arms to what they hoped would be a growing army of liberated plantation slaves. The slave rebels would then slay their masters and spread the revolution. Vesey and his cohorts planned to kill Charles Town's white men including the governor. After gaining control of the city, they would seize control of naval vessels in the harbor and escape the United States, setting sail for Haiti, a republic that had been established by rebellious slaves in 1803.

One of the conspirators, Gullah Jack, an African conjurer, provided the slave rebels with special amulets and cast spells he said would render the slave rebels invulnerable to bullets. However, frightened slaves aware of the plot feared that it would fail and that they would be executed as a result. They revealed the conspiracy to white authorities. A roundup of slaves ensued, with suspected rebels tortured into confessions, though many refused to name their co-conspirators. Vesey was captured June 22. Officials hanged Vesey and five other men on July 2, with Gullah Jack killed a few days later. Thirty-five conspirators were hanged, with twenty-two killed in a single day.

Stories circulated that between 600 to 9,000 slave conspirators remained at large. The event terrified white South Carolinians. They had convinced themselves that their slaves were childlike and wanted the firm guidance of their supposedly loving white masters. Slave owners had sometimes spoken of their chattel as members of the family and convinced themselves that their black property loved them much as a pet might love its master. The news that a coachman he trusted had entered the Vesey conspiracy rattled one wealthy Charles Town slave owner. Visiting the slave who always seemed obedient but who now awaited punishment in a jailhouse, the hurt master asked, "What were your intentions?" The slave looked coldly at his tormentor and announced to the white man that he planned "to kill you, rip open your belly, and throw your guts in your face."

White South Carolina armed itself and increased nighttime slave patrols, which roamed the woods to catch escaped slaves or those who might be carrying word of another slave revolt from plantation to plantation. In Charleston to this day, antebellum homes are ringed with fences topped with sharp spikes, a defensive measure against slaves who might climb over the fence to kill their masters. At night, many slave owners became prisoners in their own homes. Convinced that foreign black sailors had conspired with Vesey, the South Carolina legislature passed the Negro Seaman Act, which prohibited free black seamen from leaving their ships, thus imprisoning them when docked at Charles Town. Supreme Court Justice William Johnson, presiding over the federal circuit court that included South Carolina, overturned the law, noting that it violated naval treaties between Great Britain and the United States. The South Carolina state senate declared it would ignore the court ruling and would enforce the law anyway.

To justify this flagrant violation of a court ruling, the state of South Carolina dusted off a legal theory first proposed by Thomas Jefferson during the controversy over the Alien and Sedition Acts in the 1790s—a concept that came to be known as nullification. According to Jefferson, in his Kentucky Resolution, states were sovereign entities that had voluntarily entered the Union, and they retained their power not to comply with federal laws they deemed unconstitutional. The South Carolina Senate nullified Judge Johnson's decision, and the Monroe administration made no attempt to enforce it, giving the Palmetto State politicians a *de facto* legal victory.

Slavery continued to poison everything it touched, reducing African Americans to abused property and filling southern whites with fear of their human property. This paranoia only deepened in August 1831 when the deadliest slave revolt in southern history broke out in

Southampton County, Virginia, a would-be revolution led by another black preacher, **Nat Turner**. Turner led sixty slaves who shot and hacked to death about sixty white men, women and children.

Turner, a self-appointed Baptist preacher who conducted faith healings while preaching to both whites and blacks, saw himself as a prophet of God sent to Earth to bring divine wrath upon white slave owners. Since childhood, Turner claimed, the Holy Spirit regularly spoke to him and assured him that God would give him an important mission. Around 1830, Turner saw visions of a violent, bloody final struggle between good and evil, the Battle of Armageddon described in the Book of Revelation. In an ecstatic state, Turner saw combat between black angels and white demons. Turner said that angels revealed to him a scene of the crucified Christ set against a dark night sky. The next day the slave preacher encountered red spots dotting a cornfield, which he interpreted as Christ's blood. Turner took a solar eclipse in February 1831 as a sign from God that he must lead slaves in that final battle against the forces of Satan, and he started sharing his prophecies with other slaves. The uprising began August 21. The state militia aided by U.S. Naval forces and units from North Carolina obliterated the rebellion within two days. The state of Virginia executed fifty-six blacks, including Turner who died November 11. After the hanging, Turner's body was skinned, beheaded, and quartered (tied to four horses that were made to run in different directions, pulling the body apart).

A panic swept through the state. Whites murdered as many as two hundred African Americans. Whites realized as never before that their slaves were not grateful children, but people who burned with the desire for freedom, many of whom would murder their overlords in an instant should a convenient opportunity ever arise. In the aftermath of the Vesey and Turner revolts, the South transformed into a primitive police state in which mail was opened by postal authorities in search of anti-slavery literature, armed slave patrols roamed the woods at night in search of escaped slaves, and states built their own small armies in preparation for possible revolts.

The rise of a more vocal abolitionist movement in the North, backed by Quakers and by men like the journalist and activist William Lloyd Garrison of Massachusetts and the evangelist Theodore Weld of New York, only intensified white southern suspicions, not just of their possibly rebellious servants but also of northern whites who might incite them to violent resistance.

In 1835, abolitionists initiated a "postal campaign" in which they blanketed the North and South with anti-slavery tracts. Southern slave owners worried that this literature might end up in the hands of their servants and incite rebellions. The Jackson administration and Democrats in Congress contemplated passage of a federal censorship law that would ban such literature from being distributed in the mail, but, concerned about the constitutionality of such laws, the Jackson administration quietly gave the green light to local postmasters to ignore federal postal regulations, to remove suspected anti-slavery material, and to destroy it. From 1836 on, abolitionists bombarded the Congress with petitions calling for the abolition of slavery and a speedy end to the slave sales in Washington, D.C. Slave auctioneers sold human beings within hearing distance of the U.S. Capitol, which even some whites not committed to abolitionism considered a national disgrace.

The Democratic majority in the Congress required such anti-slavery petitions to be automatically tabled at the beginning of each session, thus silencing debate on the issue. This became known as the "Gag Rule." By this point, John Quincy Adams was serving in the House and he began a long crusade to end the practice. He would not succeed until 1844.

The Nullification Crisis

Slave revolts and the fear that Northerners were encouraging the overthrow of the "peculiar institution" provided the context for the explosive reaction to the 1828 tariffs. Calhoun and others were not eager to hand any powers to a federal government that might fall into the hands of abolitionists. Even as he served as Adams's vice president, Calhoun had recruited opposition to the tariffs and constructed a complicated legal argument for defying the tariffs based on the Jeffersonian concept of nullification articulated in the Kentucky Resolution. In 1828, Calhoun anonymously penned and self-published an explosive pamphlet, the *Exposition and Protest*, which echoed and expanded upon Jefferson's treatise, suggesting that the Constitution, effectively, was a treaty between nations and that it was up to each sovereign state, and not the federal courts, to determine whether a federal law violated the Constitution. Calhoun argued that a state could nullify within its borders any national law it deemed unconstitutional. The federal government could only force a state to comply at that point, he insisted, if it incorporated the law into a new constitutional amendment and convinced the states to ratify the provision. If such an amendment passed, Calhoun said, an objecting state would still reserve the right to secede from the Union. His concept of federalism had no basis in constitutional history and would have shattered the country into a crazy-quilt of conflicting laws. His ideas, if implemented, would have crippled the ability of Congress to regulate commerce and promote the general welfare, duties given it by the Constitution, thus destroying any chance of effective government at the national level. But in Calhoun's estimation, resistance to the tariff and—in the future—the defense of slavery had become paramount, even above national unity.

When Jackson, a fellow Southerner, became president in March 1829, Calhoun banked on Jackson to oppose the tariff, expecting the chief executive to propose a repeal, but the vice president miscalculated. The *Exposition*, meanwhile, sparked a fierce debate in Congress in January 1830 between Senator Daniel Webster of Massachusetts and Robert Y. Hayne of South Carolina. The initial Webster-Hayne Debate centered on the issue of sale of public lands but soon gravitated toward the doctrine of nullification. Webster powerfully argued that a nation built upon nullification had entered into a suicide pact. Only a strong union, bound together with respect for the authority of the federal government and national law, he argued, could guarantee liberty for all American citizens, in whatever state they lived. "Liberty and Union, now and forever, one and inseparable!" he proclaimed. Webster's Senate speech would be published across the country, in newspapers, periodicals, and political pamphlets. Meanwhile, South Carolina's election season in 1830 focused on the tariff issue and candidates across the state called for a nullification convention to declare the 1828 tariff void.

Jackson had on various issues been an advocate of states' rights, but he also embodied fierce nationalism. He despised challenges to his authority as chief executive of the federal government. When he found out that Calhoun—a man he hated as a potential rival in a future presidential campaign and whom he held responsible for the Eaton affair—had authored the *Exposition* and had been organizing opposition to the tariff, Jackson boiled over. The president would tolerate no further disloyalty from the vice president. He attended a gala dinner April 13, 1830, held by Democratic Congressmen honoring the late Thomas Jefferson's birthday. The event had become an annual affair, part of Van Buren's party-building efforts. Jackson sat quietly as Calhoun's allies made speech after speech defending the extreme states' rights position articulated in the *Exposition*.

After the heated oratory, the president rose to make a toast, and he sent a chill through the room as he made clear his disdain for the previous speakers. "Our federal union," he said, "It must be preserved." Someone in attendance later said those at the table turned absolutely quiet and that, "An order to arrest Calhoun where he sat could not have come with more blindingly staggering force." Shaken, Calhoun knew he had been outed as the instigator of the nullification movement, and he sensed the

president's rage. Calhoun calmed himself and responded with his own icy toast. "The Union," he said. "Next to our liberties, most dear."

To Jackson, politics were always a matter of personal honor, and Calhoun's campaign for nullification served, in the president's mind, as an act of personal betrayal. "I had too exalted an opinion of your honor and your frankness," Jackson wrote to him. Then, referring to a scene in William Shakespeare's play *Julius Caesar* where the Roman general realizes that his friend Brutus has joined a circle of assassins stabbing him to death and says, in Latin, "You too, Brutus?" Jackson wrote, "I had a right to believe you were my sincere friend, and until now, never expected to have occasion to say to you, in the words of Caesar, *Et tu Brute*." The relationship between Jackson and Calhoun turned bitter, and the vice president resigned in December 1832 in order to serve as South Carolina senator.

A few days later, a South Carolina congressman visited Jackson at the White House, told the president he would be visiting his home state, and asked if Jackson had any messages for the Congressman's constituents. "Yes, I have," Jackson said. "Please give my compliment to my friends in your state and say to them that if a single drop of blood shall be shed there in opposition to the laws of the United States, I will hang the first man I can lay my hands on engaged in such treasonable conduct, upon the first tree I can reach."

In order to appease South Carolina, Congress passed lower tariffs in 1832, but the rates were not cut enough to appease Calhoun's allies. Nullifiers dominated the state elections in 1832. In October 1832, the South Carolina legislature authorized the convening of a nullification convention. The convention met in November 1832 and nullified not only the tariff of 1828, but also the duties approved in 1832. The convention approved an Ordinance of Nullification that declared that the state would not collect duties at its ports beginning February 1, 1833. Many politicians in South Carolina spoke of using their militia to prevent the federal government from collecting the tariffs.

Many had heard of Jackson's violent temper and knew him to be impulsive and thin-skinned, but in the **Nullification Crisis**, he would surprise even his critics with his political skills. Jackson's position was clear: nullification and secession violated the United States Constitution. He issued a statement in which he declared that, "The laws of the nation must be enforced." Speaking in a message directly to South Carolinian voters, he said, "Their object is disunion. But be not deceived by names. Disunion by armed force is *treason*. Are you really ready to incur its guilt? If you are, on the heads of the instigators of this act be the dreadful consequences; on their heads be the dishonor; but on yours may fall the punishment. On your unhappy state will inevitably fall all the evils of the conflict you force upon the Government of your country . . ."

Unchecked, the crisis could have led to civil war. Jackson, however, cleverly took a two-sided approach that would assert the right of the government in Washington to enforce federal laws but also diffuse the potentially dangerous controversy over the tariff in South Carolina. He asked the Congress for a "Force Bill" that would empower him to dispatch federal troops into South Carolina to end resistance to the tariff and restore the authority of the executive branch. At the same time, the president backed another bill reducing tariffs over a long duration to levels acceptable to the South Carolina nullifiers, what came to be known as the Compromise Tariff of 1833. South Carolina rescinded its nullification of the tariff but, at the same time, declared the force bill to be unconstitutional. The issue, however, had become moot since the lower tariffs began to be collected at South Carolina ports. Both sides claimed victory. Jackson believed he had demonstrated the power of the federal government to enforce laws in the state, but nullifiers believed their threats had forced the federal government to capitulate.

Yet, the nullification doctrine was alive and well and would be used when southern states claimed a right to secede after Abraham Lincoln won the presidency in 1860. Meanwhile, Calhoun's national political ambitions had been destroyed, and he had no chance of ever securing the Democratic Party's presidential nomination in the future. Calhoun was dropped as Jackson's running mate in the 1832 re-election campaign and replaced with the ever-ambitious Martin Van Buren.

Conspiracy Theories

By the 1830s and 1840s, Americans began to distrust each other. Slave owners convinced themselves that Northerners had become so anti-slavery that they were willing to incite slaves to murder whites. Northerners, witnessing South Carolina willing to tear up the Union in order to oppose tariffs, spoke about a conspiracy of slave owners who controlled the country. Later, they argued that these slave owners wanted to spread the peculiar institution to every corner of the country, even where it had long disappeared. Conspiracy theories abounded and formed the heart of one new political movement formed in 1828, the **Anti-Masonic Party**.

The party rose after an incident in upstate New York, in a region of the state known for its intense religious fervor called the "Burned-Over District." William Morgan, a disgruntled former member of the Masonic fraternal order, mysteriously disappeared in 1826 after he planned

to publish a tell-all book revealing the shadowy organization's secrets. The issue became a statewide scandal, with Governor DeWitt Clinton, himself a high-ranking Mason, offering a $2,000 reward (about $40,000 in today's dollars) for any information on Morgan's fate or his whereabouts. A year later, a body washed up on the shores of Lake Ontario that was presumed to be Morgan's corpse. A handful of Masons would eventually be arrested and prosecuted for his kidnapping, but no homicide charges were filed because nobody had been positively identified. A court convicted the five defendants but gave them lenient sentences, outraging a public because so many judges, lawyers, others in law enforcement, and politicians were Masons themselves. Masonry had always been popular with influential elites such as George Washington and Benjamin Franklin, and publications arose that suggested the organization secretly controlled the world and sought to use that power for wicked purposes. By 1830, 140 anti-Masonic newspapers were published across the country. The Anti-Masonic Party, which called for the abolition of secret societies and secret oaths, started as a New York organization and became the chief opposition to the reigning Democrats in the state.

The party spread, and William A. Palmer won the gubernatorial race in Vermont in 1831 on the Anti-Masonic ticket. Joseph Ritner also won the governor's mansion in Pennsylvania as an Anti-Mason. The party would hold the first presidential nominating convention in the history of the United States in 1832 when it gave the nod to William Wirt, a Virginian and former U.S. Attorney General, for the presidency. Former President John Quincy Adams joined the movement and ran unsuccessfully for governor of Massachusetts as an Anti-Mason. These panics over conspiracy theories and the intense religious devotion of the era, which saw the rise of doomsday sects and new religions like Mormonism, reflected anxieties over the rapidly rising market economy in which more skilled artisans found themselves replaced by machinery, and more went from economic independence as small farmers to being wage laborers. Many sought an explanation for their uncertainty, their sense of powerlessness, and their anxiety over the future, and Masons provided an easy scapegoat. The panic over Masons eased, and the party disbanded by 1838, many of the former members joining the Whig Party, which formed after the 1832 election.

The Bank War and the 1832 Campaign

Jackson helped increase the political paranoia with his constant complaints against the "Monster" Second Bank of the United States. No issue more polarized political elites than the so-called "**Bank War**" of the 1830s.

Jackson blamed the Second Bank for investment losses in the Panic of 1819 and held a rigid belief in a specie-based currency (actual gold or silver coins, or paper money supported by precious metals). He had no trust in purely paper currency, which the Second Bank of the United States had issued in abundance at the time of the Panic. "Divorce the government from the banks," Jackson demanded.

The 20-year charter for the Second Bank was due to expire in 1836. However, Jackson's old nemesis, Kentucky Senator Henry Clay, yearned to challenge Jackson in the next presidential election. Clay and his ally, Massachusetts Senator Daniel Webster, wanted to make the bank a political issue in the 1832 White House campaign. They prodded Nicholas Biddle, the president of the Bank, to apply for a new charter in 1832. Clay suspected that support for the Bank, which could be used to finance transportation projects, might win support for his presidential bid in the largely undeveloped northwest. Knowing Jackson's volatility, Clay and Webster hoped that Jackson might emotionally respond to the issue and make a fool of himself. With Clay and Webster at the helm, Congress voted to re-charter the bank in 1832, but Jackson vetoed the legislation.

The involvement of Clay, whom Jackson saw as the "Judas" who arranged the "corrupt bargain" in the 1824 election, in this legislation only intensified Jackson's opposition to rechartering the bank. Once again, Jackson's political opponents underestimated him and his non-standard, but nevertheless eloquent, command of the language. Jackson's veto message became a classic of political rhetoric, seen by his followers as a stirring hymn to the beauties of Jacksonian democracy. The Second Bank of the United States, Jackson insisted, was illegitimate, "unauthorized by the Constitution, subversive of the rights of states, and dangerous to the liberties of the people."

Jackson attacked the Bank as being a creation of manipulative insiders, owned by shareholders from the American Northeast and British investors. "Already is almost a third of the stock [shares in the bank are] . . . in foreign hands . . . Is there no danger to our liberty and independence in a bank that in its nature has so little to bind it to our country?" Jackson wrote. The Bank, Jackson suggested, robbed the West and the South in order to enrich the eastern cities and British businessmen. People are born with unequal talents, Jackson admitted in his message, and these differences produced wealth and poverty, but he wrote the government must not play any role in exaggerating those differences. The president opposed "any prostitution of our government to the advancement of the few at the expense to the many."

Clay, Webster and Biddle received the veto message with delight. In their minds, the message revealed the president to be confused and unstable, the message itself incoherent. Biddle himself published 20,000 copies of the veto message as a campaign pamphlet, assuming it would hurt the president. Clay and his backers would be sorely disappointed. Jackson had deftly touched on all the anxieties, resentments, and hopes of the 1832 electorate. Jackson posed the bank issue as a battle between the average person and Washington insiders, rich vs. poor, hardworking farmers vs. vulture-like financiers, the virtuous South and West vs. the corrupt Northeast, and patriots vs. foreign plutocrats. Once again Jackson, the slave holding overlord of a vast plantation, successfully portrayed himself as a voice of the ordinary people battling democracy-hating aristocrats.

Clay emerged as the candidate of the anti-Jackson National Republicans. The bank issue and American policies towards Native Americans would emerge as the key issues in the campaign. Jackson had supported legislation mandating the removal of Indians to the west of the Mississippi, a position particularly popular in the southeast and the old northwest (the region around the Great Lakes). Van Buren and other allies again organized an 1832 campaign ahead of its time, maintaining card files of potential supporters to enlist their help in the campaign and their votes, creating campaign buttons, and organizing pro-Jackson clubs to run the crusade at the grassroots level. Jackson buried Clay in a landslide, beating him in the popular vote by 16 points, 54 percent to 38 percent. The president also carried almost all of the Electoral College, winning 219-49, with William Wirt of the Anti-Masonic Party winning 7 electoral votes. Jackson, however, won fewer popular votes than in 1828, and his majority in the House of Representatives slid from 59 seats to 46. He also lost control of the Senate, where he had enjoyed a narrow 4-seat advantage. His allies were now a minority by 8 seats. Jackson's divisive, often autocratic leadership style had completely divided the electorate and led to the rise of a major opposition party.

JACKSON'S SECOND TERM

The Second American Party System

By 1834, the opposition to Andrew Jackson congealed into an organized political party, the **Whigs**, a group that shared many beliefs with their Federalist forebears, including support for the federal government as a positive force that could promote American economic development.

Men like Henry Clay, Daniel Webster, and John Quincy Adams formed the core of the party, whose members saw Jackson as uneducated, erratic and destructive in his opposition to programs like building federal roads. The Whigs derived their name from those in England who had challenged James II during the Glorious Revolution in 1688. The name served as a sarcastic reference to Jackson, whom they derided as "King Andrew." The party solidly backed the Second Bank of the United States as a force that had, save for the Panic of 1819, stabilized the American economy and encouraged business development. Whigs also embraced protective tariffs, which they felt helped infant American industries get off the ground while competing against their richer and more advanced competitors in England and elsewhere in Western Europe.

The Whig Party fully embraced Henry Clay's "American System," which, as discussed in the previous chapter, called for the aggressive construction of turnpikes, bridges, canals, and, starting in the 1830s, railroads. Improved transportation, they believed, would modernize the economy, create jobs, and tie the different regions more closely together financially and culturally. Whigs also tended to draw reform-minded evangelicals who supported, on the local level, the expansion of public education, more humane prisons, and better treatment for the insane and the disabled. Many Whigs were members of the temperance movement, which sought to ban alcohol because of its role in crime and other social problems. Some Whigs also joined the movement for women's voting rights. The Whig Party received its biggest vote totals in the Northeast and the Old Northwest (states such as Ohio and Illinois, where Abraham Lincoln won election as a Whig congressman, serving from 1847-1849). Whigs tended to prevail in regions marked by industrial production and by farms owned by whites producing for the national and global market.

A chief weakness of the party was its inability to come to a consensus on slavery. Northern Whigs favored a limit to slavery's expansion west into new territories, with a minority favoring abolition, while southern Whigs defending slavery. They generally tried to avoid discussions of slavery altogether, seeing the subject as harmful to national unity. The party would splinter over the slavery issue in the 1850s but it served as the chief competition to Jackson's Democrats for two decades.

Destroying the National Bank

Jackson won, but the Second Bank of the United States still had a four-year lease on life. With the president's support eroded in the Congress, the White House worried that the Congress might try to re-charter the bank and might be able to override a veto this time. Jackson sought to hasten the bank's demise and, ignoring his supposed insistence on strictly adhering to the Constitution, he defied the will of Congress by illegally transferring federal government deposits to a collection of state banks whose officers had supported him in the 1832 race, the so-called "**pet banks**." He completed the transfers by October 1, 1833.

Biddle faced a legitimate crisis with the loss of the federal deposits and struggled to keep the Bank of the United States' books in balance. He called in all of the bank's loans to state banks who were then forced to demand immediate repayment from their private and business customers. Biddle also had national bank agents redeem all state banks notes lying within the Bank's vaults. Overall, he hoped that by provoking a credit crisis that he might turn the public against Jackson and create pressure to reverse his policies. Biddle's actions caused a ripple effect, pulling money out of circulation and provoking an economic panic in 1833-1834 that forced businesses across the country into default. The bank president again showed a knack for political miscalculation. The public blamed him and not Jackson for the economic slowdown. The panic ended when business leaders successfully pressured Biddle to end his policies; commercial activity picked up and a boom followed, particularly as a flood of silver exports from China and Mexico caused a flow of these precious metals into the United States. For this, Jackson got the credit.

Meanwhile, the circulation of federal funds in state banks enabled those unregulated institutions to make irresponsible loans, often to reckless land speculators. Inflation reared its ugly head. In the South, cotton and slave prices climbed. Wholesale prices jumped 50 percent between 1832 and 1836. Inflation only worsened as a result of the Deposit Act of 1836, which required the federal government to distribute $30 million of the $35 million budget surplus (the equivalent of $604 million of $706 million today) to the states when the Jackson administration retired the federal debt that year. The wild escalation of prices led to New York City food riots near the end of Jackson's tenure in February 1837. In New York, the cost of flour had doubled.

To combat inflation, on July 11, 1836, Jackson and Treasury Secretary Levi Woodbury issued the "**Specie Circular**," which required payment for government land to be made in silver or gold. This policy would later have disastrous consequences. For the well-off, at least, the economy still seemed to be booming, yet problems lay underneath the surface, a problem Jackson bequeathed his successor, Martin Van Buren, when he left office in March 1837.

The Heir

Jackson gave Van Buren his full blessing when the vice president sought the White House in 1836. The Whig Party, in its infancy, lacked a single national candidate. Van Buren instead faced a number of Whig regional candidates, such as Senator Daniel Webster, expected to make a powerful showing in New England; General William Henry Harrison of Ohio, who held political strength in the old northwest; Senator Hugh Lawson White of Tennessee, who represented the party's best hope in the South; and Senator Willie Person Magnum, considered competitive in the south Atlantic states. Whigs hoped they could deny an Electoral College majority to Van Buren and throw the election to the House. Worried about whether Southerners would back him, Van Buren, a New Yorker, supported a change in postal regulations that would allow states to censor abolitionist literature.

Van Buren lacked Jackson's charisma, war record, and popularity, and so the Democrats won less support in 1836 than they had under Old Hickory, but none of the regional Whig candidates posed a serious challenge. The worst side effects of Jackson's Bank War and his economic policies had not yet made themselves apparent. Van Buren won just over 50 percent of the popular vote in a five-candidate field, but he carried states in the West, the South, the North, and even in Webster's stronghold in New England. Harrison fared the best of his opponents, getting almost 37 percent of the popular vote and 73 Electoral College votes. The election turned out to be the last time a sitting vice president would prevail in a presidential election until George H.W. Bush won the White House in the 1988 presidential race.

Because 23 electors from Virginia refused to cast their ballots for Van Buren's running mate, Richard Mentor Johnson of Kentucky, he fell one vote short of the Electoral College majority needed to become vice president. Johnson's open relationship with Julia Chin, a mixed-race slave woman by whom he fathered two children, had become a campaign controversy. This would mark the only time so far in history that the Senate, under the provisions of the Twelfth Amendment, had to select the vice president. In the Senate, Johnson prevailed. At the inaugural, Jackson and Van Buren appeared together. The old general got much louder cheers than his successor. It was an ominous sign for the incoming leader. Van Buren could inhabit the White House after Jackson, but he could never assume Jackson's stature in the public mind.

HARD TIMES UNDER VAN BUREN

Jackson boosted Van Buren's rise to the White House, but he also burdened the next president with a deeply troubled economy, an unresolved diplomatic challenge posed by the successful Texas Revolution in 1836, a strengthening and growing institution of slavery and the regional tensions it provoked, and management of the final and homicidal stages of Jackson's brutal Indian removal policies. Committed to a rigid belief in limited government in all circumstances, Van Buren rendered himself incapable of responding to a brewing economic depression. His white supremacist thinking and his desire to build the Democratic Party as a national force propelled the nation further toward civil war and bloodied the nation's hands with one of its worst acts of genocide.

In his inaugural address, Van Buren promised a continuation of Jackson's policies. He stated his clear intention was to do as little as possible, insisting that the "wisest course is to confine legislation to as few subjects as is consistent with the well-being of a society and to leave as large a proportion of the affairs of man as is possible to their own management."

Van Buren, however, would be a victim of bad timing, and his administration would be primarily remembered for a severe depression that ravaged the country from 1837 to 1843. Jackson's Specie Circular, and his restric-

Whig political cartoon depicting Andrew Jackson as the tyrant "King Andrew I".

tions on paper currency, contributed to severe deflation. The money supply shrank dramatically. Forced to lower prices for their goods, farmers and businessmen saw their profits drop. Wages dropped as well, which aggravated the downward cycle. Runs on banks—in which panicked depositors raced to withdraw their uninsured deposits, emptying those institutions' vaults and driving them to close—broke out all over the country. About 40 percent of the banks in the United States shut their doors permanently during this depression, with customers losing all they held in deposits. States defaulted on their loans, and construction halted in much of the country.

A half-million workers lost their jobs nationwide, with 50,000 jobless and the unemployment rate in New York City in the winter of 1837-38 peaking at a shocking 33 percent. Many of the unemployed found themselves homeless, shivering on the streets, and without assistance as churches ran out of money and no government aid was available.

Across the country, tens of thousands of workers went on strike, and the wealthy began to voice concerns about a revolution. Unwilling to see the government play any role in relieving the poor or stimulating the economy, during the economic crisis Van Buren called for the government, already doing little, to do even less. Throughout the depression, Van Buren called for the government to maintain "severe economy," claiming that, "To keep the expenditures within reasonable bounds is a duty second only to the preservation of our national character and the protection of our citizens in their civil and political rights." Van Buren was not responsible for the policies that led to the depression. But he lacked the imagination to end or even relieve the economic misery. The voters would blame the president personally for this depression and during his term he came to be known as "Martin Van Ruin."

CONCEPTS OF RACE IN JACKSONIAN AMERICA

There is no biological basis for the concept of race. Based on random traits such as skin color and hair texture, racial categories rest on the incorrect notion that different human groups have clearly distinct biological histories, i.e., that blacks, whites and others branched off into very clearly marked, separate family trees. In fact, millions of so-called whites have relatively recent "black" ancestors, and vice versa. The concept of race rests on the mistaken idea that superficial features like color imply more important differences between these vaguely defined racial categories in terms of intelligence, work ethic, and character. The idea of race seems to have

Martin Van Buren

first developed as Europeans began their conquest of the rest of the world at the start of the 1500s and rationalized the enslavement of supposedly inferior, or even subhuman, Africans and the genocide of Native Americans.

By Andrew Jackson's time, race completely defined American society. Only whites were deemed intelligent and independent enough to function in a democracy. So-called non-whites, such as African-American slaves or Native Americans, possessing what Anglo-descended Americans considered animal-like natures, could not be allowed to participate in American life politically. Even in northern states where slavery had become illegal, African Americans were denied the right to vote. When Illinois became a state in 1818, it prohibited African Americans from living there.

By the 1820s and 1830s, white society had long puzzled over where black skin came from. Many believed that Africans were the descendants of Ham, one of the sons of Noah described in the Book of Genesis. Noah cursed Ham's descendants to be "servants of servants" because the son had disrespected his father. Many white Christians in the United States argued that Africans' and African Americans' dark skin was a sign of that curse. Black slavery, basically, was God's will, they argued.

Some Americans sought scientific explanations for perceived racial differences. From the 1500s to the early 1800s whites speculated on whether the descendants of Africans would eventually get lighter-skinned the longer they lived in more northern zones. As late as the first decade of the 1800s, Dr. Benjamin Rush, one of the signers of the Declaration of Independence, suggested that blackness represented a type of leprosy. He claimed blackness even infected southern whites surrounded by slaves. Rush, however, believed that over the decades, blackness would be cured because of what he thought was the healthier environment of North America, and he made note of cases of blacks gradually losing their dark skin color over a lifetime. Undoubtedly, Rush was referring to cases of vitiligo, a skin condition in which the body in different spots stops producing pigment. Dr. Rush experimented on African Americans to "cure" them of their blackness, and he claimed he had achieved positive results in lightening skin by bleeding test subjects and subjecting them to enemas.

By the Jacksonian era, some ministers and scientists, still accepting the Bible as the source of all scientific knowledge, struggled with answering how blacks and whites could supposedly be so different and yet both be descended from the first two humans, Adam and Eve. Many proposed the theory of polygenesis, the idea that the creation story in Genesis only referred to the origins of white people. Adam and Eve were white, according to the believers in this theory. God had created blacks, Indians and other groups separately. This idea clearly implied that only whites were truly human and that people of color were separate species and could thus be justly used as farm animals.

This rationalization for vicious exploitation came at a convenient time. Since the invention of the cotton gin, slavery had never been more important to the American economy. Southern slave owners had always argued that slavery was a "necessary evil." While slavery was regrettable, the vast lands of America could not be put to a productive use unless a large workforce was forced to do the labor. During the Jacksonian era, southern slave owners began to argue that the peculiar institution was a positive good. It kept whites from having to do the most degrading work. It also, the argument went, was good for blacks, who allegedly had been saved from African savagery through slavery and now enjoyed living in a safer, healthier white civilization. Blacks were permanently childlike, the white supremacists of the era insisted, and would be doomed forever to hunger, cannibalism, and the most primitive of existences unless placed under the firm, parent-like control of their white masters.

Van Buren was a man of his times, fully accepting the fashionable racist ideas regarding African Americans. Even though he voted against admitting Missouri as a slave state while serving as a U.S. senator from New York, he consistently accommodated slaveholders as vice president and president, not wanting to offend them for fear this might shatter the Democratic Party he had so carefully

constructed. In his inaugural address, Van Buren condemned abolitionists and as president he vowed to veto any legislation that would outlaw slavery in the District of Columbia. He supported Democrats in the House who defended the gag rule prohibiting consideration of anti-slavery petitions. When Florida statehood came up for consideration, he vigorously resisted any attempts to restrict slavery there or in any other U.S. territory.

INDIAN REMOVAL

Few aspects of American history are as shameful as the treatment of Native Americans, and a low point in that bloody relationship came during the 1820s and 1830s. By then, when much of the land west of the Mississippi was relatively uninhabited by whites and the biggest chunk of that land still lay within Mexican borders, the American government committed to a policy of Indian removal, bribing and forcing Native Americans within U.S. borders to settle west of the Mississippi River. Andrew Jackson and Martin Van Buren did not initiate Indian removal, but they saw it through to its bloody end.

John Quincy Adams's Secretary of State Henry Clay insisted that Indians were a people "destined to extinction." He dismissed indigenous people as a race "not worth preserving," "essentially inferior to the Anglo-Saxon race," and not an "improvable breed." Contemplating their possible extinction, Clay felt no sorrow but believed that "their disappearance from the human family would be no great loss." During the Adams administration, it became clear that a treaty with the Creek Indians in Georgia to swap land there for territory farther west had been drawn up under fraudulent circumstances, with representatives of the Creek bribed by both state and federal agents to make the agreement. The Creek assassinated the corrupt representatives who made the deal and then declared they were not obligated to follow it. The State of Georgia acted like nothing had happened and began surveying the Creek land in preparation for selling it to whites. The Adams administration allowed it to happen, ignoring previous treaties between the federal government and the Creek people guaranteeing the integrity of their lands.

The Creek Nation, along with the Cherokee, Chickasaw, Choctaw, and Seminole, formed what whites called **"The Five Civilized Tribes."** Federal and state government officials and Christian missionaries had previously insisted to Native Americans that as long as they remained supposed savages, they could not live peacefully alongside whites. Anglos, however, had made an implied promise to the Indians that if they "civilized," that is if they abandoned their traditional cultures and strictly conformed to white norms regarding land ownership, political organization, family structure and religion, they might win acceptance as a distinct but still welcomed people within the American nation.

Under the guidance of leaders like Guwisguwi (**John Ross**), the Cherokee in particular represented assimilation with the white majority in the extreme. They adopted a constitution based on the American model. Many within that community converted to Christianity, mastered English, and adopted Western-style clothing. Another Cherokee, **Sequoyah**, invented an alphabet for their native language, and Cherokee-language Bibles were widely distributed in Cherokee territory. Land ceased to be seen as a source of identity and increasingly as a mere commodity. Instead of holding land as a community, the Cherokee began, like their white neighbors, to divide their homeland into privately owned lots.

Like white Southerners, they started buying and selling black slaves, and some absorbed the whites' beliefs in black inferiority. They passed laws forbidding interracial marriage with those of African descent. Some Cherokee became wealthy cotton planters running large plantations. They farmed in the same style as whites and married white women. Some cultural traditionalists within the nation bitterly complained that they had so completely adopted white ways that they ceased to be real Cherokee. The nation also published a bilingual newspaper, *The Cherokee Phoenix*, and they produced goods traded on the world market, including cloth, grain, and lumber. Cherokee had accomplished what whites supposedly wanted. But to whites, no technology, no modern businesses, and no accommodation to the dominant culture would ever be enough. The Cherokee remained in white eyes congenital savages—racial inferiors who stood in the way of progress.

By Jackson's first month in the White House in March 1829, Indian removal had become largely a fact in much of the North. New York State's Iroquois mostly struggled to live on tiny reservations, and after the War of 1812, the bands in the Old Northwest suffered as a scattered and demoralized people. In the Southeast, the demands for Indian resettlement only intensified as the white populations of Alabama and Georgia increased and cotton prices rose, making land more expensive for whites and harder to obtain. Then, gold was discovered on the Cherokee land as well. About 10,000 white miners flocked to the Georgia hills within the Cherokee domain.

Always hostile to claims of sovereignty as a nation within a nation, a unique relationship with the United States government ratified through a treaty, Jackson fumed that American progress would not be sacrificed in the interests of people he dismissed as "a few thousand savages." Indian lands, he believed, belonged to whites by right of racial superiority. At the president's prompting, Congress passed the **1830 Indian Removal Act**. The law required an involuntary "exchange of lands with the Indians residing in any of the states and territories, and for their removal west of the river of Mississippi."

Chief Justice Marshall and the Cherokee

The state of Georgia began implementing Indian removal almost immediately, often at gunpoint. Cherokee leaders still retained faith in the American system and turned to the federal courts to challenge the legality of the Indian Removal Act, their lawyers arguing that previous treaties the nation had signed with the United States government (in which Washington recognized Cherokee sovereignty and control of their traditional lands in Georgia) rendered the new law moot. Uncertain of the commitment of the federal government to removal, the state of Georgia, in a series of laws, stripped Cherokee of the right to their traditional lands and invalidated laws the Cherokee had implemented to govern their territory.

Meanwhile, another legal case, involving the right of white men to live in Cherokee lands and to marry Cherokee women without licenses from the state of Georgia worked its way through the federal courts. The two cases, *Cherokee Nation v. Georgia* (1831) and *Worcester v. Georgia* (1832), reached the United States Supreme Court. The majority opinions, written by Chief Justice John Marshall, sought to define Indian rights and the political relationship between Indian bands and the state and national governments.

In *Cherokee Nation v. Georgia*, the Supreme Court ruled that it did not have jurisdiction in the case because the Cherokee were not, as they claimed, a separate "foreign" nation within U.S. borders. Marshall wrote, instead, that the Cherokee constituted a "domestic dependent nation." Marshall noted that the Cherokee still retained rights to their land until they voluntarily surrendered such property. In *Worcester vs. Georgia,* the state had arrested and sentenced to four years of hard labor seven missionaries who had refused to get required state licenses before living on Cherokee lands. At least two of the missionaries were targeted for prosecution because of their strong opposition to Georgia's Indian removal policies. The missionaries' lawsuit contended that the State of Georgia had no authority to pass laws over tribal lands.

In his majority opinion, Marshall argued that the federal government, not state governments, had the sole authority to deal with domestic, dependent nations such as the Cherokee people. He acknowledged that the exercise of conquest and purchase can give political dominion,

John Ross

but those are in the hands of the federal government and not the states. The Cherokee held a special status as a "distinct community" in which "the laws of Georgia can have no force." The U.S. Constitution gave the federal government alone the power over Indian affairs, Marshall wrote.

The Supreme Court decisions outraged Jackson, who was happy to let Georgia expel the Cherokee. Three years earlier, at his first inauguration, Jackson raised his right hand and swore to faithfully execute the laws of the United States. Now he refused to honor that oath and announced his decision to not execute the Supreme Court's decision

Sequoyah, inventor of the Cherokee alphabet

in the *Worcester* case. "[Chief Justice] John Marshall has made his decision," Jackson reportedly said. "Now let him enforce it." Jackson would let Georgia proceed in its expulsion of Cherokee and other natives, regardless of the Supreme Court ruling or standing American treaties with native people. In 1832, he ordered U.S. Army troops to aid the Georgia militia in forced expulsion of Native American tribes.

The Second Seminole War

Across the South, troops forced Indians westward at bayonet point. Not just the Cherokee, but the Creek as well became victims of white greed. White invaders claimed Indian land and often, at gunpoint, evicted indigenous people from their land before they had an opportunity to gather their belongings. Angry words sometimes provoked shootings. These violent incidents exploded into a full-scale war between the Creek and the Georgia militia in the Chattahoochee Valley in May 1836. It ended with the Georgia militia routing Creek resistance. "Enforced removal began with 14,609 Creek carried off to the Indian Territory [modern day Oklahoma], some of them handcuffed and in chains," historian Robert Remini wrote. In 1837, 5,000 more Creek had been forced westward.

After armed forces expelled his people, one Creek leader pleaded with a military officer. "You have been with us many moons. Our road has been a long one . . . on it we have laid the bones of our men, women, and children . . . you have heard the cries of our women and children . . . Tell General Jackson if the white men will let us we will live in peace and friendship." This offer was not to be heard.

Afraid of his influence, the United States Army in 1835 arrested a Seminole leader in Florida, **Osceola**, who loudly objected to removal and urged local Native Americans to hold onto their lands. After soldiers placed him in chains and locked him in a cage, Osceola, sensing the fate awaiting his people, tore out his hair and raged until he foamed at the mouth, according to white witnesses. After he calmed down, authorities eventually released him, but he would lead an uprising that came to be known as the Second Seminole War. This Jacksonian exercise in genocide proved a costly campaign in dollars and blood. Lasting seven years, from 1835 to 1842, this war against the Seminole took place mostly in murky swamps unfamiliar to American troops. The war dragged on, with the Seminole adopting guerilla tactics. Jackson told his commander, General Winfield Scott, to march toward the place where the "Indian women were collected" in order to draw Osceola and his men into an open battle and destroy his forces.

The Seminoles, women, children and all, refused to fall into a trap, and kept constantly on the move. The war, lasting through the entire term of Jackson's successor Van Buren, eventually cost the U.S. government up to $40 million and the deaths of 1,500 American soldiers. A larger number of Seminole died, some from starvation. Osceola died after a fierce battle in the Everglades. Political disunity, hunger, exhaustion, and disease eventually forced the Seminole to capitulate, and the Army would force 3,000 of them to flee west of the Mississippi River, with one-fifth of the original group of refugees dying from physical hardships during the brutal march to the distant Indian Territory.

The Trail of Tears

Even though many Cherokee and other Indians started abandoning Georgia because of the fear of white violence, bribery or discouragement, John Ross, the leader of the Cherokee, still refused to lead his people from their Georgia homeland. Van Buren now occupied the White House, but Jackson's bloody handprints were all over the tragedy that came to be known as the **Trail of Tears**, beginning in 1838. General Scott, also busy with the Seminole War, sent 7,000 white soldiers to Georgia to round up the remaining Cherokee. The soldiers were ordered to use any means, including whole-scale violence, to complete the ethnic cleansing. As with the Creek earlier, soldiers arrived and allowed no time for the Cherokee to collect their personal effects before they were coerced into a long wintertime exodus. One of the survivors, Rebecca Neugin, would be 100 years old when she was interviewed in 1932:

> When the soldiers came to our house my father wanted to fight, but my mother told him that the soldiers would kill him if he did and we surrendered without a fight. They drove us out of our house to join other prisoners in a stockade. After they took us away, my mother begged them to let her go back and get some bedding. So they let her go back and she brought . . . bedding and a few cooking utensils she could carry and had to leave behind all of our other household possessions.

The Cherokee would have little time to gather clothing that would protect them from the bitter cold they would encounter in the coming weeks. "Families at dinner were startled by the sudden gleam of bayonets in the doorway," one witness later said, "and rose to be driven with blows and oaths along the many miles of trail that led to [a] stockade. Men were seized in the fields, or

going along the roads, women were taken from their spinning wheels and children from their play." One Georgia militiaman who would later fight for the Confederacy compared the Trail of Tears to what Southerners called the War Between the States. "I fought through the Civil War and have seen men shot in pieces and slaughtered by the thousands, but the Cherokee removal was the cruelest I've ever seen."

Rousted from the only homes they ever knew, these families shivered as they groaned with hunger. White men speaking a language they did not understand yelled at terrified Cherokee children separated from their parents in the chaos. According to a white witness, John G. Burnett, soldiers forced a Cherokee couple to abandon the body of their child, who had just died.

For various people, the Trail of Tears started in different places at different times but was an approximately 1,000-mile forced march from Georgia, Alabama and Mississippi to what is now Oklahoma. Choctaw, Chickasaw, Creek, and others joined the Cherokee on this torturous trail. As the winter of 1838 started, some of the Indians began to freeze. They hungered as well. When allowed to pause, ate raw corn or pumpkins growing in the fields owned by cooperative whites. Government agents had stolen supplies meant for the Indians, with some Natives marching barefoot on ice and snow. Armed whites left the Natives with nothing, according to one witness, than "the sky for a blanket and the earth for a pillow."

Pregnant women were forced to march alongside the others, and when they could not keep up in the death march, they faced terrible consequences. A white man, Daniel Butrick, recalled seeing a soldier stab a pregnant Cherokee woman in the stomach. Other soldiers forced Native America women to drink until they became intoxicated, and the men would then gang rape them. Along the way, when soldiers decided it was time to halt the relentless drive to the Indian Territory, they forced Indians into hastily constructed stockades. These pens became hellholes of hunger and thirst, breeding grounds for cholera, diarrhea, dysentery and smallpox as the removal campaign stretched into the summer. One-third of the Choctaw forcibly moved died, some from starvation. Of the 15,000 Cherokee victims of Indian removal in the 1838-1839 Trail of Tears, about 4,000 died.

In his farewell address of 1837, Andrew Jackson piously rationalized his homicidal Indian policy. The civilized tribes, he insisted, had been "placed beyond the reach of injury or oppression, and that [the] paternal care of the General Government will . . . watch after them and protect them." It was one more lie to the continent's native peoples. Indians knew better than to rely on the tender mercies of the new, rising marketplace and an increasingly racist white society. Removed west of the Mississippi, they faced another six decades in which their lands would be stolen by fraud and warfare, and in which their peoples would be destroyed through disease, malnutrition, alcoholism stemming from despair, and deliberate extermination. The Cherokee and others would be forever insecure, wherever they dwelled.

THE AGE OF JACKSON: AN ASSESSMENT

If you were a southern white man of modest means during the 1820s and 1830s, Andrew Jackson represented the swell of democratic forces that lowered property requirements and probably resulted in you gaining the right to vote. If you were Henry Clay, Daniel Webster, or Nicholas Biddle, Jackson embodied the primitive forces afoot in the land, the unwashed ignorant masses who did not understand the rising market economy and feared it, the man who stood in the way of making the country an economic and political giant on a par with England.

If you were a white Georgian with the money to buy land, Jackson was the man who enhanced your wealth by destroying Indian nations residing within your state and opening their lands to theft. If you were a Cherokee or a Creek, Jackson was nothing less than an American Hitler, a man who guided wars of elimination, and who pursued one of the most ferocious genocides ever directed against your people. To you, Jackson was a hardhearted ruler who forced your people off of rich, fertile land and made your nation march a thousand miles to a much harsher climate, with soldiers raping and killing unarmed civilians and letting your brothers and sisters shiver and starve in a dark, deadly winter.

In spite of a lifetime of serious injury and poor health, Jackson long refused to die, writing furious letters of advice to his admirer, President James Polk, and not giving up until he was a sickly 78-year-old man at his Hermitage Plantation in Tennessee on June 8, 1845. Perhaps aware of his grave sins as a slave owner and Indian killer, Jackson summoned his black servants to his bedside and said, "I want all to prepare to meet me in Heaven . . . Christ has no respect for color." When he died, someone asked one of his slaves where he felt the iron-willed former master had gone. The black servant paused then said, "If General Jackson wants to go to Heaven, who's to stop him?"

Upon hearing of Jackson's demise, one of his many detractors, the New York merchant Philip Hone causti-

Map 11.3 The Cherokee "Trail of Tears"

Presidents, Art, and Monumental Power
in the Jacksonian Era

In the year of what would have been George Washington's 100th birthday, 1832, the Congress commissioned artist Horatio Greenough to create a sculpture honoring the first president. The artwork was ordered as the current controversial president, Andrew Jackson, was nearing the end of his first term. Jackson had raised anew a debate about the nature of the presidency and the powers of that office relative to that of the Congress.

In two years a political party, the Whigs, would form to oppose Jacksonism. Claiming the president aspired to be an all-powerful monarch and deriding Jackson as "King Andrew," the Whigs took their name from a British political party that had always defended the prerogatives of the Parliament and opposed granting the crown unlimited power.

Since the days of the Articles of Confederation, which took effect in 1781, through the ratification of the Constitution in 1789, to the days of Jackson, Americans had decidedly mixed feelings about executive power. Americans feared the presidency could assume dictatorial power, as they believed had happened under British King George III. Under the Articles, there had been no president. The Congress was given a far longer list of enumerated powers than the president in the Constitution.

Article 2 of the Constitution, which describes the duties and powers of the president, reads almost as an afterthought. Furthermore, presidents had imposed limits on the office themselves, such as the two-term tradition established by Washington when he chose, after eight years as the chief executive, to not seek the office again in 1796.

To his critics, Jackson recognized no limits to the powers of the presidency. For instance, Jackson refused to enforce the 1832 United States Supreme Court decision in **Worcester v. Georgia**, a decision which allowed whites to seize Cherokee land in that state. When Greenough's massive, 12-ton marble statue of George Washington finally arrived in the capital in 1841, Jackson had been out of office for four years, but the statue seemed a metaphor for the grotesque expansion of presidential power during his administration.

In life, Washington had struggled to inspire respect for the office of president without lending it monarchical trappings. Even during his presidency, Washington had assumed a larger-than-life presence and was endlessly memorialized on oil paintings, commemorative coins, busts, and tapestries. The mythos that grew around Washington as the "Father of His Country," including an 1800 largely fictitious biography by Parson Mason Locke Weems that depicted Washington admitting to his father that he chopped down a cherry tree because, he said, "I cannot tell a lie," made the first president seem more like an Old Testament patriarch or prophet than a mere human office holder. Even with that context, however, the new sculpture seemed over-the-top.

Greenough's sculpture drew its inspiration from a long-ago destroyed statue of Zeus from Greek antiquity. Greenough portrayed Washington as a demigod seated on a throne, partially clad in a toga, his muscled chest and left arm bare. The left arm held a sword, hilt pointing forward, as Washington was depicted holding his right arm aloft, his forefinger pointing toward heaven. The image is the opposite of democratic. It more resembled 17th or 18th century European art depicting an absolute monarch than a tribute to the president of a republic. Greenough's Washington looks more ready to strike sinful Americans with lightning bolts than, in the words of the oath of office, to the best of his ability, "preserve, protect and defend the Constitution of the United States."

The work immediately became the object of ridicule. The statue's laughable pretentiousness inspired ridicule. It scandalized many more for its semi-nudity rather than for its anti-democratic message. The Congress originally intended the statue to be displayed in the Capitol rotunda but relocated it to the east lawn of the Capitol in 1843. Moved to the United States Patent Office, then to the Smithsonian Castle in 1908, the peripatetic statue did not find its final resting place until 1964 when it was placed in what became the National Museum of American History, an unwanted artistic stepchild of a culture that at least liked to imagine it was dedicated to equality.

The reaction to the Greenough sculpture represented a healthy revulsion toward authoritarian symbols suggesting absolute power. Nevertheless, the Greenough sculpture provided a concrete illustration of an opposing authoritarian strain in American politics: the yearning for an end to inefficiencies, the partisanship, the squabbling and the petty score-settling of the Congress and the search for an authoritative leader who through charisma and will could simply solve any problem, from war against Native Americans, to banking crises, to slavery.

cally noted in his diary, "Now, to my thinking, the country has greater cause to mourn on the day of his birth than on that of his decease. This iron-willed man has done more mischief than any man alive." Others denounced Jackson as a dictator. Even to this day, however, mostly white men have written American history, and most of those white scholars have depicted Jackson as one of the giants of his age. Harvard historian and Kennedy family friend Arthur Schlesinger, Jr., in his Pulitzer-Prize winning *Age of Jackson* (published in 1945), saw in Jackson an early Franklin Roosevelt, a mostly benevolent force spreading the blessings of the franchise to poor and struggling whites and leveling the privileges of the well-to-do. Schlesinger, like so many establishment historians of his era, completely ignored Native Americans and slaves in his 523-page account. As an inconvenient truth, the Trail of Tears vanishes from Schlesinger's story of the Jackson years. In polls of historians held by his father, Arthur Schlesinger, Sr., in 1948 and 1962, and by Arthur Schlesinger, Jr. in 1996, as well as other major surveys of historians in those years, Jackson generally ranked as one of the 10 best presidents, even as high as the fifth or sixth greatest.

His image adorns the $20 bill. New Orleans named Jackson Square after him. The seventh president's name also adorns a state park in South Carolina; the city of Jacksonville, Florida; the city of Jackson, Mississippi, that state's capital; and suburbs, towns, high schools, junior highs and elementary campuses all across the country. However, more recent historians, who came of age in the wake of the 1950s and 1960s Civil Rights Movement and the American Indian Movement, have been much more critical, and Andrew Jackson is as likely to be portrayed as an Indian killer as a force for democracy. To the general public, among presidents, Jackson may not be as revered as George Washington or Abraham Lincoln, or have the passionate partisans like Franklin Roosevelt or Ronald Reagan, yet, like Thomas Jefferson, Jackson remains a polarizing but almost universally acknowledged figure of deep historical significance. Not many presidents have ages named after them.

"More than any other American, Jackson oversaw the decline and fall of the elitist gentry order established by the Framers, and its replacement with the ruder conventions and organization of democracy," wrote the scholar Sean Wilentz. "More than any other president before him,

he made the office of the presidency the center of action in national politics and government . . . Jackson and his supporters also created the first mass democratic national political party in modern history. Yet, Jackson had a very limited view of which people had a right to participate in that democracy: the white planter, the farmer, the mechanic, and the laborer . . . [T]hese classes of society form the great body of the people of the United States; they are the bone and sinew of the country."

Jackson's economic policies, however, including his war with the Second Bank of the United States and his policies tightening the money supply, injured those very same classes, triggering one of the worst depressions in American history and concentrating wealth in the hands of those same wealthy elites he supposedly despised. Meanwhile, Jackson pretended to care for people of color only in the most paternalistic way. He claimed that his Indian removal policies were designed to protect Indians from extinction, but in fact that approach only opened the door to racial mass murder.

His close associate Van Buren would in his later years not be a believer in racial equality but would at least acknowledge the dangers slavery posed to American democracy. Van Buren would run for president in 1848 as the nominee of the Free Soil Party, which opposed the spread of slavery to the western territories acquired in the Louisiana Purchase and the Mexican American War. Jackson never entertained any doubts about the rectitude of slavery.

The Democratic Party that Jackson and Van Buren created would remain a force for white racial domination, for slavery, and black disenfranchisement and segregation for decades. The two-thirds nominating rule guaranteed a white southern veto of party presidential nominees until the 1930s. Jackson appointed five southern slave owners to the Supreme Court, men such as Roger Taney of Maryland. As Supreme Chief Justice, Taney wrote the majority decision in the infamous 1857 *Dred Scott* decision that declared that the writers of the Constitution saw blacks as "beings of an inferior order, and altogether unfit to associate with the white race, either in social or political relations, and so far inferior that they had no rights which the white man was bound to respect." Jacksonian Democracy, in the end, was a fraud. White democracy in the 1830s and 1840s rested on the cruel foundation of racial dictatorship.

Chronology

1825 Completion of the Erie Canal in New York.
U.S. House of Representatives elects John Quincy Adams president. Adams appoints Henry Clay secretary of state, prompting charges of "corrupt bargain" by Andrew Jackson's supporters.

1828 Tariff of Abominations passed.
Jackson elected president.
Baltimore and Ohio Railroad chartered.

1830 Indian Removal Act.
Maysville Road Bill vetoed by President Jackson.

1831 First issue of *Liberator* published.
Nat Turner slave revolt erupts.
Alexis de Tocqueville publishes *Democracy in America.*
Cherokee Nation v. Georgia decision.

1832 Jackson vetoes the recharter of the Bank of the U.S.
Jackson signs the Tariff of 1832.
South Carolina nullified the Tariffs of 1828 and 1832.
Jackson reelected to the presidency.
Worcester v. Georgia decision.

1833 Compromise Tariff passes.
South Carolina rescinds its Ordinance of Nullification.
New York Sun becomes the first penny newspaper.

1834 Cyrus McCormick patents the mechanical grain reaper.
First strike by women laborers at the Lowell Mills.
Whig Party organized.

1836 Charter of the second Bank of the U.S. expires.
Jackson issues the Specie Circular.
Martin Van Buren elected president.
Texas declares independence from Mexico.

1837 Economic panic began a six-year-long depression.
Cotton prices plummet.

1840 William Henry Harrison elected first Whig president.

SUGGESTED READINGS

H.W. Brands, *Andrew Jackson: His Life and Times* (2006).

Andrew Burstein, *The Passions of Andrew Jackson* (2003).

Donald B. Cole, *The Presidency of Andrew Jackson* (1993).

John Ehle, *Trail of Tears: The Rise and Fall of the Cherokee Nation* (1997)

Matthew Goodman. *The Sun and the Moon: The Remarkable True Account of Hoaxers, Showmen, Dueling Journalists and Lunar Manbats in Nineteenth-Century New York.* (2008).

Kenneth S. Greenberg, *Nat Turner: A Slave Rebellion in History and Memory* (2004).

Michael F. Holt, *The Rise and Fall of the American Whig Party: Jacksonian Politics and the Onset of the Civil War* (1999).

Leon F. Litwack, *North of Slavery: The Negro in the Free States, 1790-1860* (1965).

John F. Marszalek, *The Petticoat Affair: Manners, Mutiny, and Sex in Andrew Jackson's White House* (1997).

Joanne Pope Melish, *Disowning Slavery: Gradual Emancipation and "Race" in New England, 1780-1860* (1998).

Stephen B. Oates, *The Fires of Jubilee: Nat Turner's Fierce Rebellion* (1975).

Lynn Hudson Parson, *The Birth of Modern Politics: Andrew Jackson, John Quincy Adams and the Election of 1828* (2009).

Robert Remini, *The Jacksonian Era.* 2nd ed. (1997).

___, *Daniel Webster: The Man and His Time* (1997).

___, *Andrew Jackson and His Indian Wars* (2001).

David Robertson, *Denmark Vesey: The Buried Story of America's Largest Slave Rebellion and the Man Who Led It* (2000).

David R. Roediger, *The Wages of Whiteness: Race and the Making of the American Working Class* (1991).

Alexander Saxton, *The Rise and Fall of the White Republic: Class Politics and Mass Culture in Nineteenth Century America* (1990).

Charles Sellers, *The Market Revolution: Jacksonian America, 1815-1846* (1991).

Joel H. Silbey, *Martin Van Buren and the Emergence of American Popular Politics* (2002).

William David Sloan. *The Media in America: A History.* (2002).

John D. Stevens. *Sensationalism and the New York Press* (1991).

Ronald Takaki, *Iron Cages: Race and Culture in 19th Century America* (2000).

Sean Wilentz, *Andrew Jackson.* (2005).

Major L. Wilson, *The Presidency of Martin Van Buren* (1984).

Review Questions

1. What changes in election laws expanded the number of eligible voters in federal, state and local elections, and who continued to be disenfranchised?

2. Describe the rise of the "Second Party system" and the ideologies of the Democratic and Whig Parties from the 1830s to the 1850s. How did Andrew Jackson and his supporters change the way that American politics was practiced?

3. What led to Andrew Jackson's opposition to the Second Bank of the United States? What was the viewpoint of the Bank's defenders? What was the economic impact of the national bank's closure?

4. What events led to the Nullification Crisis of 1832? What were the constitutional issues at stake and how did personal antagonisms shape the controversy?

5. Describe the relationship between Native Americans and the federal government during the presidential administrations of Andrew Jackson (1829-1837) and Martin Van Buren (1837-1841).

Glossary of Important People and Concepts

John Quincy Adams
Anti-Masonic Party
Bank War
John C. Calhoun
Cherokee Nation v. Georgia (1831)
Henry Clay
"Corrupt Bargain"
Democratic Party
The Five Civilized Tribes
Indian Removal Act of 1830
Andrew Jackson
Nullification Crisis
Osceola
Panic of 1819
"Petticoat Affair"
John Ross
Sequoyah
Spoils System
"Tariff of Abominations"
Peggy Timberlake (Margaret O'Neill Eaton)
Trail of Tears
Nat Turner
Martin Van Buren
Denmark Vesey
Whig Party

People on deck leaving England for America

Chapter Twelve

The United States in Transformation, 1830-1850

One of the favorite side trips of proper English travelers in nineteenth century America was to the backcountry South and West to witness "rough-and-tumble" fighting. These brutal struggles by working class men often ended in the backwoods equivalent of the modern knockout punch: the gouging out of the loser's eye by the victor's thumb. One such tourist watched with mesmerized horror as one combatant kept his opponent down with his knees and "fixing his thumb on his eyes, gave them an instantaneous start from their sockets. The sufferer roared aloud....The citizens again shouted with joy." These renowned local heroes hardened and sharpened their fingernails and oiled them for slickness.

The backcountry heroes bragged with great exaggeration about their abilities and accomplishments. Mike Fink, legendary boatman, daring hunter, and victorious gouger, boasted: "I'm half wild horse and half cock-eyed alligator....I can out-run, out-jump, out-shoot, out-brag, out-drink, an' out-fight, rough-an'-tumble. No holds barred, any man both sides the river...." This "spread eagle" rhetoric represented the young nation and its aggressive expansion.

The "rough and tumblers" lived in isolated, pre-modern areas in kin-based societies where subsistence agriculture was the norm. Their hard lives, limited opportunities, and uncertain futures pushed them into heavy drinking and violent sports in a competitive all-male society. In a world in which slave holding was the mark of honor and standing, poor whites sought to confirm their status as equal and free men through unbridled brutality. They could contrast their

unwillingness to allow the slightest insult with the enforced submissiveness of the slave.

By the middle of the century eye-gouging incidents began to decline as the modern world intruded on the backcountry. Bowie knives finished off more of the rough and tumbles. The invention of the inexpensive modern revolver, which easily fit into a pocket, changed the nature of frontier contests. Violence became neater and even more deadly.

In the growing cities organized spectator sports developed to counter the loneliness of urban life and preserve traditional pleasures. Steamboats and, later, railroads could carry fans to events and promote inter-city rivalries. Rising literacy and new printing technologies created the popular penny newspapers that reported sporting events. Despite the opposition of religious moralists, both workers and "slumming" upper class men flocked to "low sport" halls. There, they could watch and bet on a dog killing a pit full of rats or a sparring match between "two women who were nude above the waist."

Although it was illegal everywhere, during the 1840s and 1850s, prize fighting became the most popular spectator sport. These bare-fisted matches were almost as brutal as the frontier rough and tumbles. In one epic 1842 contest, the two fighters thrashed each other for over two and a half hours until one collapsed and died when he drowned in his own blood. Irish working class men, who honed their skills in street survival, dominated boxing. (Jews, then Italians, then blacks would replace them in the twentieth century as each group attempted to rise from the slums.) John "Old

Smoke" Morrissey, an Irish immigrant, earned enough from his matches to open his own gambling house and was famous enough to win two terms in the House of Representatives. Newspapers publicized the 1860 match of his successor, John Heenan, against the English champion, as the ultimate test of national superiority. (The match ended in a bloody two-hour draw.) The event stirred up wider publicity than the growing sectional conflict.

Organized team sports also began to capture the public fancy. Cricket clubs, spurred by English immigrants, grew rapidly. Over 24,000 attended an 1859 cricket match in Hoboken, New Jersey between an all-star American team and touring professionals. Others argued that Americans should support "a game that could be termed a 'Native American Sport.'" Boys had long taken part in impromptu bat-and-ball games in empty lots. Lower middle class men began to form clubs to play baseball, touted as "the national game." When the Brooklyn all-stars met the New York all-stars in an 1858 series, excitement reached new heights. One newspaper reported that spectators included, "a galaxy of youth and beauty in female form, who...nerved the players to their task." (New York won two of three: 22-18, 8-29, 29-18.)

The new sports, like the old, tended to encourage drinking, betting, and an absence of self-restraint, much to the dismay of religious critics. These sports, however, reflected the important changes in northern American life at a time of urbanization, immigration, beginnings of industrialization, and increased population growth.

During the first half of the nineteenth century, the United States experienced a series of rapid and often bewildering social, cultural, and economic transformations. As one of a growing number of distinguished American authors whose career became possible due to the dramatic changes occurring in everyday life, Washington Irving captured the spirit of the alterations being made to the social fabric in his 1819 short story "Rip Van Winkle"—a tale involving a man who falls asleep before the American Revolution and awakens two decades later to discover everything had changed. A prominent local portrait of George III had been replaced with the image of someone named George Washington. All of Rip's friends had died or moved away. The pace of life was now bustling.

Unlike Rip Van Winkle, Americans did not have the luxury of sleeping through the swift developments overtaking their society. From 1800 to 1860, the country expanded tremendously. In 1803, the Louisiana Purchase doubled the size of the United States. The country significantly increased in size again in 1848 with the acquisition of northern Mexico after the Mexican War. Before 1850, the U.S. also took possession of Florida, Texas, and the Pacific Northwest before completing its continental expansion with the 1853 Gadsden Purchase of southern Arizona and New Mexico. During these intervening years, the nation's population exploded. In 1790, the first U.S. Census counted 3.9 million Americans. By 1860, that number had increased nearly eight times to 31.4 million people. Northerners frequently moved to newly established farming areas further west or to the growing urban areas, indulging themselves in a variety of market activities. Meanwhile, Southerners also migrated westward to take advantage of fresh land and to cultivate cotton. Facilitating the movement of people and goods during these years of rapid territorial and demographic growth were the new steamboats, canals, and, ultimately, the railroads. Only the arrival of the Civil War in the early 1860s could temporarily stymie these revolutionary changes to American life.

NEW PEOPLE, NEW PLACES: Migration, Urbanization, and Immigration

Tremendous population increases took place during the period between 1790 and 1860, as every decade witnessed no less than 30 percent growth. During many of these years, the population consisted mainly of young, restless, and mobile native-born residents (the median age in 1820 was 16.7 years). **Alexis de Tocqueville,** a French aristocrat touring the United States to observe its experiments in prison reform who later wrote an analytical account of his travels, described a "strange unrest of so many happy men, restless in the midst of abundance," noting:

> In the United States a man builds a house in which to spend his old age, and he sells it before the roof is on; he plants a garden and lets it just as the trees are coming into bearing; he brings a field into tillage and leaves other men to gather the crops; he embraces a profession and gives it up; he settles in a place, which he soon afterwards leaves to carry his changeable longings elsewhere.

The distribution of population growth varied by state, with those lacking significant quantities of unsettled land (Delaware, Maryland, and most of New England) experiencing much slower population increases than older ones still possessing large amounts of undeveloped land, such as New York, Pennsylvania, and Georgia, though growth even in those states slowed as new states and territories further west opened for settlement.

Migration to the Old Northwest

Many members of this youthful population, facing little prospect of inheriting or acquiring land in the region of their birth, crossed the Appalachian Mountains where they found an abundance of suitable farmland. This area known as the Northwest Territory (or the Old Northwest) spanned east-to-west from the mountains to the Mississippi River and north-to-south from the Great Lakes to the Ohio River. Native American and French resistance had effectively kept the area free of settlers from British North America for most of the eighteenth century. Indeed, no U.S. settlers lived there as late as 1789. But fierce conflict between the U.S. and the region's Native American population in the 1790s opened much of what became Ohio to settlers. And they poured in. By 1800, the Old Northwest's settler population exceeded one-quarter million, and that number that would increase five-fold in the next 30 years.

The Old Northwest drew settlers from both the North and South. Migrants from New England would ultimately settle in a thick swath along the southern shores of the Great Lakes, which formed the region's northern border. Most settlers before 1830 came from states like Virginia, Maryland, and Kentucky. Drawn by cheap, fertile land, they established farms along the Ohio River and its tributaries. These folk generally came from the ranks of the South's yeoman population. **Yeomen** were landholding farmers who did not own slaves, either because they rejected the practice on principle, or they resented competing against highly capitalized plantations, or because they simply could not afford to do so. Whatever their precise reasons, the Old Northwest's southern migrants steadfastly rejected efforts to introduce slavery into their new homes and saw the absence of slavery and slaveholders as a key component to their social mobility.

This rejection of slavery did not imply a complete rejection of the southern way of life. Residents of southern Ohio, Indiana, and Illinois lived in much the same ways they had before they migrated. They farmed in a similar fashion, growing corn and raising swine for pork. They traded their produce along the local rivers, although they now worked on the northern banks or along tributaries that flowed southward into the Ohio, instead of northward. They also harbored an intense hostility to African Americans and even supported laws to prohibit their settlement in states like Ohio and Indiana. The Old Northwest would ultimately develop a complex political culture as descendants of New England migrants and southern migrants fought out the character of their social order in the mid-nineteenth century.

Urban Life

Americans flocked to the cities, and the rate of population growth there far exceeded the overall increase for the total population. In 1790, only 5 percent of the country lived in urban areas, but this statistic would reach nearly 20 percent by 1860. Older cities swelled with new inhabitants. The number of people in Charleston, South Carolina increased from 16,359 in 1790 to 40,522 in 1860, but that growth proved to be quite slow relative to other cities. During the same period, Baltimore's population increased from 13,503 to 212,418; Philadelphia's from 28,522 to 565,529; and New York City's from 33,131 to 813,669. New urban centers also emerged. Of the twenty largest cities in 1860, nine were either not yet part of the United States in 1790 (New Orleans, St. Louis, and San Francisco) or simply did not yet exist (Rochester, Buffalo, Milwaukee, and Chicago). All of these cities boasted populations over 40,000 by 1860, with nearly half containing more than 100,000 people.

The rapid influx of people into the cities created new markets as well as new opportunities for entrepreneurs willing to employ labor in new ways. In trade after trade in the nineteenth century, business owners took skilled tasks performed by specialists in their crafts and broke them up into multiple simple tasks that could be performed by low-paid, unskilled workers. A growing demand for inexpensive clothing ensured that tailors led the way in these changes. Around the turn of the nineteenth century, most Americans wore clothing made at home. Only the wealthy could afford to pay a tailor to make clothing for them. Urbanization changed this dynamic. Urban households did not produce their own clothes (or food); they depended on the market to set their needs. Enterprising tailors responded by recruiting female laborers to sew pre-cut fabric into ready-to-wear-clothing. Women workers by 1860 made up two-thirds of New York City's clothes makers, and they would constitute 25 percent of all workers in the city. At first, employers gave out piecework, which women performed on their own time in their own homes, although this practice ultimately gave way to the organization of workshops where workers could be supervised to control quality and "sweated" to increase production. New York City emerged as a manufacturing center for this new clothing. Southern planters provided one of the first markets, and the city provided inexpensive, low-quality clothing for enslaved workers. As quality improved, the city's clothing industry supplied the needs of free workers and farmers throughout the U.S., and by mid-century, even members of the affluent, emerging middle class wore premade clothing, and the shoes they wore had also been produced by a similar process.

Table 12.1

LARGEST U. S. CITIES

	1820			1860	
	City	Population		City	Population
1	New York, NY	123,706	1	New York, NY	813,669
2	Philadelphia, PA	63,802	2	Philadelphia, PA	565,529
3	Baltimore, MD	62,738	3	Brooklyn, NY	266,661
4	Boston, MA	43,298	4	Baltimore, MD	212,418
5	New Orleans, LA	27,176	5	Boston, MA	177,840
6	Charleston, SC	24,780	6	New Orleans, LA	168,675
7	N. Liberties District, PA	19,678	7	Cincinnati, OH	161,044
8	Southwark District, PA	14,713	8	St. Louis, MO	160,773
9	Washington, DC	13,247	9	Chicago, IL	112,172
10	Salem, MA	12,731	10	Buffalo, NY	81,129
11	Albany, NY	12,630	11	Newark, NJ	71,941
12	Richmond, VA	12,067	12	Louisville, KY	68,033
13	Providence, RI	11,767	13	Albany, NY	62,367
14	Cincinnati, OH	9,642	14	Washington, DC	61,122
15	Portland, ME	8,581	15	San Francisco, CA	56,802
16	Norfolk, VA	8,478	16	Providence, RI	50,666
17	Alexandria, DC	8,218	17	Pittsburgh, PA	49,221
18	Savannah, GA	7,523	18	Rochester, NY	48,204
19	Georgetown, DC	7,360	19	Detroit, MI	45,619
20	Portsmouth, NH	7,327	20	Milwaukee, WI	45,246

Source: U.S. Bureau of the Census

In places like New York City, Rochester, New York, Lynn, Massachusetts, and even as far south as Baltimore, Maryland changes in production reshaped social relations and gave rise to an urban working class. Workers' wages plummeted, especially for unskilled labor. Some skilled workers—the relatively few shoemakers who continued to make custom orders for example—could earn around $2 for a 10-hour day. Those workers that had fallen into deskilled tasks might make half or even a quarter of that. The availability of work depended heavily on the seasons. Baltimore paid laborers about a dollar a day to dredge its shallow harbor of the silt that continually poured in, a backbreaking task that provided work nine months of the year. Workers thus often faced long periods of unemployment, especially during winter months. Gender also shaped wages. Male worker often received low pay for a full 10-hour day of work, but women earned even less. Employers assumed that women's work merely supplemented the income of a male head of household and thus paid lower rates. Many of those women workers, however, lived alone, or with their children, and were the primary wage earners in their household.

A new middle class also emerged in urban areas. Although members of this group also worked for wages—and some of them earned less than skilled laborers—they distinguished themselves by performing manual labor. Instead, they worked as clerks and sales people in the elaborate showrooms and counting houses appearing in growing cities throughout the United States. These establishments embodied another development: a physical separation of working and middle class life. In the eighteenth-century, artisans generally lived and worked out of the same building. Successful entrepreneurs, however, increasingly built separate facilities for their businesses. Workshops, often located in or near working-class neighborhoods, were noisy and dirty. Offices and showrooms, like those found in Boston's Quincy Market, or along Philadelphia's Chestnut Street, were clean, quiet, and often ornate.

Living spaces underwent a similar separation. Eighteenth-century artisans often shared a home with a household that included the master's family as well as apprentices and journeymen. Over the course of the nineteenth-century, those artisan households broke into separate middle- and working-class households. The latter appeared in areas within walking distance of various places of employment and were characterized by crowded conditions (because people needed to be close to work) and high rents (again because many people needed to be close to work). Landlords met demand for housing by splitting up living quarters to hold more people. New York's Old Brewery, for example, reportedly provided residence for 1,000 people. Renters responded to climbing rents by taking in boarders or doubling up with other families. Crowded conditions within dwellings often meant that working class people spent the little time that was not dedicated to working or sleeping on the street, which made their neighborhoods appear rowdy to middle-class observers. These people increasingly lived in households that contained a single, nuclear family. Their affluence enabled these families to design homes with specialized rooms—separate bedrooms for parents and children, living rooms, dining rooms, family rooms. Guests could be entertained in the front rooms of the house, and the occupants enjoyed a level of privacy unimaginable in the colonial period (or in emerging working class neighborhoods).

What modern urban dwellers now assume to be the basics of city living—police and fire departments, regular waste removal, sewage disposal—had not yet been developed. City folk casually dropped trash in their neighborhoods to be picked over by wandering pigs and dogs. In the absence of sewage systems, people and animals urinated and defecated in the streets, which made cities foul-smelling and disease-ridden environments. Fire companies existed to put out fires, but these groups often had connections to street gangs, and rivalries among various gangs sometimes resulted in violence while buildings burned in the background. Crime became a persistent problem in the absence of professional police forces, and riots by urban crowds remained a persistent danger. Vast disparities in wealth became visible within urban populations. Although economic inequality was not by any means new, city residents increasingly became segregated along class lines. Poor people concentrated in dilapidated slums, such as New York City's notorious **Five Points**—a neighborhood famous for its poverty, brothels, and violence.

By mid-century, a number of cities initiated efforts to deliver public services designed to improve the quality of urban life. In response to outbreaks of disease—such as an epidemic of yellow fever in 1849—city governments began to build water systems to convey fresh water and to allow (for those who could afford to do so) piping water directly into their homes. Rudimentary sewer systems were developed, though service remained limited. In 1860, for example, only about 25 percent of New York City streets tied into the municipal sewer system. Cities also established formal fire departments and professional police forces, primarily to bring crowd violence under control and to patrol the neighborhoods of wealthy citizens. Along with these changes came innovations in urban transit. Animal-powered transportation—at first large horse-drawn wagons and later horse-drawn rail cars—allowed cities to begin expanding in ways not previously possible. Because these transportation services were not free, such developments accelerated class segregation within urban areas. Poor folk remained in downtown neighborhoods within walking distance of their places of employment while wealthier residents began commuting into and out of the inner cities. Some aspects of urban life common to modern Americans were thus beginning to take hold.

Immigration

As native-born Americans moved to the cities, they often reduced the number of children they had in response to the lessened need for family labor (from 1820 to 1860, the national median age increased from 16.7 to 19.4). This decline in birth rates, however, did not slow national population growth because of a large influx of foreign immigrants. Between 1790 and 1840, the United States experienced relatively little immigration when compared to the colonial period or to the decades immediately preceding the Civil War. From 1820 to 1840, only 750,000 immigrants had arrived. After 1840, however, the first of a succession of immigrant waves occurred. Over the next decade, 1.7 million migrated to the United States, followed by the arrival of another 2.6 million people during the 1850s.

The largest group of new immigrants, the **Irish**, accounted for half of the new arrivals. Fleeing a potato famine that struck in 1845, most Irish arrived in the United States with practically nothing. They clustered in urban slums—Five Points was a predominately Irish neighborhood—and disrupted labor markets through a willingness to work for near-starvation wages. Many Americans greeted the Irish with hostility. Those forced to compete with them in the labor market treated the Irish with disdain, and the Irish responded in kind. Protestants, especially in New England, expressed concern that Roman Catholic peasants would not be suited to American democracy. School reformers insisted on instilling Protestant values in the public schools, including using the Protestant King James Bible and non-Catholic forms of prayers, leading the Irish to campaign for making public financing for tuition available for parents wanting to send their children to alternative parochial (church) schools. In politics, the Irish became an influential force within the Democratic Party, primarily because they rejected the evangelical leanings of the Whig (and later Republican)

Party. In many cities, the Irish became a major force in local politics.

Prompted by a variety of push and pull factors, large numbers of Germans also immigrated to the United States between 1840 and 1860. Some left for religious reasons, while others fled their homeland after the failed democratic revolutions of 1848. Still more came for economic opportunities. Unlike the Irish, **German immigrants** generally arrived with some monetary resources. Their relative wealth allowed them more options—some established themselves in cities, while others purchased farmland in the interior regions of the country as well as many northeastern states.

Not all the new immigrants came from Europe. In California, **Chinese immigrants** arrived to participate in the Gold Rush of the late 1840s. Like the Irish, the Chinese faced considerable hostility from native-born Americans who closed the mines to the Chinese (and other non-whites), forcing many into service industries such as cooking and laundry work. State laws harassed the Chinese, while government officials often overlooked crimes committed against them (including murder).

The hostility experienced by the Irish and the Chinese, which reflected emerging tensions resulting from increased racial and ethnic diversity and economic competition, greatly complicated American politics. In the North, politicians learned to navigate within an environment charged with ethnic hatred, seeking to attract immigrant voters while also appealing to native-born voters who expressed deep hostility to the newcomers. Moreover, because foreign immigration was largely a northern affair (8 out of every 10 new immigrants settled in the North), these tensions would eventually muddle American sectional politics.

INNOVATIONS IN TRANSPORTATION, COMMUNICATION, AND AGRICULTURE

Canal Boom

The emergence of new modes of transportation after 1800 contributed greatly to the period's extensive population movement and economic development, while improved communication systems connected Americans nationally and internationally. As noted in Chapter 10, Robert Fulton's 1807 invention of the steamboat permitted the transportation of more people and goods along navigable rivers at greater speed, and, most importantly, upstream. Canals soon helped to solve another major limitation posed by the country's river network by carving "artificial rivers" where natural ones did not exist. The classic example of canal building was New York's **Erie Canal**, which ran from Buffalo on the eastern bank of Lake Erie to Albany on the Hudson River and connected the Great Lakes to New York City. Between 1815 and 1825, construction crews dug out a ditch over 300 miles long, designed locks to handle changes in elevation, and created a transportation route that offered sharply reduced shipping rates and expanded market opportunities along its length. The Erie Canal proved enormously successful; it paid for itself in seven years, and transformed upstate New York from a sparsely settled frontier region to a home for a burgeoning middle class society. Goods moved so rapidly along the canal that oysters could be shipped (on ice) from the coast and eaten Upstate, something that had never been possible before. Other states tried to replicate New York's success, but generally fell short and faced crushing debts as the new canals failed to pay for themselves with the same speed as the Erie had. Despite these problems, however, a growing network of canals in

---

Table 12.2

Immigration: 1820 to 1860

In thousands, except rate (152 represents 152,000)[1]

Period	Number	Rate
1820 to 1830	152	1.2
1831 to 1840	599	3.9
1841 to 1850	1,713	8.4
1851 to 1860	2,598	9.3

[1]Annual rate per 1,000 U.S. population. Rate computed by dividing sum of annual immigration totals by sum of annual U.S. population totals for same number of years.

Source: U.S. Department of Homeland Security, Office of Immigration Statistics, 2005 Yearbook of Immigration Statistics.

the North began to restructure the way in which goods and commerce flowed through the country. Before the emergence of canals, goods tended to flow to the west and south along the Ohio and Mississippi Rivers. With the rise of the Erie Canal and its imitators, goods now traveled eastward through the great port of New York. Canal construction did not bypass the South, but new projects tended to be relatively limited in scope and generally reinforced existing commodity flows—that is, they moved crops like cotton to port in larger quantities and with more speed than before. Southern transportation projects thus tended to accommodate growth but relative to those in the North did not really foster development.

That same pattern held for the final transportation innovation before 1860: the **railroad**. Locomotives accomplished what canals could not. They could move over steep grades and operate in areas with little water; they also permitted year-round business because they were not subject to freezing over as canals (especially in places like Upstate New York). After an initial flurry of construction in the 1830s, which was stalled by the Panic of 1837 and ensuing depression, a network of rail began emerging in the United States by the 1850s. By 1860, in fact, the nation would lead the world in railroad mile-

age. Like the canals they developed alongside, rail tended to move the flow of goods away from the westward and southward flow of the rivers and push it back toward the east. By 1860, the combination of steamboats, canals, and railroads allowed Americans who purchased tickets to travel from most any settled area of the country to most any other settled area of the country in a matter of days or even hours (if the destination was relatively close). And **Samuel F.B. Morse**'s invention of the **telegraph**, which transmitted signals across a network of electrified wires, permitted them to communicate even more quickly. By 1860, Americans had effectively conquered the physical challenges presented to them by the size of the North American continent. It had also create an enormous domestic market, allowing the United States to become less dependent on foreign exports

Advances in Agricultural Technology

These developments in transportation, combined with innovations in manufacturing, transformed American agriculture. Despite rapid urbanization, farming remained highly important. Most Americans (some 55 percent) as late as 1860 worked as farmers, and they expanded

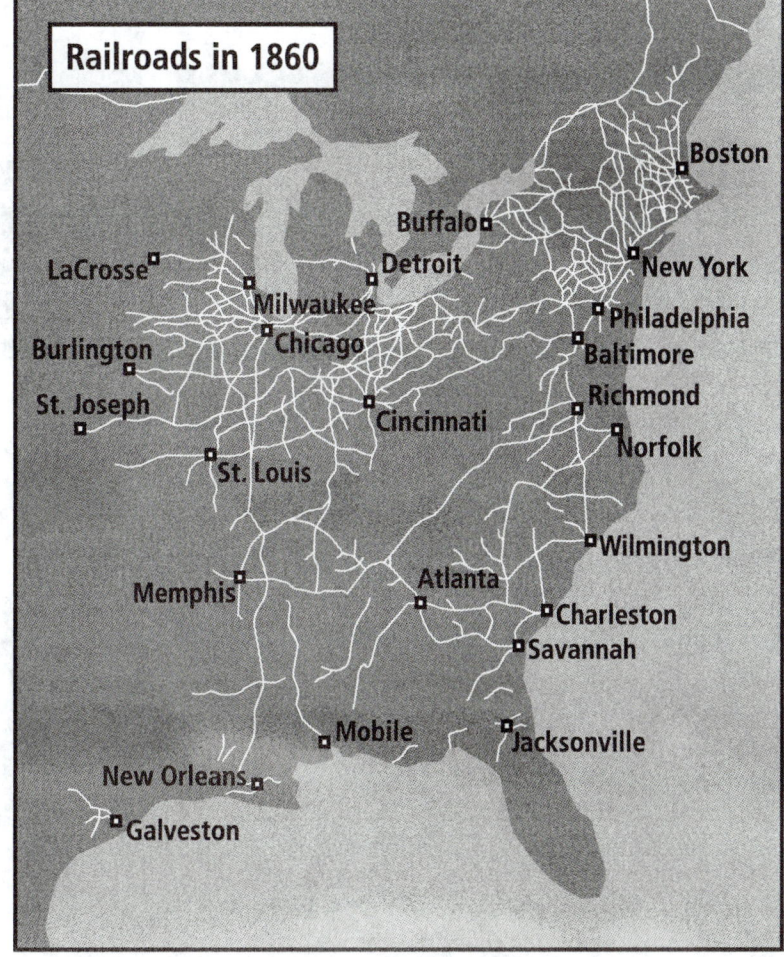

Map 12.1 The network of railroad growth, established by 1860, reinforced economic ties between the Northeast and the West.

production between 1820 and 1860. Two factors drove this expansion. First, American farmers moved onto fresh farmlands in New York and Ohio, then Indiana, then Illinois, then Michigan and Wisconsin in the North. In the South, the states differed—first Georgia and Tennessee, then Alabama, Mississippi, Louisiana, Missouri, then Arkansas and Texas—but the pattern remained the same: fresh new land brought expanded production of crops like cotton, corn, wheat, and hemp. Second, the expansion of the transportation network combined with the rise of cities and manufacturing both created new markets for expanded agricultural output and provided the means for farmers to get their products to them. Indeed, the transportation network permitted farmers to move to productive farmland, specialize in whatever crop was best suited to their region, sell their crops in distant markets, and purchase whatever they could not (or did not) produce for themselves. Farmers willing to take large risks could, if they wanted, pour all of their energy into producing a single crop and buying whatever else they needed on the market. Not all farm families did this—many hedged their bets and continued to grow crops that may not have sold as well, but would serve to feed the family if times suddenly became hard. But the expanding market opportunities pulled more and more people into their orbit with each passing year.

Finally, the expansion of agriculture and manufacturing fed off one another. In addition to the role played by urbanization and the expansion of the transportation network, mechanics and industrialists turned their attention to solving farmers' problems. Unlike their southern counterparts, northern farmers faced severe constraints on the amount of land they could cultivate, mainly because they were limited to the amount available labor, which primarily consisted of family members—hired hands were expensive and usually temporary. Southern farmers got around this problem through the use of slave laborers. Industrialists solved this problem for northern farmers by creating new machines. **John Deere** invented a new **steel plow** that cut through the tough soil of the Old Northwest, and he figured out how to mass-produce them. **Cyrus McCormick** designed a **grain reaping machine** that could harvest wheat twenty times faster than a single farmer could do. These developments transformed northern agriculture (and drew northern farmers more deeply into the market since they generally had to pay for these new machines on credit). This pattern of industrial and agricultural development, however, underscores the economic changes (and related social changes) that were playing out in different ways in the American North and South.

Samuel Morse and his apparatus for sending and receiving coded telegraph messages, with the alphabet and numbers in "Morse code."

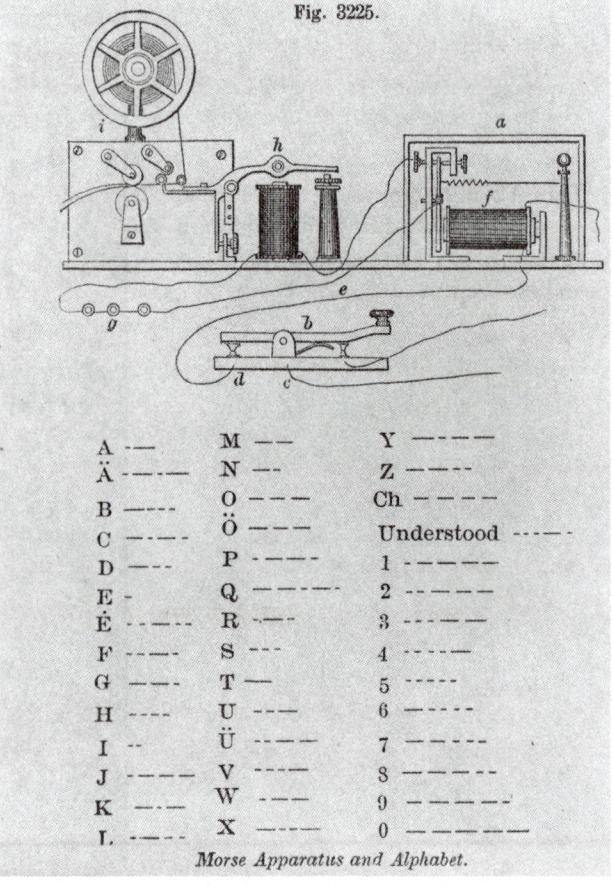

Morse Apparatus and Alphabet.

THE ANTEBELLUM NORTH

The Transformation of Northern Society

The tremendous changes made possible by increased mobility, foreign immigration, and growing urbanization, coupled with the impact of new manufacturing methods and agricultural developments, deeply shaped the development of northern social life. Although European observers such as Alexis de Tocqueville commented on Americans' dedication to equality, often portraying the United States as a "classless" society because it lacked the landed aristocracy so characteristic of the Old World, the French aristocrat also relayed his belief that the social changes produced by the rise of factories in the North threatened to create a new aristocracy:

> As the conditions of men constituting the nation become more and more equal, the demand for manufactured commodities becomes more general and extensive, and the cheapness that places these objects within the reach of slender fortunes becomes a great element of success. Hence there are every day more men of great opulence and education who devote their wealth and knowledge to manufactures and who seek, by opening large establishments and by a strict division of labor, to meet the fresh demands, which are made on all sides. Thus, in proportion as the mass of the nation turns to democracy, that particular class which is engaged in manufactures becomes more aristocratic.

This process had major social implications, de Tocqueville noted. "The workman is generally dependent on the master, but not on any particular master; these two men meet in the factory, but do not know each other elsewhere; and while they come into contact on one point, they stand very far apart on all others." The result was a situation in which neither party had any obligations to one another beyond work. "The manufacturer asks nothing of the workman but his labor; the workman expects nothing from him but his wages."

De Tocqueville observed a very real phenomenon taking place in the North—the creation of a new class structure. Although Americans never enjoyed economic equality, urbanization brought the issue into sharp relief, with the shift to new divisions of labor accelerating the trend. In New York City, a mere 4 percent of the population controlled two-thirds of the city's wealth by 1845. Meanwhile, the poor shared much less: 80 percent of Philadelphia's population in 1860 controlled a scant 3 percent of the city's wealth (the top 1 percent controlled over half of the remainder). The result was the emergence of class-segregated cities with the wealthiest families constructing lavish homes in opulent neighborhoods as destitute families scraped by on near starvation wages in households where everyone—men, women, and children—had to work.

In the old seaports, as well as the newer inland manufacturing and commercial towns, the concern for creating a classless industrial society disappeared. Vastly wealthy financiers, along with an emerging middle class of merchants, craftsmen, small shopkeepers, and professionals, lived and worked amidst the impoverished men and women who produced the ever-expanding range of consumer goods. The richest men in the old seaport cities proved to be merchants who had survived and prospered during the European wars. They continued their various import-export enterprises, with many using their profits to diversify into banking, insurance, and urban real estate, becoming even richer in the process. By the 1820s, this new capitalist elite had solidified their socio-economic and political power, becoming an entrenched, privileged class. In Boston, an extended network of well educated, urbane, and responsible families known as the Brahmins took control of the city, holding power for the rest of the century. The elite in New York and Philadelphia were less cohesive patriarchs and became more legendary for their self-serving, acquisitive, and ostentatious lifestyles than their Boston counterparts. Nonetheless, they were just as wealthy (if not more so) as their Boston brethren and just as embedded in their power. Regardless of locale, these families earned the bulk of their incomes from international commerce, profiting mainly from cotton exports and a vastly expanding range of imports.

Below the old mercantile elite were the various members of the burgeoning middle class of wholesale and retail merchants, the master craftsmen who had transformed themselves into manufacturers, and an army of lawyers, salesman, auctioneers, clerks, bookkeepers, and accountants who took care of the paperwork for the new market society. The wholesale merchants in the seaport cities who bought hardware, crockery, and other commodities from importers and then sold them in smaller lots to interior storekeepers proved to be the most prosperous and affluent members of this new middle class. Slightly below them were the large processors of farm products, such as Cincinnati's meatpackers and Rochester's flour millers, as well as the large merchants and realtors in the interior's growing cities. Another step down the middle-class ladder appeared the specialty retailers—storeowners who dealt in books, furniture, crockery, or other consumer products. Alongside this array of merchants stood the master craftsmen who had become larger-scale manufacturers

294 / CHAPTER TWELVE

of shoes, crockery, leather goods, and an ever-increasing number of consumer products once produced by a single individual helped by his apprentice helpers. With their workers busy in backrooms or in household workshops, they now called themselves shoe dealers and merchant tailors. At the bottom of this commercial world were the hordes of clerks, most of them young men who hoped to rise in the world by providing their much-needed services. These white-collar workers formed a new social class.

Americans' assessments of this divide varied. Universalist minister, Jacob Frieze, considered the emerging economic separation to be a form of oppression, as did numerous groups of striking workers. Frieze noted that even though he believed that laborers had a right to negotiate wages, their ability to do so proved to be more theoretical than actual.

> This is the manner in which *bargains* are made. The employer pays what he pleases, and no more, and will not deviate from the price he has fixed. And the laboring man, with this pittance, is also under the necessities of paying the prices made and demanded for whatever he consumes. Should he venture to complain that he cannot live comfortably, he is accused of extravagance in expending the enormous sum of *seventy-five cents a day*, and told that he should live within his income.

In an 1860 speech defending the right of factory workers to strike against their employers, presidential candidate Abraham Lincoln emphasized his belief that these new labor relations were the essence of freedom. "I am glad to see that a system of labor prevails in . . . which laborers can strike when they want to, where they are obliged to work under all circumstances, and are not tied down." The system, he continued, offered social mobility. "I take that it is best for all to leave each man free to acquire property as fast as he can. Some will get wealthy." "When one starts poor," he went on, "free society is such that he knows that he can better his condition; he knows that there is no fixed condition for his whole life."

Both Frieze and Lincoln made valid points, but Lincoln's focus on social mobility pointed to a significant feature of life in the American North—many Americans were moving into a new middle class. The previously cited numbers for Philadelphia in 1860 again provide a case in point. As noted, at the top of the wealth distribution, 1 percent of the population controlled 50 percent of the wealth, while the bottom 80 percent controlled 3 percent. However, between these two extremes lay the middle class—19 percent of the population that possessed 47 percent of the city's wealth. While they did not match

the great wealth of the truly rich and faced very real prospects of being financially ruined in the boom-and-bust economy of the nineteenth century, these individuals lived with great affluence and privilege not widely available in the eighteenth century. Members of this emerging class built private homes, featuring separate bedrooms for children and specialized rooms for entertaining guests. They prioritized the education of their children, experimented with new forms of non-corporal punishment, and placed a heavy emphasis on the values of self-control in financial transactions and sexual behavior—values that shaped the various reform movements then emerging.

Members of the middle-class identified themselves in relation to the very wealthy and against the emerging urban poor, many of whom flatly rejected their values. They often had come from small towns where they lived under considerable supervision from parents, elders, and ministers. In the cities, employers cared little about what they did while off the job, and they amused themselves with activities frowned upon by the moralists of the emerging middle class. Young workers drank heavily, fought frequently, attended theaters, watched cockfights, consumed pornography, and patronized brothels. These activities rendered urban life morally dangerous in the eyes of the middle class who soon sought to rein in such activities. These cultural conflicts became basic features of American life, showing no sign of dissipating.

Free Blacks in the Antebellum North

Along with new dimensions of class conflict, the North faced challenges on the racial front. The process of gradual emancipation that had begun in Pennsylvania in 1780 and in New York and New Jersey around 1800 had generated a class of free African Americans. Its numbers remained small. The North's free blacks made up around 1 percent of the region's population. Because African Americans moved to the cities, however, their communities became highly visible. In the North, enslaved Africans and African Americans had been spread thinly throughout the region, a practice that had inhibited the community development. With the slow emergence of freedom—the decline of slavery took decades—free blacks found urban life to be appealing because they found opportunities to build families, find work, and develop ties to their communities. All of that happened in the face of fierce hostility. Like they did immigrants, urban crowds targeted Africans Americans with violence. White crowds in Cincinnati tried to drive blacks from the city in 1842, and some African Americans suffered lynching in the New York City draft riots of 1863. State governments also lacked sympathy. Ohio and a few other northern states barred

The Middle Class and the Culture of Self-Restraint

This chapter opens with a discussion of rough-and-tumble and prize fighting that entertained Americans in the back-country and cities. Part of the spectators' enjoyment of these events came from the opportunity to drink heavily and bet freely—in other words, to live out a rejection of the expectations for self-control being propagated by middle-class ideologues and employers. Catherine Maria Sedgwick, a popular author among the middle class, provided an example of these expectations in her 1835 novel **Home***. What were the attitudes toward violence, anger, and child discipline expressed in this passage?*

The family . . . assembled in a back parlor. Ms. Barclay was at some domestic employment, to facilitate which Martha had just brought in a tub of scalding water. Charles . . . Alice . . . Mary . . . Willie . . . were busy, but the busiest was little Haddy, a sweet child of four years, who was . . . doing deadly mischief. She'd taken a new . . . kite belonging to her brother Wallace, cut a hole in the centre, thrust into it . . . her . . . kitten. . . . At this critical juncture Wallace entered. . . . In a breath he sees the kitten, and dashed into the tub of scalding water. . . .

The children were all sobbing. . . . The children saw the frown on their father's face, more dreaded by them than ever was flogging, or the dark closet with all its hobgoblins.

. . . . "Go to your own room, Wallace," said his father. "You have forfeited your right to a place among us. Creatures who are the slaves of their passions, are, like beast of prey, fit only for solitude."

"How long must Wallace stay upstairs?" asked Haddy. . . .

"Till he feels assured," replied Mr. Barclay, fixing his eyes sternly on Wallace, "that he can control his hasty temper; at least so far as not to be guilty of violence towards such a dear good little girl as you are, and murderous cruelty to an innocent animal; — till, sir, you can give me some **proof** *that you dread the sin and danger of yielding to your passions so much that you can govern them. . . ."*

The days passed on. Wallace went to school as usual, and returned to his solitude, without speaking or being spoken to. His meals were sent to his room. . . .

Two weeks had passed when Mr. Barclay heard Wallace's door open, and heard him say, "Can I speak with you one minute before dinner, sir."

"Certainly, my son" . . . .

"Father," said Wallace. . . . "I feel as if I had a right now to ask you to forgive me, and take me back into the family."

. . . . "I have only been waiting for you, Wallace; and, from the time you've taken to consider your besetting sin, I trust you have gained strength to resist it."

"It is not from consideration only, sir, that I depend on; for you told me I must wait till I could give you proof. . . . Luckily for me . . . Tom Allen snatched off my new cap and threw it into the gutter. I had a book in my hand, and I raised it to send at him; but I thought just in time, and I was so glad that I governed my passion, that I did not care about my cap, or Tom, or anything else. 'But one swallow doesn't make a summer,' as Aunt Betsy says; so I waited till I should get angry again. . . ."

"[Y]esterday, just as I was putting up my Arithmetic which I had written almost to the end without a single blot, Tom Allen came along and gave my inkstand a jostle, and over it went on my open book; I thought he did it purposely,— I think so still, but I don't feel so sure. I did not reflect then,—I doubled my fist to strike him."

"O, Wallace!"

"But I did not, father, I did not,—I thought just in time. There was a horrid choking feeling in my throat, and angry words seemed crowding out; but I did not even say, 'Blame [damn] you.' I had to bite my lips, though, so that the blood ran."

"God bless you, my son."

"And the best of it all was, father, that Tom Allen, who never before seemed to care . . . how much he hurt your feelings, was really sorry; and this morning he brought me a new blank book nicely ruled, and offered to help me copy my sums into it; so I hope I did him some good as well as myself, by governing my temper."

Source: Catherine Maria Sedgwick, **Home** *(Boston, 1835), 15-23.*

blacks from living in the states (at least on paper). Most other northern states prohibited voting by blacks and passed segregation laws. Even Massachusetts—one of the most racially liberal states in the Union—permitted separate schools for blacks and whites until the 1850s.

African Americans thus faced a hard life in the North, where they were free but by no means equal. Most members of the black community found their employment options limited to menial labor. Men worked in low status jobs as barbers and knife sharpeners. A great many went to sea, which generally meant that they had few prospects on land. Women worked as laundresses or domestic "help" (Americans of all races preferred not to be called servants). Not all African Americans labored at menial jobs. Black communities established churches whose ministers became and then trained community leaders. Organizations like the **African Methodist Episcopal Church** and other denominations provided education and social support. Black communities also supported their own newspapers. Even though northern blacks represented a small number of people, their organizations magnified their voice.

Prominent among those voices were reformers like **Frederick Douglass** and **Harriet Jacobs**. A brilliant speaker and charismatic leader, Douglass had basically taught himself to read and then escaped from slavery. By the early 1840s, he had established himself as a popular lecturer against slavery. He also wrote an autobiography that indicted slavery for its violence and corrosive impact on morality, especially for its tendency to transform men into uneducated brutes. And, he published his own news-

paper, *The North Star*. Harriet Jacobs, also a fugitive from slavery, began writing newspaper articles in the 1850s and ultimately published her own narrative, *Incidents in the Life of Slave Girl* in 1861. Her account contained harrowing (and by the standards of the time, frank) depictions of sexual abuse inflicted upon her by her master. Her work also criticized the North for its unequal treatment of African Americans.

The Changing Life of Northern Women

Harriet Jacobs wrote *Incidents in the Life of Slave Girl* with a particular audience in mind: middle-class women. Her purpose was to demonstrate that enslavement violated what they considered proper gender roles and sanctions on sexual behavior:

> [I]n slavery the very dawn of life is darkened. . . . Even the little child . . . will learn, before she is twelve years old, why it is that her mistress hates such and such a one among the slaves. . . . She listens to violent outbreaks of jealous passion, and cannot help understanding what is the cause. She will become prematurely knowing in evil things. Soon she will learn to tremble when she hears her master's footfall. She will be compelled to realize that she is no longer a child. If God has bestowed beauty upon her, it will prove her greatest curse. That which commands admiration in the white woman only hastens the degradation of the female slave.

African Americans attending church for social and religious support.

Francis Trollope on Servants and Slaves

Francis Trollope, an English woman with an aristocratic bearing, came to the United States in the 1820s hoping to establish her sons in business. Her efforts failed, and the experience embittered her. Upon returning to England, Trollop embarked on a career as a successful writer. Her first book, **Domestic Manners of the Americans** *(1832), recounted her travels in the United States. She did not like what she saw, and she found the American experiment in democracy disturbing. "Let us make a government that shall suit us all," she imagined the nation's founders' saying, "let it be rude, and rough, and noisy . . . let it interfere with no man's will, nor meddle with any man's business . . . let every man have a hand in making the laws, and no man be troubled about keeping them."*

Dealing with servants provided one of the (very) many annoyances that came with living in the United States, but her encounters with them underscored the egalitarian sentiments of American workers. She found those sentiments disgusting, and preferred the service she received from enslaved workers to be superior (although she was not proud that she did so). Trollope's travel account thus revealed not only a strong commitment of ordinary Americans to egalitarian democracy but also how slavery and freedom shaped labor relations in the pre-Civil War United States.

[I]n Ohio . . . it is more than petty treason to the republic to call a free citizen a **servant***. The whole class of young women, whose bread depends upon their labour, are taught to believe that the most abject poverty is preferable to domestic service. Hundreds of half-naked girls work in the paper-mills, or in any other manufactory, for less than half the wages they would receive in service; but they think their equality is compromised by the latter. . . .*

. . . .

I cannot imagine it possible that such a state of things can be desirable, or beneficial to any of the parties concerned. I might occupy a hundred pages on the subject, and yet fail to give an adequate idea of the sore, angry, ever wakeful pride that seemed to torment these poor wretches. In many of them it was so excessive, that all feeling of displeasure, or even of ridicule, was lost in pity. One of these was a pretty girl, whose natural disposition must have been gentle and kind; but her good feelings were soured, and her gentleness turned to morbid sensitiveness, by having heard a thousand and a thousand times that she was as good as any other lady, that all men were equal, and women too, and that it was a sin and a shame for a free-born American to be treated like a servant.

When she found she was to dine in the kitchen, she turned up her pretty lip, and said, "I guess that's 'cause you don't think I'm good enough to eat with you. You'll find that won't do here." . . .

. . . .

Trollope had a much different experience in Virginia. She travelled there by steamboat and arrived late at night. She could not stay on the boat until morning because it had to move on.

[B]ut we were instantly supplied with a dray, and in a few moments found ourselves comfortably seated before a good fire, at a hotel near the landing-place; our rooms, with fires in them, were immediately ready for us, and refreshments brought, with all that sedulous attention which in this country distinguishes a slave state. In making this observation I am very far from intending to advocate the system of slavery; I conceive it to be essentially wrong; but so far as my observation has extended, I think its influence is far less injurious to the manners and morals of the people than the fallacious ideas of equality, which are so fondly cherished by the working classes of the white population in America. That these ideas are fallacious, is obvious, for in point of fact the man possessed of dollars does command the services of the man possessed of no dollars; but these services are given grudgingly, and of necessity, with no appearance of cheerful good-will on the one side, or of kindly interest on the other. I never failed to mark the difference on entering a slave state. I was immediately comfortable, and at my ease, and felt that the intercourse between me and those who served me was profitable to both parties and painful to neither.

Source*: Francis Trollope,* **Domestic Manners of the Americans** *(4th ed., London, UK, 1832) 61-62, 153, 323.*

Jacob's account played on an emerging ethos of domesticity that prioritized modesty and female morality as the cornerstone of the domestic sphere.

Gender roles, as was the case with class and racial relations, were also going through a series of transformations. In the eighteenth century, people tended to live and work in the same place (either on farms or urban artisan households). The unity of work and home ensured that men and women labored together and socialized with one another. The breakdown of artisan households in urban areas, however, effectively separated work from home. Men increasingly left the house to go to work, and (middle class) women stayed home. Popular writers and moralists characterized this domestic sphere as the exclusive province of women and charged them with creating a morally uplifting environment in which to raise children and support their husbands. Writers, along with the demands of urban life, encouraged women to have fewer children. Women complied by abstaining from sex, using available methods of birth control (male withdrawal mainly) and resorting to chemically induced abortions. Most likely, they used a combination of such methods over the course of their lifetimes. As birthrates for native-born women declined, families became increasingly child centered. Mothers were encouraged to take the primary role in child rearing, and childhood increasingly became seen as the period in which a person's moral character was formed.

Although nineteenth-century writers tended to portray the male sphere of the market and politics and the female sphere of domesticity as completely separate worlds, the division was never so stark in reality. Women never stopped participating in the market, for example. Many middle-class women handled the finances of the household, and poor women, immigrant women, and women of color routinely labored outside the home in jobs ranging from factory work, to laundering, to sewing, housekeeping, and prostitution. Many middle-class women—an increasingly well-educated segment of society—also found employment as teachers as northern states enacted compulsory education laws in the 1850s. The overlap between the spheres, however, did not stop there. If women were truly the moral stewards of society, many believed that they had an obligation to influence the moral character of their family as well as society in general. Consequently, numerous women became involved in all manner of reform movements such as temperance advocacy, anti-prostitution efforts, and the antislavery crusade.

Popular Culture in the North

New technologies in printing, the expansion of literacy, and the emergence of cities also transformed American popular culture. The print media offered a whole new world to American readers. The combination of steam-powered presses and the telegraph left Americans awash in information, which generally came in the form of the newspaper. New presses capable of printing thousands of pages per hour forced down production costs to levels making the sale price of newspapers affordable for most people. New journals also proved remarkably easy to set up. Over three thousand papers circulated in the U.S. by 1860 (more than today), covering a wide range of subjects including politics, religion, reform, and literature. Many newspapers, especially in urban areas like New York City, reported on crimes, especially murder, in a manner generally more escapist than informative.

Print, however, did not offer the only means of entertainment. Americans also patronized a wide array of lectures, theatrical performances, and other amusements. Reformers like Frederick Douglass and Theodore Dwight Weld (an abolitionist and temperance advocate) could earn a decent living on the lecture circuit detailing the horrors of slavery and alcohol. Noted politicians such as Daniel Webster, Stephen Douglas, and Abraham Lincoln also attracted large audiences to hear their speeches and debates, which could last for hours. Intellectuals like Ralph Waldo Emerson offered public lectures seeking to explore the meaning of the new world in which Americans found themselves. Alongside reformers, politicians, and philosophers were also a number of others who later generations would dismiss as cranks. Spiritualists promised to help communicate with the dead, while **phrenologists** claimed that they could predict whether an individual had a predisposition to criminal behavior or laziness by measuring the bumps on an individual's skull. Curious Americans sometimes paid to have their own heads measured. One person who took advantage of this curiosity was **P.T. Barnum,** who unabashedly sought to enrich himself by providing the opportunity for Americans to see unusual things. His museum and traveling show gave Americans a chance to see "George Washington's Nurse" (an African-American woman who Barnum claimed was 145 years old) or the "Fiji Mermaid" (probably a monkey torso stitched to a fish's tail). Perhaps more than anyone else Barnum captured the spirit of the commercial bustle and insatiable curiosity that gripped Americans in the pre-Civil War North. The region was morphing into a much different place when compared to life in 1800, standing increasingly sharp contrast to the South, which itself was undergoing fundamental changes.

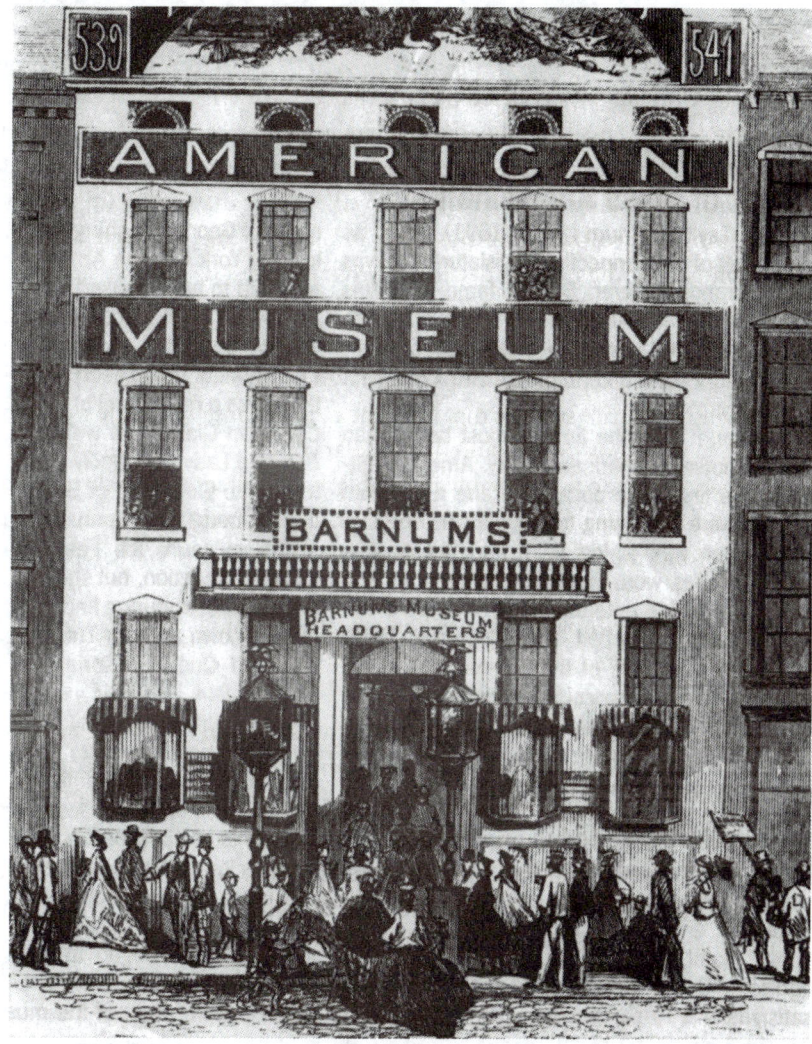

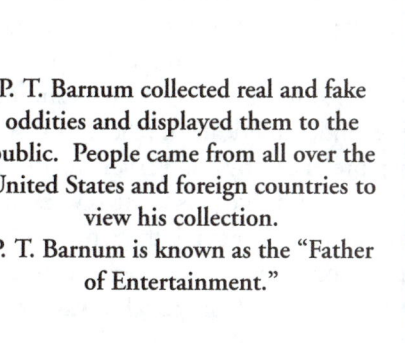

P. T. Barnum collected real and fake oddities and displayed them to the public. People came from all over the United States and foreign countries to view his collection.
P. T. Barnum is known as the "Father of Entertainment."

THE ANTEBELLUM SOUTH

When northern observers looked at the South, they tended to see a backward region. Compared to the North, the southern United States quantitatively lagged in almost every economic category. The South possessed few banks and factories, laid down far less railroad mileage, and contained a small number of cities (with the largest ones—New Orleans, St. Louis, and Baltimore—situated on the region's fringes). Ralph Waldo Emerson expressed a common sentiment when he identified the reason for what he perceived to be the South's laggard development in one of his lectures.

> Slavery is no scholar, no improver; it does not love the whistle of the railroad; it does not love the newspaper, the mail-bag, a college, a book or a preacher who has the absurd whim of saying what he thinks; it does not increase the white population; it does not improve the soil; everything goes to decay.

A few Southerners echoed these concerns. "[H]ow is it that the North . . . has surpassed us in everything that is great and good," North Carolina's Hinton Rowan Helper asked in 1857, "and left us . . . an object of merited reprehension and derision?" Helper, a Republican and an outspoken critic of slavery (both rare sights in the South), offered an atypical answer to his own question. Slavery distorted and slowed southern economic development. Other Southerners, like the New Orleans editor and early secession advocate J.D.B. De Bow, contended that slavery was central and beneficial to the South, but pleaded for more diversification. These criticisms may have been overblown. Relative to the North, the South seemed far behind, but by global standards the region ranked highly in terms of per capita income, railroad mileage, and even industrial output. Nevertheless, the most far-reaching development in the South was undoubtedly the massive increase in lands under cotton cultivation along with the corresponding spread of slavery.

Cotton and Slavery

When the United States declared independence, southern slavery remained largely confined to the regions where it had emerged in the eighteenth century. In Virginia and Maryland, a growing number of enslaved Americans worked on tobacco plantations as their masters wrung their hands over their crop's declining profitability and wondered about how they would keep their slaves employed. Planters in the Lowcountry of South Carolina and Georgia, however, kept large groups of enslaved southerners working in the rice swamps that lined the coast of those two states. Rice, however, required particular conditions to grow, and the crop, while highly profitable, had limited prospects for expansion. By 1860, however, slavery had spread beyond the Chesapeake and the Lowcounty, and reached as far west as Texas and as far North as Missouri. And the enslaved people in these regions grew new crops, like sugar (in limited amounts), and hemp (for making rope), and most especially cotton.

Cotton became the driving force behind southern economic development in the early nineteenth century. Before the 1790s, mainland North America did not have a reputation for producing the crop. Indeed, British customs officials in 1785 accused an American ship for smuggling an early cargo of cotton because they did not believe that it could be grown in the U.S. The American South, however, contained some of the most bountiful cotton land in the world, although planters did not tap into its potential until the very end of the eighteenth century. At that point, the region rapidly transformed into the center of the world's cotton production.

A growing British demand for cotton drove this change. British manufacturers devised ways to mechanize textile production (a technology that would soon spread to the U.S. North as well), but they soon found that the traditional sources of cotton did not produce enough fiber to keep their machines running. The American South, which possessed both good cotton land and an enslaved labor force, broke the bottleneck. Southern planters responded to the demand by uprooting the youth of entire committees of enslaved African Americans into the southern interior where they would be forced to grow cotton. Between 1800 and 1860, planters moved 1 million enslaved people from the East Coast to the interior. (The entire enslaved population of the U.S. amounted to around 4 million people). Cotton in the first two-thirds of the nineteenth century was by far the most important product produced in the U.S. The crop, which in the 1790s did not even amount to 3 percent of U.S. exports, made up nearly a third of exports by 1820 and over 50 percent after 1830. That output constituted nearly 70 percent of the world's cotton supply. Cotton quite simply reshaped the American South in the antebellum period.

In addition to British demand and available forced labor, a number of other factors converged to make cotton—a white fiber from which cloth is made—one of the most important crops produced in the nineteenth-century United States. First, the Black Belt region of the South (so named for the type of soil in the region) contained some of the world's best land for cotton cultivation. And the Black Belt stretched from western South Carolina to eastern Texas. Second, Americans in the 1790s solved a major problem presented by the variant of the crop that grew well in the South: the plant's seeds were deeply embedded in the fiber, and removing them by hand took so much time that doing so was not cost effective. **Eli Whitney,** a graduate of Yale College who was working as a tutor, solved this problem with the invention of the "**cotton gin.**" Whitney's machine raked the seeds out of the fiber many times faster than could be done by hand, and his machine was so simple others could easily copy it. Cotton became profitable over night. These two developments coincided with the rise of textile manufacturing in England and then in the northern United States; the expanding capacity of their operations provided a growing, and at times insatiable, market for cotton.

Cotton cultivation transformed the South. Interest in allowing slavery to die out faded away, and plans for compensated emancipation faltered in the face of rising prices for enslaved workers. (Congress's decision to outlaw participation in the international slave trade also contributed to rising prices.) Expansion also became central to the South. Unlike rice and tobacco, which had reached the limits of their ability to expand, cotton could potentially grow in numerous locations that remained untapped as late as 1820. Ambitious planters thus picked up and moved westward. Between 1800 and 1860, cotton plantations appeared in South Carolina and Georgia, then Alabama, Mississippi, and Louisiana, and finally in Arkansas and Texas. Around one million enslaved African Americans also participated in this process—generally by being ripped from established communities in Virginia and the Carolinas and forced through what some historians term the **Second Middle Passage** to work on a cotton plantation somewhere in the emerging Deep South. This population movement transformed everything it touched. Those enslaved people who were forced to migrate were often overwhelmingly young adults who lost not only their communal and family ties but also any claim to customary rights, such as private farm plots, shorter workdays, more holidays that may have been worked out between planters and enslaved workers in more established regions. Communities in older areas sometimes emptied of young people who had either been moved by planters or purchased and moved by slave traders. The effects could be seen as early as 1820. In that year, the Census reported that 11 percent of the slaves in Virginia had reached the age of 45. In Alabama, only 7 percent had done so.

This expansion was itself a consequence of a central feature of cotton cultivation: it paid. Successful planters took their profits and plowed them back into cotton production, buying more land and more slaves. Cotton output doubled every ten years, and by 1860 the crop accounted for 50 percent of the United States exports. Southerners' tendency to prioritize cotton production over other forms of economic activity proved quite rational. They sat on some of the world's best cotton land, at a time when world demand was increasing. Doing anything else with such land seemed counterproductive, although in hindsight those decisions placed the South at a relative disadvantage to the North during the Civil War era. But in the decades leading up to the war, cotton agriculture offered successful planters a reliable way of making an income. Yet the white fiber was not the only way to do so. Some planters, especially in southern Louisiana, grew sugar. In the upper South region of Kentucky, Tennessee, and Missouri—areas that tended to be more economically diversified than the Deep South—planters grew hemp, but also branched out into a range of other activities. Rice remained profitable in the Lowcountry, and even tobacco rebounded a bit in the 1850s, as producers adopted new techniques.

The Southern Social Order

Like it had in the colonial period, slavery continued to shape the South in crucial ways. Abolitionists depicted the South as a place where a handful of slaveholding aristocrats lorded over an army of slaves and pushed a large group of landless, degraded poor whites to the margin of society. That depiction, however, offered a grossly oversimplified vision of the Old South. To start, non-slaveholding whites (which accounted for around two-thirds of southern households in 1860) hardly considered themselves degraded. Most non-slaveholding households owned land, and their members tended to value self-sufficiency over deep participation in the market. A helpful way to think about the Old South—although this is just a shorthand, and this approach too is an oversimplification—is to treat it as two regions. One South formed around cotton agriculture and slavery in the region's fertile river valleys; the other South took shape around subsistence agriculture in the region's hilly uplands. Although tensions existed between representatives of these two groups, they tended to agree on the fundamental values of their society.

In South's "**Upcountry**" regions, households tended to hold few or no enslaved members, mainly because the types of crops that benefited from slave labor did not grow well in the area. Upcountry families prioritized self-sufficiency and independence above all else. Planters and outside observers often described them as lazy. Francis Anne Kemble, an English actress who had a brief marriage with a Georgia planter in the 1830s and later published her journal as an antislavery narrative, described Georgia's upcountry farmers as willfully poor and dirty:

> Have you visions now of well-to-do farmers with comfortable homesteads, decent habits, industrious, intelligent, cheerful, and thrifty? Such, however, is not the Yeomanry of Georgia. Labour being here the especial portion of slaves, it is thenceforth degraded, and considered unworthy of all but slaves. . . . These wretched creatures will not, for they are whites (and labour belongs to blacks and slaves alone here), labour for their own subsistence. They are hardly protected from the weather by the rude shelters they frame for themselves. . . . Their food is chiefly supplied by shooting the wild fowl and venison, and stealing. . . . Their clothes hang about them in filthy tatters . . . .

Kemble's main point was that slavery degraded labor (a common abolitionist theme), but the description she used here came from her husband's overseer, who worked for one of the largest slaveholders in the country (and absolutely was no abolitionist). But Kemble missed the point. Upcountry farmers—while they did not place the same value on outward appearances, as did Kemble—worked hard. They acquired land to pass down to their children and grew food to support their families. What they did not do, however, was participate regularly in the market or willingly work for other people (the essence of freedom to abolitionists). They might grow cash crops occasionally to get needed cash or earn a little extra, but they prioritized subsistence, and they showed very little interest in earning money by working for someone else. Kemble characterized this as a laziness and racial pride; Upcountry farmers considered their behavior to be an expression of independence.

In contrast to upcountry farmers, slaveholders (one-third of southern households) had become deeply enmeshed in the market, although the most prosperous worked to maintain an image that they stood above such concerns. **Planters**—the heads of households that held twenty or more enslaved members—portrayed slavery as a shelter from the market. In the North, children, the elderly, and sick or injured people became a drain on households because they could not work. Northern employers gave jobs only to the able-bodied (only to lay them off when conditions changed). Slavery offered protection and support from infancy to old age. Planters also portrayed themselves as men of honor; who stood by their word and proved ready to engage in a duel when their honor was questioned. Such "affairs of honor" and the culture of dueling involved elaborate rituals that tended to be more about managing conflict among very powerful families than they were about fighting. Such practices, however, represented the province of privilege. Only 12 percent of slaveholding households qualified as planters, although their images of plantation life have long been portrayed in popular culture as typical.

Most slaveholders lived a far different lifestyle that was not nearly so prosperous. Fully half of all slaveholding households contained five or less enslaved members (the ownership of even one slave, however, represented a considerable asset). These households lived at the mercy of the agricultural market. A single poor harvest could wipe them out. Among these families slavery offered no promise of cradle to grave protection (assuming that it did so even on the South's largest plantations). Failure could mean that a household's enslaved members would be sold into the interstate slave trade; success could well mean that new enslaved members would be purchased. Indeed, the presence of the interstate slave trade, which thrived through this entire period, deeply compromised the planter image of slavery as a shelter from the market. To slavery's critics, the South's commodification of human beings demonstrated that the market had gone too far. To enslaved Southerners, the existence of such a market remained a persistent threat.

Life under Slavery in the Old South

For the majority of Southerners before the Civil War, slavery was simply a fact of life. Human property had become deeply ingrained into the basic functioning of the Old South. Southern business transactions routinely involved the buying, selling, deeding, willing, mortgaging, and hiring of enslaved human beings. Social mobility in the Old South, moreover, depended more or less directly on the ownership of human beings (along with the ownership of land). All of these practices deeply shaped the life of the South's black population, which numbered around four million people by 1860. The vast majority of these Southerners lived on plantations owned by planters. (Planter households may have been only 12 percent of slaveholding households, but they held over half of the slaves in the region). These plantations served as home for the vibrant enslaved communities that shaped black life in the Old South.

Slavery represented a deeply oppressive human relationship, but in the nineteenth century some of the **living conditions** that slaves had to endure were improving. Nineteenth-century slaveholders faced a challenge that previous generations of slaveholders did not have to face: they were under increasing pressure to defend the legitimacy of institution as the North, England, and most other nations in the western world abandoned the practice. They also had to contend with the fact that the United States had ended its participation in the international slave trade, which meant that slaveholders could not replace dead enslaved workers with people brought over from Africa (the normative practice among slave societies in the Caribbean and Brazil). Planters responded to these pressures by articulating (and perhaps aspiring to practice) slavery as a form of **paternalism**—a relationship between planters and slaves that stressed a network of mutual obligations and a complicated mixture of love and terror on both sides. Planters argued that, in exchange for dutiful work from their slaves, they were obligated to provide upkeep and protection. Indeed, material conditions improved across the nineteenth century. Although real differences persisted between newly settled regions and older, more established ones, slave housing improved, as did diet (at least in quantity) and clothing. (However, these developments may have as much to do with the increasing value represented by enslaved property as well as an increase in material prosperity in the United States generally.) Planters also claimed that enslaved blacks were members of their household—"my family, white and black"—and as such they provided discipline (punishment), material provisions, and provisions for their spiritual care. Nineteenth-century planters, in fact, broke with their predecessors and allowed the widespread Christianization of their slaves.

The lives of enslaved Southerners remained hard. Work proved unrelenting. On cotton plantations, men, women, and children (from around the age of ten) labored in the fields under the supervision of an overseer or driver. Days could be as long as eighteen hours during harvest time. Masters, or their overseers, at times inflicted harsh punishments, often by whipping—a brutal practice that could cut deeply into a person's back and leave deep scars. Not every slave endured a whipping (advice books for planters advised using the whip sparingly), but the threat of one often worked to instill discipline through terror. Material conditions, while perhaps improved relative to the eighteenth century, were by no means lavish. Entire enslaved families lived together in small, one-room buildings that lacked flooring. Clothing consisted of one or two outfits, which were increasingly made out of the cheapest cloth produced by New England cotton mills. The diet of enslaved folk was high in calories but low in nutrients. Pork and corn were the staples. That said, studies of the heights of enslaved adults (heights are assumed to be an indicator of nutritional intake across one's lifetime) show that American slaves tended to be taller than those in the West Indies but shorter than free white Northerners. Such differences may indicate that American slaves were generally healthier than their counterparts in the West Indies, but not as healthy as they could be. Disease, although this threat was by no means limited to just enslaved people, also remained a constant threat. Crowded slave quarters and the use of traditional means for disposing of human waste brought intestinal diseases and other infections. Medical technology, in which some planters proved eager to dabble, remained rudimentary, and many enslaved people would rather face the disease than their masters' cures.

In the midst of these conditions, enslaved African Americans forged deep communal bonds. Although the vast majority of enslaved Southerners had been born in the United States, they found ways to retain aspects of African heritage. Most of these "cultural carryovers" by the mid-nineteenth century consisted of subtle things like hair styling or rhythm patterns that influenced music but had blended with European cultural influences as well. Stories told in enslaved communities passed down lessons that taught strategies for survival—trickster characters had pride of place. Christianity also swept through the communities, although it did so in two forms. One form constituted the one offered by slaveholders, who (perhaps as part of their effort to defend their institution) in the nineteenth-century had come to view slaves' religious development as part of their responsibility, and they opened their plantations to missionaries. What the planters offered, however, emphasized Biblical passages that advised accepting one's lot in life or stressed that slaves should obey their masters (as St. Paul did in the book of Ephesians). The other form consisted of the type of Christianity that enslaved people actually embraced. Self-taught (or at least informally educated) preachers emerged in the slave communities and led late-night meetings that emphasized freedom and deliverance. Indeed, Moses, the prophet who led God's people out of Egypt, became a major figure in the theology that emerged in enslaved communities.

The enslaved community and the values it reinforced formed part of a coping strategy by which enslaved folk turned back master's claims to absolute control over their bodies and minds. Most resistance took place in a relatively quiet fashion. Although outright slave revolts occurred, like **Nat Turner**'s 1831 revolt in South Hamp-

ton, Virginia, they were put down with brutal severity. Turner's revolt, which he planned as a result of spiritual visions, resulted in the deaths of sixty whites in the immediate vicinity of its outbreak. Local officials responded by putting down the uprising within a matter of days. Turner was tried, sentenced to death, and his body was cut into pieces. Eighteen other participants suffered hanging, and twelve others were sold into the domestic slave trade. All across the South, moreover, slave masters tightened discipline and supervision to guard against further uprisings. Even rumors could set off planters. In Charleston, South Carolina, word of an impending uprising spread through the white community. Historians now disagree as to whether there actually was a planned revolt, but city officials employed torture to get confessions and the rebellion (if any) was stopped.

Overt rebellion thus carried heavy consequences, and enslaved people opted for less direct forms of resistance. Acts of arson or personal violence, sometimes through poisoning remained viable approaches, as did stealing and running away. Enslaved people could also slow down work and pressure masters to respond to their demands. Some historians argue that these tactics represented a form of negotiation between planters and slaves through which both parties came to agreement about the conditions of work. That may be so, but these strategies also carried an unintended consequence. Planters frequently claimed that slavery was a form of moral uplift that took Africans (who Europeans generally considered to be uncivilized) and disciplined them so that they could survive in modern society. By disposition, they said, slaves lied, stole, and shirked work, and enslavement corrected these traits. Although these forms of passive resistance probably worked as negotiating tactics, they did so at the expense of reinforcing planter stereotypes. Of course, enslaved folk had limited options in the complex social order that had emerged in the nineteenth-century United States.

Southern Women, Black and White

As they did in the North, women's lives in the South also transformed during this period, but those changes did not work themselves out in the same ways. In the North, an ideology of separate spheres had emerged, and in some ways had enhanced female claims to power within the household. In the South, however, planter claims to paternalism had implications for gender relations primarily because it stressed the organization of a household as a unit of dependents under the authority of a father figure. Women in elite families, which were genuinely large households, did wield real power. They supervised a wide range of activities from cooking, to sewing, to cleaning, to childrearing and they could mete out punishments as effectively as any male. Planter women, however, did not achieve the level of public influence that was beginning to emerge in the North.

Planter women also faced a few other challenges. One was isolation. Plantations were spread out from one another, which rendered difficult interaction with other women beyond the household. Another challenge stemmed from the tendency of males on the plantation to use their power to take sexual advantage of enslaved women. Harriet Jacobs built much of her narrative about her experience around this issue. Frederick Douglass, who did not spend much time on the subject, hinted in his autobiography that his father also might have been his master. These observations were not just confined to slave narratives. When she arrived on her husband's island plantation, Frances Kemble "observed . . . a . . . large proportion of mulattoes." She asked why there were so many mixed-race people in such an isolated area.

> While we were still on this subject, a horrid-looking filthy woman met us with a little child in her arms, a very light mulatto, whose extraordinary resemblance to driver Bran (one of the officials, who had been duly presented to me on my arrival, and who was himself a mulatto) struck me directly. I pointed it out to Mr. [Butler], who merely answered, "Very likely his child." . . . all which rather unpleasant state of relationships seemed accepted as such a complete matter of course, that I felt rather uncomfortable, and said no more about who was like who, but came to certain conclusions in my own mind as to a young lad who had been among our morning visitors, and whose extremely light color and straight handsome features and striking resemblance to Mr. K . . . .

Mary Chestnut, an elite South Carolina women and unlike Kemble no abolitionist, also reported similar occurrences. "Any lady is ready to tell you who is the father of all the mulatto children in everybody's households but their own."

Most white women in the South, however, did not face these problems. (Or they did not do so in the same dimensions because most southern men lacked the power that came with control of a large plantation household.) The majority of southern white women lived on small farms; they received little or no education. Like rural women throughout the nation, they bore a large number of children (around six on average by 1860. They engaged in much the same work as farm women had performed since the colonial era. But they increasingly did so in new

locations since numerous households participated in the process of expansion that filled in the states in the Upper and Lower South with people of European (and African) descent.

Enslaved women also faced a hard life. They were subject to sexual abuse. They, especially on cotton plantations, faced expectations to do the exact same fieldwork as males. (Other crops, like rice however, had roles and responsibilities assigned by gender.) Work requirements extended through pregnancy, or at least to the last month. Work responsibilities resumed shortly after the birth of a child. These practices resulted in a number of miscarriages and infant deaths. Enslaved families faced, in addition to labor demands, the possibility that a family could be split up and its members sold into the domestic slave trade. To slaves, this practice represented one of the worst aspects of enslavement. Even in the absence of actual sale, enslaved mothers at times had to watch their children be punished, and they carried the responsibility for socializing their children into the institution of slavery.

SLAVE LABOR VS. FREE LABOR

During the first half of the nineteenth century, the United States manifested stark sectional differences as Americans confronted the new challenges represented by economic and territorial expansion. Some contend that the North and the South had become separate and mutually antagonistic social orders. Others posit that the two sections were substantially similar with the single exception of slavery. Historians will probably never agree on this issue, but a growing number of Americans living in the early nineteenth century certainly concluded that the North and the South were developing fundamentally different cultures. Moreover, they argued that their section represented the Founders' true vision of the United States.

Southern partisans viewed the changes taking place in the northern states as a sign of moral decline. "Oh! That vile North!" wrote Supreme Court Justice Peter V. Daniel of Virginia as he complained of the cold weather in a letter to his daughter, "it infects and spoils even that atmosphere we breathe!" In another letter, he asked, "I wonder when *the North* . . . would produce anything like these oranges! or indeed anything else that is good or decent." One of Daniel's main complaints was the incessant hustle and bustle of northern life combined with what he saw as an unseemly materialism. But beneath that criticism, Southerners generally portrayed the North's embrace of factory work and wage labor as an abdication of social responsibility. No longer were workers part of a household of a more established and powerful person who provided support and protection. They were thrown onto the mercies of the market. Worse still, those workers possessed the vote, and with every passing year carried the growing possibility that they would vote private property out of existence. Like slavery, southern partisans contended, unfree labor was not just the southern way of life—it was the foundation of all civilized social order.

Northern partisans rejected those arguments as self-serving—as indeed they were—and portrayed three developments taking place in the North as the consequence of freedom. Poet Walt Whitman captured the sentiment in his 1855 poem "A Song for Occupations": "Neither a servant nor a master I, \ I take no sooner a large price than a small price, I will have my \ own whoever enjoys me, \ I will be even with you and you shall be even with me." The absence of slavery—the "evenness" of which Whitman wrote—meant that workers were free to choose their own employers, to negotiate their own wages, to stay, quit, or even strike when they wished, to speak their minds, or to move on to somewhere else. That freedom produced material benefits: more banks, more cultivated land, more canal and railroad mileage, more factories, more immigrants—more of everything, except cotton and slaves. Like the southern counterargument, this one was self-serving. Praising **free labor** often meant overlooking real disparities in power and wealth developing in the North, where free labor really meant little more than the freedom to choose between starvation and a collection of essentially identical offers from employers for low wages, long hours, and dangerous work.

Yet along with the developments in the North came a growing number of calls to reform American society. Urbanization placed familiar social behavior such as drunkenness and crime into new perspective. New developments in religion, particularly among Protestant evangelicals, fed this reexamination, as did antebellum Americans' general willingness to experiment with new ideas. The consequence was a surge of new reform movements targeting almost every aspect of American society. This development, especially when activists addressed the question of slavery, further increased the gulf between the North and the South.

Chronology

1793   Eli Whitney invents the cotton gin, reviving slavery.

1808   Congress bans importation of slaves to the U. S.

1820   Lowell mills opened.

1822   Denmark Vesey's slave rebellion in Charleston is crushed.

1825   Erie Canal is completed.

1830   Baltimore & Ohio Railroad commences operation.

1831   Nat Turner leads violent slave revolt in Virginia.

1832   Restrictions on slaves increase in the South.

1834   Cyrus McCormick patents his mechanical reaper. Women workers strike at Lowell mills.

1837   Mt. Holyoke College for women opens. Oberlin College admits women and blacks.

1842   Knickerbocker baseball club organized.

1844   Samuel F.B. Morse sends first telegraph message.

1845   Irish potato famine starts, leading to massive immigration to America.

1845   Invention of the rotary press makes rapid printing of newspapers possible.

1847   John Deere manufactures steel plows.

1848   Failure of German revolutions increase immigration to America.

1849   California Gold Rush stimulates growth of West Coast.

1850s   Cotton boom sweeps the South.

SUGGESTED READINGS

Melvin Adelman, *A Sporting Time: New York City and the Rise of Modern Athletics, 1820-1870* (1986).

Ira Berlin, *Slaves Without Masters: The Free Negro in the Antebellum South* (1974).

Janet Farrell Brodie, *Contraception and Abortion in Nineteenth Century America* (1994).

Victoria Bynum, *Unruly Women* (1992).

Catherine Clinton, *The Plantation Mistress* (1982).

Hasia Diner, *Erin's Daughters in America: Irish Immigrant Women in the Nineteenth Century* (1983).

Paul Escott, *Slavery Remembered: A Record of Twentieth Century Slave Narratives* (1979).

Timothy Gilfoyle, *City of Eros: New York City, Prostitution and the Commercialization of Sex, 1790-1920* (1992).

Herbert Gutman, *The Black Family in Slavery and Freedom, 1750-1925* (1976).

Joan Hoff, *Law, Gender, and Injustice: A Legal History of U.S, Women* (1991).

Julie Roy Jeffrey, *Frontier Women: The Trans-Mississippi West 1840-1880* (1979).

Alice Kessler-Harris, *Out to Work: A History of Wage-Earning Women in the United States* (1982*).*

Jacqueline Jones, Labor *of Love, Labor of Service* (1985).

Lawrence Levine, *Black Culture and Black Consciousness* (1977).

Leon Litwack, *North of Slavery: The Negro in the Free States, 1790-1860* (1961).

Louise Mayo, *the Ambivalent Image: Nineteenth Century America's Perception of the Jew* (1987).

Patricia Morton, ed., *Discovering the Women in Slavery* (1995).

Lillian Schissel, *Women's Diaries of the Westward Journey* (1982).

Ann Firor Scott, *The Southern Lady* (1970).

Carol Smith-Rosenberg, *Disorderly Conduct: Visions of Gender in Victorian America* (1986).

Christine Stansell, *City of Women: Sex and Class in New York, 1789-1860* (1986).

Stephen Thernstrom, *Poverty and Progress: Social Mobility in a Nineteenth Century City* (1964).

John Unruh Jr., *The Overland Emigrants and the Trans-Mississippi West, 1840-1860* (1979).

Review Questions

1. What new social challenges were created by the rapid movement of people to the cities?

2. What were the largest groups of immigrants that came to the United States between 1830 to 1860? Why did these groups come to America and what reception did they typically receive upon their arrival? Why?

3. Describe some coping mechanisms that southern slaves used as survival techniques while in bondage.

4. Describe some of the restrictions, by law and by custom, placed on free African Americans living in the North before the Civil War.

5. How did Northerners view the South? In what ways did the South differ from the rest of the country in terms of economics, education, and culture?

Glossary of Important People and Concepts

African Methodist Episcopal Church
P.T. Barnum
Chinese immigration
John Deere
Frederick Douglass
Erie Canal
Five Points
Free labor
German immigration
Grain reaper
Irish immigration
Harriet Jacobs
Cyrus McCormick
Samuel Morse
Paternalism
Phrenology
Railroads
Second Middle Passage
Slave living conditions
Yeomen farmers
Steel plow
Telegraph
Alexis de Tocqueville
Nat Turner
Eli Whitney

FREDERICK DOUGLASS

Chapter Thirteen

THE SPIRIT OF REFORM
1820-1860

Elizabeth Blackwell's heart broke one day in 1845 as she watched her friend Mary die painfully from unknown causes in Cincinnati, Ohio. Mary moaned that "the worst part of my illness is that I am being treated by a rough, unfeeling man." Comforted by Blackwell's kind treatment, Mary told her, "You are young and strong, you should become a doctor." Blackwell later wrote that she thought about how impossible her friend's idea was: women in 1840s America did not become doctors. In any case, the 24-year-old found the human body repulsive and considered nothing in the medical profession attractive. "I hated everything connected with the body, and could not bear the sight of a medical book," Elizabeth wrote in her 1895 book **Pioneer Work in Opening the Medical Profession to Women—Autobiographical Sketches**.

In this era, across the United States, male doctors campaigned to "professionalize" medicine. The American Medical Association, founded in 1847, sought to standardize medical practice and lobbied states to pass laws requiring licenses for practicing physicians. The men of the AMA actively tried to discourage female patients from seeking care at the hands of midwives and other women healers.

Many male doctors did not think of women as intelligent, competent, or strong enough to handle the rigors of a demanding profession. Many deemed a woman seeking a job outside of the home as being unladylike. No medical schools in the country had female students. Elizabeth Blackwell, however, would break down that barrier.

Growing up, Blackwell resented that the roles of housewife or teacher represented the only respectable career option for women. Having recently experienced a failed romance,

she desired to escape the risks of love and thought entering an "absorbing occupation" might provide an escape from dreary, potentially doomed courtships.

Blackwell, born the third of nine children February 3, 1821, in Counterslip, England, grew up in a family of crusaders. Her father, Samuel Blackwell, owned a sugar refining business and became well known as an abolitionist. At a time when most parents believed in spanking their children for misbehavior, he disciplined his young ones by keeping a logbook of offenses. When a certain number of misdeeds had been recorded in the logbooks, the child had to spend dinnertime in the attic. He taught his children not to accept conventional, sexist ideas about women and made sure that his daughters received as quality an education as his sons.

The Blackwell children grew to become successful adults. Elizabeth's younger sister, Emily, would follow her into the medical profession, while older sister Anna became an accomplished poet and journalist. Another sibling, Henry Blackwell, also achieved renown as a reporter and newspaper editor and became a respected advocate for political reform with his well-known wife, suffrage campaigner and abolitionist Lucy Stone.

Worried by the political instability in England, Samuel Blackwell moved his family to New York City when Elizabeth was 11. His refinery burned down in 1836, but the elder Blackwell rebuilt the business only to see it fail financially. The clan relocated to Cincinnati in 1838. Sadly, Mr. Blackwell died within weeks of the move, leaving his widow and children in a precarious financial state during a severe economic depression from 1837-1843.

Already young adults, Elizabeth and her sisters Anna and Marian opened a school, the Cincinnati English and French Academy for Young Ladies. Elizabeth later taught in nearby Kentucky and would, in a few years, have her fateful encounter with her friend Mary. Medical schools were a fairly new idea in the late 1840s. Most doctors previously received their training by observing older physicians and providing care under the supervision of their mentors. Women occasionally underwent such an apprenticeship and practiced medicine, though without a license.

Blackwell wanted a license. Thanks to her sister Anna, Elizabeth had secured a position as a music teacher in Asheville, North Carolina, where she rented a room in a home owned by a former doctor, the Reverend John Dickson. Even as she launched a Sunday school for slaves, she voraciously read her host's medical library. Blackwell moved to Charleston, South Carolina, home of Dickson's brother, Dr. Samuel Henry Dickson. As she taught reading, she continued her informal medical training and began to apply to medical schools. Twenty-nine schools rejected Blackwell's application in 1847. Finally, she received a surprise acceptance letter from Geneva Medical College, a little-known school in rural New York State.

The acceptance letter apparently was either a joke or a mistake. The faculty mostly opposed letting Blackwell attend, but they decided to let the students vote on her admission. Students either did not take the question at hand seriously or decided to approve her in order to pull a prank on the faculty. In any case, Blackwell had opened a door at Geneva.

Professors sometimes made life hard for her, preventing her from using labs needed to perform required assignments and forcing her to sit apart from male students. Locals sometimes treated her as an immoral woman and shunned her. But her fellow students apparently treated her well. Blackwell persevered and her courage and determination won reluctant respect from professors and students.

She got the idea for her thesis by observing patients being cared for at the Blockley Almshouse, an institution for the poor in Philadelphia. Many of the patients suffered from typhus, a malady caused by the poor sanitation common in large American cities in nineteenth century. Typhus became the eventual subject of her research. Blackwell would be a pioneer in establishing the importance of sanitation in disease prevention.

She earned valedictorian honors when she received her medical degree from Geneva in 1849. She was the first woman with an M.D. degree not only in the United States, but also in the world.

After commencement, Elizabeth crossed the Atlantic to London and Paris to further her medical studies. When she returned to the United States two years later, she was determined to help other women follow her path. Blocked from practicing medicine at hospitals in New York City, in 1857 she established the New York Infirmary for Women and Children (later called New York Downtown Hospital), the first such institution run by female doctors. The infirmary added a medical college for women in 1868.

Moving back to England, Elizabeth helped create the National Health Society, earned a spot on the British Medical Registry, and became a professor at England's first medical school for women. A prolific author, she tirelessly promoted the importance of hygiene and of preventive medicine. Just as important, she inspired other nineteenth-century women who later became prominent in the medical field. She died in Hastings, England in 1910. The British humor magazine **Punch** *at one point paid the pioneer the following only-partially tongue-in-cheek tribute:*

> *Young ladies all, of every clime*
> *Especially of Britain,*
> *Who wholly occupy your time*
> *In novels or in knittin'*
> *Whose highest skill is but to play*
> *Sing, dance, or French to clack well,*
> *Reflect on the example, pray*
> *Of excellent Miss Blackwell!*

The solar eclipse that shadowed much of the United States on February 12, 1831, struck many as a portent of earthshaking change. Many speculated that the comet signaled the end of the world. The day after the eclipse, newspapers reported that preachers delivered sermons with Luke 21:25 as their key text: "And there shall be signs in the sun, and in the moon, and in the stars; and upon the earth distress of nations, with perplexity; the sea and the waves roaring." A South Carolina slave named Nat Turner believed he had just received a signal from God. Six months later, Turner launched an abortive slave rebellion that would end in the deaths of as many as sixty-five whites and the murder and execution of more than two hundred African Americans.

Generally speaking, the eclipse disappointed. The day did not grow as dark as some almanacs and astronomers had suggested. Many, however, still saw in the eclipse a powerful metaphor for a restless era of wrenching change. By 1831 many Americans fought for more humane prisons, better schools, alcohol prohibition, banning prostitution, and, most explosively, the abolition of slavery.

Historians have called the period roughly from the 1830s until the start of the Civil War in 1861 the "first age of reform." It could also be called the "age of anxiety." Before the 1830s, male success had been defined as being self-sufficient, owning a farm or being an independent businessman, but increasingly men in the larger cities ended up scrambling for low-wage jobs, living in shabby rental houses in crowded, crime-ridden neighborhoods. Working class families in Philadelphia squeezed into tenement buildings, with parents, children and other relatives crammed into a single room that lacked adequate ventilation. Families slept poorly shielded from the outside noise and the smells created by animal wastes and irregular garbage collection. Poverty, overcrowding, and the boom-and-bust economy in the first half of the nineteenth century bred a number of ills, including violent crime, a thriving sex trade, alcoholism, and urban uprisings.

Well-educated, middle class and wealthier white idealists saw this disorder and yearned for a past that never existed. They believed that the America of the eighteenth century—more rural, more Protestant, and more dominated by those of English descent—had also been a more harmonious, happy land. These same reformers, however, knew that there was no turning back the clock. They would have to find nineteenth-century means to achieve eighteenth-century ends: reinstating law, order and conformity even as they embraced the unpredictable new capitalist reality.

These reformers battled loudly against every perceived social ill, not as eclipses casting shadows on the landscape. Like the real eclipse of 1831, reform efforts often disappointed, but the reformers themselves burned as comets against a darkened sky illuminating the ugly failings of Jacksonian America. For better or worse, they tirelessly sought to leave a better country in its place.

THE TRANSCENDENTALISTS

Ralph Waldo Emerson

The poet and philosopher **Ralph Waldo Emerson** believed his generation faced a daunting agenda: nothing short of remaking the world. What did Emerson, the author of such essays as "Self Reliance," think needed reform? "We are to revise the whole of our social structure—the state, the school, religion, marriage, trade, science, and explore the foundations in our own nature."

The activists who created the First Age of Reform—such as pioneer feminists, anti-slavery crusaders, humanitarians concerned about the brutal conditions prevailing in American prisons—were too diverse to easily define philosophically. (The Second Age of Reform would come with the rise of the Progressive Movement from the 1890s to about 1920.) Most reformers from the 1830s to the 1850s believed in a benevolent God, that humanity was

perfectible, and were optimistic that humans collectively could create a society that was fair, just, and compassionate. They believed that all individuals had the obligation individually to perfect themselves and to fight social evils. Many reformers, like Emerson, belonged to the Transcendentalist Movement, which saw a divine spirit residing in all of nature and in each person and which opposed any institution like slavery that suffocated initiative and imposed conformity.

Born in Boston on May 3, 1803, the son of a well-respected Unitarian minister, Emerson was one of eight children. His father, William, died before Ralph (or Waldo, as he preferred to be called) reached his eighth birthday. As his mother took in boarders to pay the bills, Emerson enrolled in Boston Latin School in 1812 and earned financial aid to attend Harvard by serving as an aide to the college's president, John Kirkland, and by teaching children at area schools. He earned a divinity degree and, like his father, became a clergyman in the Unitarian Church. Unitarians reject the concept of God as a Trinity. They see God as a unitary being and believe in the intrinsic worth of each individual. They believe that no one holy book or individual has a unique claim to divine truth. Individuals, according to Unitarians, have the right to find the truth in their own way. Unitarianism would be a major influence on Transcendentalism.

Plagued by ill health, Emerson contracted tuberculosis and traveled to the South where he hoped the warmer weather would improve his condition. This provided his first extensive exposure to slavery. At one point he attended a church service where a nearby slave auction repeatedly interrupted the preacher's sermon. The experience solidified his revulsion to slavery. He preached for various congregations before he fell in love with Ellen Tucker of Concord, New Hampshire, and was ordained pastor of the Second Church of Boston in 1829. Ellen died of tuberculosis only 18 months into the couple's marriage, prompting a crisis of faith in Emerson and leading him to leave the ministry in 1832. Emerson became convinced that Tucker's spirit remained in his presence, and he came to believe in the indestructibility of the human soul. He traveled across Europe and met prominent authors like Samuel Coleridge. But the Jardin des Plantes in Paris, featuring plant species carefully arranged to illustrate their biological relationships, most deeply influenced him. The French garden opened his eyes to the interconnectedness of all life, including humanity, he would later say.

Living off stocks left him by his late wife, Emerson absorbed the shock of two other deaths of close family members. His brothers, Edward and Charles, both died, like Ellen, from tuberculosis in 1834 and 1836. Amid the heartache, he married Lydian Jackson, a smart, funny woman who, although she never inspired Emerson's romantic passions as Ellen had, deeply influenced his later writings. In 1835, Emerson launched a new career giving lectures across New England on topics ranging from his travels to Europe, nature, religion, and history. He became the focal point of a group of Boston intellectuals that came to be known as the "Transcendental Club." The movement drew not only Emerson but also the prominent Unitarian minister George Putnam, abolitionist leader and man of the pulpit Theodore Parker, the journalist and women's suffrage advocate Margaret Fuller, and Henry David Thoreau, a major peer of Emerson as an essayist and author. They called for greater democracy in American politics. The group split off from more conservative Unitarians in questioning the miracles attributed to Christ, insisting that the most important aspect of Jesus's ministry was his message of giving and human kinship. Emerson went further and, in a July 15, 1838, address to Harvard Divinity School graduates, he asserted that Jesus, while a great man, was not God, a belief for which he was widely condemned as an atheist.

Emerson and other **Transcendentalists** began publishing their thoughts in a journal called *The Dial*, starting in 1840. They challenged not only traditional religious beliefs but also the social and political limitations placed upon women. They were deeply skeptical about institutions such as the church and government, and doubted if meaningful change could be achieved through voting. Large institutions like churches and state and national governments, they feared, threatened individual liberties.

Transcendentalists emphasized feeling over reason. By "transcending," Emerson and his philosophical kin referred to the act of rising beyond scientific reasoning and relying on the divine spark that transcendentalists believed resided in each person. Each person, they insisted, could find a unique path to moral truth. "Trust thyself," Emerson wrote in "Self Reliance," his most famous essay. Once freed from the bonds of traditional authority, Emerson insisted, the individual enjoyed infinite potential.

Henry David Thoreau

Emerson came of age as a writer during extraordinary blossoming of literature in the United States, an American Renaissance that also included novelists and poets like Nathaniel Hawthorne (author of *The Scarlet Letter*), Herman Melville (*Moby Dick*), Emily Dickinson ("Hope Is The Thing With Feathers"), and Walt Whitman ("Song of Myself"). Emerson was friends with many of these writers, but had a particularly close and troublesome relationship with **Henry David Thoreau**.

Ralph Waldo Emerson (left) and Henry David Thoreau (right)

Thoreau grew up in Concord, Massachusetts. While a student at Harvard, he encountered Emerson's book, *Nature*, and became friends with the author. Like Emerson, Thoreau lived a life shaped by family tragedy. His older brother John, who had contributed his teacher's salary to help pay for Henry's college tuition, died painfully in Henry's arms from a case of lockjaw contracted while shaving. Only 25 years of age, Thoreau worked for a while as a pencil maker and a surveyor, joining Emerson's circle of friends.

In 1845, wishing to experience almost total isolation from society, Thoreau built a cabin on land owned by Emerson at the edge of Walden Pond. Beginning July 4, 1845, he spent 16 months in relative solitude, depending almost completely on his wits and ingenuity, as he took long strolls in the woods and read and wrote copiously about experiences he channeled into a literary masterpiece, *Walden, or Life in the Woods*, first published in 1854. Thoreau's work was somewhat disingenuous: his life in the cabin at Walden was not as completely independent as he depicted. He bought the materials he used to build the cabin at a nearby store, and his times of isolation were frequently punctuated by visits to the Emerson home where he frequently enjoyed the couple's conversation and slices of Lydian's apple pies. Nevertheless, Thoreau made an eloquent case in *Walden* that only in nature could a person find true freedom.

In an era in which people increasingly depended on others for wages and bought items like clothes and furniture that they once had constructed for themselves, Thoreau argued that by living with only necessities, one could be freed of entangling obligations. A truly independent person living in harmony with nature would not waste time that could be spent more productively gaining enlightenment, not just in order to earn money for buying objects that can never bring happiness. "Simplicity, simplicity, simplicity! I say, let your affairs be as two or three, and not a hundred or a thousand; instead of a million count half a dozen, and keep your accounts on your thumb nail," he wrote. People become owned by the objects they buy, he wrote, because of the debts accumulated in their acquisition. "Money is not required to buy the necessity of the soul," he said.

During his sojourn at Walden Pond, in late July 1846, Thoreau went on an errand in Concord and encountered a local tax collector who demanded payment of six years' worth of delinquent poll taxes. Thoreau refused to pay, objecting that his taxes would be used to help fund the United States' war with Mexico. Thoreau saw this war as unprovoked and part of a conspiracy to create new slave states out of territory seized from Mexico. (Thoreau was mistaken: the poll tax was a local levy unrelated to the war.) The sheriff, Sam Staples, arrested Thoreau, who spent a night in jail. He was freed when an unknown person, mostly likely an aunt, paid the overdue taxes, against his will. The experience inspired an essay he published in 1849 as "*Resistance to Civil Government*" (most commonly known as *Civil Disobedience*). This work found a global audience in the twentieth century, serving as a major inspiration for Mahatma Gandhi as he led India's independence movement to success in 1948 and for Martin Luther King, Jr. during the African-American civil rights struggles of the 1950s and the 1960s.

In *Civil Disobedience*, Thoreau rejected any obligation to respect any authority that commanded him to act in a way that violated his personal sense of right and wrong. "The only obligation which I have a right to assume, is to do at any time what I think is right," Thoreau said. He argued that no individual owed obedience to a government that committed evil, such as permitting the spread of slavery. Individuals owed their first allegiance to the "higher law" of God, and not to nations that violated that code.

Walt Whitman

Politics can be found in the work of other writers in this first great era of American literature. **Walt Whitman** flew in the face of the emerging discipline of the marketplace with poetry that celebrated the languid beauty of the body, spontaneity, and—most controversially—frank sexuality. At one point an advocate of temperance, he adamantly opposed the extension of slavery to territory taken from Mexico. He only gradually became an abolitionist, fearing at first that the movement alienated too many to be effective. Whitman's poems shocked readers with graphic snapshots of the often ugly urban world he inhabited, such as his horrific juxtaposition of a surgical amputation and the auction of a slave girl in one poem: "The malform'd

Walt Whitman

limbs are tied to the surgeon's table; What is removed drops horribly in a pail; The quadroon girl is sold at the auction-stand, the drunkard nods by the bar-room stove."

If the emerging industrial economy demanded rote labor and depersonalized workers, Whitman, like Emerson and Thoreau, celebrated the brotherhood of all races, declaring, "In all people, I see myself." In a society marked by ever more orderly, rigidly controlled textile mills and steel plants, and faceless, overcrowded city streets, Whitman hailed the unpredictable and chaotic in each individual. "I am large, I contain multitudes," Whitman said in his epic poem "Song of Myself." "Song" was just one of several monumental poems contained in the classic volume of verse titled *Leaves of Grass*, first published in 1855.

Herman Melville and Nathaniel Hawthorne

Herman Melville drew much of his inspiration from the transcendentalist movement, particularly its emphasis on shared humanity across racial lines. In his novels, Melville repeatedly addressed the most vexing and dangerous problem facing antebellum America: race relations. Melville based his 1855 classic novella *Benito Cereno* on a single chapter from the memoir of the Captain Amasa Delano. Delano's book, *Narrative of Voyages and Travels, in the Northern and Southern Hemispheres*, describes an 1805 encounter with a slave ship, the *Tryal*. A slave mutiny had occurred on board the ship.

Melville took liberties with the memoir and made a fictionalized version of Delano, the main character in the story. Delano is the captain of a whaler, the *Bachelor's Delight*, that happens upon a slave ship off the coast of

The Birth of American LGBT Literature

Between the 1820s and the 1850s, reform movements arose to abolish slavery, humanize prisons and insane asylums and save Americans from the scourge of alcohol. Other Americans called, usually in coded form, for sexual freedom. In an era in which keeping non-heterosexual identity in the closet could be a matter of life and death, several of the most acclaimed American writers also opened a window into gay and lesbian identity in the early and mid-19th century. They wrote what could be considered the opening chapters of LGBT literature in the United States. These writers dealt not only with sexual identity, the meaning of family, and gender roles, but also the alienation of urban life, the cruelty of slavery, the horror of war, the despair of poverty, and the puzzle of what it meant to be an American.

Born in 1819 in West Hills, New York, Walt Whitman began a journalism career writing stories for Brooklyn and New York City newspapers at age 12. By the beginning of the 1840s, Whitman moved to Long Island, teaching in a series of rural one-room schoolhouses. Whitman rejected many of the cruel practices common to education in that era, such as paddling students or striking them with canes to punish misbehavior or giving the teacher the wrong answer to a question.

A longstanding rumor has stalked Whitman that he was caught sodomizing a student in late 1840 or early 1841 in the fishing village of Southold. A mob tarred and feathered him, and banished him from the town. What is known, however, is that Whitman abruptly quit teaching after the alleged incident and resumed his career as a journalist, editor, and publisher for a number of publications, including the **Brooklyn Daily Eagle,** the **Long Islander**, and the **New Orleans Crescent**.

Whitman made his mark as a major American literary force with publication of the first edition of **Leaves of Grass** in 1855. Whitman celebrated individualism and the brotherhood of all races, declaring, "In all people, I see myself." In **Leaves**, he juxtaposed a variety of freedoms, whether emotional, sexual, or political, with the brutality of American slavery. "I wince at the bite of dogs," he wrote of slavery. "Hell and despair are upon me/crack and again crack the marksmen/I clutch the rails of the fence, my gore/dribs/thinn'd with the ooze of my/skin/I fall on the weeds and the stones/The riders . . . Taunt my dizzy ears and beat me/violently over the head with whipstocks."

In **Leaves**, Whitman blended the breathtaking vistas of the American landscape with allusions to the male form, such as in the poem "Song of Myself." By the late 1850s, Whitman became a regular feature at a Brooklyn saloon, **Pfaff's**, joining a group of young gay men who called themselves the "Fred Gray Association." These friendships inspired Whitman's most explicitly homoerotic writings, a body of work scholars would later call the "Calamus poems." In those verses, Whitman saw interpersonal relationships as inherently political. To him, the rise of the industrial, urban economy in American capitalism led men to see each other as rivals in a pitched battle for economic survival. Whitman's poetry depicted an alternative reality in which men comforted and healed each other in loving embrace.

Historians and literary scholars believe that other prominent writers published in the age of reform such as Herman Melville (the author of **Moby Dick**), Henry David Thoreau (who penned **Walden**, or **Life in the Woods**), and Emily Dickinson were likely gay or bisexual. One of the most famous recluses in American literary history, Dickinson once admitted she fled when she saw guests approaching her home. Her relationships with both men and women were often from a distance. She directed her most intense private feelings toward other women, particularly her sister-in-law Susan Gilbert Dickinson.

From her writings, it is clear that Dickinson burned with a decades-long obsessive passion for Susan. These works remained hidden from the public for decades, probably because of Dickinson's extreme shyness. Susan Dickinson, married to Emily's brother Austin, became a neighbor in 1857, and in spite of their close proximity, Emily continued her voluminous correspondence to Susan, sending her 267 poems and gazing at her through the windows of her home. Emily was inspired and tantalized by the haunting nearness of Susan, separated from her by panes of glass, "a neighbor from another world/Residing in a jar." Emily tormented herself imagining what secrets lay in Susan's heart and soul. "To be Susan/is imagination," Emily wrote. "To have been/Susan, A Dream."

Forced to hide their sexual lives, Dickinson, along with Whitman, Thoreau and Ralph Waldo Emerson were for the most part underappreciated in their lifetimes. Later generations of gays, lesbians, bisexuals, and transsexuals, however, would hail them for establishing a new American voice in literature. Whatever their intention, they served as inspirations for later generations of not just writers but also for the LGBT liberation movements of the 20th and 21st centuries.

Chile, the *San Dominick*. The later ship is in shambles and Delano decides to board the vessel. Benito Cereno is in command of the *San Dominick*, where the slaves have revolted. Cereno remains oblivious throughout the story to the pain and suffering he has inflicted on his human cargo and the role his savagery has played in provoking the uprising. Like many nineteenth-century southern slave masters, Cereno convinces himself that he has been kind to the ship's slaves. But even as Melville condemned the cruelty of slave owners but aimed much of his satiric fire at Delano. Assuming blacks to be inferior, Delano is unable throughout the novel to comprehend the ordinary human impulse towards freedom that drove the human cargo on the *San Dominick* to their rebellion.

In Melville's most famous novel, *Moby Dick: or, The Whale* (1851), Captain Ahab obsessively guides his ship, the *Pequod*, in vengeful pursuit of a giant white sperm whale that on an earlier voyage had bitten off one of Ahab's legs. Ahab ends up steering the *Pequod* and its crew to its doom. Published in a decade when white southern politicians dug in and wrecked the Union in the interest of preserving slavery, regardless of the cost in lives, Melville's novel could be read as trenchant political commentary on how the maniacal focus on white supremacy in American culture was destroying an entire society.

A contemporary of Melville's, Nathaniel Hawthorne, criticized the Transcendentalists but provided biting commentary on sexual hypocrisy and the public piety of his own Puritan forebears in his 1850 novel, *The Scarlet Letter*, which centers on the travails of Hester Prynne, who conceives a child borne of an adulterous affair in seventeenth-century New England. Prynne strives for a life of integrity even as her self-righteous Puritan neighbors shun her and her daughter. Like the Transcendentalists, Hawthorne encouraged skepticism of established authority.

Influence of the Transcendentalists

The Transcendentalists offered critiques of American culture and asked Americans to reflect more deeply on the meaning of casually tossed-off words like "freedom" and "democracy." In their novels, poems, plays, and essays, they posed difficult questions about the tyranny of consumerism, about what freedom nineteenth-century workers had when they owed their time to their bosses, and about the extent to which American society could be democratic when it sanctioned the buying and selling of black human beings.

The Transcendentalists themselves were a tiny fraction of American society. Their influence, however, far exceeded their actual numbers. Transcendentalists did not offer specific solutions, but they did articulate values that would influence the myriad reform movements from the 1820s to the 1850s. The "Reformer Generation" would be restless, determined to study and tackle every problem with an approach that combined evangelical religious zeal with new scientific methods. They saw all social problems as linked. Solving one moral crisis was impossible without solving them all. The Unitarian minister Theodore Parker was not just an abolitionist who in the 1850s helped to hide runaway slaves from bounty hunters. He also championed women's voting rights, the labor movement, prison reform, and demilitarization. One-time Congressman Gerrit Smith supported Irish independence from Great Britain, Greek independence from the Ottoman Empire, vegetarianism, women's voting rights, the abolition of secret societies like the Masons, temperance, and the liberation of slaves. These diverse crusades of these two men were typical of the antebellum reform movement.

Because so many reformers in this era opposed slavery, the impetus towards change proved anemic in the South.

Herman Melville (left)
Nathaniel Hawthorne (right)

Reform movements were strongest in New England and in the so-called "Burned-Over District" in New York, the scene of repeated religious revivals in the 1700s and 1800s, as well as in Ohio. The future Confederacy not only fiercely resisted abolitionism but virtually every other popular cause in the antebellum era. Thus, the battles to transform society took place almost entirely north of the Mason-Dixon line.

THE SECOND GREAT AWAKENING

The reform era happened amid the **Second Great Awakening**, a period of intense religious revival that swept the United States starting in the 1790s and did not taper off until the 1840s. (The First Great Awakening was in the mid-1700s). This evangelical wave saw the rapid spread of Baptist and Methodist congregations across the United States and the birth of new religious movements, such as the Church of Jesus Christ of Latter-day Saints (or Mormons) and the Seventh-day Adventist denomination. The evangelists spreading the gospel in this period tended to be post-millennialists, meaning that they believed it was the job of Christians to spread the gospel to the "four corners" of the Earth and to remold governments on religious principles, such as charity and compassion. Eventually, they believed, Christianity would prevail worldwide and usher in a 1,000-year reign of peace and freedom. Jesus would return to rule over the Earth after that "millennium."

During this period, membership in more established, traditional denominations with defined hierarchies, such as the Congregationalist and Episcopal churches, declined while more informally organized sects lacking a central governing structure and run on a church-by-church basis, such as the Baptists, flourished. These sects were, by definition, more democratic with pastors selected by church members rather than by some central authority.

The Methodists and the Baptists of this era challenged strict Calvinism: the idea that an all-powerful God preordains who is saved and who is not, regardless of the faith or deeds of an individual. The new churches preached of a loving God who wanted all to be saved. While the Baptists still insisted that faith alone, and not works, led to salvation, they taught that men and women were free to decide for themselves whether they accepted divine grace. God would welcome their repentance with open arms.

Itinerant preachers rode from town to town on horseback to bring the gospel to the most remote locations during the Second Great Awakening, holding revivals, sometimes outdoors, sometimes in hastily built structures, attracting a faithful frightened that their sins had damned them to hell. At revivals, the repentant made tearful confessions as they sought to escape hellfire. The preachers associated with these congregations tended to have less formal theological training, and more emphasis was placed on a direct emotional experience with God. Storytelling, singing, and spontaneous shouts from the faithful began to replace the rigid rituals that prevailed in Anglican and other more conventional services.

Only 50 Methodist churches could be found across the United States at the end of the American Revolution in 1783. Four decades later, there were 2,700. The number of Baptist congregations increased almost seven-fold, from about 400 to around 2,700. By the 1820s, Methodist and Baptist congregations outnumbered Congregationalist and Episcopal congregations by 3 to 1. This message, where one could choose salvation rather than passively wait for the arbitrary decisions of a distant, unknowable God, appealed to a generation that was being told they lived in a democratic age.

Saving Souls and Redeeming America

Timothy Dwight, an educator and Congregationalist minister, who served as the president of Yale College from 1795 to his death in 1817, became one of the chief architects of the Second Great Awakening. Dwight called for a sterner, more disciplined society, and he thought Jesus was the answer to problems such as increasing crime and poverty. Workers should abstain from alcohol, control their sexual behavior, and obey their bosses. Around the time of the War of 1812, Yale students formed the Moral Society to war against card games, gambling, and cursing at the campus. Soon there was a Connecticut Moral Society with thousands of members seeking to defeat sin in the world beyond the college. Another similar organization formed in Massachusetts. By the 1820s such moral societies were making use of new technology that made printing Bibles and religious tracts faster and cheaper, leading to the formation of the American Tract Society. This society published millions of copies of 167 different religious pamphlets. Wealthy businessmen, such as the banker Moses Allen, and publisher, importer, and abolitionist Arthur Tappan funded these tract societies. Tappan believed that slavery was a danger to the economy because it led white workers to disdain the hard manual work that slaves performed. In the mid-to late 1820s, these societies published about four million pages of religious literature in just two years.

Charles Grandison Finney also became an eloquent voice promoting moral purity, introducing the wide-open, spontaneous preaching style of the Baptists and Methodists to the tradition-bound Congregationalists. A lawyer from Connecticut and president of Oberlin College in Ohio from 1851-1866, Finney founded the Broadway Tabernacle in New York. He was a tireless innovator. In his sermons, often off-the-cuff, he created "the anxious bench" where sinners would sit during services as they decided whether to convert. Finney believed that saving society was inseparable from saving souls. Both were key missions of the church.

A temperance advocate, Finney would also plunge into the abolitionist movement. He fought hard to raise the status of women within society. While he was president of Oberlin College, the college would be the first in the United States to admit both African Americans and women. Finney also gave a greater voice to women within the church, encouraging them to speak out during prayer meetings. He built an evangelical army made up largely of women, who would also fill ranks of all of the era's reform programs. With parents less able to afford a viable estate to leave their children, the offspring had less incentive to stay home as long. With improved transportation, children moved away from home at an earlier age and farther away. Birth rates for white women in particular dropped throughout the nineteenth century. Meanwhile, the rise of textile mills and other industries reduced household production of items such as clothes, bed sheets, and curtains. With these changes, upper middle class and more affluent women in particular devoted more time to fighting alcohol, abusive prisons, and other moral causes.

Finney made Oberlin College a stop on the so-called "Underground Railroad" that aided runaway slaves to escape capture before the Civil War. He was a zealot for reform until his death in 1875. For the reformers like Finney, there was no true separation of church and state. Morality and law were inseparable, and building a better society inevitably meant bringing souls to Jesus. Most reformers like Finney agreed that alcohol was one of the chief threats to their twin goals of saving souls and redeeming America.

THE TEMPERANCE MOVEMENT

Drinking came to be seen as a social problem in the 1820s. In that decade, prices for alcohol dropped to 25 cents a gallon (about $5 in today's dollars), making liquor cheaper by the drink than tea and coffee. Drinking patterns changed to accommodate the new economy. Americans used to drink in small doses throughout the day, from breakfast to bedtime. By the 1820s, Americans increasingly compartmentalized their lives and crowded drinking to after-work hours, or days off. Binge drinking, in a tavern or at home alone, became much more commonplace. Americans also had firmly shifted from preferring fermented beverages such as wine to distilled drinks such as whiskey, which have a higher alcohol content. By

The Ohio Whiskey War

These ladies in Logan, Ohio, are
singing hymns in front of a barroom to aid the temperance movement. 1874.

the 1830s, doctors first began to recognize alcoholism as a medical problem and began to write about what they called delirium tremens—intense anxiety, convulsions, and hallucinations—that occur with alcoholics after a severe bout of drinking or during alcohol withdrawal. Increasing numbers of Americans supplemented their drinking with opium. Some mixed wine with opium or an opium-derived bitter tincture called laudanum, which in turn was used in a number of highly addictive medicines such as cough remedies.

Alcohol addiction haunted poor, middle-class, and rich and powerful families. One of President John Quincy Adams's sons drank himself to death, and alcoholism contributed to the suicide of another. A court declared senator and frequent presidential aspirant Henry Clay's heavy-drinking son Theodore a "lunatic." President James K. Polk's father spent much of his adult life in a haze of laudanum and alcohol.

As mills and factories began to dot the American landscape, it became harder to accommodate American drinking habits, such as the "Saint Monday" tradition of skipping the first day of the workweek to sleep off hangovers. Rich businessmen like Arthur Tappan certainly supported curbing alcohol consumption for this reason, prompting him to support the temperance movement, which sought at first to curb and eventually to prohibit alcohol sale and production in the United States.

Protestant clergy launched the American anti-liquor movement between 1810 and 1820. The New England Tract society printed numerous temperance pamphlets. Temperance organizations held alternative, alcohol-free events on holidays usually marked by drinking, such as July 4. These crusaders battled what they called "Demon Rum" by comparing the struggle against alcohol to the American colonists' struggle against Great Britain, with speakers at anti-alcohol July 4 events calling for a "second revolution." They opened "temperance hotels" where no alcohol was served, alcohol-free steamboat lines, and persuaded insurance companies to offer 5 percent discounts to ships manned by abstinent sailors. Anti-alcohol lectures, plays, and novels (including *Franklin Evans, or The Inebriate: A Tale of the Times* by Walt Whitman in 1842), reached a large audience. Meanwhile, improved ice cutting technology, transportation, and improved storage methods meant that ice could be shipped from northern climates like the Hudson Bay in Canada to American cities like New York and Philadelphia, where ice water became an increasingly popular alternative to alcohol at hotels and other public venues.

The American Temperance Society

Women provided the most enthusiastic foot soldiers for groups such as the **American Temperance Society**. They saw themselves as primary victims of alcohol abuse because of the relationship of hard drink to spousal abuse, neglect, infidelity, and the family resources husbands and male lovers often spent on liquor. Women distributed leaflets and began to speak out against alcohol, with many of these crusaders later providing leadership in the abolitionist movement. Some pursued more unconventional methods of protest. In the 1840s, one group of wives went on a sex strike, demanding their husbands stop drinking before activity could resume in the marital bed. A group of young women publicly announced that they would not marry any man who had not yet taken an abstinence pledge.

Some in the anti-alcohol campaign also exploited anti-Irish and anti-German prejudices, depicting Irish immigrants in particular as drunks by nature and suggesting that drinking was, therefore, un-American. "The Irish and the Dutch, they don't amount to much," went one popular antebellum verse. "For the Micks have their whiskey and the Germans guzzle the beer, and all we Americans wish they had never come here." ("Mick" was a common anti-Irish slur; and many called the Germans the "Dutch.") The anti-alcohol cause often overlapped with anti-immigrant politics, with many members of the Know-Nothing or American Party calling for the closing of taverns and distilleries.

Regardless of the reason, the American Temperance Society hit a chord. By 1831, the group could claim 2,200 local chapters with 170,000 members. Just three years later, the society boasted 1.25 million members. Church members still anxiously sought signs of their salvation, and preachers usefully suggested that a truly saved person would not be a drinker. Entire congregations—Baptist, Methodist, Presbyterian and Congregational—committed themselves to teetotaling (complete abstinence from alcohol). Some churches stopped using sacramental wine and expelled members who sold alcohol. This agitation worked. Hard cider consumption per person over the age of 14 dropped from an estimated 28 gallons in 1825 to 4 gallons in 1840.

Even though temperance advocates made inroads into public opinion, they had little legislative success before the Civil War. In 1838, the Massachusetts legislature passed the so-called "Fifteen Gallon" law, which forbade the sale of liquor in amounts less than fifteen gallons. The law aimed to shut down taverns but was unpopular, frequently violated, and infrequently enforced. Maine implemented a complete ban on the manufacture and sale of alcohol within its boundaries in 1851, but that law was repealed in five years. Temperance ended up being almost entirely a northern phenomenon, in part because many of the anti-alcohol campaigners also fought against slavery (and depicted drinkers as being enslaved by a cruel master, Demon Rum).

AMERICAN CRIME AND PUNISHMENT

Prison Reform

As with alcohol, religious and practical concerns prompted a push for prison reform. The Eighth Amendment to the United States Constitution, ratified in 1791, declares that "Excessive bail shall not be required, nor excessive fines imposed, nor cruel and unusual punishments inflicted." The amendment represented a reaction to abuses of British monarchs who for centuries tortured, mutilated, and executed in gruesome fashion prisoners for purely political reasons. Founders like Thomas Jefferson also worried that maiming and executing men to punish them for crimes wastefully removed needed laborers from the workforce. Jefferson and others believed that excessive criminal penalties had backfired as well. England had increased the number of crimes punishable by death from 50 in 1688 to 165 in 1765. The English penal code allowed convicts to be hanged for pickpocketing, theft of gathered fruit, or even something as specific as breaking a pane of glass at 5 p.m. on a winter's night. Juries increasingly found defendants not guilty, regardless of evidence, because they did not want to send defendants to the gallows for trivial offenses, meaning that actual criminals sometimes gained freedom.

After the American Revolution, New Jersey, New York, and Virginia reduced the number of crimes punishable by death, and in many cases eliminated other physical punishments, such as branding or cuffing the ears for minor crimes. Pennsylvania, for instance, dropped the death penalty for sodomy, burglary, and robbery in 1786, and by 1794, the state law allowed execution only for first-degree murder. Many states moved to imprisonment, public humiliation, and hard labor as punishments. Jefferson proposed a penal code for Virginia on the principle of *lex talionis* ("the law of the talon"), the idea that the punishment should match the crime embodied in the concept of "an eye for an eye." Thus, murderers who poisoned their victims would be administered poison, while rapists would be punished with castration instead of being executed. Those guilty of property crimes would be assessed years of public labor rather than hanged. Jefferson's proposals were defeated in 1785-1786, to a large degree because a

rash of horse thefts increased the public appetite for the death penalty. (Virginia would not adopt a new criminal code until 1796.)

Other alternatives to "sanguinary" punishments were tried, including banishment of criminals to remote, rural areas or beyond state lines, but this quickly was seen as impractical, a case of one state dumping its criminal population on another. Another form of punishment, subjecting prisoners to involuntary servitude, started in the late 1700s. In 1786, the Pennsylvania legislature sentenced those not guilty of capital crimes to labor as "wheelbarrowmen" chained together while toiling on state roads, mines, and other public property. Wearing distinct clothes, the convicts performed unpleasant, hard work in public view, their beards and heads shaved. Legislators hoped this spectacle would humiliate the criminal enough to curb their criminal instincts and deter those witnessing their public shaming from ever tempting a similar fate. Such punishments were also based on the notion that hard work promoted virtue. This experiment proved to be a failure. The public socialized and shared drinks with the "wheelbarrowmen" and gave them contraband while they did their chores. Many escaped and, in one humiliating instance, attempted to rob Alexander Hamilton and his wife as they were returning from the Constitutional Convention in Philadelphia.

The concept of imprisoning individuals as a punishment for crime became an increasingly preferred choice as the nineteenth century dawned. In American prisons, wardens dispatched inmates to in-house workshops where they labored as whitesmiths, toolmakers, and so on. The idea was to transform the character of prisoners by accustoming them to honest work. This approach also fell short of expectations. Riots repeatedly broke out at these poorly staffed institutions with corrupt and under-trained guards. Escapes were common, and prisoners often sabotaged equipment, used print shops to counterfeit currency, or spent most of their days learning criminal methods from their peers. Moral reformers then sought to transform the American system of criminal justice from one that simply punished to one that redeemed the moral character of the prisoners.

The Penitentiary

In the nineteenth century, prisons began to be called penitentiaries. The term came from the root word "penitent," meaning one who repents of a sin. The term reveals what reformers hoped they would get out of transformed prison systems in the early 1800s: prisoners who would leave the system regretting their crimes and thoroughly rehabilitated. In part, this stemmed from a more optimistic attitude about human nature stemming from the Enlightenment—the idea that people are born good and that bad behavior was a product of a bad environment. The prisons were designed to create a rigid setting in which bad behavior would be punished, and a better person hopefully could emerge.

Two major models of prison reform were tried in the early to mid-1800s. One model, pursued by Pennsylvania, aimed to physically isolate prisoners as much as possible during their sentences. Cells were constructed to make communication between prisoners extremely difficult, and inmates were supposed to be prohibited from communicating while they did required work. They ate only one meal a day. They could receive visitors only once a year. They could only read the Bible. The creators of this system believed that in isolation the prisoners would reflect on their past evil, realize how their misdeeds created their current hardships, and commit to compensating society with future good deeds.

Prison reformers in Pennsylvania had high hopes. "The prison is no longer a scene of debauchery, idleness, and profanity . . . but a school of reformation," declared a member of the Pennsylvania prison Board of Inspectors. Reality fell short of this rosy assessment. Perpetual isolation did have a powerful influence on prisoners' minds, but the opposite of what was intended. Instead of inspiring calm, it induced insanity in some prisoners. Meanwhile, most prisoners found ways to get around the new restrictions, communicating by tapping on pipes, sneaking in conversations with other prisoners during work time, or collaborating with guards to receive forbidden letters and other communication with the outside. Pennsylvania experienced no fewer repeat criminal offenders than other states. The Pennsylvania method also proved too expensive to be attractive to most states.

New York offered a different model, passing a series of prison reform laws in 1819 that governed the new Auburn State Prison, built three years earlier. Physical punishment was reincorporated into prison life. Guards were again allowed to use whips on unruly inmates or to throw them into irons. Prisons segregated prisoners based on the severity of their crimes and how "hardened" they were. Inmates performed physical labor in the day and experienced solitary confinement in individual cells during evenings. The warden, Elam Lynds, also cracked down on communications between prisoners, forbidding even hand signals, and imposing military discipline, requiring prisoners to march from their cells to work areas and back in lockstep. Lynds also more tightly disciplined his guards. But his biggest innovation was to contract out the prisoners as labor for private businesses.

Across the union, states imitated the Auburn System. Auburn-style prisons were cheaper than the Pennsylvania-style perpetual isolation institutions, which required greater physical distance in accommodations between each prisoner, such as separate outdoor yards for each inmate. The difference in cost for the two prison prototypes was as much as 16-1. Perhaps more importantly, the revenue the states derived from renting prisoners out as unfree labor covered two dollars out of every three it cost to imprison them.

Having unpaid workers, of course, padded the profit margins of outside firms as well, making the arrangement popular with the business community. This meant, however, that free workers faced unfair competition, and this system lost jobs for laborers outside of prison walls. Nevertheless, the Auburn system gained wide acceptability. The idea became commonplace enough that it received sanction in the Thirteenth Amendment, which abolished all but one form of slavery. "Neither slavery nor involuntary servitude, except as a punishment for crime whereof the party shall have been duly convicted, shall exist within the United States, or any place subject to their jurisdiction," said the amendment which would be ratified after the Civil War in 1865. In short, while slavery was banned forever outside American prison walls, the idea that prisoners can be subject to involuntary servitude became part of the basic law of the land.

The Almshouse

The new prisons surprisingly provided a model for how antebellum reformers tackled many social issues, from poverty to mental illness to education. All of these efforts were animated by a common desire for a comforting uniformity in a society that had suddenly become for many too loud, too crowded, too diverse, and too unpredictable. Middle class and affluent Americans craved order and predictability.

Nothing was more untidy than the urban poor. The intensely religious climate of the era meant that many reformers responded to the ragged beggars in city streets with a combination of pity and contempt. Poverty was "voluntary," some claimed, "a consequence of drunkenness, idleness, and vice of all kind," according to an official Philadelphia city report. New York officials blamed poverty on "the constant use of spirituous liquors, and the consequent waste of time." In 1821, the New York Society for the Prevention of Pauperism proclaimed that, "the paupers of this city are, for the most part . . . depraved and vicious, and require support because they are so." Alcohol abuse was chalked up as the primary cause of economic want.

This led reformers to disdain traditional charity, such as providing food to beggars. The reform generation wished to make a distinction between what they considered the "worthy" poor—the elderly, abandoned children, the sick, the crippled, and widows—and supposedly lazy deviants. In spite of the desperately low wages paid most workers and economic disasters, such as the 1837-1843 depression, many supposed experts on the poor were even critical of the sick and the aged, insisting that they should have been saving money in case of misfortune. (Most workers had to immediately spend whatever they earned and savings in institutions like banks that were uninsured by the federal or state governments were wiped out during economic downturns.) In antebellum writings about the disadvantaged, virtually no one was defined as deserving of help. The solution was not seen as pressuring business to pay better wages, or bosses to provide safer working conditions in order to prevent debilitating lifelong injuries, but to prevent the poor from indulging in vices. Many arguments for liquor prohibition centered on how banning alcohol could possibly prevent future poverty.

With the Auburn system prison as a model, cities from the 1820s to the 1840s launched a new approach to poor relief—a beggar would receive small amounts of food and cash only upon accepting confinement in an almshouse. Between 1820 and 1840, almshouses went up in 60 towns across Massachusetts while others were renovated, bringing the total of such establishments to 180. In New York, by 1835, 51 of 55 counties had established an almshouse. This approach spread through the Northeast and Old Northwest states such as Ohio and Michigan.

The almshouse was designed to provide shelter in an environment that supposedly would shield a poor person from the bad influences of a dysfunctional family, friends, and neighborhood. The elderly and others received shelter. Underage orphans and the disabled would receive care as well. The able-bodied, either voluntarily or through coercion, worked long days. As with prison workhouses, the idea was to reform bad character, in this case those individuals unlucky enough to be flat broke.

Like with the Auburn-style prisons, each minute of the day was supposed to be planned at the almshouse. The superintendent rang the morning bell at 6 a.m. Residents lined up for breakfast at the sound of a second bell and had 30 minutes for that and other meals. Late inmates missed a meal. The third bell signaled work time. Loitering, failure to follow instructions, or wasting work materials such as wood could result in solitary confinement, loss of meal privileges, or added work. The final bell rang at 9 p.m. and residents were expected to go to bed. They could only receive visitors or leave the almshouse with permission. Like prisons, the almshouses failed to rehabilitate their inmates. Conditions at these institutions dismayed inspectors. At a Clinton, Pennsylvania almshouse, staff provided the poor a diet of dirty water and pea soup while other institutions in the state lacked heat in the wintertime and, in one case, housed 32 people in a single room with poor air circulation. Criminals shared space with those who had never run afoul of the law, work opportunities turned out to be few, and some residents with jobs earned as little as $3 ($73 in today's dollars) a year. Nevertheless, the almshouse remained the preferred way to provide aid to the poor in the United States until the Progressive era in the late nineteenth century.

THE AMERICAN ASYLUM

Reformers did not always empathize with the poor, but they did with the insane. For centuries, the mentally ill were assumed to be victims of demonic possession. Many attributed insanity to immorality. By the 1700s, however, as a result of the Enlightenment, American physicians like Dr. Benjamin Rush began to attribute psychosis to brain defects, damage, or disease. As Isaac Ray, an early nineteenth-century ward of an American lunatic asylum put it, "No pathological fact is better established . . . than that deviations from the healthy structure are generally present in brains of insane subjects." Other doctors suspected that bad home environments or exhaustion of delicate nervous systems caused psychological imbalance. One New York doctor at a mental facility in the early nineteenth century listed what he thought caused his patients' mental symptoms, including poor physical health, anxiety caused by religious belief, economic problems, too much study, head trauma, frustrated ambitions, political agitation, and exposure to cold water.

Even as they speculated about the cause of insanity, doctors still had no idea how to treat the condition. Treatment facilities were primitive and grim. The first "lunatic wards" appeared in the Pennsylvania Hospital in Philadelphia in 1751 and New York Hospital in 1771. A facility exclusively for the insane did not appear until one opened in Williamsburg, Virginia, just before the American Revolution in 1773.

Stressed families usually cared for the insane, but some of the mentally ill ended up chained and manacled in what were basically prison cells. Most suffered neglect. If any treatment was provided, it consisted of being bled by a physician (having a blood vessel cut and drained or having leeches applied to the body in order to correct a supposed imbalance of body fluids suspected as a cause of mental illness). Some received copious amounts of laxatives, also for the purpose of "balancing the humors (fluids)." Sometimes doctors placed patients in a chair suspended in the air and spun at high speeds in order to induce vomiting. Other doctors plunged their wards into alternating hot and cold water because it supposedly calmed them down. Frequently, the insane found themselves confined in jails and prisons or rat-filled basements.

Dorothea Dix

No one battled harder to improve treatment of the insane than **Dorothea Dix**. Born in Hampden, Maine, in 1802, the product of an unhappy childhood, Dix grew up in the care of an abusive alcoholic father and a mentally unstable mother. Eventually, she lived with a grandparent in Massachusetts and had to care for her brothers. "I never knew childhood," she would later say. Dorothea's grandmother was wealthy, however, and Dix received an education and the social skills needed to circulate among the powerful and influential.

Impressed by her intelligence, her second cousin, the attorney Edward Bangs, helped her start a private school for girls between the ages of six and eight. Only fifteen herself, Dix taught twenty girls for three years. Dix continued teaching and writing children's books and holding classes for disadvantaged children in her home. She spent the late 1830s in England with a Quaker family deeply committed to social causes, including improving the care of the mentally ill.

Dorothea Dix

Dix's life changed at age 39 when she taught a women's Sunday school class at an East Cambridge jail. What she saw horrified her. Officials had crowded into cells the mentally ill and the mentally disabled with loud and disorderly drunks and criminals in a bad-smelling cramped space with no heat. Asked why lunatics were left exposed to temperature extremes, officials told her, "The insane do not feel hot or cold." She went to court and got a judge to issue an order requiring the jailer to provide inmates with heat and other comforts.

In 1840-1841 she traveled across Massachusetts to investigate the state's mental health-care system, finding that most town and city governments contracted with private individuals subject to no regulations who poorly cared for their wards and sometimes physically abused them. She presented a report to the Massachusetts state legislature. "I proceed, Gentlemen, briefly to call your attention to the present state of Insane Persons confined within this Commonwealth, in cages, stalls, pens!" she wrote. "Chained, naked, beaten with rods, and lashed into obedience." In the town of Medford, she reported, she found "one idiotic subject chained, and one in a close stall for 17 years." Her report persuaded legislators to increase the budget for the state mental hospital in Worcester. Dix proceeded to tour mental health facilities across the country and moved other legislatures to improve and build new hospitals in fourteen states in every region of the country.

Her efforts culminated in a proposed federal "Bill for the Benefit of the Indigent Insane," under which more than 12 million acres of federal land would have been sold to provide funds primarily for the mentally ill, but also for the care of the "blind, deaf, and dumb." Funds from the land sales would have been distributed to states for the purpose of constructing and maintaining asylums. The Congress in 1854 approved the legislation, but President Franklin Pierce saw it as an unwarranted extension of federal power into the area of social welfare, which he considered the province of the states. Pierce vetoed the bill. Dix continued to lobby for better mental health care, not just in the United States but in Europe as well, and she also battled for better and more humane prisons. "Man is not made better by being degraded; he is seldom restrained from crime by harsh measures, except the principle of fear predominates in his character; and then he is never made radically better for its influence," she said.

Hospitals for the Mentally Ill

Reformers in the 1820s sought safer environments for those who had lost their mental balance. Once again,

The Health Faddist: Sylvester Graham

Sylvester Graham had no medical degree. In his era, doctors knew nothing about germs and thought diseases were caused by bad air ("miasma") or by an imbalance of body fluids called humors that could be corrected by cutting a patient's veins and draining blood. He had attended classes but had no college degree, and even though some considered him an unreliable eccentric, Graham nevertheless found an audience and followers in the 1830s as he toured the country making speeches and writing books touting the health benefits of temperance and vegetarianism. He also caused a sensation when he began to warn his audiences about what he considered one of the worst health threats facing the nation: masturbation and excess sexual activity, even within marriage.

Born the 17th child of the elderly Reverand John Graham, Jr. in West Suffield, Connecticut in 1794, Sylvester hoped to follow a long line of ancestors and relatives in the pulpit. His father died when the younger Graham was still an infant, and his mother suffered from mental illness. He experienced poverty and instability as he moved from home, but nevertheless, in 1823, he managed to enroll in language classes at Amherst College in nearby Massachusetts. The future health advocate, however, complained of illness all his life and dropped out before graduation. For a time, he preached at a Presbyterian church in New Jersey before devoting his full energies to the anti-alcohol cause, becoming an agent and speaker for the Pennsylvania Temperance Society.

For a while, Graham was a popular speaker and began lecturing his audiences not only on temperance but on a new obsession: what he saw as the fragile nature of the human mind and the dangers of over–stimulation to a person's sanity. Not just alcohol, but meat consumption also could drive one to insanity because it over-activated the brain, he held. Graham believed that a diet of foods that were too tasty, including meat, stimulated sexual desire, and that sex drained needed mental energy. He outlined what he now called the "Graham System" for good health, advocating that men and women sleep on hard mattresses in rooms with open windows, and subsist on fresh fruits and vegetables and bread made of coarse whole grain. Spicy foods, he said, should be avoided.

*By 1829, he developed what later became known as the Graham cracker, though the original version did not include sugar. The cracker as originally designed was meant to be bland. Graham hoped it provided good nutrition without overtaxing the mind, particularly those of women and young people he saw as particularly delicate. He publications included **Discourses on a Sober and Temperate Life** and **The Young Man's Guide to Chastity**. Much of the latter work told men about the health risks he believed came with sexual pleasure generally, and masturbation in particular.*

Graham was more blunt when he barnstormed the country warning that the "filthy vice of masturbation" was polluting manhood. The "peculiar excitement of the nervous system," he said, "rapidly exhausts the vital properties of the tissues." He estimated that between 60-70 percent of 12- and 13-year-old school boys were being "almost completely ruined in health and constitution by this destructive practice." Masturbation often led to suicide, insanity or premature natural death, he said.

Other forms of sex were bad for the body too, he insisted. Sex may be necessary for reproduction, he wrote, but should best be avoided as much as possible. No one should engage in sex until their late twenties, and after marriage sex should happen no more than once a month. Graham argued that marital intercourse, although physiologically the same as any other form of sex, was the safest because it was the least exciting.

*Across America, admirers established Graham boarding houses, Graham clubs formed at college campuses, and mills ground the special, not-too-exciting coarse grain that went into the early Graham crackers. He won some famous fans such as newspaper publisher Horace Greeley. His claim that meat products hastened aging outlined in his **Treatise on Bread and Bread Making**, however, provoked a riot of area butchers and bakers when he came to speak in Boston in 1837.*

*In spite of his total lack of credentials, Graham's 1839 book, **Lectures on the Science of Human Life**, reached a wide audience. By the end of the 1840s, however, Graham remained nervous and constantly complained of ailments. He had a tense relationship with his wife, who expressed her resentments by offering up meals filled with the stimulating foods he condemned in his public addresses. Convinced he was in his last days, he began eating meat and drinking whiskey, supposedly for medicinal purposes. He died in 1851, at the age of 57, before he could complete what he considered his most important work, **The Philosophy of Sacred History**, which laid out the alleged biblical foundations for the Graham system. Graham Crackers are still produced today, though loaded with sugar and/or honey, stimulating substances Graham himself publicly shunned.*

the Auburn prison system served as a model. Doctors unlocked the chains that once confined the institutionalized insane and tried to isolate their patients from the competitive stresses of the outside world. Doctors hoped to quarantine the ill from unhealthy contact from the friends and family physicians, which were often seen as part of the problem. Patients moved to a controlled, regimented atmosphere where they would supposedly be taught how to behave and think normally. Insane asylums had been a rarity before the 1830s, but by 1860, 28 out of the 33 states had mental hospitals.

As with prisoners, isolation was seen as a key first step to rehabilitating mental patients. Mental institutions were frequently constructed in country locations or in urban locations with ample green space in hopes of shielding patients from the stresses of city life. The Pennsylvania Hospital, for instance, on a 101-acre farm two miles west of Philadelphia, was a model followed by other states. Doctors encouraged patients' relatives to not visit. Hospitals requested that family members not upset patients' routines or distract them with letters. They cut off inmates from newspapers and magazines as well.

Whips, chains, manacles, and cages began to disappear from asylums. Caregivers were encouraged to not use restraints, such as tying patients to their beds to prevent them from hurting themselves or each other, but were told to calm them by speaking in soothing, calm voices. Predictably, however, asylums fell well short of the intention of reformers. Mental hospitals remained unsafe and understaffed. Violent inmates often shared space with non-violent ones. As confinements increased in the 1840s and 1850s, overcrowding became a problem, and public attention to the mentally ill faded.

PUBLIC EDUCATION

The public school house, along with the prison, the asylum, and the almshouse, also proliferated across the American landscape from the 1820s to the 1850s. Outside the South, there was a widely shared belief that publicly funded education was one way to prevent crime and to mold good citizens. This, in part, was a legacy of Puritanism. The religious white colonists in New England saw the ability to read and understand the Bible as a key to salvation and creating a Godly commonwealth. Thus, New England became one of the first locations in the Western world with compulsory school laws.

Besides imparting basic grammar and math skills, these early schools focused heavily on religious indoctrination and made liberal use of corporal punishment for mis-

behavior. Puritans entwined religious lessons with every subject. The spelling books used starting in the 1690s in colonial Massachusetts, *The New England Primer*, taught children the ABCs with verses like, "In Adam's fall, We Sinned All/ Thy life to mend, this Book [the Bible] to attend . . . An Idle Fool is whipt at School." By the early 1800s, some New England children went to academies that received some support from tax dollars but also charged tuition. Others attended church schools. The necessity to pay tuition still limited educational opportunities for the poor. Nevertheless, the region remained one of the most literate in the world.

By contrast, high illiteracy plagued the South before the Civil War. Planters forbade slaves an education, for fear that learning might increase slaves' dissatisfaction with their status and enhance their ability to plot and carry out a rebellion. The same planters also did not care to pay taxes to educate lower-income whites. Before the Civil War, therefore, education was largely a privilege of the wealthy who could afford private tutors for their children. By the late eighteenth century, while serving as the state's governor, Thomas Jefferson advocated a public school system for Virginia, which would provide a basic education for all, but would provide more advanced education for the most accomplished pupils. Under his proposal, outlined in his 1779 "Bill for the More General Diffusion of Knowledge," local districts would establish three-year schools for white children between the ages of 7 and 10. Public schooling then would narrow to the gifted, with the top graduates of the district school able to attend three years at a higher county school and the top graduates from those campuses eligible to enter the state college. Jefferson, however, was only able to get a state university established. When a member of the Virginia legislature, Charles Mercer, proposed the establishment of a free public primary school system in 1817, Jefferson opposed the idea because it established a state board of education and included a provision that provided state funds to supplement local funds, which contradicted the former president's insistence on pure localism in education.

By the early 1800s, publicly funded "common schools" spread throughout the Northeast and in the Old Northwest (Ohio and other states carved out of the Northwest Territory). In New York, for instance, the state operated more than 7,800 common schools educating more than 400,000 students by 1825. Schools in the early 1800s made social conformity a top mission of the school curriculum. One of the chief mediums of conformity starting in the 1790s was *Webster's Blue Backed Speller*, which sought not only to standardize how Americans wrote words, but also to inspire patriotism.

The creator of the dictionary, Noah Webster, filled his text, which ostensibly was about how to spell words, with questions and answers about the duties of citizens and why the United States supposedly had the best form of government in the world. After referring to monarchy, aristocracy, and democracy, Webster's speller asked, "Is there another and better form of government than any of these?" The book then provided a handy answer: "A: There is. A REPRESENTATIVE REPUBLIC, in which people freely choose deputies to make laws for them, is much the best form of government hitherto invented."

Horace Mann and Emma Willard

A dedicated Federalist, Webster hoped that schools could forge a national identity for the new American nation, one that could transcend already brewing regional conflicts. Webster's lessons about the beauties of representative government, however, would be lost to most in a system in which school was only for those whose parents were well off enough to pay tuition at a private academy or lucky enough to find an affluent benefactor. Such a system was not fitting in an historical epic Americans believed to be devoted to the "common man." In an increasingly technological age, some businessmen could also see an advantage in a more educated workforce. The 1830s would thus see the crusade for free public primary schools open to white children everywhere in the United States. Educational crusaders like **Horace Mann** also fought for improved teacher training and, contrary to Jefferson, greater state control over local schools to ensure higher standards and better funding.

Mann, a lawyer and politician born in 1796 in Massachusetts, won election as the secretary of the newly created state board of education in 1837. He saw education for all citizens as essential for a representative democracy to thrive. Like many antebellum reformers, Mann saw social problems as deeply entwined. Education turned people into better citizens less prone to vice and other destructive behaviors. Mann believed that a better-educated public would elect honest, intelligent politicians who would effectively tackle problems such as crime, urban overcrowding, and alcoholism.

Common schools became one of the most popular ideas of the reform era. By the Civil War, 83.9 percent of white children between the ages of five and fifteen attended public school in New England, as did 72 percent in the Mid-Atlantic (New Jersey, New York, and Pennsylvania) and the Midwest (Indiana, Michigan, Ohio, and Wisconsin). Just over 67 percent of African Americans between five and fifteen in New England, and around 41 percent in the Mid-Atlantic and the Midwest also at-

tended school. The South, however, would enter the Civil War as the least educated region of the country. Only in the East South Central region of the future Confederacy (Kentucky, Tennessee, Alabama, and Mississippi) did a bare majority of white children attend school. School attendance for free African Americans was virtually non-existent in the future Confederate states.

Educators such as Emma Willard also sought to expand learning opportunities for women, teaching subjects such as mathematics, philosophy and politics that had been seen as exclusively male domains of knowledge. The Connecticut native proposed to the New York Assembly in 1819, in a report called "A Plan for Improving Female Education," the creation of a publicly funded seminary for women to match similar institutions for men. Willard's ideas horrified some legislators, especially her proposal that women be taught human anatomy, an idea some characterized as obscene. She won the support of Governor DeWitt Clinton, however. Yet, even though some saw her as a radical, Willard still believed that female education should primarily focus on preparing women for domestic duties—what today is called home economics. As a result of her lobbying, the state established the Troy Female Academy in upstate New York, which Willard ran until 1838.

THE STRUGGLE AGAINST SLAVERY

No reform campaign carried greater urgency, or had greater impact, than the campaign to abolish slavery. No reform movement generated more controversy, and none faced greater opposition from elites. Abolitionists (those demanding the complete end to slavery) represented a small minority in American society in antebellum society. They faced accusations of being traitors, of pushing the country to civil war, and, when they began to argue for black and white equality, of threatening the very existence of the white race. They faced a fury unknown to other reformers, and on many occasions mobs harassed them, beat them, destroyed their property, and even murdered them.

According to the estimate of one historian, abolitionists constituted about 1 percent of the population between 1830 and when slavery finally ended through ratification of the Thirteenth Amendment to the United States Constitution in 1865. The movement involved, at its peak, about 20,000 committed activists, but these true believers made an impact well beyond their numbers. Black and white women, often laboring in complete obscurity, formed the core of this determined group that abolitionist leader William Lloyd Garrison called "a great

William Lloyd Garrison, the leader of the militants, proposed the unconditional, universal, and immediate abolition of slavery. He founded the abolitionist newspaper, the *Liberator*.

army of silent workers, unknown to fame, and yet without whom the generals were powerless."

Many whites could not imagine free African Americans even as neighbors, much less as citizens. Some sought to expel free African Americans from the country. The **American Colonization Society (ACS)**, a group that attempted to persuade slave owners to emancipate their slaves and to resettle them in West Africa, absorbed much of the energy of the early anti-slavery movement. Robert Finley, a Presbyterian minister, founded the ACS in 1817. The ACS's approach to emancipation stemmed from racist assumptions. Finley believed in black inferiority. He thought that, because of their supposed backwardness, African Americans could never thrive as free people in a society run by whites. Finley feared that free African Americans might marry and have children with whites, which would lead to racial degeneration. ACS members feared that free African Americans inspired discontent among slaves. A majority of African Americans also bitterly rejected the idea that, upon freedom, they should be expelled from the only country they had ever known. The first slave ship bearing African-American slaves to a colony that later became part of the United States arrived in Virginia in 1619. A large percentage of African-American families had lived in the country longer than a significant proportion of white families.

Nevertheless, the ACS won support from many rich and powerful figures, including Francis Scott Key, the composer of the "Star-Spangled Banner," Richard Rush (son of Declaration of Independence signer Benjamin Rush), Supreme Court Chief Justice John Marshall, and Henry Clay, a future presidential contender who would represent Kentucky in the U.S. House and Senate. George Washington's nephew, Bushrod Washington, served as ACS's first president. The ACS secured funds from the federal government to establish Liberia, an independent West African nation intended by the society as the homeland for freed African-American slaves. The impracticality of the ACS's scheme, however, soon became apparent. Most slave owners did not want to free their human property, most freed African Americans did not want to leave the United States, and the group could never raise the money it would have taken to transport millions of human beings across the Atlantic Ocean to Africa. The ACS resettled only 12,000 freedmen in Liberia up to the 1860s.

William Lloyd Garrison

Africa Americans had always rejected the concept of white racial superiority, but the 1830s marked the first time that some notable whites seconded the idea of racial equality. That decade would mark the decline of the colonization movement and the rise of "immediatism"—the demand for complete emancipation of African-American slaves at the soonest possible date.

One of the fiercest voices for emancipation and racial equality would be **William Lloyd Garrison**, who began publishing an influential anti-slavery newspaper, *The Liberator*, on January 1, 1831. Garrison had believed in colonization at first, but African Americans in the abolitionist movement convinced him that approach represented a dishonest compromise with evil. And Garrison was no compromiser. "I will be as harsh as truth, and as uncompromising as justice," Garrison wrote in the very first issue of his paper. "On this subject, I do not wish to think, speak, or write with moderation. No! No! Tell a man whose house is on fire to give a moderate alarm; tell him to moderately rescue his wife from the hands of a ravisher . . . I am in earnest—I will not equivocate—I will not excuse—I will not retreat a single inch—AND I WILL BE HEARD."

He certainly would be. Massachusetts-born Garrison began working as a compositor and reporter for newspapers in his teens but his anti-slavery career began in 1829 when, at the age of 24, he commenced writing for Benjamin Lundy's Baltimore newspaper, the *Genius of Universal Emancipation*. Just after he joined Lundy's staff,

Garrison wrote a fiery series of articles in November of that year attacking a local shipping merchant, Francis Todd, who owned a ship called the *Francis* that transported slaves from Baltimore to New Orleans. Comparing Todd to "highway robbers and murderers," authorities arrested Garrison for libel. Found guilty, the judge fined him $50, which Garrison refused to pay. The judge confined the journalist to a jail cell; Garrison said the experience of being locked up helped him better understand slavery's bitterness. Rather than repenting for his attacks on Todd, Garrison's abolitionism deepened.

Garrison renounced colonization. African Americans were equal to whites and should receive their freedom without delay, he insisted. Garrison no doubt alienated many, even close allies like escaped slave and anti-slavery author Frederick Douglass, with his flair for the dramatic. On July 4, 1854, he publicly burned a copy of the United States Constitution, which he said had failed to abolish slavery and, through the 3/5s rule, guaranteed southern overrepresentation in Congress, and had become a "Covenant with Death, an Agreement with Hell." Garrison greatly increased the attention paid the anti-slavery movement and effectively discredited the American Colonization Society as a fraud that would never reach its goals.

David Walker

There would be no more passionate, eloquent, and informed abolitionists than those from the African-American community. Many abolitionist whites were churchgoers. But an overwhelming majority of white Christians either did not care about slavery or opposed emancipation. This fact infuriated **David Walker**, an African-American from North Carolina who had witnessed the efforts of whites in his home state of North Carolina to discourage the conversions of slaves to Christianity or to allow black participation in white churches. Born in the Cape Fear area of North Carolina to a free mother and an enslaved father, Walker inherited his mother's status and was active in the African Methodist Episcopal Church. He later moved north to Philadelphia (home to the largest free African-American community in the country at the time) before settling in Boston.

Walker saw American Christianity as a cesspool of hypocrisy. No Americans, he observed, more loudly proclaimed their faith than white Southerners. None, in his estimation, more flagrantly mocked the message of Jesus. He would later write of free and enslaved African Americans gathering together "for no other purpose than to worship God Almighty, in spirit and truth, in the best of their knowledge" being assaulted by "tyrants calling themselves [slave] patrols . . ." These patrols would "come and wait in almost breathless silence for the poor colored people to commence singing and praying to the Lord our God . . . [A]s soon as they had commenced, the wretches would burst in upon them and drag them out and commence beating them as they would rattle snakes—many of whom they would beat so unmercifully that they would hardly be able to crawl for weeks and sometimes for months."

Walker settled in Boston, establishing a used clothing shop and, although he experienced far greater freedom than in his native North Carolina, he bitterly experienced the northern hypocrisy regarding race. There, unlike in most of America, African Americans could vote but they attended segregated schools, lived in segregated neighborhoods, could find employment only in menial, low-paying jobs, could not get service in white restaurants, or even receive care in white-run hospitals.

Walker poured a lifetime of frustration and anger with white America into his groundbreaking and controversial 1829 book *Appeal to the Colored Citizens of the World, but in Particular and Very Expressly, to Those of the United States of America*. He described the white majority as "natural enemies of African Americans." Whites, he said, "have always been an unjust, jealous, unmerciful, avaricious and blood-thirsty set of beings always seeking after power and authority" who used blacks as "beasts of burden to them and their children." Walker not only argued that African Americans were equal to whites, he argued that African Americans were ethically superior because they did not reduce other human beings to commodities.

Walker appealed for African Americans to rise up in revolution against slavery. He argued that African Americans possessed an immense physical advantage over whites in terms of strength and said that 450,000 armed African-American slaves and freedmen could defeat all the white people living on the North American continent.

Southern legislatures responded furiously to the *Appeal*. Copies of the pamphlet smuggled to the South by African Americans reached some freedmen, sparking a panic. Copies were seized by southern postal authorities and police and destroyed. African Americans were arrested in port cities like New Orleans for possessing the publication. Slave states passed a wave of laws prohibiting teaching blacks to read, and slaves preaching or writing. An award of $1,000 was offered for the death of Walker and $10,000 for his capture and delivery for trial to southern authorities (more than $21,000 and $212,000 in today's dollars). Walker died, most likely from tuberculosis, just before the publication of the third edition of the *Appeal*, June 28, 1830, although rumors spread that he had been poisoned. Repeated panics over alleged slave revolt plots wracked the South for the two decades after publication of the *Appeal*. In 1831, for instance, rumor of a pending rebellion led authorities in Raleigh, North Carolina to arrest every free African American in the city.

Frederick Douglass

Walker was not alone in advocating extreme measures to end slavery. In an 1843 speech later known as the "Call To Rebellion" before the National Negro Convention in Buffalo, a former slave turned minister, Henry Highland Garnet, urged slaves to kill their masters if necessary to end the on-going exploitation of African Americans in the South. Noting the success of a revolution won by slaves in Haiti in 1803, he predicted that African-descended people would achieve mastery in other slave societies in the West.

The most famous African-American abolitionist, **Frederick Douglass,** rejected such extreme language. One of the most gifted writers and orators of the nineteenth century, Douglass had a compelling story to tell audiences in the United States and Europe when he burst upon the world scene in 1845 with publication of *Narrative of the Life of Frederick Douglass, an American Slave, Written by Himself.* Born as Frederick Augustus Washington Bailey in Maryland in 1818, Douglass was the child of a white man and a slave woman from whom he was separated as a baby. Sophia, the wife of one of his masters, Hugh Auld, taught Douglass the alphabet; and Douglass later convinced white children to give him further reading lessons. He educated himself with books he found and with newspapers. Reading opened Douglass's mind to the potential wonders of the world and all that had been denied him as a slave. He encountered the furious debates whites themselves had about the merits of slavery and for the first time heard of abolitionism.

Auld rented out Douglass's services to another slave master, William Freeland. Once there, Douglass began to teach other slaves how to read and write and held informal Sunday school classes. As word spread about Douglass, dozens of slaves began to attend his classes. Although Freeland was unconcerned, other slave masters adamantly opposed the education of their servants and, armed with clubs and other weapons, broke into one of Douglass's classes as the students were reading the New Testament, beating them and warning them to never gather for that purpose again.

In his *Life of Frederick Douglass*, he discusses how the slave owners he knew became more cruel after converting to Christianity, including one who would savagely bullwhip a slave woman as he quoted Luke 12:47 from the Christian New Testament—"And that servant, which knew his lord's will, and prepared not himself, neither did

according to his will, shall be beaten with many stripes." Douglass suggested that slave owners believed God sanctioned their role as absolute rulers over their chattel. They used the Bible to justify their theft of slaves' bodies and the fruits of their labor. Douglass so frequently blasted the rank hypocrisy of Christian slave owners that some accused him of atheism. Douglass shot back that white southern Christianity bore no resemblance to the Gospel.

When Douglass returned to the possession of Thomas Auld, his master became dissatisfied with the teenager's work and handed him over to a financially struggling and infamous "slavebreaker" named Edward Covey, who beat him daily. The beatings stopped when Douglass bested Covey in a fistfight. In love with a free African-American woman named Anna Murray, Douglass could no longer contain his desire for liberty. In 1838, he escaped. While working at a shipyard, Douglass donned a disguise as a sailor and, carrying money provided by Murray and false identification papers, he boarded a train in Baltimore, transferred to a steamboat, and then hopped another train to freedom in New Bedford, Massachusetts. He married Murray and assumed the name under which he became world famous.

Douglass spoke across the country and many whites expressed shock that an African American could be so poised and eloquent. His proclamations of racial equality provoked many whites. A mob assaulted him in Pendleton, Indiana, breaking his hand and causing a lifelong impairment, but Douglass continued to carry his abolitionist message throughout the free states.

His *Narrative* became a bestseller. He conducted a two-year speaking tour in Europe and achieved his legal emancipation when European supporters bought his freedom from Thomas Auld. Douglass began publishing his own anti-slavery newspaper, *The North Star*, in late 1847. The motto of Douglass's publication—"Right is of no Sex—Truth is of no Color—God is the Father of us all, and we are all brethren"—illustrates the degree to which antebellum reform movements overlapped and how reformers from that period saw the various struggles for social progress, for slaves, for women, for the insane, as overlapping. In 1851, *The North Star* was renamed *Frederick Douglass' Paper*. It enjoyed thousands of subscribers in the United States and in Europe and was considered one of the most influential publications in the abolitionist movement.

THE UNDERGROUND RAILROAD

Starting in the second decade of the nineteenth century, African Americans and white abolitionists created an informal network to aid escaped slaves that came to be known as the "**Underground Railroad**." By the mid-1840s, an active band of former slaves and white slavery opponents aided an estimated 100,000 African Americans fleeing their owners, not only to Mexico and to sympathetic Native American bands but also to northern states and as far north as Canada. Sometimes slaves were aided by brave free African Americans, often escaped slaves themselves, who acted as "conductors," arriving at plantations late at night and guiding escapees through the heavily guarded woods to a series of safe houses–"stations"—where they hid on the trek north. Escapees had to avoid slave patrollers—"paddyrollers" as they were called in Texas—who combed the countryside with sniffing dogs in search of vanished human property.

Escaping slaves often travelled by foot as much as 20 miles a night and lived off the land, swimming across rough waters, and improvising shelter sometimes in rain, sleet, or snow. They often escaped during Christmas season, in spite of the cold, because masters often wrote passes for their slaves during this season so their chattel could visit loved ones living on other plantations. An African American roaming at this time would not be such an unusual sight. Slaves also frequently made their escapes just after harvest time when they would be better able to grab food for their difficult journey.

According to legend, the Underground Railroad safe houses were always equipped with secret rooms where the escapees could hide. Most of the escapees stayed in extra bedrooms, barn lofts, attics, or slept on kitchen floors. Sometimes slaves quietly hid in crawl spaces for weeks while they waited to safely travel to their next station. Meanwhile, committees sprang up across the North to raise money to provide food and clothes for escapees and financial aid for the so-called stationmasters who provided their homes as shelter. These committees also helped the now former slaves find jobs in their new northern homes.

WOMEN AND THE ANTISLAVERY CRUSADE

Lydia Maria Child

By the 1830s, those calling for the immediate abolition of slavery stood apart from the racism of the larger society. For this, they often faced harsh public ostracism and were labeled immoral "race mixers." Like so many women in the abolitionist movement, **Lydia Maria Child** did not blink in the face of such pressures. Born in Medford, Massachusetts in 1802, Child was deeply influenced in her quest for learning by her brother, the Unitarian minister Convers Francis, and she pursued a career in teaching. She held a deep passion for writing, however, and immediately made a sensation with a controversial first novel *Hobomok*, published in 1824, which featured as its hero a Native American warrior who falls in love with a white woman. The 22-year-old finished the work in six weeks and established a lifelong career in letters, focusing largely on children's literature. She edited one of the country's first children's magazines, *Juvenile Miscellany*, for a decade. However, deeply influenced by William Lloyd Garrison, Child took up both the cause of abolitionism and women's suffrage and in the process destroyed her literary career.

Child, like many abolitionists in the 1830s, realized that slavery depended on the idea of white racial supremacy. She also realized that racism rested on a distorted depiction of history in which past black accomplishments were erased and black civilizations deliberately forgotten. In *An Appeal in Favor of that Class of Americans Called Africans* (1833), Child corrected the record. Pointing out the great achievements of ancient Egypt—"the great school of knowledge in the ancient world"—Child observed that the ancient Greek historians described the Egyptians of the classic period as having "black skin and frizzled hair." Similarly, she described the sophistication of African art, textiles, and poetry in nineteenth-century West Africa. She also noted the lives of accomplished people of African descent from St. Augustine, the ancient Christian theologian from modern-day Algeria, to Phillis Wheatley, a one-time slave born in Senegambia who upon her emancipation became the first published female African-American poet in United States history.

The *Appeal* was the country's first book-length anti-slavery treatise, and its thesis that blacks and whites were intellectual equals and its condemnation of racism in northern states provoked a furious backlash. Readers cancelled their subscriptions to *Juvenile Miscellany*, and she was fired as editor. Sales of her other books dropped sharply, and the Boston Athenaeum, a members-only research library, cancelled her borrowing privileges. She nevertheless became a leader in the abolitionist movement and, with her husband David Child, would become co-editor of the *Massachusetts Whig Journal*, the newspaper owned by the **American Anti-Slavery Society**.

Angelina and Sarah Grimké

Two sisters, **Angelina and Sarah Grimké**, also shocked antebellum audiences beginning in the 1830s not just because of their fiery commitment to abolition and their bold insistence on the right of women to speak out about political issues before "promiscuous" audiences including males and females, but also because of their status as the daughters of a South Carolina slave owner. The two toured as anti-slavery speakers and also authored abolitionist pamphlets like the 1836 tract *Appeal to the Christian Women of the South*.

The Grimkés' father, Judge John Faucheraud Grimké, was an iconoclast himself, supporting the idea that women should be educated. The judge appreciated the two girls' high intelligence, as did their brother, the Yale-educated Thomas Grimké. Sarah embarked on a self-study of law, and her father believed that she would have become a highly successful attorney if she had been a man.

Seventeen years older than Angelina, Sarah (born in 1792) took on the role of raising her younger sister in place of their emotionally distant, unsupportive mother who seemed completely absorbed in the task of managing the slave estate while their father presided over court. The estate's slaves lived in shabby conditions and suffered frequent whippings. The Grimké sisters later remembered hearing the blood-curdling screams of lashed slaves at the so-called "Sugar House," a corrective institution for servants in their native Charleston, South Carolina. There, whites suspended slaves by their arms and dragged them on a treadmill. The sisters' growing disgust with the violence and selfishness of slavery led them to move to Philadelphia where they converted to Quakerism in the early 1830s.

The sisters, however, became bitterly disillusioned with the Society of Friends when they were rebuked by their co-religionists after a letter by Angelina to Garrison's *The Liberator* was published. (Quakers are members of the Religious Society of Friends. To members of this religion, the words "Quaker" and "Friend" mean the same thing.) They were rebuked a second time in 1836 when Sarah tried to discuss abolitionism at a Quaker meeting.

Too many local Quakers feared that abolitionism would spark violent slave rebellions and equally violent white opposition and saw the cause as incompatible with the sect's pacifism. Yet, forming close friendships with African Americans, the Grimké sisters only became more deeply committed to the cause.

Angelina authored the *Appeal* hoping that a female audience could persuade the men in the South to abandon the "peculiar institution." "I know you do not make the laws," she wrote, "but I also know that you are the wives and mothers, the sisters and daughters of those who do." She urged the women to read widely about the subject, to pray about it, and then, finally, to actively fight human bondage. The Charleston police chief notified Angelina's mother, Mary Smith Grimké, that the author would be immediately arrested if she ever appeared in the city again. Such threats did not deter the Grimké sisters, who became speakers for the American Anti-Slavery Society and toured New York, Massachusetts, and other free states beginning in early 1837. Angelina made history in 1838 when she became the first woman to speak before a legislature as she presented in the Massachusetts state house an anti-slavery petition signed by 20,000 women.

That same year, she married another major abolitionist, Theodore Weld. While Weld was a speaker for the American Anti-Slavery Society, angry opponents often physically attacked him for speaking out against forced servitude, leading him to be labeled "the most mobbed man in America." In 1839, Weld would write one of the most graphic and powerful condemnations of slavery, *Slavery As It Is*. The book's blunt descriptions of the physical and emotional torments imposed on slaves would inspire many passages in Harriet Beecher Stowe's novel *Uncle Tom's Cabin*.

Angelina Emily Grimké (left) and Sarah Moore Grimké (right)

POLITICAL ABOLITIONISTS

Being an abolitionist was dangerous work from the 1830s to the 1850s. Black abolitionist women faced kidnappers who roamed the North to capture free blacks and sell them as slaves in the South. Physical assaults, particularly against black women, were commonplace, and assassination was always a constant threat. In spite of this risk, one of the nation's most prominent female abolitionists was an escaped slave from New York, born Isabella Baumfree, who would become famous under the name she chose for herself, Sojourner Truth. She would be controversial because of her insistence that women's suffrage should be accepted by all abolitionists, ideas she put forth in an address later famous as the "Ain't I A Woman" speech, delivered before the Ohio Women's Rights Convention in 1851.

Sojourner Truth avoided physical attacks in her public speaking career but other abolitionists were not so lucky. On November 7, 1837 in Alton, Illinois, a mob murdered an abolitionist newspaper editor, **Elijah Lovejoy**. A Presbyterian minister, Lovejoy denounced slavery from his pulpit in St. Louis and wrote fiery anti-slavery articles in the newspaper he edited, the *St. Louis Observer*. That city, located in a slave state, was bitterly divided between pro- and anti-slavery factions. In 1835, a pro-slavery throng destroyed his printing press because of his articles condemning the lynching of a free African-American man. For the safety of his family, Lovejoy moved across the Mississippi River to Alton. There, he led the College Avenue Presbyterian Church and established a new abolitionist publication, the *Alton Observer*. In the *Observer*, Lovejoy called for immediate emancipation for all American slaves, with no financial compensation for slave owners.

On November 7, 1837, pro-slavery thugs raided a warehouse where Lovejoy had hoped to conceal his printing press from determined vandals. The mob fired several shots into the building. Lovejoy and his supporters had hidden inside the building and returned fire, hitting several and killing one man. The looters set fire to the warehouse and when Lovejoy exited the building he was shot five times, killing him. The hooligans broke the press to pieces before dumping the parts in the river. The murder shocked many, and across the free states membership in abolitionist societies grew.

The variety of abolitionist media increased. Abolitionists reached school children with anti-slavery spelling books with rhymes like, "A is an Abolitionist—/A man who want to free/ The wretched slave—and to give all/ An equal liberty" and "B is a Brother with a skin/ of somewhat darker hue/But in our Heavenly Father's sight/ He is as dear as you." Anti-slavery almanacs, sometimes featuring illustrations of slaves being beaten or hanging themselves in despair, became another means of spreading the message. Abolitionism grew through the 1830s, with about 1,000 state and national anti-slavery groups including about 120,000 members nationwide active in the country at the end of the decade. The number of anti-slavery groups in Massachusetts grew from 2 in 1832 to 246 in 1838. New York went from no groups in 1832, to 369 in 1838. Even in southern-sympathizing Illinois, scene of Lovejoy's assassination, the number of abolitionist organizations went up from 3 the year of the murder to 13 the following year.

SUFFRAGISTS

The ranks of the abolitionists and the women's rights movements largely overlapped. The most famous opponents of slavery—the Grimké sisters, Theodore Weld, Lydia Child, William Garrison, and Frederick Douglass—also supported women's rights. In the early nineteenth century, women lacked not only the right to vote, they found universities and colleges closed to them. Women lost control of whatever property they held when they married. Any money earned after marriage legally belonged to their husband. They could not sign contracts without their husband's consent. The right to divorce, even from abusive, neglectful or financially reckless husbands, remained extremely limited and subject to approval in each individual case by state legislatures. If women were able to obtain a divorce from a bad husband, the children still legally belonged to the father, and mothers would not receive custody. Women who tried to physically escape abusers had no legal protection if they were held against their will, nor did the law prohibit rape within marriage.

Abolitionism rested on the idea that people should have jurisdiction over their own bodies. If this reasoning applied to slaves, early feminists argued, how could it not apply to women who essentially in the early nineteenth century represented the property of a series of men, from their fathers to their husbands to surviving male relatives if they became widowed. Abigail Kelley Foster, born in 1811, came from a middling Quaker family in Massachusetts and labored as an activist for the American Anti-Slavery Society before she became a powerful voice of antebellum feminism. Foster acknowledged the debt the women's rights cause owed to the African-American freedom struggle. "We have good cause to be grateful to the slave, for the benefit we have received to ourselves, in working for him," she wrote. "In striving to strike his irons off, we found most surely that we were manacled ourselves."

Margaret Fuller, a friend of Ralph Waldo Emerson and fellow Transcendentalist and widely read journalist, became one of the first famous feminists in American history as she advocated for women's education. Fuller, born in 1810, argued that women should be able to study any academic field or profession and not just those that conformed to contemporary gender expectations. In her 1845 work, *Woman in the Nineteenth Century*, she called for marriages to be partnerships of equals. In the book, based on Fuller's writings for the Transcendentalist newspaper *The Dial*, she went further, questioning the stereotypical expectation of how men and women should behave. "There is no wholly masculine man, no purely feminine [woman]," she argued.

The women's movement before the Civil War focused on suffrage. Without the vote and the ability to run for office, women faced an uphill battle for reform. A tea party at a home in Waterloo, New York, in July 1848 launched the women's suffrage campaign that would not reach its climax until seven decades later. Jane Hunt, a suffrage advocate born in Pennsylvania, hosted the gathering that also included **Elizabeth Cady Stanton**, Martha Wright, Mary Ann McClintock, and Lucretia Mott, all veterans of the abolitionist movement. Mott and Stanton had attended the World Anti-Slavery Convention in London in 1840 where they and other women were prohibited from active participation in the proceedings. The five animatedly discussed the political and social barriers facing women. By the end of the gathering, the five decided to organize a women's rights convention to be held in nearby **Seneca Falls** just six days later on July 19.

It was a measure of the deep political networks that had already formed and the already vast political experience of women who had fought for years for numerous reform causes that, in less than a week, the convention was able to draw about 260 women and 40 men, including Frederick Douglass. They met in the Wesleyan Chapel, hearing a series of fiery speeches. Stanton and Mott co-wrote and Stanton read to the gathering one of the most important statements in early feminism: "The Declaration of Sentiments." Modeled closely on the Declaration of Independence, the Seneca Falls statement declared, "We hold these truths to be self-evident: that all men and women are created equal . . ."

The declaration then listed, like the original Declaration of Independence, a set of grievances. Man, the declaration said, had never permitted woman to "exercise her inalienable right to the elective franchise"; he has "made her, if married, in the eye of the law civilly dead"; he has "taken from her all right in property, even to the wages she earns"; he has "denied her the facilities for obtaining a thorough education, all colleges being closed against her"; and he has "endeavored, in every way that he could, to destroy her confidence in her own powers, to lessen her self-respect, and to make her willing to lead a dependent and abject life."

Over the two-day gathering, the delegates unanimously passed a series of resolutions calling for women to enjoy greater rights in marriage and an end to gender discrimination regarding property and education, but they only narrowly approved a resolution calling for women's suffrage. Many delegates feared the idea was too radical and would frighten away potential allies. Eventually, 100 delegates signed the declaration. The document was published only in a handful of newspapers, in some cases because editors thought the statement was so ridiculous it would entertain readers. Men mocked the female delegates as unfeminine. "I want to go [home], not to the embrace of some female ward politician, but to the earnest loving look and touch of a true woman," one senator remarked. Ministers denounced the statement as

Elizabeth Cady Stanton (left)
and Susan B. Anthony (right)
as elderly women.

a rejection of God's intended role for men and women. Some signatories felt so much pressure they asked for their names to be removed.

The convention and the declaration, however, inspired a grassroots movement, with women holding local meetings, petition drives, and lobbying campaigns to persuade legislators of the wisdom of female suffrage. A National Women's Rights Convention would be held every year between 1850 and 1860.

One-time teacher, **Susan B. Anthony** of Massachusetts (1820-1906), had already campaigned for abolition, labor rights, and temperance, but she became best known for her efforts on behalf of the women's suffrage movement. Her devotion to the feminist cause stemmed in part from her frustration over not being allowed to speak at anti-alcohol rallies. She became known as the "general" of the women's suffrage campaign for her meticulous organizational skills and tireless devotion to the cause.

Such endurance would be needed. Suffrage proved to be a long struggle. Women who fought for the emancipation of slaves, and then for the voting rights of African-American men after the Civil War would be bitterly disappointed that women were not granted suffrage in the Fifteenth Amendment ratified in 1870. That amendment only gave "all male citizens" the right to vote regardless of race, color, or previous condition of servitude. Women would slowly win the right to vote in local elections state-by-state, but would not win suffrage nationally until the ratification of the Nineteenth Amendment, on August 18, 1920.

SOCIETAL ALTERNATIVES

Utopias

To many Americans, the many reform movements of the early nineteenth century, such as women's rights and abolitionism, went too far. To others, they did not go far enough. A wave of Americans withdrew from mainstream society entirely and formed utopian communities in which they experimented with new roles for men and women, new family structures, new sexual norms, and new approaches to property. In 1825, Robert Owen, an industrialist who opposed slavery, supported women's rights and was an early advocate of birth control, emigrated from Scotland and established a socialist commune in Indiana called New Harmony that at one point had more than 900 residents. Under the community's constitution, residents were responsible for providing what they needed for their private households and would invest their assets in a shared fund. Residents would work in return for goods at a community-owned store. The community, which lasted only from 1825 to 1829, drew gifted scientists (including many who would later form the National Academy of Sciences), operated quality schools, and ran a theater, but disputes over governance and money management led to the commune's collapse.

About forty utopias were established across the country based on the socialist ideas of the French thinker Charles Fourier, such as Brook Farm in Massachusetts. The United Society of Believers in Christ's Second Appearing, better known as the Shakers, created some of the most durable utopian communities. The sect split off from Quakerism. The Shakers' nickname derived from the ecstatic dances believers broke into as they were supposedly filled with the Holy Spirit. Shakers, anticipating the imminent Second Coming of Christ, practiced celibacy and lived lives of strict simplicity, reflected in a distinct music style and the furniture they built to raise funds.

Some communes became extremely controversial. Fanny Wright, an admirer of Owen, used her inheritance to establish a utopian community, Nashoba, near Memphis, Tennessee. The Scottish woman, a religious skeptic highly critical of organized religion, defended unwed mothers and generated controversy almost anytime she spoke or wrote. She planned Nashoba to be an interracial refuge for white workers, free African Americans and slaves who would work on the Nashoba property for wages and eventually purchase their freedom. She hoped this would be a model for slave owners who would adopt similar policies on their property. Rumors spread of interracial sex on the commune, and one critic described it as a "great brothel." As hostility to the community increased and funds ran out, Wright freed the slaves and used her own money in 1830 to charter a ship to transport thirty-four from the United States to Haiti.

Not even Nashoba generated as much controversy as the **Oneida Community** in upstate New York. Formed in 1848 and shaped by the religious ideas of founder John Humphrey Noyes, the community believed that Jesus had already returned to earth in A.D.70 and that the Oneida settlement would start a godly millennium free of sin and suffering. All the residents considered themselves betrothed to each other in what they called "complex marriage." Post-menopausal women in the commune and older men were encouraged to act as sexual mentors for teenagers. Monogamy was abandoned. A committee made all decisions regarding childraising and was supposed to decide who in the community could bear children, based on their supposed spiritual fitness. Nevertheless, a number of children entered the world without committee approval. The commune survived until the 1880s, but fell apart like others because of disputes over financial management as well as dissension over whether the group should continue its controversial sexual practices. The commune's businesses, including manufacturing silverware, survived into the twenty-first century.

Millerites

Thousands of Americans in the 1830s and 1840s anxiously looked for signs of the world's end in thunderstorms, earthquakes, shooting stars, eclipses, and recurring economic depressions. Many embraced a view of the Bible that was filled with yet unrealized prophecies supposedly predicting natural catastrophes, economic and political chaos, and a horrific war that would destroy much of humanity just before Jesus returned to save humanity and usher in a Millennium—a 1,000-year reign of peace on Earth. Some also believed that the Bible foretold the rise in the End Times of an evil so-called "Antichrist" who would take over the world and lead most people to reject God just before an almost-world-ending Battle of Armageddon and the "Second Coming of Christ."

William Miller, a Baptist preacher from the Burned Over District, fueled much of the End Times panic. Miller concluded, based on his interpretation of prophecies in the Biblical books of Daniel and Revelation that Jesus would return to the world to gather his followers in the sky and that the End Times would commence sometime between March 21, 1843 and March 21, 1844. In 1832, Miller traveled in the Northeast and the Midwest making ominous sermons, publishing his prophetic interpretations in a booklet, *Evidence from Scripture and History of the Second Coming of Christ, about the Year 1843: Exhibited in a Course of Lectures.* He convinced thousands of believers in New York, New England, Ohio, and Michigan that Jesus would be coming soon. Eager to renounce their entanglements with a sinful world, many followers sold all their property. Some got swept up in the hysteria and sewed special "ascension robes" in which they would rise straight to heaven without dying. As many as a half-million became "Millerites." March 21, 1844 passed with no Second Coming, and Miller, announcing he had made mathematical errors in his previous prediction, set two new dates for the return of Jesus: April 18 and October 22. When the last of these dates passed uneventfully, many felt bitter and saddened. Among Miller's followers it became known as "The Great Disappointment." Some Millerites lost their faith as a result of the failed prophecy, but others went on to found not only the Seventh-day Adventist denomination, but also the Church of God. Other Millerites later founded the prophecy-oriented Jehovah's Witnesses sect in the 1870s.

Mormons

The Church of Jesus Christ of Latter-day Saints stands as one of the most distinctly American prophecy-shaped religious movements born in the early nineteenth century. **Joseph Smith, Jr.**, another denizen of the Burned-Over District, was the son of a notably unsuccessful Vermont Baptist, who moved his family to a series of rented farms in a vain search for opportunity, ending up in Palmyra, New York in 1820, where they faced eviction. Smith's family had never been intensely religious, but hardships led Smith's mother and some of his sisters to start attending, in spite of the elder Smith's objections, an evangelical Presbyterian church. Around this time, Smith said he received two visions. The first was a pillar of light and then God himself warning him away from existing religions and telling him to await further instructions. In 1827, Smith said, an angel called Moroni appeared to him and directed him to mysterious buried gold plates inscribed in a language unknown to Smith.

With the help of this angel, Smith claimed, he translated these plates into English words that became *The Book of Mormon*. His followers then established a new faith. The revelations Smith received found an audience among those uncomfortable with many of the era's social changes, particularly the women's movement and the increased role played by women in some sects such as the Baptists. Smith preached that God had established men as the authority in each family as long as they respected women and children. He also claimed that some Native Americans descended from the so-called Lost Tribes of Israel—ten tribes from the ancient kingdom who lost their separate identity after conquest by the ancient Assyrian Empire. Smith said members of these tribes had traveled to the Americas and were preached to by Jesus after his crucifixion.

Smith's revelation stirred opposition from traditional Christians who objected to his claims of having received direct revelation from God, his insistence that his new sect was the only authentic version of Christianity, and the denomination's eventual embrace of polygamy. After trying to set up a mini-theocracy with his followers, Smith was murdered by an angry mob in Nauvoo, Illinois in June 1844. The remaining Mormons fled west, finally settling in Utah (see Chapter 14).

A TURBULENT AGE

The period of reform between the 1830s and the 1850s signaled neither the dawn of a golden age nor the first rumblings of the Apocalypse. The highest hopes of reformers were often disappointed. Reformers sought to train the poor to think like more industrious, successful people, but the economy rested on low wages, slavery, and the constant importation of surplus workers that made economic advancement extremely difficult, if not impossible for many. In spite of the reformers' good intentions, attitudes toward the poor would only harden. As the nineteenth century advanced, elites increasingly saw those who were economically struggling as biologically defective and opposed any efforts allowing them to live easier lives.

In spite of the persistence and bravery of the abolition movement, the number of slaves in the United States almost doubled between 1810 and 1860. Because of the fears generated by the abolitionist movement and events like the Nat Turner revolt, southern society actually became more oppressive, with mail censored, abolitionist literature destroyed, people hounded out of their communities for questioning the "peculiar institution," and slave patrols roaming the woods at night seeking the next leader of a bloody slave revolt.

Prison reform often turned into a rationale for exploiting convicts as slave labor. Reformers did transform many facilities for the insane into more positive environments with better care. But the mentally ill often fell victim again to neglect or abuse once the initial resolve for change ebbed. While the temperance movement curbed American drinking from its astonishing excesses of the early nineteenth century, advocates never remade the country into a teetotaling refuge. Americans continued their love affair with alcohol.

Nevertheless, antebellum reformers did launch two of the nation's most important freedom crusades: the suffrage campaign and the abolition movement. They questioned the economic powerlessness of women and drew women directly into some of the most important political controversies of the era. The feminist movement of the twentieth century can trace its roots directly to the 1830s and 1840s.

Reformers also made a dent in the country's racist ideology and for the first time made white Americans think of slavery not just in terms of how it affected them but also the evil of the institution itself. Because of the abolitionists, some whites for the first time began to acknowledge the humanity of African Americans, to talk about the rights they deserved, and to even contemplate a future in which free blacks had a place as citizens. For all their failures and shortcomings, the reformers imagined African Americans as full citizens, an idea that was nothing less than revolutionary.

Chronology

1830 Joseph Smith founds the Mormon Church. Charles Finney's religious revival meetings (through 1831).

1831 Nat Turner leads slave revolt in Virginia. Garrison first publishes *The Liberator*. Alexis de Tocqueville begins his travels through America, the basis for *Democracy in America*.

1833 American Anti-Slavery Society founded.

1837 Ralph Waldo Emerson delivers his "American Scholar" address. Mt. Holyoke opens women's college. Oberlin becomes the first coed college.

1840-1 Transcendentalists start utopian communities Hopedale and Brook Farm.

1843 Dorothea Dix issues her report on the treatment of prisoners and the insane.

1844 Joseph Smith murdered in Illinois.

1845 Publication of the *Narrative of the Life of Frederick Douglas*.

1846-7 Mormon migration to the Great Salt Lake.

1847 Frederick Douglass's *North Star* published.

1848 First women's rights convention held in Seneca Falls, New York.

1850 Nathaniel Hawthorne's *The Scarlet Letter* is published.

1851 Herman Melville's *Moby Dick* is published.

1852 Harriet Beecher Stowe's *Uncle Tom's Cabin* is published.

1854 Thoreau's *Walden* appears.

1855 Massachusetts becomes first state to end public school segregation. Walt Whitman's *Leaves of Grass* is published.

SUGGESTED READINGS

Robert Abzug, *Cosmos Crumbling: American Reform and the Religious Imagination* (1994).

Leonard J. Arrington and Davis Bitton, *The Mormon Experience: A History of the Latter-Day Saints* (1979).

Carl L. Bankston III and Stephen J. Caldas, *Public Education—America's Civil Religion: A Social History* (2009).

Andrew Barr, *Drink: A Social History of America*. (1999).

David Blight, *Passages to Freedom: The Underground Railroad in History and Memory*. (2004).

Julia Boyd. *The Excellent Dr. Blackwell: The Life of the First Woman Physician* (2013).

Paul Boyer, *When Time Shall Be No More: Prophecy Belief in Modern American Culture* (1992).

John L. Brooke, *The Refiner's Fire: The Making of Mormon Cosmology, 1644-1844* (1994).

Claudia Lauper Bushman and Richard Lyman Bushman, *Building the Kingdom: A History of Mormons in America* (1999)

Frederick Douglass, *Narrative of the Life of Frederick Douglass, an American Slave, Written by Himself* (1845).

David Gollaher, *Voice for the Mad: The Life of Dorothea Dix* (1995).

Paul Goodman, *Of One Blood: Abolitionism and the Origins of Racial Equality* (1998).

Elizabeth Griffith, *In Her Own Right: The Life of Elizabeth Cady Stanton* (1984).

Walter Harding, *The Days of Henry Thoreau: A Biography* (1966).

Julie Roy Jeffrey, *The Great Silent Army of Abolitionism: Ordinary Women in the Antislavery Movement* (1998.)

Carol Kolmerten, *Women in Utopia: The Ideology of Gender in American Owenite Communities* (1990).

Aileen Kraditor, *Means and Ends in American Abolitionism* (1967).

Gerda Lerner, *The Grimke Sisters of South Carolina: Rebels Against Slavery* (1967)

Louis P. Masur, *Rites of Execution: Capital Punishment and the Transformation of American Culture, 1776-1865* (1989).

___,*1831: Year of Eclipse* (2002).

Rebecca M. McLennan, *The Crisis of Imprisonment: Protest, Politics, and the Making of the American Penal State, 1776-1941* (2008).

W. J. Rorabaugh, *The Alcoholic Republic: An American Tradition* (1979).

David J. Rothman, *The Discovery of the Asylum: Social Order and Disorder in the New Republic* (1971).

Review Questions

1. What view of human nature did the reformers of the 1830s and 1840s share, and what social problems did they seek to address?

2. What controversies arose in the first half of the nineteenth century concerning public education for immigrants, African Americans, and women?

3. Describe the beliefs of Transcendentalism and the philosophy of its leading exponents, like Ralph Waldo Emerson and Henry David Thoreau.

4. Describe the evolution of anti-slavery thought in America in the early nineteenth century, including consideration of "colonizers," and advocates of immediate emancipation. What was the white southern response to slavery's critics?

5. What was the relationship between the anti-slavery and the women's rights movement, and what reforms were sought by nineteenth-century feminists?

Glossary of Important People and Concepts

American Anti-Slavery Society
American Colonization Society
American Temperance Society
Susan B. Anthony
Lydia Maria Child
Dorothea Dix
Frederick Douglass
Ralph Waldo Emerson
Charles Grandison Finney
William Lloyd Garrison
Grimké Sisters
Elijah Lovejoy
Horace Mann
Herman Melville
William Miller
Oneida Community
Second Great Awakening
Seneca Falls Convention
Joseph Smith, Jr.
Elizabeth Cady Stanton
Henry David Thoreau
Transcendentalism
Underground Railroad
David Walker
Walt Whitman

An engraving of settlers moving their wagon train through mountains on their way to California.

Chapter Fourteen

AMERICA EXPANDS, 1840-1850

"We feel that we cannot do our work too fast to save the Indian . . . from extinction," the missionary Narcissa Whitman wrote to her mother in an 1840 letter that revealed much conflict in her attitude to those she professed to be saving. She rightly sensed that there was not much time. "A tide of immigration appears to be moving this way rapidly. What a few years will bring forth we know not." Narcissa and her husband Marcus were among the handful of American missionaries to settle in the Oregon Country, a region in the Pacific Northwest that the United States and Great Britain jointly occupied from 1818 to 1846. When the Whitmans arrived in 1834 and established their mission near the confluence of the Snake and Columbia Rivers (close to present-day Walla Walla, Washington), the region was dominated by a diverse array of Native American groups who had been interacting regularly with fur traders and Catholic missionaries for decades. That contact had brought new economic activities, belief systems, and diseases that collectively disrupted previously established patterns of hunting and gathering, leaving many Native Americans dependent on a declining fur trade. The Whitmans planned to remedy that dependency by encouraging the adoption of farming as they also introduced them to Protestant Christianity. Narcissa reported progress to her mother: "they are becoming quite independent in cultivation. . . . Great numbers of them cultivate . . . and do their own plowing."

In the same letter, however, Narcissa also expressed frustration. She described her charges as "an exceedingly proud, haughty and insolent people," noting that they constantly demanded food and resisted what the Whitmans considered to be true Christian teachings. Narcissa expressed shock about Native American gender roles, especially the suggestion made by one that her husband, Marcus, travel without his wife, as the local Indians did. Further, in seeking to improve the lives of the natives, she also relayed her contempt of many native ways that she wished to eliminate, stating at one point about their attitude toward cleanliness: "[the Indians] are so filthy they make a great deal of cleaning wherever they go, and this wears out a woman very fast. We must clean after them, for we have come to elevate them and not to suffer ourselves to sink to their standard." In short, Narcissa and Marcus Whitman believed that their work of saving Native Americans required remaking them in the image of Protestant farmers before the inexorable tide of American settlers displaced or exterminated them.

Although the Whitmans believed themselves to be on a civilizing mission to save the Indians, they were, in fact, the first wave of the thousands of American settlers who would begin flooding the region after 1840. These newcomers expected the regions into which they moved to conform to the political, economic, and social values that had come to dominate the United States. For the Whitmans, those hopes did not work out. The Native Americans they settled among—the Umatillas, the Walla Wallas, and especially the Cayuses—proved resistant to their teachings, partly because the new missionaries did not meet the Indians' expectations. Previous missionaries, Catholics brought in by the British Hudson Bay Company, worked in a system that had encouraged Indians to become dependent on trading posts and linked religious instruction to trading. Those prospects may have been part of the reason behind the constant demands for food that so troubled Narcissa. Although the Whitmans reported success with the introduction of farming, local Native Americans adopted agriculture as only a supplemental activity and planned to continue their practices of hunting and fishing. They had little interest in becoming year-round farmers as the missionaries had desired. They also proved unwilling to reject practices like polygamy simply because the Whitmans claimed they were sinful.

As more settlers passed through the region, tensions increased. Epidemic diseases ravaged the population, and the Cayuses blamed Marcus Whitman, who was a physician by profession, for bringing the sickness. They also increasingly regarded the new missionaries—especially the Whitmans, who provided lodging to travelers on the Oregon Trail—as agents of conquest. For his part, Marcus Whitman came to accept that the Native Americans' unwillingness to embrace his definition of civilization justified their displacement, so he increasingly turned his attention to the spiritual needs of the American settlers. Tensions came to a head in September 1847 when some Cayuses attacked the mission and killed Marcus and Narcissa Whitman, along with twelve others. They also took another fifty-three people captive. Local Americans responded by pushing Indians off their lands. The United States, which secured exclusive control of the territory in 1846, established a fort on the site of the mission. By 1855, American pressure had forced all Native American groups in the area to cede their lands and move to reservations, although fighting between Indians and settlers would continue for over a decade. By then, however, Americans had established unquestioned control over the region.

The Whitmans' experience in the Oregon Country illustrated some of the central features of American expansion in the 1840s. Narcissa's insistence that she and Marcus were on a civilizing mission, for example, was a sentiment that was by no means unique to her. Numerous politicians and newspaper editors expressed similar attitudes, although at times they made more sweeping claims. John O'Sullivan, editor of the **Democratic Review**, provided one of the most famous formulations when he described American expansion in 1845 as "our manifest destiny to overspread and to possess the whole of the continent which Providence has given us for the development of the great experiment of liberty and federated self-government." In other words, God had given the United States a mission to expand throughout the Western Hemisphere and to carry its political institutions and moral values to the rest of the world. The Whitmans' experience, however, demonstrated how Americans actually implemented that mission. Like the missionaries, American settlers expected the populations living in the areas into which they

moved to conform to their standards—not just in Oregon, but also in places such as Texas and California. Moreover, the newcomers arrived in such large numbers that they quickly overwhelmed and then displaced local populations throughout western North America. From their vantage point, the Whitmans experienced one of the central developments in the mid-nineteenth-century United States: the aggressive expansion of American settlers into areas west of the Mississippi River that for a while were beyond the exclusive control of the United States. How to address the consequences of that expansion would become the central issue of American politics in the 1840s, and the choices made to address these matters would lead to war with Mexico resulting in the United States controlling an immense expanse of territory filled with rapidly changing populations.

WESTERN EXPANSION

As late as 1845, the area of North America between the Mississippi River and the Pacific Ocean fell under the formal political control of Mexico (in the present-day American Southwest), Great Britain (in the present-day Pacific Northwest), and the United States, whose western boundary extended in stepped fashion from the borders of Mexican Texas to the Pacific Northwest. Most of this area, however, remained sparsely settled by people of European descent, with effective control of many regions remaining in the hands of Native Americans. After 1820, however, Americans began moving into these regions—usually in small numbers and often as merchants, traders, and missionaries rather than settlers. These folk tended to serve as an advance guard for later groups of settlers because they sent back word of prospective sites for future settlement. By 1840, these initial waves of American migrants had established a presence in California, New Mexico, Oregon, Utah, and Texas.

After 1840, emigration from the United States into these regions accelerated. A number of factors contributed to the increase. Growing population density combined with a depressed agricultural economy made areas within the United States seem relatively less appealing. President Andrew Jackson's war with the Second Bank of the United States had in part contributed to a major financial crisis in 1837, which had reduced the national money supply by about one-third and placed enormous pressure on debtors (many of whom happened to be farmers). A collapse in the price of cotton in 1839 pulled the national economy into a deep depression that did not end until 1843. Any pressures that farmers felt after the Panic of 1837 generally became more intense after 1839. Reports from early settlers made regions outside the United States seem

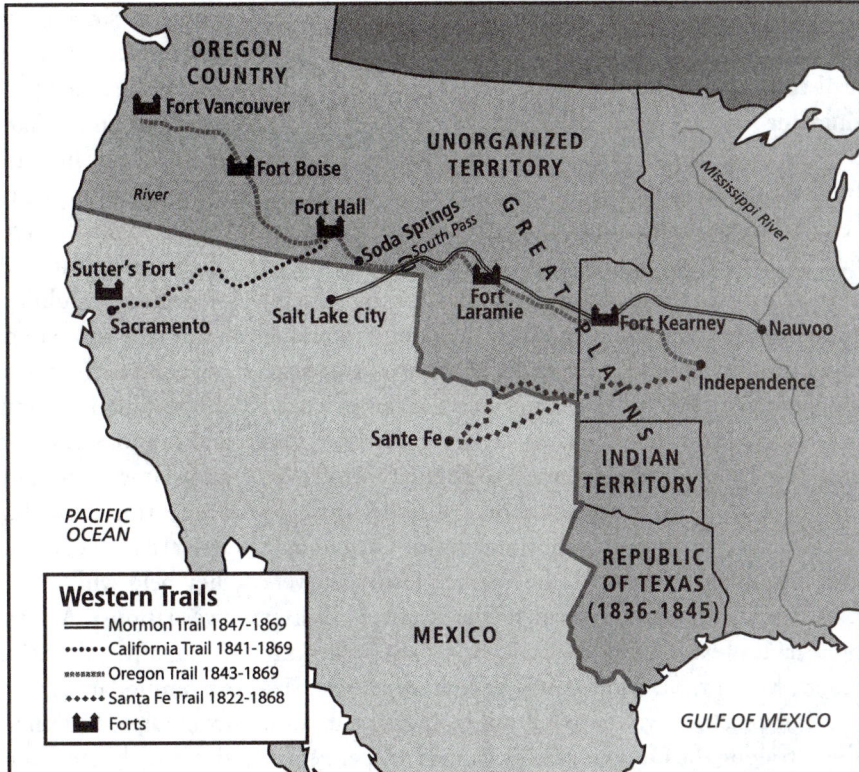

Map 14.1 Western Trails

especially attractive. An account written by two Oregon missionaries noted that the Willamette Valley, which became the primary area of American settlement in the region, was highly fertile and well suited for growing a wide range of crops. They even hinted that one farmer had managed to grow a crop of potatoes by accident, when some of the buds of his previous year's crop had fallen on the ground during harvest. Although such accounts were overblown, the more modest reports were attractive enough for prospective emigrants. "I came to this place with my wife and two children," read a letter by a new resident of Oregon that appeared in an 1843 congressional report. "We have settled ourselves, and have got plenty around us to eat and to wear, and our produce bears a good price." Pushed out of the United States by hard times and pulled by favorable reports from western lands, settlers went on the move. These migrants—with the notable exception of the Mormon journey to Utah—were by no means abandoning the United States. Moreover, within a few years they would be clamoring to be annexed by the country they had temporarily left behind.

Oregon

The Oregon Country, a territory that included the present-day states of Washington, Oregon, Idaho, and parts of Montana and the Canadian province of British Columbia, attracted only a handful of fur traders and missionaries before the 1840s, although the presence of those settlers introduced significant changes into the region. Both Great Britain and the United States claimed **Oregon** by right of discovery—the latter through the Lewis and Clark expedition of 1804-1806—but the two nations agreed in 1818 to a joint occupation for an indefinite period of time. Great Britain's presence centered on the Hudson Bay Company, which from its headquarters at Fort Vancouver (a location on the Columbia River relatively close to what would become Portland, Oregon) dominated the fur trade in western North America. The first Americans in the region likewise tended to be fur traders who had married into local Native American kinship networks and settled in the region as their careers wound down.

In the 1830s, Protestant missionaries from the United States (Marcus and Narcissa Whitman among them) moved into a region that had already experienced wrenching transformations. Native Americans in the region, such as the Cayuses, were already participating in a trade network that extended into the North American interior and along the coast of western North America when Lewis and Clark arrived in 1804. Trade with the interior brought horses; the coastal trade brought new European goods. Both brought epidemic diseases that would reduce the indigenous population from an estimated 180,000 to 40,000 over the course of the nineteenth century. The Hudson Bay Company's fur traders also introduced the region to (generally Catholic) Christianity, which Native Americans incorporated into their own belief structures. By 1840—on the eve of the first wave of expansion of

American settlers into the region—Oregon had become an area rife with tension among Native Americans stressed by diseases that neither traditional beliefs nor Christianity could adequately explain or remedy.

American migrants also made their way to Oregon. By 1840, only about 500 Americans had settled in the area, but more poured into the region over the next decade. Prospective migrants back east organized Oregon societies early in the decade and planned for the difficult trek across the continent. In 1843 alone, one thousand migrants hit the trail. By 1845, Oregon's American population reached 5,000—a number that far exceeded the some 750 British inhabitants in the region. Five years later, the 1850 Census reported a population of over 13,000. Compared to the thousands of settlers rushing into Texas at the same time, the numbers for Oregon may seem small, but journeys to the Pacific Northwest were exceedingly difficult compared to the relatively shorter sojourns to Texas, either overland or by sea. Oregon's settlers, by contrast, had to undertake an expensive, six-month trip across two thousand miles of rugged terrain. The trip along the **Oregon Trail** began in Independence, Missouri, continued across the Great Plains and through the Rocky Mountains before reaching their final destination. Settlers generally traveled in long caravans, which sometimes contained as many as one hundred covered wagons. Large groups provided safety during the arduous journey. The migrants had to bring everything they needed with them, often discovering that they had to abandon much of what they toted to lighten their loads. Life on the trail exposed travelers to all sorts of hazards. Attacks by Native Americans were always a possibility, but the settlers generally faced more mundane dangers. Animals and wagon wheels threatened to crush children. River crossings brought the danger of drowning. Moving through the mountains brought the danger of falling. Exposure to the elements remained a constant challenge. The trip was simply hard, especially for women, whose additional work on the trail stacked with the already daunting expectations for cooking, cleaning, and child rearing. Despite these obstacles, thousands of settlers successfully navigated the trail and established themselves in Oregon.

As their more numerous counterparts in Texas, settlers in Oregon expected that their new home would become part of the United States. Relations with Native Americans in the region deteriorated as they had elsewhere. Some of the Protestant missionaries who believed that they had arrived in the 1830s at the request of the indigenous population expressed frustration with their charges. Local natives rejected many of the ideas the missionaries promoted, such as the notion that people were born in

a state of sin and from birth had to be forgiven. They also refused to give up practices like polygamy. By the mid-1840s, they had also concluded that the missionaries were little more than the enablers of conquest. Missionaries did not help themselves in this regard. As settlers moved into the region, they turned their energies toward converting the newcomers and accepted the displacement of the local Native Americans. "When a people refuse or neglect to fulfill the designs of Providence," Marcus Whitman wrote to one of his relatives, "then they ought not complain at the results . . . they have in no case obeyed the command to multiply and replenish the earth [sic], and cannot stand in the way of others doing so." Settlers also clamored for annexation by the United States. Joint occupation created a very practical problem for the new arrivals: they could not establish a legal claim to the land they held while the area remained under the control of two nations. Although the director of the Hudson Bay Company, John McLoughlin, proved to be helpful and accommodating to the new settlers—despite his orders from Great Britain to discourage American settlement—the issue became increasingly urgent by the mid-1840s, and the U.S. government would respond by annexing a portion of the region.

California and New Mexico

Portions of the present-day American Southwest came into increasing contact with the United States in the decades before 1840. Prior to the 1820s, the Spanish government had regarded its colonial holdings in northern Mexico as little more than buffer zones protecting its valued possessions south of the Rio Grande from invasion by European competitors or from raids by Native American groups like the Comanche who mastered horseback riding and had developed into a significant military force on the southern Great Plains. Spain worked diligently to keep its territory closed to outsiders—even occasionally pursuing and apprehending American explorers. Spanish settlements in California, New Mexico, and Texas remained relatively isolated as a consequence. Mexican independence in 1821, however, reversed that trend, as the new government liberalized its laws, opening its northern territories to trade and, in some cases, settlement. In California, Mexico secularized (transferred from church to government control) the mission system that had extracted labor from 30,000 Native American converts, a change that mainly resulted in a shifting of the primary claim to Indian labor from the missionaries to the ranchers who sold cattle to New England merchants and businessmen in San Diego and San Francisco. American traders also worked their way into New Mexico along the

Santa Fe Trail, a route whose harsh environment coupled with hostile Native Americans, such as the Comanche, proved to be quite dangerous yet highly profitable for the caravans making the trek.

Texas

Although California and New Mexico received the attention of American merchants, Texas attracted settlers whose migration fundamentally transformed the relationship between Mexico and the United States, contributing decisively to the latter's aggressive expansion in the 1840s. Under Spanish rule, Texas had been a sparsely-settled area, primarily serving as a buffer zone against Comanche raiders and foreign interlopers. The Republic of Mexico organized the region as part of the state of Coahuila y Tejas, permitting entry to settlers under an 1824 immigration law. Even before that point, however, settlers from the United States were taking up residence in Texas. **Stephen F. Austin**, who had inherited a substantial land grant from his father, negotiated with the Spanish and then Mexican governments to secure permission to settle three hundred families along the Brazos River. Austin was the first of twenty-four *empresarios*—those persons authorized by the Republic of Mexico to recruit and accept responsibility for settlers in exchange for extensive land grants in Texas. Mexico offered favorable terms to immigrants. Farmers could claim just over 4400 acres (more if they claimed to be ranchers), although they were expected to become Mexican citizens and convert to Roman Catholicism (the state religion).

Along with some Mexicans and Europeans, Americans and their slaves (legally classified as indentured servants to comply with Mexican law banning slavery) flooded into the province. By 1830, over twenty thousand people had settled in eastern Texas. With another ten thousand arriving by 1835, the immigrant population far exceeded the Mexican population in the region. Meanwhile, newcomers often showed little interest in adopting the practices of their hosts. Despite the requirement that they do so, few immigrants truly converted to Roman Catholicism. Meanwhile, Texas's population of 5,000 African-American slaves by 1835 had moved the cotton frontier into the Mexican Republic, and the area seemed in many respects an extension of the southern United States rather than a part of Mexico.

These developments concerned Mexican officials. In 1828, General Manuel de Mier y Terán undertook an extensive inspection tour. He acknowledged that American settlers were industrious and were rapidly developing the area, but he also noted that a large number of settlers paid no heed to Mexican law (which he admitted had not

been rigorously enforced). "Official documents that I have obtained," Terán wrote to Mexico's President, Guadalupe Victoria, "prove that more than two thousand foreigners are living on the best lands on the border. None of them has requested permission." "If it is bad for a nation to have vacant lands and wilderness," he wrote in another part of the letter, "it is worse without a doubt to have settlers who cannot abide by some of its laws. . . . They soon become discontented and thus prone to rebellion." Terán's statement proved prescient. In 1830, the Mexican government responded to his report by instituting a prohibition on American immigration and renewing its laws against slavery. Settlers still came by the thousands, and tensions mounted between the newcomers and their Mexican hosts. Relations between the settlers and the Mexican government reached a breaking point when **General Antonio López de Santa Anna** seized power. In 1834, Santa Anna named himself dictator of Mexico, replaced a federal constitutional system that had allowed significant autonomy to states like Coahuila y Tejas with a centralized governance, and began crushing his opposition in many rebellious regions of Mexico with brutal military force.

Anglo settlers in Texas, along with a number of *Tejanos* (Mexican Texans) showed their willingness to resist by first refusing to pay customs duties, then by skirmishing with Mexican troops, and finally by declaring independence on March 2, 1836. By this time, Santa Anna had arrived in Texas to suppress the rebellion personally. His force of several thousand troops laid siege to the Alamo (Mission San Antonio de Valero) in San Antonio where 187 rebels resisted for two weeks until they were wiped out in a final assault. Near Goliad, Mexican troops captured and then executed another 350 rebels under orders from Santa Anna. **Sam Houston**, a protégé of Andrew Jackson chosen to command the regular Texas rebel army, turned around the bleak string of defeats and retreats at the Battle of San Jacinto, an engagement in which Houston took advantage of Santa Anna's decision to split his forces and managed to capture the Mexican leader. To gain his release, Santa Anna signed agreements acknowledging Texas independence, with the entire Rio Grande serving as the national border. After removing Santa Anna from power upon his return to Mexico City, a new group of Mexican government officials rejected these audacious claims. Since the Spanish period, the border of Texas had always been viewed as the Nueces River, which meets the Gulf of Mexico at Corpus Christi. The Republic of Texas's claim, however, extended the border about 300 miles further south and encompassed a large slice of New Mexico including the important trading town of Santa Fe. Regardless of border considerations, the Mexican government refused to recognize Texas independence in

The Alamo.
San Antonio, Texas

the first place, though financial constraints and the need to suppress other revolts closer to the capital precluded mounting another major military expedition into Texas.

After its successful revolt against Mexico, Texas experienced a new flood of immigration. Between 1836 and its annexation by the United States in 1845, over 100,000 settlers arrived in the **Republic of Texas** (mostly from the United States). Some of these immigrants were surely drawn by reports of good farmland in the region. "What can the husbandman desire more," asked an English observer. Texas had plentiful wood, water, and land well suited for both farming and livestock. "Nature has lavished her [Texas's] bounties with the munificence of an indulgent parent; it only remains for man to show himself worthy of her favors by the due application of his energies, mental and corporal, and the temperate use of the means of enjoyment placed it his disposal." The government of the new republic, however, made Texas appealing by offering land on favorable terms. Heads of households could receive a grant of 1,280 acres of land, and the relative proximity of Texas to the United States rendered this offer even more enticing.

Despite the influx of new settlers, the Texas Republic faced a host of challenges. Mexico refused to recognize its independence generally and its claim to a border at the Rio Grande specifically. In 1842, Santa Anna (now back in power) launched two raids into Texas to probe the Republic's defenses, twice capturing San Antonio before withdrawing. Ongoing hostilities with Mexico contributed to a growing distrust of the *Tejano* population. Although some prosperous families managed to intermarry with Anglos and thereby retain their status in the region, others lost their land holdings and other economic resources either by intimidation or fraud. Rela-

tions with Native Americans, especially the Comanche, remained tense. The republic's first president, Sam Houston, sought to establish peaceful relations by marking a border between his constituents and the Comanche. His successor, Mirabeau B. Lamar, however, rejected that approach and sent troops deep into Comanche territory, an act that led to a war that lasted from 1838 to 1841. Just as Texas's leaders were divided over how best to deal with the Comanche, they split over the prospect of annexation by the United States. Houston's faction supported the idea; Lamar's faction favored continued independence and expansion westward into California. Texas voters strongly favored annexation, but concerns within the United States about the prospects of war with Mexico and especially the sectional dispute caused by the slavery expansion issue delayed annexation until 1845.

The Mormon Exodus

Although most migrants to Texas and Oregon hoped that their new homes would eventually be annexed by the United States, **Mormons** took to the trails in the hope of leaving the nation permanently. Since their emergence in upstate New York in the 1820s, adherents to the Church of Jesus Christ of Latter-day Saints had experienced resentment and harassment from their non-Mormon neighbors. Mormon communities under the leadership of the church's founder and prophet, Joseph Smith, Jr., had emerged in Ohio and Missouri, but many values of the Latter-day Saints ran counter to those of their neighbors. Under the stewardship of patriarchal church leaders, Mormon settlements practiced economic cooperation, which allowed them to undercut the prices of nearby farmers. On election days, Mormons voted in a bloc for candidates favored by church leaders. Most controversially, Smith's religious teachings, including polygamy (publicly condemned by early Mormons, but privately practiced as many suspected), were unacceptable to most Americans. When coupled with the economic and political power of their tight-knit communities, Mormon religious and cultural practices bred deep resentment among non-Mormons. The resulting conflicts ultimately drove them to western Illinois where they established a new settlement at Nauvoo along the Mississippi River. The city quickly boasted over ten thousand inhabitants and featured an impressive temple. Nauvoo's time as one of the fastest growing towns in the nation proved to be short-lived. Tensions over Smith's autocratic leadership emerged within the Latter-day Saint community, while recurring friction with non-Mormons produced a series of crises that culminated with Smith's murder in 1844 by a violent mob.

Mormon leaders concluded that they needed to leave the United States, ultimately selecting Utah's Great Basin region, a remote area in Mexican territory that had been essentially ignored. The region's remoteness made it especially attractive to Mormon leaders who sought to build their own society free from the interference of hostile neighbors. In 1847, the Mormons' new leader, **Brigham Young**, led a group of more than 2,000 settlers along what became known as the Mormon Trail, which branched off the Oregon Trail and terminated between the shores of the Great Salt Lake and the foothills of the Wasatch Mountains. Thousands of additional Mormons arrived each year thereafter. Under church direction, settlers divided land and water rights while building a community centered on their religious values, which by this time included the open practice of polygamy. Though the goal of the Mormon migration was to leave the United States, the nation they fled annexed their territory in 1848 along with the rest of northern Mexico after the Mexican American War.

The surge of settlers pouring out of the United States transformed the balance of political and diplomatic power in the region. Native Americans who had managed to accommodate small numbers of settlers found themselves pushed off the land. Great Britain and Mexico found that the growing number of migrants, combined with the certainty that more would surely come, rendered their claims to territory in western North America more tenuous with each passing year. Outside of Utah, the demands of settlers to be annexed by the United States would be embraced by a number of politicians, particularly within the Democratic Party. Their responses would transform American politics and ultimately lead to war with Mexico.

Joseph Smith's original temple, Nauvoo, IL.

MANIFEST DESTINY AND THE POLITICS OF EXPANSION

During the 1840s, territorial expansion became the central issue of American politics. The movement of settlers into Texas and Oregon created a new set of pressures that turned politicians' and voters' attention away from the disputes over banking, tariff rates, and funding infrastructure projects that had dominated party politics in the previous decade. Though these issues certainly did not disappear from the political landscape, they just became relatively less pressing concerns. By the middle of the decade, the parties divided primarily over the speed and scope of American expansion. Democrats favored a rapid expansion, calling at times for the annexation of substantial portions of Canada and Mexico—some of them even advocated expansion throughout the entire hemisphere. Whigs, who themselves accepted the inevitability of American expansion, favored a more cautious approach that they hoped would avoid conflict with other nations and reduce the prospect for political instability at home. The Whigs lost this struggle. In 1844, the Democrats regained the presidency and endorsed a series of aggressively expansionist policies that ultimately led the United States into a war with Mexico.

Horace Greeley and the American Bison

One of the more interesting experiences that mid-nineteenth-century settlers encountered as they traveled from the eastern United States to Oregon, Utah, and California involved their initial contact with the astonishingly large number of American Bison (buffalo) that lived on the Great Plains. These prolific, robust animals which fed on the abundant grasses found in the area sustained the hunting culture of many Native American groups, including the Sioux, Comanche, and Apache. In these excerpts from a travel memoir, Horace Greeley, editor of the **New York Tribune,** described his experience with the buffalo as he traveled from New York to San Francisco. As you read, pay particular attention to how he viewed these creatures, and ask yourself whether his attitude—assuming that it was widely shared—might explain why the American Bison became nearly extinct by 1900:

I would rather not bore the public with the buffalo. I fully realize that the subject is not novel. . . . Yet I insist on writing this . . . promising then to drop the subject. . . . All day yesterday, they darkened the earth around us, often seeming to be drawn up like an army in battle array on the ridges and adown there slopes a mile or so south of us—often on the north as well. . . .

They are moving northward, and are still mainly south of our track. Whenever alarmed, they set off on their awkward but effective canter to the great herds still south. . . . This necessarily sends those north of us across our roads often but a few rods in front of us, even when they had started a mile away. . . . Of course, they sometimes stop and tack, or, seeing us, sheer off and cross further ahead, or split into two lines; but the general impulse, when alarmed, is to follow blindly and at full speed, seeming not to inquire or consider from what quarter the danger is to be apprehended.

What strikes the stranger with the most amazement is their immense numbers. I know one million is a great many, but I am confident we saw that number yesterday. Certainly, all we saw could not have stood on ten square miles of ground. Often, the country for miles on either hand seemed quite black with them. . . . Consider that we have traversed more than one hundred miles in width since we first struck them, and that for most of this distance the buffalo have been constantly in sight, and that they continue for some twenty-five miles further on—this being the breadth of their present range, which has a length of perhaps a thousand miles. . . . I doubt whether the domesticated horned cattle of the United States equal the numbers. . . .

. . . [A] party of our drivers . . . went back seven miles on mules last evening, to help get our rear wagon out of a gully into which it had mired and stuck fast. . . .[T]hey found the road absolutely dangerous from the crowds of buffalo feeding on either side, and running across it. . . they were often in great danger of being run over and run down by the headlong brutes. They were obliged to stand still for minutes, and fire their revolvers right and left, to save their lives and their mules.

The superintendent of this division, Mr. Fuller, had a narrow escape day before yesterday. He was riding his mule on our road . . . when a herd of buffalo north of the road were stampeded by an emigrant train. . . . A slight ridge hid them from Mr. F's sight to till the leader came full tilt against his mule, knocking him down, and going over him at full speed. Mr. F of course fell with the dying mule, and I presume lay very snug by his side while the buffaloes made a clear sweep over the concern—he firing his revolver rapidly, and thus inducing many of the herd to shear off on one side or the other. He rose stunned and bruised, but still able to make his way. . . .

Two nights ago, an immense herd came down upon a party . . . camped just across the creek from [Greeley's location], and, (it being dark) were with difficulty prevented from trampling down tents, cattle, and people. Some fifty shots were fired into them before they could be turned. And now our stationmaster has just taken his gun to scare them off so as to save our mules from the stampede.

Source: Horace Greeley, *An Overland Journey from New York to San Francisco in the Summer of 1859* (New York, 1860), 86-90.

Part of the Democratic Party's political strength rested on the ability of its partisans to articulate the expansionist impulse emerging in the early 1840s. Foremost among Democratic ideologues was **John O'Sullivan**, editor of the *Democratic Review*. "[O]ur country," he wrote in 1839, "is destined to be the great nation of futurity." By that awkward phrase, he meant that the United States had broken decisively with the past. The American population came from a multitude of European nations, and it had no legacy of aristocracy and no history of bloody conflicts with other countries. O'Sullivan insisted that in the United States the past was unimportant; all that mattered was its boundless future. Freed from the historical baggage carried by other nations, Americans enjoyed the opportunity to build a country on the principle of political equality. That principle represented more than simply a formal foundation of government. Equality was a universal value—"a self-evident dictate of morality"—and the United States held an obligation to share it with the rest of the world. For O'Sullivan, fulfilling that obligation entailed expansion. "[W]ho will, what can, set limits on our outward march," he asked. "Providence is with us." All of this led to a sweeping conclusion:

> [T]he boundless future will be the era of American greatness. . . . [T]he nation of many nations is destined to manifest to mankind the excellence of divine principles; to establish on earth the noblest temple ever dedicated to the worship of the Most High. . . . Its floor shall be a hemisphere. . . , and its congregation an Union of many Republics, comprising hundreds of happy millions. . . governed by God's natural and moral law of equality, the law of brotherhood of peace and good will amongst men.

In his later writings, O'Sullivan would coin the phrase **"manifest destiny"** to convey his sense of a God-given American right to expand throughout the Western Hemisphere and to carry political institutions and moral values to the rest of the world.

Very little written by O'Sullivan, however, proved to be new. Americans already believed strongly that the founding of the United States represented a major break with the past. Thomas Paine had made that point on the eve of independence. The conflict with Britain, he wrote, "[t]is not the concern of a day, a year, or an age; posterity are virtually involved in the contest, and will be more or less affected even to the end of time." O'Sullivan's words in some ways echoed those of Thomas Jefferson's First Inaugural Address (1801), which noted that Americans possessed "a chosen country, with room enough for our descendants to the thousandth and thousandth generation." And Jefferson's own vision of the United States as an expanding "empire of liberty" was hardly unique to him. The idea of mission stretched deep back into the American past. John Winthrop, the first governor of Massachusetts, hoped that his colony would become a "city upon a hill" as an example for others to emulate. Winthrop, of course, did not share the relatively more secular, expansionist vision articulated by O'Sullivan, but the latter built on the theme pronounced on the *Arbella* more than two hundred years before.

What O'Sullivan and his fellow writers added to this sense of mission and expansion was a sense of ethnic and racial destiny. Speaking of the possibility that California may be annexed, O'Sullivan made the point bluntly: "The Anglo-Saxon foot is already on its borders. Already the advance guard of Anglo-Saxon immigration has begun to pour down upon it, armed with the plough and the rifle, and marking its trail with schools, colleges, courts and representative halls, mills and meeting houses." In a later essay, he cautioned against annexing all of Mexico, believing its population to be ill suited for republican government. "Are there probably as many men in the whole Mexican Republic competent to exercise the elective franchise with the intelligence of the average American citizen as there were righteous men in Sodom when she was destroyed?" O'Sullivan asked, referring to the story from Genesis in which God promised not to destroy Sodom if it contained ten righteous persons (it did not). "If so, the number of the righteous in that fated city must have been exaggerated. Beyond a question, the entire Mexican vote would be substantially below our national average both in purity and intelligence." Incorporating Mexicans into the Union, he asserted, would require a much stronger government than that which Americans were accustomed, and establishing that would undermine American values. His discussion in some ways echoed the sentiments of Narcissa Whitman who saw herself as coming "to elevate" the Indians in a way that would not require her "to sink to their standard."

Even if not entirely new concepts, and despite their being chauvinistic by modern standards, these ideas struck upon a powerful chord in American politics. As Americans poured into Texas and Oregon, settlers in these regions and politicians back home clamored for annexation. The process, however, would play out in a way more convoluted and far more violent than O'Sullivan envisioned.

The Tyler Presidency

Despite the calls of ideologues like John O'Sullivan, expansion as a political issue developed quietly in the early

1840s, catching a number of political leaders by surprise when it finally burst upon the scene toward the middle of the decade. National politics in the early 1840s revolved around many of the same issues that had dominated the previous decade, especially banking. Taking advantage of the national economic depression, Whig nominee William Henry Harrison and his party finally won the presidency and control of Congress in 1840 with a solid victory over Martin Van Buren and the Democrats. In an effort to counter the charges of critics that he was too old to serve, the 68-year-old Harrison delivered a two-hour-long inaugural address on a frigid morning without a hat or overcoat. Perhaps weakened by the speech and definitely worn down by the constant demands of office seekers at the beginning of his presidency, Harrison contracted a severe cold that developed into pneumonia. He died within a month of taking office, introducing a number of complications into domestic politics. Harrison's successor, **John Tyler,** quickly came into conflict with Henry Clay and other Whig leaders in Congress. A Virginian with a political career as a state legislator, governor, and congressman before election to the U.S. Senate, Tyler had been a supporter of Andrew Jackson before breaking with Old Hickory over the nullification crisis. In the 1830s, he joined a faction of southern Whigs who rejected what they perceived as the president's hostility to states' rights. Party leaders selected Tyler as the vice presidential nominee in 1840 to balance the ticket geographically (though born in Virginia, Harrison had long resided in the Old Northwest and thus was considered a Northerner by the general public). No one expected Tyler to become president. The new chief executive soon showed that he did not share the priorities of other Whig leaders. Henry Clay, believing that Tyler would either follow his lead or could be forced into doing so, led a repeal of the Independent Treasury Act—a law passed in 1840 with the support of the Van Buren administration to manage the national money supply in the wake of the destruction of the Second Bank of the United States—and shepherded a new national bank bill through Congress. Tyler vetoed it. In response, all but one member of his cabinet resigned. A stalemate between the Whig-dominated Congress and the president over economic policies such as banking and tariffs consumed the remainder of Tyler's presidency.

In foreign policy, Tyler proved more successful. Secretary of State Daniel Webster, the only member of Harrison's original cabinet not to join the 1841 mass resignation, completed negotiations on the **Webster-Ashburton Treaty** in 1842. Uncertainty over the border between the U.S. and Canada had generated a number of conflicts in the late 1830s, including the burning of a U.S. steamship by Canadians, a retaliatory arrest of a Canadian in New

John Tyler

York, and a related refusal by British officials not to return a group of American slaves who had mutinied on board a New Orleans-bound ship that sailed to the Bahamas. The resulting treaty settled the border between the United States and Canada in eastern North America (from Maine to what is now the state of Minnesota), provided for the extradition of the jailed Canadian, and secured American cooperation in suppressing the African slave trade. With his work finished, Webster resigned in 1843.

Tyler also pushed for the admission of Texas, although without much initial success. A substantial number of Texans, most notably Sam Houston, had favored annexation since the Lone Star Republic's declaration of independence in 1836. President Andrew Jackson, who extended diplomatic recognition to the fledgling nation, opposed annexation on the grounds that doing so would likely lead to war with Mexico. With the certainty that Texas would enter the Union as a slave state ensuring that annexation would be a politically sensitive issue that threatened to intensify sectional divisions, neither party exhibited much interest in the annexation issue. Looking for a way to revive his political fortunes and exploiting rumors that Great Britain planned to use its influence and financial support to entice Texas to end slavery and thus block the institution's expansion, Tyler entered into secret negotiations with the Lone Star Republic. John C. Calhoun, Tyler's newest Secretary of State and one of the South's most outspoken defenders, completed negotiations on an annexation treaty in 1843. He then promptly poisoned the issue with a public letter to a British official extolling the virtues of slavery, stating that protecting the institution required that the United States incorporate Texas. Calhoun's outspokenness alienated Northerners in both parties, and a Whig-dominated Senate happily rejected the treaty.

Daniel
Webster

James K.
Polk

The Election of 1844

Despite the defeat of his Texas annexation efforts, Tyler displayed a keen sense of the direction of American politics. The 1844 presidential election would soon demonstrate that expansion had become the dominant issue. Henry Clay received the Whig Party nomination, running on a platform that did not mention expansion, focusing instead on the party's signature issues: support for a new bank, a protective tariff, and the belief that the chief executive should defer to the will of Congress. Tyler thought his push for Texas annexation would provide him with enough support to build a third party, but his hopes did not materialize. Democrats ultimately embraced the issue, but they found a relatively unknown candidate from within their own ranks to run for office. Former President Martin Van Buren had expected to secure the party's nomination and return to the office he had lost in 1840, but, like Tyler, his hopes were dashed. Van Buren had strongly opposed Texas annexation, especially after the issue had become linked with the expansion of slavery. Southern Democrats supported continuation of a convention rule requiring that the party's nominee receive the support of two-thirds of the delegates. Van Buren could not generate enough support, and the nomination eventually went to **James K. Polk** of Tennessee.

A former Speaker of the House and governor of Tennessee, Polk unified the Democratic Party around the expansion issue by calling for the annexation of more territory than just Texas. In addition to standard objections to protective tariffs and national banks, the party's platform called for the annexation of Texas and exclusive occupation of the entire Oregon Territory. Polk's linking of Texas and Oregon removed expansion from the realm of sectional politics (for a brief while) and provided the Democrats with a winning political strategy. Expansion's

resonance with voters caught the Whigs off guard and even forced Clay to switch positions on Texas annexation, stating that he could support the incorporation of Texas if the act could be accomplished without war. The election results were very close, with Polk edging Clay by less than 40,000 votes while carrying 15 of 26 states. Historians still debate the factors that produced the narrow margin of victory, but most point to Clay's changing position on Texas annexation which alienated some key voters, especially anti-slavery abolitionists who bolted to support James Birney, the nominee of the **Liberty Party**—a third party that grew out of abolitionist church congregations primarily in New York and New England. In western New York, Birney siphoned enough abolitionist support from Clay to allow Polk narrowly to win a plurality and thus all of New York's electoral votes. This result became the difference in the national election, which had far-reaching implications as Polk would soon lead the country into a morally questionable war with Mexico, triggering a series of political crises that a dozen years later culminated in the outbreak of the American Civil War.

The Annexation of Oregon and Texas

Pledging to serve only one term as president, James Polk carried out his agenda with single-minded tenacity. By the time he left office, he had secured the exclusive occupation of a substantial portion of the Oregon Territory, completed the annexation of Texas, and taken possession of one-third of Mexico through military conquest. Soon after taking office, the new president moved quickly to secure Oregon. In his 1845 Inaugural Address, Polk asserted that the United States' claim to Oregon "is 'clear and unquestionable,'" and he noted that American settlers were "preparing to perfect that title by occupying it with their wives and children." Polk thereby gave public support to an issue that had become dear to expansion-minded northern Democrats who had rallied around the slogan **"54-40 or Fight!"**, insisting that Great Britain must cede all of Oregon (which meant giving up the entire west coast of Canada) or go to war. Polk never intended to pursue matters that far. In late 1845, he asked Congress to terminate the joint-occupation agreement while notifying Great Britain that he would be willing to seek a compromise. The British government, which had already concluded that Oregon would be difficult to hold should the situation escalate, agreed to open negotiations. Discussions proceeded quickly. By mid-1846, the Senate voted by a large margin to ratify a treaty setting the border between the United States and Canada at the 49th parallel. Polk's willingness to negotiate—especially when compared to the lengths he would go to secure Texas—left some northern Democrats disappointed, accusing him of duplicity.

The process of annexing Texas began before Polk took office. Outgoing President Tyler read the 1844 election results as an endorsement of his policy and bypassed a two-thirds vote in the Senate by asking both houses of Congress for a joint resolution accepting annexation. Congress complied a few days before Polk delivered his inaugural address, which portrayed annexation as a peaceful process that involved only Texas and the United States. American expansion, he stated, would simply "extend the dominions of peace over additional territories and increasing millions." Other nations, he continued, should view annexation "not as the conquest of a nation seeking to extend her dominions by arms and violence, but as the peaceful acquisition of a territory . . . with the consent of that member, thereby diminishing the chances of war and opening to them new and ever-increasing markets for their products." Polk's statement echoed the sentiments of writers like O'Sullivan who insisted that the United States represented a break from a past marred by bloody wars of conquest.

Not surprisingly, Mexico's government rejected this assessment of American intentions, believing peaceful expansion felt like aggression. Although deeply divided, Mexican leaders proved determined to resist, so Polk let the conflict escalate. A few weeks after his inauguration, Mexico broke off diplomatic relations. The Mexican ambassador issued a public denunciation of annexation before returning home. A month later, Mexico's president, José Joaquín de Herrera, announced that a state of war existed. Texas's annexation continued despite the increasing tensions. In July 1845, Texas voters overwhelmingly voted to join the United States, and Polk ordered General **Zachary Taylor** and his troops to Corpus Christi to de-

fend American claims. The president also moved a naval squadron to the Gulf of Mexico and sent a diplomat, John Slidell, to Mexico City on the pretext of a peaceful settlement. Slidell's offer from Polk only raised tensions further because it asked Mexico to give up even more territory. Polk offered to give Mexico $25 million in exchange for Texas as well as Mexico's territorial holdings in New Mexico and California. The land for which Polk asked amounted to approximately one-third of Mexico's territory and included what would become the future states of Texas, California, Utah, and Nevada along with parts of the present-day states of New Mexico, Arizona, Colorado, and Wyoming. Mexico's leaders considered the deal flatly unacceptable. Beleaguered by press rumors that he intended to sell out the country and cede territory, President Herrera refused to meet with Slidell. By January 1846, one of Herrera's generals, Mariano Paredes, had driven Herrera from office and taken the presidency. Paredes would be the first of four presidents to take power in 1846, a sign of volatile political instability among Mexico's leadership.

Despite the internal divisions, Mexico's leaders agreed that ceding territory was unacceptable, though Polk continued to press the issue. In March 1846, General Taylor, on orders from Polk, marched his troops to the northern bank of the Rio Grande close to three hundred miles into land claimed by Mexico. A tense standoff between Mexican and United States forces then ensued, ending when Mexican cavalry, responding to American efforts to block access to the Rio Grande, crossed the river in late April and engaged American dragoons under the command of Captain Seth Thornton, killing 16 and capturing 49. War with Mexico had begun. Word of the incident, known thereafter as the **Thornton Affair**, soon reached Washington. Within a few days, Polk secured a declaration of war from Congress. Although he informed Congress that Mexico's decision to attack American troops on American soil forced his hand, the president had already received word from Slidell that Mexico would not give up any territory without a fight, leading him to prepare his war message.

Congress greeted Polk's assertion that a state of war now existed between the United States and Mexico with enthusiasm, and the body promptly passed a bill authorizing the president to call for as many as 50,000 volunteers to carry out the war effort. Despite the large margins of the votes (173 to 14 in the House and 40 to 2 in the Senate), questions about the legitimacy of Polk's actions remained. A number of Whigs wondered whether the president's aggression forced Mexico into a position in which its leaders would feel compelled to go to war. That concern raised the issue of whether the president could use his authority as commander-in-chief to take Congress' power to declare war by maneuvering troops in a manner that made armed conflict all but certain. Democrats proved willing to gloss over this issue. One Representative summed up the position well: "a state of war exists. . . . I hold it to be no part of my duty to inquire how this war originated. . . . It is enough for me . . . to know that it exists. . . to arrive at the conclusion. . . that our only course is to conquer peace by a vigorous prosecution of the war just commenced." Whigs proved more conflicted. All but 14 of 78 Whigs voted for the war declaration because they did not want to follow the example of the Federalists whose opposition to the War of 1812 had left them open to charges of disloyalty. But Whig congressmen frequently qualified support that continually questioned the wisdom and propriety of the conflict. A Kentucky Whig who reluctantly voted to declare war expressed the point well during the course of the debate, protesting against "the unfounded statement that Mexico began this war." He then recounted the events leading up to the Thornton Affair and concluded that "our own President. . . began this war. He has been carrying it on for months. . . ." The ensuing conflict, which grew directly out of the politics of Manifest Destiny, would last for another two years and soon thereafter begin to fundamentally transform the United States.

THE MEXICAN AMERICAN WAR

Although overshadowed by the American Civil War occurring a dozen years later, the Mexican American War remains a highly significant event as the first major conflict fought by the United States on foreign soil, and the first war—thanks to the invention of the telegraph and developments in printing technology—to become the subject of regular, daily reporting. News of the latest developments allowed American readers to experience the war in new ways and fueled continuing debates about the legitimacy of the conflict and the wisdom of its management. Numerous military officers, including Robert E. Lee and Ulysses S. Grant who later opposed each other as commanding generals during the Civil War, received their first combat experience fighting against Mexico. The war also radically redrew the border between the United States and Mexico, but the peace settlement ultimately reached in 1848 represented only one of a number of possible outcomes shaped by domestic political considerations as well as with social and political developments inside of Mexico.

The war's initial phases proceeded swiftly. By February 1847, less than a year after the conflict began, the United States had taken effective control of the territory that Polk had offered to purchase from Mexico. New Mexico and California fell quickly. General **Stephen W. Kearny**, upon receiving orders to invade northwestern Mexico, marched the troops under his command from Missouri to Santa Fe. When his force arrived in August 1846, Mexican soldiers retreated, allowing Kearny to take control of the city unopposed. The general then split his forces into three groups. One force remained to occupy New Mexico. Another marched southward with orders to take El Paso before joining up with other American units. The final, and smallest group, rode with Kearny to California. After a grueling trek lasting from September 1846 to December 1846, requiring travel through the harsh Mojave Desert, Kearny arrived in California with one hundred worn-out troops just in time to participate in the final stages of military operations there.

Events in California had moved rapidly in the months before Kearny arrived. In June 1846, a small group of American settlers, upon hearing about the declaration of war, staged the **Bear Flag Revolt** by capturing a small Mexican garrison in Sonoma and declaring California a republic. A few days later, a small force of American troops under the command of Captain John C. Frémont arrived to claim California for the United States. When American naval forces under the command of Commodore Robert F. Stockton learned of the revolt, they began operations against Monterey, the capital of California. By August 1846, the United States had taken control of northern California. Capturing southern California proved a bit more difficult. In Los Angeles, *Californios* (people of Mexican descent born in California) organized and, for a while, managed to push back the advancing American forces. Nevertheless, Kearny's beleaguered troops arrived just in time to assist in the capture of Los Angeles. By January 1847, the United States had gained control of California.

In contrast to commanders in New Mexico and California, General Zachary Taylor faced significant resistance as he pushed his troops deeper into Mexico. In May 1846, Taylor moved his forces to break the Mexican army's siege of Fort Texas at what is now Brownsville. A larger contingent of the Mexican Army of the North, under the command of Mariano Arista, intercepted him. The two sides engaged on May 8, 1846 at the Battle of Palo Alto. Taylor's troops' use of highly mobile artillery units outmaneuvered Arista's forces, which withdrew to a more defensible location and received reinforcements. On the next day, the two sides engaged again at the Battle of Resaca de la Palma, which largely involved hand-to-hand fighting. The battle ended in a rout when U.S. cavalry troops captured the Mexicans' artillery. Taylor followed up these victories by crossing the Rio Grande and invading Mexico. Command of the Mexican military was again

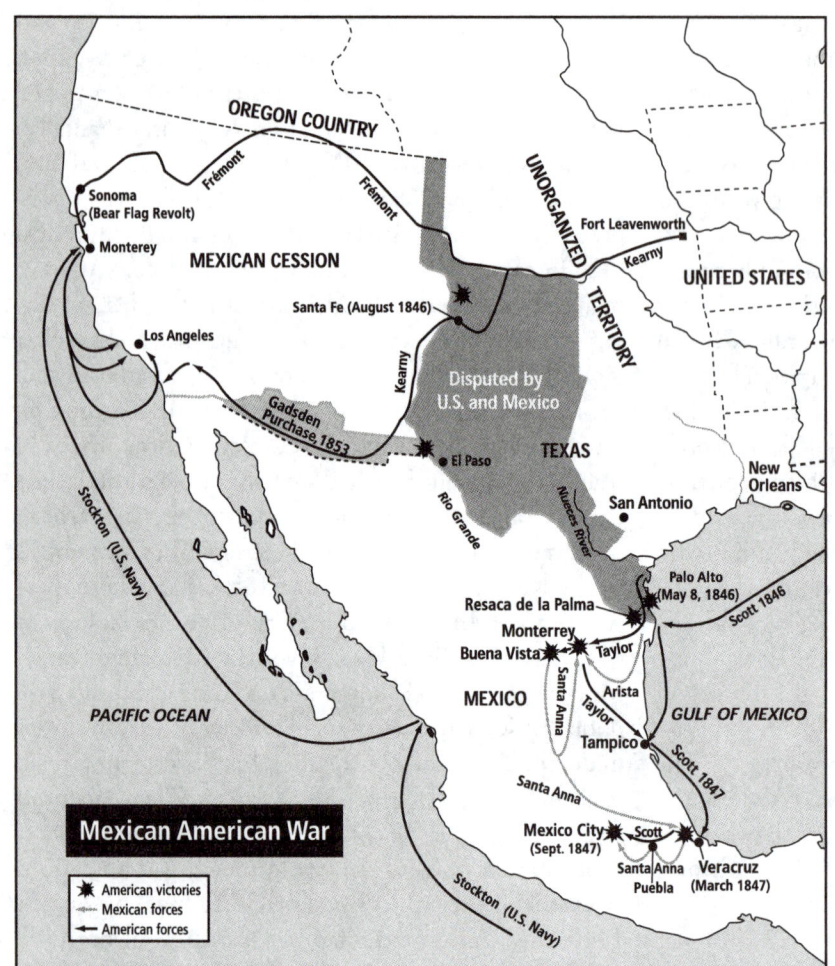

Map 14.2 Mexican American War

under the control of General Antonio López de Santa Anna, who had been in exile but had returned promising to reverse Mexican losses and claiming (insincerely) that he had no interest in retaking the presidency.

Santa Anna ordered the Mexican Army of the North, now led by General Pedro de Ampudia, to retreat to Saltillo where it would become part of a line of forces defending the nation's interior. Eager for a victory and commanding troops tired of retreating, Ampudia opted instead to hold the fortified city of Monterrey, located fifty miles northeast of Saltillo. On September 21, 1846, Taylor attacked the city with a force of 6,000 troops who lacked experience in urban warfare. The 9,000 Mexican defenders inflicted heavy casualties as Taylor's forces attempted to move through the city on streets exposed to fire from all directions. By the third day of the Battle of Monterrey, however, American troops learned to move from building to building by cutting through walls. These tactics forced Ampudia to seek a cease-fire, leading to an eight-week truce followed by the evacuation of Mexican troops. Neither Polk nor Santa Anna was happy by this turn of events. Polk ordered Taylor to break the truce, and the general complied by capturing Saltillo. Santa Anna relieved Ampudia of his command and marched

with 20,000 troops (many of whom deserted along the way) northward from central Mexico. On February 22, Santa Anna's assembled force of 15,000 men attacked Taylor's 4,700 troops who had entrenched themselves in a mountain pass. During the resulting two-day Battle of Buena Vista, Taylor's forces were almost routed. Both sides suffered heavy casualties. The battle might have continued beyond February 23, but Santa Anna received word of political instability in Mexico City, leading him to withdraw his forces so he could reclaim the presidency. Taylor's victory left the United States in control of northern Mexico and established the general as a national hero.

Meanwhile, the war continued. Despite the occupation of New Mexico, California, Monterrey and Saltillo, Mexico's leaders remained determined to resist the invasion, although they remained divided among themselves. Mexico's presidency changed hands nine times during the course of the war, which rendered negotiations even more difficult. Mexican leaders also had to contend with popular uprisings as well as U.S. forces invading central Mexico, threatening the capital, Mexico City. In March 1847, General **Winfield Scott** landed 12,000 troops and supplies near Veracruz, Mexico's primary port, safely outside the range of the city's defenses without suffering any casualties, completing the first major amphibious landing in U.S. military history. With the assistance of fire from naval vessels, the general laid siege to the city, which surrendered twelve days later.

Leaving behind garrison troops and many incapacitated by a yellow fever outbreak, General Scott advanced on Mexico City with 8,500 men. His forces outmaneuvered and routed Santa Anna's army to capture Puebla, the country's second largest city, on May 1, 1847. The general's experience with Puebla underscored the complexity of the central Mexico invasion. Hostility to Santa Anna within the city led its leaders to surrender without any opposition, and Scott wanted to ensure that his troops' actions did not turn that hostility against them. The general remained careful throughout his entire campaign not to alienate the local populace. "The people," he ordered, "must be conciliated, soothed, or well treated by every officer and man of this army, and by all of its followers." Scott required that the army pay for any supplies it took, worked to ensure that his largely Protestant soldiers did not disparage Roman Catholicism, and harshly disciplined soldiers who refused to comply with his orders. Despite these efforts, guerrilla units continually harassed the American supply lines between Veracruz and Puebla. Rather than stretch his supply lines further, Scott opted in August 1847 to purchase supplies from non-hostile locals and proceed with his mission. After a few battles fought in the outskirts of Mexico City, including an assault on Chapultepec Hill against a force that included valiant teenage cadets defending their military academy located on the site, Scott's army triumphantly entered the Mexican capital on September 13, 1847. A month later, Scott's forces defeated Santa Anna's effort to cut off their supply lines at Puebla and brought an end to major combat operations between regular forces. Scott and Taylor then maintained the occupation while U.S. and Mexican diplomats worked out a treaty, a process that would not be completed until May 1848. In the meantime, fighting continued as the forces of both generals faced regular attacks by guerrillas.

Opposition to the War

As the war dragged on, opposition to the conflict in the United States grew. In Congress, opposition from Whigs remained relatively tempered. Antislavery Whigs, such as Ohio's Joshua Giddings, denounced the war as a murderous land grab fought by the government on behalf of slaveholders. Most Whigs, however, continued the line of criticism they had employed at the beginning of the war, blaming Polk for starting the conflict and usurping Congress's war making power. A young Abraham Lincoln, then serving

his only term in the House of Representatives, proposed a set of "spot resolutions" demanding that Polk prove that the Thornton Affair took place on American soil. The resolutions went nowhere. The Whigs tread carefully for a number of reasons. They drew lessons from the experiences of the Federalists, of course. The fact that Generals Taylor and Scott were Whigs also muted their criticism of the war's progress. Questions remained, however, about the war's objectives. Northern Democrats took the lead on this front by expressing their frustration with Polk and their party's leadership through support for the Wilmot Proviso (see Chapter 15)—a proposed amendment to a war funding bill that, if passed, would have prohibited slavery in any territory acquired from Mexico. Their efforts would reopen the sectional conflict and move the nation toward civil war.

Outside of Congress, intellectuals and antislavery advocates opposed the war. Transcendentalist philosopher **Henry David Thoreau** spent a night in a Concord, Massachusetts jail because he expressed his opposition to the war by refusing to pay his taxes. He would have stayed longer, but a relative paid his fines. Thoreau used his experience to write one of his most significant essays, "Resistance to Civil Government," where he argued the best way to challenge unjust laws was to withdraw one's support for the government and suffer the consequences. "If a thousand men were not to pay their tax bills this year, that would not be a violent and bloody measure, as it would be to pay them, and enable the State to commit violence and shed innocent blood." Following this course, Thoreau noted, would likely lead to imprisonment, but "the true place for a just man is . . . a prison." Thoreau's ideas would later be embraced by the likes of Mohandas Gandhi and Martin Luther King, Jr. Opposition to the war went beyond small circles of intellectuals. A set of resolutions passed in 1847 by large margins of the Massachusetts legislature echoed the rhetoric of numerous antiwar publications: "such a war of conquest, so hateful in its objects, so wanton, unjust and unconstitutional in its origin and character, must be regarded as a war against freedom, against humanity, against justice, against the Union."

Treaty of Guadalupe Hidalgo

The war and occupation continued while both sides negotiated a settlement. Over the course of the conflict, Polk increased his demands for territory. He now wanted all Mexican land north of the twenty-sixth parallel, proposing to draw a straight line from the mouth of the Rio Grande across Mexico. Others in his party advocated taking possession of the entire country. Whigs like Henry Clay and Daniel Webster advised taking no territory beyond the Rio Grande. Polk eventually backed away from his larger demands and settled for the portions of northern Mexico that he had originally offered to purchase. This would achieve one of his main objectives—to secure ports on the west coast of North America to gain better access to Pacific markets. Racist concerns that the United States could not absorb a huge mass of Spanish-speaking Catholics considered by Anglo-Americans to be inferior also entered his decision. So did the inability of the U.S. Army to stop guerrilla attacks, convincing Polk that the densely populated areas of Mexico would be exceedingly difficult to hold. The main reason, however, may have been that Polk took what he could get when his envoy, Nicholas Trist, sent him a draft of the **Treaty of Guadalupe Hidalgo**. At one point, Polk became so frustrated with the slow pace of the peace talks that he recalled Trist, but the diplomat ignored his orders and completed his negotiations. In the treaty, Mexico, in exchange for $15 million, ceded one-third of its territory, giving up claims to Texas as well as land that would later become the future states of California, Nevada, Utah, and portions of the modern-day states of New Mexico, Arizona, Colorado, and Wyoming. (Five years later, the United States would secure the area of New Mexico and Arizona south of the Gila River through the Gadsden Purchase.) Polk sent the treaty to the Senate for ratification. After efforts to expand or reduce the size of the Mexican Cession were defeated and a provision protecting the validity of Mexican land grants in the ceded territory was removed, the Senate ratified the treaty officially ending the war.

Consequences of the Mexican American War

Though James Polk served only four years in office (he pledged to serve just one term and took pride in keeping his promises), the war he pursued against Mexico had many far-reaching consequences. His actions had a decided hu-

man cost, as the war brought 13,000 American and 16,000 Mexican casualties. Meanwhile, the conflict set the stage for another 750,000 American deaths because disputes over whether slavery would expand into the newly acquired territories contributed greatly to the American Civil War. For people west of the Mississippi, however, life changed drastically as a consequence of the peace.

Mormons, for example, found their effort to abandon the United States compromised by the Mexican Cession, which included almost all of what they claimed as the Kingdom of Deseret. They petitioned Congress to convert all of Deseret into a U.S. territory, but Congress refused and created a smaller, but still sizable, Utah Territory in 1850. Brigham Young, leader of the church, received an appointment as governor of the new territory, and other officials in the church were also given high posts. Although expected (and required) to have a republican government, Utah was run more like a theocracy in which elected officials rubberstamped decisions made by Mormon leaders. Federal judicial officials, "gentiles" (non-Mormons) appointed by the president, complained that Young and his followers had established a Mormon court system that allowed them to evade federal law. Tensions between Latter-day Saints and the federal government escalated as eastern politicians continued to denounce Mormonism as a "relic of barbarism." Young declared martial law in anticipation of a federal invasion. Then, in September 1857, in the midst of war hysteria, a wagon train of settlers from Missouri and Arkansas passed through the region and clashed with Mormons in Cedar City when locals refused to provision the emigrant party as they traveled toward California. A group of Mormon militiamen then attacked the settlers at a clearing known as Mountain Meadows in southern Utah, disguising themselves as Paiute Indians. After five days of skirmishing, the militiamen believed their true identify was revealed

PLUCKED:

THE MEXICAN EAGLE BEFORE THE WAR!   THE MEXICAN EAGLE AFTER THE WAR!

Contemporary American cartoon boasting over the United States' victory in the Mexican American War.

and decided to wipe out the travelers. Convincing the emigrants that the governor offered them safe passage, 120 of them were subsequently ambushed and murdered in the infamous Mountain Meadows Massacre. By the time of the assault, President James Buchanan had already sent 2,500 troops along with a new territorial governor. Young vowed to resist, but the troops moved slowly and winter slowed them even more. The delay provided time for negotiations, and the two sides worked out a tense accommodation in which Young stepped down from the governorship, federal troops would maintain a continuous presence, and the Mormon Church and its practice of polygamy would be left alone (at least for a while).

Life in California changed almost overnight. In May 1848, the same month that the Mexican American War officially came to an end, news of a gold strike in California reached San Francisco and spread rapidly through press reports. A few months later, people began pouring into California from all over the world—the United States, Europe, Latin America, and even China. The non-Native American population increased from 15,000 in 1848 to over 92,000 by 1850 to nearly 224,000 by 1852 as a result of the **California Gold Rush**. Many of these newcomers soon realized that gold prospecting offered few people the opportunity to get rich. A few early seekers could make their way panning for gold individually, but the opportunities for making the most lay in the hands of people who could mobilize the labor required to build sluices that could redirect rivers so miners could dig in exposed river bottoms. More opportunity for profit lay in the hands of people (or more likely corporations) that could use hydraulic mining to blast away hillsides to access the gold stored within. Most miners had no such capability and either moved on or became employees of these emerging enterprises. Others found ways to profit in selling supplies to miners, as the rapid increase in population sent the prices of basic goods and services skyward. American attitudes toward race also influenced a person's ability to mine for gold. American miners excluded Chinese and Mexicans (including *Californios*) from working in the mines, even as they forced some Native Americans to work for them essentially as slaves.

The flood of settlers exerted a harsh impact on both Native Americans and *Californios*. In 1845, California's Indian population may have been as high as 150,000. By 1855, that population had been reduced to around 50,000, and it would ultimately decline to about 30,000. A number of factors explain the losses. Disease, of course, extracted a terrible toll. Early California law expressed great hostility toward Native Americans, establishing a system of indentures and a network of legal triggers designed to ensnare them in forced labor. Other laws

permitted the killing of Indians who ran away, and extant records demonstrated that white Californians killed at least 4,500 Native Americans between 1845 and 1880. By 1860, most surviving Indians had been driven out of the areas of white settlement.

Meanwhile, numerous *Californios* found themselves stripped of their land. Although the Treaty of Guadalupe Hidalgo originally contained a provision stating that the United States would honor land grants made by the Mexican government, the Senate struck it out. Consequently, numerous landholders of Mexican descent, though U.S. citizens by the treaty, found themselves beset with problems. Migrants, especially those who opted for farming rather than mining, moved on to *Californios*' lands with impunity and forced them to defend their claims in court. American common law, however, demanded a level of precision in the delineation of property lines more than Mexican land grants employed, and even successful legal defenses, which took years and were expensive, tended to eat away at an estate's value. As a group of *Californios* petitioners to Congress explained, "some, who had at one time had been the richest landholders today find themselves without a foot of ground, living as objects of charity—and even in sight of the many leagues of land, which . . . they once called their own." So in California a process of dispossession quite similar to what was already occurring in Texas was beginning to play out.

The increasing movement of people from the eastern United States to the nation's new holdings in California and Oregon also transformed life on the Great Plains, which lay between the East and the new West. This largely unanticipated development undermined the Indian removal policy established in the 1830s. Federal policy makers had generally assumed that the majority of territory west of the Mississippi—an area that included the present states of Oklahoma, Kansas, and Nebraska but also extended far beyond the borders of those areas—would be permanently, or at least indefinitely, Indian Country. The new policy drew a sharp line between United States and Native American sovereignty, provided for the federal regulation and supervision of trade between whites and Indians, and assigned territory with clear boundaries to Indian nations among whom the federal government kept peace.

This arrangement began to fall apart in the 1840s when the Indian Territory became a corridor for Americans headed for Oregon, Utah, or California. As the number of migrants increased, they disrupted game migrations and trampled the crops of Native American farmers. Such actions increased tensions on the Plains, but Native Americans contributed to the escalation by demanding tolls and raiding wagon trains for livestock.

Isabella Leaves New York City

Isabella Baumfree Van Wagenen, who renamed herself Sojourner Truth, lived an interesting life. Born in Ulster County, New York, in 1797, Truth spent the first thirty years of her life enslaved to Dutch speaking families. The state's emancipation law ultimately freed her, and Truth reacted by successfully suing the owner of her son, Peter, for his freedom. She and Peter then moved to New York City, although they lost contact with each other when he found work as a sailor. A deeply religious woman, Truth joined the Kingdom of Matthias, a religious community headed by two self-proclaimed prophets, Elijah Pierson and Robert Matthews. The Kingdom failed with Pierson's death and accusations that Matthews and Truth had murdered him. Truth was acquitted, but the experience left her broke.

The selection here deals with Truth's failure to rebuild her savings and decision to change her name, to leave New York City, and to begin a career as a lecturer on religious topics and reform. She would soon become well known as an advocate for abolition and women's rights. But her decision to leave turned on her discomfort with the economic changes taking place in the U.S. North. Although her response was in no way representative to that of other Americans, her analysis provides insight into the competitive economic climate that had taken hold in places like New York City, as well as some of the reasons why Americans went on the move.

[Isabella] commenced anew her labors.... [S]he toiled hard, working early and late, doing a great deal for a little money, and turning her hand to almost any thing that promised good pay. Still, she did not prosper; and somehow, could not contrive to lay by a single dollar for a 'rainy day.'

When this had been the state of her affairs some time, she suddenly paused, and ... inquired within herself, why it was that, for all her unwearied labors, she had nothing to show; why it was that others, with much less care and labor, could hoard up treasures for themselves and children? ....

... [S]he came to the conclusion, that she had been taking part in a great drama, which was, in itself, but one great system of robbery and wrong. 'Yes,' she said, 'the rich rob the poor, and the poor rob one another.' True, she had not received labor from others, and stinted their pay, as she felt had been practised against her; but she had taken their work from them, which was their only means to get money, and was the same to them in the end. For instance—a gentleman where she lived would give her a half dollar to hire a poor man to clear the new-fallen snow from the steps and sidewalks. She would arise early, and perform the labor herself, putting the money into her own pocket. A poor man would come along, saying she ought to have let him have the job; he was poor, and needed the pay for his family. She would harden her heart against him, and answer—I am poor, too, and I need it for mine.' But, in her retrospection, she thought of all the misery she might have been adding to, in her selfish grasping, and it troubled her conscience sorely....

Her next decision was, that she must leave the city; it was no place for her; yea, she felt called in spirit to leave it, and to travel east and lecture.... [S]he informed Mrs. Whiting, the woman of the house where she was stopping [staying], that her name was no longer Isabella, but Sojourner; and that she was going east. And to her inquiry, 'What are you going east for?' her answer was, 'The Spirit calls me there, and I must go.'

She left the city on the morning of the 1st of June, 1843 ... she 'remembered Lot's wife,' and hoping to avoid her fate, she resolved not to look back till she felt sure the wicked city from which she was fleeing was left too far behind to be visible in the distance; and when she first ventured to look back, she could just discern the blue cloud of smoke that hung over it, and she thanked the Lord that she was thus far removed from what seemed to her a second Sodom.

Sojourner Truth, **Narrative of Sojourner Truth, Emancipated from Bodily Servitude by the State of New York in 1828** (Boston, MA, 1850), 98-99.

The federal government tried to manage the situation in the early 1850s by negotiating a series of treaties. Negotiators hoped to establish a system of roads along the Oregon and Santa Fe Trails, providing safe passage for American migrants while delineating the boundaries of Indian Territory. The effort failed. Native Americans had little interest in ceding land that they had been told belonged to them forever, and migrants and settlers tended to disregard the demarcation lines anyway.

Tensions between settlers and Native Americans were by no means confined to the Great Plains. Texas claimed all Indian land within its borders and then worked at removing or exterminating its native population. In Oregon, Washington, and Utah, settlers claimed land

Table 14.1	Westward Expansion, 1815 - 1850	
New Free States	New Slave States	Territories (1850)
Indiana, 1816	Mississippi, 1817	Minnesota
Illinois, 1818	Alabama, 1819	Oregon
Maine, 1820	Missouri, 1821	New Mexico
Michigan, 1837	Arkansas, 1836	Utah
Iowa, 1846	Florida, 1845	
Wisconsin, 1848	Texas, 1845	

before Indians had ceded title to the federal government, a step required by federal law. By the 1850s, policy makers began discussing new solutions to what was often termed the Indian question: reservations. In the words of Indian Affairs commissioner Edwin Lea:

There should be assigned to each tribe for a permanent home, a country adapted to agriculture, of limited extent well-defined boundaries within which all . . . should be compelled to remain until such time as their general improvement and good conduct may supersede the necessity of such restrictions. In the mean time, the government should cause them to be supplied with stock, agricultural implements, and useful material for clothing; encourage and assist them in the erection of comfortable dwellings, and secure to them the means of facilities of education, intellectual, moral, and religious.

In the 1850s, this new policy went into effect unevenly. Native Americans who moved to reservations either faced problems with encroaching settlers or found they could not eke out a living on the land they were assigned. Another two decades and no small amount of warfare would pass before the federal government would achieve full compliance with its new policy. But the new direction of the federal Indian policy was clear shortly after the Mexican American War. Lea summed up the trajectory in 1852. "When civilization and barbarism are brought in such relation that they cannot coexist together, it is right that the superiority of the former be asserted and the latter compelled to give way." Lea, in words that could have been written by the disillusioned missionary Marcus Whitman, saw "no matter of regret that so large a portion of our territory has been wrested from its aboriginal inhabitants and made the happy abode of an enlightened and Christian people."

Following the conclusion of the Mexican American War, therefore, the process of settling the Trans-Mississippi West by Anglo-Americans proceeded at full pace, and the new inhabitants reshaped their new homes in the image of the East. They established farms and started mines— gold, silver, copper, and zinc among others. They took over the cattle industries that had been dominated by *Tejanos* and *Californios* as well as New Mexico's sheep industry. These activities would fuel American economic and industrial development and help transform the nation's economy in a matter of decades. But before then, American politicians would have to confront the immediate political problem presented by the conclusion of the war: what was the status of slavery in the Mexican Cession.

MORE LAND, MORE PROBLEMS

Narcissa Whitman wrote to her mother on the eve of the United States emergence as a continental republic. In the space of a decade, the United States would double its territory and spread across the North American continent. New settlements emerged rapidly in Texas, Oregon, Utah, and California, and the United States aggressively pursued these claims even to the point of war. Although the United States made war against both Mexico and Native American groups, the United States established a vision of itself as a peaceful actor on the world stage. American expansion did not happen out of a desire for conquest, and defenders of the war can point to the fact that the United States paid for the territory it acquired in 1848. Expansion stemmed from a desire to spread American political and social values that had something to offer the rest of the world. But those values contained an expectation that others would conform to them and accommodated the displacement of those people unwilling or unable to do so. The rapid expansion proved to be a major economic boon to the economy, but in the short term the acquisition of new territory opened up a new conflict over slavery that would ultimately split the Union.

Chronology

1818 United States and Great Britain agree to joint occupation of the Oregon Country.

1819 Adams-Onís Treaty.

1821 Mexico gains independence from Spain.

1824 Mexico opens Texas to immigrants.

1830 Mexico prohibits further American immigration to Texas and reaffirms its antislavery laws.

1834 Antonio López de Santa Anna becomes dictator of Mexico.

1836 Texas declares independence from Mexico. General Sam Houston secures Texas independence by defeating Santa Anna at the Battle of San Jacinto.

1841 John Tyler (Whig) becomes president.

1842 Webster-Ashburton Treaty.

1844 Joseph Smith, Jr. founder of the Church of Jesus Christ of Latter-day Saints (Mormons), is killed.
James K. Polk defeats Henry Clay.

1845 The United States annexes Texas.
Polk sends General Zachary Taylor to Corpus Christi, Texas, to defend the U.S. new claims.

1846 United States and Great Britain end joint occupation of the Oregon Country and establish a border at the 49th parallel.
The Thornton Affair.
The Bear Flag Revolt.
U.S. troops occupy New Mexico.

1847 U.S. troops gain control of California.
Battle of Buena Vista.
General Winfield Scott invades Mexico takes Veracruz, Puebla, and then Mexico City.
Brigham Young leads the first group of Mormon migrants to Utah.

1848 Treaty of Guadalupe Hidalgo.
Gold discovered in California.

SUGGESTED READINGS

Randolph B. Campbell, *An Empire for Slavery: The Peculiar Institution in Texas, 1821-1865* (1989).

John Mack Faragher, *Women and Men on the Overland Trail*, 2d. ed. (2001).

Michael Golay, *The Tide of Empire: America's March to the Pacific* (2003).

Stephen L. Hardin, *Texian Iliad: A Military History of the Texas Revolution* (1996).

Thomas R. Hietala, *Manifest Design: Anxious Aggrandizement in Late Jacksonian America* (1985).

Reginald Horsman, *Race and Manifest Destiny: The Origins of American Racial Anglo-Saxonism* (1981).

Stephen G. Hyslop, *Bound for Santa Fe: The Road to New Mexico and the American Conquest, 1806-1848* (2002).

Robert W. Johannsen, *To the Halls of Montezumas: The Mexican War in the American Imagination* (1985).

Irving Levinson, *Wars within War: Mexican Guerrillas, Domestic Elites, and the United States of America, 1846-1848* (2005).

James M. McCaffrey, *Army of Manifest Destiny: The American Soldier in the Mexican War, 1846-1848* (1992).

Laton McCartney, *Across the Great Divide: Robert Stuart and the Discovery of the Overland Trail* (2003).

Frederick Merk, *Manifest Destiny and Mission in American History: A Reinterpretation* (1963).

Michael A. Morrison, *Slavery and the American West: The Eclipse of Manifest Destiny and the Coming of the American Civil War* (1997).

David M. Pletcher, *The Diplomacy of Annexation: Texas, Oregon, and the Mexican War* (1973).

Paul W. Reeve, *Making Space on the Western Frontier: Mormons, Miners, and Southern Paiutes* (2006).

Joel H. Silbey, *Storm over Texas: The Annexation Controversy and the Road to Civil War* (2007).

Anders Stephanson, *Manifest Destiny: American Expansionism and the Empire of Right* (1995).

John David Uhruh, *The Plains Across: The Overland Emigrants and the Trans-Mississippi West, 1840-1860* (1979).

William E. Unrau, *The Rise and Fall of Indian Country, 1825-1855* (2007).

William Earl Weeks, *Building the Continental Empire: American Expansion from the Revolution to the Civil War* (1996).

Steven E. Woodworth, *Manifest Destinies: America's Westward Expansion and the Road to Civil War* (2010).

Review Questions

1.   Describe the concept of manifest destiny. How did this idea shape American expansion in the mid-nineteenth century?

2.   How did the experience of Mormon migrants differ from that of other migrant groups? What did the other emigrants from the United States have in common?

3.   Discuss the significance of Texas annexation to American politics during the 1840s. Why did the annexation of Texas become such an important issue?

4.   What was the significance of race in American expansion?

5.   Evaluate American expansionism in the mid-nineteenth century. Do you believe that the territory gained through expansion justified the costs, moral or otherwise?

Glossary of Important People and Concepts

Stephen F. Austin
Bear Flag Revolt
California Gold Rush
Empresario
"54-40 or Fight!"
Treaty of Guadalupe Hidalgo
Sam Houston
Stephen W. Kearny
Liberty Party
Manifest Destiny
Mormons
Oregon
Oregon Trail
John O'Sullivan
James K. Polk
Republic of Texas
Antonio López de Santa Anna
Santa Fe Trail
Winfield Scott
Henry David Thoreau
Zachary Taylor
Thornton Affair
John Tyler
Webster-Ashburton Treaty
Brigham Young

Depiction of John Brown before his Execution

Chapter Fifteen

EXPANSION, SLAVERY, AND SECESSION: The Road to Civil War

In 1835, Harriet, an enslaved woman from Virginia, arrived on the edges of American settlement with her master, Lawrence Taliaferro. Taliaferro brought her to the environs of Fort Snelling (present-day St. Paul, Minnesota) to wait on his family while he worked as an Indian agent for the United States. Although the area in which she settled was included in the territory closed to slavery under the Missouri Compromise, Harriet was not the only enslaved person living at the post. She met her husband, Etheldred (or Dred) Scott, an enslaved man bound to John Emerson, one of the post's surgeons. Life at Fort Snelling for the enslaved couple proved different from residence on a plantation. Although Emerson purchased Harriet from Taliaferro, Dred and Harriet Scott seemed to have had an atypical level of autonomy. After marrying in a civil ceremony, their master would frequently leave them alone at the post, sometimes for weeks at a time. Yet, they were not free. Emerson ultimately moved Dred, Harriet, and the couple's two children back to St. Louis.

When John Emerson died in the mid-1840s, Dred and Harriet Scott sued his widow, Irene Emerson, for their freedom. Missouri's judicial system had been relatively accommodating to slaves who had been taken into free territory. Previously, judges had recognized the freedom of slaves who had resided with their masters in Illinois (where Dred had lived with John Emerson for a few years prior to living in Minnesota), and had even freed an enslaved woman named Rachel who had lived at Fort Snelling. By the time their case reached the state supreme court in 1852, however, the judicial attitude toward freedom for slaves taken by their masters into free territory had changed. In the words of the judge speaking for the court:

> Times now are not as they were when the former . . . decisions on this subject were made. Since then not only individuals, but States, have been possessed with a dark and fell spirit in relation to slavery, whose gratification is sought in the pursuit of measures, whose inevitable consequence must be the overthrow and destruction of our government. Under such circumstances it does not behoove the State of Missouri to . . . gratify this spirit.

Dred and Harriet Scott's case had become caught up in the growing rift between the North and South over slavery, and the presiding judge said that he was overturning the court's previous practice because he did not want to give any encouragement to antislavery sentiment. This moment proved to be just the beginning of the politicalization of their case. Five years later, when the United States Supreme Court heard the Scotts' appeal, the judges and lawyers involved used the decision to strike at the antislavery movement and to rule the Missouri Compromise unconstitutional, an act that helped move the United States closer to secession and civil war.

THE POLITICAL DIVIDE OVER SLAVERY EXPANSION

Victory in the war with Mexico greatly increased the United States' total area but also resulted in renewed conflict over the expansion of slavery. Tensions between the North and South began escalating soon after the war began and became unmanageable by the end of the 1850s. The renewed sectional conflict, in fact, fulfilled the predictions of two of the war's critics. South Carolina Senator **John C. Calhoun**—the South's most prominent proslavery spokesman—likened Mexico to a forbidden fruit, which would bring death to those who consumed it. Ralph Waldo Emerson, a preeminent New England intellectual and opponent of slavery, sounded a similar note. "Mexico will poison us," he wrote in his journal. The war would undermine the Union's stability by shattering a network of legislative compromises and political alliances that had contained the nation's sectional tensions since the 1820s.

Before the war, mainstream politicians, both Whigs and (especially) Democrats, managed sectional conflict in two ways. First, they worked to maintain a balance of power between slave states and free states by ensuring that the Union contained an equal number of both. The admission of Missouri set the pattern. That state (a slave state) entered the Union alongside Maine (a free state). Congress also prohibited the expansion of slavery into federal territory north of Missouri's southern border (36°–30' latitude). The next six states fit the pattern: the admission of Michigan in 1837 (free) followed on the heels of Arkansas's (slave) admission in 1836. Florida and Texas, both slave states, joined in 1845; the next two states—Iowa and Wisconsin—prohibited slavery.

Admitting states in this manner preserved the South's political power, even though its relative share of the Union's population declined steadily. As late as 1800, about half the total population lived in the South. By 1820, its share had fallen to 45 percent. In 1860, its share dropped to 35 percent. These proportions, in fact, overstate the South's share because the Constitution's Three-Fifths Clause reduced the number of enslaved persons that could be counted when determining a state's representation in the House. But the Constitution also gave each state two senators, and the policy of maintaining an equal number of slave and free states allowed southern politicians to protect their section's interests in that chamber.

The second way politicians managed sectional conflict came through their efforts to keep the slavery issue off the national agenda. Both the Democratic and Whig Parties consisted of national political coalitions that depended on the cooperation of their northern and southern wings to remain competitive. Sectional issues like slavery undermined the alliances on which that cooperation rested, and politicians thus had an incentive to keep slavery out of national politics. Democrats worked feverishly, if ultimately ineffectively, to do so. Indeed, Martin Van Buren of New York and his numerous northern allies supported purging the mail of antislavery literature and the "gagging" of abolitionist petitions in Congress, and party leaders pressured rank and file members to keep any antislavery leanings they may have had under wraps. Whigs, whose organization contained outspoken opponents of slavery like Ohio's Joshua Giddings and New York's William Seward, as well as committed defenders of slavery like Georgia's Robert Toombs and Alexander Stephens, proved more tolerant of diverse views, but their need to work together created an incentive to push slavery out of national politics.

Together, the practice of admitting an equal number of slave and free states and the dynamics of party politics combined to give the South a disproportionate amount of political power. The section provided more than half of all appointed federal officers. Southerners, for example, provided over 60 percent of the men appointed to serve as Supreme Court justices between 1789 and 1860. And that Court, perhaps not coincidentally, stated on a number of occasions in the 1840s and 1850s that slavery was, in almost all cases, a matter of local, and not national, concern.

The South's entrenched political strength, however, appeared to critics as less a way to protect valid minority interests than a way for a "**Slave Power**" to use its lock on the federal government to protect and expand slavery. From the perspective of disgruntled northern politicians, both Whigs and Democrats, the South seemed always to prevail, winning on Indian removal and the admission of Texas. Now, Southerners threatened to extend slavery into all of the territory acquired from Mexico.

Slavery Expansion: Four Alternatives

On August 8, 1846, David Wilmot, a first-term congressman from Pennsylvania, provided his discontented northern colleagues with a rallying cry when he attached a rider to a Mexican American War funding bill. The **Wilmot Proviso**, as it became known, stated "as an express and fundamental condition" that "neither slavery nor involuntary servitude" would be permitted in any territory acquired from Mexico. The bill, with Wilmot's attached amendment, passed through the House with an 85 to 80 vote that split along sectional lines, but the bill died in the Senate. Martin Van Buren's allies, who had grown weary of southern demands, promptly reintroduced the proviso in the next session. Wilmot articulated what became known as the **free soil position**—the argument that all federal territory should be closed to slavery. Northern politicians who became free soilers did so for a variety of reasons stemming from a combination of sincere opposition to slavery, discontent with southern domination of the political system, a desire to protect northern family farms from economic competition with slave-based plantations, and simple, vulgar racism on the part of those who wanted to keep blacks out of the West altogether.

Whatever the motivations, the emergence of the free soil position signaled that the consensus for handling slavery at the national level had broken down. Columbus Delano, an Ohio Whig, expressed the sentiment on the House floor in January 1847:

> Let me say . . . to the South, in all kindness and candor. . . . Never, never shall you extend your institution of slavery one inch beyond its present limits. . . . Go on. . . . Conquer Mexico, and add to the territory, but we will make it free. . . . If you drive on this bloody war of conquest to annexation, we will establish a cordon of free States that shall surround you; and then we will light up the fires of liberty on every side, until they melt your present chains, and render all your people free. This is no idle boast. . .

Southerners agreed and responded with horror to the Wilmot Proviso. Free soil advocates like Delano spoke as if the South blighted the nation, as if Southerners (or at least slaveholders) were unworthy of reaping the full benefits of American citizenship. That attitude offended their sense of honor as much as the policy threatened their section's political and economic interests. Their politicians countered by insisting that all federal territory should be open to slavery.

In February 1847, South Carolina's John C. Calhoun, then serving in the Senate, provided a forceful articulation of this position, which has been cumbersomely labeled the "**common property doctrine**." Because federal territory had been acquired through the participation of all the states, Calhoun argued, it belonged to them in common. Moreover, because all citizens possessed equal rights under the Constitution, citizens from every state had a right to enter that territory and bring their property with them. Calhoun and his allies argued that the Wilmot Proviso was unconstitutional because it deprived a portion of U.S. citizens of the right to enter federal territory with their (human) property. If Northerners refused to respect the South's rights under the Constitution, then secession might be the appropriate response. Georgia's

Robert Toombs made the point clearly in 1849, as a House divided deeply along party and sectional lines struggled to nominate a speaker:

> I do not . . . hesitate to avow before this House and the country and in the presence of the living God, that if by your legislation you seek to drive us from the territories . . . purchased by the common blood and treasure of the whole people, and . . . thereby [attempt] to fix a national degradation upon half the states of this Confederacy, I am for disunion. . . . From 1787 to this hour the people of the South have asked nothing but justice—nothing but the maintenance of the principles and the spirit which controlled our fathers in the formation of the Constitution. Unless we are unworthy of our ancestors, we will never accept less as a condition of union.

Between these irreconcilable positions, moderate politicians struggled to find a middle ground. President Polk, Secretary of State James Buchanan, and Senator Stephen A. Douglas of Illinois advocated extending the Missouri Compromise line (36°–30' latitude) to the Pacific. The position had a number of merits. It represented a (literal) extension of existing policy toward slavery in the territories that had functioned effectively since the 1820s, and it lacked ambiguity by clearly laying out the areas open and closed to slavery's expansion. Sectional partisans rejected the suggestion. Under the terms of the common property doctrine, the policy was unconstitutional and therefore unacceptable (although a number of proponents of this position had supported the Missouri restriction in the past). Free soil adherents rejected the policy because much of the territory acquired from Mexico would fall on the southern side of the line, thus excluding their constituents from the fruits of any victory.

A potential extension of the Missouri Compromise line also competed with a second option, the so-called "**popular sovereignty**" doctrine. Senator Lewis Cass of Michigan, an aspirant to the 1848 Democratic presidential nomination, put forth this final position, which called for letting settlers decide for themselves the future of slavery in the territories. Cass contended that democratic, self-governing territorial legislatures should regulate their own internal affairs (including slavery). Three aspects of Cass's position made it especially appealing to Democratic politicians. First the emphasis on territorial self-governance meshed well with their belief that most policy should be made locally. Second, popular sovereignty had the added benefit of getting the question of slavery out of Congress and giving responsibility for its solution to someone else. Finally, the policy had a useful amount of ambiguity. Cass purposely refused to state precisely when a territorial legislature would make its decision concerning the future of slavery, and his reluctance enabled Democrats who might disagree sharply over the timing of the crucial vote to rally around him.

Each of these four positions (free soil, common property, extension of the Missouri Compromise line, and popular sovereignty) had emerged in fully articulated form by the end of 1847, before the war with Mexico had even ended. Congress achieved very little in the course of this debate. The war appropriations bill, which had been defeated after Wilmot attached his rider, squeaked through Congress (without the proviso) at the close of the next session. An effort to organize the Oregon Territory had stalled because it had become enmeshed in the debate over slavery's expansion. No one seriously thought this area in the present-day Pacific Northwest would become slave territory, but politicians used the issue to position themselves for the real struggle that would occur when the war with Mexico finally ended.

The Growing Political Crisis over Slavery

The war officially ended with the Treaty of Guadalupe Hidalgo in February of 1848, but Congress proved too divided to act on the slavery expansion issue. As the months dragged on, the situation unraveled until politicians faced what they believed to be a crisis that threatened the Union's continued existence. The deadlock that emerged in the previous Congress created time that nurtured sectional animosity and allowed debate to spread from the future of slavery's expansion in the territory acquired from Mexico, to its status in the District of Columbia, and to include argument over the reach of the Constitution's Fugitive Slave Clause. Politicians faced those issues within a context that simultaneously pushed them to move quickly (because settlers were pouring into California) while encouraging them to drag their feet (because of the impending presidential election). These factors further intensified the deadlock, leading a significant number of southern leaders to respond by seriously contemplating secession. With these prevailing pressures, the stage was set for a potentially great political compromise.

By 1848, slavery had become a problem for Congress in no fewer than three ways. One aspect of the problem involved slavery's legality in the District of Columbia. Under the Constitution, Congress possessed vast authority over the District. Many Northerners had long advocated that Congress contemplate outlawing the institution there—slavery in the capital of a government professing to be devoted to freedom tended to make the United States

appear hypocritical in the eyes of the world. Abolitionist petitions on this subject had occasioned the House Gag Rule during the 1830s, but the House had since lifted that rule. As sectional tensions intensified, some northern politicians revealed their willingness to push the issue.

Another problem centered on the capture of fugitive slaves. Under the Constitution, slave holders and the slave catchers they hired had a right to pursue runaway bondsmen into the free states and to return them to slavery. Congress passed a law regulating this practice in the 1790s, but that legislation provided no procedures for proving whether a captured runaway was the actual person being sought. With some justification, critics argued that the law provided cover for kidnappers. Northern states responded with legislation requiring slave catchers, among other procedures, to prove the status of the people they captured in a jury trial. In 1842, the Supreme Court in *Prigg v. Pennsylvania* ruled those laws unconstitutional, but the Court also said that the federal government could not require state officials to participate in the apprehension of fugitive slaves. A number of northern states responded by ordering their officials not to comply, which effectively made apprehension of alleged fugitives impossible. Southerners considered these actions to be a breach of constitutional obligations and demanded that Congress pass legislation to fix the issue.

Of course, the major issue remained the future of slavery's expansion into the federal territories. The matter was already complicated by the four competing solutions, and became further muddied by politicians in the various camps who did not trust one another. At one point, a group of senators labored hard to push a bill organizing the Oregon, California, and New Mexico territories through their chamber. The bill allowed the Supreme Court to settle the issue of slavery in those territories, and the compromise it embodied represented the product of months of false starts and weeks of deliberation. In the House, however, northern and southern representatives united to kill the bill without debate. No one knew how the Court would have ruled, but both proslavery and antislavery advocates found common ground in not trusting the justices.

A further complication came with the discovery of gold in California, which had occurred a few weeks before the Treaty of Guadalupe Hidalgo had reached Washington. At war's end, California's population (excluding Native Americans) reached 15,000. Two years later, the U.S. Census reported over 92,000 residents, as gold-hungry settlers and those who supplied and serviced the miners flocked into the area. The province's stunning growth meant that it could bypass the territorial phase and enter the Union as a state. If that occurred, California would, without question, enter as a free state given the strong anti-slavery feelings of a majority of its inhabitants. This development would break the sectional balance in the Senate because no corresponding pro-slavery area existed to become a slave state. Southerners, therefore, pushed for delay.

The Election of 1848

Stalling, in fact, proved to be the order of the day in 1848, as politicians positioned themselves for the upcoming presidential election. Although Congress managed to pass a bill organizing the Oregon Territory, it failed to do so for California and New Mexico. Some of this failure resulted from Whigs and Democrats not wanting to work together as the election neared because a solution would have deprived them of issues while helping the other side. Unfortunately, the election brought little clarity. The Democrats nominated **Lewis Cass**, indicating that a majority of them embraced the popular sovereignty position. At the same time, however, President Polk began pushing extension of the Missouri Compromise line as the only solution. Thus, the favored position of Democrats remained unclear.

Whigs also cloaked themselves in ambiguity. They ran without a platform position on slavery and passed over their most prominent national figure, Henry Clay of Kentucky, in favor of General Zachary Taylor. Although he had distinguished himself as a commander of the American forces during the Mexican American War, Taylor was an unknown in politics—he belonged to no political party and had never cast a vote in an election. The circumstances of his nomination added little clarity. A Louisianan whose family owned more than one hundred slaves, Taylor received most of his support in the nominating convention from southern Whigs, but his principal advisor was William Seward of New York—an open and forceful advocate of abolition. Exactly how Taylor would come down on the issue of slavery's expansion thus remained anyone's guess.

A number of northern politicians had grown weary of this ambiguity and bolted in favor of a new organization—the Free Soil Party. Formed in August 1848, the new party attracted three very different groups of antislavery politicians. New York's "Barnburner" Democrats—a faction led by former President Martin Van Buren—formed one of these groups. Barnburners, who had received their name from a story about a farmer who solved a rat infestation by setting his barn on fire, nursed a list of grievances against the national party. Van Buren's loss of the 1844 Democratic nomination and President Polk's subsequent favoring of the "Hunkers"—a rival

faction in state politics—symbolized southern domination of the party. Barnburners embraced the Wilmot Proviso and looked for like-minded allies. They found support among the "Conscience Whigs," a Massachusetts political faction that had formed around Van Buren's nemesis, former president (and recently deceased) John Quincy Adams. Conscience Whigs had long squared off against rivals they found to be too conciliatory toward the South—a group including so-called "Cotton Whigs" as well as the majority of Democrats. However when Taylor's nomination began to appear likely, they bolted and followed Adams's son, Charles Francis Adams, into an alliance with the Barnburners. Members of the Liberty Party, which had run in 1840 and 1844 on a platform of abolishing slavery in the District of Columbia, stopping the expansion of slavery into the western territories, and ending the interstate slave trade and racial discrimination, rounded out the Free Soil Party's membership.

In the 1848 election, the Free Soil Party received 10 percent of the popular vote but no electoral votes. Such a performance doomed the party's prospects to become a permanent, competitive organization, but its impact proved decisive in the election. The party overperformed in New York where it captured over 25 percent of the popular vote, helping Taylor win a plurality with 48 percent of the state's vote. Victory in New York provided "Old Rough and Ready," as Taylor was known, with enough electoral votes to win the election.

Not only did Taylor prove to be no better than Polk in solving the issues before Congress, the situation only unraveled further on his watch. Southerners, especially Whigs like Robert Toombs, had hoped that the new president would take their position on the sectional issues before them. After all, Taylor was a Southerner who owned a substantial number of slaves. Such a hope, however, proved to be misplaced. William Seward, one of the party's strongest opponents of slavery, assumed a role as unofficial advisor within Taylor's administration, and his influence soon became apparent. To end the issue quickly, he made a bold proposal that only worsened sectional discord. In addition to the prompt admission of California as a free state, he wished to create a large second free state ("New Mexico") out of the remaining lands acquired from Mexico. Southerners felt betrayed. Before and immediately after the election, John C. Calhoun had tried to build a southern political alliance, but his efforts failed for a variety of reasons—a general distrust between Democrats and Whigs, a specific distrust of the ambitious Calhoun, and the Whigs' hopes for Taylor. As Taylor's views became clear, Southerners became united in outrage. Talk of secession became widespread across the region, as historian David Potter noted: "From the pulpit, from the editorial sanctum, from state legislatures, from party conventions, from mass meetings, there poured out a steady stream of sermons, editorials, resolutions, speeches, and joint statements, all warning of the immediate possibility of disunion." Taylor promised to resist all challenges to the Union, but numerous observers were concerned that the nation might soon fall apart.

The Compromise of 1850

In January 1850, Senator Henry Clay of Kentucky embarked on an ambitious plan to solve the crisis. Over the years, Clay had developed a reputation as the Great Compromiser (this term did not carry the same negative connotations in the mid-nineteenth century that it does now). His record supported that image. Clay had engineered the Missouri Compromise and brokered the agreement that reduced tensions between South Carolina and the Jackson administration during the Nullification Crisis. Now, in January 1850, he proposed a set of resolutions that would address all of the outstanding sectional issues, which boiled down to five basic points:

1. California would join the Union as a free state;
2. Congress would organize the remaining Mexican session lands as federal territories (Utah and New Mexico) with popular sovereignty to decide the fate of slavery in each territory;
3. Congress would amend the Fugitive Slave Law to

satisfy southern complaints about its effectiveness;
4. Congress would abolish the slave trade—but not slavery—in Washington, D.C.;
5. Texas would cede much of its western territorial claims in exchange for assumption of its public debt by the U.S. Treasury.

By April 1850, Congress had bundled Clay's resolutions into a single, or omnibus, bill, which meant that accepting any one proposal required compromise on others. Northern partisans who wanted the prompt admission of California as a free state, for example, would also have to accept a revised fugitive slave code. Many Northerners considered that section of the bill unconscionable because alleged fugitives would be brought before a federal magistrate to decide whether they would be released to the custody of a slave catcher. The proposed law contained none of the safeguards that many northern states deemed essential to determining whether that person was, in fact, a runaway slave, such as a jury trial with the opportunity for alleged fugitives to testify or at least a habeas corpus hearing that required masters to prove their case. To make matters worse, under the terms of the bill, judges would receive ten dollars in compensation for court costs if they returned a person to slavery, but only five dollars if they did not. Critics charged that the difference amounted to a tacit bribe. Also troubling to many Northerners was a provision enabling federal marshals to compel citizens to participate in posses to hunt for runaway slaves. Refusals

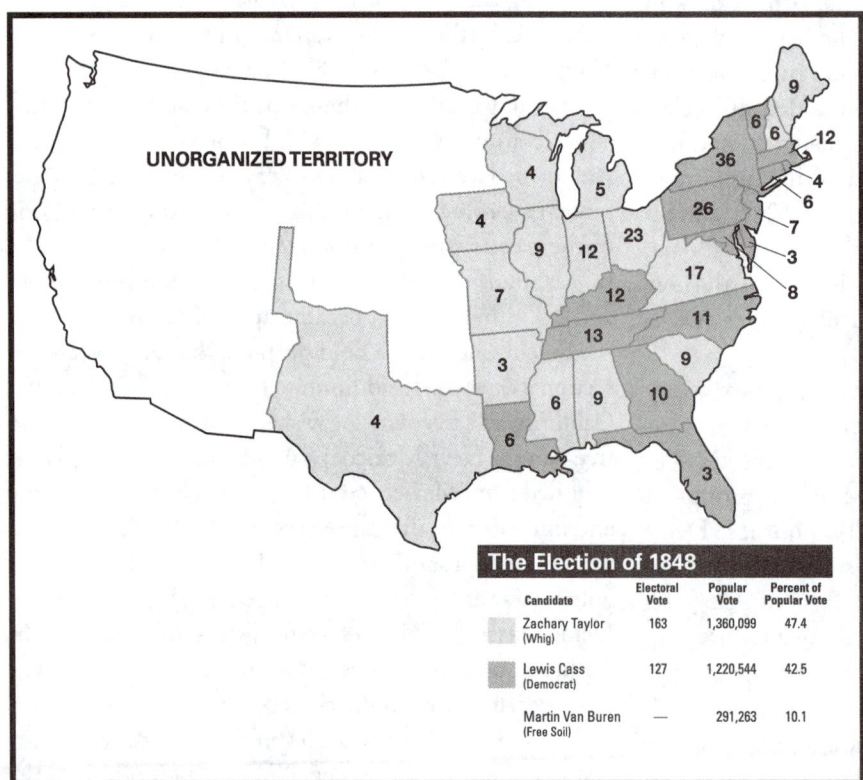

Map 15.1 The Election of 1848

The Election of 1848			
Candidate	Electoral Vote	Popular Vote	Percent of Popular Vote
Zachary Taylor (Whig)	163	1,360,099	47.4
Lewis Cass (Democrat)	127	1,220,544	42.5
Martin Van Buren (Free Soil)	—	291,263	10.1

Harriet Tubman Takes Joe to Canada

Abolitionist Harriet Tubman escaped from slavery in 1849 and spent the 1850s helping other enslaved people escape as well. Working with the Underground Railroad—a network that aided fugitive—Tubman returned to the South repeatedly and escorted enslaved people to freedom. The passage here shows the arbitrary treatment that prompted people to flee as well as the difficulties involved in such an undertaking.

...[A]fter the passage of the Fugitive Slave law, [Harriet] said, "I wouldn't trust Uncle Sam wid my people no longer; I brought 'em all clar off to Canada."

Of the very many interesting stories told me by Harriet, I cannot refrain from telling to my readers that of Joe....

Joe was a noble specimen of a negro, and was hired out by his master to a man for whom he worked faithfully for six years.... At length this man ... determined to buy him at any cost.... Joe passed into the hands of his new master.

... Joe was somewhat surprised when the first order issued from his master's lips, was, "Now, Joe, strip and take a whipping!"....

"Mas'r," said [Joe], "habn't I always been faithful to you?..."

" No, Joe; "I've no complaint to make of you; you're a good nigger, and you've always worked well; but the first lesson my niggers have to learn is that I am master, and that they are not to resist or refuse to obey anything I tell 'em to do....

Joe thought it best to submit.... [B]ut as he drew his clothes up over his torn and bleeding back, he said, "Dis is de last!" That night he took a boat and went a long distance to the cabin of Harriet's father, and said, "Next time Moses comes, let me know".... One fine morning Joe was missing ... [he] made part of Harriet's next party, who began their pilgrimage from Maryland to Canada....

Their adventures were enough to fill a volume; they were pursued; they were hidden in "potato holes," while their pursuers passed within a few feet of them; they were passed along by friends in various disguises; they scattered and separated, to be led by guides by a roundabout way, to a meeting-place again.... they came at last to the long bridge at the entrance of the city of Wilmington, Delaware. The rewards posted up every-where had been at first five hundred dollars for Joe, if taken within the limits of the United States; then a thousand, and then fifteen hundred dollars.... The long Wilmington Bridge was guarded by police officers, and the advertisements were everywhere. The party were scattered, and taken to the houses of different colored friends, and word was sent secretly to Thomas Garret.... Thomas Garrett is a Quaker....

...He engaged two wagons, filled them with brick layers... and sent them across the bridge.... The guards saw them pass, and of course expected them to recross the bridge. After night fall... the same wagons went back, but with an addition to their party. The fugitives were on the bottom of the wagons... And so they made their way to New York. When they entered the anti-slavery office there, Joe was recognized at once by the description in the advertisement. "Well," said Mr. Oliver Johnson, "I am glad to see the man whose head is worth fifteen hundred dollars." At this Joe's heart sank. If the advertisement had got to New York ... he thought he was in danger still.... When told how many miles, for they were to come through New-York State, and cross the Suspension Bridge, he was ready to give up. "From dat time Joe was silent," said Harriet; "he sang no more, he talked no more; he sat wid his head on his hand, and nobody could 'muse him or make him take any interest in anyting." They passed along in safety, and at length found themselves in the cars, approaching Suspension Bridge [that crossed Niagara Falls into Canada]....

The cars began to cross the bridge....

....

Harriet knew by the rise in the center of the bridge, and the descent on the other side, that they had crossed "the line." She sprang across to Joe's seat, shook him with all her might, and shouted, "Joe, you've shook de lion's paw!" Joe did not know what she meant. "Joe, you're free!"....

She has seen Joe several times since, a happy and industrious freeman in Canada.

to do so could result in a $1,000 fine. The fugitive slave portion of Clay's bill represented a significant concession to the South, which would greatly increase the power of the federal government at the expense of the states (in this case, the northern states), thus attacking the principle of states' rights in order to protect the institution of slavery from outside interference. In order to receive that part of the deal, southern partisans would have to accept California's admission as a free state, breaking the sectional balance of power in the Senate that had served as an important element of the South's power within the federal government.

The bill's remaining provisions fell into a similar pattern of compromise. Clay's proposal on the District of Columbia closed slave markets in the nation's capital, but otherwise left the institution untouched. His handling of Texas did much the same thing. The Lone Star State became smaller but would be relieved of its public debt in exchange for reduced borders. Because so few citizens lived in the Utah and New Mexico Territories, the bill deferred the matter of slavery's potential expansion into these areas by adopting the principle of popular sovereignty. The location of the border between those two territories, however, may have hinted at a future settlement, for it ran roughly along the same latitude as the Missouri Compromise line and created the impression that the North may get Utah and the South, New Mexico.

Congress debated the omnibus bill for another four months before voting it down in July 1850. A number of factors explained the result. President Taylor, who thought the Wilmot Proviso should provide the basis for settling the issue of slavery in the territories, opposed the bill and thus left Clay deprived of crucial administration leadership. The senator had also built up a large number of enemies over the decades, and they saw defeat of his omnibus bill as their last opportunity to extract revenge. Further, a general unwillingness to compromise existed among sectional partisans in Congress. A significant number of both northern and southern politicians believed the bill gave up too much to the other section, so they decided to vote against the entire bill. All of these factors ensured that Clay's compromise effort would fail. After months of fierce debate, the sectional issue remained unresolved, and secession still remained a viable threat. In fact, nine southern states sent 175 delegates to a convention in Nashville, Tennessee in June 1850 to discuss the appropriate response to the sectional crisis. Although some called for secession, more moderate attendees stifled their efforts. The Nashville Convention eventually endorsed an extension of the Missouri Compromise line and resolved to meet again in November to discuss the South's options in case Congress failed to act as they wished.

Almost immediately after the defeat of the omnibus bill, however, a series of events worked to defuse the

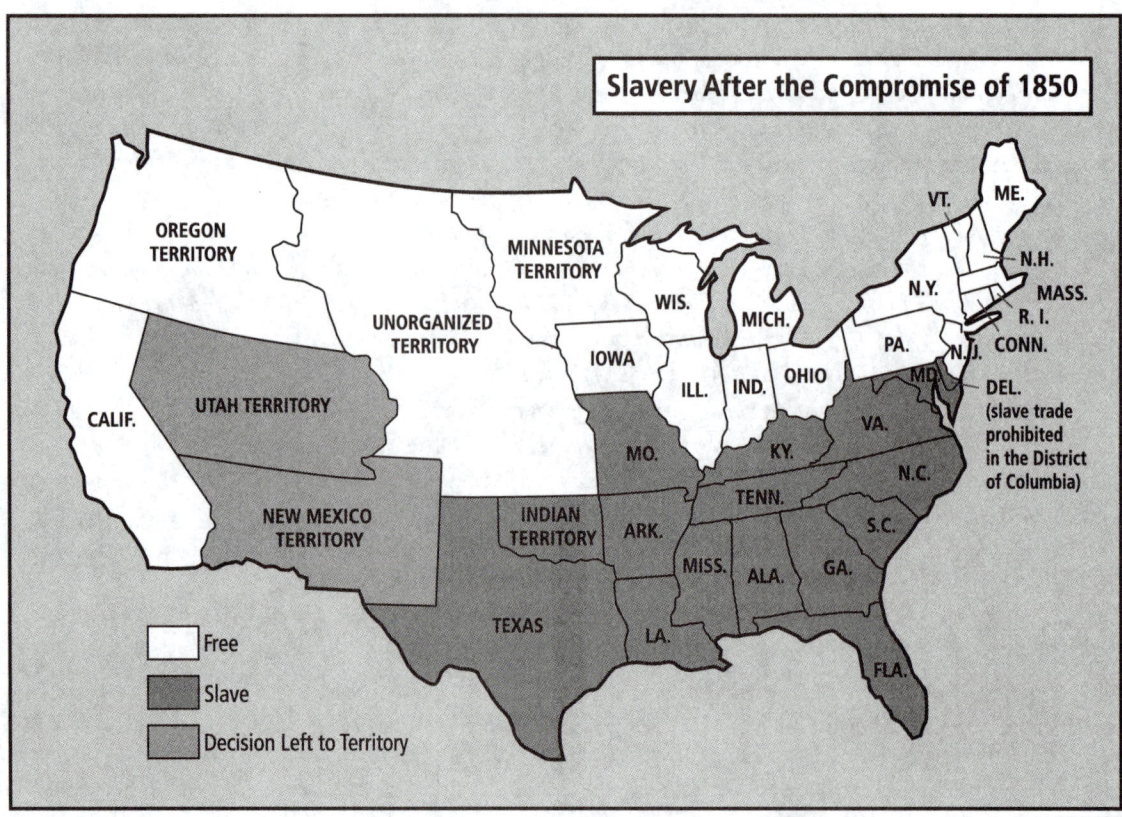

Map 15.2 **Slavery after the Compromise of 1850**

crisis. In July 1850, President Taylor died after contracting cholera. His successor, **Millard Fillmore,** supported Henry Clay's compromise bill. Congress also experienced changes in its leadership, as the three figures who had dominated the institution passed from the scene. John C. Calhoun had died in March 1850, the same month in which he left his deathbed to hear his speech against the compromise delivered on the Senate floor (he was too weak to read it himself). Clay left Congress shortly after the defeat of the omnibus bill to recover from exhaustion and the effects of tuberculosis (from which he eventually died in 1852). Daniel Webster, who had supported the compromise from the beginning, became Fillmore's Secretary of State, a position from which he would enforce the elements of compromise after it was passed. As these congressional veterans left the scene, new leaders emerged. Some were sectional partisans determined to defend their regions' interests at all costs. Others were dealmakers, including Senator **Stephen Douglas** of Illinois. Like Fillmore, Douglas was eager to put the sectional crisis to rest—largely because he thought the political furor distracted from issues that he considered to be more important, especially railroad construction and the economic development of the western territories.

With Clay and Fillmore's blessing, Douglas used his considerable knowledge of legislative process to work around the sectional impasse. He broke up the omnibus bill into five separate bills (one for each of the numbered points discussed on the previous page) and built a shifting majority around each bill. Douglas's strategy allowed him to rely on a combination of northern Democrats and Whigs to pass the bill for California statehood, while he found enough northern Democrats to join with Southerners to pass the Fugitive Slave bill. Douglas repeated this process for the other three components of the collective agreement soon to be known as the **Compromise of 1850** that he believed would bring a final settlement to the sectional disputes over slavery. A more accurate interpretation would be that the senator found a way for his colleagues to stop arguing for a while. As historian David Potter noted, Douglas had not achieved so much of a compromise as he had engineered an armistice.

But in 1850, the temporary nature of the compromise was not evident. Douglas, Fillmore, and their allies considered it to be a permanent arrangement. The Fillmore administration certainly worked hard to enforce its provisions. In his new role as Secretary of State, Daniel Webster ensured that anti-compromise Whigs received no patronage from the administration. Abolitionists railed against the **Fugitive Slave Law of 1850,** urging people to resist. Some abolitionists even advocated violence. When an early attempt to enforce the law in Christina,

Franklin Pierce

Pennsylvania, produced a riot that left a slave owner dead and a few others seriously wounded, the administration responded by issuing forty-one indictments for treason. The government's case ultimately fell apart—opposition to the Fugitive Slave Law, even when violent, hardly amounted to the constitutional definition of treason as war against the United States—and no one was convicted. In 1851, the administration ensured that Thomas Sims, a Georgia runaway who had been apprehended in the abolitionist stronghold of Boston, Massachusetts to be returned to his owner. Court proceedings took place under guard, with Sims being surrounded the entire time by nine armed men. A force of three hundred men surrounded Sims as he was moved from the courthouse to a waiting ship bound for Georgia. A similar scene would be repeated in Boston three years later when the same court ordered runaway Anthony Burns to be returned to slavery in Virginia. An estimated crowd of 50,000 showed up at the docks to show their displeasure with the judge's decision. (Both men eventually returned to Boston—Burns after abolitionists succeeded in purchasing his freedom for $1,300, and Sims after escaping again in 1863.) In the long term, these incidents convinced many Northerners that the federal government had fully committed itself to the defense of slavery. In the short term, however, these events tended to make the antislavery movement, or at least its more radical elements, appear to be the

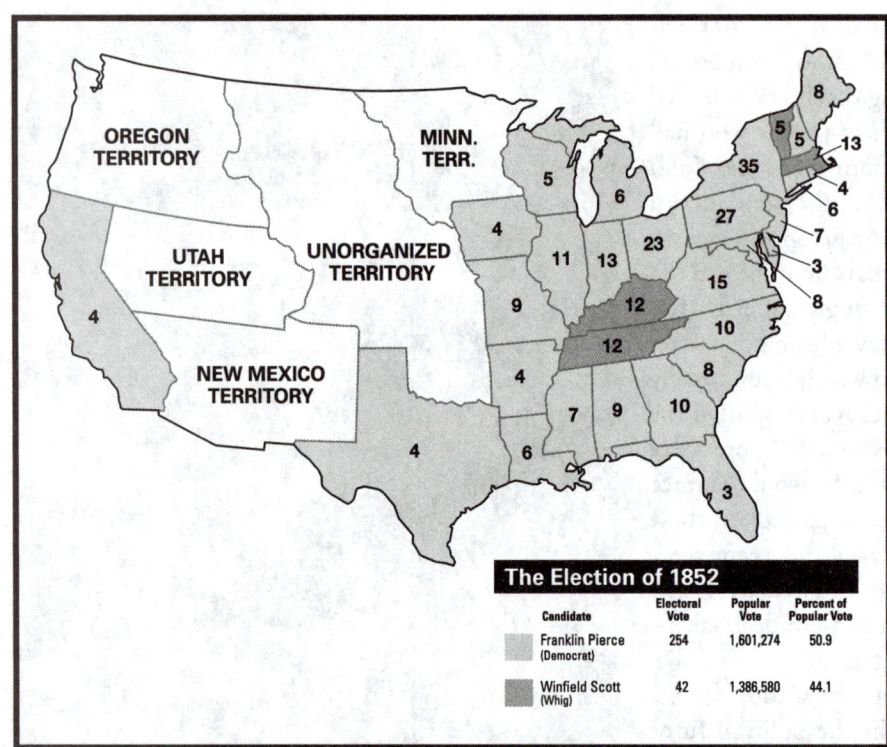

Map 15.3 The Election of 1852

The Election of 1852			
Candidate	Electoral Vote	Popular Vote	Percent of Popular Vote
Franklin Pierce (Democrat)	254	1,601,274	50.9
Winfield Scott (Whig)	42	1,386,580	44.1

enemies of law and order—a perception that tended to leave them marginalized. Southern secessionists likewise found themselves isolated. The sequel to the Nashville Convention failed to materialize. By 1851, sectional tensions for the first time since 1846 had subsided, and Americans hoped they could turn their attention to other matters.

THE END OF SECTIONAL HARMONY

Decline of the Whigs

Stephen Douglas quickly capitalized on the emergence of sectional peace. His faction within the Democratic Party—the "Young America" movement—took the initiative in setting the agenda for the nation. Young America advocates sought aggressive territorial expansion, free trade, and support for internal improvements. They succeeded in getting one of their own, **Franklin Pierce** of New Hampshire, the Democratic Party's nomination for president in 1852, after which he crushed the Whig candidate, General Winfield Scott. Pierce received nearly 51 percent of the popular vote, carrying 27 of 31 states and captured 254 of 296 electoral votes. Democrats also picked up 30 seats in the House, which secured them a two-thirds majority. The election of 1852 demonstrated that the Whigs had ceased to be a nationally competitive party. Divisions that had emerged during the crisis that led to the Compromise of 1850 had torn the party apart.

Its northern and southern wings no longer trusted one another, while its northern ranks were also riddled with internal conflict over how to deal with slavery. Yet, the sudden decline of the Whigs was just one signal that American politics were moving in a new direction, one that tended toward continued sectional conflict. Indeed, Pierce would ultimately find himself mired in it—and the developments taking place during his term ensured little prospect existed for a long-term settlement between the North and South.

One development that undermined the Whig Party reflected the changing face of the northern electorate. For most of the first half of the nineteenth century, the vast majority of the American population had been native born. During the 1840s, however, large numbers of immigrants arrived in American port cities. (Nearly three million arrived between 1845 and 1854, more than triple the number of immigrants coming in the preceding ten-year period.) In 1850, nearly 10 percent of the U.S. population was foreign born; by 1860, that proportion increased to 13 percent. Most of these newcomers settled in the northern states. The foreign-born population of Massachusetts increased from 16 percent in 1850 to 21 percent in 1860 and rose from 13 to 18 percent in Illinois during the same period. By 1860, 25 percent of the entire nation's immigrant population lived in New York City. The foreign-born population also increased in the South, but the proportion was small in comparison with the North. Arkansas, Florida, Georgia, Mississippi, Virginia, and both Carolinas each had foreign-born populations

Harriet Beecher Stowe, author of *Uncle Tom's Cabin*

under 3 percent. These currents of immigration brought large numbers of impoverished Irish Catholics (along with other migrants, especially Germans) into areas previously dominated by Protestants primarily of English descent. Many Protestant voters felt culturally and economically threatened by these demographic changes and demanded greater restrictions on immigration.

Uncle Tom's Cabin

The new political dynamic introduced by immigration competed with continuing concerns over slavery within substantial segments of the northern electorate. Although Douglas, Fillmore, Pierce and others believed that the Compromise of 1850 had settled the matter, the slavery issue remained salient. One sign confirming this was the northern public's reaction to **Uncle Tom's Cabin**, an immensely popular novel published by Harriet Beecher Stowe in 1852. A daughter of the influential, reform-minded minister Lyman Beecher, Stowe found inspiration for her book in the Fugitive Slave Law of 1850, which horrified her and fellow abolitionists. The novel contains two storylines. One subplot involves Eliza, a slave who fled from a Kentucky plantation upon learning that her infant son had just been sold to a slave trader. Her story includes a dramatic escape across the frozen Ohio River (with her child in her arms), meetings with politicians who become moved to renounce their support for the Fugitive Slave Law, and confrontations with armed slave hunters. The second storyline involves Uncle Tom, a loyal, deeply Christian slave sold to the same trader who had purchased Eliza's child, though he refused to run away. Tom's initial

sale took him deeper into the South as he was transferred from owner to owner. Along the way he meets a variety of masters and enslaved people who recount their experiences. At one point, Tom is almost set free—his freedom being the dying wish of a girl he had befriended during his travels—but his prospects of freedom end when the girl's father is killed in a drunken brawl. Instead, the man's widow sells Tom, and he eventually lands on the plantation of the abusive Simon Legree, who kills him when he tries to protect two exploited enslaved women. Tom dies in the arms of the son of his original master who had tracked him down with the intent of purchasing him and bringing him home. Throughout the novel, Stowe emphasizes that, although there may have been examples of decent slaveholders, the system of slavery offered no protection from the worst ones—and the entire institution was therefore morally bankrupt.

After being published in serialized form in the *National Era*, *Uncle Tom's Cabin* sold 300,000 copies in its first year of release as a single volume book. Not all readers embraced her goals, as numerous minstrel shows produced racist, bastardized versions of her narrative. (Minstrel shows were live performances featuring white actors wearing "blackface" makeup in which they imitated black dialect, black music, and told often racially-charged jokes.) Nevertheless, her novel effectively took arguments that abolitionists had been making for years and presented them in a narrative framework that northern readers found more accessible. The success of her work contributed greatly to a further transformation of northern attitudes toward slavery, clearly demonstrating that there remained a significant amount of interest in the subject.

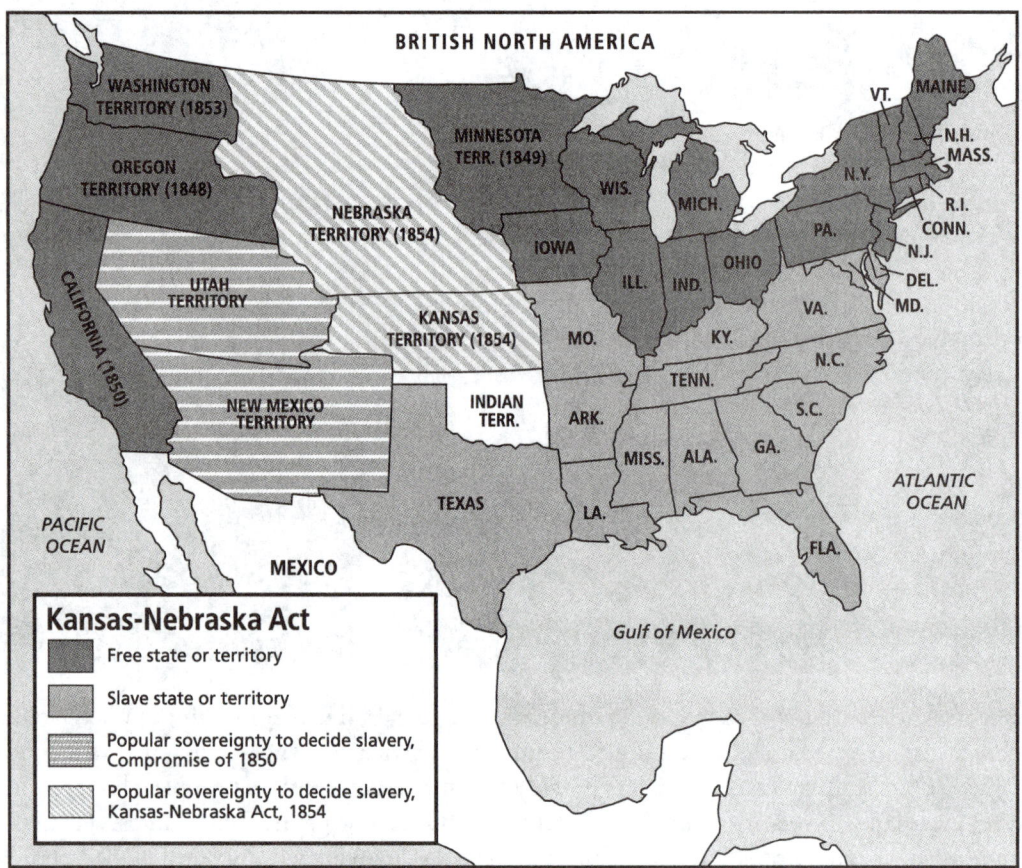

Map 15.4 Kansas-Nebraska Act

The Ostend Manifesto

Southern expansionists had also not lost their interest in the slavery issue, wishing to secure more territory for slaveholders. In 1854, three pro-expansion American diplomats to Europe appointed by the Pierce administration met in Belgium and composed the **Ostend Manifesto**—a diplomatic dispatch supporting the view that the United States should annex the Spanish colony of Cuba, which in the early 1850s was experiencing yet another in a recurrent series of uprisings. Cuban instability, the diplomats argued, posed a threat to the United States, to which the nation should respond by either purchasing the island for no more than $120 million or by "wresting it from Spain if we possess the power." Such an acquisition would have provided the United States with more slaveholding territory since the institution had long been legal in Cuba. The proposal went nowhere, but it did carry some intended consequences when its contents became public. First, the interest in Cuba created an impression that American expansion had now been linked specifically to the expansion of slavery. Second, the Pierce administration had demonstrated its susceptibility to political pressure from proslavery Southerners determined to protect and extend their institution. By the time that the Ostend Manifesto came to light, however, American politicians were concluding that the compromise effort had failed as they had begun to square off over the expansion of slavery into Kansas.

The Kansas-Nebraska Act

Although the success of *Uncle Tom's Cabin* and the controversy over the Ostend Manifesto hinted that the sectional crisis had not been resolved, Stephen Douglas remained convinced that the compromise measures he ushered through Congress in 1850 had settled the dispute between the North and the South. In 1854, however, he inadvertently reopened the conflict through his effort to secure a railway route that would link San Francisco, California, to Chicago, Illinois. As a leader of the Young America faction of Democrats, Douglas held a deep interest in expansion and economic development. The construction of a transcontinental railroad route furthered both of those goals. As an ambitious politician based in Chicago, he knew this project would benefit both his home state and his own prospects for higher office. However, the "Little Giant" (as the portly, five-foot-four-inch-tall senator was nicknamed by contemporaries) did not operate in a vacuum, and the concessions that he made along the way moved the United States' sectional conflict to an unprecedented level of acrimony.

The main challenges that Douglas faced involved beating back competing corridors favored by other politicians while dealing with the fact that much of his route passed through unorganized territory—the remaining Louisiana Purchase lands north of the 36°30' latitude where Congress had banned slavery as a result of the 1820 Missouri Compromise. Before he could move forward, Douglas needed to convince Congress to organize this area. Getting such a bill approved required him to court leading southern Democrats who demanded that the proposed legislation explicitly repeal the Missouri Compromise's prohibition on slavery's expansion. Realizing that such a drastic shift would alienate northern supporters of his plan, Douglas proposed dividing the region into two separate federal territories—Kansas Territory to the immediate west of Missouri, and the larger Nebraska Territory encompassing the lands to the north of Kansas—with popular sovereignty to determine the fate of slavery in each territory. Douglas expected trouble, predicting that the change would raise "a hell of a storm," but he also fully expected Kansas to become a free state. The senator believed that the flow of northern settlers combined with the local soil and climate would retard widespread cotton cultivation, thus preventing slavery from taking hold in Kansas.

As Douglas predicted, the introduction of his bill produced a major uproar in the North. Ohio's Salmon Chase and Joshua Giddings, along with Charles Sumner of Massachusetts, released "an Appeal from the Independent Democrats" to the press. The three politicians accused Douglas of violating a sacred pledge to stop slavery's expansion and warned that the proposed **Kansas-Nebraska Act** would cut the Union's free territory in half. The "Appeal" shifted the terms of the sectional debate by linking both Douglas and popular sovereignty to the expansion of slavery—a charge from which the "Little Giant" never fully recovered. Douglas moved the bill through the Senate by a 37 to 14 vote, before Alexander Stephens (the future Vice President of the Confederacy) guided the measure through the House by a 113 to 100 margin. President Pierce signed the Kansas-Nebraska Act into law a few days later, further cementing his image among northern abolitionists as a tool of slaveholding interests.

The Know Nothings

The passage of the Kansas-Nebraska Act transformed American politics. Its passage severely weakened the Democratic Party's northern wing. Before 1854, northern and southern Democrats had been roughly balanced with neither section dominating the party. The House of Representatives that passed the Kansas-Nebraska Act, for example, contained 67 southern Democrats and 91 northern Democrats. After the 1854 congressional elections, however, Northerners made up only 25 of the 88 House Democrats. Although the party regained a majority in the House by 1856, Democrats would remain numerically dominated by Southerners for years to come. The declining number of northern Democrats coincided with larger shifts in the northern electorate. By 1854, northern voters shifted their allegiances as they looked to organizations capable of responding to new concerns that now seemed to be most important.

One of these concerns grew out of the reaction against the growing number of immigrants moving into the North. Anti-immigrant sentiment—or nativism—had spawned its own political movement by 1854, finding its vehicle in the **American Party**. Five years earlier in New York City, local workingmen with nativist views had founded a secret fraternal organization officially known as the "Order of the Star-Spangled Banner" but soon acquiring the nickname of "Know Nothings" because of their vow to say "I know nothing" if ever asked any details about the group. During the early 1850s, the Know Nothings chose to organize politically in order to advance their views, entering state and national politics under the American Party label. Strongly anti-Catholic and convinced that Irish Catholic immigrants would undermine American democracy and hand control of the country to the Pope, the Know Nothings supported the expulsion of all poor immigrants, a ban on any foreign-born person from ever voting or holding elective office, and requiring an immigrant to live 21 years in the United States before they could become a citizen. Taking advantage of the declining power of both the Whigs and northern Democrats, and building on the anxieties generated by the increasing number of immigrants that had arrived in the last decade, the new party captured 62 seats in the House during the 1854 congressional elections. Despite its early success, the Know Nothings ultimately proved to be an ineffective national force for two reasons. First, nativism's strength faded as it moved westward from states like New York, Pennsylvania, and Massachusetts and toward states like Illinois and Indiana, which were hungry for settlers. Second, the American Party faltered on the slavery issue. Initially, the Know Nothings' leadership sought to build a southern wing, often identifying abolitionists as a threat to the Union. By 1855, however, the party fragmented when its leaders refused to take a stand against slavery's expansion. The renewed fear of slavery's expansion strongly competed with nativism for the attention of northern voters.

The Rise of the Republican Party

The new **Republican Party** which formed in the North from the ashes of the Whig Party and attracted a sizeable number of northern Democrats, eventually proved to be the political organization that best responded to that growing angst. Politically shrewd, Republican leaders accommodated nativist voters by focusing their critique on immigrant groups who were not likely to vote for their candidates anyway. (Republicans, for example, wrote off the Irish who generally distrusted the party's Anglo-Protestant orientation and support for issues like temperance.) The issue that motivated the Republicans was slavery, although they were by no means an abolitionist organization. Some of the new party's members, like William Seward and Salmon P. Chase, favored immediate emancipation, but they also worked alongside members like Abraham Lincoln who could tolerate slavery's continued existence for an indefinite period as long as the institution was not allowed to expand. Despite these internal differences, opposition to slavery's expansion became the core principle uniting all Republicans.

The key element in the Republican Party's antagonism toward slavery's expansion lay in the conviction that the absence of slavery had made the North's "free labor" system superior to the South in every way. To Republicans, the phrase "free labor" denoted workers' ability to labor for employers of their own choosing, to earn and save their wages, to move at will, and to speak their minds. Free-labor capitalism in the North had produced a society that had more railroad mileage, banks, land under cultivation, investment capital, cities, and manufacturing than the South. In highlighting this contrast, Hinton Helper of North Carolina, a rare southern Republican, wrote in his book, *The Impending Crisis of the South*, that "if eight entire slave States . . . and the District of Columbia . . . were put up at auction, New York could buy them all, and then have one hundred and thirty-three millions of dollars left in her pocket! Such is the amazing contrast between freedom and slavery." Sustained progress, however, depended on the continuous expansion of free farmers into fresh land, and slavery's expansion stood in the way.

The Republicans' vision proved remarkably influential as it came together in the mid-1850s. The party attracted northern Whigs looking for a new political home, such as Abraham Lincoln and William Seward who brought with them a Protestant sensibility and an admiration for Henry Clay. A great many northern Democrats also joined the new party. Voters in New Hampshire, which had been a Democratic stronghold since the days of Jackson, transformed their state into a Republican bastion in 1854, and they never looked back. Former Democrats like

Salmon Chase rose to positions of leadership within the Republican Party whose receptiveness further contributed to the decline of northern Democrats.

The emergence of the Republicans, combined with the growing dominance of the South within the Democratic Party, intensified the sectional conflict. Southerners saw Republicans as a revolutionary force that would destroy the Union. They considered free labor to be little more than a mask for all sorts of radical reform—free love, abolition, socialism. Free labor also accommodated the brutal exploitation of white workers, since employers hired and discarded them at will. This system of "wage slavery" kept people mired in poverty, even as it gave those same people the right to vote. Southern propagandists argued that the electorate would one day vote private property out of existence. Slavery, they continued, provided a fundamental stability that the North lacked. Thus, by the mid-1850s, northern and southern views of their sections had hardened into mutually antagonistic worldviews.

Republican electoral strategy further intensified this dynamic because the party's strategists determined that they could win a national election by carrying the North. Their plan began with their portrayal of the federal government in general, and Stephen Douglas in particular, as a tool of a Slave Power conspiracy to expand slavery into both the West and the North. Republicans only needed to convince a majority of northern voters to believe them. Events over the next few years would give their theory an increasing air of truth, especially since southern politicians feeling increasingly embattled took actions perceived to be increasingly aggressive.

"Bleeding Kansas"

Events in Kansas soon provided Republicans with an opportunity to develop their narrative. Land-hungry settlers poured into the new territory when it opened in 1855. Most of these folk cared little for sectional politics; they came to farm, but sectional partisans cared deeply about the future of Kansas. William Seward predicted that the North's advantage in population would deliver a free state. Other leaders took affirmative steps to ensure that their side would determine the fate of slavery in the territory. The New England Emigrant Aid Company settled a few thousand antislavery activists. Proslavery interests met the challenge, as thousands of "Border Ruffians"—proslavery activists from neighboring Missouri—spilled into Kansas to cast illegal ballots in the first territorial election and intimidate northern settlers. Within months, both factions had organized their own governments. By 1856, the two sides were engaged in open warfare.

Republicans labeled this turn of events "**Bleeding Kansas**," even if the fighting itself up to this point tended to be relatively bloodless. They effectively highlighted selected events to make their case that the "Slave Power" was restraining democracy with violence. Two incidents, in fact, made their job easy. On May 21, 1856, pro-slavery settlers attacked Lawrence, Kansas, which free-state settlers claimed as their capital, setting fire to the Free State Hotel (a fortified structure used by the Massachusetts Emigrant Society to welcome arriving anti-slavery settlers) and destroying two printing presses. That act, according to Republicans, showed proslavery advocates' willingness to squelch free speech to protect their institution. Further, an event taking place the next day in Washington, D.C., revealed that the violence was not limited to Kansas. During congressional debate over the events in Kansas, three days earlier, Republican Senator **Charles Sumner** of Massachusetts had delivered a vitriolic speech denouncing slavery while lambasting slaveholders and pro-slavery politicians, specifically insulting South Carolina Senator Pierce Butler, who had no opportunity to respond because he was home recovering from a stroke. Representative Preston Brooks, one of Butler's relatives, avenged his kinsman by savagely beating Sumner on the Senate floor while he worked at his desk, knocking Sumner unconscious. Brooks soon resigned his seat, but the voters in his district easily reelected him. Not only did his constituents look favorably upon his actions, people from across the South sent him new canes to replace the one he broke on Sumner. Meanwhile, Senator Sumner left Congress for three years to recover, with Massachusetts keeping his seat vacant to remind onlookers of the "Slave Power's" quick resort to force when challenged. The Republicans' developing narrative required them to downplay the violent tendencies on their own side. For example, Henry Ward Beecher, an influential minister and brother of Harriet Beecher Stowe, sent rifles to Kansas in boxes labeled Bibles ("Beecher's Bibles"). Meanwhile, **John Brown**, a white abolitionist who concluded that violence offered the only means of ending slavery, led his sons to the banks of Pottawatomie Creek, Kansas, where they killed five proslavery settlers with machetes, setting off a guerilla-style war for the remainder of the year until President Pierce stationed over a thousand federal troops in Kansas to restore order.

The Dred Scott Case

Republican electoral strategy began showing dividends in the 1856 election. John C. Frémont, a famous western explorer and veteran of the Mexican American War, secured the first Republican presidential nomination, running on a platform opposing the expansion of slavery and embracing as its slogan: "Free soil, free labor, free speech, free men, Frémont!" Pennsylvania's James Buchanan, an established politician whose foreign assignments had allowed him to sit out most of the sectional controversies, took the nomination for the Democratic Party, which supported popular sovereignty and the proslavery faction in Kansas. Buchanan won the presidency with 45.3 percent of the popular vote and 174 votes in the Electoral College; Democrats also regained 48 seats in the House, which placed them back in the majority. Although Frémont lost the election, the returns gave Republicans hope. Frémont won 11 of the 16 free states. Meanwhile, in the House of Representatives, Republicans established themselves as the major opposition party, claiming 44 seats and nearly absorbing the American (Know Nothing) Party's loss of 48 seats. In fact, if the anti-Democratic vote had not been split between the Republicans and Know Nothings, Buchanan may well have lost the presidency. The new party, therefore, pushed on, soon benefiting from the actions of overreaching proslavery Democrats.

Within days of Buchanan's inaugural address in which the new president predicted the end of sectional controversy, the Supreme Court renewed the conflict. Buchanan remarked in his speech that the Court was about to issue a ruling that would settle the question of slavery in the territories. The case, **Dred Scott v. Sandford** (1857), grew out of lawsuits filed by Harriet Scott and her husband, Dred, initiated in the 1840s to secure their family's freedom on the basis of being brought into the free territory of Minnesota despite the congressional ban on slavery there as part of the 1820 Missouri Compromise. After losing in Missouri state courts, the Scotts moved their case into federal court where their suit became transformed from a relatively straightforward freedom claim into a case that would finally define Congress's power over slavery in the territories. In early March 1857, Chief Justice Roger B. Taney issued the Court's official opinion. His sprawling, confusing, and decidedly proslavery opinion contained two major rulings. First, because he believed that African Americans historically "had no rights which the white man was bound to respect," the Constitution did not recognize any blacks, whether enslaved or not, as a citizen of the United States. Consequently, the federal courts had no jurisdiction in the case. Nevertheless, Taney continued to issue a second major ruling: that the portion of the Missouri Compromise restricting slavery north of the compromise line was unconstitutional because Congress had no right to ban slavery in any federal territories.

Republicans led the attack against the ruling, linking the Court to the "Slave Power conspiracy," emphasizing the fact that southern Democrats dominated the tribu-

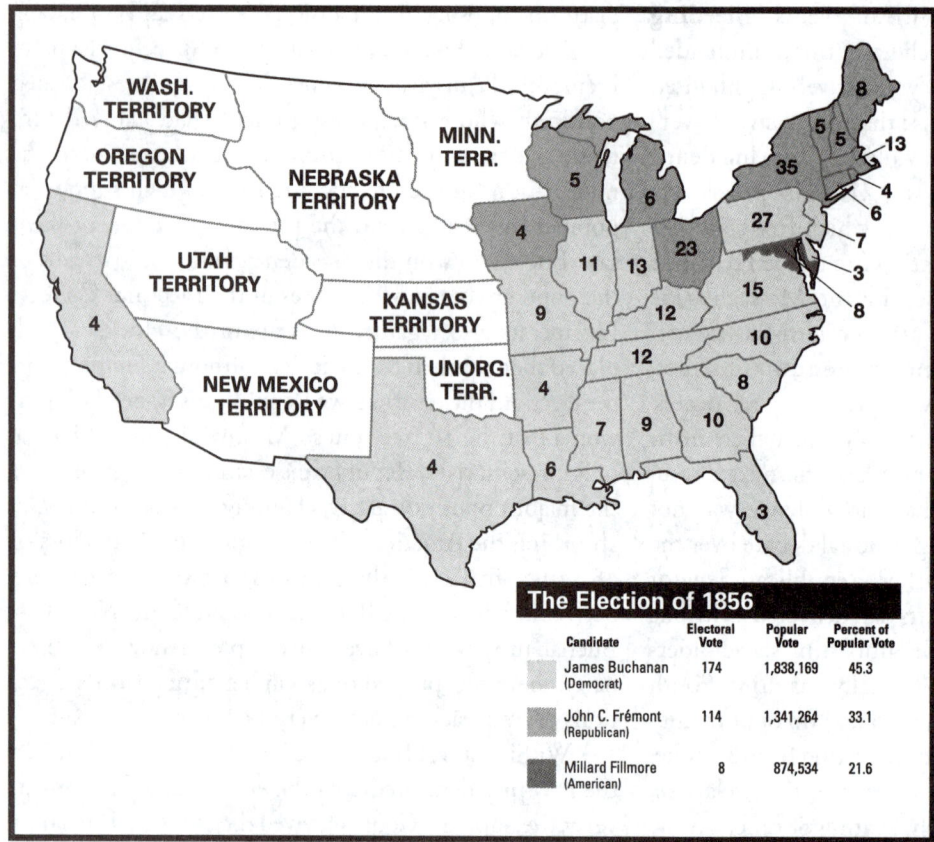

Map 15.5
The Election of 1856

The Election of 1856			
Candidate	Electoral Vote	Popular Vote	Percent of Popular Vote
James Buchanan (Democrat)	174	1,838,169	45.3
John C. Frémont (Republican)	114	1,341,264	33.1
Millard Fillmore (American)	8	874,534	21.6

nal. Of the Court's nine justices, seven belonged to the Democratic Party, five were Southerners, and four were slaveholders (though strongly proslavery, Chief Justice Taney had not personally owned slaves for decades). Yet, only the Court's two non-Democratic members—John McLean (a Republican) and Benjamin Robbins Curtis (who remained a devoted Whig)—dissented. The remaining justices all agreed with Taney that Dred Scott and his family should remain enslaved, although they did not agree on exactly why. Some even wrote elaborate opinions that contradicted Taney's reasoning, if not the Chief Justice's conclusions.

Rather than settling the issue, the *Dred Scott* decision deepened regional distrust. The decision seemed to imply that Congress was powerless to limit the expansion of slavery anywhere. Some slavery opponents wondered if the Supreme Court would later rule that state bans on slavery violated a master's property rights. The decision fed the worst suspicions of those who believed that the country secretly was ruled by a "slave power" that wanted to see the peculiar institution spread from coast to coast. It also greatly undermined the popularity outside of the South for President Buchanan, who the public perceived as enthusiastically supporting the controversial ruling.

The Lecompton Constitution

The bonds between Southerners and northern Democrats became severely strained at the next crisis point, emerging only a few months after the *Dred Scott* decision. Kansas once again became the source of the trouble. Although free-state residents outnumbered them by at least two to one, proslavery settlers, thanks to votes cast illegally by border ruffians in both 1855 and 1857, controlled the officially recognized government in the territory. In 1857, the legislature called for a convention to be held in Lecompton, Kansas to draw up a state constitution, provided for the election of delegates through a process that all observers knew to be rigged, and permitted the finished product to advance without a referendum. All of these moves guaranteed that Kansas would have a proposed state constitution favored by the territory's proslavery minority.

When the territorial governor resigned in disgust, President Buchanan appointed Robert J. Walker (a respected Democrat born in Pennsylvania but who long resided in Mississippi) to be the territory's new governor. Walker urged free-state settlers to participate in the election of delegates, but they refused, thus all the convention's seats fell into the hands of proslavery settlers. Believing he had Buchanan's support, Walker insisted that any constitution be subject to a referendum, which, he knew, would have doomed any proslavery document in any fairly conducted process. The Lecompton Convention drew up a constitution that explicitly protected slavery. Although initially hesitant, the delegates authorized a public referendum on their work, but in a contrived manner that ensured that the process would not be fairly conducted. Rather than subject the constitution to the usual method of an up-or-down vote, the convention forced voters to choose between two constitutions. Both versions explicitly protected slavery, the only significant difference was that one permitted Kansas to participate in the interstate slave trade while the other did not. Free-state Kansans denounced the process as a sham; Walker resigned in protest; and Kansas voters chose the option allowing participation in the interstate slave trade. (An investigation later concluded that close to half these votes were cast illegally.)

Northern observers, both Democrat and Republican, agreed that the entire process producing the **Lecompton Constitution** was pure folly, and they reacted with disgust when Buchanan proposed that Congress accept the document and admit Kansas as a slave state. Stephen Douglas argued that the Lecompton Constitution reduced popular sovereignty to little more than a joke and led the opposition. Buchanan warned him that Democratic administrations enforced party discipline by crushing those who broke ranks, citing examples as far back as Andrew Jackson's administration. Before storming out of the White House, the senator told Buchanan "to remember that General Jackson is dead." Douglas could not stop the bill's passage in the Senate, but his supporters in the House of Representatives joined with Republicans to defeat the bill after a fierce debate that included an open brawl on the House floor. Southerners, who had regarded Douglas as an ally, now treated him as a traitor. The Senate stripped him of his leadership positions, and Buchanan tried unsuccessfully to replace him as a candidate for his seat in the upcoming 1858 election.

The Rise of Lincoln

Although some Republicans toyed with the idea of embracing Douglas as one of their own—he was after all the most prominent politician in the North—Illinois Republicans understood that the senator would remain a committed Democrat so instead they nominated Abraham Lincoln, a successful lawyer and frustrated politician, to run against Douglas. A former Whig who had retired from politics after serving a single term in the House of Representatives during the late 1840s, Lincoln reentered politics as a Republican when the Kansas-Nebraska Act reopened the issue of slavery's expansion. During his fa-

mous 1858 "House-Divided" speech in which he accepted his party's nomination for the Senate, Lincoln argued that the Democratic Party's leadership (specifically naming Douglas, along with Franklin Pierce, James Buchanan, and Roger B. Taney) had conspired to force slavery into the territories and might attempt to reintroduce slavery into the northern states. Their plan had begun with the Kansas-Nebraska Act, and, abetted by the *Dred Scott* decision, would continue unless stopped by organized Republican opposition. In Lincoln's words:

[T]his government cannot endure permanently half slave and half free. I do not expect the Union to be dissolved. . . . It will become all one thing, or all the other. Either the opponents of slavery will arrest the further spread of it, and place it . . . in the course of ultimate extinction; or its advocates will push it forward, till it shall become alike lawful in all the States, old as well as new—North as well as South.

Douglas, of course, rejected Lincoln's charge that he was the chief architect of an effort to transform slavery into a national institution, though he had no moral qualms about slavery's continued existence in the South or even the institution's expansion into places where settlers genuinely wanted it. He would have many opportunities to defend himself because he and Lincoln engaged in a series of seven joint debates across the state before voters went to the polls (to choose their state legislators who would actually decide who the next U.S. Senator from Illinois would be).

The 1858 **Lincoln-Douglas Debates** did little to aid Lincoln's short-term prospects—the Democrats would narrowly retain control of the Illinois legislature and reelect Douglas—but they played a powerful role in establishing Lincoln as a national political figure while also intensifying the post-Lecompton divisions in the Democratic Party. Using a common accusation against antislavery politicians, Douglas tried to portray Lincoln as an advocate of racial equality. An end to slavery, Douglas predicted, would place black and white Americans on equal footing and even permit interracial marriage. Lincoln responded that he did not intend to "introduce political and social equality between the white and the black races." He agreed with his opponent that African Americans were "not my equal in many respects—certainly not in color, perhaps not in moral or intellectual endowment." Yet Lincoln insisted that accepting inequality did not therefore mandate slavery: "[I]n the right to eat the bread, without the leave of anybody else, which his own hand earns, [a black American] is my equal and the equal of . . . Douglas, and the equal of every living man." By modern standards Lincoln took a racist position, but his stance in 1858 established him as a moderate figure within the Republican Party capable of appealing to a wide range of voters across the northern electorate who detested slavery while holding no great sympathy for African Americans.

The Harpers Ferry Raid

Over the next two years, relations between the North and South continued to deteriorate. The Panic of 1857, a short but severe economic downturn, forced businesses to close, threw hundreds of thousands of workers onto the streets, and pushed crop prices down. Yet the crisis confined itself to the North; the southern economy remained relatively unscathed. Southerners took their uninterrupted prosperity as a sign of the superiority of "King Cotton" and the institution of slavery that sustained it. In Congress, Southerners blocked a tariff bill that Republicans believed would have boosted the economy and put people back to work. They also blocked bills supported by both Republicans and northern Democrats. Southern maneuvers—supported at times with Buchanan's veto—killed a proposed railroad to the Pacific, grants of land to agricultural and mechanical colleges, and a Homestead Act that would have provided free land to settlers. These actions gave the South some short-term victories, but they further alienated northern voters in a way that would benefit the Republicans in 1860.

Just how distant the North and South had moved from each other became clear in late 1859, when John Brown resurfaced to lead an attempted insurrection among the South's enslaved population. Brown planned to capture the federal arsenal in Harpers Ferry, Virginia (now West Virginia), arm the slaves who he believed would flock to join him, and grow his force as he pushed further into the South. Although he received financing backing from a group of wealthy white abolitionists inspired by his actions in Kansas, Brown received little support from northern blacks. Frederick Douglass, who befriended Brown, thought the plan was suicidal and that the attack would "array the whole country against us." Brown attacked with a force consisting of eighteen men, capturing the nearly unguarded arsenal before armed locals and state militia pinned them down. U.S. Marines, under the command of future Confederate generals Robert E. Lee and J.E.B. Stuart, captured Brown after storming the building near the arsenal where he and the others were held up. Within a few months, Virginia had tried and hanged Brown and six of his comrades for treason against the state.

The reaction to Brown's execution in December 1859 underscored the Union's growing sectional divisions.

Southerners welcomed the hanging. Believing that Brown had attempted to open a race war within their section, they feared his effort would not be the last by radical abolitionists. In the North, however, concerns about Brown's sanity gave way over the course of his trial to a portrayal of the man as a martyr for the cause of freedom. His execution triggered the ringing of church bells, gun salutes, and commemorative sermons across the North. This behavior horrified Southerners, who considered Brown to be little more than a murderer, and politicians responded by maneuvering for advantage. Democrats condemned the mourning of Brown's death as the product of minority sentiment and organized anti-Brown meetings. Republicans distanced themselves from the abolitionist's violence, but compared him to the southern "filibusterers" who had emerged during the 1850s seeking to expand slavery by capturing territory in Latin America. One of them, William Walker, took over Nicaragua for a while. Brown had simply changed the focus from slavery to freedom.

The Election of 1860

Increasing sectional tensions finally split the Democratic Party in 1860. By that point, most other national institutions had already divided along sectional lines. In 1844, the Methodist and Baptist churches both separated into northern and southern branches. Nearly ten years later, the Whig Party had fallen apart, leaving some Southerners politically homeless and creating an opportunity for the Republican Party to emerge during the mid-1850s. Northern and southern Democrats, however, had managed to hold their party together until they met in April 1860 to nominate a presidential candidate. Stephen Douglas had established himself as the frontrunner by the time the convention opened, but southern delegates, who controlled enough votes to deprive Douglas of the two-thirds majority required to secure the nomination, demanded that the party include in its platform a uniform federal slave code for all U.S. territories. Douglas and his supporters, however, refused to consider the request. Southern delegates promptly walked out, eventually forming their own convention to nominate John C. Breckinridge of Kentucky (Buchanan's vice president) for the presidency on a platform that included the federal slave code provision. Before adjourning, the remaining northern Democrats nominated Stephen Douglas on a platform endorsing popular sovereignty as the best approach to the issue of slavery in the territories.

Republicans emerged from their Chicago convention in May 1860 more unified than their opponents. The main problem leading into their meeting involved the

John Brown: Traitor or Martyr?

In 1859, John Brown, a white abolitionist who believed that slavery would only end through violence, led an unsuccessful attempt to start a slave revolt by capturing the federal arsenal at Harpers Ferry, Virginia (now West Virginia). Southerners denounced him as a traitor who sought to foment a race war.. Many moderate northern politicians—such as future president Abraham Lincoln—who opposed slavery's expansion but rejected immediate emancipation—worked hard to distance themselves from Brown and his violent methods. A growing number of Northerners, however, viewed Brown in a positive light, as a man who sacrificed his life to end slavery. The painting by Thomas Hovenden that begins this chapter depicts an apocryphal story in which Brown asked an enslaved woman, rather than a southern clergyman, to pray for him upon his execution. Notice that Hovenden depicts Brown stopping to kiss an enslaved child, which one could read as an expression of racial equality. The antislavery poet John Greenleaf Whittier saw an even deeper meaning, believing that Brown's actions were driven by a deep and sacrificial Christian love that would eventually overwhelm southern oppression:

> John Brown of Ossawatomie spake on his dying day:
> "I will not have two strive my soul a priest in Slavery's pay.
> But let some poor slave-mother whom I have striven to free,
> With her children, from the gallows-stair put up a prayer for me!"
>
> John Brown of Ossawatomie, they led him out to die;
> And lo! A poor slave-mother with her little child pressed nigh.
> Then the bold, Blue eyes grew tender, and the old harsh face grew my,
> As he stooped between the jeering ranks and kissed the negro's child!
>
> The shadows of his storming life that moment fell apart;
> And they who blame the bloody hand for gave the loving heart.
> That kiss from all its guilty means redeem the good intent,
> And around the grisly fighter's hair the martyr's aureole bent!
>
> Parish with him the folly that seeks through evil good!
> Long live the generous purpose unstained with human blood!
> Not the raid of midnight terror, but the thoughts which underlies;
> Not the borderer's pride of daring, but the Christian's sacrifice.
>
> Nevermore may yon Blue Ridges the Northern rifle hear,
> Nor see the light of blazing home/on the Negro spear.
> But let the free-winged angel Truth there guarded passes scale,
> To teach that right is more than might, injustice more than mail!
>
> So vainly shall Virginia set her battle in array;
> In vain her trampling squadrons knead the winter snow with clay.
> She may strike the pouncing eagle, but she dares not harm the dove;
> And every gate she bars to Hate shall open wide to Love!

Source: John Greenleaf Whittier, "Brown of Ossawatomie," in **The Writings of John Greenleaf Whittier: In Seven Volumes** (London: MacMillan, 1889), 4: 106-107.

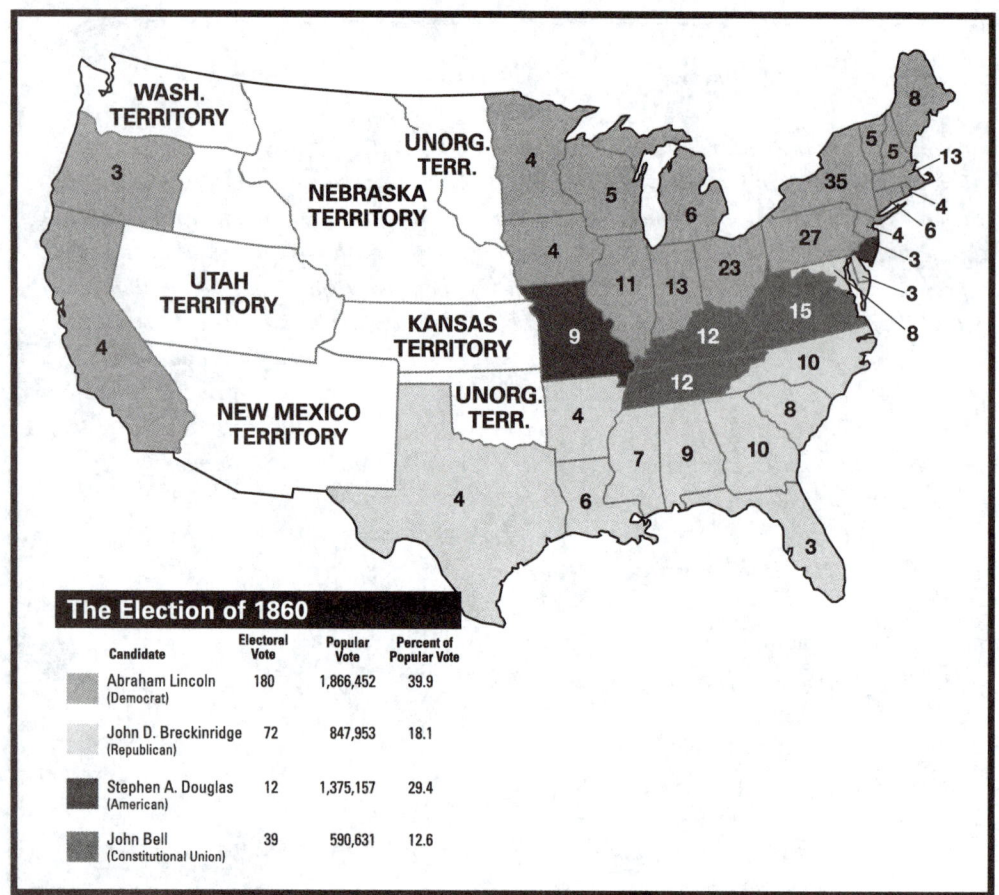

Map 15.6 The Election of 1860

The Election of 1860			
Candidate	Electoral Vote	Popular Vote	Percent of Popular Vote
Abraham Lincoln (Democrat)	180	1,866,452	39.9
John D. Breckinridge (Republican)	72	847,953	18.1
Stephen A. Douglas (American)	12	1,375,157	29.4
John Bell (Constitutional Union)	39	590,631	12.6

public's perception that some of their leading candidates were too radical. William Seward, for example, an avowed abolitionist who argued that the existence of a higher law trumped the Constitution. Democratic Senator Jefferson Davis of Mississippi charged that John Brown had found his inspiration in such talk, and the charge resonated with many voters, especially those supporting one of Seward's many Republican rivals. Ohio Senator Salmon P. Chase, who had built his reputation by challenging the Fugitive Slave Law, likewise seemed too radical for a national electorate. Other candidates proved too affiliated with the Know-Nothings, too willing to compromise with the South on slavery matters, or seemed too openly opportunistic to secure the nomination. As the convention worked through the list of potential nominees, Abraham Lincoln emerged as a figure worthy of serious consideration. Although his debates with Douglas had given Lincoln some national exposure, few observers thought he had much of a chance going into the convention. After performing well on the first ballot, his managers effectively sold him to the delegates as a self-made man who had worked hard to transform himself from a poor farm boy to a successful lawyer. Most importantly, he was a moderate on the slavery issue who nonetheless would not waver in his opposition to the extension of slavery into the territories. By the third ballot, Lincoln had secured

the nomination, and the party rallied behind him with enthusiasm.

Lincoln, however, ran for election only in the North. Most southern states refused to put his name on the ballot. Indeed, the election of 1860 proved to be nearly two separate elections. In the South, Breckinridge squared off against John Bell of the **Constitutional Union Party**, an organization consisting of former Whigs from the Upper South whose main goal was to seek further compromise between the two regions. By helping to deprive Republicans of enough electoral votes to win the election, they hoped Bell would emerge victorious in the House of Representatives. In the North, Lincoln and Douglas faced off. Douglas nearly worked himself to death during the election campaigning for himself (an unprecedented move in 1860), traveling through the North and South to tell voters that he was the only national candidate with the prestige and ability to end the sectional crisis. Republicans and southern Democrats both rejected this argument; his support for the Kansas-Nebraska Act led Republicans to believe that he was a tool of the Slave Power while his opposition to the Lecompton Constitution and his articulation of the Freeport Doctrine made him appear duplicitous to Southerners. A rash of corruption scandals in the Buchanan administration simply added to Douglas's troubles. Republicans in contrast unified behind Lincoln. William Seward, Lincoln's main rival for the nomination, and his supporters campaigned vigorously for Lincoln. His supporters delivered an estimated 50,000 stump speeches during the campaign.

Despite the crowded field of candidates, Abraham Lincoln emerged victorious in the presidential race. Though he received slightly less than 40 percent of the popular vote, Lincoln carried every free state—seventeen in all—to win a majority (58 percent) of the Electoral College votes. Breckinridge (18 percent of the popular vote) carried eleven of the fourteen slave states. Bell won the other three slave states, all located in the Upper South. Meanwhile, Stephen Douglas received nearly 30 percent of the national popular vote, but only won Missouri. Coinciding with the Republicans securing control of the Senate and maintaining their advantage in the House, these results all added up to a decisive electoral victory for Lincoln and his party.

THE END OF COMPROMISE

Lincoln's triumph moved the sectional crisis into a new phase. Southern partisans had long warned that the election of an antislavery president would lead to secession. Within weeks of Lincoln's election, South Carolina made good on the threat. Mississippi, Florida, Alabama, Georgia, Louisiana, and Texas followed suit over the next two months. By January 1861, these states had organized the Confederate States of America, with Jefferson Davis of Mississippi chosen to be its first (and only) president. The Confederacy's new vice president, former congressman Alexander Stephens of Georgia, minced no words about the immediate cause of the tumult. Debate over "the proper status of the negro in our form of civilization" had brought the South to this point, he noted, but the new government made possible by secession rested "upon the great truth, that the negro is not the equal of the white man; that slavery . . . is his natural and normal condition." Secession mania did not sweep the entire South. Citizens outside of the Deep South, in states such as Virginia, North Carolina, Maryland, and Kentucky, waited to make their decisions, as Lincoln had not yet taken office.

Even though seven southern states had already announced that they had seceded and formed the Confederate States of America, political leaders on both sides still hoped for compromise. Outgoing President James Buchanan, who believed that secession was unconstitutional but also held the view that the federal government had no legitimate authority to compel a state to stay in the Union against its will, did nothing to help the situation. Though he refused to recognize the Confederacy and supported the continued occupation of federal property in rebel states wherever possible, he also allowed federal property to fall into rebel hands in places where they were not tenable. Federal troops, for example, continued to control **Fort Sumter** in Charleston, South Carolina because its commander, Major Robert Anderson, though a Virginian, remained loyal to the United States. Anderson moved his soldiers into the fort, whose location on an island in the mouth of Charleston Harbor continued to control the city's port. By contrast, General David Twiggs, a Georgia native who commanded federal troops stationed in Texas, surrendered his headquarters in San Antonio and the forts under his command when pressed by Confederate agitators, in exchange for the peaceful departure of his men from the state. (Twiggs later became a major general in the Confederate army.)

Before his March 1861 inauguration (a full five months after his election), Abraham Lincoln deliberately kept a low profile. Not yet holding office, the president-elect did not wish to make the sectional tensions worse, especially since he did not yet possess any power to respond. The situation in the winter of 1860-1861 looked bleak. Along with the states that already announced that they were leaving the Union, a number of others lay on the brink of secession. Virginia, North Carolina, Tennessee, and Arkansas—all slave states—rejected the initial call for disunion, but voters in those states who remained deeply wary of Lincoln and the Republicans could be turned rather easily. Many voters in the border states of Kentucky, Maryland, and Missouri were also sympathetic to secession. Political leaders moved cautiously, but tensions escalated, nonetheless, especially in the vicinity of Fort Sumter.

As the winter dragged on, compromise efforts failed. Neither side could agree on the future of slavery's expansion. Senator John J. Crittenden of Kentucky, a former Whig and Know Nothing who most recently supported the Constitutional Union Party, brought forward the most notable conciliatory proposal. The so-called **Crittenden Compromise** offered to end the secession crisis with a package of constitutional amendments and congressional resolutions designed to entice the South back into the Union peacefully: "Unrepealable" amendments would have permanently guaranteed the existence of slavery in the states where it currently existed while extending the Missouri Compromise line to the California border, allowing slavery south of that boundary. Other proposed amendments would prohibit the abolition of slavery in Washington, D.C. and provide compensation to owners of fugitive slaves. The congressional resolutions pledged fidelity to the federal

Table 15.1 Overview of the Sectional Crisis

Event	Year	Effect
Wilmot Proviso	1846	A rider to an appropriations bill proposed by Representative David Wilmot of Pennsylvania at the beginning of the Mexican-American War. The Proviso stated that any territory acquired from Mexico should be closed to slavery. The Wilmot Proviso was never approved.
Compromise of 1850	1850	The Compromise of 1850 was a series of five bills dealing with the spread of slavery to the territories and other lingering national issues dealing with slavery. California was entered as a free state, New Mexico and Utah were allowed popular sovereignty, and a new stronger Fugitive Slave Act was established. It satisfied neither North or South and planted the seeds of future conflict.
Election of 1852	1852	Franklin Pierce of New Hampshire crushed the Whig candidate, General Winfield Scott. The election of 1852 demonstrated that the Whigs had ceased to be a nationally competitive party.
Kansas-Nebraska Act	1854	A law drafted by Stephen Douglas, passed by Congress, and signed by President Franklin Pierce that organized the territory that became the states of Kansas and Nebraska. Controversy surrounded the law because it repealed the Missouri Compromise restrictions on slavery in the northern Louisiana Purchase lands, and the reaction against that repeal brought about the organization of the Republican Party.
"Bleeding Kansas"	1855 to 1856	Refers to the violence surrounding the settlement of Kansas, which encompassed the activities of Missouri "Border Ruffians," the actions of John Brown, and the mini-civil war that broke out in the territory between pro- and anti-slavery forces during the mid-to-late 1850s.
Election of 1856	1856	Presidency won by Democrat James Buchanan of Pennsylvania, but a surprisingly strong showing by John C. Fremont, the nominee of the recently formed Republican Party in the North, set the stage for the 1860 election.
Dred Scott Case	1857	An 1857 Supreme Court decision that held African Americans were not citizens of the United States and that Congress possessed no power to limit slavery's expansion into the federal territories. Republicans used the case as evidence that a Slave Power Conspiracy had captured the federal government.
Lecompton Constitution	1857	A document that tried to bring Kansas into the Union as a slave state. The entire process was riddled with fraud, and the effort was defeated – despite the support of President Buchanan – by the combined efforts of Stephen Douglas and the Republicans. Kansas would ultimately enter the Union as a free state in 1862.
John Brown's Raid	1859	John Brown unsuccessfully attempted to start a slave revolt by capturing the federal arsenal at Harpers Ferry, Virginia. He was captured and executed for treason, but many Northerners regarded him as a martyr.
Election of 1860	1860	Abraham Lincoln received around 40 percent of the popular vote. He had carried every free state – seventeen in all. Lincoln's name was not on a ballot in a single southern state, however population growth in the North allowed Lincoln to be elected. The election was a decisive victory for Lincoln and the Republicans.
Fort Sumter	1861	Fort Sumter is best known as the site upon which the shots initiating the American Civil War were fired.

Fugitive Slave Law and condemned northern state laws that impeded the return of runaway slaves, but also took into account northern criticisms by suggesting a modification of the national law so judges received the same compensation regardless of their decisions in fugitive slave cases. The compromise failed. Congress tabled the proposal in December 1860, about two weeks after being introduced.

Many of Senator Crittenden's proposals reemerged at a Peace Conference that convened in Washington in February 1861. This convention proposed a constitutional amendment that, like the Crittenden Compromise, permitted the expansion of slavery (again below the Missouri Compromise line). For President-elect Lincoln and most Republican leaders, some of the proposals were open to negotiation, but not the continued expansion of slavery. If they made such a concession, their victory in the 1860 election (a mandate against the further expansion of slavery, in Republican eyes) would be meaningless. Without such a concession, however, the seceded states would not willingly submit to federal authority.

Lincoln summed up the impasse in his First Inaugural Address (March 4, 1861): "One section of our country believes slavery is right and ought to be extended, while the other believes it is wrong and ought not to be extended. This is the only substantial dispute." Lincoln professed, likely in all honesty at the time, "no purpose . . . to interfere with the institution of slavery in the States where it exists." He also accepted the Fugitive Slave Law, but he reasserted that secession was the immediate issue, not slavery's future: "I hold that in contemplation of universal law and of the Constitution the Union of these States is perpetual." The Constitution, Lincoln argued, did not contain a "provision . . . for its own termination." No state had the right to break with the Union on its own. "Secession," Lincoln's stated, was "the essence of anarchy." He thus pledged to hold on to the federal property, including Fort Sumter, to assure mail delivery, and to maintain the Union. "In doing this there needs to be no bloodshed or violence, and there shall be none unless it be forced upon the national authority."

Lincoln made two crucial rhetorical moves in this address. First, his portrayal of the conflict as one over the perpetuation of the Union rather than the future of slavery allowed him to push federal claims in a way that would not instantly alienate voters (and potential secessionists) in the Upper South and the Border States. He also gave assurances that the Union would not be the aggressor if violence broke out: "In your hands, my dissatisfied fellow-countrymen, and not in mine, is the momentous issue of civil war. The Government will not assail you. You can have no conflict without being yourselves the aggressors. You have no oath registered in heaven to destroy the Government, while I shall have the most solemn one to 'preserve, protect, and defend it.'"

Lincoln's words were immediately put to the test. Shortly after he delivered his address, the new president received word that Fort Sumter was running out of supplies. Control of this well-fortified outpost located in Charleston's harbor had been a point of contention ever since South Carolinians claimed they were leaving the Union. Buchanan refused to give it up, and the garrison's commander, Major Robert Anderson, had ratcheted up the tension when he moved his forces into the fort in December 1860. Before Lincoln took office, an effort in January 1861 to reinforce the garrison had failed. Confederate officials then indicated that further efforts would be considered an act of war. Lincoln's most obvious options were not desirable. He could send reinforcements, but that move would precipitate war and make the federal government appear to be the aggressor, despite assurances in his just-delivered inaugural address. He could also authorize the fort's surrender—an action that would certainly be read as a sign of weakness as well as a tacit admission of the legitimacy of secession. These alternatives put Lincoln in a box, and neither choice was desirable to him.

Lincoln demurred for a few weeks until he could find a preferred solution to his predicament. Eventually, he brilliantly opted to resupply the fort, but without reinforcements. He notified the governor of South Carolina of his intentions, assuring the official that only provisions, and not armed men, would be arriving on supply ships. This plan removed Lincoln from his bind while placing the ball squarely into the Confederacy's court. If the southern leadership allowed supplies to land, the action would be interpreted as an acknowledgement of federal control of the fort, not to mention allowing the federals to maintain possession of the fort for several months into the future. If they ordered an attack, the Confederacy would basically assume responsibility for starting the war. The Confederate national government, under pressure from the press and prominent secessionist politicians, opted for the latter course. After 33 hours of bombardment, Major Anderson surrendered Fort Sumter. The Civil War had begun.

Chronology

1846   Mexican American War begins.
        Wilmot Proviso proposed.

1848   Treaty of Guadalupe Hidalgo.
        Gold discovered in California.
        Zachary Taylor wins the election of 1848.

1849   The Know Nothings form in New York City.

1850   Nashville Convention meets.
        President Zachary Taylor dies.
        Millard Fillmore becomes president.
        Compromise of 1850 passes.

1851   After a highly-publicized trial in Boston,
        Thomas Sims is returned to slavery

1852   Franklin Pierce elected president.
        Harriet Beecher Stowe publishes *Uncle Tom's Cabin*.

1854   Ostend Manifesto written.
        Kansas-Nebraska Act passes.
        Whig Party collapses.
        American Party captures 62 House seats.
        Republican Party organizes.

1855   Kansas Territory opened to settlement.

1856   Lawrence, Kansas, attacked by "Border ruffians."
        Caning of Senator Charles Sumner.
        James Buchanan elected president.

1857   *Dred Scott* decision issued by the Supreme Court.

1858   The Lincoln-Douglas Debates take place.
        Lecompton Constitution rejected.

1859   John Brown attacks the federal armory at
        Harper's Ferry, Virginia.

1860   Abraham Lincoln wins the 1860 presidential
        election.
        7 Lower South states announce they are
        seceding from the Union

1861   Confederate States of America organized
        Confederate attack on Fort Sumter
        4 Upper South states join the Confederacy

SUGGESTED READINGS

Austin Allen, *Origins of the Dred Scott Case: Jacksonian Politics and the Supreme Court, 1837-1857* (2006).

Ray A. Billington, *The Protestant Crusade, 1800-1860: A Study of the Origins of American Nativism* (1938).

David Herbert Donald, *Charles Sumner and the Coming of the Civil War* (1961).

Jonathan H. Earle, *Jacksonian Antislavery and the Politics of Free Soil, 1824-1854* (2004).

Nicole Etcheson, *Bleeding Kansas: Contested Liberty in the Civil War Era* (2004).

Don E. Fehrenbacher, *The Dred Scott Case: Its Significance in American Law and Politics* (1978).

Eric Foner, *Free Soil, Free Labor, Free Men: The Ideology of the Republican Party before the Civil War* (1970).

William W. Freehling, *The Road to Disunion*, 2 vols. (1990-2007).

William E. Gienapp, *The Origins of the Republican Party, 1852-1856* (1987).

C.C. Goen, *Broken Churches, Broken Nation: Denominational Schisms and the Coming of the American Civil War* (1985).

Holman Hamilton, *Prologue to Conflict: The Crisis and Compromise of 1850* (2005).

Stanley Harold, *Border War: Fighting over Slavery before the Civil War* (2010).

Michael Holt, *The Political Crisis of the 1850s* (1978).

Robert W. Johannsen, *Stephen Douglas* (1973).

Bruce Laurie, *Beyond Garrison: Antislavery and Social Reform* (2005).

Bruce Levine, *Half Slave, Half Free: The Roots of Civil War* (1992).

William A. Link, *The Roots of Secession: Slavery and Politics in Antebellum Virginia* (2003).

James M. McPherson, *Battle Cry of Freedom: The Civil War Era* (1988).

Russell McClintock, *Lincoln and the Decision for War: The Northern Response to Secession* (2008).

Michael A. Morrison, *Slavery and the American West: The Eclipse of Manifest Destiny and the Coming of the American Civil War* (1997).

David M. Potter, *The Impending Crisis, 1848-1861* (1976).

Leonard Richards, *Slave Power: The Free North and Southern Domination* (2000).

Brian Schoen, *The Fragile Fabric of Union: Cotton, Federal Policies, and the Global Origins of the Civil War* (2009).

Joel Silbey, *Storm over Texas: The Annexation Controversy and the Road to Civil War* (2007).

Elizabeth R. Varnon, *Disunion! The Coming of the American Civil War, 1789-1859* (2008).

Review Questions

1.   Discuss the significance of the Wilmot Proviso. Why did the debate over slavery's expansion become the central question of American politics during the 1850s?

2.   Discuss the Compromise of 1850. What were the components of the compromise and why did it fail to produce a lasting peace between the North and the South?

3.   Why did the Kansas-Nebraska Act transform American politics?

4.   Republican politicians argued that the federal government had been captured by a conspiracy of slaveholders determined to force slavery's expansion (i.e., the "Slave Power"). To what degree was this position accurate? How much of this view was political rhetoric designed to mobilize northern voters?

5.   Evaluate the South's decision to secede from the Union. Based on your reading of this chapter, why did states of the Deep South decide to secede? Were they justified in doing so? Why or why not?

Glossary of Important People and Concepts

American Party/Know Nothing
"Bleeding Kansas"
John Brown
Lewis Cass
Common Property Doctrine
Compromise of 1850
Constitutional Union Party
Crittenden Compromise
Stephen Douglas
Dred Scott Case
Millard Fillmore
Fort Sumter
Free Soil position
Freeport Doctrine
Fugitive Slave Law of 1850
Kansas-Nebraska Act
Lecompton Constitution
Lincoln-Douglas Debates
Ostend Manifesto
Franklin Pierce
Popular Sovereignty
Republican Party
"Slave Power"
Charles Sumner
Uncle Tom's Cabin
Wilmot Proviso

ABRAHAM LINCOLN

Chapter Sixteen

THE AMERICAN CIVIL WAR
1861-1865

Future United States Supreme Court Justice Oliver Wendell Holmes, Jr. was twenty years old when he enlisted to fight in the Civil War. He would emerge from the conflict physically scarred by his experiences. After taking a bullet to the chest at the Battle of Ball's Bluff in October 1861, Holmes returned to service only to be shot in the neck and left for dead at the Battle of Antietam in September 1862. He recovered again and returned to his unit only to be shot in the foot eight months later at the Battle of Chancellorsville. Although originally wishing to have his foot amputated so he could go home, he bravely finished out his commission. In addition to his physical wounds, the war left a lasting impact on Holmes mentally. Each year until his death, he drank a glass of wine to observe the Battle of Antietam—the single bloodiest day of the war. Other soldiers, who may not have shared Captain Holmes's wish for amputation, returned home from the conflict with missing limbs. Jonathan M. Allison, a Union corporal who lost his right arm at the Battle of Resaca in May 1864, described himself and others like him as "living monuments of the late cruel and bloody Rebellion." A New Hampshire minister, speaking decades after the conflict had ended, reminded his listeners that one need only "count the empty sleeves" to know the cost of the conflict. Southerners, of course, suffered as well, and they would have to cope with the fact that they had lost the war. John Sitgreaves Green, a quartermaster in the Confederate army, was wounded by a "sabre-cut of excruciating, continued agony." He suffered

for the rest of his life, becoming addicted to both opium and alcohol. His family ultimately placed him in an asylum, where the doctors had become quite familiar with veterans struggling with the war.

Just as the conflict altered the lives of Holmes, Allison, and Green, the Civil War simultaneously wounded and transformed the United States. Although few expected the fight to last as long as it did, the conflict pulled a huge number of Americans into its vortex. Approximately half of the North's military-age population entered military service, while between 75 and 85 percent of draft-age white men fought for the South. A large number of these men died—over a quarter of a million Southerners and close to four hundred thousand Northerners. Though the North would emerge from the war an economic powerhouse, the South, by contrast, was left significantly damaged for decades, losing two-thirds of its wealth. The former Confederate states also lost their central economic institution: slavery. The Civil War did not begin as a crusade to end slavery. Indeed, President Abraham Lincoln labored hard in the early phases of the war to present the struggle as one devoted solely to preserve the Union. When the fighting stalemated, however, freeing the slaves became a major northern military objective. Ultimately, the federal victory saved the Union, but not as it had been. The nation that survived the conflagration would be, in many ways, changed forever.

ADVANTAGES FOR THE UNION AND CONFEDERACY

Nothing about the outcome of the American Civil War was inevitable. Although the North won, this result was far from clear in April 1861. Hindsight allows observers to focus on particular features of the North and South, identifying relative strengths and weaknesses to explain the Union victory or the Confederate defeat, but no single factor could predict how the war turned out. Both the North and the South possessed an array of advantages and disadvantages that may have changed the course of the war if events had broken in slightly different ways. At the beginning of the conflict, many factors benefited the South. As the war dragged on, however, the North's sizeable material advantages would contribute greatly to the ultimate Union victory.

Northern Economic Advantages

American economic productivity had increased significantly over the first half of the nineteenth century, fundamentally transforming many aspects of life in the United States. These developments, of course, did not play out in a uniform way across the nation. By 1861, a host of economic changes had left the North better positioned for a prolonged military conflict. Economic historians have noted that the South, if considered as an independent country and measured on a per capita basis, actually ranked in the top ten of the world's nations in railroad construction, pig iron production, and textile manufacturing—placing the region on par with such industrializing contemporaries as France and Germany. Nevertheless, the South's manufacturing sector remained far less developed than the North's. Though approximately 110,000 people worked in southern factories, northern factories employed about 1.3 million. On the eve of secession, workers in the North produced over 90 percent of the iron, textiles, and firearms produced in the U.S. Northern economic advantages did not end with manufacturing; the section also held three-quarters of the nation's farm acreage and about four-fifths of its wheat production. By war's end, these advantages allowed the Union to field some of the best-equipped soldiers in the history of the world.

Despite being outproduced by their northern counterparts, southern manufacturers worked diligently to sustain the war effort. Virginia's secession gave the Confederacy control of the Tredegar Iron Works, one of the largest iron manufacturers in the country. Iron producers in states like Georgia and Alabama emerged as well. These companies, supported by the Confederate Ordinance Bureau under the leadership of a transplanted northerner, General Josiah Gorgas, ensured that Confederate soldiers remained adequately supplied with weapons and ammunition throughout much of the war. Other supplies, however, proved harder to access. Worn out (or non-existent) shoes and irregular uniforms were common among Confederate soldiers. Food also ran short for both civilians and soldiers. Plantation managers proved slow to shift away from cotton production to foodstuffs. Moving supplies from one part of the South to another, moreover, proved difficult, increasing the burden of sustaining the war effort over the long term.

None of these factors guaranteed certain victory for the Union. The North's greater industrial and agricultural capacity became a significant asset only as the war dragged on. In the earliest phases of the conflict, the Union experienced difficulties in distributing what its farms and factories produced. Consequently, the military relied upon private contractors who gouged the government on everything from railroad rates to firearms. Merchants and manufacturers fulfilled unprecedentedly large orders for military equipment by cutting corners. Cavalry troops took shipments of sick and dying horses. Soldiers were issued poorly made uniforms, shoes, blankets, and other items (popularizing the term "shoddy" for cheap materials made with scraps) that wore out after a few weeks of use. Many months passed before Edwin M. Stanton, Lincoln's second Secretary of War, and the Union's quartermaster general, Montgomery Meigs, could master the logistical challenges involved in turning the North's productive potential into a definite military asset.

Another economic challenge faced by governments in both the North and the South centered on how to pay for the conflict. Citizens in both regions were averse to taxes, and neither side possessed a national banking system. The response in both sections was to resort to printing paper money, a policy choice that threatened to foment ruinous inflation. The Union tempered this tendency by backing the value of its "greenbacks" with an income tax on certain salaries. The Confederacy never adequately dealt with the issue, and by the end of the war, its currency had become essentially worthless.

Manpower Disparities

The Union also possessed an advantage in numbers. Around nine million people lived in the South (less than one-third of the total U.S. population in 1860). Almost four million of those Southerners were slaves and thus ineligible for military service. The North, by contrast, had a population of twenty-two million people, and it would ultimately field an army of over two million soldiers, including 200,000 African Americans.

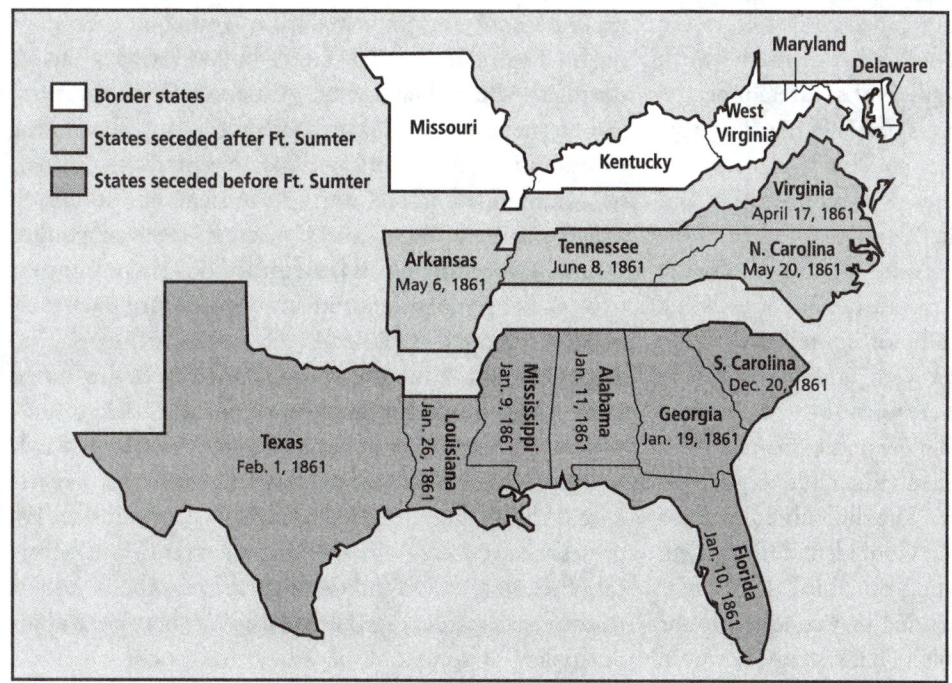

Map 16.1 The Slave States and Secession. West Virginia seceded from Virginia and joined the Union in 1863.

Sheer numbers, of course, did not ensure victory. Entire communities existing in the North, in fact, preferred (or even openly supported) the Confederacy, especially in the border states of Missouri, Maryland, and Kentucky. New soldiers also needed to be organized, trained, and led. As the Union mobilized, the number of raw recruits swelled to over 500,000. The regular army, which only had a force of 13,000 in 1861, became quickly overwhelmed. A lack of experienced, capable officers severely plagued the North. The development of an officer corps that could decisively defeat the Confederate military—particularly in the politically essential eastern theater—took years of bloody trial and error. Even with training and effective leadership, the North's larger population did not translate into overwhelming numbers on the battlefield, since some troops needed to be deployed in the Far West to manage tensions with Native Americans and significant numbers of soldiers were needed to garrison areas under federal control. The Union's sizeable population, however, did allow its army to fulfill those tasks while consistently outnumbering Confederate forces on the battlefield by about a third (a significant but not overwhelming advantage).

As with its manufacturing capacity, the South utilized its limited manpower resources effectively. By the end of the war, the Confederacy fielded 900,000 soldiers, a number that included nearly all of the men eligible for military service (about half of the North's eligible men served in Union armies). The South's forces also enjoyed the advantage of excellent military leadership. A majority of the U.S. Army's most talented and experienced officers during the antebellum period happened to be Southern-

ers. When their states joined the Confederacy, most resigned their commissions to command Confederate forces. Some of these commanders became legendary. Robert E. Lee, who eventually led the main Confederate army based in the politically critical Virginia region, would batter larger Union forces so soundly and repeatedly that many of his northern counterparts believed him to be unbeatable. General Thomas "Stonewall" Jackson, one of Lee's subordinates, became known for his bravery and his ability to outmaneuver larger enemy forces. Because of their previous military service, these men were well placed to move into critical leadership positions early in the war. By contrast, Ulysses S. Grant, the Union general who would ultimately defeat Lee and secure the North's victory, was not even in the army when the war began. Along with other emerging officers who helped him win the war, Grant had to work his way through the ranks before being given an important field command.

Southern Geographic Advantages

Another advantage that the Confederacy possessed came from its geography. The South comprised 750,000 square miles of territory including the Appalachian Mountains and immense woodlands. Preventing secession meant invading and conquering this territory, a strategy that also threatened to stoke Confederate morale since soldiers would be fighting in their home territory. Moving through the South also proved to be a challenge. Although the amount of railroad construction measured on a per capita basis was second only to the North (who led the world in this area), the South's 9,000 miles of rail proved to be woefully underdeveloped compared to the North. While the North had built an extensive network consisting of 22,000 miles of railway that interconnected most of the region, southern rails basically ran from cotton planting districts to coastal and interior ports. Its rail system had not been designed to move people and products from one part of the South to another. This situation inhibited the distribution of food within the South, but it also complicated the movement of invading armies who found the rails to be of limited usefulness. Travel along roads likewise proved difficult, especially in wet weather that quickly transformed dirt roads into mud pits that bogged down soldiers on the march. Both the roads and railroads remained vulnerable to guerrilla attack throughout the conflict. The difficulties involved in invading the South provided Confederate forces with the advantage of merely holding out until the North's leadership (or populace) concluded that conquering the South was not worth the trouble. That strategy, however, ran counter to the notion of a short war.

Executive Leadership: Abraham Lincoln and Jefferson Davis

Presidential leadership shaped the war effort in crucial ways for both sides. At first glance, the Confederacy appeared to have the man best suited to the occasion. Mississippi's **Jefferson Davis**, the first (and only) president of the new government, brought a great deal of experience to his post. A successful cotton planter, Davis had served a brief stint in the House of Representatives, two terms in the Senate, and four years as Secretary of War under President Franklin Pierce. He also possessed military experience, having graduated from West Point then serving briefly under his future father-in-law, Zachary Taylor, during the Black Hawk War. Although he left the army to become a planter, Davis later gave up his House seat to serve in the Mexican War. Attaining rank of colonel, he commanded troops during the siege of Monterrey and the Battle of Buena Vista, where he received a bullet wound to the foot. Davis later turned down a promotion to brigadier general, choosing instead to return to civilian life and resume his political career.

Abraham Lincoln, in contrast, came into office with a very limited military and political background. He served briefly in the army during the Black Hawk War but claimed no special knowledge from the experience. Unlike Davis, Lincoln had failed to translate his professional success—as an Illinois lawyer—into political office. He served only a single term in the House of Representatives during the late 1840s where he was an outspoken opponent of the war with Mexico.

Once in the White House, however, Lincoln proved himself to be flexible, patient, and a tenacious leader. Partisan politics—except perhaps for a brief moment following the attack on Fort Sumter—continued unabated throughout the war years, and Lincoln faced a constant barrage of criticism from both enemies and allies. Democrats, despite the secession of the region that had provided the party's dominant wing in the 1850s, remained a political force, and the party offered consistent opposition to Lincoln and the Republicans. Even so, secession and war left the party internally divided. Moderate Democrats opposed secession and supported the war, even as they bitterly second-guessed nearly every aspect of the manner in which Lincoln handled the conflict. A smaller faction of largely border-state Democrats, the so-called "Copper-

President Abraham Lincoln and his cabinet: (left to right) Postmaster General Montgomery Blair, Secretary of the Interior Caleb B. Smith, Secretary of the Treasury Salmon P. Chase, President Lincoln, Secretary of State William H. Seward, Secretary of War Simon Cameron, Attorney General Edward Bates, and Secretary of the Navy Gideon Welles.

Confederate President Jefferson Davis and his cabinet: (left to right) Attorney General Judah P. Benjamin, Secretary of the Navy Stephen M. Mallory, Secretary of the Treasury C.S Memminger, Vice President Alexander Hamilton Stephens, Secretary of War Leroy Pope Walker, President Jefferson Davis, Postmaster John H. Reagan, and Secretary of State Robert Toombs.

heads," loudly opposed the war. Although they were not generally disloyal, Copperheads pushed for a negotiated settlement and would willingly accept an independent southern republic. For the most part, Lincoln regarded such opposition as legitimate and never moved to suspend elections or to restrain speech or actions that were not openly disloyal. Although he showed little tolerance for disloyalty, Lincoln usually just endured the charges that he was a "tyrant," pressing forward to achieve his goals.

Republicans did not refrain from criticism of the president even though he came from their ranks. Like the Democrats, Republicans split over the best way to conduct the war. One faction, the Radical Republicans led by Senator Charles Sumner of Massachusetts and Representative Thaddeus Stevens of Pennsylvania, demanded that the war result in both emancipation and the establishment of racial equality. The more numerous moderate Republicans, on the other hand, were willing to stop well short of those goals. Some of them questioned whether emancipation was a legitimate war aim. Lincoln thus had to maneuver among these factions along with opposition Democrats and a rebellious South.

Lincoln's capacity to lead an often divided North emerged early in his presidency as he worked with a cabinet that contained members with deep connections to both major factions within the Republican Party. Salmon Chase, Secretary of the Treasury, was an Ohio politician who spoke for the Radicals and repeatedly pressed the president to move quickly toward ending slavery. Secretary of State William Seward of New York, although outspoken in his opposition to the peculiar institution, represented moderate Republicans who urged the president to move cautiously, if at all, toward emancipation. Both Chase and Seward possessed far more political ex-

perience than Lincoln; they had both been senators and state governors. Most of their colleagues in the cabinet could also boast more experience than the new president. Seward, in fact, planned to be the real power within the administration and thought he could reduce the inexperienced Lincoln to a figurehead. Immediately upon taking office, Seward began working toward a settlement of the secession crisis and even promised his southern contacts that Lincoln would abandon Fort Sumter. As his intrigues fell apart, he proposed that Lincoln start a conflict with Mexico as a way to reunify the country around a foreign enemy. Lincoln declined but did so in a way that allowed Seward to save face while definitely affirming that he, as president, would be the one making the major policy decisions. Seward soon became one of the president's most loyal supporters, and Lincoln became without question the dominant figure in his administration. He also proved willing to replace appointed officials whose performance inhibited the war effort. Lincoln removed his first Secretary of War, Simon Cameron, who had been awarding military contracts mainly as a way to enrich himself rather than to properly supply the army. Cameron's replacement, Edwin M. Stanton, cleaned up the department. Freely intervening in matters of military strategy, the president also regularly removed unsuccessful generals, even when he liked them personally or when they were popular with the public.

Lincoln's ability to make decisions that he thought were right and then endure whatever criticism followed came paired with a keen sense of political timing. He worked by making a series of small decisions that tended to open the way for bigger ones. Lincoln's handling of the Fort Sumter crisis, for example, allowed the president to portray the South as an aggressor, thus better enabling him to call for state troops to put down the rebellion. He would move toward emancipation in the same way. Such a combination of skills, along with the genuine emergency presented by the war, helped Lincoln to become the most powerful and innovative president of the nineteenth century.

Jefferson Davis, by contrast, seemed more ill suited for his office as the war dragged on. He intervened in military strategy, as did Lincoln, but his choices tended to be ineffective or worse. Playing favorites with his generals and fighting with his subordinates, Davis's pride would not permit him to let insults pass, and he had little patience for those he disliked. The Confederate Cabinet, which for political reasons included neither opponents of secession nor its most outspoken advocates, proved weak relative to Lincoln's. Limited by the Confederate Constitution to a single, six-year term, Davis had little practical incentive to build alliances, leaving him politically isolated over time.

Davis also proved reluctant to delegate authority, and his government consequently gave little attention to the challenges that emerged on the home front as the South's social order unraveled. The decentralized nature of the Confederacy compounded his difficulties. Southern governors regularly invoked states' rights doctrine to oppose many Confederate national policies, such as conscription. Despite his long list of pre-war accomplishments, the struggle ultimately overwhelmed Davis. The advantage of national leadership thus went to the Union, but like the other factors thus far discussed, Lincoln's ability was by no means the sole factor in bringing about the North's victory.

Diplomacy during the Civil War

A key to victory for both sides lay in international diplomacy. Confederate leaders correctly viewed diplomatic recognition by Great Britain, France, and other European powers as an important step toward establishing their new republic. Insisting that the Civil War was a strictly domestic affair, Lincoln and Seward worked laboriously to keep these European nations neutral. As with most other important factors dealing with the war effort, the North and the South in the diplomatic realm possessed both advantages and disadvantages. The northern electorate's relative discomfort with slavery tended to be more in line with European public sentiment, which had long turned against the institution. But European governments in the 1860s were largely monarchies, thus public opinion had limited impact. A number of Lincoln's tactics, such as blockading southern ports, raised questions as to whether the conflict was merely a domestic affair. Any distaste toward slavery, moreover, had to be weighed against the

fact that the South possessed a valuable commodity—cotton. Control of that vital resource gave the Confederacy a great deal of potential leverage in international diplomacy.

Confederate leaders placed high hopes in cotton. "You dare not to make war on cotton," Senator James Henry Hammond of South Carolina told his northern colleagues a few years before secession. "Cotton is king." What he meant was that factory systems in the North and in Europe were so dependent on the South's staple that they could not afford to isolate themselves. A war on cotton threatened economic depression abroad, leading to closed shops and protests from angry displaced workers. Hammond and other southern leaders had a point. Southern cotton accounted for more than half of U.S. exports in 1860. Those exports provided nearly all of the cotton used by factories in France and Russia and three-quarters of the fiber consumed in Great Britain.

As the war began, the Confederate government implemented "King Cotton Diplomacy" in an effort to pressure European powers for recognition. Although southern leaders acted reasonably given their region's power in the world cotton market, the strategy backfired as it ran afoul of a number of unintended consequences. First, the South experienced a few bumper crops during the 1850s. European textile manufacturers—who were quite aware of the potential for instability in the U.S.—had thus built up stockpiles that provided a cushion from the shock. Second, the factory owners searched for and cultivated replacement sources of cotton (an understandable reaction given the drop in southern exports of the staple from nearly four million bales in 1860 to almost nothing in 1862). By the war's end, a defeated South would reenter the world cotton market, not as a dominant producer but as one major player among several others including Egypt and India.

Although the limits of cotton as a diplomatic tool had become clear by mid-war, northern military and diplomatic strategy prevented the Confederacy from correcting itself. The Union's key tool lay in its blockade. One of the early military strategies considered by the Lincoln administration was the **"Anaconda Plan"** proposed by venerable General Winfield Scott. The strategy called for the Union to blockade southern ports while simultaneously advancing down the Mississippi River—a process that would slowly squeeze the South into submission. The plan was ultimately rejected in favor of a more aggressive approach, but the blockade became a major feature of the war effort. The Union ultimately built enough ships to effectively limit trade along the southern coast, with the exception of several successful swift craft known as "blockade runners." When Confederate leaders decided to bring cotton back to market, the blockade largely

General Winfield Scott

Map 16.2 The Anaconda Plan

stopped them (except for a few hundred thousand bales exported through Texas to ports in northern Mexico). It continued to deprive the South of sorely needed imports.

The Union blockade, however, posed a diplomatic problem. According to international law, the tactic constituted an act of war among countries. Lincoln, meanwhile, continued to assert that the federal government was not engaged in a formal war because such a declaration would amount to tacit recognition that the South was an independent nation. He insisted that his government was putting down a domestic rebellion. If that were the case, however, a blockade was not a legal tactic, and foreign powers need not respect it. Nevertheless, the British government overcame internal divisions among its high officials and ultimately decided to adhere to the blockade's provisions anyway, remaining neutral throughout the conflict. Again, this was not an inevitable turn of events. Relations between the U.S. and Great Britain became quite tense in late 1861 when a U.S. Navy frigate stopped a British mail packet vessel, the *Trent*, off the northern coast of Cuba, removing two Confederate diplomats in violation of international law. Though a few politicians on both sides of the Atlantic talked seriously about the potential for war, cooler heads prevailed, and Lincoln eventually ordered the release of the Confederate emissaries. In these dealings, the president's ambassador to the United Kingdom, Charles Francis Adams (son of John Quincy Adams) proved to be a great asset, working

effectively with the members of England's foreign policy establishment. Though Lincoln succeeded in securing European neutrality, the true key to stopping the southern independence movement lay in producing clear-cut victories on the battlefield, yet significant Union military successes were rare during the first year of the conflict.

THE WAR BEGINS IN EARNEST, 1861-1862

The Confederate firing upon Fort Sumter created a public clamor for war in both the North and the South. Both sides expected the conflict to be short-lived. Lincoln responded to the fort's surrender by requesting 75,000 troops from the states for ninety days of service (later calls sought larger contingents of soldiers for longer terms, usually three years). Many volunteers formed distinctive regiments in communities across the North. Wealthy New Yorkers and Ohio farmers organized their own units, as did Irish and German immigrants. These new soldiers brought with them essentially no military experience and a wide array of uniforms—ranging from blue, to gray, to red, to multi-colored "Zouave" stylings that copied outfits worn by famed North African units in the French Army. Organizing and equipping these troops—numbering 700,000 by 1862—with standardized gear took time. Meanwhile, volunteers also poured into the Confederate ranks. By Lincoln's first call, the South had already mo-

A sketch of a group of Zouaves, April 17, 1862.

bilized 60,000 men, and the Confederate Congress had authorized a total force of 100,000. Like their Yankee counterparts, Confederate armies also required organization and equipment—a process that produced inevitable delays. Meanwhile, the northern and southern publics both clamored for the one big battle that would force the other side to capitulate, but that never occurred. Within a year, the Union and Confederacy found themselves locked in a struggle with no end in sight. Although the Union won numerous strategically important battles in the West and at sea, its forces failed—at times spectacularly—in the politically important Eastern Theater centered in the area between Washington, D.C. and the Confederate capital of Richmond, Virginia.

The First Battle of Bull Run (Manassas)

As the Union army prepared for battle, Lincoln debated his strategic options. Despite persistent calls from the northern press to move quickly and capture Richmond, supposedly to bring the conflict to an abrupt end, most military commanders and political leaders remained skeptical that the war would be short. General Scott's Anaconda Plan, for example, was designed to take time—the ultimate goal being to isolate the South, cut its economic ties to the rest of the world, and then wait for secessionist leaders to lose their legitimacy. Such a policy, Scott argued, would minimize wartime deaths and limit destruction while perhaps paving the way for a smooth reconciliation. Editors denounced this plan as too timid and demanded immediate action. Concerned that the terms of some of the initial recruits were about to expire, Lincoln proved sensitive to these demands and hoped that an early victory in Virginia would help bring a rapid end to the war. Thus, he ordered General Irvin McDowell, commander of the 35,000 troops stationed in

the Washington, D.C. area, to attack amassing Confederate forces assembling in northern Virginia.

McDowell, a career staff officer with no experience commanding troops in combat, decided to attack the 20,000 Confederate troops defending Manassas Junction (a railroad intersection located 25 miles southwest from the national capital). His objective was to force rebel troops to withdraw deeper into Virginia, thus making Washington less vulnerable to attack. The general's battle plan seemed sound in theory, but its execution required experienced troops and officers. When McDowell told Lincoln that his forces were not ready, the president responded by reminding him that both sides were "all green alike." He thus pressed forward with 30,000 men, although delayed supply wagons, a continuous need to organize newly arrived troops, and his soldiers' lack of familiarity with marching slowed his advance. By the time Union troops arrived at Manassas Junction, the Confederate commanding officer, General P.G.T. Beauregard, was prepared to meet the attack. McDowell's slow march, combined with intelligence provided by the South's spies in Washington, had provided plenty of advanced notice. Beauregard reinforced the positions that he anticipated McDowell planned to attack and summoned General Joseph E. Johnston to bring his force of 11,000 soldiers from Harpers Ferry to reinforce him. McDowell took Beauregard's new positioning in stride and revised his plan accordingly. In anticipation of Johnston's movements, he ordered General Robert H. Patterson to tie down Johnston's forces. Patterson, however, failed in his mission, and Johnston's troops soon joined the fight.

The battle—called **First Manassas** by the Confederacy (who tended to name battles after the nearest settlement) or **First Bull Run** by the Union (who often named battles after the nearest body of water)—took place on July 21, 1861, when McDowell sent 10,000 troops against a weak point in the Confederate lines. Although

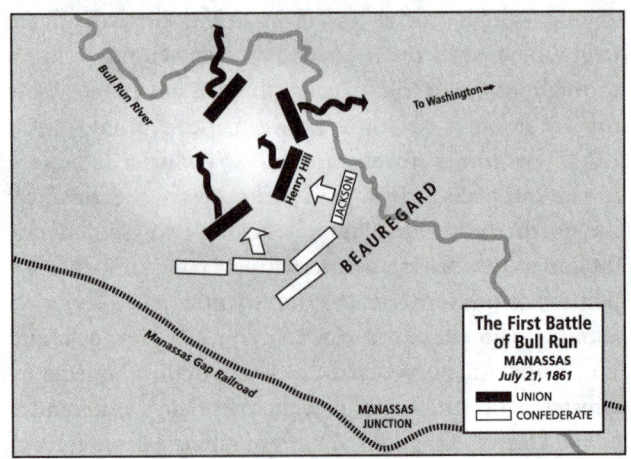

Map 16.3 The First Battle of Bull Run

enemy fire and their own officers' inexperience slowed their advance and hampered their coordination, Union troops initially drove the Confederates from their positions, forcing them into retreat. Then, the battle turned against them as Colonel (soon to be General) **Thomas J. "Stonewall" Jackson** earned his nickname by rallying his troops and stopping the Union advance. Both sides spent the afternoon slugging it out until Beauregard gained access to Johnston's troops and ordered a counterattack. Advancing with a shrill battle cry known as the "rebel yell" that terrified McDowell's men, the Confederates pushed the exhausted Union forces back. Their retreat quickly turned into a panicked flight as many soldiers dropped everything they carried, even fleeing through crowds of spectators who had come from Washington to watch the battle (one northern congressman in the chaotic scene was actually captured by advancing Confederate troopers). The First Battle of Bull Run thus ended in a humiliating Union defeat.

The battle produced a number of important consequences. In theory, the South's victory opened the way for a Confederate advance toward Washington, which, if attempted, might have ended the war more quickly in the South's favor. In July 1861, however, both Johnston and Beauregard believed that their forces were in no condition for an immediate follow-up on their victory. Their troops were disorganized and out of supplies, rainy weather made travel difficult, and McDowell immediately began positioning fresh troops between Manassas and Washington. The Confederate triumph did succeed in slowing Union efforts to invade Virginia, bolstering southern confidence and instilling a deep-seated suspicion among the northern public that perhaps the Confederates were simply superior warriors. In the North, although the defeat proved jarring, President Lincoln and his supporters responded with renewed resolve. Immediately following the battle, Lincoln placed General George B. McClellan in command of federal troops in Washington and signed bills authorizing the enlistment of a million men for three-year terms. What proved to be an agonizingly long war had just begun.

McClellan Takes Command

Though he eventually demonstrated himself to be a lackluster battlefield commander, Lincoln's promotion of **George McClellan** to head the main Union army initially made sense. Born to a prominent Philadelphia family and educated at West Point (where he graduated second in his class), McClellan had enjoyed successful military and civilian careers by the time he rejoined the United States Army. He served as an engineering officer during the Mexican War, taking from the experience a deep appreciation of flanking maneuvers and siege tactics. McClellan also admired General Scott's efforts to avoid alienating civilian populations and the strict enforcement of discipline among his troops. Following the war, he taught at West Point and undertook various observation missions in Europe. McClellan left the service in 1857 to work as the president of two railroad companies—a job that gave him a great deal of logistical experience. His list of accomplishments gave McClellan a considerable amount of confidence. "I can do it all," he told Lincoln when the president expressed concerns about the general's increasing workload.

That quip would become a glaring overstatement, but Lincoln's new general did succeed in completely reorganizing the main federal army. McClellan combined the forces that had been under McDowell's command with a number of troops in Virginia to form the Army of the Potomac. Retraining his soldiers from scratch, he drilled the men constantly and reviewed their progress regularly, a process that built up morale. The general enforced discipline, coming down hard against drunkenness and absences without leave. McClellan fortified the capital behind a network of fortifications protected by heavy artillery. As press reports lauded his changes, he reveled in his newfound prestige, telling his wife in a letter that he was so esteemed that he could be named dictator if he wished.

Beyond his ego, McClellan had one major failing: he almost never believed his forces were ready to face the enemy. The general's cautiousness led to constant delays, creating tension with Lincoln and other military commanders. (Lincoln once complained that McClellan suffered from a "perpetual case of the slows.") The general and Winfield Scott quickly became embroiled in an argument over whether to follow the Anaconda Plan or McClellan's idea to build an invasion force of greater than a quarter-million men to crush the South in one massive offensive campaign. McClellan won the dispute; Scott resigned, and by November 1861, McClellan was general-in-chief of the Union's armies. His relationship with Lincoln became very tense. The general, politically a Democrat, held the president in low regard, casually describing him as a "baboon" and "gorilla" in letters to his wife. Once, when Lincoln came to see him at his residence, McClellan decided to go to bed rather than meet his commander-in-chief. In response to what he regarded as McClellan's foot dragging, Lincoln drew up his own plans to attack Virginia and ordered operations to begin in February 1862. McClellan countered with a long critique and finally presented his own plans—the first he had ever submitted in writing. Lincoln deferred to

President Abraham Lincoln visits with Union commander George B. McClellan at Sharpsburg, Maryland after the Battle of Antietam to urge the general to pursue Robert E. Lee's retreating army. October 3, 1862."

his general because at least he had received a commitment to attack. Even so, McClellan did not begin his advance until mid-March 1862, moving with his characteristic caution.

The War in the West

Although McClellan's Army of the Potomac made little headway in the East, which, because it contained both capitals, was the most politically important theater of the war, Union forces had considerable success in the strategically critical Western Theater. There, armies fought for control of the continent's major rivers, which provided access to numerous potential targets. Union control of the Mississippi River would effectively split the Confederacy in two. In addition to producing a few early victories, the West became the proving ground that groomed the Union commanders who would ultimately win the war, especially **Ulysses S. Grant**. Like McClellan, Grant had been an officer in the regular army who had returned to civilian life before the outbreak of the Civil War. Yet his career—whether military or civilian—had not been nearly as impressive. Grant graduated in the middle of his class at West Point. He served as a quartermaster during the Mexican American War, earning recognition for bravery

and skilled horsemanship delivering dispatches under fire. After the war, the Army promoted Grant to the rank of captain and assigned him to a remote northern California post where rumors of heavy drinking forced his resignation. Grant then spent most of the 1850s failing at a variety of civilian jobs. Working in a relative's tannery when the war began, he promptly volunteered, taking an assignment training new soldiers while lobbying for a field command. Grant ultimately received one, attaining the rank of colonel and, along with other commanders such as William Tecumseh Sherman and Phillip Sheridan, developed the aggressive tactics that would secure Union victory.

Although Grant achieved some minor victories by the end of 1861, his successes in early 1862 elevated his reputation as an outstanding offensive commander. In February 1862, Grant coordinated his land forces with naval gunboats and captured Fort Henry, a Confederate outpost that controlled access to the Tennessee River (mastery of this waterway cut off Memphis, Tennessee, from the rest of the state and opened a route into northern Alabama). About a week later, Grant's forces surrounded nearby Fort Donelson, which protected the Cumberland River and provided direct access to the farms and vital manufacturing centers near Nashville, Tennessee. With these triumphs, Grant secured his reputation as an aggressive field officer. When Fort Donelson's commander asked for surrender terms, Grant offered none, "except unconditional and immediate surrender." The strategy paid off, as the force of about fifteen thousand capitulated. Grant received a promotion to major general, and the press began to jovially state that the "U.S." in his initials stood for "unconditional surrender."

Grant's next major battle demonstrated the new general's ability to recover from setbacks and drive his men to ultimate victory in the face of horrific conditions. Moving his army (now numbering nearly 50,000 men organized into six divisions) southward down the Tennessee River, Grant's new goal became securing control of the railways connecting western Tennessee with the eastern Confederacy. By the beginning of April, Grant's men had set up camp next to Shiloh Church, a small settlement in southwestern Tennessee near the border with Alabama and Mississippi. Grant left his encampment largely unfortified and focused on drilling his soldiers. (He had a reputation for focusing more on what he planned to do rather than what the enemy intended to do against him.) Consequently, the Confederate Army of Mississippi, under the command of General Albert Sidney Johnston, took the Union troops by surprise on the morning of April 6, 1862. The attacking force turned out to be somewhat disorganized because Johnston and one of his subordinates, General P.G.T. Beauregard, had not coordinated their battle plans. Nonetheless, they still managed to undertake a punishing assault, leading many new Union recruits to retreat while other federal units faced nearly complete destruction. Grant and his division commanders had not expected any attack that day. Still recovering from a fall off his horse, Grant did not reach the front until a few hours after the fighting began. General Sherman, however, stepped into the fray and appeared all along the front to rally the troops. Even so, by the end of the day, the Union army was forced to fall back two miles from its original position. Grant remained undeterred. When Sherman remarked that they had had "the devil's own day," the general simply replied, "Yes. Lick 'em tomorrow though."

And he did. During the previous day's fighting, Albert Sidney Johnston had been killed, depriving the South of one of its best generals. Fresh Union troops arrived, giving them a sizable numerical advantage not immediately apparent to Beauregard, Johnston's successor. Grant's forces advanced, recaptured the ground lost the day before, and forced the Confederates to withdraw. The encounter proved costly in terms of human life. With nearly 25 percent of the combatants for each side either killed or wounded, the Battle of Shiloh produced more American casualties than the total number lost in combat during the American Revolution, the War of 1812, and the Mexican American War combined. The hard fight convinced Grant that defeating the Confederacy would be a long and bloody task. His performance at the beginning of the battle, combined with the unprecedented number of casualties, raised questions about his abilities as a commander. Lincoln, however, rejected calls for his removal—"I can't spare this man; he fights." Grant followed his victory at Shiloh by capturing the railroad junction at Corinth, Mississippi before moving against Vicksburg, Mississippi, which by the end of 1862 became the last Confederate fortress along the Mississippi River.

The War at Sea

The Union commanders in the Western Theater were not the only ones to secure major gains for the North. Union naval commanders quickly made headway against the Confederates along the coasts and the high seas. The Union Navy, in fact, dominated conflicts at sea, despite impressive efforts on the part of the Confederacy to break its power.

As the Union worked to tighten its blockade, Flag Officer David Farragut, a Virginian who opposed secession and kept his post in the U.S. Navy, sailed his fleet into New Orleans in April 1862 and captured the city (a move that left Vicksburg isolated). Congress responded by elevating him to the newly created rank of admiral.

Because the Confederacy began the war with no navy and did not have the shipbuilding capacity to match the Union, Southerners concentrated on building a few highly powerful vessels. Most notably, Confederates bolted iron plating onto the wooden hull of the *Merrimack*—a scuttled U.S. Navy frigate—to construct the world's first "ironclad." Outfitted with concealed cannons and a battering ram, Confederates hoped that the modified vessel, renamed the *C.S.S. Virginia*, could sink wooden blockade ships with impunity as cannon balls harmlessly bounced off its reinforced metal frame. The *Virginia* performed as planned on March 8, 1862, when it emerged unscathed after destroying two Union frigates and running another aground in Hampton Roads at the mouth of the James River. The U.S. Navy, however, had already developed its own ironclad, the *U.S.S. Monitor*, which soon arrived in the Hampton Roads area. The two ships then fought each other to a standstill, leaving both crews deafened from the sound of cannonballs striking their ships' iron

The *Monitor* and the *Merrimack*

Depiction of the *Monitor* engaging the *Virginia*, originally the warship *Merrimack*, in Hampton Roads

plating. Although the battle ended inconclusively, the North had negated the *Virginia's* impact and soon built another fifty ironclads. (Confederates scuttled the *Virginia* in mid-May when the Union regained control of its base in Norfolk, Virginia.)

During the war, Southerners also experimented with prototypes for submarines and contracted with the British shipbuilders John Laird Sons and Company to construct specialized ramming vessels ("Laird Rams") to destroy Union blockaders and swift "commerce raiders" (most famously the *C.S.S. Alabama*) to harass northern merchant ships on the high seas. Union diplomats finally convinced the British government to put a stop to this practice by 1863.

McClellan's Failed Peninsular Campaign

While commanders at sea and in the West pushed forward, George McClellan continued dragging his feet. The general had reorganized, resupplied, and trained a powerful army which did not move. Lincoln pressed him, at one point even relieving him from post as general-in-chief so he could concentrate on what the president hoped would be a frontal assault on Richmond. McClellan, however, opted for an indirect, less heavily defended route. In March 1862, he moved the Army of the Potomac by water from Washington, D.C. to the Virginia peninsula flanked by the York River, Chesapeake Bay, and the James River. From this staging area, he planned to move westward

against Richmond, but the logistics involved produced delays. Moving his force and its equipment required four hundred ships and took several weeks. Meanwhile, McClellan continued to exercise excessive caution. By early April, McClellan had 100,000 men in position facing only 17,000 Confederates on the peninsula after most of its defenders withdrew to protect Richmond. Rather than overwhelming the rebels, McClellan ordered a siege. He had been duped by the Confederate commander, John Magruder, who deceptively marched his small forces back and forth, deployed fake cannons, and spread false rumors to create the illusion that he commanded far more soldiers than he actually possessed. Lincoln pressed McClellan to attack, but the general waited until his artillery was fully in place. When finally ready to advance, McClellan learned that Magruder's troops had completely withdrawn from the peninsula.

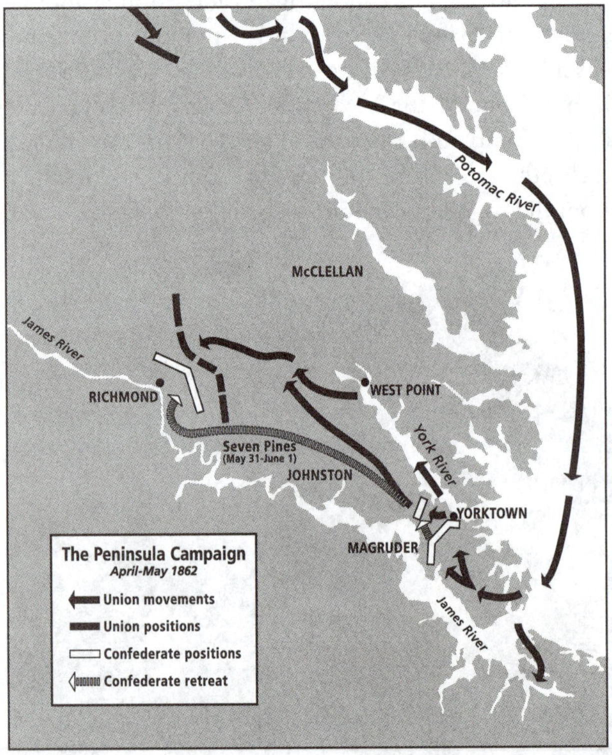

The Army of the Potomac then slowly moved toward Richmond, but upon arrival at his destination McClellan believed his men were outnumbered and thus refused to attack Confederate forces under the command of General Joseph E. Johnston. McClellan called for reinforcements, but Stonewall Jackson prevented their arrival by tying them up in Virginia's Shenandoah Valley following a series of dizzying maneuvers that left the larger Union force divided and ultimately defeated. As McClellan maneuvered his forces in an effort to besiege Richmond, Johnston launched a surprise attack on May 27. The resulting Battle of Seven Pines (Fair Oaks) ended inconclusively, but the conflict left McClellan shaken and Johnston badly wounded, soon to be replaced by General Robert E. Lee.

Lee's promotion transformed the conflict. A member of Virginia's elite related by marriage to George Washington's family, Lee would soon become one of the greatest military leaders of his generation. McClellan thought him unsuited to the task of command and predicted that he would be a timid leader. Instead, Lee proved willing to accept great risks, and he quickly took the offensive. In the Seven Days' Battles (June 25–July 1), Lee drove McClellan from Richmond and back to the peninsula. As the Union forces fell back, McClellan telegraphed Secretary of War Edwin M. Stanton and blamed the government for his defeat "because my force was too small." He also stated: "You have done your best to sacrifice this army," but an alert telegraph operator left that line out of his message. In August 1862, a frustrated Lincoln ordered McClellan to withdraw from a defensive position on the peninsula and return to Washington. He then reduced the size of McClellan's command by transferring three corps from his army to General John Pope's Army of Virginia.

Map 16.4 The Peninsula Campaign

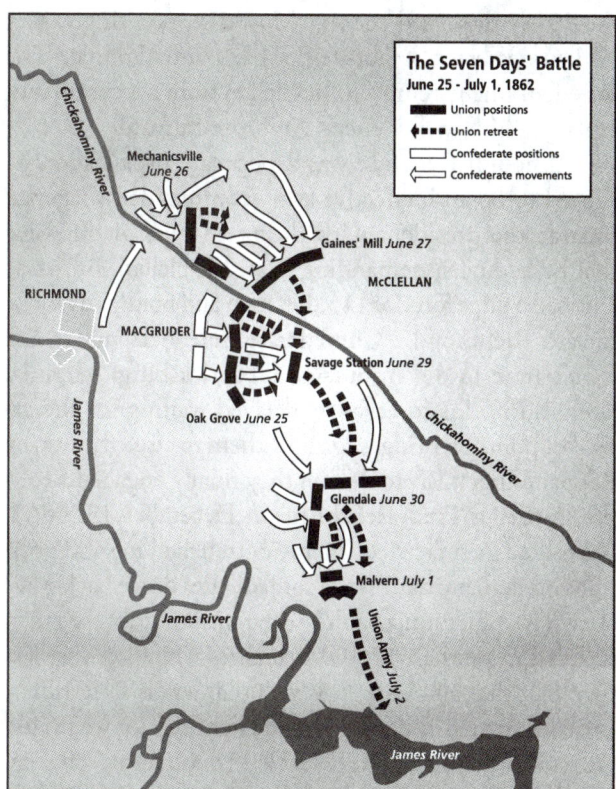

Map 16.5 The Seven Days' Battle

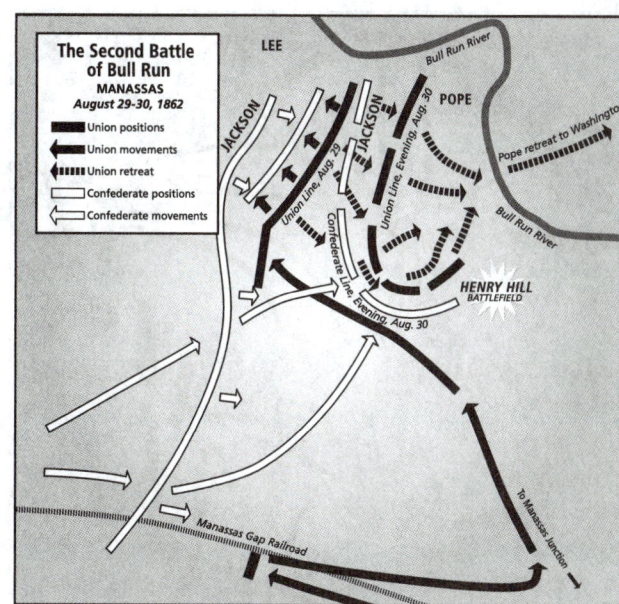

Map 16.6 The Second Battle of Bull Run

Stalemate

Although he had been successful in the Western Theater, Pope—a career officer from Kentucky—proved to be no match for Lee and his Army of Northern Virginia. Pope's troops operated in the Shenandoah Valley, charged with protecting the capital and relieving pressure on McClellan while he remained on the peninsula. Thus, in August 1862, Lee faced two large Union forces: the withdrawing Army of the Potomac, which lay to the east of Richmond, and Pope's Army of Virginia situated to the north. Lee decided to strike before the two units could link up. With McClellan tamed, the Confederate general went after Pope, who Lee believed to be indecisive. Lee split his force, ordering "Stonewall" Jackson to flank Pope's army from behind, a feat that Jackson performed well. His troops captured a major Union supply depot at Manassas Junction, which drew Pope's full attention. The Union commander committed the majority of forces to an attack on Jackson, but as he did so, Lee slammed into one of Pope's relatively unprotected flanks. The ensuing battle, Second Bull Run (or Second Manassas) fought August 28–30, 1862, resulted in a Union defeat with heavy losses. The Confederate victory helped to create the impression that Lee was unstoppable. Lincoln responded to Pope's failure by sending him to Minnesota where he would spend the remainder of the war contending with the Sioux Nation. The Army of Virginia was then merged

with the Army of the Potomac, still under the command of McClellan.

In spite of his limitations as a field commander, George McClellan would prove (with a degree of luck) that Lee was beatable at the **Battle of Antietam** (Sharpsburg), fought on September 17, 1862. Lee planned to follow up his victory at Second Bull Run with an invasion of the northern states, which would allow him to capture needed supplies and possibly create a demand for peace that would influence upcoming congressional elections. To carry out these goals, Lee again split his command. His main force moved northward through western Maryland, while the other moved against the federal arsenal at Harpers Ferry (located in present-day West Virginia at the convergence point with the borders of Virginia and Maryland). McClellan, however, had been tipped off. One of Lee's subordinates had inadvertently dropped his copy of the invasion plans, which were soon discovered by Union scouts. Upon receiving this information, McClellan responded by sending the Army of the Potomac to crush Lee's divided force, but his troops were somewhat delayed moving through mountainous terrain while being harassed by smaller Confederate units. By the time McClellan caught up to Lee, the latter had gathered most of his forces near Sharpsburg, Maryland, and received waves of uncoordinated attacks from McClellan's forces throughout the day. The fighting resulted in the war's bloodiest single day—actually the bloodiest day in all American military history. A quarter of Union soldiers engaged in the battle (over 12,000) were casualties, while a little over 10,000 Confederate soldiers (approximately one-quarter of those engaged) were killed or wounded. The battle itself was a tactical draw. Lee's losses, however,

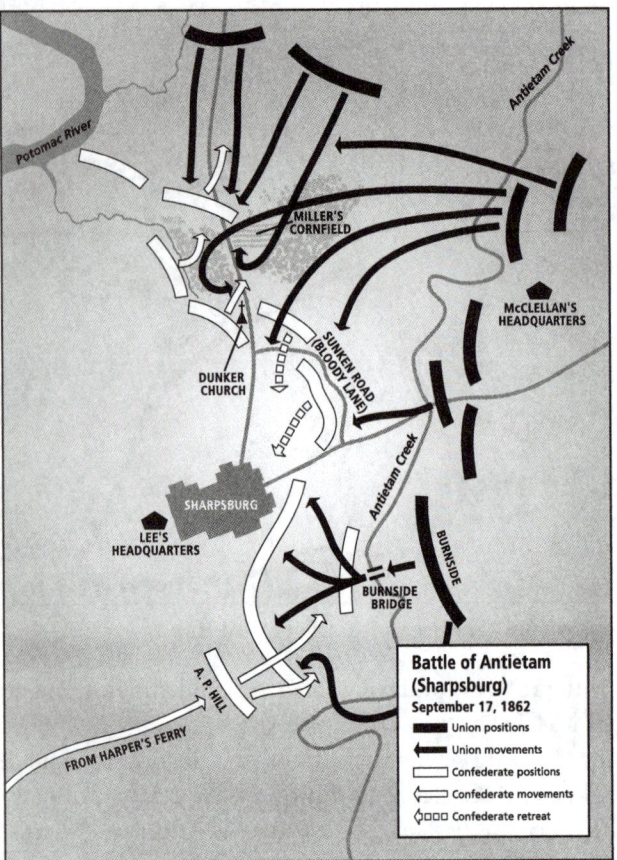

Map 16.7 Battle of Antietam

forced him to withdraw from Maryland, so the Union claimed victory. Lincoln by this point had become completely disillusioned with McClellan. The general's forces had outnumbered Lee's army nearly two-to-one, and he passed on several opportunities during the battle to crush the widely dispersed enemy. Most disappointingly, McClellan neglected to pursue Lee back into Virginia. The president finally removed McClellan from his command, replacing him with General Ambrose Burnside.

Although Burnside was a popular corps leader, he proved to be an ineffective army commander. Eager to provide the president with the rapid type of offensive that he had been demanding from McClellan, Burnside amassed a huge force of 115,000 men and boldly advanced toward Richmond. Confederate defenders under Lee found time to dig in outside Fredericksburg, Virginia, while Burnside's forces were delayed waiting for the arrival of pontoon bridges to allow them to cross the nearby Rappahannock River. When they finally engaged Lee at the **Battle of Fredericksburg** on December 13, 1862, Burnside's men faced an enemy entrenched in solid positions on high ground. The Confederates drove back wave after wave of Union assaults, seven in all. Ambrose's men suffered more than 12,600 casualties while Lee lost less than half that amount. "It is well that war is so terrible," Lee commented as he watched the fighting, "or we should grow too fond of it." The defeat left Union morale shaken. "All think Virginia is not worth such a loss of life," wrote one Union soldier in a letter to home. "Why not confess that we are worsted," he continued, "and come to an agreement?" Lincoln, who described himself as being in "a worse place than Hell," removed Burnside but faced renewed questions about his leadership. Rumors swirled that his cabinet would be reorganized—Salmon P. Chase,

Tending to the wounded on the Antietam battlefield.

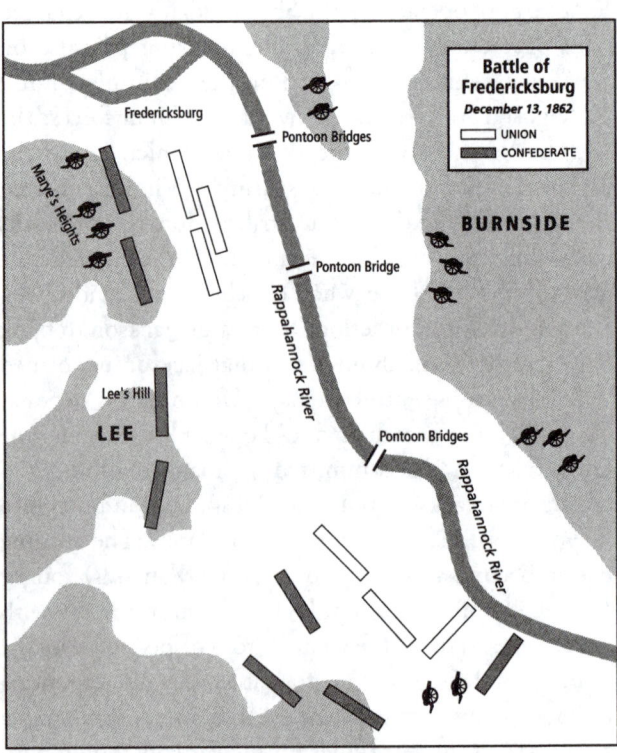

Map 16.8 Battle of Fredericksburg

in fact, tried to use the defeat as a way to force Seward out of the cabinet. Lincoln outmaneuvered him, and Chase felt compelled to offer his resignation (which the president refused to accept).

By the end of 1862, Union war prospects looked bleak. Although it had won significant battles on the high seas and in the West—victories that removed Confederate forces from Kentucky and almost all of Tennessee—the fighting between Washington and Richmond had brought nothing but defeat and frustration. A succession of Union commanders had no luck defeating the Confederacy as Lee's Army of Northern Virginia proved thus far to be the dominant force in the Eastern Theater. The astonishing numbers of casualties, although inviting doubts about Lincoln's abilities as a war leader, opened the way for a transformation in northern war aims from a fight solely to save the Union to one also including the death of slavery. Lee's success, in fact, ironically put the survival of slavery at greater risk, as Lincoln and his cabinet reached the conclusion that emancipation was a necessary war measure. Even so, the end of the war remained a long way off, and Union victory at the end of 1862 was far from certain.

WARTIME TRANSFORMATIONS

By the end of 1862, the Civil War had already brought significant changes to both the North and South. Reflecting on the Battle of Shiloh, which produced over 23,000 casualties, Ulysses Grant wrote that one could "walk across the clearing in any direction stepping on dead bodies without a foot touching the ground." Sherman remarked "the scenes on this field would have cured anybody of war." Shiloh proved to be just the beginning. The Seven Days' Battles brought an additional 36,000 casualties; Second Bull Run, 25,000; Antietam, 23,000; and Fredericksburg, 18,000. Troops fighting in Tennessee closed out the year at the Battle of Stones River (December 31, 1862), which resulted in another 19,000 killed and wounded. Soldiers wrote home describing the bodies that they had seen in the aftermath of battles—mangled, swollen, decapitated. Numerous soldiers returned home as amputees. Future battles would bring more casualties. Chancellorsville in May 1863 cost nearly 30,000; Gettysburg a few months later brought more than 50,000; Chickamauga took almost 35,000 casualties. Civil War deaths due to combat and diseases ultimately exceeded a half million, with the most likely estimate being around 750,000. A recent approximation based on comparisons of census data taken from before and after the war, however, argues that the traditionally-cited number is too low because military records, especially those from the South, undercounted

the number of casualties. Updated estimates, which are gaining rapid acceptance among historians, raise the total number of deaths to approximately 750,000. Whatever the actual figure, however, the scale of the Civil War, in terms of mobilization and total casualties unleashed a host of transformations throughout government and society.

The Civil War and State Power

Wartime demands significantly altered the role of government for both adversaries. In the North, the war made a number of actions possible that previously had not been politically feasible. Republicans in Congress, for example, took advantage of secession to drive through a number of measures that had been blocked by Democratic opposition during the 1850s. Before the end of 1862, Congress enacted the Homestead Act, which offered farmers an opportunity to claim 160 acres of land if they actually lived on the property and made substantive improvements. Congress also raised tariffs, authorized a transcontinental railroad, created a national banking system, and established land grant colleges. Such policies would ultimately provide a legal and social foundation for the postwar industrial economy, but the most immediate transformations to impact the North and South were those changes directly tied to the war effort.

Both the Confederate and Union governments passed conscription laws to address their manpower demands. In April 1862, the Confederate Congress passed the first draft law in American history. The U.S. government reciprocated the following year. For the most part, the intent of these laws was to use the threat of the draft to encourage men to enlist voluntarily. While the vast majority of soldiers in both armies continued to be volunteers, the policies nevertheless generated significant hostility from the public. Both sides also allowed individuals the option of hiring a substitute, giving rise to the popular assertion that the conflict was a "rich man's war, but a poor man's fight." A host of scholars have worked to debunk that claim, as there are plenty of examples of wealthy people heading off to the front. Substitution, moreover, gave officials the option of keeping skilled people in civilian life where their work—such as in food production and manufacturing—was critical to sustaining the war effort. Still, the perception remained that the policies were manifestly unfair to the poor, especially in the case of the Confederate law that, for a while, permitted planters with twenty or more slaves to stay home and manage their plantations.

Another considerable expansion of state power—especially in the North—involved the suppression of civil liberties. Although President Lincoln willingly endured

The Enrollment Act of 1863 allowed drafted men to purchase an exemption or to furnish a "substitute" in lieu of their own service. This illustration dramatizes the unfairness of the measure to the economically disadvantaged showing the bust of one man, "I'm drafted" in contrast to that of an obviously more well-to-do young man, "I ain't." 1863.

Democratic Party opposition (the Democrats actually gained 32 House seats in the 1862 congressional elections), he had his limits. Lincoln worried a great deal about Maryland, which, although its legislature voted not to secede, had enough hostile elements within the state to cause him to take drastic measures there. Losing control of Maryland would result in the nation's capital being surrounded by hostile territory, and, in early April, Confederate sympathizers in Maryland attempted to thwart a Massachusetts unit's efforts to reach Washington, D. C. Likewise, states such as Kentucky, with its long border along the Ohio River, offered huge potential disadvantages to the Union war effort if they fell into Confederate hands. Thus, in late April 1862, Lincoln ordered the suspension of the writ of **habeas corpus,** thus authorizing warrantless arrests of citizens (though the Constitution seemed to imply that only the legislative branch could curtail habeas corpus, Congress sanctioned Lincoln's actions in early 1863). During the course of the war, 30,000-50,000 citizens, most residing in the Border States or active war zones, were incarcerated at one time or another. The president personally ordered very few arrests. Instead, he and his subordinates gave vague dictates to military officers and federal marshals to arrest those accused of giving aid and comfort to the enemy or otherwise engaging in "disloyal practices." In

the vast majority of the cases, those arrested were not detained for their political speech. A major exception was ex-Congressman Clement Vallandigham, one of the "Copperhead" leaders whose opposition to the war had crossed the line to open disloyalty. (Though General Burnside, not Lincoln, ordered Vallandigham's arrest in May 1863, the president eventually deported him to the Confederacy. He returned to the North unmolested a year later.) By far, most were arrested for trading or communicating with the enemy, blockade running, undertaking fraudulent sales to the U.S. government, selling alcohol to Union soldiers, and hindering the draft or interfering with voluntary enlistments. Lincoln firmly believed his power to be a short-term war measure. In 1863, he professed in an open letter that he saw little chance "that the American people will, by means of military arrest during the rebellion, lose the right of public discussion, the liberty of speech and the press, the law of evidence, trial by jury, and Habeas Corpus, throughout the indefinite peaceful future . . . any more that . . . a man could contract so strong an appetite for emetics during temporary illness, as to persist in feeding upon them through the remainder of his healthful life." Although the policies of conscription and the suppression of civil liberties proved temporary, they nevertheless represented some of the most aggressive uses of power by a national government in American history.

Emancipation

The most far-reaching exercise of state power, emancipation, by no means proved to be temporary. Before the war, only radicals and fear-mongers seriously believed that the federal government possessed authority under the Constitution to end slavery in the states. Faced with potential trouble in the slaveholding Border States and opposition from a northern electorate that was not particularly sympathetic toward African Americans, Lincoln worked hard in the early phases of the war to keep the conflict focused on the preservation of the Union. As he wrote Horace Greeley, editor of the widely read *New York Tribune*, "My paramount object in this struggle is to save the Union. . . . What I do about slavery, and the colored race, I do because I believe it helps to save the Union; and what I forbear, I forbear because I do not believe it would help to save the Union." By the time of his letter to Greeley, however, Lincoln had privately concluded that the saving of the Union required ending slavery.

Lincoln's effort to keep the war focused on preserving the Union proved to be politically problematic. Slavery's role in bringing about secession was no secret. Confederate leaders, such as Vice President Alexander Stephens of Georgia, freely admitted that slavery formed a "cornerstone" of their government, and the South had acted to fix a wrong turn made by Thomas Jefferson when he declared that "all men are created equal." Abolitionists and Radical Republicans also saw the war as inseparable from slavery. Frederick Douglass, however, insisted that the price of secession had to be emancipation. Some Union commanders ordered their soldiers to free any slaves found in the areas under their control. Lincoln moved cautiously. He floated the possibility of gradual emancipation and colonization to border state politicians (with no success) and avoided sudden moves that might alienate Unionists in those areas. He even ordered his commanders not to free slaves in their jurisdictions while reserving the right to order emancipation in the future.

Events on the ground, however, ran ahead of the president. Slavery unraveled as Union armies pushed into the South, and enslaved blacks—perhaps as many as 500,000—left plantations to seek freedom in the Union army encampments. By 1862, Union policy, influenced by commanders and politicians who saw no good in turning slaves back, moved to accommodate this movement. Federal law initially defined such runaways as "contrabands" and forbade returning them to the South. Within a matter of months, Congress had moved from that point to confiscation, a policy that freed the slaves of anyone who supported the Confederate war effort. By this time, Congress, with Lincoln's support, had imposed a compensated emancipation on the District of Columbia.

By the summer of 1862, Lincoln himself was ready to connect the war effort directly to emancipation. In July, he shared with his cabinet a draft of the **Emancipation**

Fugitive slaves—"Contrabands"—came into the union lines and were employed as laborers. Contrabands on Mr. Foller's farm, Cumberland. May 14, 1862.

Proclamation, an executive order ending slavery in all areas not under Union control by a specific date (ultimately January 1, 1863). His proclamation transformed the nature of the war. No longer would the conflict be solely concerned with preserving the Union—although that goal remained significant. The war now also became a war to end slavery. Militarily, the promise of freedom would hopefully induce slaves to run away to Union lines if an opportunity presented itself, further weakening the Confederate rebellion. Diplomatically, Lincoln's proclamation would be a master stroke, making it impossible for England and France to lend substantial support to the Confederacy without directly promoting the survival of slavery. By the 1860s, slavery was deeply unpopular among the public in Great Britain and France where voting rights had recently expanded. Voters in neither country would have tolerated their governments giving diplomatic, much less military, aid to a slave republic fighting against an emancipating army. When Lincoln presented the document, however, his cabinet advised caution, suggesting that he wait for a significant Union victory before releasing the order to the public. Otherwise, in the wake of McClellan's unsuccessful Peninsular Campaign, Lincoln could be open to the charge that he acted out of desperation, a move that might bring the South some sympathetic European support. Lincoln agreed, waiting until Lee's retreat after the Battle of Antietam to issue the presidential order.

News of the Emancipation Proclamation brought a mixed response among abolitionists. Some criticized its limited nature since the document only promised to legally end slavery in the areas of Confederate control. Others, however, viewed the document as the first step toward full emancipation and helped to fulfill its promise in transforming the meaning of the war.

The proclamation's inclusion of an authorization for the use of African-American soldiers further cemented the idea that the Civil War was becoming a crusade for freedom in a very literal sense. Even before Lincoln had issued his order, Secretary of War Stanton began enlisting former slaves from the sea islands of South Carolina, overturning a federal prohibition on black soldiers in place since 1792. Service in the Union Army struck at the heart of the southern slave regime. Frederick Douglass regarded that as a good reason to enlist. "Every negro-hater and slavery lover in the land," he wrote in 1863, "regards the arming of negroes as a calamity and is doing his best to prevent it." One good way to deal with an enemy, he continued, was to "find out what he does not want and give him plenty of it." Military service also provided African Americans with an opportunity to claim a right to citizenship:

It has been the fashion in this country—even in some of our northern cities—to assault and mob colored citizens, for no other reason than the ease with which it could be done. We have it in our power to do something towards changing this cowardly custom. When it is once found that the black man can give blows as well as take them, more congenial employment will be found than pounding him. The black man, in arms to fight for the freedom of his race, and the safety and security of the country, will give his countrymen a higher and better revelation of his character. We have asked . . . for a chance to fight the Rebels; to fight against slavery and for freedom. That chance is now given us.

Ultimately, 178,000 African Americans served in the war. Many did so at great cost, as 37,000 died in the conflict—a greater proportion of deaths than those suffered by their white counterparts. Black soldiers served in segregated units and endured unequal pay (until 1864) while often performing monotonous support work such as garrison duty. By 1863, however, African-American troops began making significant military contributions after Major Robert Gould Shaw's 54th Massachusetts Regiment made headlines launching a gallant but futile attack on Fort Wagner, which protected the Charleston, South Carolina harbor. Ultimately, black soldiers and sailors gave Union commanders an incredible boost in manpower and many performed well in battle (during the war, twenty-five African Americans were awarded Congressional Medals of Honor for outstanding feats of valor on land and at sea). Confederate troops reacted viciously to the use of black soldiers and sometimes killed the ones

they captured on the spot. The **Fort Pillow Massacre** demonstrated how far such resentment could go. In April 1864, Confederate forces under the command of General Nathan Bedford Forrest (who later served for a time as the main leader of the postwar Ku Klux Klan) overran the fort's garrison then captured and killed over two hundred of the black troops who had defended the post.

Everyday Life during Wartime

As the fighting raged, the war transformed many aspects of everyday life for both civilians and soldiers. At home, the economics of daily life became more challenging. In the North, inflation pushed prices up 80 percent over the course of the war. While wages failed to keep pace, labor unrest—strikes punctuated with the rapid use of strikebreakers—followed. Southerners had an even more difficult time. Hemmed in by the blockade and burdened with a flood of paper money, the southern economy faced rapid inflation. Prices increased by 9,000 percent. Shortages of goods, such as salt and coffee, were common. Basic staples, such as butter and flour, cost a small fortune.

Economic and social tensions in both regions also generated a number of riots. Shortages of food in the South brought a wave of bread riots in Alabama, North Carolina, and even in the Confederate capital of Richmond. The largest riot, however, occurred in the North. In July 1863, economic discontent combined with resentment toward conscription and emancipation produced the **New York City Draft Riots**. The incident began when a crowd of largely Irish, working-class protestors, especially outraged by the draft law's provision allowing individuals to purchase an exception for $300 (a year's salary for the average worker), stormed a draft office. Four days of

The War in America: the Conscription in New York.
Blindfolded men are drawing slips from a cylinder. 1865.

rioting followed, and much of the violence targeted New York City's free black community. New York's Colored Orphan Asylum was burned to the ground. Although the children escaped, the riots resulted in the deaths of over 100 people, including ten African Americans who were lynched. Militia and regular army soldiers eventually arrived to restore order in the city.

Everyday life remained challenging for soldiers as well. Although they endured harrowing battles, soldiers spent much time on the march and even more in camps where life was monotonous and potentially deadly. Camps were often unsanitary and frequently lacked fresh drinking water, leading to soldiers succumbing to such diseases as typhoid and dysentery. Food quality also tended to be poor (over the course of the war, this improved for Union soldiers while becoming worse for Confederate troops).

Soldiers' medical needs quickly overwhelmed the capabilities of military physicians. Crowded camps filled hospitals with soldiers exposed for the first time to the measles and mumps, joining their comrades suffering from typhus and dysentery. Combat created soldiers wounded by devastating new weapons. In earlier wars, soldiers used muskets—weapons with a relatively short range (about 100 yards), slow rate of fire, and not much accuracy. Tactics built around those weapons led soldiers to fire massive volleys at one another (timed so that some soldiers were firing as others reloaded) before moving in to fight at close quarters with bayonets. Early in the Civil War, however, new weapons with rifled barrels could be loaded much more rapidly and fired accurately up to 800 yards, but Union and Confederate battlefield tactics did not change as rapidly as the technology, resulting in massive casualties. Those who were not killed outright, like Corporal Jonathan Allison, often lost a limb in surgical procedures designed to stop the spread of infection. Such men became, in Allison's words, "the living monuments of the . . . cruel and bloody Rebellion."

Some soldiers faced capture. Initially, the Union and Confederate armies agreed to exchange their respective prisoners of war. (Neither side possessed the capacity to house the number of captives that battles between such large forces made possible.) That system broke down when Confederate officials refused to recognize black soldiers as legitimate prisoners of war. Both sides then kept prisoners in crowded and unsanitary prison camps. Southern camps, which like the rest of the South, suffered from a lack of food and medicine, became particularly horrid places to be held. At **Andersonville**, Georgia, the worst of all camps of the era, thirteen thousand men died during their internment. The war thus touched almost every aspect of American life, and the experience left deep scars—both physically and socially—that would take a long time to fade.

Women on the Home Front

War also brought new roles for women. In the North, thousands of women served as nurses. Many women participated in the work of the United States Sanitary Commission, the chief agency through which northern women helped the war effort. Volunteer workers ran its thousands of auxiliaries, collecting clothing, food, and medicine. "Sanitary Fairs" were organized whose fundraising strategies included lavish galas that benefited directly from the growing economic inequality accelerated by the war, which helped to provide cleaner camps, healthier diets, and improved medical care for Union soldiers. Such work expanded female influence in the public sphere and

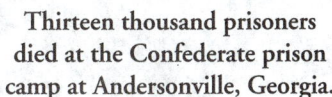

Thirteen thousand prisoners died at the Confederate prison camp at Andersonville, Georgia.

built upon work carried out by women in the antebellum reform movements. Elizabeth Cady Stanton and Susan B. Anthony founded the National Women's Loyal League, enabling them to continue the struggle for the abolition of slavery and securing women's rights in the context of the war effort. Northern women took over many of the remaining male jobs in teaching and, for the first time, gained positions in government offices and stores, as a result of the wartime manpower shortages. Many of these women, whose husbands and fathers were away in the army, would have been destitute without these new jobs.

Just like the women in the North, southern women likewise found new roles thrust upon them. They formed patriotic societies and collected supplies for the soldiers. But they suffered far worse shortages and more severe losses of manpower, resulting in greater hardships. Wealthy women ran plantations—some of the largest economic enterprises in the nation before the war. Plantation mistresses often had to manage their slaves at a time when slavery was disintegrating. As stealing, dawdling, and even sabotage by restless slaves was increasing, soldiers exhorted their wives to take charge. "You may give your Negroes away," one weary mistress wrote her husband in 1864, "I cannot live with them another year alone." Poor women often became saddled with heavy fieldwork while their male relatives went off to fight. As in the North, women also found work as teachers. In Richmond, many women nicknamed "government girls" found work in offices of the Confederate bureaucracy.

Many women, North and South, suffered the loss of their husbands, lovers, and sons and had to learn to make do without them. "I have not read my bible since Charlie died, " one bereft southern woman wrote, "My tears and feelings seem frozen. I know, I feel but one thing, I am alone, utterly desolate."

Women on the Battlefield

Not only did women do most of the work in volunteer civilian agencies like the Sanitary Commission, but thousands also worked as nurses in army hospitals. Florence Nightingale in the 1854 Crimean War had elevated the nursing profession, previously defamed as menial or morally dubious. Many still worried that the rough and bloody atmosphere of a military hospital was no place for a gentle, respectable young woman. The Union appointed the famed reformer Dorothea Dix as superintendent of nurses. She insisted that her nurses be over thirty years old, "plain in appearance," and unadorned by jewelry. Eventually, 3,200 women met these requirements and served as northern army nurses, the first professional nurses in American military history. Perhaps the most fa-

mous of them, Mary Ann "Mother" Bickerdyke, crusaded tirelessly to improve the health of the soldiers and won the admiration of the normally ornery General Sherman.

Others were volunteers on the battlefield. A small, pretty woman in a bonnet and a bright red bow named **Clara Barton** arrived at Antietam with a wagonload of bandages and medicine. She worked tirelessly through the battle comforting the wounded and aiding the surgeons. One of the latter called her, "the true heroine of the age, the angel of the battlefield." She continued her efforts through most of the war. Later, she worked to identify the remains of the POWs at Andersonville and, eventually, founded the American Red Cross. "Michigan Bridget" Divers who attached herself to her husband's cavalry regiment became famous for her courage and coolness under fire in removing wounded men from the battlefield. She also picked up a fallen soldier's weapon and fought alongside the men.

At least one woman, **Mary Walker**, served as a surgeon in the Union army. When the Confederates captured the pants-wearing Walker, they expressed astonishment "at the sight of a thing that nothing but the debased and depraved Yankee nation could produce." Walker was awarded the Medal of Honor for her battlefield and prison camp medical services. (Congress rescinded the decoration two years before her death in 1917 but restored the medal in 1977.)

Clara Barton was called, "the true heroine of the age, the angel of the battlefield." She later founded the American Red Cross.

Nurses and the Union War Effort

The Civil War mobilized Americans on a scale never before seen, and the harrowing number of casualties created a demand for nurses to heal the sick and wounded and also to comfort the dying. Working with the military or through private organizations such as the United States Sanitary Commission, women like Dorothea Dix, a reformer long committed to the creation of asylums for the mentally ill, Clara Barton, the future founder of the Red Cross, and Louisa May Alcott, later to be author of the novel, **Little Women***, devoted themselves to the cause of nursing. This passage, taken from an early history of the United States Sanitary Commission, underscored both the perceived importance of this work and also the way in which it had grown out of earlier reform projects.*

Much has been said and written upon the part taken by American women in supporting the National cause during the war, but the full extent of the influence they exerted, can hardly be understood, without adverting to the peculiar position which they occupy in a democratic society like ours. Women, in history, have often been the inspirers of men, rarely their fellow workers. The power which they wielded in the late war, was due to the exercise of those gentler, domestic virtues, which find their birthplace, and ordinarily their only sphere of action, within the narrow limits of home. The influence of these qualities has been little observed in other wars; here, exceptional circumstances, arising from the peculiar structure of our society, first gave an opportunity for a development on a vast scale, of that same tender, generous spirit of devotion on the part of the woman to those who are suffering in the cause of their country, as was excited by the needs of their own kindred. Of course, this spirit of zeal and devotion was not created by the war, for it had long manifested itself in an organized form, in every part of the country, where any of the countless forms of human suffering required succor. But the peculiarity is, that here, organizations for such benevolent purposes, had been for a long time under the control and management almost exclusively of women. The admirable plans arranged by them for conducting such societies, and the wonderful success, which had attended these schemes, both in their organization and practical result, first suggested the employment of their extraordinary zeal for kindred purposes on a much larger scale, and in a novel field of labor. The Commission was convinced in the intelligent zeal and devotion of these women, in their habit of persecuting benevolent labors by organized effort, and in their general familiarity with the principles and methods, which ensure success in such undertakings, it had discovered a precious source for a regular, systematic, and bountiful supply of all that the soldier could need in the way of voluntary and supplemental aid. It was its constant effort during the war, so to direct their zeal in this work, and so to instruct them in regard to their labors, that the greatest possible practical benefit should result to the soldier. It was wholly unnecessary to stimulate this zeal, or urge to self-denying labor, in so sacred a cause. The intense feeling of nationality, characteristic of all classes, the ardor of which no reverses or discouragements could chill, burned with tenfold intensity in the hearts of the women of the country. Denied a participation in the actual toils and dangers of the strife, they eagerly sought to manifest the depth of their sympathy, by work suited to their sex. If they cannot leave those they loved in battle, they could, almost before its smoke it cleared away, bite up their wounds, minister to their sufferings, and set them an example of heroic courage, patience and self-sacrificing devotion, which would inspire them with fresh and undying enthusiasm for the cause.

Source: Charles J. Stillé, *History of the United States Sanitary Commission, being the General Report of Its Work during the War of the Rebellion* (Philadelphia: J.B. Lippincott, 1866), 170-172.

The Confederate army was slower to allow "decent" white women to serve as nurses. At first, only slave women performed this task in army hospitals. Eventually, however, white women from "good families" volunteered and were authorized to work as nurses. One of the southern surgeons admitted he preferred the women to the "rough country crackers" who had been performing that duty and who did not "know caster oil from a gun rod."

Black women helped the Union army by working as laundresses and unofficial nurses. Hundreds of others hid Union soldiers and helped them to escape. Some were punished for bringing food to Union prisoners. Susie King Taylor, who had learned how to read and write, was recruited by Union officers when she was 14 years old to teach freed slaves. She married a black sergeant and served alongside him as a nurse and laundress. She also confided, "I learned to handle a musket very well while in the regiment, and could shoot straight and often hit the target." Harriet Tubman not only worked as a nurse and cook for the Union army, she also served as a spy, utilizing her "invisibility" as a black woman to learn important information about troop movements.

Harriet Tubman Serves in a War for Freedom

Historians debate whether the Civil War began as a war to save the Union or as a war to end slavery. For Abolitionist Harriet Tubman, a formerly enslaved African-American woman who spent the 1850s helping other people escape from slavery, the war was always about freedom. Her 1868 narrative recorded how she served throughout the conflict.

"I'd go to de hospital ... early eb'ry mornin'. I'd get a big chunk of ice ... and put it in a basin, and fill it with water; den I'd take a sponge and begin. Fust man I'd come to, I'd thrash away de flies, an' dey'd rise, dey would, like bees roun' a hive. Den I'd begin to bathe der wounds, an' by de time I'd bathed off three or four, de fire and heat would have melted de ice and made de water warm, an' it would be as red as clar blood. Den I'd go an' git more ice ... an' by de time I got to de nex' ones, de flies would be roun' de fust ones black an' thick as eber." In this way she worked, day after day, till late at night; then she went home to her little cabin, and made about fifty pies, a great quantity of ginger-bread, and two casks of root beer. These she would hire some contraband to sell for her through the camps, and thus she would provide her support for another day; for this woman never received pay or pension, and never drew for herself but twenty days' rations during the four years of her labors. At one time she was called away from Hilton Head, by one of our officers, to come to Fernandina, where the men were "dying off like sheep, "from dysentery. Harriet had acquired quite a reputation for her skill in curing this disease.... At another time, we find her nursing those who were down by hundreds with small-pox and malignant fevers....

When our armies and gun-boats first appeared in any part of the South, many of the poor negroes were as much afraid of "de Yankee Buckra" as of their own masters. It was almost impossible to win their confidence, or to get information from them. But to Harriet they would tell anything....

Gen. Hunter asked her at one time if she would go with several gun-boats up the Combahee River, the object of the expedition being to take up the torpedoes placed by the rebels in the river, to destroy railroads and bridges, and to cut off supplies from the rebel troops. She said she would go if Col. Montgomery was to be appointed commander of the expedition. Col. Montgomery was one of John Brown's men, and was well known to Harriet. Accordingly, Col. Montgomery was appointed to the command, and Harriet, with several men under her ... accompanied the expedition....

Harriet describes in the most graphic manner the appearance of the plantations as they passed up the river; the frightened negroes leaving their work and taking to the woods, at sight of the gun-boats; then coming to peer out like startled deer, and scudding away like the wind at the sound of the steam-whistle. "Well," said one old negro, "Mas'r said de Yankees had horns and tails, but I nebber beliebed it till now." But the word was passed along by the mysterious telegraphic communication existing among these simple people, that these were "Lincoln's gun-boats come to set them free." In vain, then, the drivers used their whips, in their efforts to hurry the poor creatures back to their quarters; they all turned and ran for the gun-boats. They came down every road, across every field, just as they had left their work and their cabins; women with children clinging around their necks, hanging to their dresses, running behind, all making at full speed for "Lincoln's gun-boats."

....

This fearless woman was often sent in to the rebel lines as a spy, and brought back valuable information as to the position of armies and batteries; she has been in battle when the shot was falling like hail, and the bodies of dead and wounded men were dropping around her like leaves in autumn; but the thought of fear never seems to have had place for a moment in her mind. She had her duty to perform, and she expected to be taken care of [by God] till it was done.

Several other women operated as spies for both sides, including society hostess, Rose O'Neal Greenhow, a close friend of former president James Buchanan. She was arrested and deported to England, only to drown in a shipwreck trying to smuggle gold to the Confederacy. **Belle Boyd** carried messages and spied for Stonewall Jackson. She later made quite a career for herself on stage, recounting her dramatic adventures.

Both in the North and the South (although more in the former) there were a number of women who dressed as men and fought in the war. The best research has uncovered 150 women soldiers. Several of these were promoted to sergeant, a few to lieutenant, and one even became a captain. Albert D.J. Cashier, whose real name was Jennie Hodgers, fought in numerous battles from 1862 to 1865. After the war, she collected a pension for disabled soldiers and was active in the Grand Army of the Republic, the Union veterans' organization. Her sex was not discovered until 1911 when she broke her leg and had to be treated by a physician.

While the efforts of these soldiers are interesting, the work of the women nurses had greater significance in advancing the professional status of nursing in America. After the war, nursing veterans started training programs, wrote textbooks, and even administered hospitals. Nursing became an important profession for women although the job description continued to include such menial activities as cleaning, doing laundry, and cooking for patients.

THE TURNING POINTS OF 1863

Gettysburg

In 1863, the war's momentum fundamentally changed. Although the end of the conflict remained far off, the Union achieved two crucial victories at Gettysburg, Pennsylvania, and Vicksburg, Mississippi, that turned the tide forever in its favor. Those victories did not come quickly. After the Battle of Fredericksburg, Lincoln replaced Ambrose Burnside with General Joseph Hooker, an aggressive corps commander. The president did not hold Hooker in high regard, particularly because the general was reputed to favor establishing a dictatorship. Lincoln gave him the command anyway. "Only those generals who gain successes, can set up dictators," he wrote to Hooker. "What I now ask of you is military success, and I will risk the dictatorship." In the spring of 1863, Hooker took a force of 125,000 men across the Rappahannock River in a flanking maneuver designed to move behind Robert E. Lee's forces. Anticipating Hooker's movements, Lee moved to intercept the Army of the Potomac in a heavily wooded area near Chancellorsville, Virginia. Though outnumbered two-to-one, Lee skillfully used his knowledge of the local terrain to his advantage, even dividing his forces further by sending Stonewall Jackson to strike at Hooker's right flank. Jackson's surprise attack combined with Lee's frontal assault wilted the Union lines. Although the Union troops rallied, they ultimately retreated after bearing over 17,000 casualties. By comparison, Lee lost 13,000 men, none more important than Jackson who died of wounds received when accidentally shot in the dark by a nervous Confederate sentry after returning from a reconnaissance mission. Despite this major blow to the Confederate high command, military historians consider the **Battle of Chancellorsville** (April 30—May 6, 1863) a masterpiece. To this day, war colleges cite Lee's perfor-

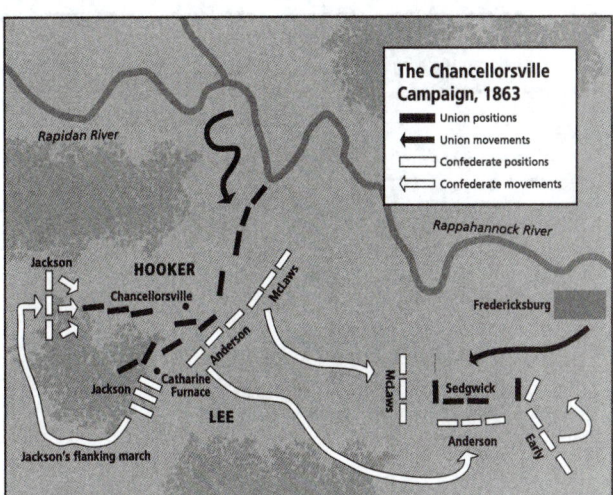

Map 16.9 The Chancellorsville Campaign

mance as a textbook example of how an aggressive general can use the terrain to negate numerical disadvantages.

Lee soon decided to capitalize on his victory at Chancellorsville by invading Pennsylvania and destroying the Army of the Potomac on Union soil. He believed that moving his army northward would relieve pressure on Richmond and allow the Army of Northern Virginia to live off the land in an area that had not been a scene of regular fighting. If successful, his actions might also make Lincoln's government appear weak, bolster peace sentiment in the North, and hasten an end to the war. Though Hooker moved his forces between Lee's army and Washington, D.C., Lincoln did not believe his general was moving rapidly enough to intercept Lee's forces and soon replaced him with George G. Meade, a seasoned corps commander whose army intercepted Lee at Gettysburg, a crossroads town in southwestern Pennsylvania. The next

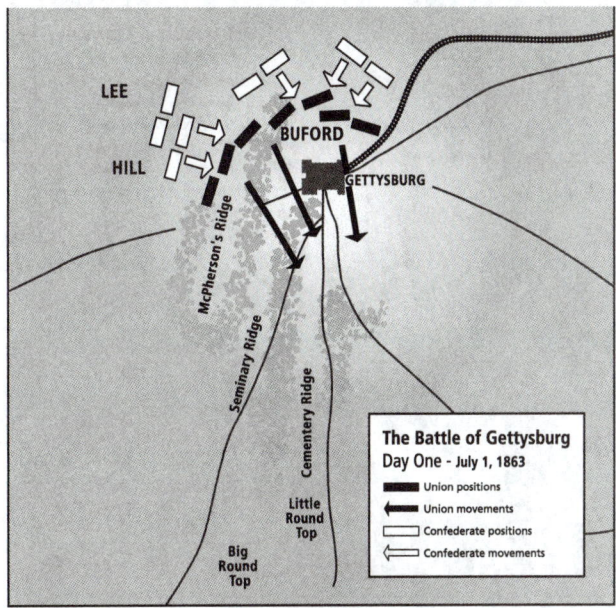

Map 16.10 Battle of Gettysburg, Day One

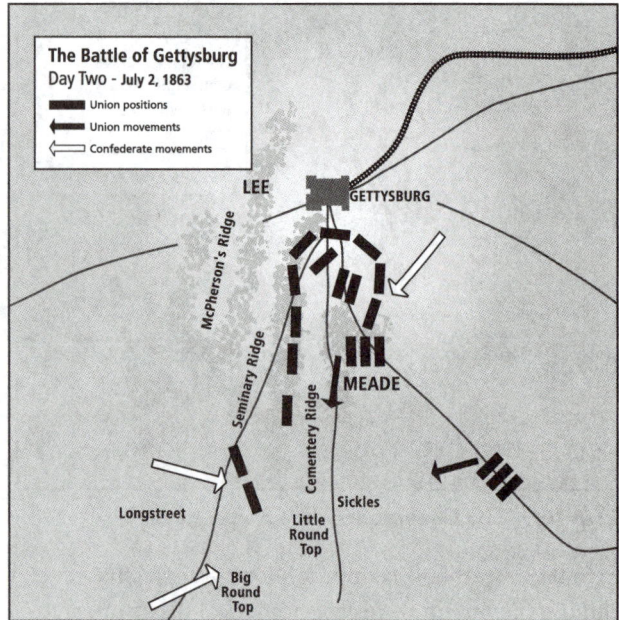

Map 16.11 Battle of Gettysburg, Day Two

three days of fighting would largely determine the final outcome of the war. On the first day, Lee's forces held the edge, but Meade's men were able to retreat to the high ground overlooking the town. By the second day, additional troops from each army arrived on the scene, and the Union had tightened its defenses. Though outnumbered, Lee launched massive attacks on Meade's fortified flanks, but units at each position, fighting desperately, managed to hold their ground. On the third day, Lee made one final attempt to break through the Union lines. Believing in the ability of his men to do whatever he asked of them and determined to make Gettysburg the decisive battle of the war, Lee boldly (many would later say fool-

ishly) launched one final massive frontal assault on the Union center—the ill-fated "Pickett's Charge"—which resulted in over 10,000 casualties before the attack dissipated before a withering rifle and cannon fire. Fought between July 1 and July 3, 1863, the **Battle of Gettysburg** became the bloodiest battle of the entire war. Lee lost over 23,000 men, almost one-third of his army. Though victorious, Meade suffered more than 23,000 casualties, or one-fourth of his total forces. As a result of the heavy casualties sustained, the general (to Lincoln's great dismay) chose not to pursue Lee's battered army when the defeated general reluctantly ordered his men to retreat on the Fourth of July.

The Vicksburg Campaign

On the same day that Lee retreated from Gettysburg, the Confederate defenders of **Vicksburg, Mississippi,** surrendered to Ulysses Grant's army. The general had been trying to capture the fortified city since March 1863, proceeding against the city through a process of trial and error, embracing a new approach after the preceding one failed. By the end of April, Grant had managed to get his troops onto Vicksburg's side of the Mississippi River. He then moved inland to attack the city from behind (along the way he captured the state capital of Jackson). The general's assaults on Vicksburg toward the end of May, however, inflicted heavy losses on his troops while failing to breech the city's defenses, so Grant ordered a siege on May 25. Confederate defenders held on for over forty days, but Grant's position kept them cut off from reinforcements, and their supplies dwindled. On July 4, 1863, Vicksburg surrendered, and Grant captured an army of nearly 30,000 troops. The Union now had complete control of the Mississippi River. Lincoln, who had questioned Grant's strategy, now promoted him to major general and sent him an apology. "I now wish to make the

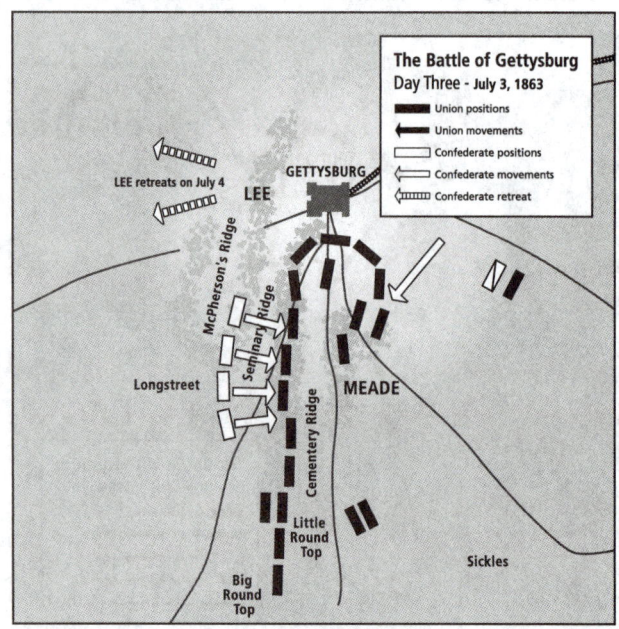

Map 16.12 Battle of Gettysburg, Day Three

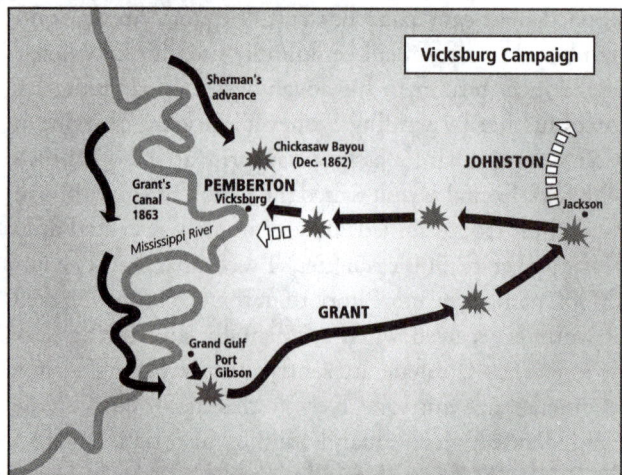

Map 16.13 Vicksburg Campaign

personal acknowledgement," the president wrote, "that you were right, and I was wrong."

By 1863, momentum in the war had definitely shifted. Union victories at Gettysburg and Vicksburg placed the South on the defensive. Lee would never again have a chance to push into Union territory, and Grant's achievement had cut the Confederacy in half. The meaning of the war had also undergone a significant shift. Although Lincoln initially had worked to present the conflict as a struggle to save the Union, he had come to link the war to a higher purpose—the protection and expansion of freedom. In his Gettysburg Address, delivered as part of a dedication for a cemetery for Union soldiers who had died in that battle, Lincoln noted that "these dead . . . have not died in vain." They, and others like them, had died for a cause; they gave their lives so "that this nation, under God, should have a new birth of freedom—and that government of the people, by the people, for the people, shall not perish from the earth."

Chickamauga and Chattanooga

Even after the decisive Union victory at Gettysburg, the end of the war lay in the distant future. Meade's decision not to pursue Lee into Virginia permitted Lee an opportunity to regroup and gather strength. Grant, moreover, paroled the troops that he captured in Vicksburg, allowing them to return home. Keeping them as prisoners of war would have slowed down his forces, plus Grant hoped that the return of defeated troops would sap Confederate morale. Instead, many former prisoners joined new units; some of them even returned to battle in time to fight Grant's force again at the Battle of Chattanooga in eastern Tennessee. Indeed, southern resolve remained strong. Confederate forces defeated a Union army under the command of General William Rosecrans at the Battle of Chickamauga (September 19–20, 1863). The fighting, which resulted in over 35,000 casualties combined, forced Union troops to retreat into Chattanooga where the Confederates placed them under siege. Grant, now in command of all Union troops in the West, soon arrived to save them. His forces managed to open supply lines to the besieged city. The fighting culminated toward the end of November when Grant's troops broke the siege and forced the Confederate forces out of Tennessee. As it settled into its winter quarters, the Union army was now positioned to push its way into the Deep South. Grant had earned his way to the top. When the fighting picked up again, Grant would be general-in-chief of all Union armies. Lincoln had finally found his man.

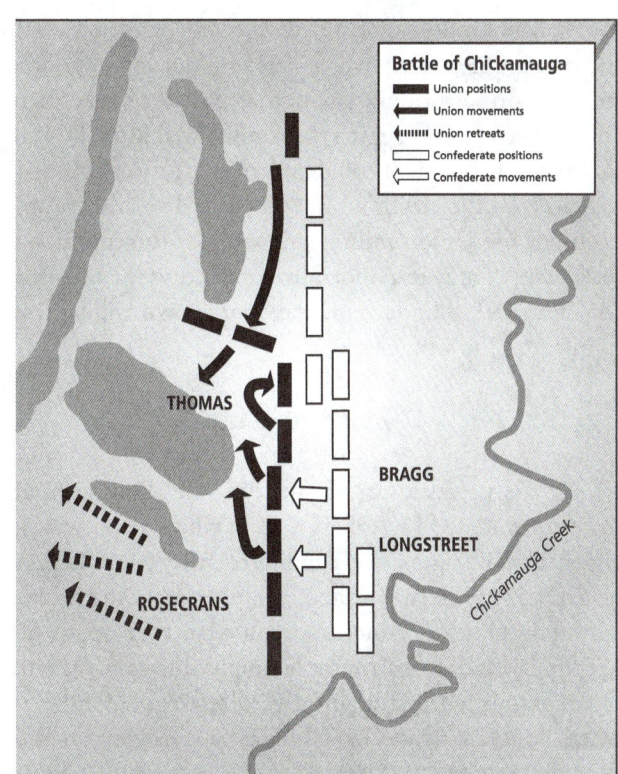

Map 16.14 Battle of Chickamauga

TOWARD UNION VICTORY, 1864

Although the Union had won significant victories in 1863, the war remained far from over. The situation did not look good for the Confederacy, of course, after its crippling losses at Gettysburg and Vicksburg. Despite criticism of the Davis administration and the state of the war effort from the Confederate press, southern resolve remained firm. The Confederate armies still contained experienced soldiers, albeit in reduced numbers, which remained very capable in the field. Southern military objectives still

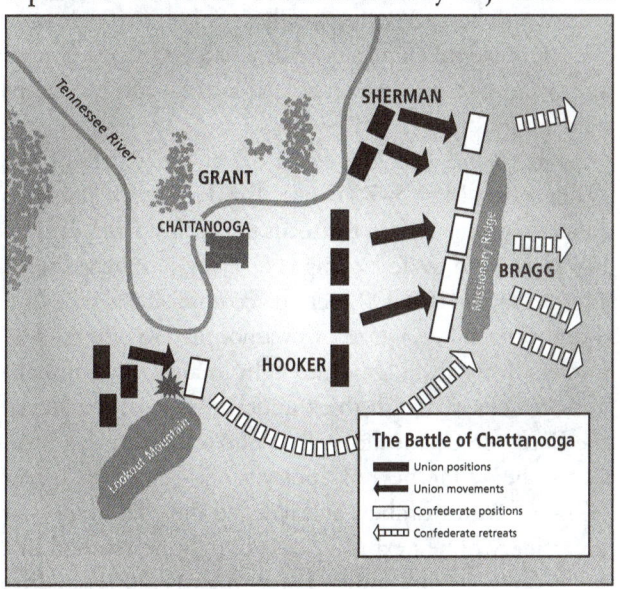

Map 16.15 The Battle of Chattanooga

sought recognition of Confederate independence, but the strategy now centered on holding out long enough to turn northern public opinion against the war. Such an effort required dragging the conflict well into 1864 so that antiwar sentiment could undermine the Republicans' prospects in the election of 1864. Faced with such opposition, the Union military, now under the command of Ulysses Grant, responded by conducting the war in a way designed to undermine the South's own willingness to carry on the struggle.

Grant versus Lee

Unlike his predecessors, Grant did not allow himself to be intimidated by Robert E. Lee, who had become a larger than life figure in the minds of many commanders in the war's Eastern Theater. He ultimately instructed his subordinates to concentrate on what they might do against Lee rather than what he might do against them. Grant employed a straightforward strategy: "Find out where your enemy is. Get at him as soon as you can and keep moving on." He described this strategy as "simple enough," but it probably worked in 1864 and 1865 for two primary reasons. One involved the position of Union forces. Although the Army of the Potomac had failed to dislodge Lee's Army of Northern Virginia from the Richmond area, Union forces under the command of William T. Sherman (one of Grant's most trusted subordinates) were ready to push from Tennessee into the Deep South. Grant planned to trap Lee between his and Sherman's armies and crush him. The second reason stemmed from the North's relative abundance of men and equipment. Grant could "keep moving on" because he could replace whatever he lost after any particular battle. Lee could not. (Grant also had accepted as early as Shiloh that defeating the South would entail a great deal of bloodshed.) Grant's approach soon put Lee on the defensive—but his troops paid a high price.

Grant and Lee first faced off at the Battle of the Wilderness (May 5–7, 1864). Breaking with previous generals, Grant shifted the focus in the East from capturing Richmond to destroying Lee's army, and he gathered a force of over 100,000 men to accomplish the task. An outnumbered Lee, whose army amounted to only 61,000 soldiers, forced the Union to fight in a largely uninhabited area covered with thick underbrush near the site of the Battle of Chancellorsville. The terrain in this location—the Wilderness of Spotsylvania—deprived Grant of his superior numbers and reduced the effectiveness of his artillery. The next three days of fighting resulted in a costly draw. Grant's suffered more than 17,000 casualties while Lee lost over 11,000 men before the Union general

Photograph of General Grant taken by famous Civil War photographer Mathew Brady at Cold Harbor.

broke off the attack.

Rather than withdrawing after the Battle of the Wilderness, however, Grant kept moving as he planned to maneuver around the Army of Northern Virginia and force Lee to fight in terrain more hospitable to his forces. Grant planned to take control of a nearby crossroads, which would effectively place his army between Lee and Richmond—a shift that would surely draw the Confederate commander out of the Wilderness. Unfortunately, Union forces did not move quickly enough to prevent some of the Confederates from beating them to the crossroads and entrenching. The ensuing Battle of Spotsylvania Court House lasted from May 8 to May 21. Nearly two weeks of sporadic fighting brought another 32,000 casualties (over 18,000 of them among Grant's men) while the Union tried to break the Confederate defenses. Again, the Union commander broke off the attack and attempted to maneuver for a better position. When Grant's forces captured a crossroads at Cold Harbor, which lay about ten miles outside of Richmond, reinforcements for both sides arrived and the Confederate defenders quickly constructed a seven-mile line of defenses. The subsequent fighting lasted from May 31 to June 12, with much of the heaviest fighting occurring on a June 3 frontal assault by Grant's troops. The combat produced little but dead and wounded bodies for the Union, with casualties numbering nearly 13,000 (compared to a little over 4,500 for Lee's forces). Grant regretted his decision, later stating: "No advantage whatever was gained to compensate for the heavy loss we sustained."

Grant pressed on, shifting his objective from defeating Lee in the field—although the previous month of fighting had reduced the size of Lee's army by over 45 percent—to putting pressure back on Richmond. He now moved against Petersburg, a city that served as Richmond's principle source of supplies. With this maneuver, Grant effectively pinned Lee down because the fall of Petersburg would rapidly produce the fall of Richmond and the Confederacy's retreat. Lee's forces responded by digging in, forcing Grant's forces (after an assault on the city failed) to besiege to the city. Soon, the two armies sat deployed in more than 30 miles of trenches and engaged in fighting that anticipated the type of warfare later seen in France during World War I. The siege lasted from June 1864 to March 1865. The war in the East had stalled again.

Sherman's March to the Sea

While Grant led the fight against Lee in Virginia, General **William Tecumseh Sherman**, his trusted subordinate, moved an army of nearly 100,000 men from Tennessee into northern Georgia. His goal was to crush the Confederate force under the command of General Joseph E. Johnston and to capture Atlanta. Sherman's success in securing the city, followed by his destruction of large portions of the Georgia plantation belt, would ultimately undermine southern morale and hasten the end of the war.

Although his force outnumbered Johnston's, Sherman hoped to avoid a frontal assault against his enemy. Instead, he proceeded by moving his forces along the Confederate flanks. Such maneuvers forced Johnston to either fight from a disadvantaged position or to vacate to a better location. Johnston tended to opt for the latter course, a tendency that Jefferson Davis found highly troubling. This strategy allowed Sherman to move toward Atlanta with a minimal number of casualties, but he did not always adhere to his strategy. At the Battle of Kennesaw Mountain (June 27, 1864), Sherman ordered a frontal attack because he thought Johnston had stretched himself out too thin in the course of his maneuvers. He was wrong, and the Confederates quickly fought him off, inflicting about 3,000 casualties in just a few hours of fighting, while only suffering 1,000 casualties in the process. Like Grant, Sherman did not allow defeat to stop him. By early July, the Union general had forced Johnston to withdraw to Peachtree Creek (a site three miles outside of Atlanta). Johnston planned to assault Union troops as they crossed the creek, but Davis removed him from command and replaced him with John Bell Hood, a general who the Confederate president hoped would be more aggressive.

Hood largely followed the plans of his predecessor, except he attacked after the Union troops crossed Peachtree Creek. His attack hit the Union lines hard, but they withstood the assault, forcing the Confederates to fall back. A few days later, Hood tried again at the Battle of Atlanta (July 22, 1864) to drive Sherman from the vicin-

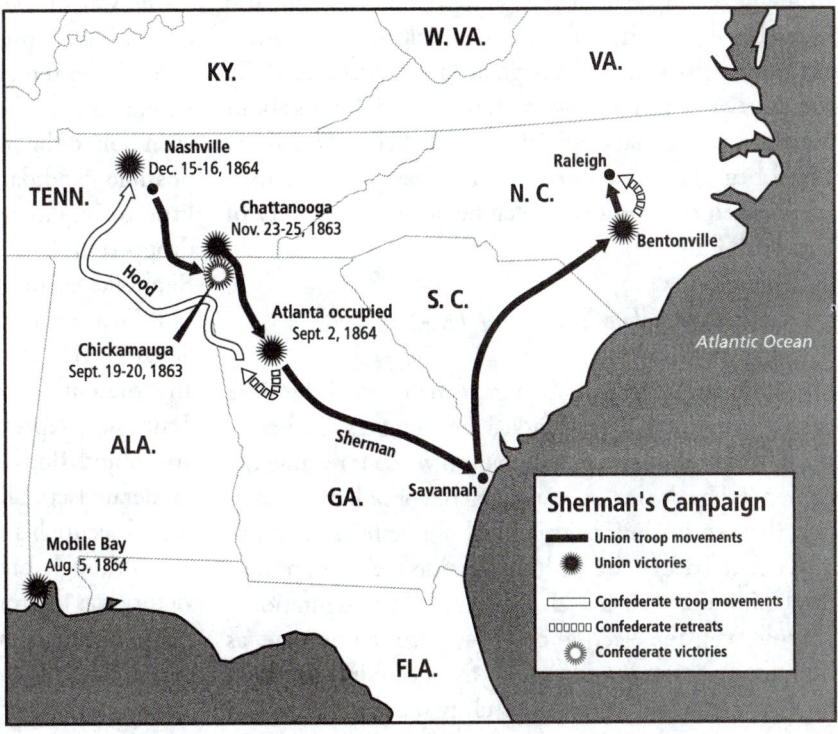

Map 16.16 Sherman's Campaign

ity, this time by sending troops around the Union general's rear flank. The effort failed, and the Confederate forces suffered heavy casualties (nearly 8,500 to the Union's 3,641). Sherman responded by placing the city under siege, a process that took time because his troops had to gain control of the rail line supplying the city. Cavalry raids failed to do the job, so Sherman ultimately moved his entire army to capture the line. After Hood pulled his troops out of Atlanta, the city surrendered on September 2, 1864. Sherman notified Lincoln on September 3, and the news probably saved the president's election as many Northerners felt that the fall of Atlanta meant that the war would soon be over.

Though General Hood ordered all public buildings and property to be destroyed before Confederate troops withdrew, William Sherman made the devastation of Atlanta complete by torching most of the city before following up on his victory with his famous "**March to the Sea**" (November 15—December 21, 1864) during which his army advanced 250 miles from Atlanta to Savannah along the Atlantic Coast. As they moved, Sherman's troops lived off the land. Union officers were ordered to destroy or confiscate any property that could be used to support the rebellion. The march left a path of devastation in its wake. Soldiers took 5,000 horses, 4,000 mules, 13,000 cattle, nearly 5,000 tons of corn, and over 5,000 tons of fodder. They also destroyed 300 miles of rail line and a great number of bridges. Overall, the destruction amounted to $100 million (well over one billion in current dollars). Sherman embarked on this march for a number of reasons. He wanted to undermine southern civilians' willingness and capability to support the war. He also wished to demonstrate that the Confederacy was powerless to stop his army. Although he faced resistance along the route, and both Grant and Lincoln had doubts about his strategy, Sherman reached Savannah before December 25. "I beg to present you as a Christmas gift," Sherman telegraphed the president when he arrived, "the City of Savannah."

The Election of 1864

On August 23, 1864, while Grant maintained the siege against Petersburg, Lincoln asked the members of his cabinet to endorse a sealed memorandum without reading the contents. The document contained the president's prediction that "this Administration will not be reelected" and a pledge to "cooperate with the President elect as to save the Union between the Election and the inauguration." Lincoln won the election of 1864, but the outcome, as his memo demonstrated, was far from certain. Although Grant's aggression against Lee ultimately won the war,

few Northerners could see that result in the summer of 1864. What citizens saw instead was a general—many in the press called him a butcher—who in the space of a month had produced 60,000 casualties before getting stopped by Lee. To make matters worse, a Confederate unit under the command of General Jubal Early came within five miles of Washington in July 1864. There was no real threat to the city, but many northern observers had concluded that the quickest way to end the war entailed voting Lincoln out of office.

Although deeply divided among themselves, northern Democrats united against Lincoln. Since the outbreak of the fighting, the party was divided into war and peace factions. War Democrats, like Governor Horatio Seymour of New York, sought a negotiated peace that would bring the South back into the Union without further bloodshed. Peace Democrats, led at the convention by politicians such as Clement Vallandigham (who had returned from Canada after his failed effort to run for governor of Ohio *in absentia*), advocated peace at all costs. These two factions struck a compromise and nominated General George B. McClellan, a War Democrat, and Thomas H. Seymour, a Peace Democrat and one-time governor of Connecticut. Peace Democrats also wrote the party platform, despite McClellan's outspoken support for continuing the war effort until the South agreed upon reunification (the ex-general opposed the Emancipation Proclamation, arguing that it served as an impediment to reunion). Grant's high casualties against Lee's forces in Virginia strengthened McClellan's support among the public.

Meanwhile, the Republican Party became divided as the war dragged on. Radical Republicans, who were beginning to push for constitutional amendments to consolidate the gains made on behalf of emancipation, remained critical of Lincoln for moving too slowly. Some even bolted the party and temporarily rallied around the possible candidacy of John C. Frémont. Lincoln did little to ingratiate himself to the Radicals. Indeed, he dropped his Vice President Hannibal Hamlin (a Radical Republican from Maine) in favor of **Andrew Johnson**, a War Democrat from Tennessee. Johnson, a former U.S. Senator who refused to resign when his state seceded and presently was serving as the military governor of Tennessee, represented a political fusion in the Upper South and Border States between War Democrats and moderate Republicans. Lincoln hoped that such support would secure his re-election.

Although Lincoln eventually won the election, his victory was far from certain. By the fall of 1864, however, events began to shift in his favor. Frémont, whatever his criticism of Lincoln, reacted with horror to the Democratic Party's peace platform, which he believed threatened to restore slavery to the Union. Rather than stay in the election and risk a McClellan victory, he pulled out of the race. Without Frémont splitting the Republican vote, McClellan had little chance of winning. Lincoln garnered only 55 percent of the popular vote but received 212 of 233 Electoral College votes.

THE WAR ENDS

By the beginning of 1865, the Union was poised for victory as Ulysses Grant continued to besiege Robert E. Lee's forces at Petersburg and William Sherman prepared to march northward from Savannah to help crush Lee's army. The Confederacy's days were clearly numbered.

Sherman's army began their trek toward Virginia in January 1865 with an overland campaign through the Carolinas. Union troops were able to move through the region as easily as they had rampaged through Georgia. Along the way, Sherman hoped that the impact of his march—especially as it moved through South Carolina, the state in which the war began—would undermine southern morale. The general divided his 60,000 troops into three groups whose movements had been planned to confuse the enemy. By mid-February, Sherman had forced the surrender of Columbia, the state capital of South Carolina. Union troops had stripped the city of valuables and left it burning (although who started the fires remains a matter of dispute). Less than a week after Columbia's surrender, the vital port of Wilmington, North Carolina also capitulated. Sherman later defeated Johnston at the Battle of Bentonville (March 19–21), a rout of smaller Confederate forces that left little opposition between Sherman and Virginia.

As Sherman moved northward, Grant kept the pressure on Lee at Petersburg. A winter in the trenches had left the 50,000 Confederate defenders in poor shape. Disease and desertion had further thinned their ranks. Supplies ran short, and Lee's efforts to break the Union's pressure had failed. By the end of March, Lee found himself facing not only Grant, but also a force under the command of General **Phillip S. Sheridan**, who had just completed a Sherman-style march through the Shenandoah Valley. Sherman too was on his way with another army. Lee made one final effort to break the Union siege and regain the initiative on March 25. He failed with his troops suffering 4,000 casualties while Grant's army, which itself suffered around 1,000 casualties, moved into a better position.

On April 1, Union troops broke through the Confederate lines. Both Petersburg and Richmond surrendered on the following day. Jefferson Davis fled the city, although Union troops would capture him about a month later. Lee too evacuated the city, hoping that he

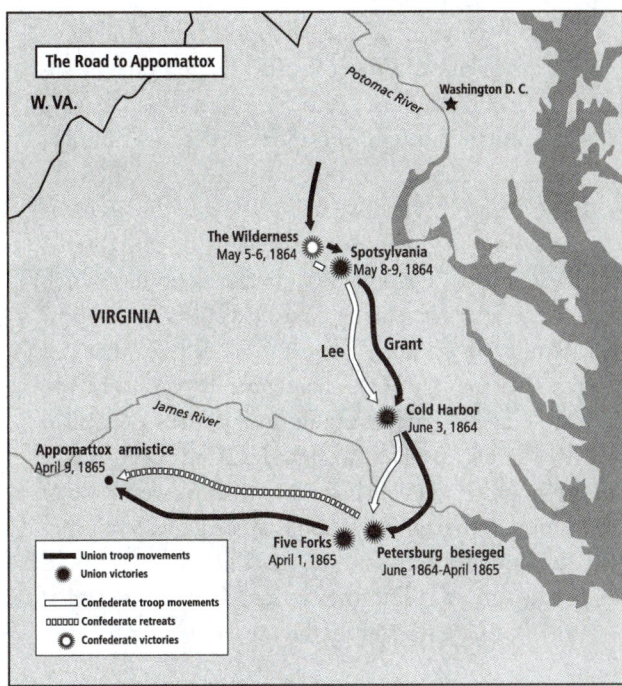

Map 16.17 **The Road to Appomattox**

could join the Confederate forces that were still fighting in North Carolina. But as Grant had done before the siege of Petersburg, he again pursued Lee with tenacity. Within days, Lee's efforts to escape had failed, and his army was surrounded on nearly all sides by Union troops. Reluctantly, but to avoid needless bloodshed, Lee surrendered to Grant at **Appomattox Court House** on April 9, 1865. A few weeks later, General Johnston surrendered to Sherman in North Carolina. Though sporadic skirmishing continued for another month among die-hard Confederates and those yet to hear the news of Lee and Johnston's surrenders, the war had finally come to an end.

During the war's final weeks, Lincoln delivered his Second Inaugural Address, which looked solemnly to the nation's future. The conflict, he noted, now progressed in a manner that was "reasonably satisfactory and encouraging to all." He made no predictions but had "high hopes for the future." Lincoln then moved to a discussion of slavery, which all observers at the outset of the conflict "knew…was somehow the cause." Neither side, however, could have predicted "that the cause of the conflict might cease with or even before the conflict itself should cease." Both had sought "a result less fundamental and astounding." Yet, the struggle proved to be bigger than either side—perhaps one that could be explained only by trying to discern divine will:

> The Almighty has His own purposes. "Woe unto the world because of offenses; for it must needs be that offenses come, but woe to that man by whom the

offense cometh." If we shall suppose that American slavery is one of those offenses which, in the providence of God, must needs come, but which, having continued through His appointed time, He now wills to remove, and that He gives to both North and South this terrible war as the woe due to those by whom the offense came, shall we discern therein any departure from those divine attributes which the believers in a living God always ascribe to Him? Fondly do we hope, fervently do we pray, that this mighty scourge of war may speedily pass away. Yet, if God wills that it continue until all the wealth piled by the bondsman's two hundred and fifty years of unrequited toil shall be sunk, and until every drop of blood drawn with the lash shall be paid by another drawn with the sword, as was said three thousand years ago, so still it must be said "the judgments of the Lord are true and righteous altogether."

Lincoln, however, did permit himself briefly to consider the future. "With malice toward none… let us strive on to finish the work we are in, to bind up the nation's wounds,…to do all which may achieve and cherish a just and lasting peace among ourselves and with all nations."

With that brief statement, Lincoln summed up the magnitude of the conflict and offered a hint of vision for the post-war Reconstruction era. Most significantly, the war brought an end to slavery. By the end of 1865, the United States would ratify the Thirteenth Amendment, which abolished slavery and indentured servitude in all the states and every U.S. territory, thus expanding and embedding the Emancipation Proclamation into the United States Constitution. The conflict also fundamentally transformed both the North and the South. The North emerged from the war as an economic powerhouse and the region's interests were now firmly wedded to national policy. The war left the South economically devastated—it would not recover for decades—and politically weakened, although it was by no means rendered impotent. As he delivered that address, Lincoln and Congress were already engaged in the process of developing a plan for Reconstruction, and the president tended to favor a strategy that would have rapidly restored the South to the Union.

Whatever plans Lincoln may have had, he had no chance to carry them out. Less than a week after Lee's surrender to Grant at Appomattox Court House, **John Wilkes Booth**, a Confederate sympathizer from a prominent Maryland acting family, assassinated Lincoln while he relaxed watching a comedic play in a Washington, D.C., theater. The difficult work of Reconstruction would then fall into the hands of the recently selected Vice President Andrew Johnson and Republicans in Congress. Johnson would prove to be a starkly different leader than his predecessor. Though a Unionist, the new president was also a Southerner who carried a deep hostility toward both planters and free blacks. Had Johnson and Congressional Republican leaders agreed on Reconstruction policies, then the transition to peacetime would have been much smoother, but their disagreements would add to the tumult of the postwar period.

As Johnson and his contemporaries prepared to move forward, they faced a continuation of a variety of lingering issues. One involved the persistent bad blood between veterans of the war. Although Lincoln had suggested "malice toward none" and "with charity for all," memories of the war would endure in both regions. Soldiers, like the amputee Jonathan Alison, gave up a great deal in the war, and they struggled with the idea of a rapid reunion with those they considered rebels and traitors. Debates over the place of African Americans in American society would also continue. Although the Civil War brought an end to slavery in the United States, what freedom meant remained an open question—and one that would not be settled for decades to come.

Confederate General Robert E. Lee (left) and Union General William Tecumseh Sherman (below)

Table 16.1	Major Battles of the Civil War, 1861 - 1865		
Battle or Campaign	Date	State	Outcome
Battle of Fort Sumter	April 12, 1861	South Carolina	Confederate victory; first battle of American Civil War
First Bull Run	July 21, 1861	Virginia	Confederate victory that bolstered southern confidence
Fort Henry Fort Donelson	February 6, 1862 February 11-16, 1862	Tennessee	Union victory that gave the North control of strategic river systems
Battle of Shiloh	April 6-7, 1862	Tennessee	Union victory
Seven Days Battles	June 25-July 1, 1862	Virginia	Standoff; halted Union General McClellan's advance on Richmond in the Peninsula Campaign
Second Bull Run	August 29-30, 1862	Virginia	Confederate victory
Antietam	September 17, 1862	Maryland	Standoff; halted Lee's first advance into the North
Fredericksburg	December 13, 1862	Virginia	Confederate victory that revived morale of Lee's army
Chancellorsville	April 30-May 6, 1863	Virginia	Confederate victory; Confederate General Thomas "Stonewall" Jackson killed
Gettysburg	July 1-3, 1863	Pennsylvania	Union victory; halted second Confederate advance into the North
Vicksburg	May 18-July 4, 1863	Mississippi	Union victory; Union gained complete control of the Mississippi River
Chattanooga	August – November 1863	Tennessee	Union victory
Chickamauga	September 19-20, 1863	Georgia	Confederate victory
Battle of Fort Pillow	April 12, 1864	Tennessee	Confederate victory; Confederate troops under General Nathan B. Forrest massacres black soldiers
Battle of the Wilderness	May 5-7, 1864	Virginia	Standoff; Union and Confederate forces suffer huge losses; Union General Grant continues advance toward Richmond
Battle of Spotsylvania Court House	May 8-21, 1864	Virginia	Standoff; Union and Confederate forces suffer huge losses
Cold Harbor	May 31-June12, 1864	Virginia	Confederate victory; Lee repulses Grant
Battle of Petersburg	June 9, 1864	Virginia	Confederate victory; Beauregard defeats Butler
Battle of Kennesaw Mountain	June 27, 1864	Georgia	Confederate victory; Johnston repulses Sherman
Battle of Atlanta	May-September, 1864	Georgia	Union victory; Union General Sherman captures Atlanta
Sherman's March to the sea	November 16-December 21, 1864	Georgia	Union victory; Sherman's forces destroy southern infrastructure along a wide path
Battle of Bentonville	March 19-21, 1865	North Carolina	Union victory; Sherman defeats Confederates
Appomattox Court House	April 9, 1865	Virginia	Lee was surrounded and surrendered formally to Grant

Chronology

1861   Confederate States of America formed
with Jefferson Davis named president.
Firing on Fort Sumter begins Civil War.
Lincoln calls up militia and suspends habeas
corpus.
First Battle of Bull Run.
Trent Affair endangers U.S.-British relations.

1862   The *Monitor* battles the *Merrimac*.
McClellan's failed Peninsula Campaign.
Battle of Shiloh.
Second Battle of Bull Run.
Battle of Antietam.
Battle of Fredericksburg.
Confederacy institutes military draft.
Homestead Act passed.
Morrill Land Grant College Act passed.
Union Pacific Railroad chartered.

1863   Lincoln issues Emancipation Proclamation.
Congress enacts military draft.
Battle of Chancellorsville.
Battle of Gettysburg and surrender of Vicksburg.
Battles of Chickamauga and Chattanooga
New York City Draft Riots erupt.
Food riots break out in the South.

1864   Ulysses S. Grant named head of all Union armies
Fort Pillow Massacre.
Battle of the Wilderness.
Battle of Cold Harbor.
Battle of Atlanta.
Siege of Petersburg.
William T. Sherman's "March to the Sea"
through Georgia.
Lincoln reelected.

1865   Lee surrenders at Appomattox.
Thirteenth Amendment abolishes slavery.
Lincoln assassinated.

SUGGESTED READINGS

Iver Bernstein, *The New York City Draft Riots* (1990).

William C. Davis, *Jefferson Davis: The Man and His Hour* (1991).

David Donald, *Lincoln* (1995).

Drew Gilpin Faust, *This Republic of Suffering: Death and the American Civil War* (2008).

Joseph Glatthaar, *Forged in Battle: The Civil War Alliance of Black Soldiers and White Officers* (1990).

Doris Kearns Goodwin, *Team of Rivals: The Political Genius of Abraham Lincoln* (2006).

Herman Hatttaway, *Shades of Blue and Gray* (1997).

Elizabeth Leonard, *Yankee Women: Gender Battles in the Civil War* (1994).

Glenn Lindend and Thomas Pressly, *Voices From the House Divided* (1995).

William McFeely, *Grant* (1981).

James McPherson, *Abraham Lincoln and the Second American Revolution* (1990).

—— *Battle Cry of Freedom* (1988).

—— *For Cause and Comrades* (1998).

—— *The Negro's Civil War* (1965).

Louise Mayo, *The House Divided: America in the Era of Civil War and Reconstruction* (2009).

Reid Mitchell, *The Vacant Chair: The Northern Soldier Leaves Home* (1993).

Mark Neely, *The Fate of Liberty: Abraham Lincoln and Civil Liberties* (1991).

—— *The Last Best Hope of Earth: Abraham Lincoln and the Promise of America* (1993).

Alan T. Nolan, *Lee Considered: Robert E. Lee and Civil War History* (1991).

Stephen Sears, *George B. McClellan: The Young Napoleon* (1988).

Wendy Hamand Venet, *Neither Ballots nor Bullets: Women Abolitionists and the Civil War* (1991).

Ronald C. White Jr., *Lincoln's Greatest Speech: The Second Inaugural* (2002).

T. Harry Williams, *Lincoln and His Generals* (1952).

Garry Wills, *Lincoln at Gettysburg* (1992).

C. Vann Woodward, ed., *Mary Chestnut's Civil War* (1982).

Review Questions

1. What were the relative advantages held by the North and the South in the Civil War and the weaknesses suffered by each side?

2. What challenges did the Union and the Confederacy face in manning, funding, and supplying their armies, and what was the reaction to conscription in each region?

3. What factors shaped the attitude of European powers towards the American Civil War?

4. What issues shaped how and when Abraham Lincoln issued the Emancipation Proclamation?

5. How did perceptions of President Lincoln vary and evolve during the course of the Civil War?

Glossary of Important People and Concepts

"Anaconda Plan"
Andersonville
Battle of Antietam
Appomattox Court House
Clara Barton
John Wilkes Booth
Belle Boyd
First Battle of Bull Run
Battle of Chancellorsville
Jefferson Davis
Emancipation Proclamation
Fort Pillow Massacre
Battle of Fredericksburg
Battle of Gettysburg
Habeas corpus
Thomas J. "Stonewall" Jackson
Andrew Johnson
Abraham Lincoln
March to the Sea
George McClellan
New York City Draft Riots
Phillip S. Sheridan
William Tecumseh Sherman
Vicksburg siege
Mary Walker

Chapter Seventeen

A BROKEN PROMISE OF FREEDOM: Reconstruction, 1863-1877

On April 9, 1865, Confederate General Robert E. Lee, the commander of the Confederate Army's largest and most resilient fighting force, surrendered to Union General Ulysses S. Grant, ending the Civil War. With the war concluded, the nation awaited Abraham Lincoln's ideas on how to piece the country back together again. The president gave a hint two days later, delivering a fateful speech in which, for the first time, he called publicly for granting full citizenship and the right to vote to at least some African Americans—"the very intelligent, and . . . those who serve our cause as soldiers." In the audience, an embittered, Confederate sympathizer named John Wilkes Booth grimly vowed, "That's the last speech he will ever make."

Just 27 years old, Booth had been plotting against Lincoln for months. Born in Maryland, Booth supported the South throughout the Civil War, but his enthusiasm never moved him to enlist in the Confederate Army. A heavy drinker, Booth acted for a living but never quite measured up to the talent or fame of his older brother Edwin Booth, the most admired Shakespearean performer of his generation. Booth despaired as it became clear the South would lose the war and resolved as early as August 1864 to rid the country of its "false president."

Booth hoped he might snatch southern victory from the jaws of defeat by kidnapping Lincoln and holding him hostage until the North agreed to recognize Confederate inde-

pendence. After stalking the chief executive in early 1865, he decided that kidnapping the tall, strong, and always guarded president would be too difficult. Frustrated, he resolved instead to kill Lincoln after hearing the president's April 11 call for what Booth termed "nigger citizenship." He had already gathered around him a gang of conspirators, which met at a Maryland tavern owned by Mary Surratt. The clique now planned to murder Lincoln and other top administration figures.

The conspirators included Mary's son John Surratt, a Confederate spy; another Confederate agent, George Atzerodt; David Herold, a pharmacist in Washington, D.C.; and Lewis Powell, a veteran of the Confederate Army. Powell was assigned the task of killing Secretary of State William Seward while Atzerodt was to kill Vice President Andrew Johnson. Always seeking the center stage, Booth assigned himself to kill Lincoln.

*April 14 was Good Friday, a day when Christians commemorate the crucifixion and death of Jesus. For much of his presidency, Lincoln had trouble sleeping and often seemed depressed. Yet, the awareness that the Civil War was winding down lifted the president's spirits. "His whole appearance, poise, and bearing had marvelously changed," his friend, Illinois Senator James Harlan later remarked. The First Couple planned to spend the evening forgetting about their troubles, attending a lighthearted comedy—***Our American***

Cousin—at Ford's Theater. The Lincolns convinced a friend, Major Henry Rathbone and his fiancée to accompany them. They took a carriage ride that afternoon and after Mary commented on his happy mood, Lincoln remarked, "I consider this day the war has come to a close."

That night, the Lincolns received a standing ovation to the tune of "Hail to the Chief" when they entered the colorful presidential box decked in red, white, and blue bunting and a big portrait of George Washington. The Lincolns and their friends laughed at the misadventures on stage when Booth, who often performed at the theater, arrived and worked his way upstairs to where the honored guests sat. Lincoln's lone bodyguard, an incompetent police officer named John Parker who had been repeatedly disciplined, had abandoned his post at intermission to grab some drinks at the nearby Star Saloon.

Unimpeded, Booth entered the box and shot the president in the back of the head at close range at a pre-planned moment when as the audience loudly laughed during a particularly funny scene. Lincoln fell forward, already unconscious. Mary Lincoln screamed as Booth stabbed Rathbone on the arm and pushed him aside before leaping from the box. A spur on one of Booth's boots got caught on a flag decorating the box. The assassin broke a leg as he landed on the stage. He still managed to yell at the confused audience, "Sic Semper Tyrannis!" (the state motto of Virginia, which translates as "Thus Always to Tyrants!") before limping to the exit and leaping on a horse he had intentionally left outside the theater.

The other conspirators were unsuccessful in carrying out their assigned tasks. Lewis Powell came the closest to achieving his goal of killing William Seward. After arriving at the Secretary of State's home, Powell pretended that he was delivering medicine and forced his way to the Seward's upstairs bedroom. The Secretary was convalescing from a broken jaw and shattered arm he suffered after being thrown from a carriage. Powell stabbed Seward repeatedly and then escaped, only to be captured later. George Atzerodt lost his nerve and got drunk instead of attacking Andrew Johnson at the vice president's hotel room. Meanwhile, Lincoln was carried to the home of William Petersen, a German tailor, located across the street from Ford's Theater, and placed in a bed not long enough to fully accommodate his tall frame. He died the next morning. Looking upon the president's body, Secretary of War Edwin Stanton said either, "Now he belongs to the angels" or "Now he belongs to the ages."

Booth evaded capture and Union troops did not corner him until April 26, when they discovered the assassin in a barn on a northern Virginia tobacco farm. Booth refused to surrender. Soldiers set fire to the barn, but a soldier shot Booth, who was carried out of the building still alive. Staring at his hands, he reportedly muttered, "Useless . . . useless" before he died. After a brief trial, the federal government executed Powell, Herold, Atzerodt, and Mary Surratt

John Wilkes Booth

on July 7. John Surratt escaped to Canada and then to England before he was arrested. In 1867, a jury failed to convict him of conspiracy to murder the president and the conspirator lived to the age of 72. Lincoln became the first of four U. S. presidents to die through gun violence. His death caused shock and profound grief across the North. The assassination added to the fears and uncertainty that many Southerners felt as they wondered what postwar life had in store for them.

When Abraham Lincoln delivered his Gettysburg Address on November 19, 1863, he expressed his hope that from the horrors of the Civil War the nation would experience a "new birth of freedom." The war indeed ended slavery. Though the Thirteenth Amendment was not ratified until December 1865, the year of the war's end, under terms of Lincoln's Emancipation Proclamation, the vast majority of the country's slaves were legally freed beginning January 1, 1863. African Americans soon hoped to start the long, hard struggle to move from being slaves to exercising their rights as citizens.

During the postwar period, while African Americans felt joy at their liberation, many southern whites would repeatedly conspire to claw back much of former slaves' newly won freedom. As African Americans experienced this difficult transition, the nation as a whole, and the defeated South in particular, faced a major rebuilding of many of its political, social, and economic institutions— what came to be known as "Reconstruction"—a daunting task for which neither section was prepared.

Five generations lived on Smith's Plantation, Beaufort, South Carolina, 1862.

As the war concluded, the federal government endeavored to reconstruct the South while reviving a shared sense of American identity between the regions. Daunting obstacles loomed as leaders sought to create a "New South." About 750,000 Americans died in the war, the highest death count for any military conflict in the nation's history. About 290,000 out of a population of 5.5 million southern whites in the eleven Confederate states died in the war. Virtually everyone south of the Mason-Dixon Line separating the regions knew someone killed in the conflict. These soldiers died for a failed cause, leaving a mourning population angered and resentful toward the federal government. As the Union troops gained control over southern territory, many local whites saw them not as fellow citizens but as conquerors.

The white South had lost the labor of not just the war dead and the severely injured, but also the approximately 4 million slaves freed by Lincoln's proclamation. White Southerners had defined those black humans as property. The financial investment in those flesh-and-blood assets had, by the time of Lee's surrender, reached more than $10 trillion in today's money, wealth lost forever to the former masters. At the same time, on top of the destruc-

tion normally expected by mass, mechanized warfare, northern troops had torched some southern cities and towns, as well as plantations and farms, to deny supplies to the enemy and break the Confederate will to fight. To impede the ability of the Confederate Army to move troops, weapons, and supplies, Union forces also wrecked the South's relatively small network of railroads—vital infrastructure that the South would need to bounce back from the war. The damage impoverished the region. Overall, some economists estimate that the value of southern property dropped 75 percent from 1861, the year the war began. If rich Southerners took a massive fiscal hit from the war, poor Southerners faced hunger, with many of their hardscrabble farms looted or destroyed while others decayed from neglect as the male owners served in the Confederate military

Upon emancipation, most African Americans in the South dreamed of becoming landowners and independent farmers, but they began life as freedmen with no land and, except in rare cases, no money. With the tiny southern industrial base shattered from the war, the primary jobs remaining for most African Americans involved working on land owned by their old masters, although the details of that relationship, post-emancipation—including wages—remained unclear. Before and during the Civil War, ten of the southern states had legally prohibited teaching African Americans how to read and write, arithmetic, and other basic skills that would have greatly aided their quest for financial independence. After the war, southern white landowners wanted to keep African Americans working at low wages, or even no wages, and stood in the way of blacks seeking education as a pathway to a better future. Additionally, the South suffered from the highest rates of white illiteracy in the country. Before the war, southern elites had shown little interest in spending tax money on educating their hard-luck white neighbors. Rebuilding the southern economy on the basis of freed laborers proved devilishly difficult with such a poorly educated workforce in an atmosphere of mass poverty and with an elite contemptuous of universal public education.

As poisonous as race relations had been before the war, racism in many ways actually intensified when the war ended. Whites believed their loved ones had died in a war over slavery and blamed African Americans for their losses. They saw black liberation, and the citizenship and voting rights soon won by the black community, as coming at their expense. As violent as slavery had been, slave owners often restrained themselves from killing or permanently disabling their expensive property. Now that African Americans represented replaceable free workers, that restraint disappeared, and white violence against blacks escalated.

During the Reconstruction Era, from 1863 until the northern political leadership essentially gave up on reforming the South in 1877, the federal government would be asked to involve itself in aspects of southern life where it had never ventured, finding itself, for the first time, operating schools, providing aid and legal services to the poor, and defending voting rights for the previously disenfranchised. For African Americans, the era opened with great hope, but in less than 15 years it came crashing down in a reign of terrorism and dashed dreams.

ABRAHAM LINCOLN AND RECONSTRUCTION

The Hesitant Emancipator

From the time that the first shot of the Civil War was fired at Fort Sumter, African Americans knew that the outcome of the conflict would seal the fate of the "peculiar institution." African Americans supported the cause of the Union in myriad ways, understanding that a northern

Abraham Lincoln

victory would lead to the abolition of human bondage. In his classic work *Black Reconstruction in America, 1860-1880*, the scholar W.E.B. Du Bois notes that as many as a half-million slaves escaped their southern masters during the Civil War, a movement he called "The General Strike." This loss of labor gradually undermined the southern wartime economy. Slaves who remained often served as spies for northern troops and saboteurs wrecking Confederate farm production and military equipment. Abolitionist leader Frederick Douglass, an escaped slave, repeatedly urged the U.S. military to recruit African-American soldiers and to assign them to combat duty. No group in America, he argued, held a more passionate interest in defeating the southern slave owners. "Let the slaves and the free colored people be called into service, and formed into a liberating army, to march into the South and raise the banner of emancipation among its slaves," Douglass declared. President Lincoln, however, initially resisted this message and, to Douglass's great exasperation, delayed making the end of slavery in the Confederacy a war aim until almost two years into the conflict.

Abraham Lincoln was in many ways a product of his time. Born in Kentucky, a slave state, he lived most of his adult life in Illinois (a northern state heavily settled by southern whites), and married the daughter of a slave owner. He absorbed many of the racist ideas common among most white people in the first half of the nineteenth century (although some abolitionists in Lincoln's time did believe in racial equality). Lincoln publicly expressed a belief in black inferiority, though his words have to be placed not only in the context of his times, but also in consideration that he was a politician seeking to win the votes of whites hostile to the idea that African Americans shared full humanity with whites. Throughout his political career, he had opposed the spread of slavery to new U.S. states and territories. He condemned slavery, which he called a "monstrous injustice," as physically cruel and as a type of theft, which stole the fruits of labor from its victims. Lincoln further predicted in 1858 that the Union could not forever remain "half slave" and "half free."

Yet, until his presidency he always stopped short of calling for abolition in all the states. He angered Frederick Douglass and other anti-slavery crusaders when he proclaimed in his First Inaugural Address: "I have no purpose, directly or indirectly, to interfere with the institution of slavery in the States where it exists." These comments led Frederick Douglass to dismiss the new president as an "excellent slave hound," referring to the dogs used to track down escaped slaves. As late as an August 22, 1862 letter to the abolitionist Horace Greeley, less than four months before he issued his Emancipation Proclamation, Lincoln wrote, "My paramount object in this struggle is to save the Union, and is not either to save or to destroy slavery. If I could save the Union without freeing any slave I would do it, and if I could save it by freeing all the slaves I would do it; and if I could save it by freeing some and leaving others alone I would also do that."

Lincoln also sent mixed signals regarding his racial views and what rights African Americans should enjoy if they were free. In one of his speeches delivered during the Lincoln-Douglas Debates taking place during his 1858 campaign against Democrat Stephen Douglas for his Senate seat, Lincoln stated: "I will say then that I am not, nor ever have been, in favor of bringing about in any way the social and political equality of the black and white races—that I am not nor ever have been in favor of making voters or jurors of negroes, nor of qualifying them to hold office, nor to intermarry with white people; and I will say in addition to this that there is a physical difference between the white and black races which I believe will forever forbid the two races living together on terms of social and political equality." Still, during the same campaign he told a different audience, "Let us discard all this quibbling about this man and the other man—this race and that race and the other race being inferior, and therefore they must be placed in an inferior position . . . Let us discard these things and unite as one people . . . declaring that all men are created equal."

Lincoln's contradictions stem from his attempts to appeal to a Republican Party united in opposing the spread of slavery but divided on abolitionism and uncertain on what to do with African Americans should they be emancipated. For most of his political career, he expected that slavery would eventually vanish, though he was unsure how, and—believing that African Americans lacked the intellect to compete and thrive in a white-majority country—he favored "colonization," a scheme in which freedmen would be sent to their African ancestral homeland. Most African Americans rejected this plan as unfair and cruel. As far back as the early 1600s, many black families arrived in the British colonies that became the United States. Many black families had lived in North America longer than many white families. Most black Americans had never seen their ancestral homeland. "We live here—have lived here—have a right to live here, and mean to live here," as Douglass wrote in an 1849 editorial for his abolitionist newspaper *The North Star.*

Lincoln also proposed in 1862 a gradual emancipation scheme that would have taken 31 years to fully implement and would have provided financial compensation for slave owners for their freed human property but offered nothing to the freedmen for their unpaid work. Rather than a "slave hound," however, Lincoln represented a work in progress regarding human bondage and the status of free blacks in America. African Americans lobbied, pressured, and by their valor in the Civil War, pushed Lincoln towards an increasingly more just position on ending slavery and, eventually, African-American citizenship.

The Start of Reconstruction: The Emancipation Proclamation

The performance of African-American troops in the Union Army greatly influenced Lincoln's views on race. Four slave states—Missouri, Kentucky, Delaware, and Maryland—remained in the Union, but most of their residents had no desire in 1861 to abolish slavery. Lincoln feared the pro-Union slave owners would interpret the arming of black men as a prelude to emancipation. These fears became less important as the war turned out to be much harder than most Northerners expected, the casualties escalated, and the number of white volunteers sagged. Lincoln knew he could not spare potential military manpower. As military frustrations piled up, he also realized that he had to quickly change the tone of the war and boost morale. The stubbornness of southern resistance in the war had dramatically enhanced support for abolition in the North. Lincoln sensed a political advantage in transforming the war into not just a struggle to preserve the union but a crusade for human liberty. The thousands of slaves who began flocking to the Union lines in hope of freedom and who indicated a willingness to serve pushed Lincoln in a new direction. The president was also heartened by Union military's ability to secure control over large portions of the pro-Union slave states. In April 1862, he signed a law that immediately freed the 3,000 slaves within Washington, D.C., but a more dramatic step lay in the future.

Lincoln waited until a military victory so it would not appear he made the decision for emancipation out of desperation. The Union victory at the Battle of Antietam opened that door. On September 22, 1862, he announced the Emancipation Proclamation, which declared, as of January 1, 1863, "all persons held as slaves within any State or designated part of a State, the people whereof shall then be in rebellion against the United States, shall be then, thenceforward, and forever free." The proclamation also specified that emancipated slaves "will be received into the armed service of the United States to garrison forts, positions, stations, and other places, and to man vessels of all sorts in said service."

The proclamation was far from universally popular. Major Charles J. Whiting, a Union Army cavalry officer from Maine, complained bitterly about fighting in a "damned abolition nigger war." Yet, the proclamation changed the politics of slavery in the North; and the border states of Delaware, Maryland, Kentucky, and Missouri soon acted to end chattel servitude on their own before the Civil War ended. The proclamation furthermore marked the beginning of Reconstruction, and the war became a rolling revolution that destroyed the old southern economy and the relationship between the races there, battle by battle. The first phase of this key turning point in American history—"Wartime Reconstruction" or "Military Reconstruction"—began as a moral crusade. African Americans flocked to Union Army and Navy recruitment centers to serve. Nearly 200,000 African Americans enlisted in the Union military during the Civil War, and they made up about 10 percent of the northern Army. They performed with valor.

African American combat performance eroded racism among white soldiers. As one white solider put it, "I've been one of those men who never had much confidence in colored troops, but these doubts are now all removed, for they fought as bravely as any." The service of black soldiers convinced one Illinois man that it was "safer to trust 4,000,000 loyal negroes" than "8,000,000 disloyal whites" and that, therefore, "the faithful and patriotic negro soldiers have richly earned . . . suffrage." Lincoln became another convert, abruptly ending his talk about colonization.

Radical Republican Opposition to Lincoln

Even as Lincoln and other northern political leaders struggled with how to define the political status of black freedmen in the post-war world, they wrestled as well with the future status of states that had seceded and had been brought back by the Union Army. Lincoln's Republican Party not only controlled the White House, but also controlled both chambers of Congress. The Republican majority emerged in 1861 because, as the eleven states that formed the Confederacy left the Union, their Democratic-dominated congressional delegations resigned. At first, no consensus formed among Republicans on the requirements for reunion (if any) that should be imposed on the states retaken by northern troops. Conservative Republicans in the Congress advocated minimal change. Southern states should be readmitted, the conservatives argued, minus slavery but still firmly in the hands of the wealthy planters, politicians, and businessmen who had dominated the region before the war. Conservatives saw blacks as morally and intellectually unfit for citizenship and could see little role for them in the postbellum South other than providing physical labor. They viewed wealthy Southerners as the natural leaders of the region. To the conservatives, national reunification trumped all other issues, even if that unity came at the expense of the freedmen.

So-called **Radical Republicans** (those adamantly in favor of abolition and securing civil rights for freed slaves) recoiled at this thought. Led by Senators Benjamin Wade of Ohio and Charles Sumner of Massachusetts and Representative **Thaddeus Stevens** of Pennsylvania, the Radicals believed that the Conservative Republican approach would return men they saw as traitors to power in the South. Radicals also feared that should the former Confederate states re-enter the Union too quickly, the Republicans might lose their congressional majority and even the White House to the Democrats in the upcoming 1868 elections.

The Republican Party, which had formed only in the mid-1850s, did not exist in the South prior to the Civil War, therefore, Radicals wanted time to build the party in the southern states before allowing them back in the Union. Radicals believed they could recruit pro-Union white Southerners into the party, but to have any chance of success, they needed freed slaves to join as well. Freedmen had an obvious reason to back the Republican Party, the party of Lincoln and the Emancipation Proclamation. However, for the freedmen to be active parts of a new southern Republican Party, the Radicals would have to change state and federal laws to grant citizenship to African Americans and to give black men the right to vote. Such dramatic reforms would take time. Political calculations aside, men like Stevens and Sumner saw black voting rights (suffrage) as a matter of justice.

Radical Republicans also knew that African Americans could not defend their political rights without economic independence. If blacks were left as landless workers dependent on their former masters for their livelihoods, the white landowners could pressure African Americans to not vote or to vote as the landowner wished. Many Radical Republicans, therefore, also pushed for redistributing land in the South, seizing land from wealthy families that had supported the rebellion and giving it to freedmen who could then become independent farmers. Radicals also wanted to secure loyalty oaths from former Confederates before allowing them to vote or run for office. Stevens declared that true reconstruction must "revolutionize southern institutions, habits, and manners. . . . The foundation of their institutions . . . must be broken up and relaid, or all our blood and treasure have been spent in vain."

As with emancipation, Lincoln positioned himself as a moderate. Like the Radicals, he wanted to provide African Americans education and believed in at least limited black suffrage. However, he did not want to break up the large plantations for the benefit of freedmen. Agreeing with the Conservatives, Lincoln placed a premium on reconciliation between the white North and South. He wanted to reassure white Southerners that they would not be punished for secession and the war and that they were welcomed back in the Union. Once true unity had been achieved, he hoped, maybe then other reforms could be pursued. With this mindset, Lincoln formulated plans he hoped would be consistent with his pledge in his Second Inaugural Address delivered in March 1865, to guide Reconstruction with "malice toward none, with charity for all."

On December 8, 1863, Lincoln shared his vision for the postwar order with the issuance of his Proclamation of Amnesty and Reconstruction, in which he provided pardons for those who had fought for or otherwise supported the Confederacy (with the exception of top Confederate political and military officials). The president's proclamation established a process for how states that left the Union could rejoin, stipulating that when the number of voters in a state applying for readmission who swore loyalty to the Union and its laws (including the Emancipation Proclamation) equaled 10 percent of the number of people from that state who voted in the 1860 presidential election, then the people there could hold statewide and local elections and revise their state's constitution to abolish slavery. That state could then apply for readmission and hold congressional elections.

Lincoln's plan generally met with enthusiastic approval in the North. The war was not yet over, but the public was tiring of conflict, and the proposal—which came to be known as "the **Ten Percent Plan**"—seemed to offer a rapid path to reunification once the shooting stopped. Radical Republicans, on the other hand, saw the Ten Percent Plan as a betrayal, as did African American leaders like Frederick Douglass. The plan made no mention of African-American political rights. No requirements that southern blacks be recognized as citizens, have the right to vote, or any other freedom other than the right not to be bought and sold were included. Abolitionist leader Wendell Phillips argued that the amnesty program "makes the negro's freedom a mere sham." Douglass said that the plan would "hand the Negro back to the political power of his master, without a single element of strength to shield himself from the vindictive spirit sure to be roused against the whole colored race."

Lincoln's Ten Percent Plan hit a roadblock erected by members of his own party. Henry Davis, a Maryland representative, and Senator Benjamin Wade collaborated on a Reconstruction bill that set a much higher bar for southern states seeking readmission. The **Wade-Davis Bill**, passed July 2, 1864, would have required a majority of the state's white citizens to swear loyalty to the Union before it could be considered for re-entry. Only when that happened, could a state hold a constitutional convention to write a new state constitution that prohibited slavery and barred Confederate officeholders and military veterans from serving in elective office. Under the bill's provisions, a resident of a former Confederate state would not be allowed to vote until they took a so-called "ironclad oath" that they had never willingly aided the Confederate cause.

Lincoln pocket vetoed the measure. Under the Constitution, while the Congress is in session, a president has ten days (excluding Sundays) to decide whether to sign a bill or veto it. If he or she declines to sign it without issuing a veto, the bill becomes law. If the Congress is in recess, as it was after passage of the Wade-Davis legislation, the bill fails if the president does not sign it. Lincoln believed the law would have undermined the Union-friendly governments established in the states already under federal control—Tennessee, Louisiana, and Arkansas. Radical Republicans fiercely criticized the president. Wade and Davis issued a "Manifesto" in which they accused Lincoln of unconstitutionally usurping Congress's power, but Lincoln's sound victory over his Democratic Party opponent in the November 1864 election, Union General George McClellan, limited any political damage caused by this conflict within the Republican ranks.

The Thirteenth Amendment

Despite divisions within the Republican Party, Lincoln and the Congress made an epic break with the American past. Lincoln spent much of the final months of his life not only leading the war effort, but also ending slavery once and for all across the union. Lincoln had finally become an abolitionist. He worried that the conservative Supreme Court might overturn the Emancipation Proclamation on the ground that the president had exceeded his Constitutional powers with this act. Such a court reversal would re-legalize slavery in the southern states then under Union control.

Lincoln and his allies in the Congress, including Senator John B. Henderson of Missouri, pushed for a Constitutional amendment abolishing slavery permanently in all U.S. states and territories. An early version of the amendment died in the House in the summer of 1864, falling short of the required two-thirds majority. After winning re-election in November 1864, Lincoln lobbied intensely for passage of the **Thirteenth Amendment**, one of the shortest and simplest in the Constitution, and which in its final form said in its first section, "Neither slavery nor involuntary servitude, except as a punishment for crime whereof the party shall have been duly convicted, shall exist within the United States, or any place subject to their jurisdiction." The Congress passed the amendment on January 31, 1865 and the necessary three-fourths of the states ratified it as of December 6, 1865, almost eight months after Lincoln's death.

The Thirteenth Amendment forever changed the lives of African Americans, but it contained one unforeseen loophole. The amendment, which marked the first time that "slavery" was ever explicitly mentioned in the Constitution, allowed involuntary servitude as a punishment for a crime. Southern states would later exploit that clause. Local law enforcement would soon arrest African Americans on dubious grounds and the courts would sentence these defendants to toil without pay for wealthy landowners or to perform uncompensated work on public projects, thus allowing a continuation of slavery under a thin disguise.

A NEW LIFE FOR AFRICAN AMERICANS

General Sherman Promises "40 Acres and a Mule" to Former Slaves

With the ruling Republican Party at odds with itself, the Congress and the White House could not agree on what to do with the slaves who had escaped from behind Con-

federate lines or had been liberated by the Union Army. Such freedmen posed a dilemma for military commanders. The freedmen needed food and protection from possibly vengeful southern whites, and desired a chance to earn an independent living. Still facing the Confederate enemy, the Army was reluctant to devote resources to serve as a social agency helping one-time slaves adjust to their new lives. With no clear directions from Washington, D.C., Union generals concocted policies under the pressure of war regarding the employment of freedmen, with different generals experimenting with wildly different solutions.

In New Orleans in 1862, prior to the Emancipation Proclamation taking effect, the army initially felt overwhelmed by the slaves who flocked to their camps and ordered the escaped slaves to go back to their masters. Slaves, however, resisted this, and General Nathaniel Banks improvised a new plan where the black work force, though not yet free, received wages from the military for the work they did on their masters' properties. The masters, now more like employers, were obligated to provide meals and shelter. The slaves had to sign one-year contracts with their "employers" and could only change who they worked for after completing that term.

General William Tecumseh Sherman took a far more revolutionary approach. After leading a force of 60,000 troops that punched through the heart of the Georgia Plantation Belt, and Sherman had, by September 1864, seized the city of Atlanta. Whenever his force arrived in a given area, slaves ran towards the men in blue and sought protection. "They flock to me, old and young, they pray, they shout, and mix up my name with Moses . . . as well as Abraham Lincoln," Sherman wrote from the field. Secretary of War Stanton traveled to Georgia to confer with the general and urged him to meet with a group of freedmen in Savannah. The gathering, attended by about 20 men mostly from the clergy, convened on January 12, 1865. The ministers were asked what slavery had meant to them. One of the ministers, 67-year-old Garrison Frazier told Sherman that life in bondage meant masters "receiving . . . the work of another man, and not by his consent" and he said he dreamed of a day when his people would "reap the fruit of our own labor."

While possibly moved by the minister's words, Sherman was primarily motivated by the practical necessities of running the Union's western forces when on January 16, the general announced Special Order No. 15, in which the military seized the Georgia Sea Islands, the South Carolina low country, and part of northern Florida's Atlantic Coast, that had been abandoned by Confederate owners. Sherman set aside this rice-producing land for black settlement. Freedmen families could apply for use of 40 acres. Upon request, the military also loaned each family an army mule. Sherman may have only intended what came to be known to some as "Sherman land" as a temporary expedient to get freedmen back to work and producing crops, but African Americans jumped at the opportunity to become landowners.

By June 1865, 40,000 freedmen had taken up Sherman's offers and, using their farming expertise, soon were successfully cultivating about 400,000 acres. About 1,000 freedmen occupied Skidaway Island, off the Georgia Coast, and declared Ulysses L. Houston, who had participated in the meeting with Sherman in Savannah, the "black governor." Freedmen would get little opportunity to celebrate their achievements. By the fall of 1865, Lincoln had died, and Andrew Johnson, a one-time slave owner possessing no sympathy for African American aspirations, reversed Special Order No. 15 and ordered the Sherman Land returned to the previous white owners. Sadly, Special Order No. 15 would be one of the few substantial attempts to address black poverty. Sherman's directive became the first of many broken promises made to African Americans in the Reconstruction Era.

The Freedmen's Bureau

At the Civil War's end, African Americans in the old Confederacy remained in limbo. They were no longer property but they held little or no property themselves. They possessed meager resources with which to start their lives as freedmen and their white neighbors had little interest in aiding them. Any assistance would have to come from Washington, D.C., which posed a further problem. Prior to 1865, the federal government had never provided direct aid to the poor, even during the brutal depression that occurred from 1837 to 1843. The U.S. government had spent no money on public schools and no tradition yet existed of the federal government tackling poverty, illiteracy, or workers' rights. Yet, these were precisely the type of social services freedmen would need to get a firm start on their new lives.

In their last major collaboration, President Lincoln and Congress engaged in a bold, unprecedented experiment. Congress provided direct aid to the former slaves with the March 3, 1865 passage of a bill creating the Bureau of Refugees, Freedmen, and Abandoned Lands, better known as the **Freedmen's Bureau**. The War Department operated the Bureau, which would be staffed by U.S. Army personnel. At first, the Bureau provided relief not just for freedmen but also whites left destitute and homeless by the war. The Bureau tended to basic needs for its clients such as food and clothing. Congress also gave the Bureau authority over land owned by individuals who could not be traced, either because they were missing in action from the war, or they were Confederates who fled before the advance of Union armies. The Bureau could then lease 40 acres of abandoned land to former slave families for three years at a rate of 6 percent of the value of the land per year. After the three years, the freedmen enjoyed the option of purchasing the tract at its full value.

The most important part of the bill gave the agency responsibility for "all subjects relating to refugees and freedmen." This broad mandate allowed the Freedmen's Bureau to educate African Americans by establishing schools across the South, which, in turn, led to dramatic

The Freedmen's Bureau by A.R. Waud. An army officer representing the Freedmen's Bureau stands between armed groups of white Americans and African Americans. 1868.

increases in African-American literacy rates. The Bureau also became a legal aid agency. As former slaves became free workers, landowners offered them contracts with confusing wording that deliberately locked them into years of service in return for miserably low wages. Most freedmen still lacked the education to understand what they were being asked to sign. Army lawyers began to review the contracts and help freedmen renegotiate the terms. Finally, the soldiers assigned to the Bureau became the blue shield protecting African Americans from white vigilante violence. Crimes against blacks, including rape, assault, robbery, and murder escalated during Reconstruction. Law enforcement would only rarely arrest any white person for these crimes even when the identity of the suspect was widely known. Grand juries routinely failed to indict whites for crimes against freedmen and, if a trial were ever held, white defendants would not be found guilty. Law enforcement officials themselves often participated in the crimes. As the violence mounted, the Bureau began to hold such assailants accountable, presiding over military trials for such suspects.

All of these federal interventions on behalf of the freedmen outraged southern whites, but the Bureau's schools may have been the most subversive example of Reconstruction Era social engineering. Most southern whites convinced themselves that black men and women could not learn beyond a basic level and insisted that formal schooling would only inspire black discontent with their economic and social plight. African Americans enthusiastically embraced education. "The free people are aroused to the possibility of educating their children," observed William H. Horton, the Sub-Assistant Commissioner for the Freedmen's Bureau in Dallas, Texas, two years after the Emancipation Proclamation.

Black schools received funding from federal allocations to the Bureau, and from northern charitable societies. When Republicans began winning control of state governments in 1868, they also provided money for black education. Within a month of the arrival of Union troops, more than 1,000 black boys and girls sat at school desks in Richmond, Virginia, the schooling provided by white and black churches. Learning became contagious, with children returning home and teaching their parents the alphabet.

Teachers—white and black, male and female, often inspired by religious faith—trekked South to teach under the most difficult, and sometimes physically dangerous, circumstances. Even with these hardships, by 1870 the impoverished African-American community in the Old Confederacy pooled their meager resources and expended more than $1 million to build schools, buy classroom supplies, and pay teachers. These schools helped train a generation of post-slavery African-American political, cultural, and spiritual leaders.

Sharecropping

Much of the drama during Reconstruction occurred in places other than Washington, D.C. In this era, the southern economy dramatically evolved. Lacking money and without land, freedmen fought to become independent farmers. "They appear to be willing to work, but are decisive in their expressions, to work for no one but themselves," an officer with the South Carolina Freedmen's Bureau reported in 1866. With the experiment in Sherman Land aborted early in Reconstruction, most freedmen were forced to labor for their former masters. Two systems of farm labor arose in the South to replace slavery: farm tenancy and sharecropping.

In spite of their continued poverty, many African Americans at first greeted their new circumstances with hope. Landowners improvised new systems of labor because they had lost their workforce, but they would rig the system to ensure maximum benefit for themselves while maintaining tight control over their workers. Under tenancy, the landowner divided his property into lots rented by the freedmen who owned the crops that they grew. The tenant farmers were not limited to growing only cash crops like tobacco and cotton, and could devote some land to growing food for the family. At the end of the growing season, the freedmen sold the crops and used the proceeds to pay off the rent, which was often one quarter of the crop. Such farmers believed they had taken a mighty step from slavery. They were no longer subject to the lash. They controlled, to a larger degree, their own work schedule. The husbands and fathers in freedmen families were thrilled if their wives could tend to the children rather than working in the fields and if their children could attend Freedmen Bureau schools rather than toil.

Under sharecropping, the freedmen owned virtually nothing, but instead signed contracts to obtain everything not necessary to grow the crop on credit from the landowner. Whereas the planter usually provided seeds, planting equipment, and work animals such as mules, the growers borrowed to purchase food, clothing, medicine, and others life essentials. At harvest time, sharecroppers typically were contracted to receive one half of the proceeds from the crops they had grown that year. The problem with both tenant farming and sharecropping was that landowners and sometimes owners of nearby country stores (often the same individuals) held local monopolies on providing credit and thus charged exorbitant interest, sometimes 50 or 60 percent, on all the items the freedmen borrowed since the beginning of the year.

When these costs were subtracted from the share of the crop, and when unscrupulous landowners lied about the profits received from crop sales or the amount borrowed, the freedmen usually ended up in debt. Their contract required sharecroppers to work off the last year's debt and then the freedmen had to borrow again for all their necessities for the coming year. Essentially, sharecroppers never got paid for their labor, a situation heartbreakingly close to life under slavery.

Sharecropping became a cancer that ate at the southern economy. Greedy landowners, thinking only in the short term, insisted that the sharecroppers devote more acres to cash crops and less to food production. This aggravated a worldwide glut of cotton, which caused prices of that commodity to tumble. As their incomes fell, poor and struggling white farmers who owned their land eventually could not pay their mortgages and were sucked into tenancy and sharecropping as well. This meant the South could not produce a consumer base that might have sparked industrial development, leading much of the region to languish in poverty.

Celebrating Freedom

African Americans celebrated their liberation in myriad ways, public and private, in manners great and small. As the historian Leon Litwack observed, upon realizing the day of emancipation had arrived, African Americans in Athens, Georgia, erected a liberty pole and danced and sang around it, while more than 4,000 black men and women marched through the streets of Charleston, South Carolina, wildly cheered by about 10,000 mostly African-American spectators. The parade featured a mule-drawn cart with a coffin draped with the message, "Slavery is Dead." Resentful whites made such open celebrations of black freedom dangerous. When freedmen celebrated emancipation in the streets of Huntsville, Texas, an angry white man on horseback rode up to the crowd and swung a sword at an African-American woman, slicing her in half. Annie Row, a former slave interviewed in the 1930s, remembered her childhood at a Rusk County, Texas, plantation. "Marster Charley," she said, received a letter informing him of his son John's death in the Civil War. The loss of his child and the imminent disappearance of the fortune he had invested in slaves proved too much for him to bear. He "started cursing the war, and he picked up the hot poker and said, 'Free the niggers, will they, I'll free them.' Then he hit my mammy on the neck, and she started moaning and crying and dropped to the floor ... He took the gun off the rack and started for the field where the niggers were working. ... But the good Lord took a hand in that mess, and the master hadn't gone far in

the field when he dropped all of a sudden ... He couldn't talk or move, and they toted him in the house. The doctor came, and the next day marster died."

Some white landowners living in remote rural communities kept news of the emancipation from their African-American workforce, which kept them toiling as slaves for years. In some cities, Union troops arrived and announced to the freedmen that their chains had fallen, but when they moved on to the next front, local whites placed them back in bondage. Slavery thus died a slow death in the South.

When it came, African Americans acted upon their freedom. African Americans sought autonomy in their political and spiritual lives. After slavery, African Americans formed their own religious establishments across the South, including new African Methodist Episcopal (AME), Baptist, and Methodist churches—black churches led by black preachers supporting the dreams of black congregations. These churches became hotbeds of political activism, as ministers urged their flock to fight for full citizenship, including the vote, the right to serve on juries, and the right to run for office. When African Americans won citizenship and the right to vote, black preachers recruited candidates and urged church members to register to vote and to show up on Election Day.

Hence, for the next 100 years, whites targeted black churches for terrorism because of their role in resisting white supremacy. From the 1860s through the June 17, 2015 mass shooting at Emanuel AME Church in Charleston, South Carolina (which once claimed famous slave rebel Denmark Vesey as a member), black churches suffered arson and bombings while white assassins slew ministers and congregants. The black church also became the launching pad for many of the twentieth century's most important African American political figures, including civil rights leaders Martin Luther King, Jr., Ralph Abernathy, and Jesse Jackson.

The African-American Family during Reconstruction

Slavery had represented not only an act of kidnapping and the theft of black bodies and black wages, but also an assault on the black family. Out of self-interest, slave owners had tried to keep together slave couples that fell in love and sought to not split slave parents from their children. Slave "marriages" had no legal standing because recognizing such unions would interfere with what southern states assumed was the absolute authority slave owners held over their flesh-and-blood possessions. Yet, slave couples built lives together and informally married, improvising ceremonies such as "jumping the broom" to mark the occasion. Nevertheless, because of debt, the loss of a lawsuit, the need for cash, or to display their power, owners sometimes split up slave families, selling children, spouses and other relatives away from their loved ones.

Whites who broke up slave families assured themselves that black human beings quickly forgot such attachments and pain. Even after emancipation, southern whites refused to acknowledge that African-American couples could fall in love and desire a lifetime relationship with each other. "Now what does the Negro know about the obligations of the marriage relation?" wrote former U.S. senator and ardent secessionist Robert Toombs in the *Atlanta Constitution* in 1871. "No more, sir, than a parish bull or village heifer."

Such whites were in for a shock when African Americans rebuilt their families after emancipation. "It was commonly thought that the negroes, when freed, would care very little for their children, and would let them die for want of attention, but experience has proven this surmise unfounded," one white observer from a former plantation-owning family, David G. Barrow, wrote in 1881. Freedmen proved their devotion in several ways. They sacrificed all they could to see that their children got an education and provided for them as best they could even though they were denied decent wages. In large numbers, they flocked to authorities to have their marriages sanctified and legally recognized. Freedmen raced to Union Army chaplains wanting the legal protections for their relationships that marriage provided. Army chaplains later reported that they could have performed freedmen marriages around the clock in the final days of the war. In 1864, the War Department authorized Freedmen Bureau agents to preside over freedmen marriages as well.

One of the more poignant tasks faced by too many freedmen was piecing together families broken under slavery. Freedmen started newspapers and these publications filled with advertisements bought by money-starved husbands, wives, and parents seeking kin who had been sold away, sometimes decades earlier. A northern reporter touring the postwar South later wrote of meeting an exhausted middle-aged African American in North Carolina. The freedman's feet ached and his heart did as well. He had walked about 600 miles believing his wife and children had been sold there four years earlier but he had not yet finished his quest. Freedmen made these epic journeys and sometimes never reunited with their loved ones. In other cases, they discovered with heartbreak that partners they had considered husbands or wives had started new romantic relationships at their next master's property.

Andrew Johnson, 1866.

PRESIDENTIAL RECONSTRUCTION UNDER ANDREW JOHNSON

Lincoln's Unfortunate Successor: Andrew Johnson

A dramatic decline in the quality of leadership befell the country when Lincoln died and Vice President **Andrew Johnson** took power. If diplomacy defined Lincoln's approach to leadership, divisiveness defined Johnson's. If Lincoln worked well with rivals and sometimes won them to his side, Johnson needlessly made enemies. If Lincoln could handle brutal criticism and stay focused, Johnson was thin-skinned and easy to anger. If Lincoln grew in his worldview and became more tolerant and supportive of black rights as he aged, Johnson remained a white supremacist who could see no place for former slaves than as the tightly-controlled servants of their supposed white superiors. With a reputation as a heavy drinker and a combative personality, Johnson provoked Republicans in Congress, and he became the first president to be impeached. At a time when regional and racial relationships were at their most delicate point, he was remarkably ill suited to occupy the White House.

Johnson grew up in poverty in Raleigh, North Carolina. Strapped for cash, his widowed mother Polly apprenticed Andrew to a tailor so he could learn a profession. At age 15, he ran away, eventually settling in Tennessee where he perfected his tailoring skills and became a successful businessman. Johnson's new home shaped his political destiny. Greeneville sat in Eastern Tennessee, in the foothills of the Appalachian Mountains, a terrain not suited for the establishment of large plantations run by wealthy landowners and worked by armies of slaves. Whites in eastern Tennessee in general were poorer and far less likely to own slaves than their western neighbors. This region would oppose secession, and many there would fight for the Union during the Civil War.

Johnson married and ran a successful tailor shop, investing his profits in real estate, and owned up to nine slaves. Now a prosperous man, and one who seemed to relish an argument, Johnson plunged into politics and climbed up the state's political ladder, along the way winning races for the U.S. Congress, for governor, and in 1857, the United States Senate. Johnson always positioned himself as the voice of the common folk speaking out against the recklessness and greed of the wealthy.

Throughout his political career, Johnson vigorously defended slavery, insisting that the Constitution guaranteed property rights, including slaves. He denied that the federal government or even states had the right to abolish slavery. He frequently expressed the deep-seated racism that would shape his policies towards freedmen during his presidency, including his lack of support for anything but token voting rights for African Americans. While serving in Congress, Johnson argued, "the black races of Africa were inferior to the white man in point of intellect—better calculated in physical structure to undergo drudgery and hardship—standing as they do, many degrees lower in the scale of gradation . . . than the white man."

Johnson infuriated most white Southerners by his actions after Abraham Lincoln won the 1860 presidential election. When most of the slaveholding states, including Tennessee, seceded from the Union, Johnson became the only U.S. senator from a Confederate state to remain loyal to the Union and remain in office. For Johnson, the regional conflict was about the survival of the Union, one he hoped would still preserve and protect slavery. "Damn the negroes," he once said. "I am fighting these traitorous aristocrats, their masters."

Johnson's loyalty to the Union caught Lincoln's attention. At the end of Johnson's Senate term, the president appointed him to serve as the military governor of Tennessee, where much of the state including the eastern section had returned to Union control. Johnson played a surprising role in promoting black enlistment in the Union Army, with 20,000 African-American soldiers enlisting from Tennessee, but his relationship with African Americans would only go downhill from there. Because Lincoln faced a tough re-election bid in 1864, Republican leaders wanted to add a pro-Union Democrat to balance the ticket. Lincoln convinced Johnson to join him as running mate under a temporary "National Union Party" label. The ticket prevailed, and this placed Johnson next in line to the presidency.

Johnson's Reconstruction Plan

When Johnson became president after John Wilkes Booth's murder of Lincoln, he stepped into a power vacuum. Congress would be in recess for most of the time between April 1865 and the next session in December. Lincoln and the legislative branch had been unable to reach a consensus on Reconstruction policy, so there was no official plan on the table. Johnson saw an opportunity, and he asserted his authority as chief executive to implement his own road map to national reconciliation. His approach would be a disaster.

In spite of Johnson's condemnations of wealthy slave owners as greedy traitors, the new president decided he needed the southern elites to restore order and to keep what he feared were potentially lawless African Americans in their place, under white control where they could not start a race war. Johnson generously handed out pardons to top Confederates. African-American leaders including Frederick Douglass met with the new president, hoping to win his support for black voting rights. Johnson could not take seriously the African-American aspirations for fair treatment, equal opportunity, and especially, voting rights, insisting that poor southern whites had lost more in the war than any other group while African Americans had gained the most. To grant black voting rights would only provoke deeper racial tensions. Johnson also believed that supposedly childlike former slaves would meekly vote as their one-time masters instructed them, which would only strengthen the dominance of the old planter class that had caused the Civil War. Douglass scoffed at the notion, pointing out that African Americans had been deeply loyal to the Union and had suffered at the hands of those planters. Blacks would be the most likely political counterbalance to pre-war white elites. Johnson did not budge from his opposition to a constitutional amendment enfranchising African Americans, arguing that voting rights were a state matter. The president did not take kindly to being challenged by a black man. After the conference, Johnson ranted about Douglass and his compatriots. "Those damned sons of bitches thought they had me in a trap. I knew that damned Douglass; he's just like any nigger and he would sooner cut a white man's throat than not."

Johnson's Reconstruction plan—what came to be known as "Presidential Reconstruction"—prioritized readmission of the southern states into the Union over even a minimal nod to African-American rights. Johnson set a low bar for readmission. He viewed emancipation as a mistake but felt it was too late to reverse course on that issue, so his plan required states seeking readmission to ratify the Thirteenth Amendment. Under Johnson's scheme, the interim governors that the president had appointed would have to convene state constitutional conventions. These conventions had to officially renounce their state's right to secede. Because Johnson wanted to punish those who had bankrolled the rebel war against the Union and discourage those who might fund future treason, returning states also had to renounce their war debt. Johnson did not make black suffrage a requirement. He did, however, support extending token voting rights for freedmen, first granted to those who served in the Union Army, then to literate African Americans holding personal property between $200-$250 (about $3,300 to $4,100 in today's dollars). Such policies would leave most African Americans disenfranchised. Once states met these requirements, they could hold congressional elections and resume their old status in the Union. The region would remain a land of, by, and for white men alone. He still required those Confederate supporters who owned $20,000 or more in property (about $313,000 today) to personally apply to Johnson for a pardon. Those pardons, and full restoration of property minus slaves, flowed easily from President Johnson's pen.

Rather than being relieved at Johnson's lenient terms, southern leaders saw the plan as a sign of Johnson's weakness and sought to restore the South as close to its pre-war condition, and African Americans in as close a condition to slavery, as legally possible. Johnson, in turn, responded to this continued southern resistance passively, which would provoke a backlash from even moderate Republicans.

The Black Codes

Seeing Johnson's leniency as a sign of weakness, delegates to the state constitutional conventions in mid-1865 clearly expected they would face no consequences if they ignored Johnson's requirements for re-admission. Mississippi declined not only to repudiate its Confederate war debt, but also even to ratify the Thirteenth Amendment abolishing slavery. (Although the amendment went into effect across the United States when ratified by three-quarters of the states in December 1865, Mississippi would not get around to approving it until 2013.) Other states also refused to repudiate their debts. Regardless of this intransigence, Johnson not only appeared ready to accept the old Confederacy back in the Union, he continued to

defend their interests, for instance vetoing a bill in 1866 admitting Colorado as a state, insisting that no such move should be made until the South was completely represented in the Congress.

As new and still unreconstructed governments took power in southern states, Johnson remained indifferent as they implemented a series of cruel limits on African-American freedoms that came to be known as "**Black Codes.**" Each former Confederate state passed a different set of laws that applied only to black people, but most of these codes included provisions that harshly punished "vagrancy," or lacking what the local authorities decided was adequate employment. Under the Black Codes, African Americans had to carry documents written by whites certifying that they had jobs, which echoed the

Above, a satirical cartoon by Thomas Nast that blames the Democratic Party for anti-black violence in the South. Nast mocks what he sees as the three wings of the Democratic Party. From the left, Nast depicts an Irish immigrant, a Confederate soldier and a greedy Wall Street investor. The three stand on a dead African-American soldier from the Union Army. In the background, black schools and orphanages are in flames. This illustration appeared in an 1868 edition of *Harper's Magazine*.

written passes slaves had to carry when they traveled.

Black Codes in some states required African Americans to work from sunrise to sundown. Upon freedom, many African-American families celebrated the freedom to allow women, who as slaves had been forced to leave offspring each day with grandparents or other relatives too old to labor, to stay with and care for their own children. In Texas and Louisiana, the Black Codes mandated that all members of a freedman family, including young children, were required to work.

The Black Codes in many cases prevented African Americans from developing job skills and business experience that would take them off the farm. Even though African Americans had acquired many skills under slavery, working for instance as blacksmiths, saddle makers, animal trainers, leather craft workers, or even distillers, some states now banned African Americans from having any job other than working in the fields. Mississippi even outlawed African Americans from owning or renting farmland, thus requiring them to be field hands toiling for white people. In South Carolina, the state forced African Americans to pay annual taxes between $10 and $100 (between $163 and $1,634 in today's dollars) if they worked at any occupation other than servant or farm laborer.

In Florida, courts could order a freedman who violated a labor contract to be whipped and sentenced to one year of uncompensated labor. Black Codes prohibited African Americans from serving on juries and all-white juries without fail found African Americans charged with vagrancy guilty and sentenced them to work without wages for white planters or the local government. African Americans could also be forced to perform unpaid work if they failed to show proper respect to a white person, for instance looking them straight in the eye or not bowing or failing to bow quickly enough.

At a time of intense white violence against African Americans, many freedmen were denied a right to self-defense and were banned from owning firearms. At the same time, states across the South also did not allow African Americans to testify against whites in court. Since African Americans were often the only witnesses to crimes whites committed against the black community, such laws meant that these crimes went unpunished. The most mean-spirited of these Black Codes, in states like North Carolina, allowed courts to take stewardship of black orphans or of children whose parents supposedly could not adequately care for them and hand them over to white "guardians," who then exploited them as servants. Under this form of legal kidnapping the guardians were allowed to whip or use other physical punishments against black minors. African Americans who worked so hard

to put families back together after slavery now saw white authorities seizing control of their loved ones again by the thousands.

Many whites embraced terrorism to beat their former servants back into a position of subservience. According to research by historian Barry Crouch, former Confederates murdered about 1 percent of all African-American men from ages 15 to 49 in Texas from the years from 1865 to 1868. Another scholar, Eric Foner, noted that age or gender did not shield African Americans from beatings, torture, or murder. Whites in Bosque County, Texas, during the first years of Reconstruction raped a black girl, castrated a black boy, and whipped another child to death without legal consequences. In Limestone County, Texas thugs seized Jo Brooks and hacked off her arms for no reason other than her black skin. "Damn their black souls, they're the things that caused the best blood of our sons to flow," one white man exclaimed in Mississippi.

The Black Suffrage Issue in the North

Racism still warped northern society, but many whites there had embraced black emancipation as a sacred cause for which their fathers, husbands, sons, and other loved ones had given their lives. Northern whites watched in horror as the Black Codes robbed African Americans of the freedom they had just won at so high a cost.

Yet, southern leaders refused to accept the consequences of wartime defeat. They believed that their continued resistance would incur no consequences from the Johnson administration. Even though some of the states applying for readmission had failed to meet Johnson's minimal requirements, the former Confederate states held Congressional elections in the fall of 1865 and sent to Washington, D.C. a delegation dominated by leaders of the failed rebellion including 15 former officers in the Confederate military and 25 officeholders from the Confederacy, prominent among them the former Confederate Vice President Alexander Stephens. African Americans had not been allowed to vote or run for office in those elections.

Northern voters were furious at the prospect of men they saw as traitors returning to power. Even moderate Republicans worried that returning southern states controlled by the Democratic Party to the Union too quickly threatened Republican Congressional majority. When the Congress convened in December 1865, a majority voted not to accept the credentials of the 80-member southern delegation and sent them back home.

CONGRESSIONAL RECONSTRUCTION

Moderate and Radical Republicans in the Congress temporarily bridged their differences during Andrew Johnson's presidency. Both factions blamed Johnson for continued southern intransigence. Rather than reconciling the regions, the president had deliberately or through incompetence reinforced regional grievances. The alliance between moderate Republicans and their Radical peers began with the refusal to seat the southern delegation and deepened in 1866 as Johnson vetoed two bills enjoying broad support.

The law creating the Freedmen's Bureau in March 1865, specified that the agency would cease operations one year after the Civil War ended. That deadline loomed in the spring of 1866, but it became clear that the Bureau had become a critical lifeline for African Americans in the South and that much work remained undone. Majorities in both houses of Congress passed a bill extending the life of the agency, but Johnson vetoed it, arguing that the federal government had no constitutional mandate to provide education or financial assistance to the poor and that Congress should pass no major legislation as long as the old Confederate states were unrepresented. An attempt to override Johnson's veto by the required two-thirds majority barely failed.

Johnson's relationship with Congress had already soured, and he did not improve matters when, speaking to White House visitors on George Washington's birthday, he improvised a speech in which he compared Radical Republican leaders like Representative Thaddeus Stevens of Pennsylvania and Charles Sumner of Massachusetts to Confederate leaders, accusing them of dividing the Union. Johnson made a split with Congress inevitable when he vetoed the 1866 Civil Rights Act, the nation's first civil rights bill, which aimed to undo the Black Codes widely despised by the Republican majority in Congress. The bill defined all born in the United States, except for Native Americans not taxed, as citizens due "the full and equal benefit of all laws . . . as is enjoyed by white citizens." The proposed legislation specified that African Americans had the right to sue, to testify in court, and to enter into contracts, and that states could not give unequal punishments for violating the law based on race. Johnson again wielded his veto pen, claiming that state citizenship was not a federal matter.

Given the clear human rights abuses unfolding in the South, Johnson's March 27 veto shocked even the moderates in Congress, who had become partners with the Radicals. The Congress overrode the veto in April. In July 1866, Congress again passed another bill extending the life of the Freedmen's Bureau, prompting yet another

Johnson veto which the House and Senate promptly overrode. Power clearly passed from the White House to the House and Senate, thus beginning the third and most significant phase of Reconstruction, Congressional or Radical Reconstruction.

The Fourteenth Amendment

Fearing that the Supreme Court might overturn its 1866 civil rights legislation, congressional Republicans fought to permanently enshrine the legislation's principles. In April 1866, moderate Republicans proposed the **Fourteenth Amendment**, destined to become one of the most important and complicated additions to the U.S. Constitution. The amendment for the first time specified that all born in the United States, and naturalized immigrants, were not only citizens of the United States but also of the state in which they lived. This clause undid the Supreme Court's infamous *Dred Scott* decision, which held that the writers of the Constitution never intended African Americans to be citizens and viewed them as "beings of an inferior order . . . altogether unfit to associate with the white race . . . and so far inferior, that they had no rights which the white man was bound to respect."

The Fourteenth Amendment not only guaranteed African-Americans rights but also specified that as citizens they enjoyed the same "privileges and immunities" as white citizens, and could not be denied "life, liberty, or property without due process of law." All citizens, it said, were due "equal protection under the law." No longer could a state legally target African Americans, requiring only blacks to carry proof of employment, for instance, or prohibiting only them from testifying in court. In response to the elections that took place in the former Confederate states in the fall of 1865, the Fourteenth Amendment prohibited anyone who violated a military or civil oath by participating in the rebellion from holding elective or military office in the future unless specifically allowed by a two-thirds vote of Congress. States were also prohibited from repaying their Confederate war debt.

Finally, although the amendment did not specifically grant voting rights for African Americans, it did allow Congress to reduce a state's representation in the federal legislature by the proportion of African-American men 21 years and older represented in that state's total population if that state disenfranchised black men. Cynicism lay behind the wording of this section. Many white northern voters still adamantly opposed black suffrage, and some states outside of the South still denied African Americans the franchise. The black population, however, still overwhelmingly resided in the old Confederacy. In states like Vermont and Maine, the black population amounted to less than 1 percent while in several southern states the African-American population exceeded 40 percent. African Americans were a majority in Mississippi and South Carolina. After ratification of the Fourteenth Amendment, southern states rejoining the Union would suffer a major penalty in terms of political power if they denied black voting rights while the impact on a northern state blocking black suffrage would be minimal. Republicans supporting the amendment, meanwhile, knew they would gain politically by promoting black voting in the South. Congress passed the Fourteenth Amendment by the required two-thirds vote on June 13, 1866, and three-fourths of the states ratified it less than two years later.

Johnson's Failed "Swing Around the Circle"

Tennessee ratified the Fourteenth Amendment on July 19, 1866, and became the first southern state to satisfy Congress's expectations for readmission. Ten former Confederate states remained unreconstructed. As black rights advanced, the mood got uglier in the South, and President Johnson added kindling to the fire by touring the country that summer in a large circular route. On this grand "swing around the circle," he denounced Radical Republicans and the Fourteenth Amendment while promoting the congressional candidacies of fellow conservatives. Johnson wanted to win a presidential term in his own right in 1868, but he realized that he was in deep political trouble since Democrats regarded him as a traitor and Republicans saw him as an obstacle to their Reconstruction program. Johnson hoped that if he elected allies to the next Congress, he might use that foundation

to build a third political party that would nominate him for president. Like many Johnson initiatives, this effort proved a disaster.

Race riots stained the summer of 1866. Violence wracked Charleston, Richmond, and Atlanta, with particularly appalling bloodshed as well in New Orleans and Memphis. In Memphis, African American Union soldiers and freedmen forced the release of a black man arrested on dubious grounds, sparking white fury and a riot that claimed the lives of 46 African Americans (including two children) as well as a white policeman and a firefighter. Rampaging whites burned down much of the African American part of town, torching schools, churches and homes. In New Orleans, chaos reigned when black workers paraded, demanding voting rights during a state constitutional convention, sparking an upheaval that slew 48 and wounded 166 in an incident a congressional investigation later labeled a massacre of African-American civilians.

Rather than using his high office to unite the country, Johnson exploited the tragedies, attempting to blame his radical political enemies for the melees even as he showed complete indifference to the loss of African-American lives. In speeches delivered in August and September, he compared Radical Republican leaders like Thaddeus Stevens and Wendell Phillips to Satan, to Judas Iscariot (the Biblical betrayer of Jesus) and to the Confederate rebels. As a result of his angry outbursts, Johnson probably lost more votes for his allies than he won. Republicans, now solidly anti-Johnson, gained more than a two-thirds majority in both the House and the Senate, meaning they could (if they maintained unity) override any Johnson veto

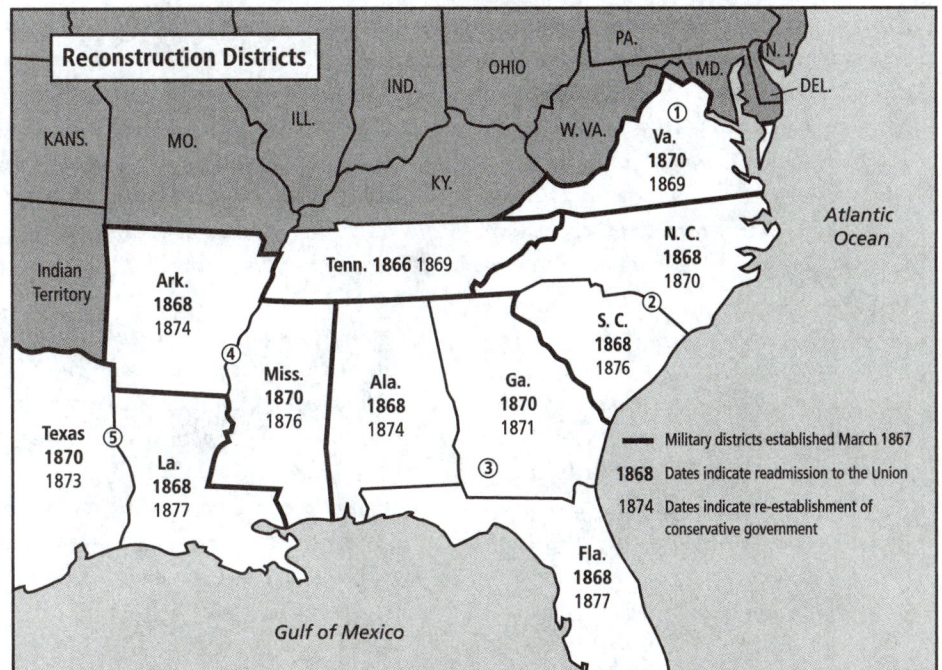

Map 17.1 Reconstruction Districts

STEPHEN SWAILS:
A VOICE FOR BLACK RECONSTRUCTION

Perhaps no man more completely embodied the fears of southern whites during the Reconstruction Era than Stephen Atkins Swails. Of mixed-race heritage (with a black father and a white mother), Swails was a war hero who became one of the first African-American officers in the U.S. Army. Though derided by ex-Confederates as a so-called "carpetbagger" (a Northerner who moved to the South after the Civil War), he could not be intimidated by white threats and violence. Swails worked for the Bureau of Refugees, Freedmen and Abandoned Lands, commonly known as the "Freedman's Bureau"—an agency run under the supervision of the U.S. Army that provided education, legal aid, and other services to the former slaves to aid them in their transition from slavery to freedom. The Freedman's Bureau became a focus of hatred for bitter, unrepentant Confederates. During Reconstruction, Swails enjoyed a remarkably successful political career. Terrorist groups such as the Ku Klux Klan, horrified by the "race mixing" that the Swails family represented, arose during the period to silence the voice of politically empowered black men such as this northern transplant.

Born in 1832, Swails spent his first two years in Columbia, Pennsylvania, a town with an unusually large African-American population (about 32 percent) where black men experienced an unusual degree of prosperity in business. The size and success of the town's black community, however, sparked increasing resentment among whites. In 1834, a year that witnessed race riots erupting across the North, violence shattered the town, with a white mob destroying a lumber business owned by Stephen Smith, Columbia's most prominent African-American entrepreneur. White violence prompted a black exodus that included the Swails family, which moved to nearby Manheim. Receiving a modest education, Stephen Swails worked for a time as a waiter in Cooperstown, New York and got married. However, he felt restless, so when the Civil War started in 1861, he wanted to join the crusade to end slavery. Swails eventually signed up with the Massachusetts 54th Regiment, with all-black enlisted men led by a white abolitionist colonel, Robert Gould Shaw.

Although initially turned down for a promotion because of his black heritage, he earned the rank of First Sergeant. The 54th achieved fame for bravely spearheading an ultimately ill-fated assault on Fort Wagner near South Carolina on July 18, 1863. Due to Swails's bravery under fire and the huge losses suffered by the regiment, the unit's new commander, Colonel Edward N. Hallowell, named him acting Sergeant Major. In February 1864, Swails fought bravely at the Battle of Olustee, where he received a head wound. After the fight, Colonel Hallowell recommended to Massachusetts Governor John Andrew that Swails be promoted to Second Lieutenant. The governor approved the request, but the U.S. Army initially refused to recognize Swails's new rank because of his race. Under pressure from Andrews and Hallowell, however, the Army finally relented, making Swails one of the first black officers in United States Army history.

*After the war, Swails remained in South Carolina, serving as an agent for the Freedmen's Bureau in Charleston. Even though many former Union soldiers decided to settle in the South after the Civil War, Swails was one of the few African-American soldiers to do so. To meet congressional requirements for readmission to the Union, South Carolina held a state constitutional convention in 1868, and African Americans were allowed to participate. Williamsburg County picked Swails as its delegate. The convention gave African Americans the right to vote. The large black population in the state briefly made African Americans a powerful constituency, giving Swails a chance to lead. He had moved to Kingstree, South Carolina, in 1868 and won election as mayor, an office he held for the next eleven years. Swails also edited a newspaper, **The Williamsburg Republican**. He represented his district in the South Carolina State Senate until 1878, serving three terms as Senate Pro Tempore. Along the way, he became a delegate to the Republican National Convention three times and served as a presidential elector in the Electoral College. No black man had ever achieved such political stature in the Palmetto State.*

South Carolina, however, descended into a nightmare of violence as the curtain fell on the Reconstruction Era. White Democrats essentially staged an insurrection to end Republican rule of their state and to return African Americans to a condition of political and economic powerlessness. Hundreds of Republicans, mostly African Americans, died or were injured in an orgy of racial violence between 1876-1877. A white mob tried to murder Swails, who decided to resign from the state senate rather than leave his four children fatherless.

Through his Republican Party connections, Swails managed to secure positions with the United States Postal Service and the Treasury Department in Washington, D.C. After a lengthy absence, he returned to Kingstree where he died in 1900, as a largely forgotten man, buried in an unmarked grave in Charleston. In 2006, after research by a local history buff uncovered his remarkable career, activists erected a five-foot-high granite monument to the memory of this overlooked hero of one of the country's most troubled epochs.

of congressional legislation. The election threatened to make President Johnson a bit player in the ongoing drama of Reconstruction.

The Reconstruction Acts of 1867

By March 1867, moderates and Radical Republicans largely agreed that Johnson's policies were a failure, and they decided to hit the reset button and to begin the process all over again. They passed the **Reconstruction Acts of 1867**, four laws under which the southern state and local governments created under Johnson in an atmosphere of terror and without black participation would be replaced. The legislation placed the ten unreconstructed states under direct military rule and were divided into five military districts, each under the authority of an Army general whose first task was to impose law and order.

Once violence ended in a military district, the army would initiate voter registration. The law required each state to hold new constitutional conventions, with the delegates to be elected by male citizens age 21 and older registered to vote. The law required that African Americans must be allowed to register, cast ballots, and run for the delegate slots. Men who had been major military or political officials in the Confederacy would not be allowed to participate in the constitutional convention delegate elections. The law also set requirements for these conventions. Each of the ten states was required to grant voting rights for all adult male citizens 21 years of age and older regardless of race, and to ratify the Fourteenth Amendment. Once all these requirements were met and the voters approved the new state constitution, that state could then hold elections and apply for readmission to the Union.

Unlike Lincoln's 10 Percent Plan and Johnson's program for Reconstruction, the Reconstruction Acts dealt directly with the political status of African Americans post-emancipation. Blacks would have the legal right to vote, and for a time the Union Army would ensure that those rights were respected. However, like its predecessors, the congressional plan did not address the freedmen's poverty and landlessness. African Americans would continue to be economically vulnerable and subject to financial pressure to not assert their political rights. Reaching his desk only 10 days before the end of the 1867 regular Congressional session, Johnson had the opportunity to pocket-veto the first Reconstruction Act but instead decided to grandstand, issuing a veto with an angry denunciation, only to see the Congress override the veto that same day. Johnson had been sidelined, and by this time many Radicals sought to eliminate him from the political process in Washington completely.

The Impeachment of Andrew Johnson

The authors of the Constitution deliberately made it difficult for the Congress to remove high-ranking federal officials, such as a president, vice president, cabinet member, or federal judge. Under Article II, Section 4 of the Constitution, the House of Representatives is given the power to impeach such officials for "Treason, Bribery, or other High Crimes and Misdemeanors." The role of the House in such cases is similar to that of a grand jury in a criminal case. The House determines if sufficient evidence has been presented to justify **impeachment**, and it takes a simple majority in the lower chamber to move the case forward. An impeachment is, therefore, similar to a grand jury indicting a defendant. Guilt has not been determined and an impeached official does not yet have to leave office. The Senate must then hold an impeachment trial. The accused official can present a defense through lawyers, while the "prosecution" is handled by House managers, members of the lower chamber who act as prosecutors. The Senate acts as the jury, with the Chief Justice of the Supreme Court presiding over the trial to rule on legal issues. The Senate must vote by at least a two-thirds majority to remove a president or other officials from office.

Johnson still worried congressional Radicals. Even if the large Republican congressional majority severely limited his ability to block Republican Reconstruction plans, Johnson remained commander-in-chief. This gave him authority over the Freedmen's Bureau, an agency that the U.S. Army administered and Johnson had wanted to destroy. The president had authority over Secretary of War Edwin Stanton with whom he had battled over policy. Stanton frequently allied with the Radicals on Reconstruction matters. Radical and moderate Republicans both trusted Stanton and feared Johnson would fire him and replace him with someone sympathetic to the former slave owners.

With this conflict between Johnson and Stanton in mind, Congress passed the **Tenure of Office Act** over the president's veto in March 1867. The law prevented the president from firing any officeholder in the Executive Branch who had been approved by the Senate until that body approved a replacement. Johnson would not be deterred in his attempt to dump Stanton and made two legal arguments against the act. First, Lincoln had appointed Stanton and not Johnson. Based on the precise wording of the law, Johnson believed the law did not apply to him in this particular case. Second, the law violated the Constitution's "separation of powers" doctrine. If the law stood, the president would not be able to fill the executive branch with individuals he trusted for advice and to implement policy. Congress would be interfering with the functioning of the Executive Branch, which was designed to be equal with the federal legislature. Johnson wanted to challenge the constitutionality of the law. He suspended Stanton from his position on August 12, 1867, while the Senate was in one of its lengthy recesses. Johnson named General Grant as Stanton's interim replacement, hoping to tap into the former Union commander's popularity.

Radical leaders believed that they held the upper hand and, when Congress reconvened, they declared Stanton's firing violated the Tenure of Office Act and voted to reapprove Stanton as Secretary of War. Grant desired the presidency in 1868, and he had no motive for helping out the politically unpopular Johnson, so he resigned as Stanton's temporary replacement. Johnson refused to give ground, firing Stanton on February 21, 1868. To prevent being physically removed, Stanton barricaded himself in his office for the next three months, only occasionally sneaking off to visit his home. The House of Representatives, out of patience with Johnson, approved eleven charges of impeachment against him, including firing Stanton, not enforcing Reconstruction laws passed by Congress, libeling members of Congress by denouncing them as traitors, and bringing into "disgrace, ridicule, hatred, contempt, and reproach the Congress of the United States." The House overwhelmingly voted for impeachment March 24, 1868, by a margin of 126-47, a coalition that included many moderates.

The president's fate now rested with the Senate, where many Senate moderates there doubted that Johnson's actions rose to the level of "high crimes and misdemeanors." Several senators believed that Johnson was on trial not because of a serious breach of law but because he disagreed with the Congress on Reconstruction. To force a president from office under such circumstances, they worried, would weaken the presidency to the point that future chief executives fearing impeachment and removal would hesitate to challenge the Congress on policy matters, even if a president viewed acts of Congress as unconstitutional. Furthermore, by the time his trial began March 4, Johnson had slightly less than a year left in his term. Some questioned the value of taking so drastic a step when the president had so little time left in office.

In addition to their concerns over what precedent the impeachment might set, moderates who did not care much for Johnson, strongly disliked his potential replacement even more. At the time of Lincoln's assassination, there was no process for replacing a vice president who rose to the White House. The country had to wait until someone was elected vice president the next election. With no vice president in place, and by a law earlier passed by the Congress, the person next in line was Senate President Pro Tempore Benjamin Wade, a Radical whose support for African American and women's rights, placed him at cross-purposes with more conservative Republicans. "There are Republican [news]papers that believe the president guilty of crime and favor impeachment, but they hate the idea of Mr. Wade becoming Acting president," a writer for the *Cincinnati Gazette* noted. The Senate reached its verdict May 16, with 35 voting for conviction and 19 for acquittal, exactly one vote short of the two-thirds majority required for Johnson's removal from office. Johnson would stay president, but his influence over events had completely evaporated. Stanton, meanwhile, resigned as Secretary of War that same month.

The Fifteenth Amendment

During congressional Reconstruction, Republicans wanted to permanently secure an African-American voting base in the South. Widespread poverty, however, would play a role in hindering black political rights. If the Fourteenth Amendment represents one of the most complicated additions to the U.S. Constitution, the **Fifteenth Amendment** proved to be one of the briefest yet most poorly worded. On the surface, the amendment seemed to guarantee African-American suffrage, but the amendment's authors unintentionally opened the door to poll taxes and literacy tests.

The Fourteenth Amendment pressured only states with large African-American populations—specifically those that had formed the former Confederacy—to adopt black suffrage. The Fifteenth Amendment eliminated this inconsistency, as it would apply equally to all the states. The brief first section declared: "The right of citizens of the United States to vote shall not be denied or abridged by the United States or by any state on account of race, color, or previous condition of servitude." The amendment passed the House and the Senate February 25-26, 1869. A handful of Radical Republicans, most notably Charles Sumner, voted against it because they believed the amendment did not go far enough to safeguard black voting rights. These concerns turned out to be prophetic. By February 3, 1870, three-fourths of the states had ratified the amendment.

Unfortunately, the amendment did not guarantee the right to vote to all U.S. men age 21 and older. It only prohibited states from barring a citizen from voting for three specific reasons, leaving the door open for states to later contrive any other reason for denying suffrage. Georgia pioneered one such method by passing the first poll tax in 1877. Poll taxes were not large by today's standards, upwards of $2 (about $38 in 2016 dollars). But they were unreachable particularly for sharecroppers who rarely received cash payments for their work. Polls taxes spread throughout the South from the late 1870s until Texas finally implemented one in 1902. By themselves, poll taxes cut black voting by half in the South. Because such laws could not directly refer to race, they applied to whites as well. White political participation in the South dropped to a third between the 1880s and the 1930s. Other states required literacy tests, designed to be difficult or impossible to pass, beginning in the 1890s. This requirement disproportionately affected African Americans, since, even more than two decades after slavery, African Americans had been denied equitable access to education and upwards of 60 percent still could not read or write.

The passage of the Fifteenth Amendment caused an unfortunate rift between movements for the African American rights and women's rights. Women such as Lucretia Mott, Elizabeth Cady Stanton, and Sojourner Truth had heroically fought against slavery for decades and saw the spirit of radical reform in Reconstruction as opening the door to women's suffrage. Mott, Stanton, and Truth fought to include women's voting rights in the Fifteenth Amendment. They could not prevail against men like Frederick Douglass and women like longtime abolitionist Lucy Stone who argued that asking to enfranchise both African Americans and women at the same time was too much and could end up politically dooming both efforts. In particular, southern white women fighting for voting rights argued that it was an injustice that they were denied the franchise while it was held, technically at least, by African-American men.

Republican State Governments

For a brief time, black voting dramatically changed southern politics. With some whites still disenfranchised because they had not met the loyalty requirements of the Fourteenth Amendment, and others boycotting elections that included black voters, Republicans took control of the governments in all the former Confederate states, ushering in (for a short while) one of the most progressive, modernizing, and democratizing periods in the region's history. African Americans flocked to the Party of Lincoln, and comprised eight of ten Republicans in the South, but the party had two other important constituencies.

Northerners who moved South at the end of the war, migrating from a region already dominated by the Republicans, carried their party loyalties with them. Southern Democrats later villainized this group, the smallest within the Republican Party, as "**carpetbaggers**." Such migrants were stereotyped as lowlife con artists who, living on the margins in their home states, stuffed their few possessions in a cheap carpetbag, and headed South, where they

hoped to con their way to riches and political office. In fact, carpetbaggers were mostly teachers and missionaries associated with the Freedman's Bureau, Union veterans, and respectable businessmen who felt a humanitarian urge to teach freedmen and poor whites, to spread the Gospel, or who saw the South as a place ripe for economic development. A large number remained committed to the South and lived there past the end of Reconstruction. Even though they were the smallest Republican faction, Northerners took the initiative in forming local Republican Party organizations. Their leadership, however, soon passed to a much larger Republican Party demographic that Democrats derided as "**scalawags**."

The origins of the term "scalawag" are controversial but evidence suggests that the word came into use in the early 1800s and referred to worthless livestock. The term transformed into an insult directed at supposedly worthless people, a description southern Democrats thought applied to southern Republicans. Democrats smeared scalawags as ignorant, uneducated, and prone to crime, reflective of the party elite's disdain for the poor. While scalawags included many poor whites, non-slaveowners or owners of few slaves, who struggled to raise crops on hilly, hard-to-farm land, a large number came from the economic middle and some were elites. About 40 percent of them held public office at some level before the war. Many had been Whigs or pro-Union Democrats before the first shots were fired at Fort Sumter. They supported government investment in internal improvements such as building bridges and roads and bringing back a centralized banking system. Frequently, scalawags simply resented the power and the arrogance of the old slave owner class.

These three groups catapulted the Republicans to dominance in elections selecting delegates to the state constitutional conventions. Republicans made up 75 percent of the delegates at these conventions. Later southern-sympathizing historians like William A. Dunning, who taught at Columbia University in the late 1800s and early 1900s, promoted a racist myth still prevalent among many today that this period marked when the South temporarily came under "negro rule," the government falling under the control of corrupt and unqualified officials placed into power by ignorant, enfeebled freedmen. This interpretation not only insultingly misrepresented African Americans, it was also inaccurate in terms of numbers. Only 258 African Americans served as delegates in the southern constitutional conventions out of 1,027 overall. The so-called scalawags comprised six out of ten convention delegates. In the Reconstruction era, only two African Americans reached the United States Senate—Hiram Revels and Blanche Bruce—and only sixteen served in the U.S. House, with almost half of that number from South Carolina, a state with a large African American population. Only in South Carolina, did African Americans win a majority in a chamber of a state legislature, the state's House of Representatives. Although African Americans played a significant part in shaping subsequent reforms, this era reflected not African American but a different type of southern white rule.

Rather than ushering in an era of unprecedented waste, fraud, and abuse born of African-American immorality and incompetence, African Americans helped turn the Reconstruction Era into one of the most-forwarding looking in southern history. The constitutional conventions dropped property qualifications for voting or holding office, and shielded homes from seizure in bankruptcy proceedings. In nine former Confederate states, laws were passed that protected married women's property rights for the first time. The number of elective statewide offices expanded, changes that increased the voice of poor whites in their government. In state after state, the southern Republicans made a priority of creating the first viable, widely attended public school systems. Although segregated, these provided education for African Americans. South Carolina implemented its first-ever compulsory school attendance law.

The most important innovations involved the public schools. Southern-born whites, even in the Republican Party, would not countenance black and white children sitting together in classrooms. So except in a small district in New Orleans, these schools were racially segregated. All ten states covered in the Military Reconstruction Acts provided public schools for blacks and whites between the ages of five and twenty-one. By the 1870s, around half of children received regular education in South Carolina and Mississippi, with numbers ranging from 30 percent to 40 percent in Georgia and Alabama.

Finally, Republican state legislatures tried to modernize and stimulate the southern economy as well, subsidizing railroad construction. This move proved controversial because of the taxes required to fund the subsidies, especially when an economic depression in the 1870s left many of these railroad lines unfinished. Taxes and spending did dramatically increase when Republicans controlled the southern state governments, as they tried to address the many issues that the antebellum slave-owning planter class had ignored, such as education, public health, and developing industry and infrastructure. Reconstruction Republicans tried to accomplish all this with what was still largely a one-crop economy devastated by war, a planter class set on obstruction, and a profoundly undereducated population. It was remarkable that the Republican Reconstruction governments accomplished as much as they did with so few resources in such a short time (roughly from 1868 to 1874).

The Acquisition of Alaska

Even as it struggled to exercise its full authority over the unreconstructed states, the federal government expanded the American borders and took tentative steps towards the imperialist empire building that would commence full-throttle at the end of the nineteenth century. The purchase of Russian America, soon to be designated by

The first African American Senators and Representatives in the 41st and 42nd Congress of the United States, by Currier and Ives, 1872.
(Left to right) Senator Hiram Revels of Mississippi, Representatives Benjamin Turner of Alabama, Robert DeLarge of South Carolina, Josiah Walls of Florida, Jefferson Long of Georgia, Joseph Rainey and Robert B. Elliot of South Carolina.

Secretary of State William H. Seward as the **Alaska Territory**, provides one of President Johnson's few clear-cut achievements. The company contracted to run the colony for Moscow was rapidly losing money even while the Russian government feared a military conflict with the ever-expansive British Empire. The Russians did not know if it could adequately defend their North American possession against their European rival even as they encountered resistance from indigenous people. Seward concluded a treaty with the Russian envoy on March 19, 1867, to buy Alaska, about 500,000 square acres of real estate, for $7.2 million (just over $123 million today). The president presented the agreement to the U.S. Senate for ratification the following day. One newspaper ridiculed the Alaska purchase as "Johnson's Polar Bear Garden" and for years it was famous as "Seward's Folly." Because of its vast oil and gas resources and the military value of its geographic position in the North Pacific, the purchase, then at two cents an acre, has since generally been seen as a lucky gamble.

THE PRESIDENCY OF ULYSSES S. GRANT

Grant Administration Scandals

After Lincoln's death, **Ulysses S. Grant** stood as the Union hero of the Civil War, and there was little chance he would not be elected the next president of the United States. On May 20, 1868, just four days after the Senate acquitted Johnson of impeachable offenses, the Republican National Convention opened and quickly handed Grant the party's nod. The badly divided Democrats, tarnished by the Civil War and the continued resistance to Reconstruction in the South, took twenty-one ballots to nominate a bland former New York governor, Horatio Seymour. That November, Grant won twenty-six of the thirty-four states and crushed Seymour by a 214-80 margin in the Electoral College.

Grant was well meaning but politically inexperienced and completely unqualified for the presidency, relying on men he trusted but who often took advantage of him or otherwise let him down. His presidency unfolded during a period of record fortunes made by reckless and unscrupulous men while governmental ethics were rarely policed. One irony of the corruption charges made against Reconstruction Era governments in the South is how clean most were compared to what unfolded across the North and the West at the same time. Grant's administration reflected the period's relaxed ethics. Though never directly blamed for the numerous scandals that unfolded during his eight years in the White House, the former military commander made astonishingly bad choices for his cabinet and Grant suffered from guilt by association. At the Treasury Department, officials accepted bribes from distillers to falsify records on how much liquor they manufactured and distributed, in order to avoid paying federal taxes. One 1874 estimate placed the federal revenues lost to the so-called "Whiskey Ring" at $15 million in taxes (about $318 million today.) As negative as the reactions

Map 17.2   The Election of 1868

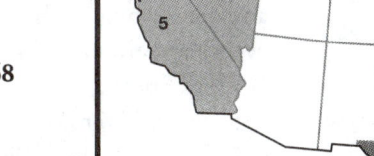

The Election of 1868			
Candidate	Electoral Vote	Popular Vote	Percent of Popular Vote
Ulysses S. Grant (Republican)	214	3,012,833	52.7
Horatio Seymour (Democrat)	80	2,703,249	47.3
Nonvoting states (Reconstruction)			

were to these incidents, the **Crédit Mobilier Scandal** of 1872 stands as the biggest and most complicated scandal to rock the Grant White House. The Lincoln Administration in 1864 had chartered the Union Pacific Railroad to build a transcontinental line, providing $100 million for the project and $60 million in low-interest loans (an astronomical $3 billion today when accounting for inflation.) Much of this money was not spent on railroad building. The Union Pacific Company Directors set up a shell company they called Crédit Mobilier, supposedly the subcontractor that would actually build the railroad. Receiving payments from Union Pacific, Crédit Mobilier used the cash to buy stock in Union Pacific at below-market value and then sold the shares publicly at greatly inflated values. The Union Pacific directors split the proceeds among themselves. This financial shell game may have eventually generated more than $877 million at 2016 values. Beginning in 1867, before Grant became a candidate for president, the railroad company sought to prevent this theft from becoming public and to sway

Congress to pass more legislation favorable to Union Pacific. They sold shares of Crédit Mobilier stock to House and Senate members at discount rates. An 1872 report made these bribes public, prompting a Congressional investigation of 13 of its members for involvement in the scandal. Grant had no personal involvement, and since both parties were implicated, he did not have any baggage from this particular scandal to carry when he ran for another term in 1872. These tawdry affairs eroded Grant's influence within his own party.

The Ku Klux Klan

Even with the swirl of controversy over scandals and foreign affairs, Grant could never direct his attention far away from the South. There, an organization soon channeled unfocused white cruelty and rage at freedmen into a more precisely defined political and economic agenda aimed at crushing the Republican Party in the South, ending all northern occupation of the region and putting black people "back in their place" as tightly controlled and powerless farm and manual labor.

In December 1865, six bored young men, mostly college educated and former Confederate officers, gathered in Pulaski, Tennessee, a place filled with old slave plantations on the state's mid-southern border. They decided to kill time by forming a fraternity devoted for a brief time to pulling pranks and drinking. The group soon dubbed itself the **Ku Klux Klan**, derived from the Greek word *kuklos* (meaning circle) and "clan" (spelled with a "k" for alliterative effect). As the Klan expanded beyond its original membership, it developed secret rituals, initiation rites, and code words to be used in greetings. Some started wearing sheets or similarly ghostly outfits because Klansmen thought this clothing would frighten allegedly superstitious freedmen. As they turned political, seeking to roll back black freedoms, the Klan grew the largest in counties without large African-American populations, and before long the "Invisible Empire" penetrated almost every southern state. Former Confederate General Nathan Bedford Forrest of Tennessee emerged as the Klan's original Grand Wizard.

The Klan, the Knights of the White Camellia, and similar groups served as goons for big planters to enforce sharecropping contracts. They beat and whipped African Americans who dared speak up to white growers. The Klan sought to suppress any incipient black revolt by assaulting and even murdering "uppity" freedmen who expressed pride and independence. The Klan waged war on all three major factions of the southern Republican Party, not just freedmen but also carpetbaggers and scalawags. Among so-called carpetbaggers, black and white teach-

A cartoon depicts President Ulysses S. Grant as a circus acrobat being pulled down by several figures in his administration implicated in the "Whiskey Ring" scandal. Multiple scandals marred Grant's presidency. Illustration from an 1880 edition of *Puck* magazine.

A Thomas Nast cartoon, "Worse than Slavery" from *Harper's Weekly* in 1874, portrays the sinister alliance of violent terror organizations— the so-called "White League" and the Ku Klux Klan—that bullied and murdered African Americans in the South during Reconstruction. Armed with guns and knives, the two groups shake hands above a frightened family of freedman. A lynched African American looms in the background. Such organizations sought to frighten away African Americans from seeking an education or exercising their just-won right to vote.

ers, seen as dangerous outside agitators, drew the most intense Klan fury. Even if instructors stuck to the ABCs in the classroom, teaching black children in the 1860s and 1870s was an act of political dissent. The planter class whites and their Klan enforcers knew teachers reinforced the black demand for economic justice. They responded by disrupting classes and intimidating students, torching schoolhouses, threatening teachers that they would be burned alive if they did not leave town immediately, and by raping and hanging teachers who stayed.

Republican politicians and activists (including Freedman's Bureau agents) who registered African Americans to vote became the most numerous Klan victims. The list of Republican public officials assassinated by the Klan included state representative Richard Burke of Alabama, Republican state judge George Ashburn of Georgia, and state representative James Martin and state Senator B.F. Randolph of South Carolina. A political dispute instigated a Klan massacre of Republicans in Colfax, Louisiana, April 13, 1873. The killings took place after a racially charged gubernatorial race the previous year. Democrats in Colfax Parish formed a militia to do battle with the mostly African-American state militia and overthrow the local government. On Easter Sunday, the white militia,

the Klan, and members of the Knights of the White Camellia amassed in a 300-man force and attacked the courthouse. After gaining control of the building, whites hunted black members of the state militia and African-American residents. Eventually, 150 African Americans and three whites died in the battle. The Klan literally got away with murder because the general white community protected them, or feared them too much to speak out.

The level of violence forced the Grant Administration to act. In 1870-1871, at Grant's behest, Congress passed a series of three laws known as the "Ku Klux Klan" or "Enforcement" Acts. The laws enforced the Fourteenth and the Fifteenth Amendments by making, for the first time in the republic's history, interfering with voting a federal crime and gave the federal government the power to prosecute such violations. Under the law, the president could declare a county to be in a state of insurrection, impose martial law, and suspend the writ of *habeas corpus* in those places. (Under *habeas corpus*, authorities cannot detain suspects indefinitely without presenting legal justifications in court.) The three laws went into full effect in nine upcountry South Carolina counties, prompting 800 Klan members to flee the state. Under these statutes, the U.S. Army arrested thousands of

Klansmen. Courts convicted hundreds and sent sixty-five Klansmen to prison. Klan membership dwindled.

By the mid-1870s, the Klan's usefulness had passed because they had largely achieved their goals. Federal troops began to withdraw from the South, removing the force protecting African-American civil rights. The Democratic Party began taking control of the former Confederate states. Most freedmen had been reduced to sharecropping. The Klan itself disappeared by the end of Reconstruction in 1877, to be replaced by smaller, local terrorist cells that operated under names like the White League or designated themselves as "rifle clubs." The Klan would return in much bigger form as not just an anti-black group, but also an anti-immigrant, anti-Catholic, anti-Jewish, anti-alcohol, and anti-women's rights organization in 1915.

The Santo Domingo Affair

The acquisition of Alaska during Andrew Johnson's presidency also provided a jumping-off point for further American imperialist adventures. European empires began to see China and the rest of the Pacific Rim as a treasure trove of easily exploited labor and natural resources. As early as 1861, thirty-seven years before the Spanish-American War, William Seward advocated starting a war with Spain to gain control of Cuba as a way to heal North-South conflict with the tonic of shared militarism. Seward also spoke of buying Hawaii, Samoa, or the Fiji Islands. **Santo Domingo**, now known as the Dominican Republic, also sat high on Seward's expansionist wish list, and he lobbied for its annexation. He encountered strong resistance, however, from whites who might have loved to seize foreign lands and their riches but, echoing anxieties in the 1830s and 1840s about conquering Mexican territories, many politicians and opinion makers did not want to add the dark-skinned, non-English-speaking in Cuba and the other lands to the American population. *Harper's Weekly* insisted that it would be impossible to make citizens of "a people wholly alien from us in principles, language, and traditions, a third of whom are barbarously ignorant."

Administrations changed but ambitions to take over Santo Domingo did not. That nation's president, Buenaventura Báez, had hoped to personally profit from selling his nation to the highest bidder, regardless of the consequences to his people. Santo Domingo already produced much of the coffee and sugar Americans consumed and, if the nation were conquered by one means or another, the cost for those products would drop for American consumers. Santo Domingo annexation would provide the United States a plantation for tobacco, chocolate, and tropical fruits, all grown by pitifully low-wage

Horace Greeley, c. 1872.

labor. Again, racism trumped greed as opponents of a Santo Domingo expansion warned about the dangers posed by its largely African-descended and Catholic natives.

Grant was undeterred and dispatched his secretary Orville Babcock and General Rufus Ingalls to negotiate an annexation agreement with President Báez. A proposed annexation treaty offered $2 million (about $38 million today) for Samaná Bay (also on the island of Hispaniola). In an unwise move politically, the agreement also included a provision that would allow Santo Domingo to apply for U.S. statehood. Grant sent the treaty to the Senate on January 10, 1870. When Babcock spoke on behalf of the treaty to the Senate in March 1870, it provoked fury. The Senate had not been consulted about the negotiations in advance. Babcock treated the Senate with arrogance and, when some objected to the treaty, became threatening. Treaties must receive a two-thirds majority from the Senate to be approved, and the Santo Domingo pact failed in a 28-28 tie on June 30.

The 1872 Presidential Election

Grant's actions in the Santo Domingo Affair opened a rift within the Republican Party by the end of his first term. Carl Schurz, a Senator from Missouri, led a revolt against Grant in 1870. By the time of the 1872 election, Charles Sumner of Massachusetts, who had opposed Grant on Santo Domingo annexation, joined him. Aware they could not block Grant from winning re-nomination at the Republican Party Convention, they formed the Liberal Republican Party, which held a convention in

Cincinnati, Ohio in May 1872. Prominent Republican newspaper editors like Horace White of the *Chicago Tribune* and Horace Greeley of *The New York Tribune* joined the splinter group. The **Liberal Republicans** professed disgust at the myriad Grant administration scandals. They also deemed many of the Reconstruction policies pursued since Lincoln as failures. Liberal Republicans were unimpressed with the results of black voting in the South, which they believed had placed unqualified men in office and had worsened racial tensions. The splinter party nominated Greeley for president.

Democrats, still crippled by their association with the southern rebellion, decided to merge with the Liberal Republicans and nominate Greeley and his running mate, Governor Benjamin Brown of Missouri, for president and vice president as well. The effort was doomed to fail, with Grant winning by a landslide. He carried the popular vote by a nearly 56 percent to 44 percent margin. The Electoral College gap was wider, 286-66, though Greeley died only 24 days after the election and his freed electors were scattered among various third party candidates.

Strangeness aside, this election marked an intensification of the women's suffrage movement as Victoria Woodhull and her allies formed the Equal Rights Party, which nominated the feminist Woodhull for president as a protest against female disenfranchisement. The Equal Rights Party nominated Frederick Douglass, a strong backer of women's suffrage, for vice president. Douglass ignored the symbolic gesture because of his urgent hope that Grant would earn another presidential term. The party advocated the right of women to file for divorce. Woodhull campaigned although she was barred from serving as president because of her gender and because she had not yet reached the constitutionally mandated age of 35. Her campaign consisted of a series of protests aimed at heightening consciousness about the women's suffrage cause, which would not reach fruition until 1920.

The Panic of 1873

Jeopardizing both Republican dominance of the political landscape and the continuation of Reconstruction in the South, a sharp economic downturn in 1873 enveloped the United States and soon the world. This depression, which lasted five years, had multiple causes. What became known as "**The Panic of 1873**" began on September 18, 1873, when Jay Cooke & Company announced it could not pay off railroad bonds after its Northern Pacific Railroad project fell apart. Investors began to dump railroad portfolios. In days, 5,000 investment firms went bankrupt and stock prices plummeted. On September 20, the New York Stock exchange suspended trade for the first time

ever as top stocks tumbled. The Grant administration tried to calm nerves by buying $13 million in railroad bonds to revive confidence in what seemed like a collapsing industry, but the move failed. The post-Civil War economy seemed to be unraveling.

Reckless real estate speculation resulting in artificially inflated land prices triggered a collapse of property values. When land speculators could not pay loans, banks failed, leading panicked Wall Street investors to dump stock. Across the country, retail stores, laundries, and restaurants closed. Manufacturing output markedly declined. Flour, cotton, and iron mills shut their doors. The unemployment rate hit 25 percent in New York City. Civil War veterans and others formed armies of the unemployed who tramped across the country in desperate search of work.

Strikes broke out across the country. Rejecting charity as an undesired alternative, workers and the unemployed formed the Committee for Safety in New York City in December 1873, demanding that the city create public jobs to provide relief. They planned a massive rally drawing thousands in Tompkins Square Park leading to a march on city hall where they would present demands and called for the city to spend $100,000 on a Labor Relief Bureau to offer public works jobs. Conservative newspapers spread the rumor that jewel-stealing radicals in Paris bent on destroying capitalism had funded the committee. The committee decided to not march on city hall but simply stage a January 13, 1874, demonstration at the park. The city revoked a permit for the rally, but 7,000 showed up anyway. Armed with clubs, police charged into the peaceful crowd, beating demonstrators and even patrolling nearby streets on horseback where they assaulted pedestrians unlucky enough to be nearby.

In 1874, Congress finally responded with a bill to increase the money supply as a means of stimulating the economy, but Grant vetoed it. Congress tried a much more conservative approach in early 1875 with passage of the Specie Resumption Act, under which the government bought back currency with gold, further tightening the money supply, but boosting its value. The move benefitted the wealthy and stabilized the investment climate but still left millions unemployed or struggling.

Retreat from Reconstruction

The economic spiral had immediate political consequences. The Republicans held the White House, the Congress, and most of the nation's statehouses. The public blamed them for the depression. In 1874, for the first time since before the Civil War, Democrats won a majority in the House of Representatives. Republicans held onto the Senate, but a conservative Democratic majority in the lower chamber spelled doom for any more dramatic efforts to reconstruct the South.

Reconstruction by this time had languished. Due to recent appointments, the Supreme Court by 1873 had shifted in a conservative direction. The justices strictly narrowed the application of the Fourteenth Amendment in a set of 1873 decisions called the Slaughterhouse Cases. The Court ruled that Fourteenth Amendment only barred states from denying the equal protection of the law to all citizens but did not pertain to individual acts of discrimination. In a subsequent case, *Minor v. Happersett* (1875), Virginia Minor sued after she was denied voter registration in Missouri because of a state law that limited the franchise to men. The Court ruled that voting rights were not one of the privileges of citizenship protected by the Fourteenth Amendment and that states could regulate who qualified to vote, a decision reinforced by the 1876 *United States vs. Reese* decision, which held that the Fifteenth Amendment did not guarantee an absolute right to vote, but only set limits on the grounds on which the states could limit suffrage.

Meanwhile, Grant began to privately say that the Fifteenth Amendment had been a mistake. "It had done the Negro no good, and has been a hindrance to the South, and by no means a political advantage to the North," he told his cabinet. In this atmosphere of retreat, it was not surprising that the Republican control of southern states slipped. In the old Confederacy, so-called "**Redeemer**" Democrats accused Republicans of spending too much, raising taxes too high, and of having handed the region over to corrupt and incompetent "negro rule." By 1870, all eleven former Confederate states had reentered the Union, and the Redeemers had gained control of the state governments in Tennessee, Virginia, North Carolina, and Georgia. The Redeemer rollback of reform picked up pace after the 1873-1878 depression started, as Republican control ended in Texas, Alabama, and Arkansas between 1873-1874.

Democrats gained control of the Texas legislature in 1873 and stripped Republican Governor Edmund J. Davis of many of his powers. Beginning in 1875, "the Mississippi Plan"—the label given to describe the use of armed gangs, strategic murders, threats, and bribes to prevent African Americans from voting, brought Redeemers to power in that state. In an 1875 election in one black majority county there, not a single African American voted. A massacre of blacks in Vicksburg may have claimed as many as 80 lives. Whites followed similar tactics in South Carolina, where as many as 150 African-American politicians and voters fell to white assassins. The Grant administration lost the will to intervene on behalf of its southern black constituents. Mississippi fell completely in the hands of the Redeemers by the fall of 1876. Going into November of that year, Republicans only held the governorships in Florida, Louisiana, and South Carolina.

The 1876 Presidential Election

It is perhaps fitting that so violent and scandal-ridden an era as Reconstruction should end in one of the most corrupt and controversial presidential elections in United States history. The ballots closed on November 7, 1876, but the disputed final results were not determined until March 2 of the following year, the announcement coming only two days before the new president was to be sworn in. During the five-month interim, the two major parties accused each other of attempting to steal the election. Some Southerners threatened another civil war if the Democratic candidate was not declared the winner, and terror gripped African Americans that they would be re-enslaved if Republicans lost.

Grant's influence within his party had waned and, even though he likely could have secured a third nomination, Grant's association with scandals and the ongoing economic depression worried Republicans that he would lose to the Democrats in the fall. Instead, Republicans settled on a compromise candidate, Ohio Governor Rutherford B. Hayes, an ally with the 1872 Liberal Republican faction whose nomination seemed a rebuke to the corruption of the sitting administration. Hayes told southern friends that he was skeptical of the president's Reconstruction policies. The Democrats also nominated a reform-minded governor, Samuel J. Tilden of New York, who also was a critic of Grant's actions in the South.

Operatives from both parties stuffed ballot boxes, and, in the South, Democrats sometimes placed armed gangs near courthouses to keep Republicans from voting. Tilden clearly won the popular vote, 4,288,546 to 4,034,311, but both parties claimed that they had won the electoral votes in four states: in Oregon where one elector had been replaced when his credentials were challenged, and the three southern states that still had Republican governors and where Union troops still protected black voters. Minus the tally from those states, Tilden had won 184 Electoral College votes, one short of victory. Hayes would have to win all 20 unresolved votes to win the White House. The Constitution states that Congress receives and tallies Electoral College votes before it certifies the results, but it had recently adopted rules that granted members of the House or Senate the power to challenge any Electoral College votes. The House, controlled by Democrats, could block Hayes from winning, and the Senate, controlled by Republicans, could deny Tilden the one remaining vote he needed for victory.

Revisionist History:
Creating the "Lost Cause" Mythology

Before President Rutherford B. Hayes withdrew the last of the Union troops from the South in 1877, white Southerners who had supported the Confederacy during the war began concocting legends about the Civil War and Reconstruction that came to be known as the "Myth of the Lost Cause." The Lost Cause mythology portrayed the leaders and soldiers of the Confederacy as virtuous people in a sinful world and closer to God than their materialistic "Yankee" combatants.

After the Civil War, Lost Cause mythologists insisted that southern slaves had been treated lovingly like family members by their masters. Confederate defeat, the mythology insisted, emanated from the wiles of Satan or was God's test of faith, similar to the travails endured by the Hebrews during their forty years in the desert after leaving Egypt. Pastors like Episcopalian cleric Randolph McKim compared the suffering of Confederate leaders like General Robert E. Lee to that of Jesus on the cross. In any case, the legends insisted, the Confederate soldiers had been braver and smarter and had lost only because the northern states were richer, more populous, better-armed, and more ruthless. Promoters of the Lost Cause portrayed men who waged war on their country not as traitors but as patriots and heroes.

By the end of Reconstruction, white Southerners observed annual memorial days for fallen Confederates. Meanwhile, groups such as the Sons of Confederate Veterans, established in 1889, and the United Daughters of the Confederacy (UDC), organized in 1894, dedicated themselves to spreading the Lost Cause Gospel nationwide.

The UDC raised money to build and maintain at least 700 Confederate monuments honoring the Lost Cause across the United States. Most rose on the national landscape during the peak of segregation, voting restriction laws like the poll tax, and lynching between the 1890s and the 1930s, and during the struggles over desegregation in the 1950s and the 1960s.

Mildred Lewis Rutherford, the historian general of the UDC from 1911-1916, declared in one speech "The Negroes under the institution of slavery were well-fed, well-clothed, and well-housed. How hard it was for us to make the North understand this!" In another speech, she asked whether African Americans had benefitted from freedom since the war. "As a race," she said, "unhesitatingly no!"

The UDC also tried to erase the memory of the many white Southerners who, along with slaves, resisted the Confederate government. In 1911, a monument went up at the Cooke County Courthouse in Gainesville, Texas, the scene of a mass hanging of 42 suspected Union supporters by backers of the Confederacy in 1862. The inscription at the bottom of the Gainesville monument reads, "No nation rose so white and fair/None fell so free of crime." Monuments also went up in southern states that stayed in the Union, such as Kentucky, Missouri, and West Virginia, the latter of which broke off from Virginia to stay in the Union.

Even historians like William Dunning at Columbia University in New York took up the Lost Cause. Many of Dunning's graduate students wrote public school textbooks that were used across the United States. These books portrayed pre-Civil War abolitionists as deranged fanatics unconcerned about tearing the country apart. These historians described freemen as ignorant, unintelligent, and childlike, and completely unprepared to become citizens. The "Dunning School" also falsely claimed that terrorist groups like the Klan had saved the South from "Negro rule," an era of supposed black domination marked by political corruption and incompetence.

These scholars gave credibility to the UDC, which held annual history essay contests. A Seattle student won a UDC "loving cup" for her pro-KKK essay. The scholars also influenced American popular culture and inspired the hit 1915 silent film **The Birth of a Nation**, *which depicted black Union soldiers as rapists and the Klan as southern saviors; and the novel* **Gone with the Wind**. *In Margaret Mitchell's novel, she describes the freedmen as "creatures of small intelligence" who handled their right to vote "like monkeys or small children . . . they ran wild." As the historians Warren Beck and Myles Clowers noted, "More Americans have learned the story of the South during the Civil War and Reconstruction from Margaret Mitchell's* **Gone with the Wind** *than from all of the learned volumes on this period."*

Gone with the Wind *was adapted into a highly popular movie in 1939. Confederate monuments became a political controversy in recent years. Neo-Nazis rallied in Charlottesville, Va., on August 11-12, 2017, to protest the proposed removal of a Robert E. Lee statue. An anti-monument protestor, Heather Heyer, was murdered by one of the white nationalists. In the last two years, statutes of Lee and other Confederate heroes have come down in Austin, Baltimore, Dallas, New Orleans, and other cities.*

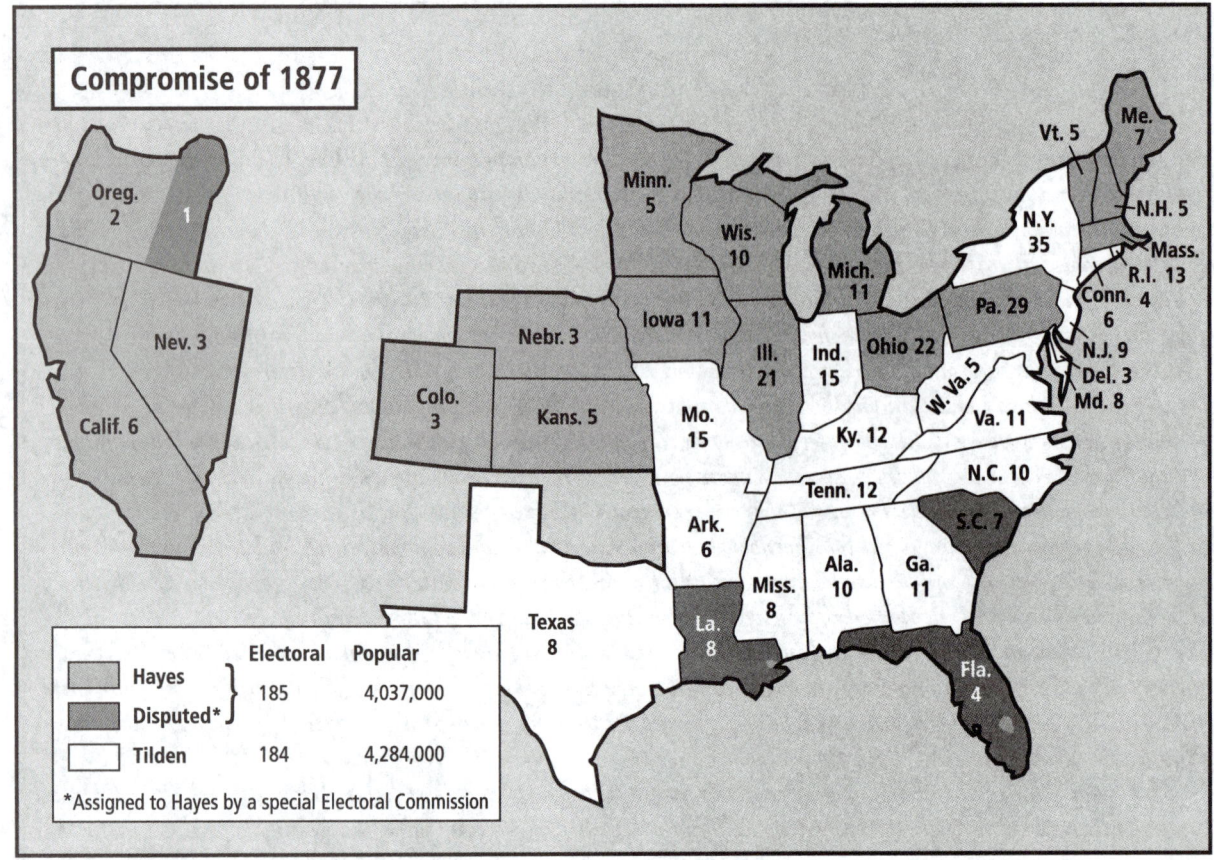

Compromise of 1877

	Electoral	Popular
Hayes } Disputed* }	185	4,037,000
Tilden	184	4,284,000

*Assigned to Hayes by a special Electoral Commission

Map 17.3   The Election of 1876

To resolve this logjam, the Congress voted to create a special Electoral Commission, designed to be as balanced as possible in such a hyper-partisan environment. The commission featured five Republicans and five Democrats from the Congress and five justices from the Supreme Court. Congress picked four justices, two Democratic and two Republican appointees and left it to the Court to pick a fifth member to round out the 15-member commission. Both parties expected Justice David Davis of Illinois, a genuine independent, to become the last member of the commission, but the night before the Congress approved the commission's creation, the Illinois Legislature named Davis to the United States Senate. (Voters did not directly elect senators until the Seventeenth Amendment, ratified in 1913). Congress established the commission anyway. Instead of Davis, a Republican, Joseph Bradley, filled the last seat, leaving the commission with eight Republicans and seven Democrats. Predictably, the commission voted 8-7 along strictly party lines to award all twenty disputed electoral votes to Hayes, and thus Hayes edged Tilden by a 185-184 count in the Electoral College.

Throughout this crisis, southern newspapers ran headlines like "Tilden or War!" Yet, the reaction to the commission's decision turned out to be mild. Some historians believe that the waters had been calmed behind the scenes through the so-called "**Compromise of 1877**" in which, in return for Democrats agreeing to accept Hayes as president, Hayes would withdraw troops protecting the Republican state governments in Louisiana, South Carolina, and Florida. After the election, the Union troops were withdrawn, bringing a final, fitful end to Reconstruction. As one Louisiana freedman put it, "The whole South—every state in the South—has got into the hands of the very men that held us as slaves."

RECONSTRUCTION: THE TURNING POINT THAT NEVER TURNED

The Compromise of 1877 brought black dreams in the South to a crashing halt. After Reconstruction, sharecropping, which left black farmers in an endless cycle of debt and poverty, became their typical destiny. As Redeemers assumed control of southern states, they rolled back state spending and many reforms Republicans had enacted. Black schools vanished in many places, and the remaining schools struggled with meager funds. Meanwhile, segregation in the following years would become a new means of enforcing white supremacy. What came to be known as "Jim Crow" aimed at preventing poor blacks and whites from making common political cause.

When Union troops withdrew, enforcement of the Fourteenth and Fifteenth Amendments vanished, making citizenship for African Americans largely symbolic and voting rights almost entirely fictitious. Northern whites disillusioned about progress in the South looked the other way. The states north of the Mason-Dixon line and on the West Coast would, from the 1880s until World War I, experience an unprecedented wave of immigration primarily from Northern and Southern Europe, and from China and Japan. Americans of Northern and Western European descent in the North and West saw these new-comers as racial aliens, as inferiors. Anti-black racism had never disappeared in the North. Now it spiked again along with anti-immigrant prejudice, and northern whites empathized to a greater degree with the bigotry of their southern neighbors. Northern whites largely responded with apathy as southern lynchings of mostly black men, women, and even children became a weekly spectacle of violence that sometimes drew an audience of thousands.

The South, meanwhile, became a nation within a nation. It remained deeply rural as the North became more industrial. Its society was defined by the divide between black and white, while the North and the West became ever more diverse. The South remained poorly educated as public schools advanced on the other side of the Mason-Dixon line. As voting rights and democratic participation expanded in the North and West, the South increasingly blocked voting and the Democrats suffocated dissent in the South until one-party rule began to collapse in the 1960s. Technically, the United States became a single nation again between 1863-1877. In reality, the South in many ways increasingly became a land unto itself, cut off from the dramatic changes enveloping the other states in the emerging industrial age.

Chronology

1863 The Emancipation Proclamation goes into effect and Lincoln issues his Proclamation of Amnesty and Reconstruction.

1864 Lincoln pocket vetoes Wade-Davis Bill.

1865 The Freedmen's Bureau is established.
The Civil War ends.
Lincoln is assassinated.
General Sherman issues Special Order No. 15.
Black Codes enacted by southern legislatures.
Thirteenth Amendment is ratified.

1866 Congress passes Civil Rights Act and extends the life of the Freedmen's Bureau.
The Ku Klux Klan founded.

1867 Congressional Reconstruction Act.
U. S. purchases Alaska from Russia.
Congress passes Military Reconstruction Acts, Tenure of Office Act.

1868 President Johnson is impeached but acquitted.
Fourteenth Amendment ratified.
Ulysses S. Grant elected president.

1870 Ratification of the Fifteenth Amendment.
Last four southern states admitted to the Union.
Enforcement Act.

1871 Ku Klux Klan Act.

1872 Grant re-elected president.

1873 Financial panic leads to five-year depression.

1875 Whiskey Ring scandal further discredits Grant administration.
Civil Rights Act.

1876 Disputed presidential election of Hayes vs. Tilden.

1877 Electoral commission awards presidency to Rutherford B. Hayes.

SUGGESTED READINGS

Paul H. Bergeron, *Andrew Johnson's Civil War and Reconstruction* (2011).

Josiah Bunting, *Ulysses S. Grant* (2004)

David M. Chalmers, *Hooded Americanism: The History of the Ku Klux Klan* (1987)

Richard Nelson Current, *Those Terrible Carpetbaggers: A Reinterpretation* (1988)

David Herbert Donald, *Lincoln* (1995).

Ellen Carol DuBois, *Feminism and Suffrage: The Emergence of an Independent Women's Movement in America, 1848-1869* (1978).

W.E.B. Du Bois, *Black Reconstruction in America, 1860-1880* (1935).

Eric Foner, *Reconstruction: America's Unfinished Revolution, 1863-1877* (1988).

Herbert G. Gutman, *The Black Family in Slavery and Freedom, 1750-1925* (1976).

Richard L. Hume and Jerry B. Gough, *Blacks, Carpetbagger, and Scalawags: The Constitutional Conventions of Radical Reconstruction* (2008).

Leon F. Litwack, *Been in the Storm So Long: The Aftermath of Slavery* (1980).

Louis P. Masur, *Lincoln's Hundred Days: The Emancipation Proclamation and the War for the Union* (2012).

Eric L. McKitrick, *Andrew Johnson and Reconstruction* (1960).

Michael Perman, *Emancipation and Reconstruction, 1862-1879* (1987)

Michael Phillips, *White Metropolis: Race, Ethnicity, and Religion in Dallas, 1841-2001* (2006).

Roger L. Ransom, *Conflict and Compromise: The Political Economy of Slavery, Emancipation, and the American Civil War* (1989).

Roger L. Ransom and Richard Sutch, *One Kind of Freedom: The Economic Consequences of Emancipation* (1977)

Hannah Rosen, *Terror in the Heart of Freedom: Citizenship, Sexual Violence, and the Meaning of Race in the Postemancipation South* (2009).

Jean Edward Smith, *Grant* (2001).

Kenneth M. Stampp, *The Era of Reconstruction, 1865-1877* (1965).

Mark Wahlgren Sumners, *A Dangerous Stir: Fear, Paranoia, and the Making of Reconstruction* (2009).

___.*The Ordeal of the Reunion: A New History of Reconstruction* (2014).

Hans L. Trefouse, *Andrew Johnson: A Biography* (1989).

Wyn Craig Wade, *The Fiery Cross: The Ku Klux Klan in America* (1987).

Review Questions

1. What was the Emancipation Proclamation and why did Lincoln word the document the way he did?

2. How did freedmen respond to news of their emancipation?

3. Describe the three major phases of Reconstruction—Wartime (under Lincoln), Presidential (under Johnson), and Congressional. What were the goals for each phase? How successful were they? How and why did each phase end?

4. Explain how sharecropping worked. How was it that sharecroppers were never able to escape debt?

5. Describe the Southern backlash to black political gains, including the rise of the Ku Klux Klan.

Glossary of Important People and Concepts

Alaska purchase
Black Codes
"Carpetbaggers"
Compromise of 1877
Crédit Mobilier Affair
Fifteenth Amendment
Fourteenth Amendment
Freedmen's Bureau
Ulysses S. Grant
Impeachment
Andrew Johnson
Ku Klux Klan
Liberal Republicans
Abraham Lincoln
Panic of 1873
Radical Republicans
Reconstruction Acts of 1867
Redeemers
Santo Domingo Affair
"Scalawags"
Thaddeus Stevens
Ten Percent Plan
Tenure of Office Act of 1867
Thirteenth Amendment
Wade-Davis Bill

APPENDIX A

Declaration of Independence

Congress, July 4, 1776

When, in the course of human events, it becomes necessary for one people to dissolve the political bonds which have connected them with another, and to assume, among the powers of the earth, the separate and equal station to which the laws of nature and of nature's God entitle them, a decent respect to the opinions of mankind requires that they should declare the causes which impel them to the separation.

We hold these truths to be self-evident: That all men are created equal; that they are endowed by their Creator with certain unalienable rights; that among these are life, liberty and the pursuit of happiness; that, to secure these rights, governments are instituted among men, deriving their just powers from the consent of the governed; that whenever any form of government becomes destructive of these ends, it is the right of the people to alter or to abolish it, and to institute new government, laying its foundation on such principles, and organizing its powers in such form, as to them shall seem most likely to effect their safety and happiness. Prudence, indeed, will dictate that governments long established should not be changed for light and transient causes; and accordingly all experience hath shown that mankind are more disposed to suffer, while evils are sufferable, than to right themselves by abolishing the forms to which they are accustomed. But when a long train of abuses and usurpations, pursuing invariably the same object, evinces a design to reduce them under absolute despotism, it is their right, it is their duty, to throw off such government, and to provide new guards for their future security. Such has been the patient sufferance of these colonies; and such is now the necessity which constrains them to alter their former systems of government. The history of the present King of Great Britain is a history of repeated injuries and usurpations, all having in direct object the establishment of an absolute tyranny over these states. To prove this, let facts be submitted to a candid world.

He has refused his assent to laws, the most wholesome and necessary for the public good.

He has forbidden his governors to pass laws of immediate and pressing importance, unless suspended in their operation till his assent should be obtained; and, when so suspended, he has utterly neglected to attend to them.

He has refused to pass other laws for the accommodation of large districts of people, unless those people would relinquish the right of representation in the legislature, a right inestimable to them, and formidable to tyrants only.

He has called together legislative bodies at places unusual, uncomfortable, and distant from the depository of their public records, for the sole purpose of fatiguing them into compliance with his measures.

He has dissolved representative houses repeatedly, for opposing, with many firmness, his invasions on the rights of the people.

He has refused for a long time, after such dissolutions, to cause others to be elected; whereby the legislative powers, incapable of annihilation, have returned to the people at large for their exercise; the state remaining, in the mean time, exposed to all the dangers of invasions from without and convulsions within.

He has endeavored to prevent the population of these states; for that purpose obstructing the laws for naturalization of foreigners; refusing to pass others to encourage their migrations hither, and raising the conditions of new appropriations of lands.

He has obstructed the administration of justice, by refusing his assent to laws establishing judiciary powers.

He has made judges dependent on his will alone, for the tenure of their offices, and the amount and payment of their salaries.

He has erected a multitude of new offices, and sent hither swarms of officers to harass our people and eat out their substance.

He has kept among us, in times of peace, standing armies, without the consent of our legislatures.

He has affected to render the military independent of, and superior to, the civil power.

He has combined with others to subject us to jurisdiction foreign to our constitution, and unacknowledged by our laws, giving his assent to their acts of pretended legislation:

For quartering large bodies of armed troops among us;

For protecting them, by a mock trial, from punishment for any murder which they should commit on the inhabitants of these states;

For cutting off our trade with all parts of the world;

For imposing taxes on us without our consent;

For depriving us, in many cases, of the benefits of trial by jury;

For transporting us beyond seas, to be tried for pretended offenses;

For abolishing the free system of English laws in a neighboring province, establishing therein an arbitrary government, and enlarging its boundaries, so as to render it at once an example and fit instrument for introducing the same absolute rule into these colonies;

For taking away our charters, abolishing our most valuable laws, and altering fundamentally the forms of our governments;

For suspending our own legislatures, and declaring themselves invested with power to legislate for us in all cases whatsoever.

He has abdicated government here, by declaring us out of his protection and waging war against us.

He has plundered our seas, ravaged our coasts, burned our towns, and destroyed the lives of our people.

He is at this time transporting large armies of foreign mercenaries to complete the works of death, desolation and tyranny already begun with circumstances of cruelty and perfidy scarcely paralleled in the most barbarous ages, and totally unworthy the head of a civilized nation.

He has constrained our fellow-citizens, taken captive on the high seas, to bear arms against their country, to become the executioners of their friends and brethren, or to fall themselves by their hands.

He has excited domestic insurrections among us, and has endeavored to bring on the inhabitants of our frontiers the merciless Indian savages, whose known rule of warfare is an undistinguished destruction of all ages, sexes, and conditions.

In every stage of these oppressions we have petitioned for redress in the most humble terms; our repeated petitions have been answered only by repeated injury. A prince, whose character is thus marked by every act which may define a tyrant, is unfit to be the ruler of a free people.

Nor have we been wanting in our attentions to our British brethren. We have warned them, from time to time, of attempts by their legislature to extend an unwarrantable jurisdiction over us. We have reminded them of the circumstances of our emigration and settlement here. We have appealed to their native justice and magnanimity, and we have conjured them, by the ties of our common kindred, to disavow these usurpations, which would inevitably interrupt our connections and correspondence. They, too, have been deaf to the voice of justice and of consanguinity. We must, therefore, acquiesce in the necessity which denounces our separation, and hold them, as we hold the rest of mankind, enemies in war, in peace friends.

We, therefore, the representatives of the United States of America, in General Congress assembled, appealing to the Supreme Judge of the world for the rectitude of our intentions, do, in the name and by authority of the good people of these colonies, solemnly publish and declare, that these United Colonies are, and of right ought to be, FREE AND INDEPENDENT STATES; that they are absolved from all allegiance to the British crown, and that all political connection between them and the state of Great Britain is, and ought to be, totally dissolved; and that, as free and independent states, they have full power to levy war, conclude peace, contract alliances, establish commerce, and do all other acts and things which independent states may of right do. And for the support of this declaration, with a firm reliance on the protection of Divine Providence, we mutually pledge to each other our lives, our fortunes, and our sacred honor.

JOHN HANCOCK

BUTTON GWINNETT
LYMAN HALL
GEO. WALTON
WM. HOOPER
JOSEPH HEWES
JOHN PENN
EDWARD RUTLEDGE
THOS. HEYWARD, JUNR.
THOMAS LYNCH, JUNR.
ARTHUR MIDDLETON
SAMUEL CHASE
WM. PACA
THOS. STONE
CHARLES CARROLL OF CARROLLTON
GEORGE WYTHE
RICHARD HENRY LEE
TH. JEFFERSON
BENJ. HARRISON

THOS. NELSON, JR.
FRANCIS LIGHTFOOT LEE
CARTER BRAXTON
ROBT. MORRIS
BENJAMIN RUSH
BENJA. FRANKLIN
JOHN MORTON
GEO. CLYMER
JAS. SMITH
GEO. TAYLOR
JAMES WILSON
GEO. ROSS
CAESAR RODNEY
GEO READ
THO. M'KEAN
WM. FLOYD
PHIL. LIVINGSTON
FRANS. LEWIS
LEWIS MORRIS

RICHD. STOCKTON
JNO. WITHERSPOON
FRAS. HOPKINSON
JOHN HART
ABRA. CLARK
JOSIAH BARTLETT
WM. WHIPPLE
SAML. ADAMS
JOHN ADAMS
ROBT. TREAT PAINE
ELBRIDGE GERRY
STEP. HOPKINS
WILLIAM ELLERY
ROGER SHERMAN
SAM'EL HUNTINGTON
WM. WILLIAMS
OLIVER WOLCOTT
MATTHEW THORNTON

APPENDIX B

The Constitution of the United States of America

PREAMBLE

We the people of the United States, in order to form a more perfect union, establish justice, insure domestic tranquility, provide for the common defense, promote the general welfare, and secure the blessings of liberty to ourselves and our posterity, do ordain and establish this Constitution for the United States of America.

ARTICLE I.—THE LEGISLATIVE ARTICLE

Section 1. All legislative powers herein granted shall be vested in a Congress of the United States, which shall consist of a Senate and a House of Representatives.

House of Representatives: Composition, Qualification, Apportionment, Impeachment Power

Section 2. The House of Representatives shall be composed of members chosen every second year by the people of the several States, and the electors in each State shall have the qualifications requisite for electors of the most numerous branch of the State Legislature.

No person shall be a Representative who shall not have attained to the age of twenty-five years, and been seven years a citizen of the United States, and who shall not, when elected, be an inhabitant of that State in which he shall be chosen.

Representatives and direct taxes shall be apportioned among the several States which may be included within this Union, according to their respective numbers, *which shall be determined by adding to the whole number of free persons, including those bound to service for a term of years and excluding Indians not taxed, three-fifths of all other persons.* The actual enumeration shall be made within three years after the first meeting of the Congress of the United States, and within every subsequent term of ten years, in such manner as they shall by law direct. The number of Representatives shall not exceed one for every thirty thousand, but each State shall have at least one Representative;

and until each enumeration shall be made, the State of New Hampshire shall be entitled to choose three, Massachusetts eight, Rhode Island and Providence Plantations one, Connecticut five, New York six, New Jersey four, Pennsylvania eight, Delaware one, Maryland six, Virginia ten, North Carolina five, South Carolina five, and Georgia three.

When vacancies happen in the representation from any State, the Executive authority thereof shall issue writs of election to fill such vacancies.

The House of Representatives shall choose their Speaker and other officers; and shall have the sole power of impeachment.

Senate Composition: Qualifications, Impeachment Trials

Section 3. The Senate of the United States shall be composed of two Senators from each State, *chosen by the legislature thereof,* for six years; and each Senator shall have one vote.

Immediately after they shall be assembled in consequence of the first election, they shall be divided as equally as may be into three classes. The seats of the Senators of the first class shall be vacated at the expiration of the second year, of the second class at the expiration of the fourth year, and of the third class at the expiration of the sixth year, so that one-third may be chosen every second year; and if vacancies happen by resignation or otherwise, during the recess of the legislature of any State, the Executive thereof may make temporary appointments until the next meeting of the legislature, which shall then fill such vacancies.

No person shall be a Senator who shall not have attained to the age of thirty years, and been nine years a citizen of the United States, and who shall not, when elected, be an inhabitant of that State for which he shall be chosen.

The Vice President of the United States shall be President of the Senate, but shall have no vote, unless they be equally divided.

The Senate shall choose their other officers, and also a President *pro tempore,* in the absence of the Vice President, or when he shall exercise the office of President of the United States.

The Senate shall have the sole power to try all impeachments. When sitting for that purpose, they shall be on oath or affirmation. When the President of the United States is tried, the Chief Justice shall preside: and no person shall be convicted without the concurrence of two-thirds of the members present.

*Passages no longer in effect are printed in italic type.

Judgment in cases of impeachment shall not extend further than to removal from the office, and disqualification to hold and enjoy any office of honor, trust or profit under the United States; but the party convicted shall nevertheless be liable and subject to indictment, trial, judgment and punishment, according to law.

Congressional Elections: Time, Place, Manner

Section 4. The times, places and manner of holding elections for Senators and Representatives shall be prescribed in each State by the legislature thereof; but the Congress may at any time by law make or alter such regulations, except as to the places of choosing Senators.

The Congress shall assemble at least once in every year, and such meeting *shall be on the first Monday in December, unless they shall by law appoint a different day.*

Powers and Duties of the Houses

Section 5. Each house shall be the judge of the elections, returns and qualifications of its own members, and a majority of each shall constitute a quorum to do business; but a smaller number may adjourn from day to day, and may be authorized to compel the attendance of absent members, in such manner, and under such penalties, as each house may provide.

Each house may determine the rules of its proceedings, punish its members for disorderly behavior, and with the concurrence of two-thirds, expel a member.

Each house shall keep a journal of its proceedings, and from time to time publish the same, excepting such parts as may in their judgment require secrecy; and the yeas and nays of the members of either house on any question shall, at the desire of one-fifth of those present, be entered on the journal.

Neither house, during the session of Congress, shall, without the consent of the other, adjourn for more than three days, nor to any other place than that in which the two houses shall be sitting.

Rights of Members

Section 6. The Senators and Representatives shall receive a compensation for their services, to be ascertained by law and paid out of the treasury of the United States. They shall in all cases except treason, felony and breach of the peace, be privileged from arrest during their attendance at the session of their respective houses, and in going to and returning from the same; and for any speech or debate in either house, they shall not be questioned in any other place.

No Senator or Representative shall, during the time for which he was elected, be appointed to any civil office under the authority of the United States, which shall have been created, or the emoluments whereof shall have been increased, during such time; and no person holding any office under the United States shall be a member of either house during his continuance in office.

Legislative Powers: Bills and Resolutions

Section 7. All bills for raising revenue shall originate in the House of Representatives; but the Senate may propose or concur with amendments as on other bills.

Every bill which shall have passed the House of Representatives and the Senate, shall, before it become a law, be presented to the President of the United States; if he approve he shall sign it, but if not he shall return it with objections to that house in which it originated, who shall enter the objections at large on their journal, and proceed to reconsider it. If after such reconsideration two-thirds of that house shall agree to pass the bill, it shall be sent, together with the objections, to the other house, by which it shall likewise be reconsidered, and if approved by two-thirds of that house, it shall become a law. But in all such cases the votes of both houses shall be determined by yeas and nays, and the names of the persons voting for and against the bill shall be entered on the journal of each house respectively. If any bill shall not be returned by the President within ten days (Sundays excepted) after it shall have been presented to him, the same shall be a law, in like manner as if he had signed it, unless the Congress by their adjournment prevent its return, in which case it shall not be a law.

Every order, resolution, or vote to which the concurrence of the Senate and House of Representatives may be necessary (except on a question of adjournment) shall be presented to the President of the United States; and before the same shall take effect, shall be approved by him, or being disapproved by him, shall be repassed by two-thirds of the Senate and House of Representatives, according to the rules and limitations prescribed in the case of a bill.

Powers of Congress

Section 8. The Congress shall have power

To lay and collect taxes, duties, imposts and excises, to pay the debts and provide for the common defense and general welfare of the United States; but all duties, imposts and excises shall be uniform throughout the United States;

To borrow money on the credit of the United States;

To regulate commerce with foreign nations, and among the several States, and with the Indian tribes;

To establish an uniform rule of naturalization, and uniform laws on the subject of bankruptcies throughout the United States;

To coin money, regulate the value thereof, and of foreign coin, and fix the standard of weights and measures;

To provide for the punishment of counterfeiting the securities and current coin of the United States;

To establish post offices and post roads;

To promote the progress of science and useful arts by securing for limited times to authors and inventors the exclusive right to their respective writings and discoveries;

To constitute tribunals inferior to the Supreme Court;

To define and punish piracies and felonies committed on the high seas and offenses against the law of nations;

To declare war, grant letters of marque and reprisal, and make rules concerning captures on land and water;

To raise and support armies, but no appropriation of money to that use shall be for a longer term than two years;

To provide and maintain a navy;

To make rules for the government and regulation of the land and naval forces;

To provide for calling forth the militia to execute the laws of the Union, suppress insurrections, and repel invasions;

To provide for organizing, arming, and disciplining the militia, and for governing such part of them as may be employed in the service of the United States, reserving to the States respectively the appointment of the officers, and the authority of training the militia according to the discipline prescribed by Congress;

To exercise exclusive legislation in all cases whatsoever, over such district (not exceeding ten miles square) as may, by cession of particular States, and the acceptance of Congress, become the seat of the government of the United States, and to exercise like authority over all places purchased by the consent of the legislature of the State, in which the same shall be, for erection of forts, magazines, arsenals, dock-yards, and other needful buildings;—and

To make all laws which shall be necessary and proper for carrying into execution the foregoing powers, and all other powers vested by this Constitution in the government of the United States, or in any department or officer thereof.

Powers Denied to Congress

Section 9. *The migration or importation of such persons as any of the States now existing shall think proper to admit shall not be prohibited by the Congress prior to the year 1808; but a tax or duty may be imposed on such importation, not exceeding $10 for each person.*

The privilege of the writ of habeas corpus shall not be suspended, unless when in cases of rebellion or invasion the public safety may require it.

No bill of attainder or ex post facto law shall be passed.

No capitation, or other direct, tax shall be laid, unless in proportion to the census or enumeration herein before directed to be taken.

No tax or duty shall be laid on articles exported from any State.

No preference shall be given by any regulation of commerce or revenue to the ports of one State over those of another; nor shall vessels bound to, or from, one State, be obliged to enter, clear, or pay duties in another.

No money shall be drawn from the treasury, but in consequence of appropriations made by law; and a regular statement and account of the receipts and expenditures of all public money shall be published from time to time.

No title of nobility shall be granted by the United States; and no person holding any office of profit or trust under them, shall, without the consent of the Congress, accept of any present, emolument, office, or title, of any kind whatever, from any king, prince, or foreign state.

Powers Denied to the States

Section 10. No State shall enter into any treaty, alliance, or confederation; grant letters of marque and reprisal; coin money; emit bills of credit; make anything but gold and silver coin a tender in payment of debts; pass any bill of attainder, ex post facto law, or law impairing the obligation of contracts, or grant any title of nobility.

No State shall, without the consent of the Congress, lay any imposts or duties on imports or exports, except what may be absolutely necessary for executing its inspection laws: and the net produce of all duties and imposts, laid by any State on imports or exports, shall be for the use of the treasury of the United States; and all such laws shall be subject to the revision and control of the Congress.

No State shall, without the consent of Congress, lay any duty of tonnage, keep troops or ships of war in time of peace, enter into any agreement or compact with another State, or with a foreign power, or engage in war, unless actually invaded, or in such imminent danger as will not admit of delay.

ARTICLE II.—THE EXECUTIVE ARTICLE

Nature and Scope of Presidential Power

Section 1. The executive power shall be vested in a President of the United States of America. He shall hold his office during the term of four years, and, together with the Vice President, chosen for the same term, be elected, as follows:

Each State shall appoint, in such manner as the legislature thereof may direct, a number of electors, equal to the whole number of Senators and Representatives to which the State may be entitled in the Congress; but no Senator or Representative, or person holding an office of trust or profit under the United States, shall be appointed an elector.

The electors shall meet in their respective States, and vote by ballot for two persons, of whom one at least shall not be an inhabitant of the same State with themselves. And they shall make a list of all the persons voted for, and of the number of votes for each; which list they shall sign and certify, and transmit sealed to the seat of government of the United States, directed to the President of the Senate. The President of the Senate shall, in the presence of the Senate and House of Representatives, open all the certificates, and the votes shall then be counted. The person having the greatest number of votes shall be the President, if such number be a majority of the whole number of electors appointed; and if there be more than one who have such majority, and have an equal number of votes, then the House of Representatives shall immediately choose by ballot one of them for President; and if no person have a majority, then from the five highest on the list said house shall in like manner choose the President. But in choosing the President the votes shall be taken by States, the representation from each State having one vote; a quorum for this purpose shall consist of a member or members from two-thirds of the States, and a majority of all the States shall be necessary to a choice. In every case, after the choice of the President, the person having the greatest number of votes of the electors shall be the Vice President. But if there should remain two or more who have equal votes, the Senate shall choose from them by ballot the Vice President.

The Congress may determine the time of choosing the electors, and the day on which they shall give their votes; which day shall be the same throughout the United States.

No person except a natural-born citizen, *or a citizen of the United States at the time of the adoption of this Constitution,* shall be eligible to the office of President; neither shall any person be eligible to that office who shall not have attained to the age of thirty-five years, and been fourteen years a resident within the United States.

In case of the removal of the President from office or of his death, resignation, or inability to discharge the powers and duties of the said office, the same shall devolve on the Vice President, and the Congress may by law provide for the case of removal, death, resignation, or inability, both of the President and Vice President, declaring what officer shall then act as President, and such officer shall act accordingly, until the disability be removed, or a President shall be elected.

The President shall, at stated times, receive for his services a compensation, which shall neither be increased nor diminished during the period for which he shall have been elected, and he shall not receive within that period any other emolument from the United States, or any of them.

Before he enter on the execution of his office, he shall take the following oath or affirmation: —"I do solemnly swear (or affirm) that I will faithfully execute the office of President of the United States, and will to the best of my ability preserve, protect, and defend the Constitution of the United States."

Powers and Duties of the President

Section 2. The President shall be the commander in chief of the army and navy of the United States, and of the militia of the several States, when called into the actual service of the United States; he may require the opinion, in writing, of the principal officer in each of the executive departments, upon any subject relating to the duties of their respective offices, and he shall have power to grant reprieves and pardons for offenses against the United States, except in cases of impeachment.

He shall have power, by and with the advice and consent of the Senate, to make treaties, provided two-thirds of the Senators present concur; and he shall nominate, and by and with the advice and consent of the Senate, shall appoint ambassadors, other public ministers and consuls, judges of the Supreme Court, and all other officers of the United States, whose appointments are not herein otherwise provided for, and which shall be established by law: but the Congress may by law vest the appointment of such inferior officers, as they think proper, in the President alone, in the courts of law, or in the heads of departments.

The President shall have power to fill up all vacancies that may happen during the recess of the Senate, by granting commissions which shall expire at the end of their next session.

Section 3. He shall from time to time give to the Congress information of the state of the Union, and recommend to their consideration such measures as he shall judge necessary and expedient; he may, on extraordinary occasions, convene both houses, or either of them, and in case of disagreement between them, with respect to the time of adjournment, he may adjourn them to such time as he shall think proper; he shall receive ambassadors and other public ministers; he shall take care that the laws be faithfully executed, and shall commission all the officers of the United States.

Section 4. The President, Vice President and all civil officers of the United States shall be removed from office on impeachment for, and on conviction of, treason, bribery, or other high crimes and misdemeanor.

ARTICLE III.—THE JUDICIAL ARTICLE

Section 1. The judicial power of the United States shall be vested in one Supreme Court, and in such inferior courts as the Congress may from time to time ordain and establish. The judges, both of the Supreme and inferior courts, shall hold their offices during good behavior, and shall, at stated times, receive for their services a compensation which shall not be diminished during their continuance in office.

Jurisdiction

Section 2. The judicial power shall extend to all cases, in law and equity, arising under this Constitution, the laws of the United States, and treaties made, or which shall be made, under their authority;—to all cases affecting ambassadors, other public ministers and consuls;—to all cases of admiralty and maritime jurisdiction;—to controversies to which the United States shall be a party;—to controversies between two or more States;—*between a state and citizens of another state*;—between citizens of different States;—between citizens of the same State claiming lands under grants of different States, and between a State, or the citizens thereof, and foreign states, citizens or subjects.

In all cases affecting ambassadors, other public ministers and consuls, and those in which a State shall be party, the Supreme Court shall have original jurisdiction. In all the other cases before mentioned, the Supreme Court shall have appellate jurisdiction, both as to law and fact, with such exceptions, and under such regulations, as the Congress shall make.

The trial of all crimes, except in cases of impeachment, shall be by jury; and such trial shall be held in the State where said crimes shall have been committed; but when not committed within any State, the trial shall be at such place or places as the Congress may by law have directed.

Treason

Section 3. Treason against the United States shall consist only in levying war against them, or in adhering to their enemies, giving them aid and comfort. No person shall be convicted of treason unless on the testimony of two witnesses to the same overt act, or on confession in open court.

The Congress shall have power to declare the punishment of treason, but no attainder of treason shall work corruption of blood, or forfeiture except during the life of the person attained.

ARTICLE IV.—INTERSTATE RELATIONS

Full Faith and Credit Clause

Section 1. Full Faith and credit shall be given in each State to the public acts, records, and judicial proceedings of every other State. And the Congress may by general laws prescribe the manner in which such acts, records and proceedings shall be proved, and the effect thereof.

Privileges and Immunities; Interstate Extradition

Section 2. The citizens of each State shall be entitled to all privileges and immunities of citizens in the several States.

A person charged in any State with treason, felony or other crime, who shall flee from justice, and be found in another State, shall on demand of the executive authority of the State from which he fled, be delivered up, to be removed to the State having jurisdiction of the crime.

No person held to service or labor in one State, under the laws thereof, escaping into another, shall, in consequence of any law or regulation therein, be discharged from such service or labor, but shall be delivered up on claim of the party to whom such service or labor may be due.

Admission of States

Section 3. New States may be admitted by the Congress into this Union; but no new State shall be formed or erected within the jurisdiction of any other State; nor any State be formed by the junction of two or more States, or parts of States, without the consent of the legislatures of the States concerned as well as of the Congress.

The Congress shall have power to dispose of and make all needful rules and regulations respecting the territory or other property belonging to the United States; and nothing in this Constitution shall be so construed as to prejudice any claims of the United States, or of any particular State.

Republican Form of Government

Section 4. The United States shall guarantee to every State in this Union a republican form of government, and shall protect each of them against invasion; and on application of the legislature, or of the executive (when the legislature cannot be convened) against domestic violence.

ARTICLE V.—THE AMENDING POWER

The Congress, whenever two-thirds of both houses shall deem it necessary, shall propose amendments to this Constitution, or, on the application of the legislatures of two-thirds of the several States, shall call a convention for proposing amendments, which, in either case, shall be valid to all intents and purposes, as part of this Constitution, when ratified by the legislatures of three-fourths of the several States, or by conventions in three-fourths thereof, as the one or the other mode of ratification may be proposed by the Congress; *provided that no amendment which may be made prior to the year one thousand eight hundred and eight shall in any manner affect the first and fourth clauses in the ninth section of the first article*; and that no State, without its consent, shall be deprived of its equal suffrage in the Senate.

ARTICLE VI.—THE SUPREMACY ACT

All debts contracted and engagements entered into, before the adoption of this Constitution, shall be as valid against the United States under this Constitution, as under the Confederation.

This Constitution, and the laws of the United States which shall be made in pursuance thereof; and all treaties made, or which shall be made, under the authority of the United States, shall be the supreme law of the land; and the judges in every State shall be bound thereby, anything in the Constitution or laws of any State to the contrary notwithstanding.

The Senators and Representatives before mentioned, and the members of the several State legislatures, and all executive and judicial officers, both of the United States and of the several States, shall be bound by oath or affirmation to support this Constitution; but no religious test shall ever be required as a qualification to any office or public trust under the United States.

ARTICLE VII.—RATIFICATION

The ratification of the conventions of nine States shall be sufficient for the establishment of this Constitution between States so ratifying the same.

Done in Convention by the unanimous consent of the States present, the seventeenth day of September in the year of our Lord one thousand seven hundred and eighty-seven and of the Independence of the United States of America the twelfth. In witness whereof we have hereunto subscribed our names.

GEORGE WASHINGTON
President and Deputy from Virginia

New Hampshire	*New York*	*Delaware*	*Pennsylvania*
JOHN LANGDON	ALEXANDER HAMILTON	GEORGE READ	BENJAMIN FRANKLIN
NICHOLAS GILMAN		GUNNING BEDFORD, JR.	THOMAS MIFFLIN
	New Jersey	JOHN DICKINSON	ROBERT MORRIS
Massachusetts	WILLIAM LIVINGSTON	RICHARD BASSETT	GEORGE CLYMER
NATHANIEL GORHAM	DAVID BREARLEY	JACOB BROOM	THOMAS FITZSIMONS
RUFUS KING	WILLIAM PATERSON		JARED INGERSOLL
	JONATHAN DAYTON	*Maryland*	JAMES WILSON
		JAMES MCHENRY	GOUVERNEUR MORRIS
Connecticut		DANIEL OF ST. THOMAS JENIFER	
WILLIAM S. JOHNSON	*North Carolina*	DANIEL CARROLL	
ROGER SHERMAN	WILLIAM BLOUNT		
	RICHARD DOBBS SPRAIGHT		*South Carolina*
	HU WILLIAMSON	*Georgia*	J. RUTLEDGE
Virginia		WILLIAM FEW	CHARLES G. PINCKNEY
JOHN BLAIR		ABRAHAM BALDWIN	PIERCE BUTLER
JAMES MADISON, JR			

THE BILL OF RIGHTS
The first ten Amendments (the Bill of Rights) were adopted in 1791.

AMENDMENT I.—RELIGION, SPEECH ASSEMBLY, AND PETITION

Congress shall make no law respecting an establishment of religion, or prohibiting the free exercise thereof; or abridging the freedom of speech, or of the press; or the right of the people peaceably to assemble, and to petition the government for a redress of grievances.

AMENDMENT II.—MILITIA AND THE RIGHT TO BEAR ARMS

A well-regulated militia being necessary to the security of a free State, the right of the people to keep and bear arms shall not be infringed.

AMENDMENT III.—QUARTERING OF SOLDIERS

No soldier shall, in time of peace, be quartered in any house without the consent of the owner, nor in time of war, but in a manner to be prescribed by law.

AMENDMENT IV.—SEARCHES AND SEIZURES

The right of the people to be secure in their persons, houses, papers, and effects, against unreasonable searches and seizures, shall not be violated, and no warrants shall issue but upon probable cause, supported by oath or affirmation, and particularly describing the place to be searched, and the persons or things to be seized.

AMENDMENT V.—GRAND JURIES, SELF-INCRIMINATION, DOUBLE JEOPARDY, DUE PROCESS, AND EMINENT DOMAIN

No person shall be held to answer for a capital, or otherwise infamous crime, unless on a presentment or indictment of a grand jury, except in cases arising in the land or naval forces, or in the militia, when in actual service in time of war or public danger; nor shall any person be subject for the same offense to be twice put in jeopardy of life or limb; nor shall be compelled in any criminal case to be a witness against himself, nor be deprived of life, liberty, or property, without due process of law; nor shall private property be taken for public use without just compensation.

AMENDMENT VI.—CRIMINAL COURT PROCEDURES

In all criminal prosecutions, the accused shall enjoy the right to a speedy and public trial, by an impartial jury of the State and district wherein the crime shall have been committed, which district shall have been previously ascertained by law, and to be informed of the nature and cause of the accusation; to be confronted with the witnesses against him; to have compulsory process for obtaining witnesses in his favor, and to have the assistance of counsel for his defense.

AMENDMENT VII.—TRIAL BY JURY IN COMMON LAW CASES

In suits at common law, where the value in controversy shall exceed twenty dollars, the right of trial by jury shall be preserved, and no fact tried by a jury shall be otherwise reexamined in any court of the United States, than according to the rules of the common law.

AMENDMENT VIII.—BAIL, CRUEL AND UNUSUAL PUNISHMENT

Excessive bail shall not be required, nor excessive fines imposed, nor cruel and unusual punishments inflicted.

AMENDMENT IX.—RIGHTS RETAINED BY THE PEOPLE

The enumeration in the Constitution, of certain rights, shall not be construed to deny or disparage others retained by the people.

AMENDMENT X.—RESERVED POWERS OF THE STATES

The powers not delegated to the United States by the Constitution, nor prohibited by it to the States, are reserved to the States respectively, or to the people.

PRE-CIVIL WAR AMENDMENTS

AMENDMENT XI.—SUITS AGAINST THE STATES
[Adopted 1798]

The judicial power of the United States shall not be construed to extend to any suit in law or equity, commenced or prosecuted against one of the United States by citizens of another State, or by citizens or subjects of any foreign state.

AMENDMENT XII.—ELECTION OF THE PRESIDENT
[Adopted 1804]

The electors shall meet in their respective *States*, and vote by ballot for President and Vice President, one of whom, at least, shall not be an inhabitant of the same State with themselves; they shall name in their ballots the person voted for as President, and in distinct ballots the person voted for as Vice President, and they shall make distinct lists of all persons voted for as President, and of all persons voted for as Vice President, and of the number of votes for each, which lists they shall sign and certify, and transmit sealed to the seat of the government of the United States, directed to the President of the Senate;—the President of the Senate shall, in the presence of the Senate and House of Representatives, open all the certificates and the votes shall then be counted;—the person having the greatest number of votes for President shall be the President, if such number be a majority of the whole number of electors appointed; and if no person have such majority, then from the persons having the highest numbers not exceeding three on the list of those voted for as President, the House of Representatives shall choose immediately, by ballot, the President. But in choosing the President, the votes shall be taken by States, the representation from each State having one vote; a quorum for this purpose shall consist of a member or members from two-thirds of the States, and a majority of all the States shall be necessary to a choice. And if the House of Representatives shall not choose a President whenever the right of choice shall devolve upon them, before *the fourth day of March* next following, then the Vice President shall act as President, as in the case of the death or other constitutional disability of the President.

The person having the greatest number of votes as Vice President shall be the Vice President, if such a number be a majority of the whole number of electors appointed; and if no person have a majority, then from the two highest numbers on the list the Senate shall choose the Vice President; a quorum for the purpose shall consist of two-thirds of the whole number of Senators, and a majority of the whole number shall be necessary to a choice. But no person constitutionally ineligible to the office of President shall be eligible to that of Vice President of the United States.

CIVIL WAR AMENDMENTS

AMENDMENT XIII.—PROHIBITION OF SLAVERY
[Adopted 1865]

Section 1. Neither slavery nor involuntary servitude, except as a punishment for crime whereof the party shall have been duly convicted, shall exist within the United States, or any place subject to their jurisdiction.

Section 2. Congress shall have power to enforce this article by appropriate legislation.

AMENDMENT XIV.—CITIZENSHIP, DUE PROCESS, AND EQUAL PROTECTION OF THE LAWS
[Adopted 1868]

Section 1. All persons born or naturalized in the United States, and subject to the jurisdiction thereof, are citizens of the United States and of the State wherein they reside. No State shall make or enforce any law which shall abridge **the privileges or immunities** of citizens of the United States; nor shall any State deprive any person of life, liberty, or property, without **due process of law**; nor deny to any person within its jurisdiction the **equal protection of the laws**.

Section 2. Representatives shall be apportioned among the several States according to their respective numbers, counting the whole number of persons in each State, excluding Indians not taxed. But when the right to vote at any election for the choice of Electors for President and Vice President of the United States, Representatives in Congress, the executive and judicial officers of a State, or the members of the legislature thereof, is denied to any of the male inhabitants of such State, being twenty-one years of age and citizens of the United States, or in any way abridged, except for participation in rebellion, or other crime, the basis of representation therein shall be reduced in the proportion which the number of such male citizens shall bear to the whole number of male citizens twenty-one years of age in such State.

Section 3. No person shall be a Senator or Representative in Congress, or Elector of President and Vice President, or hold any office, civil or military, under the United States, or under any State, who, having previously taken an oath, as a member of Congress, or as an officer of the United States, or as a member of any State legislature, or as an executive or judicial officer of any State, to support the Constitution of the United States, shall have engaged in insurrection or rebellion against the same, or given aid or comfort to the enemies thereof. Congress may, by a vote of two-thirds of each house, remove such disability.

Section 4. The validity of the public debt of the United States, authorized by law, including debts incurred for payment of pensions and bounties for services in suppressing insurrection or rebellion, shall not be questioned. But neither the United States nor any State shall assume or pay any debt or obligation incurred in aid of insurrection or rebellion against the United States, or any claim for the loss or emancipation of any slave; but all such debts, obligations and claims shall be held illegal and void.

Section 5. The Congress shall have power to enforce, by appropriate legislation, the provisions of this article.

AMENDMENT XV.—THE RIGHT TO VOTE
[Adopted 1870]

Section 1. The right of citizens of the United State to vote shall not be denied or abridged by the United States or by any State on account of race, color, or previous condition of servitude.

Section 2. The Congress shall have power to enforce this article by appropriate legislation.

AMENDMENT XVI.—INCOME TAXES
[Adopted 1913]

The Congress shall have power to lay and collect taxes on incomes, from whatever source derived, without apportionment among the several States, and without regard to any census or enumeration.

AMENDMENT XVII.—DIRECT ELECTION OF SENATORS
[Adopted 1913]

Section 1. The Senate of the United States shall be composed of two Senators from each State, elected by the people thereof, for six years; and each Senator shall have one vote. The electors in each State shall have the qualifications requisite for electors of (voters for) the most numerous branch of the State legislatures.

Section 2. When vacancies happen in the representation of any State in the Senate, the executive authority of such State shall issue writs of election to fill such vacancies: Provided, that the Legislature of any State may empower the executive thereof to make temporary appointments until the people fill the vacancies by election as the Legislature may direct.

Section 3. This amendment shall not be so construed as to affect the election or term of any Senator chosen before it becomes valid as part of the Constitution.

AMENDMENT XVIII.—PROHIBITION
[Adopted 1919; Repealed 1933]

Section 1. *After one year from the ratification of this article the manufacture, sale, or transportation of intoxicating liquors within, the importation thereof into, or the exportation thereof from the United State and all territory subject to the jurisdiction thereof, for beverage purposes, is hereby prohibited.*

Section 2. *The Congress and the several States shall have concurrent power to enforce this article by appropriate legislation.*

Section 3. *This article shall be inoperative unless it shall have been ratified as an amendment to the Constitution by the legislatures of the several States, as provided by the Constitution, within seven years from the date of the submission thereof to the States by the Congress.*

AMENDMENT XIX.—FOR WOMEN'S SUFFRAGE
[Adopted 1920]

Section 1. The right of citizens of the United States to vote shall not be denied or abridged by the United States or by any State on account of sex.

Section 2. The Congress shall have power to enforce this article by appropriate legislation.

AMENDMENT XX.—THE LAME DUCK AMENDMENT
[Adopted 1933]

Section 1. The terms of the President and Vice President shall end at noon on the 20th day of January, and the terms of the Senators and Representatives at noon on the 3rd day of January, of the years in which such terms would have ended if this article had not been ratified; and the terms of their successors shall then begin.

Section 2. The Congress shall assemble at least once in every year, and such meeting shall begin at noon on the 3rd day of January, unless they shall by law appoint a different day.

Section 3. If, at the time fixed for the beginning of the term of the President, the President-elect shall have died, the Vice President-elect shall become President. If a President shall not have been chosen before the time fixed for the beginning of his term, or if the President-elect shall have failed to qualify, then the Vice President-elect shall act as President until a President shall have qualified; and the Congress may by law provide for the case wherein neither a President-elect nor a Vice President-elect shall have qualified, declaring who shall then act as President, or the manner in which one who is to act shall be selected, and such persons shall act accordingly until a President or Vice President shall have qualified.

Section 4. The Congress may by law provide for the case of the death of any of the persons from whom the House of Representatives may choose a President whenever the right of choice shall have devolved upon them, and for the case of the death of any of the persons from whom the Senate may choose a Vice President whenever the right of choice shall have devolved upon them.

Section 5. Section 1 and 2 shall take effect on the 15th day of October following the ratification of this article.

Section 6. This article shall be inoperative unless it shall have been ratified as an amendment to the Constitution by the Legislatures of three-fourths of the several States within seven years from the date of its submission.

AMENDMENT XXI.—REPEAL OF PROHIBITION
[Adopted 1933]

Section 1. The eighteenth article of amendment to the Constitution of the United States is hereby repealed.

Section 2. The transportation or importation into any State, Territory, or Possession of the United States for delivery of use therein of intoxicating liquors, in violation of the laws thereof, is hereby prohibited.

Section 3. This article shall be inoperative unless it shall have been ratified as an amendment to the Constitution by conventions in the several States, as provided in the Constitution, within seven years from the date of submission thereof to the States by the Congress.

AMENDMENT XXII.—NUMBER OF PRESIDENTIAL TERMS
[Adopted 1951]

Section 1. No person shall be elected to the office of President more than twice, and no person who has held the office of President, or acted as President, for more than two years of a term to which some other person was elected President shall be elected to the office of President more than once. But this article shall not apply to any person holding the office of President when this article was proposed by the Congress, and shall not prevent any person who may be holding the office of President, or acting as President, during the term within which this article becomes operative from holding the office of President or acting as President during the remainder of such term.

Section 2. This article shall be inoperative unless it shall have been ratified as an amendment to the Constitution by the legislatures of three-fourths of the several States within seven years from the date of its submission to the States by the Congress.

AMENDMENT XXIII.—PRESIDENTIAL ELECTORS FOR THE DISTRICT OF COLUMBIA [Adopted 1961]

Section 1. The District constituting the seat of Government of the United States shall appoint in such manner as the Congress may direct:

A number of electors of President and Vice President equal to the whole number of Senators and Representatives in Congress to which the District would be entitled if it were a State, but in no event more than the least populous State; they shall be in addition to those appointed by the States, but they shall be considered for the purposes of the election of President and Vice President, to be electors appointed by a State; and they shall meet in the District and perform such duties as provided by the twelfth article of amendment.

Section 2.   The Congress shall have power to enforce this article by appropriate legislation.

AMENDMENT XXIV.—THE ANTI-POLL TAX AMENDMENT
[Adopted 1964]

Section 1.   The right of citizens of the United States to vote in any primary or other election for President or Vice President, for electors for President or Vice President, or for Senator or Representative in Congress, shall not be denied or abridged by the United States or any State by reason of failure to pay any poll tax or other tax.

Section 2.   The Congress shall have power to enforce this article by appropriate legislation.

AMENDMENT XXV.—PRESIDENTIAL DISABILITY, VICE-PRESIDENTIAL VACANCIES
[Adopted 1967]

Section 1.   In case of the removal of the President from office or his death or resignation, the Vice President shall become President.

Section 2.   Whenever there is a vacancy in the office of the Vice President, the President shall nominate a Vice President who shall take office upon confirmation by a majority vote of both Houses of Congress.

Section 3.   Whenever the President transmits to the President pro tempore of the Senate and the Speaker of the House of Representatives his written declaration that he is unable to discharge the powers and duties of his office, and until he transmits to them a written declaration to the contrary, such powers and duties shall be discharged by the Vice President as Acting President.

Section 4.   Whenever the Vice President and a majority of either the principal officers of the executive departments or of such other body as Congress may by law provide, transmit to the President pro tempore of the Senate and the Speaker of the House of Representatives their written declaration that the President is unable to discharge the powers and duties of his office, the Vice President shall immediately assume the powers and duties of the office as Acting President.

Thereafter, when the President transmits to the President pro tempore of the Senate and the Speaker of the House of Representatives his written declaration that no inability exists, he shall resume the powers and duties of his office unless the Vice President and a majority of either the principal officers of the executive department{s} or of such other body as Congress may by law provide, transmit within four days to the President pro tempore of the Senate and the Speaker of the House of Representatives their written declaration that the President is unable to discharge the powers and duties of his office.   Thereupon Congress shall decide the issue, assembling within forty-eight hours for that purpose if not in session.   If the Congress, within twenty-one days after receipt of the latter written declaration, or, if Congress is not in session, within twenty-one days after Congress is required to assemble, determines by two-thirds vote of both Houses that the President is unable to discharge the powers and duties of his office, the Vice President shall continue to discharge the same as Acting President; otherwise, the President shall resume the powers and duties of his office.

AMENDMENT XXVI.—EIGHTEEN-YEAR-OLD VOTE
[Adopted 1971]

Section 1.   The right of citizens of the United States, who are eighteen years of age or older, to vote shall not be denied or abridged by the United States or by any State on account of age.

Section 2.   The Congress shall have power to enforce this article by appropriate legislation.

AMENDMENT XXVII.—VARYING CONGRESSIONAL COMPENSATION
[Adopted 1992]

No law varying the compensation for the service of the Senators and Representatives shall take effect until an election of Representatives shall have intervened.

APPENDIX C

PRESIDENTIAL ELECTIONS

Year	Name	Party Vote	Popular Vote	Electoral College Vote
1789	George Washington			69
1792	George Washington			132
1796	John Adams	Federalist		71
	Thomas Jefferson	Democratic-Republican		68
1800	Thomas Jefferson	Democratic-Republican		73
	John Adams	Federalist		65
1804	Thomas Jefferson	Democratic-Republican		162
	Charles C. Pinckney	Federalist		14
1808	James Madison	Democratic-Republican		122
	Charles C. Pinckney	Federalist		47
1812	James Madison	Democratic-Republican		128
	George Clinton	Federalist		89
1816	James Monroe	Dmocratic-Republican		183
	Rufus King	Federalist		34
1820	James Monroe	Democratic-Republican		231
	John Quincy Adams	Democratic-Republican		1
1824	John Quincy Adams	Democratic-Republican	108,740	84
	Andrew Jackson	Democratic-Republican	153,544	99
	William Crawford	Democratic-Republican	46,618	41
	Henry Clay	Democratic-Republican	47,136	37
1828	Andrew Jackson	Democrat	647,286	178
	John Quincy Adams	National Republican	508,064	83
1832	Andrew Jackson	Democrat	687,502	219
	Henry Clay	National Republican	530,189	49
	Electoral votes not cast		2	
1836	Martin Van Buren	Democrat	765,483	170
	William Henry Harrison	Whig	550,816	73
	Hugh White	Whig	146,107	26
	Daniel Webster	Whig	41,201	14
	Total for the 3 Whigs		739,795	113
1840	William Henry Harrison	Whig	1,274,624	234
	Martin Van Buren	Democrat	1,127,781	60
1844	James K. Polk	Democrat	1,338,464	170
	Henry Clay	Whig	1,300,097	105
1848	Zachary Taylor	Whig	1,360,967	163
	Lewis Cass	Democrat	1,222,342	127
	Martin Van Buren	Free-Soil	291,263	
1852	Franklin Pierce	Democrat	1,601,117	254
	Winfield Scott	Whig	1,385,453	42
	John P. Hale	Free-Soil	155,825	
1856	James Buchanan	Democrat	1,832,955	174
	John Fremont	Republian	1,339,932	114
	Millard Fillmore	Whig-American	871,731	8
1860	Abraham Lincoln	Republican	1,865,593	180
	John C. Breckinridge	Democrat	848,356	72
	Stephen Douglas	Democrat	1,382,713	12
	John Bell	Constitutional Union	592,906	39
1864	Abraham Lincon	Unionist (Republican)	2,206,938	212
	George McClellan	Democrat	1,803,787	21
	Electoral votes not cast		81	
1868	Ulysses S. Grant	Republican	3,013,421	214
	Horatio Seymour	Democrat	2,706,829	80
	Electoral votes not cast		23	

1872	Ulysses S. Grant	Republican	3,596,745	286
	Horace Greeley	Democrat	2,843,446	
	Thomas Hendricks	Democrat		42
	Benjamin Browns	Democrat		18
	Charles Jenkins	Democrat		2
	David Davis	Democrat		1
1876	Rutherford B. Hayes	Republican	4,036,572	185
	Samuel Tilden	Democrat	4,284,020	184
	Peter Cooper	Greenback	81,737	
1880	James A. Garfield	Republican	4,453,295	214
	Winfield S. Hancock	Democrat	4,414,082	155
	James B. Weaver	Greenback-Labor	308,578	
1884	Grover Cleveland	Democrat	4,879,507	219
	James G. Blaine	Republican	4,850,293	182
	Benjamin Butler	Greenback-Labor	175,370	
	John St. John	Prohibition	150,369	
1888	Benjamin Harrison	Republican	5,447,129	233
	Grover Cleveland	Democrat	5,537,857	168
	Clinton Fisk	Prohibition	249,506	
	Anson Streeter	Union Labor	146,935	
1892	Grover Cleveland	Democrat	5,555,426	277
	Benjamin Harrison	Republican	5,182,690	145
	James B. Weaver	People's	1.029,846	22
	John Bidwell	Prohibition	264,133	
1896	William McKinley	Republican	7,102,246	271
	William J. Bryan	Democrat	6,492,559	176
	John Palmer	National Democratic	133,148	
	Joshua Levering	Prohibition	132,007	
1900	William McKinley	Republican	7,218,491	292
	William J. Bryan	Democrat	6,356,734	155
	John C. Wooley	Prohibition	208,914	
	Eugene V. Debs	Socialist	87,814	
1904	Theodore Roosevelt	Republican	7,628,461	336
	Alton B. Parker	Democrat	5,084,223	140
	Eugene V. Debs	Socialist	402,283	
	Silas Swallow	Prohibition	258,536	
	Thomas Watson	People's	117,183	
1908	William Howard Taft	Republican	7,675,320	321
	William J. Bryan	Democrat	6,412,294	162
	Eugene V. Debs	Socialist	420,793	
	Eugene Chafin	Prohibition	253,840	
1912	Woodrow Wilson	Democrat	6,296,547	435
	William Howard Taft	Republican	3,486,720	8
	Theodore Roosevelt	Progressive	4,118,571	86
	Eugene V. Debs	Socialist	900,672	
	Eugene Chafin	Prohibition	206,275	
1916	Woodrow Wilson	Democrat	9,127,695	277
	Charles E. Hughes	Republicn	8,533,507	254
	A.L. Benson	Socialist	585,113	
	J. Frank Hanly	Prohibition	220,506	
1920	Warren Harding	Republican	16,143,407	404
	James M. Cox	Democrat	9,130,328	127
	Eugene V. Debs	Socialist	919,799	
	P.P. Christensen	Farmer-Labor	265,411	
	Aaron Watkins	Prohibiton	189,408	
1924	Calvin Coolidge	Republican	15,718,211	382
	John W. Davis	Democrat	8,385,283	136
	Robert La Follette	Progressive	4,831,289	13
1928	Herbert Hoover	Republican	21,391,993	444
	Alfred E. Smith	Democrat	15,016,169	87
	Norman Thomas	Socialist	267,835	
1932	Franklin D. Roosevelt	Democrat	22,809,638	472
	Herbert C. Hoover	Republican	15,758,901	59
	Norman Thomas	Socialist	881,951	
	William Foster	Communist	102,785	

1936	Franklin D. Roosevelt	Democrat	27,752,869	523
	Alfred M. Landon	Republican	16,674,665	8
	William Lemke	Union	882,479	
	Norman Thomas	Socialist	187,720	
1940	Franklin D. Roosevelt	Democrat	27,307,819	449
	Wendell Willkie	Republican	22,321,018	82
1944	Franklin D. Roosevelt	Democrat	25,606,585	432
	Thomas E. Dewey	Republican	22,014,745	99
1948	Harry S. Truman	Democrat	24,179,345	303
	Thomas E. Dewey	Republican	21,991,291	189
	Strom Thurmond	Dixiecrat	1,176,125	39
	Henry Wallace	Progressive	1,157,326	
	Norman Thomas	Socialist	139,572	
	Claude A. Watson	Prohibition	103,900	
1952	Dwight D. Eisenhower	Republican	33,936,234	442
	Adlai Stevenson II	Democrat	27,314,992	89
	Vincent Hallinan	Progressive	140,023	
1956	Dwight D. Eisenhower	Republican	35,590,472	457
	Adlai Stevenson II	Democrat	26,022,752	73
	T. Coleman Andrews	States' Rights	111,178	
	Walter B. Jones	Democrat		1
1960	John F. Kennedy	Democrat	34,226,731	303
	Richard M. Nixon	Republican	34,108,157	219
	Harry Byrd	Democrat		15
1964	Lyndon B. Johnson	Democrat	43,129,566	486
	Barry Goldwater	Republican	27,178,188	52
1968	Richard M. Nixon	Republican	31,785,480	301
	Hubert H. Humphrey	Democrat	31,275,166	191
	George Wallace	American Independent	9,906,473	46
1972	Richard M. Nixon	Republican	47,170,179	520
	George McGovern	Democrat	29,171,791	17
	John Hospers	Libertarian		1
1976	Jimmy Carter	Democrat	40,830,763	297
	Gerald R. Ford	Republican	39,147,793	240
	Ronald Reagan	Republican		1
1980	Ronald Reagan	Republican	43,904,153	489
	Jimmy Carter	Democrat	35,483,883	49
	John Anderson	Independent candidacy	5,719,437	
1984	Ronald Reagan	Republican	54,455,074	525
	Walter F. Mondale	Democrat	37,577,137	13
1988	George Bush	Republican	48,881,278	426
	Michael Dukakis	Democrat	41,805,374	111
	Lloyd Bentsen	Democrat		1
1992	Bill Clinton	Democrat	43,727,625	370
	George Bush	Republican	38,165,180	168
	Ross Perot	Independent catdidacy	19,236,411	0
1996	Bill Clinton	Democrat	45,628,667	379
	Bob Dole	Republican	37,869,435	159
	Ross Perot	Independent catdidacy	7,874,283	0
2000	George W. Bush	Republican	49,820,518	271
	Albert Gore Jr.	Democrat	50,158,094	267
	Ralph Nader	Green Party	7,866,284	
2004	George W. Bush	Republican	62,040,610	286
	John Kerry	Democrat	59,028,439	251
	Ralph Nader	Green Party	463,653	
2008	Barack Obama	Democrat	66,882,230	365
	John McCain	Republican	58,343,671	173
2012	Barack Obama	Democrat	60,459,974	332
	Mitt Romney	Republican	57,653,982	206
2016	Hillary Clinton	Democrat	65,844,610	227
	Donald Trump	Republican	62,979,636	304

APPENDIX D

Members of the Supreme Court of the United States

Chief Justices	State App't From	Appointed by President	Service
Jay, John	New York	Washington	1789-1795
Rutledge, John*	South Carolina	Washington	1795-1795
Ellsworth, Oliver	Connecticut	Washington	1796-1799
Marshall, John	Virginia	Adams, John	1801-1835
Taney, Roger Brooke	Maryland	Jackson	1836-1864
Chase, Salmon Portland	Ohio	Lincoln	1864-1873
Waite, Morrison Remick	Ohio	Grant	1874-1888
Fuller, Melville Weston	Illinois	Cleveland	1888-1910
White, Edward Douglass	Louisiana	Taft	1910-1921
Taft, William Howard	Connecticut	Harding	1921-1930
Hughes, Charles Evans	New York	Hoover	1930-1941
Stone, Harlan Fiske	New York	Roosevelt F.	1941-1946
Vinson, Fred Moore	Kentucky	Truman	1946-1953
Warren, Earl	California	Eisenhower	1953-1969
Burger, Warren Earl	Virginia	Nixon	1969-1986
Rehnquist, William H.	Virginia	Reagan	1986-2005
Roberts, John G., Jr.	Maryland	Bush, G. W.	2005-

Associate Justices			
Rutledge, John	South Carolina	Washington	1790-1791
Cushing, William	Massachusetts	Washington	1790-1810
Wilson, James	Pennsylvania	Washington	1789-1798
Blair, John	Virginia	Washington	1789-1796
Iredell, James	North Carolina	Washington	1790-1799
Johnson, Thomas	Maryland	Washington	1791-1793
Paterson, William	New Jersey	Washington	1793-1806
Chase, Samuel	Maryland	Washington	1796-1811
Washington, Bushrod	Virginia	Adams, John	1798-1829
Moore, Alfred	North Carolina	Adams, John	1799-1804
Johnson, William	South Carolina	Jefferson	1804-1834
Livingston, Henry Brockholst	New York	Jefferson	1806-1823
Todd, Thomas	Kentucky	Jefferson	1807-1826
Duvall, Gabriel	Maryland	Madison	1811-1836
Story, Joseph	Massachusetts	Madison	1811-1845
Thompson, Smith	New York	Monroe	1823-1843
Trimble, Robert	Kentucky	Adams, J. Q.	1826-1828
McLean, John	Ohio	Jackson	1829-1861
Baldwin, Henry	Pennsylvania	Jackson	1830-1844
Wayne, James Moore	Georgia	Jackson	1835-1867
Barbour, Philip Pendleton	Virginia	Jackson	1836-1841
Catron, John	Tennessee	Jackson	1837-1865

*ActingChief Justice; Senate refused to confirm appointment.

| McKinley, John | Alabama | Van Buren | 1837-1852 |
| Daniel, Peter Vivian | Virginia | Van Buren | 1841-1860 |

Nelson, Samuel	New York	Tyler	1845-1872
Woodbury, Levi	New Hampshire	Polk	1845-1851
Grier, Robert Cooper	Pennsylvania	Polk	1846-1870
Curtis, Benjamin Robbins	Massachusetts	Fillmore	1851-1857
Campbell, John Archibald	Alabama	Pierce	1853-1861
Clifford, Nathan	Maine	Buchanan	1858-1881
Swayne, Noah Haynes	Ohio	Lincoln	1862-1881
Miller, Samuel Freeman	Iowa	Lincoln	1862-1890
Davis, David	Illinois	Lincoln	1862-1877
Field, Stephen Johnson	California	Lincoln	1863-1897
Strong, William	Pennsylvania	Grant	1870-1880
Bradley, Joseph P.	New Jersey	Grant	1870-1892
Hunt, Ward	New York	Grant	1873-1882
Harlan, John Marshall	Kentucky	Hayes	1877-1911
Woods, William Burnham	Georgia	Hayes	1880-1887
Matthews, Stanley	Ohio	Garfield	1881-1889
Gray, Horace	Massachusetts	Arthur	1882-1902
Blatchford, Samuel	New York	Arthur	1882-1893
Lamar, Lucius Quintus C.	Mississippi	Cleveland	1888-1893
Brewer, David Josiah	Kansas	Harrison	1889-1910
Brown, Henry Billings	Michigan	Harrison	1890-1906
Shiras, George, Jr.	Pennsylvania	Harrison	1892-1903
Jackson, Howell Edmunds	Tennessee	Harrison	1893-1895
White, Edward Douglass	Louisiana	Cleveland	1894-1910
Peckham, Rufus Wheeler	New York	Cleveland	1896-1909
McKenna, Joseph	California	McKinley	1898-1925
Holmes, Oliver Wendell	Massachusetts	Roosevelt T.	1902-1932
Day, William Rufus	Ohio	Roosevelt T.	1903-1922
Moody, William Henry	Massachusetts	Roosevelt T.	1906-1910
Lurton, Horace Harmon	Tennessee	Taft	1910-1914
Hughes, Charles Evans	New York	Taft	1910-1916
Van Devanter, Willis	Wyoming	Taft	1910-1937
Lamar, Joseph Rucker	Georgia	Taft	1911-1916
Pitney, Mahlon	New Jersey	Taft	1912-1922
McReynolds, James Clark	Tennessee	Wilson	1914-1941
Brandeis, Louis Dembitz	Massachusetts	Wilson	1916-1939
Clarke, John Hessin	Ohio	Wilson	1916-1922
Sutherland, George	Utah	Harding	1922-1938
Butler, Pierce	Minnesota	Harding	1923-1939
Sanford, Edward Terry	Tennessee	Harding	1923-1930
Stone, Harlan Fiske	New York	Coolidge	1925-1941
Roberts, Owen Josephus	Pennsylvania	Hoover	1930-1945
Cardozo, Benjamin Nathan	New York	Hoover	1932-1938
Black, Hugo Lafayette	Alabama	Roosevelt F.	1937-1971
Reed, Stanley Forman	Kentucky	Roosevelt F.	1938-1957
Frankfurter, Felix	Massachusetts	Roosevelt F.	1939-1962
Douglas, William Orville	Connecticut	Roosevelt F.	1939-1975
Murphy, Frank	Michigan	Roosevelt F.	1940-1949
Byrnes, James Francis	South Carolina	Roosevelt F.	1941-1942
Jackson, Robert Houghwout	New York	Roosevelt F.	1941-1954
Rutledge, Wiley Blount	Iowa	Roosevelt F.	1943-1949
Burton, Harold Hitz	Ohio	Truman	1945-1958

Clark, Tom Campbell	Texas	Truman	1949-1967
Minton, Sherman	Indiana	Truman	1949-1956
Harlan, John Marshall	New York	Eisenhower	1955-1971
Brennan, William J., Jr.	New Jersey	Eisenhower	1956-1990
Whittaker, Charles Evans	Missouri	Eisenhower	1957-1962
Stewart, Potter	Ohio	Eisenhower	1958-1981
White, Byron Raymond	Colorado	Kennedy	1962-1993
Goldberg, Arthur Joseph	Illinois	Kennedy	1962-1965
Fortas, Abe	Tennessee	Johnson L.	1965-1969
Marshall, Thurgood	New York	Johnson L.	1967-1991
Blackmun, Harry A.	Minnesota	Nixon	1970-1994
Powell, Lewis F., Jr.	Virginia	Nixon	1972-1988
Rehnquist, William H.	Arizona	Nixon	1972-1986**
Stevens, John Paul	Illinois	Ford	1975-2010
O'Connor, Sandra Day	Arizona	Reagan	1981-2006
Scalia, Antonin	Virginia	Reagan	1986-2016
Kennedy, Anthony M.	California	Reagan	1988-2018
Souter, David H.	New Hampshire	Bush, G. H. W.	1990-2009
Thomas, Clarence	Georgia	Bush, G. H. W.	1991-
Ginsburg, Ruth Bader	New York	Clinton	1993-
Breyer, Stephen G.	Massachusetts	Clinton	1994-
John Roberts	Maryland	Bush, G. W.	2005-
Alito, Samuel A., Jr.	New Jersey	Bush, G. W.	2006-
Sonia Sotomayor	New York	Obama	2009-
Elena Kagan	New York	Obama	2010-
Gorsuch, Neil	Colorado	Trump	2017-
Kavanaugh, Brett	Maryland	Trump	2018-

Notes: The acceptance of the appointment and commission by the appointee, as evidenced by the taking of the prescribed oaths, is here implied; otherwise the individual is not carried on this list of the Members of the Court. Examples: Robert Hanson Harrison is not carried, as a letter from President Washington of February 9, 1790 states Harrison declined to serve. Neither is Edwin M. Stanton who died before he could take the necessary steps toward becoming a Member of the Court. *Chief Justice Rutledge is included because he took his oaths, presided over the August Term of 1795, and his name appears on two opinions of the Court for that Term.

[The foregoing was taken from a booklet prepared by the Supreme Court of the United States.]

**Elevated.

APPENDIX E

ADMISSION OF STATES INTO THE UNION

State	Date of Admission	State	Date of Admission
1. Delaware	December 7, 1787	26. Michigan	January 26, 1837
2. Pennsylvania	December 12, 1787	27. Florida	March 3, 1845
3. New Jersey	December 18, 1787	28. Texas	December 29, 1845
4. Georgia	January 2, 1788	29. Iowa	December 28, 1846
5. Connecticut	January 9, 1788	30. Wisconsin	May 29, 1848
6. Massachusetts	February 6, 1788	31. California	September 9, 1850
7. Maryland	April 28, 1788	32. Minnesota	May 11, 1858
8. South Carolina	May 23, 1788	33. Oregon	February 14, 1859
9. New Hampshire	June 21, 1788	34. Kansas	January 29, 1861
10. Virginia	June 25, 1788	35. West Virginia	June 20, 1863
11. New York	July 26, 1788	36. Nevada	October 31, 1864
12. North Carolina	November 21, 1789	37. Nebraska	March 1, 1867
13. Rhode Island	May 29, 1790	38. Colorado	August 1, 1876
14. Vermont	March 4, 1791	39. North Dakota	November 2, 1889
15. Kentucky	June 1, 1792	40. South Dakota	November 2, 1889
16. Tennessee	June 1, 1796	41. Montana	November 8, 1889
17. Ohio	March 1, 1803	42. Washington	November 11, 1889
18. Louisiana	April 30, 1812	43. Idaho	July 3, 1890
19. Indiana	December 11, 1816	44. Wyoming	July 10, 1890
20. Mississippi	December 10, 1817	45. Utah	January 4, 1896
21. Illinois	December 3, 1818	46. Oklahoma	November 16, 1907
22. Alabama	December 14, 1819	47. New Mexico	January 6, 1912
23. Maine	March 15, 1820	48. Arizona	February 14, 1912
24. Missouri	August 10, 1821	49. Alaska	January 3, 1959
25. Arkansas	June 15, 1836	50. Hawaii	August 21, 1959

APPENDIX F

POPULATION GROWTH

Year	Population	Percent Increase
1630	4,600	
1640	26,600	478.3
1650	50,400	90.8
1660	75,100	49.0
1670	111,900	49.0
1680	151,500	35.4
1690	210,400	38.9
1700	250,900	19.2
1710	331,700	32.2
1720	466,200	40.5
1730	629,400	35.0
1740	905,600	43.9
1750	1,170,800	29.3
1760	1,593,600	36.1
1770	2,148,100	34.8
1780	2,780,400	29.4
1790	3,929,214	41.3
1800	5,308,483	35.1
1810	7,239,881	36.4
1820	9,638,453	33.1
1830	12,866,020	33.5
1840	17,069,453	32.7
1850	23,191,876	35.9
1860	31,443,321	35.6
1870	39,818,449	26.6
1880	50,155,783	26.0
1890	62,947,714	25.5
1900	75,994,575	20.7
1910	91,972,266	21.0
1920	105,710,620	14.9
1930	122,775,046	16.1
1940	131,669,275	7.2
1950	151,325,798	14.5
1960	179,323,175	18.5
1970	203,302,031	13.4
1980	226,542,199	11.4
1990	248,718,301	9.8
2000	281,421,906	13.1
2010	308,745,538	9.7

GLOSSARY OF IMPORTANT PEOPLE AND CONCEPTS

Adams, Abigail (1744-1818): The wife and perhaps most influential advisor of John Adams (the first vice president and second president of the United States) and mother of the sixth president John Quincy Adams.

Adams, John (1735-1826): Massachusetts lawyer and politician who served as a member of the Second Continental Congress and on the committee that drafted the Declaration of Independence, and who later won election as the first vice president and second president of the United States.

Adams, John Quincy (1767-1848): Son of John Adams who became the 6th President of the United States in 1825. He also served as a diplomat, member of the U.S. House and Senate, and Secretary of State under James Monroe (during which time he developed the principles behind the Monroe Doctrine).

Adams, Samuel (1722-1803): Massachusetts politician who served in the First Continental Congress in Philadelphia in 1774 and the Second Continental Congress in 1776 where he signed the Declaration of Independence. He was a cousin of the nation's second president, John Adams.

Adams-Onís (Transcontinental) Treaty: Treaty by which Spain finally ceded Florida to the U.S. for $5 million, which was payment to American citizens for damages done to them by marauding Seminoles. Treaty also established the boundaries of the Louisiana Purchase with Spain along its Borderland territories all the way up to the 42nd parallel in the Pacific Northwest. For such terms the U.S. agreed to relinquish its demands for Texas.

Adena and Hopewell: Mound building cultures of Native Americans that existed in the Ohio River Valley from about 100 B.C. to about 700 A.D.

African Methodist Episcopal Church: Founded by the Reverend Richard Allen (1760-1831) in Philadelphia in 1816, this African-American sect originated among members of the Free African Society, established in 1787.

Alaska purchase: Secretary of State William H. Seward negotiated the 1867 purchase of Alaska from Russia for $7.2 million. Though often ridiculed as "Seward's Folly" for its sizeable expense for a land mostly of ice and tundra, the land proved to be invaluable to American security and a provider of immense resource wealth in the form of gold, oil, and natural gas.

Albany Plan of Union: Plan put forth in 1754 by Massachusetts Governor William Shirley, Benjamin Franklin and others calling for an intercolonial union to manage defense and Indian affairs.

Alien Act: Part of a two-pronged High Federalist attempt to destroy their opposition, the Democratic-Republican Party, by curtailing immigrant voting potential by extending the naturalization period from 5 to 14 years, thus effecting the Jeffersonian party by denying it of the future citizens' vote.

American Anti-Slavery Society: The first national abolitionist organization established in 1833.

American Colonization Society: An anti-slavery organization founded in 1817 by anti-slavery reformers, calling for a gradual emancipation and removal of freed blacks to Africa.

American (Know Nothing) Party: A nativist political organization that came together in New York in 1843 but rose to prominence in response to the influx of immigration to the United States after 1845.

American System: The name Clay gave his economic program for the country's post-war development that called for government funding and promotion of the nation's infrastructure, a national bank, and protective tariffs to help promote domestic manufacturing.

American Temperance Society: Antebellum temperance organization established in Boston in 1826. Within ten years, over a million members nationally had voluntarily taken a pledge to abstain from drinking alcoholic beverages.

"Anaconda Plan": The original war plan to crush the Confederate rebellion, devised by Union General-In-Chief Winfield Scott in 1861. It called for a major thrust by ground troops along the path of the Mississippi Valley to bisect the southern states and a naval blockade of southern ports to deprive the Confederacy of badly needed manufactured supplies and revenue from cotton sales.

Andersonville: A Confederate military prison in Sumter County, Georgia, where about 25 percent of just under 50,000 Union prisoners, or about 13,000, died from hunger, disease, and exposure to unsanitary conditions in just 14 months from February 1864 to the end of the Civil War the next spring.

Andros, Edmund: Imperious governor of the Dominion of New England who enforced James II's will over an especially harassed and targeted Puritan New England, whom James especially despised, holding the sect responsible for his father's death.

Annapolis Convention: Commercial meeting where delegates formally called for a larger convention to consider ways of refining or replacing the Articles of Confederation.

Anthony, Susan B. (1820-1906): A feminist leader from Massachusetts who spent much of her life promoting women's suffrage, the abolition of slavery, and temperance.

Anti-Federalists: The label given to the diverse group of opponents to ratification of the U.S. Constitution. Though unable to defeat ratification, many of their concerns with the document were included in the Bill of Rights.

Antietam, Battle of: The bloodiest single-day battle in American history, fought between the Union and Confederate armies on September 17, 1862 near Sharpsburg, Maryland, resulting in a total of 23,000 casualties (including 3,654 dead). The battle ended the first unsuccessful Confederate invasion of the North.

Anti-Masonic Party: Formed in 1827 in opposition to the presumed power and influence of the Masonic order.

Appomattox Courthouse: Near the site of the last battle fought by Robert E. Lee's Army of Northern Virginia against Union General Ulysses S. Grant, the courthouse became the scene of Lee's surrender April 9, 1865.

Arnold, Benedict (1741-1801): An American general during the Revolutionary War who switched sides and ended up a British officer by the end of the conflict.

Articles of Confederation: The first formal constitutional document for the United States of America, approved by the states in 1781.

Atlantic Slave Trade: The forced transport of 12 million slaves from Africa to the New World from 1500-1800.

Austin, Stephen (1793-1836): American *empresario* who established the first Anglo colony of settlers in Texas upon reaching an agreement with Mexican authorities to settle 300 immigrant families in the eastern section of the province.

Aztecs: A group of Native Americans that developed a highly sophisticated civilization in central Mexico.

Bacon's Rebellion: After years of growing acrimony between the planter elite of Virginia and the colony's freedmen, rebellion brought about the end of indentured servitude in the Chesapeake. African slavery would be the permanent labor force on the tobacco plantations.

Bank of the United States: Part of the Hamiltonian agenda to assert greater governmental control over the new Republic's economy and finances by establishing a national bank that would print and back a national currency and regulate other banks as well as make loans to individuals and companies.

Bank War: The controversy over renewing the charter of the Second Bank of the United States during the administration of President Andrew Jackson.

Barbary Pirates: North African corsairs operating out of Tripoli who harassed both European and U.S. shipping in the Mediterranean.

Barnum, P.T. (1810-1891): An American entertainment producer and creator of the most popular 19th-century circus called "The Greatest Show on Earth."

Barton, Clara (1821-1912): An American nurse, humanitarian, and (in 1881) the founder of the American Red Cross, noted for her heroic services for the Union military during the Civil War.

Bear Flag Revolt: Rebellion in California staged by a group of American settlers upon hearing of the outbreak of war between the United States and Mexico.

Bill of Rights: The first ten amendments to the U.S. Constitution adopted to enumerate and protect basic civil liberties for American citizens.

Black Codes: Laws passed by the newly-elected southern white governments during presidential reconstruction (under the Johnson administration) that virtually re-enslaved southern blacks, making a mockery of the war's purpose, especially in the eyes of Radical Republicans and many northern whites.

Bladensburg races: Derisive name given to Battle of Bladensburg after defeat of poorly trained troops led to British burning Washington, D.C.

"Bleeding Kansas": A term describing the violence surrounding the settlement of Kansas. The term encompassed the activities of the border ruffians of Missouri, the actions of John Brown, and the attack by Preston Brooks on Charles Sumner on the floor of the U.S. Senate.

Board of Trade: Panel of officials set up in 1696 in England to try and regulate colonial trade and politics on behalf of the Crown.

Booth, John Wilkes (1839-1865): The child of renowned stage actor Junius Brutus Booth, and the brother of famed Shakespearean actors Edwin and Junius Booth, who on April 14, 1865, assassinated President Abraham Lincoln.

Boston Massacre: A violent confrontation between an angry street mob and a group of British soldiers on March 5, 1770. The crowd began throwing snowballs containing rocks, and the terrified soldiers panicked, and fired into then. Five died, including Crispus Attucks, a man of African and Native American heritage. Six others suffered injuries.

Boston Tea Party: A protest action against the British Parliament's 1773 Tea Act carried out by a group of Massachusetts colonists December 16, 1773. Protestors dumped 342 containers of tea worth approximately $18,000 into Boston Harbor.

Boyd, Belle (1843-1900): A Confederate spy born in what is now West Virginia, she provided information on Union troop movements to Confederate Generals Thomas "Stonewall" Jackson and Turner Ashby.

Braddock, Edward: British general sent by the king and Parliament to drive the French out of the Ohio River Valley. Accompanying Braddock's 3,000 British regulars on this mission was a contingent of 2,500 colonial militia, commanded by George Washington.

Brown, John (1800-1859): A white abolitionist who became convinced that slavery would only end through violence. In 1856, John Brown and his sons killed a family of proslavery settlers in Kansas. Three years later, Brown unsuccessfully attempted to start a slave revolt by capturing the federal arsenal at Harpers Ferry, Virginia (now West Virginia). He was captured and executed for treason, but many Northerners regarded him as a martyr.

Bubonic Plague: A disease that devastated Europe in the 14th century, killing about one-third of the continent's population during the 1360s and 1370s.

Bull Run, First Battle of: The first major battle of the Civil War, fought on July 21, 1861, which resulted in a Confederate victory and shattered northern overconfidence that the Union forces would win a quick and easy victory over the South.

Bunker Hill, Battle of: British General Thomas Gage's armies faced encirclement by Massachusetts militiamen who occupied the high ground overlooking the Boston peninsula and, after receiving reinforcements, he decided to risk an assault on American troops led by Colonel William Prescott on ridgetops called Bunker Hill and Breed's Hill on June 17, 1775. The British scored a Pyrrhic victory, suffering more than 1,000 dead and wounded.

Burgoyne, John (1722-1792): British general who commanded forces in Canada in 1776 and 1777. In 1777 he was forced to surrender after the Battle of Saratoga.

Cabot, John: A Venetian sea captain who explored North America for England in 1497 and 1498 in search of the Northwest Passage.

Calhoun, John C. (1782-1850): A South Carolina politician known for his articulate defense of the southern states' rights and slavery.

California Gold Rush: Massive wave of settlers to California from the United States, Europe, Latin America, and China after the discovery of gold in 1848.

Camden, Battle of: A major battle fought in the interior of South Carolina in 1780 resulting in a crushing victory for Lord Cornwallis's forces over colonial troops led by Horatio Gates.

"Carpetbaggers": Name given to all northern whites who migrated south allegedly to take advantage of a prostrated southern people and economy. Most carpetbaggers were northern male and female school teachers who came to the South to help educate the freedmen, not unscrupulous opportunists.

Carrying trade: American trade ships carrying the trade of European and U.S. producers were an important part of growing American economy after 1790.

Cass, Lewis (1782-1866): Democratic senator from Michigan who championed popular sovereignty as the best alternative to the growing sectional differences over slavery expansion. After receiving his party's nomination for president, he lost the 1848 race to Zachary Taylor.

Chancellorsville, Battle of: Fought between April 30 and May 6, this Civil War battle in Northern Virginia was part of an offensive launched by Union General John Hooker designed to bypass Confederate forces in Fredericksburg in part of a general campaign to capture the southern capital in Richmond.

Charles I: English King who granted the charter giving the Puritans the right to settle in Massachusetts Bay.

Chase, Samuel (1741-1811): Federalist Supreme Court Justice who Jeffersonians in Congress impeached but failed to remove for his anti-Republican diatribes from the bench.

***Cherokee Nation v. Georgia* (1831):** The United States Supreme Court in 1831 ruled that, because the Cherokees were not a foreign nation but a "domestic dependent nation" and had a relationship to the U.S. like a "ward to its guardian," the Cherokees did not have standing to argue their case in the federal courts.

Child, Lydia Maria (1802-1880): American abolitionist and women's rights advocate whose writings challenged traditional views of white supremacy and asserted racial intellectual equality, which produced a strong backlash among many in the antebellum North.

Chinese immigration: The first large group of Chinese immigrants came as part of the late-1840s and early-1850s Gold Rush to California where they frequently experienced nativist hostility to their presence.

"City upon a Hill": Metaphor used by John Winthrop illustrating the Puritan vision of the Massachusetts Bay Colony to be not only a refuge for persecuted Puritans but also a model Calvinist community whose prosperity, it was hoped, would convince England to change its ways.

Clark, George Rogers (1752-1818): Virginia militia leader whose captures of Kaskaskia and Vincennes solidified colonial control over the Northwest Territory leading to the eventual ceding of the region to the United States after the American Revolution.

Clay, Henry (1777-1852): A Kentuckian member of Congress, speaker of the House, senator, and secretary of state who played an instrumental role in forging the Missouri Compromise and the Compromise of 1850. Clay would be a principal founder of the Whig Party, formed to oppose Democratic President Andrew Jackson.

Clinton, Henry (1730-1795): A general appointed commander-in-chief of the British forces in North America in 1778, who led a successful invasion of South Carolina in 1779, and captured Charleston in 1780, but waited too long to dispatch his fleet to rescue General Charles Cornwallis in Yorktown, Virginia, resulting in the decisive British defeat there October 17, 1781.

Clovis Point: A tool that was far superior to European and Asian choppers and scrapers developed by Native Americans of the Paleo-Indian period.

Columbian Exchange: A term used to describe the exchange of animal and plant life between the Old and New Worlds that was sometimes deliberate and sometimes inadvertent.

Columbus, Christopher: An Italian sailor who accidentally "discovered" North and South America when he was sailing westward across the Atlantic looking for a water route to Asia.

Common Property Doctrine: An alternative to the Wilmot Proviso articulated by John C. Calhoun and asserting that all federal territory should be opened to slavery.

Common Sense: A provocative pamphlet written by radical journalist and author Thomas Paine and published in January 1776 that characterized King George III as a tyrant, argued the 13 North American colonies should seek independence from Great Britain, and urged the colonists to think of themselves as belonging to a single American nation.

Compass: An important navigational instrument invented by the Chinese that contained a magnetic needle that always pointed toward the north.

Compromise of 1850: Congressional agreement originally proposed by Henry Clay to settle the sectional dispute over slavery once and for all by passing separate laws allowing for the following: California to join the Union as a free state; the remaining Mexican session lands to be organized as federal territories (Utah and New Mexico) with popular sovereignty to decide the fate of slavery in each; the Fugitive Slave Law to be amended to satisfy southern complaints about its effectiveness, the abolition of the slave trade in Washington, D.C.; and Texas would cede much of its western territorial claims to help form the New Mexico Territory in exchange for assumption of its public debt by the U.S. Treasury.

Compromise of 1877: Informal agreement made by Republican and Democratic Party leaders to resolve the impasse produced by the disputed election of 1876, resulting in the election of Republican Rutherford B. Hayes as president in return for allowing the Democrats to gain control of the final three unredeemed states in the South and other concessions.

"Connecticut Compromise" (or "Great Compromise"): The key agreement worked out, in early July 1787, between delegates from large and small states at the Constitutional Convention in Philadelphia, over the allocation of representatives in the two houses of the proposed national legislature and the division of powers between the two houses.

Constitution of the United States: The charter establishing a new national government, defining its institutions (branches), and specifying their legal powers and responsibilities. After ratification was accomplished in 1788, the new federal government began operating under the terms of the Constitution in early 1789.

Constitutional Convention: The political convocation held in Philadelphia between May 14 to September 17, 1787 that drafted the United States Constitution.

Constitutional Union Party: A short-lived political organization that emerged during the presidential election of 1860, mainly of former Whigs, of Southerners who emphasized allegiance for the Union.

Convention of 1818: Accord for the purpose of rapprochement between England and the U.S. whereby both nations agreed to the 49th parallel as the northern boundary of the American-controlled Louisiana Territory all the way to the Rocky Mountains while setting up a "joint-occupation" system of the Oregon Territory.

Cornwallis, Lord Charles (1738-1805): British general who served as commander of the British army in the South after the conquest of Charleston in 1780, but allowed his forces to be trapped between the Americans and the French in the 1781 Battle of Yorktown. He surrendered his large forces, ending the American Revolution with a defeat for Great Britain and independence for the United States.

Corps of Discovery: Official name of the Lewis and Clark expedition to survey Louisiana Purchase territory and Oregon Country to the Pacific Ocean.

"Corrupt Bargain" (1824): The accusation of Andrew Jackson and his supporters that Henry Clay agreed to use his influence as Speaker of the House to procure enough votes necessary to elect John Quincy Adams the sixth President of the United States in exchange for Clay's appointment as Secretary of State.

Cortés, Hernán: Spanish conquistador who subdued the Aztec empire.

Coverture: Legal doctrine under which married women lost their independence and legally became part of their husband's person.

Crédit Mobilier Affair: A Grant administration scandal involving the siphoning off of millions of dollars in government funds to a "dummy company" to build the Union Pacific Railroad.

Crittenden Compromise: Effort by some congressional leaders to avert the outbreak of civil war following Abraham Lincoln's election as president by offering to end the secession crisis with a package of constitutional amendments and congressional resolutions designed to entice the South back into the Union peacefully, including the passage of unrepealable amendments permanently guaranteeing the existence of slavery in the states where it currently existed and extending the Missouri Compromise line to the California border, allowing slavery south of that boundary.

Dartmouth College v. Woodward: One in a series of post-war landmark cases of the John Marshall Supreme Court in which the Court's ruling reflected the Federalist position of the power of the federal government over that of the states.

Davis, Jefferson (1808-1889): A Mississippi politician who at various times served as congressman, United States senator, secretary of war, and, during the Civil War, as President of the Confederate States of America. An ardent believer in white supremacy and slavery.

Deere, John (1804-1886): The inventor, in 1837, of the steel plow, which replaced the more fragile and less powerful wooden and cast-iron plows. By 1857, his factory was producing 10,000 plows a year.

Deism: The "religion" of many of the Enlightenment *philosophes* who believed in a Supreme Being (God) but not in Christianity.

Democratic Party (1832 --): The oldest political party in the United States, the Democrats can trace their origins to Thomas Jefferson's Republican Party, which formed in the 1790s.

Democratic-Republicans: Party name assumed by the opponents of Hamilton and his followers. Leaders became Thomas Jefferson and James Madison, and eventually the party's ideology became that of Jeffersonianism.

Dias, Bartolomé: Sailor who rounded the Cape of Good Hope and saw the Indian Ocean for the first time.

Dickinson, John (1732-1808): A Philadelphia lawyer who became a political leader during the Revolutionary War era who, even though he had consistently opposed separation from Great Britain, enlisted in the American military when the war started.

Disestablishment: The process of removing ties between churches and state governments in the decades following the American Revolution.

Dix, Dorothea (1802-1887): A social reformer who served as the Union Army's Superintendent of Female Nurses during the Civil War (1861-1865), she devoted much of her life to humanizing the treatment of the insane.

Dominion of New England: Created by James II to impose tighter royal control over England's North American empire, especially the New England colonies, whom James perceived as potentially the most dangerous to royal authority.

Douglas, Stephen (1813-1861): An Illinois politician who emerged a prominent Democratic politician in the 1850s.

Douglas embraced the popular sovereignty position, which he defended in his successful bid for reelection to the U.S. Senate in 1858 (in which he defeated Abraham Lincoln) and his unsuccessful run for the presidency in 1860 (in which he lost to Lincoln).

Douglass, Frederick (1818?-1895): An escaped slave who became an eloquent leader in the abolitionist movement. His classic 1845 memoir, *Narrative of the Life of Frederick Douglass, an American Slave*, energized the northern anti-slavery forces.

Drake, Francis: English explorer and privateer who became the foremost mariner of the Elizabethan Age.

***Dred Scott* Case**: An 1857 Supreme Court decision that held African Americans were not citizens of the United States and that Congress possessed no power to limit slavery's expansion into the federal territories.

Lord Dunmore [John Murray, 4th earl of Dunmore] (1730-1809): Royal governor of Virginia at the outbreak of the American Revolution. In 1775 he issued a famous proclamation declaring martial law in the colony and promised freedom for the slaves of rebels who left their masters and supported the English cause.

Edwards, Jonathan: Perhaps the most famous of the Great Awakening's evangelical preachers who delivered "fire and brimstone" sermons with such passion that people reacted physically to the imagery presented in his emotion-charged perorations.

Electoral College: The process for electing U.S. presidents established by the Founding Fathers at the Constitutional Convention.

Elizabeth I: Queen of England during the late stages of the English Reformation and during England's first American colonization attempts.

Emancipation Proclamation: A decree issued by President Abraham Lincoln that declared free as of January 1, 1863, all slaves living in territory still in rebellion against the Union.

Embargo Act (1807): Jefferson pushed through Congress the Embargo Act that forbade all American ships from leaving U.S. ports while denying foreign vessels access to American ports and trade.

Emerson, Ralph Waldo (1803-1882): The son of a Unitarian minister, Emerson was an author, anti-war activist and leader of the Transcendentalist movement, which argued that humans were innately good but could become corrupted through institutions like the church and government. In essays like "Nature" and "Self Reliance," Emerson stressed the need for intellectual independence from majority opinion and derided the American emphasis on materialism.

Empresario: Title given to American, European, and Mexican entrepreneurs who contracted with the Mexican government to settle families in various assigned sections of Texas in an effort to bolster the population of the province.

Encomienda System: A system designed to meet labor shortages in which the Spanish government rewarded *conquistadors* by giving them title to vast tracts of land and allowing them to enslave Native Americans.

Enlightenment (The "Age of Reason"): An eighteenth-century philosophical movement that emphasized the use of reason to reevaluate previously held doctrines.

Episcopal Church: Post-Revolution name adopted by American members of the Anglican Church after breaking away from the Church of England.

"Era of Good Feelings": Period during James Monroe's presidency in which the Federalist Party dissolved, though partisan rancor was replaced by factionalism within the Republican Party and sectional differences over slavery.

Erie Canal: This canal provided the first relatively rapid transportation across the Appalachian Mountains.

Fallen Timbers, Battle of: 1794 defeat of Native Americans in Northwest Territory that led to decade of relative peace there.

Federalist Papers: A series of 85 essays written by James Madison, Alexander Hamilton and John Jay in defense of the proposed United States Constitution, then being considered for ratification by the states.

Federalists: Supporters of the Constitution who favored its ratification.

Fifteenth Amendment: A Reconstruction-era amendment that prohibited states from interfering with the right to vote based on "race, color, or previous condition of servitude."

"54-40 or Fight!": Slogan used by American expansionists demanding that the U.S. government settle with the British for an Oregon Country boundary no less than the 54° 40' line (deep into present-day British Columbia).

Fillmore, Millard (1800-1874): A New York politician who succeeded Zachary Taylor to the presidency following his death in 1850. As president, Fillmore supported the provisions of the Compromise of 1850 and signed each one into law.

Finney, Charles Grandison (1792-1875): A fiery evangelical Christian preacher who played a leading role in the religious revivals that began in the first decade of the 19th century and peaked in the 1830s and 1840s. Finney rejected the strict Calvinist doctrine that God predestined who would be saved and who would be damned. Finney preached that God wanted all to achieve salvation.

Five Civilized Tribes: The Indian peoples—Cherokee, Choctaw, Chickasaw, Creek and Seminole—originally living in the Southeastern United States (in Georgia, Alabama, Mississippi, Tennessee and Florida) deemed to be "civilized" by their white neighbors.

Five Points: a New York neighborhood famous for its poverty, brothels, and violence.

Fort Pillow Massacre: One of the worst war crimes of the Civil War committed by members of a cavalry division under the command of Confederate General Nathan Bedford Forrest against captured African-American troops near Henning in western Tennessee on April 12, 1864. After the fall of Fort Pillow, Forrest's men killed over 200 black troops who had surrendered.

Fort Sumter: Fort located on an island near the mouth of Charleston, South Carolina's harbor that became the scene of a national crisis in early 1861 when federal troops refused to surrender their post to Confederates. The Civil War began when Confederates fired upon the fort.

Fourteenth Amendment: A Reconstruction-era amendment ratified in 1868 that officially made the freedmen U.S. citizens while prohibiting the states from denying such individuals all the rights and privileges guaranteed any citizen of the United States.

Franklin, Benjamin (1706-1790): A Pennsylvania politician, author, scientist, and diplomat who would be present for many of the most important events in early American history, including the writing of the Declaration of Independence, the negotiation of the peace treaty with Great Britain ending the Revolutionary War, and the writing of the United States Constitution.

Fredericksburg, Battle of: A Civil War battle fought in Virginia between December 11 and 15, 1862, which resulted in heavy Union casualties and ended a Union drive toward the Confederate national capital in Richmond.

"Free Labor": An antebellum Republican shorthand for what made the North superior to the South. The phrase denoted the ability of Northerners to choose their own employers, places of residence, and political views.

Free Soil Position: A policy proposal in the 1840s and 1850s, most famously articulated in the Wilmot Proviso, that all federal territory be closed to slavery.

Freedmen's Bureau: First federally-sponsored and funded welfare agency created during Reconstruction to help the freedmen adjust to their new status while providing education, protection, and other services.

Freeman, Elizabeth (?—1829): An African-American woman who sued for her freedom in Massachusetts following the American Revolution and won. Her case led to the disappearance of slavery in Massachusetts.

Freeport Doctrine: Name given to Senator Stephen Douglas's answer to Abraham Lincoln's query during the Lincoln-Douglas Debates about what, if anything, opponents in a western territory could do about slavery in their territory given that the Supreme Court's *Dred Scott* decision forbade the banning of slavery in any federal territory. Much to the anger of many pro-slavery Southerners, Douglas responded that a territory's residents could refuse to enact and enforce territorial legislation supporting the institution of slavery, including punishment for aiding and abetting runaways.

French and Indian War (1754-1763): The last of the Anglo-French colonial wars and the first in which the fighting began in North America. The war ended with France's defeat and loss of its North American empire.

Frobisher, Martin: An English explorer who brought back iron pyrite (fool's gold).

Fugitive Slave Law: Passed as part of the Compromise of 1850, this federal legislation bolstered efforts to aid slave owners recover their runaway slave property.

Fulton, Robert (1765-1815): An engineer and inventor often mistakenly believed to be the inventor of the steamboat, Fulton actually was the first person to put a workable design to the test. Fulton tested the first steamboat he constructed, the *Clermont*, on the Hudson River in New York in 1807.

Gallatin, Albert: Republican Secretary of Treasury under Jefferson and Madison. Put U.S. on path to paying off debt until War of 1812 disrupted it.

Garrison, William Lloyd (1805-1879): An anti-slavery journalist who in 1831 began publication of *The Liberator*, an anti-slavery newspaper that continued publication through the end of the Civil War in 1861.

Gates, Horatio (1727-1806): An American general during the Revolutionary War (1775-1783) who won a major victory against the British in two battles near Saratoga, New York in 1777, but later suffered a crushing defeat in South Carolina at the Battle of Camden in 1780, ending all talk of him replacing George Washington as commander of the Continental Army..

Genêt, Citizen Edmund: French Girondist emissary sent by the revolutionary republican government to enlist American aid for France's war effort in Europe, disregarding with blatant contempt the official U.S. position of neutrality.

George III (1738-1820): The British monarch during the time of the American Revolution who supported the policies of prime ministers such Frederick North who sought to relieve Britain's budget crisis by shifting some of the costs of empire to the barely-taxed American colonists.

Georgia Trustees: Organization of prominent British gentlemen who governed Georgia from 1732-1752, limiting landholding and banning slavery in the colony.

German immigration: Generally more prosperous than other immigrant groups, large numbers of Germans came to America in the 1840s and 1850s and established themselves as successful family farmers and tradesmen.

Gettysburg, Battle of: Major Civil War battle taking place July 1-3, 1863, in southeastern Pennsylvania in which Confederate General Robert E. Lee's forces were defeated by George Meade's Union Army. A major turning point of the conflict, Lee's army could no longer mount offensive operations and remained on the defensive for the remainder of the war.

Gilbert, Sir Humphrey: The driving force behind England's overseas explorations under Elizabeth I. He, like Cabot, wanted to find a Northwest Passage.

Glorious Revolution: Parliamentary insurrection in 1688 against James II's attempt to rule England as an absolute monarch. The event marked the end of the English monarchy's power, establishing England as a constitutional monarchy.

Golden Age of Piracy: The period from 1716-1726 which saw a rapid rise in illegal attacks on shipping and a great disruption of commerce in the Atlantic Ocean and the Caribbean.

Grain reaper: Cyrus McCormick's mechanical invention, patented in 1834, that revolutionized grain harvesting in the United States.

Grant, Ulysses S. (1822-1885): General-in-chief of the Union Army by the end of the American Civil War (1861-1865), Grant won credit for the North's victory and was able to ride his popularity to two terms in the White House (1869-1877).

Great Awakening: Tremendous religious revival that emerged during the colonial period against the traditional Puritan theology of predestination. Salvation was now open to all and God's message was delivered in a most passionate and direct way to all those wanting his grace and redemption; evangelism became the most important feature of this revival.

Great Migration: The name given to the 14,000 plus Puritans who came to New England in the 1630s and 1640s, fleeing persecution and eventual civil war in their homeland.

Greene, Nathanael (1742-1786): A major general in the Continental Army who became Washington's most trusted subordinate and later won fame in his own right for his command of the Continental Army in the southern states.

Grenville, George (1712-1770): Served as British Secretary of State and most powerful government minister during the French and Indian War (1754-1763), Grenville served as prime minister from 1763-1765. It was his administration that pushed through the Parliament the Stamp Act in February 1765.

Grimké Sisters: Sarah (1792-1873) and Angelina (1805-1879) were born and raised on a plantation owned by their slave-owning father but became notable abolitionists and advocates for women's rights.

Guadalupe Hidalgo, Treaty of: Peace treaty signed in February 1848 that ended the Mexican American War.

Gutenberg, Johannes: A resident of Mainz, Germany who is credited with inventing the modern printing press that used moveable type.

Habeas corpus: The constitutional right through which a prisoner can ask a court to be released unless the jailing authority presents sufficient grounds to justify continued detention.

Haitian Revolution: The successful slave revolt of the early 1790s in the French colony of Saint-Domingue on the island of Hispaniola that resulted in the establishment of the Republic of Haiti.

Hakluyt, Richard: English author whose late 16th century writings generated support for English efforts to colonize the Americas.

Half-Way Covenant: Compromise in Puritan New England that allowed children and grandchildren of church members to be baptized without having to undergo a conversion experience.

Hamilton, Alexander (1757-1804): Leading American statesman and politician after 1789 whose early career included key contributions to the Continental Army and the ratification of the Constitution. As the first Secretary of the Treasury, Hamilton used his position to strengthen the powers of the central government by having the government play a direct role in the nation's economic development.

Harrison, William Henry: Territorial governor of Indiana who led militia to defeat Native Americans at Prophetstown.

Headright System: In order to attract more settlers to Jamestown for tobacco growing, the Virginia Company offered 50-acre land grants as incentives to newcomers. Those already living in the colony received two head-rights if they agreed to grow tobacco rather than other crops on their farms or engage in other enterprises.

Hemings, Sally (1773-1835): A mulatto slave owned by Thomas Jefferson who in all probability had an intimate relationship with the future president and bore him six children.

Henry, Patrick (1736-1799): A Virginia planter, attorney, riveting speaker and fierce advocate of American independence in the 1770s. Henry opposed the Constitution adopted in 1787, believing it violated the principle of states' rights.

Henry the Navigator, Prince: Portuguese leader who supported efforts to explore parts of the world previously unknown to Europeans.

Hessians: The popular name given to German mercenaries fighting for the British Army during the American Revolutionary War (1775-1783).

House of Burgesses: In 1619 the Virginia Company granted Jamestown colonists the right to form a legislative assembly, which its elected members called the House of Burgesses. This body represented the first gathering in the New World of an elected representative government, even though the majority of Burgesses were members of the plantation elite.

Houston, Sam (1793-1863): Former Tennessee congressman and governor who became the victorious general of the

Texas Revolution and served as the first elected president of the Republic of Texas. He later served as a U.S. Senator and Governor of Texas.

Howe, William (1729-1814): The general who took over the position of commander-in-chief of the British forces in the American Revolution (1775-1783) from Thomas Gage but who resigned after being unable to defeat George Washington after three years in the position.

Hudson, Henry: An English sea captain who explored and claimed for the Netherlands the Delaware Bay, New York, the Hudson River, and Hudson Bay.

Humoralism: Mistaken but widespread medical theory in the colonial period that the body consisted of four substances or "humors" that must be kept in balance for a person to be healthy

Hutchinson, Anne: Perhaps the most legendary of Puritan New England's dissenters, who challenged the fundamental tenets of the Puritan faith, most notably predestination.

Impeachment: The process specified in the U.S. Constitution whereby the House of Representatives can indict a federal government official in cases of "bribery, treason, or other high crimes and misdemeanors." Those impeached are to be tried by the U.S. Senate, with a two-thirds majority needed to convict and remove the officeholder from his position.

Implied powers: Federal government powers not specifically stated in the Constitution; Federalists believed the Constitution granted these and Republicans did not.

Impressment: A serious affront to American neutrality by the Royal Navy of abducting American sailors from American vessels into the British Navy. Typical policy of the British navy during times of war to ensure the manpower needs of their navy.

Inca: A sophisticated Native American civilization in modern Peru that developed a social welfare system to care for the physically handicapped, the mentally ill, and individuals suffering from chronic illnesses.

Indentured Servitude: Indentured servants were poor, dispossessed Englishmen, desperate for work, who contracted with the Chesapeake planters to come to Virginia and work for a specific time until they had fulfilled their debt obligation to their planter-employer. Once the contractual obligations had been met, the individual became "free."

Indian Removal Act of 1830: A law adopted by Congress that gave the president authority to negotiate treaties with Indian nations living east of the Mississippi for their removal and settlement west of the river.

Indian Slave Trade: Lucrative commerce in the Carolinas whereby the English traded guns and ammunition to Native Americans in exchange for captives from rival Indian groups. These prisoners, often women and children, were then exported out of the Carolinas.

Internal improvements: Projects designed to improve a country's infrastructure (such as the construction of roads, bridges, and harbors) to facilitate the movement of people and goods.

"Intolerable Acts": A series of harsh laws passed by the British Parliament in 1774 in response to the Boston Tea Party. Also known as the "Coercive Acts," these measures closed Boston Harbor to all commerce until the colonists compensated the East India Company for the destroyed tea; rewrote the Massachusetts Bay Colony's charter to expand the royal governor's limited powers, limited town meetings to once a year; and moved the trials to England for royal officials charged with crimes.

Irish immigration: The largest immigrant group to come to America during the 1840s and 1850s, the Irish largely came to America to escape starvation after a blight destroyed much of the potato crop in the mid-1840s. Generally poor and Catholic peasants, the Irish experienced much hostility from nativists who resented their presence in America.

Iroquois Confederacy: A powerful Indian confederation in western New York and important party in the rivalry between the Dutch, French, and English in America.

Jackson, Andrew (1767-1845): Seventh President of the United States, serving from 1829-1837. Favoring low tariffs, reduced federal support for internal improvements, and strongly opposing the national bank, Jackson's policies provided the initial foundation for the Democratic Party.

Jackson, Thomas J. "Stonewall" (1824-1863): A veteran of the Mexican American War (1846-1848), Jackson was renowned as a brilliant commander in the Confederate Army during the Civil War (1861-1865).

Jacobs, Harriet (1813-1897): Born a slave, Jacobs would later author a searing memoir of her experiences in North Carolina, including warding off the sexual advances of her married master, in the autobiography *Incidents in the Life of a Slave Girl*.

James I (1566-1625): English king who granted the London Company's charter to establish Virginia. The Jamestown settlement and James River were named in his honor.

Jamestown: Name given by the Virginia Company to their colony founded in 1608 on the James River in present-day Virginia. Named after King James I of England who had granted the company its charter.

Jay's Treaty (1795): After several years of dealing with British violations of American neutrality, Washington sent John Jay, Chief Justice of the Supreme Court, to England. Jay was only able to secure modest concessions and a guarantee of no war "in the immediate future" between the two nations.

Jefferson, Thomas (1743-1826): A Virginia politician, inventor, writer, principal author of the Declaration of Independence, the founder of the Republican Party, the second vice president and third president of the United States.

Johnson, Andrew (1808-1875): A pro-Union but anti-black-suffrage Tennessee politician who served in the U.S. House, the Senate, as governor of his home state, as vice president under Abraham Lincoln and, following Lincoln's murder in April 1865, as president from 1865-1869.

Joint-stock companies: Businesses owned by shareholders whose individual stake was based on the proportion of total stocks owned. Beginning in the 1600s, English joint-stock companies raised large amounts of working capital to finance explorations, settlements, trading expeditions, and privateering campaigns in the New World.

Judicial Review: The principle that the courts have the final say in the interpretation of laws.

Judiciary Act of 1789: Act of Congress that established a Supreme Court with six members along with thirteen district courts and three circuit courts of appeals. The legislation made it possible for certain cases to be appealed from state courts to federal circuit courts.

Junto Society of Philadelphia: Similar to the famous salons that became the gathering places for Europe's Enlightenment intelligentsia, Franklin and his equally progressive friends developed such a community in Philadelphia, which by the middle of the 18th century was not only colonial America's most populous city but, thanks to its Quaker heritage, the most tolerant and welcoming of new ideas and their free expression.

Kansas-Nebraska Act: A law drafted by Stephen Douglas, passed by Congress, and signed by President Franklin Pierce that organized the territories of Kansas and Nebraska. Controversy surrounded this law because it repealed the Missouri Compromise restriction, and the reaction against that repeal brought about the organization of the Republican Party.

Kearny, Stephen W. (1794-1848): American general who marched troops overland to secure control over New Mexico and California during the Mexican American War.

Key, Francis Scott: American lawyer who wrote "The Defense of Fort McHenry" while watching Battle of Baltimore; later became the U.S. national anthem.

King Philip's War: The bloodiest Anglo-Indian conflict in American colonial history, ironically one of the few initiated by Native Americans. The Wampanoag chief Metacom (whom the English called "King Philip") led his tribe against the Puritans in 1675 and because the Puritans did not expect such an uprising, Metacom's braves succeeded in winning many encounters and each victory brought new Indian allies. Eventually the Puritans defeated Metacom and his forces, the result of Puritan alliances with other tribes, ironically the Pequot.

Ku Klux Klan: A white supremacist group that aimed to destroy the Reconstruction-era Republican Party in the South, to force the withdrawal of Union troops from the region, and terrify African Americans into not voting or demanding better working conditions.

Lafayette, Marquis de (1757-1834): French nobleman who served as a major general in the Continental Army during the American Revolution. Journeying back to Europe to negotiate increased French aid, he returned to help entrap British troops under General Cornwallis at Yorktown.

La Salle, René-Robert Cavelier, Sieur de: French explorer and colonizer who hoped to extend France's presence in North America into the Southwest, territory claimed but not colonized by Spain.

Lecompton Constitution: A document that tried to bring Kansas into the Union as a slave state. The entire process was riddled with fraud, and the effort was defeated—despite the support of President Buchanan—by the combined efforts of Stephen Douglas and the Republicans. Kansas would ultimately enter the Union as a free state in 1861.

Lexington and Concord: The first military engagements of the American Revolutionary War. The battles marked the outbreak of open armed conflict between Great Britain and its thirteen colonies in North America.

Liberal Republicans: Anti-Grant faction within the Republican Party that allied with Democrats in the 1872 election in an unsuccessful attempt to deny Grant a second term as president. They condemned the scandals of the Grant era, favored civil service reform, and sought an end to the Republicans' Reconstruction policies.

Liberty Party: The first antislavery party formed in 1840.

Lincoln, Abraham (1809-1865). An Illinois politician who served as president from 1861 to his assassination in 1865. Before 1860, Lincoln, a successful lawyer, served a single term in the House of Representatives. In 1858, he lost a contest for the Senate to Stephen Douglas, but then defeated Douglas in the 1860 presidential election. As president, Lincoln shepherded the United States through a bitter Civil War.

Lincoln-Douglas Debates: A series of seven debates held across Illinois during the 1858 U.S. Senate race between Democrat Stephen Douglas and his Republican challenger Abraham Lincoln. Though Douglas won re-election, the debates gave Lincoln national name recognition and greatly elevated his chances for the Republican presidential nomination in 1860.

Locke, John: Political philosopher whose ideas about representative government and individual liberties became influential in England and America.

London or Virginia Company: The consortium of private merchant/capitalists who formed a joint stock company to try to establish a mainland colony in North America. Their enterprise was for personal and collective profit, not for the greater glory of God and King.

Long Island, Battle of (Aug. 27, 1776): The first major battle between the Continental Army, under General Washington, and the British army commanded by General William Howe, and the largest battle of the war in numbers of troops engaged.

Louisiana Purchase (1803): The greatest purchase/acquisition of foreign territory in U.S. history. Jefferson purchased from France for $15 million all of French Louisiana, doubling the size of the United States.

Lovejoy, Elijah (1802-1837): A Maine native, minister and abolitionist newspaper publisher assassinated for his anti-slavery views. In 1833, he began publishing the *St. Louis Observer*, which ran articles critical of slavery.

Lowell, Francis Cabot: American who toured English factory towns before the War of 1812 and copied the machines he saw in operation, bringing such knowledge back to the U.S.

Lowell Girls: Nickname given to the young single women who labored in the Lowell Mills under the "Waltham System."

Macon's Bill Number 2: Passed by the Madison administration in 1810, which allowed for the resumption of trade with France and Great Britain but allowed the president to re-impose sanctions on whichever country refused to respect U.S. neutrality, while authorizing trade with the other. Madison hoped such a measure would prevent war, which was likely by 1810 with either France or Great Britain.

Madison, James (1751-1836): Virginia statesman who helped draft the U.S. Constitution, authored the Bill of Rights, formed the Democratic-Republican Party along with Thomas Jefferson, and served as the 4th President of the United States from 1809-1817 (was president during the War of 1812).

Magellan, Ferdinand: Spanish explorer who found an ocean route to Asia and led the first expedition to circumnavigate the earth.

Malthus, Thomas: English political economist who maintained that the world's population would eventually outstrip the world's food supply causing global famine and all manner of socio-political problems.

Manifest Destiny: The belief held by many nineteenth-century Americans that God ordained that the United States spread across the North American continent.

Mann, Horace (1796-1859): The leader of the Common School movement, which aimed at providing every child a tax-supported basic education.

March to the Sea: Union General William Tecumseh Sherman's offensive through Georgia to the Atlantic Ocean during the Civil War in 1864 in which, by destroying cities, railroads lines, and farms, he hoped to demonstrate to Southerners that the Confederate government could not protect them.

Marbury v. Madison: Supreme Court case in which John Marshall established the precedent of judicial review by overturning a section of a law of Congress for the first time based on its unconstitutionality.

Marion, Francis (1732-1795): Leader of Patriot partisan troops against Tories and British troops in the Carolinas during the American Revolution.

Maroon communities: Towns and villages built by runaway slaves in remote areas of South America and the Caribbean islands.

Marshall, John: Marshall was Supreme Court Chief Justice from 1801-1835. During his tenure, he established the concept of judicial review. The Marshall Court, in a series of landmark decisions, further strengthened the balance of power within the federal government and thus the system of checks and balances. The Marshall Court in an overwhelming majority of cases heard decided in favor of the federal government over the states.

Mather, Cotton: One of the most famous and respected Puritan ministers; the author of over 400 books, one of which was a strong defense of the Salem witchcraft trials.

Maya: Native American culture of Central America who developed a system of complex mathematics, created a form of hieroglyphics, and studied astronomy. They discovered the number zero long before Europeans and could accurately calculate the beginning of solar eclipses.

McClellan, George B. (1826-1885): Commander of the Union Army of the Potomac until fired by Abraham Lincoln after the Battle of Antietam. In 1864 he became the Democratic Party nominee for president but lost to Lincoln.

McCormick, Cyrus (1809-1884): The inventor of the mechanical harvester, which used features of other men's designs, first patented in 1834. He began manufacturing his model three years later and opened a large factory to produce his machine in Chicago in 1847.

McCulloch v. Maryland: 1819 case in which the Supreme Court upheld the constitutionality of the Second Bank of the United States.

Melville, Herman (1819-1891): A former sailor turned author who wrote such classics as *Moby Dick: or, The Whale* (1851) and *Billy Budd* (published posthumously in 1924), works that satirized American self-righteousness, zealotry, and obsession with wealth.

Middle Passage: Name given by slave traders to the journey on slave ships from Africa to the New World.

Midnight Appointments: Last minute federal judge appointments by President Adams after Federalist election losses in 1800.

Miller, William (1782-1849): An evangelist active in upstate New York who gathered followers in the 1830s and 1840s after he announced that the second coming of Jesus Christ would happen between March 21, 1843, and March 21, 1844.

Missouri Compromise: The first in a series of several compromises to come in an attempt to avoid civil war over the issue of slavery expansion. Missouri was admitted as a slave state along with Maine as a free state, thus preserving the balance of power in the Senate. All territory above Missouri, above the parallel 36°30' was to be free; territory below Missouri's southern boundary was assumed to be open to slavery by Southerners.

Monroe Doctrine: Promulgated by the Monroe administration and largely the handiwork of Secretary of State John Quincy Adams that declared the U.S. to be not only opposed to any attempts by the European powers to reclaim or expand their New World empires but that the U.S. spoke for all the nations of the Western Hemisphere. Any attempt by any "outside" powers to expand their empire would be met with harsh reprisals from the U.S.

Monroe, James (1758-1831): 5th President of the United States. During his two terms as president, the Federalist Party disappeared, leading to Monroe's tenure to be labeled the "Era of Good Feelings."

Mormonism: The religious ideas laid out between the 1820s and the 1840s by Joseph Smith who claimed to have received revelations from angels who led him to discover gold plates in the hills of New York State written in an ancient language that he translated into *The Book of Mormon*. Smith's followers would establish the Church of Jesus Christ of Latter-day Saints. Mormons believe that Joseph Smith was a divinely inspired prophet, and that the *Book of Mormon* is the word of God on equal standing with the Bible.

Morse, Samuel: Inventor of the telegraph in 1836, which allowed Americans to spread information across many parts of the nation almost instantaneously. The system involved the transmission and reception of electrical impulses along a connected wire using a standard code.

"Mosquito fleet": Name given to U.S. Navy by critics of Jefferson's plan to shrink size and scope of the fleet.

National Union Party: A third-party coalition formed by conservative Republicans, northern Democrats, and other Unionists to represent a compromise between the Radical Republicans and the Democrats while supporting Andrew Johnson's policies.

Navigation Acts: A series of English laws starting in 1651 that tried to capture colonial trade to make sure that it benefited the mother country first and foremost.

Newburgh Conspiracy: An abortive plot by officers in the Continental Army in 1783 to overthrow the Confederation Congress and establish a military government headed by George Washington or, if he refused, General Horatio Gates, if promised bonuses were not paid.

New Jersey Plan: Plan sponsored by William Paterson at the Constitutional Convention that greatly favored granting the small states a disproportionate share of power in the Congress.

"New Lights": Those colonial Protestant ministers who embraced the theology and evangelism of the Great Awakening, insisting that they were not challenging Calvinist or Puritan orthodoxy but rather opening up the potential for salvation to all mankind. New Lights also maintained that formal seminary training in Protestant theology was not necessary to spread God's work and redemption.

New Netherland: The Dutch colony incorporating Manhattan Island and outposts along the Hudson River Valley until seized by the British in 1664 and renamed New York.

New Orleans, Battle of (January 1815): A decisive American War of 1812 victory over British troops in January 1815 that ended British hopes of gaining control of the lower Mississippi.

New York City Draft Riots of 1863: A mostly Irish-immigrant protest against conscription in New York in July 1863 that escalated into a racial riot that had to be quelled by federal troops.

North, Lord Frederick (1732-1792): A British Prime Minister deeply loyal to King George III and serving before and during the American Revolution (1775-1783). A personal friend of the king, Lord North tried unsuccessfully to be a moderating influence as tensions between the British government and the American colonists escalated in the early 1770s.

Nullification Crisis: A conflict between South Carolina's political leadership and President Andrew Jackson over a tariff law, which went into effect in 1832, imposing taxes on foreign-made goods.

Ohio Company: A private company owned and financed by wealthy Virginia planters, among them George Washington, who wanted to acquire the Ohio River Valley area for both tobacco cultivation and land speculation, as well as to penetrate the lucrative Indian fur trade of the region.

"Old Lights": Name given to those conservative members of colonial Protestant sects opposed to the Great Awakening, its message of salvation open to all, and they were especially contemptuous of the evangelical style of preaching.

Olive Branch Petition: Written largely by John Dickinson declaring the unchanging loyalty of the American colonists to the king but demanded that the Parliament cease what the Congress saw as oppressive measures such as the so-called "Intolerable Acts." The king never responded to the petition.

Oneida Community: A utopian settlement established in 1848 by socialist John Humphrey Noyes and his followers in upstate New York.

Opechancanough: Powhatan's brother who succeeded Powhatan as chief of the Algonquian Confederacy and who was determined to rid the Chesapeake of the English menace.

Orders in Council: British decrees authorizing the British navy to seize any foreign ships attempting to trade with France, which resulted in the seizure of scores of U.S. merchant ships caught trading with French West Indian possessions.

Oregon: The territory occupying present-day British Columbia and the states of Washington, Oregon, and Idaho that lured thousands of American immigrants during the 1840s and 1850s. Originally jointly held by the U.S. and England, the area was divided at the 49th parallel by joint agreement in 1846.

Oregon Trail: A vital northwestern trade route that also brought thousands of immigrants westward to the Oregon Country during the 1840s and 1850s.

Osceola (1804?-1838): A military leader of both white and Native Americans who directed the resistance of the Seminole Indians during the Second Seminole War (1835-1842) to the U.S. Army's attempts to remove that people from their land in Florida.

Ostend Manifesto: A proposal by American diplomats stationed in Europe to acquire Cuba, by purchase or conquest, providing more territory for the United States.

O'Sullivan, John (1813-1895): Influential pro-expansion editor who popularized the belief that it was America's "manifest destiny" to spread from coast to coast.

Otis, James, Jr. (1725-1783): A Massachusetts politician and lawyer and an early advocate of American independence who coined the phrase, "Taxation without Representation is Tyranny," which became a rallying cry of the American resistance to British authorities in the 1760s and 1770s.

Paine, Thomas (1737-1809): Radical pamphleteer and author of *Common Sense*, advocate of American independence and supporter of the French Revolution.

Panic of 1819: The first "depression" in American economic history caused by the decline of European demand for American goods in the aftermath of the Napoleonic Wars.

Panic of 1837: A financial crisis triggered by the collapse of banks involved in railroad speculation resulting in a seven-year-long economic depression, business failures, and high unemployment.

Paris, Treaty of (1783): Agreement between Great Britain and the United States, signed in Paris on Sept. 3, 1783, formally ending the war and stating British recognition of American independence.

Paternalism: Describes the attitude of masters who believed that holding the slaves was in the bondsmen's best interest, often referring to them as children needing constant protection, supervision, and discipline.

Paxton Boys: A 1763 uprising of backcountry Pennsylvania settlers hostile towards Native Americans and towards coastal elites who controlled the provincial government.

Penn, William: A former aristocrat and son of one of England's most decorated naval heroes, Penn converted to the Quaker faith in 1667 and emerged as one of the faith's most important leaders after Fox. Penn obtained from Charles II a charter to establish a colony in North America to be a refuge for his persecuted Quaker brethren.

Pequot War: First in a series of conflicts between Puritan New Englanders and their Native American neighbors. Puritan militia slaughtered over 400 innocent Pequot women, children and old men in this "war." Even the Puritans Indian allies were shocked by the Englishmen's ferocious brutality in annihilating the Pequot.

"Petticoat Affair": The daughter of a Washington tavern owner, Margaret O'Neill Timberlake "Peggy" Eaton (1799-1879) played a central role in a sex scandal during the administration of Andrew Jackson in 1829.

Philipsburg Proclamation: An announcement of British policy relating to slaves in the South issued on June 30, 1779 by General Sir Henry Clinton, the British commander, as part of his preparations for the campaign to reconquer the southern states.

Phrenology: A pseudo-science popular in the early 19th century based on the idea that various "organs" within the brain housed different "faculties" and that these organs were located underneath the scalp causing unique bumps. A trained phrenologist supposedly could tell how intelligent, honest or reliable a person was by massaging the skull and interpreting its topography.

Pierce, Franklin (1804-1869): A New Hampshire politician who served as president from 1853 to 1857. Support for the South—especially the Ostend Manifesto and the Kansas-Nebraska Act—marked his presidency, and Pierce became distinguished as a "northern man with southern principles" by his critics.

Pilgrims: The Separatist Puritans who left Holland and established the Plymouth Colony in 1620.

Pitt, William: One of England's prime ministers who took charge of his majesty's government and war effort in 1757 completely changing the British war focus and ultimately bringing victory and the greatest empire in world history to Great Britain.

Pizarro, Francisco: Spanish conquistador who subdued the Inca empire.

Pocahontas (c. 1595-1617): Daughter of Powhatan who occasionally acted as an intermediary between her father and the Jamestown settlers. Captured by the English, she eventually married John Rolfe.

Polk, James K. (1795-1849): Tennessee congressman and governor elected the 11th President of the United States in 1844. His expansionist beliefs and policies ultimately led to war with Mexico in 1846.

Pontiac's Rebellion (1763-1765): Conflict between a confederacy of Native American groups led by the Ottawa chief Pontiac against the British occurring after the conclusion of the French and Indian War.

Popular Sovereignty: An alternative to the Wilmot Proviso asserting that settlers in a federal territory should decide whether a territory should be open or closed to slavery.

Powhatan: Leader of the indigenous Algonquian tribes that lived in the Chesapeake area and who had formed a large Indian confederacy to keep other tribes out of the area. Powhatan hoped to form a trading partnership and possible military alliance with the English at Jamestown. Smith was receptive to such arrangements.

Praying Towns: Name given to those Indian communities whose inhabitants had converted to Christianity and thus were to be exempt or protected from Puritan reprisals. Very few Puritans, even among the clergy, believed in "saving" the Indians of the region.

Primogeniture: Traditional colonial-era practice of granting inheritances only to the oldest male heir.

Princeton, Battle of (January 3, 1777): Clash between the Continental Army and British units in and around Princeton, New Jersey, resulting in a minor American victory. Washington's triumph at the Battle of Princeton further demonstrated the Continental Army's abilities and reinforced the impact of the Battle of Trenton on Patriot morale.

Proclamation Line of 1763: Royal decree that upset many colonists because of its restrictions against legal settlement past the Appalachian Mountains.

Proclamation of Neutrality: George Washington's announcement that the U.S. would remain neutral during European war in the 1790s.

Proprietary Colony: A colony in which one person or a small group of private individuals held ultimate power, including the right to appoint a governor.

Protestant Reformation: A religious upheaval during the 1500s that shattered the religious unity of Europe.

Pueblo Revolt: 1680 uprising by Pueblo Indians against the Spanish that held off Spanish settlement until 1692.

Puritans: One of the most important and largest groups of English migrants coming to North America in the 17th century, proving to be pivotal in the shaping of the American creed.

Putting-Out System: An early form of manufacturing in which industrialists delivered raw materials for workers to craft into finished products at home to be picked up upon completion.

Quakers (The Society of Friends): A radical Protestant sect that emerged in Reformation/Civil War England. Founded by George Fox in the 1640s, Quakers believed more in a way of living in the temporal world than in any specific religious doctrine. For their "strange" beliefs, the Quakers became, along with English Catholics, one of the most proscribed Christian sects in English history.

Quasi-War: The undeclared naval war between the United States and France (1798-1800) begun by the seizure of American ships by French privateers after the signing of Jay's Treaty.

Radicals Republicans: Opposed to President Abraham Lincoln and Andrew Johnson's Reconstruction policies from 1863-1868, the Radicals believed the South should be punished for their "treason" and that the freedmen should become full-fledged United States citizens and their new status protected by the federal government.

Railroads: Two decades after steam-powered locomotives first emerged in Great Britain, the Baltimore and Ohio Railroad in 1830 became the first commercial rail line in the United States. By the start of the Civil War three decades later, railroads had become the second most used form of transportation for the movement of people and goods in the United States behind only the steamboat.

Raleigh, Sir Walter: Half-brother of Humphrey Gilbert who was the financial backer for the Roanoke Colony, which disappeared in 1590.

Reconstruction Acts of 1867: Represented the end of Presidential Reconstruction and the beginning of Congressional or Radical Reconstruction. These laws restarted the political process in the South, with the 10 unreconstructed southern states divided into five military districts administered by Army generals.

"Red Sticks": Creek Indian prophets who allied with Tecumseh and believed in his Pan-Indian movement as the best way to hold off white America from taking over the lands and destroying the Native American way of life.

Redeemers: The antebellum elite who sought to end "Yankee domination" and regain political power in the South after the Civil War.

Renaissance: A flowering of knowledge in the 14th and 15th centuries that led to development of new technology important in overseas navigation and exploration.

***Report on Manufactures*:** Alexander Hamilton's December 1791 report to Congress calling for federal government aid to American industry in the form of high tariffs, national bank loans, and subsidies to encourage the production of manufactured goods.

***Report on the Public Credit*:** Alexander Hamilton's 1790 report to Congress relaying the amount of the young republic's public debt and proposed that the nation's debt obligations be paid in full to whoever held government bonds and other securities at the time regardless of when and where they were acquired.

Republic of Texas: Declared during the Texas Revolution of 1836, the Republic existed for ten years until the United States annexed Texas in 1845.

"Republican Mothers": The concept of recognizing the importance of elevating and educating women so they could impart proper virtues to the children of the post-Revolutionary era.

Republican Party: A political organization that emerged in response to a growing belief among antebellum Northerners that the federal government and Democratic Party had been captured by politicians who wanted to force the expansion of slavery throughout the United States. The party focused on the non-extension of slavery in the 1850s and on keeping the South in the Union in the 1860s.

Rhode Island System: Early manufacturing capitalists such as Slater wanted to avoid being stigmatized by the Jeffersonians of creating horrible factory towns rife with poverty, blight, and class tensions. Slater and other early industrialists moved their operations to rural areas, creating "factory villages," which employed local farm women and children. At the same time, Slater and others rented land to local farmers for them to provide food for their factory workers.

Roanoke: The first serious English attempt to settle in the New World, whose inhabitants vanished without a trace in 1590 and became known as the "Lost Colony."

Rolfe, John (1585-1622): Jamestown settler whose successful efforts at tobacco cultivation led to the massive Virginia tobacco boom. He later married Pocahontas and was killed in one of Opechancanough's attacks in 1622.

Ross, John (1790-1866): The leader of the Cherokee people who tried to assimilate his people to white culture as a means of preserving his nation's land and resource rights in their native Georgia and Alabama.

Rush-Bagot Agreement (1817): First in a series of agreements between Great Britain and the U.S. The accord recognized the Great Lakes as the natural boundaries between the U.S. and British Canada while completely demilitarizing the lakes.

Sacking of Washington, D.C.: The 1814 British burning of government buildings in the nation's capital before the failed attack on Baltimore.

Saint-Domingue: French sugar colony on Hispaniola whose slaves successfully revolted in the late eighteenth century, leading to the establishment of the Republic of Haiti.

Salem Witchcraft Hysteria: People were executed for being "witches," the result of the resentment and hostility that had emerged in Salem and other Massachusetts towns born of economic frustration, especially among young males, who believed their economic advancement and security (land ownership) was being stymied by widowed landowners and others. Conservative Puritan leaders believed the presence of witches reflected the sinful behavior of many of the community's inhabitants.

Salutary neglect: British policy of lax governmental oversight and relatively light enforcement of the Navigation Acts in the years prior to the Seven Years' War.

San Lorenzo, Treaty of: 1795 treaty between U.S. and Spain that guaranteed American right to trade through New Orleans.

Santa Anna, Antonio López de (1794-1876): Mexican general whose military coup and declaration of a centralist government provoked resistance in many parts of Mexico and led to the Texas Revolution in which his forces were defeated and the Republic of Texas declared.

Santa Fe Trail: A lucrative southwestern trade route running through Santa Fe, New Mexico.

Santo Domingo Affair: The attempt by the Grant administration in 1869 to annex the present-day country of the Dominican Republic.

Saratoga, Battles of (Sept. 19 and Oct. 7, 1777): The first large-scale, strategically crucial military victory of American forces over a British army. The American victory sustained the Patriot cause and led directly to French intervention in the war.

"Scalawags": A term given during the Reconstruction Era in the 1860s and 1870s to southern whites who had supported the Union during the Civil War and the Republican Party during Reconstruction.

Scott, Winfield (1786-1866): The commander of the United States Army during the Mexican American War between 1846-1848. His military renown led to his nomination for president by the Whig Party in 1852, in which Democrat Franklin Pierce soundly defeated him.

Second Bank of the United States: Chartered in 1816, the Second B.U.S. had even more direct regulatory power over the nation's fiscal and monetary policies than the original bank. The principal purpose of the Second B.U.S. was the same as the first: to help stimulate economic growth while simultaneously stabilizing the nation's financial and monetary system.

Second Continental Congress: Delegates from the colonies that convened in May 1775 after the outbreak of fighting in Massachusetts between British and American forces.

Second Great Awakening: Series of religious revivals in the first half of the nineteenth century that showed great emotionalism in large public meetings.

Second Middle Passage: Enslaved people who were forced to migrate in the Deep South.

Sedition Act: A measure pushed through Congress by the High Federalists to destroy the Democratic-Republican Party by denying its members the right of free speech and press to criticize the Federalist Party. The act set jail terms and fines for persons who advocated disobedience to federal law or who wrote, printed, or spoke out against any person or policy of the federal government.

Seneca Falls Convention of 1848: A women's rights gathering held July 19-20, attended by Lucretia Mott, Elizabeth Cady Stanton, Frederick Douglass and others to "discuss the social, civil and religious condition and rights of women." Stanton authored a *Declaration of Sentiments* that demanded women receive the right to vote.

Separatists: English Puritans who believed the Church of England was beyond redemption and thus to avoid its corruption, true believing Calvinists (Puritans) must separate themselves completely from its popery and Catholic sinfulness. This particular sect of Puritans left England, ultimately establishing the first Puritan colony in North America at Plymouth in present-day Massachusetts. Also became known as the Pilgrims.

Sequoyah (1770?-1843): The child of a British father and a Cherokee mother, Sequoyah reached adulthood illiterate, but in 1821 he devised a written language for the Cherokee language that used 86 characters. The Cherokee Nation adopted Sequoyah's system, which had a character for every syllable in the language.

Shaman: A member of a Native American group believed to have the ability to access the spiritual world in order to perform such tasks as healing the sick, influencing the weather, and predicting the future.

Shays's Rebellion (1786-1787): A 1787 armed rebellion of debt-ridden farmers in western Massachusetts whose protests against foreclosures for failure to pay state taxes culminated in an attack upon the federal arsenal at Springfield, Massachusetts. State militia ultimately put down the rebellion. The inability of the federal government to provide any aid to the government of Massachusetts became an argument for supporters of the movement to replace the Articles of Confederation.

Sheridan, Phillip S. (1831-1888): A Union major general during the Civil War (1861-1865) who successfully drove the Confederates out of Virginia's fertile Shenandoah Valley and destroyed farm land in an offensive in August 1864 that aimed to cut Robert E. Lee's Army of Northern Virginia from food supplies.

Sherman, Roger (1721-1793): Delegate from Connecticut at the Constitutional Convention who brokered the Great Compromise concerning representation of the states in the Congress.

Sherman, William Tecumseh (1820-1891): One of the most perceptive and innovative generals in the Union Army during the Civil War, William T. Sherman embraced total war tactics during his "March to the Sea" across Georgia to the Atlantic Ocean in 1864. Sherman believed that undermining the morale of southern civilians would be a key to northern victory, so he directed his men to live off the land and to take food supplies from the Confederate-owned farms they seized and to destroy what could not be taken.

Slater, Samuel (1768-1835): English apprentice who brought his knowledge of British textile manufacturing to the United States, allowing for the establishment of the first American textile mill in Rhode Island in the early 1790s.

Slave Codes: Laws created in the English mainland colonies of North America between 1690 and 1715 in response to the massive importation of slaves into the Chesapeake and Carolina regions. Characterized by their consideration of slaves as mere property to be treated as a degraded workforce, the codes reflected the harsher and more impersonal treatment of slaves in the colonies when compared to the seventeenth century.

Slave coping mechanisms: The various means by which slaves psychologically endured their captivity, ranging from the use of music and religion for emotional release to dependence on family members for support.

Slave living conditions: While provided with the basic necessities of life in terms of food and shelter, slaves frequently received quantity of food over quality and living area providing basic protection from the elements but limited privacy and comfort.

"Slave Power": A theory, most fully developed by Republicans in the 1850s, that a conspiracy of slaveholders had captured the federal government and were using its power to expand slavery into the West and perhaps into the North.

Smith, John: Member of the original 104 settlers who established Jamestown who survived the first winter and eventually took charge of the colony. The other colonists came to resent Smith for imposing a harsh regimen of work and discipline for the sake of survival. Had Smith not imposed his will, the colony would have self-destructed and England might have given up on establishing a North American colony.

Smith, Joseph, Jr. (1805-1844): The founder of the Church of Jesus Christ of Latter-day Saints or the Mormon religion.

Sons of Liberty: Originally called The Loyal Nine, this group of Boston merchants and artisans organized in the summer of 1765 to oppose to the Stamp Act.

Spoils System: The practice of removing political opponents from positions in the federal government and replacing them with loyal party members.

Squanto: Pokanoket Indian leader who forged an alliance with the Pilgrims in order to have Pilgrim assistance in freeing their tribe from Narragansett domination.

Stamp Act: Revenue law passed by Parliament in March 1764 and due to take effect in November of that year that placed a tax on printed materials in the colonies leading to a storm of protest and the legislation's repeal in early 1766.

Stanton, Elizabeth Cady (1815-1902): An abolitionist advocate of women's suffrage from New York, Stanton authored the "Declaration of Sentiments" adopted at the Seneca Falls Convention in 1848 that called for women to have the right to vote.

Steel plow: John Deere's 1830s invention that allowed for easier and more efficient cutting of the soil.

Steuben, Frederick Wilhelm Von (1730-1794): Prussian officer hired by the American Continental Army who professionalized that force, teaching them European drills, precision marching and providing discipline during the long, bitter winter the soldiers spent in Valley Forge in the winter of 1778. The Baron also wrote a comprehensive set of training instructions and standard regulations, which was published by Congress in 1779 and served as the U.S. Army's official manual until 1812.

Stevens, Thaddeus (1792-1868): A member of the United States House of Representatives from Pennsylvania who supported abolition before and during the Civil War and who became a leader of the Radical Republican faction during after the War.

Stono Rebellion: A major slave insurrection among South Carolinian slaves assisted by the Spanish promise of arms and sanctuary against the colonies' rice planting elite. Rebellion was crushed but henceforth South Carolina rice planters enforced strict slave codes on all their bondsmen.

Strict Constructionist: One who prefers a narrow interpretation of the Constitution, favoring the view that the federal government can only perform acts specifically listed in the document.

Sugar Act: Legislation passed by Parliament in 1765 that lowered the tariff on foreign molasses entering the colonies, in effect changing the nature of the tax from one designed to regulate commerce to one that generated revenue for the crown.

Sumner, Charles (1811-1874): Abolitionist lawyer and orator from Massachusetts who became a Radical Republican leader in the U.S. Senate. His caning on the floor of the Senate in 1856 by a South Carolina congressman following an incendiary anti-slavery speech outraged many in the North and heightened further sectional tensions.

"Tariff of Abominations": The 1828 federal tariff condemned by South Carolinian radicals who decried the high rates on foreign manufactures. Arguing that high tariffs only benefited New England industrialists at the expense of southern agriculturalists who had to pay higher prices for manufactures and possibly suffer foreign retaliation against American farm commodities, South Carolinians would eventually attempt to nullify it along with the 1832 Tariff, which maintained the high tax rates on foreign imports.

Tariff of 1816: The first "real" protective tariff passed in U.S. history, raising the duties on many foreign manufactured and raw goods to 35 percent ad-valorem. Such protectionism would eventually lead to sectional discord as the South opposed what it perceived as "Yankee favoritism" by the federal government.

Taylor, Zachary (1784-1850): American general who gained fame leading troops in northern Mexico during the Mexican American War. After receiving the Whig Party nomination, he was elected the 12th President of the United States in 1848 but died two years later.

Tea Act: Law passed by Parliament in 1773 to help the ailing British East India Company and generate revenue for the British Crown. The law authorized the company to bypass colonial middlemen and sell directly to consumers resulting in a lower overall price despite the continued existence of the Townshend Tea Tax. Colonial displeasure with the legislation led directly to the "Boston Tea Party."

Tecumseh: Shawnee Indian, who along with his brother the Prophet, forged the largest Indian confederation in U.S. history against white America. Tecumseh's efforts at promoting a Pan-Indian movement proved successful as he united all the tribes from the Great Lakes to the Gulf of Mexico along the Mississippi River Valley.

Telegraph: By 1836 allowed Americans to spread information across many parts of the nation almost instantaneously. The telegraph transmitted and received electrical impulses along a connected wire using a standard code.

Ten Percent Plan: Abraham Lincoln's wartime Reconstruction Plan whereby a presidential pardon would be given to all southern whites (excluding Confederate government officials and high-ranking military officers) who took an oath of allegiance to the United States and accepted the abolition of slavery. Further, any state where the number of white males over 20 years old who took this oath exceeded 10 percent of the eligible voters in 1860 could establish a new state government that would be recognized as legitimate.

Tenskwatawa ("The Prophet"): Shawnee leader and brother of Tecumseh who tried to rally Native Americans to embrace native culture while resisting American westward expansion.

Tenure of Office Act of 1867: Bill passed by Radical Republican-controlled Congress designed to further strip President Andrew Johnson of his power by making it illegal for him to remove any cabinet member without Senate approval. Johnson defied the act by attempting to fire Secretary of War Edwin M. Stanton, which became the pretext for Johnson's impeachment and Senate trial in 1868.

Thoreau, Henry David (1817-1862): A former schoolteacher, abolitionist and philosopher, he wrote *Resistance to Civil Government or Civil Disobedience* (published in 1849) in which he argued that a moral person has an obligation to resist unjust laws.

Thornton Affair: Border skirmish between U.S. and Mexican troops that led President James Polk to ask Congress for a declaration of war against Mexico.

"Three-Fifths Compromise": The key agreement worked out, in August 1787, between delegates from northern (some antislavery) states and southern (slaveholding) states, at the Constitutional Convention in Philadelphia. Three-fifths of the slave population was added to the population of free people to be used in allocating representatives by state in the lower house of Congress.

Timberlake, Peggy [Margaret O'Neill Eaton] (1799-1879): Daughter of a Washington hotel owner whose second marriage to Andrew Jackson's close friend and Secretary of War, John Eaton, gave rise to the "Petticoat Affair." As a result of Jackson's defense of her honor, several members of his Cabinet were replaced.

Tocqueville, Alexis de (1805-1859): French author and historian whose four-volume book *Democracy in America* (published between 1835 and 1840) still ranks as one of the most perceptive portraits of American social and political life in the early 19th century.

Tories: One of the names given to Americans who remained loyal to the British crown during the War for Independence (1775-1783).

Townshend Revenue Act: Law passed by Parliament in 1767 that levied import taxes on colonial imports of paper, glass, paint, lead, alcohol, and tea.

Trail of Tears: President Martin Van Buren sent a 7,000-man military force under General Winfield Scott to round up the Cherokees and prod them at bayonet point out of Georgia. Soldiers arrived during the winter of 1838 and gave Cherokees mere minutes to gather their families and possessions before they were forced to march westward. About a quarter succumbed to exposure, exhaustion and disease.

Transcendentalism: The philosophical, literary, and political movement arising in the 1830s and 1840s and exemplified by the works of Henry David Thoreau and Ralph Waldo Emerson. Transcendentalists believed in the inherent worth of every individual, opposed slavery and believed that the authentic life lived in harmony with nature.

Turner, Nat (1800-1831): The leader of a major slave revolt in Southhampton County, Virginia, in August 1831.

Tyler, John (1790-1862): Virginia governor, congressman, and senator elected vice president on the Whig ticket with William Henry Harrison in 1840. With Harrison's sudden death after only one month in office, Tyler became the first vice president to assume the presidency upon the death of a president.

Uncle Tom's Cabin: An antislavery novel written by Harriet Beecher Stowe in 1852. The novel sold enormously well and helped distribute abolitionist arguments beyond the ranks of the already converted.

Underground Railroad: A secret network of abolitionists, free blacks and escaped slaves who assisted African Americans escaping bondage in the South during the 1840s and 1850s. "Conductors" directed slaves to safe houses where they could eat, rest and hide from slave patrols, and provided them the quickest routes to free territory.

U.S.S. Chesapeake: U.S. naval ship fired on by British ship in 1807, led to rising tensions with Britain and an embargo.

U.S.S. Constitution: Flagship of U.S. Navy that led blockade of Barbary Pirates and won important victories of British in War of 1812.

Valley Forge: Site in eastern Pennsylvania, roughly 30 miles from Philadelphia, selected by General Washington for the Continental Army's winter quarters in 1777-1778 and remembered from then on for the suffering of soldiers during the winter. Diseases common to military camps—such as typhoid and dysentery—killed hundreds of weakened men. Ultimately Valley Forge became a symbol of perseverance as well as suffering, but the army endured many of the same problems each winter for the rest of the war.

Van Buren, Martin (1782-1862): Eighth President of the United States, serving from 1837-1841, Van Buren became the main architect behind the formation of the Democratic Party by the end of Andrew Jackson's presidency.

Vesey, Denmark (1767?-1822): Free African American who planned a massive slave revolt in Charleston, South Carolina in 1822 until word of the plot was leaked to the authorities who arrested, convicted, and executed Vesey and fellow conspirators.

Vicksburg, Siege of: A military engagement, from May 18-July 4, 1863, considered a major turning point in the Civil War that allowed Union General Ulysses S. Grant to split the Confederacy in half and to give the North control of the Mississippi River.

Vikings: People from Scandinavia led by Leif Erickson who established colonies in Canada long before Columbus "discovered" the New World.

Virginia and Kentucky Resolutions: Pair of resolutions authored by James Madison and Thomas Jefferson protesting passage of the Alien and Sedition Acts by the Federalist-dominated Congress.

Virginia Plan: Plan drafted by James Madison and sponsored by Edmund Randolph at the Constitutional Convention that greatly favored granting the larger, more populous states a disproportionate share of power in the Congress.

Wade-Davis Bill: The Radical Republicans' counter-proposal to President Abraham Lincoln's "10 percent plan." Lincoln's plan would have allowed a former Confederate state to be eligible for readmission to the Union once 10 percent of the number of voters in that state who participated in the 1860 presidential election swore loyalty to the Union. The Radicals' proposal called for all southern whites to take an "iron-clad" oath that they had never taken up arms against the United States government before they would be eligible to vote or hold office. The Radicals also proposed requiring 50 percent of a state's white population to swear their allegiance to the United States before that state would be eligible for re-admission.

Walker, David (1785-1830): An African-American abolitionist who in 1829 published his anti-slavery pamphlet *Appeal to the Colored Citizens of the World,* a document that called for African-American slaves to use any method, including violence, to win their freedom. Walker also harshly criticized the American Colonization Society, which advocated relocating freed American slaves to Africa.

Walker, Mary (1832-1919): An abolitionist, temperance advocate and campaigner for women's suffrage who served as a surgeon and alleged spy for the Union during the Civil War and became the only woman to date to receive the Congressional Medal of Honor.

Waltham System: Labor system/force used by the Boston Associates in their various factory towns. Lowell and company used exclusively young, single, rural women as their principal workforce.

War Hawks: Name given to those Congressmen, primarily from the South and West, who agitated for war against Great Britain to uphold national honor.

Warren, Mercy Otis (1728-1814): Sister of James Otis, Jr. who became a well-known political writer and pro-American propagandist during the Revolutionary War.

Washington, George (1732-1799): The commander of the American Continental Army during the Revolutionary War and the first president of the United States. Washington participated in the First and Second Continental Congresses, which aimed to coordinate resistance to British tax policies in all of the colonies. He vigorously supported the Constitution's ratification. He was elected president unanimously and took office April 30, 1789.

Webster-Ashburton Treaty: Signed in 1842, this agreement between the U.S. and England settled the border between the United States and British-held Canada in eastern North America (from Maine to what is now the state of Minnesota) and secured American cooperation in suppressing the African slave trade.

Whig Party: Political party organized in the mid-1830s by Henry Clay and other opponents of Andrew Jackson's policies. The Whigs supported high tariffs on foreign manufactured goods, federal sponsorship of internal improvements, and maintenance of the national bank.

Whiskey Rebellion: A 1794 uprising among western Pennsylvania farmers against Hamilton's excise tax on "spirits," which they believed to be "illegal."

Whitefield, George: Evangelical English disciple of Methodism founder John Wesley who came to the colonies to preach a similar message to that of Edwards—that the ability to be saved was now an individual matter and that God no longer predestined your ultimate fate. Evangelical preachers such as Whitefield and Edwards found their greatest audiences among the colonies' lower classes.

Whitman, Walt (1819-1892): A notable journalist and poet from New York whose 1855 collection of poems, *Leaves of Grass*, shocked contemporary readers with its frank celebration of the human body and sexuality. His use of free verse in poetry was considered innovative.

Whitney, Eli (1765-1825): American inventor best known for developing the first cotton gin in 1793.

Williams, Roger: The first among several dissenters who emerged within the first decade of the Puritans' presence in New England. Williams, a minister, had been a "closet" Separatist, whose true sentiments emerged after coming to Massachusetts. He began preaching his "heresy," which challenged the colony's quasi-theocratic structure. Most disturbing to the colony's governors and elders was Williams' advocacy of religious toleration and the separation of church and state.

Wilmot Proviso: A rider to an appropriations bill proposed by Representative David Wilmot of Pennsylvania at the beginning of the Mexican-American War, the Proviso stated that any territory acquired from Mexico should be closed to slavery. The proposal reopened sectional conflict.

Winthrop, John: Leader of the Massachusetts Bay colony and responsible for holding the saintly religious together through some very challenging early years. Winthrop was governor from the moment the Puritans sailed until his death in 1649.

Yeoman farmers: Landowning small farmers who dominated the Upcountry regions of the South where they practiced mixed agriculture with limited contact with the region's cotton markets.

Yorktown, Siege of (Sept. 28-Oct. 19, 1781): The decisive military engagement of the war in the South, which led directly to the British decision to accept the independence of the United States. The loss of Cornwallis' army of some 7,000 men was the final blow to the British war effort in North America.

Young, Brigham (1801-1877): An early convert to Mormonism in 1823, Young acted as a missionary for the Church of Jesus Christ of Latter-day Saints. By 1841, he ranked second in authority within the church only to the founder of Mormonism, Joseph Smith.

John Peter Zenger: New York newspaper editor whose 1735 trial set a precedent in favor of freedom of the press in America.

Index